H. W. TILMAN

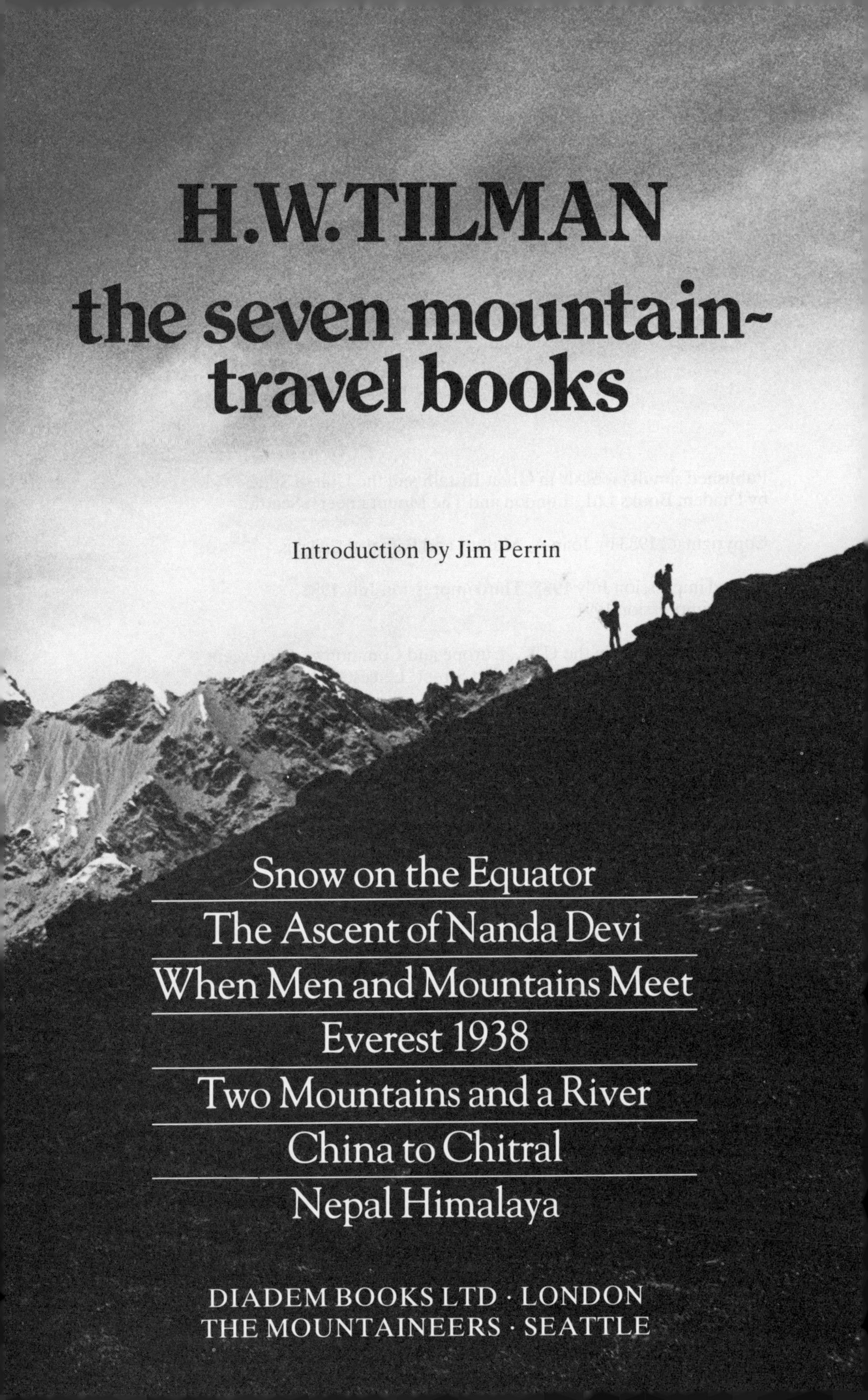

H.W. TILMAN

the seven mountain-travel books

Introduction by Jim Perrin

Snow on the Equator

The Ascent of Nanda Devi

When Men and Mountains Meet

Everest 1938

Two Mountains and a River

China to Chitral

Nepal Himalaya

DIADEM BOOKS LTD · LONDON
THE MOUNTAINEERS · SEATTLE

Published simultaneously in Great Britain and the United States
by Diadem Books Ltd., London and The Mountaineers, Seattle

Second impression July 1985; Third impression July 1988,
Fourth impression 1991

All trade enquiries in the U.K., Europe and Commonwealth (except
Canada) to Cordee, 3a De Montfort Street, Leicester, England

All trade enquiries in the U.S.A. and Canada to The Mountaineers,
306 2nd Avenue West, Seattle, Washington 98119, U.S.A.

British Library Cataloguing in Publication Data:
Tilman, H. W.
    The seven mountain-travel books.
    1. Mountains   2. Mountaineering – voyages and travels
    I. Title
    910.09 143   GB501

    ISBN 0-906371-21-X (UK)

Library of Congress Catalog Card Number 83–61865
    ISBN 0-89886-074-1 (US)

Production by
Chambers Green Limited, Tunbridge Wells, Kent

Printed in Great Britain by
St Edmundsbury Press Limited, Bury St Edmunds, Suffolk

Contents

Photographs in the Text

Illustrations used at the beginning of each book

Illustrations between pages 320 and 321

School and War; African travels; Nanda Devi, 1936; Everest Reconnaissance 1935; Everest, 1938; Albania, 1943; Italy, 1945.

Illustrations between pages 640 and 641

Rakaposhi Expedition, 1947; Central Asia, 1947–48; Langtang Himal, 1949; Annapurna, 1950; Everest approaches, 1950.

The copyright holders wish to thank the following for permission to use photos not drawn from the Tilman collection: Mike Banks, John Cleare, Pam Morrison, The Royal Geographical Society, Dr. and Mrs R. Scott Russell and Doug Scott.

INTRODUCTION

by Jim Perrin

More than in any other genre the effect of travel writing depends on personal response to the author. Half an hour of Doughty's quirky pomposity is enough for anyone not intent on sleep; D. H. Lawrence might just entice you into the intoxication of a sunny afternoon; there are very few whom you would take willingly to the uttermost parts of the Earth, but H. W. Tilman belongs in this latter category. The re-publication of the seven titles collected together in this volume has long been overdue, for Tilman is unsurpassed as a mountaineering author, and can hold his own with any travel writer in the language.

These seven books are a form of restrained autobiography covering the years 1919–1952[1]. *Snow on the Equator* can be read as an idiosyncratic account of the author's attempt to find his personality, or more simply as a fascinating thirties African travelogue. *The Ascent of Nanda Devi* and *Everest 1938* are as close to conventional accounts of expeditions to big mountains as Tilman could countenance, and have long been regarded as classics of their kind. *When Men and Mountains Meet* covers a pre-war trip to the little-known Assam Himalaya and goes on to describe Tilman's Second World War experiences. The three books dealing with his post-war travels – *Two Mountains and a River, China to Chitral, Nepal Himalaya* – are those on which his fame will probably rest and are descriptions of an extraordinary series of individual peregrinations through every major range of the Himalaya and Central Asia.

The personality of the author is central to the matter of travel writing, yet that of Tilman, despite a painstaking biography[2], remains enigmatic and elusive. The boat on which he was sailing for the Antarctic disappeared in the South Atlantic six years ago in a season of storms. The tragedy became apparent when the boat failed to arrive at any likely port of call. For Tilman it was a curiously apt and romantic ending, setting the seal on the legend of his life.

Far too many, on the evidence of the numerous apocryphal tales which have collected about him, have pre-judged Tilman as the slightly 'blimpish' and austere monomaniac conqueror of peak, ocean or Asian col – an unconsciously humorous misogynist cast in a sterling British Imperial mould.

---

1 A number of Tilman's expeditions with Shipton are recorded in the latter's books – notably the Rishi Gorge exploration (1934), Everest Reconnaissance Expedition (1935) and the Karakoram/ Shaksgam explorations (1937). See Bibliography for details.

2 *High Mountains and Cold Seas* by J. R. L. Anderson (Gollancz, 1980).

Such a judgment is manifestly incorrect. There is little point in recapitulating on the events of a life already well recorded in the Anderson biography. Instead this preface may best serve as the *character*, in the eighteenth-century sense of the word, of a slightly anachronistic, yet profoundly civilised and intelligent man for whom such a gesture is entirely appropriate.

In a way, the manner and timing of his death, so tragic for his young fellow-sailors, was for him a blessing. In the last conversation I had with him before he sailed for the Antarctic, he confessed that he felt himself to be getting feeble now, and that he would not mind if he did not come back from this trip – this said quite matter-of-factly, and with not a trace of self-pity. Pam Davis, his niece and probably the person closest to him in his last years, put it thus: 'The way he went – it just couldn't have been better. It was just absolutely perfect. The idea of him being ill or nursed was unthinkable. The pity of it was that those boys went too, but at least he wasn't in charge – it was their expedition, and their boat, on which he'd been invited along.'

Tilman was a lifelong bachelor and reputedly a misogynist, which gave rise to the usual run of unfounded gossip and wrong-headed speculation, as well as the reputation of humourlessness. Some months before he sailed on his last voyage, I asked him why he had never married. He replied, grinning hugely to himself at my presumption, 'I've had my peccadilloes, but the trouble with women is, they get in the damned way.' There's nothing the least sexist about this reply – an adventurous woman could give the same response about men. A marital partner, family commitments and the like would have acted as constraints upon the pattern of life he came to discern in the twenties, and seeing this, he wisely and unselfishly – for there is an element of moral choice here as well as working out a mode of individual integrity – disciplined himself and forwent the pleasures along with the responsibilities of marriage. He was certainly aided in this decision by the close relationship he enjoyed throughout his life with his sister Adeline who had been left, after the break-up of her marriage, with two small daughters who grew particularly close to their uncle and possibly regarded him in the light of a rather distant, but fascinating and romantic father-figure. His needs for female companionship and support were amply fulfilled through Adeline, with whom he went dancing, for whose children he brought back presents – African stools, elephant tails – from his trips, and with whom he eventually made his home in Wales. Tilman was, in his own way, a family-orientated man and one who blossomed amongst the company of relations and close friends.

His attitude to women was rather that of an old-fashioned courtesy. Although he could and did appreciate simple, honest ribaldry on his Asian trips, impropriety towards his family was a different matter. Pam Davis has a recollection of accompanying him to the 20th anniversary celebrations of the liberation of Belluno in the Dolomites. After introducing Pam, then a strikingly handsome woman in her early forties, to his old partisan friends as his niece they were shown, amidst a good deal of nudging and winking, to a double hotel bedroom. Pam recounts how she strove to suppress laughter as he furiously rounded on his hosts to insist, thunderously and with piercing blue eyes, 'She is my niece!' I have to add that such an unamused reaction would have been occasioned only by his strict sense of family propriety.

Which brings us back to the point of his reputed humourlessness. Such an accusation is crass beyond belief. Tilman was the funniest man I ever met and for proof of that assertion you need do no more than dip into any one of the books contained in this volume. They are laced with self-mockery, continual ironic reflection, moments of high farce, and a due sense of the ridiculousness inherent in so many of our actions.

One of his chief joys in conversation was to send up the accepted image of himself mercilessly. I remember asking how many of the stories which grew up about him were apocryphal. 'By far the greater number,' he replied, 'but there is one which is substantially true. It was on an expedition in the thirties. We embarked at Tilbury, and I am said to have stayed on deck until we rounded the North Foreland, whereupon I was heard to mutter the words, "H'm, sea!" After this I went below decks and was not seen again until we hove in sight of Bombay. I then came on deck once more and was duly heard to utter the words, "H'm, land!" It is asserted that these were the only words I uttered on the entire voyage, which is more or less the truth of the matter, and the reason, quite simply, is that I could not stand the other chaps on that trip.'

At which point the conversation dissolved into alcoholic chuckles. The occasion on which he told me this anecdote sticks in my mind. After the death of his sister in 1974 he lived on by himself in their fine old house, Bod Owen, looking out over the Mawddach Estuary to Cader Idris. Although completely self-sufficient, he was undoubtedly lonely at times and relished company. Visitors were received in the morning, and those not arriving punctually at 10 would incur his tolerant wrath. On the February morning of this particular conversation, we sat round a log fire in his study, dogs grumbling at the usurpation of their hearth rug by other feet, and talked. How he could talk! He would fence with quotations, and if you could quip back at him from Johnson, Hazlitt, Montaigne, Jane Austen or – his especial delight – Robert Surtees, he would rock with glee and come back at you with another equally apposite tag. At 11, punctually, he served acrid coffee from tiny cups of old porcelain, always with the admonition, 'None of your instant muck here, Perrin, though I'm damned if you can get anything decent hereabouts these days.'

To anyone who knew him personally and who was receptive to his brand of ironic humour, he was a source of amusement and delight, an excellent raconteur and a quick-witted, kindly adversary. But this was the lighter side for his humour, as you would expect from this distinguished old soldier, was a strategy which presupposed a serious world-view. The general run of his humour is towards irony, and Tilman's irony, which frequently has about it something of a Swiftian *saeva indignatio*, is a way of coping with a world the moral stability of which was thoroughly eroded throughout his lifetime, and shattered by the effects and implications of two world wars.

Tilman went to war a month before his eighteenth birthday. He was wounded in the thigh shortly afterwards, but was back in action in time to see the start of the Battle of the Somme. In the next six months over a million soldiers were to die, 420,000 of them British, and dying as much through the fault of a cold-eyed, antediluvian British High Command as by German machine-gun fire. Tilman was a first-hand witness to this slaughter channelled between two bitter winters. Thirty years after the event, he wrote:

> . . .after the first war, when one took stock, shame mingled with satisfaction at finding
> oneself still alive. One felt a bit like the Ancient Mariner; so many better men, a few of
> them friends, were dead:
> > And a thousand thousand slimy things
> > Lived on; and so did I.

How those lines must have haunted a man who had seen the limbs of the wounded and dying twitch and writhe in the mud of the Somme, and whose own life was to take on some of the archetypal resonance of Coleridge's poem.

The experience of the Great War coloured Tilman's later attitude in two important ways. Firstly, it put him out of all patience with whiners, complainers, and malingerers – how could a man who had seen death and suffering at first hand so early in his life have fellow-feeling for such people? Secondly, and perhaps more importantly, it put him out of all patience with England. The dreams of soldiers who spent their days in muddy trenches, waterlogged craters, or out in the winter snow, are probably accurately expressed in Max Plowman's poem *When It's Over*, which I heard Tilman quote on several occasions. There are the aspirations of the lotus-eater:

> I shall lie on the beach
> Of a shore where the rippling waves just sigh,
> And listen and dream and sleep and lie.

Or, more constructively, those of the soldier who will

> . . . get out and across the sea,
> Where land's cheap, and a man can thrive.

Which is what Tilman did in 1919, joining that astonishing exodus from England which was to make travel-writing the characteristic literary genre of the twenties and thirties.

Strong ties of family and affection held him from making a complete break, but there was little attraction in a formal and strictured society to a man who, for three years, had experienced the camaraderie of an army at war. The comradeship of the bush, the expedition, the trek, became a substitute for the lost friendships of war, and the ingenuous hospitality and occasional insubordination of the natives he employed or travelled with gave him a fair parallel to the officer's responsibility for his men. And somehow, the fact of war itself seemed to register against that society sufficiently to make him critical of it. In *Nepal Himalaya* he writes:

> Like Tibet, Nepal has always sought isolation and has secured it by excluding
> foreigners, of whom the most undesirable were white men. A man fortunate enough to
> have been admitted into Nepal is expected to be able to explain on general grounds the
> motives behind this invidious policy and, on personal grounds, the reason for such an
> unaccountable exception. But now that the advantages of the Western way of life are
> becoming every day less obvious no explanation should be needed. Wise men
> traditionally come from the East, and it is probable that to them the West and its ways
> were suspect long before we ourselves began to have doubts.

Tilman's interest in, and affection for, the native characters he meets on his travels is everywhere apparent in his writing. In fact, he gives far more attention to characterising his Sherpas, for example, than to fellow Europeans who share his adventures. Even Eric Shipton, probably his closest associate in his explorations, emerges as a shadowy figure by contrast to Tensing, Da Namgyal, Pasang Kikuli, Nukku, Naiad Shah or Mir Hamza. It is worth quoting a recollection by Sherpa Norbu[1] who, at the age of 62, was cook to the Changabang expedition of 1974. Of all his many expeditions, the most memorable to Norbu were those undertaken with Tilman in the thirties:

Tilman was always first away in the morning, carrying a load in excess of the standard Sherpa load. He always arrived first at the day's destination. Sometimes he would run along parts of the route. He would have tea brewing by the time the rest caught up with him and then he would praise those who had made good time, and yell and scream at those he thought had been lazy or lacking in some way. On at least one rest day he made all his Sherpas a cake. Tashi, the Sherpa who was translating all this for me, was made to repeat this fact several times. He was always the first to cross turbulent streams, pass hard rocky sections, and shoulder awkward loads.

Another Sherpa remembers him as 'the strong little sahib who ate the same food as us and carried heavier loads'. Soldiers who served with him have similarly respectful recollections of his toughness and courage. A bombardier from his battery in the Western Desert during the Second World War recalls being told by Tilman to 'Stay 20 paces behind and step exactly where I do' – only realising, when told after a certain distance to relax, that they had been crossing a minefield. Dr John Ross, who was parachuted behind enemy lines in the Dolomites with Tilman, wrote that 'He was a wonderful companion in dangerous situations, and almost worshipped by the partisans and the troops.'

Part of the winning of such respect surely lay in the matter-of-fact, unheroic manner in which he treated danger. If it lay there athwart the path it was merely a problem which one should use one's intelligence to face or circumvent, but it was nothing to raise the emotional tempo about. His attitude to mountaineering also has a cool rationality. For him it is

Not war, but a form of amusement whose saner devotees are not willing to be killed rather than accept defeat.

Indeed, Tilman was less interested in the 'bagging' of a particular peak than in the viewing of new territory. At the beginning of the Nanda Devi expedition he writes that:

I sailed in the hope and expectation that we would be permitted to try Kangchenjunga, mainly because for me it would be new ground.

He doesn't bewail the fact when they are restricted to Nanda Devi, which he had seen two years before, but his preference is left in no doubt – not the conquest, such as it is, but the exploration is his primary stimulus.

Tilman, both through his character and his writings, was in the best sense an educative force in my life. From him I learnt – something I never managed to pick up through six years at universities – that great intelligence can be allied to great humility; that the best courage is quiet and seamed with humour; that what is left unsaid can, to the attentive ear, speak loudly

1 As recorded by Alan Hankinson in *Changabang* (Heinemann, 1975)

enough; that there is a value in moral discipline and perhaps a beneficent God in Heaven, who looks down on such as Tilman and blesses them for their curiosity and gratitude in Creation. As an aside, I remember Tilman once asking me what I was giving up for Lent, which rather flustered me, so I turned the question back at him: 'Oh, I thought of giving up conversation,' he replied, 'but then the dogs might get to feel deprived.'

He was shorter than average in height, and because of back injuries stood ramrod straight. In later years he was a little deaf. His gaze was direct, and his eyes and mouth constantly wrinkled with a gentle inward laughter. He smoked a perpetual pipe, liked his domestic routine to run with clockwork precision – his niece once threw a spoon at his head when he suggested there might be something untoward in dinner's being five minutes late – and enjoyed good food and wine. He was virtually vegetarian, and simple in his tastes. In matters of diet his thinking was in line with most modern medical and nutritional theory, and processed foods give rise to some of the most acid comments in his books. His appetite was at all times healthy:

Without wishing to boast I think the feat of eating a large mugful of pemmican soup at 27,200 ft. performed by Lloyd and myself, is unparalleled in the annals of Himalayan climbing and an example of what can be done by dogged greed.

To him, civilised behaviour precluded the overt expression of emotion, but he nevertheless felt deeply for people, places, histories. He was particularly attached to animals and they to him, whether they were horses, yaks, dogs or cats – especially cats, one of which he adopted in the course of the war in the Western Desert. I once told him of Boswell's meeting with Rousseau, at which the French philosopher had suggested that a love of dogs showed a servile nature, whilst a love of cats was the true sign of a democratic spirit. He roared with laughter at this, and said that his liking for the beasts was so inordinate that I should put him down as a communist.

There was an eccentric mingling of generosity and parsimony about his character, and except when grey with pain from his back, at which times he could be abrupt, he was always even-tempered and considerate of others' feelings in everything he said or did. He was something of a Luddite, and a little out of tune with many mechanical contrivances of the modern world – the tuning of a television was beyond him, and according to his niece he could not understand the knitting of a patterned sweater. For all that, his ability as a surveyor was marked, and his navigational instinct and expertise little short of genius. Of him as a writer I shall have more to say in the appendices. I end here by stating that no-one who met him at first hand was unaffected by the strength, uprightness, and firm purpose of his character. He could inspire extremes of affection or inadequate rage. His books are his fittest memorial, and to this reader at least are the best of their type yet written. It seems apt to borrow for the conclusion of this memoir Boswell's summing-up from *The Life of Johnson* – Tilman's favourite book throughout his life:

. . . a man whose talents, acquirements and virtues, were so extraordinary that the more his character is considered, the more he will be regarded by the present age, and by posterity, with admiration and reverence.

SNOW ON THE EQUATOR

Snow on the Equator

First published by G. Bell and Sons Ltd., 1937

Contents

Contents

CHAPTER ONE

Ten Years' Hard

'"Young soldier, what will you be,
When it's all over?"
"I shall get out and across the sea,
Where land's cheap and a man can thrive."'

— Max Plowman

To those who went to the War straight from school and survived it, the problem of what to do afterwards was peculiarly difficult. A loss of three or four years upset preconceived plans, and while the War was in progress little thought was devoted to such questions. Not that there was no opportunity for thinking, for there was ample time for that during solitary night watches at observation post or gun line; during periods of what was euphemistically called 'resting' behind the lines; or, where most of us went sooner or later, in hospital. No, the reason was because making plans seemed rather a waste of time. Either the War would go on interminably, in which case one was already arranged for, or, in the other alternative, consolation might be found in the philosophy of Feeble, that 'he who dies this year is quit for the next.'

Coming home, then, from the Rhine in April 1919, with what the polite friend might call an 'open' and the candid a blank mind, it was not altogether surprising that in August of the same year I found myself on a cargo-boat bound for East Africa, or B.E.A. as it was then called. My destination was simply accounted for by the fact that I had drawn a farm, or rather a square mile of land, in a lottery for ex-servicemen; and the conveyance, because that seemed to be the quickest way of getting there. And since our destination was believed to be a place where, speaking metaphorically, pearls could be picked up on the beach, it was impossible for one to be on the spot too soon.

When the War had ended there were so many Colonials and others awaiting repatriation, or anxious to begin new jobs abroad, that passages were at a premium. The shipping offices were besieged, and had waiting-lists miles long. One was told dark stories, which I am sure were libellous, of the necessity of bribing the clerks if one's name was to appear in the first few thousands. To avoid this indefinite delay, seven of this impatient horde, including myself, were impetuous enough to pay thirty-five pounds for the privilege of a passage to Mombasa on the S.S. ——. Five of us were quartered in a steel deckhouse on the poop, flanked on either side by a pen of live sheep, and immediately below was the lascar crew's galley, whence the fumes of cooking never ceased rising. At all seasons of the year the striking thing about the Red Sea, and one that is taken for granted, is the heat, but in August, and in a steel deckhouse with no fans, even Shadrach, Meshach, and Abed-nego might have remarked on it.

British East Africa – Kenya as it now is – occupies a central position on the east coast of Africa astride the equator. It has undergone many changes since starting life as a chartered company, becoming first a Protectorate and then a Colony, and as such assuming the name it now bears. Its neighbours, too, have changed. It marches on the south what was formerly German East Africa and is now British Mandated Territory of Tanganyika, while on the north it is now bounded by Italian territory instead of Abyssinian. West is Uganda, which still stands where it did, and on the east is the sea, one of the few unchanging things left in a changing world.

In the closing years of last century British interests in East Africa, represented mainly by missionaries and the Chartered Company of British East Africa, were centered in Uganda. In 1893 the Imperial Government took over from the company, and the favourable reports of administrators like Lugard and Portal, the pressure of missionary influence at home, and fear of French designs in the Sudan, combined to bring about the construction of the Uganda railway from Mombasa on the coast to Kisumu on the eastern shore of Lake Victoria. An East African Protectorate was declared in 1902, and the healthy, fertile uplands lying beyond the arid coastal belt, which the railway had now reached, began to attract the attention of a few enterprising pioneers. The higher and better parts were uninhabited except for the nomadic Masai, who so dominated the country that the other tribes, for peace's sake, confined themselves to the forest and bush. Grants of land in the Highlands, as they were called, were made to individuals and companies (a small matter of five hundred square miles to one of the last), and there was some talk of making the Highlands a Jewish National Home – Palestine not being available at that time. By 1914 there were a few hundred settlers, mostly engaged in cattle farming and coffee growing, and Nairobi was already a place of some importance as the capital of the Protectorate.

Prior to the War, Nairobi had some notoriety on account of occasional ebullitions of high feeling on the part of the settlers against the too fatherly attitude of the Government. After the War it was notorious for another reason. Lurid stories were told of the guile and rapacity of those who lay in wait in the Nairobi bars to separate the new settler from his capital, so that the innocent and fearful, like myself, hardly dared to have a drink, kept both hands in their pockets, and passed through the town as quickly as possible. So it came about that in October (the voyage having lasted for six weeks) I was viewing from the top of a tree the square mile of land which was to be my home for the next ten years. This unusual method of inspection was adopted because heavy bush, through which there were no paths, for there were no inhabitants, prevented access to it; and from a tree on a neighbouring ridge a much better notion of its features and possibilities could be got than by submerging oneself in a sea of bush and fighting a way across.

I knew nothing about land, and less about farming it, but the climate of this district was said to be good both from a coffee-growing and a health standpoint. I could see for myself that the land was watered by several

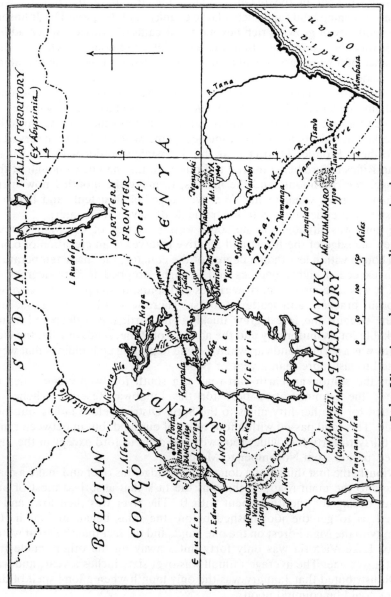

Lake Victoria and surrounding territories

streams and one large river, while the growth of forest and bush on it clearly indicated that the soil was good. True, it was in the back blocks fifty miles from the railway, a journey of three or four days for ox-wagons, which were then the only means of transport; no Europeans had grown anything there before, and the clearing of the land would be an expensive business; but all that weighed light in the balance against the ardour of the pioneer, the thought of owning land (and such a large chunk), and, to quote Dr. Johnson, 'the potentiality of growing rich beyond the dreams of avarice.' When added to this was the knowledge that the financial conditions attached to the acceptance of it were easy, it will be understood that I was not long in making up my mind.

Another settler who had arrived here in August was in occupation of some land about one and a half miles from where I proposed to make my home. B. was a newcomer to the district and to farming, but not the B.E.A., since he had worked in Nairobi for a short time before the War. He had then served in the Northern Frontier District near the Abyssinian border with the King's African Rifles before being moved to France, so that he knew enough of the language, the conditions, and the natives, to make the month I now spent with him of great value to me. We lived together in a tent, and began a friendship that ended only with his tragic death seven years later.

The land was situated on the south-western slopes of the Mau Forest, between the edge of the forest and a native reserve, at an elevation of 6,500 feet. Though within less than a degree of the equator, the shade temperature seldom exceeded eighty degrees and at night dropped to fifty degrees or lower. It was a country of narrow ridges and spurs, of steep valleys, covered with bush, bracken, and scattered forest. There was little or no grass, and near the streams the forest grew thickly. The earth was a deep red loam, remarkable for its uniformity and the absence of stone, sand, or clay, the lack of which was a severe handicap when it came to putting up buildings that were expected to last more than a year or two.

From the station an earth cart-road ran south for twenty-one miles to Kericho, the administrative post for the Lumbwa Reserve, whence it continued for another fifty miles to the Sotik District before fading out into the blue. This road passed within four miles of our land, but in between ran a river, thirty to forty feet wide, too swift and deep to ford except in the 'dry weather' period from November to March.

Obviously the first thing to be done was to bridge this river and make a road of access to the main road, so this was the task that absorbed most of our energies during the month I spent with B. The river was then low, and it behoved us to get the job finished before the rains began in March. Its proximity to the Mau Forest on the one hand, and the fact that the great water mass of Lake Victoria was only forty miles away on the other, made the district a wet one. The average rainfall was over sixty inches a year, and was so well distributed that January was the only month when a long spell of dry weather could be counted upon.

We built a fearsome structure of four spans of twelve feet, carried on clumsy but solid wooden piers. Single logs were tied together with iron dog-spikes, and the whole pier coiled round with barbed wire in much the same way as the drunken 'Brugglesmith' bound himself to his stretcher as he gyrated down the street pulling the bell-wire after him. Barbed wire is more conveniently used for fencing than for lashing bridge piers. Large quantities had been used recently for the long and elaborate fences stretching from Switzerland to the sea, but, the demand for wire for this purpose having fortunately ceased, miles of it could now be bought for an old song, and that, of course, was our sole reason for using it. We found it just as intractable and spiteful to handle here as it had been in France.

The steep river-banks were heavily wooded, so that timber for the bridge was plentiful, but we had to rely entirely upon the natives for expert knowledge about the suitability of different types of tree. Much bitter experience was needed before we acquired this very necessary knowledge ourselves, and, meanwhile, for any building operations of ours, the natives naturally selected trees with an eye to their proximity, or the ease with which they could be felled, rather than for their powers of resistance to water or white ants. So that this first bridge of ours lasted only for a year, and most of our earlier huts and sheds were devoured standing by the all-pervading termite. Until we built a steel and concrete bridge over a similar river bounding the property on the other side, communications were always liable to interruption. The fate of every cart that left, or was due to return, was a source of anxious speculation until we knew whether it was across the bridge or in the river, while during every spell of wet weather and the accompanying spate in the river it was the usual thing to walk down to the bridge of an evening to see if it was still there.

Feeling a slightly less vivid shade of green after my month with B., I returned to Nairobi, and a week later started again for what I now liked to call my estate, taking with me an assortment of carts, ploughs, harrows, tools, household gear, and food. Having hired some oxen and their drivers at the station, the two light carts (army transport carts ex-German East) were loaded up, the oxen inspanned, and B.'s place reached four days later. The bridge was not quite finished, but it was solid enough for B. to cut the silk ribbon, as it were, and declare the bridge open. The carts crossed in triumph at the run, with the oxen, encouraged by fierce cries and whip-flourishing from the drivers, leaning hard against each other and away from the rushing water.

Word was now passed round by B.'s boys that another white man wanted labour, and soon I had a small gang at work clearing a track through the mile and a half of bush to my future home. I took up my residence in a tent on the highest land of all, and started the gang, which had now increased to fifty, cutting the bush on a long, gently sloping hillside where I proposed turning the first furrow. Other boys began training oxen to make up the necessary teams, and this was a process which forcibly suggested to the inexperienced onlooker a bloodless bull-fight. Unless one was both callous and nimble it was advisable to be busy elsewhere while this was in progress. A good deal of beating and tail-twisting was necessary to produce results, for an ox has a very effective trick of lying down and remaining down when asked to do anything unusual. Before things got to that stage, even before the animal had been captured and yoked, there woud be many fierce rushes which put the fear of death into the clothed, booted, and clumsy white man, but only amused the naked and agile Lumbwa.

Meantime, accompanied by one or two boys armed with 'pangas', or machetes, to clear a way, I began to find out how my land lay, and soon discovered that there were more eligible sites for a house than where the tent was now pitched. A sheltered position, room for a garden, a view, and water near at hand, were the essentials, and there was more than one place where all these could be had. As I grudged spending time or money on a house while the more important work of development remained to be done, the house was to be only a mud and wattle affair, so that no great harm would be done if it turned out to be in the wrong place. Two, in fact, were built in different places before I was satisfied I had found the best, and before I began to build, many years later, something more substantial.

The first had all the stern virtue of simplicity – a single square room without doors or windows. That is to say, there were two apertures, a larger one for the door and a smaller one for the window, but nothing that needed opening or shutting. A small veranda was cunningly built on in front, where in the daytime I fed, because the living-room was too dark. It was fitted with a chair and table by the simple expedient of driving into the ground four stakes which supported small straight sticks. The floor was of earth, of which one advantage was that you could light a fire on it, or, when I had reached a more advanced stage of civilisation and could spare the tin, a brazier. Close as we were to the equator, the altitude made the nights cool enough for a fire to be welcome all the year round.

There were, however, one or two drawbacks to an earth floor. Bracken and creepers grew up through it as if they were being 'forced', and had to be cut down frequently; it became dry and dusty, so that the boy sweeping it with an improvised bracken broom lowered it by several inches a month. (It was not wise to tell him to be less vigorous, or the floor might not have been swept at all.) Moreover, it held a great attraction for the hens, who liked coming in to scratch holes in which they could enjoy a dust bath and lay eggs. Encouraged by these ideal conditions, the jigger flea made its appearance. This is a very small insect which burrows under toe-nails and finger-nails, where it is only discovered by the intense irritation it sets up. It has then to be extracted by digging round it with a needle, an operation which is only complete when the whole insect, with its newly formed egg-sac, has been removed. Houseboys, hens, and dogs are the main sources of flea-infection, but in this district the jigger did not seem to find conditions very congenial. A liberal sprinkling of the earth floor with some disinfectant like Jeyes' (which the boys called 'cheese') , or even water, kept them in check, while with a wood floor they were practically unknown. The jigger, or chegoe, is indigenous to South America, and is supposed to have been brought over to the west coast of Africa in the sand ballast of a ship early in the last century. From there, within a short time, it spread across Africa to the east coast.

Of the plagues and pests usually associated with the tropics we were singularly free; at least, of those which annoy man; but with crops and livestock it was quite another matter. Mosquitoes were rare, while those few we had were not infected with malaria. It was too cold for scorpions. Hornets and snakes were only occasional visitors. I remember killing a puff adder in the garden, and nearly being killed by a bright green snake sitting in a coffee-bush which I had just started to prune; and many years later, after the petrol age had dawned, I found a puff adder enjoying the lingering warmth on the cylinder head of a car when I opened the bonnet in the morning. But the number seen or killed on the farm annually could be counted on one hand, and, though the natives were mortally afraid of snakes, even dead ones, I never heard of anyone, European or native, being bitten.

The white ant was always with us, but it, fortunately, is not carnivorous, and feeds exclusively on any wood stuck in the ground or in contact with the ground. It never comes to the surface, so that the posts, the rafters, and even the thatch of a house, can be honeycombed with ants without any visible sign of their activities except a few bits of earth, like wormcasts, on the outside of the wood. Certain woods – cedar, for instance – they will not touch, but most posts have to be sunk in concrete. Nor is the wood of a roof or ceiling resting on a brick wall safe, for the ants find a way up to it through the wall between the bricks. The worker termites, which do all the damage, are white, and cannot stand the light of day, hence the earth which they stick on the outside of a post to keep their runs dark.

More ferocious are the black soldier or safari ants, and the red, tree ants, which attack anything living that comes in their way, but an occasional visit from safari ants is not without benefit to a grass hut, to which they give a very thorough spring cleaning. The roof of a grass hut and the mud walls harbour an astonishing variety of insects, of which the least revolting are the spiders and the most obscene a great, fat, white slug. None of these obtrude on one if left alone, and the only indications of their presence are mysterious rustling noises at night, a slight but constant shower of sawdust sent down by the borer beetles, bits of grass dislodged by some restless slug, and occasionally the arrival of some kind of insect in person on the bed or in the soup. But that unpleasantness can be avoided by using a ceiling-cloth or sleeping under a mosquito net, while the safari ants can be relied upon to clear the whole lot out periodically.

If their visit takes place in the daytime, little inconvenience is caused, for one simply vacates the house and waits until they have cleaned up the livestock. The houseboy may make futile attempts to deflect their line of march with barriers of hot embers, but if the army is in strength this is a useless expedient. A few hours after taking possession they will have devoured every live and dead insect in the hut and passed on their way.

At night it is a different matter. The first indication of trouble is an intensification of the rustling sounds in the roof, but this warning may go unheeded and, presently, if not under a net, one is awakened by a sharp stab in the arm or some more sensitive spot, or by one of the fat slugs, smothered with ants, dropping from the roof on to one's face. You must then 'stand not upon the order of your going,' but make a dive for the door, picking up several hundred ants off the floor *en route*, and, when well clear of the marauding host and its far-flung scouts, tear off your pyjamas and proceed to pull off the numerous ants which have now got their fangs well buried in all the most inaccessible parts of your body. If you have had time to rescue some blankets and a camp-bed, all is well, for on several occasions I have been thus driven out and spent the rest of the night bedded down in a store or tool-shed.

Bats were another source of disturbed nights. Three or four might find their way into the room at the same time, where they seemed to delight in brushing past one's face as close as possible. The thought of being touched by their clammy wings and mouse-like, flea-ridden bodies was revolting, and I found it impossible to sleep so long as one remained fluttering about. I used to light the lamp and lie in bed holding a ·22 rifle, to pot them off one by one whenever they settled and hung head downwards from a beam, as sooner or later they did. A quicker and more sporting method was to bag them flying with a tennis racquet.

While on the subject of pests, one of a more serious, widespread, and devastating kind, amounting, in fact, to a plague, should not escape notice. This was the invasion of Kenya and neighbouring East African territories by the desert locust, which began in 1928 and continued for three or four years. The southern deserts of the distant Sudan were their source of origin, but once a swarm is allowed to lay eggs and hatch out it multiplies itself in a way which defies arithmetic. So serious was the destruction of food crops, both native and European, that at one period the export of foodstuffs was forbidden for fear of famine. It was no uncommon thing to see a swarm take a whole day to pass overhead, veiling the sun as it went, or for a swarm to settle and strip two or three hundred acres of maize or wheat in a very short time. Coffee was about the only green stuff they appeared not to eat, but they did almost as much damage by settling on it and breaking the branches with their weight. There were stories of their eating even the thatch of a roof, one man, it was said, having his roof eaten over his head while he was in his bath. But perhaps such stories were apocryphal.

My second dwelling was a more elaborate affair, built on another site, and finished not a moment too soon, for the old hut collapsed the day I moved into the new one. This house was another wattle and daub structure, but it consisted of two big six-sided huts connected by a veranda, open to the front. It had a fireplace of sun-dried bricks, and a wood floor made from planks cut by the small circular saw which was now in use at B.'s place. (B., who had worked at a saw-mill, got a lot of fun out of slicing up big logs. His main trouble was to prevent boys putting their hands on it to see if it was going round.) From the house I could command a view of the whole planted area of the farm, but, in spite of this encouragement to do so, I did not adopt the practice of 'farming from the veranda,' a common East African failing. Across the valley of the Itare River one looked over the green, broken, but uninteresting country of the Lumbwa Reserve, and beyond to the low wall of the Kisii Hills bounding the western horizon, hills which were washed to a deep indigo after the storms which broke on them had passed away.

The reason for the dullness of the view across the Reserve was, I think, a complete absence of trees; a common feature, sooner or later, of all native

Reserves. It is brought about by their system of cultivation and their goats. Each family will clear an acre, or half an acre, of new land every season for their crop of maize or wimbi (a small millet), while the innumerable goats see to it that no seedling trees survive to replace those thus annually destroyed. In the more populated parts of the Reserve it was a source of wonder as to where the natives collected enough sticks for fuel, and for the light fencing which they put round the fields to keep out the ubiquitous goat. As these goats produce neither milk nor hair, and as they are used for food only on the occasion of certain festivals, they are in themselves almost valueless. Their chief function is to figure as a form of currency in such transactions as the purchase of wives or cattle, in the payment of fines, or in the feeing of the witch-doctor. The destruction of trees, of course, encourages 'wash', denudes the soil of humus, and may even affect the rainfall. The evil is obvious, and, though something is being done to repair the damage by encouraging tree-planting, the root of the evil is difficult to remove without considerably altering the native's mode of living.

The most attractive part of the view, at any rate to me, was in course of time, the neat parallel rows of alternating coffee-bushes and shade-trees stretching away from below the house for half a mile. Most pleasing of all was it when in blossom, with the white flowers set off against the rich dark green of the leaves, or, six months later, when promise had come to fruition, and the bright red cherry-like berries weighed down the branches. It sounds magnificent and it looked magnificent, but in later years it became an increasingly infrequent sight. Hail might knock off all the flower, or even prevent the trees flowering; the flowers when formed acquired an unfortunate habit of not 'setting'; and, if the fruit did appear, it presently acquired a nasty way of turning black and dropping off long before it had reached the cherry-ripe stage. In the six, seven, or even eight months between flower and harvest there was so much that might happen, and so much that did.

During our first few years most of our energy and capital were devoted to the growing of flax. This commodity was fetching a very high price at the end of the War, and for the first year or two after it. Our mouths watered when we heard of one lot of Kenya flax which sold for £400 a ton, and calculations of profit based on a price of £200 a ton seemed fair, and were undoubtedly attractive. When estimating profits, it should be a safe rule to halve the probable returns and double the estimated expenses, but we were to find that even then two and two sometimes made three.

Eager to take advantage of the high price, we worked feverishly to clear, stump, plough, and sow as many acres as possible. My first year I got in fifty acres, while in succeeding years the acreage sown to flax, if not always reaped, was near a hundred. The snag about flax-growing is that, though the growing of it is fairly simple, the harvesting is not the end of one's troubles, but only the beginning. The ripe stalks have all to be pulled up by the roots by hand, dried on the field in stooks, and stored in a barn. When the weather is favourable – that is, not too much sun and not too much rain – it is taken out and spread thinly and evenly, almost stalk by stalk, on grass, to undergo what is called 'dew-retting'. This process takes ten to fourteen days, according to the weather, during which time it has to be turned frequently. If there is too much rain it goes mouldy, while too much sun weakens the fibre. After that it is stooked again, tied in bundles, and once more stored in a barn until it can be scutched. With ten or fifteen acres of ground covered with retted flax, ready to carry, the awaiting of the necessary dry day in the middle of a wet spell was a most wearing business for the poor farmer, when every day longer that it remained out meant a serious deterioration in quality and loss in value.

For the scutching, machinery is needed, and it was nearly three years after I started that the first flax was scutched at B.'s and shipped home to England. During this time we had watched the market for flax drop first to £200 and then to £100 at which figure my first lot was sold. Then the rot set in, and before another year was out we were receiving only £50 a ton, a lower price than we had previously obtained for our tow, a by-product of the scutching process. A few farmers in Kenya were ruined by flax, and most lost money by it; especially those who, like my neighbours B. and his partner, had put money into flax machinery. I was fortunate myself, but unless the machinery had been put up it would not have been any use growing flax.

However, even from the beginning, neither my neighbours nor myself had banked entirely on flax, because there were several factors besides the fickleness of the market and the vagaries of the weather which made it an uneconomic crop for us. The yield was low (about half that which is obtained in Europe), a tropical sun weakened the fibre and made it a poorer quality, and we found that it was impossible to crop the same land more than twice. This meant that, to maintain the acreage, fresh land had to be cleared and broken every year, adding greatly to the cost of production; and, apart from that, it was an immoral proceeding in that it partook more of mining the land than farming it, taking good out of it and putting nothing back – exactly what the natives were doing in their Reserve on the other side of the river.

Coffee was the alternative crop, and, after the first year, twenty or thirty acres were planned annually, so that, when flax was finally dropped, five years later, there was a substantial acreage of coffee, the oldest of which was just coming into bearing. Entitled now to call myself a planter, which sounds so much more dashing than farmer, I felt that a mud and grass hut was hardly worthy of my new status. The planter's bungalow of the novelist is generally spacious, if not luxurious. Even the assistant manager's bungalow is 'trim', and, in both, servants in spotless white hover silently at their master's elbow. Only planters who have lost their job through drink or women, and have very nearly 'gone native', are allowed to live in grass huts, and to have their gin poured out by a boy attired in a blanket.

So I began my third and last house. It was built of burnt bricks made on the spot, roofed with corrugated iron, and possessed the usual amenities – a floor, a ceiling, doors, glass windows, cupboards, and, not least, a fireplace and a brick chimney. When it was completed with living-room, two bedrooms, veranda, and built-in kitchen, so astonished and impressed were the houseboy and the cook that they demanded a rise in wages and a uniform.

The method of construction was original. I put the roof up first on poles, and then, when the walls were built, taking the poles away, I lowered the roof on to the wall-plate. The reason for this was that the bricks of the inside walls were only sun-dried and not burnt, and so the walls had to be protected from rain as they were built, while in the first place the roof had to serve as a covering for the kiln in which the bricks were burnt. The new house, and therefore the brick-kiln, was sited immediately behind the old one; so close that I had to sit up throughout one night to see that the red-hot wall of the kiln did not set fire to the grass roof of the old house in which I was still living.

Had it caught fire, I might have said with some truth that the new house rose phoenix-like from the ashes of the old. Nevertheless, something of the sort did take place, because when all was ready the old house was abolished almost as rapidly as the felling of a chimney, and there the neat, but not too spacious, bungalow of the novelists stood revealed in all its glory.

The house and my faith in its solidity were severely tested shortly after I moved in. The whole Colony was put into a state of alarm by a severe earth tremor – a mild earthquake, in fact – which at one place opened cracks in the earth and brought down dwellings. The effect was less violent in our district, but sufficiently frightening. It happened in the early hours of the morning, when I was awakened by a sort of roar, rather like that of an approaching train. At this ominous prelude dogs barked, cocks crowed, cattle lowed, and then the bed began to shake violently. For what seemed like a minute, but what was probably only a few seconds, I lay in bed wondering what would happen next. Then there was a loud crash, and I streaked for the open spaces, while the roar receded in the distance. That was the finish of it, and after a decent interval of time, when confidence was restored, I returned to the house to find an inch crack opened in the upper half of the wall over my bed, and a big rhino horn, whose proper place was on the wall, now on the floor. The fall of that had made the crash which lent wings to my flight.

At the end of one year in my new house, and ten on the farm, I sold out. Many were the changes that had taken place in that time. New settlers had come, old ones had gone. In a small community such as ours, births, marriages, and deaths become almost family affairs. Communications had improved greatly, particularly with the station, the negotiation of which road had interested us perhaps more than anything else. The motor-car and the lorry were now the normal form of transport, and the ox-wagon almost an anachronism. The road had been widened, re-graded, drained, but it was still unmetalled, so that a prolonged wet spell soon gave rise to quagmires from which, if entered, it was impossible to escape. Chains for the wheels were a *sine qua non* on any journey, no matter how fine the weather appeared, while in wet weather shovels, pangas, planks, old sacks, rabbit-netting, or even a block and tackle, were all items of equipment that would be carried by the prudent driver. I remember on one occasion, through neglect of some such precaution, having to put my waterproof under a spinning back wheel for want of anything handy to make it grip. That was the last service it rendered.

For those ten years, except for an annual shooting excursion and one brief visit to England, I had kept my nose to the grindstone. I saw no one else except at week-ends, so that, in spite of the efforts of kind neighbours, there was some danger of my becoming as mossy and as difficult to uproot as some of the bigger trees which had taken us days to stump; of developing into the sort of person who in another planting community is called a 'hill-topper'; a man who had lived by himself for so long that he dreads meeting anyone, and therefore builds his house on the top of some hill, so as to have timely warning of the approach of visitors to escape into the safety of the neighbouring bush.

Another impelling motive for change of scene was that the daily routine of attending to planted coffee was much less congenial to me than the earlier struggle to carve a home out of the forest and to tame the wilderness; to watch the landscape – a waste of bush and jungle, but a familiar one – change daily under one's eyes; to see a new clearing here, a shed there, paths and roads pushing out in all directions, while seeds, which one had oneself planted, grew into big trees big enough to make timber.

I already had some land in the Sotik, thirty miles further from the railway, where this absorbing task could be tackled afresh; where with a newly acquired partner there would be no danger of becoming enslaved by the farm. If either wanted a holiday, it could be taken; all that was needed between the two of us was the sort of understanding that John Jorrocks had with his huntsman, James Pigg, to wit, 'that master and man should not both get drunk on the same day.'

CHAPTER TWO

Buffaloes – and False Teeth

'For now I am in a holiday humour.' – Shakespeare

It has been hinted that during this first ten years the treadmill on occasion ceased to revolve, and a number of brief excursions were made. By way of comparison, it will be interesting to recall some of these before going on to tell of the more distant tours which I was able to make as a result of the excellent arrangement come to between my partner and myself, as narrated at the end of the last chapter.

Possibly the most urgent desire of the newcomer to a country of big game is to go out and kill something. Fortunately for most, this unsporting blood-lust is soon satiated. The pursuit may be abandoned altogether, or reserved solely for dangerous game, which is a less one-sided affair, or perhaps forsaken for hunting with the camera. One of the many compensations for living in East Africa, if any are needed, is the facility for indulging these desires. I refer particularly to the low cost, for if, on these trips of three or four weeks which we made, we spent £5 over and above the cost of a shooting licence (£10), we thought it an expensive holiday. At the other end of the scale is the visitor, whose licence cost him £100, who may spend up to £100 a month while out on safari, and who, having collected a number of trophies, will be faced by a thumping bill for the mounting of them.

As a newcomer to B.E.A. I was no exception. I was bent on slaughter, and read with avidity every book on hunting that I could lay my hands on; Neuman, Selour, Stigand, and Bell were my mentors. Neuman, who from his skill with the rifle was called by his boys 'Risasi moja' (one cartridge) or 'Nyama jango' (my meat); Selous, who was not only a mighty hunter, but naturalist, pioneer, and soldier, meeting a soldier's death in German East when he was over sixty; Stigand, soldier too, and administrator, who was always careful to insist on the difference between 'hunting' and 'shooting' – the one in which wits, skill, and endurance are needed to track down and bring to bag the quarry in thick bush or forest, while for the other, which can only be done on the open plains, skill with the rifle is the sole requisite. And lastly Bell – 'Karamoja Bell,' Karamoja being the name of his stamping-ground in Eastern Uganda – who used to kill his elephants with a .266 rifle, a very small bore, at times standing on something resembling a surveyor's plane-table to enable him to see over the long grass into which he had followed them.

On the farm there was no outlet for this pent-up desire, for there was little game except wild pig and bush buck, while the growth was too dense to allow any chance of shooting these. I think, in all the years spent there, the total bag was a leopard, a serval cat, and a wild pig. The leopard was tracked down, surrounded, and despatched (when he broke) by several hundred natives armed with spear and shield, at the cost of a badly torn scalp. B. and I were present, armed to the teeth, but were not called upon to do anything bold except to put back the scalp and sew it up. Our antiseptic methods were not thought much of, and our dressing was replaced by one of cow-dung, which was equally, possibly more, effective.

The pig was run down and bayed by a dog of mine, and finally killed by natives with spears, after the dog had received several deep gashes. I was again in attendance, but was not present at the death, as the pace was far too hot, even had I not been encumbered with a rifle, which hooked itself on to every branch and creeper in sight. The serval cat did fall a victim to my prowess, but even that was not unaided, for it was shot at night sitting in a tree, having been chivvied there by the same dog. The serval cat is a handsome spotted beast much bigger than a cat, though this particular one was black and was an unusual example of melanism.

Living alone on a farm in its early stages of development allowed of few holidays. On a farm 'the master's eye is worth a cartload of dung,' but preaching the gospel of hard work to fifty or more natives day after day was an uphill task, and the time soon arrived when the sight of a boy turned one's stomach. Very likely my presence had the same effect on them, and it was then time to go away for a few days.

The nearest hunting-ground was the Mau Forest, the home of bush buck, elephant, buffalo, the rarely seen bongo, and the giant forest hog. It was only three days' march away, and the difficulties of the ground, the wariness of the game, and the wetness of the climate, made it a place where anything that was bagged was fully earned. Needless to say, little was bagged; all that I can claim in some half-dozen visits are three bush buck. But it was a fascinating place, possessing all the attractiveness of the unknown. It was unsurveyed, and its innermost recesses were known only to a few Wanderobo – thought by some to be the aboriginal inhabitants of the country – though many of the Wanderobo are now natives who have left their own tribes to live in the forest to be free from the restraints of tribal customs. They depend for food on seeds, roots, wild honey, and whatever they can snare or kill.

One might walk, or rather crawl, quietly and stealthily through bamboo thickets, beds of giant nettles, and dripping undergrowth, or perhaps follow warily the broad track stamped out by an elephant, from dawn to dark, seeing no living thing, and hearing nothing but the distant chatter of a monkey or the cry of a hornbill. Another time, a bongo might offer a chance too fleeting to take, or a herd of buffalo would stampeed with a fearful crash while one crouched, rooted to the spot, in a tangle of bush too thick to see through; or one followed all day a herd of elephant, looking for the shootable bull which was not there. It is a curious thing that, though elephants were hardly ever shot in the Mau, where, in consequence, shootable bulls should have been numerous, I never saw even so much as the spoor of anything but cows and immature bulls. The local Lumbwa had a story of some fabulous monster of a bull elephant which roamed the Mau, whose tusks were so long and heavy that he was unable to raise them clear of the ground, but they were never able to show me the tracks, surely unmistakable, of this father of all elephants. The natives of most districts where there are elephants have similar tales to tell.

The forest had a great attraction for the Lumbwa, the local natives, who are not merely drawers of water and hewers of wood, but who are fully endowed with the instincts of the hunter and the warrior. The leopard incident was typical of them, and in the spacious days of raid and counter-raid they are said to have given even the Masai as good as they got. They enjoyed exercising their skill as trackers; they found roots and barks, valuable as medicines, which could be obtained only in the Mau; there were choice bamboos for making bows and quivers; and lastly there was always the chance, however remote, of meat.

And so for trips to the forest they were useful allies, except for an ineradicable prejudice against the carrying of loads. Most African natives – that is, all except the pastoral tribes – will carry a load of 50lbs or 60lbs. on their heads and make no bones about it. But the Lumbwa, although agriculturists, are at heart aristocratic stockowners, and refuse to burden themselves with loads. As a favour they will carry up to 20lbs., but even this must be carried under the arm or on the shoulder as though it were merely a parcel. Their women, perforce, will carry enormous loads, but the men of the tribe are warriors and will not so far demean themselves. Indeed, I think had it been to a place less attractive to them than the forest, or to anywhere where they might have been seen by the men of some other tribe, they would not have consented to carry even 20lbs.

The forest then was handy, and offered great rewards, but in it the shooting, or rather hunting, was of the sort that would only appeal to the experienced connoisseur, to whom the difficulties to be overcome are more important that the prize. For more fun and less work, for seeing game in vast numbers, for plenty of meat, for hides to make into 'reims'[1] and yoke-strops, and for the chance of a lion, we had to go further afield. What we termed loosely 'The Plains' was only a small portion of a vast area stretching for hundreds of miles along the Kenya-Tanganyika border. It is the home of the wandering Masai, with their hundreds of thousands of head of cattle; it carries, perhaps, more game to the square mile than anywhere else in the world, so that undoubtedly it is the place for the man who wants to 'shoot' rather than 'hunt'. More interesting by far, and where, after one trip to the Plains, we always went, was the country lying between the Kisii Hills and the beginning of the Plains proper – broken bush country, where the game was less numerous and more difficult to get, but where the possibilities of surprise lurked behind every bush and in every donga.

The Plains had the advantage of being easily reached and easily traversed. There we could take a light cart pulled by six oxen in charge of a couple of boys, and wander anywhere at will. It was possible to travel with a cart in the bush country, but movement was restricted to where the cart could go, and, if the best ground was to be reached, porters had to be taken as well – an unfortunate necessity this, because they had to be fed, which task of feeding them was an ever-present threat to our peace of mind. We carried some maize meal for them, but relied largely upon supplementing it with meat; and how the beggars grumbled if large and fequent supplies of it were not forthcoming, and how we hated the job of getting it!

Shooting while on the march, however favourable the opportunity, is not advisable, because it means generally that the march comes to a sudden end, the porters insisting on camping at the kill. Having reached our destination, therefore, one of us, attended by the hungry horde, would have to go out and shoot something. A moderate shot at all times, I found that, when followed by an expectant crowd, the little proficiency I had was sadly impaired. It was rather like a nervous and unskilful golfer driving off in front of a critical swarm of caddies, but there the audience are entirely disinterested as to the result of the shot, while here the case was far otherwise. It was not really vital whether our men stuffed themselves with meat or not, though it did keep them in good heart and enabled them to do long marches, but anxiety to get the job over, and, perhaps, to impress them with the deadliness of the white man's rifle, commonly resulted in some very poor shooting. I had a fellow-feeling for prehistoric man, whose life, with that of his family, depended on his hunting prowess. It must have been a wearing, hand-to-mouth existence, though, no doubt, the hard alternative of success or starvation, kill or die, would have a remarkably beneficial effect on one's abilities. 'Depend upon it, Sir, when a man knows he is to be hanged, it concentrates his mind wonderfully,' was the opinion of Dr. Johnson.

If the presence of these expectant mouths waiting to be filled had no good effect upon myself, the effect it had upon our quarry was positively bad. The porters we took on these longer excursions were not natural hunters like the Lumbwa, but men of the Kavirondo tribe, who more than fulfil the popular

1 Rawhide thongs.

notion of what an African should be. Jet black, muscular, with squash nose and full lips, clumsy, cheerful, and noisy – all flashing teeth and loud-voiced talk. They had no idea of moving quietly or of making themselves inconspicuous. They would maintain a running commentary in their quiet conversational tone – that is to say, much louder than I could shout – and would gesticulate wildly with both arms to draw my attention to some buck long after I had seen it myself.

Under such conditions a stalk was out of the question, and the shot had to be taken at much longer range than is desirable for clean shooting. The buck, whatever it was, or zebra, if hit, was probably not killed, and would only be brought to bag after a long chase lasting possibly till dark accompanied by a fusillade of shots that disturbed all the game for miles around. Such experiences, the antithesis of good sport, disgusted by their clumsiness and cruelty, but the porters cared nothing about that so long as they got their meat. Great was the rejoicing when this was assured, and the man who grumbled loudly at carrying 50lbs. along a good path in broad daylight, would stumble home in the dark under a load of 80lbs. of meat with the best will in the world.

While one of us was performing this unpleasant duty, the other was free to take a quiet stroll with a shot-gun to spy out the land, to look for the fresh spoor of some larger game, or to pick up some unconsidered trifle for our own table. Most of the buck, and even zebra, are good eating, while for the porters size is the criterion, not quality; but for ourselves we preferred a tasty guinea-fowl or pigeon, or the delicious meat of one of the smaller antelopes like duiker, dik-dik, or reedbuck.

We were not always thinking of our own stomachs, or even those of the porters, to the exclusion of everything else, as the foregoing might seem to imply. On our first safari to the bush country our ambitious hopes were fixed upon elephant. At that time the cost of a licence was less than it is at present, and the value of the ivory more, so that the one balanced the other, while an elephant with good tusks more than paid expenses. The restrictions, however, with which a licence to shoot an elephant was hedged about were so many that, when we came into close contact with our first herd, we were more worried by the legal aspects than by the elephants. No cow elephant could be shot, and only those bulls carrying tusks of over 30lbs. weight each, while the penalty for infringing these conditions was the forfeiture of the ivory and the licence.

We followed the fresh tracks of a small herd, eventually coming up with them in long, ten to twelve feet high grass – elephant grass, as it is called. Dotted here and there were flat-topped thorn-trees, from the top of which we had our only chance of seeing our quarry. Even from that vantage-point only the tops of their heads and great backs showed above the sea of grass like a whale breaking the surface. To our inexperienced eyes it was difficult enough to tell cows from bulls, much more so to judge the ivory, whose presence was only betrayed by an occasional gleam of white.

What with fear of the elephants and fear of the Game Laws, we suffered a deal of nervous wear and tear while we barged about submerged in the grass sea or watched expectantly from the branch of some thorn-tree, bitten the while by ferocious tree ants. How we avoided blundering into or being charged by some peevish cow, or, through sheer nervousness, shooting some undersized beast, remains to me a mystery. In the end we had to give it up without ever having had a view sufficiently clear to justify a shot.

Plodding despondently homewards, as we won clear of the long grass, we were astonished by the sight of a few stragglers evidently on the way to join the herd. They were moving slowly up the opposite bank of a small stream, and, with respect for the Game Laws still uppermost in our minds, we took up a post of observation some fifty yards from where they would pass. It was fascinating to watch them gliding along so quietly and majestically; to see one pause, put up his trunk to wrench off a great branch from some overhanging tree, strip off and stow away pieces of bark and leaves, drop the pealed branch, and move on again. Then a cow would pass, shepherding her calf in front of her with none too playful taps of her trunk.

There was nothing of outstanding size amongst them, but an obvious bull came to a stand right opposite us, broadside on, offering a perfect target. 'We do it wrong, being so majestical; to offer it the show of violence,' was certainly how we felt about it, but he seemed warrantable, and I had with me a new heavy rifle which I was itching to try on something worthy of its weight. One shot between eye and ear dropped him stone dead, leaving us aghast at the suddenness of it and feeling like murderers with an 'outsize' corpse on our hands. Now that the irrevocable deed was done we were less confident that the ivory was up to the required standard.

The disposal of the body was taken out of our hands by the porters and other natives, men, women, and children, armed with knives, and baskets for the spoil, who seemed to drop out of the sky like so many vultures, possessing, like them, the same uncanny instinct for a corpse. There and then they lit fires and signified their intention of camping on the spot until the meat was finished. Elephant meat is held in high esteem by most natives, who have a belief that by eating it in sufficient quantity they will acquire something of the animal's strength and stature. The cutting up and the subsequent scramble were a revolting sight, frequent fights taking place *inside* the body for the titbits. We had read somewhere that the foot and the best end of the trunk were considered delicacies, but the two nostril holes running through the round of trunk which later appeared on the table were altogether too life-like for the squeamish, while the foot was of exactly that texture and toughness one would expect of a pad of flesh which has to receive and absorb the jar of several tons. Perhaps it had not been hung long enough.

The following day we cut out the tusks. On the ground they looked far more imposing than in the elephant's head, the reason being that a third of the length is embedded in the skull. The part inside the head is hollow, but the size of the hollow decreases until, near the tip, the tusk is solid; the older the elephant the greater is the solid part. We were still rather worried about the weight, and, having no spring balance with us, we were constantly picking them up and balancing them against an imaginary 30lbs. When finally weighed, they went nearly 50lbs. each, so that I was able to keep them but it was nothing to shout about, for a good average pair would go 70lbs., while tusks of 100lbs. are still obtainable. The biggest tusk known is in the Natural History Museum, Kensington, and weighs 226½lbs., and is 10ft. long. A large African bull elephant stands over 11ft. at the shoulder, and weighs about 6 tons.

On the hills of those parts there were, besides elephants, one or two herds of buffalo. These beasts, however, are so wary that you have to be very skilful or lucky, sometimes both, in order to get one. Except in the very early morning and late evening, they seldom leave the shelter of the bush or forest in which most of the day is spent. Day after day we left camp long before the eastern sky had begun to pale, but never did we bring anything back to breakfast except a raging hunger. Whether the buffalo in question had any inkling of our murderous intentions is doubtful, but that they had a profound contempt for us the following regrettable incident seemed to show.

We had at length tired of these fruitless peep-o'-day excursions, and given orders to our Lumbwa cook to be called at a more civilised hour next morning. Imagine, then, our wrath when at the very same time, a full hour before dawn, the wretched boy came creeping into the tent where we slept. We were both awake instantly, but before the storm broke, while we collected our thoughts and sought for words violent enough to express them, the rash youth held up a warning hand and whispered the single word 'Mbogu'. Cautious and hurried whispering elicited the information that the buffalo herd was grazing almost in the camp. Apparently a boot thrown out of the tent could not fail to hit one, and luckily, the porters were too petrified to stir.

My first thoughtless impulse was to strike a match, but B., hearing me fumbling, hastily stopped me. Then I remembered that my heavy rifle had been taken down to be packed away in its case, and that the only ammunition handy was soft-nosed. (A buffalo has a very tough hide, so that to make sure of sufficient penetration it is advisable to use a solid bullet – that is, a bullet encased in nickel – whereas the soft-nosed bullet has the soft lead tip uncovered.) The same thought had evidently struck B., for he was on the floor, routing about in the haversack which contained his ammunition, cursing softly but vehemently. Afterwards I learnt what the trouble was. B. had false teeth, which in the dark and confusion he had mislaid, and he was now trying to distinguish between solid and soft-nosed bullets in the dark, without being able to bite them.

Finally he got outside, armed, if not to the teeth, at any rate sufficiently, but his diatribes, my oaths, and our dilatoriness had disgusted our callers, and they were gone. We dressed and followed, but it was no use; we had lost our chance. Had our Lumbwa esquire been a Sancho Panza he would no doubt have observed: 'When they bring you the heifer be ready with the rope.'

This humiliation quite spoiled our trip. B. could not, so to speak, get his teeth out of hs head, while my well-meant reminders of the seaman's rule, 'A place for everything and everything in its place', did nothing to solace him. No doubt we had been over-cautious, for at such close quarters any bullet – possibly a charge of buck-shot – would have sufficed.

A very dense strip of bush along the banks of a big river in these parts exercised on me a sinister attraction. It was a veritable warren – not for rabbits, but for rhinos. For hard work coupled with fearful excitement, a few hours in the rhino warren took a lot of beating. The bush was so dense that ingress and progress were only possible by following game tracks, and, once inside, visibility was restricted to a few yards. In such a place, if following tracks, it was almost impossible to keep the wind right, and usually the only warning of the close proximity of a rhino would be an appalling, explosive splutter, like the sound of some gigantic soda syphon in action. There might be a fleeting glimpse of a great grey bulk before the noise of his crashing flight receded in the distance, leaving the hot silence of the bush again undisturbed but for the buzz of a fly and the beating of one's own heart. We never got a shot, and a little of that sort of thing went a long way, but it was a satisfying moment for me when, in a cooler but equally thick place, I dropped a forest rhino at ten yards' range with one shot from a little .256 rifle. Forest rhinos have much longer horns than their fellows of the Plains; this one had a front horn of 36 inches. A rhino weighs about 3 tons, but a shell from a 6-inch gun could not have been more deadly than that tiny bullet.

One of these same bush rhinos gave us a night almost as agitated as the night of the buffalo, but him we had no wish to kill even had it been possible, for it was too dark to shoot. We were camped near a water-hole and, foolishly enough, right astride a very obvious well-used rhino path. About midnight the camp was roused by the familiar sound of the giant soda syphon going off: an alarming sound at all times, in spite of its familiarity, but much more so at night. Some unknown hero from the porters' tent went out to blow up the dying fire while we lit our lamp. Neither had any effect. The most alarming snorts and stampings continued to outrage the peace of an African night.

B. and I took the precaution of loading our rifles, but it was raining, we could see nothing, so we remained in bed – unwisely, I thought, because if the rhino did decide to charge through the camp to reach the water-hole, he would very likely vent his fury on the tent in passing. Rhinos have very poor eyesight, so that the tent would have offered the most tempting target. It was comforting to reflect that the porters' tent was bigger than ours. Meantime, they were very unhappy, and one by one they piled into our tent for moral support, and B.'s dog, a big Rampur greyhound, had all his hackles up but was far too frightened to bark. There was nothing we could do. Our combined voices could not have produced a noise equal to the rhino's, or one that would have any intimidating effect. Indeed, shouting was an experiment we did not care to try, as it might have had the opposite effect. So we just sat still, and at each explosion of the perambulating syphon smiled a wan and sickly smile.

We endured this unhappy situation for a tense hour, until it apparently dawned on the angry, spluttering rhino that a slight deviation from his normal route would take him to the water without walking through our camp. This he must have done, for we heard no more.

This dog of B.'s – Bruce, as he was called – came to an untimely end soon afterwards. He went off hunting on his own and was never seen again, although we waited for a day to scour the country and to send back to the last camp. Probably a leopard got him. He was not destined for a long life, anyhow, for he was an inveterate sheep-killer and, in a country where every native owned sheep and goats, and in those days usually carried a spear, it was a wonder that no one had put a spear into him before this. Still, he was a great loss to B., for he was a handsome dog, with some very endearing ways. You had only to say to him: 'Laugh, Bruce,' and he would bare his teeth and wrinkle up his nose in a dreadful grin. Less amusing was a trick he had of stealing food. My house was nearly two miles from B.'s, but very often Bruce would come over in the night, break open my ramshackle larder, and treat himself to a snack of a couple of loaves and a dozen eggs. Peace to his memory, for at least he lived dangerously!

Returning home from these excursions, it was exciting to see how the flax had grown, or how the last planting of young coffee seedlings had 'taken', but we had, invariably, to steel our minds against the recital of a chapter of accidents by the head boy whom we had left in charge; the oxen that had strayed or died, the boys that had deserted; how the plough had broken the day we left, and had done no work since. So ran the tale, while other less obvious items, such as disease in the cattle or the coffee, we had the fun of finding out later for ourselves.

Perhaps, when I mentioned a fiver as our total outlay for these expeditions, I was under-estimating, and, on looking backwards and taking into account that which was done and more that was not done in our absence, I suspect that this was so. But, whatever the cost, it was money well spent.

CHAPTER THREE

Kilimanjaro: Kibo and Mawenzi

'So, and no otherwise hillmen desire their hills.' – Kipling

AT first sight few places would appear to offer less scope for mountaineering than tropical Africa – mountaineering, that is, in the full sense of the word; by which I mean climbing on ice, snow, and glaciers, as well as rock. But in fact there are three widely separated regions where such climbing is to be had; in two of them on isolated peaks, and in the third on a range of snow peaks. In the course of the next few years, by taking full advantage of the working agreement reached at the end of Chapter One, and by meeting someone of a like mind to myself, who had as yet also escaped being 'shut up', I was able to visit all three.

Kilimanjaro, 19,710 feet, is an extinct volcano lying about 180 miles south-east of Nairobi, just inside the Tanganyika border. The boundary between Kenya and Tanganyika, which is elsewhere a straight line, bulges out to the north to include Kilimanjaro in Tanganyika Territory, or German East Africa, as it was when the boundary was delineated. The story is commonly related (and, whether true or not, it has too firm a hold now to be given up) that when the boundary was fixed according to the Treaty of 1890, Kilimanjaro was specifically included in Germany territory, at the cost of an unstraight line, so that the German Emperor might have the gratification of possessing the highest mountain in Africa.

It was first seen in 1848 by the two missionaries Rebmann and Krapf, and was climbed for the first time by Hans Mayer and Ludwig Purtscheller in 1889. High though it is and capped with ice and snow descending as low as 16,000 feet on the south-west and to 18,500 feet on the north side, the great bulk of the mountain is more impressive than its height, for to travel round the base would involve a journey on foot of several days. The enormous base detracts from the apparent height, and this detraction is accentuated by the squat, pudding-like dome of Kibo, the highest summit. In fine weather Kibo can be seen from Nairobi, when the haze rising from the hot intervening plains blots out the lower slopes, leaving the white dome suspended in mid-air like a cloud. The Masai, who inhabit the plains between Nairobi and the mountain, call Kibo 'Ngaje Ngai' – the House of God.

On the last day of February 1930, S. and I forgathered at Nairobi, whence we left by car for the mountain. S. who, like myself, was a coffee planter, had a farm north of the railway about 160 miles from mine. In the middle of it was a great tooth of granite, which soared up for about 200 feet – an eyesore to a planter, but to those of the Faith better than water in a thirsty land. S. had worked out several routes up it to which I was later introduced.

From Nairobi the road runs south through the Southern Game Reserve – vast plains, sparsely dotted with thorn-trees a few feet high, and at this season of the year, towards the end of the dry weather, burnt almost bare of grass. Nevertheless, these plains support great quantities of game, together with two or three hundred thousand head of Masai cattle. These Masai are pastoral nomads, who in former days overran the whole of East Africa, but are now confined to their Reserve, which includes part of the Game Reserve. They number only about 22,000 and, since they have at their disposal over 200 acres per head, there is room for them, their cattle, and the game. All the land, of course, is not equally good, but they follow the best grazing according to the season. They live in low huts of hides plastered with cow-dung, built contiguously in the form of a circle, inside of which the cattle are put at night for safety from lions, and, in former days, hostile tribes. The Masai village, or *manyatta*, inevitably becomes in a short time a quagmire of trampled mud and cow-dung, infested with myriads of flies. The diet of the Masai consists almost exclusively of blood and milk, the blood being obtained by bleeding their cattle. They do not work except tend their herds and flocks, and they have the frank manner and independent bearing that befit such a life. Although clean in person, they live in the utmost squalor, have no morals as understood by us, and are complete savages; but their bravery is proverbial, and they are savages of a rather glorious type.

The road across the plains was at that time more or less as nature had made it. Little improvement had been attempted except to put 'Irish' bridges across the sandy beds of the water-courses. These take the form of a concrete causeway across the beds of the numerous dongas, which for most of the year are dry, but which on occasion can become formidable rivers within a matter of minutes. For crossing the sand beds of these dongas when dry the 'Irish' bridge is most useful, but the way into and out of these river-beds was always a strain on the car and one's nerves; I remember one, where the front wheels started climbing out before the back wheels had finished going down.

The road between these fearsome places was seamed and scored with parallel ruts and transverse cracks, sometimes a foot wide; the pace was therefore circumspect, so that the man who was not driving had leisure to admire the game which was to be seen on either hand. There a rhino would be grazing peacefully two hundred yards from the road; here the head of a giraffe might stare at us superciliously from over the top of a thorn-tree not twenty yards away, before the owner of it glided away in his strange, undulating gallop; and once we stopped the car to inspect through field-glasses a lion lying under a bush a quarter of a mile from the road. When we got out in order to go closer, he got up and walked away with his tail twitching contemptuously.

We reached Longido (130 miles) after dark, and stopped there for the night. There was a rest house, and hard by is Mount Longido, a conical scrub-covered hill rising straight from the plain to a height of 8,500 feet. It was the scene of heavy fighting at the commencement of the War in East Africa in 1914.

Next day a run of 120 miles over a better road took us to Marungu, a little place on the south-east slopes of the mountain at an elevation of about 5,000 feet above the sea. We had driven round two sides of the mountain – the west and south sides – on which there is a considerable area devoted to coffee-growing by both natives and Europeans. The volcanic soil is deep and rich, the climate warm, while water furrows can be led everywhere from the innumerable streams descending from the forested slopes of the mountain above. At Marungu there is a small hotel where we put up, dumped our surplus kit, and arranged for twelve porters and a donkey to accompany us next day.

When the Germans were in occupation here they built two huts on the mountain; one at 8,500 feet, which is called Bismarck, and another at 11,500 feet, called Peter's Hut, after Dr. Karl Peters, the notorious German explorer, whose efforts to extend the German sphere of influence to Uganda, when matters there were still undecided, did not stop at opening the private correspondence of his British rivals. These huts, particularly the lower ones, are in fairly frequent use by visitors to Marungu, which is popular as a health resort for people condemned to live in hot, unlikely places like Tanga, on the neighbouring coast. Apart from the great altitude, there is nothing to stop the more energetic from going to the top, because on Kibo there are no climbing difficulties whatsoever. Perhaps that is putting it too strongly, for on any mountain much depends on the weather, and on Kibo in thick weather the finding of the summit presents more difficulties than usual. The reason for this will be apparent later, but, I suppose, up to 1930 at least twenty people had made genuine ascents, and a few others, like ourselves, ascents which were only technically invalid.

Leaving Marungu, the track to Bismarck follows a broad spur at an easy gradient. On every hand are the huts, banana groves, maize and coffee fields of the natives, the lower slopes at this point being thickly populated and well cultivated by the Wachagga, who seem to have a good working knowledge of the art of irrigation. At about 7,000 feet the cultivation comes to an end on the fringes of the forest zone. Inside the forest it is dark and gloomy; the undergrowth is thick; streams abound, and the trees are typical of those found in 'rain forest'. These are evergreen, the species numerous, trees of all sizes and shapes struggling together for space and light. Elephants abound, but are protected, and near the Bismarck hut their tracks lie everywhere, making the finding of the path to the hut difficult.

This is a substantial structure of stone situated near the upper limit of the forest zone. Little more than four hours were needed to reach it, and that evening, after we had settled in, we climbed to a point clear of the forest to enjoy a good view of Mawenzi, a fantastically weathered peak of red volcanic rock, 17,000 feet high, separated from the higher but less interesting Kibo by a wide, flat saddle of shale. It looked difficult, and if the climbing of Kibo was a duty, that of Mawenzi promised to be a pleasure.

Rain fell heavily in the night, but we got away soon after seven to a fine morning, and reached Peter's Hut in four hours, just in time to avoid a sharp hailstorm. The path lay over bare and boggy moors, where we saw for the first time the curious plants peculiar to the Alpine zone in the tropics. This zone lies between 10,000 and 14,000 feet, and the most remarkable plants found there are the giant groundsel and the giant lobelia. The first is like an enormous cabbage stuck on top of a thick stem six to eight feet high, while the lobelia is a long, columnar, feathery, green stalk, very unlike an ordinary lobelia. Besides these there are Alpines, balsams, heather-like bushes, and withal many more birds than are seen in the rather lifeless forest.

The hut was a small wooden building with a tin roof and a very efficient stove, for which we had brought a supply of wood. Not unreasonably, the porters, whose quarters were distinctly airy, complained bitterly of the cold, while the little white donkey voiced the sentiments of all with a series of discordant brays, and looked very much out of place. The walls of the hut were sadly disfigured by the names of the many parties who had penetrated thus far, and who were not willing to have it forgotten.

In the night there was a heavy thunderstorm, and, judging from the solid banks of cloud below and to the south, we feared that the 'long rains' were about to break. The rainy season generally sets in towards the end of March – slightly earlier, perhaps, in Tanganyika than in Kenya, because the rain spreads up from the south with the advance of the south-west monsoon. This unusually early onset of the rains foreboded for us not only unpleasant conditions on the mountain, but the possibility of getting stranded on the way home by rivers in flood.

Nearing the 16,000-foot saddle, and within a mile of the hut, we came upon snow. Our head porter and guide, one Solomon, who had been very near to the top of Kibo, if not on it, pointed out our destination, the Hans Mayer Caves, across the saddle. It looked about half a mile distant, but it took us an hour to get there, and we realised the height was beginning to tell. The porters, who were anxious to dump their loads and get back from these inhospitable wastes to the comparative comfort of Peter's Hut, went well, and we did our best, but our little white dapple had the legs and lungs of us all.

The cave, like most caves, still seemed to be the home of many winds unreleased by Æolus, but we made ourselves fairly comfortable, and prepared for an early start next day. I had a slight headache, due to the altitude, but S. was fit enough. The donkey and all the porters had gone down except Solomon and one companion, who suffered together silently. There is nothing, I think, except cold which will reduce an African native to speechlessness, and that unusual state of affairs is perhaps accounted for by the impossibility of talking intelligibly with chattering teeth.

We started at 4.30 a.m. in thick weather and falling snow. The route at first lay up snow lying thinly on scree at an easy angle. The climb is devoid of interest from a mountaineering point of view, so the reader is, for the moment, spared the arduous mental exertion of following the party up the perilous knife-edge ridges, stone-swept gullies, and precipitous faces which abound so plentifully in descriptions of a climb. On top of Kilimanjaro is a great flat-bottomed crater, possibly a mile across at its longest diameter, filled with ice and snow – what the Germans called on their map the Credner Glacier. On the rim of the crater is the summit, or summits, for on this great circumference there are numerous snow hillocks or bumps of varying height. The rim is gained by a notch at its lowest point, which is close on 19,000 feet, and then the climber turns left-handed to follow the crater-wall round to the south and west, passing over several of these bumps, until the highest of all, Kaiser Wilhelm Spitze, is reached.

At half past ten we gained the first of these points, Gillman Point, in a mist, where, digging in the snow, we found a cairn and a visitors' book. Solomon, with the wisdom of his namesake, now declared he had had enough, so we parked him there to await our return, and pushed on, well knowing that the official summit was still far off, though very little higher. I was not feeling very well myself; in fact I was being sick at frequent intervals; but we ploughed slowly on through waist-deep snow, presently reaching the top of another bump, which later we judged must have been Stella Point. Yet another top loomed vaguely through the mists some distance ahead, but I am obliged to confess that its challenge aroused little interest in us, and, after debate, we turned in our tracks. We picked up the patient Solomon, now the colour of a mottled and overripe Victoria plum, and at twelve o'clock started down.

When a party fails to get to the top of a mountain, it is usual and convenient to have some picturesque excuse – preferably some objective reason for turning back, such as the dangerous state of the snow, the approach of bad weather, or falling stones, so that a story of failure makes better reading than one of success, while a chorus of praise resounds to the party's display of sound judgement and its unselfish renunciation of a victory easily within its grasp. If the story of our failure has lost something in the telling, it is owing to an unfortunate propensity, perhaps only temporary, for truth, and the reason for our retreat was the more prosaic and not uncommon one – inability to go any further.

During our flounderings in the vicinity of the summit the weather was so thick and the sun so effectually hidden that we had both discarded our snow-glasses, the better to see where we were going. When we got back to the cave about two o'clock our eyes began to smart, then to hurt, until by evening they were firmly closed and exceedingly painful. We were completely snow-blind. The pain made the night a wretched one, but by morning our eyes were on the mend. It snowed all that day, during which we slept, pottered about near the cave, and discussed our next move . . . A stern sense of duty prompted some half-hearted talk of finishing what we now suspected was the uncompleted task of climbing Kibo, but the fresh snow which had fallen, and the bad weather, gave us a good excuse for going down to the warmth and comfort of Peter's Hut. No one was more delighted at this decision than the faithful Solomon, though it would be idle to pretend that we ourselves acted upon it with any great show of reluctance.

It was raining hard when we arrived there at noon next day, which so disgusted us that we almost abandoned hope of Mawenzi, and talked of retreat from the mountain. However, that evening the weather appeared more promising, so we decided to wait. March 8th, however, was another day of mist and rain. At night there was another violent thunderstorm, but, rendered desperate by inactivity, we resolved to attempt Mawenzi next day, be the weather what it might.

The two of us left the hut at 3.15 a.m. and reached the saddle between Kibo and Mawenzi soon after dawn . . . At least, we assumed the slight lessening of the gloom was the dawn, for a dense mist shrouded everything, and we sat there waiting for a clearing to disclose the whereabouts of our peak. This was presently vouchsafed us, and at eight o'clock we were sitting at the foot of the north-west face of Mawenzi waiting impatiently for another clearing to give us some hint as to where to start. No clearing came so we roped up and began poking about tentatively at the foot of the rocks. The peak had been climbed twice before, and we were looking for a couloir which was the key to the ascent. We entered a chimney which looked invitingly simple, but were soon brought to a stand and an ignominious retreat by the ice and snow with which the rocks were plastered.

This check seemed to rouse us from our defeatist attitude, just as an insult may goad the most placid into determined activity. We dumped our rucksacks at the foot and started again, and at nine o'clock we reached the foot of a promising-looking gully. The whole mountain was iced, the rock rotten, snow falling, and it was still misty, but in defiance of these bad conditions we continued the climb. Four short rock pitches divided by stretches of steep snow landed us at the foot of a subsidiary gully coming down from the left. This seemed to be the line of least resistance, so we turned up it, and, after a severe struggle, reached the top of one of the several jagged teeth which decorate the summit ridge. The time was about two o'clock. We could now see that it was not the highest of them, for this lay at the head of the main gully. It is called Wissmann Spitze on the German map. Descending rapidly into the main gully, we climbed a steep snow slope, and gained the summit at four o'clock.

No view but the half-seen snows of Kibo greeted us, but now, as ever, the joy of difficulties overcome was ample reward. We had no time to waste, and hastily began the descent, where, in the course of climbing down one of the rock pitches via S.'s shoulders, I lost both hat and snow-glasses, which went spinning down the gully. We reached the foot of the rocks before dark, and, not stopping to look for my property, raced down the 3,000 feet to Peter's in the gathering gloom, fearful lest we should miss the hut.

Breakfast at Bismarck, lunch at Marungu, marks the rapidity of our retreat next day. We paid off and dismissed the porters; Solomon, wise as ever, forgetting to return a heavy overcoat which S. had lent him. Our fears about the effect of the early rains upon the road were fully confirmed, and we learnt that the direct road to Nairobi was now impassable. The only alternative was to follow the old Mombasa road east via Taveta to Voi on the railway, 200 miles the wrong side of Nairobi and only 100 miles from Mombasa. From there we could try the new road which follows roughly the alignment of the railway, or, if the worst came, go back by train.

All went well as far as Voi, which was reached in one day without incident. Trouble began next morning at a river, where the bridge, only an 'Irish' one, had been washed away. Luckily there were a gang of natives at work on the road, who pushed us across the fifty yards of flooded river while the water swirled over the floorboards of the car. We bowled merrily along a road on which lay many pools. These we took as they came at full speed, careful trials having assured us that the bottoms were hard. At midday we had the misfortune to encounter one that refused to be rushed. It was deep and soft, and the car settled down with the back axle sitting firmly on the ridge between the ruts, while the wheels revolved helplessly in a liquid mud bath of nauseous colour and smell. All the usual expedients of jacking up, digging out, and strewing branches were tried, without any result but to plaster us in mud from head to foot. There was nothing to be done but wait upon the event, and presently a lorry came along and pulled us out of the slough. Proceeding with more caution, we reached that night Makindu, a station on the railway, where we heard that ahead of us there were a dozen cars and lorries waiting for a flooded river to subside. At that time the Mombasa-Nairobi road was very popular with transport agents, the Government having been foolishly persuaded to spend some money on making it passable. This resulted in a serious loss of traffic to the railway (a familiar story), but the *status quo ante* was speedily restored when the Government withheld funds for the road's upkeep, allowing it to revert to its former state. S. was in a hurry to get home, so boarded the train next morning, while I arranged for an open truck to receive the much-enduring car – a necessary arrangement, but one that seriously upset the expedition's balance-sheet. I ran the car on to the truck, but we did not get hitched on to a goods train until evening. We chugged away through the night, myself sitting in the car, too cold to sleep, and imagining I was back in the draughty cave in Kibo. When dawn came we were running across the Plains we had traversed a short fortnight ago: then, bare brown veldt, now a fresh green carpet on which the drifting herds of game grazed contentedly, hardly deigning to watch our dragon-like progress.

CHAPTER FOUR

Kenya Mountain

'Behind that leader, who gave me hope and was a light to me.' – Dante

THE mountain which gives its name to the Colony is a magnificent isolated peak rising out of a plain, of a general elevation of 6,000 feet, to a height of 17,040 feet. It lies about 130 miles north of Nairobi by road, and within a few miles of the equator. The base of the mountain rivals that of Kilimanjaro in size, the drive round it by road being a journey of over 100 miles. The lower slopes of Kenya are forested, like those of Kilimanjaro, and both are extinct volcanoes, but there the likeness ends, for the two summits are as different as the dome of St. Paul's and the spire of Salisbury. This illustration is only used to emphasise the contrast; the dome of St Paul's would pass as a likeness to Kibo, but there is nothing spire-like about the peak of Kenya. Rather is it a great jagged tower, buttressed by a number of equally jagged ridges, while between the ridges the rock faces of the tower are festooned with snow and hanging glaciers.

The mountain is a very old volcano, judged by geologists to have been at one time 3,000 feet higher. No trace of the original crater remains, while the peak itself consists of the rock which in past ages consolidated into a 'plug' and sealed up the volcano. This rock is of a peculiar type which was given the name 'kenyte' by the late Professor Gregory, after whom one of the glaciers on Kenya has been named. The same sort of rock has been found on Mount Erebus, in the Antarctic. It is not as reliable as it might be from a climber's point of view, but it is infinitely better than the loose volcanic 'tuffs' found on some of the neighbouring lesser peaks, such as Sendeyo, whose rock is similar to the rock of Mawenzi. There are a dozen named glaciers, but some are only small hanging glaciers, while none are to be compared for size with Alpine glaciers.

The peak was first seen in 1849 by Dr. Krapf, a German working for a British missionary society. His story was received in Europe with incredulity, for at that time the existence of snow mountains in equatorial Africa was regarded by many as an impossibility. Already, in November 1849, Krapf had seen Kilimanjaro, and in December of the same year he writes from Kitui, 'I could see the "Kegnia" more distinctly, and observed two large horns or pillars, as it were, rising over an enormous mountain to the north-west of Kilimanjaro, covered with a white substance.'

Fifty years passed before it was climbed by Sir Halford Mackinder and his two Alpine guides, César Ollier and Joseph Brocherel, in 1899. This feat was the more remarkable when it is remembered that the railway to Nairobi was only under construction, that the tribes between there and the mountain were in a very unsettled state, and that food-supplies had to be brought up from Naivasha, 50 miles away. The summit is crowned by twin peaks to which Mackinder gave the names of Batian and Nelion. Batian, which is the higher by about 40 feet, Mackinder's party climbed direct, omitting Nelion's altogether. This climb from their high camp to the summit, a matter of 2,000 feet, took six hours, and a like time was spent on the descent.

It was another thirty years before the second successful attempt was made, though many parties tried. In 1929 Messrs. Shipton and Wyn Harris reached the summit of Batian, having first traversed over the top of Nelion. Their route followed that of Mackinder's up the south-east face of Nelion, but on nearing the lower summit Mackinder's party had traversed beneath it and across the steep, tough ice of the hanging Diamond Glacier, whereas the later party took Nelion in their stride. The new route involved difficult rock climbing, but that would be preferred by an amateur party to the three hours of step-cutting on steep ice which the traverse of the Diamond Glacier demanded of Mackinder's guides.

The twin peaks were named by Mackinder after the man who was then *laibon*, or chief witch-doctor, of the Masai, and his brother. Batian – or Mbatian, as it should be written – was not only a witch-doctor, but a man of great influence over his tribe, and a prophet. He is said to have prophesied the coming of the white man to Kenya even before Europeans had been there, and another of his prophecies was that a great snake would come, stretching from the sea right across the land, and with its coming the supremacy of the Masai would cease. The Masai believe that Batian's 'great snake' is the railway. Two lesser peaks are named Sendeyo and Lenana, after Batian's sons, and the story of Batian's death and the disputed inheritance bears a close resemblance to the story of Isaac and Jacob. The brothers and their supporters fought together for many years, until, in 1902, Sendeyo the elder was beaten and sued for peace with Lenana his brother, who had cheated him out of the succession. It was a happy thought of Sir Halford Mackinder's to use names whose music sounds even clearer now amongst the dull cluster of disharmonious European names which have been sprinkled lavishly over the remaining peaks, glaciers and valleys.

Not long after our return from Kilimanjaro I heard from S. that the coffee had managed so well in his absence that he was now ready to carry out a plan which he had long had in mind. This was nothing less than a traverse of the twin peaks of Kenya by ascending the west ridge and descending by the 1929 route. I was quite agreeable, and, whether we succeeded in carrying out this ambitious plan or not, we expected to put in a very good fortnight playing about on the mountain. This time our rendezvous was Nakuru, a town 100 miles west of Nairobi, where we forgathered towards the end of July. S.

brought with him one of his farm boys named Saidi, to cook and make himself generally useful. His normal occupation was driving a tractor.

Nanyuki, our jumping-off place at the foot of the mountain, was 240 miles away, but we were anxious to get there in the day. At least one of us was, for S. was burning with impatience to be on the mountain, while I, who had to drive, would have been content to reach it in two. We left Nakuru at half past four in the morning in rain and mist, and lost some precious time by missing the way in the fog and going for some miles down the wrong road. By the time we had breakfasted at Naivasha the weather had improved, and, as we climbed the steep, rough road up the escarpment out of the Rift Valley, the parched country looked, as was usual there, as though it did not know what rain was.

An hour was spent in Nairobi collecting some food and necessaries, but we left again at midday with 140 miles still to go. It remained dry until we pulled into Nanyuki at six o'clock, but while we were enquiring the whereabouts of the farm from which we had arranged to take transport, there was a heavy shower. The farm was only a mile or two out, but the road to it consisted

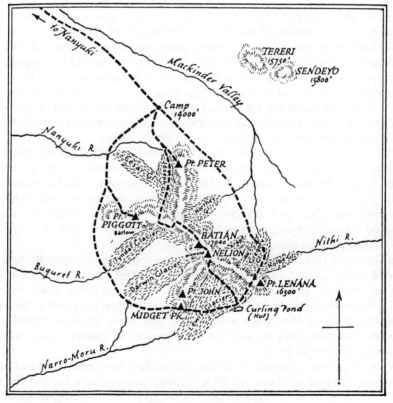

Mount Kenya

mainly of two enormous ruts, out of which it was essential to keep the wheels. The rain was fatal to a safe negotiation of this atrocity, and, after several hairbreadth escapes, we landed fairly in both ruts, the car sitting firmly down on the axles. It was almost dark, so we abandoned ship and walked on to the farm, where we slept.

Next morning was a busy one. The car had to be rescued with a team of oxen, and our impedimenta made up into 50 lb. loads, but at one o'clock we started with five pack-ponies, led by six boys, to carry our ten loads. The way led through homely grass glades surrounded by cedar forest, where a rhino, standing in the middle of one, looked as unreal as a dragon would have done. We had to pass within 200 yards of him, but he elected to run away instead of stampeding blindly through the caravan – a contingency that one should always be prepared for in the presence of these eccentric beasts. Having steered safely past this Scylla, we nearly got foul of Charybdis in the shape of a big bull elephant standing at the edge of the forest. The ponies got very jumpy, but he too moved quietly away and allowed us to settle into our camp just inside the forest. A heavy storm just missed us, so that we spent a happy evening under the cedars sitting round a noble fire. No elephant or rhino came to disturb the peace of the night – a peace which was broken only by the distant snapping of a bamboo, where, perhaps, some elephant moved and by the slow, shrill, long-drawn cry of the tree hyrax – that unforgettable sound which for me embodies all the mystery and charm of Africa.

Next morning our march continued through the forest zone, the Kikuya pony-men beating tins and shouting to give timely warning of our approach to any rhino, buffalo or elephant within earshot. On the west and north side of the mountain, the forest is of a drier type than the 'rain' forest of Kilimanjaro, which is found again on the wetter eastern slopes of Kenya. Cedar-trees predominated amongst olive and podocarpus; all valuable for timber, but the first-named especially so because it is the pencil cedar.

The trees, growing scanty and stunted, yielded at length to bamboos, which in turn faded away as we reached the beginning of the moors of tussocky grass, heath, and giant groundsel. Here one of the ponies had to be relieved of its load, and, before we reached the caves which were our objective, everyone was tired and the boys mutinous. The cave which the natives annexed was very good; ours was wet; but there was no lack of groundsel, which makes an excellent fuel.

In the night two of the ponies ran away, so that some reorganisation was needed before we got away at half past ten with three ponies, one of which I now led, while S. and three of the boys carried the remaining loads. Our way lay up the broad Mackinder Valley, and as we marched we gazed at the peak, filling the head of the valley and looking like some glorious cathedral. A cloudless blue sky, with the sunlight sparkling on the glaciers, gave vigour to the black outlines of its rock.

We took up our quarters in another convenient cave near the head of the valley, at a height of about 14,000 feet. Saidi we kept with us, but the boys and the ponies we sent down to the lower camp with instructions to visit us occasionally for orders. In spite of the height, there was still plenty of senecio (giant groundsel) for fuel, and it was needed, because the night was clear and cold, with the thermometer registering some six degrees of frost.

Our first task was to reconnoitre the west ridge, and to do this we made ascents of two rock aiguilles of about 16,000 feet. The comfort and conveniences of our base had to be paid for by a rather laborious climb up a steep, dry boulder-strewn watercourse, which had to be ascended and descended every day going to and returning from the scene of our activities. The climbing of these two rock peaks, Dutton and Peter – which, by the way, were first ascents – made a satisfying and not too difficult first day, and showed us that the west ridge could be reached from a col at its foot. The col lay at the head of the Joseph Glacier, and the problem of reaching it, and the nature of the ridge above it, were the questions to which we devoted the second day.

Leaving camp at seven, we reached the snout of the glacier at half past eight. Some step-cutting was necessary to gain a lodgment on the glacier, up which we then went as far as the foot of an ice couloir leading to our col. Here we took to some rotten and rather difficult rock on its left bank, and reached the col before midday. The col was narrow, and sitting astride it, à cheval, we gazed with fascination at the terrific view of the west face of the mountain. Below the almost vertical cliffs of the pinnacled west ridge were two hanging glaciers which seemed to cling there in defiance of all laws of gravity. Below them again, the rocks, which were swept by the ice falling from these glaciers, curved steeply to the Tyndall Glacier, a thousand feet below us. The little we could see of the lower part of our proposed route up the ridge was not encouraging. An upward traverse over steep ice and snow-covered rock led to a notch between what we called the Grand and Petit Gendarme, and everything depended on our ability to turn the former by a traverse on the north side, which we could not see, in order to gain the ridge above it. What lay beyond we could not tell, and it seemed doubtful whether we should get far enough to learn.

Sitting on the col, while the mists boiled up and shrouded the ridge from our straining eyes, we debated whether to attack it the next day. We had seen as much of the route as we ever would, steps were cut up to the col and would not last more than a day or two, and the weather seemed settled. The only advantage of delay was to acclimatise more, for, though we now reaped the benefit of the acclimatisation received on Kilimanjaro, we should probably be fitter still after another day or two, and the obvious difficulties of the ridge plus the altitude would call for all our reserves. A natural desire to put it at once to the test carried the day, and we decided to make our bid next morning. It would be August 1st, but, though the fact that this was also S.'s birthday was not given any undue weight, it would be a very nice birthday present if we pulled it off.

We were up at 3 a.m. on this eventful morning, left camp at 4.30 a.m., and were at the foot of the Joseph Glacier at dawn. Our steps were intact, so we mounted rapidly, this time taking to the rocks on the opposite side of the ice couloir, which brought us to the col at a point nearer to the foot of the west-ridge. We were there by 8 a.m., and sat on its knife-edge for a breather with our legs dangling over the Tyndall Glacier below.

We roped up and began climbing, with S. leading, as he did from here to the top. The traverse across the south flank of the Petit Gendarme took time and care. The rocks were steep, exposed, and plastered with ice and snow, which had to be chipped or scraped away before foothold could be found on the rock beneath. We moved one at a time, crossing a series of rock ribs which effectually concealed from us what lay ahead. We liked the whole thing so little that there was some talk of retreat, but we agreed that we should at least gain the notch before admitting that we had bitten off more than we could chew.

This was at length reached by an ice couloir just before midday, when the usual mists began to envelop the peak and the upper part of our ridge. A halt was called to munch some chocolate before going on to have a look at the traverse on the north side of the Grand Gendarme. As the rocks on that side were dry and free from snow, and as the memory of what we had just climbed was fresh in our minds, we both preferred going on to going back. Some difficult rock had to be overcome before we succeeded at last in turning the Grand Gendarme and gaining the ridge once more above it, and twice the leader had to accept a shoulder from the second man wedged in a crack below. We were confronted now by a succession of pinnacles, none so imposing as the Grand Gendarme, but one or two gave just as much trouble to surmount. No turning movement below these was possible, for the ridge now fell away almost sheer on both sides, so that each had to be taken as it came.

Snow began falling lightly, but, as this seemed a daily occurrence of an afternoon, we were not unduly alarmed by it; indeed, so preoccupied were we with the climbing that it passed almost unheeded. We had now got to the point where the north-east ridge abutted against the west ridge, which here turns southwards towards the summit, almost horizontally. Climbing along the crest on unstable rocks, we were presently faced by a great gap in the ridge into which it was impossible to climb. Conscious that by so doing we were denying ourselves the possibility of retreat, we lowered ourselves down into it.

Crossing the icy crest of the cap, more ridge-work followed, the rock being now of a hard columnar formation which was very pleasant to handle. A patch of difficult ice just below the summit delayed but did not stop us, and at 4.15 we climbed, tired but elated, on to the summit of Batian. Except for the brief halts on the col and below the Grand Gendarme, we had been climbing continuously for twelve hours.

S. was familiar with the route down on the south-east side, but there were a bare two hours of daylight left, so, allowing only time to swallow each a small tin of meat essence, we began the descent. Crossing the Gate of the Mists between Batian and Nelion, we lost much valuable time by having to cut steps in hard, sticky ice. Nelion was climbed, and, without pause, we started down the other side. Things now began to happen. First the point of my axe was twisted clean off, and then, as I was descending a rock pitch with the axe hitched in the rope round my waist, a slip, which was immediately checked, jerked the axe free and it shot down the slope bound for the Lewis Glacier. At the same time S. was attacked with violent spasms of vomiting, which could only be attributed to the meat essence. Each bout of sickness necessitated a long halt and made him progressively weaker.

Our pace slowed, the light began to fade, and the rocks became almost too cold to handle. A bivouac was suggested, for with one man axeless, one sick, and both tired, it was becoming questionable whether we could continue to climb safely, but a bitter east wind springing up banished all thoughts of a bivouac, and the light of the moon which sailed out from behind some cloud encouraged us to persevere. Very slowly and cautiously we climbed down, using the rope to lower ourselves wherever possible. The most vivid impression that remains in my mind of this grim ordeal is how S., in the feeble state he was, not only climbed, but led the way unerringly and safeguarded his companion.

At about 9 p.m. we descended by means of a final 'rappel' on to the frozen snow of the Lewis Glacier, whence, unroping, we began the trudge up to Point Lenana, a snow ridge which had to be crossed on the way back to our camp some four or five hours' march away. Now that the tension was over we realised how exhausted we were. The gentle slope of hard snow in front of us appeared quite insuperable, and we now remembered that there was a hut lower down the glacier near a place called the Curling Pond. For this we headed, where, on reaching it about 10 p.m., we lay and shivered until the first streak of light encouraged us to start once more for our camp. S.'s sickness had passed off, and we got there by 8 a.m., when we promptly turned in and spent the rest of the day in bed. Our return home with the milk did not seem to surprise the faithful Saidi, nor did he display much curiosity as to what we had been doing since we left camp the previous morning. What did astonish him, I think, was our hunger, which took several days to appease.

This climb took such a lot out of us that little more was done until August 5th, when we climbed Sendeyo, a very striking rock peak on the opposite side of the Mackinder Valley. The rock was volcanic tuff, very hard on the hands and apt to give way at a severe look. Most advantageously placed for photography as we were, it was disappointing that the mists came down earlier than usual over the main peak and remained down.

On the following day we made a first ascent of Point Piggott, 16,350 feet. It was thus named by Professor Gregory after an officer of the B.E.A. Company who had assisted him in his expedition. Gregory, who visited the mountain in 1892 on a scientific expedition, was the first to reach the glaciers. A glacier was named after him by Mackinder.

Piggott is a peak that is nearly all ridge, a continuation, in fact, of our west ridge, but cut off from the main peak by the col from which we began our climb. The real summit of Piggott lies at the north-east end of the ridge and thus overlooks our col, but it was too steep to tackle from there. We gained the summit ridge further to the west after some difficult climbing, and the summit itself was not reached until 1 p.m. The mists were late in forming that morning, so that we were rewarded with glorious views of the west ridge and face, together with a great expanse of territory below us. The dark green of the forest merged into the wide grey-green sea of the plains, a vague, shadowy surface streaked with the darker lines of bush growing by the watercourses. This was bounded on the north by the Loldaika Hills, beyond which the green changed to brown, and the brown to yellow, as the arid sandy wastes which stretch to the Abyssinian Highlands took possession. To the south, cloud hid all but the loftiest of the Aberdares, allowing us no glimpse of Kilimanjaro, 200 miles away, which once or twice has been seen from high up in Kenya.

Our descent was enlivened by a variation which at first promised well, but later involved us in a long rappel; and on the way to camp we passed the skeleton of a buffalo at about 15,000 feet. We got home in a snowstorm at five o'clock, pretty tired.

In the night there were ten degrees of frost. We lay long in bed and had an easy day looking for a tarn which, from the top of Piggott, had attracted us by its brilliant, emerald-green colour.

On the 8th we made a grand circular tour of the peak, passing to the west of Piggott, and by Two Tarn Col to the Lewis Glacier, which we crossed to get home again by four. Near Point Lenana we found a thermometer dropped by S.'s party in 1929; the height was about 16,000 feet and the minimum reading was thirteen degrees – nineteen degrees of frost. The extreme cold which we had felt, after our return from the traverse of the peak, even inside the hut, made us doubt the accuracy of this reading. We left a thermometer of our own in the same place to be collected later. The ponies were to come up for us on the 10th, so the 9th was devoted to the climbing of what we called Midget Peak, a very pointed and precipitous little rock needle on the south side of the mountain, which only lack of time had prevented us having a go at on the previous day. We fully expected the climbing of it would afford some amusement, nor were we disappointed.

We reached it by the same route at 9.30 a.m., and started climbing by a gully in which there was rather more snow and verglas on the rocks than we liked. Higher up the difficulties increased, progress became slow, and snow began falling steadily. I suppose we should have turned back, but mist hid the summit and we expected every pitch would prove to be the last. S. led over several critical steps, one of which, a sloping ice-ledge, I had later particular reason to remember.

A great block crowning the summit was reached soon after one o'clock. Mist hid everything, the snow fell more heavily, and we immediately began the descent, feeling some concern at the condition of the rocks, rendered doubly difficult now by the fresh snow. Crossing the sloping ledge with more haste than caution, the new snow came away and I with it. What happened then I do not know, for my next recollection is standing with S., who was now about eighty feet above me. My first question was true to form, because on the stage, when the heroine recovers from her faint, she usually gasps out, 'Where am I?' before once more relapsing into semi-consciousness and the arms of her beloved. With me it was no idle question, because I had a very strong impression that we were on Kilimanjaro, an illusion only dispelled by repeated assurances to the contrary from S. Physically I seemed to be all right, but mentally I was all wrong – perhaps the jerk of the rope had knocked me senseless. Nor were my mental anxieties any less when I found that this descent of mine by a new and very quick route was of no use, because I had reached an impasse and had to climb back to join S., assisted by the rope.

A second attempt to traverse the iced-up ledge was successful, and the descent continued over rocks which seemed to become colder and more difficult every minute. Wherever it was possible, we roped down on a doubled rope, making eight or nine in all of these rappels. Had the descent continued much further we should have run out of rope, because we had to cut 18 inches or more off each time to make a rope ring through which to pass the climbing-rope. We were singularly ill equipped for this travesty of climbing, necessary though it was, since we had with us not even a pocket-knife, so that the rope had to be hacked through with a sharp stone.

However, we got down, still with some rope in hand, collected the ice-axe and rucksack which we had left at the foot, and trudged heavily up the Lewis Glacier for the third time, in soft new snow. (This glacier, by the way, was named after a Professor Lewis, an American geologist who accomplished some revolutionary work in the study of glaciers.) It was not altogether a surprising thing that I now began to feel as though in the course of the day I had come into violent contact with something hard: in addition, both of us were very wet, and neither of us was strong-minded enough to deviate from our route to collect the thermometer left near Point Lenana. It was probably buried deep under snow anyway, and no doubt it still lies there, taking temperatures which no one will ever read.

On the 10th we did nothing but lament the fact that the ponies would not arrive until evening, for we now realised that we had very little food left to see us down. Three came up, and on the 11th we made a double march to our first camp at the edge of the forest, which was reached at five o'clock in rain. We had nothing left to eat but a small quantity of one of those food beverages which are a household word. Perhaps we had insufficient, but we began to suspect that the claims made for it were as hollow as our stomachs. This camp in the forest, which should have been doubly pleasant to our senses, starved by many days lived amongst rock and snow, was for us merely an irksome delay before the satisfying of our more animal wants.

We were horribly weak as we crawled feebly down next day to the farm from which we started. Bacon and eggs there at 10.30 a.m., and lunch and beer at noon, were partial restoratives, after which we settled our accounts, and left for home.

This was, I think, the most satisfying fortnight either of us ever spent or is ever likely to spend in Africa. On Kenya is to be found climbing at its best. There is no easy route up it, but much virtue may be got from a mountain without climbing it. For those who are not compelled to answer its challenge, let them camp near the solitudes of its glaciers, to gaze upon the fair face of the mountain in sunshine and shadow, to watch the ghostly mists writhing among the crags and pinnacles, and to draw strength from her ruggedness, repose from her aloofness.

Few are the countries that, having no traditions, have in their stead such a symbol and an inspiration.

CHAPTER FIVE

Business and Pleasure

'It [hunting] was the labour of the savages of North America,
but the amusement of the gentleman of England.' – Samuel Johnson

Two of Africa's snow mountains had now been visited, and both had given to us great delight, but before we could round off our experiences on the third a hiatus of more than a year elapsed. For most of 1931 I was alone on the farm while S. was out of the country, but towards the end of the year I got away again, armed once more with a rifle instead of an ice-axe.

My excuse was an invitation from a friend, D., who occupied the next farm. 'Owned' the farm would be more correct, for he very seldom occupied it. Much of his time was spent on safari, for, like Nimrod, he was a mighty hunter to whom little came amiss but whose main preoccupation was elephant.

He had lately succeeded in following his favourite pursuit at someone else's expense by getting himself appointed a temporary Vermin Control Officer, or V.C.O., but this 'bureaucratese' requires some explanation. Like the A.D.C., who so interested the snobs of Handley Cross until they discovered that the letters implied a connection with drains and not with the Army, so, possibly, the municipal rat-catcher is referred to officially as the V.C.O. But the term vermin may include much more than rats or mice, for, just as weeds are a plant in the wrong place, so vermin are animals (of any kind) living where they are not wanted. In East Africa there are many such, and to the list of common vermin animals such as elephant, buffalo, lions, rhinos, or zebra have from time to time to be added should they become dangerous to the lives or injurious to the property of the natives. The calling of them vermin, which means that they can be shot without restrictions, is only temporary and local, and as soon as effective steps have been taken the usual shooting restrictions apply as before. These stipulate that only males can be shot, and limit the number of those which can be killed by the licence-holder in the year.

D.'s appointment was for the control (not the extinction) of a herd of about two thousand elephants. The herd's main stamping-ground was a valley (let us call it the Gubba) some thirty miles long, itself uninhabited, but situated in the middle of thickly populated country. The former dwellers in the Gubba had been driven out by the depredations of the herd, so that a large tract of fertile land had been lost to the native Reserve concerned. This was bad enough, but the herd might have been left in peace had it confined its wanderings to the valley instead of using it as a base from which to roam in all directions, moving to and from other feeding-grounds, doing enormous damage to the natives' crops *en route*.

A single elephant might easily destroy a quarter-acre plot of maize or bananas in a night, far more, or course, being trampled down than are actually eaten. The diameter of the foot of a full-grown bull is a good eighteen inches; the circumference, therefore, is nearly five feet, so that, allowing four of these meat plates to each, as we must, the devastation wrought by the passage of only a few of the two thousand can be imagined. The unfortunate natives, having no firearms, applied to the District Commissioner for protection, and D.'s appointment was the result. His orders were to drive the herd into some country on the other side of a big river thirty miles to the south-east – country occupied by a pastoral tribe who gave no hostages to fortune by growing crops. It was hoped that the elephants, with a little persuasion, would remain there, and one of the methods afterwards employed to effect this was more successful than seems likely. A wide and deep trench was dug for a length of about five miles on the near side of the river by their accustomed crossing-place, and it was not until a section of this fell in, through neglect on the part of the chief responsible for it, that the elephants began to find their way back.

This was the general idea; the tactics were left to D., whose plan was to harass them severely in and around the Gubba to get the main body moving, and kept moving, in the required direction. Like mankind, elephants follow their leaders and are creatures of habit, so this was not so difficult as it sounds; their appointed exile was also one of their familiar haunts, and in their forays from the valley they kept mostly to time-honoured paths. By shooting some of the more independent-minded, and by closing the paths with a dead elephant or two as a warning to others, D. hoped to confine them to beyond the river.

When I recived his invitation to join him for a fortnight he had been at work on this for some months, and had moved all but about two hundred, which clung obstinately to their old haunts. In effecting it he had endured much, for the country is hot, wet, and unhealthy, while the harassing had not been all on one side. Thirty elephants had fallen in the campaign, and as time went on the survivors resented it more and more, and became increasingly cunning. The stubborn remnant comprised mainly immature bulls, and cows with calves at foot, who on that account were loth to travel and were less complaisant when hustled.

Provided with shooting licence, a double-barrel .470, and a .256 rifle, I joined D., and we left for the Gubba in a battered Ford car buried under a mountainous load of kit. Very many decrepit bridges, not an inch wider than the wheel-track of the car, with nothing to keep the wheels on and every inducement wet and greasy mud could provide to make them slip off, were sufficient to occupy our minds for the drive of three hours. At the end of that time we stabled the car under a grass shelter and set about collecting porters to carry our stuff to D.'s old camp in the Gubba, on the other side of a ridge eight miles away.

This camp site was a charming one, perched high above the floor of the valley, sheltered amidst a clump of trees, and watered by a clear stream whose source was a spring near the top of the ridge. From the door of the tent we commanded several miles of the valley, while from a small spur half a mile away the field of view was even greater. The only drawback to an otherwise perfect situation was the waist-deep grass, concealing many boulders, whose presence made worse the cold, wet job of stumbling sleepily out of camp in the half-light of dawn, and increased the possibility of falls and damaged rifles.

The elephant kept to the valley bottom, which was only a mile across, and fairly open except for a dense strip of bush on either side of the stream or series of muddy water-holes that lay in the middle of it. In places this strip almost filled the valley floor; at others it narrowed to a few yards; but it was nowhere penetrable except by following game tracks. It consisted largely of euphorbia-trees, which gave the bush a sinister aspect. Better known as the candelabra-tree, a name which well describes the shape, this is a dismal grey giant cactus. It is much disliked by the natives on account of the property the sap has (or is said to have) of blinding a man. The bushmen of South Africa use the juice of a euphorbia for poisoning their arrows.

Besides lesser game, the valley was the home of a herd of buffalo, and D. had seen tracks of rhino. Less tangible but more to be feared than these, were the tsetse fly, carrier of sleeping-sickness. The fly lives in thick bush, seems to require shade, and is never far from water. There are two principal specia, *glossina palpalis* and *glossina morsitans*; the former is the carrier of sleeping-sickness while the other infects cattle with a fatal disease called 'fly'. It is now thought probable that their rôles are interchangeable. For us the only way of avoiding this pest was to leave the bush before eight in the morning and not to enter it again until lae in the evening.

While coming along in the car we had noticed recent tracks of elephant, and, after making camp, D. interviewed some local natives in order to bring his knowledge up to date – he had been away from the district for some weeks with a bad attack of fever. Meanwhile I took a light rifle and strolled along the hillside, where I saw some reedbuck and a herd of waterbuck. The reedbuck was Chandler's variety, which in spite of its name is never found near reeds but on stony hillsides. We wanted meat – or I have no doubt our porters did – but I did not shoot, because the locals reported that the buffalo herd was at this end of the valley and a shot might spoil our chances of bagging one. As a result of being shot at, elephant and buffalo are now the wariest of game, and the sound of a rifle, even at a distance, is enough to make them leave the locality. For this reason there is much to be said in favour of a light rifle, the report of which does not disturb a whole district as does the roar of a big double-barrel rifle.

Next morning D., who was still convalescent, stayed in camp, when I turned out at five, again carrying only a light rifle, to wander slowly up the valley skirting the edge of the bush. I was very much on the *qui vive*. According to the natives, an elephant which D. had wounded was still hereabouts. I saw nothing until at seven o'clock, as I was about to turn for home and breakfast, out of the corner of one eye I caught a glimpse of what looked like the tail of an elephant disappear into the bush. The wounded elephant had been looming large in my imagination – an imagination quickened by a lack of food – to the exclusion of all else. I had only the little .256 rifle, so instead of closer investigation I returned at once to camp for a heavier weapon. On the way I shot two kongoni for our meat-hungry porters. Having seen nothing of the buffalo or their spoor, I concluded the natives had been mistaken when they told us the buffalo were in this part of the valley.

After some food D. accompanied me back to the scene of my ignominious flight. He was a bit sceptical, and rather thought I had been seeing things, and now I was not so sure myself, for my glimpse had been but a fleeting one, and of only a tail at that. It was therefore a surprise for both of us when we found from the spoor that the tail I saw was not an imaginary one, and that it belonged, not to an elephant, but to a buffalo.

It was then too late in the day to do anything, because the buffalo would be lying up in the bush. I kicked myself for having missed such a chance, and no doubt D. wanted to kick me too for my unwary shots at the kongoni. However, even if the buffalo were alarmed they would not stir before evening; we were therefore back again at sunset. Our perseverance was rewarded by a hurried snapshot which D. took, and missed, at a big bull running across a grass glade. That was all we saw.

Next morning we were out again from five to nine to find the herd had moved down the valley, whither, in the evening, we followed them – but they had gone too far.

This bare recital illustrates the difficulty of getting a shot at wary game even though their whereabouts are more or less known. We knew where they were, had devoted two days to them, and had had only one very slim chance; all very dull, possibly, to read about, but great fun in the doing. The pursuit was full of interest – indeed, excitement, since in this type of country you can never tell what you may not meet round the corner.

Meanwhile our native intelligence department had definitely located the elephant in a stretch of very bad bush some ten miles down the valley, towards which we now moved camp. It had rained hard every night since our arrival, and we had barely packed the sodden tents before it started again. It was a wet, warm, and exhausting march, mainly because the floor of the valley was compounded of black cotton soil, of which vile, sticky stuff our boots picked up several pounds at each step. Camp was not reached until afternoon.

The valley here was much wider, so that to be within striking distance of the bush we had to camp in a far less pleasing spot almost in the bottom, where mosquitoes were troublesome. A side valley, the Aru, came in close to the camp, and we were about two miles from where we expected to find the elephant.

That evening we went down to the bush but found no spoor, and on the way home D. was tempted by a roan antelope with a very good head. The wind was setting away from the bush, nor had we seen any sign of the elephant, so he risked disturbing them and loosed off. After a stern chase and a second shot the big roan was brought to bag, and we got back to camp long after dark with the head.

Three days had thus passed without any hostilities in the warfare against the elephant, but this morning we were to have an affair of outposts. Down in the bush by six, we soon came on fresh spoor, and a little later heard elephants trumpeting. For an hour we manœuvred in dense bush, trying hard to keep a chancy wind right and to get a sight of something. The tension increased every minute. We were all keyed up, and had almost had enough, when, suddenly, thanks mainly to a very good Lumbwa tracker of D.'s, we found ourselves regarding a solitary bull elephant standing in a little clearing twenty yards away, offering an easy shot. He had very poor teeth, but that did not matter. D. promptly fired both barrels, but failed to drop him, and then followed a most startling conjuring trick. The elephant vanished instantaneously into the bush with a fearsome crash, and in his place stood a rhino, weaving his head to and fro in a puzzled but threatening manner.

It must have been immediately behind the elephant, and it was very strange that these two great beasts should have consorted together in this manner. I was told by D. of a case where the body of a rhino he had shot had been moved a distance of two hundred yards by some elephants. It is not uncommon to see herds of antelope mixed up with kongoni, wildebeeste, and eland, grazing happily together, but in their case it is probable that other animals like to be near the kongoni, which are of a particularly alert and watchful nature, in order to have timely notice of the approach of any danger.

We stood facing each other for a matter of minutes until the rhino showed signs of wishing to investigate the cause of the disturbance, upon which D. fired again. He, too, disappeared with a crash little less loud than that of his companion, leaving us there in the thickest of bush with a wounded elephant and a wounded rhino on our hands, and the rest of the elephant herd all round us.

With infinite caution we slowly followed the rhino spoor through dangerously thick stuff for a hundred yards. The sound of a long-drawn breath stopped us as if shot, but the bush was so dense that some minutes passed before we could make out the form of a rhino facing us, not ten yards away. D. fired, stepping hastily back as he did so. The rhino fell and got up again, but, taking D.'s place, I finished it off.

The removal of one possible source of unpleasantness made us feel slightly easier. We advanced to examine the rhino, and were at once struck by the fact that the horn now seemed much smaller than that which had menaced us in the first place, which we had remarked as a particularly fine specimen. A cry from the tracker made us both jump, for we were still rather on edge, but, looking round, we saw him pointing, and there, a few yards from him, lay the body of another rhino. There were two, and this was the elephant's companion whose last breath it was we had heard.

It was an unfortunate affair, because we had no wish to kill a rhino, much less two, but from the time of firing at the elephant no other course was open to us, and, considering all other things, we were well out of it. Having taped the long horn, which measured thirty-one inches, we decided to get out of the bush and leave the wounded elephant till next day. The tsetse fly were becoming active, and we had had a busy morning and no breakfast.

The shortest way home led through a long stretch of bush, through which we passed with some apprehension by means of game trails. Much spoor indicated the presence of the whole herd, and D. knew from experience that when alarmed they could remain uncannily and deceptively quiet. It was eerie work in the gloom of the euphorbias, and when an elephant passed like a wraith not thirty yards from us, we froze instinctively in our tracks. He was moving fast and quite noiselessly. All we saw was a momentary glimpse of his ribs. As he passed behind us he got our wind, whereupon there was one loud crash as he changed direction, and then silence. The fright was mutual.

We returned to the scene at dawn next day with some porters to chop out the horns, and, having started them on this, we took up the spoor of the elephant.

The porters did not relish being left alone with the dead rhinos; even the thought of five tons of meat failed to cheer them. They imagined the surrounding bush to be alive with elephants, and, admittedly, this time they had more grounds for their fears than was usual. True, the elephants were no longer there, but twenty-four hours ago they had been, and to a native this was almost the same thing and quite sufficient cause for alarm. These particular natives, of an agricultural and not very intelligent tribe of Nilotic negroes, had an ingrained fear of the bush. Even if they could be persuaded to enter it, they were quite useless at finding their way about or moving quietly. On the other hand, D.'s tracker, who was a Lumbwa, was perfectly at home in it, and coolness itself when there was dangerous game about. We could always rely on him for that extra pair of keen eyes and sensitive ears which are so essential for hunting of this kind.

There was one exception amongst the porters: a man whom D. had told off to accompany me. He was an oldish man, not much use as a tracker, a complete clown, the butt of the camp, and apparently insensible to fear. He seemed to cherish a private grudge against all large game, and was never happier than when in pursuit of them. Carrying a light spear, he would barge about, quite unconcerned, in horrible proximity to elephant and buffalo; and to less ardent fire-eaters like myself seemed inconveniently eager to come to close action in the shortest possible time.

To return to the chase; our hopes were soon dashed. We could find no blood spoor, and the tracks soon became inextricably mingled with those of the herd, which had apparently left the bush and gone up to the Aru Valley during the night. They must have passed close to the camp. This wounded elephant was subsequently found dead by some natives not far from where he was hit.

In the afternoon we went up a hill overlooking the Aru Valley. The bush was less dense here, and towards evening we spotted the great black backs of the buffalo grazing slowly up. The herd kept inside the bush, but presently two glorious bulls moved out into a glade. This was not what we were there for, but I at any rate was not on duty and the chance was too good to miss. As a guest, I was to take the first shot, and after a long and very careful stalk we got within seventy yards of the biggest bull. Unluckily, when the time came to shoot I was behind D., and it was too late to change places, for the bull was already suspicious. Had we been sure of the wind and the buffalo we might have bandied politeness like the Gentleman of the Guard at Fontenoy, but, as it was, D. rightly took his chance and dropped the bull with a shot in the chest. The herd stampeded in a flash and no second chance offered.

The horns were a fine pair, old and gnarled, and over thirty-six inches long. Not content with that, D. also wanted the skin, which is highly prized by the natives, who will gladly give a heifer in exchange for one. They like buffalo hide for making their shields. Only the Lumbwa and the Clown were with us, but the shot soon drew a horde of men, women, and children, carrying baskets in anticipation of free meat. In spite of this willing assistance, it was dark before the long job of skinning was finished, and when the crowd understood that the skin had to be carried back to camp that night they melted away as a crowd does at the announcement of a silver collection. The skin was very big, a good inch thick over the shoulders, and, of course, wet, so the weight was enormous. In addition, it had to be carried over two miles of rough going – to our porters a disagreeable thought, but not so disagreeable as the idea of leaving the remnants of the carcase to others – humans or hyenas.

D.'s determination, backed by a forcible manner, prevailed, so that soon a gang of ten were staggering along under a strong sapling round which the skin was draped. We had to stay with them every step of the way or the precious hide would have been thrown to the hyenas forthwith. We rested when they rested, which was often, and it was two hours later before the party, now almost mutinous, arrived in camp. However, they had contrived to bring some meat as well as the skin, and when this was sizzling over the fire they ceased reviling the oppressor and began blessing their benefactor.

The following morning D. attended to cleaning the trophies while I walked over to a distant hill across the valley, known to D. as Lion Hill. A month back he had come across eleven lions near this hill, but very wisely left them alone. No such sight rewarded me for a long, hot walk, and when I got back to camp I was disgusted to find D. had gone up the Aru on fresh news of the elephant. But I missed nothing. He had not been able to get near them, but had loosed off a few rounds to keep them on the move. This was effective, for the next day we learnt that they had retreated up the Gubba again, whither we must now follow.

So ended the first round with honours easy, or perhaps slightly in our favour, for the elephants were on the run and badly frightened. Regarded merely as a shooting trip it had been more than successful, but D. in his capacity of V.C.O. would have to be discreet about that side of the business, and we hoped that the next round would make up for any remissness on our part, as indeed it did.

CHAPTER SIX

Business and Pleasure

'And o'er unhabitable downs,
Place elephants for want of towns.' – Swift

WE were glad to exchange the heat and smells of the valley camp for the cool freshness of our old eyrie on the hillside; the porters' larder, which was now overstocked with rhino and buffalo meat, was an offence in the eyes of heaven if not in those of our men. A native never throws anything away or leaves anything behind; old tins, old bottles, old clothes, and old meat – especially old meat – are their delight, so that, as a safari proceeds, and one fondly imagines the loads to be getting lighter, the reverse is the case. All the old rubbish which has long since been thankfully discarded will be found, if one troubles to look, packed carefully away in the loads as treasured possessions, and, in addition, there will be samples of meat and bits of skin, in every stage of decay, from all the animals that have been shot since the safari started.

The morning after our return we sat on Observatory Hill, as we had named the little spur close to the camp, raking the valley bottom with our glasses. We sat there till nearly eight o'clock, and just as we were about to give up D. spotted five cows moving up the valley. We dashed down in hot haste, but by the time we had picked up their spoor they had already retired to the thickest cover against the heat of the day.

The evening was another blank. Nothing was moving, and we concluded that the main herd were now past our camp and near the head of the valley, probably on the way out.

After nearly a year's experience of his herd, D. and his tracker knew their habits and the country in which they moved like a book, and could predict with uncanny certainty their probable movements. Our next attempt to come to grips was based on this knowledge, and was very nearly successful.

Ten miles up, the valley narrowed to a neck through which the herd must pass on the way out. Here the hills came down steeply on each side, and between them was less than a quarter of a mile of short grass and thorn-trees. Above and below the neck was the abominable bush in which it was so difficult to move or see, but if we could only catch them crossing the open ground in daylight we could probably kill three or four and frighten the others out of the Gubba for good.

Such was our plan, but now a boy brought news that some of the elephant D. had already driven out were beginning to come back across the river. This called for prompt action, and meant that we could not stay here much longer but must get away to the river to stop them from filtering back to rejoin the small herd of 'die-hards' which had been leading us such a dance.

The upshot was the next morning we returned to the car, and sent the porters on with the main camp to a known camp site by the river. We ourselves, the Lumbwa tracker, and the Clown, with a light camp, made a long detour by car to a place as near to the neck as we could approach. We got there by midday, parked our bus under a shady thorn-tree, and walked over to the neck some two miles away. We were pleased to find by the absence of spoor that the elephant had not yet passed, and we sat there expectantly until dark, but nothing came. Talking things over that night under our tree, D. took a gloomy view of our chances, because the odds were heavily in favour of their coming through in the night.

We were up at four and on the ground by five, only to find our fears realised. The herd had passed in the night and was now probably in the sanctuary of the bush. We followed hot-foot, hoping to come up with them feeding near the edge. But it was too late; there was not a sound, and we saw nothing.

Afterwards we found that at one point the herd must have been just inside the bush when we passed outside quite unsuspectingly. Such a thing was disconcerting, not to say alarming, for normally a feeding herd can be readily detected by the crash of breaking branches, the squealing, and the noise of stomach-rumbling. Here we had passed within a few yards of them without being aware of it, so that if they had got our wind a sudden charge by some angry cow would have caught us off our guard.

They had beaten us again, but as a last gambler's throw we arranged that I should return to the neck and that D. would fire some random shots in the hope of frightening them back towards me. This was done, and D. told me afterwards that they had got into a fine state of panic, but it was too late in the day to expect them to leave the shade of the bush and nothing broke in my direction.

While waiting there for something to happen I heard first a single shot and then the sounds as of a brisk battle from D.'s heavy rifle, and though I was eager, like Napoleon's well-drilled marshals, to march to the sound of the guns, I dared not leave the neck unguarded. At ten o'clock I gave it up and returned to the car, where I learnt from D. that he had enjoyed a more interesting morning than I had. After his first shot to get the elephant moving he had actually seen one, and fired some ineffective shots at long range; on the way home he had tried for an impala, that most graceful of antelopes, and also had two snap shots at a leopard. What a thoroughly mixed bag it would have been if he had got all three.

The scene now shifts to the river for the last act, to that part of it near the elephants' crossing-place on which all their routes converge. Like most African rivers, there was on both banks a narrow strip of dense bush, but outside this the country was more open. It was hilly and broken, covered with short grass and scattered thorn-trees, allowing a range of visibility of a good hundred yards – on the whole much easier country for our purpose than the Gubba.

It is a common mistake to camp too near to the intended hunting-ground.

Our camp, therefore, was pitched two miles from the river, but, even so, the elephant down by the ford were noisy enough during the night to be heard by us – perhaps they had got our wind even at that distance. The scent and hearing of an elephant are most acute. One very experienced elephant hunter considers that they can scent a man at a greater range than any other animal – perhaps at six hundred yards or more – but that they cannot sight anything at more than fifty yards, even though it is on the skyline.

Next morning we made a long round, heard one scream, but saw nothing; while from two o'clock till seven we were out again further up the river. Coming home we again heard one, when we ran for a couple of miles, but failed to come up with them.

For several days now I had been having trouble with a knee that had gone completely stiff so that I had to walk with one leg a 'swinger'. This 'dot and carry one' was a painful business, and, plodding home after this exhausting day, I tried to convince D. of what was now crystal clear to me, that to camp two miles from our scene of action was carrying caution to absurd lengths. 'Two b—— miles of b—— absurdity' was the text on which I preached. It made no impression on D., who had not got a dud leg, but I forgave him because he had an excellent theory, which, moreover, he carried into practice, that in order to keep fit on safari you must do yourself rather better than when at home. The bottles which exemplified this theory travelled in company with a syphon in a specially constructed four-gallon petrol tin with a hinged lid, and when this was under the table between us we soon forgot tired legs, stiff joints, and elephants that behaved like will-o'-the-wisps.

In the old days in South Africa, before fear of man drove them into thick bush and forest, the elephants were hunted on ponies; a pony that was staunch in the presence of elephant, and would allow one of the old elephant-guns (a young cannon like a 4-bore) to be fired from off its back, was a thing of great value. Nowadays a stout pair of legs are more useful. It was, I think, the celebrated hunter Stigand, whose opinion of the scenting powers of elephant I have just quoted, who reckoned that, failures included, every elephant killed had cost him one hundred miles of walking.

We repeated the round next morning, and yet once more in the afternoon. Towards evening we climbed a hill overlooking the ford and sat there listening to the very noisy mob down below in the bush. Suddenly, from directly behind us, came one shrill, solitary trumpet. Our chance had come.

Heading away from the bush, we had not far to go before we located about a dozen elephants, mostly cows and young bulls in fairly easy country. Cows are, of course, protected in the ordinary way, but for our purpose a dead cow was as effective as a dead bull.

Taking advantage of their short range of vision, and troubling only to keep the wind right, we got to within fifty yards before being seen. The biggest of the cows then swung round to face us, ears stuck out and trunk erect, looking indeed 'wiciously wenomous', as John Jorrocks would have said. D. fired, and she came for us at the shot. I fired and turned her, and D., taking advantage of the broadside presented as she swerved, poured in more lead. He was taking no chances. Meanwhile I succeeded in dropping two more, and D. one, before the rest broke for the river, where we hoped that their panic might infect the others and carry the whole lot over.

D. thought that these may have been some of our friends from the Gubba in search of a quieter neighbourhood, or possibly forerunners of the main body. The ivory was all small, but it was then too late to cut it out, so we returned for it early next day. On the way down we were disappointed to hear a pandemonium still raging at the river; it was evident there was an agitated discussion in progress, but what the upshot would be we could not tell.

Before leaving camp we had given the word to pack. My leave was at an end and D. was willing to give the elephant a breathing-space so that this last lesson might sink in. He had also a chance now of fulfilling a commission given him by some learned body in England engaged in research work, which was to obtain for them the fœtus of an elephant.

Neither of us knew the first thing about an elephant's interior arrangements, nor had we gone closely into the means of preservation and despatch beyond providing ourselves with a five-gallon drum of methylated spirits. This drum we had solemnly carted about with us from camp to camp, much to the chagrin of the porter who had to carry it. Our men were curious as to the contents, and from the way we cherished it thought it must be some potent spirit, as indeed it was: but had we explained the base uses to which it was to be put they would have been more than ever convinced of our madness. This drum was about twelve inches in diameter and eighteen inches deep, and our plan, beautiful in its simplicity, was merely to remove the lip, drop in our specimen, and solder it up.

However, there was now no time to waste; the cows had been dead for twelve hours and we set about our grisly task. In one of them we found what we wanted, and, having imbued the boys with some of our recently kindled enthusiasm for science, they extracted it with the greatest care. When at last it was laid at our feet for inspection, we found it measured about four feet by two and weighed every bit of two hundred pounds. Our five-gallon drum, which was standing open-mouthed in readiness, looked rather foolish – our own mouths must have stood open in sympathy. The problem of getting a quart into a pint pot seemed, in comparison, simple, but D. was not to be beaten by a trifle like that, and bethought him of a forty-gallon oil-drum now lying empty on his farm seventy miles away. He forthwith decided we must go there, quickly, specimen and all. The mild objections to having the repulsive mass lying at our feet as a fellow-traveller for that distance, which I raised, were brushed contemptuously aside.

By now it was nine o'clock, and getting warm. Already the air bore to the sensitive nostril something more than a hint that speed was essential if our gift was to be at all acceptable to science. A stretcher of branches was rigged up, and six of our stoutest porters hoisted the whole thing on to their shoulders. Grass and leaves were then strewn over it to protect it from the sun and to keep off the flies, and the cortege started at a most unfuneral pace for the car. In spite of frequent relays of porters we did not get there until midday, but camp had already been struck and everything was ready.

The elephant in embryo was slid gently from the stretcher into the box-body of the car, which it almost filled, while to avoid doing it any damage our kit was festooned round the bonnet and the wings. D. took the wheel and off we sped over a shockingly bad road. After an hour D. succumbed to an attack of fever, so that I had to take over the driving. I am never fond of driving a car with the critical owner of it sitting beside me as a passenger, and now everything conspired to make the position an unenviable one. Neither of us was feeling very amiable. It was a disgustingly hot day, our kit kept dropping off, and the other passenger at the back was beginning to make its presence felt. The luckless driver could do nothing right; if I hit the innumerable ruts and pot-holes too hard I was accused of lack of skill or deliberately attempting to break up the car; if, on the other hand, I drove too carefully, I was rated for allowing our unique specimen to go bad on our hands, thus showing a pitiful lack of enthusiasm for the great cause of scientific research in which we were now enlisted as humble but active pioneers; moreover, it was pointed out that if such a fate did overtake our precious burden, our names, mine particularly, would stink for ever in the nostrils of biologists with a stink far worse than that from which we were now shrinking.

At four o'clock, when we were about half-way, we reached an Administrative Post, where there was a hospital for natives, the doctor of which was a friend of D.'s. We stopped for advice, thinking, not unnaturally, that here was something after their own hearts. The experts there were interested but pessimistic. Accustomed only to seeing paltry specimens tucked comfortably away in little glass bottles, the Brobdingnagian scale of ours seemed to deprive them of any imagination or inventive resource they may have had. They talked learnedly but vaguely of formalin injections, but were unable to say off-hand how many pints or gallons would be needed, and at length hinted broadly that they had neither formalin nor time to waste. Meanwhile the passenger at the back, for whose benefit we had stopped, complained loudly of the delay, so, thanking them, but with our faith in the usefulness of doctors shaken, we drove on desperately. It was 'night or Blücher', the oil-drum or the grave.

We got in without further adventure about dark, and called urgently for boys and lights to assist at the obsequies or the pickling. The Thing had stood the journey fairly well, but looked a bit wan in the light of the lanterns. A friend who was present had the hardihood to suggest that it had been hung a shade too long – a piece of facetiousness that struck me as dangerous in view of D.'s choleric mood.

It was ticklish work getting it into the drum, with D. hopping about and cursing everybody in his anxiety lest at the last moment his flawless specimen should receive some irreparable injury. To say it was poured in would be an exaggeration – insinuated, perhaps, describes it better; but, anyhow, in it went, and now all depended upon our precious five gallons of methylated spirits.

The suspense was frightful, as this was swallowed in the cavernous depths of the big drum, and agonising were our doubts as to whether the spirit would be sufficient to cover everything. Happily it sufficed, and with a last affectionate glance at the dreadful Thing inside we popped the lid on and sealed it up. We went to dinner, proud of the day's work and our unique specimen, with our appetites unimpaired by memories of its recent past or fears for its future.

I left next day, and that was the last I saw of D. and the oil-drum for some time. I often wondered how it had fared on the long journey of seventy miles to the station, five hundred miles in the fierce heat of a steel truck to the coast, and yet fiercer heat of the Red Sea; and even more did I wonder what the biological consignee thought of it. The true story is shrouded in mystery, and I fear it will never be revealed. Perhaps the drum was never delivered, because, shortly after, I read in a paper of a truck on the Uganda Railway being derailed by the explosion of an oil-drum. I had an uneasy feeling that there might have been some connection.

Later I heard that D. had controlled his vermin so well that his services were no longer needed and he lost his job. All had been rounded up and banished to beyond the river except for a remnant of 'die-hards' which still clung stubbornly to the Gubba. I believe he even found a solution to another problem in practical biology, but it was probably one of less formidable dimensions than ours.

CHAPTER SEVEN

Ruwenzori – The Mountains of the Moon

'And with Cæsar to take in his hand
the army, the empire, and Cleopatra,
and say, "All these will I relinquish if
you will show me the fountain of the Nile." '
                                          – Emerson

THE rifles were oiled and packed away, and, after the rather forced gaieties of an African Christmas, I took the ice-axe from its corner preparatory to joining S. on his farm. We had in mind a journey to Ruwenzori in January of 1932, that month being specially picked because in most parts of East Africa it is the driest. The forethought went unrewarded.

The Ruwenzori range seems to me to combine the greatest geographical and historical interest of any part of Africa; true, historically, Egypt must take pride of place, but somehow I have never been able to regard Egypt as part of Africa; it seems more akin to Asia, though it is so inseparably connected with the Nile, a connection that is expressed in the aphorism: 'The Nile is Egypt and Egypt is the Nile'. These Ruwenzori mountains are the birthplace of the Nile, the Fons Nilus of the ancients, and their existence was for more than two thousand years a field for discussion, speculation, and endeavour by Egyptian, Greek, Roman, Hindu, Arab, and European. The discovery by Stanley in 1888 of this range of mountains whose snows feed the two lakes from which the greatest of the Nile branches takes its source, brought to an end the long quest for the sources of this classic river.

The first hint we have that their existence was known in very early times is a verse in Æschylus which speaks of 'Egypt nurtured by snow', and Aristotle in the fourth century B.C. mentions the 'Mountains of Silver, the source of the Nile'. The Greeks themselves were active in trade and exploration on the Upper Nile and round the East African coast, but they were probably only followers in the footsteps of Arabs, Phœnicians, Egyptians, or even Hindus. Speke, when preparing for his journey which culminated in his discovery of the Ripon Falls, where the Nile leaves Victoria Nyanza, secured his best information from the Hindu sacred books, the Puranas: 'All our previous information,' he says, 'concerning the hydrography of these regions originated with the ancient Hindus, who told it to the priest of the Nile; and all those busy Egyptian geographers . . . in solving the mystery which enshrouded the source of their holy river were so many hypothetical humbugs. The Hindu traders had a firmer basis to stand upon, through their intercourse with the Abysinians.' The Puranas trace the course of the Nile to a great lake, mention Zanzibar, Lake Tanganyika, the Karagwe Mountains (in Uganda), and Unyamwezi, the Country of the Moon.

Under the settled rule of the Roman Empire the Greek merchants in Egypt prospered, and we read of one of them, Diogenes, who, returning from a voyage to India, landed on the east coast at Rhaptum (Pangani, near Tanga ?); thence he claimed to have travelled inland for a journey of twenty-five days until he arrived in the vicinity of 'two great lakes and the snowy range of mountains whence the Nile draws its twin sources'. He was told that the Nile united its head streams at a point north of the great lakes, whence it flowed through marshes to the Blue Nile and so to Egypt. The time taken – twenty-five days – rather invalidates his story of having seen the snow mountains unless it was Kilimanjaro or Kenya that he saw (and there, of course, there is no lake), but the information he brought back, from whatever source derived, was amazingly accurate, and was evidently based on something more than guesswork. The story is told by Ptolemy, the great Greek geographer writing about A.D. 150, and he it is who has received the credit for the theory of the origin of the Nile, which was not proved until seventeen centuries later.

It is from him that we get the name Mountains of the Moon, for on his map he called the Karagwe Mountains 'Lunæ Montis finis occidentalis', and, for the confusion of subsequent explorers and geographers, Kilimanjaro is shown as Lunæ Montis finis orientalis. This classical tradition that 'the sources of the Nile were to be found in two lakes whose waters were fed by the snow melting on the Mountains of the Moon, south of the equator', was handed down unchallenged. Mediæval maps and descriptions, Arab and European, reproduce the Mountains of the Moon and the equatorial lakes in spite of a complete lack of any confirmation of their existence.

When Krapf and Rebmann discovered the mountains of Kilimanjaro and Kenya in 1848, it was at once thought that these were Ptolemy's Mountains of the Moon, although there is no lake near either of them, nor are they in any way connected with the Nile basin.

In 1861 Speke discovered the Mfumbiro volcanoes, a group of volcanic peaks 12,000 feet to 14,000 feet high lying between Lakes Kivu and Albert Edward, and claimed that these were the Mountains of the Moon. He was on surer ground, because a tributary of the Kagera River, one of the most remote sources of the Victoria Nile, rises here, but there is a fatal objection in that there is no snow on any of these peaks, which thus fail to answer Ptolemy's description.

In the twenty years preceding Stanley's discovery of Ruwenzori in 1888, many explorers had traversed the same country and sailed upon the waters of Victoria, but none had suspected the near presence of this region of snow and ice, hidden as it was in the clouds and vapours which are a persistent and dominating feature of the range. Indeed, in 1875, when circumnavigating Victoria, Stanley himself was camped on the eastern slopes and relates, without comment, the assertions of the natives that above him there were mountains of extraordinary size and of a shining whiteness; and it was only on a later journey, in 1888, that he was vouchsafed the almost incredible vision of these snow mountains, practically on the equator, which by then had become almost fabulous. 'While looking to the south-east and meditating upon the events of the last month, my eyes were attracted by a boy to a mountain, said to be covered with salt, and I saw a peculiar-shaped cloud of a most beautiful silver colour which assumed the proportions and appearance of a vast mountain covered with snow. Following its form downwards, I became struck with the deep blue-black colour of its base, and wondered if it portended another tornado; then, as the sight descended to the gap between the eastern and western plateaux, I became for the first time conscious that what I gazed upon was not the image or semblance of a vast mountain, but the solid substance of a real one, its summit covered with snow.'

To these mountains Stanley gave the name Ruwenzori, as being that by which they were most widely known amongst the natives of the surrounding regions. It was, naturally, only an approximation to the sound they uttered when questioned by Stanley on the subject. Amongst the natives whom we employed on the mountain, the word, or our way of uttering it, had no meaning whatsoever. This is only to be expected, because the numerous tribes who live near the mountains probably have, and in those days certainly had, very little intercourse. Even those living on the same side of the range have different languages and mix very little, while those on opposite sides might as well be in different worlds for all they know or see of each other. Nor would any native think of giving a name to the whole range, but would only name, if at all, some particularly prominent peak.

Stanley attributed the obscurity, in which the mountains seemed to be always wrapped by cloud, to vapours exhaled from the surrounding plains saturated by rain and then exposed to the fierce heat of an equatorial sun. The rainfall to the east of the range is about 60 inches annually; on the west it is heavier, while on the northern slopes it is said to reach 200 inches.

Stanley's opinion that Ptolemy's Mountains of the Moon had at last been identified did not go unchallenged. Some learned pundits maintained that Kenya and Kilimanjaro were the mountains in question, and, as has been seen, Ptolemy did call the last-named Lunæ Montis finis orientalis, presumably in the belief that a great range stretched for five hundred miles from Ruwenzori in the west to Kilimanjaro in the east. But neither Kilimanjaro nor Kenya is remotely connected with the Nile basin, and the only argument in support of this contention is that these two mountains are far more likely to have been seen by very early travellers than the inaccessible Ruwenzori range.

Others identified the Mountains of the Moon with the Mfumbiro volcanoes, in accordance with Speke's notion, and yet others accepted the explanation advanced by the German explorer, Dr. O. Baumann. He discovered that one source of the Kagera, mentioned above as the main tributary of the Victoria Nile, was situated in the mountains of Missosi ya Mwesi, north-east of Lake Tanganyika. This name does in fact mean the 'Mountains of the Moon', the surrounding country is known as Charo cha Mwesi, or the Lands of the Moon, and the people of it are Mwana ya Mwesi, the People of the Moon. That this romantic title should actually be applied to the mountains of this country by the natives was at least a strange coincidence, but their insignificant altitude and comparative unimportance incline one to the belief that it was nothing more, or, perhaps, the mistaken transference of the name by ancient geographers to mountains more worthy of it.

The mountains of Abyssinia are also competitors for the title and are not without their backers, but to the plain man it seems clear enough that the only mountains answering in all respects to Ptolemy's description are those which we now call Ruwenzori. To argue otherwise appeals strongly to the upholders of lost causes, of whom there is never any lack, and no doubt to the end of time people will be found maintaining stoutly that Bacon wrote Shakespeare's plays, that the earth is flat, or that the Ruwenzori Mountains are not Ptolemy's Mountains of the Moon. But it is time to leave this interesting but profitless speculation and to recount briefly the history of the more recent exploration of Ruwenzori, wherein ascertainable facts take the place of cloudy theory.

The first to penetrate the mountains was Stanley's assistant, Lieutenant W. G. Stairs. He approached from the west, and reached an altitude of about 10,000 feet. In 1891 Dr. F. Stuhlmann made a five-day excursion up one of the western valleys, attaining a point not far below the snow-line which he estimated to be 13,300 feet. He it was who recognised that Ruwenzori was not a single mountain, but a range, and who accurately described the successive zones of vegetation from foothills to snow-line. Four years later G. F. Scott Elliott, a naturalist, made several journeys from the west, and was the first to find a route from the east up the Mobuku Valley, by which route all subsequent successes were achieved, save that of a Belgian expedition, which climbed the peaks from the western side in 1932.

The closing years of the last century were years of stress and turmoil for Uganda, for it was at that time gradually being brought under British administration. The country was in a very disturbed state, and no more exploration was done around Ruwenzori until 1900, when C. S. Moore ascended the Mobuku Valley to a height of 14,900 feet and was the first to reach the glaciers lying at its head. He confirmed Stuhlmann's observations, which distributed the peaks amongst four main groups. Three other parties, including that of Sir Harry Johnston, the exceedingly versatile High Commissioner of the Uganda Protectorate, followed him in the same year, and another a year later, so the route was becoming well known.

Transport problems, too, were very much simpler than formerly. In 1902 the Uganda Railway was opened to the east side of Lake Victoria, and steamers ran from railhead to Entebbe, the capital of Uganda on the northwest shore of the Lake, only 200 miles from Fort Portal, at the north end of the range. Moreover, with the crushing of the insurrection of 1897, the country was rapidly pacified, and travellers could move about with some sense of security.

In November 1905 the mountains were attacked for the first time by a party of mountaineers, but on this occasion the weather proved to be a sufficient defence. Douglas Freshfield, A. L. Mumm, with the guide Moritz Inderbinnen, reached the head of the Mobuku Valley, but were prevented by persistent rain from doing more than reach the snows. Early in the following year a party sent out by the British Museum to study the flora and fauna of Ruwenzori spent several weeks in the Mobuku Valley. A. F. Wollaston (an experienced mountaineer and explorer) and H. B. Woosnam climbed a small peak on the ridge west of the valley, and so reached a height of over 16,000 feet.

It was left to the Italians to achieve not only the first success, but a success so sweeping that little was left to be done afterwards, and mountaineering expeditions of the same nationality have upheld the reputation then gained for thoroughness of organisation on the mountains of Alaska and in the Himalaya. From what has been said it will be clear that, when the Duke of Abruzzi took his large and well-equipped expedition out in the summer of 1906, little was known of the mountains except the best line of access; the position, number, and height of the snow peaks were only guessed at, estimates of the last ranging from 16,000 feet to 18,000 feet.

Apart from climbing the highest peaks, the objects of the expedition included a survey of the range and the study of geology, glaciology, botany, zoology, and meteorology. To carry out this ambitious programme there were twelve Europeans, including six scientists, four guides, a photographer, and a cook. The magnitude of the undertaking and the skill required to organise it can be gathered from the fact that over 300 porters were employed – a generous figure, but modest when compared with the numbers of some recent Himalayan expeditions – German, French, Italian, and British. Experience rather suggests that the success of an expedition is an inverse ratio to its magnitude, but to this the Duke of the Abruzzi's party was a marked exception. A dozen snow peaks, including Margherita, 16,815 feet, and Alexandra, 16,749 feet, the two highest, were climbed for the first time, while on some the ascent was repeated several times for purposes of survey. An accurate map of the peaks, glaciers, and high valleys was made, a mass of meteorological and other observations collected, and a wealth of botanical, zoological, and geological information gathered and specimens brought back.

That all this work should have been accomplished in the course of six weeks is the more remarkable when the handicap of 'Ruwenzori weather' is taken into account. Perhaps this expedition was more favoured by the weather than most, but from their records it appears that there were few days when the peaks remained clear after eight in the morning, while for the whole of June and the first week of July bad weather predominated. The only fine spell was in the second week in July, when the retreat from the higher valleys had already begun.

It was twenty years later before the highest peaks of Ruwenzori were again climbed, this time by an English party led by Dr. Noel Humphreys. In these two successful expeditions the extremes of size almost meet. Dr. Humphreys was accompanied by one other European and perhaps twenty porters; nevertheless, not only were the principal summits climbed, but a great deal of exploratory work was done in untouched country at the northern end of the range.

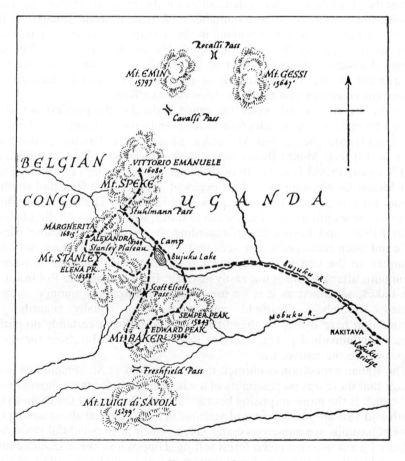

Ruwenzori

Before passing on to our attempt on the peaks, which was the third successful one, it may be well to outline roughly the size and position of Ruwenzori. In the last Ptolemy's guess was not far wrong, for it lies about a half degree north of the equator. The general direction of the range is north and south, and it consists of six snow mountains or groups of peaks separated from each other by lower ridges uncovered by snow. The length of the entire snowy range is about eleven miles; extending north and south of this are perhaps twenty miles of high but vegetation-covered ridges; and beyond again are the low foothills. At the southern end is Lake Edward, at the northern Lake Albert, and on the western side lies the trough of the western branch of the Great Rift Valley. Flowing through this trough from Lake Edward to Lake Albert is the Semliki River, into which river and its two lakes flows all the drainage from the northern, southern, western, and even eastern slopes of the Ruwenzori massif. Thus the White Nile issuing from Lake Albert is fed almost entirely by the waters from Ruwenzori, while Lake Victoria and the Victoria Nile is altogether a separate and independent system.

Another remarkable fact is that, although the range constitutes the most considerable group of snow mountains in Africa, a group situated in the middle of the continent and running in the direction of the main axis, yet it does not form part of the main watershed. The divide between the Nile and Congo drainage systems lies west of the Semliki River and is the western escarpment of the Great Rift. It is prolonged southwards through the Mfumbiro volcanoes and the west shore of Lake Kivu.

Of the six groups into which the range is divided the greatest is that of Mount Stanley, which includes four peaks over 16,000 feet, amongst them the two highest, Margherita and Alexandra. Mount Speke has two peaks, both over 16,000 feet; Mount Baker comes next with Edward Peak, 15,988 feet, and Semper, 15,843 feet. North of these are the two groups of Mount Emin and Mount Gessi, comprising four peaks of about 15,700 feet, and south is Mount Luigi di Savoia, with three peaks of 15,200 feet. The five passes which separate the six groups are, from north to south, Roccati, Cavalli, Stuhlmann, Scott Elliott, and Freshfield. Disregarding the lesser peaks, whose names have not been mentioned, one sees that the early explorers have not been forgotten in the system of nomenclature adopted. The practice of naming mountains after persons is not easily justified. Even a name like Robinson, in the Lakes, sanctified as it is by use, sounds incongruous amongst such as Scafell, Saddleback, Fairfield, and many more equally beautiful. In extenuation here it may be urged that there are almost certainly no native names for individual peaks, many of which are not visible from the lower slopes where the natives live.

The Italian expedition confirmed the observations of Stuhlmann and Scott Elliott that there was no possibility of a volcanic origin for these mountains, a fact which is the more surprising because around the base of the chain to the south and east are many traces of volcanic activity. Dotted about among the eastern foothills are numerous crater lakes, which form delightful turquoise-coloured gems in a rich green forest setting. Hippos love these secluded little lakes, while the surrounding forest is the home of a wonderful variety of birds and animals – both small and great, of which last class the rhinoceros alone is absent. Here, then, are traces of volcanic action, but to the south are volcanoes themselves – the Mfumbiro volcanoes, of which one is still active. Surrounding these are many miles of lava-covered ground with numerous crater lakes. To the north and east of Ruwenzori earth tremors are frequent, and of the few days I have spent at Fort Portal not one has passed without an earth tremor of some kind.

The glaciers of the range are small and are gradually receding. They have no real basins, but resemble ice-caps from which depend numerous ice-streams. The most striking feature of the snow regions is the number of the cornices, most of which assume an appearance peculiar to this region. The formation looks very like a section of an ostrich feather fan. None of the glaciers descend lower than 14,000 feet, the snow-line being about 700 feet higher. Above 14,000 feet rain generally falls as snow, but doesn't lie long.

Any traveller familiar with snow mountains is quick to notice two unusual features of Ruwenzori's glacial streams. They are comparatively small and, owing to an absence of the usual detritus, are very clean. Much melting of the glaciers is no doubt prevented by the almost permanent mist which covers the range, but that this does take place in some small degree is easily seen from the slight variation in volume of the streams, whose flow gradually rises as the daily sun exercises what slight power it has in these mist-covered regions, and diminishes again at night. The absence of silt is accounted for by the fact that the glaciers are almost stationary, and so grind no detritus from the rocks beneath them, being, as already noticed, more in the form of ice-caps crowning the summits and high ridges than ice-streams flowing down a valley. In spite of this apparently slight degree of melting, a great volume of water flows from the range to feed the White Nile. The range, by reason of its great extent and height, forms a large condenser upon which the hot, moist air drawn up from the surrounding plains is precipitated as snow, mist, or rain. A multitude of valleys scarring the slopes discharge this water again into neighbouring rivers. Stanley counted sixty-two rivers flowing from the mountains into the Semliki from the southern and western slopes alone.

The upper slopes of Ruwenzori, from 10,000 feet to the snow-line, comprise a world of their own – a weird country of moss, bog, rotting vegetation, and mud, on which flourish grotesque plants that seem to have survived from a past era; the vegetation of some lost world inhabited by dinosauria, pterodactyls, and mammoths. Here are seen gaunt giant groundsel crowned at the top with spiky heads like half-eaten artichokes; tough, leafless shrubs with white everlasting flowers called helichrysum; grey, withered, and misshapen tree heaths, tumescent with swollen growths of moss and lichen oozing moisture; monstrous freaks of nature bred from the union of mist and morass; a slimy barrier serving to enhance and make more desirable the fresh purity of the snows which lie beyond.

Such are the Mountains of the Moon – vying not with the austere splendour and sublimity of the Alps or the Himalaya, but by their position, mystery, traditions, and matchless scenery, ranking, surely, amongst the wonders of the world.

CHAPTER EIGHT

The Approach to Ruwenzori

'A barren detested vale, you see, it is:
The trees, though summer, yet forlorn and lean,
O'ercome with moss, and baleful mistletoe.'
– Shakespeare

WE left Turbo by car on the morning of January 9th and, leaving the squat bulk of Mount Elgon on our right, headed for the high granite obelisk seen in the distance marking the position of Tororo, on the Uganda border. The Uganda roads have a well-deserved reputation, so that we sped rapidly along, dropping gradually until Jinja was reached about tea-time.

Jinja is a little town on the shores of Lake Victoria close to the Ripon Falls, where the Nile issues from the lake to begin its long journey to the sea. The falls were discovered by Speke in 1862, who thus solved the problem of the position of one of the Nile sources. They are only about 20 feet high, but even without the romantic associations of the river it is an impressive sight to see the great volume of water sweeping over the falls to run through a gorge and disappear round a wooded bend a mile lower down. Above the falls are pools and shallows in which crocodiles and hippos laze, while immediately below, the water seems to be alive with big Nile perch, 30 lbs. to 40 lbs. in weight, trying ceaselessly but vainly to jump up the falls.

In addition to its romantic situation, Jinja is celebrated for a nine-hole golf-course lying close to the lake shore, the grass of which is kept short by the hippos which emerge nightly from the lake to graze. There is a local rule about hippo foot-marks, which are treated in the same way as rabbit scrapes at home, where the ball can be lifted without penalty. One of these hippos was such a regular visitor that he was known to the people of Jinja, indeed of Uganda and even further, as Horace. A usual way of entertaining visitors was to drive down to the links in the evening to watch Horace enjoying his supper. There was a story current when we were there that one party, which had dined not wisely but too well, went down with the avowed intention of pulling Horace's tail. One of the 'pot valiant,' boldly leaving the car, advanced towards the hippo, but Horace, also feeling playful, came for the man and chased him back to the car, taking a large piece out of something more than the slack of his breeches *en route*. The party were too happy to notice much amiss until someone discovered the presence of quantities of blood, and, after returning hastily to the town, they spent a long time in persuading a doctor that he was not being made the victim of a drunken leg-pull. The upshot was that the would-be humorist spent a month or so in hospital.

Until 1928 the Uganda Railway, so called, perhaps, because it never entered Uganda, stopped at Kisumu, on the east shore of the lake. Now, the main line enters Uganda to the north, crosses the Nile by a bridge just below the Rippon Falls, and terminates at Kampala, 80 miles away. The bridge also carries a road, but before that was built travellers by road were obliged to cross an arm of the lake by a rather cranky ferry running at very infrequent intervals. Thanks to the bridge, no time had to be wasted by us on the ferry, and we pushed on that evening, reaching Kampala at seven after a run of 250 miles.

We were ready for an early start next day in order to cover the remaining 200 miles to Fort Portal in good time, but we were delayed until seven waiting for a mechanic who we had agreed to take out to a car stranded 75 miles out. It was a case of assisting a damsel in distress, so the delay was suffered gladly by one of us, and by the other without impatience.

At four we reached Fort Portal, where we put up at a small hotel. It is the centre of the Toro district of Uganda, a district more favoured by spoil and climate than the rest of the Protectorate. The altitude is about 5,000 feet, the rainfall well distributed, and the soil a fertile, volcanic ash. Coffee is the main European crop, but bananas, citrus fruits, maize, wheat, potatoes and other vegetables, all flourish. To live in this garden is pleasant and simple, but to earn money from it is a different matter, for its remoteness is a severe handicap. To export anything involves 200 miles of road haulage and 800 miles of rail before one starts paying for sea carriage, so that only high-priced crops can justify themselves, and coffee, unfortunately, can no longer be put in that category.

Outside the township, on a neighbouring eminence, are the houses which comprise the palace of the King of Toro, or the Kabaka, who rules his country with the assistance of a Prime Minister and a Council of Elders, advised when necessary by the District Commissioner, who lives in Fort Portal. The thatching of the houses of the palace and the neat reed fences surrounding them are evidently the work of real craftsmen.

Fort Portal lies at the northern end of the Ruwenzori range, and only two miles north-west is the brink of the steep escarpment which plunges down 2,000 feet to the floor of the Western Rift Valley, through which the Semliki River winds. It is called the Semliki, but it is in reality the head waters of the White Nile. Across the bare, brown, sun-scorched plain at the bottom, broken only by the silver coils of the river, is the steep opposing wall of the Rift, crowned on top with the outer fringes of the Congo forest and forming the Congo–Nile divide, the watershed of Africa.

We spent a busy morning buying blankets, cooking-pots, and cigarettes for the porters, and interviewing the District Commissioner, from whom we got a letter to a native chief, who lived at the entrance to the Mobuku Valley, invoking his aid. Which things done, we drove south for 45 miles, reaching the Mobuku River at midday.

We hoped to find our chief somewhere in the neighbourhood, but the task promised to be difficult, for, to our surprise, the whole of the native population of Uganda seemed to be gathered there. We learnt that a bridge across the Mobuku was being built; an operation that had been in progress for the past two years. Several times it had almost reached completion, only to be washed away by the river coming down in flood. That day H.E. the Government of Uganda, who was on tour, had come in person to inspect progress; hence the assembled multitude.

Contrary to all expectations, we did find the needle in the haystack of humanity and gave the chief the D.C.'s letter, but that was all, for under the circumstances we could not expect to receive much attention.

We had another stroke of luck when we found amongst the crowd at the bridge a local settler, or, since he was the only one, *the* local settler. He lived a few miles up the Mobuku Valley, and he it was who had been Dr. Humphrey's companion in 1926. We were invited to make his house our headquarters and offered every assistance.

The farm was seven miles away, whither we at once proceeded along a very narrow and tortuous farm track. Driving away from the vicinity of the bridge when it was apparently the duty of everyone to be present, we had the guilty feeling of playing truant, while even the car registered a protest by puncturing a tyre. While we were perspiringly jacking it up to effect a change, two very smart and impressively large cars came round a bend, the leading one flying a small Union Jack. By pulling off the road a little they could have squeezed past, but we realised that this was hardly to be expected, so, fearful of delaying the ceremony at the bridge and feeling like the blundering hero of some Bateman drawing – the bluejacket who spat on the quarter-deck – we hastily kicked the jack away to manhandle the car off the road into the bush. It was a good car, but we blushed for its dingy paint and battered wings festooned with kit, and as the gubernatorial procession filed past in slow and shining solemnity it seemed to us that the bush was the only place for it.

Rather shaken by this little incident, we finished changing the wheel, and pushed on, only abandoning the car where the road came to an abrupt end below a steep hill. On top of this hill were some thatched huts belonging to the farm, and, having procured some boys to assist with the baggage, we toiled up to them.

The D.C.'s letter bore fruit. Very early next morning there arrived at the huts a great crowd of volunteers eager to accompany us, indeed, we had difficulty in persuading them that we wanted only a few. After much haranguing on both sides we picked out fourteen of the toughest-looking and finally got away about midday. Thirteen of the men carried 50-lb. loads, while the duty of the other was to go ahead with a panga (a heavy bush knife) to open up the overgrown track.

Some of these natives, Bakonjo, living on the lower slopes of the mountain knew what lay ahead, as they had been up to about 13,000 feet, with previous parties. They were a cheerful, willing lot, as tough as they looked, and well suited to carrying 50-lb. loads over the difficult country we presently reached. They had little equipment and less clothing, and were delighted to receive the blanket and vest issued to them out of the expedition's slender resources. Their most treasured personal possessions, chief of which was a pipe and tobacco, were carried in a little fur pouch slung from the neck. Another very important item of equipment carried by many was a cigar-shaped package of leaves closely wrapped and bound up against the weather. Inside was a sort of moss or lichen, which seemed to have the faculty of smouldering away happily without any air for days on end. When a light was wanted, the package was unwrapped and a few breaths soon blew the smouldering tinder to life.

The day was fine and hot as we marched through banana groves by the river before ascending a steep and narrow spur to a camping-ground called Bihunga. This was a small level spot on top of the spur at an altitude of about 7,000 feet.

Here cultivation ceases, and 1,000 feet higher thick forest is reached. Before burying ourselves in this, we stopped for a last look at the outside world to see beyond the green foothills a wide, flat expanse of light brown, almost yellow, country, a monotony of colour only relieved by the pale blue of a distant lake. The whole was bounded by the gentle, rounded summits of the Ankole Highlands. The sun still shone, but on entering the forest we were unaware of it, nor were we to see it again for many days. We climbed steeply to a pleasant little forest clearing called Nakitawa, where we camped. It was only one o'clock, but nothing, not even bribes, would induce the porters to go a step further. We realised there were also disadvantages in having men who had been up before, for they knew the time-honoured camping-grounds and used them in undeviating ritual, at whatever time they were reached.

From this point it was a matter of fighting one's way rather than marching, and every day the work became more severe. The track – or rather the line we followed, for track there was none – plunged headlong into deep valleys, only to climb the opposing slope with uncompromising abruptness. The Mobuku was already behind us, and now we crossed its greater tributary the Bujuku, up the valley of which our route lay.

Overhead, tall trees wrapped about with a tangle of creepers formed a dense canopy which shut out the light; underfoot was a matted carpet of undergrowth – ferns, brambles, fallen bamboos, giant nettles (said to be capable of making even an elephant sit up), and dead trees – over which we sometimes crawled, sometimes crept beneath on all fours, and sometimes had to cut a way through with the panga. The pace was painfully slow, but it was something that the porters could advance at all, balancing their loads on their heads, walking barefoot along the green and slimy trunk of some fallen giant many feet above the ground, or lowering themselves down steep and slippery cliffs of earth; torn by thorns, snatched at and caught by creepers, stung by nettles, plastered with mud, and everlastingly wet.

Through a window in the living green wall of our prison we saw for a brief moment the ice peaks of Stanley and Speke, filling the head of the valley, before they vanished once more in wreathing cloud. From now on 'Ruwenzori weather' prevailed, so that, but for one other occasion, this was the only time the peaks revealed themselves to us betweeen dawn and sunset.

We camped that night under a dripping, overhanging cliff at about 9,500 feet at almost the upper limit of the forest zone. As forest it compared ill with the clean, straight-growing cedar and the podocarpus giants of the Mau or the forested slopes of Mount Kenya, for a few indifferent prodocarpus were the only trees that looked as if they would make timber. The forest zone is succeeded in turn by a short but dense belt of bamboo, and then, above 10,000 feet, by a forest of tree heaths. This is a thick stand of leafless trees of a uniform height of 20 to 30 feet, made grotesque by waving beards of lichen hanging from every branch, and by the mossy growths covering the trunks.

The going, however, was very much better in this forest of tree heaths. The gradient was slight, with little to hinder progress except the soft and spongy ground, so that the camping-place of Kigo was reached by midday. We were welcomed by a cold drizzle, which made the porters the more resolute to stop where they were in spite of our protests at the shortness of the march.

Beyond the tree heaths we found an even stranger country, where solid earth disappeared altogether under an overburden of moss or fallen and rotting giant groundsel (senecio). Thick groves of these grow on every hand; they are from 12 to 20 feet high, and thick in proportion, but can easily be pushed over with one hand, so that in the groves themselves there are many more trees lying than standing. So rotten are these fallen trunks that they will not support the weight of a man, with the result that forcing a path through the labyrinth presented by senecio forest, growing as it does out of a morass, is laborious to the point of exhaustion.

By way of variety one can make a less slimy but perhaps more strenuous way through the suggestively named 'helichrysum' bushes; this is a pink and white flowered 'everlasting', growing nearly as high as a man. It is stiff, tough, wiry, trying to both clothes and temper. Its pretty flowers, like coloured paper, which do a little to brighten a drab landscape, make insufficient amends for a harsh, stubborn, unyielding nature. Over all a clammy mist hangs like a pall, and a deep silence broods. Even the innumerable brooks and rivulets are hushed as they flow deep below ground level in a narrow trench of moss – moss that seems to breed wherever the mist touches, on tree, plant, earth, or rock.

Such was the nightmare landscape across which we toiled on our fifth day, and such is the nature of all the high valleys below the snow-line, giving to Ruwenzori a mystery and strange beauty that has not its likeness in any other land. A country that only the language of Lewis Carroll could paint, the natural habitat of Snarks and Jabberwoks and jub-jub birds. A slough, but not a Slough of Despond, for were not the Delectable Mountains at hand?

CHAPTER NINE

The Ascent of Ruwenzori

'Round its breast the rolling clouds are spread.' – Goldsmith

WE camped in a damp but welcome cave at about 13,000 feet, hard by the Bujuku Lake, a mournful, shallow mere which, with its fœtid, mud-lined shores, was in harmony with the desolate landscape surrounding it. But from the cave our eyes lingered, not on this, but on the grim precipices across the valley below the snows of Mount Baker, on the serrated ridge of the Scott Elliott Pass, and the peaks and glaciers of Mount Stanley. This, however, was a view which was seldom, if ever, seen in whole except for a minute or so at dawn or dusk, so that we were usually compelled to trust to fleeting glimpses of rock and ice, peak and ridge, seen through the writhing mists, and in imagination link the whole together.

Our first plan had been to carry all our own food and kit to an advance base near the Scott Elliott Pass – a pass lying between Mount Stanley and Mount Baker which we hoped would give us access to both mountains. It was some time before the mist cleared sufficiently for us to identify the pass, and from that distance it looked as though the approach to it might prove too much for our porters. We had already sent eight of these down, retaining six with us in the cave. They were comfortable enough and moderately content, but were so daunted by the appearance of things higher up that it seemed advisable to leave them out of our calculations and shift for ourselves. On account, therefore, of this alteration in our plans the afternoon of our arrival at the cave was a busy one, sorting out food and kit for ourselves for five days, and making it up into two loads of 40 lbs. We intended to establish our camp on the Stanley plateau, from there climb Margherita and Alexandra, move our bivouac nearer to Mount Baker and climb that before returning to the cave to refit. We had yet to discover that as the hare must first be caught, so, on Ruwenzori, the peak must first be found.

We left camp at eight on the morning of the 17th, with two men carrying our loads. Skirting the lake-shore, we climbed through senecios, reached the rocks, and at about 15,000 feet came upon the site of a former bivouac. It was now eleven o'clock, and, as snow was beginning to fall, we sent the men back to the cave, shouldered our 40-lb. packs, and climbed slowly upwards. About one o'clock we reached the foot of the Elena Glacier, and, climbing now on snow at an easy angle, we presently reached the yet flatter slopes of the Stanley Plateau. The weather was thick, so that our sole guides were infrequent glimpses of the rocks of the Elena and Moebin Peaks close on our left. By three o'clock we were completely at a loss as to our whereabouts, so we pitched our little tent in what we imagined was a sheltered spot, and prayed for the mist to lift. At sunset the longed-for clearing came, showing, to our amazement, our camp pitched almost on the divide. A few hundred steps up a snow-slope, and we were brought to a stand as much by a view which held us spellbound as by the sudden falling away of the ground at our feet. Far to the west and below us, through a rift in the driving clouds, we could see the dark green, almost black, carpet of the Congo Forest, upon whose sombre background was traced a silvery design by the winding Semliki River. To the south showed a lighter patch, where the waters of Lake Edward reflected the last light of day; but in a moment sinking sun and rising mist merged all but the snow at our feet in a once more impenetrable gloom.

Of more practical value to us than this wonderful sight was the exposure for a brief minute of a snow ridge to the north leading up to a peak which we knew must be Alexandra. In spite of the conditions, we had pitched camp in a position well placed for an attempt on this peak, and we turned in with unjustified complacence, for it was more by good luck than good management. It snowed all night and was still snowing at dawn, so that the clearing from which we had hoped to refresh our memories never came. When we started at 7.30 to try to 'hit off' the ridge which we had seen the previous evening, visibility was limited to about ten yards, and, after wandering perplexedly for two hours amongst a maze of crevasses, we returned to camp. Caution was needed, as tracks were obliterated by fresh snow almost as soon as they were made.

The persistent snow soon found the weak spots in our little tent, which was not well adapted either for sheltering two men or for use on snow. Pools of water soon accumulated on the floor, limiting the area at our disposal, an area already made small by an inconvenient centre pole, so that it became increasingly difficult to keep our sleeping-bags dry. In the evening another clearing in the mist caused us to dash out, but we only got as far as the foot of the ridge before gathering darkness compelled us to return.

On the third day it was still misty but the snow had stopped falling. Assisted by our tracks of the previous night, which in places were still visible, we reached the ridge and began climbing. Except for one awkward cornice and the uncertain quality of the snow, the climb was not difficult, the summit (16,740 feet) being reached by midday. There was a patch of rock on top where we found a cairn in which were records left by the Duke of the Abruzzi in 1906 and Dr. Humphreys in 1926. We sat there till 2.30 p.m., but caught only passing glimpses of the neighbouring summit of Margherita. Camp was reached at 4 p.m., when a brief clearing enabled us to wring out our sleeping-bags and bale the tent. Our success on Alexandra, combined at sunset with another remarkable view of the Congo and a sight of the Margherita ridge, sent us to bed in a more or less contented frame of mind.

More snow fell in the night, but we turned out at 7.30 a.m. and were rewarded by seeing Margherita clearly for five minutes. By the time we had got under way, the mist had re-gathered, so that in a short time our ideas as to position and direction became as nebulous and woolly as the mist itself. The crevasses seemed more numerous and the mist thicker than on our first attempt, but, after groping about for some hours, we saw looming before us what was undoubtedly a ridge. At the foot of it was a steep rock buttress, which we managed to turn on the right, traversing back above it to the left. Hopes ran high as we reached the crest of the ridge and began to follow it, but next moment we stood dumbfounded, staring, Crusoe-like, at footprints in the snow. Such was our bewilderment that wild and impossible conjectures of another party on the mountain flashed across our minds before we realised the unflattering truth that these were our tracks of the previous day, and that we were climbing Alexandra for the second time.

We crept back to camp with our tails well down, to pass a rather miserable night, depressed as much by our failure as by the state of the tent, whose contents, including our sleeping-bags, were now sopping wet. By now our food was almost finished, but before our forced descent on the morrow we determined to make one more attempt to reach the summit of Margherita.

By three in the morning we were so cold in our wet sleeping-bags that we gave up trying to sleep, brewed some tea, and prayed for dawn. Camp was struck, the sodden loads packed, and at six we moved off down the glacier, dumping the loads near the foot of the Stanley Plateau. Then, in a last desperate resolve to find the Margherita ridge, we turned north again. The usual mist prevailed, while the width and frequency of unbridged crevasses made vain any attempt at following a compass course, which in any case could only have been an approximation.

These repeated changes of direction enforced on us by the crevasses tried our tempers severely; every change gave rise to heated argument, during which each of us would fall to drawing little maps in the snow with ice-axes to illustrate our respective theories.

Once more a rock buttress loomed up. It was viewed with suspicion and tackled without enthusiasm, while every moment we expected to come once again upon our old tracks. In this we were delighted to be disappointed, and at eleven o'clock we reached the summit of an undoubted peak, but which we could not tell. It was snow-covered, so there could be no records to find; all to be done was to wait for the mist to clear. This we did, sitting in a hollow scraped in the snow.

The climb had been an interesting one but not difficult. The ridge and the summit were draped with cornices of a strangely beautiful feathery appearance. Very little melting appears to take place at these heights, so it is possible that this formation is due to wind rather than rapid alterations in temperature. On the other hand, the presence of numbers of large ice stalactites under the cornices suggests a considerable range of temperature.

Unless another night without food was to be spent on the glacier, our departure had to be timed for 3 p.m. A searching wind began to lessen our interest as to what peak we were on, threatening to drive us off its summit with our knowledge unsatisfied. Time after time the swirling mists seemed to be thinning. Repeatedly we would take off our snow-glasses in the hope of finding a tangible clue in the sea of fog, only to be baulked by fresh clouds rolling up from some apparently inexhaustible supply. Repeatedly we were disappointed, but at last a clearing came. It lasted hardly a minute, but it was long enough for us to see and recognise the familiar summit of Alexandra, and to realise from its relative position that we must be on Margherita (16,815 feet).

It was sheer luck to have hit off the ridge on such a day, so that we were almost jubilant as we started down. Helped by our outgoing tracks, we reached our rucksacks at 4.30 p.m., and, stopping only to swallow a mouthful of raw pemmican, we hit out for the cave. In spite of mist and gathering gloom we found the route, quitted the snow for the rocks, slid and slithered down moss-grown slabs, and soon were fighting our way through the senecios above the lake. Burdened as we were with water-logged packs and exhausted by our previous efforts, our condition was such that our progress was governed more by the impulse of gravity than by our legs. So with one mind we steered straight for the mud of the lake-shore, knowing that it would be soft, but doubting whether a quicksand itself could be worse than the senecio toils in which we were struggling.

It was not a quicksand, but a very fair imitation, and, withal, very evil-smelling; 'Here, therefore, they wallowed for a time, being very grievously bedaubed with dirt; a Christian, because of the burden that was on his back, began to sink into the mire.' Frying-pan and fire, devil and deep sea, Scylla and Charybdis, all seemed weak comparisons for the horns of our dilemma. Finally we took once more to the senecio forest – perhaps because it did not smell – and by nightfall reached the cave and the welcome warmth of a roaring fire.

Although, on the march, no words could be bad enough for the senecio, or giant groundsel, in camp we sang a different tune. To all appearances it looks as likely to burn as cabbage-stalk, but, dead or alive, wet or dry, it burns almost as well as birchwood. Without it life in the high valleys of Ruwenzori, where the sun is hardly ever seen and where to move a yard from camp is to be soaked, would be almost unbearable; at any rate to natives, to whom sitting over a fire, or even in the smoke of a fire, is meat and drink.

After devoting a day to food and rest, and the drying of clothes and sleeping-bags, we set out for Mount Speke in thick weather on January 23rd. As it lies to the north of the Bujuku Lake, our line of march lay up the valley towards the Stuhlmann Pass at its head. In an attempt to cut short the struggle with vegetation and morass we tried to break out of the valley by climbing the cliffs of its eastern flank, but we were repulsed by the moss-covered slabs. After several great strips of moss had peeled away, almost taking us with them, we continued up the valley, at last reaching the snow above the pass. We roped up, more from ingrained orthodoxy than necessity, and climbed an easy snow slope to Vittorio Emmanuele (16,080 feet), gaining its summit at half past ten. From this vantage-point, almost the centre of the range, we should have seen, but for the mist, most of the snow peaks and their glaciers. For three hours we sat there waiting patiently for a clearing. At half past one the mist did lift a little, giving us a glimpse of a summit along the ridge to the north, which appeared to be higher than ours. Whether it was or not, it gave us an excuse for getting warm, so we raced off along the ridge, climbed three small intervening hillocks, and reached the top of the fourth unnamed peak. Dr. Humphreys was of the opinion that this summit was higher than Vittorio, which is officially the highest, an opinion with which we were inclined to agree. The point is only of academic interest, however, for not one of the four is worthy of the name of 'peak'.

We started back at half past two in a curious mixture of thunder and snow, reaching camp in two hours. We tried more short cuts on the way, and at least had the melancholy satisfaction of proving once again that if mossy slabs are not ideal for ascents, they are excellent for descents, if effortless speed is the main consideration.

Our six porters, who were in a fair way to becoming troglodytes, began to hope that the madness which had driven us to these inhospitable wastes had now spent itself, and that with a return to sanity there would be a return to a warmer climate. Whether man could be eternally happy in the heaven, paradise, or nirvana offered by the several religions has always seemed to me doubtful (for, after all, bliss is only appreaciated after spells of misery), and here were these natives, enjoying what I imagine to be a native's idea of heaven, with nothing to do but eat, drink, sleep, and draw their pay, and yet counting the days until they could return to work, women, and taxation. Since the only obligation they were under was to remain passive, and desertion would involve being active, it was not difficult to persuade them to wait a little longer, as we were able to assure them that one more day would suffice to exorcise the devil which possessed us.

That day, January 24th, we proposed to devote to the climbing of Mount Baker direct from our base camp – a much more formidable task than the climbing of Speke although it was the lower of the two, being only 15,986 feet. Our original plan had been to attempt it by the ridge, leading up from the Scott Elliott Pass, but the shattered, ice-glazed rocks of that ridge presented a very forbidding appearance. The alternative was to climb it by the north face from a point in the Bujuku Valley lower than our camp site. We started very early to see what we could do.

'Reculer pour mieux sauter' may sometimes be sound strategically, but it calls for high morale in those called upon to practise it, and there is no more trying a way of starting an ascent than by a descent. Our route began with a descent of the valley for a good half-mile. It was not as though we could just run down. On the contrary, every foot of it had to be fought for in the depressing knowledge that every foot so gained was a foot lost on the mountain, so that it was with mingled feelings of relief and dismay that we at last found ourselves at the foot of the lower cliffs of Baker, which bound the south side of the valley, faced by a climb of what was now more than 3,000 feet. The lower part of the cliffs were, of course, sheathed in moss, a fact which, after our experiences of yesterday, caused us to approach them with misgivings and climb them with caution, the more so because we knew it was seldom possible to safeguard the party with a rope belay. As we slowly gained height, the moss gave place to less treacherous but more difficult ice-glazed rock, while the mist clinging to the face made it impossible for us to choose the best line of ascent. Just below the crest of the east ridge of Baker the rocks steepened. Several attempts were made before we finally overcame these, and, after four hours of continuous climbing, hoisted ourselves on to the snow-covered ridge.

Turning westwards, we followed the ridge at an easy angle over three lesser summits, reaching Semper Peak (15,843 feet) at about one o'clock. Here we found a cairn containing the records of the all-too-thorough Italian party, but we derived some satisfaction from having made a new route. To the south, a quarter of a mile away, was the top, Edward Peak (15,986 feet), and almost as we reached it we enjoyed the novel and pleasing experience of the mists melting away in the middle of the day. Looking across to the Stanley Plateau, where we had played at Blind Man's Buff for four days with Alexandra and Margherita, we found it difficult to imagine that anyone could have had any trouble in finding them. The whole scene stood revealed, and took on a fresh aspect in this almost unnatural sunlight. As dawn dispels the weird shapes and half-seen horrors of the night, so the Mubuku Valley became a smooth and smiling pleasance; the vile tangle of its spongy floor became a firm green lawn, the dark and desolate waters of the mere sparkled gaily, the slimy mud of its shores looked like hard yellow sand. The snow peaks themselves took on a milder aspect, and with the clouds filling and blotting out the lower valleys, which might have destroyed the illusion by their emptiness, we might have been amongst one of the homely lesser ranges of the Alps, instead of the mysterious Mountains of the Moon.

Encouraged by this fair scene, and momentarily forgetful, perhaps, of what the smiling faces of the valleys concealed, we planned an ambitious return journey by a complete traverse of Mount Baker, with a descent towards the Freshfield col which divides Mount Baker from Luigi di Savoia, the southernmost peak. From the col we would drop down into the unnamed valley between Mount Baker and Mount Stanley, on the south side of the Scott Elliott Pass, returning to the Bujuku Valley and our camp over this last-named pass. It meant a long day, and was rather a shot in the dark, but it took us into fresh country, and, in spite of the prudent adage, we preferred the unknown to the known evils of the mossy slabs up which we had come.

After half an hour's rest on the summit we began the descent of the south ridge towards Freshfield col at about two o'clock. Realising too well that every step south was taking us further from home and lengthening our forthcoming struggle in the valley, we decided to cut matters short by descending from the ridge into the valley before reaching the col. The steeper snow below the ridge lay insecurely on top of ice and needed care, but we were soon off the glacier, encountering the less obvious but greater perils of steep rock covered with a type of moss new to our experience, which was almost imperceptible. The rock itself looked bare, and seemed reasonably trustworthy, until a sudden skid provoked closer inspection and revealed the presence of the new enemy.

The slope which fell away at our feet was steep and convex, so that we could not see what lay between us and the valley floor. In the nature of things some sort of steep wall was to be expected near the bottom, and so it was found. It was so steep that but for the assistance of the hated helichrysum which grew out of it we could never have tackled it, and must have returned to the ridge to descend by the much longer way of the Freshfield col. The helichrysum grew in profusion on the face of the cliff, clinging there with all the toughness and tenacity that we knew so well and had so often cursed – a toughness we now had occasion to bless. It was at once an enemy and friend; one moment we were reviling it as heartily as ever for holding us back, and the next giving thanks as we used it for a 'Thank-God-handhold' in the descent of some steep rock wall. But for its aid many such places would have defeated us, while the only toll it exacted for me the loss of a wrist-watch and for S. a sprained shoulder.

Once we were down on the valley floor there began what we had expected and feared – a long fight against the giant groundsel, helichrysum, chaotic boulders, and the approach of night. The valley was closely shut in between the high containing walls of the lower cliffs of Mount Baker and Mount

Stanley. Debris falling from the slopes of these mountains filled the valley, and in one place had dammed it to form two lifeless tarns which deepened the melancholy aspect of this grim defile.

Approaching the foot of the Scott Elliott Pass, the impeding vegetation gave way to scree, but we had to summon all our flagging energies in an effort to reach the col quickly, to see something of our way down the other side before darkness descended and left us benighted. We pressed on, and, as we topped the ridge, there was just light enough to see the Bujuku Lake below, and at our feet a narrow gully which seemed to offer a practicable route.

Hurrying down this as fast as safety permitted, we joined battle once more with senecio forest and helichrysum, in which I suffered the additional loss of my camera and the irreplaceable exposed film which it contained. We reached the lake-shore in a darkness which, though 'hellish', did not 'smell of cheese', like the cupboard which the half-drunk James Pigg thrust his head into in mistake for the window. It smelt instead like a sewer as we began floundering along the margin of the lake, sinking to our knees in the noisome mud at every step. On this occasion we preferred it to the senecio, and resigned ourselves, more or less happily, to long wallowing in the slough, because with the water to guide us we were sure of our direction. Presently a boy who had heard our shouts met us with a lamp, and in a short time we were sitting by the fire discussing food and the day's adventures.

In the morning we packed up and bade farewell to the friendly cave which we had come to look upon as home, so warm was its welcome on our belated returns from long, wet days. By promising the porters extra baksheesh we persuaded them to double march all the way, for our road lay downhill and the trail was already broken. They were eager to get back certainly, but it needed a pretty strong incentive to goad them into this fierce activity.

Their labours finished, these six worthies received, besides the blankets and clothes, eleven shillings each, with which they were well pleased. A full month's work on farm or road would not have brought them in as much as this, the fruits of only sixteen days' absence. Now they could return in affluence to their villages, willing and able to astonish the stay-at-homes with tales of hardship and peril amidst the mysterious snows.

The boy we had deputed to keep an eye on the car, left by the roadside, met us with the news that all was well. This was a great relief because it was quite on the cards that some elephant had stepped on it or that it had been destroyed by a bush fire. Not only was all well with it, but, according to the boy, rather better than well, because a swarm of bees had settled in the box-body. He was surprised when we told him that we did not want them, that we did not even want the car so long as the bees were in possession, but that we would come along again as soon as the present tenants had left. I had experienced swarms of bees in cars before, and I have yet to own a car that will go fast enough in these circumstances.

We were not there to see what wiles he employed to eject them, but when we got down later the swarm had gone but for a few bewildered stragglers. Most natives, if not exactly bee-keepers, encourage bees by hanging up hives made from hollowed logs in trees near their huts; while in the forest, they have an extraordinary keen nose for the honey which is often found in hollow trees and crannies in the rocks. Naked as they are, their boldness and indifference to stings when dealing with the rightful owners would startle the gloved and netted apiarist. Before loading up we held a snake inspection, for it has already been recorded how on another occasion a puff adder, one of the deadliest snakes, was found dozing peacefully on the cylinder head.

In spite of the long exposure to sun, rain, and curious natives, the car consented to start, and we bowled along cheerfully to Kampala and home, giving thanks for the twin blessings of snow mountains on the equator and the means of getting to them. It is interesting to recall that the Abruzzi expedition, as recently as 1906, spent more time in getting from Kampala to the foot than we did on the mountains – thanks to a road and a car. Even to such light-hearted coffee-planters as ourselves, the time involved without such transport could not have been spent away from the farm without some twinges of conscience, to say nothing of the extra cost a caravan of porters would have entailed. Delightful though the slow-moving porter safari may be, giving opportunities of seeing the country, the natives, and the game which no traveller by car ever has, it is but a means to an end, and the loss of these things is compensated for by the more memorable days spent in high places, among the solitudes of ice and snow.

CHAPTER TEN

The Gold Rush

'The narrowing lust of gold' – Tennyson

UNTIL 1931 the search for precious metals in Kenya had attracted little general interest. The accepted theory seemed to be that, in the Highlands at any rate, any valuable minerals that might exist were buried deep beneath great deposits of volcanic soil, so that to look for them was a waste of time. No doubt a few enthusiasts were not so easily put off, but generally more attention was paid to the neighbouring territory of Tanganyika, which was comparatively rich in minerals, and where promising alluvial diggings were already being exploited. In Kenya in 1923 gold was found in the Lolgorien area south of the Sotik, and a mild 'rush' took place to peg claims. In view of the later history of this particular area, it is difficult to understand why this interest so soon evaporated; the majority who went down there returned disgusted, and in only two places was serious development work undertaken. Ten years later it was becoming apparent that those who took part in that rush were as blind as they were easily discouraged.

Early in 1931 reports of rich finds in the Kakamega district, near the north-east corner of Lake Victoria, began to circulate. At first the stories met with the usual scepticism, in spite of the fact that the Colony was then sinking fast into the trough of the depression when people were more inclined to snatch at straws, most of them being in a fair way to financial drowning. The stories continued, losing nothing in the telling, and interest spread so rapidly that in a year or even less there were few people in the Colony who had not either been to Kakamega or joined some syndicate which was prospecting there.

Napoleon has been fathered with a great many trite aphorisms, so no harm will be done in attributing to him another – 'Fortune is a fickle jade, so when she knocks at the door be quick to open' – a saying which S. and I sometimes think we neglected to our cost. A friend whose farm was not far from S.'s was one of the syndicate which made the original discovery at Kakamega, so that during my periodic visits to S. we used to hear a good deal of what was being found there, and still more of what might be found. In our foolishness, or possibly wisdom (for every seeker was not a finder), we accepted these tales with some reserve, chaffing the enthusiastic teller about holes in the ground and the futility of throwing money down them. It was right and proper enough to desert our respective farms for several weeks of mountaineering, but we simply could not afford to waste a week playing at prospecting.

So in a superior way we remained unmoved, even pitying the poor boobs who left their farms to try their luck. In 1932 the excitement became intense, the 'strike' seemed to be extending, and the rush was no longer confined to settlers of Kenya, as people from South Africa, the Rhodesias, and even America had begun to take a hand. Towards the end of that year the population of the 'field' was over a thousand whites – more than the number of farmers in the whole of Kenya – money was flowing into the country, and many companies were being formed. The Government had employed an eminent geologist[1] to report on the possibilites, and it was the publication of his report in 1932, which recommended, *inter alia*, the opening of other and wider areas to prospectors, that did much to bring this about.

Gold fever is a very infectious complaint, particularly so when the source of infection is comparatively close and easily accessible; here was no ocean to cross, no snow passes, no thirsty desert to overcome, only the trouble of a day's ride in a car. That I was not infected the first year seems to argue the tranquil mind of the philosopher or the apathetic insensibility of a blockhead. For most of the following year I was out of the country, but when I returned towards the end of it to find the Kakamega gold-field now, more than ever, the all-absorbing topic, I was prepared to listen to the voice of the charmer. This more receptive frame of mind was due to no sudden access of wisdom (or foolishness), but because I had given up coffee-planting and was for the moment at a loose end.

I soon learnt that, of the friends and acquaintances I had, sane or less sane, the few who were not already on the spot were financially interested. As related to me casually, I was, at first, rather impressed by the mysterious and important nature of these interests, since in my ignorance I invested the holders of them with the glamour and power commonly associated with the mining magnates of the Rand. Closer enquiry, however, revealed that the

1 The late Sir Albert Kitson

majority of holdings consisted of a fractional share in some syndicate whose modest capital of £100 (nominal) was mostly represented by 'call money' which might or, more likely, might not be forthcoming on demand. In all cases, poverty of capital was offset by richness of title, and he would be a cold, calculating, mean-spirited man who questioned the stability or doubted the future prosperity of the 'Find Gold Syndicate', 'Amalgamated Black Cats', 'Blue Reefs Consolidated', and a hundred others similarly named.

Half a dozen friends or a group of neighbouring farms would combine to float one of these, sending the man who had last seen a golden sovereign or knew quartz from coal to the field to commence operations. For the rest, it was very like backing horses; the stakes were not too big, there were a number of attractively named runners from which to choose, and, though the financial results were usually the same, at least one had a longer run for one's money. When the means of the backers were considered (for by now the resources of most people in Kenya were at a very low ebb), it was surprising how long some of these runs did last; but the sanguine hopes of the majority had first to be completely quenched before a halt was called, while the more prudent or less confident had either to meet the calls for more money or make up their minds to cut their losses.

Since I was now drifting without moorings, it was not long before I was drawn into the current which was setting stronger than ever in the direction of the gold-field. I started up-country, flattering myself that I was going into it with my eyes open, and that if it came to throwing money away I was no mean performer and could manage to dispose of my few assets unaided by any fancy-named syndicate.

For those whose notions of a gold rush have been coloured by the *Trail of '98*, it will be disappointing to hear that in these degenerate days the gold-field was reached either in the speedy and unromantic comfort of a car, or, in those cases where gold-fever temperature had risen to dangerous heights, by the yet swifter aeroplane. If the road was dry it could be reached in a long day's run from Nairobi, but when I, at last, set out to try my luck, rain compelled me to stop a night at Kisumu, on the shore of Lake Victoria. This was formerly a place of some importance, being the terminus of the Uganda Railway and the port for Uganda, to and from which passengers and produce were brought by steamer across the lake. With the extension of the railway to Uganda in 1928, Kisumu lost its importance and retained only its heat, mosquitoes and ramshackle appearance. Now, however, this town, moribund a year ago, had entered upon a new lease of life owing to the fact that it was the nearest station on the railway for the gold-field, which was only forty miles away. Many of the inhabitants of Kisumu had not even to leave home, for the lucky owner of shop or hotel had his gold-mine under his hand. They were reaping a rich harvest from this new field of activity, a harvest well earned by any who had had the hardihood to remain.

The scene at the hotel was animated. Outside stood a row of cars, most of them ready for the knacker's yard, their box-bodies crammed with camp-kits, picks, shovels, and prospecting tools, with a further miscellany slung on running-boards and wings; while inside the bar their owners forgathered to swap the latest rumours and lies from the field. A new gold-field, like a war, breeds rumour 'painted full of tongues', where facts become lost in a sea of conjecture or impenetrably disguised by distortion and exaggeration. It is commonly said that 'there are three kinds of liars – liars, damned liars, and mining engineers'; for the last 'prospector' might well be substituted, as nowadays the mining engineer's talents in this direction are limited, or have only a negative quality, owing to the conditions under which he works – all companies enjoining upon their employees the silence of a clam.

Among the motley crowd of enthusiasts, amateur and professional, there were the usual accompanying tipsters whose advice was not entirely disinterested. I had not been there five minutes before being buttonholed by a man who was anxious to do me a good turn by selling me some alluvial claims for £500. He was not at liberty to disclose either the names of his partners or the whereabouts of the claims without some tangible proof (£50) of my bona fides, but those were details of little moment in view of the wealth of picturesque information placed at my disposal concerning the past earnings of the claims and their potential yield in the future. The hard-bitten air which on entering Kisumu I had tried to assume had evidently not carried conviction – I must have appeared both opulent and innocent.

Next morning I drove out to the field and began a search for the 'Lucky Strike Syndicate', one of the 'favourites'. I was not thinking of backing it, but I had an introduction to the manager and hoped to acquire some practical knowledge of the ways of the treasure-hunters. The area open to prospecting began about twenty miles out of Kisumu, and one at once began to see on either side of the road numerous 'pegs' (posts carrying galvanised plates on which were painted the details of the claim), and many direction-boards pointing the way to such promising places as the 'Moonshine Reef' or 'De Profundis', so that the passing mining magnate on the look-out for valuable properties would have no excuse for missing them. Unluckily, the object of my search was more retiring, and many were the potential El Dorados I visited before running it to earth.

I spent three valuable days here obtaining elementary notions of the art of washing a pan of 'dirt', the first essential for a prospector, and a general insight into conditions on the field.

To late-comers like myself the difficulties in the way of acquiring claims by pegging seemed to be considerable. Almost every available bit of land was taken up, or, if vacant, so hemmed in by claims as to be useless. There was no map to be had showing existing claims, because the officials in charge of survey and registration could not possibly keep pace with the rate at which pegging was being done. According to the mining laws governing 'reef claims', no pegging could be done unless a 'discovery of gold reef in place' had been made, which meant that before pegging a claim some reef, vein, or 'leader' actually carrying gold had to be found. The ignorant novice, finding almost every square yard pegged, immediately fell to kicking himself for arriving too late on what was seemingly a 'Tom Tiddler's ground'. If traces of gold *had* been found on every claim pegged, he argued, then the country must be simply oozing gold. But such impressions were deceptive, because this salutary rule had gone by the board, and most of the pegging now in progress was what is termed 'blind' – that is, without the making of any real 'discovery' but in the hopes of making one. The motive behind this was, of course, to gain time, and to prevent anyone else having a look, and was a practice to which there was no effective check.

In the matter of 'alluvial claims', where the gold is won from the beds of rivers and streams, the rules are different, for a likely strip of river-bank could be claimed and pegged before any work was done on it. All the earlier discoveries had been of alluvial gold, and it was this type of mining that in the first year or two yielded for some lucky people extraordinarily good returns. As by now practically every foot of stream or river was either in process of being worked or had been worked out and abandoned, attention was concentrated on prospecting for reefs – the reefs from which, in theory, all the alluvial gold had come.

The result of this demand for what was no longer to be had put a value on claims *qua* claims, regardless of whether anything had been found on them or not, with the result that the enterprising early birds were reaping their proverbial, if unjust, reward. It was eighteen months now since gold had first been found here, nor had there been any new or startling discoveries to account for the present 'rush'; but it was just before Christmas, and the middle of the dry season, circumstances combining to swell the normal influx with a crowd of curious sightseers who came to scoff and stayed on to dig. Outsiders of all nationalities were there, but the bulk of the prospectors and miners were the farmers, settlers, clerks, and shopkeepers of Kenya, who were the less reluctant to leave their jobs because, in the depressed conditions then prevailing, they had nothing to gain by sticking to farm, shop, or office.

For my own part, staking a claim was less important than finding a place where I could make a home and find occupation for the next few months. It did not take many days of prowling round to convince me that the cheapest way of supplying this modest need of a desirable residence on top of a profitable gold-mine was to find some claim-owning friend with whom I could join forces. Since pretty well the whole population were up there, I was pretty sure of finding someone suitable, and after a week my search came to an end.

It was late one evening when I finally tracked down the man I was looking for. To reach his camp I had to abandon the car and ford the wide Yala River. D. was a man whose sanguine spirit was not easily subdued, a fact which I already knew, so that when I found him stretched out on his camp-bed I was not surprised to find that his attitude did not betoken despair but merely that he was feeling the effects of a late night at whisky poker. This sounded promising, quite in keeping with the character of the gold-digger which D. could already claim to be. It would be pleasant to add that D. had settled his gambling debts with gold-dust and nuggets, but a regard for truth constrains me to admit that the stakes were the unromantic shillings and cents. My arrival roused D. from his lethargy, and, hearing what I wanted, he at once dragged me off to have a look at his claims, although by that time the sun was almost down.

D. (even he of the elephants), who was a late aspirant for fortune like myself, had only been there a month. This surprised me, as he was the type that would be first in the field on a thing like this, and the last to leave. Moreover, he had previously been part owner of a gold-mine in Tanganyika, but perhaps that was an experience bitter enough to enable him to withstand the renewed temptation for so long. Be that as it may, he had now made up for lost time and had already pegged a block of ten claims round a 'discovery' which really did show some 'colour'. What was more, the country for a mile round was still unpegged, a fact which might have aroused suspicion, but which, in our ignorance, seemed to be a special dispensation of Providence in our favour – one of those rare instances when the race was not to the swift. In addition to these favourable circumstances, he was in the act of grabbing twenty alluvial claims on the Yala River, which, if size was any criterion, could easily hold the wealth of the Indies.

We knew each other well, so there was no difficulty in coming to terms, with the result that before we got back to the tent I was half-owner of one promising mine, of any others we might take the trouble to discover, and a collection of picks, shovels, 'pans', 'dollies', earth-augers, and other tools, which the cynic might think were the most valuable part of our property.

CHAPTER ELEVEN

Amateur Prospectors

'A thirst for gold,
The beggars vice which can but overwhelm
The meanest hearts.'
                                        – Byron

THE formation of this new and powerful combine, which for the moment we forbore naming, was honoured that night in the usual fashion, and no time was wasted in getting to work. Next morning at dawn the partners went down to the Yala to measure and peg out their alluvial claims. A layer of gravel and sand under both banks was known to be gold-bearing, so presumably the same held good for the gravel under the present river-bed. It was, therefore, only a matter of selecting from the few promising places still unclaimed. Difficulties enough would come later with the working, for the 'pay-dirt' was eight feet below the surface of the banks, while the river itself was a good hundred feet wide and six feet deep. For the present we ignored this, trusting that later someone with sufficient capital would come along to work our claims on a percentage basis, or even buy them outright.

These hopes were never realised. Our claims were examined, but the test bore-holes showed that they were not rich enough to warrant the heavy expenditure necessary to win the gold. On the banks eight feet of overburden had to be removed to reach the underlying gravel, while to reach that in the river-bed itself the river would have had to be diverted. Alterations of the landscape on this scale were not to be undertaken lightly, for, although the man of money might, and in some cases did, say, like another Hotspur proposing to turn the Trent, 'I'll have it so, a little charge will do it,' there was a Glendower in the shape of the Government which, though it did not actually forbid, insisted on the river being restored eventually to its original course and all the excavations filled in when the gold had been won. A hard condition this, unpalatable, and unprofitable to mining Hotspurs, and one which saved more parts of the river than ours from violent hands.

My recollections of that first day are of the junior partner swimming about in the river at one end of one hundred and twenty feet of chain, played by the senior partner, like a tired tunny-fish, of washing pans of 'pay gravel' brought up by the auger from under eight feet of foul-smelling overburden, and finally of returning late to camp through a deluge of rain. It was a hard day but an interesting one, for the kick we got out of watching the specks of gold trailing after the black sand as we steadily 'panned' the gravel more than repaid us for our toil.

After another day or so of this promiscuous bathing and mud-larking, when a thousand feet of both river-banks had been pegged we turned our attention more than willingly to the reef claims – there one could at least keep dry.

These were the claims under which we hoped to expose, by deep trenching or shaft sinking, a body of goldbearing rock. The rock is usually, not necessarily, quartz – that which Spaniards call *madre de oro*, or 'mother of gold' – and the reef may outcrop at the surface or lie buried at a depth of hundreds or even thousands of feet. (On the Rand, in the Village Deep Mine, gold is being mined at 7,600 feet below ground level.) Near the surface the ore body may be only a few inches thick – what is termed a 'leader' or 'stringer' – but if this is found to be carrying gold it is always worth while following, as it may lead to the mother lode, of which it is an offshoot. If the reef outcrops, well and good, but more usually the only indications to guide one in the search for the reef are bits of quartz lying about on the surface – 'floats', which have to be traced if possible to their sources. Sometimes there are not even any 'floats' to be found, and then samples of the subsoil have to be taken at close intervals to be washed for traces of gold. As the traces in the sample increase or diminish, so the prospector knows whether he is getting 'colder' or 'warmer' in the game of hunting the elusive reef.

D.'s original discovery was an outcrop of rock in which there were thin veins of quartz. Having crushed the rock in a 'dolly' (an iron pestle and mortar) and having washed the fine sand so obtained in a prospector's pan, one got a fair-sized 'tail' of gold; that is to say, a fine streak of the yellow metal tailing behind the residual sand owing to its greater weight, and showing up unmistakably against the black bottom of the pan. Perhaps not 'unmistakably', as I remember one sample of quartz which showed tremendous 'tails' of some heavy yellow stuff – a find which made us almost sleepless with excitement until an assay showed it to be, not gold, but some metal of no value.

However, there was no deception about this first discovery, from the quartz veins of which gold was found in every sample, with 'tails' of sufficient size to fill us with the wildest hopes. Unfortunately, the quartz veins, which were few and small, petered out very quickly; nor did we ever succeed in finding the reef from which they must have come.

This early and very partial success went to our inexperienced heads. We did not realise its unsubstantial nature, and so left a more thorough investigation to the future, while we embarked upon a policy of 'pegging' as much of the surrounding unclaimed country as we could, with the object of having something worth while to offer the company which, we confidently expected, would sooner or later come along., This area was all part of a vast tract pegged by a man who later found that he had swallowed more than he could digest, and who for some reason, probably financial, had failed to register the claims. This meant that he had no rights over them, with the result that several people, including D., had taken advantage of his faulty title.

We were so confident of the latent possibilities that we regarded every chance white man who showed himself in the neighbourhood as a dangerous rival – an object of suspicion and hatred. Our days were laborious, our nights uneasy. Christmas Day itself brought to us neither peace nor goodwill, for on the previous evening we had happened upon the 'discovery peg' of some wandering Dutchman, which so wrought upon us that we proclaimed our 'goodwill toward men' by searching feverishly for something to justify the placing of a 'discovery peg' close to his, so as to prevent his encroaching any further on what we regarded as our preserves. Thus did the gold bug arouse the envy, hatred, and malice of two mild, kindly disposed coffee-planters, for I think we were quite prepared to jump his claim, shoot him, and bury him in his own trench had we not already sampled his 'discovery' and found it barren.

Our daily routine was to leave camp at daybreak armed with an entrenching-tool, a geologist's hammer, a magnifying-glass, and a pan, and accompanied by two boys carrying pick, shovel, earth-auger, and food. An eye-witness might well have mistaken us for a party of gravediggers attending the funeral of one of their fellows. We proceeded with bowed head and measured step, our eyes glued to the ground searching for likely looking stones. Quite literally, no stone was left unturned. Any arousing interest were broken, to be examined with the magnifying-glass for traces of free gold. The promising bits of quartz were put in separate bags, with notes as to where they had been found, before being taken home for crushing and testing. The note specifying the place of origin was important, because more experienced prospectors than ourselves had been known to carry home a load of samples, prove one to be carrying gold, and then find themselves unable to remember its place of origin. The methodical examination of every piece of quartz with the pocket lens for visible gold was a rite seldom omitted, and, although none was ever seen, the search never lost its interest or excitement. But the most exciting part of the day came when, back in camp, all the samples were crushed and panned. This was the decisive test, for quartz may be rich in gold and yet show no trace of it even under a magnifying-glass. We worked sitting on boxes outside the tent, one of us pounding away at the quartz in the iron 'dolly', the other carefully washing the fine dust in the pan. Usually, of course, silence or a groan of despair showed the result to be negative, but occasionally a triumphant yell announced the presence of a 'speck' or, rarely enough, a palpable 'tail' amongst the fine black sand in the pan.

This washing and crushing had to be done with scrupulous care. It was easy to overlook specks, but easier still to see some that were not there. Neglect to clean very thoroughly after each trial the dolly, pestle, sieve, and pan was a fruitful source of trouble. Specks of gold from one successful sample might be left over and turn up again in the next, which, though in reality completely barren, was now made to appear gold-bearing. Much extra work and eventual disappointment were the result, because at least ten more negative tests were necessary before the culprit was compelled to admit that he was the victim of his own carelessness, and that the successful pan had been unwittingly 'salted' by himself.

If a sample giving a 'colour' was found, the procedure was to return to the place next day to try to discover from where the bits of surface quartz or 'floats' had come. If they appeared to lie more plentifully in one particular spot than another, a long narrow trench running at right angle to the general 'strike' of the field would be sunk, in the hope of cutting the reef itself or being directed to it by the finding of some 'leader' or 'stringer'. As previously explained, these are the narrow veins of quartz an inch to eighteen inches thick which at some geologically distant period welled up to the surface from the molten reef below.

It is a fascinating game – so fascinating that even after months and years of continual disappointment a trivial find will fire the prospector afresh with all his old enthusiasm. It is a game which is often played out under conditions of extreme heat, cold, and discomfort. Not that we had much to complain about on that score, for, although we were on the equator, we were 5,000 feet above sea level, and the heat was by no means unbearable.

The country in which we thus 'fossicked' about was thickly populated and well cultivated – two factors which made prospecting easier in some respects. At this season, the dry weather, the crops of maize and kaffir corn had been harvested, the land was being broken in preparation for the long rains, so that there were large areas of stubble and newly cleared land which were easier to examine for surface indications than the bush. The inhabitants were only too pleased to have work and pay without the necessity of leaving their Reserve to look for it, while from our point of view the natural fertility of the country made the feeding of the labour a simple matter. There was one drawback, a serious one for prospectors, in such homely and pleasant surroundings, namely, the necessity of obtaining from the owner of the land permission to dig a trench or even to drive in a post. Even if operations were begun in the middle of a dense patch of bush on the steep bank of some stream, in a place obviously useless for cultivation, before many hours had elapsed some native would turn up demanding compensation for the bush which had been cut down.

One could well understand their reluctance for having cultivated land defaced by trenches, but, by a strange perversity, the most promising place for opening a trench would inevitably prove to be the site of some hut or in the midst of a banana grove. To remove a few banana-trees, which could be replaced in eighteen months, was as sacrilegious an act as the cutting down of a whole avenue of immemorial oaks, and the value placed on them put even the prospective gold-mine to shame. In most places, either on cultivated or uncultivated land, the owners were reasonable enough; only too pleased, in fact, to be paid for allowing a trench to be dug and then filled in, for the filling in of trenches after they had served their purpose was obligatory. If the trench happened to cut a reef which justified further investigation, it would still be filled in, but a shaft, occupying perhaps only a pace ten feet by twelve feet, could be sunk instead.

There were fixed rates of compensation for everything; so much for trenching, so much for the ground occupied by one's tent or hut, so much for the trees and grass used in building a hut. Money was asked and paid for putting in a peg or for making a six-inch hole with an earth-auger, no matter where, while the unlikeliest bit of land soon found an owner who was just about to start its cultivation. Thus encouraged, the natives became 'compensation-minded', and found in us and other prospectors scouring their country a source of revenue that a Chicago racketeer might have envied.

After six weeks of strenuous work we had pegged and registered forty claims. Of the two operations, registration was the more difficult. Many forms had to be filled in and many maps drawn (all in triplicate) before being submitted to the Mining Office at Kakamega for inspection and approval. The passing and registration of these claims in less than three separate visits to the office was unusual, and rather suggested some oversight on the part of the inspector, for the details required were many and the scrutiny severe.

Since these excursions to the growing town of Kakamega added a little variation to life, and gave us an opportunity to collect our mail, they were not entirely unwelcome.

The post office for this mining population of one thousand was a tin shed ten feet square. It was under-staffed, yet overcrowded by a staff consisting of an Indian babu and his native assistant, of whose qualifications for the post, except for a disarming grin, it would be rash to say anything. Add to this that many of the letters bore strange foreign names in the difficult spidery writing affected by the continental nations – whose owners had no English – and it will be readily understood that the scene when the mail arrived was more amusing for the onlooker than for the participant. Outside, sweltering in the sun, was a seething queue of angry miners; while inside, the babu, ankle deep in mail, sorted with slow, maddening, methodical deliberation, trampling underfoot halfpenny circulars and registered letters with calm indifference.

Having played an active part in this drama of the mail delivery or having got the worst of a wordy battle with the Commissioner of Mines, it was a relief to be able to turn to places in Kakamega where the *tempo* of life ran more smoothly – to a recently constructed hotel where, at immoderate expense, a much needed restorative could be obtained. Emerging from the hotel, bemused but once again benevolent, there were several interesting things that one might see before returning home. It was but a step from the bar to the strategically placed stockbroker's office, resembling very much a hen-coop on wheels, where one gazed with solemn interest at the latest share prices displayed outside on a blackboard. Further down the very bumpy earth street were the many stores which had sprung up in this town of mushroom growth, where every mining tool imaginable could be bought, or at least priced. Here were cunningly constructed sluices for alluvial mining, small stamp batteries for crushing quartz, pumps, windlasses, and even crash helmets to safeguard the miner's skull when grovelling in the bowels of the earth. More important and exciting than anything else, however, were our periodic visits to the assayer's office, either taking in fresh samples or learning that our hopes of yesterday had again proved barren – a verdict which sent us home long-faced and wondering whether the fellow could find gold in a sovereign.

As pressure of work grew less we turned our attention to securing a better home. The approach of the rainy season necessitated more adequate protection than that afforded by a tent. Mosquitoes were troublesome at our present camp by the river; moreover, the tent had been so long in one position that rats and jiggers had become a plague.

The jiggers preferred me as a host rather than D., and before long I was having four or five extracted daily, or nightly, for the irritation is so intense that sleep is impossible until the offending insect has been removed. Natives are very quick at spotting them and taking them out, but they seem curiously indifferent about attending to their own feet, for it is not uncommon to see a boy minus a toe or two as a result of neglected jiggers. The rats had more affinity for D., so that he, too, had many disturbed nights. Under these afflictions I was eager to be gone, but D. was a keen fisherman who liked to spend his evenings ringing the changes fruitlessly with flies, spoons, meat, dough, and locusts, and he was loath to leave the river. There were plenty of fish there, but a stick of dynamite seemed to be the only lure they understood. However, it solaced D. greatly to thrash the water. There were no elephants here to chase, and the reef that we were chasing was proving even more elusive than our friends of the Gubba. I think we might have been camped by that river yet had not a rat contrived one night to get inside D.'s mosquito net. He and the rat were of one mind about getting out, but his anxiety to be first was fatal to the net, the bed, and almost the tent – everything, in fact, except the rat. We moved next morning.

Our new home was on high ground at the other end of our claims; too far from the river for D.'s peace of mind. Here, in the course of three or four weeks, we built a three-roomed mud and wattle house thatched with grass. Its size and elegance astonished the natives, who were now convinced that the lumps of barren quartz we were so assiduously collecting must be the source of our new wealth now made so unmistakably evident. The house finished, I made it my business to start a flower and vegetable garden, since it now seemed likely that there woud be time to raise and eat a quick-growing crop like peas before we sold out for a few thousands and went elsewhere. Our hopes were still pitched pretty high, but we recognised that it was necessary to develop our holdings a little, and so provide something more tangible than hope before asking the prospective buyer to pay us a visit.

Another amenity was added by the discovery and opening up of a new route to the main road, a route which made it possible to keep the car on the same side of the river as ourselves. Hitherto, this had sat, forlorn and unhoused, on the far bank of the river, as if discarded by someone in a fit of pique, and, though a two-mile walk, followed by the removal of boots, socks, and trousers, to reach one's garage may at first amuse, it soon becomes a bore, and with the advent of the rains the river would become unfordable.

D.'s greed for claims was still unsatisfied. He argued that it was impossible to have too much of a good thing. I disagreed, partly on account of the cost of registration (£1 per claim), but also, and more particularly, because no one but ourselves had yet shown the slightest interest in this part of the country. This neglect puzzled me, for, although I might agree with D. that in enterprise and acumen we were in a class of our own, it did seem a little odd that of all the people scouring the country for claims not one had thought it worth while putting a peg in anywhere near us. We argued and debated our future course of action with the earnestness due to its importance, and, like the tribe of whom Gibbon writes, we took counsel together when drunk to give our resolutions fire and when sober to give them moderation. Finally, we pegged ten more claims and then devoted our dwindling resources to development work.

Having settled this momentous question, D. departed to his farm, leaving me to prove our claims. Only a dozen boys were employed, but, as there was work going on in five widely separated places, supervision, sampling, and further prospecting kept my days fully employed. In the evening I cultivated my garden.

As a result of five months' work we found and exposed five different quartz reefs, only one of which carried gold, and that a miserable two and a half pennyweights to the ton (which, of course, was not good enough). In large-scale mining such as on the Rand, a value of five pennyweights, or less with the present price of gold, is considered profitable, but, for a small reef, a value of ten pennyweights is the least that can be entertained. This bearing reef was a peculiar one, and our experience with it was typical of the disappointments which in gold-mining are the rule and not the exception. The 'floats' which were found on the surface near by gave a surprisingly rich 'colour' when panned. After digging many trenches in various places the reef was at last struck, and proved to be a good solid affair about three feet thick and lying almost vertically like a wall. Samples of rock were taken at different places, and on both faces, along the exposed portion, pounded up, mixed well together, and assayed, with the poor result stated.

It was, therefore, time to face facts; the glamour of mining was wearing thin, and the stick of our rocket-like hopes had almost come down to earth, but, before throwing our hand in, it was decided to sink a shaft alongside the bearing reef in the hope that it would 'improve at depth'. The hoary and oft-quoted adage that a reef is often richer lower down – so comforting and alluring a theory to the discoverer of a large but barren reef – must be responsible for many deep and abortive holes in the ground. Fortunately for us, we had not far to dig before finding a very convincing reason for stopping.

The shaft was sunk close to the reef, and at a depth of forty feet I thought it would be a good plan to make a horizontal drive to see how the reef was getting on. We drove for ten feet, which should have been enough to cut it, but there was no vestige of reef, not even the odd lumps and the small 'stringers' which are usually found in the vicinity of a large body of quartz. To make sure, we drove for twenty feet clean through where it should have been, but it had already petered out.

From the safe distance of his farm D. would not acknowledge defeat; he seemed to think I had temporarily mislaid or overlooked the three-foot thick wall as one might a collar-stud. But, backed by another disappointing assay, I was firm, for in this game it is fatally easy to allow hope to triumph over experience, and one lucky but unfair sample from a richer part of the reef is enough to start one sinking deeper again. Though there are many stories of men missing fortunes which another stroke of the pick or a foot deeper shaft would have revealed, less is heard of the fortunes which have been lost through not knowing when to stop. There was a provision in the prospecting regulations which, though not inserted for the express purpose, did something to insure against this tendency to go on trying till the last cent had been spent. Before a prospecting licence was granted, a deposit of £25 had to be made, so that when a man did reach the end of his tether there was always this amount in reserve to pay his debts and see him out of the field.

We had not reached that stage yet, and I thought it was time to notify D. that I for one had no intention of reaching it. In this he very unwillingly acquiesced, but he did not return for the celebration of the last sad rites, which took place only six months after the project had been born. The filling in of the shaft and the numerous trenches was depressingly like a burial, even though it were only our hopes that were being interred. He did come back later while I was still winding up our affairs (I was in no hurry to quit, having nowhere to go; also the vegetables were coming on nicely), and managed by eloquence and a brazen forehead to persuade our nearest neighbours, not unappropriately named the 'Golden Goose Syndicate,' to pay us £25 for the privilege of further investigating our claims. They were driven to this magnanimity by sheer desperation, because, although they had an area much larger than ours, they had not found even so much as a 'float' that gave any 'colour'. We could at least show them something better than that, and that we had lost nothing in the showing – indeed, the rich pans we found for them, and D.'s convincing eloquence, made me wonder why we were selling at all.

Before we left, the fever and excitement had died down, leaving in its place a healthier feeling of strong hopefulness. Like ourselves, most people began to realise that reef-chasing on this field was no game for the poor; for it was only here and there a man struck a rich, easily worked pocket and did well out of it. Big companies, able to take a longer view, had now entered the field, and, satisfied with the prospects, were quietly buying options on claims. The prices offered led one to suppose that they were actuated by pity rather than a desire to acquire something of value, but as a rule the seller had little development to show and was not in a position to wait.

No doubt the successful gold-digger must always be a gambler, with a philosophy of life resembling that of the Australian opal-gouger: 'Live in hope, if you die in despair.' Possibly a few years hence my friend D. and kindred spirits will shake their heads, cursing fate and pusillanimous partners, when they read of the riches found underlying the claims which they once had held and had abandoned.

CHAPTER TWELVE

Kilimanjaro Alone

'For solitude sometimes is best society,
And short retirement urges sweet return.'
– Milton

FEELING not much sadder and very little wiser after our experiences, we returned together to the Sotik, D. to his farm and myself for a few days' rest and relaxation, while deciding on my next move. During this visit a gymkhana took place in which, for my sins, I was given a ride in the big race. The distance was one and a half miles, and as we entered the straight a herd of oxen strayed on to the course. The rest of the field passed in safety, but I was not so fortunate. My mount, lying last and galloping full split, hit one broadside on, and I was catapulted over the horse's head. I slid along on my face several yards, 'biting the dust' in a very literal fashion – bit it to such a purpose, in fact, that most of my teeth were unshipped.

With a very sore mouth, and hardly able to talk intelligibly, I fled to Nairobi, and left again almost at once for Kilimanjaro. There were several reasons for this, chief among them being, perhaps, the temporary shortage of teeth and some diffidence about appearing in public, but also a desire for a return match with this mountain, for it will be remembered that in 1930 we did not accomplish all that we should have done.

At the risk of perhaps needless repetition, it is advisable to mention again that the summit of Kibo, which is the main peak of Kilimanjaro, consists of an ice-filled crater some 800 yards in diameter divided in the middle by a low ridge running east and west. The rim of the crater is the actual top of the mountain, the highest point on this long circular wall lying on the south side and named Kaiser Wilhelm Spitze. Between the point at which the crater wall is first reached and this highest point, a distance of perhaps 600 or 700 yards, are three other peaks, points, or bumps of varying heights, all slightly lower than Kaiser Wilhelm Spitze itself. These several points were always the cause of much heartburning.

In appearance they are all very similar, and in thick weather or soft snow the climber is quite happy to stop at the first, second, or third reached, on the false assumption that that is the summit. In 1930 we had to contend with both these handicaps, so, when the mist prevented us from seeing any point higher

than the one on which we stood, we were satisfied with what we had done –
the more so because we had not breath or energy for any more. Since that
time a newly formed Mountain Club, with good intentions but with
deplorable taste, has removed what little difficulty (and therefore fun) there
was to be had by labelling each point with a small iron name-plate, so that the
weary aspirant has no longer any adequate excuse for self-deception.

At each of these name-plates there is a receptacle of some kind for records,
so that for the conscientious mountaineer on Kibo a card-case is a necessity. It
was the omission to leave our full quota of cards in 1930 that I now wished to
repair. As S. was not available, I had to go alone, and although solitary
climbing is not in accordance with sound mountaineering practice,
Kilimanjaro is, perhaps, a mountain where this vice can be indulged in with
more safety than usual. There are no technical climbing difficulties apart from
those consequent on the great altitude, while it is well provided with huts. A
new one has been built at 16,000 feet, the jumping-off place for the summit,
and to this it is possible to take a heavily laden caravan of porters. In 1930 we
took a donkey there. All this extraneous assistance hardly gives the mountain
a fair chance, so this time I decided to dispense with at least some of it and to
carry what I wanted myself. I suppose, to be logical, I should have sternly
avoided the huts, but I was content to follow the very sound maxim of the
ancients: 'Nothing in excess'. With a companion it might have been rather
different, for discomfort can be borne with greater equanimity if shared by
others.

Leaving Nairobi by car, in August, I found the road less rough and the
plains greener than when we drove this way in 1930. My first objective was a
place called Namanga, about 100 miles from Nairobi, whither I had been
commissioned to take a new driving pinion for the back axle of a car whose
owner was stranded there. Namanga has usurped the place of Longido as a
halting-place on the way to Tanganyika, for there is a comfortable rest-house
there which is much patronised. One of the advertised attractions for visitors
is a close view of a herd of elephants which haunts some neighbouring bush.
For large parties it is advisable to reserve accommodation, and, since there is
no mail or telegraph service to Namanga, this is done by means of the nightly
broadcast from Nairobi wireless station. If the visitors desire to see elephants,
this request is usually included, so that the message heard after the nine
o'clock news may run something like this: 'Manager Namanga rest-house.
Party of six arriving tomorrow. Elephants required.'

I got there about four o'clock and found my stranded motorist. He was on
his way to the coast for a fortnight's holiday, but four days of it had already
been passed here, so that even the elephants had begun to pall. He was all
joy, like a prisoner who has been reprieved, when he heard I had something
for him. I handed over the spare part amidst an embarrassing accompaniment
of compliments and thanks for a very trivial service. I went in for a cup of tea
while the castaway wrestled with his back axle, and, on coming out again,
perceived at once that all was far from well. Curses and lamentations filled the
air, and I was soon told with excusable heat and emphasis that the part I had
brought did not fit the car. I was not to be blamed for that, but as 'the first

bringer of unwelcome news hath but a losing office', and as I could see that my presence at Namanga that night would be like an irritant in the wound, I pushed on. Driving slowly onwards in the darkness until about eight o'clock, I eventually came to some natives camped by the roadside round a large fire. Since I was to sleep out, one place was as good as another, so, pulling the car off the road, I got them to boil some water for tea and then curled up to sleep in the box-body of the car.

Next day I reached Marungu, putting up at the same little hotel where I had been previously received by the kind German host and his wife. The beautiful simplicity of my plan and its attendant advantages were now fully appreciated, for, instead of spending the remainder of the day haggling with greedy porters over wages, rations, clothes, packing and weighing loads, I had nothing to do but loaf about, inspect critically the local coffee *shambas*, and drink beer. In the morning, having packed a rucksack with sleeping-bag, warm clothing, and seven days' food, I told my astonished host to expect me when he saw me and walked off into the forest.

My load was quite heavy enough for me, weighing some 40 lbs. – a weight that did not include that of a tent which I had wanted to take in order to spend a night on the top. The weather was bad. A fine rain fell, while higher up the mountain was shrouded in mist. Showers of water dripped from every branch, so that it was not long before I reached the comparatively happy state of being unable to get any wetter. It is the long-drawn-out process of getting wet that is unpleasant, and when saturation point is reached one ceases to care. Approaching Bismarck Hut, one passes through grass glades, where the path was faintly marked and much confused by numerous elephant tracks. For ten panicky minutes I was astray and completely at a loss, and, in view of my earlier scorn for huts, it was astonishing how anxious I was to find one, how relieved when I did.

As I reached it in good time – at one o'clock – I had the whole afternoon to collect fuel and dry clothes. Next day was a repetition of the first – mist and rain – but once clear of the forest there was little difficulty in sticking to the path. This mounts by what the French guide-books call *une pente insensible*, but at that height, carrying a heavy load, I was by no means insensible of it.

There was a sharp frost that night at Peters's Hut, giving promise of better things to come, and, soon after leaving the hut next morning, I passed out of the mist and cloud below and emerged into blazing sunshine under a cloudless blue sky. The height was 13,000 feet.

Approaching the 'saddle' at nearly 16,000 feet, I saw a herd of twenty-seven eland. These are the largest of all the antelopes; they weigh as much as 1,000 lbs. and the meat is very tender and juicy. Both sexes are horned, those of a bull averaging 25 inches, and they stand five to six feet high at the shoulder. They are so gentle by nature that they can be domesticated, and in one instance at least have been trained for draught purposes. Butter made from eland's milk is said to be of exceptional quality. Their normal habitat is the open plains at heights of 5,000 feet to 6,000 feet, but so far as one could tell the eland up on the 'saddle' at 16,000 feet were in no way different, except for apparently shaggier hair. This particular herd seemed to be subsisting very happily on a diet of little more than shale, and were very shy.

Looking at the two peaks of Kibo and Mawenzi and recalling our visit of 1930, I was amazed to see the very striking difference in conditions which now prevailed. The present year of 1933 had been an exceptionally dry one throughout East Africa, so that the snow on Kibo scarcely descended further than Leopard's Point, just below the lip of the crater. Mawenzi was completely bare of snow. The steep snow gully up which we had kicked steps was rust-red rock, with the result that neither as a climb nor as a peak did it look so attractive as when draped in snow and ice.

The local Mountain Club, which has marked Kibo's hoary head with tin insults, has done the mountain a further disservice by building a new hut a few hundred feet above the Hans Meyer Caves. It seemed to me that camping out for the sake of camping was neither useful nor beneficial, and, as there was a roof available, pointless. Backed by such specious reasoning, by the well-remembered draughtiness of the caves, and hoping to mortify the flesh next night by sleeping on the top, I condescended to make use of the hut. Near it there was another herd of eland, and if only the Mountain Club would domesticate these, and supply the hut with milk and butter, nothing would be wanting to the improvement of Kilimanjaro but a motor road.

The unusual absence of snow on the lower slopes made it difficult to find water. I had to search in nooks and crannies of the rocks above the caves before I could scrape together enough old snow for my wants. Next morning, carrying a light load consisting of sleeping-bag and two days' food, I started for the top before sunrise – at about half past five. In normal years the snow lies as low as 17,000 feet, but now I toiled up loose scree until Leopard's Point, just below the crater rim, was reached. Leopard's Point is a little rocky knoll on top of which lies the desiccated remains of a leopard. I have never heard any explanation of how it came to be there, but presumably it went up of its own volition. A similar curiosity is the buffalo skeleton high up on Kenya, but that lies at a place nearly 3,000 feet lower than the leopard on Kibo.

It was delightful weather here, clear, sunny, windless. Below, at the 12,000 feet level, was a billowing sea of cloud which broke against the mountain, sending up wisps of mist like spray, which were in turn quickly dispersed by the sun. I seemed to be alone on an island detached from the world, floating in space on a sea of cloud.

The crater wall was gained at about 19,000 feet without any difficulty, under conditions much different from those of my first visit. The snow was hard and not even continuous, for in places it had melted away, leaving the bare rock exposed, while the whole of the crater, the rim and its several 'peaks', lay clear and glistening in the vivid light. I looked down a short, easy snow-slope to the flat snow-covered floor of the crater, and across to the opposite wall half a mile away. Now begins the slow and arduous perambulation of the rim, passing over the sequence of 'bumps' – they are really little more – each honoured with the name of 'point'. In the order reached they are Gillman Stella (our furthest in 1930), Hans Meyer, Kaiser Wilhelm Spitze (the true summit), and one beyond it called Furtwängler.

Taken together, the names, with one exception, provide an awful example of what mountains have to suffer in the way of nomenclature. I have not discovered who Gillman was; Hans Meyer, who was the first to climb the mountain, deserves to be remembered, but whether that can be said of the fourth name is open to doubt. Furtwängler, I am told, was the first to use skis on Kibo.

The earnest mountaineer sheds a card at each, and at Kaiser Wilhelm Spitze, which I reached at midday, there is a receptacle for records somewhat resembling, and almost as big as, a deed-box. In this are a miscellany of personal records, a Union Jack, and a Bible. Records can be found on all the points if the trouble to search for them in the snow is taken. There are few who would not take this trouble, for, however much one may despise the custom of leaving one's name on a mountain, it is at any rate one which furnishes an ever welcome excuse for a rest.

Furtwängler is about one hundred yards beyond the summit, and at first seemed higher, but a change of view-point showed it to be obviously lower. I sat there for some time, enjoying the sense of aloofness which the dense curtain of cloud below gave me, but the mist now began to prevail in its battle with the sun, which was presently hidden by a veil. No longer had it the power to disperse the upshooting jets torn from clouds as they broke against the mountain, and these, gradually coalescing, produced a slight but persistent fall of sleet.

Descending one or two hundred feet of snow and rock on the inner slope of the rim, I reached the crater floor and began casting about for a place in which to spend the night. A rather inadequately overhanging rock was soon found, and, having dumped my sack there, I walked across to the north side of the crater to inspect a secondary and very perfectly formed crater. At the top the diameter was about 400 yards across, at the bottom 200 yards. Sulphurous fumes rose from the lip, and pieces of sulphur lay about.

After taking photos and collecting some of the sulphur, I returned to the bivouac to turn in about 4.30, after a little food had been forced down. I was beginning to feel the effects of altitude, and suffered slightly from nausea and lassitude, but it was very noticeable that these symptoms were not nearly so well marked as in 1930, substantiating the well-known fact that acclimatisation is retained to a certain degree over long periods. In 1930 I was sick at 17,000 feet, sick most of the way up, and on top suffered from excessive willingness to sit down, whereas this time it was only after some hours on top (having also carried a load there) that I felt there was a remote possibility of losing my breakfast, but actually did not.

As soon as the sun sank behind the western wall, which it did quite early, and a thin wind began stirring, the deficiencies of my bivouac became apparent. I built a low stone wall to break the force of the wind, but wind is like water, and, though an imperfect barrier may check the ingress of some, that which enters spurts through with redoubled force. However, the night passed sufficiently well, half sleeping, half shivering, without complaint, for it would be unbecoming to criticise the hospitality of the mountain after sneering at that offered by man.

Dawn, nevertheless, was very welcome. I rose, cold and stiff, packed up, and crossed the crater floor in the direction of Leopard's Point. In places the snow in the crater had assumed a most curious formation, standing up in thin sheets like the leaves of a book lying open on its back. Each leaf was about six inches apart, and two feet high, and was too fragile to support the book. They had to be broken down before solid footing was reached.

This formation appears to have some affinity with the *nieves penitentes*, or 'snow penitents', of the Andes; so called from a supposed resemblance to cowled Penitent Friars. The name would have no sense if applied to the Kilimanjaro formation, but in the Andes, where it consists of fields of cones or pyramids of snow set close beside each other, slightly hooked at the top, and four or five feet in height, the name is more applicable. In his book *The Highest Andes*, Fitzgerald says the effect is produced by the combined action of sun and wind upon the frozen mass of snow-field, the crystalline parts, upon which the sun has little melting power, remaining erect in this strange fashion. I believe that no really satisfactory explanation for this phenomenon has yet been given, but it seems probable that since this formation is seen only in snow found within the tropics it may be due to the peculiar effects of a vertical, or almost vertical, sun. The great ice pinnacles found on Himalayan glaciers is another formation for which it is not easy to account.

Romping down the slope from Leopard's Point was a pleasant change, and, arriving at the top hut about eight, I had breakfast there before pushing on to Peters's, where the night was spent. Lunch next day was eaten at Marungu with mine host, who was with difficulty convinced of the fact that thirty hours ago I had been on the summit.

Hoping to reach Nairobi in the day, I made an early start, and, soon after leaving Marungu, passed my stranded motorist of Namanga. He was still on his way to the coast to enjoy the three remaining days of his fortnight's holiday.

I failed to reach Nairobi, and spent the night in the car in the middle of the Game Reserve. As I sat at dusk by the fire, listening to the mournful cry of a hyena, the rays of a sun, which for me had already set, picked out, high up in a darkening sky, Kilbo's snowy dome.

CHAPTER THIRTEEN

A New Way Home

'In all matters before beginning a diligent preparation should be made.' – Cicero

MEDITATION and solitude upon the top of Kilimanjaro had not clarified my thoughts as I had hoped, so that when I got back to Nairobi I was still undecided as to my next movement. The lure of gold was still very strong, and but for a certain happening I might have again responded to the call. A large tract of country bordering the north shores of Lake Victoria had been reserved for private prospecting – a welcome departure from the usual custom of granting sole prospecting rights over vast areas to companies. As yet, however, it had not been declared open, and no one was allowed to prospect there until it was. Meanwhile, the spending of a weekend duck-shooting near the lake had led to D. and I travelling by road across a large part of this new area, and on our return journey a large number of quartz samples had, by some strange chance, found their way into the car. But the wicked do not always flourish, and so it was with us, for every sample we tested proved to be barren.

That decided me. I concluded (wrongly, I now believe) that it was not worthwhile hanging about until this new area was opened, and made up my mind to go home for a time. Being in no particular hurry, this seemed the opportune moment for carrying out a scheme with which I had been toying for some time, namely, the finding of an alternative to the usual east-coast route to Europe. I have no great liking for steamer travel at any time, and I was heartily sick of this route, but the alternative had to be at least as cheap – cheaper if possible – a consideration that rather narrowed the field of choice. Journey by air was out of the question; travelling via the Sudan and the Sahara by car, though doubtless exciting, would also be expensive, and in any case I was not in love with motoring, even in a desert. This overland journey had at that time been done by several parties in cars, and it required not only money, but also the mechanical ability to cope with the breakdowns that would be certain to occur. Walking, on the other hand, was cheap, and was, moreover, a method by which I was certain of arriving somewhere, but would need more time than even I could afford, so I compromised finally on the humble but ubiquitous push-bike. Having thus simply settled the means of locomotion, the route and the ultimate destination had to conform. The sudd, swamp, and water of the Nile route gave little scope for cycling, and little knowledge of geography was needed to realise that if I meant to go home overland all the way, it entailed the crossing of the Sahara. That is all very well for cars and camels, but there are waterless stretches of three or four hundred miles which made the idea of riding a bicycle across it absurd, apart from the impossibility of riding at all in sand. So there remained the west coast, and to that I determined to go, and from there take ship. The precise point on the coast at which I would aim could be decided later, when I knew more about it.

It will be seen, then, that this plan of riding to the west coast was arrived at by a series of logical steps, based on the premise that I wanted to get home. In addition to many less complimentary reasons ascribed to it, one friend suggested that the real motive was the possibility of selling bicycles to advantage on the west coast; this I have less hesitation in mentioning because, unlike the other reasons, it implies a modicum of lucidity or normality. But in fact I had two very good reasons, namely, to get home and to see the country, for ever since gazing down upon the Congo forest from the top of Ruwenzori I had longed to travel through it. I have been at some pains to make my motives clear lest this proposed journey should appear to be in the same category as many projects whose only object is notoriety. Had notoriety been sought, I might have ridden the bicycle backwards, or at least have done the thing properly and started from Mombasa, on the east coast, with the back wheel in the Indian Ocean under a battery of cameras. I particularly wanted to avoid cycling in Kenya, first because the road through it was already so familiar that the idea of 'push-biking' along it gave me no pleasure at all; and secondly, because, as I myself was known there, the notice that my appearance would attract was very distasteful to me. It may seem strange that a man riding a bicycle should attract attention, but in tropical Africa a white man thus occupied is very conspicuous indeed, the more so if he carries a pack on his back, more kit on the handle-bars, and sleeps by the roadside at night under nothing more substantial than a mosquito net.

I decided, therefore, to start from Kampala, in Uganda, the furthest point west reached by the Uganda Railway, and on September 14th I boarded the Uganda Mail at Nairobi on my way to England, unencumbered except for a rucksack. The railway journey is interesting, embracing, as it does, an extraordinary variety of scenery – desert, bush, forest; native villages and European farms, mountain and plain, rivers and lakes. Perhaps the most striking feature of all is the deep, wide gash of the eastern arm of the Great Rift Valley, down into which the line drops and then crosses some forty miles west of Nairobi. It was of peculiar interest to me because ten days later, in the Belgian Congo, I was to cross the western arm.

In structure the two are alike – steep scarps containing a broad flat valley – and in both are found lakes and volcanoes. These two branches are parts of a single rift system which begins south of the Zambezi and extends northwards to the Sudan and Abyssinia, a distance of 2,000 miles. North of Lake Nyasa the Rift divides, its two arms enclosing the great mass of Lake Victoria, which is the only East African lake that does not lie in the floor of one or other of the two Rift Valley branches. In the western arm are the lakes of Tanganyika, Kivu, Edward, and Albert; in the eastern, Natron, Naivasha, Elmenteita, Nakuru, Hannington, Baringo, and Rudolph. Some geologists go so far as to link up the African Rift with that of the Red Sea, and its extension northwards to the Dead Sea and the valley of the Jordan.

Until 1928 the Uganda Railway terminated at Kisumu, a port on the eastern extremity of the Kavirondo Gulf of Lake Victoria. A branch line was then built from Nakuru to the Uasin Gisha Plateau and the northern highlands of Kenya, being subsequently extended into Uganda as far as Kampala. This is now the terminus, and the northern branch has become the main line.

Before reaching Kampala the railway crosses the Nile by a bridge just below the Ripon Falls, where the river issues from the lake. Here is the little town of Jinja, with its remarkable hippo-infested golf-course, the sight of which from the train brought back memories of our journey to Ruwenzori. Thirty-six hours after leaving Nairobi the train landed me at Kampala, where I spent one day choosing a bicycle and buying stores.

Kampala is the commercial capital of Uganda, twenty-five miles from

Entebbe, the official capital. It is the seat of the Kabaka (the native king of Buganda), and is built, like Rome, upon seven hills, which form the respective centres for business, the king and his parliament, the Church Missionary Society, the Roman Catholic Mission, and the residential area.

The Baganda, the natives of the Buganda Province which gives its name to the whole Protectorate, are probably the most advanced and intelligent natives of East Africa. Few ornaments are worn, mutilation of the features or cicatrisation is not practised, and the body is completely clothed, formerly in cloth made from bark, but now in cotton sheeting, made up in the form of a long nightgown reaching to the ankles. It is called a *kanzu*, and is no doubt a result of Arab influence. Dressed in this, with a little white skull-cap, a native is far more becomingly garbed than in the European dress which they increasingly affect. They are skilful potters and weavers of mats, music means a great deal to them, and an additional mark of culture is the attention they have always paid to road-making – an interest very unusual among so-called savage tribes. In fact, the Baganda are very different indeed from the Masai, Lumbwa, Kikuya, Kavirondo, and other East African tribes, having little in common with them except their colour.

This traditional interest in road-making has been maintained and encouraged by a happy combination of circumstances resulting mainly from the system of administration in force at the present day – the system which is known as 'indirect rule'; that is to say, as much of their former power and responsibility as possible is left in the hands of the native king and his chiefs. In the matter of roads this system works in the following way to produce remarkable results. By an old-established native custom the peasants are obliged to work for so many days a year on objects of public importance – roads, bridges, or rest-houses – and nowadays the chiefs take a greatly increased interest in seeing where and how this involuntary labour is spent, not only in the public capacity of chief, but in the private capacity of a car-owner; for, thanks to cotton growing, Mr. Ford, and 'hire-purchase', most of the chiefs own motor-cars.

Cotton is the most important product of Uganda, and on it the prosperity of the natives mainly depends. This prosperity is by no means constant, but, combined with the excellence of the roads, it has been sufficiently great in the past to have had a very stimulating effect upon the bicycle trade, as it is the ambition of every native to own one. Kampala is the centre of this trade – which brings me back to my own reason for being here.

For me, the purchase of a bicycle presented some little difficulty. As I had not ridden one since pre-War days, my knowledge of the 'points' of one of these machines was a little rusty. Complicating the issue still more was the fact that the trade in Kampala was in the hands of wily Indians, so that my simple purchase soon resolved itself into a struggle wherein I tried to avoid getting 'stuck' with something which had been lying in stock during the three years' depression, deteriorating rapidly in the equatorial climate. One of this fraternity was as plausible as a horse-coper, and, while telling me the age of the stock of his numerous competitors, showed with pride the date of manufacture stamped on his own. If the date was correct it meant that the bicycles had only left the factory a short month ago. Certainly it was possible they had been sent out by the unusual and expensive way of air mail, but a simpler explanation seemed to be that the man was a liar. That this was correct the sequel showed. Passing the same shop later in the day with a bicycle bought elsewhere, I went in to get some valve tubing. While measuring a piece, which I pocketed without examining, my friend expressed his sorrow that I had had the oldest bicycle in Kampala planted on me, and doubted its ability to carry me much further than the outskirts of the town. The bicycle I still have, but his precious valve tubing was perished when I bought it.

The bicycle finally purchased was an ordinary English make costing £6. I might have had a Japanese one for £2, but I felt that here at any rate was a case where 'Buying British' was sound policy for more reasons than that of patriotism.

The question of spare parts gave me some anxious thought, as it was extremely unlikely that any would be obtainable after leaving Kampala. It occurred to me that unless I took a complete spare bike I might as well take nothing at all, so nothing it was, except for a couple of spare inner tubes. In the event, this attitude of faith and hope was rewarded, for in the course of a fairly rough 3,000 miles no vital part either dropped off or broke. On returning home I mentioned this fact to the makers, hoping, in my simple way, that they would be so pleased with my unsolicited testimonial that they would give me a new bicycle. However, behaving with true British phlegm, they managed to contain their enthusiasm within due bounds, so that all I received was a kind little note expressing the pleasure it gave the firm to hear of what had been no doubt an agreeable and satisfactory journey.

I took the two inner tubes because I imagined – quite wrongly, as it happened – that punctures would be an everyday occurrence. I did find that inner tubes could be obtained at one or two places *en route*, but spare parts were not to be had.

My ideas about the route were vague. I could get no maps of the Congo or the country north and west of it; the only one I possessed was a small-scale map of the whole African continent torn out of the back of a magazine. I decided to make first for Stanleyville, in the heart of the Congo, thereafter steering for any port that could be reached between Accra in the north and Benguela in the south. This gave me a sufficiently wide target of about 1,500 miles at which to aim, so that my plans had the very desirable quality of elasticity.

My luggage consisted of a rucksack containing 20 lbs. weight of food, spare shirt, shorts, camera, and other necessities, with a small roll of bedding made up of a light sleeping-bag, mosquito net, and ground-sheet carried on the handle-bars, bringing the total weight up to 30 lbs. An eiderdown sleeping-bag, out of place though it may seem on the equator, served the purpose well. At heights of 8,000 and 9,000 feet on the Uganda-Congo border I slept *in* it, and in the sweltering lowlands through which the greater part of my route lay I slept *on* it. A tent, though desirable, was too heavy to carry.

The small amount of food taken from Kampala was, of course, exhausted in a few days, and for the rest of a journey of more than two months I relied mainly on the country. What could be had naturally depended on the presence of natives and their standard of living, which was not extravagantly high. Bananas were the main stand-by, particularly a big, coarse variety which, when roasted in the ashes, was very excellent and satisfying. Two of these were enough to give one the sensation of having dined. In Uganda and parts of the Congo bananas are the staple food, and the natives are said to distinguish two hundred varieties. There are three main classes: the female banana, which is cut green, cooked and served mashed, or dried and made into flour; the male banana, which is used for beer-making; and lastly the sweet banana, which we know, eaten raw as a fruit or baked green. The leaves of the banana provide plates, wrappings for food, and umbrellas.

Other articles which sometimes appeared in my dietary were eggs, potatoes, and occasional fruit-oranges or pawpaw. The last is delightful, resembling a small marrow in shape and tasting like a canteloup melon. The flesh contains a ferment which is capable of digesting meat, while even the leaves wrapped round meat are said to make it more tender. With a drop of lemon-juice and some sugar it makes an even more delightful approach to breakfast than grapefruit, but unfortunately, like the mango, it is too perishable to export to Europe. On this vegetarian diet (I had nothing else) I kept pretty fit. True, I lost two stone in weight, but it must be remembered that cycling on the equator is rather heating. Before leaving, a boy offered to come with me as a servant. I told him he could, but as I was not going to buy him a bicycle he must run behind the whole way. He refused this generous offer, but I think he was quite capable of doing it. In Kampala they still tell the story of some native sports which were held there, of which the great event was a Marathon race. The runners, some fifty in number, were accompanied by several Europeans on bicycles to see fair play. After the lapse of a few hours they re-entered the stadium in a compact body, just as they had left it, all cheering and shouting. They thought it far more fun to stick together; they could see no sense in racing. As for the unhappy cyclists, it was several hours later when they straggled in in ones and twos, dead-beat to a man.

After a preliminary canter round Kampala in the evening to assure myself that I could still ride, I was up very early next morning in order to be clear of the town before anyone was about. I was still dreadfully afraid of being stared at, and, although my sensitiveness on this point soon wore off, had I known what I was to suffer in this respect later the trip would have been abandoned forthwith. At the last moment, aghast at the weight imposed upon the back wheel, I removed the roll of bedding from the carrier to the handle-bars, and so weighty was the impression my full rucksack made on me that I considered the tearing off and scrapping of such superfluities as gear-case, mudguards, and even bell. Fortunately I was in too much of a hurry to be off to put this foolishness into effect, so I mounted and pedalled slowly westwards out of the town on the first stage of my long journey.

CHAPTER FOURTEEN

Through Uganda

'Let the blow fall soon or late,
Let what will be o'er me.
Give the face of earth around,
And the road before me.'
— R. L. Stevenson

As the sun swung up over the horizon and began to play upon my back, where the weight of the rucksack was now making itself felt, I began to have misgivings about the effect upon myself of riding all day under a tropical sun and of the additional 30 lbs. weight upon the bicycle, and it was borne upon me that this first day would be a crucial one. But, as has already been said, the Uganda roads are good, so that at sundown that evening, after I had reeled off nearly 60 miles without any sign of imminent collapse on the part of the bicycle or myself, I regarded the remaining 2,950 miles with less respect.

For the first two or three days the scenery was typical of Eastern Uganda: an endless succession of low conical hills clad in dense forest, unbroken except for scattered banana groves, while between the hills lay wide flat bottoms through which flowed sluggish streams whose water was concealed beneath vast swamps of papyrus grass. The road switchbacked amongst the hills and was carried across the swamps on long causeways. A rather bright and shiny green, common alike to the cultivated banana patches, the tropical jungle, and the swamps, coloured the whole landscape.

My choice of camp the first night on the swampy shore of Lake Victoria was not a happy one. It was close to the depot of a road gang, whose huts I thought could be used as cover if rain fell, but mosquitoes abounded, forcing me to seek the shelter of my net as soon as the sun went down at six o'clock. My evening meal was taken under its protection.

While in Uganda and the Eastern Congo, I made it a rule not to sleep in native huts or rest-houses. (The last are thatched mud and wattle huts put up and maintained by the local headman for the use of officials on tour and other travellers. With the advent of the motor-car and the consequent abolition of the old slow-moving porter safari, they are falling into disuse.) The reason for this self-denial was the prevalence in those parts of the fever tick (*ornithodorus moubata*), the carrier of spirillum or relapsing fever. This tick infests native huts, rest-houses, and old camping-grounds, and its bite may result in a fever even more unpleasant than malaria. As a compromise, I camped when possible near to huts or rest-houses, but only for cover in case of rain. Sickness induced either by tick bites or by chills was a mischance that I could ill afford and did not care to contemplate.

The natives were always horrified at my sleeping out, and it was not easy to make them understand my reasons for it. On two occasions in Uganda, I heard lions grunting at night, but there was little to fear from them, while there was a good deal to fear from the tick-infested huts. The headman of the village near which I camped usually insisted on lighting an enormous fire near me and providing a couple of men armed with spears to act as a bodyguard. What prowling perils they warded off I cannot tell, but they successfully warded off my sleep by their loud and ceaseless chatter. All natives are inveterate talkers; a taciturn African is a freak; the result, possibly, of illiteracy. Cattle, goats, and women – in that order – are the staple topics, while their conversational tone is a hearty roar.

It may be thought rash, even foolhardy, to travel thus unarmed, sleeping outside in a country abounding in dangerous game, but the lightest weapon that would be worth while carrying to stop a lion or an elephant would weigh at least 10 lbs., and long and expensive formalities would have had to be gone through in order to take a rifle into foreign colonies.

I think the risk run from big game is slight provided you leave it alone. Of course, if you hunt it you may have reason to agree with that Frenchman who wrote in a natural history book of some animal (I forget which), 'Cet animal est tres méchant, quand on l'attaque il se défend.'

There have been cases recorded of unprovoked assaults by rhino, elephant, or buffalo, but it is generally found that the animal had been shot at and wounded by someone else previously, and therefore bore a grudge against any human being.

A man-eating lion is less common than a man-eating tiger (tigers, of course, are not found in Africa), but in Uganda there are occasionally outbreaks of man-killing by lions, and in Kenya there is the historic case of the man-eaters of Tsavo. The incidents are related in a book called *The Man-eaters of Tsavo*. They occurred at Tsavo, between Mombasa and Nairobi, when the railway-line was being built. Some thousands of coolies from India were employed on the construction of the line (for in those happy days the African native, except for a few Swahili porters from the coast, did not know what work was), and for weeks on end their camp was terrorised by a number of lions, which killed and carried off one or more coolies almost every night. Many efforts were made to kill or drive away the marauders, whose raids were threatening to put a stop to the building of the line by frightening away all the labour. One of these attempts is worth relating.

Three Europeans sat up one night for the lions in a railway carriage, leaving the door open through which to shoot. They must have dozed, for the first thing they knew was that a lion was shut inside the carriage with them, the weight of his spring having rocked the carriage and slammed to the door behind him. The carriage was fitted for sleeping, with two berths below and two above. The lion then proceeded to stand on the chest of a man in the lower berth while he seized the man above and then jumped out through the opposite window with his victim in his mouth.

Stories of the railway and the game are the more amusing on account of the incongruity of the two, but the railway runs through over two hundred miles of country set apart as a Game Reserve, and more game is perhaps seen from the train than from anywhere else. In the early days, when the Colony was small and the atmosphere more happy-go-lucky, it was not difficult to persuade the driver to stop while the passengers killed a buck, or took part in a lion hunt.

Nowadays lions are rarely seen from the train, the majority of the so-called lions reported by excited travellers new to the country being merely inoffensive and smelly hyenas. On one famous occasion the train was charged by a rhino, and the attention of the railway authorities ought to be drawn to the fact that the train in question must have been grossly overcrowded, as twenty people at the very least claim to have been sitting in the actual carriage against which the rhino dashed himself. There is another good story of a telegram which was received at Nairobi from the heroic babu in charge of the telegraph office of some station down the line. It ran, 'Three lions on platform, station-master in water-tank, please wire instructions.'

Lions are a popular subject in the business of big-game photography for the cinema which enjoyed such a vogue recently, the reason being that lions are more easily photographed than any other game. By the simple expedient of providing free meals of buck or zebra daily, the lions of a district are soon attracted to the spot, and after a few weeks of that sort of treatment they become almost tame.

On the Serengeti Plains, a famous shooting-ground, some wag has put up a notice-board with the following warning: 'Notice to Sportsmen. Shout before you shoot; these lions are accustomed to be fed.'

More common than the lion and more feared by the natives is the leopard, for this bold and cunning beast is quite capable of raiding a hut for the sake of a sheep or goat. Dogs, too, are very frequently taken by leopards, but a man is very unlikely to be attacked unless the animal is wounded or cornered.

On the whole, I think I ran little risk in travelling so improvidently through the haunts of lions, leopards, elephant and buffalo, nor was I ever molested by any of these fierce beasts. My immunity was due no doubt to the common-sense attitude which on this occasion I adopted; similar to that of the Johannesburg Jew in the early days who, when his pals asked him why he never went lion-hunting, replied that he saw no reason to, because he hadn't lost any.

I was now three days out from Kampala, and approaching the district of Ankole in Western Uganda. To reach it I had traversed the populous cotton-growing districts of Mengo and Masaka, where the road was seldom without traffic of some sort – lorries taking cotton to Kampala, a few natives on bicycles, and hundreds on foot carrying their raw cotton to the local Indian trader who lived in a ramshackle tin shanty by the roadside. On leaving that country, and almost until the west coast was reached, I had the road pretty much to myself. Once or twice a week a lorry might be met, but I do not remember seeing more than two bicycles, and neither of those were in motion. The constant stream of natives met with during the first few days put a great strain on my politenes. I had little breath to waste on shouting the usual greeting of 'Jambo,' and, owing to my heavy load and lack of practice, too much punctiliousness in returning salutes by hand resulted in a sudden swoop across the road, followed by some paralysing moments while I strove to regain my balance and my dignity. The heat, too, was very great, in spite of an elevation of between 3,000 and 4,000 feet. I felt it more on these first few days in Uganda than at any other time, partly, I suppose, because I was not yet hardened.

In Ankole the country changes to open, rolling, grassy downs almost bare of trees. It is higher, and therefore cooler, than Eastern Uganda. The natives consist of a ruling race, the Hamitic Banyankole, who are all pastoralists, and an inferior Bantu strain who do the agricultural and menial work for their superiors. The cattle of Ankole, said to number nearly five million head, are remarkable for the enormous horns they carry. Forest or bush are conspicuously lacking, a fact which doubtless accounts for the absence of the tsetse fly, for broad belts of the surrounding wooded country are infested.

This open country was preferable to the bush, forest, and swamp through which I had passed, but it had its drawbacks. If there were no tsetse fly, there were plenty of the harmless but more annoying kinds, as is generally the way in a cattle country. Against this minor plague there was no protection, and short of dismounting I was completely at their mercy, for I was still insufficiently familiar with my mount and the queer distribution of weight to be able to ride with one hand while employing the other to swat flies.

Mbarara, 180 miles from Kampala, was reached on the third day. It is the capital of Ankole and the place of residence of the native king and his prime minister, or Katakiro, though I am ashamed to say that of more interest to me was the fact that there was some beer to be had. From a road engineer I managed to learn something about my route. At that time there were two roads from Uganda to the Congo, both passing to the north of the great barrier presented by the Ruwenzori range. One of these went to Butiaba and by boat across Lake Albert, and the other further north still, via Rejaf in the Sudan. Neither of these was any use to me now, as I was too far to the south, but I learnt that a motor road was being built to pass south of Ruwenzori between Lakes Edward and Kivu to link up with the Belgian road from Lake Kivu to Stanleyville. It was not yet complete, but I was told that by leaving it at Kabale, the last administrative post in Uganda, I could get into the Congo by following the old caravan track, which, though it would involve much pushing up and walking down, would take me through very interesting country.

I was now fairly amongst the Ankole highlands, whose main features are rolling downs, swamp-filled valleys, and very little cultivation; a vast grazing-ground for huge herds of long-horned cattle, and many head of antelope, zebra, and other game. At a place called Lutobo, I found a delightfully situated rest-house, perched, like most of its kind, on the highest available hill, up which I was not too proud to hire a slave to push the bicycle. It was well kept and clean, but for safety I slept on the short-cut grass lawn outside, where I was glad to use the inside of my sleeping-bag for the first time, the height being now over 6,000 feet. The only food to be had was an enormous wooden bowl of milk, but had it been a month later I might have had strawberries and cream, for there was a vegetable garden in the compound with a large strawberry bed. As yet none were ripe.

Near Kabale the country became very broken, and the road wound about through steep shut-in valleys where I did as much walking as riding. Kabale is the administrative centre for the Kigezi district, in the extreme south-west corner of Uganda. The District Commissioner lives there, and, wishing to get some more information about the caravan track I proposed following, I went to consult him. There was a long uphill grind to reach the seat of authority, which was built on an eminence truly Olympian. Added to the toil was some nervousness about the reception I would receive at the hands of the Presence, for I must have looked, even at this early stage, uncommonly like a 'down and out.' But my reception was cordial, and the expenditure of so much energy amply repaid by the receipt of much useful information concerning the difficult country between Kabale and the Congo.

Before leaving the town I managed to obtain, in exchange for East African shillings, a few hundred Belgian francs. By this time it was midday, but I pushed on, and a mile from the town turned off the road according to instructions. I was at once faced with a three-mile hill of appalling steepness up which, I confess, I bribed a small boy to push the bicycle. The midday heat was blistering, and I felt it would require all my remaining energy to get myself and the rucksack to the top. The descent was steep, but led to a deliciously cool-looking lake called Bunyoni. I crept down this with both brakes jammed on hard.

The lake had to be crossed, and while negotiating for the charter of a dugout I found time for some food and a bathe. The water was surprisingly cold (far too cold for crocodiles), the altitude being over 6,500 feet. Bunyoni is the largest of the lakes of the Ankole highlands, being fifteen miles in length. It is very narrow, dotted with many small islands, and lies in a cup whose sides are steep and heavily wooded.

The long hour's sail across the lake was a restful interlude which I spun out as long as possible by having yet another bathe before landing. My crew of three, who had to do the paddling, anxious to make the voyage as short as possible, pointed out several desirable harbours, but I was firm, insisting on being taken to the place advised by the District Commissioner, which was at the extreme end of one arm of the lake. A break in the reed fringe was our only port, and, having landed, one of the paddlers rather surprisingly volunteered to push the bicycle up another long steep hill to a rest-house called Behungi. This climb, long though it was, made very little impression on the high walls of the deep depression in which the lake lay. I could see the track making short zigzags up the steep sides, and, learning that there was worse country ahead, I engaged my volunteer for another bout of pushing on the morrow.

My rations here consisted only of another giant bowl of milk. I turned in alongside a large fire, for it was very cold, but about midnight a heavy drizzle drove me to the shelter of the *banda*, with all its dire possibilities of lurking fever ticks.

The boy and I set off next morning while it was yet dark. Walking was to be my portion for some time, so there was no immediate need of light. The hills surrounding the lake were over 8,000 feet high, covered in their upper parts with dense bamboo forest, which was the home of numerous elephant and buffalo. Their spoor was everywhere, but we saw nothing of the animals themselves or of the human inhabitants of this jungle – a race called Bativa, savage, semi-pygmies, who are said to have practised cannibalism in the not distant past.

From the rim of the bowl, and looking towards the Congo, there was a prospect as rich in colour as it was wide in extent. Far below, shimmering in the heat, stretched a reddish-coloured plain of lava, studded with little crater lakes of an intense turquoise blue, and ringed about with mighty volcanic peaks. Of these the huge bulk of Mahavura filled the foreground, its flanks covered with thick scrub almost to the rocky summit. It is the third highest of this remarkable group of volcanic peaks known as the Mfumbiro volcanoes. The name Virunga is sometimes applied to them, but that is merely a local native name for a mountain. Karisimbi, 14,780 feet, is the highest; one of them, called Nino Gonga, 11,386 feet, lying nearer to Lake Kivu, is still active. The several peaks extend in a chain east and west across the thirty-mile floor of the Rift Valley, and form the divide betwen the Nile and Congo basins. The largest affluent of Lake Victoria, and therefore of the Victoria Nile, the Kagera River, rises on the east; northwards the drainage falls into Lake Edward, which is the source of the Semliki River and the White Nile; while southwards and to the west the drainage is into Lake Kivu, whence it flows into Lake Tanganyika and the Congo River system.

On the top I dismissed my follower; prematurely, as it happened, for the descent to the plain was as arduous as the ascent, as at times the bicycle had to be carried bodily. On the lava plain the going was indescribably bad. The track, which was studded with lumps of rough lava, traversed a sort of natural slag heap, winding amongst small craters and volcanic cones; twelve miles of agonised bumping over rasping lava before I reached the frontier post of the Belgian Congo. It was a 'post' in the literal sense of the word. There was nothing there (and I thanked heaven for it) but a wooden post, silent and uninquisitive, stuck upright in the ground – no customs official, no police, not even a human being.

It was exactly a week since I had left Kampala.

CHAPTER FIFTEEN

Lake Kivu to Stanleyville

'Where are forests hot as fire,
Wide as England, tall as a spire.'
— R. L. Stevenson

I sat there contemplating what had been done and what remained to do, wondering whether my tyres were as badly frayed as my temper; and there, in a weak, unguarded moment, I was tempted and fell. My self-imposed rules for the journey allowed of no assistance in the way of lifts, and hitherto my firmness of mind had not been severely tested. If, after leaving Mengo, I met more than one lorry every other day the road seemed congested. But now, while I was ruefully examining my tyres, the devil appeared in the guise of an Indian lorry-driver bound for Lake Kivu. He at once offered me a lift. Concern for my tyres silenced the haughty refusal hovering on my lips, and instead I asked him how far the horrible surface continued. On being told nearly to Ruchuru, the first Belgian post twenty miles away, I accepted his offer. It was flagrant cheating, but it is the only instance to be recorded, and I excused it on the grounds that it was necessary to save the tyres.

It was a rougher ride in the lorry than it would have been on the bike, so that I was not sorry to dismount when we reached the Lake Kivu-Stanleyville road, two miles short of Ruchuru. I ought now to have turned north for Stanleyville, but as Lake Kivu, which I was anxious to see, was only fifty miles away, I turned south. We had got clear of the lava plain, and for a brief space I was once more in a country where man could live and cultivate. Near by Ruchuru there were several European coffee plantations whose appearance was the more startling following so hard upon the arid waste of lava over which I had come.

I stopped that night half-way between Ruchuru and the lake, at a Mission run by the White Fathers, where I was very hospitably received. It lay at the foot of one of the volcanoes, Mikeno (14,385 feet), a very striking peak whose summit consisted of a curved rocky fang. There was no vestige of a crater, as it had apparently been eroded away. Away in the south-west a lurid glow in the sky marked the activity of Nino Gonga – a fittingly baleful beacon to light such a desolate landscape.

The run from here to Kisenyi, on the lake-shore, was a well-balanced mixture of pain and pleasure. At first I regretted heartily the curiosity which had involved me in a hard grind in white lava dust along a road which wound amongst a chaos of lava boulders where dreary-looking trees and bushes struggled for existence. There were no huts, no villages, no water, no life. It is a fantastic country – part of what the Belgians call the Albert National Park. This is a big tract which has been set aside as a Game Reserve, where it is hoped that the fast-vanishing African gorilla, which, appropriately enough, haunts the wooded slopes of the volcanoes, may now have a chance to survive.

Near Lake Kivu there is a swift transition from desert to fertility. Lava boulders give place to a rich soil of volcanic ash which supports a dense population made up of natives called Wahuta. The womenfolk of these people outdo the Lumbwa, Masai, or Kikuyu women in the amount of wire which they coil about their ankles. The weight carried must amount to several pounds per leg, producing an appearance suggestive of elephantiasis.

The surface of the road also changed for the better, the low watershed had been crossed, and I free-wheeled for nearly ten miles down to Kisenyi and the lake. The little port of Kisenyi, where I stopped the night, contained a white population of about a dozen, mostly Greeks. In Kenya and Uganda the Indian storekeeper is ubiquitous, but in the Congo his place is taken by the Greek. These two races seem able to thrive where the Englishman or the Belgian would starve. Possibly the secret lies in what it would be polite to call simple living, and in making full use of the natural resources of the country. This last point was well exemplified by my Greek host. I had put up at a little place kept by one of these Greeks which was styled rather grandiloquently The Lido – a name to which it had some claim, because the white sandy beach was not fifty yards away. My attention was drawn to this when I asked my Greek friend if I could get a bath. He looked at me as though I had made a joke in rather doubtful taste, and pointed out, quite rightly, that there was a perfectly good lake just outside his door!

When I came to act on this hint I was surprised to find that Kisenyi was as careful to observe the proprieties as Margate, so that I was compelled to borrow a bright red horror from my host and thus spoil an otherwise perfect bathe. The firm, clean, sandy beach shelved steeply into cool, limpid water, and but for the wretched entangling garment that bathe would have been hard to beat. Even so, it ranks high in my list of classic bathes, for the life-giving water closed over my head to drown the fatigues and sweeten the memories of the last ten days.

Lake Kivu was discovered in 1894 by Count Gotzen. It is 5,000 feet above the sea, and in depth second only to Lake Tanganyika, which is the deepest of all the African lakes. Its green, fertile shores rise in places to 10,000 feet, wooded islands lend their beauty to its calm blue surface, its waters abound in fish, while hippos and crocodiles are entirely absent. It is considered by some to be the most beautiful of the African lakes; indeed, the Kisenyi bay has been compared to the Bay of Naples, but in my opinion it lacks the charm and the colour of the Kenya lakes, Naivasha, Nakuru, or Elmenteita.

I was now faced with the long stretch of 650 miles to Stanleyville. In a direct line, the town is only about 300 miles north-west of Kivu, but the road leads north, passing west of Lake Edward, Ruwenzori, and the south end of Lake Albert, reaching to Irumu before it at last turns west and heads for

Stanleyville. While retracing my steps to Ruchuru, and for a day's journey beyond that place, I was riding along the trough of the western Rift Valley.

At Ruchuru, a small administrative post, the road takes a bend to the west, crossing the floor of the Rift to its western wall, which is formed here by the Kabasha escarpment. After leaving Ruchuru, cultivation ceased, and I rode through uninhabited country of open grassy plains on which herds of topi roamed. Wherever there was water the long grass was trampled into lanes with the tracks of hippo.

Not knowing for where the road was heading, and having no map, I was surprised and disquieted by this westerly bend. I had expected it to follow the valley, but on this new alignment it was with inexorable perversity making for a long range of high hills instead of running parallel to them as before. Towards evening I came to a few huts, which were the first habitations I had seen since leaving Ruchuru, so that when I perceived that the road meant to climb those high hills I decided to defer that pleasure and to camp.

I found that I was at the establishment of a native game warden and his underlings, for the country through which I had been travelling was another part of the Albert National Park. Approaching the huts, I had myself seen the freshly broken branch of a tree denoting the presence of elephant, and the natives now assured me that both these and lions were plentiful. The game warden urged me to share his hut, but, mindful still of the spirillum ticks, I preferred the dangers without to those within. In the end I tried both. Quite early in the night heavy rain drove me into the hut, and then, later on, by flooding the floor, drove me out again. I endured lying on the floor in a pool until three in the morning, when, the rain having stopped, I had some food and started pushing the bike up the escarpment in the dark, lions or no lions. Some light would have been agreeable, but it was by no means necessary, for I knew that the wet and heavy road surface with the formidable climb would prevent any riding for some time. Dawn came at six to find me still pushing, and it was after nine before the climbing of the first step of the escarpment enabled me to start pedalling again. When it was light enough to see, I found that I was on a well-made road zigzagging backwards and forwards up the rocky escarpment. This road up the 8,000 feet Kabasha escarpment is a remarkable piece of engineering. It climbs nearly 4,000 feet in less than twenty miles with a gradient of nowhere more than one in twenty.

The bleak uplands on top of the escarpment were sparsely inhabited. The few natives I did meet either fled at sight or crouched behind a bush – evidently a being on two wheels was to them something in the nature of a sign and a portent. Late the same evening I came to the first Belgian rest-house – what they call a *gîte d'étape* – but, still playing for safety, I slept outside by a roaring fire. It had been a gruelling fifteen-hour day, with fifty miles made good, twenty miles of it on foot.

If the spirillum tick is susceptible to cold, I should have been safe enough in the *banda*. Judging by the high altitude vegetation such as bamboo and bracken which flourished there, I estimated the height at 8,000 feet. The native crops were potatoes and wimbe, the altitude being too high for maize or bananas.

Every road must go downhill sometimes, and next morning I had twenty-five miles of coasting. I passed a signboard which said forty-seven miles to Lubero, and, though I had no notion what Lubero was, I was cheered by this mute guide. There is a charm, rarely attainable in these ordered days, of travelling blindly, in profound ignorance of the country ahead, but it was comforting to know that one was on the way to somewhere. Little help could be got from the natives. Most of them knew nothing of the country outside their immediate neighbourhood, and no amount of interrogation could instruct me how far it was to any place beyond the next village, or where to make for to spend the night.

Luberto proved to be the centre of a thickly populated district. The natives were engaged mainly in growing potatoes of the European variety, which I was told were sent by road to Stanleyville and thence as far as Leopoldville, near the Congo mouth.

Pushing on through pleasant, healthy, fertile country, I stopped the night with a young American missionary from Texas. He had chosen a difficult place for his activities, having to contend not only with the heathen, but also the Roman Catholics, whose missions greatly preponderate in those parts. Every village almost had its church, in the shape of a grass hut surmounted by a cross, while every child seemed to bear a crucifix round its neck. It was a pleasant enough country in which to work. It was comparatively cool, free from fever, and capable of growing most kinds of European fruits and vegetables, many of which appeared at our meal that night. Being an American – a Southerner at that – and a man who had been living alone for some time, my host had a good deal of pent-up conversational steam to blow off. He was commendably frank about the local natives, and had not allowed enthusiasm for his mission to blind him to their faults. They were the Bananda, a poor, timid, undersized race, who, like the Wakamba of Kenya, had the custom of filing their teeth to a point. This custom, which makes a normally ugly face look ten times worse, is supposed to denote cannibal tendencies. Why it should is not quite clear to me, because no human flesh, not even a cyclist's, could possibly call for sharper teeth to chew than African chicken or goat. The nearest approach to human flesh that I have sampled is monkey, and that is not in the least tough.

The end of these cool, healthy uplands was now in sight, and next day, from the edge of another escarpment, I beheld, far below me, a smooth expanse of dark olive green stretching away into the distance, flat and unbroken, like the sea. It was the Congo forest, reaching westwards to the sea and extending to four degrees north and south of the equatorial line. That afternoon I entered what was to be my environment for the next fortnight. Within this tract of low-lying virgin forest, terrifying in its silent immensity, the atmosphere is that of a hothouse, sapping the energy of both mind and body. The only road crossing this sea of vegetation in which I was now submerged stretches endlessly before one like a thin red band at the bottom of a canyon of living greenery. The dark wall of foliage towers up on either hand for nearly two hundred feet, to arch and almost meet overhead, as if to reclaim for the forest the pitiful strip that man has wrested from it. As I watched the narrow red ribbon of road unwind slowly in front of my wheel, I felt as though I had been doomed to ride endlessly along the bottom of some enormous trench out of which it was impossible to climb.

The only break in the oppressive monotony were the villages, the huts of a road gang, and the rivers. The villages and the *cantonniers*, as the huts of the road gangs are called, are merely two single lines of huts spread along either side of the road. At the villages there is also a narrow strip of cultivation, perhaps thirty yards deep, overshadowed at the back by the dark wall of the forest, appearing thus envious at yielding even that insignificant patch to man, its enemy.

This is 'ribbon development' *in excelsis*. Everything centres on the road. Away from it is nothing human, except here, in the part called the Ituri Forest, a few pygmies, who live by hunting and who come into the villages to barter skins and meat for maize and bananas.

A very short stature of four feet or less, broad and flattened nose, prognathous chin, long arms and short legs, are the characteristics of these curious people. But, however inferior physically they may be, they are more mentally alive than the average negro. On the other hand, they live in the most primitive manner possible, in huts little better than the nests which gorillas make for themselves, and they are entirely ignorant of agriculture or of any industry but hunting. Though living a life similar to the Wanderobo of the Kenya forests, the Congo pygmies differ from them very notably in that they are by no means shy of other natives or Europeans, and will come readily into the villages for purposes of barter.

This part of the Congo forest called the Ituri is also the home of that strange animal the okapi, whose existence was first made known by the skins brought in by pygmies. It is allied to the giraffe – its fore-arms and thighs are striped like a zebra's. The horns, which are found ony on the male, are covered with skin except on the tips.

The roadside population, which must comprise practically the whole, is complementary to the road; without the one there could not be the other. As the road was made, so the road-makers settled or were planted alongside – the only possible arrangement both for administration and trade in a country so inhibitive to movement. In the Congo, near towns or favoured areas, this 'ribbon development' had produced a long, continuous strip of life and activity, which in this primitive community has all the material advantages and none of the æsthetic drawbacks which a like development has at home. The huts may be dark, dirty, and, according to Western standards, only fit to be burnt, but darkness is rather pleasant in a country of blinding sunlight, the dirt is more apparent than real, and they are at least habitations adapted to the owners and their environment. The dignity of the Congo forest and the 'poor but honest' simplicity of its villages have not yet been menaced by bungaloid growths, corrugated iron, petrol pumps, and kiosks.

The villages, occurring every ten or fifteen miles, and rivers, form welcome breaks in the deadly monotony of the forest. Under the canopy of the forest, a network of rivers, great and small, which are at once a means of, and a barrier to, communication – tributaries of the mighty Congo – flow sluggishly between low banks, through valleys which are almost imperceptible, so uniformly flat is the surrounding country.

The first of the big rivers (and there were many), to which I came was also called the Ituri. It was reached at the end of a long day in country which for the last twenty miles had appeared to be uninhabited. The reason for the absence of villages, which I only discovered later, was that this tract was infested with elephants. No indication was given that I was approaching a large river. There was no warning descent; the road merely came to an end, terminating with the forest, on the brink of a quarter of a mile stretch of muddy. slow-moving water. At first I was at a loss how to cross, until I spotted a wire hawser spanning the river and on the far side a number of canoes. This first ferry was typical of many by which I crossed on the Kivu-Stanleyville road. It consisted of half a dozen dugout canoes supporting a rough plank platform big enough to hold a lorry. This contraption was attached to the wire cable by a pulley wheel, and, once it had been poled out into the stream by the crew, the force of the current, striking it at an angle, was sufficient to take it across.

By dint of shouting I got the ponderous affair manned and brought slowly across for its disproportionate freight. It seemed rather like chartering the *Queen Mary* to take one across the Channel. I learnt later that single canoes were provided for the conveyance of travellers on foot and idiots on bicycles. They were a good deal quicker than the ferry, and native passengers were carried free. The charge for the ferry made to lorries varied with the size of the river from three francs to ten.

I put up my net close to the huts of the ferrymen and was soon sound asleep. Much to my disgust – for I was very tired – I was presently awakened by the lights and hooting of a lorry. In England we are slowly being educated to accept the nightly roar of traffic as one of the amenities of civilisation, but it seemed a bit hard to suffer in the same way in the depths of the Congo. Anyhow, I am pretty sure it was after the legal hour for blowing a horn. My thoughts and imprecations on the menace of an advancing civilisation, capable already of disturbing the peace of an African night, were trite but malevolent, but I might have remembered that, had there been no such things as petrol engines, there would have been no road through the Congo. No animal transport, except perhaps elephant, could work there. In the end civilisation had the last and best laugh, for long before dawn I was again roused with a start from a deep sleep, to hear pandemonium raging on the far side of the river. A herd of elephants had come down to drink, and the squealing, trumpeting, and crashing of branches made further sleep impossible.

Reverting for a moment to transport, it is interesting to note that the Belgians have established an elephant farm and have taken in hand, with some success, the training of African elephants for draught purposes. Hannibal was the last to use the African elephant, which, unlike the Indian elephant, was thought to be too intractable to submit to harness until the Belgians, 2,000 years later, once again demonstrated the contrary.

In 1929 the herd under training numbered about seventy, while some thirty had already been sold for agricultural purposes. Two are said to be able to draw a load of four tons fifteen miles, or plough an acre of land in a day. I remember one morning in the Congo spotting an elephant advancing down the road towards me. I was rather astonished, though there was no particular reason why an elephant should not come out of the forest to walk on the road, but I hastily prepared to waive any right of way. It was not until he got nearer that I saw he was trundling a cart behind him. I felt he was in more need of sympathy than his fellows who had fallen to a bullet.

In spite of a chill white mist hanging over the river early next morning, and the evil colour of the water, I was sorely tempted to bathe. But I refrained now, as I did until the Atlantic was reached, on account of the risk of acquiring some disease. The bilharzia parasite, producing an almost uniformly fatal disease, breeds in the many low-lying rivers in the tropics. Even walking about in bare feet provides an excellent opportunity of picking up hook-worm. Denying myself bathing and being unable to drink any but boiled water were severe deprivations for a man taking violent exercise in the atmosphere of a Turkish bath.

I was now well to the north of the Ruwenzori range, and almost level with Lake Albert, both of which, of course, were lying well to the east of my line. Before reaching Irumu the Stanleyville road branched off, but I was not sufficiently interested to push on to see this considerable town, which is the headquarters of the Kilo district, a rich gold-mining area.

Mambasa, a small administrative post, I also passed without stopping, although there was a gîte d'étape. I managed, however, to buy, or rather beg, a loaf of bread, which was a very infrequent luxury, for it was only obtainable in places where there were Europeans, who, naturally, were not often willing to part with bread for their own use. In Kenya, whether on the farm or on safari, I never had any difficulty in getting a boy to turn out good bread; his yeast was made from sugar and a potato in a bottle which was always exploding, while his oven consisted of an empty four-gallon petrol tin.

If I could, I avoided stopping at the rest-house of these administrative posts, where there were generally one or two European officials or traders. I found it was much easier to have one's simple wants in the way of food, wood and water supplied at a village, or even at a cantonnier. Sometimes one had occasion to regret this preference, as, for instance, the night on which I scorned the attractions of Mambasa. Having ridden on till almost dark and failed to find a village, I had to 'doss' down near one of these cantonniers. As soon as I turned in a ngoma, or dance, with drum accompaniment began just outside my mosquito net. In spite of my protests, it was kept up with maddening persistence and repetition until after midnight. I was chagrined to learn that it was not in honour of my arrival, but was merely an anticipatory celebration of payday, which was due the following day. I could not help cherishing a hope that some of them, especially the band, might be disappointed.

The question of finding a billet for the night or a place for the midday halt was ever a chancy one. In spite of the height of the trees which bordered the road – great 150-feet giants of mahogany, palisander, and cotton-trees, which overtopped a lower stratum of palms, tree ferns, and wild bananas, entwined and bound together with creepers – the midday sun beat through unmercifully. I used to start at the first faint streak of light just as soon as there was enough of the road visible to ride, and carry on until midday, when I had a two hours' halt before going on again until the sun went down at six o'clock. Even for the midday halt a village was better than the shade of the forest, because there one could get a fire to boil water without the trouble of making one, and pass the time of day with the natives.

I soon became adept at rapidly summing up the possibilities of any village; what the chances were of finding bananas, eggs, or fruit. But appearances, however promising, were usually deceptive. The bananas would be unripe, or possibly only of the cooking variety, the eggs would be too ripe, and the fruit-trees barren. Some of the villages seemed to have been provided with a few orange, lemon, or pawpaw trees by a paternal Government, but the treatment these received was a good example of the weakness of collective ownership. None of the trees was cared for, and the natural desire of each man to forestall his neighbour commonly resulted in any fruit that might form being picked before it was ripe.

On deciding to halt, the first thing I did was to call out for a chair, and it was a source of continual surprise to me to find that most villages in the Congo could produce a home-made chair, sometimes even a table. The chair was usually modelled in the style of a deck-chair, with a skin for the seat, and in it the owner seemed to spend more time than exponents of the gospel of hard work would approve. In Kenya a native would despise such a thing: not that he believes in hard work – far from it – but that he would be far more comfortable squatting on his hams, that agonising posture which a native seems able to assume and enjoy for an indefinite period.

These Congo natives were certainly far more advanced than those of East Africa, no doubt because they have been for a longer period in contact with Europeans. Instead of the primitive bee-skep-shaped, windowless huts common to East Africa, whose single aperture can only be entered on all fours, the huts along this Congo road are rectangular. They have windows which can be closed with shutters, doorways which can be entered without stooping, and a veranda in front where the owner lolls at ease in his deck-chair while he encourages his womenfolk to get on with the work. Roofing is always a difficulty, as there is no grass in the forest, and I was consulted by a missionary I met on the road as to how he could roof his house. It seemed strange to me to be in Africa and to be without grass – Africa's almost never-failing roofing material. All I could devise was to try growing some long-strawed wheat. The natives overcome the difficulty by using a particular kind of broad leaf cunningly pinned or laced together. It is satisfactory, but does not last long. The thatch is prepared on the ground in foot-wide trips of the length of the roof, the whole strip being then lifted bodily into position. The absence of grass is, of course, responsible for an absence of cattle. Goats and chickens are common, while, in many villages, lean razor-backed pigs, looking more like hyenas than pigs, can be seen.

When I had been accommodated with a chair and when I had bought whatever was going in the way of food – bananas, sweet potatoes, or eggs – a fire would be brought from the nearest hut and what simple cooking there might be I attended to myself. Unless a native has had a lengthy training, food has little association in his mind with cleanliness, while, in addition, he can be counted upon to bungle the simplest job such as making tea or boiling an egg. It is possible to train natives into very good cooks and servants, but the task is often a heart-breaking one, requiring more time and patience than a man living alone on a farm can devote to it. When the trouble is taken, it often happens that the boy leaves for another job just when he has learnt how one likes things done.

On the principle of 'what the eye doesn't see the heart doesn't grieve for,' I would advise a man living alone on a farm to avoid his kitchen, or the grass hut which answers to that name. He might find, as I did, the cook or one of his friends combing his woolly, ghee-dressed hair with one of the best forks, or straining the soup or the coffee through a sock. When I remonstrated mildly with the cook about the last, he was quite hurt. My fuss he thought unnecessary, because, as he pointed out, indignantly but correctly, he was using not one of my clean socks, but only an old, dirty one.

On my leaving a village in the morning the present of a few cents to the headman, and to those who had brought wood and water or loaned me a chair, made everybody happy. Throughout the Congo they were hospitable and friendly, in spite of my poverty-stricken appearance and singular mode of travel, for, in tropical Africa, as in India, there is a tendency amongst natives to despise a white man who does any work with his hands, or walks instead of riding in a car. A smattering of education seems to accentuate this tendency, so that the victims of the educational system in vogue begin to look on physical effort as not only beneath a white man's dignity, but beneath their own.

While more than 200 miles from Stanleyville I got my first puncture, and, as it occurred at the hottest time of the day, it was impossible to make a patch stick. During my struggles the rubber of the pump connection, which was slightly perished, fused solid in the heat, rendering the pump useless – a calamity which produced visions of pushing the bike for 200 miles to Stanleyville before finding another pump. However, my luck was in, for after walking only five miles I came to a big village of about four hundred inhabitants, all Mohammedans. It was a sort of Mohammedan oasis in a wilderness of pagans and semi-Christians, ruled over by a man who called himself an Arab, a descendant probably of Arab slavers. His name was Saili bin Salim (on his head be peace). He was very hospitable. He put a newly built hut at my disposal and caused some of his men to rig up a bed of sticks and branches inside. This was a timely act, because no sooner had I arrived than a most violent storm began. It continued most of the night, and was accompanied by terrific thunder and lightning, wind and torrential rain.

Strangely enough, there was a bicycle in this village, and the owner of it, learning that a fellow-cyclist had arrived, brought it along next morning to compare notes. More surprising still was the fact that there was also a pump; less surprising, and more in accord with natural laws, was the fact that it did not work. I could not make out his standing. He may have been cyclist by appointment to the local sultan or merely his bicycle-slave, but he was certainly equal to his job. He showed me a trick which I might have known myself, one which made me independent of pump connections. This was to apply the business end of the pump directly to the valve, over which was placed a piece of wet rag. Pumping was a slow business, but the trick worked and kept my tyres hard, but at Stanleyville I bought another pump connection.

The fierce rain of the night had made the surface so 'holding' that only walking was possible until after 7 a.m. Even then I had constantly to stop to clear the wheels of mud before they would turn round. A fierce sun soon dried the surface, enabling me to reach that afternoon the junction of the road which comes in from Rejaf in the Sudan. Pushing on, I stopped for the night at Avakubi, a small post on the winding and twisting Ituri River which had again to be crossed. It was now much wider, and the ferry journey across took half an hour.

There was a solitary trader with a native wife here, off whom I borrowed a loaf of bread before repairing to the rest-house. The trouble with these places is that they are always bare of furniture, compelling one to sleep on a brick or brick-hard mud floor. By sending out one could sometimes collect a chair – less frequently, a bed, the latter being either of split bamboo, which makes hard lying, or of rope, which is soft but dirty.

The road between Avakubi and Stanleyville was of much older construction. The villages were more numerous than heretofore; more land had been won from the forest, and some rice was grown.

My next billet was in a fly-ridden village where I had made for me, in the open, a rather elaborate bedstead of sticks, with a thick mattress of banana leaves to soften its asperities. I looked forward to a good night on this, but it was not to be. Soon after dark a thunderstorm blew up, so that I had to forsake my comfortable couch for the refuge of a hut. The loss of the bed was no great matter, but it was difficult to rig up my mosquito net in the hut in darkness. This was one of the few places since leaving Uganda where mosquitoes were troublesome: even when I turned out just before 4 a.m. to light the fire they were still numerous and very vicious.

Now that Stanleyville was near I became absurdly impatient to reach it. It marked a definite stage on my journey, and it was there I hoped to resolve my anxieties as to whether it was possible to reach the coast by road. This impatience manifested itself by very early starts, short midday halts, and late finishes, which combined to give me some very restless nights. It is about this stage that there appears in my diary a severe diatribe on the wretched camps I was enduring – a reflection that was made more pointed when I remembered the delightful camps we sometimes enjoyed on our shooting safaris. 'Tied to the road with a bike,' I wrote, 'there is no choice, but what rotten camps I have had; differing only in degrees of badness, but having the worst feature in common – a gaping crowd which cannot be escaped and which is wearing me out.' In certain places the crowds became almost unendurable, giving me a faint notion of what men like Mungo Park in West Africa, or, later on, Joseph

Thomson in East Africa, had had to endure for months, or even years. Those men travelled alone, without an army of porters and armed guards, relying for permission to travel – nay, even for life itself – upon the goodwill of the natives, a goodwill which sometimes could only be bought by the cheerful suffering of all kinds of familiarities and indignities – with never a moment's privacy.

After twenty-one days on the road I rode into Stanleyville on a blistering hot afternoon, endeavouring to assume an air of nonchalance, as though riding in from close by for an afternoon's shopping. The effect was rather spoilt when I fell off in the main street with the bicycle on top of me. I was very tired.

CHAPTER SIXTEEN

North to Bangui

'Turn, turn my wheel! Turn round and round,
Without a pause, without a sound.' – Longfellow

I SOUGHT out a small hotel the proprietor of which was a Portuguese. Much to my surprise, it had a bath – a vast cement sarcophagus – for, mindful of my experience at Kisenyi, I fully expected to be told that there was a nice big river just outside, as indeed there was, the Congo itself, which is about a mile wide here.

The Congo, 3,000 miles long, is the seventh longest river in the world, and the fact that it was a mile wide at this point 1,000 miles from its mouth, was very impresssive. It is navigated by steamers of 500 tons between here and Leopoldville, distant 200 miles from the coast. The journey takes eleven days coming up-stream, and nine going down. A mile above Stanleyville navigation is prevented by the Stanley Falls, but the gap of 80 miles is bridged by a railway, while beyond, vessels of 150 tons ply as far as Kindu, 200 miles away. From there by means of rail and river (still the Congo, although called the Lualaba) it is now possible to reach the east coast via Lake Tanganyika and the Central Railway; the west coast by the Benguela Railway; and Cape Town by railway via Elisabethville. That town is the centre of the rich mining district of Katanga, on the Belgian Congo–Northern Rhodesia border. Copper is the chief product, but uranium ore, the source of radium, is also mined there.

Stanleyville had a half-begun, half-finished sort of air. The trade depression was then being felt severely; everything seemed to be in a state of suspended animation. There were great wide avenues beautifully planted with ornamental trees, which bore grandiloquent names such as 'The Avenue of the Grand Duke,' but which contained either nothing at all, or perhaps a solitary grass hut.

I spent the day looking round the town, removing some of the sand and grit from the bearings of the bicycle, changing a tyre, and procuring some information from the British Consul about my next immediate objective. I could, of course, have reached the coast by river steamer, but as the fare was over 1,000 francs – of which amount I was 800 francs short – it was satisfactory to learn that there was an alternative route, albeit a long one. This alternative road led north to Bangassu, in French Equatorial Africa, before it turned westwards through the French Cameroons, to finally reach the coast at a little port called Kribi. This information was not all available at Stanleyville; all I could learn there was that there was a road as far as Bangassu, so to Bangassu I determined to go.

Like the Kivu-Stanleyville road by which I had come, this road to Bangassu and beyond was of recent construction. Since the War, communications in all parts of Africa have been extended with extraordinary rapidity. Kipling, in one of his stories, affirms that 'transportation is civilisation,' and if it is as simple as that, then the nations of Europe, however mixed their motives, are rapidly civilising Africa.

I intended having two days' rest at Stanleyville, because a painful boil seemed to hint that something of the sort was advisable. There was, however, little of interest in the town, and the boil was not on a part vital to a cyclist, so I pushed on again after only one. My Portuguese host very kindly got up himself to give me an early breakfast, and speed me on my way with a present of oranges. This was not the only instance of Portuguese kindness which I shall have to record.

At the next halt I watched with interest a local chair-making industry. The wood used was, I think, mahogany, the design original and beautifully simple. There were no legs, only two pieces of wood. The piece for the back, about 4 feet long and 18 inches wide, was slightly hollowed, with a horizontal slit a foot from its lower end through which the second piece was passed. One end of the latter rested on the ground behind the back as a support, the other end, also slightly hollowed, forming the seat. The finished article was comfortable and very good to look at.

Assisted by a moon just past the full, I was making very early starts, and the following day I took the road soon after 4 a.m. Once the sun rose above the horizon little grace was allowed. Minute by minute the heat increased, becoming within a short two hours so gruelling that the flesh grew weary and the spirit drooped at the bare thought of the yet distant noontide.

About eleven o'clock a loud report indicated a flat tyre. It was more of a burst than a puncture, and proved to be the first of a rapid series, until I discovered the cause. The tyres bore the words 'inflate hard,' an injunction I was following too faithfully, allowing nothing for the expansion of the air inside caused by the increasing heat. The spare tubes came in handy now, for, with the high temperature, it was quite impossible to make a patch stick in the daytime, another tube had to be fitted, and any patching repairs made at night.

My old acquaintance the Ituri River, cropping up again after a change of course, welcomed me with a pest which was new to me and which made it difficult to suffer with patience a long wait for the ferry. It was a very small bluish fly which settled on the bare skin and drew blood. As I was wearing no socks or stockings, and my shirt-sleeves were rolled up, I was an easy prey, and soon legs and arms were streaked with blood. I met it again later on, but it seemed to occur only in the vicinity of rivers.

I was now north of the equator, having already twice crossed it, and, although the sun was well to the south, the temperature seemed to be increasing, due no doubt to a gradual fall in the country, which was now only about 1,500 feet above sea level.

The next place I reached of any note was Buta, 200 miles north of Stanleyville. It boasts two banks and some half-dozen trading houses, and it is connected by road with Rejaf, in the Sudan. It is the highway which is used by cars travelling from Uganda to Nigeria or the Sahara. In spite of the comparative importance of Buta, I was unable to change my Belgian Congo francs for French Congo francs, or to obtain any quinine or tobacco. Situated as I was, I regarded these two as essentials – particularly the quinine, which was at length provided by a Government hospital, but only after I had filled in more forms than would have been necessary had I been getting buried. For my pipe I was reduced to using disintegrated *caporal* cigarettes. I was told (and it was the truth) that no banks existed between here and the coast, but I managed to pick up some French money from a Greek storekeeper. He came from Cyprus, and when he discovered that I was English, and therefore a fellow-subject, he not only changed my money but generously gave me a lot of oranges.

Soon after leaving Buta, I made an unnecessarily long halt at midday in a little wayside store kept by a 'coast boy,' a native of Nigeria and therefore another fellow-subject. He delighted in airing his pidgin-English, and, being of more than average intelligence, also spoke French, Swahili, and Bangalla, the language used in the northern part of the Congo. Swahili, the lingua franca of East Africa, was at length beginning to fail me as a conversational medium. Up to Stanleyville it had served me well.

A sufficiently belated start was further delayed by the discovery of a flat back tyre just as I was going to mount. It was a burst almost too big to patch, and I cursed my stupidity for not having changed the tube when I changed the tyre at Buta. 'A new cover deserves a new tube' is as sound a rule for cyclists as for motorists. Remembering the struggle I had had in removing the back wheel, I did not welcome a repetition, so I put patch over patch, with an all-embracing one over everything for luck, and rode off in fear and trembling. I need not have worried. That remarkable bit of work lasted the remaining 250 miles to Bangassu, where I was able to buy another tube.

Still going north and slightly west, I rejoiced to see the forest giving way gradually to more open country. I felt like a swimmer coming to the surface after prolonged submersion. The road was becoming more hilly, too, offering me at odd times distant views which did something to compensate me for the extra pushing thus entailed. Otherwise my field of vision was restricted, as before, to the road. The country was covered in elephant grass 10 feet high, which was just as difficult to see over as the 150 feet high walls of forest.

As forest gave way to grassland, the cultivated areas became more extensive. The palm-oil tree, whose products, together with cotton and sesame, are exported, was seen for the first time. Sesame, a small oil-producing seed, used sometimes as a relish with bananas, is a highly concentrated food-stuff.

Hunting, however, seemed a more popular industry than agriculture, for nearly every native carried some sort of weapon – the less wealthy or more conservative a sort of cross-bow, the others an antiquated firearm. Game was apparently plentiful, and there were no restrictions, but, although the long grass makes hunting difficult, thereby prolonging the animal life and the industry, yet when the grass is burnt off in the dry weather the harassed game must fall an easy prey to the multitude of hunters. No game will survive long in these conditions.

At the village at which I stopped, the headman insisted on providing me with a guard of two arque-busiers. I assumed, mistakenly as it turned out, that this was because I was back in a game country, but he later explained that it was not so much the dangerous game he feared as the thieving propensities of his fellow-villagers. I like to think that he misjudged them, for I lost nothing here nor anywhere else. Once, when I dropped a spanner, a boy chased me for a mile to return it.

The crossing of another large river brought me to Bonda, another trading centre, surrounded by extensive cultivation – oil palms, cotton, and sesame. On leaving Bonda, taking advantage of a good road and a heavily overcast sky, I put in a very long day during which I covered 80 miles. This distance was only done by carrying on until a too late hour – a folly for which I paid with a poor billet where there were very few bananas and no eggs. As these were my mainstays, both dinner and breakfast would not have embarrassed an ascetic, while, to make matters worse, at the latter cheerless meal, taken in candlelight, I made the pleasing discovery that a tyre was flat and the pump missing. No doubt it had been shaken off at one of those many places where it had been a matter for surprise that anything, including the rider, had been left on.

My mood was one of the deepest gloom as I trundled the bike slowly along. I was very empty, and I was uncertain whether I should have to push it for 1,000 miles or only 100 miles before finding another pump. Five miles on, I saw an obvious mission perched on a high hill half a mile from the road, where a passing boy told me that the missionary had a bicycle. I went up there, to have matters soon put right and to be given a meal by the Norwegian missionary and his wife. It was one of the Basle Missions. Apart from the relief of being once more mobile, I found it refreshing to be on a hill again and to look out upon surrounding country after so many days' confinement in a tunnel of vegetation.

A little further on was Monga, which, although the French Boundary is another 50 miles north, is the last post in Belgian territory. I discovered that there was a customs barrier here, in charge of a Belgian official to whom I should have to present myself for examination. I was rather conscience-stricken and not a little worried, because I had been travelling in the Congo for three weeks and was now about to leave it without having made my presence known to anyone officially. The official concerned was rather shocked when I made this confession, but, to my surprise, accepted the fact cheerfully and passed me through without any fuss. I left the Belgian Congo with a very favourable impression of at least one official. I was soon to learn that, in the French colonies, the way of the stranger was hard, being the subject of a tiresome official scrutiny which in the Belgian had been conspicuously absent.

The frontier between the Belgian Congo and French territory is the Ubangi River. The French colony, called by them Afrique Equatoriale Française, or A.E.F. for short, comprises a very large area stretching over twenty-seven degrees of latitude. In such a vast area conditions must necessarily vary greatly, but in the Ubangi-Shari province which I traversed they are similar to those in the northern Congo. The total white population in 1926 was 2,500, and the natives numbered over 3,000,000, two-thirds of which occupied the relatively remote northern provinces of Chad and Ubangi-Shari.

I reached the Ubangi River and the frontier on a sweltering hot afternoon, hot enough to provide reasonable mortals with every excuse for sleep. French officialdom, however, was very wide awake. The canoe in which I crossed had barely grounded before I was surrounded by a cloud of black myrmidons demanding that I should present myself forthwith before the respective heads of the administration, the customs, and the police. On a hot afternoon, after a 60-mile ride, I found it an overpowering welcome. As I was aware that my streaming face and shabby shirt would not make a good impression, I asked for time to put on the clean shirt kept for such emergencies. But no respite was allowed. I had to present myself as I was, all dust and sweat, to explain in halting French whence I had come, whither I was going, and even more vital questions, such as my mother's maiden name and the Christian names of both my parents. (I am told that this is done to find if one has any remote German connections.)

M. le Commandant at the bureau was polite and helpful, but all this information had to be laboriously entered on various forms before I was given a *laissez-passer*. At the customs they were less polite and not at all helpful. The 'big shot' was not at the office, and when I suggested going away to look for food and lodging before returning later, his black henchmen would not hear of it, but promptly impounded the bicycle, the rucksack, and myself. When the chief did come at five o'clock, he was rather peeved at being expected to transact business at that hour. We were not at all *en rapport*, and in the end the vileness of my French and the lateness of the hour so exasperated him that he detained me there over the week-end while he laboriously filled in the necessary forms for one bicycle in transit – what he called a *vélocipède*.

There was a European-owned store here where I was lucky enough to find a pump to be able to change both tyres. But that was not done till next day, as at the moment I wanted food and drink. Having procured with some difficulty a bottle of beer and a few eggs, I repaired to the rest-house in the dark, where a boy volunteered to bring wood and water. As there was no chair and no bed, a brick floor was again my portion. Pending the arrival of the wood and water, I tackled the beer-bottle. The top refused to budge, so, losing what little temper the customs officer had left me, I tried to knock the neck off, with the result that the whole thing exploded, leaving behind nothing but a cut finger, a mess upon the floor, and a fragrant memory. I forgot how many francs it had cost – enough, anyway, to preclude the possibility of buying another.

There was nothing remarkable in the tiny station of Bangassu except the rudeness of the customs man, the inhospitality of the half-dozen inhabitants, and a diminutive racecourse with the most hair-raising bends I have ever seen. There is a racecourse at Darjeeling which is circular – all bend and no straight – but this one seemed to be all straight, with the bends right angles. I saw no horses, but further north, where the country is drier and more open, they are common. Since leaving Ankole, the only livestock I had seen had been goats and pigs, but I had been told some cows were kept on a farm near Stanleyville to supply the town with milk. Most of the goats seemed to be of a very good type. Three kids to one nanny goat was a common sight, and at one or two places I was given goats' milk, a luxury never had in Kenya, where goats swarm.

After two nights on the brick floor of the rest-house I was ready, anxious almost, to start for my next objective. This was Bangui, a town lower down the Ubangi River, but only to be reached by traversing 500 miles of road of unknown quality. I had been warned not to expect such good roads after leaving the Belgian Congo, where the road had fully justified the good accounts I had heard of it. Motor traffic, for which the road was made, cannot expect much better, and the fact that on a cycle one could average between 50 miles and 60 miles a day for 1,000 miles through a small corner of the Congo is striking testimony to the energy and skill which went to its making. To carry a road over escarpments, across many big rivers, and multitudinous small streams, through swamps and dense forests, aided only by a scanty and half savage population, is a task worthy of a General Wade or a Macadam. In the Congo the trunk roads are confined to the north-east corner; in the centre and west the rivers, helped out by short stretches of rail, are the only means of communication between distant places. In a relatively short time much development has been accomplished, but as yet only the fringe has been touched. Further expansion depends on more roads and more railways, the provision of which must be necessarily a slow and costly business, owing to the difficulties of the terrain and the sparse population. In an area of 918,000 square miles there are only 9,000,000 natives, whereas in Nigeria, which is less than half the area, there are 20,000,000. However, the Congo is better off in this respect than French Equatorial Africa, where for the same area there are only 3,000,000 natives.

In passing from Belgian to French territory, little change was to be noted, nor was it to be expected by the mere crossing from the south side of the Ubangi River to the north. The natives and the scenery appeared the same, and I longed in vain for some break in the ever recurring ridge and valley covered with the same long elephant grass, which was by now almost as monotonous as the forest. The road was slightly worse, but at first by no means bad, although later it deteriorated. The French seemingly had less regard for grading than the Belgian engineers, charging their hills in a very uncompromising manner. This neglect of grading gave rise to much 'wash', producing a surface scored and rutted with deep channels. In Uganda, and possibly in the Congo, too, the system used for the making of a road is to dig two trenches, each about two feet wide, the width of a wheel-track apart. These are then filled with big stones, and the whole surface of the road, not much wider than the wheel-tracks, is then covered with murram. This murram is a sort of red gravel which seems to form the subsoil, almost without a break, from Uganda to the west coast. When well beaten down it makes a fair surface. (The best going for a bicycle was generally, not on the road, but on a footpath made and worn smooth by native use, which carefully avoids the road on account of the unkindliness of murram for bare feet.) This system ensured that the portion of road which carried the weight of traffic was well ballasted, and was at the same time economical.

The Belgians employed permanent labour, established in the *cantonniers*, for road maintenance, but the French seemed to rely only upon the villagers. Judging by the state of the road, and by the few gangs I saw at work, this system was inefficient and unpopular. With each gang there was an askari, or native soldier, armed with rifle and bayonet to back the authority of the headman who carried a mighty whip. A minor point that interested me was that between Bangassu and Bangui there were no kilometre posts. I knew not whether to repine or rejoice. Long before Stanleyville was reached, it had become a debatable point whether the advantage of knowing the length of the day's run outweighed the accumulatively depressing effect of counting them.

Little change was discernible either in the natives, their huts, or their mode of life, but there was one variation which affected me personally – namely, that Swahili was no longer understood. The officials at Bangassu had assured me that most of the village headmen could talk French – a fact that I am prepared to believe, but it was not the sort that I could understand. As my own is of 'the pen of my aunt's gardener' variety, the fault, perhaps, was not entirely theirs. As my wants were few and simple I managed well enough, but much of the interest of travel is lost if one cannot talk to the inhabitants.

Another not unimportant change for me was that bananas seemed now to be grown only as a luxury, for the staple food was manioc, or cassava. This is a tuber which has to be prepared for eating by fermentation and drying. The first process seemed to be never-ending, as every village stank like a bag of maize meal which has got wet and gone bad.

My second day in A.E.F. saw a marked deterioration in the road and a great reduction in the number of villages, the last fact probably accounting for the bad road. Not even the most perfunctory attempt at grading had been made, as the guiding principle appeared to be that valleys, of which there were many, existed only to be crossed. The end of a gruelling day found me in a disgustingly dirty village. A boy who spoke Swahili, having served in East Africa during the War, advised me to go to a mission a little further on, and this I did. I had avoided missions so far except on two occasions, partly on account of the difficulty of making an early start without disturbing my hosts, and partly because, having contributed nothing to missions in the past, it seemed unfair for me to make use of them now. It was another of the Basle Missions kept by a Norwegian and his Swiss wife, who received me very kindly. They had a small, frail-looking child, and they told me that they had buried four other children there, a fact which was eloquent enough testimony to a villainous climate. From the Congo to the Cameroons there is little to choose from in the way of climate; most of the country is under 2,000 feet, very hot, and the rainfall heavy.

During the course of the evening, I heard a good deal about the country from the missionary, who spoke English well. I was told that the construction of the road had advanced to this point only in 1925, and that the natives were still rather wild and intractable. Among other unpleasant traits was some skill in the use of poisons, while they had a burial custom which struck me as being more revolting than cannibalism. They boiled the corpse gently until only the bones were left, the resulting soup being then drunk by the sorrowing friends and relatives. These kind people (I mean the missionaries, not the soup-drinkers) gave me a lot of dried bananas, an excellent sustaining food, to take with me. These are prepared by baking ripe bananas until they are quite brown and tough, in which state they will keep indefinitely. At this mission work was regarded as second only to prayer. There were one hundred acres of coffee demanding attention from the mission's adherents, with the result that the day began early, thus allowing of my leaving before seven without making myself a nuisance to my hosts.

The following night I enjoyed yet more hospitality at the camp of three French gold prospectors. From the comfort of their quarters, their dinner, and the two bottles of St. Julien which accompanied it, I concluded that they were employed by a wealthy company and were not free-lances. It rained and thundered furiously in the night, and was still so doing when I left before dawn. The road was mostly under water, but I found good going on a native footpath on the far side of the deep drainage ditch which lined the road. It cleared about midday, when I reached Bambari, a small trading centre where there was a store and a cotton ginnery. Here the flood of hospitality, which had set in at the mission, reached its height, almost overwhelming me.

I stopped at the store, the only one of its kind between Bangassu and Bangui, hoping to get some bread. The owner was a Portuguese. He had no bread to sell, but gave me a small roll gratis. Touched by this kindness, I thought to repay it by buying a bottle of his red wine, but, not to be outdone, the man from Portugal then invited me to lunch. On the veranda of his hut there were two fellow-guests, a Russian and an Italian, who had come to buy cotton, although at the moment they were drinking whisky. It was a hot day (they were all that, but this one was what John Jorrocks would have called 'uncommon 'ot') but, in spite of that and the time of day, I was invited to help myself. They braced themselves to see me knock back a neat tumblerful, for foreigners seem to expect an Englishman to mop up whisky like water at any hour of the day or night. Possibly this is because they fail to differentiate between Englishmen and Scotsmen, the latter, of course, being far the more numerous of the two in these outlandish places. Another curious thing is that out in Africa most foreigners – Frenchmen, Belgians, Greeks, Portuguese – drink whisky, whereas at home probably none of them would think of touching it. It is perhaps less expensive for them in Africa than in their own countries, but, besides that, they regard it as the most suitable drink for a hot climate; I remember a Frenchman becoming quite lyrical over its properties, both medicinal and convivial.

Well, there were my friends, waiting goggle-eyed with apprehension for the Englishman to swallow unblinkingly, in the national manner, a terrific dose of whisky, and great was their astonishment, amounting almost to horror, when he refused to take any. This refusal cost me a good deal of prestige which a glass of port, accepted as the lesser of two evils, did little to restore. With the arrival of a Belgian, a Frenchman, and the Portuguese storekeeper's brother, the party was complete, so that when we gathered round the table, Russian, Frenchman, Belgian, Italian, two Portuguese, and an Englishman, but for the more convivial atmosphere prevailing we might have been mistaken for a meeting of the League of Nations Assembly.

The meal was tremendous. It began with a sort of olla podrida, passed on to the flesh of some unknown animal, followed that with duck, salad, and a sweet, and ended with some pungent Roquefort cheese. We drank a rough red wine and 'topped up' with coffee laced with more whisky. It would have been impolite to ask, but I was curious to know whether this was my host's usual midday meal, or whether it was a banquet specially prepared to facilitate a deal in cotton which he apparently concluded satisfactorily by an exchange of signatures with the Italian; whatever it was, I for one could say, 'Fate cannot harm me – I have dined today.'

By four o'clock, I had recovered the use of some of my faculties and rode gently on for fifteen miles, musing on life's vicissitudes. The village where I finally fell off was the home of the local chief, who lived in dignified seclusion behind a tall reed fence. He did not show himself to the stranger within his gates, sending me instead a present of six bad eggs, but with this exception the natives here seemed quite uncivilised. They brought wood and water before I asked for it, and put an empty hut at my disposal, which, now that I was beyond the tick-infested area, I was not afraid of using. In addition to the snack which I had had for lunch, that was a red-letter day for other reasons. Since leaving Bangassu I had seen only two lorries, both of them in Bambari, the scene of the orgy. Here, in the village, I noticed a bicycle, and, still a little muddled, half expected to see a sign, 'Teas and Accommodation for Cyclists.'

Next day I passed through a small administrative post called Gumari, where, anxious though I was to avoid officialdom, I was trapped by an officious native clerk into paying a visit to the commandant. This clerk who accosted me was so curious and suspicious that he considered it his duty to introduce me to M. le Commandant, who was busy hearing cases in the court. To create a diversion I sent him to the market to find some oranges, playing thus all unknowingly into his hands, for presently he returned with a great basket full of oranges which he declared were a present from the commandant. I could hardly ignore this, untrue though I felt it to be, and was led meekly to the Presence. The course of justice was suspended while the commandant took me away to be introduced to his wife and family; my plea for mercy, or at least a respite, on the grounds of dirtiness, was of no avail, because he himself sported a three-day beard. Neither he nor his wife had any English, but we drank beer and battled away for an hour or more before I could decently escape. Outside, the black promoter of sociability amongst the whites was still waiting for me, carrying the *fons et origo malorum*, of which I could only take away a dozen – the sole fruits of two hours' delay.

The lost time was made up by the cutting short of my midday halt. This happened to be at a rest-house, a building which usually ensured for one a little privacy, but here the crowd showed no respect even for that. They invaded it and refused to be driven out, so that I was forced to flee. The crowd nuisance was aggravated or mitigated according to the degree of control exercised by the headman – or *capita*, as he was called – of the village. He was responsible for the rest-house and for the providing of anyone who occupied it with wood and water, so that the occupant had some official standing. Some of these headmen had their people well in hand, but others were completely ineffective. There was an amusing example of the former type that same night when the headman of the village at which I stopped, seeing a woman going past with a load of wood, commandeered it for my use. Pleased with this show of authority, he turned to continue his chat with me, but no sooner was his back turned than the old woman recommandeered her load. Unfortunately, before going far she was spotted by the irate headman, who gave chase and dealt out summary punishment. The custom was to pay the *capita* a fixed rate for supplying wood and water – a very satisfactory arrangement no doubt for him, but highly unsatisfactory for the hewers and drawers of these necessities.

As I drew near to Bangui I was again seized with the same feverish impatience which beset me approaching Stanleyville. A sequence of long days was brought to an end with twelve hours of almost continuous riding in which nearly 80 miles were covered. I arrived in a deluge of warm rain.

CHAPTER SEVENTEEN

Westwards to the Atlantic

'Men to holloa and men to run him.' – Masefield

BANGUI boasted a small hotel whose proprietor was not too proud to receive me as a guest in spite of my ruffianly appearance – an appearance perhaps best described as travel-stained. The beer (which was iced) exceeded my wildest expectations, but the bath was an anti-climax. For this, a boy conducted me to an outhouse with a bare floor but no sign of a bath. On my telling the boy to hurry up and bring it, he pointed with smiling satisfaction to the ceiling, whence hung a small perforated bucket. Pulling a string, he released on me a feeble, short-lived shower, of the same temperature as, but of considerably less violence than, the storm in which I had arrived.

It was a Sunday evening, and it seemed to me that the whole of the European population of Bangui, numbering about three hundred, were assembled on the terrace outside, drinking *apéritifs* and talking as only Frenchmen can talk. I had forgotten there were so many white people in Africa, and that some of them could be as noisy and as voluble as the natives.

Bangui is the second town in importance in French Equatorial Africa. The capital town is Brazzaville, on the opposite bank of the Congo to Leopoldville, which is the capital of the Belgian Congo. From Bangui down to Brazzaville is ten days' steaming by river steamer. In addition to this outlet by river there is a road to Yaunde, in the French Cameroons, 740 miles away. A transport company has a contract with the Government to maintain a fortnightly lorry service on this road for the conveyance of mails and passengers, the journey taking five days and costing three thousand francs. Owing to Bangui's remote situation, its trade is comparatively small, so that the population consists mostly of officials. A big military aerodrome and a wireless station lend it some importance. The climate is warm and not particularly healthy, as the town is situated on the river-bank itself; rather unnecessarily in my opinion, because, less than a mile away, are some hills 200 or 300 feet high, where the residential quarter could have been built with advantage.

I spent two days resting here. On the afternoon after my arrival, while I was 'taking mine ease in mine inn,' Falstaff-like, my tranquillity was rudely shattered by a very brusque French policeman who wanted to know why I had not yet reported my arrival. His manner was so peremptory that I was a bit short with him, and both of us began to get heated. My passport and the *laissez-passer* which had been given me at Bangassu failed to pacify him, and he intimated that the debate, now very warm, would be continued at the local lock-up. Luckily, my host, who was standing by, seeing how things were going, suggested a drink. Quickly taking the hint, I ordered unlimited iced beer, which soon had a cooling effect upon the wrath of the policeman, who presently began pledging the Entente Cordiale, whose existence he deplored having momentarily forgotten.

I made an early start when I left Bangui. I breakfasted off some hard-boiled eggs and red wine which I had had placed in my room, with the result that I soon began to feel queer – it takes a Frenchman to drink red wine at dawn. I felt weak and muzzy all morning, but fortunately the road was flat and ran perfectly straight through forty-five miles of oil palm forest. I lunched at the hut of a War veteran who had fought in the Cameroons campaign. He repaid the interest I showed by mending my shirt, both sleeves of which had come adrift where they had been chafed by the rucksack straps.

Stopping that night at a little post called Mbaiki, I had occasion to reconsider the low opinion of French officials which I had formed. I was treated in a way that more than atoned for the little unpleasantness at Bangui, but my benefactor, although in charge of the district, was an army officer, not a civilian. In the less settled parts of French Equatorial Africa the administrtion is in the hands of the army, and Mbaiki was the headquarters of a district in charge of a captain who was the local Pooh-Bah – Judge, Policeman, Commandant,. and Lord High Muck-a-Muck. He had with him half his company of native soldiers (askaris), while the other half under two white subalterns was stationed in other parts of the district.

As soon as he heard of my arrival he sent along a camp-bed and an invitation to dinner. He had served in France during the War and in most parts of French Africa since, so that in listening to him the evening passed very pleasantly. He spoke no English, and as my French might be described as passive rather than active, he had to do most of the talking. According to him, their best recruiting-ground was the Province of Lake Chad, west of the Sudan, the natives of the country round Bangui or nearer the coast being of little value as soldiers. The native soldiers, he told me, greatly looks forward to doing a tour of duty in France (I presume he meant in peace-time), and if a man's record is good he can serve for fifteen years, after which he is entitled to a pension of eighty francs – the equivalent of about two shillings a month, an amount seemingly insufficient to keep a man in tobacco, but on which a native can live quite comfortably.

Although the dinner was not in the grand Portuguese manner, it was ample. In place of coffee we drank citronella tea, an infusion made from a grass which is here planted extensively by the roadside as a border to check 'wash.' The tea is a pleasant, mildly lemon-flavoured drink supposed to have medicinal properties. It is a curious fact that while there are several varieties of 'tea' which in addition to being quite pleasant to drink are also reputed to be 'good for one,' that which is drunk almost universally is the one that has no pretensions to being anything but mildly poisonous. Either we are difficult to please or have a deal of innate perversity.

The broken, hilly country of long grass with scattered forest continued unaltered, failing by its monotony, like the Congo forest, to arouse any feeling but dislike. If the scenery was the same, the road surface was full of variety, claiming, with the many hills, a single-minded devotion from the traveller. That day there was one particularly vile stretch of sand-surfaced road on which I executed many 'voluntaries.'

It was about this time, too, that my popularity as a public spectacle was at its height. On the second night from Bangui the natives invaded my quarters and would not be ejected. They fought for front seats, while I took my food like a lion at the Zoo but without the protecting bars. That was bad, but next day this staring business reached a climax, so that for the next forty-eight hours I thought I had reached a country of Bedlamites. It sounds merely funny now, but at the time it nearly drove me frantic; possibly my sense of humour was becoming a little blunted now that I had acted the part of a travelling circus for so long.

The trouble started at a midday halt, where a crowd gathered to see the bicycle and to watch me eat. It need hardly be said that that was nothing unusual; indeed, by now I was quite accustomed to eating and drinking, getting up and going to bed, watched by an astonished crowd like the Grand

Monarchy at a levee. This time, however, when I re-started, the crowd started, too, so that I pedalled down the road surrounded by the whole village, laughing and yelling like madmen. Thinking they would soon tire, I rode fast to shake them off, only to be easily caught up with on the hills. Nothing would induce them to stop. Scowls, threats, curses, and attempts to ride them down only made them more excited. Long before the human pack began to tire and tail off, hunted and hunters had reached another village, whose people, incited by the approaching cry, were not slow to catch the infection, and turned out fresh and fit to take up the running. Changing foxes in the middle of a run is the huntsman's *bête noir*; but what would the fox think – what could I think – of changing packs?

I had to stop somewhere; I could not go on riding all night; but at the first village where I pulled up the mob exceeded all others in size, curiosity, and determination. Bear gardens, bargain counters, jumble sales, are all weak similes with which to liken the scene in that rest-house (what irony to call it that!). Goaded at last to desperation, I ran amok with a stick, and, having cleared a passage, rode off in the gathering darkness to camp foodless, but in peace, by the roadside.

On the following morning this harassing pursuit flared up again for a time, until it stopped, almost as suddenly as it began, at a village where I was received with a quiet which was, by reason of its contrast, well-nigh stunning. A few grave elders were the only ones to approach, the common herd attending strictly to its business, and when I thought the notables had gazed their fill, a mild 'Allez-vous,' was sufficient to disperse them.

The reasons for this extraordinary outbreak are obscure. The only theory I have is that these particular villages had only recently been built and occupied by natives brought in from some outlying district. As has already been noted, the administrative policy in the Congo and in parts of A.E.F. is to collect the natives in villages along the roadside, in the first place to make the road, thereafter for its maintenance, and to facilitate the work of the district officers. For unless the natives are within reach of a road they are to all intents and purposes non-existent from an administrative point of view, so difficult is movement away from the road. It is understandable that to a raw native the astounding spectacle of a white man carrying a load, riding along miraculously balanced on two wheels, was not likely to be repeated in his lifetime, so that it was worth more than a passing glance. Imagine the case of a black man in native dress stalking into a village in England to stand, say, on one leg, leaning on a spear, in the attitude beloved of Nilotic negroes. How the children would guy the poor fellow, chivying him to the next village, while even their elders might leave their beer for an unguarded moment to know the meaning of it.

That these particular natives were scarcely human – people who, according to Darwin, had not long come down from their trees – could be inferred not only from their odd sense of humour, but also from their huts, which were of that primitive beehive type last seen by me on top of the Kabasha escarpment. The villages appeared to have been constructed only recently. They were big, dirty, rather miserable-looking places, all as like as peas, with the huts arranged in two well-spaced parallel lines. They had obviously been laid out to order, while the fact that as yet there were no banana-trees or pawpaws was an indication of their recent origin. Lean, long-snouted, black pigs ran about scavenging like pariah dogs.

Rather more than half-way to Yaunde is Berbarati, an administrative post, where I stopped for the night. It was a fairly big place, with a rest-house and a store at which, however, I could buy nothing. Returning disconsolate to the rest-house, I was met by a boy bearing a basket of oranges with the 'compliments of M. le Commandant.' This was a familiar gambit, but in the circumstances an invitation to a meal, or the offer of even a loaf of bread, would have been more than welcome. Half expecting something of the kind, I put on my spare shirt and walked round to pay my respects, but the only invitation I received was one to produce my passport forthwith.

The following day I reached Gombola, on the border between A.E.F. and the French Cameroons, where curiously enough there is a customs barrier. We are not quite so stupid in the management of our East African Colonies. True, the three adjacent territories of Kenya, Uganda, and Tanganyika has each its separate, expensive, and jealous government, but there is at any rate a customs and postal union.

I had been warned of the *douanier* in charge at Gombola when I was at distant Bangui, where they said he was mad. Sane custom officials can be awkward enough, but imagination boggles at the thought of being examined by a mad one. I therefore assumed what I thought was an ingratiating manner, but on approaching the enemy with the utmost trepidation, we almost fell on each other's necks. There is a proverb to the effect that 'like draws to like the whole world over,' which is perhaps some explanation of the favour I found, but I prefer to think that he only feigned madness the better to carry out his disagreeable duties, and that, like Hamlet, he 'knew a hawk from a hand-saw.' Indeed, when I told him where I had come from and what I was doing, I thought he was going to kiss me, but he thought better of it, and, instead, passed me and my bicycle through at a cost of forty centimes in as many seconds, giving me a bunch of bananas three feet long into the bargain. While talking he told me that on an average he examined only two vehicles a day, but he managed to fill his leisure hours with gardening and bird-shooting. He also assured me that the road through the Cameroons was so perfect that I should just *rouler* (French, I suppose, for free-wheel) to the coast. At that I mounted hastily, thinking that perhaps my informants at Bangui were right after all.

On crossing this artificial frontier, I found no marked change of scenery. Further west the country became more hilly and the elevation gradually increased, until at Yaunde a height of 2,500 feet above sea level was reached. There was one minor but rather curious difference, which was that, once I had entered the Cameroons, I no longer found chairs in the villages. For the midday halt I therefore reverted to the roadside, gaining in privacy and losing nothing in comfort. My first halt in this way was shared by a Polish lorry-driver who spoke excellent American. He was bound for Yaunde, still 300 miles away, and offered me a lift, which I was obliged to refuse, for it had now become a point of honour with me to finish the journey unaided. From the first he had, I think, entertained doubts as to my sanity – doubts which this refusal fully confirmed.

Batouri, which I reached a day later, was the first administrative post in the Cameroons, and, knowing by now the vigilance of the French authorities, I took the trouble to report my arrival to M. le Commandant. The Polish lorry-driver who preceded me there must have talked, because I was received with the soothing manner reserved only for the very rich or the very eccentric. Even my proffered passport was waved aside.

The Cameroons were, of course, a German colony before the War, and are now under French and British mandates. The French portion is very much larger than the British, comprising 166,489 square miles against 34,236 square miles, the respective populations being two million and seven hundred thousand. The name 'Cameroons' is derived from a river which was called by the early Portuguese navigators the Cameroes River, meaning the river of prawns.

In the Cameroons I first began to hear 'pidgin' or 'coast' English spoken. The usual greeting was now 'Morning' instead of what had always sounded to me like 'Bon soir.' As this expression was used regardless of the time of day, I found it a bit disconcerting to be greeted with 'Bon soir' at dawn. 'Pidgin' English, which has for long been the lingua franca of the west coast, has now spread far inland; it was used by the Germans, and is used now by the French traders, who could not get on very well without it. I believe the Germans, with their usual thoroughness, had published a German-'Pidgin' dictionary. I myself felt the need of something of the kind, for this curious jargon is not so easy to understand as might be imagined, even for an Englishman. There are familiar words which mean something else, such as 'chop' meaning food, and 'dash' a present. The last word is also used as a verb, for when one gives a boy a tip one speaks of 'dashing' him. 'Lib,' which I suppose is the west coast way of pronouncing 'live,' is a very hard-used word – 'him no lib' means 'it is not here' and 'him lib for die' means 'he is going to die.'

The approaching completion of any important stage on the journey always filled me with nervous impatience and now I was becoming all worked up at the proximity of Yaunde, which marked, if not quite the end of the journey, at least the end of all difficulties. I had been on the road now for forty-five days, and I congratulated myself that I was crossing Africa at its waist, so to speak, south of the great bulge, thereby saving myself an extra thousand miles.

My starts became earlier and earlier. On November 1st I was on the road so early that, being unable to see the road properly, I took three spills in quick succession. Dawn brought with it a storm which burst on me and which, with the perversity of storms, travelled in the same direction as the road, so that I rode all day through rain and mist over a wet, heavy surface. At the unusually early hour of 3.30 p.m., when I reached a small administrative post, I decided to call it a day. I found shelter in a good rest-house where there was a table, several string beds, and a caretaker who spoke 'pidgin,' so that after a meal eaten off a table I turned in early, anticipating a good night on a bed. It was good until midnight, when a lorry drew up to disgorge three missionaries. Their leader woke me by flashing a torch in my face and began a shorter catechism as to who I was and what I was doing. He then reviewed briefly his own antecedents, told me his late arrival was due to a broken bridge, and proceeded to unfold his plans for the immediate future. I tried to discourage his proposal to pass the rest of the night at the rest-house by pointing out the lateness of the hour and the probabilities of my disturbing them when I started at 4 a.m. But that was simply playing into the hands of this masterful man, for I was quickly informed that he himself was getting up at 3.30 a.m., and would I mind leaving the table clear for him to celebrate Mass before they left. At that hour I was awake myself. As the Church still snored, I got up to start breakfast even at the risk of upsetting the time-table. When the zealot did wake, the sight of my eating eggs provoked him to fury. He routed out his two companions with scant ceremony, shouted to his boys to load the lorry, and presently the whole party had disappeared, furious and fasting, in a metaphorical cloud of smoke.

On the following day, helped by a moon near the full, I started even earlier to do fifty miles before halting at midday. Determined to make a day of it, I pushed on again at one o'clock, disregarding the fierce sun, and at five o'clock entered upon a long stretch of flat, swampy country where there were no villages but plenty of mosquitoes. It was dark before I found a village where I hoped to get some food. My plan was to take advantage of the moon and ride all night, but, fortunately, while I was still eating it began raining hard, thus obliterating the moon and with it my fatuous proposal. I found quarters for the night in the hut of a very helpful mission boy who, with his family, vacated half their hut to leave it at my disposal, but I was too restless to sleep much. At 1 a.m. I breakfasted, shaved, and put on my best shirt in anticipation of Yaunde, bestowing the old one on my host. By 2 a.m. I was on the road again – a road made soft and sticky by the rain.

There was a grain of method in this seeming madness because, the day being Saturday, I was anxious to reach Yaunde by midday before the post office closed down for the week-end. A moment's reflection would, however, have reassured me, for in French Colonies the week-end habit is not observed with the scrupulousness that with us would almost make the stranger think we were observing a religious festival.

Within a hundred miles or so of Yaunde kilometre posts again began to line the road. As I rode along in the moonlight I seemed to pass a great many of them, but it was too dark to read the figures, and I forbore to dismount, hoping that the surprise would be all the greater when dawn came. I got my surprise all right, but it was not the pleasant one I expected and I was shaken to find that I had covered only some twenty miles and that there were another fifty to do. While having a second breakfast I almost decided to take it easy, for I was getting very feeble, the road seemed to be getting worse, and it was doubtful whether I could reach Yaunde that day, much less by midday.

Soon after I had started again, almost reconciled to another night out, the road suddenly began to improve. My flagging energies revived, to receive further stimulus from the sight of the road gang who were responsible for the greatly improved surface. There were several hundred men drawn up in columns of fours, advancing slowly, tamping down the newly laid murram with heavy wooden logs. The logs rose and fell together with a glorious thud which shook the ground, the time being taken from a two-man band which marched in the rear, one man playing a sort of Jew's harp, the other a wooden drum. I could not help reflecting how much better this was in many ways, for the nerves and for employment, than our confounded pneumatic drills.

This excellent hard surface continued all the way. Pedalling like one possessed, I rode a desperate race against time, dismounting at last, limp and wet with sweat, outside the Yaunde post office on the stroke of twelve – to find it did not close until five o'clock.

Waiting for me was a cable telling me to get in touch with the representatives of an old-established west coast firm of Liverpool. At Yaunde, Kribi, Duala, and on the voyage home, I enjoyed their hospitality and assistance.

Yaunde is the administrative capital of the French Cameroons, connected by a railway to Duala, the principal town and port 200 miles away. This was formerly the capital, but when the railway was extended inland to Yaunde the French were wise enough to transfer the seat of administration. It is situated on the central plateau in a hilly, well-wooded region, 2,300 feet above sea level. Considering it is only four degrees north of the equator, the climate is pleasant, while fever is almost absent. Compared with the coast itself it is a health resort, and it is much frequented by people from Duala on that account. The European population numbers about two hundred and fifty. There are many well-built, red-tiled bungalows for the officials and an imposing residence for the Governor of the Cameroons. It was interesting to see the unpretentious, democratic site chosen for this building, befitting that of the representative of a republic. It was in the town, with its main entrance opposite to a football ground on which the natives of Yaunde played with much noise every evening. Until then Government House had always conjured up for me a vision of a place set at a respectful distance from the town in the dignified seclusion of its grounds of many acres, so surrounded with trees that all one knew it by was the sentry-box at the gate. This idea is seen at its best or worst in Uganda, where Government House and its satellites have a town of their own (where nothing so plebeian as a shop is allowed), twenty-five miles from the real capital.

The railway terminates at Yaunde, which is thus the collecting centre for the native produce of a large area. Palm oil, palm kernels, cocoa, ground nuts, are brought here to be despatched to the coast, either by the State-owned railway to Duala or by road to Kribi, a smaller port a hundred miles south of Duala. This road, in spite of its narrowness, is a thorn in the flesh of the railway by reason of the number of lorries which ply on it in competition. There is no road to Duala, although the Government are constantly being urged to build one, but as they own the railway their reluctance is very natural.

At Yaunde there are some dozen trading-houses, four of them British. They are all engaged in the same line of business, buying native produce for export, and distributing for native consumption cotton goods, hardware, salt, dried stockfish, wine, and tobacco. Cheap red wine is a very popular drink. The same concerns are found at all the principal trading-centres between Yaunde and the coast, while in important places like Yaunde or Duala some of the bigger ones have three or four branch shops in charge of natives, placed at strategic points to tap the native custom.

Wishing to finish the journey to the sea by road, I decided to go first to Kribi before embarking as arranged at Duala. After three days' rest, I began the last stage inauspiciously by losing myself in the not very extensive suburbs of Yaunde. After two months of Hobson's choice in the matter of roads the offer of more than one proved too embarrassing. With a drop of 2,300 feet in front of me I anticipated hopefully that I should now *rouler* to the coast as the eccentric *douanier* had promised, but for the first thirty miles at any rate the road was uphill. Later, when it did begin to descend, the surface was so bad, owing to the lorry traffic and the fact that it was the end of the rainy season, that there was very little free-wheeling at all. As one would expect, the population between Yaunde and the coast is denser (or less scanty), the cultivation more extensive, and the natives more prosperous than in the interior. Some lived in houses, as distinct from huts (I saw several of two stories built of timber), all of which had well-made doors and shuttered windows.

I stopped the night at the house of a local chief in which were three well-furnished rooms. The chief made me a present of eggs (good ones), a compliment which I returned with a 'dash' of five francs. His two intelligent-looking sons both spoke good French and were eager to know what East Africa was like.

At Lolondorf next day, about half-way to the coast, the road becomes so narrow and tortuous that traffic is allowed to move only in one direction. In the morning, until midday, it moves up from the coast, and in the afternoon it leaves Lolondorf for Kribi. If a lorry fails to reach Lolondorf before midday or Kribi before midnight it has to stay where it is, under penalties.

Soon after leaving Lolondorf I was caught by a storm and by the midday exodus of lorries for Kribi. I very willingly left the road to them, for there were about a dozen lorries in the convoy, all driven by light-hearted natives. To be passed by them on a narrow road was a shattering experience.

I took shelter in a hut whose owner was a garrulous old negro in the Uncle Tom tradition. He was busy making a fishing-net, and talked away without looking at his work while his fingers 'netted' automatically. It reminded me of the Kikuyu women I had seen walking in the streets of Nairobi with their fingers busy weaving string bags. I saw the same sort of thing in a village near Bangassu, but there they were weaving mats; men, women, and children, all carrying a piece of mat and weaving it, whether lying, sitting, standing, or walking.

Uncle Tom's remark that 'the rain done finish' was right. I pushed on and had a long, pleasant run through the cool of the evening, coming out at last fairly upon the coastal plain – I had left the hills for good. I found shelter for the night in a hut belonging to a highly 'civilised' citizen who told me he had spent several years in New York working in a laundry. He was very reticent and, to my disappointment, I could get nothing out of him, for it would have been curious to know his reasons for returning, and his opinion of life in this west coast village compared with life in New York – as extreme a contrast as could be imagined.

Only fifty miles remained to be done, but as yet there was no hint that I was approaching the sea. Many days back I had pictured to myself some distant, dramatic glimpse of the Atlantic – something like that of the Pacific which rewarded stout Cortez and his men 'silent upon a peak in Darien,' but no such vision was vouchsafed me. The first I saw of the sea was round the corner of a tin shed in Kribi itself.

Kribi is a small town at the mouth of a large but unnavigable river. There is no harbour, so that ships have to lie out a mile and a half to discharge into surf boats. (The surf on this coast is nothing like so heavy as it is further north outside the Bight.) Kribi's palmiest days were before the War, during the rubber boom, when wild rubber from the forests of the southern Cameroons formed the bulk of the Colony's exports.

The bungalow at which I stopped shared with the lighthouse a small spit of land almost surrounded by river and sea, so that it received what little cool air there was stirring, but, in spite of that, it was sizzling hot.

I came out on the coast on the other side of Africa fifty-six days after leaving Kampala. November 10th was the actual day of my arrival, so that I was just in time to see Kribi 'going gay,' Armistice Day being an official holiday in French Colonies. All the European residents, numbering about fifty, were invited to a dance, while for the natives a programme of sports was arranged, where the great event was a race for war canoes from the bar to the river-mouth. The crews of the six canoes taking part were drawn from different tribes, and the bitterness of their rivalry was excelled only by that of their respective supporters.

Although the crowd lining the shore seemed to find it exciting enough, the race itself was in the nature of a procession, but the real fun started when the winners paddled round the inner harbour, showing off and chanting songs of victory. This ill-timed jubilation was altogether too much for two of the losing crews, who promptly fell upon them, and a fierce naval battle began. Hardwood paddles were broken on harder heads, the crowd on land threw stones and bottles at each with rare impartiality, and finally the canoes capsized, the late occupants swimming ashore to continue the fight on land. Things were really warming up when the native police intervened, chasing away the more active participants and leaving only the greybeards of the rival clans to continue the warfare with vituperation that would have made a fish-wife envious. I was told that this little fracas was the usual custom after the annual canoe race (a more virile form of Boat Race night activities), and it seemed to me a peculiarly appropriate one for Armistice Day.

Harmony was restored in the afternoon when the whole of native Kribi, dressed in European finery, paraded the streets to the music of the town band. These brass bands, peculiar to the Cameroons towns, are a relic of the German days. At Yaunde there was a very grand one dressed in uniform, but it confined itself entirely to pre-War airs – not for sentimental reasons, but because there had been no one to teach them any others.

Two days were spent at Kribi, mostly in the sea, before I mounted the bicycle once again to ride north to Edea, eighty miles away. In that little market town on the Yaunde-Duala line the bell was rung for the last time in Africa and our Odyssey came to an end. From there to Duala there was no way but by rail. I slept by the road for the last time, ten miles short of Edea, riding in at six in the morning to find my prospective host already in the thick of produce buying. At that time of year the produce offering seemed to be mostly cocoa, which was, I imagine, less nauseating to handle at that hour of the morning than palm oil. It was an animated scene, as all the rival stores on opposite sides of the street were hard at it, while the street itself was thronged with natives bringing in produce. The cocoa-beans were brought in baskets as head loads. The load was weighed and examined for dryness, the owner being then offered a price which he either accepted at once or tried to better at one of the rival stores. It was not a pleasant job for the buyers, whose tempers at times must have been sorely tried. The patience shown and the long hours worked by these west coast traders, in a climate inimical to patience or work, impressed me profoundly.

Edea stands on a big river, the Sanaga. Just above the town are the falls, which I saw at their best – a full river pouring a vast volume of water over a straight drop of 130 feet. A few hundred yards below the falls the river flows round an island in two channels, spanned by two mighty bridges, carrying the railway. These were built before the War, and the story goes that the German engineer who built them was later told off to destroy them to delay the British advance when we invaded the Cameroons in 1915. To the astonishment of all, the bridges were found intact, for the father could not bring himself to compass the destruction of his own children.

The bicycle and I brought our labours to an end by taking the train to Duala, a journey of about three hours. Duala is not on the sea, but is situated twenty-three miles up the wide estuary of the Wuri River; opposite, on the north side of the estuary, lie the British Cameroons and the great mass of the Cameroon mountain, an extinct volcano, towering to 13,000 feet. From the upper part of the town one can see in clear weather both the Great and Small Cameroon mountains, and the 9,000 feet peak on the island of Fernando Po.

There are about a thousand Europeans and two thousand five hundred natives in the town, which is divided roughly into three parts. The European part, known as Bell, where Germans have been responsible for the general lay-out, boasted many fine avenues and buildings. Evidences of similar careful planning and readiness to spend money can be seen in the ex-German port of Der-es-Salaam, on the east coast. Lagos, the principal British port on the coast, seems to have grown up fortuitously, for it is a hotch-potch mixture compared with the orderliness of Duala.

I had a few days to wait for a ship, but the time passed pleasantly enough exploring the town and sleeping off the somnolence induced by the west coast delicacies of palm oil chop and ground nut stew. Very excellent dishes they are, too, but in my opinion more suitable for the Arctic than the tropics. As

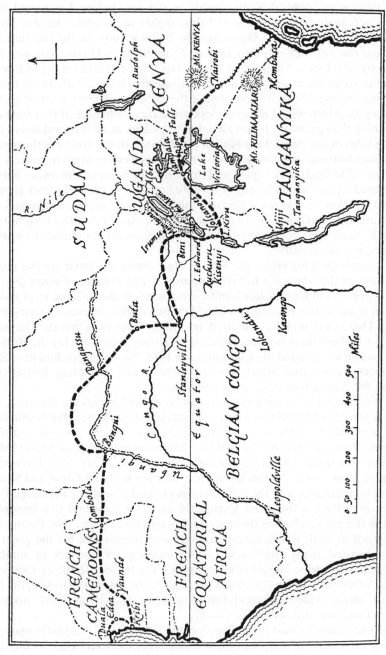

The route taken across Africa from east to west

their eating necessitates the revivifying effects of much gin, meals in which they figure are serious affairs. On the coast, the day set aside by custom for their consumption is Sunday, just as at home we in England on the same day celebrate the solemn rites of roast beef and Yorkshire pudding.

While waiting for a ship I had leisure to think over the journey which was now ended – a not very eventful journey of 3,000 miles across Africa. Satisfaction at getting across was tinged with disappointment at the extraordinary sameness (I had almost said 'tameness') of the scenery of the western half of the journey as compared with the variety seen in the eastern; once the central highlands have been crossed and left behind, the monotony of forest and long grass is all-embracing. Neither is there the great diversity of peoples one meets with in East Africa, where the tribes, differing widely in dress, features, customs, and modes of life, combine with the ever-changing scene to make travel in Kenya, Uganda, or Tanganyika a constant delight. But in spite of the complaint of monotony, which might also be levelled at travel in the desert or the Arctic, for that man who travels by his own exertions no day can be dull and no journey without an abiding interest.

A surprise, perhaps another disappointment, was the comparative ease with which the journey had been done. From what has been said, it should be clear that the sole requisite for success was ability to follow the advice of James Pigg to 'keep tambourine a-roulin.' This absence of difficulty and danger may be disappointing to others, too, for the tradition of Darkest Africa dies hard. Ten or fifteen years earlier such a ride would have been difficult enough, if not impossible, and even to-day the road is but a slender thread, and Africa, a vast country in which, away from the road, one can still find the Africa of boyhood's dreams – the dreams inspired by Rider Haggard, Selous, Stanley. Mechanical transport has a great deal for which to answer, but even if we use it there is no reason why we should not deplore it. Modern methods of transport (perhaps I might be allowed to exclude the push-bike) have abolished the hardships of African travel, and with them most of the joys, too – the joys of the march, the camp, the cheery porters. Very wisely was it said, 'All travel is dull exactly in proportion to its rapidity.'

My ship came up the river and I prepared to embark by buying myself a coat and a pair of trousers. I was glad that ships tie up alongside a quay at Duala, thus allowing my faithful 'grid' to be wheeled on board instead of suffering the indignity of being hoisted through the air like so much inanimate freight. Sailing-day arrived, bringing with it for me the mingled feelings of most 'last days.' Countries, if lived and worked in long enough, have a queer way of making a man feel an affection for them, whether they have treated him well or ill. For fourteen years – a fifth of our allotted span – Africa had been my task-mistress, and now I was leaving her. If she had not given me the fortune I expected, she had given me something better – memories, mountains, friends.

We dropped down the river whose muddy waters were soon to be lost in the clean blue immensity of the sea, while the Cameroon mountains, showing faintly astern, waved to me Africa's last farewell.

THE ASCENT OF NANDA DEVI

The Ascent of Nanda Devi

First published by Cambridge University Press, 1937

Contents

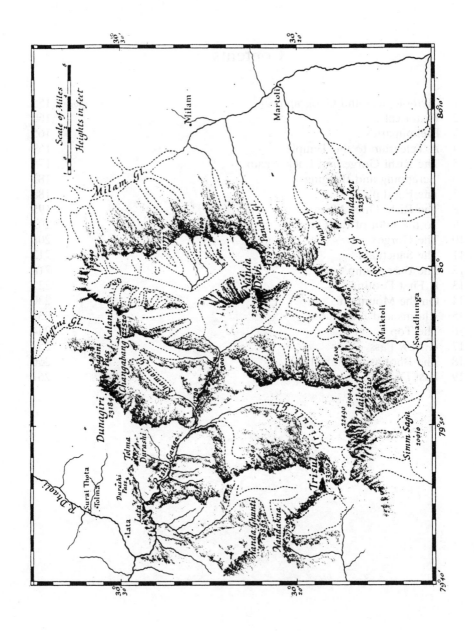

CHAPTER ONE

Mythological and Geographical

IT is questionable whether the story of a successful attempt on a new peak will be as acceptable as a story of failure; at any rate to lovers of mountains or to those who know one end of an ice-axe from the other. These will perhaps be more inclined to echo the words of David's lament and cry, 'Tell it not in Gath, publish it not in the streets of Askelon.'

If an account of the climbing of Everest is ever written, I take leave to doubt whether it will be as widely read as have been the stories of successive failures. For, say what one may, when the summit is reached some of the mystery and grandeur surrounding a peak hitherto untrodden by man is lost; and a book recounting the fall of one of the giants will be bought—or by mountaineers more likely borrowed—with misgiving and read with loathing. But so complex is our make-up that the pleasure which success brings far outweighs any remorseful pangs, and friends, even mountaineering friends, congratulate the triumphant party sincerely instead of damning them heartily. And, as if that was not enough, pressure of various kinds results in the members of the expedition putting on record their experiences so that all profit by them, and the invincibility of yet another great mountain is thereby imperilled. Perhaps when the millennium dawns, of the writing of books there *will* be an end, at least of mountaineering books; if there are then any unconquered peaks remaining, come what may, successive generations will think them still unconquered to the end of time.

Stories of unsuccessful climbs are in a different category. The splendour of the mountain is undimmed or even enhanced, and the writer can be trusted to see to it that the honour of man is, at the lowest, not diminished. But having now hinted at the motives impelling the writing of this account it is time to cut the cackle and come to the 'osses; for it would puzzle a conjuror to explain satisfactorily a habit (not confined to mountaineers) of believing one thing and doing another.

Before leaving for the Himalaya in May, I was asked by an otherwise intelligent man whether it would be summer or winter out there when we arrived. This is mentioned in no critical spirit, but only to show that what one man assumes to be common knowledge may be known only to very few. A banker, for instance, popularly supposed to be without a soul, may know nothing and care less about mountains, but be deeply interested in music or literature; and, conversely, mountaineers may not know the most elementary principles of banking or, possibly, grammar.

To some the Himalayas may be only a name vaguely associated perhaps with a mountain called Everest: to geologists they provide a vast field for the starting and running of new hares; to other learned men, glaciologists, ethnologists, or geographers, the Himalaya are a fruitful source of debate in which there is no common ground, not even the pronunciation of the name; while to the mountaineer they furnish fresh evidence, if such were needed, of the wise dispensation of a bountiful Providence. For, lo, when the Alps are becoming too crowded, not only with human beings but with huts, the Himalaya offer themselves to the more fanatical devotee—a range of fifteen hundred miles long, containing many hundreds of peaks, nearly all unclimbed, and all of them so much higher than the Alps that a new factor of altitude has to be added to the usual sum of difficulties to be overcome; and withal to be approached through country of great loveliness, inhabited by peoples who are always interesting and sometimes charming. Here seemingly is a whole new world to conquer, but it is a world which man with his usual perversity, flying in the face of Providence, has reduced to comparatively small dimensions: for what with political boundaries, restrictions, and jealousies, the accessible area is less than one-third of the whole. And though European travellers and climbers may grouse about this state of affairs, Europeans are, I suppose, largely to blame. For with the present state of the outside world before their eyes the rulers of Tibet, Nepal, and Bhutan can scarcely be blamed, and might well be praised, for wishing their own people to have as little as possible to do with ourselves.

Sikkim, Kashmir, and Garhwal remain open to travellers, though the first two are not without their restrictions; restrictions which we were to experience. Garhwal is a small district almost in the centre of the Himalayan chain and lying about two hundred miles north-east of Delhi. It is divided into British Garhwal and the native state of Tehri Garhwal, but here we need trouble ourselves only with the first, which did not come under British control until after the Nepalese War of 1815. Originally the country was in the hands of a number of petty chieftains, each with his own fortress or castle; the word 'garh' itself means a castle. In the early years of the nineteenth century it was overrun by the Ghurkas, who, not content with this acquisition, extended their ravages down to the plains and thus came into collision with the ruling Power and brought about the Nepalese War. In the early stages of the war we reaped our usual crop of defeats and disasters, but in the end (and up to the present this also has been usual) we muddled through and drove the Ghurkas back within their present boundaries; and, as a slight reward for the trouble to which we had been put, we annexed the greater part of Garhwal for ourselves. It is roughly rectangular, about a hundred miles from north to south and fifty from east to west, and diagonally across the northern half runs the Himalayan chain. In this short section of the range there are two peaks over 25,000 ft., including Nanda Devi (25,645 ft.), the highest peak in the Empire, and over a hundred lesser peaks all over 20,000 ft. To the east lies Nepal, on the west is the native state of Tehri Garhwal, and north is Tibet. The Tibetan border runs on the north side of the highest axis of elevation, the northern slopes of the range merging into the high Tibetan plateau, and south of the range are the foothills running down to the plains of British India. It is noteworthy that the watershed lies near the Tibetan border on the north side of the line of highest elevation, which would naturally be expected to form the watershed. The rivers have either cut back through the range or the country has been elevated since the existence of the rivers.

There are three main rivers flowing roughly south, cutting through the range at right angles, and between these river valleys are the chains containing the highest summits, forming, as it were, spurs thrown out from the main range. From east to west the rivers are the Gori, the Dhauli, and the Alaknanda. The last two flow into the Ganges, the Alaknanda constituting one of its main sources, and at the head of all three valleys are high passes leading into Tibet. Between the Gori and the Dhauli lies the range containing Nanda Devi, and at its southern extremity this range bends round to the west towards Trisul (23,360 ft.), and culminates in Nandakna (20,700 ft.), and Nanda Ghunti (19,983 ft.). Some ten miles north of this abrupt westerly bend another spur of approximately equal length branches off, its western extremity marked by Dunagiri (23,184 ft.). Between these two short parallel spurs is a yet shorter one composing Nanda Devi itself, so that we have here a sort of reversed letter 'E', the short middle stroke representing Nanda Devi, the longer top stroke the Dunagiri, and the bottom stroke the Trisul massif. But that is not all; subsidiary spurs branch off from Trisul and Dunagiri and converge upon the middle stroke, thus almost encircling Nanda Devi with a ring of mountains.

The space between the foot of Nanda Devi and its ring-fence of giant peaks, in extent some two hundred and fifty square miles, contains many lesser peaks and ridges, an extensive glacier system, rock, scree, and, surprisingly enough, grass slopes of wide extent. The whole is known as the Nanda Devi Basin or, more felicitously, the Sanctuary, a name first bestowed on it by Mr Ruttledge of Everest fame, who in the following passage graphically describes the unique situation of the mountain:

'Nanda Devi imposes on her votaries an admission test as yet beyond their skill and endurance. Surrounded by a barrier ring, 70 m. long, on which stand twelve measured peaks over 21,000 ft., and which nowhere descends lower than 18,000 ft., except in the West, where the Rishi Ganga river, rising at the foot of Nanda Devi, and the sole drainage of 250 sq.m. of ice and snow, has carved for itself what must be one of the most terrific gorges in the world. Two ridges converging on the river form as it were the curtain to an inner sanctuary within which the great mountain soars up to 25,645 ft. So tremendous is the aspect of the gorge that Hindu mythology described it as the last earthly home of the Seven Rishis—here if anywhere their meditations would be undisturbed.'

The Rishis mentioned here were seven wise men, Hindu sages, and they are now said to be represented by the seven stars of the Great Bear.

The superstitions, myths, and traditions relating to mountains, are most of them interesting and some beautiful. The mountains of Garhwal are particularly rich in such stories, because Garhwal is the birthplace of the Hindu religion, the traditional home of most of the gods of the Hindu Pantheon, and the terrestrial scene of their exploits. Every mountain and river, almost every rock and pool, is associated in legend with the life of some god.

Of the population of Garhwal, the orthodox among the immigrant Brahmans and Rajputs worship the five great gods, Vishnu, Siva, Devi, the Sun, and Ganesh, the elephant-headed god of wisdom. The bulk of the people, Khasiyas, a race of a caste lower than the Brahmans or the Rajputs, but yet generally allowed to be also immigrants from an Aryan source, adore principally the mountain god Siva; while the Doms, less than a fifth in number of the rest and believed to be the aborigines of the country, propitiate the local gods and demons who were in existence long before the coming of the Brahmans and Hinduism. But all, even the hillman such as the Bhotia, who has little respect for things sacred, finds a common subject for reverence in the majesty and aloofness of the snowy ranges. At any sudden revelation of one of these giants, the home of one of the deities, coolie and priest alike will fold their hands and with bowed head utter a word of prayer.

Nor is worship at the high places of Himachal, 'the abode of snow' sacred to the Hindu gods, confined only to the nearer inhabitants. From all parts of India pilgrims make their way annually to this Hindu 'Palestine' to 'acquire merit' by enduring the privations of the road, and, by worshipping at the shrines, to receive forgiveness for past sins and assurance of future happiness.

At Kedarnath Siva, or Mahadeo, the god of everything destructive and terrible, is the object of adoration; at Badrinath the temple is dedicated to the benignant Vishnu, and a third famous shrine is found at Gangotri. All three lie amongst the great group of mountains which separate the valleys of the Bhagirathi and Alaknanda, rivers which unite lower down to form the Ganges.

At Kedarnath the tradition is that the god in the form of a buffalo took refuge from his pursuers the Pandavas (a tribe of the Dasyus who represent the original black race as opposed to the fair Aryans). For further safety he dived into the ground but left his hinder parts exposed, and a mountain there, in shape something like the less dangerous end of a buffalo, is still an object of adoration. The remaining parts of the god are worshipped at four other places along the Himalayan chain; the arms at Tungnath, the face at Rudrnath, the belly at Madmaheswar, and the head at Kalapeswar. Together these five places form the 'Panch-Kedar', and to visit them in succession is a great ambition of the Hindu devotee, but one, I imagine, which is not often accomplished. I have in mind particularly Madmaheswar, which lies up a valley that few plainsmen would care to penetrate.

Bigoted followers of Siva or Vishnu visit only the temple dedicated to their respective god, but the great number of pilgrims make the round of as many of the sacred places as possible. Badrinath probably receives the most, and derives from its fifty thousand annual visitors a far greater revenue than that of Kedarnath. Badrinath also has its five sacred places, the 'Panch-Badri', comprised within the Holy Circle of Badrinath, which extends from the shrine of Kanwa to the summit of Nanda Devi, on which there is a lake, the abode of Vishnu himself. The Bhagirathi, which is a lesser stream than the Alaknanda, has a greater reputation for sanctity, but it does not attract as many pilgrims as do the sources of the Alaknanda, particularly the fall of Bhasudara. The temple of Gangotri is ten miles below the place where the Bhangirathi issues from the snout of the Gangotri glacier, a very holy spot called Gaumukh or the 'Cow's Mouth'. It is here that, according to Hindu mythology, the heaven-born goddess first descended upon earth. Water from the river at Gangotri, sealed in flasks by the priests, is taken to the plains as being of great value.

Of the exact meaning of Nanda Devi, or rather of 'Nanda', it is not easy to get any precise information. According to one interpretation it means the 'Blessed' or 'Revered' Goddess, but if there is anything in a story I was told it means the goddess Nanda. Nanda was the daughter of a Kumaon king (Kumaon is a division of which Garhwal is part, and was formerly a separate native state) whose hand was demanded in marriage by a Rohilla prince. He was refused, and war followed, a battle taking place near Ranikhet. Nanda's kingly father was defeated and the future goddess fled and, after many vicissitudes, took refuge on the top of Nanda Devi. There are two other mountains in the vicinity in which the name 'Nanda' occurs. Nanda Ghunti to the west has already been mentioned and this, I was told, means 'The halting-place of Nanda'; it is only 19,893 ft. high and was probably used as a stepping stone to Nanda Devi itself. To the east is Nanda Kot (22,500 ft.), which means 'The stronghold of Nanda', and south is Trisul, 'The Trident', a defiance to any rapacious Rohillas.

Amongst the local natives this belief that the mountains are the abode of gods and demons is less strong than it used to be. In 1830 Mr Traill, the first Commissioner, accompanied by local coolies, crossed a pass between Nanda Kot and Nanda Devi. The story goes that he suffered severely from snow-blindness, which the coolies attributed to the wrath of the goddess, and they affirmed that he only recovered after making an offering at the temple of Nanda Devi at Almora. The story may not be strictly accurate, but only a pedant would have it otherwise.

In 1855 the same route was taken by Adolph Schlagintweit, and of this crossing Mr A. L. Mumm in *Five months in the Himalaya* related the following. A promise of additional pay and a rich offering to Nanda Devi had to be promised before any coolies could be persuaded to start. On top of the Pass, 'Schlagintweit commenced taking observations but was disagreeably interrupted by three of the hardiest men being seized with epileptic fits . . . A cry rose up that Nanda Devi had entered into them and Adolph, fearful lest the seizure might spread further, took aside two Brahmans whom he had with him, and after pointing out that he had given Nanda Devi all that they had demanded, and that this unpleasant scene was only the result of their own folly in calling on the goddess at every difficult place on the way up, ordered them to put a stop to it at once. This they achieved, partly by prayers, and partly by putting snow on the head of the sufferers, the latter remedy being, in Adolph's opinion, the more effective of the two.'

A later traveller, W. W. Graham, in 1883 had trouble with the local natives when he attempted to approach Nanda Devi by the gorge of the Rishi. His men all deserted, ostensibly on the grounds that the gorge was infested with devils. But in 1934 when Mr Shipton and the writer penetrated the gorge our Dotial and Bhotia coolies evinced no superstitious fears, though they, of course, are not really local men. Some men from the Dhauli valley whom we employed did desert, but I think the devils they feared were more tangible— the devils of discomfort and hard work. In 1936 we took a few coolies from a village at the very mouth of the Rishi Ganga and for them superstition either did not exist or was overcome, and this was the more remarkable because they came up the Rishi and joined us at the foot of the mountain, unaccompanied by any European.

On the other hand, shortly after our return, a local correspondent of a well-known Indian newspaper published a report to the following effect. In 1936 the monsoon rainfall was exceptionally heavy in the United Provinces and Garhwal, and on August 29th, after a severe storm, the Pindar river, which is fed by the glaciers of Nanda Kot and Trisul, rose many feet and wrought considerable havoc in the village of Tharali; a village, by the way, through which we had passed on the way to the mountain some weeks before. Forty lives were lost, several houses destroyed, and many cattle drowned. It was on the same day, August 29th, that we climbed the mountain and thus provoked the anger of the goddess, who immediately avenged, blindly but terribly, the violation of her sanctuary.

CHAPTER TWO

Historical

THE reader who blenches at the chapter heading will be pleased to hear that it is not necessary to recall the history of previous attempts on the mountain because there have not been any. For fifty years the problem which engaged the attention of many experienced mountaineers was not how to climb the mountain but how to reach it. But as the approach to the mountain was not the least serious of the problems which we had to face, perhaps it will not be out of place to outline briefly the story of these attempts, although they have already been recounted very thoroughly in Mr Shipton's *Nanda Devi*.

The truism that we climb on the shoulders of our predecessors is sometimes forgotten, and it is difficult to exaggerate the importance of the part which earlier failures play in the final success. The Himalayan peaks over, say, 23,000 ft. which have been climbed at the first attempt can be numbered on the fingers of one hand, and even if the present climb be cited to the contrary, the answer is that we had the inestimable advantage of knowing where to make our efforts and how to get there—knowledge gained for us by our forerunners. And apart from previous experience on the actual mountain there is the vast fund of accumulated knowledge of high climbing in general to draw upon; for though experiences may be 'the name men give to their mistakes' it does not lessen their value to those who are willing to learn.

The earliest expedition was that of W. W. Graham in 1883, who was accompanied by two Swiss guides and who hoped to reach the mountain by way of the Rishi gorge. This river, as has already been said, drains the whole of the Nanda Devi Basin. It has two sources at the snouts of the two glaciers encircling the north-east and south-west sides of the mountain, and the streams from these glaciers unite at the foot of the west ridge. From this point the river, by now a formidable torrent, flows west through a gorge or series of gorges until after a distance of about eight miles it joins the Dhauli river near the village of Rini. Graham's party started to follow the river up from near its junction with the Dhauli, but were stopped almost at once by the difficulty of the terrain; nor to this day has anyone succeeded in passing the lower portals of the gorge.

Repulsed here Graham and his two guides, Boss and Kaufmann, moved round to the north and, after an unsuccessful attempt on Dunagiri, learnt from shepherds that there was a way into the Rishi *nala* over the northern containing wall which avoided the insuperable difficulties of the lower four miles. 'On the evening of the second day', Graham wrote, 'we reached a lovely little table-land called Dunassau (Durashi). The last day's route had been extremely wild running along the southern face of the ridge, sometimes with a sheer drop to the river below—some 7000 to 8000 feet. Such wild rocks and broken gullies I had never met before.' Here most of their coolies deserted, but they pushed on: 'Occasionally we had to hang on to a tuft of grass or a bunch of Alpine roses, and I do not exaggerate when I say that for half the day's work hand-hold was as necessary as foot-hold.' Several days of this sort of work brought them to a place where they were finally stopped by the smooth cliffs of the north side and inability to cross the river to the more accommodating south bank. The desertion of their remaining coolies put an end to their hopes and they abandoned their loads and struggled back as best they could.

In 1905 Dr Longstaff, a name for ever associated with mountain exploration in Garhwal, attacked the problem from the opposite side. In that year he and two Italian guides, the Brocherel brothers, were in the Gori valley to the east of the Nanda Devi massif with designs on East Nanda Devi (24,300 ft.). This mountain is the highest of the encircling peaks and from it extends that short ridge, the middle stroke of the reversed letter 'E', which links it with Nanda Devi itself. Starting from Milam in the Gori valley Longstaff's party got on to the rim of the Basin at the foot of the south-east shoulder of the lesser Nanda Devi, at a height of 19,100 ft. They were thus the first ever to look down into the mysterious sanctuary; but the descent looked formidable, nor was it their objective. It had been a close thing, but the Sanctuary remained inviolate.

In 1907 Dr Longstaff returned to the attack with a strong party which included General Bruce, Mr Mumm, and three Alpine guides. Their first attempt was by what Dr Longstaff called the 'back door', the route which Graham had learned of from the shepherds. Half-way up the gorge from Rini on the north side of the river, and a couple of thousand feet above it, there are two hanging valleys. Here is valuable grazing to which, in the summer, are brought the sheep and goats from many neighbouring villages, some enterprising but unknown shepherd of a bygone age having found a remarkable route to these alps, or Kharaks, as they are called locally. The route involves the crossing of a 14,000 ft. pass which in late spring is still snow-covered, and a rather hair-raising, or since sheep form the bulk of the travellers, wool-raising, traverse across a mile of cliffs. The pass, however, was found to be still blocked by snow, so the party moved round to the north and east of Dunagiri and proceeded up the Bagini glacier in an attempt to cross the northern wall of the Basin, the top stroke of our reversed 'E'. There was a pass at the head of this glacier which according to the map then in use should have led into the Basin, but this region of ice and snow had of course not been included in the survey, and though the map did credit to the maker's imagination it was apt to mislead. The map of Garhwal in use up to 1936 was made from a survey in 1868 which was, rightly, only carried up to the snow-line, and above this, not so rightly, it was largely filled in by guess-work. There is nothing but praise and thankfulness for the accuracy of the surveyed portion, but for the unsurveyed part we should all prefer to have a map which, like the crew of the *Snark*, we can all understand, 'a perfect and absolute blank'.

In 1934 we had the same experience as Dr Longstaff's party in other parts of Garhwal. From an explorer's point of view it may seen inconsistent and ungracious to gird at inadequate maps, for it is the explorer's job to fill them in. But this is only a plea for blanks instead of fancy; blanks, of which there are, alas, but few remaining, thanks to the energy of the Indian Survey. At the present moment a new survey of Garhwal is in hand, and this year (1936) we had the advantage of a provisional new issue of the old map incorporating the results of much private and official work done in Garhwal in recent years. Is it not time to start a Society for the Suppression of Abolition of Maps and Guide Books, not necessarily confined to the Himalaya? With the accumulation of exact knowledge comes the desire to put it to use, and we shall presently have a Five-Year Plan for the Himalaya and learn that the Sanctuary is one of those eligible sites 'ripe for development'. To show that this is not completely idle fancy I might mention that 'Pilgrimage by Air' is, if not an actual fact, at least an advertised one. The following appeared in *The Times* dated from Delhi this year: 'An aerodrome among the Himalayas, 10,500 ft. above sea-level, is being constructed by the Air Transport Company here to cope with the pilgrim traffic to the Badrinath shrine, sacred to the Hindus. The present terminus (long may it remain so) of the air route to the shrine is situated at Gauchar, about 70 miles from Hardwar. The return journey between Hardwar (*sic*) and Gauchar takes about eight weeks by road, and could be done in twelve hours by rail.' The words in parenthesis are the author's. For Hardwar, in the last sentence, I suggest read Badrinath; we have been told the distance is seventy miles, and four weeks for the single journey is a little slow even for a pilgrim travelling on his hands and knees or measuring his length on the ground at every step, as some of them do.

To return to our exploring party on top of the Bagini pass; they found, after crossing the pass and descending another glacier, that they had got into the Rishi gorge at the point reached by Graham and were still separated by three miles of cliff from the Inner Sanctuary. Shortage of food compelled them to hurry with all speed down the Rishi instead of attempting to force this upper passage, and they finally emerged by the 'back door', which was now clear of snow. After a rest they came up the Rishi once more and Dr Longstaff with two of the guides (the Brocherel brothers) climbed Trisul, going from a camp at 17,500 ft. to the top in one day—an amazing *tour de force* which is not likely to be repeated.

Trisul was climbed on June 12th, and the 14th saw Dr Longstaff and two Gurkhas trying to force a way up the south bank of the Rishi. Foiled here, they crossed to the north side by a natural rock bridge and camped near the entrance of the Rhamani torrent down which they had come on the previous journey recounted above. The height was 11,700 ft., and the next day they climbed to 13,500 ft. up the cliffs of the north bank, but found this side even less encouraging than the other. In view of the difficulties and at the instance of other plans still to be carried out, no further attempt was made to penetrate the grim defile and Dr Longstaff rejoined his party in the lower Rishi.

In 1932 Mr Ruttledge, who as Deputy Commissioner of the Almora district had had opportunities for studying the problem of Nanda Devi and the Basin both from distant Almora and from journeys to the east and north, thought that he had discovered a breach in the outer rampart. About half-way round the southern rim from Trisul to East Nanda Devi the surrounding wall falls to its lowest elevation, about 18,000 ft. or slightly less. From a distance this depression seemed a likely place for a crossing of the wall, but rising as it did from a deep and steep valley very little of the approach to it could be seen. Accompanied by Emil Rey, an Italian guide, and six Sherpa porters, Mr Ruttledge went up the Maiktoli valley to get a closer look, but from beneath so forbidding was the aspect of the proposed pass that not even a closer inspection was required.

'We were brought up all-standing by a sight which almost took our remaining breath away. Six thousand feet of the steepest rock and ice . . . Near the top of the wall, for about a mile and a half, runs a terrace of ice some 200 feet thick. Under the pull of gravity large masses constantly break off from this terrace and thunder down to the valley below, polishing in their fall the successive bands of limestone of which the face is composed. Even supposing the precipice to be climbable, an intelligent mountaineer may be acquitted on a charge of lack of enterprise if he declines to spend at least three days and two nights under fire from this artillery. As alternative, there is a choice of three knife-edge arêtes, each one excessively steep, sometimes overhanging in the middle and lower sections, on which even the eye of faith, assisted by powerful binoculars, fails to see one single platform large enough to accommodate the most modest of expedition tents.

'The jury's verdict was unanimous; and so vanished the last hope of a straightforward approach to Nanda Devi; and the goddess keeps her secret.'

Prior to this Mr Ruttledge had made two previous attempts. One in 1926 accompanied by Dr Howard Somervell and Major-General R. C. Wilson, when an approach by the Timphu glacier to the north-east was tried but found to be even more hopeless than that by the south or west. And again in 1927 with Dr Longstaff, when the lowest point of the wall, 17,000 ft., at the head of the Nandakini valley to the south-west was reached. Further progress was barred by bad weather, but this approach would but have led into the lower Rishi Ganga and not into the Basin.

In 1934 Mr Shipton and the writer with three Sherpa porters went to Garhwal, having as our main objective the entrance and mapping of the Basin. As with a man making a second marriage, hope triumphed over experience, and by Dr Longstaff's advice we directed our attention to the Rishi gorge. The gorge was passed and a month was spent exploring and mapping the Promised Land of the Basin, and in the autumn a second journey was made to complete the work. On this second occasion a way out was found over the low depression in the southern wall but, of course, in the reverse direction to that which Mr Ruttledge had intended, and in consequence a much simpler affair.

In the course of the six weeks spent in the Basin we had ample opportunity to study the mountain from every side. As a result of this study, having exhausted all other possibilities, we concluded rather unhopefully that a lodgement could be effected on the south ridge, but it seemed unlikely that the ridge would 'go'.

We took a camp up the south-east glacier to within striking distance and, fully expecting that a closer acquaintance would only strengthen our first impressions, we devoted a day to the ridge. We reached a height of about 20,000 ft. and found it easier than we expected, which only goes to show the value of an oft-quoted piece of mountaineering advice by Dr Longstaff, that 'you must go and rub your nose in a place before being certain that it won't "go"'. It was a perfect autumn day and we sat for some time on our airy perch, following in imagination a route up the ever-steepening southern ridge, and fascinated by the grand sweep of the horse-shoe cirque at the head of the glacier, a 3000 ft. glacis of glittering ice. Despite our height and the clear day we were not well placed for judging the difficulties of the ridge above our heads. We were looking at it *en face*, we were too close, and the whole was very much foreshortened, but with due allowance for this our opinion was summed up by Mr Shipton in *Nanda Devi* as follows: 'The ridge was certainly showing signs of becoming more difficult but for the next few hundred feet there did not appear to be any insuperable obstacles, and we came to the definite conclusion that if a well-equipped party were to spend a couple of weeks over the job there was a good chance that the ridge could be followed to the summit. It would be no easy task and the party would have to be supremely fit and competent.'

Two things may be noted in this brief summary: first, that Sherpa porters made their first appearance in Garhwal in 1927 with Mr Ruttledge, for it was not until after the earlier Everest expeditions that the possibilities of these men were realised. The first travellers in Garhwal, like Traill and Graham, had only the local natives as porters, and these could only be relied upon below the snow-line, and not always then. Later their place was taken by European guides, an infinitely stronger substitute but a monstrously expensive one. Secondly, that the parties become successively smaller, ending with two Europeans and three Sherpas, for with a problem such as the approach to Nanda Devi the advantage lies obviously with the smaller party. I might add that in the last case smallness was dictated almost as much by motives of economy as of mobility.

When attempting a high mountain the party may have to be larger, but how much larger, if any, is a debatable point, and we still have what for convenience may be called 'Big-endians' and 'Little-endians' with us in the mountaineering world. A great deal must depend on the peak to be tackled, but there is no question which is the best for purposes of mountain exploration as opposed to an attack on single peak. It may be thought that the expedition to be described, comprising eight Europeans, was a successful reversion to type, but apart from the number of climbers (actually seven) there was nothing big about it and in the course of the narrative it will appear that there is every justification for classifying it as small.

CHAPTER THREE

Preliminaries

WHEN an expedition is on foot a certain amount of preliminary work, proportionate to the size, has to be done. For some the whole of the winter may be all too short for this, while, on the other hand, I think the preparations for our two-man show in 1934 could, if necessary, have been completed in one day. However, for those concerned with the organisation of something which intends calling itself an 'expedition', the winter is a busy time, and since it is the custom to be very reticent about plans, the organisers meet and go about their business with the air of conspirators. One reason for this is that it is annoying, or ought to be, to read in the Press of what an expedition is going to do before it has even started; nor is it any consolation to know that the information bears as much relation to fact as an official communiqué did during the War.

The notion of a British-American expedition to the Himalaya was first mooted in America, and plans were very far advanced before any climbers on this side were approached. The objective was Kangchenjunga, the third highest peak in the world, and preparations were on a correspondingly large scale. It was not until February 1936 that W. F. Loomis came to England to collect four climbers, more equipment, and, most important of all, to apply to the Indian Government for permission to go. This was cutting it rather fine, for no one, least of all a Government, likes to be bounced into making quick decisions, and if they are so bounced the decision is usually unfavourable. Fortunately we were warned that such might be the case and we selected Nanda Devi as a second string for our bow. Here, as has been explained, there were no political complications, and moreover, for this objective, we had the goodwill of all who had had anything to do with the mountain.

Meanwhile, Loomis, having drawn up two equipment lists, one of rather staggering dimensions for Kangchenjunga and a more modest one for Nanda Devi, returned to the States, leaving me to collect our Nanda Devi requirements and to await the result of our application before ordering the rest.

The British party was now complete and comprised, in addition to the writer, T. Graham Brown, F.R.S., an eminent physiologist, who has climbed in the Alps for many years and who was one of the party which in 1934 climbed Mt Foraker (17,300 ft.), a difficult peak in Alaska, for the first time; N. E. Odell, a geologist, who in 1924 climbed twice to Camp VI (27,000 ft.) on Everest, and who, in addition to the Alps, has climbed in Spitsbergen, Labrador, and the Rockies. And lastly Peter Lloyd, another experienced Alpine climber with many fine guideless ascents to his credit, and a brilliant rock climber.

How many of the original American members would go was still uncertain and much depended on what our objective was to be. It was decided that the party should assemble in India at the end of June, as this was the earliest by which most of them could arrive. This was of course unusually late, for at that time the monsoon would already be active, but according to the experience of two German expeditions this would be no disadvantage for Kangchenjunga. July and August were said to be the most favourable months; the reason given being that prior to the monsoon particularly severe winds were the rule. For Nanda Devi the advantages of climbing during the monsoon were not very obvious, indeed anyone who had seen the mountain and knew the conditions in the gorge would consider that our chance of success was in consequence materially diminished.

It was important that one of us should go out to India in advance to collect porters and arrange transport, so I decided to leave in March, hoping that before then we should know whether we were going to Sikkim or Garhwal, seven or eight hundred miles apart. But it was not to be, and when I sailed at the end of the month, accompanied by only part of the food and equipment, the oracle at the India Office had not yet spoken. For my part I sailed in the hope and expectation that we would be permitted to try Kangchenjunga, mainly because for me it would be new ground. But correspondence with the others gave me the impression that they were prepared for a refusal with a most Christian-like resignation; in fact, I suspected they might even welcome it. To them both mountains were new, but there was more freshness and originality about Garhwal and Nanda Devi. Kangchenjunga is seen by everyone who goes to Darjeeling, various parties have prowled around it, and it has received three full-dress assaults, and possibly to their minds it was getting a bit moth-eaten. And moreover, though both mountains gave us an equal chance of putting up a good show, there was vast inequality in the chance of getting to the top; Kangchenjunga is probably as formidable as Everest.

We tied up at Calcutta on a Monday, and a blacker day, in both senses, I have seldom experienced. The first letter to be opened informed me, with regret, that the British-American Himalayan Expedition would not be permitted to enter Sikkim to attempt Kangchenjunga; like most oracular pronouncements no reasons were given. It seemed a pity to have to accept this fiat without some protest, but there was nothing to be done except write a 'forlorn hope' of a letter asking for reconsideration and the reply to that was merely an official 'raspberry'.

I now went round to see the Customs, for the Indian Government very generously allow expeditonary equipment to come in free of duty. We had already written asking to be accorded this privilege, but unfortunately no instructions had yet been received from Simla, so nothing could be disembarked. Feeling a bit subdued, I thought it was time to enlist some local aid and began hunting up the few people I knew in Calcutta. All were either in England or Darjeeling and, feeling more like a pariah every minute, I slunk away to a hotel. On the way I noticed one or two people staring rather hard and, looking down, I discovered a dark blue sea of ink the size of a plate on an otherwise spotless white coat. At the hotel I handed it over to a boy telling him to get busy with milk, lemon juice, india-rubber, and any other ink-remover he knew. An hour later it was brought back, but not by the same boy, and one soon understood why, for the last state was worse than the first, the inky sea being now suffused over half the coat, and though the deep rich blue had paled to a watery grey the effect was still too bizarre for me to carry off.

My suitcase had now arrived, and in it another exciting discovery awaited me in the shape of the havoc wrought by an uncorked bottle of ink. Few things had escaped unmarked, and for the next few days I must have looked a bit mottled because in a temperature of 100 degrees colour is apt to run. But soon a wire from Simla allowed me to land and store the equipment and to escape from the Turkish bath of Calcutta in April to the freshness of Darjeeling.

The question was what to do, for now there was no preparatory work to be done in Sikkim, and the others would not arrive in India for nearly two months. There was the possibility of making a journey into the Basin to form a dump, but I had only a small amount of the food with me and, further, there was always the chance that bad weather might prevent the main body getting through and necessitate a change of plans—we should look uncommonly foolish if all our food was inside the Basin and we outside unable to reach it. Nor was it weather alone that might bring about this contingency; the first burst of the monsoon might break the slender thread of the route through the gorge by rock-falls or by washing off from the underlying slabs the thin covering of earth and grass upon which one depends mainly for holds. The most useful way of spending the time seemed to be to go into Sikkim with a few Sherpa porters to test their abilities, and then to take them up with me to Garhwal at the end of June.

For a stay of more than a fortnight in Sikkim a pass has to be obtained from Gangtok, the capital, and, being in a hurry, I was unwise enough to wire for this without explaining my intentions. The name must have aroused suspicion, for the reply was a request for full particulars of my intended journey; evidently I was regarded, figuratively, as the thin end of a British-American wedge. Telegrams were abandoned in favour of the typewriter and various other people were written to for assistance in this crisis. As a friend remarked, if the pen is mightier than the sword, the typewriter is mightier than the ice-axe. All Himalayan expeditions should carry one, even if it means leaving their ice-axes behind.

After a week's delay I started with four Sherpas, obtained only with difficulty. Even in England it had been clear that good porters would be hard to come by, and this was found to be true enough. The Everest expedition had of course skimmed the cream, a French expedition had taken thirty Sherpas to the Karakoram, and there was a small British party in Sikkim with another twenty. In consequence it was difficult to scrape together even four, and two of these were complete novices. On the eve of a long-delayed start a cable was received saying that Loomis would arrive in Bombay on May 21st, and asking if a journey into the Basin would be done before the monsoon began. A reply was sent advising him to wait and come out with the others, and then we made a double march from Darjeeling which put me well beyond the reach of any more cables.

After an all too brief but peaceful fortnight on the glaciers south of Kangchenjunga, I began worrying about what was happening and decided to return to Darjeeling, where we arrived on the 21st. Sure enough there was a letter to say that they had not been able to get in touch with Loomis to stop him and that he would be in Bombay on the 21st. Something had to be done, and now, contrary to previous notions, I thought it might as well be done in Garhwal. If we went straight there and moved fast we might be able to take some loads into the Basin and get back in time to organise the main party as well. By doing this we should have fewer loads to take in after the monsoon had started, and the party would therefore be less cumbersome; during this Sikkim trip the weather had been such as to remind me forcibly how unpleasant conditions might be in the monsoon, so that the fewer coolies we then had with us the better. I forgot how many wires I sent to Bombay, for I did not know where Loomis was and feared he might have already started for Sikkim. The American Consul, all the Travel Agencies, and the Shipping Line, seemed a wide enough net, and next day I had the satisfaction of knowing that I had caught him.

We arranged by wire to meet in Ranikhet on May 28th.

Some arrangement had now to be made about the Sherpas. Of the four, I had already decided that only one was worth a place on a serious show; this was Pasang Kikuli, who was quite outstanding. He had been to Everest in 1933 and carried to Camp V, where he got slightly frost-bitten hands, but having been treated with oxygen suffered no ill-effects. He had also been twice to Kangchenjunga and was on Nanga Parbat in 1934, where he was one of the five porters to get down alive from the highest camp, six porters and three Europeans dying on the mountain. It was strange that he should have been overlooked by the Everest and other parties, but their loss was our gain, and he turned out to be a treasure. When the time came for me to leave Darjeeling no more porters had come in, so I took two of the original four, one of course Pasang Kikuli, and left instructions for four more to be sent up later when there might be some more likely candidates available. Pasang's companion was one Pasang Phuta. A good average porter but with no outstanding qualities except a disarming grin. The Americans called him a bit 'dumb', and anyone who knew Pasang Phuta would not need to be told that this is a briefer way of saying that he was not highly endowed mentally.

CHAPTER FOUR

A Telegram to the Temple

RANIKHET, whither we were now bound, is a hill station in the United Provinces. From Kathgodam, thirty-six hours' journey by train from Calcutta, it is reached by a good road of fifty miles. Numerous buses ply on this fifty-mile stretch of road and competition is so fierce that the fare is only three shillings, luggage included, and perhaps an extra sixpence for the doubtful privilege of sitting next to the driver.

Ranikhet is 6000ft. above sea level, and the relief on reaching it and breathing the pine-scented air, after a journey by rail through the sweltering plains, has to be felt to be believed. On many days of the year this feeling of having left hell and arrived somewhere near heaven is intensified by the sight of a hundred and more miles of snow peaks: distant, it is true, but near enough to stagger by their height and fascinate by their purity. At this time of year though, before the monsoon, they are seldom seen to advantage, owing to the dust haze which drifts up from the plains.

Apart from the view there are no distractions for the casual visitor to Ranikhet, and this was as well, because we had no time to waste. We had to get up the Rishi gorge, into the Basin if possible, and I had decided that we must be back by June 25th, in order that we could have things well in hand before the others arrived. Normally, it would take eighteen days to get there, not allowing for any delay *en route*, and in this case delay was almost inevitable. The food and equipment which I had brought out was still on the way up from Calcutta by goods train and none of the American consignments had yet arrived, so that the only loads we could take were coolie food, which could be bought locally; that is rice, atta (wheat flour), and satu, for feeding the local coolies on the way in and the Sherpas while on the mountain. Satu is the same thing as the Tibetan tsumpa—barley, or wheat, which has been parched and then ground into meal. It has one great advantage in that it needs little or no cooking; you can put it in tea and make it into a thick paste, or moisten it very slightly with water and mould it into a cake; it can even be eaten dry, but that is not a method I can honestly recommend. It also makes an excellent porridge, and, if there is a little milk to help it down, tastes more like food than some of the shavings and sawdust sold as cereals. This food could be bought at Joshimath, nine marches from Ranikhet, so there was no need to take any coolies until Joshimath was reached. These men I proposed getting from Mana, a little village in the extreme north-west of Garhwal near the Tibet border. It was only twenty-one miles from Joshimath, and men from there had been up the Rishi with Shipton and me in 1934, and their stoutness and rock-climbing ability were beyond all question.

If delay was to be avoided these arrangements had to be made before we left Ranikhet, because it would take time to collect 900 lb. of food and to get the men down from Mana to Joshimath. Fortunately this could be done. There is a telegraph line to Joshimath, and a wire and a money order to a man in the bazaar there set on foot the collecting of the food. There remained the problem of the porters. Mana is twenty-one miles from Joshimath, and to go up there, find the men, and return would take a good three days. But the problem was solved in a rather unlikely way by invoking the aid of the priesthood.

The telegraph line does not stop at Joshimath but follows the Pilgrim Road up to Badrinath, which is only three miles short of Mana. Of Badrinath, the Mecca for fifty thousand Hindu pilgrims, something has already been said. It consists of a temple, a number of pilgrim rest-houses, and shops, situated in an open valley on the right bank of the Alaknanda river, only twenty-five miles below the Mana Pass into Tibet. The fall of Bhasadura, one of the sacred sources, where 'the Ganges falls like the thread of a Lotus flower', is not far away, and there are bathing pools in the river, and thermal springs, which are all efficacious in cleansing believers of past offences.

The temple, however, is the centre around which the life of Badrinath revolves during the short pilgrim season between May and October. Badrinath is 10,280 ft. above the sea, and during the winter snow lies everywhere, the temple is closed, and the officials, shopkeepers and others migrate to a less inhospitable clime. The temple is close to the river. It has a very modern appearance, but the foundation dates from the eighth century and the first building is said to have been erected by Sankara Acharya, the great Hindu reformer. This building and several subsequent ones are believed to have been destroyed by avalanches but, considering its situation, this is difficult to understand unless great changes have taken place in the formation of the surrounding country. The idol in the main temple is of black stone, stands about three feet high and is clothed with rich brocade, and wears a tiara of gold in which is a large diamond. The dresses and ornaments are reputed to be worth at least ten thousand rupees. The idol is served daily with two meals, and after a decent interval has elapsed the food is distributed amongst the pilgrims, many of whom are too poor to feed themselves. Offerings are of course made by the pilgrims in cash, kind, or ornaments, according to their means; strict accounts are kept by the treasurers, and the business affairs of the temple are in the hands of a secretary. Other members of the temporal council for the affairs of the Badrinath temple are the Bhotias of Mana, so that this village is intimately connected with its larger neighbour.

At the height of the pilgrim season the scene in the one narrow street of Badrinath brings back memories of *Kim*. Wealthy babus in 'jhampans', or dandies, carried by four sweating coolies, the more economically minded in long cylindrical baskets carried by only one; old men and women of all classes arriving on foot travel-stained and weary, clutching their pilgrim's staff; all welcomed by a roll of drums nicely proportioned in length and loudness to the probable state of the pilgrim's purse; naked fakirs smeared with ashes, long-haired saddhus, blind and deformed beggars thrusting their wooden bowls under the nose of every shopkeeper in the bazaar, getting here a little flour or a handful of rice, there some spices or salt, and nowhere a refusal; all these jostle each other in the narrow stone-flagged street between the open-fronted shops where yak-tails and Manchester cottons, musk and cheap photographs lie huddled together; and over all, aloof, watchful, stand the snows of Himachal where the gods live.

To find amongst all this a Post and Telegraph Office savours of banality if not impropriety, but to us it proved invaluable. In 1934 Shipton and I had twice visited Badrinath and made the acquaintance of the Rawal or Priest of the temple (to give him his full title, His Holiness the Rawal Pandit Basudeva Numbudri), a high-caste Brahman from Southern India. This custom of appointing a Brahman from the south as the Rawal of a temple in the northernmost confines of India dates back to about A.D. 800, when the great Hindu reformer, Sankara Acharya, drove out encroaching Bhuddism from Garhwal and took measures, of which this was one, to maintain the purity of the restored religion. It was this same Sankara who preached the efficacy of the pilgrimage to the holy places of the Himalaya. I was now reminded of this friend in need and felt confident that a wire to him, asking for a dozen Mana men to be sent to Joshimath on June 6th, would be all that was needed.

One more day was spent in Ranikhet having a big tarpaulin made up, buying a few necessities, and arranging for a bus. In the course of the day a reply came from Joshimath assuring us that the food would be ready. None of our equipment had yet arrived, a fact which made it the more easy to travel as light as we intended. My sleeping bag, which had an inner and outer lining, would do for both of us, the tarpaulin would cover the food, the two Sherpas, and ourselves, while extra clothing was not wanted as we would not be going above 14,000 ft.

So on May 30th, two days after arriving, we started out, the party consisting of two Sherpas, a 10 lb. Cheddar cheese, and ourselves. The cheese was one out of a case of six which I had luckily brought up from Calcutta in my own compartment to spare them the prolonged suffering of a ten-day journey by goods train in the hot weather.

From Ranikhet you can get a flying start in a bus, and this dropped us fifty miles away at a place called Garul, where the road ended, by half-past ten in the morning. The height of this place is only 3000 ft., and Gwaldam, where we stopped for the night, is over 3000 ft. higher and ten miles away. It was fairly cool, thanks to a dust cloud which hid the sun, but otherwise this march can be a trying one. At Gwaldam a bungalow welcomes the traveller. That and a few unhappy looking tea bushes are the only remaining evidence of a once flourishing tea estate. It rained hard in the night, but next day we were permitted to remain dry until two o'clock, when it began again with some violence. A fair interval persuaded us to push on from the village where we were sheltering to the next stream, and there we got our tarpaulin rigged just before another deluge began. It was open at both ends, and when the four of us were lying cheek by jowl there was a foot or two to spare at each end—on fine nights the outer berth was very desirable. Rain in Garhwal may be heavy, but usually it seems to be unaccompanied by wind and the tarpaulin kept us dry very effectively.

When reading accounts of travel in Garhwal the peculiar nature of the country should be borne in mind. The whole country is an intricate tangle of valleys and ridges with their attendant ravines and spurs, which, even in the foothills, are all on a scale undreamt of in this country. The stages of a march may seem short, but involving, as most of them do, a rise of 3000 ft. or more and an equally great descent, they are quite long enough. It is possible to be in a valley not more than 3000 ft. above the sea, the home of a vegetation which is almost tropical, and at the same time to be within fifteen miles of snow-clad peaks 20,000 ft. high.

The following story seems to me to provide as apt an illustration of the country now as it did then. 'In the reign of Akbar, that prince demanded of the Raja of Srinagar (the ancient capital of Garhwal) an account of the revenues of his raj and a chart of his country. The Raja being then at court, repaired to the presence the following day and in obedience to the commands of the king presented a true statement of his finances and a chart of his country by introducing a lean camel and saying: "This is a faithful picture of the territory I possess—up and down and very poor." The king smiled at the ingenuity of the thought and told him that from the revenues of a country produced with so much labour and in amount so small, he had nothing to demand.' It was over the humps and hollows of the camel's back that we had now to pass.

There are three possible routes from Ranikhet to Joshimath and we took the most easterly, which is the one generally used and one which has been frequently described. It is supposedly the shortest, but that is doubtful, for it certainly involves more climbing than the other two. There are three big valleys between Garul and Joshimath, all running from east to west directly across the route; the valley of the Pindar river which comes from the south of Nanda Kot, the Nandakini from the slopes of Trisul, and the Bireh Ganga from Nanda Ghunti; and naturally the farther east and the nearer the mountains these are crossed, the higher are the intervening ridges.

The most westerly route is the Pilgrim Road, which avoids crossing any of these valleys by following the main valley of the Alaknanda. It is usually shunned by expeditions, at any rate on the outward journey, on account of the risk of picking up dysentery, cholera, or malaria; curiously enough these diseases seem to lose their terrors when the expedition is on the way home. It is provided with bungalows at every stage and a variety of food can be bought, which perhaps explains the curious fact noted above; whereas on the route we took there is only one bungalow and no food. We had brought from Ranikhet for our own use rice, lentils, and flour, sufficient to last until Joshimath, but the Sherpas, expecting to be able to buy at every village, had brought very little. For most of the way all they could get was barley flour, and it became quite pathetic to hear them asking, hopefully but vainly, at every house they passed for wheat flour.

Eggs and milk were our desideratum, but this was a much fonder hope than that entertained by the Sherpas for their atta. The absence of eggs is understandable because to Hindus hens are unclean and are seldom kept, for in some ways the Garhwali is a very orthodox Hindu. Sometimes one comes across ex-soldiers who have served the British Raj in the Garhwal Rifles who have so far lost caste that they are sufficiently abandoned to keep hens. The rarity with which milk could be got is less easily explained. Every village possessed livestock in abundance, cows, water buffalo, goats; and one could not help thinking that it was the will to help which was lacking, not the ability.

This wet night in a forest glade was a dismal one owing to a new brand of midges, new at least to me. An ordinary midge observes regular hours and knocks off as soon as darkness sets in, but here they carried on business all night long without intermission—if you left your head out you were driven frantic, and suffocated if you put it inside the sleeping bag.

Next day we crossed a pass on the ridge between the Pindar and Nandakini valleys at about 10,000 ft. and dropped down through oak and rhododendron forest and grassy alps to Kanol. It was just too late in the year to see the rhododendrons in flower, which are at their best early in May; they are found between 8000 and 10,000 ft., and this route is particularly rich in this gorgeous kind of forest—gorgeous when in flower, but at other seasons drab and grey. It rained again all the afternoon, and an inside that was far from well added to my gloom; but apart from that we had good reason to be pleased because we were already a day ahead of time. It required a desperate effort next day to retain this lead, for the usual bridge over the Nandakini had gone, and a long detour, five miles up stream and five down again, had to be made. Then we got into trouble crossing a smaller river, where the bridge consisted of the usual two pine logs and flat stones in between. Those with experience are careful to stick to the logs, but Loomis trusted to the stones, which naturally slipped through and in he went, losing both topee and ice-axe. Pasang Kikuli recaptured the topee after an exciting race down stream, and we wasted half an hour at the pool below the bridge while Loomis stripped, tied on the climbing rope, and searched the bottom for the axe. The loss of this axe led to the loss of another, nor was the topee destined to live much longer.

We finally made the appointed stage late that evening, wet, weary, and cold, the result of a very violent hailstorm which we had encountered. In my infirm state I was glad to find shelter in a sort of rest-house; it had a mud floor and no furniture, but a roof and an excellent fireplace made up for these deficiencies.

The next obstacle was the Bireh Ganga, across which we were relieved to find there was still a bridge albeit with little to spare between it and the surging water. I began to wonder how we would fare six weeks later when the river would certainly be very much higher. Our camp that night was amongst some large erratic boulders near the village of Kaliaghat, and a convenient rock overhang preserved our fire from what was now the inevitable afternoon rain. It seemed that the monsoon had already broken, but we talked ourselves into believing that this was merely the 'chota Barsat', the little rains, which are supposed to precede the monsoon proper.

The last and highest ridge was yet to be crossed, that between the Bireh Ganga and the Alaknanda valley in which lies Joshimath itself. The way over this ridge is by the well-known Kuari Pass, 12,400 ft., which is usually crossed on the second day's march from Kaliaghat. We, however, put on steam and reached Dekwani, the camping place at the foot of the Pass, by midday, and went up and over in the afternoon.

Dekwani is a grazing ground just above the tree-line and 1000 ft. below the Pass, and that day there must have been at least a thousand sheep and goats present. It lies on a route which is much used by sheep and goat transport into Tibet. This route follows the Dhauli valley down from the Niti Pass (16,600 ft.) and, leaving the valley short of Joshimath, crosses the Kuari Pass and so reaches the southern valleys of Garhwal. It is a route favourable to such a form of transport because it is high and cool, there is plenty of grass, and few villages. Grain is the usual commodity carried going up to Tibet and salt and borax on the return. A sheep can carry about 20 lb. and a big goat 30 lb., so that a flock of one hundred, which is a small one, can shift a ton or more. The saddle bags are made of coarse wool or hemp strengthened with leather, and are carefully balanced on the back and secured by what corresponds to a breastplate and a crupper; there is no girth. When halted the saddle bags are stacked into a high wall which affords some shelter to the drovers.

We halted at Dekwani to have some food and pass the time of day with the sheep drovers. They were inclined to be surly and took time to thaw out; in fact when the Sherpas borrowed their fire to boil some water they spat ostentatiously and muttered imprecations. A little tobacco soon mollified them, for these Bhotias are inveterate smokers, smoking stuff which looks for all the world like plum pudding, and smoking charcoal rather than nothing at all.

From Dekwani we were on top of the Pass in fifty minutes, but of the glorious view which often rewards the early morning traveller there was no sign. Lowering clouds and mist veiled the horizon in all directions and when, an hour later, we camped below the tree-line these burst in furious squalls of wind and rain. In the evening when the rain stopped we were able to appreciate the best camping ground we had yet had. A smooth flat carpet of grass to lie on, a sparkling brook at our feet, unlimited firewood for the gathering, and at our backs the shelter of a mighty cedar. As if that was not enough, the clouds lifted, and for a moment, before darkness fell, the great bulk of Hathi Parbat, the 'Elephant Mountain', loomed up across the valley, and far to the northwest the shapely white cone of Nilkanta seemed to stand alone in a darkening sky.

Next day we reached Joshimath, a day in advance of the time appointed for the Mana men. Of these there was no sign—and the telegraph line to Badrinath was broken.

CHAPTER FIVE

The Rishi Gorge and Back Again

JOSHIMATH is a village of some importance on the Pilgrim Road to Badrinath and two marches short of that place. It is 6000 ft. above sea level and 1500 ft. above the confluence of the Alaknanda and Dhauli rivers. At the junction is the temple, so often seen at the place where two rivers meet, built on a tongue of rock between the two. This is known as the 'prayag', and the shrine and the few huts are called Vishnuprayag. There are five such 'prayags' at the five sacred confluences of the Alaknanda. The river here, and for a few miles up, is called the Vishnuganga. A flight of stone steps leads down to the water, which is cold, swift, and deep, and in it the pilgrims bathe ceremonially, hanging to chains and ringbolts to avoid being carried away. Even with this precaution several lives are said to be lost every year. The long zigzag path from Vishnuprayag to Joshimath is cut into steps faced with stones.

The temple, or rather collection of temples, is built round a courtyard and is of great antiquity. Some of them are in a state of dilapidation owing, it is said, to an earthquake, but the temples of Vishnu, Ganesh, the Sun, Navadevi, and Narsinha are in fair preservation.

The idol of Vishnu is of black stone, well carved, and about seven feet high. That of Narsinha is reputed to have an arm which diminishes daily, and when it falls off the road to Badrinath will be closed by a landslip and a new temple will be erected at Tapoban, seven miles up the Dhauli valley from Joshimath. The legend giving rise to this forecast is that Vishnu, in his man-lion incarnation of Narsinha, visited the palace of an early Raja of this region and asked the wife of the absent prince for food. Having partaken he lay down on the bed of the Raja, who found him there on his return from the chase and struck him on the arm with his sword. Instead of blood, milk flowed from the wound, and the startled Raja, sensing that he must have struck a god, asked that his crime might be punished. The deity disclosed himself, and having ordained that the Raja must leave the pleasant vale of Joshimath, added: 'Remember that this wound which thou hast given me shall also be seen on the image in thy temple, and when that image shall fall to pieces and the hand shall no more remain, thy house shall fall to ruin and thy dynasty shall disappear from amongst the princes of the world.'

In one of the Hindu writings is the following:

> The road to Badri never will be closed
> The while at Joshimath Vishnu doth remain;
> But straightway when the god shall cease to dwell,
> The path to Badri will be shut to men.

There is a dâk bungalow at Joshimath for the use of travellers and the Rawal of Badrinath has a large house here in which he resides during the winter months. The streets are paved with stone flags and the houses are neatly built with squared stone and roofed with shingles or heavy slates; they are usually of two storeys. The ground floor being devoted to a store or shop while the family live above. Traders, cultivators, and temple officials make up the population of about five hundred.

There are two bazaars, where all native foods can be bought; the Sherpas at last got all the atta they wanted and we were able to replenish our stock of sugar, rice, and lentils, and make ourselves sick on the local sweetmeats, which are very good indeed. There were far too many flies about for the fastidious, but, in Garhwal, if you eat only what the flies have not touched then you go hungry. The flies are no doubt worse in Joshimath and along the Pilgrim Road generally, but it would not be right to ascribe this wholly to the pilgrims and their small regard for sanitary rules. All the villages of Garhwal, even up to 7000 and 8000 ft., are plagued with flies, but as a good part of the Pilgrim Road lies in a comparatively low and hot valley they are naturally more numerous in villages on the Road. Chamoli, for example, twenty-five miles below Joshimath, is only 3000 ft. above the sea.

Malaria, dysentery, and cholera, though not exactly rife, are nevertheless prevalent along this Road in the summer. A great deal has been done by the Government to combat this by piping down a clean water supply to the villages, enforcing sanitary rules, and placing a Medical Officer in charge of the Road. Cholera was active in Joshimath and neighbouring villages when we returned there a fortnight later and the Medical Officer, who was then in Joshimath, told us how difficult it was to control, particularly in the outlying and more inaccessible villages to which it sometimes spreads. Bodies are left unburied by the banks of streams which carry infection to lower villages, and the terrified inhabitants migrate, panic-stricken, to other places, taking the infection with them. Corpses are left to rot in the houses and the sick lie untended.

The pilgrim season was in full swing and Joshimath was alive with devotees of all ages and all classes, men and women, rich and poor. To an outsider their demeanour gave the impression that this pilgrimage was more of a disagreeable duty than a pleasure, that the toil and hardships of the road were supported with resignation rather than accepted joyfully as a means of grace—incidents on the road to heaven. But this downcast air may rightly be attributed to the awe and terror which most must feel in the presence of such strange and prodigious manifestations of the power of the gods. Savage crags, roaring torrents, rock-bound valleys, hillsides scarred and gashed with terrific landslides, and beyond all the stern and implacable snows—all these must be overwhelming to men whose lives have been passed on the smug and fertile plains, by sluggish and placid rivers, with no hill in sight higher than the village dunghill.

Nor is it remarkable that they should attribute the faintness felt in the rarefied air of Badrinath and Kedarnath to the influence of superhuman powers; or believe that the snow wreaths blowing off the Kedarnath peak are the smoke of sacrifice made by one of Siva's favoured followers, or that the snow banner flying on Nanda Devi is from the kitchen of the goddess herself.

The accomplishment of such a journey by such men must be a tremendous fact in their lives, something to remember when all else has faded. To reach the temple alone is a sign of divine favour, for the gods turn back those with whom they are displeased. The daily exercise, the months of frugal living, the hill air, the sacrifice of time and money, all these must play no small part in the moral and physical regeneration of the pilgrims; and if this salutary discipline of mind and body were to be enjoyed there would perhaps be the less merit. For the mountaineer, it is to be feared, though he penetrate to the ultimate *sanctum sanctorum* of the gods, there is, like the award of the Garter, 'no damned merit about it'—his enjoyment is too palpable.

By midday of June 6th the telegraph line to Badrinath was working and an exchange of telegrams brought the good news that the porters would be down next day. Meantime our 900 lb. of food was ready, half here and half at another village, so that all was set for a start on the 8th, and only a day had been lost. In the perverse way the weather sometimes has, both of these days spent sitting idle in Joshimath were gloriously fine.

Fourteen men from Mana arrived in the evening, among whom were three who had accompanied us in 1934, and on the 8th we did a short march to Tapoban, where the balance of the food was collected and three more local porters enlisted. One of these men, hailing from Bompa, a village higher up the Dhauli, was an amusing character. His name was Kalu and he had chits from previous expeditions in which he appeared to have distinguished himself by going high on Trisul. He was a shameless cadger with an ingratiating manner, and a habit of placing both palms of his hands together as if in prayer whenever he spoke to you. As a mountaineer he thought no small beer of himself, particularly if the conversation should turn to Trisul as it always did if he was taking part in it, and then he would slap his chest like a gorilla, and cry out in a loud voice what great feats Kalu had performed and what greater he was about to do. For all that he worked so well on this trip that at the end I placed too much faith in him and was let down.

At Tapoban we had a fortunate meeting with two British officers out on a shooting trip, who invited us to use their camping ground and join their mess, an invitation we were not slow to accept, as I knew from previous experience that on these shooting trips the doctrine of 'living on the country' is not

carried to extreme lengths. But for this chance meeting and the existence of a
hot spring, Tapoban would have left nothing but evil memories. The flies
were unusually fierce, and as soon as they stopped work at dusk the midges
began, and at dawn the reverse process took place.

The hot spring I mentioned is up a little side valley a couple of hundred
yards from the road. There is a stone tank about ten feet square and three feet
deep, into which gushes a stream of water at a temperature of about 90
degrees. The water is clear and sparkling, and has no taste. Close by is a
shrine and a hut for its guardian, an emaciated hermit whose hair reached
almost to the ground. On this occasion he was absent and we could lie in the
bath at ease, increasing the pleasure by running a few yards to a brook where
the water was as cold as the bath was hot, and smelt deliciously of wild mint.

A more detailed description of our route may be left for the moment;
sufficient to say that after one more vile night of midges in the warm valley we
began the climb to the 14,000 ft. pass where flies and midges ceased from
troubling. On our way up we met a flock of sheep, and the shepherd was
understood to say that one of his sheep had fallen over a cliff and it was ours
for the carrying. The Mana men soon found it, skinned it, and went on their
way rejoicing; it certainly looked fresh enough, but there was suspiciously
little sign of it having suffered a fall. In camp that night when Loomis and I
had, after some argument, come to a decision about the respective merits of
grilled chops and boiled neck, the inquest was resumed, and we were calmly
informed that the sheep had died through eating a poisonous plant. Somehow
or other mutton chops ceased to allure and we generously gave our share to
the Sherpas. I should hesitate to accuse them of using this stratagem to bring
about such a desirable result, but they showed no reluctance to accept
fortune's gift and suffered not the slightest ill-effect.

We crossed the pass, now clear of snow, and got down to the Durashi
grazing alp. There were no sheep there and we had the place to ourselves, the
Mana men finding shelter in some caves, ourselves under the tarpaulin, and
the Sherpas in a stone hut used by shepherds. It required a certain lack of
imagination to sleep in this hut, because the roof of enormously heavy stones
was only supported by some singularly inadequate pieces of wood, one of
which was already cracked.

We woke to a wet morning and did not leave till nine o'clock, though this
was not much later than usual, for the Mana men are very independent and
dislike being hurried. After a leisurely breakfast, the pipe (they had only one)
would be passed round several times before they even thought of hinting at a
readiness to begin packing up, and unless there was some urgent reason for an
early start it was useless to try and hurry them. It was the same on the march;
they knew how far they were going and took their own time getting there,
sitting down whenever they felt the need for a pipe, which was frequently, and
remaining there till all had smoked enough.

The pipe has a ritual of its own: it is a water pipe with a stem about two feet
long which is carried by one man; another carries the bowl, a clay affair the
size of a jam dish; the bamboo mouthpiece, also two feet long, is carried by a
third, the tobacco by a fourth, and the flint and steel by a fifth. If there is any

straggling on the march it is some time before the whole is assembled and yet longer before the thing is fairly alight; unless there happens to be a fire handy, when they simply put a burning brand on top of the bowl and leave it there. These dilatory habits are somewhat exasperating, but the men are withal so active and sturdy and reliable that it is impossible to find fault, and if a special effort is required they can and will move quicker than most. Nor is there ever any trouble about making up their loads and deciding who will carry what, a blessing which only those who have travelled with African porters can really appreciate. In their case this unenviable task of apportioning loads usually begins with a free fight and ends with the abandonment of the heaviest load.

Between Durashi and the lower grazing alp of Dibrugheta lies an easy grass pass involving an ascent of 1000 ft. from Durashi and a descent of 3000 ft. to Dibrugheta. The ridge which is crossed by this pass was, by Dr Longstaff, aptly named 'The Curtain'; away from the pass towards the Rishi the ridge rises and the grass slope changes to enormous slabs of smooth, grey rock, which jut right out to the river and completely hide the lower part of the gorge, like the fire curtain on some vast stage.

We sat for some time on the ridge waiting in vain for a view up the gorge to Nanda Devi. Then the Mana men, having had their smoke, took it into their heads to build two enormous cairns and to dedicate them to Loomis and myself, first asking our names, which the scholar amongst them then wrote in Urdu on a stone with a piece of charcoal. This cairn building and stone balancing is the national pastime amongst Tibetans and kindred people such as Sherpas, who are likewise Bhuddists, and these Bhotias who, though nominally Hindus, possibly came from Tibet originally and have maintained a connection with that country ever since. They will run up a noble cairn out of the most unlikely material in a very short time, and crown the whole with stones of diminishing size, skilfully balanced, one on top of the other.

Meanwhile it had started raining again, but the cairns had to be finished off, and in no slovenly manner either, before we were allowed to go on. Rain on the march was to be particularly dreaded at this time, because although the flour and rice were put up in Willesden canvas bags these would not stand a prolonged soaking, and the food was going to be left for six weeks or more before being eaten.

At Dibrugheta we were once more down among birch and pine forest and the Mana men made themselves elaborate huts roofed with birch bark. This invaluable material has many uses. We have all heard of birch-bark canoes, here we were using it for thatching, and it was strongly recommended to me by a former traveller in these parts as a substitute for tobacco, though after trying it I decided that this was a joke in rather bad taste. The Mana men were full of beans this evening, and when they had finished their meal the lads amongst them started throwing lighted brands on the roof of each other's huts, and the whole mob roared with delight when someone's hut was burnt down.

The next camp beyond Dibrugheta is the Cave Camp and here all hands can be accommodated in caves. That is true at least of a party of reasonable size such as ours was then, but it puzzled us to know what we should do when the main body of fifty or more came, because of tent sites there were none. Loomis and I slept that night on a mattress of bags of food to escape the adamantine hardness of the cave floor.

We made the first small food dump here where it was dry, and where it was beyond the reach of those in the villages who might be curious to know what we had done with so much food. It was now the 13th and it was time to think of turning back. But things were going well, the farther we got the food the better, and above all I wanted to have a look at the difficult part of the gorge to see if the route would still 'go'. It was conceivable that since 1934 a fall of rock or the disappearance of some grass or trees from the cliff faces would have made the gorge impassable. One of the charms of the route then discovered was the weakness of some of the links in it and the absence of any alternatives. We therefore decided to go on for another three days, long enough to take us beyond all difficulties and to the threshold of the Promised Land.

Our march that day took us to what had been our base camp in 1934, a pleasant camp under a big rock overhang on the south side of the Rishi Ganga, which can be crossed here by a natural bridge. Before dropping down to the crossing of the Rishi, the glacier-fed torrent of the Rhamani, coming down from the north, had to be crossed. At this time of year it was not a serious obstacle, but for all that it was no place to cross without the support of the third leg which an ice-axe provides. Accordingly as soon as I had crossed, instead of waiting for the rope, I foolishly threw my axe back for Loomis, whose own axe, it will be remembered, had been lost. The bank on that side was steep and high and, instead of landing on top, the axe hit a boulder and bounced back into the river. Loomis made one unavailing grab and then jumped into the river after it, and the net results of two pieces of foolishness was the loss of his topee and my ice-axe.

After carrying an axe for some days one feels lost at first without it, but in the Rishi, where it is better to have both hands available rather than one hand and an axe, it was really more of a hindrance than a help. The loss of the topee might have been serious for anyone with a sensitive skull, but none of us found such things necessary in Garhwal, which is outside the tropics and in about the same latitude as Cairo.

The natural bridge over the Rishi, which is formed by an enormous boulder, caused some delay. All loads had to be lowered down to it and on the boulder itself a rope was necessary because the branches, which in 1934 we had placed there as ladders, had all gone. However, all got safely over and there we were only two days from the Basin, with ten loads of food, and a dry overhang under which to sleep.

From this point the way lies straight up the south wall of the gorge to a height of about 1500 ft. above the river, and from there pursues a horizontal or slightly downwards course—what we call a traverse. The first 400 or 500 ft. out of the river bed are steep and exposed, and the climber is disquietingly dependent on branches of trees and tufts of grass for his safety. No further difficulty is encountered until the beginning of the traverse. From a grass terrace a rock chimney leads up to what we called the 'Slabs', smooth rock sloping upwards at such an angle, that with a load on, it is difficult to stand up with any confidence. These slabs form the floor of a wide gully, which just below here plunges down to the Rishi at a much steeper angle. Above the slabs is a rock wall which can be climbed on the left by men without loads, and these can then be hauled directly up the wall.

We arrived at this place and found the slabs dry, and Loomis and I, who were in rubbers and had only moderate loads, got up without a rope. The Mana men go barefoot and most of them climb like cats, but here only a few of them, and neither of the Sherpas, despised the aid of the rope. Loads were dumped and some of us climbed to the top of the wall and began hauling while the others remained below to tie on. It is a slow job at the best, and I climbed down again to hasten matters, as I wanted to get finished before the rain started; we had a rope 120 ft. long so that both ends could be used—tying a load on one end while the other was being hauled up. To superintend this I was standing on a narrow ledge about twenty feet above the floor of the gully and, thick-headedly enough, almost under the rope. Things then happened quickly. Gazing at an ascending load I was petrified to see a large flake of rock, probably loosened by the rope, sliding down the wall straight for me. Whether it hit me, or whether I stepped back to avoid it, is only of academic interest because the result was the same, and next instant I was falling twenty feet on to the slabs, head first and face to the wall, for I distinctly remember seeing it go past. Hitting the slabs I rolled for a bit and then luckily came to rest before completing the 1400-odd feet into the river.

In a minute or two I was able to sit up and take notice, and having told the load-haulers to get on with it, crawled up the slabs to a more secure place and assessed the damage. A sprained shoulder and thumb, a bruised thigh and a cracked rib, and a lot of skin missing was the sum total. None were serious, and it might have been much worse; in which case, I thought, the last lines of a little verse about the man who tried to hurry the East would not have been inapplicable: 'And the end of the fight is a tombstone white with the name of the late deceased, and this epitaph drear, "A fool lies here who tried to hurry the East."'

It was necessary to get moving before stiffness made this impossible, so with a rope on and some men shoving behind, I was got up to the top of the wall, and when the loads were all up we started for Halfway Camp, which was still a mile distant.

Next day Loomis went on with the men and dumped all the remaining loads at Pisgah Camp within sight of the Sanctuary, and returned the same day to Halfway Camp. I lay in camp and felt sorry for myself, wondering how I was to get back, for the slightest movement was difficult, tomorrow was the 17th, and we were due in Ranikhet on the 25th.

With Pasang Kikuli assisting I started very early next morning, in advance of the others, who caught us up at the 'Slabs'. These were difficult for me because both arms were useless, but the Mana men were very solicitous and skilful and before midday we reached the overhang by the Rishi. After an hour's rest we pushed on over the bridge, which had now been made easier by placing trees there, and Cave Camp was reached the same day.

Another double march followed, Kalu and the Mana headman taking care of me. The 3000 ft. climb up to the 'Curtain' ridge from Dibrugheta was enlivened by a violent hail storm and we were so perished with cold that, on arrival at Durashi, Loomis and I shared the stone hut with the Sherpas, caring little whether the roof fell in or not. Still marching double stages we crossed the pass and got down to flies and the Dhauli valley next day, and on the 20th reached Joshimath, not omitting to wallow for an hour in the hot spring at Tapoban in the hope that it would ease my battered limbs, which, when they realised they were not likely to get any rest, began to respond to this 'healing by faith' treatment.

Here we paid off the Mana men, giving them a liberal tip at which they grumbled loudly for, unlike the Sherpas who do this sort of work more for its own sake than for the money, they are out for all they can get and value their services highly. For all their complaining, they let it be understood that they would be willing to come with us again next month, despite our illiberal notions about baksheesh. Kalu had already engaged himself, and had undertaken the collection of another ten loads of coolie food, assuring me that I could rely on him to have it ready waiting for us, an assurance I was foolish enough to accept.

Now that the Mana men had gone, Loomis and I had no one to carry our loads, and for me it was painful enough to get along at all, without having to carry a load. We combed the bazaar for a coolie, but at ten o'clock gave it up and left in pouring rain and in a very sour mood. It was late evening before we camped amongst the pines not far below our old camp site. On the 22nd we crossed the Kuari, went on through Kaliaghat and down to the Bireh Ganga. The bridge was down but a repair gang were at work on it and, after a short wait, two logs were got into a sufficiently stable position to cross with the aid of a rope. Spray was dashing over the logs and Pasang Phuta was rash enough to try it in rubber shoes, slipped on the wet wood, and hung suspended with his load in the water and his head not far off it. He was soon rescued from this undignified and perilous position and we pushed on and camped in the gathering dark some way above the river.

We seemed to be getting into a defiant sort of mood and evinced a growing determination to reach Ranikhet in five days from Joshimath, cost what effort it might. Next day we crossed the ridge, got down to the Ramni bungalow at midday and, encouraged by hearing that the bridge on the direct route was repaired, crossed the Nandakini and trudged the 2000 ft. up to Kanol, camping at six o'clock in a field.

I was rapidly recovering under this treatment, but Loomis was not well; yet on the following day we eclipsed all previous efforts and covered what are normally three stages, reaching the Gwaldam bungalow at half-past seven at night. We learnt that the Ranikhet bus left Garul at five in the morning, and we toyed with the idea of leaving Gwaldam again in the small hours to catch it. But in the night there was tremendous rain and it was so jolly sitting once more in a chair with a roof over our heads and a fire at our feet that we consigned this particular bus to the devil and strolled down to Garul like gentlemen late in the forenoon. By paying rather more than the usual fare we persuaded another bus to start and got back to Ranikhet on the evening of the 25th, twenty-eight days after leaving it.

CHAPTER SIX

'Scrapping and Bagging'

THANKS to the goodwill of the Forest Service we had been given the use of the Ranikhet Forest Bungalow, and here we installed ourselves to begin work and to await the arrival of the others. It is a big building of eight rooms, with a wide verandah running round two sides which made an ideal place for the reception of the flood of cases which was about to engulf us. Furthermore, it is one of the most pleasantly situated bungalows in Ranikhet and commands a complete panorama of the snows from the Kedarnath peaks in the west to Nepal in the east.

We were told that the weather had been atrocious ever since we left, the monsoon having set in exceptionally early. Comparing notes it seemed that the weather had been less severe where we were, farther north, and personally I did not consider monsoon conditions really established in the north until we returned to Joshimath on the 20th. However, there was no doubt about it then, for it rained all the way back and, except for a short break, continued to rain throughout our stay in Ranikhet; so much so that the later arrivals never got a glimpse of a mountain until we reached the Kuari Pass. During this brief fine spell Loomis and I, and Arthur Emmons, the second of the American contingent to arrive, had some clear views of the Range. The side of Nanda Devi which can be seen from Ranikhet is that by which our attempt was to be made, and after studying it through glasses and telescope we could only express a pious hope that it was not so bad as it looked.

Emmons, who joined us on the 28th, had done some climbing in Alaska and was one of the party which in 1932 climbed Minya Gonkar (24,900 ft.), a peak in the south-west of China near the Tibet border. While at the highest camp on this mountain Emmons had been severely frost-bitten in both feet, which he was fortunate not to lose altogether. He was still able to climb, in fact he had since been to the Alps; but he was not able to go high because frost-bite is very apt to recur in a limb which has already been attacked. He was to take charge of the base for us and carry out a survey.

Most of the food and equipment had now arrived, and although a considerable quantity of food was purposely left at Delhi, we yet had far more than we could use, due mainly to preparations having been made on a Kangchenjunga scale for a party of twelve. This was not such a happy position as it may sound. Some stoicism was required for the scrapping of so much good food, and even with only three present whose tastes need be considered, it was hard to satisfy everyone. It was all the more important therefore to get this job done before any other members of the party arrived, further to darken counsel by urging the claims of their pet foods.

Without wishing to appear over-righteous I may say that I was indifferent to what we took so long as it was food and not chemicals, and gave value for weight. That this attitude involved no self-sacrifice I might add that in my opinion all tinned foods tasted the same, and that if we had to take a hundred pounds of tinned meat the proportion of ham, tongue, chicken, roast beef, bully beef, or even sardines was of no consequence. And the same might be said of cereals, of which we had a weird and wonderful assortment of every hue and texture, but which in the end all boiled down to porridge. Tinned jams too are more distinguishable by colour than by taste and, when these came up for selection, I put in a mild plea on behalf of honey to the exclusion of all jam, a plea which received more favourable hearing because its advocate had taken no part in the fierce contests which raged over, say, oatmeal versus hominy grits, and corned beef against roast beef. Having fixed the total weight of food required and deducted what I considered the essentials, namely all the pemmican, cheese, biscuit and, if possible, honey, that we had with us, plus sugar at the rate of half a pound a day a man, the remaining weight was then apportioned between meat, cereals, sweet-stuffs, and miscellaneous, and Loomis and Emmons filled the lists in detail, tossing up, presumably, for first pick. The method might not have been approved by a dietician, but the results were satisfactory and nobody groused about the food, at least not until circumstance compelled us to jettison a lot more.

Saving weight was to my mind all-important, and this doctrine found ready backers amongst the others, especially those who had climbed in Alaska or British Columbia, where porters as understood in the Himalaya are non-existent, and everything has to be carried on the climber's back. When porters *are* available, as in this case, it may seem immaterial whether we took forty or fifty, apart from the small extra cost. But the route up the Rishi is difficult for heavily laden porters and a slip might have serious consequences, so that every coolie in excess of the minimum was an added responsibility. It was not like climbing on a mountain with a few Sherpas, when Europeans are roped to the porters and able to look after them. Roping together large numbers is not very practicable nor can you festoon three miles of cliff with fixed ropes, and in most of the places where a slip might occur no safeguards are possible.

When a large amount of tinned food is taken the packing is no small proportion of the total weight. For example, 30 lb. of bully beef packed in 1 lb. tins, or sometimes ½ lb. tins, weighs nearly 40 lb.; it is seldom safe to allow less than one-fifth of the total for packing, and more often it is a fourth. We saved what weight we could by bulking where possible, and things like cereals and dried fruits were put in waterproof bags. In only one instance did our zeal for saving weight outrun discretion, when a certain much advertised drink in powder form was put in bags and promptly coagulated into a stiff, glutinous mass. To some of us it was more palatable in this toffee form than as a drink.

When the remainder of the party arrived, the results and implications of this scrap and bag policy were regarded with mixed feelings. 'Scrapping and bagging' became a stock jest and dark hints were thrown out that the leader of the 'scrap and bag' school should himself be scrapped, or at any rate bagged. It was a job for a Fisher and I am afraid that unlike him none of us were sufficiently 'ruthless, and remorseless'.

The weight suggested for our personal gear, including sleeping bag and boots, was 35 lb. Boots were included among gear to be carried, because for the approach march everyone used the highly unorthodox footwear of rubber shoes, usually without socks too, until beyond Joshimath, and some of the more impious wore them on to the glacier. If the weight was kept down to this poundage per person each Sherpa could carry his own kit of 25 lb. and his Sahib's, and the Sahibs would march unladen, at least as far as Joshimath. In practice this was unsatisfactory, for most people then proceeded to burden themselves with a private rucksack and another 20 lb. or more of personal belongings. Very little of this extra stuff was used, but was dumped at various places from Tapoban onwards and later solemnly carried back again. It is rather a problem deciding what you must take and what you can leave behind, but it is amazingly simplified when you know that you have to carry it all yourself.

The Sherpas' personal effects wanted a lot of overhauling to keep them within the stipulated weight, and in *their* case it was possible to be dictatorial. But, despite the severest scrutiny, when we arrived in the Basin one of them suddenly appeared wearing a wholly unauthorised and very unexpeditionary pair of trousers, another a favourite pair of buttoned boots.

To conclude, this overlong dissertation on weight, I should add that on the day before starting, when most of the others were out or too preoccupied, Charles Houston and I had a glorious hour amongst the 'kitchen' and 'miscellaneous junk' loads, which resulted in the scrapping of most of the innumerable articles included for the time-honoured reason that 'they might come in useful', and the reduction of our eating utensils to a mug and a spoon apiece.

The four additional Sherpas arrived on July 3rd. One of them, Nuri, had been with me in Sikkim, two I had looked at in Darjeeling and turned down on the score of age. These were Da Namgyal and Nima Tsering, who were both on Everest in 1924 but who now seemed, from one cause or another, to be past any really strenuous work, as indeed the event proved. The fourth was Kitar, who had an extraordinary record of expeditionary work to his credit but who did not seem to us a very likeable type of Sherpa. He had been on the Everest expeditions of 1922, 1924, and 1933, Kangchenjunga expeditions of 1929, 1930, 1931, and Nanga Parbat of 1934 when he, Pasang Kikuli, and three others were the only survivors of the eleven high-camp porters.

The remainder of the party, excepting Odell, arrived on July 6th and included Graham Brown, Peter Lloyd, and Charles Houston. The last named was the third American, and had organised the attempt on Mount Foraker in which Graham Brown had taken part. Odell, in the tradition of learned professors, was last, and we were still one American short. This was Adams

Carter, who on this particular date was believed to be in Shanghai, rather a long way from Nanda Devi. Apparently there had been some misunderstanding, and he was under the impression that we were not going to tackle the mountain until after the monsoon. I thought it would be hardly worth his while to come, but in this I reckoned without his resource or the possibilities of air travel. Anyhow, we sent him a cable to the effect that we were starting on the 10th, and that if he could not reach Ranikhet within a fortnight of that date, he might as well stay in Shanghai.

Odell, who was intending to do a lot of geological work, and who as a scientist lent seriousness to our otherwise frivolous proceedings, had gone to Simla and was not to arrive until the 8th. This was a source of worry to me, who had to arrange the transport, for it was credibly reported that he was accompanied by a mountain of luggage, would probably acquire more scientific instruments in Simla, while others of the same genus were said to be converging on Ranikhet from various parts of Europe and America. Meantime we had to tell the coolie agent with whom we were dealing exactly how many coolies we required, for these Dotial porters have to be sent for from some distance and would have to start in advance of us. Making a guess, I mentally devoted two coolies to the service of science, and prayed fervently that the reports were exaggerated and that the instruments on the way would arrive too late; as happily they did.

The Dotial porters do not come from Garhwal but from Doti, a corner of Nepal bordering on the Almora district, which perhaps accounts for some of their toughness. They are a class of professional porters and most of the carrying in Garhwal is done by them: an exception to this is on the Pilgrim Road, where the men who carry the dandies all come from the native state of Tehri Garhwal. They are very strong and the normal load for a Dotial on a good road is 80 lb.

In 1934 Shipton and I employed eleven Dotials to carry from Ranikhet to the entrance of the gorge, and, when eight coolies from the Dhauli villages deserted, these men stood by us, added all but two of the abandoned loads to their own, and carried 80 lb. over the 14,000 ft. pass when it was still deep in snow. Their behaviour then had left me with a very high opinion of their qualities, and though, on that occasion, we did not take them over the most difficult part of the gorge, I was confident of their ability to tackle it.

Yet there was a risk in relying entirely on them, because amongst the large number we proposed taking there were likely to be some who were not equal to difficult climbing, and coming, as they do, from a comparatively low, hot country, the cold and wet conditions we expected to encounter in the gorge might knock all the stuffing out of them. The Mana men, on the other hand, could climb anything and were pretty well impervious to weather, the result of living part of the year at 10,000 ft. and most of it at yet higher altitudes tending their flocks. But on the last trip they had told me that we could not get forty Bhotias because not many would be willing to come on an engagement of only three weeks' duration, being at this season more profitably employed trading with Tibet. I therefore decided to rely mainly on Dotials and to leaven the lump with a few Mana men.

For this purpose thirty-seven Dotials paraded in the bazaar on July 7th and, having been signed on and given an advance of pay, were instructed to meet us at Garul on July 10th. Two of these were of the gallant eleven of 1934, and one, Aujra, appointed himself as headman, but on the understanding that he would carry a load. The aid of my friend the Rawal of Badrinath was again invoked, and I asked him to send ten Mana men to meet us in Joshimath on the 19th.

But for this man Aujra we employed no headman, cooks, or other idlers, but each Sahib had a Sherpa allotted to him as servant. There were seven of us, and only six Sherpas, so Pasang Kikuli was detailed to look after Graham Brown and myself while the others had each a Sherpa. This was not so unselfish as it appears, because Pasang could and did attend to the needs of two better than his fellows could look after one, doing most of the camp work into the bargain. Da Namgyal was chosen for Odell and proved to be the perfect 'gentleman's gentleman'; and this was most fitting because Odell was the only one amongst us capable of doing his man credit and of upholding the white man's prestige. By talking to Da Namgyal very loudly and clearly in English, Odell at once arrived at a complete understanding, and thenceforward he was attended by a perfect valet who, with a little encouragement, would have pressed his master's shorts and polished the nails of his climbing boots.

To Da Namgyal the rest of us were rather low and common, scarcely Sahibs in fact; the Americans, especially at first, were rather impatient of too much attention, and I must say it is a bit corrupting to have your boots put on and your pipe lit for you. However, I noticed that before long they acquiesced not unwillingly in the ways of the country and were as ready as the rest of us to shout 'koi hai' on the slightest pretext.[1]

Nima Tsering, who was large and tough-looking, was given to Loomis who was even larger, so that if necessary he could be repressed. He turned out to be our second best man in spite of his age and the effects, as they told me in Darjeeling, of a life-long belief that 'beer is best'. Fortunately, or unfortunately from some points of view, Garhwal is 'dry', at least I have never, or seldom, come across any beer in the villages, though that might be because the search was not diligent enough. Had it been there I am sure the Sherpas would have found it, but we never had any trouble from them on this account. Nima was as strong as a horse and very ready and active, with a prodigious grin in front and a magnificent pigtail behind. He was the only one of our six to wear a pigtail, and I confess to being prejudiced in favour of Sherpas who do wear one, if only because it may mean that they have not been enervated by long residence in Darjeeling.

Pasang Phuta, who, as I have remarked, was a bit bovine, and Nuri, who was small and frail, were allotted to Lloyd and Houston respectively because they seemed least in need of assistance. Emmons took Kitar because he was not travelling with the main body, but was riding to Joshimath by the Pilgrim Road to save his feet and needed someone reliable with him. Kitar knew the

1 'Koi hai' means 'anyone there?'—the usual way of calling a servant.

ropes, having been to Garhwal some years ago with Mr Ruttledge and again, only a month previously, with an Austrian traveller.

All was now set for a start. On the evening of the 9th two lorries came up to the bungalow and were loaded with our 2500 lb. of stuff to facilitate an early start next morning. To save weight nearly all the loads were packed in gunny bags instead of boxes. These served the purpose well enough and managed to last out the wear and tear of a rough journey; the only disadvantage was that when anything was wanted they had first to be unstitched and then sewn up again: we carried a supply of twine and packing needles. It speaks well for the honesty of our men that although very little was under lock and key nothing was stolen.

A mass of surplus kit and equipment was now carried over to a neighbouring bungalow and stored there against our return. For this and many other kindnesses we were indebted to Mrs Browne, an old resident of Ranikhet, who has travelled extensively in Garhwal and as far as Tibet. Carter's kit and a small tent were left here ready for him should he arrive, and Mrs Browne undertook to take charge of him and see him started on the road to Joshimath. It had rained without pause for the last forty-eight hours and next morning, when we piled ourselves and the Sherpas into the lorries, it looked like continuing for another forty-eight. No one was there to see us off—a few words of chaff passed with Emmons—and so we started with hopes which no rain could quench.

CHAPTER SEVEN

The Foothills

THE fifty miles of road between Ranikhet and Garul are carved for the most part out of abrupt hillsides and are as full of kinks as a wriggling eel. The heavy rain had started many small landslips, and rounding everyone of the innumerable bends I half expected to find the road completely blocked. Nor was it comforting to reflect that only yesterday a lorry from Kathgodam had slipped off the road and gone down the *khud* with fatal results. Such gloomy thoughts must have been roused by a too early and too heavy breakfast, and it was with a feeling of having been delivered from a great peril that I got down at Garul at midday.

Our thirty-seven Dotials were all present and correct, one or two capitalists sheltering under battered umbrellas, for it continued to rain cheerfully. The thirty-seven loads were dumped in the mud and presently these were adjusted to the satisfaction of all, the headman, having successfully palmed off most of his on to the more complacent of his followers, contenting himself with an umbrella and a canvas bucket, perhaps with a view to being prepared for both contingencies—flood or drought. There was some talk of stopping for the night at a dâk bungalow two miles away, the headman arguing with some cogency that it was raining (a fact which might have escaped our notice) and quoting the time-honoured rule that the first day's march should be a short one. To this I replied that if we only marched in fine weather we should not march at all, that they had already marched for two days from Ranikhet so that it was not their first day, and as for ourselves, though it was kind of him to think of us, we would for once make an exception to the rule.

Gwaldam was therefore our destination, ten miles away and a long climb, and it must have been a portentous sight for the Garulians to see this long caravan sliding and slipping out of their muddy village, most of us brandishing an ice-axe in one hand and an umbrella in the other, some draped in green oilskin cycling capes, and one even crowned with a sou'wester. I remembered the march to Gwaldam in 1934 as a decidedly grim affair, for it was a grilling hot day in May, and when we finally crawled into the bungalow we were more dead than alive. Today nobody seemed to feel it much, not even those who had only recently stepped off a ship, and the slowest of the porters was in by half-past six. There is much to be said for travelling in the monsoon.

The Gwaldam bungalow is a poor place, at least for a party of six; its best feature is the magnificent view which of course we were not to see, save only for a patch of snow which, through a break in the clouds, appeared for a moment high up and seemingly belonged to no earthly mountain. Nor were we more favoured with material things; the usual inquiry for eggs and milk met with the usual reply.

The Dotials had been asking questions about the route, and, hearing that the bridge over the Nandakini was again down, had mapped out a new route for us some distance to the west of the more usual way. Accordingly next morning, when we dropped down through a forest of noble 'chir' trees (*Pinus longifolia*) to the Pindar river, instead of crossing it, we turned west and marched down the valley to a place called Tharali. Here the river was crossed by a wire suspension bridge and the camping ground, a green flat on the river bank, was pointed out to us. It was too public and looked too wet to be very inviting, and since the march had been but short we asked if there was nothing better ahead. There is only one answer to such a question, even should there happen to be a stream round the next corner, and we were hastily assured that there was no water for at least ten miles. For once the liars who told us this did us an inestimable service, for, in consequence of believing them and stopping there, we got three dozen eggs on the spot and two dozen more next morning. Blessings on Tharali! And the more pity that it should have been singled out for vengeance by the flooding of the Pindar river. No doubt the more pious Garhwali considered that Tharali was doubly damned and deserved all it got, not only for keeping the unclean hen but, worse still, for selling the product to the defilers of the shrine of the Blessed Goddess.

The camping ground belied its wet appearance, the sun shone for a brief interval, we broached a 10 lb. cheese of perfect maturity, bathed in the icy Pindar, and were the subject of much amiable curiosity on the part of young Tharali.

It rained again at night and in the early morning, but we got away in good time, for it was advisable to inculcate good habits while the expedition was in its infancy. The usual routine was for me to get up about five and rout out the Sherpas, or rather two of them, for the others seldom came to life until much later. Nima was very good and was generally out first to light the fire, with Pasang Kikuli a close second ready to cook the food I gave him. A great beaker of tea all round was the first thing and then, while the porridge was cooking, Pasang and I started making the chapatties. Pasang was an artist at this and what is more he always washed his hands before getting to work. The mathematically perfect circles of thin dough which he cleverly slapped down on to the hot plate were the envy and despair of all who tried their hands at this game of skill. The amateur's effort was of any shape, varying from an ellipse to something resembling the map of England, that is if it ever reached such an advanced stage; more often it was beaten to fragments or slipped out of the hands on to the ground before ever it was ready for the neat backhander which should, but seldom did, spread it flat on the iron plate. The beaker of tea and the noise we made whacking away at chapatties were the signal for the others to 'rise and shine', though precious little 'shining' was done after the first few days.

When our breakfast was off the fire the Sherpas started cooking theirs—at this stage of the journey usually a vast mountain of rice and a mouth-blistering sauce containing 100 per cent chillies to help it down. Some might have preferred the breakfast order reversed, Sherpas first and Sahibs last, but as it was we had a pleasant interval for digestion, smoking a pipe, writing up diaries, or any other odd job before having to pack up and march.

Today we turned north up a pleasant side valley through more pine forest, and then west again, heading for a gap in the ridge. Camp was made on a delightful green terrace set amidst oak trees, three miles beyond the last village and 8000 ft. up. Odell and I were in first, and while waiting for the porters we stripped and walked back down the road to a nearby waterfall for a bathe. Odell was out of luck; he was surprised by a bevy of ancient beldames and was forced to flee in confusion pursued by a volley of Garhwali Billingsgate.

It began to rain as the porters arrived and all our seven tents had to be pitched for their accommodation. We slept three in a tent, the Sherpas five, the Dotials seven, and those who were left over sought shelter in some shepherds' huts close by. One function of a tent is to keep out rain, but we were now beginning to suspect that the makers of our tents were not aware of this. Every seam dripped, and, where the guys joined the fabric, rivers flowed out to collect on the floor into young lakes, which were summarily dealt with by stabbing a hole in the ground-sheet with a knife. These tents were not made in America, but poor Houston, who was responsible for them and who, under the sheltering roof of the forest bungalow, had waxed eloquent over the impeccable behaviour of the same type in Alaska, came in for some merciless chaff. 'Were they equally good in snow?' we asked, 'and was the rain in Alaska very dry?' And an insect common in Garhwal, though hitherto unknown to science, was discovered for Houston's benefit—a flying leech, which we assured him would fly through these precious tents as easily as the drops of rain.

The mention of insects constrains me to add the following. The seven tents were in two sizes, 6 ft. × 7 ft. and 7 ft. × 8 ft., but in appearance all were alike and now, having given them out to the Dotials, I suddenly called to mind a little roadside incident I had witnessed only that morning. Two Dotials were resting by the wayside, one of them subjecting an indescribably dirty shirt to a close scrutiny, while his companion, sitting behind, did a like office for his head. I kept this disturbing memory to myself and there and then went out, armed with an indelible pencil, and marked with a large 'S' the tents used by ourselves and the Sherpas.

While on the subject of tents I may say, to anticipate matters, that on the mountain the tents were severely tested and behaved very well.

Next day's march took us down to the Nandakini river, about ten miles down stream of the old route, at a place called Ghat. It was not a long march; indeed the stages on this route seemed to me much easier than those of the other, and the Pindar-Nandakini watershed was crossed at a height of only 8900 ft. instead of 10,000 ft. From the pass we followed a delightful river, in which we bathed, down to its junction with the Nandakini; bathing was rapidly becoming an obsession and we did it again in the Nandakini, across which Houston swam, greatly to the astonishment of the natives.

At Ghat a dâk bungalow was in the last stages of construction; there were no doors or windows and the debris which always accumulates during building operations lay thick on the floor—but for all that we occupied it, most of us, even Houston, preferring to be dry though dirty. There was nothing interesting to eat here, and though a man went down to the river at dusk with a net the hopes thus aroused were not fulfilled. Mahseer are found in these bigger rivers where the water is not too cold.

At breakfast next morning we were entertained by a party of strolling minstrels, two bold-looking hussies who sang and an insignificant little man playing a drum with his fingers. We gave them a rupee, which was apparently far too much, for they were quite beside themselves with delight and I feared they would follow us up the mountain.

The Nandakini was crossed by a permanent bridge and for four hours the road zigzagged steadily up a steep slope bare of trees. From the top there was an uninterrupted view up the valley, where the river slowly uncoiled itself like a silver snake between the dark olive green of the forested slopes, flecked with sunshine and shadow. We gazed for a long time, waiting vainly for the great white dome of Trisul to reveal itself at the valley head, while a wandering shepherd beguiled the time for us with the music of his pipe.

The road now contoured the hillside, converging gradually towards the old route and finally joining it in the little village of Ramni, where we took up our quarters in the same ramshackle bungalow.

A Garhwal village is, at any rate from a distance, a very delightful and humanising incident in the Himalayan landscape. It is generally built on a spur or half-way up the slope of a hill, so that the cultivation extends both above and below. Regard must of course be had to the water supply, and this should preferably be from two sources, so that the low-caste Doms shall not foul the water of their betters the Biths (Brahmans and Rajputs). The houses are of stone and are two-storeyed and in front is a stone courtyard bounded by a low stone wall. It is here that the threshing, winnowing, and weaving are carried on. Fruit trees are sometimes planted round the courtyard, peach trees in the higher valleys and bananas or plantains in the lower.

The village with its solid stone houses, sometimes having the walls white-washed, surrounded by terraced fields, has a very satisfying appearance—an appearance of comfort, warmth, and prosperity that is many times accentuated for the traveller who first views it after many weeks above the tree-line.

It rained during the night, and in the morning we climbed in dank mist through dripping rhododendron forest to the top of the ridge at nearly 11,000 ft. Between Ramni and Kaliaghat, the usual halting-place, is a delightfully situated grazing alp called Shim Kharak. I had pleasant recollections of camping there in 1934, but hearing a report that the bridge over the Bireh Ganga was down, we decided to push on and camp closer to the river, so that we could learn the truth of this report and if necessary begin building operations.

We camped a mile short of the bridge and 500 ft. above the river, and Aujra, the headman, went on down to look at the bridge. He reported that the bridge, a tree-trunk affair, was still standing, but that the river was almost lapping it. This news made us very uneasy; it was fine at the moment, but if it rained in the night the bridge would probably go.

Sure enough it rained all night and was hard at it next morning when we hurried down to the river expecting the worst. From half-way down we caught sight of the river through the trees, and there was the bridge with the water a clear two feet below it. It seemed doubtful whether Aujra had gone to the bridge yesterday or merely drawn on his imagination, but I was too thankful to press the inquiry, and rather felt it was a job one of us ought to have done. Had the bridge gone we should certainly have been held up for a day or more, for it would have been no easy matter to throw fresh logs across the forty feet of rushing water.

Climbing up the north side of the valley we could see where the river widened out into the Gohna Lake, the result of a great landslip which occurred in 1893, damming up the Bireh Ganga until a lake of many square miles was formed. At first reports from the local headman that a mountain had fallen were ignored, but when the place was visited by Lieut.-Col. Pulford, R.E., Superintending Engineer, it was found that a succession of slips had formed a dam 900 ft. high, 11,000 ft. wide at the base, and 2000 ft. wide at the top. His opinion was that nothing would happen until the water topped the dam and, in spite of other experts holding contrary views, this opinion was adopted and acted upon, and in the event was triumphantly justified.

An engineer was put on to watch the rise of the water and a light telegraph wire erected for the purpose of warning the towns and villages down the Ganges valley. The danger limits of the expected flood were marked out by masonry pillars beyond which the inhabitants were warned to retreat. Suspension bridges were taken down and pilgrim traffic diverted to other routes.

Final calculations predicted that the flood was not to be expected until August 1894, and on August 25th the water began to trickle over the dam and at midnight it collapsed with an appalling crash. The flood lasted until the morning of the 26th, when it was found the lake had fallen 390 ft. Only one life was lost, but much damage was done all down the river, the town of Srinagar being swept away. From the permanent lake which now exists, the water escapes over the sound remains of the huge barrier.

The enormous grey scar on the hillside above gave us but a faint notion of the cataclysmic nature of the event. The steepness of the valleys, the nature of the rock, and the heavy rain combine to make landslips a frequent occurrence and the maintenance of roads a task of Sisyphus.

It was still drizzling when we reached Kaliaghat at midday and camped amongst the giant boulders, the Dotials boldly and, as it chanced, unwisely deciding to use the spare tents instead of walking a mile to the village. After a fine afternoon it began again in earnest that night, and was raining heavier than ever when we got up. Breakfast was cooked under difficulties, or, to be accurate, under an umbrella. When this dismal rite was over, the flood continued unabated and the porters were averse to starting, saying that a river at the foot of the Kauri Pass would be unfordable. They had already abandoned the tents and taken refuge in a derelict cowshed, and since everyone was wet and miserable we made their faint-heartedness an excuse for 'lying at earth', as Mr Jorrocks would express it, when the weather was too bad for hunting. This decision cost us Rs 37, a day's pay for the Dotials, and the words 'milksops' and 'sissies' were freely bandied about in self-accusation, but it is difficult to conceive a process better calculated to promote universal misery than striking water-logged tents and packing up soaking bedding in a deluge of rain.

We lay in our tents all day watching the drips and rivulets, stabbing holes in the floor to keep the lakes at a reasonable level, and blessing our stars that we were the right side of the Bireh Ganga. It was a day for song if ever there was one; on such a day, pent up in a leaking tent, the most mournful hymns have been found to have a very composing effect. But we were singularly deficient in this useful accomplishment and I do not remember a single chorus. Perhaps we were too serious-minded and certainly the ship was heavily freighted with learning. In one tent you could listen to a discussion on geology or, if not a discussion, at any rate a monologue; in another poetry was not only discussed but also written, while in a third medicine would be the theme, for we boasted no less than two doctors in embryo, and one *ci-devant*. It was possible to have a fellow-feeling for Walpole, the Prime Minister, who said that he always encouraged the guests at his table to talk bawdy because that was a subject in which everyone could join.

So many would-be doctors were rather a thorn in the flesh at times, because there was a ban on unboiled water and it was impossible to drink out of a stream unless they were out of sight, and then it was done furtively and with a sense of guilt. Even some apples which we got in Joshimath, straight off a tree, were subjected to the indignity of a potassium permanganate bath; I suppose they deserved it for not moving with the times, and omitting to grow a cellophane wrapper as well as a skin.

Meantime it is still raining, as it was when this digression started, and so it continued for a second night until by dawn it had rained itself out. After crossing another 11,000 ft. ridge above Kaliaghat we dropped again to the stream which had to be forded. The approach to it was down the loose debris of a comparatively recent landslide, flanked on the right by the horribly unstable-looking precipice of yellow rock off which the slip had broken. The road crosses the river below a waterfall issuing from a gorge which is almost a cave, and which Loomis compared to the Bee Rocks of *The Jungle Book*. Normally this ford is only ankle-deep but now it was impracticable, and we had to cross by a fresh place a hundred yards down stream where the bed widened. The previous day even this would have been impassable, as the porters had feared.

On the far side we passed many clumps of bamboo and, partly for old times' sake, and to amuse the others, I got the Sherpas to gather some young shoots, which we had cooked for dinner. On one occasion in 1934 bamboo shoots had been our 'manna'. We enjoyed another gastronomic treat that day when we found wild strawberries almost as large as a cultivated variety.

And talking of gastronomy, we ourselves provided a gastronomic treat for the leeches that were here in considerable numbers. It has always puzzled me what these creatures live on in the normal course of a dull life, and whether blood is a necessity. The banquets provided by human beings must be of rare occurrence in the dense, wet, tropical forests which are their usual habitat. We had met a few in the lower country earlier in the march, but it was curious to find so many here at an altitude of over 9000 ft. Leeches have always been associated in my mind with hot, wet climates, but I suppose no one from the forests of Assam or Burma, where there really are leeches, would admit that we had seen any; half a dozen on one's feet in the course of a march would to them appear negligible. We found our footgear, or rather lack of footgear, namely rubbers and no socks, as satisfactory as any for combating these revolting beasts. One generally noticed them at once on shoe or bare leg and could pull them off before they had a good hold, whereas boots, socks, and puttees will not prevent them from getting at the feet; the leech on them is harder to spot, and, once in, it is not discovered until the boots are removed in camp and found to be full of blood and gorged leeches.

Now began a long, steep grind to the 12,400 ft. Kuari Pass, but today we were bound only for Dekwani, the grazing alp 1000 ft. below the ridge. When we were here in June the air resounded with the bleating of sheep, and white flocks covered the hillside, but now the place was empty of life except for some choughs and a questing hawk. This camping ground is just above the tree-line and in consequence rather bleak; instead of pitching their tents the Dotials retired to the woods to sleep—only the Europeans were hardy enough to endure the rigours of the ". . ." tents.

When we passed this way in 1934 we made a special effort to be on top of the Pass at dawn and virtue was for once rewarded by the unsurpassed panorama of the Garhwal Himalaya, which is seen from here in fair weather. But that was in May, and now in this month of rain and mist not much was to be expected, so we were content to be up there by eight o'clock. There was a lot of cloud to the north but all was not hidden and to the majority of our party, who had not yet seen a Himalayan mountain, the little that remained was a breath-taking revelation. Dunagiri to the north-east claimed pre-eminence of beauty and of stature, and her perfectly proportioned shape shone dazzlingly white in a frame of massive cloud. Across the Dhauli valley the great bulk of Hathi Parbat stood up like an iceberg from a sea of vapour, while to the north, near Badrinath, the country was bathed in sun and the warm glow of a glacier there was for all the world like pink snow.

For long we looked, trying with camera and cinema to capture some record of the changing scene, and then, having added each a stone to the cairn which guards the Pass, we began the long and easy descent. The grass merged into pine forest and 1000 ft. lower, where two tracks diverged, Pasang Kikuli and I turned west for Joshimath while the bandobast[1] went on down to Tapoban.

1 Bandobast—a useful term meaning organising or the organisation itself.

CHAPTER EIGHT

The Rishi Once More

It was July 19th when we reached Joshimath and inquiries for Emmons in the bazaar elicited the information that, arriving two days ago, he had gone up to Badrinath and was expected back that day. Having collected the mail, we repaired to the dâk bungalow and half an hour later Pasang Kikuli reported that he could see Emmons and Kitar riding up from Vishnuprayag, the temple at the junction of the Dhauli and Alaknanda rivers, 1500 ft. below Joshimath.

A little later he and Kitar arrived and we swopped news. He had thoroughly enjoyed his journey along the Pilgrim Road, particularly the day spent at Badrinath, where he was very kindly received by the Rawal, and shown the Temple, the hot spring, and the steps leading down to the frigid waters of the Alaknanda, where the pilgrims bathe ceremoniously, clinging to a ringbolt.

The next to arrive was a wire from Carter saying that he was leaving Ranikhet that day, so that here were two members of the party who had not allowed the grass to grow, however leisurely may have been the progress of the main body.

Finally, in the evening, ten Mana men arrived with the chest-slapping Kalu. Kalu I had hoped was up the valley at Tapoban collecting food, but here he

was with the Mana men and, seemingly, rather the worse for wear. I soon
learnt that, if we were relying on him to find coolie food, we might whistle for
it; the month that had elapsed since he left us had apparently been spent at
Mana or Badrinath, and from his blear-eyed look very ill-spent. I hurried
down to the bazaar to see what could be done, but the man I had dealt with
previously was away and all that his underling could promise was one load of
atta. Here was a pretty kettle of fish, for it might take two or three days to
collect the ten loads we wanted and the prospect of further delay was
maddening. Returning to the bungalow, I gave the Mana men sufficient
rupees and told them to scrape together all the food they could find in the
bazaar. The result was beyond expectation, and two hours later they had got
together eight loads of atta and two of rice.

Early next morning two Dotials and Phuta came in from Tapoban as
arranged, and I spent the morning again in the bazaar buying odds and ends
for them and the Bhotias. The Mana men are Bhotias and the name gives
some indication of their origin, for Tibet was known as the land of Bhot.

The Garhwal Bhotias number about five hundred, divided between the
villages of Mana and Niti. They themselves claim that they are Hindus who
crossed the Himalaya into Tibet many generations ago, and after a long
sojourn there, during which presumably they intermarried, they returned to
their present home. They are not identical with Tibetans, but they are of a
Mongolian type, sturdy, thick-set, with olive complexions sometimes tinged
on the cheeks with a ruddy glow. The men wear a long blanket coat of
homespun reaching to the knees, over trousers of the same material, which
are tight at the ankles, baggy above, and tied at the waist like pyjamas. None
of them are fanatical about cleanliness.

The village of Mana is 10,500 ft. above the sea and is set on a boulder-
strewn slope, where the low stone houses of the village seem as natural as the
great erratic blocks which litter the hillside. It overlooks the Alaknanda river
at its confluence with the Saraswati and only a few miles below the glacier
source of the first-named. The shrine at this river junction is called
Keshoprayag and is sacred to Vishnu. Immediately above here the Saraswati
flows through a very remarkable cleft, the walls of which almost touch above,
the river flowing heard but unseen several hundred feet below. Some
cultivation of barley and buckwheat is carried on and there is one tree, of
which the Mana people are rightly proud; but sheep, goats, and the Tibetan
trade are their main interest.

The trade from Mana is neither so extensive nor so lucrative as that carried
on over the eastern passes from the Milam valley in Almora. The Mana Pass
is 18,650 ft. and comparatively more difficult than the others, and the trade
seems to have fallen off considerably in recent years. Here, as in Milam, the
Tibetan Jongpen sends an official to Mana to ascertain whether there is any
disease amongst men or cattle before declaring the Pass open for the summer.
The official is given a stone (who determines the size I have not learnt) and
the Bhotias undertake to forfeit its weight in gold if any disease be introduced
into Tibet. A licence to trade has to be paid for in cash or kind, and a
commission is exacted on all deals. The chief exports are food-stuffs of all

kinds, cloth, sugar, spices, tobacco, and dried fruits; and the imports salt, borax, wool, ponies, dogs, jubus (a cross between a yak and a cow), rugs, Tibetan saddles, tea, butter, gold, yak tails, and horns.

Now that we were about to leave the habitation of men, our porters had to be supplied with a few extras, both luxuries and necessities, and it was interesting to compare the respective wants of our three different breeds.

The Bhotias' needs were hard to satisfy either in variety or quantity. They evidently believed in doing themselves well if someone else footed the bill, and seemed not to have heard anything about pipers and the tunes they played. Eight pounds of tobacco was their first demand, cut down by me to four; then half a dozen different spices were selected and equal quantities red and black lentils. Ghee was the next item, and several shops were visited before a superfine quality was found, and then I had to put in another demurrer as to quantity, for good ghee is more expensive than butter. Several 2 lb. cakes of jaggery wrapped in leaves were next added to the growing pile; it is unrefined sugar like solidified treacle and indistinguishable from their tobacco. Tea and salt were bought after another wrangle over quantities, for they seemed to think they were fitting out for a year.

That met, if it did not satisfy, their wants, and I wondered apprehensively whether the Dotials had the same generous notions about what was requisite for their well-being. Fortunately the headman himself had not come, no doubt only because he realised that something might have to be carried back, and the two men he had sent had not been properly coached. When asked what they wanted, they were quite at a loss, and tea, sugar, salt, and tobacco had to be pressed on them. The Sherpas' needs were similar to the Bhotias', except that they took cigarettes instead of tobacco, and made no attempt to take advantage of having *carte blanche* to get what they wanted.

While this was going on, Loomis and Lloyd arrived, having come in to see the sights of the metropolis, and at one o'clock we all started back together carrying the morning's purchases, ten loads of coolie food, and some apples for ourselves. There is a small orchard at Joshimath and earlier in the year peaches of enormous size can be had.

Before leaving, arrangements were made for Carter's possible coming, and instead of turning Kalu off, as he deserved, I gave him the job of waiting here to take charge of Carter when he arrived and, with the help of another Mana man, to follow us into the Basin. He was very repentant, praying constantly with his hands palm to palm, and seemed pleased at having this responsibility put upon him.

We reached Tapoban at three o'clock and, jealous of the others who had spent the morning wallowing in the hot bath, we three lost no time in visiting it. To our annoyance the hermit was there sitting outside the hut, his long hair reaching to the ground, and his eyes fixed vacantly on the stone tank. It is *infra dig.* to strip in front of natives, but I got rid of him by the simple expedient of holding out a four-anna piece and pointing to the hut. His mind was not as blank as his face, for he at once understood, got up and went into his hut, and I placed the money on the stone thus vacated. When we had done boiling ourselves and dashing from the hot to the cold and back again, he came out of the hut, took up the money, and resumed his contemplation of the infinite.

The camping place at Tapoban is on a grass plateau the size of a tennis court, which has the appearance of having once been part of a fort. Close by are three very old and completely neglected shrines, beautifully built of massive stone put together without any mortar. They are said to date back to A.D. 800. The only inhabited building nearby is a school for the children of the neighbouring villages. After school hours it serves the purpose of an inn, for I remember we slept in it in 1934 and now it sheltered the Mana men. Some slight re-adjustments of loads were made here when most of us found we had brought too much, and some articles of food found to be in excess were also left. From these we made up an assortment of food for Carter's use, and the whole was handed over to the care of the schoolmaster.

It was important that the Dotials and the Mana men should get on well together, but I had always had a lurking fear that this pious hope would not be realised—that in fact it might be far otherwise. The Bhotias did not strike one as being good mixers, although they were friendly enough with the Sherpas, but I think they despised the Dotials and resented the fact that we were employing them instead of Bhotias. I watched them when they first met that evening and, though neither side was effusive, they talked together a little, in a distant manner, like two strange dogs smelling round each other. Once the ice was broken I hoped that good relations would be established, but an incident next morning showed that of this there was little likelihood.

The Mana men were as usual the last to start, and as they were coming up the road to collect their loads they met the Dotials starting off, already laden. Unfortunately one of the Dotials had taken one of the food loads which the Mana men had brought yesterday from Joshimath—a handy compact bag of 60 lb., very comfortable to carry. The Mana men had marked all their loads and promptly claimed this one. The Dotial refused to give it up and both sides gathered round to join in the argument. We were still at the camp, but the row attracted our attention and I hurried down to see what was happening. All loads had been downed and the more hot-tempered on both sides were shouting and grimacing and threatening each other with fists and sticks. The headman, instead of pacifying them, had got his face about an inch off the head Bhotia's, shouting away with the best. A first-class riot seemed imminent. They were so excited that little attention was paid to me, but with the arrival of one or two Sahibs we managed to separate them, and giving the Mana man his load sent them off out of the way. The Dotial who had been the most aggressive in flourishing his stick I paid off and sacked on the spot, 'pour encourager les autres', and in the heat of the moment overpaid him to the extent of Rs 7. Perhaps this was lucky, because without that accidental inducement he might have refused to go home alone and would probably have been backed up by his fellows. He was the strongest of the Dotials and a good man, and I was sorry to lose him.

Later, when I caught up with the Mana men, I gave them a talking to, and declared fiercely that at the least sign of trouble they would all be sacked—a piece of bluff which to have had called would have been exceedingly inconvenient. For the next day or two I lived in constant dread that some triviality would blow up the smouldering fires, and took care not to leave them alone together on the march. There were no rows but there was no cordiality, and the notion previously entertained, that the Mana men would extend a helping hand to a Dotial in difficulties, was obviously false—they were more likely to push him down the *khud*.

Our route that day followed the Dhauli valley, and the aspect of this valley differed widely from those mild and beautiful valleys which we had crossed on the way to Joshimath. Here the scene was grander and sterner, in places almost savage, and no imagination was required to guess that close behind the steep enclosing walls lay the ice, rock, and snow of high mountains. The Dhauli river rises near the Niti Pass and its course down to Tapoban is almost one great gorge, through the bed of which the water roars and rages with incredible violence. It is milky white with glacial deposits.

Four miles above Tapoban, where the road crossed by a stout cantilever bridge from the south to the north side of the river, the Rishi Ganga flows into the Dhauli. We looked with newly awakened interest at the grey rushing waters that were a living witness to the mysterious Basin, and at the gorge above which still kept its secrets.

Beyond this we recrossed to the south bank of the Dhauli by a rather amateurish suspension bridge, the flimsy flooring sagging and swaying a few feet above the boiling water that dizzied the eye to look upon. Frail though it was, it was comforting to feel that two-foot wide flooring underfoot, unlike the home-made bamboo bridges of Sikkim, where one shuffles one foot after the other along two slippery bamboos, clinging affectionately to the handrail the while.

After crossing the bridge we climbed up from the river to the village of Lata, the porters sweating hard and resting frequently under a hot sun, which we noticed was surrounded by a wide halo. Lata is no place to camp at if it can be avoided, but the next water is a long way up the hill, and the need of shelter and food for the coolies make it advisable to stop near a village if there is one. One very remarkable fact about this village was that there were three eggs in it, but even this paled before the yet more remarkable fact that the owner wanted half a rupee (about *9d.*) for each of them.

Lata was the last link with the outside world, and from now on we and our fifty-three porters were dependent for food and shelter on what we carried. We could not afford to waste any days now, for when the porters are not marching they still eat. They were consuming nearly one hundred pounds of food every day and the number of days we could keep them was dictated by the food we had. Of course the longer their services were available the farther, within limits, we could push our base, and any time wasted meant that we should have to dismiss them before this goal was reached.

Bad weather might hold us up, as it had at Kaliaghat, and it was with gloomy foreboding that we observed the sun halo, but the next day turned out as fine as any we had had. The road climbed almost without break for 5000 ft. to Lata Kharak, which was to be our camping ground. It is a grassy hollow just above the tree-line, which here is over 12,000 ft.; birch trees and rhododendrons are the only trees able to grow at this height, the pine having given up the struggle a little lower down. One variety of pine which grew here, the 'chir' or *Pinus longifolia*, is a most useful tree because, being full of resin, it burns like a torch, and a few slivers of it make excellent kindling. Pasang Kikuli generally carried some, and with it a fire could be started under the worst conditions. Rhododendron makes a good fire too, but it is not easy to start.

The Dotials were on their mettle today and out to show the Mana men what they could do, with the result that they climbed this 5000 ft. in five hours and were in camp by half-past twelve; the Bhotias took it easy, as they usually did, and were not up until two o'clock. A chill wind and mist are the rule at this camp but today it was fine and warm. The Mana men retired to the woods to sleep, despising tents at this moderate altitude even had tents been available, as they were not. The Dotials occupied all there were, probably more with a view to depriving the Mana men of them than from any renewed faith in their weather-resisting powers.

It was wet when we got up at half-past five, but when we started two hours later this had turned to fine mist. The crest of the ridge overlooking the Rishi valley from the north is first gained at a height of about 13,000 ft., and then the path traverses along the north side, ascending gently, until it crosses the ridge by the 14,000 ft. Durashi Pass. From the Pass views of peaks both to north and south should be obtained, but though we sat there an hour to give it a chance, the mist refused to lift. From here a sensational traverse leads across a mile of some of the steepest and most rugged cliffs imaginable. At first glance a man would despair of getting himself across, let alone a flock of sheep, but every summer many hundreds of sheep and goats are taken over it, and back again in the autumn with young lambs at foot. In May, when there is snow and ice about, step-cutting is necessary, but when the snow has gone all is plain sailing and it is merely an airy walk.

At the further end of the traverse is much dead juniper wood, and those who know the scarcity of fuel at Durashi add as much of this as they can carry to their loads. The traverse ends in a long steep gully full of loose stones, and at the bottom of this I waited to see the porters come down, thinking that someone might get hit by a stone. I need not have worried—not even a pebble was dislodged. A steeper but shorter gully was then climbed and there below us lay Durashi, but no tinkle of sheep bells reached our ears, and the place was apparently deserted. The Bhotias accounted for this by saying there was not enough grass, but I think it more likely that the shepherds had been driven out by excessive rain; sheep had certainly been there recently.

We had already reduced the loads appreciably by eating, and now we were able to pay off five Dotials, which made a useful reduction in the number of mouths to be fed. I had expected some trouble in selecting the five victims, but two of them chose themselves by being sick and the other three made no bones about going. The Dotials are much more amenable than the Bhotias; when Loomis and I were here in June I had tried to send some of the Mana men back because there were no longer any loads for them, but it only led to trouble. They presented a united front and said that all would go on or all would go back, so we had to submit to paying and, what was more important, feeding four unnecessary men.

The march between Durdashi and Dibrugheta is short, and again, as in June, we lingered long on the 'Curtain' ridge, expectant of a view, for on a clear day Nanda Devi herself is visible. The mist however was thicker than ever and even the Dibrugheta alp immediately below us was hidden. From the ridge to the alp is a drop of some 3000 ft. down an excessively steep grass slope, and the few who now remained faithful to rubber shoes had some very unhappy moments, which were accentuated when it began raining. At the bottom is a stream, and the way out up the opposite bank lies over steep rock clothed with a thin layer of mud, grass, and other vegetation. Here it went hard with the rubber school and the porters with awkward loads, one of whom had to have his load carried up piecemeal. This was an unlucky Dotial carrying a load, part of which consisted of tent poles, the most troublesome and impracticable tent poles that ever were. Each pole weighed 4 lb. and was in two sections, each four feet long; one section telescoped into the other but at the slightest provocation telescoped out again. If carried horizontally they caught on every projection near the path, and if carried vertically they bruised either the man's head or his backside. The seven poles made up half the load and the other half was something just as unwieldy but rather less necessary, a glacier drill. This is a scientific instrument and not, as one might suspect from its presence in a mountaineering party, some device to facilitate glacier travel. Of its subsequent history all that need be said is that like the immortal Duke of York's men it 'was marched right up the hill, and then marched down again'.

Having disentangled ourselves from these perplexities we emerged on to the small plateau of the Dibrugheta alp, an emerald gem in a sombre setting of dark green pines. The flowers which, earlier in the year, make this meadow a Joseph's coat were past their best, only a few white anemones remaining to set off the rich crimson of the potentillas. Of greater interest than these to the materially minded were the wild shallots which mingled with them.

It was raining too hard when we arrived for a due appreciation of our surroundings. As Dr Johnson said, 'the noblest prospect is improved by a good inn in the foreground', and no time was lost by us in thus augmenting the beauty of the scene. The tents were pitched, the loads stacked on top of a flat rock and covered with a tarpaulin, and at last a fire was started under a sheltering canopy of umbrellas. At dark the rain ceased, fresh logs were piled on, and we sat round enjoying the blaze like so many salamanders. Then the moon rose, outlining for us in a silver silhouette the summit of Niti peak and emphasising the black profile of the 'Curtain' which towered above us, while, across the dark cleft of the Rishi, pinnacle upon pinnacle of rock was etched against an indigo sky.

CHAPTER NINE

To the Foot of the Gorge

THE sheep track which we had so far followed ends at Dibrugheta and from here to the foot of the gorge and through it the going becomes progressively difficult; the first stage from Dibrugheta to the Cave Camp gave the Dotials a taste of what was in store for them higher up. It might be said of them as of the crew of a more famous expedition:

> The danger was past—they had landed at last,
> With their boxes, portmanteaus, and bags:
> Yet at first sight the crew were not pleased with the view,
> Which consisted of chasms and crags.

The march begins in a brutally abrupt manner with a stiff climb of 1000 ft. through grand pine forest. We were off before eight on a fine morning and an hour later had cleared the pines and were sitting on the ridge getting a first sight of our objective, Nanda Devi. The lower part was hidden in cloud, giving an added effect of height. Gazing with wonder at the great wedge of the summit, supported on the south-west by a fearfully steep sort of flying buttress, all who were looking at the mountain for the first time were profoundly impressed. In the immediate foreground ravines and ridges alternated with rock walls and grass slopes to confuse the eye, until in the distance a great grassy shoulder screened the whole of the upper gorge.

The porters went well and by eleven o'clock we reached what Shipton and I had christened 'Rhubarb Gully', a gully with a stream running down it, full of lush vegetation, including a quantity of wild rhubarb. The porters like to eat the tops of this when it has gone to seed, but the stems stewed with sugar are every bit as good as the cultivated variety. We ate them whenever we could.

We continued our march, groping our way through thickets of rhododendron, balancing along narrow ledges of rock, and stepping gingerly over the smooth water-worn slabs of the ravines, until we reached the most critical piece of the day. This was a smooth cliff several hundred feet high, liberally provided with holds in the shape of grass and short furze. Although I had been up and down it five times I never was fond of it, disliked it especially coming down, and dreaded it when wet. Luckily today the rain was holding off and everyone made a special effort to get there before it started. The Mana men in their bare feet simply romped up, and most of the Dotials seemed equally at home, but the little man carrying the tent poles broke down completely. He could not face it, and even after dumping his load he had to be shepherded all the way up, Emmons and I keeping an eye on him from behind while a Dotial in front held his hand. His load was again brought up piecemeal.

There followed a trying half mile over a chaotic scree of enormous blocks, amongst which we dodged and climbed, coming frequently to an impasse. The Cave Camp, reached at three o'clock, consists of one big cave with a very uneven floor and a through-draught which by means of a vent at the back draws the smoke of a fire right through the cave, thoroughly fumigating the occupants. We appropriated this, the Bhotias found another cave, and the Dotials pitched tents in the most unlikely places. There is ample juniper wood here, rhubarb grows luxuriantly, and the cave is dry, so that altogether it is a refuge not to be despised.

In June we had dumped a bag of atta and a bag of rice here and we were relieved to find the atta was only slightly affected by damp. For food on their return journey we now left some atta for the Dotials and some rice for the Bhotias. The Dotials had asked for nothing but atta and this was their sole food, morning and night, in the form of chapatties; nor could they use rice had they wanted it, because they had no cooking pots except the shallow iron bowl in which chapatties are baked.

So far everything had gone well; true, it had rained most days, but this had neither damaged the loads nor depressed the spirits of the porters. But on Sunday, July 26th, the tide of fortune seemed to be on the turn. It rained heavily in the night and in consequence we made a late start, not getting away until nearly nine o'clock. Our destination was the old Base Camp, hereafter called the Bridge Camp, on the south bank of the Rishi, and to get there we had to go over the big grass shoulder and cross the Rhamani torrent which lay beyond. Neither in 1934 nor in June this year had we experienced much trouble in crossing this stream provided it was tackled before afternoon. It is fed by a glacier and like all such streams it increased in volume as the day wore on, reaching its maximum at evening, owing to the melting of the glacier as the warmth increased. With this in front of us then, it was desirable to make an early start, but having failed to do this I tried to keep the porters moving and was not unduly worried about the river.

We reached the top of the grass shoulder at midday, when the mist which had been hanging about all morning turned to rain. This was fortunate in a way because the ridge was a favourite halting-place for the Mana men, who loved to sit there and smoke. On fine days there is a magnificent view of Nanda Devi and the gorge. We were quickly driven off by rain, which increased in intensity as we descended to the Rhamani until it became so blinding that it was difficult to find the crossing-place. It was essential to hit off the right place because the Rhamani flows in a miniature box canyon and in that place only was it possible to climb out on the other side.

When we finally reached the river at one o'clock it was running fast and high and looked very uninviting. Loomis and I waded out, tentatively, hand in hand and tied to a rope. We got about half-way and then turned back, for it was over our thighs, or at any rate mine, and running too fast for the porters to be expected to face it. Various futile expedients were tried, such as pushing big boulders into the water. This was the Sherpas' idea, but I think it was more for the pleasure of seeing a boulder go in than from any thought-out plan. A boulder of anything less than five hundredweight would not stand against the current, but there were plenty of big ones about and the Sherpas managed to roll one of nearly half a ton down the bank into the water and the prodigious splash it made was greeted with happy cries—it was a comfort to know that someone was getting some fun out of our predicament. Operations then ceased, for even they were not capable of standing on this and dropping another of equal weight on the far side of it, and so on until the fifty feet of rushing water were bridged.

We cast up and down the bank, but fifty yards either way was all that could be made before cliffs barred further progress. Meantime we were all very wet and cold and it was at last borne in upon us that we must wait here for better times. The word was given to camp, and soon the already water-logged tents were pitched on the narrow bed of shingle, and the Bhotias, as was their way, had found a snug cave some way above the river. It was more annoying to be stopped because once across the Rhamani it was no great distance to the Bridge Camp.

Within an hour of our arrival the river appeared to rise another foot but after that it began to drop a little. Our camp was quite safe because we were six or seven feet above the water, but it was puzzling to know whether the rise was caused mainly by rain or was merely due to the melting of the glacier. If the rain had brought it about we might be here for a day or two, for there was no sign of it stopping, but we hoped that most of the rise was normal, in which case we should be able to get over early in the morning.

We found an overhang that gave enough protection to keep a fire going, and after a hot meal we felt more cheerful, though the outlook was gloomy enough. Before dark I had a talk with the Dotials and told them I wanted four more to return from here. The headman approved of that and though he confessed to being sick himself he did not ask to be one of the four. This sudden illness was probably diplomatic, but had he been at death's door he could not have looked a greater picture of woe, squatting under a tattered umbrella with his head enveloped in a pink shawl. On that I went to bed, but the noise of the river, which seemed to have a note of malice in it, made sleep difficult. Just as I was dozing off, a head was thrust through the tent door and a torrent of words rose high above the roar of the river. It was one of the Dotials, the most vocal of them, a demagogue with a fearful rush of words to the mouth. By his tone I guessed he had not come to tuck me in and say 'goodnight', but it was some time before I grasped the gist of his tirade—they were all going home.

He had chosen the best time for belling the cat because I was not sufficiently awake to be interested and could only tell him to take his face out of the door and shut both. The news was disturbing but was not taken very seriously, and I thought that tactful handling and a lower river would bring about a change of mind.

It rained all night and was still drizzling at dawn when I went outside to have a look at the river. It was still pretty high, but better than yesterday, and routing out Loomis I got him to hold the rope while I went over. We then hauled the rope taut and made fast at each end, spanning the stream, and I hoped that this little surprise arranged for their benefit, would put fresh heart into the Dotials. Early morning bathing in glacier streams might be enjoyed by the hardy souls who break the ice in the Serpentine, but for my part I made a beeline for the kitchen fire to still my chattering teeth.

Here Nima pointed with glee to a great slab of rock which had peeled off the rock of the overhang in the night, falling flat on the fireplace. Another piece now threatened to do the same, but Nima was blowing away at the fire quite indifferently. A Sherpa blowing up a fire is a rare spectacle. He has only to put his head down, and after a few well-directed and long-drawn blasts, which scatter wood and ashes in all directions, a fire which is seemingly past praying for will burst crackling into life; and for dealing with fires, and all that fires imply, food, drink, and warmth, which in this sort of life seem almost as important as life itself, they possess equally useful adjuncts in hands which can lift up live coals and boiling saucepans, and in eyes and lungs which are impervious to smoke.

The Dotials were now stirring, but when they saw the rope across the river it was not greeted with the joyous and enthusiastic shouts that we expected, and presently my eloquent friend of last night was reaffirming their determination to have nothing to do with the river. I told him the river was lower, there was a rope to hang on to, and that all the loads would be put across for them, and on that he retired to take the sense of the meeting. After breakfast the Bhotias descended from their cave and their resourceful minds soon hit on the right method for roping the loads over, putting our scientific brains to shame. Several of them went across by the fixed rope and took up a position on a rock ten feet above the water; others took up a position high up on a cliff on our side immediately opposite. Two 120 ft. climbing ropes were slung across and soon the loads were being tied on and hauled over as fast as they could be carried up the cliff. The fact that the taking-off place was much higher than the landing-place made the hauling quite light work.

The Dotials helped us in getting the loads up instead of sulking as might have been expected, and from this I argued they were going to change their minds and come with us. No loads fell in, the last went over, and then the remaining Bhotias and Sherpas crossed followed by the Sahibs.

It was beginning to rain again when I turned to make a last fervent appeal to the Dotials before crossing myself. The headman, still under his umbrella and wrapped closer than ever in his pink shawl, looked yet more disconsolate and took no interest in the proceedings. I asked for a few to cross, even if only to carry our loads to the Bridge Camp, but the only response to all entreaties was that they were frightened of the river, and that they wanted to be paid off and dismissed. It was time to play the last card, a card that I fondly hoped would be a trump, and I pointed out that all the money was now on the other side so that they would have to cross anyhow to get their pay—to which the reply was, that I could go across and fetch it back.

For a moment it looked as if they would go home without their pay, but bribing one of them with the gift of my umbrella, I persuaded him to cross with me hand in hand. The rupees were unpacked and, sitting by the river with Pasang holding the umbrella over us, we counted out the money due. The transaction was soon completed, for the envoy was too cold and wet to argue about it, and we were spared the importunites of the whole mob for more baksheesh, and the abuse of the headman at receiving none. The man recrossed and with no more ado the Dotials climbed out of the river bed and disappeared in the driving rain.

We discovered much later, on the way back in fact, that they took it out of the Mana men by eating or taking away all the rice left at the Cave Camp, which was two days' rations for the Mana men, a mean act which might have had serious consequences for anyone less tough and less able to look after themselves than the Bhotias.

It was time to consider our own position. Our porter strength was now sixteen instead of forty-eight, but by increasing the Sahibs' loads to 60 lb. we could reckon on shifting about twenty full loads. We still hoped to reach the Bridge Camp that day, and if everyone piled on a bit extra all the loads might be got there in two journeys. The route followed the precipitous bank of the Rhamani down to its junction with the Rishi, a distance of about half a mile. Just above the junction was the natural bridge across the Rishi formed by a giant boulder, but the short approach to the bridge was a sheer wall and loads had to be lowered down. The rock of the bridge too was smooth and slippery, as was the descent on the far side, but all these places had been made easy, if not very safe, when we were here in June by fixing branches as ladders. The camp was only a couple of hundred yards upstream from the crossing-place.

The Bhotias seemed in good heart, rather pleased, I imagined, at the defection of the Dotials, and carrying very big loads we cautiously began the descent to the Rishi. It was infernally steep and slippery, but we got down to a point close above the bridge without incident, dumped the loads there under a tarpaulin, and went back for the remainder. It seemed to me that if we went right on to the camp with this lot it would, under the prevailing weather conditions, be difficult to make anyone turn out again.

By midday everything was assembled at the dump. The loads had then to be carried down to the roping-up place and Loomis and I went down first to receive them as they were lowered. The first load to come down however was received, not by us, but by the Rishi. Apparently Phuta slipped while approaching the dump, which was about 100 ft. higher up; he managed to stop himself rolling, but his load shot down the slope, just missed the party who were busy tying loads on, flew past Loomis' head, and on into the river. I was still lower down and just caught sight of a two-gallon tin of paraffin and the fragments of an oxygen cylinder spinning through the air before they hit the water. I was not sorry to see the oxygen thus taken off our hands, for clearly the time had come for some more scrapping, but the loss of the paraffin could be ill afforded. [The oxygen apparatus had not been brought to assist climbers, but for use in case of illness or frost-bite.]

After this Phuta, very shaken and frightened, was lowered down and parked out of harm's way near the bridge. Then the loads began to arrive, not unaccompanied by small stones, and soon there were enough assembled for the Mana men to start carrying them across the bridge. It was desperately cold work standing there in the pitiless rain and the first fine enthusiasm of the men was evidently on the wane. Once they had carried a load over and dumped it under a convenient overhang it became increasingly difficult to make them leave the shelter for another journey.

At long last everything was down and all hands turned to carrying across the bridge. Bridge is not quite the word for a place where you first had to climb down a wet slab putting all your weight on a branch of wood—a branch for the apparent security of which no one could see any valid physical reason—then to step across a narrow gap with the river roaring and boiling twenty feet below, traverse across another slab and finally descend to *terra firma* by another branch. But by now the Mana men had had enough and began drifting away to a cave which one of them had discovered on the Rhamani side, and in which he had started a fire. The Sherpas were still good for a bit, and with them we started carrying loads up the south bank of the Rishi to the camp site, which was quite close. It consists of a big overhang which is usually bone-dry but where now there was hardly a dry spot. At four o'clock we called it a day; there were still a number of loads by the bridge, but we had enough for our immediate needs and the call of hot tea and food was too insistent.

The chronic state of wetness of our clothes, sleeping bags, and tents did not make for cheerfulness as we discussed the turn which events had taken. For the moment our star was not in the ascendant, but the situation was by no means bad. By cutting down weight a little, only one relay would be necessary and no load need be more than 60 lb.; nor had I any fear of the Bhotias leaving us in the lurch, for they had worked like Trojans until cold and wet finished them. Indeed in one respect the loss of the Dotials could be borne philosophically, if not cheerfully, in that I felt our responsibilities were considerably lightened, and there was now no doubt of our having sufficient food for the porters. I still think it was the river which upset the Dotials and that in good weather we could have got them up the worst part of the gorge, now immediately ahead of us, though some of them might have needed a lot of assistance.

Against these meagre benefits was the fact that it was going to take us longer to reach the mountain and that there would be less time available for climbing it, and, moreover, that from now onwards we ourselves would have to carry heavy loads—not the best preparation, I thought, for heavy climbing. If we did, it would be 'magnificent but not war', that is we would be exhausting ourselves before ever the mountain was reached. In most Himalayan expeditions the object is to spare the climbers any work at all until on the mountain in order to conserve their strength, and here were we proposing to carry 50 or 60 lb. loads over difficult country for the next ten days or more. The alternative of Sherpas and Mana men, meant that the extra time required would not leave us enough food to finish the job. These preconceived ideas were upset and our policy justified by the event.

For all that, I felt that my misplaced confidence in the Dotials had let the party in for this and would not have been surprised to hear some hard things said. But there was not a word of reproach and the aim of all seemed now, more than ever, to be to spend themselves rather than spare.

CHAPTER TEN

The Gorge

THE day after these memorable events dawned fine, and having discussed the position and decided on a plan, we started sorting out loads and rebagging the food. Food was almost the only item on which much weight could be saved, so it was arranged that only enough for forty days should be taken on from here. Having fixed the amount of each kind, it was easy to fill in the varieties, for by now we knew our likes and dislikes. Even so it was a long job which was only just finished before the rain began again at ten o'clock.

One other way in which weight was saved was the abandonment of two pressure cookers. Their scrapping did cause us some heart-burning, since it was from here onwards that their need would be felt. Cooking at high altitudes becomes difficult owing to the low temperature at which water boils; even at 15,000 ft. this temperature is 85 degrees instead of 100 degrees and of course it decreases as you go higher. Tough things like rice, lentils, beans, or dried vegetables will not cook properly at these temperatures, but the difficulty is got over by using a cooker that cooks by steam under pressure, and in which, I think, even a pair of boots would be made edible. It is a thing like a heavy saucepan with a steam-tight lid, fitted with a safety valve, and a whistle which can be adjusted to go off when the desired pressure is reached. We had two of them, and they were left behind with less reluctance because, so far, we had used hardly any rice or lentils—perhaps Loomis and I had had a surfeit of them on the earlier trip.

By the time this work was finished the Mana men had brought everything up from the bridge, and although they were rather expecting to have the day off we persuaded them to make the trip. The plan was to carry some loads as far as the foot of the 'Slabs' and to return here for the night, and at midday we all moved off in drizzling rain carrying 60 lb. loads. It was about 1500 ft. up to the 'Slabs' and the first few hundred feet immediately above camp were as steep and exposed as any part of the route. Numerous birch trees growing out of the cliff face were of great assistance, and provided the branch did not break or the tree pull out bodily it was impossible to fall.

At the top of this bad stretch was a short rock pitch known to us as the 'Birch Tree Wall', where considerable amusement could be had watching the efforts of the purists to climb it *with* a load on and *without* a pull from above.

The difference of climbing without or with a load is not always realised; when bowed down under a load places, which otherwise would not be given a thought, appear to bristle with difficulties and have to be treated with the utmost respect. The centre of gravity has shifted so much that balance has to be learnt afresh and any slight movement of the load may have very untoward results. The Bhotias carry their loads by shoulder straps as we do, but the Sherpas and the Dotials use a head strap which must be far more unsafe for any delicate climbing. On this trip we had brought light carrying-frames provided with a belly band which did much to obviate the risk of a load shifting. They were very successful but, without careful adjustment and judicious padding, at the end of a long day one's back felt as though it had been flagellated.

For the remaining thousand feet there was little difficulty but much labour, and it was with sighs of relief that we dragged ourselves up to the cairn, built in 1934, which marks the end of the climb. From here we descended slightly to a wide grass ledge lying at the foot of a rock wall, and a short way along this we dumped the loads under a little overhang. Taking a couple of Mana men, a quantity of light line, and some rock pitons, I went on up the shallow rock chimney leading to the top of the wall and the foot of the 'Slabs'. We secured the rope at the top of these by means of the pitons so that it hung down the full length of the 'Slabs', affording invaluable assistance to a laden man. This done, we started back and reached the Bridge Camp in an hour, thoroughly wet, but very pleased with our day's work.

Next morning, the 29th, was again fine, and we took advantage of it to do some much-needed drying before packing up. The 'Slabs' were reached by ten-thirty and the slow business of getting the loads up began. Some were busy carrying up the 'Slabs' from the dump while others attended to hauling them up the wall. Luckily the rocks were dry, everyone worked with a will, and by one o'clock all were got up without incident.

From here it took nearly two hours to cover the mile to Halfway Camp with half the loads; the route is intricate, involving much up and down work, and there are one or two bad places. The height of this camp is about 13,000 ft. and it is sited on a very uneven boulder-strewn ridge on which the making of tent platforms is hard work.

It was almost three o'clock when we reached it, and it would have been pleasant to devote the rest of the day to making ourselves comfortable. The Sherpas and the Mana men were of this opinion and lost no time in getting to work digging out boulders and levelling sites. It seemed a pity to disturb them, but I had to remind them that the remainder of the loads had still to be brought from the 'Slabs'. It took some time to overcome their passive resistance to this suggestion but finally all, less Graham Brown and Emmons, started back for a second load.

When put to it the Mana men can move at tremendous speed over rough country, and on this occasion we were left toiling hopelessly in the rear. Knowing their leisurely way, one could only surmise that they had gone mad, but there was method in this madness because the first on the scene had the pick of the loads. There was not much to choose as far as weight went, but we still had our old friends the tent poles with us, and there were other loads which vied with them in popularity, such as a sack of miscellaneous junk of which the *least* angular part was the needle-pointed tripod legs of a plane table; and there were several sacks of sugar which had got wet and started to sweat, so that the shirt of anyone unlucky enough to carry one became like a treacle paper for catching moths.

Better time was made on this second journey, camp being reached soon after five. Graham Brown and Emmons had delved out a tent platform and it was not long before the Sherpas had us all comfortably housed. I say the Sherpas, because at work such as this they are in a class by themselves. No boulder is too big for them and no trouble too great, and when they set to work on a tent platform they remind me of so many terriers digging away at a rat hole.

We were blessed with another fine morning, so that it seemed as though fortune had relented and was smiling on us again. Whilst we were tackling these two difficult stages of the gorge, one of which was now completed, dry weather was an inestimable boon. Of the two I think that over the upper half of the gorge is the worse. There is no place so awkward that loads have to be taken off and roped up, but there are many which are very exposed, which cannot be made safe, and where a slip would be fatal.

Today we reversed the procedure, taking the camp forward and leaving the rest of the loads to be fetched next day. A gully of smooth water-worn slabs had first to be crossed, where the rubber-footwear school could for once tread with more confidence than those clad in orthodox nailed boots. A gently descending terrace brought us to the crux of this part of the route, a place which in 1934 had earned the name of the 'mauvais pas', and for which, at least on my part, familiarity had bred no contempt. Here the general angle steepens until, when standing, you can touch the slope with your elbow. A narrow grass ledge leads to a projecting nose of rock which has to be rounded and then, with no pause, a short steep chimney leads down to another narrow ledge. This continues for about fifty yards of varying degrees of difficulty until finally a high rock bulge is surmounted and the security of a wide terrace reached. The whole distance is so great that there is no means of securing anyone engaged on this traverse, nor is any encouragement derived from the prospect below, where the steep rock and grass slope continues relentlessly to the river a thousand feet below.

The Mana men crossed unperturbed and did not even bother to wait for us at the other end. I took off my shoes and made the Sherpas take off theirs—an advisable precaution, because the trouble with these sort of places was that as more people went over them so they got worse. Many of the footholds were grass tufts and by the time the last man used them they were reduced to a small sloping rugosity of slippery earth. One or two of the Sherpas were unable to negotiate the rock nose and Pasang enjoyed himself carrying their loads for them; he was always ready with a helping hand for the weaker. We made three journeys over the 'mauvais pas' and on each were lucky enough to have it dry; when wet it is hazardous, and once in 1934 when there was a covering of fresh snow it became a nightmare.

Descending by easy grass terraces the route approached the river and the Pisgah Buttress, the last defence of the gorge, and so called because from it can be seen the Promised Land of the Sanctuary. It is a great buttress of rock which springs sheer from the river and then slants less steeply upwards for 2000 ft. The original route in 1934 dropped almost to the river before turning to ascend the gully and grass spur flanking the buttress; but the Mana men have improved on this, and now, by what we called the 'Mana variation', the old route is joined high up the grass spur so that descent to the river is avoided.

This 'variation' we took and, though in places rather exposed, it saved us a lot of hard work. From where the routes joined we climbed a slope almost bare of grass. Working over to the left, we gained a grass terrace backed by a high wall, up which we climbed by means of a rock staircase. On top were slabs, overlapping like tiles on a roof, but set at a moderate angle, and these took us up to another grass terrace, where we rested before tackling the final problem. This was a vertical rock wall only about ten feet high, and a little overhanging chimney was the solution. With a load on, it was a severe struggle, but there were plenty of willing hands above and below. From here to the ridge of Pisgah was long and steep, and Nuri's condition began to cause us some anxiety. He was going slower and slower and at last gave out altogether, so we relieved him of his load and told him to come on at his own pace.

It was nearing two o'clock as we approached the crest of the ridge, but the sun still shone in a clear sky and as we finished the climb and stepped round a rock boss out on to the ridge, Nanda Devi stood there in all her majesty, the cloud veil for once rent aside. All eyes were drawn to the south ridge on which our hopes centred and we prayed that the face which it hid might be less grim than the profile.

Camp was but a short distance away and we took up our quarters on a ledge in front of the low cave in which Loomis and the Bhotias had dumped the seven bags of food in June. It would not hold a tent and sites for these had to be made, a task that the Sherpas set about in their indefatigable manner, digging out and heaving down phenomenal lumps of rock which in their descent threatened to demolish the Mana men who were camped below.

Some of the food bags that had been left here were found to be damp; we turned them all out, spread the flour and satu in the sun, and rebagged it in dry bags. Only about five pounds from each bag had to be thrown away.

Nuri had to be helped into camp and our united medical talent did their best to diagnose his case without much success.

The days spent at Pisgah camp we shall not easily forget. Apart from the view of Nanda Devi, which is probably more striking from here than from anywhere else, a good part of the northern Basin lies spread out below one like a coloured map. In the middle is the great main glacier which terminates in a hundred feet ice wall from beneath which the Rishi rushes; on the left are smooth grass downs broken only by the white moraine of the Changabang glacier; on the right are the variegated rocks, rust red, yellow, and black, of Nanda Devi's pedestal, while in the far background the kindly grass runs up to warm-coloured scree, the scree merges into glacier, and high over all towers the crenellated snow wall of the Basin.

During the two days spent here we were privileged to see all this not only under a bright sun and blue sky but also by the light of a full moon. Even when we had done admiring the miracle of colour performed at sunset, the distant snow-white wall would be suffused with the delicate pink flush of the afterglow; and then as this faded, snow blending with greying sky as the stage was darkened, the curtain rose gradually on yet a third scene. The grey of the sky changed to steely blue, and the snow wall, at first vaguely outlined, shone out clearly like white marble as the moon sailed up from behind a screen of jet-black rock.

The last day of July dawned fine and after a more leisurely breakfast than usual we started back for Halfway Camp. Nuri, who was a very sick man, and three Sahibs remained behind, as there were only nineteen loads to be fetched. The Mana men again set a furious pace and as we were descending the 'variation' we could see them on the 'mauvais pas'. Going flat out, we did the journey in an hour and they must have beaten us by nearly fifteen minutes. It would be interesting to enter some of those men for the Guides' Race at Grasmere where, I feel sure, they would astonish the natives.

Travelling unladen after a week of heavy packing, one felt as if walking on a different planet, perhaps Mars, where the force of gravity is but half that of the earth. Even so the 'mauvais pas' was treated with respect, and on the return journey, grievously burdened as we were, with much more.

We were back soon after one o'clock, observing on the way the beautiful sky phenomenon of an iridescent cloud. The border of a high patch of cirrus cloud appears coloured like a rainbow, the red and green being particularly clear. Until recently their origin was not known, but it is now believed that these coloured patches are fragments of unusually large and brilliant coronae, a corona consisting of a number of concentric rings, rainbow-coloured, which are sometimes seen round the sun or moon when it is covered by a thin cloud veil. It is caused by refracted light from the ice particles which form high cirrus cloud and differs from a halo in having a much smaller radius and a reverse order of colours, blue near the sun and red farthest away. Coronae can be seen frequently round the moon and no doubt they form often round the sun, but owing to the intensity of the light they can only be observed under favourable conditions. I have seen both iridescent cloud and sun halos several times in the Himalaya but nowhere else.

A sun halo is usually regarded as heralding the approach of bad weather, but the period between the omen and the event is indefinite. It seemed to be hardly ever less than a day, but sometimes there was no change in the weather for several days; indeed it was often difficult to see any connection at all between halos and weather. If a corona round the moon is observed and the diameter contracts, it shows that the water particles are uniting into larger ones which may fall in rain; conversely, an expanding corona indicates increasing dryness. The open side of a halo is believed by some to foretell the quarter from which bad weather may be expected. Like most weather signs, halos and coronae are not infallible.

However, the rain, which had held off for so long at this critical time, and now could no longer hinder us, started again the same afternoon. It was with relief and thankfulness that we saw the last load brought into camp and realised that the gorge was now behind us and the way to the mountain lay open.

CHAPTER ELEVEN

The Sanctuary

IN 1934 the next camp from here was close to the snout of the South glacier, but it seemed improbable we should be able to get as far as that with the first loads because we had to return to Pisgah the same day. However, I had a lingering hope that we might, and accordingly made a fairly early start.

Most of the precious time thus gained was wasted before we had gone fifty yards. Close to camp was a broad band of smooth slabs set at an angle of about 30 degrees, caused by the slipping away of the surface soil and the exposure of the underlying rock. The Mana men waltzed across this with no more ado than crossing a road, indeed it was not unlike crossing a road but, of course, less dangerous, and then they sat down on the far side to see how we, the eminent mountaineers, would fare. It was not a prepossessing place to look at and the first few tentative steps soon convinced us that this time appearances had not deceived us. The wretched loads were of course the trouble, for with those on one had not the confidence to stand up boldly and plank the feet down. Each man took the line that seemed good to him, but all got into difficulties, and then was seen the comic sight of seven Sahibs strung out over the slabs in varying attitudes, all betraying uneasiness, and quite unable to advance. The Mana men, having savoured the spectacle to the full and allowed time for the indignity of our situation to sink in, came laughing across the slabs to our aid and led us gently over by the hand like so many children.

Fighting a way down through a heavy growth of bush, we crossed a stream, contoured the other side of a valley, and rounding a high ridge set our faces towards the south. We were now fairly within the Sanctuary, but there was another hour of very rough going over scree and boulders before we trod the grass downs for which we were all longing. After so many days traversing a country so hopelessly askew as that of the Rishi valley, our ankles had developed a permanent flex, and great was now the relief and joy of getting them straight again, of walking without having to hold on, and without watching the placing of every step.

Keen as we were to reach the old camp near the glacier, it was difficult if not useless to drive the Bhotias. All that could be done was to push on as fast and as far as possible, and hope that, in their own good time, they would follow; but it was exasperating to look expectantly back and see them sitting like so many crows on some distant ridge over a mile back. At last about two o'clock, when still some one and a half miles from the glacier, I felt that they would not follow much longer, and sat down to wait for them.

A cold wind blew up the valley, but there was a sheltered grass hollow close by a stream which would make a delightful camp. There was no juniper wood at hand, but we had passed some half a mile back and I knew there was more in front. When the Mana men came, an effort was made to get them to push on a little, but they assured me there was no water for a long way. Two of them had been here in 1934, and when it came to pitting their memory for a country against mine I was quite prepared to give them best; but later we found that this particular piece of information, which I was not prepared to dispute, was a flat untruth. However, it had been a long march, so we dumped the loads and hurried back, reaching Pisgah about five o'clock. Nuri had been left in camp but appeared no better for the rest, and we wondered how he would manage tomorrow when camp had to be moved. It had been yet another fine day despite the omens of the sky, and again from our vantage point we watched the pageant of setting sun and rising moon, beyond the means of a painter, either in words or colour.

We had carried extra-heavy loads on the first journey, hoping that on the second there would be little left but our personal kit, but when the porters had made up their loads it was so arranged that we had each a tent to shoulder: Nuri was able to travel but of course without a load.

All felt slack, the result of our efforts yesterday. Emmons had gone off at the first streak of light to set up his plane table, but when we joined him at his station half-way to camp he told us he had not been able to fix his position. I was not surprised, because from inside the Basin this is by no means easy. To effect it you have to be in a position to see and recognise three known triangulated peaks, all at the same time; and owing to cloud and mist you may have to wait many hours on some bleak and wind-swept spot before this happy event occurs, and when it does you probably mistake one of the peaks and get a completely false result. Before going out to Garhwal in 1934, we had some instruction in plane-table work in Richmond Park, but somehow conditions in the Basin seemed quite different.

Loomis and I reached camp long ahead of the others and impatiently raided the dump for cheese and biscuits, which were still our daily lunch and of which we never tired. On their arrival no time was lost in getting up the tents, for the same cold wind was blowing and presently a drizzling rain set in. The height of this camp was about 14,000 ft. and now for the first time the Mana men condescended to sleep in the despised tents. I confess to some disappointment at this evident sign of degeneration. In 1934, in much the same spot, they appeared quite happy in the lee of a large boulder. Did they but know what our tents were like, their hardihood in proposing to sleep in them might have been admired, but since they expected to find shelter in them their softness was to be lamented. Were the Mana men becoming 'sissies' like their employers?

This camp site was a delicious change after the cramped asperity of the quarters to which we had now been long accustomed, and it was difficult to say which gave us most pleasure, the space, the flatness, or the absence of rock. Below our little hollow the rounded slope curved gently down to the southern branch of the Rishi and the contrast between the opposite bank and our own was as great as it might well be, and could be adequately summed up in the words 'frowning cliffs' and 'smiling downs'. On our side wide slopes of short, sweet grass extended in all directions; a herd of cattle grazing on some distant rise or a flock of sheep coming over the hill would have caused no surprise, so peaceful was the scene. But across the river, savage, reddish-brown cliffs, seamed with dry gullies, rose sheer from the river, presenting a seemingly unbroken alternation of buttress and gully along four straight miles of river frontage; and beyond these the snow and rock of the western ridge of Nanda Devi loomed vaguely in the swirling mists.

It was now August 2nd, and we still had food to feed the Mana men for another five days. Within that time we had to establish a base camp as high up the mountain as we could. The South glacier consists of two main branches which join almost at the snout, one coming in from the south and the other, with which we are concerned, from the south-east. In 1934 we went up this South-East glacier by the true left bank, that is, the side farthest from the mountain, and some two miles up we had found a very pleasant camp at about 16,000 ft.—a sheltered grass flat tucked away behind the moraine and watered by a spring. From this camp we had crossed the glacier, there half a mile wide, and by means of a scree slope gained a serrated rock ridge which, higher up, curled round and merged into the south ridge of Nanda Devi.

It was on this serrated ridge at a height of about 18,000 ft. that we hoped to find a site for a base camp, but the immediate problem was whether to make for the old camp on the far side of the glacier or to go up the unknown right bank. The grassy flat and the spring were very great attractions, but it was more than doubtful if they could be reached in a day from our present camp, so far below the glacier snout. On the other hand by hugging the mountain on the right bank the way would be shortened, and only one camp would be necessary between Sanctuary Camp, where we now were, and the proposed base camp. We decided to eschew the delights of the 1934 camp and to take our chance on the unknown right bank, time being a more important factor than soft lying and spring water.

We got off at eight on the 3rd, all, including Nuri, carrying loads, most of them 60 lb. We had not gone half a mile before coming to a delightful stream of clear water, flanked by an acre patch of dry juniper wood, the sort of camp one only finds in dreams. I was rather ashamed at not having remembered it myself, but I had no doubt that the Mana men knew of it and could not refrain from asking them how they reconciled this with their statement of two days ago, and whether perhaps the stream and the juniper had both come into existence within the last two years. They had lied, and knew that they had lied, but they were not the least abashed, and laughingly replied that we had gone quite far enough that day and they were not to be blamed, indeed we ought to be grateful to them for furnishing such a good excuse for stopping.

About an hour from camp we came to another of our 1934 camp sites, the one near the snout of the glacier. Cached under a rock were a bag of satu and a spring balance. I opened up the satu and, finding that beneath a hard core the inside was still good, was cautious enough to dry it, rebag it, and add it to our reserve.

Opposite this camp is a tremendous avalanche cone of snow which has slid down one of the gullies of the opposing cliffs and formed a permanent bridge over the Rishi. When it first fell it must have dammed the river, but now this flows underneath it by a passage which it has burrowed out for itself. We crossed by this and climbed up the hard snow of the avalanche for a couple of hundred feet before leaving it for the grass of an old moraine. This took us close under the ciffs at the base of the mountain to a corner where their general direction changed from south to south-east. Here the moraine petered out and we had to commit ourselves to the hummocky, boulder-strewn surface of the South-East glacier. Still hugging the cliffs, we advanced slowly, either on the glacier or in the trough lying between it and the cliffs; on these a wary eye had to be kept, for at one point there was a continuous fall of stones that necessitated a wide detour.

At about midday we halted on top of one of the miniature ice-mountains of the glacier to take stock of our position and to allow the Mana men to catch up, for they were finding it heavy going in bare feet on the rough surface of the glacier, though it was seldom that they had to tread on ice. We eagerly scanned the ground ahead, between the glacier and the base of the mountain, for some suggestion of a camp site, but it was clear that grass flats and springs formed no part of the landscape on this side. Half a mile up was a high bank of talus which looked as though it might conceal something, so, leaving the others, Graham Brown and I pushed on to investigate. When opposite the bank we dumped our loads, got off the glacier, and climbed on to the top of the bank by a stone gully. Following up along the edge we came first to a stream and then to a dry flat of sand and mud lying between moraine and cliffs. It appeared to be clear of stone-falls, so we decided it would do and hastened back to call up the others. Pasang dashed ahead, and before Graham Brown and I had reached the foot of the stone gully he was coming down from the glacier carrying both our loads and his own!

By two o'clock everybody was in and, after a long rest, we started back, satisfied at having found in this wilderness of rock and ice such a comparative oasis, but fearing that it might yet prove too far from where we hoped to put our base camp. While we rested here a herd of bharal, or wild sheep, was seen traversing at a gallop the yellow cliffs nearly 1000 ft. above us and stopping occasionally to utter a sort of shrill whistle. On the grass downs of the Sanctuary there are at least two large herds, but this time we did not come across them. Had we seen any, the sight of so much fresh meat walking about might have made us regret our decision against bringing rifles, but to disturb a peace, which for them has never been broken, would be almost sacrilege, nor were a rifle and ammunition worth their weight for the sake of supplementing an ample diet with an occasional haunch of venison. Shooting for the pot may in some circumstances be necessary, but in the Sanctuary both sentiment and expediency are strongly opposed to it. It has been proposed that the Government of the United Provinces make this a sanctuary in fact as well as in name, and it is to be hoped that the game here will continue to enjoy by law the immunity hitherto conferred on them by reputed inaccessibility.

At this Moraine Camp, as it was subsequently known, there was of course no fuel. The limit of height for the invaluable juniper bush is about 14,000 ft. and the height of this camp was 15,000 ft. It was essential to keep our small stock of paraffin, now reduced to 6 gallons, for use on the mountain, so arrangements had to be made to bring wood up to here and on to the next camp, which we hoped would be our base. I wanted to stock the base camp with fuel for three weeks and use no paraffin at all there.

On August 4th we were able to make a start by bringing up two full loads of wood and the rest of us made what small additions of fuel we could to the loads which had still to be carried from Sanctuary Camp. As soon as we reached the new camp at one o'clock it began to rain heavily and a recess under the cliffs had to be burrowed out in order to light the fire. As far as space and flatness went, it was almost as good as the last camp; with all seven tents pitched, and a neat pile of loads under their tarpaulin, it had a most business-like appearance. In fact some were so attracted by it that there was a suggestion that it should be made our base.

It was I think this proposal—no more than a proposal—that led to a very happy evening and, as we realised later, a very timely one. Loomis apparently, had been carrying, buried in the recess of his kit, a small flask of Apricot Brandy, and, on the grounds that we had now reached what could, might, or ought to be our base camp, he was moved to produce it.

The secret had been well kept and when, supper over, our mugs, contrary to custom, were returned to us clean, we assumed that someone was going to make a brew of cocoa. Judge then of our surprise and pleasure when instead of that flaccid beverage this small bottle of beautiful amber liquid appeared, and was with due reverence uncorked. One's sense of smell gets a bit blunted in the course of an expedition—it has to—but grateful, oh most grateful, was the aroma of that Hungarian nectar which by some subtle alchemy overcame the fetid atmosphere of the tent. The flask was small and our pint mugs, seven in all, were large, but Napoleon brandy itself could not have been sipped with such gusto or lingered over so lovingly.

As the brandy was good so it was potent, and that distant country Alaska, of which we had already heard more than a little, assumed, along with its travellers, new and terrifying aspects. The already long glaciers of that frozen land increased in length, the trees which seemingly burgeon on these glaciers grew branches of ice, the thermometer dropped to depths unrecorded by science, the grizzlies were as large as elephants and many times as dangerous, and the mosquitoes were not a whit behind the grizzlies in size or fierceness, but of course many times more numerous. And amid all these manifold horrors our intrepid travellers climbed mountains, living the while on toasted marshmallows and desiccated eggs, inhabiting tents similar to ours, and packing loads which to think of made our backs ache. To echo and amend Dr Johnson, 'Claret for boys, port for men, but Apricot Brandy for heroes.'

CHAPTER TWELVE

The Base Camp

THE morning following this debauch we sent all the Mana men down the valley for fuel. The Sherpas and ourselves set out with the intention of finding a base camp, carrying 60 lb. and 40 lb. respectively: as the height increased we should find this quite enough, for we hoped to get somewhere near 18,000 ft., which would be higher than most of us had ever been.

We pursued the same tactics as yesterday, keeping where possible in the trough between the glacier and the cliffs, sometimes being forced out on to the glacier. Progress was rather laborious, but in an hour and a half we reached the foot of the scree slope up which Shipton and I had gone in 1934, and this was now the scene of a regrettable incident, nothing less than the loss of one of our scientists. On the way up the glacier Odell, either through excess of zeal or insufficiency of load, had led the field at a rare pace and the field had got rather strung out. By the time we plodders had reached the foot of the scree he was out of sight. I told him that we had to turn up a scree slope but, perhaps in the traditional absence of mind of the professor, or, more likely, because his eyes were glued to the ground after the manner of geologists and prospectors, he had steamed past without noticing it. We sat there for some time wasting valuable breath, which we should presently need, shouting for him, but with no effect.

I forget what load he was carrying. It may have been, and poetic justice demanded that it should have been, the unmentionable glacier drill; but I hardly think it was, because I remember we were flattering ourselves that that would be dumped at Moraine Camp where there was what seemed to be, at least to our ignorant minds, a fair sample of Himalayan glacier within a stone's throw, waiting to be drilled.

Anyhow we wrote Odell off for that day at least and addressed ourselves to the task presented by the steep scree. It was not as loose as scree can be, but it was loose enough to make it very hard work for the man in front, whose feet sank down several inches at every step. We rejoiced to see a stream of water coming down, indicating that we might find water on top of the ridge. We had had some doubt about this and later it was disappointing to see that the source of this stream was a good 500 ft. below the crest.

It took over two hours to climb the 1500 ft. to the top, and, before it was reached, rain, which presently turned to snow, began to fall. We gained the crest at a notch just below the fantastically weathered 'coxcomb' of crumbling yellow rock which gave the ridge its serrated appearance and also its name, for we now preferred the 'Coxcomb', *tout court*, to the former 'Saw-tooth' or 'Serrated' ridge.

Where we stood the ridge runs roughly east and west. On the south side, up which we had come, is the South-East glacier, one branch of which flows round the eastern foot of the ridge from its head beneath the southern slopes of East Nanda Devi, Nanda Devi itself, and the mile of snow ridge connecting the two. These slopes, together with the south ridge of Nanda Devi, make up a tremendous cwm, comparable, though on a lesser scale, to the West Cwm of Everest. From our position on the ridge then it will be understood that we looked down on to the upper névé of the South-East glacier and across it to East Nanda Devi. Had our erratic (I use the word in its strict sense of 'wandering') scientist continued his course up the right bank of the glacier, we would now have seen him on the glacier below us; but this we neither hoped nor expected, and I mention it merely in an attempt to explain the topography.

We now turn west along the crest of the ridge until driven off it by the steep and jagged rocks, below which we traversed on the north side. There was no sign of water, nor did it appear likely that we should find any higher up. The only alternatives for a base camp were on the névé of the glacier 200 or 300 ft. below us or near the source of the stream which we passed on the way up. The former would have been a fairly frigid spot for a base camp and the presence of water was problematical; the advantages were its height and the fact that the whole of our proposed route up the mountain would be in view. On the south side of the ridge the camp would be on shale, which is as preferable to ice for sleeping on as a feather bed is to a 'donkey's breakfast'. Also water was plentiful; but against this was the 500 ft. plug up to the ridge and the fact that the mountain would not be in view at all, though some of us thought this was a point in its favour. Emmons was the only one who preferred the glacier site. As he would have to spend most of his time there his opinion carried weight, but he was overruled, and I hope he was duly grateful.

While this discussion was going on, we were getting colder and wetter, so we dumped the loads under the 'Coxcomb' wall, covered them up, and hurried back. These loads contained nothing that we could not do without at the base, and we could therefore leave them here to be picked up when we returned this way to establish Camp I. Plunging and scree-riding down the southern slope, we reached the bottom in about twenty minutes, where we found a note from Odell saying that he had left his load and gone back to camp.

We followed him there, arriving at half-past three, and were mightily surprised to find Carter. We had calculated that he could not get here for another two days and I am afraid our first reaction was a feeling of relief that the Apricot Brandy had been drunk last night. Kalu was with him, his damaged reputation somewhat mended, and two other coolies, one from Mana and one from Lata—an acquisition of strength which would have been more welcome had we not got to feed them. The Bhotias got back later with big loads of wood.

The morning of the 6th was as unpleasant as it could be, raw, wet, and misty. The Sherpas, less Da Namgyal, and the Sahibs, got away with loads by nine o'clock, but the Bhotias were extremely reluctant to leave their tents. They disliked the glacier travel and made anxious inquiries about the route, but luckily I was able to assure them that it was free from ice or snow. Even so, much patience was required, but at last, an hour later, they made up their loads of fuel and started. Da Namgyal remained in camp because his cough was troubling him. He had suffered from this almost from the start and every night we would hear him coughing in the most distressing way; he must have made sleep difficult for his tent-mates, who were probably relieved when I sent him down.

The Mana men needed coaxing on the way up and I was fearful lest they should jib; indeed on one occasion when I had got too far ahead they were so long in coming that I went back to look for them, fully expecting to find that they had had enough. However, they brightened up when we reached the scree slope and I could point out our destination, nor were they long in reaching it. We were joined here by Odell, who had retrieved yesterday's error and was now carrying two loads. The others passed us on the way down, but by three o'clock the last of us were back at the Moraine Camp, having dumped the loads and the wood on a fairly flat site close to the highest water. Into the remainder of the short afternoon we crowded the writing of letters and the further weeding of our kits, for tomorrow the Base Camp would be occupied and the Mana men dismissed.

A wonderfully fine morning greeted us on this important day. On account of the Mana men there was no time to waste since they had to carry loads to the Base Camp, receive their pay, and then get down to the wood and warmth of Sanctuary Camp because they would be without tents.

More kit was left here, things that we should not need on the mountain and things that never should have been brought. Odell and I had some harsh words over the glacier drill, because in making up the loads for the men this had been left out on the assumption that it would stay here, an erroneous assumption, because we now learnt that what to our uninstructed minds appeared to be a perfectly good bit of glacier was to the scientific mind beneath contempt. The glacier down here was too old, worn, and decrepit to yield the desired results; its temperature at depth—'the be-all and the end-all' of our hopes, the sum of our ambition, that which we had left England to find—this could only be taken where it was young, fresh, and unsullied by a covering of stones. The glacier drill went with us.

We made good time and reached the new camp at half-past eleven and immediately began paying off all the men, except Kalu, who was to stay with us in place of Da Namgyal, whose job was to go back with the Bhotias as far as Joshimath, where he could have a week or ten days' rest. Then having collected six men from Lata village he was to return up the gorge, bringing our mail and two loads of coolie food, and to arrive at the Base Camp by September 1st.

Kalu was overjoyed at being promoted to the ranks of the Sherpas, though I take leave to doubt whether the joy was mutual. He indulged in a little of his customary chest-thumping but retained sufficient presence of mind to claim Da Namgyal's high-altitude clothing and boots, which Da Namgyal was very loth to surrender. That important point settled in his favour, Kalu then made the round of the Sahibs, praying diligently, and cadging tobacco. He was the most inveterate smoker I have ever met and would smoke charcoal, paper, or old rags if there was nothing else. Now that the Mana men were leaving he was without a pipe, but he got over that in a very ingenious manner. He made a long sloping hole in the earth like the adit of a miniature mine, and then sank a vertical shaft to cut this at the lower end. The shaft was filled with tobacco, or in Kalu's case anything inflammable, and the smoker's mouth was applied to the mouth of the adit. It gives, I imagine, a very cool smoke, and does away with the tiresome necessity of carrying a pipe about, and to this day I regret that I did not get Kalu to try the same method during his very brief residence on snow.

The paying off of the Mana men took place under circumstances very different to the last pay-day, even if only because it was a fine hot day instead of a pouring wet one. These men had done all, and more, than was expected of them. We could be liberal ungrudgingly, and we parted, at any rate on our side, with feelings of esteem and almost affection. They are the most likeable of men and in character not unlike the Sherpas; given the opportunity, they might in time become as useful on a mountain as the Sherpas, but if that was ever the case I should hate to have the paying of them. For once they now appeared satisfied with what we gave them, true they asked for more, but only as a matter of form, and the demand was not pressed very hard. Many and profound were their salaams, and then they ran down the scree, laughing and shouting like schoolboys on a holiday. To them we owed a lot.

It was a great satisfaction to be here. We felt that at last after nearly a month, or in some cases two months, of preparatory drudgery the stage was set and the supernumeraries dismissed; or like a builder who, having finished the prosaic task of digging the foundations, was about to begin the more exciting job of erecting the walls. To be rid of all coolies and to have no one but the Sherpas and ourselves to look after gave a new feeling of confidence, for, capable though the Bhotias are of taking care of themselves, they can yet be a source of worry. It is one of the drawbacks of Himalayan climbing that coolies should be necessary, but I think that anyone who has travelled with the better type of Sherpa would like to have them along with him whether necessary or not, just for the fun of their companionship.

We had good reason to be pleased with the result of all this preliminary work. We were not more than a week behind schedule, we had a comfortable Base Camp stocked with a month's food and three weeks' wood fuel, and everybody except two of the Sherpas was in good health and spirits. None of us had had any sickness on the way up, apart from a few septic sores. Loomis was the worst sufferer in this respect, but his were now practically healed, thanks to Houston's assiduous attention.

There were too many unknown factors for us to gauge with any accuracy our chances of getting to the top, but at this stage we were decidedly hopeful. The view of the south ridge from Pisgah had rather dashed us, but a closer, though fleeting, look from the 'Coxcomb' ridge *en face*, even with due allowance for foreshortening, had been encouraging. But if the first appearance had proved to be false, common sense might have told us that the other need not be true. That this was so we were presently to learn.

CHAPTER THIRTEEN

A First Footing

I HAVE always admired those people who before ever reaching a mountain, perhaps even before seeing it, will draw up a sort of itinerary of the journey from base camp to summit—a complicated affair of dates, camps, loads, and men, showing at any given moment precisely where A is expected to be, what B will be doing, what C has had for breakfast, and what D has got in his load. It always reminds me of the battle plans an omniscient staff used to arrange for us in France, where the artillery barrage and the infantry went forward, hand in hand as it were, regardless of the fact that while there was nothing whatever to impede the progress of the barrage, there were several unknown quantities, such as mud, wire, and Germans, to hamper the movements of the infantry.

Parallels drawn from warfare are apt, and difficult to avoid, but they assort very ill with the spirit of mountain climbing; yet any programme that includes a human factor is liable to go amiss, and in our case almost every factor was unknown. Moses himself, who was no mean organiser, could hardly cope with a problem of movement which included such imponderables as the route, the state of the snow, the rate of climbing, the weather, the porters, and the powers of acclimatisation of a party only two of which had been over 17,300 ft. before.

In the final stages of a climb, when the unknowns have been greatly reduced, a time-table is essential, but we made no attempt to elaborate any such miracle of organisation and foresight at this early hour. We might have succeeded in keeping in step for one day, but, as will appear, the second and third days would have played the devil with it.

The first thing to do was to find a Camp I and take up everything we should need on the mountain, including food for twenty-five days, leaving at the Base Camp a week's extra food and twenty days' food for Emmons, who was stopping there. We had the advantage of knowing that there were no difficulties up to 19,000 ft., so we were able to start without waiting to reconnoitre. We completed our loads from the dump on the ridge and continued traversing below the 'Coxcomb', the Sherpas carrying 60 lb. and ourselves 40 lb., which we found was as much as we could well manage at this height.

We kept as high as possible under the rock wall, over some very loose ground, and as soon as the ridge beyond the 'Coxcomb' looked feasible we edged up to the left to get on to it. To do this a patch of snow had to be crossed, but even at the late hour of midday it was in fair condition, a fact we noted with premature satisfaction. On the crest of the ridge we were once more on rock and at one o'clock we reckoned the height at 19,000 ft. This was gauged by taking a clinometer reading to the top of what was known as 'Longstaff's Col', a col on the rim of the Basin at the foot of the shoulder of East Nanda Devi. It is not a pass, or at least it was not then, because it had not yet been crossed, but in 1905 Dr Longstaff and his two guides, the Brocherels, had stood on this col and were the first to look down into the inner Sanctuary. To quote Dr Longstaff: 'Below us was an extraordinary chaos of wind-driven cloud, half veiling the glaciers which surround the southern base of Nanda Devi. Above was the vast southern face of the great peak, its two summits connected by a saddle of more than a mile in length. From this spot the mountain strangely resembles Ushba, and the likeness must be even more striking from the West. Directly from the col rose the southern ridge of the eastern peak by which we hoped to make the ascent.'

By now none of us were feeling very strong and it was time to look for a camp site, for there was nothing suitable in the immediate vicinity. While we were admiring the view or, less euphemistically, resting, Houston and Loomis went up about 300 ft. and reported there was a possible site. When we got to it, it appeared so uninviting that I went up still higher, hoping to find something better. But there was not the vaguest suggestion of a tent platform, the rock of uniform steepness sloped away to the névé of the glacier on the one side, on the south was a precipice, and the ridge in between was too narrow and broken even to climb, much less furnish a platform. It now began to snow, so we fell furiously to digging out and buiding up three platforms on the proposed site. At the end of an hour's hard work, we had three passable platforms, one big enough for the two-man bivouac tent and two for the larger 6 ft. × 7 ft. tents. This done, we stowed the loads under a convenient ledge and hurried back to the Base Camp at half-past four. The height of this Camp I was 19,200 ft.

At breakfast next morning what may have been a spontaneous and was certainly an almost unanimous desire for an off-day found expression. It happened to be a Sunday, so we may have felt that some recognition of this was due, or perhaps a mental itinerary had persuaded us that we had more time in hand than would be needed to complete the job. It was so tempting to divide the remaining 6000 ft. into three lifts of 2000, allot a couple of days to each and one day to get down, and so climb the mountain in a week. Poor Maurice Wilson, who tried to climb Everest alone and die on the glacier from exhaustion, had much the same notion; but for him the problem was even simpler, for he did not worry much about height and estimated his task in terms of distance—a mere seven miles from Rongbuk monastery to the top.

A fine, sunny morning made some of us regret the waste of a good day, but a wet afternoon made amends. It may have been a wise resolve physiologically, but tactically it was a mistake, because experience shows that there are usually enough involuntary rest-days due to weather without adding any voluntary ones. The time was spent pleasantly enough smoking too much, eating too much, and in too much group photography—the results of these alone, portraying as they do what looks like a blackguardly group of political refugees (politics according to taste), are ample condemnation of off-days. Loomis and Emmons relieved me of the catering for the day and I have grateful recollections of some inspired hominy cakes. The Sherpas had rigged up a very effective roof for the kitchen out of the bit of tarpaulin and the ponderous steel tent poles, which now almost justified their existence, but which, I am glad to say, were not to go any higher. We had three light aluminium poles for use on the mountain and, though they were fragile enough to look at, they stood up uncommonly well.

Early in the night the rain turned to snow and when we woke next morning there were six inches of snow at the camp, and the glacier below was white down to 14,000 ft. It was still snowing hard, so we sat tight and towards midday the wind got up and very soon a blizzard was blowing from the south-west. Conditions were rather miserable, the kitchen roof blew away at intervals or collapsed under the weight of snow, and even when up afforded little protection to the fire or to anyone working there. To add to our worries Kitar and Nuri were now on the sick list. Nuri had never recoverd from his attack at Pisgah and daily looked more fragile and more anxious; clearly we could strike him off the strength. Kitar had complained of his stomach at Pisgah, but after being dosed had said no more about it. I noticed he always took the lightest loads he could and we thought he was a bit of a 'lead-swinger', but in this we maligned him.

Meanwhile we lay in our tents thinking sorrowfully on sundials and their sententious advice about the passing moment and the lost day that never returns, and vowing with many oaths that we would go up to Camp I on the morrow, blizzard or no blizzard. It was still snowing and blowing in gusts when we turned out, but there were breaks in the flying scud and a brighter patch of light in the murky sky assured us that the sun had risen even if the cock had not crowed.

This day we meant to establish Camp I, but only ourselves were to sleep there, the Sherpas returning to the Base Camp and bringing up the final loads on the following day. The loads had to be dug out from under a canopy of snow and it was half-past nine before we began plodding heavily up to the ridge in the soft new snow. On the north side of the 'Coxcomb' the snow was deeper and we were forced to take a lower route, changing the lead every ten minutes. This route took us on to the névé of the glacier, where we had a sorry time floundering in soft snow, and were finally led into what appeared to be a bottomless pit. At this point there was some discussion whether we should keep down a little longer or at once strike up over the snow-covered rocks to the ridge. It seemed to me rather like debating the advisability of walking in the ditch or on the road, but the luckless man in the lead, although up to the neck in snow, still evinced a strange preference for the lower route. Pasang, however, who happened to be next, had no doubt about it and struck out boldly for the rocks, where the rest of us speedily followed. Our ruffled feelings caused by this ignominy soon recovered on the better going afforded by the ridge, and by two o'clock we had reached our goal.

The snow had stopped by now and the wind died away, but the diminutive platform buried under snow and the complete absence of any drips of water from the rocks formed a very discouraging welcome. All hands fell to clearing away the snow, and at almost the first dig one of our two precious Bernina shovels went down the *khud*. These Berninas are light collapsible shovels of aluminium which are invaluable for digging tent platforms in snow. The business end of this one was improperly secured and at the first thrust came off the handle, went over the edge of the platform, and so down the snow slope to the glacier 500 ft. below. This was the second, but neither the last nor the most aggravating, occasion on which we learnt that the laws of gravity were much the same on Nanda Devi as elsewhere.

Owing to the accident of the ground, the three platforms were of necessity at considerable intervals apart, and to pass from one to the other was quite a climb. The job of cooking was assigned to the middle tent, of which Odell and myself were the unlucky occupants, on the specious pretext that it was most handy. Our system of allotting tents was a haphazard one and the only guiding principle was that of frequent changes. The object of this was to avoid any tendency to form cliques and it was beneficial in various ways. If a man knows that his martyrdom has only to be endured for a night or two running, he can tolerate good-humouredly the queerest little idiosyncrasies of his stable-companions. Some of us talked too much or too loudly, some did not talk enough, some smoked foul pipes, some ate raw onions, some *never* washed, some indulged in Cheyne-Stokes breathing, and one even indulged in Cheyne-Stokes snoring. I should explain that this form of respiration afflicts one at high altitudes and only occurs during unconsciousness. Short bursts of increasingly violent panting, as though the victim was suffocating, rise to a crescendo and are succeeded by complete stillness as if the man has died, although a quickly recurring spasm convinces the other occupants of the tent that this unfortunately is not so. The devastating effects of this sort of thing when combined with snoring can be imagined. But these singularities, which, if endured for too long, might lead to murder, were, by our system of musical chairs, matter only for frank criticism or even amusement.

The unfortunate necessity of cooking, from which we seem to have wandered, was on the mountain a very simple routine. All that it implied was boiling the porridge and beating up the dried milk in the morning, and in the evening boiling the pemmican. No more was allowed, and in the fullness of time (such is habit), no more was expected—I was going to say 'desired', but that perhaps would be putting it too strongly. It sounds simple enough, but the production of these sybaritic repasts needed first the presence of a Primus stove in the cook's tent. Moreover, this stove had to be lit and kept alight in the teeth of all the devils which seemed at once to take possession of it, causing it to splutter, smoke, lick the tent roof with a devouring flame, do everything in fact except burn. Perhaps I exaggerate, for all were not like this, the outbreaks were few, and with skilled and sympathetic handling need not occur at all. Still there the beastly thing was in the tent, room had to be made for it, patience exerted on it, the fingers burnt by it, the nostrils assailed by it, and its fumes swallowed. To have to do and suffer thus was excellent moral discipline, but it should only be taken in small doses and the stove should change tents as frequently as the personnel.

Cooking was only the penultimate duty of the cook; before this came the providing of water and after it the dishing out into seven expectant mugs— enamel ones that is. Here both skill and expedition were required, for if there was expedition and no skill the tent floor received the most liberal helping, and, if the converse held, the pemmican congealed before the other tents got their ration. Practice, as always, makes perfect, and it was astonishing what prodigies of pouring were performed from any height, at any angle, and, if need be, in the dark.

The provision of water was at Camp I a simple matter except on this first night when everything was under snow. Thereafter there was a useful drip from some nearby rocks and a cunning distribution of pots in the morning assured the evening supply. Higher up it was not so easy, and ice or hard snow had to be dug out in sufficient quantity. The melting of this takes longer than the boiling, and some judgment is needed to know what amount of water different types of snow will yield. The hapless cook lights his stove, puts the snow on to melt, and while this is doing takes off his boots and gets into his sleeping bag. He then discovers that a heaped saucepan of snow has yielded a teacupful of water, and perforce leaves his warm bag, puts on his boots, and collects more snow—not only in the saucepan but also in his imperfectly laced boots and socks. An attempt was made to enact that the tent doing the cooking should also distribute the food to the other tents, but this seemed to Odell and me (at that moment anyhow) a monstrous arrangement akin to sweated labour, or like making the condemned man dig his own grave.

Next morning was fine and cold but did not look promising. The party split up, three went down to the dump to help the Sherpas and were also commissioned to look for the shovel, Graham Brown and Houston were to prepare a fourth tent platform against the arrival of the Sherpas, and Odell and myself had the more interesting job of reconnoitring for the second camp. Immediately above us there appeared to be about 800 ft. of rock and snow ridge similar to that on which we were, and beyond was a steep snow arête, which continued for possibly 500 ft., before flattening out into a convenient snow saddle, the very place, we thought, for Camp II.

It was indeed the very place for a camp, but it was not Camp II that we put there but Camp III, and it was five days later before it was occupied.

How hopelessly out we were in these glib estimates, due to foreshortening, was apparent in a very short time, and henceforth we took very little on trust. For 700 or 800 ft. we mounted steadily, taking a line just below the crest of the ridge on the east side of it, for on the western it was precipitous. It was by no means similar to the ridge below, being decidedly steeper and very much looser. In fact when we came to carrying loads up here it became a nightmare owing to the danger from loose rocks, nor was it possible to escape the danger by keeping to the crest, so sharp and broken was it. If I am ever guilty of using the phrase 'firm as a rock' again, I shall think of this ridge and strike it out.

Above this horrible section the rocks were snow-covered and before going any farther we sat down for a long rest at what was subsequently known as the 'roping-up place', for from this point onwards a rope was essential. Both of us were feeling the effects of altitude here, though later in the day, when we got higher, we felt it less; perhaps we were taken out of ourselves by the more interesting and difficult climbing in the same way that a man will cease being sea-sick if the ship is sinking—having something better to think about. Between 19,000 ft. and 20,000 ft. seemed to be the critical height and both the old hands and the newcomers suffered from extreme lassitude, and one or two from headaches and slight nausea. Personally I was astonished at the speed with which those who had not been high before did acclimatise, and how comparatively mild their symptoms were. In 1935 four of us, crossing a pass of only 17,000 ft. from Sikkim into Tibet, suffered extremely, and although carrying no loads were quite incapable of keeping pace with our transport which, since it included some yaks, was not exactly devouring the ground. Such discrepancies are difficult to explain and a great deal has yet to be learnt about acclimatisation. Houston collected all the data he could to help in this object and persuaded most members of the party to submit to keeping a very detailed and indecently intimate record of their day-to-day symptoms and feelings. The keeping of such records in the cause of science is I suppose very praiseworthy, and since questions had to be answered and symptoms noted in that grim interval between awakening and getting out of one's sleeping bag, it showed amazing restraint and commendable determination in all who undertook the task. To be confronted morning after morning, at that unseasonable hour, with such questions as how one had slept, and what one at that moment desired, would compel most people, including the writer, to try to be funny at the expense of truth. Psycho-analysis, medical examinations, oxygen masks, *et hoc genus omne*, seem a far cry from mountaineering as understood by Whymper, Leslie Stephen, Mummery and the giants of the past.

The effects of the recent blizzard were felt on this upper section, because there was a lot of fresh snow which had to be cleared away before steps could be cut in the underlying harder snow or ice. For some way it was a straightforward upward traverse just below or sometimes on the crest of the ridge, but presently a double cornice warned us off the crest just when this course had become most desirable owing to the increasing angle of the snow slope.

On one pitch the snow beneath the cornice was so steep and deep that, instead of steps, a continuous track had to be scraped and stamped out, and at the farther end of this critical passage a hole had to be flogged through another cornice, crowning a short lateral rib, which crossed our line at right angles. Having successfully emulated the camel, we were rewarded by a good stance, where one man could anchor the party with an axe belay while the other essayed a traverse across some rotten rocks, covered with snow and verglas. Thanks to a loose rock, the leader here came unstuck and shot down some distance before being stopped by the rope secured round the second's axe driven deeply into the snow.

After this, in every sense *moving* incident, we regained for a short space the security of the ridge only to be driven off again by a cornice under which another long traverse had to be made. Early in the day our ambitions had been fixed on the snow saddle; at the roping-up place the snow arête leading to it would have contented us; and, as the difficulties increased, so our hopes receded down the ridge, until now we were aiming at what looked like a rock platform, only 100 ft. above us and still 300 ft. from the foot of the arête. Even this we were destined not to see.

This last traverse took longer than we expected, because once more a continuous track had to be beaten out while the overhang of the cornice did its best to shove us off. By the time we had finished this, snow was falling, and it was three o'clock, so we decided to call it a day. We were probably 1500 ft. above Camp I and, considering the route, it was clear that this would be a long enough carry when laden. The fact that in all the distance we had come there was no suitable place for a tent was disturbing, but we had strong hopes of the top of the rock bulge now just above us.

We got down at five o'clock to find the others back and four Sherpas ensconced in the fourth tent. No Bernina shovel had been found and another similar accident had occured. A full tin of tea, left on the platform outside one of the tents, had for some unexplained reason gone over the edge. The only witnesses to this tragedy were Graham Brown and Houston, who were working on another platform and suddenly noticed it rolling down the slope; and it was the more serious because, but for an ounce, this was all the tea we had left. I think that the only drink worth having on a mountain is one which will quench thirst, and that things like cocoa and patent drinks, which pretend to be food as well, are not worth their weight. After all, the bulk of the food, like pemmican and porridge, is slops and what is really wanted is something to eat, that is chew, and something to drink, not an anaemic mixture of the two. Even the Americans, traditionally hostile to tea and addicted to cocoa and kindred drinks, came round to this point of view and felt the deprivation as much as the tea-swilling British.

We were rather wet and miserable and by nightfall it was snowing hard, a state of affairs which gave us more concern on account of the lost tea than for its effect on the mountain; every flake that fell buried it deeper and lessened the already remote chances we had of finding it.

Lloyd and Carter were still feeling the altitude here and Kalu and Phuta were both sick, so they were detailed to go down and look for the tea. Four full-grown men poking about in the snow of a glacier for a 1 lb. tin of tea sounds like mountaineering with Alice in Wonderland, but it seemed natural enough at the time and it gives some measure of how we felt our loss. In a few days the Americans, who have not been brought up on tea, were talking about it as they might of whisky in the days of Prohibition, so that the hell of unfulfilled longing which the wretched Englishmen endured can well be imagined.

Five of us carrying 20 lb., and Pasang and Nima carrying 40 lb., set out to find Camp II. The 700 ft. up to the roping-up place were purgatorial, particularly for the leader, for the task of finding the best route and at the same time treading delicately, like Agag, to avoid launching great rocks on to those below was very wearing. The slightest mistake in placing a foot would inevitably send down a stone and a too vigorous use of the hands would have brought a large piece of the arête about one's ears. In places it was impossible to avoid crossing back above those behind, and the only thing to do was to wait until they were clear. I nearly bagged Odell this way, but he managed to duck and the rock went over his head.

At eleven o'clock it began snowing again. We climbed on two ropes of three and four, with a Sherpa in the middle of each, and by half-past one had reached almost to yesterday's highest point. The old steps were of great use, but all had to be cleared again of snow and, laden as we were, we moved with great caution, particularly on the traverse leading to the needle's eye, which was petrifying for the performer though probably amusing enough for the onlooker. At the thinnest part of the traverse a protruding ice bulge enforced the adoption of almost a crawl to get by, and, if the attitude was not sufficiently humble, the load jammed under the bulge, greatly to the embarrassment of its bearer and the diversion of the second man who, fortunately, at this critical juncture, had a secure axe belay in a niche beneath the cornice.

Just before the upper traverse there was perhaps room for a small bivouac tent, so, leaving the others there in case nothing better was found, Odell and I crossed the traverse to investigate the platform which we had failed to reach the previous day. The movement round the projecting nose of rock covered with snow of doubtful integrity was a delicate one, but we were rewarded by finding on top of the nose a place which with a little work could be made to hold one tent, possibly two. It was a slightly sloping snow-covered ledge measuring about 6 ft. x 20 ft. set in the angle of a sheer rock wall, which enclosed it on two sides. On the third side was the way by which we had come and the fourth fell away steeply to the glacier now nearly 2000 ft. below. At first sight it looked as though we had entered a cul-de-sac, but a little search disclosed a snow ledge outside the rock wall furnishing an exit almost as perfunctory as the entrance.

It was now late, so without bringing the others up we dumped our two loads there and all went down together. We got back to Camp I wet through and found Emmons had come up to see what was happening. When he went down he took with him Kalu, the great chest-thumping Kalu who had already had enough—perhaps he wanted to get back to somewhere where he could dig holes in the ground for a pipe. The all-important matter of finding a place for Camp II had been settled and we had learnt that at any rate two of the Sherpas were fairly safe climbers. Pasang was particularly steady and Nima too was good but a bit light-hearted in his management of the rope. On the whole therefore it had been a day of gains, but against this was Kalu's defection, Phuta's sickness, the weather, and failure to find the tea. I must have been feeling a bit hipped myself, a state of mind which in politer society than that of our own we would have called 'sanguinary-minded', for the last entry in my diary runs: 'Still snowing 7 p.m. and we still cooking.'

CHAPTER FOURTEEN

On the Mountain

OUR plan now was for two of us to occupy Camp II or the Gîte, as it was appropriately called, and on the following day, while those two went up higher to look for a Camp III, two Sherpas would join them at the Gîte. We assumed that a site for Camp III would be found on the snow saddle, and on the third day the Sherpas would assist in establishing the two Sahibs there while two more of us in turn occupied the Gîte.

It was a fine morning on the 14th, but we did not get away until 10 a.m. Graham Brown and Houston, who were going to sleep at Camp II, had to pack up the bivouac tent and their own gear and then someone dropped a mug down the *khud* and Houston very sportingly went down after it. The task looked hopeless in all the new snow, but he got it. Odell stayed in camp to catch up with his geological notes, but six of us started with Pasang and Nima.

At the roping-up place Carter went back as he had not yet acclimatised, and from there we climbed on three ropes, Lloyd and Nima, Pasang and myself, and Graham Brown, Houston, and Loomis. As usual the steps had to be cleared of snow and in places they were now not very reliable, but by cutting deep in they held sufficiently well. The passage round and up the projecting nose below the Gîte roused so much misgiving that we talked of putting a fixed rope there. But it was an awkward place to fix anything and in the end familiarity bred sufficient contempt for us to do without. A rope of two can move quicker than one of three, so Lloyd and I got there well ahead of the others and Pasang and Nima began making a platform; it now looked as though there would just be room for the bivouac tent and a big one. When they had finished I took them down on my rope, Lloyd waiting for the others, who had not yet arrived. By six o'clock it was snowing again.

The journey to Camp II, though now a daily routine, was never boring however unpleasant it might be in other ways. The unstable rocks of the lower half still lay in wait to punish any carelessness, and on the upper section the daily snow-fall made it at least look like a new ascent.

The next day all started except Phuta and, when we reached the roping-up place, we descried what looked like two flies crawling up the steep snow arête above the Gîte. These of course were Graham Brown and Houston, and we watched them anxiously, making ribald remarks about their rate of progress and their frequent halts. The fact that we were ourselves sitting down eating chocolate by no means lessened our enjoyment of this spectacle and certainly increased the flow of wit. We felt like dramatic critics eating their chocolates in the stalls, and sharpened the pencils of our wit accordingly.

It was a fine day for a change and the bright sun on the snow sapped our energy. We were up by 2 p.m. and having seen the tent pitched, for which there was just room enough, and Pasang and Nima safely established there, Lloyd and I went down, while Odell and Loomis waited to hear the news from above. An hour later Graham Brown and Houston got back to Camp II, and reported that there were a couple of hundred feet of difficult climbing before the snow arête was reached, that this was steep and long, but that a good site for a camp had been found where the arête merged into the broad saddle. They had felt the sun even more severely than we had.

We got down to Camp I at four o'clock and Phuta requested that he might go to the Base Camp that evening. It was no use keeping him, so I gave him a chit to Emmons and sent him down. There were now five of us at Camp I, two Sahibs and two Sherpas at Camp II, and Emmons, Kalu, and three Sherpas at the Base Camp.

Next day, the 16th, two more Sahibs had to occupy Camp II, and at half-past nine we all started, Odell and I carrying our personal kit and some odds and ends. Some student of human nature has remarked that 'no one can do an act that is not morally wrong for the last time without feelings of regret', but now I was doing the climb from Camp I to Camp II for the fifth and last time and can very positively refute that statement. Of course devout Hindus might say that in climbing Nanda Devi we *were* committing an immoral act and that would account satisfactorily for my absence of regret.

Before reaching the roping-up place, we were bothered by seeing two tents still standing at the Gîte and it looked as though no move was in progress. Later we made out somebody on the arête but could see only two instead of the four we expected. We puzzled our heads over this and made many wild conjectures. If Graham Brown and Houston were not moving up to Camp III there would be some congestion at the Gîte, but Odell and I were determined to sleep there, even if it meant four in a tent. We could not face yet another ascent from Camp I.

It was no use speculating, and as Odell was going slowly, and I was not unwilling to do the same, he and I went along together while the other three pushed on as fast as they could to find out what the matter was. We two continued in leisurely fashion, not arriving until three o'clock. Perhaps we were carrying heavier loads; Odell certainly was, for he was cluttered up with hypsometers, clinometers, and thermometers, and was so attached to certain favourite but unnecessary articles of clothing that his personal kit was a portentous affair—nor was Da Namgyal there to carry it as he should have been. I remember particularly a hideous yellow sweater, a relic of the War, which weighed more than the five Shetland woollies carried by us all; and at the highest camp he produced a hat which none of us had ever seen before and which, I suppose, had some attributes peculiarly fitting it for wear at 24,000 ft.

The mystery of the two tents was solved by a note and the presence of both Sherpas. Nima was sick and Pasang was completely snow-blind. The note told us that they had gone up with food and kit and asked us to bring on the tent and their sleeping bags. Loomis and Lloyd had already left with these when we arrived and half-way up the snow arête they were met by Houston and Graham Brown. For these four it was a hard day.

Houston's note went on to say that the necessary dope for alleviating snow-blindness had been unaccountably left at Camp I, and suggested that strong tea should be tried in the interim. Tea was at a premium, for we were carefully conserving our solitary ounce for higher up, but we brewed some and did what we could for Pasang, who was in considerable pain. He was lying on his face in the tent and quite unable to open his eyes, but by forcing the lids apart we managed to get some tea in. This treatment was continued until the medicine arrived two days later, but had little effect; nor had the medicine either for that matter, and, though we did not then suspect, Pasang was now out of the hunt.

It was not easily understood how he had managed to get such a severe attack. Yesterday had been very bright and sunny but no one noticed him with his glasses off, nor were these any different from Nima's which were perfectly efficient. While he was preparing the platform here, I noticed he was working without glasses and it must have been then that his eyes were affected, although the platform was in shadow and there was more rock than snow. But a rarefied atmosphere makes the light more dangerous in this respect and we read that on Everest in 1924 Norton was snow-blind merely from the glare off rocks. In 1930 Shipton and I climbed Kilimanjaro (19,700 ft.), and on snow near the summit we both took off our glasses to see where we were, for there was a thick mist and not a sign of the sun. Nevertheless that same night we both went snow-blind and suffered great pain, but in twenty-four hours it passed off without any treatment and this led me to think that Pasang's would do the same.

When Lloyd and Loomis returned, we agreed that they should please themselves whether they came up tomorrow with the little that was left at Camp I to bring. They would not be able to sleep here because Odell and I would still be in residence. Another tent, more food, and our own kits had to be carried to Camp III before we could move up, and for reasons of acclimatisation it was a sound plan to sleep two nights at a camp before going on to the next.

When they had gone, we took stock of our surroundings. These consisted of blank rock wall and thin air in equal proportions; there were about four feet of terra firma between the two tents and one could walk, without a rope, for about ten paces round the corner where the exit lay. All view of the ridge was cut off and only a little of it immediately below the Gîte was visible, but to the east a wide field of vision included East Nanda Devi, 'Longstaff's Col' now well below us, a great crescent of fluted ice wall on the rim to the south of it, and, beyond, the beautifully proportioned Nanda Kot. The height was about 20,400 ft.

Having brewed the tea for Pasang's eyes and drunk some ourselves, we tried to instil some life into Nima, who seemed very lugubrious and lethargic—in much the same frame of mind as a passenger in the last stages of sea-sickness, who having prayed long and earnestly for the ship to sink has almost abandoned hope that it will. I think they had not eaten since they got there, so we made him light his stove and cook some pemmican, which the Sherpas relish far more than we do. They were in the roomy 6 ft. x 7 ft. tent while we occupied the small bivouac tent vacated by Graham Brown and Houston, who had taken up one of the larger ones. We graciously allowed the Sherpas to remain in the enjoyment of their luxurious quarters, but this generosity will not be counted unto us for righteousness because the atmosphere in their tent was such that no tent at all would have been preferable.

I forget the exact dimensions of our tent, but it was very long and narrow and the two occupants lay, literally, cheek by jowl—that is if the human face has a jowl; or is it confined to pigs? It was admirably suited to Odell, who is also long and a bit narrow, and I think this was the first night that he was able to lie at full length since he had left Ranikhet. On this expedition we were experimenting with air beds as insulation when lying on snow, instead of the usual rubber mats, half an inch thick and 3 ft. x 4 ft. The extra room they took up was very noticeable in a small tent and apart from that they were not altogether successful. Punctures were numerous and unless they amounted to bursts, as they sometimes did, they were not easy to locate; situated as we were, the method of plunging them into a bath and watching for bubbles was seldom practicable. If your bed did go flat, it was a serious matter because no protection at all was afforded, and the result was a cold and sleepless night. Again, if you blew them up too hard you rolled off, and if they were too soft you were in contact with the ground and therefore cold. The Sherpas used to blow them up as if they were blowing up a dying fire, with the result that one bounded about like a pea on a drum, and if two people sat on it when in that state the whole thing exploded. Pasang got a lot of amusement out of the operation of blowing up and deflating beds by making them produce discordant noises like ill-played bagpipes. Now that only two of the Sherpas were left, and those two incapable of raising even a zephyr, we had to blow our own up, and this process provided yet another example of the perfection of natural laws which can even legislate for the remote association of a mountaineer and an air bed; as we gained in altitude and lost breath, the beds required less air to fill them owing of course to the diminution of pressure.

There was a storm in the night but, packed as we were, it was easy to keep warm and difficult to keep cool. Pasang was still blind and very sorry for himself, but Nima was brighter and offered to come with us to Camp III. Odell and I took a tent and paraffin, and Nima 40 lb. of sugar. Care was required on a short stretch above the camp and an upward traverse on rather shaky snow took us on to the ridge. We left it again where it suddenly stood on end and got into trouble on the rocks which would, when climbed, bring us out above this steep bit which had so frightened us. Odell led over a steep ice-glazed traverse which Nima and I resolved mentally to have nothing to do with, and when he was securely placed we had ourselves more or less pulled up in a direct line.

We were now at the foot of the steep snow arête which was such a prominent feature from below, and we settled down to kicking steps up it very slowly and methodically, the steps made by our forerunners having vanished. It was a narrow ridge, but we were able to stick to the crest, or slightly on the Rishi side, which was now less steep than the east side, though both fell away sharply, and the upward angle was 40 or 45 degrees; it will be remembered that from Camp I to Camp II the route lay always on the east flank and that the Rishi side was a precipice. As might be expected after the persistent falls of the last week, there was a lot of fresh snow to kick through before solid footing was obtained, and when we reached the tent at Camp III Graham Brown told us exactly how many of these steps we had kicked out, he having counted them. As far as I remember, the figure was disappointingly small for we felt that it must be something astronomical, but in sober fact there were only about 700 ft. of snow ridge. Approaching the tent, the angle eased off and we found it pitched snugly under the shelter of a steep snow bank.

It was after midday, but Graham Brown and Houston were still in bed and evidently intended 'lying at earth' after their efforts of yesterday. Going back we rattled down in an hour, and this time reversed our upwards procedure by descending the very steep snow patch in order to avoid the rocks. Nobody had come up from below, Pasang was still blind, we both had slight headaches, it was snowing again, and there was a big sun halo; but all this was forgotten in the warm glow of self-righteousness induced by our virtuous activity.

Having thus acquired enough merit for the time being by working while others slept, we sat about next morning until Graham Brown and Houston came down from Camp III for more loads. We found it such a pleasant occupation that we sat about some more until the other three came up from Camp I. As soon as the first man's head appeared round the corner of the bulge below us, a shout went up to know if they had found the tea. They had no tea, but they brought the zinc-sulphate medicine and we now hoped that Pasang's recovery would be speedy; at present his eyes were as firmly closed as ever. Nima too had relapsed into his former state of misery, but even yet we did not despair of getting some useful work out of these two. There was still a load to come up from Camp I, so it was arranged that Carter and Nima should go down tomorrow for this and as much more food as they could carry.

At three o'clock four of us started back for Camp III, Odell and Houston on one rope, Graham Brown and myself on the other. We had the advantage of the steps made by them on the way down and, in spite of heavy loads, were up in two hours. Our tent platform was ready for us, so the others had not been so idle yesterday as we thought, and it was pleasant to have some room again, room outside as well as in. I was sorry we had not got a cat to swing.

As Odell and I lay that night with our cheeks and our jowls at a reasonable distance apart, we wondered happily whether the three below were suffocating in the bivouac tent or succumbing to asphyxiation in the overripe atmosphere of the Sherpas'.

We flattered ourselves that the height of this camp was about 21,500 ft. but, if it was, it seemed highly improbable that from here we could put a bivouac within striking distance of the summit. It postulated a carry of 2000 ft. at the very least, 2500 would be better, and on the difficult going below we had not done a carry of more than 1500. The climbing was likely to get harder rather than easier and, of course, the increasing altitude would slow us up progressively. Repeated trials with the hypsometer made things appear even more discouraging by giving Camp III a height of only 21,200 ft., and though we knew by now that this instrument was, to put it mildly, subject to error, we had perforce to accept the lower figure in making future plans.

The question of the height of our camps bothered us a lot and, quite early on, the hypsometer had earned for itself an opprobrious name of a like sound which may not be printed. For some reason or other we omitted to bring an aneroid barometer graduated for reading height; possibly our numerous scientists scorned an instrument which even the half-wits of the party could read. I remember in 1934 Shipton and I, having no scientific training, took with us an aneroid barometer out of an aeroplane. I think it cost ten shillings at one of those miscellaneous junk shops in Holborn. Our Sherpas conceived a great affection for it and called it 'Shaitan', probably because we consulted it so frequently. It worked very well until we dropped it. But this hypsometer, or boiling-point thermometer, while not giving us any very precise information, afforded everyone a lot of fun and the scientists food for thought. The results it gave were always interesting, sometimes amusing, and seldom accurate. For example, after several hours of exhausting climbing in what we foolishly thought was an upward direction, it was startling to learn that we had in reality descended a hundred feet from where we started. The learned scientists explained with bland assurance that such vagaries were to be expected, and were accounted for quite simply by the presence of a 'column of cold air', the unlearned oafs on the contrary thought that it must be something to do with 'hot air', and plenty of it.

But there is generally some use to be found for the most unlikely things, and so it was with the hypsometer. It had as part of its equipment a small bottle of methylated spirits, and when we ran out of solid methylated for priming the stoves, this came in very handy. Priming a stove with paraffin is both noisome and inefficient.

On the 19th Graham Brown and Houston went down again to Camp II for loads while Odell and I went to spy out the land higher up. At the point we had reached, our ridge had widened out into a great hog's-back, so wide that it was in reality the south face, though up the middle of this face a ridge was still discernible, and 1000 ft. higher up it again stood out prominently. We struck straight up the middle of the face over what we called the 'snow saddle', avoiding the steep bank above the camp by a short traverse to the left. The snow was in good condition and the angle of slope about 30 degrees for the first 700 ft., after which it began to steepen. Above this was a sort of glacis of snow-covered rock lying at an angle of 45 to 50 degrees. In the steep places outcrops of rock appeared through the snow. This broad glacis appeared to stretch upward for 1000 ft. until it narrowed again to a sharp ridge. On our immediate right was a forbidding gully, a trap for falling stones and ice, and beyond that the tremendous cirque which forms the connecting ridge between East Nanda Devi and Nanda Devi itself. Some two or three hundred yards to the left was a wide shallow depression, scarcely a gully, and on the far side of it the horizon was bounded by a very bold and steep ridge, probably the same which we had looked at from Pisgah.

We attacked the glacis in the centre and worked upwards and to the left, making for what looked like a slight ridge overlooking the shallow gully. As we mounted, the angle grew steeper and the climbing more difficult. At first a good covering of snow overlay the rocks, but presently this became thinner and the outcrops of rocks more numerous. For mountaineering as well as geological reasons we were keenly interested to reach the first of these outcrops, for the line we should take, and our progress, depended greatly upon its quality. We hoped that at this height it might have changed to something more honest than the treacherous rock of the lower ridge, and that the strata might lie in a more favourable direction. Technically it may have differed, but for a climber it was substantially the same crumbling yellow stuff upon which no reliance could be placed, and though the dip of the strata was now more in our favour, little comfort was to be derived from that on rock of such rottenness.

When we had climbed about 500 ft. from the foot of the glacis, it became apparent that the supposed ridge we were making for was no ridge at all. To go straight up was still possible, but with loads on it would be both difficult and dangerous, for nowhere was there enough snow for an anchorage with an axe, or any rock round which a rope could be belayed. We decided to traverse to the left and go for the shallow gully which appeared to offer a safe route on snow for at least 1000 ft. But shortly after putting this resolve into practice, we contrived to get ourselves into such a mess on the ice-glazed face of a rock outcrop that all our attention was concentrated on getting out of it, and instead of continuing the traverse to the left we were compelled to embark upon a long and tricky traverse in the opposite direction. By sticking wherever possible to snow, and avoiding any rock like the plague, we worried a way back down the glacis until we rejoined our earlier track.

A lower route was obviously the best line for the gully, but it was now too late for any more and we hurried back to camp, where we arrived in time to avoid the start of a blizzard. Two days had elapsed since the warning of the sun halo.

Lloyd and Loomis had come up here to sleep after only one night at Camp II in defiance of our self-imposed rule of two at each camp. No one, however, with experience of the Gîte would doubt their wisdom in making that camp an exception to the rule.

The results of our reconnaissance were mainly negative but not without value. It was clear that a route directly up the glacis should only be tried as a last desperate resort, and also that whichever way we went it was going to be a painfully long carry before a place where a tent could be pitched would be found. The conclusions were that further reconnaissance was needed, that the most promising line was the broad gully, and that in any case it would be advantageous to move the present camp to a new site at the foot of the glacis.

CHAPTER FIFTEEN

Alarms and Excursions

THE night was cold and windy and no one turned out until nine o'clock. Lloyd and Loomis started out to have a look at the way to the gully, and the rest of us went down to Camp II for loads. All the tracks down had to be remade after the blizzard and we had long ceased to expect any tracks to last for twenty-four hours. To anticipate, they did not last so long today, and when we returned in the afternoon all were once more obliterated.

We found Pasang still blind and Nima not well, and it was pretty clear that neither would be any use. Nima's single journey to Camp III, the highest reached by any of the porters, was but a dying kick. The almost total failure of the Sherpas is easily explained, for, as I have pointed out, we had to take the leavings of several other expeditions. The only two I expected to go high were Pasang and Kitar. Of the others three were past their best and one was too young and inexperienced. Pasang of course was unlucky to be struck down with snow-blindness, but it cannot be said that it was not his own fault. Kitar was a victim to disease.

The medicine seemed to be having little effect on Pasang's eyes, and Nima's cheery grin was a thing of the past. That they should both go down was now the best course, but this was not possible until Pasang could see something. Apart from their rather miserable mode of existence at the Gîte, I was anxious to have them safely down at the Base Camp before we lost touch with them entirely by going higher up the mountain. We left them there, alone now, in the big tent, having told them that two of us would come down again tomorrow, and we started back, Carter with us, taking the small bivouac tent. Carter had a note which he had found at Camp I telling us that Emmons had moved the Base Camp down to the foot of the scree slope and that he was busy with the plane table, but only Kalu was able to help him by carrying loads.

It was cold and windy when we reached Camp III in a flurry of snow. There was a halo round the sun and two mock[1] suns, and I have seldom seen a more ominous-looking sky. The report of the reconnoitring party was more cheering than the weather. Taking a line below and to the left of ours, they had reached a point from where they could see into and up the gully. They had not

---

1 Mock suns are coloured images of the sun which appear on either side of the sun and at the same altitude. They probably result from the intersection of two halos and are fairly common in high latitudes.

got into it, but they reported that it could be reached by a route which lay almost entirely on snow, and that the going up the near side of it looked straightforward enough. Like us, they had seen no promise of a camp site higher up, and it was agreed to move this camp to the top of the snow saddle and to press the attack by the gully.

It was a quiet night in spite of all the signs of approaching storm, but the morning of the 21st dawned dull, misty, and snowy. We had a late breakfast and spent the morning in one tent discussing ways and means. Now that the thing was to be put to the test, it was clear that some difficult decisions would have to be made, and the upshot of our talk was that the responsibility for these decisions was put upon the writer. The too frequent use of the word 'I' in this narrative will not have escaped the notice of the reader. The reason for this is that up to now I may have had most to say in our affairs; but that was merely through the accident of my being the only one who knew the country or the porters. We had no official leader, and managed very well without, until at this crisis the need was felt for some kind of figurehead.

After a cup of cocoa additional to our lunch which, by the way, was usually a slab of chocolate and nothing else, Lloyd, Carter, and I went down again to Camp II for more loads, and the others took a first instalment of loads up to what would presently be Camp IV.

Pasang and Nima still appeared to be immovable, but I told them that two of us would come down again tomorrow and see them safely over the worst of the route to Camp I. Until they were down they were merely a source of anxiety, and, after tomorrow, we expected to be out of reach. We climbed up again in one and a quarter hours and it was satisfactory to see that our time on the snow arête became faster, indicating that we were still acclimatising and not deteriorating. The other party had found a good camp site on the snow saddle near the foot of the glacis, and had dug out one tent platform.

The sunset was again threatening, with greasy-looking cigar-shaped clouds hanging low over East Nanda Devi, a greenish watery haze to the west, and, to the south, black banks of cumulus tinged with copper.

We woke to find the tent shaking and banging to the blasts of a fierce blizzard. The wind was coming out of the south-east, some snow was falling, but it was impossible to tell what was new snow and what was drift, for outside was nothing but a whirling cloud of driving snow. The three tents were close together and guyed to each other for mutual support. Six of us occupied the two big ones and Carter was by himself (a doubtful privilege under these conditions) in the small bivouac tent, pitched on the weather side. Odell, Lloyd, and I held the baby in the shape of the Primus stove, but it was conceivable that the inconvenience of fetching ice and breathing paraffin fumes was outweighed by the advantage of getting the food hot without having to fetch it. Going from the comparative warmth of the sleeping bag and the tent out into the blizzard was a breathtaking experience. Breathing was almost impossible facing the wind, and nothing could be handled without mittens, while the act of leaving or entering the tent by the small sleeve entrance required the quick co-operation of all, unless the inside was to be covered with a layer of snow.

There was nothing to be done but lie in our bags, with one eye on a book and the other on the furiously flapping fabric and the quivering tent pole. The pole was of very light aluminium and we were rather nervous about it, but it stood the strain well, as did the tents, for which we forgave them all our past discomforts. At five o'clock, when we cooked our evening pemmican, conditions were unchanged. The wind still maintained a steady roar with occasional gusts of gale force, and we discussed the advisability of sleeping with windproofs on in case the tent went in the night. However, we pinned our faith to the fabric and did not resort to these extreme measures.

Morning brought no change in these unpleasant conditions, and we wondered whether it was blowing as hard at the Gîte and how the Sherpas were faring. Anyhow, with the direction of the wind as it was, the rock wall would stop them being blown off their ledge.

The snow was being blown away as soon as it fell, and round our tent it had not accumulated to any great depth. The other big tent had not fared so well and there was a high bank of snow around it by morning. The pressure of this snow had reduced the space inside by half, so that the unfortunate residents were sleeping almost on top of each other. They had the consolation of knowing that their tent was now securely anchored. Carter too, in the bivouac, was experiencing trouble in keeping the snow-laden walls off his face.

Another weary day of inactivity and torpor passed, but towards evening the wind began to moderate and we were able to get outside, clear the accumulated snow away from the doors, and attend to the guys. Snow was still falling lightly and a leaden pall hid everything but the snow at our feet and three forlorn-looking tents.

Followed another cold and stormy night, but the morning of Monday the 24th dawned fine, calm and sunny. Had it been black as night, we would not have complained, for stillness was all we asked for after the battering of the last two days. The loss of this valuable time was disturbing, and though it may seem strange that two days in bed could be anything but beneficial, there was no doubt that the strain and the inaction had done us harm physically. Nor could we tell what effect the blizzard might have had on the snow of the upper slopes. It was imperative now to push on with all speed, and surely after such a snorter we might expect several days of fine weather.

These blizzards which we experienced, three of them lasting for thirty-six, twelve, and forty-eight hours respectively, all came from between east and south-east. Monsoon weather in the hills generally comes from between south and west, but these storms may have been deflected by the mountain. Such blizzards are more to be expected prior to the break of the monsoon, and during two previous monsoon periods in the Himalaya, one in Garhwal and one in the Everest region, I do not recollect one of any severity. This year the monsoon broke early and ended late, and was exceptionally severe in the United Provinces and Garhwal.

At nine o'clock Lloyd and I started out for Camp II in accordance with our promise to the Sherpas, the fufilment of which the blizzard had compelled us to postpone. We left to the others the cold work of breaking out the tents from their frozen covering and digging out the buried stores, preparatory to carrying one big tent and the bivouac to the new Camp IV site. Five of us were to sleep up there tonight in readiness for carrying up a bivouac for the first summit party next day.

The presence of a lot of powder snow made conditions on the arête bad, and we both felt weak and got progressively weaker as we descended. Arrived at the Gîte, we were surprised to find it empty; evidently the Sherpas had tired of waiting for us and left early. It was comforting to know that the tent had weathered the storm, that Pasang's eyes must be better, and that we ourselves had not to descend any father. Indeed, we were now in such a state of languor that our chief concern was how on earth we were going to get up again. We lolled about on the ledge, assailed by a violent thirst, feeling complete moral and physical wrecks; and it was evident that two days and nights in our sleeping bags had taken more out of us than a hard day's work.

The Sherpas had taken the stove and cooking pot with them, but there was some food here and we opened a tin with an ice-axe—not for the sake of the food but for the tin, in which to catch the elusive drips from the rock wall. We had to sleep at the higher camp that night, so at midday we summoned up all our resolution and, taking with us all the food that was left here, we crawled weakly away from the Gîte.

I should be ashamed to say how long it took us to get back to Camp III, but by the time we arrived we were feeling better and our strength was beginning to return. Graham Brown and Carter, who were spending the night here, came down from Camp IV just as we arrived and informed us that up there it was perishing cold. Carter thought his toes were slightly touched with frost-bite.

Adding some more food to our loads, Lloyd and I went off once more and an hour of steady plodding brought us to the new camp. They had evidently started late that morning owing to the frozen tents, and, when we got up, the second tent was just being pitched. There was a bitter wind blowing and Loomis was inside attending to his feet, which also had been slightly affected by cold.

In spite of the cold, it was difficult to turn away from the astonishing picture painted by the fast-sinking sun. Nanda Kot still shone with dazzling purity like an opal, and beyond to the east was range upon range of the snow peaks of Nepal, looking like rollers breaking in white foam on a sunny sea. From the snow slope falling away out of sight at our feet, the eye swept across a great void till arrested by the castellated ivory wall of the Sanctuary, dominated by Trisul, up which the shadows were already stealing. And to the west was the dark chasm of the Rishi gorge, the clear-cut outline of the 'Curtain', and the blue-green swell of the foothills.

The height of Camp IV we estimated to be 21,800 ft., and with five of us here and food for nearly a fortnight we were in a strong position. If we could push a bivouac up another 2000 ft., the summit would be within reach, and, big 'if' though this was, the time had come to make the attempt. Of the five now at this camp, it was not difficult to decide which two should have the privilege of first shot. Odell was going very well and his experience, combined with Houston's energy, would make a strong pair. Assuming that we could place the bivouac high enough tomorrow, they were to have two days in which to make their attempt, and on the third day a second pair would take their place, whether they had been successful or not. The form shown tomorrow would indicate which two would have the second chance, and, provided the weather held, it might be possible to send up a third pair.

The 25th broke fine, but it was ten o'clock before we had made up our loads of 15 lb. each, which included food for two men for six days. During the blizzard, not very much snow had actually settled, and since then sufficient time had elapsed for this new snow to consolidate. We found it in good condition. After gaining some height by kicking steps, we approached the gully by a long traverse where steps had to be cut and great care exercised. The snow covering grew thinner and we came to an uncomfortable halt on the steep lip of a minor hollow, cutting us off from the main gully. This was the farthest point reached by Lloyd and Loomis, and they had seen that this difficult little gully could be avoided by working round the head of it, 200 ft. higher.

We sat here for a little, but it was no place for a long sojourn without prehensile trousers. There was not enough snow to afford a step, much less a seat, and the angle of the rock was such that mere friction was of no avail— boots, hands, and ice-axe were all needed to prevent the beginning of a long slither which would only end on the glacier 6000 ft. below. Turning up the slope, the next few feet were of the same precarious nature that Odell and I had experienced on the glacis, but this was as yet the only part of the route where we had to forsake the security of the snow for the uncertainty of the rock. Once over this, we settled down to a long steady grind, kicking and cutting our way up very steep snow, and having rounded the head of this minor hollow, we took a line up the true left bank of the broad gully.

We were climbing on two ropes, so by changing the leading rope and also the leading end of each rope, the work was divided among four. It was a beautiful day, but in our perverse way we were not content, and were captious enough to wish the sun obscured so that we could climb in more comfort. Nanda Kot, 22,500 ft., sank below us and we began to cast jealous eyes on Trisul, which still looked down upon us majestically from its height of 23,400 ft. Meantime we began to search the snow above us for the slightest break in the relentless angle of the slope which might afford a site for a tent. We were tempted momentarily by the broken outline of the skyline ridge away across the gully, but we decided it was too far off and the approach to it too steep.

As we gained height, the curve of the face to our right grew rounder and narrower and the central ridge was beginning to stand out again like the bridge of a Roman nose. We edged over towards it, thinking that the rocks might provide easier going than the snow, and aiming for the foot of a rock tower where there might be a platform. Knowing by now the sort of rock we might expect, it was curious that we should so think, but such was the distorting effect on our minds of five hours of laborious step-kicking. The change of course was for the worse and we had some awkward moments before we dragged ourselves to the foot of the tower, to find it sloping away as steeply as the rest of the mountain.

The time was now three o'clock and our height something over 23,000 ft., practically level with Trisul. Loomis had an attack of cramp, but when he had recovered we turned our attention to the rock tower at our backs, on top of which we hoped to find better things. Lloyd did a grand lead up a steep rock chimney with his load on and was able to give the rest of us some much needed moral and, in my case, physical encouragement with the rope. This took some time and it was four o'clock before we were all on top of the tower, where there was barely room for five of us to stand, much less pitch a tent. Looking up the ridge, it was impossible to say where such a place would be found, but it was sufficiently broken to offer considerable hope. Meantime three of us had to get back to Camp IV and at this time of the afternoon of a bright sunny day the snow would be at its worst. With the assent of all, it was decided to dump our loads here leaving Houston and Odell to shift for themselves. It seemed a selfish decision at the time and it seems so now; no doubt we could have cut it a bit finer and yet got down before dark, but it was likely that they would not have to go far before finding a bivouac, and, in any case, with sleeping bags and warm clothing they could not come to much harm.

We learned afterwards that they had an uncommonly busy evening. They had to climb another 150 ft. before even the most imaginative could discern the makings of a platform, and then they had to make two journeys up and down with the loads. It was dark before they were finally settled.

Oblivious of this activity and the curses which were being bestowed, rather unjustly, on us for our premature desertion, we climbed hastily but cautiously down, reaching the camp at sundown. There was no sign of Graham Brown and Carter, so we assumed they were having a day off at Camp III.

Discussing the results of this day's work, we decided the bivouac was about 23,500 ft., probably too low for an attempt on the summit, but as high as we could push it in the day. We thought they would probably move it higher tomorrow and make their bid on the following day. The closer view of the upper part of the mountain which we had obtained had not made it look any easier, and it was a puzzle to make out where exactly the peak lay. I began to fear we had not allowed them enough time, but now it was too late to alter plans.

Next day was fine, but mist shrouded the upper mountain from our anxious gaze. We felt slack, and took the morning off before going down to Camp III to give Graham Brown and Carter a hand with their loads. As their tent was the one which had been half-buried by the blizzard, it took them a long time to dig it out, so we returned before them and prepared a platform.

The 27th was to be for us at Camp IV another day of idleness. That at least was the plan, but the event was different, and for some of us it was a day of the greatest mental and physical stress that we had yet encountered.

I had been worrying all night over the waste of this day, trying to devise some scheme whereby the second pair could go up at once to the bivouac. The trouble was that a second tent was essential, and having seen something of the extraordinary difficulty of finding a site even for the small tent, to go up there on the slim chance of finding a site for the big one as well was incurring the risk of exhausting the party to no purpose. While we were having breakfast, debating this knotty point and wondering how far the summit party had got, Loomis disclosed the fact that all was not well with his feet, the toes being slightly frost-bitten, and that henceforward we should have to count him out. The loss of carrying power knocked the scheme for a second tent on the head and a few moments later we had something else to think about.

We had just decided they must be well on the way to the top when we were startled to hear Odell's familiar yodel, rather like the braying of an ass. It sounded so close that I thought they must be on the way down, having got the peak the previous day, but it suddenly dawned on us that he was trying to send an S.O.S. Carter, who had the loudest voice, went outside to try and open communications, and a few minutes later came back to the tent to announce that 'Charlie is killed'—Charlie being Houston. It was impossible to see anyone on the mountain, but he was certain he had heard correctly. As soon as we had pulled ourselves together, I stuffed some clothes and a bandage into a rucksack and Lloyd and I started off as fast as we could manage, to be followed later by Graham Brown and Carter with a hypodermic syringe.

It was a climb not easily forgotten—trying to go fast and realising that at this height it was impossible to hurry, wondering what we should find, and above all what we could do. The natural assumption was that there had been a fall, and that since they were sure to be roped, Odell was also hurt, and the chance of getting a helpless man down the mountain was too remote to bear thinking about. As if to confirm this assumption, we could get no answer to repeated calls on the way up.

Remembering our struggles yesterday on the ridge and in the chimney, we took a different line and tackled a band of steep rock directly above us, in between the gully and the ridge. It proved to be much worse than it looked and, when we had hauled ourselves panting on to the snow above, we vowed that the next time we would stick to the gully, which here narrowed and passed through a sort of cleft in the rock band.

The time was now about two o'clock, and traversing up and to the right over snow in the direction of the ridge, the little tent came in sight not thirty yards away. Instinctively we tried almost to break into a run, but it was no use, and we advanced step by step, at a maddening pace, not knowing what we should find in the tent, if indeed anything at all. The sight of an ice-axe was a tremendous relief; evidently Odell had managed to crawl back. But when another was seen, conjecture was at a loss. Then voices were heard talking quietly and next moment we were greeted with, 'Hullo, you blokes, have some tea.' 'Charlie is ill' was the message Odell had tried to convey!

Lloyd and I experienced a curious gamut of emotions; firstly and naturally, of profound relief, then, and I think not unnaturally, disgust at having suffered such unnecessary mental torture, and, of course, deep concern for Houston. While we swallowed tea, tea that reeked of pemmican but which I still remember with thankfulness, we heard what they had done and discussed what we were to do.

They had devoted yesterday to a reconnaissance. Following the ridge up they found, at a height of about 500 ft. above the bivouac, a flat snow platform capable of holding two tents comfortably. Beyond that the climbing became interesting and difficult, but they had reached the foot of a long and easy snow slope leading up to the final rock wall. Here they turned back, having decided to move the bivouac next day to the higher site. Both were going strongly, but early that night Houston became violently ill, and in the cramped quarters of the tent, perched insecurely on an inadequate platform above a steep slope, both had spent a sleepless and miserable night. Houston attributed his trouble to the bully beef which both had eaten; Odell was unaffected, but it is possible that a small portion was tainted and certainly the symptoms pointed to poisoning of some kind.

Houston was still very ill and very weak, but it was he who suggested what should be done, and showed us how evil might be turned to good. It was only possible for two people to stay up here, and his plan was that he should go down that afternoon and that I should stay up with Odell, and thus no time would have been lost. We demurred to this on the ground that he was not fit to move, but he was so insistent on the importance of not losing a day and so confident of being able to get down that we at last consented.

We all four roped up, with Houston in the middle, and started slowly down, taking frequent rests. We struck half-right across the snow and joined the gully above the rock band according to our earlier resolution, and there the two men anchored the party while Lloyd cut steps down the narrow cleft, which was very icy. Houston was steady enough in spite of his helpless state of weakness, and having safely negotiated this awkward bit, we kicked slowly down to the left and found our up-going tracks. Presently Graham Brown and Carter hove in sight, and I imagine their amazement at seeing four people coming down was as great as ours had been at the sight of the two ice-axes. When we met, Lloyd and Houston tied on to their rope and continued the descent, while Odell and I climbed slowly back to the bivouac.

This illness of Houston's was a miserable turn of fortune for him, robbing him as it did of the summit. Bad as he was, his generous determination to go down was of a piece with the rest of his actions.

CHAPTER SIXTEEN

The Top

SCENICALLY the position of the bivouac was very fine but residentially it was damnable. It was backed on two sides by rock, but on the others the snow slope fell away steeply, and the platform which had been scraped out in the snow was so narrow that the outer edge of the tent overhung for almost a foot, thus reducing considerably both the living space and any feeling one yet had of security. Necessity makes a man bold, and I concluded that necessity had pressed very hard that night when they lit on this spot for their bivouac. Odell, who had had no sleep the previous night, could have slept on a church spire, and, as I had Houston's sleeping bag and the extra clothing I had fortunately brought up, we both had a fair night. Odell, who was the oldest inhabitant and in the position of host, generously conceded to me the outer berth, overhanging space.

The weather on the 28th still held and without regret we packed up our belongings and made the first trip to the upper bivouac. The snow slope was steeper than any we had yet met but, at the early hour we started, the snow was good and in an hour we reached the spacious snow shelf which they had marked down. It was about 20 ft. × 20 ft., so that there was room to move about, but on either side of the ridge on which it stood the slope was precipitous. After a brief rest the increasing heat of the sun warned us to be on the move again and we hurried down for the remaining loads. The snow was softening rapidly under a hot sun nor was this deterioration confined only to the snow. We already knew, and it was to be impressed on us again, that at these altitudes a hot sun is a handicap not to be lightly assessed.

Guessing the height of this camp, aided by the absence of the hypsometer, we put it at about 24,000 ft. Trisul was well below us and even the top of East Nanda Devi (24,379 ft.) began to look less remote. The condition of the wide belt of snow which had to be crossed, the difficulties of the final wall, and the weather were so many large question marks, but we turned in that night full of hope, and determined to give ourselves every chance by an early start.

We were up at five o'clock to begin the grim business of cooking and the more revolting tasks of eating breakfast and getting dressed. That we were up is an exaggeration, we were merely awake, for all these fatigues are carried out from inside one's sleeping bag until it is no longer possible to defer the putting on of boots. One advantage a narrow tent has, that at lower altitudes is overlooked, is that the two sleeping bags are in such close proximity that boots which are rammed into the non-existent space between them generally survive the night without being frozen stiff. It worked admirably on this occasion so that we were spared the pangs of wrestling with frozen boots with cold fingers. Frozen boots are a serious matter and may cause much delay, and in order to mitigate this trouble we had, since the start, carefully refrained from oiling our boots. This notion might work well enough on Everest in pre-monsoon conditions where the snow is dry, but we fell between two stools, rejoicing in wet feet down below and frozen boots higher up.

By six o'clock we were ready, and shortly after we crawled outside, roped up, and started. It was bitterly cold, for the sun had not yet risen over the shoulder of East Nanda Devi and there was a thin wind from the west. What mugs we were to be fooling about on this infernal ridge at that hour of the morning! And what was the use of this ridiculous coil of rope, as stiff as a wire hawser, tying me for better or for worse to that dirty-looking ruffian in front! Such, in truth, were the reflections of at least one of us as we topped a snow boss behind the tent, and the tenuous nature of the ridge in front became glaringly obvious in the chill light of dawn. It was comforting to reflect that my companion in misery had already passed this way, and presently as the demands of the climbing became more insistent, grievances seemed less real, and that life was still worth living was a proposition that might conceivably be entertained.

This difficult ridge was about three hundred yards long, and though the general angle appeared slight it rose in a series of abrupt rock and snow steps. On the left was an almost vertical descent to a big ravine, bounded on the far side by the terrific grey cliffs that supported the broad snow shelf for which we were making. The right side also fell away steeply, being part of the great rock cirque running round to East Nanda Devi. The narrow ridge we were on formed a sort of causeway between the lower south face and the upper snow shelf.

One very important factor which, more than anything, tended to promote a happier frame of mind was that the soft crumbly rock had at last yielded to a hard rough schistose-quartzite which was a joy to handle; a change which could not fail to please us as mountaineers and, no doubt, to interest my companion as a geologist. That vile rock, schist is, I believe, the technical term, had endangered our heads and failed to support our feet from the foot of the scree to the last bivouac. It was a wonder our burning anathemas had not caused it to undergo a geological change under our very eyes— metamorphosed it, say, into plutonic rocks. But, as had been said by others, there is good in everything, and, on reflection, this very sameness was not without some saving grace because it meant that we were spared an accumulation of rock samples at every camp. A bag of assorted stones had already been left at the Glacier Camp, and I tremble to think what burdens we might have had to carry down the mountain had the rock been as variegated as our geologist, and indeed any right-minded geologist, would naturally desire.

Thanks to the earlier reconnaissance by him and Houston, Odell led over this ridge at a good pace and in an hour and a half we had reached the snow mound which marked the farthest point they had reached. It was a ridge on which we moved one at a time.

In front was a snow slope set at an angle of about 30 degrees and running right up to the foot of the rock wall, perhaps 600 or 700 ft. above us. To the west this wide snow terrace extended for nearly a quarter of a mile until it ended beneath that same skyline ridge, which below had formed the western boundary of the broad gully. On our right the shelf quickly steepened and merged into the steep rock face of the ridge between East Nanda Devi and our mountain. We were too close under the summit to see where it lay, but there was little doubt about the line we should take, because from a rapid survey there seemed to be only one place where a lodgement could be effected on the final wall. This was well to the west of our present position, where a snow rib crossed the terrace at right angles and, abutting against the wall, formed as it were a ramp.

We began the long snow trudge at eight o'clock and even at that early hour and after a cold night the snow was not good and soon became execrable. The sun was now well up. After it had been at work for a bit we were going in over our knees at every step, and in places where the slope was steeper it was not easy to make any upward progress at all. One foot would be lifted and driven hard into the snow and then, on attempting to rise on it, one simply sank down through the snow to the previous level. It was like trying to climb up cotton wool, and a good deal more exhausting, I imagine, than the treadmill. But, like the man on a walking tour in Ireland, who throughout a long day received the same reply of '20 miles' to his repeated inquiries as to the distance he was from his destination, we could at any rate say, 'Thank God, we were holding our own.'

The exertion was great and every step made good cost six to eight deep breaths. Our hopes of the summit grew faint, but there was no way but to plug on and see how far we could get. This we did, thinking only of the next step, taking our time, and resting frequently. It was at least some comfort that the track we were ploughing might assist a second party. On top of the hard work and the effect of altitude was the languor induced by a sun which beat down relentlessly on the dazzling snow, searing our lips and sapping the energy of mind and body. As an example of how far this mind-sapping process had gone, I need only mention that it was seriously suggested that we should seek the shade of a convenient rock which we were then near, lie up there until evening, and finish the climb in the dark!

It is noteworthy that whilst we were enjoying, or more correctly enduring, this remarkable spell of sunshine, the foothills south and west of the Basin experienced disastrous floods. As related in the first chapter, it was on this day that the Pindar river overflowed sweeping away some houses in the village of Tharali, while on the same day nineteen inches of rain fell at the hill station of Mussoorie west of Ranikhet.

We derived some encouragement from seeing East Nanda Devi sink below us and at one o'clock, rather to our surprise, we found ourselves on top of the snow rib moving at a snail's pace towards the foot of the rocks. There we had a long rest and tried to force some chocolate down our parched throats by eating snow at the same time. Though neither of us said so, I think both felt that now it would take a lot to stop us. There was a difficult piece of rock to climb; Odell led this and appeared to find it stimulating, but it provoked me to exclaim loudly upon its 'thinness'. Once over that, we were landed fairly on the final slope with the summit ridge a bare 300 ft. above us.

Presently we were confronted with the choice of a short but very steep snow gully and a longer but less drastic route to the left. We took the first and found the snow reasonably hard owing to the very steep angle at which it lay. After a severe struggle I drew myself out of it on to a long and gently sloping corridor, just below and parallel to the summit ridge. I sat down and drove the axe in deep to hold Odell as he finished the gully. He moved up to join me and I had just suggested the corridor as a promising line to take when there was a sudden hiss and, quicker than a thought, a slab of snow, about forty yards long, slid off the corridor and disappeared down the gully, peeling off a foot of snow as it went. At the lower limit of the avalanche, which was where we were sitting, it actually broke away for a depth of a foot all round my axe to which I was holding. At its upper limit, forty yards up the corridor, it broke away to a depth of three or four feet.

The corridor route had somehow lost its attractiveness, so we finished the climb by the ridge without further adventure.

The summit is not the exiguous and precarious spot that usually graces the top of so many Himalayan peaks, but a solid snow ridge nearly two hundred yards long and twenty yards broad. It is seldom that conditions on top of a high peak allow the climber the time or the opportunity to savour the immediate fruits of victory. Too often, when having first carefully probed the snow to make sure he is not standing on a cornice, the climber straightens up preparatory to savouring the situation to the full, he is met by a perishing wind and the interesting view of a cloud at close quarters, and with a muttered imprecation turns in his tracks and begins the descent. Far otherwise was it now. There were no cornices to worry about and room to unrope and walk about. The air was still, the sun shone, and the view was good if not so extensive as we had hoped.

Odell had brought a thermometer, and no doubt sighed for the hypsometer. From it we found that the air temperature was 20 degrees F., but in the absence of wind we could bask gratefully in the friendly rays of our late enemy the sun. It was difficult to realise that we were actually standing on top of the same peak which we had viewed two months ago from Ranikhet, and which had then appeared incredibly remote and inaccessible, and it gave us a curious feeling of exaltation to know that we were above every peak within hundreds of miles on either hand. Dhaulagiri, 1000 ft. higher, and two hundred miles away in Nepal, was our nearest rival. I believe we so far forgot ourselves as to shake hands on it.

After the first joy in victory came a feeling of sadness that the mountain had succumbed, that the proud head of the goddess was bowed.

At this late hour of the day there was too much cloud about for any distant views. The Nepal peaks were hidden and all the peaks on the rim, excepting only Trisul, whose majesty even our loftier view-point could not diminish. Far to the north through a vista of white cloud the sun was colouring to a warm brown the bare and bleak Tibetan plateau.

After three-quarters of an hour on that superb summit, a brief forty-five minutes into which was crowded the worth of many hours of glorious life, we dragged ourselves reluctantly away, taking with us a memory that can never fade and leaving behind 'thoughts beyond the reaches of our souls'.

If our thoughts were still treading on air, the short steep gully, swept by the avalanche bare of steps, soon brought us to earth. We kicked slowly down it, facing inwards and plunging an arm deep into the snow for support. Followed another exhausting drag across the snow, hindered rather than helped by the deep holes we had made coming up, and then a cold hour was spent moving cautiously, one at a time, down the ice and the benumbing rocks of the long ridge above the bivouac. We paused to watch a bird, a snow pigeon, cross our ridge and fly swiftly across the grey cliffs of the ravine beneath the snow terrace, like the spirit of Nanda Devi herself, forsaking the fastness which was no longer her own.

At six o'clock we reached the tent and brewed the first of many jorums of tea. After such a day nothing could have tasted better and our appreciation was enhanced by our long enforced abstinence. There was but a pinch left and we squandered it all recklessly, saving the leaves for the morning. Food was not even mentioned.

We paid for this debauch with a sleepless night, to which no doubt exhaustion and a still-excited imagination contributed. Each little incident of the climb was gone over again and again, and I remember, in the small hours when the spark of life burns lowest, the feeling which predominated over all was one of remorse at the fall of a giant. It is the same sort of contrition that one feels at the shooting of an elephant, for however thrilling and arduous the chase, however great has been the call upon skill, perseverance, and endurance, and however gratifying the weight of the ivory, when the great bulk crashes to the ground achievement seems to have been bought at the too high cost of sacrilege.

It was very cold next morning when we packed up and started down. Near the bottom of the gully we were met by Lloyd and Loomis, who were coming up to help us down and who were overjoyed when they heard that success had crowned the efforts of the whole party. Houston and Graham Brown had already gone down and we decided to stop the night at Camp IV. There were still three or four days' food left in hand but Loomis and Carter were both troubled with their feet, which must have been touched with frost the day Camp IV was occupied. Lloyd was going stronger than ever and it was much to be regretted that we could not make up a second party.

The weather, which during this crucial period had been so kind, now broke up and on the morning of the 31st it was blowing half a gale out of a clear sky. Lloyd, Loomis, and I started some time before the other two, all carrying heavy loads because we left nothing but the two big tents, some snow-shoes, and two pairs of crampons or ice-claws. The snow-shoes had been lugged up to assist us on soft snow and the crampons for use on hard snow, but the slopes were, of course, all too steep for snow-shoes, and the only time we might have used the crampons was now when they had been abandoned.

It was bitterly cold, and the snow on the arête was hard and dangerous—the mountain had not finished with us yet. We started to descend in the usual way, plunging the heel in at each step with a stiff leg. When one or two 'voluntaries' had been cut, we should have taken warning that the snow was not right for such tactics, but we were all pretty tired and in a hurry to get down, and it is in such circumstances that care is relaxed and the party comes to grief. Fortunately before this happened we had another warning which could not well be ignored. The leader's heels went from under him and he slid down the slope pulling the second man after him until checked by the rope belayed round the end man's axe, which fortunately held firm. We all felt rather ashamed of ourselves after this exhibition and abandoned that method in favour of the slower but safer one of cutting steps and moving one at a time, which should have been adopted at the start.

There was another slip, quickly checked, when one of the snow steps above the Gîte gave way, and we reached this camp in a chastened frame of mind and hoping that the mountain had now exhausted its spite. After a brief rest we pushed on, unroped gladly when we were off the snow, and picked our way with great caution down the unstable rocks to Camp I. On the way we noticed with concern that Odell and Carter were still high up on the arête and moving very slowly.

We found here Graham Brown and Pasang. The former's leg was troubling him, so he had spent the night here where there were still two tents, and Pasang had come up from below to take his load. We heard that Graham Brown and Houston too had narrowly escaped disaster on the previous day by the breaking of a step above the Gîte. Pasang had completely recovered his sight, but he was not yet his former bright self, for I think he felt keenly the disability which prevented him from helping his Sahibs at grips with the mountain.

It was now midday and after a drink of cocoa, which served only to bring home to us the loss we had suffered, we continued the descent. The cocoa so wrought upon Lloyd that, with a desperation born of thirst, he turned aside to prosecute a last and unsuccessful search for the tea. On the Coxcomb ridge I met Phuta going up to help Pasang and was shocked to hear that Kitar had died in the night. We got down to the new Base Camp at the foot of the scree at two o'clock and but for the melancholy news of Kitar's death there was nothing to mar our contentment. Twenty-one days had elapsed since we left.

CHAPTER SEVENTEEN

A New Pass

HOUSTON had almost recovered, Da Namgyal was there, still coughing, but obviously bursting to lay out Odell's pyjamas. He had brought with him six men from Lata, the mail, and one or two luxuries which had been scrapped at the Bridge Camp. Best of all, one of our old Mana men had come with them bringing a letter of greeting and a present from the Rawal of Badrinath—an enormous basket of apples, nuts, potatoes, and other vegetables, than which nothing, not excepting a tin of tea, could have been more acceptable. After living as we had been, any fresh food is the greatest luxury imaginable; many of our idle hours had been passed in devising the sort of meal for which each of us most longed, and in every imaginary menu fruit bulked large. We were deeply touched by this kindly and thoughtful act on the part of one who had already helped us in every way he could. Fortunately some of the party were able to visit Badrinath on the way back and thank our benefactor personally.

Not the least of our delights was that of being, if not on grass at any rate on the sort of soil which looked as if, with very little encouragement, it might grow grass, and that did in fact support some moss and scant herbage. To our starved senses it looked like an oasis and smelt divinely. Fresh water to drink in unstinted measure, a wood fire to look at, bare feet on warm earth, the cry of a marmot, such were the simple things which now gave us unbounded pleasure. Some averred that the air felt and tasted differently, and on the mountain they went so far as to claim that this difference could be felt on going down from Camp III to Camp II; but speaking personally, provided of course one sits still, I would not undertake to say whether the air I was breathing was that of 10,000 ft. or 20,000 ft.

While we were on the mountain Emmons had not been idle, having almost completed a plane-table survey of the South-East glacier and its tributaries. He had further made a valiant and almost successful attempt to reach the top of 'Longstaff's Col', accompanied only by the inexperienced Kalu. Kalu apparently had worked very well and was once more in the mood for chest-beating. In the midst of these activities he, Emmons, had had two sick men to look after, Kitar and Nuri. Kitar got steadily worse in spite of all that could be done for him in the way of medicines and special food, and on the night of the 30th he died. He was buried before we got down, and on his grave the Sherpas built a large cairn and fenced it about with a ring of stones. He sleeps amongst the mountains to which he had given of his best, to which his long record of service is eloquent testimony. He had probably served on more major expeditions than any other Sherpa living. Nuri was still with us, but more wasted and woebegone than ever, and so weak as to cause us some anxiety. The other porters had recovered, Pasang his sight and Nima his cheery grin.

By the evening it was snowing hard, but that did not prevent Emmons and Houston from preparing for us, and serving, a supper that put to shame any previous efforts. Odell and Carter had not yet arrived but, knowing our geologist by now, we were not unduly worried and thought they might be spending the night at Camp I. However, as darkness fell they came down the scree, soaked to the skin and dog-tired. It was too late now for the mountain to strike back.

September 1st was a day of luxurious idleness devoted to settling plans for our return. I was bent on attempting to force a new route out of the Basin by 'Longstaff's Col' and Houston was keen to come too, despite the fact that it was imperative for him to be in Ranikhet by the 13th, and no one could tell how long it would take us. Of the others, all were anxious to see Badrinath of which they had heard so much, and Emmons wanted another day or two in the Basin to complete his survey.

On the 2nd the various caravans got under way; first to leave was Nuri, carrying no load, for in his feeble state he wanted a long start. He was followed by Graham Brown, Lloyd, and Odell, with a most ambitious programme which entailed double-marching all the way—we called them the 'express'. Then Loomis and Carter pushed off with most of the porters carrying the surplus gear—they were the 'slow freight'. Emmons and Kalu then departed, bound for the other side of the glacier, after a moving display of chest-thumping by Kalu. If he got safely across the glacier he would have something to thump about, for his load was of staggering dimensions. Finally

Houston, Pasang, and I left about midday in a snow storm, travelling as light as possible and bound for a bivouac at the foot of the snow slope below the Pass.

The 'express' and the 'slow freight' seem to have changed rôles soon after starting, the 'express' having trouble with its feet. Ranikhet was reached in the reverse order to that of leaving the Basin, and some time behind schedule.

We three followed up the true right bank of the glacier and crossed it when it began to curve round at the foot of the Coxcomb ridge. We were armed with a plan, drawn by Emmons, showing us where he had made his bivouac, but we misled ourselves by assuming his progress was as slow as our own and, failing to find it, camped on snow, all in one tent, some way below it. The height was about 17,500 ft., the col is 19,200 ft., so we made preparations for a very early start. We took a gloomy view of our chances of getting over on account of the snow which had fallen that day and was still falling that night.

We were up at 3.30 a.m. and left at five on a fine morning, creeping along at the foot of a rock wall. The snow was soft, filling us with alarm and despondency, but once we were clear of the rocks it hardened up and soon we had to scrape out steps with our ice-axes, The slope steepened rapidly and we made for an outcrop of rock over to our right, where we thought we would be more comfortable and which would, when scaled, led us to the foot of a snow rib set at a slightly easier angle than the rest of the face. We had studied the approach to this col long and earnestly from our camps on the mountain in all conditions of light and shadow; always hoping for, but never receiving, some slight hint that it was not really as steep as it looked. Coming up last night we had caught a distorted glimpse of it through snow and swirling mists, when it looked ridiculously easy, but now, as every step brought us closer under it, our first impressions were not only confirmed but deepened.

After tentative essays to effect a lodgement on the rock bulge in two different places, we decided there was too much verglas on the rock for safety, and retreated stealthily to the snow. We climbed up till level with the top of the rocks and then began traversing across above the outcrop in order to gain the snow rib. The snow of the traverse was horribly deep and loose and, with no supporting snow below but only rock, conditions seemed ideal for an avalanche. It was with considerable misgiving that we crept slowly and cautiously across it, but the rib was temptingly close and the alternative route straight up the snow to our left was minatory in its steepness. The sun, which was now well over the wall above us, added to our anxiety, but the snow held, and once astride, literally astride, the rib we breathed more freely. For the first few feet of this the snow was rather worse than that which we had experienced near the top of Nanda Devi, and for every step up we sank down two. After tremendous exertions we struggled up a few feet and then began to find solid bottom. A prolonged bout of step-kicking landed us on top of the col at eleven o'clock.

For most of the way up the weather was clear and there was a magnificent view of our ridge on Nanda Devi seen in profile. I had brought a camera solely for the purpose of taking this invaluable picture, but it was stowed away in the bottom of my rucksack which was in turn part of a load, strapped to a carrying frame. Once we were fairly committed to the difficult part of the climb there was little inclination or opportunity for getting it out; but that is a feeble excuse and with a little trouble the thing could have been done—but I kept on putting off the evil moment. Now, of course, when we sat down exhausted on the top of the pass the whole mountain had disappeared in the mist. Had we been higher I might cite this as a fair sample of high-altitude mentality, but since we were only 19,000 ft. the less said about it the better. One lesson at least it teaches, which is not to carry your camera in a rucksack, and the corollary to that is a small, light camera.

Our field of view was restricted to within a hundred yards of where we sat, but we had looked at the pass and its neighbourhood so long and frequently that we knew, or thought we knew, the topography of it. We were on the eastern rim of the Basin at the foot of the long shoulder which runs up to East Nanda Devi. To the south the rim climbs for a thousand feet to form the fluted ice wall which towers above the main arm of the South-East glacier. From somewhere on this ice wall and outside the Basin, a ridge extends eastwards linking Nanda Kot with the Nanda Devi group. On this ridge, between Sanctuary wall and Nanda Kot, there is a pass, called Traill's Pass after the first Commissioner of Kumaon, whose administration lasted from 1815 to 1835. He was also the first to cross this pass in 1830, and it has been suggested that his object was not mountain exploration but to find a short cut between the Pindar valley and Milam which would be useful for commercial purposes. The pass is 17,700 ft. high, and whatever his object it was a very remarkable feat for one who was not a mountaineer and who lived almost before the dawn of mountaineering. Since then it has been crossed in 1855 by Adolph Schlagintweit as related in Chapter One, in 1861 by Colonel Edmund Smyth, and again in 1926 by a party which included Mr Hugh Ruttledge. The Pass leads to the Pindari glacier and from there to Ranikhet is a short and easy route, so it was attractive to us for that reason as well as for the few time which it had been crossed.

On the east side of the col, or what might now be truly be called the Pass, a slope of rock and snow, decidedly less steep than the Basin side, led down to the Milam valley. This was a known and suitable route for us to take, but we had not yet given up hope of finding and crossing Traill's Pass, although the heavy mist was a severe handicap. Our very distant surveys from high on Nanda Devi had led us to think that the ridge on which the Pass lay was not far from where we now sat, and we thought that by traversing to our right we might arrive somewhere in the vicinity of the Pass without losing much height—a consideration which in our then feeble state of mind and body seemed of paramount importance. We sat there for an hour waiting for a clearing in which we might see something of what lay between us and the Pass. No clearing came, so we began traversing blindly.

After we had been going for two hours on steep, soft, and rather unsafe snow, the mist was as thick as ever and we appeared to be getting nowhere except, possibly, into trouble. We gave up traversing and began casting about for a tent site, and in the process we were driven lower and lower down the slope. When there was still no sign of a suitable platform and it was getting late, we decided to go straight down to the glacier, although we knew that this probably meant the abandonment of Traill's Pass. We were all very tired and made a sorry job of the descent, getting into trouble in a long ice runnel which was like a water-course full of ice. I was in front of the others and, after one or two involuntary glissades, had half made up my mind to forsake the firm but dangerous going in the icy channel for the safe but laborious snow-plodding on the bank above. My mind was made up for me by a boulder which came spinning down and which I only just managed to dodge. With more haste than dignity I scrambled up the bank. We finally camped at about half-past five on what was almost a grass sward a few hundred feet above the Lwanl glacier. For once Pasang seemed to have had enough.

Talking things over that night we reluctantly gave up an attempt on the Pass and decided to go home via the Milam valley. Having lost so much height we were not in the right trim for facing a climb up again and, though the valley route might be longer, in the weather and snow conditions prevailing it was conceivable that once more the longest way round might be the shortest way home.

Next morning, lightened by the scrapping of the Primus stove and some paraffin, we descended to the glacier, crossed it to the north side and followed it down to below the snout. There was the usual stream, here only in its infancy, issuing from the glacier, but, mindful of the ways of these streams, I decided that we would do well to get on the Ranikhet side of it while we could. I therefore forded it without much difficulty, but Pasang, seeing a likely-looking line of country ahead and sniffing the fleshpots from afar, went off at score down the north bank where Houston, for his sins, followed him. Walking along our respective banks of the river we came soon to the grazing alp of Narspati which lies under the northern slopes of Nanda Kot. Looking back, the whole head of the valley was filled with the magnificent bulk of East Nanda Devi, seen with advantage from a fresh angle and no longer overshadowed by its namesake, which was now hidden away behind it. West of the glistening pile of Nanda Kot, with its familiar table-top, was the long low ridge which we should then have been crossing by Traill's Pass. It was much farther away from our pass than we had imagined nor did the Pass look by any means a walk-over.

There were here a few stone huts on both sides of the river, but on the north side there was also a well-marked path, along which I watched Pasang disappearing with envy. On my side the river lapped the foot of the moraine of a big glacier coming down from Nanda Kot, and soon I was blaspheming and boulder-hopping along this in a very evil frame of mind. Presently the going became so bad that I decided to climb 200 ft. up to the top of the moraine, where I thought I would find better going or even the path, which I was convinced must exist from the evidence of the stone huts. But this exhausting climb was to no purpose, I had merely exchanged boulder-hopping on a slope for boulder-hopping on the razor-backed moraine top, and my already sour temper grew worse as I thought how the other two must be enjoying my antics from the security of their path.

Having won clear of the boulders of the glacier I did find a sort of path and, hurrying along to catch up, I at length saw the others waiting for me on the opposite bank. It was impossible to carry on any conversation above the roar of the river, which was now a formidable torrent, but they were complacent enough to suggest by signs that I should try to cross it, at which I shook my head with terrific violence and signalled a counter suggestion that it was time they joined me. Then I remembered that Houston was carrying all our chocolate and by pointing to my mouth I got him to throw some over. We lunched amicably but distantly and then pursued our divided but parallel courses.

I could see what was happening on their steeply sloping bank much better than they could and, while my path steadily improved, I could see that there was trouble ahead for them in a series of big landslides, which could only be circumvented by using another path much higher up. They failed to spot this path and presently got spread-eagled on the almost vertical earth cliff left by the landslide. I gesticulated wildly to indicate that they must go up, but they seemed to think I was merely 'registering' enjoyment of their discomfiture, as perhaps I was, and paid no attention.

Finding themselves at last completely baffled they climbed wearily up and found the track, and we all started legging it for Martoli, the first village and the place where our respective paths would, in the fullness of time, unite. More trouble of the same sort awaited them round the next bend and, seeing this, I pushed on, leaving them to it, bent on vindicating my judgment by arriving before them, but never imagining it would be so thoroughly vindicated as it was.

While yet some three miles from Martoli and with no sign of my rivals on the other bank, I suddenly came upon a tributary river, and was dismayed to find the path turning off at right angles to follow up this side valley for one and a half miles, where it crossed the river by a bridge and then came back down the other side for a like distance, before once more following the main valley down to Martoli. This extra three miles was an unexpected blow for I imagined that they would soon be gloating over my receding back as I toiled up this side valley, getting farther from Martoli every minute. However, there was no help, though all was not yet lost and, putting on all steam, an hour and a half later I was back in the main valley, very much hotter in mind and body and scanning the opposite slopes eagerly for signs of my pursuers. There was nothing to be seen and it seemed hardly possible that they could be already out of sight ahead. I noticed that as it approached Martoli the opposing slope grew steeper and steeper, and below the village, which was perched high up on my side, the river flowed through a deep gorge—nor was there a bridge nor any sign of a path leading to a bridge.

Reflecting that this would give them something to think about, I pushed on and reached Martoli at three o'clock.

CHAPTER EIGHTEEN

The Bhotias of Martoli

MARTOLI is one of the main trade routes between India and Tibet and is the last village but one (which is Milam) on the Indian side of the border. Situated on a high spur between the Gori and Lwanl rivers, 11,000 ft. up, it is a bleak and desolate spot, surrounded by high hills and swept by piercing winds. It is occupied by a population of about two hundred Bhotias. 'Occupied' is the word rather than inhabited, because these people only come up here in the early summer with their sheep, and go down again in October to pass the winter at Munsiara and other villages lower down the Gori valley. All food has to be brought up, for nothing is grown there except a little mustard and potatoes; but the grazing is excellent, and juniper and rhododendron bushes supply fuel. The houses are solidly built of stone and roofed with heavy slate, and are usually in the form of a hollow square surrounding a flagged courtyard.

About these most interesting people, the Bhotias, and their trade with Tibet, much could be written, but I must attempt only a brief sketch. As has been said, the Bhotias are of Mongolian extraction and speak a dialect akin to Tibetan. Bhot or Bod is really the same word as Tibet, but the people of Garhwal and Almora seldom use either of these names when referring to the country north of them, but call it Hundes. They have been Hinduised to a certain extent and worship not only Tibetan deities but also the gods of the Hindu pantheon. But they are not very orthodox Hindus, and the caste system is interpreted as it suits them. In the matter of food they are quite ready to eat with Tibetans, which would be defilement to strict Hindus, but which is probably of advantage to the Bhotias in their trade relations; nor did the Garhwal Bhotias show much scruple about eating any of our foods. Of their character it can be said that they are cheerful, hardy, industrious (at least the women), honest, hospitable, charitable, and a thoroughly likeable people. Nor are they the wild uncivilised barbarians that is sometimes thought. Their houses are well built and have some pretence to architecture; they are shrewd traders, willing to be educated, and have produced such men as Rai Kishen Singh Bahadur, the famous Pandit 'A.K.' of the Indian Survey, and one or two others who have earned a name for themselves in the exploration and mapping of Tibet.

The Bhotias enjoy a monopoly of the trade with Tibet, which appears to be a lucrative one in spite of the many taxes imposed by the Tibetans. The route from Milam to Tibet involves the crossing of three passes between 17,000 and 18,000 ft., all of which have to be crossed in one day because there is no grazing in between. The two chief markets to which the Bhotias of this valley resort are Gyanema and Gartok. The latter is a journey of five days or ten when travelling with sheep. In the spring the local Tibetan official visits Milam and, having first assured himself that there is no epidemic disease in the Bhotia villages, he levies a general toll before declaring the passes open. Further taxes are paid in Tibet. At one time the Indian Government decreed that no taxes were to be paid to the Tibetans, but when the Tibetans replied by closing the passes, the Bhotias were so hard hit that at their request the decree was rescinded. Tibet produces very little grain and is largely dependent on imports from India; wheat, barley, rice, therefore, are the chief articles carried in by the Bhotias, but sugar, tobacco, brass, copper, and iron are also taken. In return they bring from Tibet wool, salt, borax, yaks' tails, ponies, and of these the wool is by far the most important. The figure of 400 tons of wool for the year 1907 is an impressive one when the route and the means of transport are considered. The Bhotia traders and their households come up to Milam and Martoli in the spring and establish depôts there, and in the course of the summer they make two or three journeys into Tibet. In the early autumn they begin sending their wool, salt, and borax to centres in the southern valleys, and by early November Milam and Martoli are once more deserted. Goats and sheep are the principal carriers, but yaks, jibbus, and mules are sometimes used. No fodder is carried for these, and in consequence the greater part of each day must be devoted to grazing. Marches are therefore short, seldom exceeding six or seven miles.

There is romance in trade and not least in this carried on in the grim defiles and over the stern passes of the Himalaya.

And now to continue the story of our strange antics on this the first day of our return to the habitations of man. I sat down beneath a low stone wall in the middle of the village to avoid the wind and to await the event. A crowd soon began to gather, as it would in an English village if someone dropped out of the skies, and a barrage of questions was fired at me. Their own knowledge of the country to the west stopped at the grazing alp of Narspati; beyond was hearsay, and they found it difficult to believe that anyone could have come over the icy barrier which lies west of this; if I *had* flown there they could not have been more surprised. When I had got it into their heads that we had come from Joshimath, climbing Nanda Devi on the way, they were profoundly impressed and showed an insatiable curiosity about our experiences on the mountain. Time and again they asked me if we had seen the goddess on top of the mountain, and when I was obliged to confess that we had noticed nothing but snow they seemed loath to believe it, and returned to the charge with suggestions that we must at any rate have seen the house in which the goddess dwelt. My boots, ice-axe, rope, clothes, face, and beard were all appraised and commented upon, fortunately in a language which I could not understand, and having thus provided them with considerable free instruction, entertainment, and amusement, I thought it was their turn and hinted that a little food and drink would not come amiss. Enormous thick chapatties, some blistering hot curry, and Tibetan tea, were soon forthcoming, and the clumsy way I handled the curry with my fingers amply repaid the donor.

A wet mist now blew up the valley and the whole party adjourned to a low, stone, windowless building, and the noise inside made it unnecessary for them to tell me it was the village school. Fifty diminutive Bhotia infants, boys and girls, were turned out, and the schoolmaster with one or two favourite pupils did the honours. He was a man of the world, and to impress upon me that at least one man in Martoli was not an ignorant savage he sent over to his house for a Thermos flask, of all things. It was full of very hot Tibetan tea, flavoured with red pepper, and at the moment I could not have too much to drink. But before I was allowed to start every man in the crowd had to stick his fingers down the mouth of it, not to enhance the flavour of the tea, as of course it did, but to assure himself that there was no deception about this modern miracle. While I was drinking, the favourite pupils were put through their paces, the most advanced had to write a sentence in Hindustani (in Roman characters I was relieved to find), and to this I had to write a suitable reply which the unfortunate scholar had then to read aloud for the edification of the audience. He passed the examination with far more credit than I did.

I found these mental exercises rather exhausting and welcomed a diversion in the shape of some 'chang' which one of my well-wishers brought along. This is a thin whitish beer made from barley and no Tibetan is ever far away from it. Just as we were settling down happily to some solemnish drinking a cry went up outside and we all trooped out to investigate. The excitement was caused by the strange spectacle of two men clinging like flies to the cliffs on the far side of the gorge. At first I thought it must be two enthusiasts of the Martoli Mountaineering Club, if such there was, enjoying a little practice on the local crags, but soon, in the failing light, I realised that it was Houston and Pasang looking for some means of reaching the haven where they would be, and, at almost the same moment, that they were not at all likely to find it. I was told that the bridge was a mile below the gorge and that they were way off the path to it. I suggested that someone should go over and show them the way, but it was obvious that nothing would be done, for it was now almost dark—besides there was a lot of beer left. We returned to the school.

When the party broke up I was not allowed to take up quarters on the earth floor of the school as I hoped. Under the guidance of the schoolmaster we stumbled in the dark through narrow lanes between house walls, colliding several times with what seemed to be the town band, a gang of youths who paraded the village after sundown, singing and beating a sort of tattoo on drums. Presently we turned through a narrow tunnel and emerged in a large courtyard about thirty yards square, and, stumbling first over a yak and then over some goats, I was led up a stone staircase and into a little room which seemed to be a kind of store. There were bales of wool, sheepskins, skins of bharal and musk deer, baskets of grain, and a couple of hand-dressed mill-stones. There was a primitive oil lamp and a carpet was spread on the floor, so I hung up my hat and took possession. Then the genial Bhotia who was my host arrived, bringing with him my supper of curry and rice and a few intimate friends to watch me dispatch it. This done I distributed tobacco and one of them produced some fiery home-made brandy. It had been too hard a day for me to shine socially and, when I nearly fell asleep where I sat, they took the hint and withdrew.

My host insisted on sleeping in the store with me, rather, I hope and believe, to ensure that nobody stole anything from me than that I should appropriate anything of his. He spent half the night measuring out rations of flour to one of his drovers who was going on a journey next day, and he was up before four to see the sheep loaded with their saddle bags. This activity did not disturb me, for I was too tired, nor did the bales of wool, which I had remarked with concern, discharge the clouds of fleas that I expected.

I was out at daylight next morning to have a look round but was not earlier than the women, who had already settled down to their endless task of weaving, seated round the courtyard at their twelve-foot lengths of cloth in the making, darting the shuttle through, and pressing the woof home with flat wooden staves. The spinning of thread for the weaving is done by the men and the children, who are never without a hank of wool on one wrist, which they spin into thread on wooden spindles, as naturally as breathing, and half-unconsciously like a woman knitting.

The village is, as I have said, on a high bluff in the angle between the main Gori river and the tributary Lwanl stream down which we had come. To the north the valley is open and grassy, and nine miles away is Milam, the last village on the road and a much more important one than Martoli. Walking out of the village that morning, towards the end of the spur, I could look down on to the bridge over the Lwanl 400 ft. below, and beyond it to the white ribbon of road leading up the valley to Milam, whose position was indicated by the shining Milam peak. Down this road and across the bridge came flock after flock of white sheep and goats, bringing their burdens of wool, salt, and borax, from distant Tibet. Some took the valley road below the village but many climbed the steep zigzag track up to Martoli, and as they gained the flat plateau on which the village stands they were met by the band of last night and escorted to their owner's house in triumph with tap of drum. The patient plodding yaks and the jostling sheep, many of them lame and all of them tired, seemed to take fresh heart; it was for all the world like a footsore regiment being played into billets after a long march.

There was no one to play the two weary, belated wanderers in. I spotted them on the far side of the river accompanied by a third man, evidently a guide. They came slowly up the hill, wading knee-deep amongst a sea of sheep, and when Pasang saw me sitting there, trying hard to suppress a malicious grin, he had the grace to look sheepish himself. Perhaps I have dwelt too long on this incident, but to me at the time it afforded more amusement than it may when set down on paper, because so often the boot is on the other leg—it is the Sherpa who hits off the best route and the Sahib who is the fool.

We all returned to my lodging, where we ate eggs and potatoes and Houston told of their adventures. They had left the track which they should have followed because it turned up the hill away from the river and the village, and they were further betrayed by the sight of a man coming down from Martoli towards the river, whom they rashly assumed to be making for a crossing place. By dusk they were deeply involved on the cliffs above the gorge where I had seen them, and when they had extricated themselves they had to go back up the valley for a good half mile before finding a camping place. In the morning they chanced upon a shepherd who took them to the bridge by a short cut.

While we were breakfasting a man, a girl, and a baby came into the courtyard, and while the man played on a drum with his hands, the baby being parked at his side, the girl danced and sang in a blood-curdling falsetto. She hardly moved off the flat stone on which she stood and expressed more with her hands and her body than with her feet. Occassionally she stopped to pass round the hat in the form of the shovel-shaped basket which is used for winnowing, but her performance impressed by its sustained effort more than by its beauty. However, it seemed to be appreciated by the weaving women, the idlers, and by a small party who, having slaughtered a sheep, were busy cutting it up alongside the man holding the drum and the baby. Nor did the sheep, goats, yaks, cows, and mules, sunning themselves on the warm stones of the courtyard, show any violent symptoms of dislike. Contributions of grain, rice, and bits of wool found their way into the basket and we, with mistaken generosity, added a four-anna piece. This was fatal, because the girl promptly took up a position close to Houston, who was foolishly sitting outside, and gyrated in front of him till he was dizzy and fled inside for refuge.

We did not want to leave the protection of our room until this dangerous dancing girl had gone, but she showed no signs of stopping and it was time to think of starting, although the hospitable Bhotias wanted us to stop and make another night of it. We tried to hire two porters to carry our loads, but no one would come for less than the outrageous rate of Rs 3 a day and, like the Mr Ramsbottom in the song 'Runcorn Ferry' who would 'sooner be drownded than done', we continued to carry our own packs. Then came the question of settling with the good people of Martoli for my board and lodging and the food we had bought, and in that I am afraid my host's trading instincts overcame his geniality; not in the amount asked, for that was only Rs 3, but in a little comedy that was acted for our benefit. Having nothing else, we tendered a five-rupee note, and after a prolonged absence our host returned with the sad news that there was no change in the village. We offered him a 120 ft. climbing rope in full settlement, but as this would not do we took back the five-rupee note. That worried him a lot and off he went again to return at last with one rupee. We were hard-hearted enough to refuse this, and the whole farce was re-enacted and that time one and a half rupees were forthcoming. It was a consummate piece of acting, but by now we had tumbled to it, so, pocketing our five rupees, we shouldered our packs, said goodbye and walked off, when of course he at once produced, quite unabashed, the two rupees change.

Turning our backs on Martoli and the mountains we marched down the valley towards the plains.

CHAPTER NINETEEN

Last Days

THE short, sweet grass of the Martoli spur was soon left behind and the road grew ever rougher as the towering walls of the valley closed in upon the river, so that soon we were marching through a wild and savage gorge out of which we were not to escape until the second day. The gorge of the Gori, or 'white' river, rivals the Rishi gorge in its stark and gloomy grandeur and surpasses it in length and continuity. For twenty miles there is scarcely any break in the precipitous nature of either bank of the river, and in this distance the fall is about 4000 ft. The river runs with such violence and rapidity that for many miles it is nothing but a series of cascades and rapids. The rough track is nowhere level, climbing up and down, crossing and recrossing the river as it avoids impassable rock faces and seeks a way over the many torrents that come leaping down the sides of the great gorge. At one point, thinking we had already seen the last of snow for many a month, we were astonished to find ourselves walking over a huge avalanche cone of hard, dirty snow. Considering the time of the year and the altitude of only about 9000 ft., the presence of this snow is a convincing witness to the little sunlight that reaches the bottom of this deep and narrow cleft, and the depth of the winter snowfall.

There were no villages in the gorge, indeed no habitations of any kind, and at five o'clock, in pouring rain, we found shelter in a big cave. There were already five travellers and drovers in it who occupied the best pitch, and who did not invite us to join them round their fire. However, when Pasang asked them for some tea one of them gave us a handful of the stalks they use as tea and refused indignantly to take any of our sugar in exchange. At dusk six more wayfarers arrived and, finding the ground floor occupied, took possession of a second storey reached by a difficult rock climb up a slab. We thought it was now time to put out a 'House Full' notice, but in this we were mistaken, for, after dark, five more men came in and found a niche for themselves in yet a third storey.

When we woke to another wet morning most of the hotel guests had already left, apparently without any breakfast, and by half-past five we were left in sole possession and with a feeling that we were disgracefully late risers. We regretted this laziness because we had planned to touch some of our fellow lodgers for some atta, to make the chapatties for which our hearts yearned. We breakfasted austerely off satu.

All that morning the gorge continued to amaze us with its ruggedness and the road by its makers' ingenuity. It was carried backwards and forwards across the river on spidery bridges, it was carried up slabs on wooden stairs, across cliff faces, on cunningly built stone revetments, and through tunnels carved out of solid rock. The gloominess and the severity of the scene, the rain and the eternal roar of the river, became oppressive, so that we were glad when the gorge at length opened out, and the track climbed up out of the valley to a gentler land of villages and fields.

We stopped at the village of Munsiari, where we were able to buy some flour and some rice, but we were worried about the state of our purse because we had only a few rupees, apart from a note for Rs 100, which was as valuable in these parts as waste paper. Even at this short distance from the mountains the peasants were as different from the frank, self-sufficient Bhotias of Martoli as chalk from cheese. We seemed to have nothing in common, and they displayed not the slightest interest or curiosity in us or our doings. And this, I think, without any implications of self-importance on our part, can only be attributed to the apathy of ignorance.

We were both by now terribly footsore and we learnt later that the rest of the party suffered in the same way. It may have been due to the cold and wet feet we frequently had on the mountain or to the wearing of several pairs of socks for a long period, and now that we had gone back to rubbers we felt like penitents condemned to walking in shoes full of peas or pebbles. In spite of this we sturdily refused to put on climbing boots again, even though this refusal meant an extra 5 lb. weight on our backs. Walking through hot valleys in heavy climbing boots is as incongruous as it is tiring, and for me it had become a point of honour to return to Ranikhet shod with the same rubbers in which I had started, although there was now little but the soles remaining.

Our loads, of which to relieve us we had not yet been able to hire a coolie, weighed us down and made us limp the more, but for all that it was difficult not to enjoy every minute of this march. The trees, the grass, the paddy fields, the birds; the streams in which we bathed and which, on one memorable occasion, provided us with a meal of fresh-caught fish.

The streams were not always so friendly, for one of them nearly cost Houston his passage which we were racing to catch. At a place of evil memory called Tejam, we camped in a field of wheat-stubble by a big river called the Ramganga, and it is difficult to say which were the most trying, the villagers or a small venomous fly known locally as 'mora'. The villagers adopted what we found on this march to be their usual *non-possumus* attitude in the matter of food, but an ex-soldier of the Kumaon Rifles came to the rescue with some rice and milk. In all our travels in Garhwal it was always the reservist, usually of the Garhwal or the Kumaon Rifles, who was the most willing to help and the ablest. While talking to him we learnt the unexpected news that the bridge over the river was down—had been down in fact for two years. There did not appear to be the remotest chance of fording it, but he told us that two miles up there was a ford. To offset our relief he was careful to add that it was a difficult ford and that sometimes the water was up to a man's neck. Provided it did not rain in the night, he thought we might get across and volunteered to come with us to lend a hand. After paying him for the rice and milk we had only one rupee left, and, as we should have to travel for at least two more days before there was any hope of changing our Rs 100 note, we could not afford to pay him for any services rendered and had to decline his offer.

From the colour of the river, a lovely turquoise, we judged it not to be a glacier-fed stream, but in this we were mistaken, for we found later that it rises under the southern slopes of Nanda Kot. A heavy thunderstorm up the valley soon changed the colour to mud and we were concerned to hear the thunder growling away for most of the night. It was raining in the morning, and when we set off at seven it got steadily worse. The path was ill-defined, but having made what we thought was a liberal two miles we began to look for the ford.

The path appeared to terminate at the water's edge at a place where the river momentarily slackened the pace of its current, and on the far side we thought we could make out a continuation of the path. Much against our wishes we concluded that this must be the ford, but it looked so uninviting that, before trying it, we went a bit farther up stream. We could see no path, so we sent Pasang on to try higher up while Houston and I went back to what we now feared was the ford. Linking hands we took to the water, but had not covered more than a few yards out of the necessary fifty before we were up to our waists and hard put to keep our feet on the bottom. We turned back, convinced that there must be some mistake, for the water there would be up to a giraffe's neck let alone a man's.

While we were in the water we saw two men striding along the path who beckoned to us to come back. They were going to the ford they said and advised us to follow, and on they went again at a furious pace. They were active, long-legged beggars, with a minimum of clothing, and they carried a little bundle of short bamboo sticks, and clutched in one hand a great bamboo pole about 8 ft. long. I assumed this must be a necessary item of equipment for crossing the ford, and thought dismally how singularly ill-provided we were for pole-jumping with ice-axes 3 ft. long. However, there was not much time for thought as we had practically to run to keep them in sight; I imagined that they were as nervous as we were that the heavy rain, which still persisted, would make the river unfordable, possibly for several days.

We picked up Pasang, and a mile farther up they turned down towards the river and began removing the little surplus apparel they had preparatory to business. It was a curious place and the obvious one for a ford, for the river ran over a bed of shingle flats perhaps 300 yards wide. The water flowed in four separate channels, divided by banks of shingle, and the crossing of the first two of these was so easy as to make us think that it was all over bar shouting. The sight of the third soon dispelled this impression, and we watched with anxiety while our long-legged and half-naked friends tackled it. It was not very deep, just over the knees, but the speed of the current made one gasp. Their technique was instructive but quite impossible for us to emulate with the heavy loads we had. They took a diagonal line down stream, not attempting to stem the current, and went as fast as they could, lifting the foot clear of the water at every bound. In a few moments they were safe on the far side, laughing at us as we advanced slowly and fearfully into midstream hand in hand. The effort required to maintain any footing was tremendous and it was difficult to keep the point of an ice-axe on the bottom to support one. Houston cast off from us and attempted to finish at speed, as they had done, but in the deepest part he lost his footing and I thought he was gone, but after rolling right over he struggled up again and reached the bank. Pasang and I were still ten yards from the shore and making very heavy weather of it, so I was mightily relieved when one of the bamboo merchants dashed in and caught me by the hand. We were soon over the rest, and I was so thankful to have the Ramganga behind us that I bestowed on our deliverers nearly all the tobacco I had left.

Travel in the Himalaya involves sooner or later the bridging or fording of rivers, and it is surprising what can be crossed with an axe, a few straight trees, and a good eye for a likely place for a bridge; and when fording, how great is the assistance obtained from a rope, an ice-axe, and the mutual support of two or more persons. In dangerous rivers it is advisable to carry the load so that it can easily be slipped off, for though a load helps to keep your feet on the bottom, once that footing is lost the same load would be a fatal handicap.

Two more days of hard going, getting daily more footsore, and we reached Kapkot in the valley of the Sarju river on the route to the Pindari glacier. This is a deservedly popular tourist route, well provided with dâk bungalows, the last of which is but a mile or two from the glacier snout. The one-horse village of Kapkot seemed in our eyes a wealthy metropolis, for there were several native shops and a big dâk bungalow pleasantly situated on a green lawn above the river, and shaded by an enormous banyan tree.

The caretaker of the bungalow was not much impressed by our appearance, and indeed if we were to be taken at our face value this was quite understandable. Very grudgingly he opened one of the rooms for us and began, metaphorically, to count his spoons; but when he asked where our coolies were, and we were obliged to confess that the faithful but dishevelled Pasang was the sole member of our suite, he seemed half inclined to shut it again. We had no cash at all now except for the Rs 100 note, and, large though Kapkot appeared to us, we doubted whether the combined population could find change for this amount. If this, as we expected, proved true, then our creditors would be asked to accompany us on the march until we were, as it were, solvent; nor did we allow this consideration to make us stint ourselves in the orders we gave to the caretaker for the provision of food. However, when we did produce the note as an earnest of good faith the eyes of the caretaker shone with a sudden geniality, and he hastened to assure us that change would be found. His former surliness was forgotten, he became profoundly respectful, and bustled about throwing open doors, setting chairs and tables, attending to our wants in every way he could.

Being now on the well-ordered Pindari glacier route it was from here on nothing but roses, roses, all the way. At the next halt Bageswar, the Rawal of the temple, a fine type of Indian gentleman of the old school, very dignified and erect in spite of his age, sent us with his customary generosity a present of

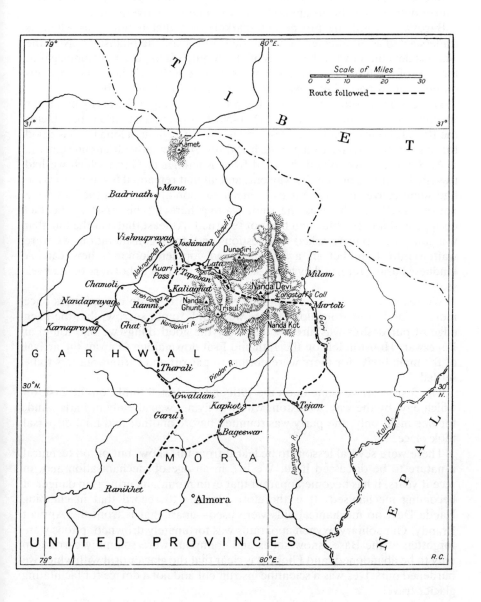

Scale of Miles

0   5   10   20   30

Route followed ─ ─ ─ ─ ─ ─

fruit; a party who were also stopping at the bungalow pressed upon us a loaf of bread and an enormous fish out of the Sarju river, while the khansama in charge of the bungalow served up a four-course dinner. I had been this way before and had promised Houston that at Bageswar we would get a five-course dinner, but this disappointment he generously overlooked.

Bageswar is not the prosperous market town that it once was when its traders acted as middlemen between the Bhotias and the plainsmen. Now the Bhotias deal direct with the banias of Haldwani, Tanakpur, and Ramnagar at the foot of the hills. The bazaar consists of solid well-built houses with shops on the ground floor, but it was sad to see so many of these shut up.

There is a very old temple here; the present building, which is by no means the first, is said to date back to A.D. 1450. It is over this that our benefactor the Rawal, Poona Sahib, presides, a man who throughout a long life has stood for unswerving loyalty to the British Raj under very difficult circumstances.

At Someswar we joined the road from Ranikhet to Garul which we had travelled over in a bus on the way out, and all that remained for us now was to find some conveyance. The *deus ex machina* soon appeared in the guise of a native chauffeur who was, he said, waiting here for his master who had disappeared into the blue and had not returned. At least that was the tale that was told to us, but we asked no questions and, for a consideration, we were wafted into Ranikhet in a high-powered, opulent-looking, new car. A kindness Pasang returned by being sick all over the rich upholstery of the back seat.

We reached Ranikhet on September 12th and took up our quarters once more in the Forest Bungalow, where we found, to our sorrow, that the keen edge of our desires was already dulled by the good things we had found at Bageswar. Houston left on the 13th and I sat down alone to await the arrival of the main body, for there were porters to pay off and various matters to be settled.

The first to arrive came in on the 19th and the last, I think, on the 21st, on which day, by the way, Houston, who was flying, was already in Paris. And, for one night only, the party was reunited before another and final dispersal took place.

There were several lessons to be learnt from this show, but of too technical a nature to be discussed here. We live in an age of mechanisation and, in recent years, it has become apparent that even mountaineering is in danger of becoming mechanised. It is therefore pleasing to record that in climbing Nanda Devi no mechanical aids were used—apart that is from the Apricot Brandy. Our solitary oxygen apparatus was fortunately drowned, pitons were forgotten at the Base, snow shoes and crampons were solemnly carried up only to be abandoned, and I hope it is clear that the glacier drill with which we burdened ourselves was a scientific instrument and not a device for facilitating glacier travel.

Another interesting point is that the age limit for high climbing, previously put at 35, seems to have expanded, for our party was of all ages from twenty-two to over fifty, but I do not want to imply that either of these extremes is the best. Porters for high camps were found to be not indispensable, and a certain amount of hard work and hard living on the march up did not incapacitate anyone for work on the mountain. Even stranger was the fact that men of two different nations could work together under trying conditons in complete harmony and without jealousy.

It was but a short three months that we had met, many of us as strangers, but inspired by a single hope and bound by common purpose. This purpose was only achieved by team-work, team-work the more remarkable on account of the two different nationalities; and though these two nations have a common origin they are for that reason more critical of each other's shortcomings—as relationship leads proverbially to ill-feeling. The Americans and ourselves do not always see eye to eye, but on those rare occasions when we come together to do a job of work, as, for example, in war or in the more serious matter of climbing a mountain, we seem to pull together very well.

Where each man pulled his weight each must share the credit; for, though it is natural for each man to have his own aspirations, it is in mountaineering, more than in most things, that we try to believe

> The game is more than the players of the game,
> And the ship is more than the crew.

WHEN MEN AND MOUNTAINS MEET

When Men and Mountains Meet

First published by Cambridge University Press, 1946

Contents

Part 1 PEACETIME

Part 2 WARTIME

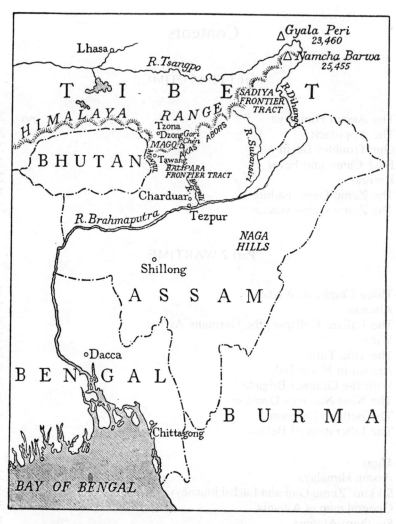

SKETCH MAP TO ILLUSTRATE ASSAM HIMALAYA

Part 1

PEACETIME

CHAPTER ONE

The Assam Himalaya

THE total length of the great Himalayan chain from Nanga Parbat in the west to Namcha Barwa in the east is some 1,500 miles. Of this the Assam Himalaya, as defined by Burrard and Hayden in their standard work, *Sketch of the Geography and Geology of the Himalaya*, occupy about 450 miles. These, however, include the Himalaya north of Bhutan; if we consider only that part of the chain between Assam and Tibet the length is about 250 miles.

Of all the Himalaya these are the least known, and it is not difficult to understand the reason. From the Assam-Bhutan frontier for a distance of 250 Miles eastwards to the Brahmaputra valley there is only one way over the Himalaya to Tibet, or even as far as the main range, and the existence of this route was not even suspected until the opening years of the present century. Between the last tea gardens and rice fields of Assam and the crest of the Himalaya is a wide belt of heavily forested foothills inhabited for the most part by savage tribes—Miji Akas, Silung Abors, Daflas. The reputation of these tribes, the difficult country, and an extremely heavy rainfall, discouraged closer inquiry until it was gradually realised that between the Bhutan-Assam frontier and the Bhareli river, a distance of some 40 miles, the country was not occupied by violent men inimical to strangers, but by peaceful tribes allied to the Bhutanese called Mönba, Sherchokpa, and others. Through the interest and exploration of various Political Officers from Assam, this corridor, known as Mönyul, was slowly opened up. Through it have passed travellers like Col. F. M. Bailey and Major H. T. Morshead in 1913 and Kingdon Ward in 1935 and 1938.

The journey of Bailey and Morshead in 1913 was extremely interesting, for it cleared up one of the outstanding problems of Asiatic exploration. It was only in 1912 that the discovery of Namcha Barwa by Morshead and the determination of its height as 25,445 ft. had surprised the geographers, who

275

had thought that there could be no peaks above 20,000 ft. north of Assam. A year later Morshead and Bailey discovered the great gorge between Namcha Barwa and Gyala Peri, 23,460 ft., by which the Tsangpo forces its way through the Himalaya to become the Dihang and later the Brahmaputra of Assam. The question of where the Tsangpo flowed after leaving Tibet was the most interesting problem of Asiatic exploration in the last decade of the nineteenth century. Several well-known 'pundits', native explorers and surveyors employed by the Survey of India, had been engaged on its solution. Three of the most famous were Nain Singh, A.K., and Kinthup. In 1884 Kinthup was dispatched from India to Tibet with orders to cast marked logs of wood into the waters of the Tsangpo in the hope that they might be recovered in the Brahmaputra later on. This rather fond hope came to nothing.

It is interesting to note that the discovery of a great peak, or rather two great peaks with only 14 miles between them, at the point where the Tsangpo breaks through to the plains, confirmed a conjecture of Burrard and Hayden who, in the the first edition of their book, 1907, wrote: 'The Sutlej in issuing from Tibet pierces the border range of mountains within 4½ miles of Leo Pargial, the highest peak of its region; the Indus when turning the great Himalayan range passes within 14 miles of Nanga Parbat, the highest point of the Punjab Himalaya; the Hunza river cuts through the Kailas range within 9 miles of Rakaposhi, the supreme point of the range. It will form an interesting problem for investigation whether the Brahmaputra of Tibet has cut its passage across the Himalaya near a point of maximum elevation.'

In their journey in 1913 Bailey and Morshead entered Tibet from Assam by following the course of the Dihang until they were stopped by the gorge east of Namcha Barwa. By a detour to the north they rejoined the river, the Tsangpo as it is called in Tibet, and followed it down past Namcha Barwa to a point less than 30 miles from the place at which they had left it. After this they moved west along the Tibetan side of the Himalaya and returned to Assam by the Mönyul corridor route.

In 1935 and again in 1938 Kingdon Ward travelled extensively in Mönyul and on the Tibetan side of the Assam Himalaya bringing back many new plants and seeds and much new geographic knowledge.

In 1934 and 1936 Messrs Ludlow and Sherriff, starting from Bhutan, travelled through Mönyul into south-eastern Tibet, also collecting plants and seeds.

The position then in 1939 was, that of the mountains themselves little or nothing was known except that the major peaks, that is, those over 20,000 ft., had been fixed trigonometrically from the plains of Assam. Even the Assam-Tibet frontier had not been defined. It was assumed that it followed the crest line of the main range until in 1912 it was discovered that Mönyul, which is south of the Himalaya, was being administered by Tibetans. In 1913, by some arrangement between the Governments concerned, all the districts south of the Himalaya were ceded to India, but nothing was done to administer the ceded territory, which remained, until 1939 at least, to all intents Tibetan.

Just to the east of the Mönyul corridor, or 'Tibetan Enclave' as it might be called, lies a group of some dozen peaks over 20,000 ft. Only four bear names, which are all Tibetan in origin: Gori Chen 21,450 ft., Kangdu 23,260 ft., Chiumo 22,760 ft., and Nayegi Kansang 23,120 ft. These were the mountains which I hoped to explore, and some of which I hoped to climb. Nothing is known of them and nothing has been written about them, for unlike many other parts of the Himalaya they have no place in the religious history of India. No temples or shrines adorn the banks of their rivers, no pilgrims visit them, no traditions enrich them.

I like to think I can see as far through a brick wall as most people, and in the latter part of 1938 it seemed clear to me, as to many others, that war was inevitable. This affected my plans for 1939. Shipton was returning to the Karakorams to continue the work which we had begun in 1937, and I should very much have liked to join him. But we should be extremely isolated, almost beyond recall in fact, and Shipton's plans necessitated staying out the following winter. I was not so abandoned yet as to consider being beyond recall an advantage. Moreover, the War Office, after twenty years of deep thought, had just remembered they had a Reserve of Officers, of which I was one, and had announced a scheme for their training. I decided therefore that by August 1939 I must be home. This ruled out the Karakoram, and my choice fell upon the Assam Himalaya as being the most accessible and the least known region for exploration.

This would be my sixth visit to the Himalaya, and though occasionally I had qualms about such indulgence, I had so far managed to stifle them without any severe struggle. The appetite grows as it is fed. Like the desire for drink or drugs, the craving for mountains is not easily overcome, but a mountaineering debauch, such as six months in the Himalaya, is followed by no remorse. Should such a feeling arise then one may echo Omar's *cri de cœur*,

> Indeed, indeed, Repentance oft before
> I swore—but was I sober when I swore?

Having once tasted the pleasure of living in high, solitary places with a few like spirits, European or Sherpa, I could not give it up. The prospect of what is euphemistically termed 'settling down', like mud to the bottom of a pond, might perhaps be faced when it became inevitable, but not yet awhile. Time enough for that when the hardships common to mountain travel—the carrying of heavy loads, the early morning starts, living or starving on the country— were no longer courted or at any rate suffered gladly.

Having fixed upon the Assam Himalaya as my objective, I had to decide how to get there and what to do there. Obviously the greatest prize for a mountaineer was Namcha Barwa, and a very useful job could be done making a reconnaissance with a view to climbing it another year. It would be necessary to get permission to enter Tibet, but even if one were not allowed to go to Namcha Barwa, the best approach to the Gori Chen group, my second string, was from the Tibetan side. Indeed, when these tentative plans were made on the way back from Everest in July 1938 I was not aware of any other way.

Passport difficulties are not confined to what we call the civilised world. For some of the lesser known parts of Asia entrance is even more troublesome; Tibet is a case in point. Most of the stock of good will of the Tibetan Government as well as the patience of the Indian Government in evoking it is used up by the Mount Everest expeditions. A favoured few can sometimes get in by using the direct-approach method, and one or two omit all formalities and just go in, presenting the Tibetans with a *fait accompli*. The difficulty about this is that if the Tibetans authorities resent this intrusion, the invader is easily checkmated by the local headman who will be told to refuse his unwelcome guest all means of transport. Exceptions have been made. On the way back from Mount Everest in July 1938 I met at Tangu in north Sikkim a party of German scientists led by a Dr Schaefer. They were officially working in Sikkim, but by a direct approach to a high official from Lhasa, who happened then to be just on the other side of the border, they were invited into Tibet where they spent several months. Strange stories of their behaviour were current when I came across them again in a train in India the following July. They must have got home just in time.

For the necessary permission I applied to Mr B. J. Gould (now Sir Basil Gould), British Resident in Sikkim. He had recently been to Lhasa on an official visit and was as well liked by the Tibetans as by the numerous British mountaineers whom he had helped so often. He had been instrumental in obtaining permission for the last two Mount Everest attempts. At that time he was at Yatung in the Chumbi valley, for which place I started immediately on reaching Gangtok, the capital of Sikkim. It is a two-day march with a rise of 2,000 ft. to the Natu La (14,000 ft.). Having finished my business I returned to Gangtok in one day, as I was pressed for time, taking 15½ hours for the 43 miles including halts. I mention this to show that though men coming off Mount Everest are usually in very poor condition, often with dilated hearts, recovery does not take long.

Mr Gould was not very hopeful about either permission for my own journey or for another Mount Everest attempt. Apparently some emphasis had been laid on the fact that 1938 was to be the last time we should ask, and a dispute over the Tibet-Assam boundary (Mönyul as mentioned above) was in progress.

This setback made it essential to visit Shillong, the pleasant hill capital of Assam, 5,000 ft. up, where Sir Robert Reid, then the Governor, afforded all possible help. In northern Assam the frontier tracts are what are called Excluded Areas. The one with which I was concerned was the Balipara Frontier Tract which is administered by a Political Officer drawn from the Assam Police who is directly responsible to the Governor. The tract is divided by an 'Inner Line' into administered and unadministered territory, of which the latter is by far the larger portion. The administered territory corresponds roughly to the short strip of plain between the Brahmaputra and the foothills; the unadministered comprises all that from the foothills to the Tibetan border which is supposed to follow the MacMahon line of 1914. The tribes to the north of the Inner Line, Daflas, Akas and Miris, are primitive people with no desire to respond to the soothing influences of civilisation. They receive subsidies contingent on their good behaviour, and for many years they have given us no trouble. Occasionally the Political Officer has to visit them (with a strong escort) to settle disputes, generally by mild persuasion, sometimes by force. The hill tribes are allowed to cross the Inner Line for peaceful purposes, trade or work, but no plainsmen may cross it without a special permit. Few, of course, wish to. As Mr Churchill once remarked when questioned about the efficacy of anti-shark measures in the Pacific, that 'H.M. Government was entirely opposed to sharks', so the tribesmen of those parts are entirely opposed to strangers.

The H.Q. of the Political Officer for the Balipara Frontier Tract was at Charduar, 20 miles north of the Brahmaputra. Permission to cross the Inner Line and to proceed to the Gori Chen area on the Tibetan border was readily obtained, and the Political Officer promised assistance in finding the necessary porters for the first stage of the journey.

All therefore was set for the 1939 campaign; it remained to decide what form this should take. Should it be mountaineering alone, or should I try to bring back something more substantial than a feeling of 'something attempted, something done' by collecting enough data for the making of a map? Would this necessarily add to the conviction, of which I was already assured, that the time had been well spent? Hitherto I had played no very active part in the more technical side of the three expeditions in which map-making had been the main object; in fact, I had on occasion regarded these activities rather as a benign but not too patient uncle might regard his nephews playing trains on the table on which he was shortly expecting his lunch.

Of course, as Lord Conway said, 'in all high mountain climbing there is an element of exploration'; and since the Gori Chen group was as yet unvisited this element would be considerable. But nowadays the explorer who brings his modest offering to the temple of science (may its worshippers increase) in the form of a dirty, illegible sketch, or an incoherent verbal description, is thought a little uncouth. Shipton's whole-hearted conversion to the side of the big battalions was of long standing; and I might have to forgo my admiring sympathy with Mummery, one of my heroes, who in the preface to his *Climbs in the Alps and Caucasus* expressed himself thus: 'I fear no contributions to science, or topography, or learning of any sort are to be found sandwiched in between the story of crags or seracs, of driving storm or perfect weather. To tell the truth, I have only the vaguest idea about theodolites, and as for plane tables, their very name is an abomination. To those who think with me, who regard mountaineering as unmixed play, these pages are alone addressed.' If you can call mountaineering an act of violence, which I think you can, then Mummery's forcibly expressed philosophy is greatly strengthened by a dictum of G. K. Chesterton (another of my heroes), who was admittedly no mountaineer, but who certainly had the root of the matter in him when he wrote: 'Almost any act of violence can be forgiven on this strict condition— that it is of no use at all to anybody. If the aggressor (or mountaineer) gets anything out of it, then it is quite unpardonable. It is damned by the least hint of utility or profit.'

This time I had to reckon with another factor which forbade my taking such a detached view as formerly about the 'scientific' side of an expedition. In the absence of a suitable companion I proposed going alone with a few Sherpa porters. Who they would be I could not tell, so that I might easily find when I arrived that I was unable to do as much climbing as I had hoped. Moreover, without a companion to act as stimulant or counter-irritant it would be an advantage to have something to occupy the mind in the many hours sometimes necessarily spent in camp. On a long expedition the active mind becomes dull, the dull becomes cataleptic. I decided, therefore, to modify my high principles and attempt a modest survey with one of Mummery's abominations, a plane-table—but not too much zeal.

CHAPTER TWO

The Approach

I reached Darjeeling on 5 April 1939 to collect my Sherpas. Owing to the many expeditions in the field that year, all of which had bespoken their porters early, good men were hard to come by. There were two German parties, an American party bound for K2, a Polish party going to Nanda Devi East (which they climbed), and Shipton's Karakoram party. Under the Hitler regime German mountaineers were extremely active in the Himalaya. They spent a lot of time and money and lost many climbers and porters, sometimes through bad luck, more often, perhaps, through bad judgement. To lose porters is a heinous offence, and, in my opinion, their use of an aeroplane for dropping stores to their camps on Nanga Parbat deserved a place in the same category.

Our centre of operations was a long way from the starting point. The route led through villages where porters were an unknown quantity, into a region where we could obtain nothing once we had arrived. I therefore had to cut to a minimum the number of mouths to be fed. I took three of the few porters available: Wangdi Norbu, an oldish but very capable and experienced man, who had been to Kamet with Smythe and also to Mount Everest in 1933; Nukku Sherpa, a young and very active porter, who had been with us in the Karakoram in 1937 and to Mount Everest in 1936 and 1938; Thundu, a dark horse, with no major expeditions to his credit, but recommended by the other two.

In 1939 the Himalayan Club instituted a system of grading porters. The graded men were to be called 'Tigers', a name which is not very suitable but one which has stuck owing to having been used of the 1924 Mount Everest porters who went highest. Certainly there are two qualities which the Sherpa shares with the tiger, strength and courage, but he is not a fighting man like his compatriot the Ghurka. The chosen men, the choice being based on the recommendation of leaders of expeditions, had a badge of a tiger's head and were entitled to 8 annas a day more than other porters for work above the snow-line. In 1939 there were a dozen of them, of whom Wangdi was one.

Travelling by rail from Silliguri on the eastern Bengal line we reached Rangapara on the north side of the Brahmaputra Valley on 8 April where we were met by Capt. Lightfoot, the Political Officer, and taken to Charduar by car. Charduar is a small post on the Inner Line consisting only of the Political Officer's bungalow and a few native houses and shops. A detachment of the Assam Rifles is stationed at Lokra on the Bhareli river 2 miles away, but the nearest place of any importance is Tezpur on the Brahmaputra, 21 miles away by earth road. The banks of the great river for 30 miles back are flat and covered with tea gardens and rice fields. It is less than 400ft. above sea-level here; the climate, except in the short winter season, is hot and steamy, and the rainfall about 100 in. Beyond the last tea garden to the north is the beginning of the dense forest running up into the hills. Presumably the forest at one time extended farther south until cleared to make room for tea gardens; for it is upon the 'red bank', which was old forest land, that most of the gardens are planted. Very few, and those inferior, are found on the grass land near the Brahmaputra where the soil is alluvial, light and sandy.

For the next two days we packed our stuff into suitable loads, bought rice and some oddments in Tezpur, and collected 600 silver rupees for paying the local porters. One evening we went down to the Bhareli river to fish. It was a magnificent stretch of water whose sources I hoped soon to see far to the north in the glaciers of Gori Chen. Across the river was the Forest Reserve, the home of elephant and rhinoceros. In the north lay the heavily forested foothills, the territory of the Miji Aka who, according to Lightfoot, had not yet entirely given up raiding the plains for slaves.

On the wireless came news of the Italian invasion of Albania and the mobilisation of the Italian fleet. I felt I ought to be going the other way, but I hardened my heart and arranged to leave on the 11th. Lightfoot promised to send a runner if war started.

Two bullock carts left early with our fifteen loads for the camping ground, known as Tiger Flat, at the edge of the plains and the beginning of the foothills, 25 miles away. There we were to pick up twenty-five men of Lightfoot's porter corps, Nepalese, whom he was good enough to lend. The extra ten were for carrying food for the others because the country over which we had to travel for the first five marches is uninhabited at this season. We left after lunch in a car which took us as far as the Belsiri river which was unbridged. Farewells were said, we took to our feet, and once more turned our backs on the civilised world.

At five o'clock we reached Tiger Flat, a clearing on the edge of the forest. Close by there was another European in camp, a Game Warden. The camp was evidently semi-permanent. Sweet peas were growing outside a grass hut, three elephants (tame ones) were tethered hard by, and the Game Warden himself was standing by the bank of a small river feeding the fish which were

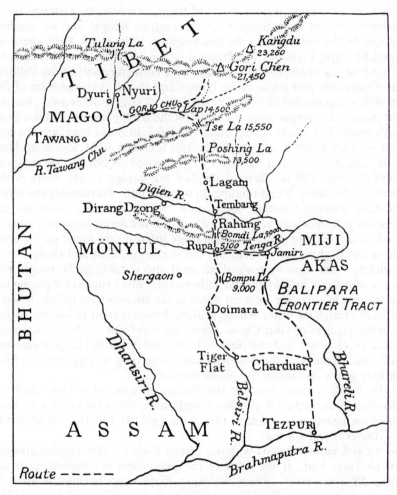

SKETCH MAP TO ILLUSTRATE ASSAM HIMALAYA

(not to scale)

apparently also tame. Over a drink the local picture was painted for me by my host who seemed as tough a denizen of the forest as the elephant and rhino, whose welfare was his care. From him I received a nicely balanced mixture of hope and fear. Mosquitoes were the first forest denizens about which I sought information. As soon as we had reached Charduar I had begun administering prophylactic doses of quinine to the three Sherpas and myself. Quinine, though a sovereign remedy, could not compare as a prophylactic with the modern drug mepacrine. We had only a bottle of 100 quinine tablets with us, as I assumed we should not be in malarious country for more than two nights; and since it was the tail end of an unusually dry season I imagined there would be few mosquitoes about. My fears were laughed at by my informant. Admittedly, there were a few mosquitoes, but they were a harmless variety, and he had forgotten how long it was since he had been troubled with malaria.

The talk then turned not unnaturally to elephants; for the whole foreground as we sat outside the tent was occupied by three vast backsides adorned with ridiculous little tails. One of them was a cow in season, and it seemed that the previous night a rogue elephant who haunted the vicinity had caused considerable panic by his efforts to make her closer acquaintance. Shots had been fired without effect. 'Elephants were more numerous than mosquitoes. Bhotia traders going north with caravans of grain and salt had been killed by elephants, greedy for a concentrated meal of grain seasoned with salt in place of their everyday unseasoned bark and branches. If I had any grain or salt with me it would be advisable to bury it deep or plant it high in a tree. Otherwise if they winded it we should be raided for a certainty. If I had an elephant rifle (I had a .22) I should sleep with it by my side with both barrels loaded.'

It was getting dark, so hastily drinking as much whisky as politeness allowed, I made my excuses and hastened back to camp, uneasy in mind, ears well cocked, seeing elephants behind every tree as I went. We had, of course, a number of loads of rice and atta, also some salt, but I did not fancy starting to bury it at that time of night with the help of four ice-axes, and most of the trees were of the straight-boled, high-branching variety. However I thoughtfully passed the news on to the Sherpas so that I should not be the only one to spend an anxious night, and after reconnoitring a route up the only likely-looking tree in the neighbourhood I turned in.

Sure enough it was a wretched night—due solely to mosquitoes. I comforted myself with the thought that as the country was not inhabited they were not likely to be infected with malaria, forgetting a standing camp which Lightfoot's porter corps had not far away, and the frequent passage of natives up and down the road. Rising early, after a night of heat and bites, I was surprised to find the Nepalese coolies had already gone leaving behind most of the loads. I was assured an elephant would come for these, and sure enough, like a rabbit out of a hat, a great mountain of wrinkled flesh presently walked into the clearing, dragging after it by its trunk a great length of chain stout enough for a ship's cable. A wizened little anatomy of a man climbed up its foreleg to make fast on its back a vast padded mat such as you see in gymnasiums, and then the loads were passed up and built into a neat pile.

Wangdi and I exchanged astonished glances as the twelfth 60 lb. load went up, followed by two more men and the 50-odd feet of mooring chain. Whereupon practically the whole of our outfit swayed off into the forest borne upon that one capable back. Here at last was the solution to all transport problems. Yaks, zos, goats, mules, ponies, donkeys, men might be all very well for picnics, but for serious business let us have elephants. It was with fresh respect for Hannibal that I followed admiringly in the wake of that ludicrous, swaying rump, stepping out at a good four miles an hour in the effort to keep pace.

Marching through forest, climbing hardly at all, we camped on a shelf above a wide stony river bed near a village of grass huts called Doimara. There was no sign of life, no pigs rooted, and no dogs barked. I thought at first that some frightful plague had wiped everyone out or that the Miji Akas had been doing business in a big way, but a Tibetan agent from the porter corps camp, who had come with us for the day, told me that Doimara was only occupied during the winter months. Everyone had retired to his mountain village before the onset of the rainy season. Achoong, the Tibetan, translated our 'purwana' (passport) into Sherchokpa for the benefit of the raja of Rupa three marches on. I bathed in a pool where I was astonished to see on the cliff 4 ft. above the deep water a well-carved Buddha. There were fewer mosquitoes here, though we were still less than a thousand feet up, but in the daytime there was a new amusement in the form of blister flies or 'dimdams'. Every bite resulted in a blood blister with which our hands were soon covered. The coolies used some kind of oil, citronella I think, with effect.

Beyond this we climbed steadily, another day's march sufficing to put us beyond the reach of the dimdams and mosquitoes. The porter corps marched well in a most military manner, signals for the regulation halts being given by whistle, a procedure which amused the Sherpas, who prefer to take their halts according to their inclination and the amenities of the place. On the fifth day we started early and began climbing in earnest. We soon left the maples, oaks and birch behind, and, nearing the top of the pass, the Bompu La (c. 9,000 ft.), entered rhododendrons and bamboo through which ran many old elephant trails. While waiting for the porters to come up I climbed trees in the hope of seeing the snows, but there was too much haze. On the north side pines and juniper appeared almost at once, but unlike the trees of the dense rain-forest of the south were neither festooned with moss nor half-buried in undergrowth. We descended a lovely valley through blue pines and grassy glades to camp on a flat, shaded, grassy spur—an ideal camp site—half a mile from the Sherchokpa village of Rupa. The country reminded me of Garhwal, but the houses were of wood like Swiss chalets: the heavy beams supporting the roof were morticed to the uprights, the projecting piece being heavily notched. The gable end was decorated with a black and white machicolated pattern, and from it hung something very like a carved phallus with hairs tied to it.

Rupa was a poor, ugly, dirty village, and the Sherchokpa inhabitants were fully in keeping with it. Who they are it is not easy to say. They speak a language of their own, but they are very similar to the Mönba of the rest of

Mönyul. Maize is the principal crop, but, as they do not irrigate, all crops seemed light. After I had waited in vain all afternoon for the so-called raja, Tsari Bhutia, to appear, Mahomet had to go to the mountain. I found him a shifty looking fellow who claimed not to understand Wangdi when he spoke Tibetan, but he promised to have porters by the following evening to take us to Rahung, two marches away, at 8 annas a day. The raja returned my visit in the evening bringing with him a chicken and six eggs, for which I gave him snuff and a tablet of quinine—the exchange rate seemed to be in our favour. Many of the natives were suffering from malaria which they presumably contract in villages like Doimara where they spend half the year.

The next day was a holiday. I was still very uneasy at having started at all, and half hoped that a runner from Lightfoot would catch us before we went on, bringing definite news of war or peace. I realised that I would be lucky to get any mail beyond this, for it would be passed from village to village. The Government porters were going back tomorrow (they were then busy devouring a goat I had bought them for 2½ rupees), so having written some letters I wandered down to the river, bathed, and watched some men fishing with long bamboo poles. They used a bait like a piece of carrot, and in place of a hook a running noose on the line just above the bait. I can commend this method to those who find fishing with a hook too easy; several big bronze-coloured fish had a go at the 'carrot' but all escaped. There was the usual cane bridge over the river with the less usual feature of a complete cane-ring support, which made the crossing much easier than did the rope bridges of Sikkim and Ladakh which have only a handrail. In the evening the raja took snuff with me again and warned us of the 'badmash' below the Himalaya, meaning presumably the Abors or possibly the abominable Snowmen.

We left on the 17th. Instead of our well-disciplined porter corps marching to the sound of the whistle, we were accompanied by eight men armed with bows and arrows, four women whose privilege it was to carry the heavier loads, and three small boys aged about eight, who nevertheless carried a full 60 lb. and smoked their bamboo pipes like the men. Passing through Rupa where Tibetan influence was evident from the number of mani walls and chortens, we followed a northern tributary of the Tenga river in whose valley Rupa lies. This lesser valley, the Dikong Ko, leads up to the Bomdi La (9,000 ft.) which we had to cross. After two hours' march the pines gave place to rain-forest, trees coated with moss, and everywhere ferns and flowering shrubs.

At our first halt before entering the rain-forest there were some cattle, and one strange-looking beast, marked black and white, like a Friesian, with a fine head. They called it 'guru' and I took it to be a domesticated wild ox allied to the gaur of India. We sat here for an hour while our troop of tatterdemalions drank beer which they make on the spot by pouring water into a bamboo jar of fermenting maize. They seemed to have little provision for the road but this handy article and a few maize cobs or puffed maize. Their clothes were no richer than their fare—a scant piece of cotton cloth was all they wore, except for one gentleman who sported a bit of what looked like a bear skin. Watching these scarecrows sucking away at their bamboo pot put me in mind of that sixteenth-century toper's lament, 'I cannot eat but little meat, My belly is not good', with its haunting refrain:

> Back and side go bare, go bare;
> Both foot and hand go cold
> But, belly, God send thee good ale enough,
> Whether it be new or old.

One of the women, 'a fair hot wench in flame-coloured taffeta', whose hair hung down to conceal a very attractive face, asked Wangdi in her uncouth tongue for a cigarette. Wangdi gave her one and in reply went through the motions of sleeping with her in eloquent sign language, which so shocked her that I fully expected Wangdi would receive a clout on the ear. These people pierce the lobes of their ears and then distend them with wooden rings like the Wa Lumbwa who used to work for me in Kenya. The songs they sang while marching, too, were in a rhythm reminiscent of Africa.

We camped high up, an hour below the Bomdi La. It was cold, but luckily fine; for our friends had no blankets and did not trouble to build any shelters. I was early on the pass only to be disappointed once more by a blanket of mist and smoke seen through a dense bamboo screen. Unlike the Bompu La both sides seemed wet; it was not until we were down to about 5,000 ft. that we came again upon grass and pines. We descended to the valley of the Digien river which, like the Tenga, runs from west to east to join the Bhareli. It is very steep-sided, more like a Sikkim valley; on some of the ridges were pine, on others deciduous trees, and forest fires were burning on all sides.

After we had paid off our mixed Rupa troop along came the raja of Rahung, a comic-looking youth who talked animatedly in a Hindustani that only Wangdi could understand. We at once started bargaining for porters for the short march to Tembang, which was the last village, or rather town, at which we could hire porters for the long stretch to our proposed base in the Gorjo Chu. Wangdi's opening gambit was to tell him that I was the Political Officer's younger brother—an inexactitude weighty enough to help us to come to terms at 9 annas; the raja insisting, meanwhile, that any attempt to bilk them would be reported at once to the aforesaid brother.

We left early with a rather larger proportion of children to carry the loads. A halt was called for food in Rahung, a village remarkable only for pigs, dirt, and goitres. It is smaller than Rupa, with the usual dilapidated chortens and mani walls. There is a direct route to Tembang, not shown on the ¼ in. O.S. map, which crosses the Digien by a cane bridge 500 ft. below the village. This, like the Rupa bridge, was built on the same three-strand principle as suspension bridges elsewhere in the Himalaya but with the local modification of a stout bamboo hoop every 3 or 4 ft. completely containing the three main cables. The women of the party had their loads carried across by the men—a courtesy which was not done for chivalrous motives, but because it is taboo for women to carry loads across bridges.

A steep climb of 2,000 ft. brought us by midday to Tembang where we camped by a spring under some trees just beyond the town.

CHAPTER THREE

Our Troubles Begin

TEMBANG is a biggish Mönba village built on a commanding spur with steep sides. Round it there is a wall approached by two flights of stone steps. In spite of its apparently strong position it is liable to be raided by the Miji Aka, its nearest neighbours to the east, to whom the people of Tembang pay tribute. From here two routes lead to Tibet. The most frequented goes via Dirang Dzong, the Se La, and Tawang. This last place is a very important monastery on the direct road to Tibet and, in particular, to Lhasa. Theoretically Tawang is in Assam, but it is controlled from Tsona Dzong in southern Tibet. In turn it controls Dirang Dzong and the whole of Mönyul. Mr Kingdon Ward, who has travelled extensively in Mönyul, in a paper read to the Royal Geographical Society described the position thus: 'The political status of Dirang Dzong is ambiguous. The surrounding country is ruled by two Tibetan dzongpens appointed from Tawang. They collect the taxes, listen to complaints, and maintain law and order without the help of a single soldier or policeman. The Mönbas, who seem never to have struck a blow for themselves, are almost servile. They have definitely thrown in their lot with Tibet, and where Tibet cannot help them—as for instance against the Akas to the east—they buy immunity. The Bhutanese ignore them; the Tibetans rule them; the Akas fleece them; and the British have, or had up to quite recently, forgotten them.'

The other route north, which is more to the east and skirts the country of the Abors, goes by the Poshing La, the Tse La, and the district called Mago. This was the route I wished to follow since it led direct to the Gorjo Chu, where we proposed making our base. I was told the Dzongpen of Dirang Dzong was in the village, so after disposing of a present of 'chang' (local beer brewed usually from barley but in this case from maize), which looked and tasted like sour pea soup, I went down to meet him. Dressed in the usual dirty maroon-coloured Tibetan 'chupa', embroidered felt boots, and cheap Homburg hat, from below which bespectacled eyes stared impassively, he looked like bureaucracy personified. Obstruction oozed from him. It was obviously no use telling him I was the Political Officer's brother or even the Emperor of China's son. However, over a flagon of arak we got down to business. A number of the village elders were present including the headman, or 'gambo'.

We exchanged snuff and arak amicably enough for several hours, but whenever the conversation was steered back to porters a deadlock was reached. They all insisted that it was far too early for the Poshing La, which was never open until June and which would be deep in snow. The dzongpen, who would not have to exert himself at all in the matter, kept harping on the other route via Dirang Dzong, which he hoped, I suppose, I should eventually have to follow, sprinkling a few rupees on the way. In fact, there was no sense in his suggestions, because if the Poshing La were closed so would be the passes on the western route. The upshot was that I persuaded the 'gambo' to give me a guide to the Poshing La next day to see if it were open or not. It was a two-day march there, but I hoped we might get there and back in three.

Next morning, the 30th, Nukku and I packed for three days and went up to the village where Wangdi had preceded us to find a victim for the sacrifice. Overnight the 'gambo' had repented and washed his hands of the whole affair—an inapt metaphor, for this was quite the filthiest village I had ever seen. While the discussion was proceeding in the narrow midden of a street, I looked up and saw far off, floating on a white bed of cloud, a still whiter snow peak. The natives called it Sherkhang Karbo; by its bearing I thought it might be Kangdu (23,260 ft.), east of Gori Chen. This encouraging glimpse of the snows was the first vouchsafed me.

After two hours' vehement eloquence from Wangdi, a man called Dorje consented to risk his life with us for a consideration. We got away by ten o'clock, and after five hours of up-and-down work reached Lagam (9,000 ft.), where we camped. Here there were a small wooden monastery, a yak or two, and some hens. The solitary lama who looked after the Gompa brought us wood and lugubriously volunteered some information about the Poshing La. From the map, which at this point becomes sketchy, it looked about 10 miles with a rise of 4,000 ft.

We hoped to make the double journey in one day. My diary calls this an exhausting and exasperating day. It might have gone much further than that without misrepresentation, and perhaps still kept within what Swinburne considered 'language of the strictest reserve' when he called Emerson a 'hoary-headed and toothless baboon'. We were off by half-past five carrying only lunch, a sweater, and a rope. A rope, if you please! which goes to show how successfully the Tembang men had wrought upon our imagination with their account of the Poshing La in April. In forty minutes we had gained the ridge 2,000 ft. above us, and then for seven and a half hours we followed an uneven, seesaw crest through silver fir, rhododendron, and thick writhing mist which allowed us tantalising glimpses of the valleys on either side. After two hours, going flat out, when we must have been well over 10,000 ft., we dumped the rope which was obviously going to be unnecessary: it seemed impossible there could be any snow pass within several days' march. Two hours later, still going fast, I asked Dorje how far it was to the pass and was told it was now just about as far as yesterday's march. I thought he was being purposely discouraging.

Having lost some height we again began to climb steadily. Our hopes rose with the ground, and presently we came upon a 'chorten' and some prayer flags, the usual signs of a pass. I asked Dorje confidently if we had arrived; he replied that we were nearly half-way. The track then descended to a pond in a grass glade, and a hut, beyond which we saw in the mist a grassy shoulder crowned by what looked like a cairn. This *must* be it, I thought—this wretched man Dorje does not want us to get to the pass. Dumping the rucksack containing our food, Nukku and I started for it with a rush, but Dorje, who then came up, advised us to moderate our ecstasies, for the pass was still as far distant as the spot at which we had dumped the rope. After that we toiled on sullenly. I was rapidly acquiring a headache due to the height and the exertions of our unrelenting progress. It was now midday; halts and inquiries became more frequent—sure signs of distress; moreover, if we were to get back to Lagam before dark it was time to think of turning. At length we came upon the first snow in the form of deep drifts, whereupon Dorje eagerly assured us that if there was snow here it must be lying feet deep on the pass. He said the fact was inescapable; everyone knew that snow here indicated much more snow there. I felt sure he quoted himself some hoary rhyming couplet to this effect: 'If at this point snow you find, Put the Poshing La out of mind.' This riled me, because if we failed to set foot on the pass itself Dorje would infallibly paint a gloomy picture on our return to Tembang and our exertions would have been all in vain. I determined to get there if it took all day. If need be we would sleep at the pond which seemed to be the only water on the ridge. Dorje himself had a headache by now—a piece of intelligence which I found not displeasing, reflecting that we had not come so far and so fast altogether in vain. Nukku seemed as fresh as ever.

At long last we came to a really steep rocky rise up which we scrambled, hardly daring to hope this was the pass. There was no doubt about it this time. You could feel the unmistakable free air of a pass beginning to stir. At half-past one we stood on the Poshing La (*c.* 13,000 ft.), and even Dorje had to admit that there was no snow worth talking about. Having come to a clear understanding with him on that all-important point, Nukku casually remarked that we would now return to Lagam. 'Sez you', said I, but this choice piece of sarcasm fell upon deaf ears, for the Sherpas have not had our advantages of a good modern education. A cold, clammy mist enveloped us, and there was nothing to keep us, so down we went back to the pond for food and rest. At three o'clock we set off for Lagam. As is often the way on a descent there was a great deal of climbing: at least it seemed so to me, for the gentlest rise reduced my pace to a feeble crawl, and very soon I felt sick and 'sold out', as the New Zealander likes to express it. Darkness overtook us as we began the 2,000 ft. drop to Lagam. We had taken only six hours coming home, 13½ for the double journey.

By half-past ten next morning we were back to Tembang, and that afternoon, which was fine and hot, we reopened negotiations for porters with the headman. He began by politely hinting that the Tibetan translation of our Government permit, which invoked the help of all whom it might concern in the matter of food and transport, was not the same as the original copy with its official stamp. However, after 'great argument about it and about', Wangdi brought things to a satisfactory conclusion, the bargain being for twenty-two men to carry our things and their food to Mago in five days for 4 rupees each. At this point I retired to my sleeping bag feeling very queer. As we had been sitting in the hot sun drinking the arak which inevitably accompanies these dickerings, I blamed this indiscretion for my sickness. Nukku had gone to lie down as soon as we got in, but I thought that was only due to fatigue. This was the 22nd, ten days after our camp at Tiger Flat, just about the last day that we might expect malaria to develop.

We had arranged to start on the 24th, but this was now impossible. On the 25th I was better but weak, but both Nukku and Thundu were suffering from unmistakable malaria. I had feared this from the first. I doled out quinine, of which we still had a fair supply, but the Sherpas put more faith in a great jorum of 'chang' which they had sent them daily. The headman now seemed anxious to be rid of us. He talked of his having to go to Dirang Dzong and pressed me to name a day for our start. This was not possible, for Nukku was worse and I was no better. However, on the 28th, after a night of sweating, I felt well for the first time for a week, and as Nukku, too, was on the mend, I ordered the porters for the 30th. Thundu even in full health was not exactly a ball of fire; now he did nothing whatever and I thanked God for Wangdi, who did all the camp work as well as fighting our wordy battles with the headman.

On the last day of April we pushed the two cripples off early, carrying nothing but their own kit, which I had already gone through like a destroying angel purging away the dross. I also jettisoned some of my own, in my zeal overlooking the fact that amongst the jetsam was our bottle of quinine with still some thirty tablets. Then Wangdi and I sat expectantly amongst the loads for an hour and a half, by which time the 'gambo' arrived with a few men and the tidings that no more were to be had. I had expected something like that would happen and I blamed myself for not having asked for twice as many men as we really wanted. Putting a smiling face on it we accompanied the headman through the noisome streets of the village, feeling about as charitably inclined as an old-time Liverpool crimp with a commission to complete the crew of a notoriously ill-found ship. It would have been unwise to have offered more pay, and difficult for us, who had not been there, to paint in glowing colours the delights of the Gorjo Chu to men who had.

At half-past ten we were obliged to start with sixteen greatly overloaded men instead of the twenty-two we needed. They were carrying 60 lb. of our stuff and 25–30 lb. of food for themselves. Luckily it was only 8 miles to Lagam. For my part when on trek I am not averse to starting slowly and easing up as I go on, and we surely did that on this occasion. The short climb of 2,000 ft. up to Lagam monastery took us three hours, the last man getting in at half-past seven.

This was the last inhabited place on our route until we reached our destination. We had been told we might possibly get an extra porter or so here, but there was still only the old Lama, who was polite but quite firm in his refusal to join us. To pass the time while Wangdi was talking to him I made an inventory of the interior of the Gompa. This is what I then wrote: 'A carved and painted beam divides the altar from the rest. In the left-hand corner housed in a crudely wooden box is a prayer wheel 4 ft. diameter, turned by hand. A bell rings at each revolution. The altar consists of two stone ledges running right across. On the lower, eighteen brass bowls of water, two trumpets, and an earthenware Tibetan teapot. On the extreme right an empty Castrol tin, a beer tin (Barclays), a varnish tin, and four beer bottles (empty). On the upper shelf eighteen more brass bowls, several brass vases, a china bowl, a brass Tibetan teapot, and in the centre a white cloth-covered box carrying three small brass Buddhas and a brass stupa. In the carved and painted wall behind the altar are niches holding painted clay images. Tucked away out of sight behind the prayer wheel a big wooden Buddha. In front a piece of black stone (meteorite?), weight about 20 lb., shaped like a blunted rhino horn stood on end. On a wooden bench to the right a "dorje" or "thunderbolt", a bell, prayer book, cymbals, two trumpets, and a large flat drum like a tambourine supported by a cord to the ceiling like a punch-bag. Both side walls frescoed but spoilt by age. Hung on a line in front of altar are coloured paper, coarsely woven ceremonial scarves, and several mealie cobs.'

Although we were to camp short of the Poshing La I rather feared the next day's march—a short march which you know is more tiresome than a long one you don't know. The porters had gone all right yesterday but would they go to-day? We were so near Tembang that desertion would be simple. All such fears proved groundless. The men were cheerful, marched well if slowly, and, apart from showing some inclination to halt for the night at the first 'chorten', made no bones about reaching the pond and hut, short of the pass, in 10½ hours. Moreover, the sun shone. Strolling along the ridge through the vivid scarlet, cream, and orange rhododendrons we enjoyed some pleasing glimpses of the not very distant hill clearings made by the Miji Akas, and through the trees to our left ridge after ridge of blue hills stretching to the distant Bhutan frontier.

That night just after turning in there was a very violent storm of thunder, wind and rain, in which Wangdi heroically went out to secure the ground sheet over our heads. This seemed to be the signal for a break in the weather, which steadily deteriorated as we approached the mountains.

Starting before seven next morning, in the hope of getting a view from the pass, I reached the summit in two hours, but was easily beaten by the mist. The descent on the north side was easy, the men were going well, and at midday we all halted for a meal of maize 'satu', which is roasted flour and can be made from barley, wheat or maize; in Tibet barley is the most generally used, as it is the only cereal which will ripen at such heights. Here it was generally maize.

At this halt Wangdi succumbed to a sudden attack of fever. He then seemed to recover and rushed on ahead by himself to the bottom of the hill where presently I found him lying. Fortunately, the camping place of Samjung was only half a mile away, so I relieved him of his load and we went on together, arriving just in time to avoid the evening storm. With Wangdi out, Thundu doing nothing, and Nukku little more, the outlook was bleak.

The camp at Samjung was by a pleasant stream, the Sangti Chu, which comes down from the Tse La. This was the 15,500 ft. pass between us and the Gorjo Chu which we had to cross next day. Samjung is just under 13,000 ft.; it was appreciably colder than the Poshing La camp: no rhododendrons were in flower and there were no Alpines to be seen.

The night was wet, and in the morning (3 May) we were shocked to find there had been a heavy fall of snow. It could not have come at a more inconvenient time, but for me the shock was mitigated by finding that Wangdi had recovered overnight. Fortunate it was for us during the evil days ahead that Wangdi's malaria was of a different type to ours. Almost every other day about noon, as regularly as a clock, he would come to me, shivering violently, to tell me, apologetically, that he was going to bed, and an hour or two later he would be up and about apparently none the worse. I am not expert in these matters, but I believe his was a benign tertiary form while ours was malignant.

His recovery was happily timed, for that morning all his forceful personality was needed to persuade the Mönba men to move. They were as reluctant to start as we were to wait, but in the end Wangdi prevailed. We still had with us our friend Dorje, of Poshing La fame, with his valuable but sometimes irritating habit of looking facts in the face, but we could have dispensed with him that morning because, besides telling us precisely how far it was to the pass, he went beyond his office to prophesy, Cassandra-like, more snow. How I hated the man—as the great Lord Halifax remarked, 'Nothing hath an uglier look than reason when it is not of our side.'

The Mönba men had Tibetan felt boots but no snow glasses, so that, within reason, snow would be more tolerable than bright sun. In the end we had both; for during the long seven-hour trudge to the pass the sun shone dazzlingly, and on top we encountered a mild blizzard. The forest ceases south of the Sangti Chu, and we followed the hidden track through stunted birch and juniper, which, at a touch, discharged on our heads the contents of their snow-laden branches. Soon we were clear of this, marching on a bare, gently sloping field of snow whose skyline ridge was always just in front of us, ever receding as we advanced.

Seven hours of dogged plodding brought us to the top at three o'clock. With hardly a pause, for it was now snowing hard, we pushed on down easy slopes into the wide, bare valley of the Gorjo Chu. The stream, which was small, was crossed by a plank, and in half an hour we reached the sheep fold called Lap (c. 14,500 ft.) consisting of some stone huts, one of which had a weathertight roof. It had been a trying march for all. The Mönbas had the loads, and we our fevers; Thundu lagged far behind, Nukku seemed listless, and my stomach celebrated our arrival by again 'selling out'. By the evening all but four of the Mönbas were suffering from snow-blindness which I treated with a mixture of castor oil and cocaine. It was not as efficacious as I had hoped, but next morning although most of them were semi-blind, the pain had been reduced to more bearable limits.

I now had to decide what to do. Lap was at the very useful height of 14,500 ft.; there was shelter here; the Gorjo Chu valley led north-east in the direction of Gori Chen. These facts seemed to mark it out for our base. From it we could push a dump of food to the head of the valley from where we should be in a position to explore the Gori Chen group, and then having learnt more about the lie of the land we could carry out journeys to the higher mountains to the north-east. All this, of course, depended on how soon, if at all, we could get rid of our fever. Thundu was certainly getting worse, Nukku seemed fit but lethargic, Wangdi was all right except for his occasional midday bout, while I myself fondly imagined I had already recovered. We had no drugs for treatment, but as there was no chance of reinfection I hoped the fever would run its course and finish. Meantime I paid off the Mönbas, who announced their intention of going on next day to the twin villages of Nyuri and Dyuri known collectively as Mago. The Tembang people seemed to have close connections with Mago, which lies on the road to Tibet. I decided that it might be useful to make contact with our nearest neighbours and to go along with them, taking Wangdi but leaving the others to recuperate.

CHAPTER FOUR

Base Camp and Fever

SNOW was falling when we left at 8 a.m. on 4 May. A little had fallen the day before in the Gorjo Chu and that did not look as if it would lie long, but now all was white and I was sorry for the snow-blind Mönba men, some of whom had to be led by the hand on this march. The track followed the north side of the river until, after about four hours, it plunged steeply into thick forest and began climbing to the Chera La. It was snowing heavily when we crossed the pass at one o'clock. We dropped steeply, first through rhododendron and then into magnificent pine forest to the gorge of the Dungma Chu. We crossed this by a bridge and at three o'clock reached Dyuri, a little 'drokpa', or herd village, consisting of about nine wooden huts in a sea of mud. On the other bank of the Dungma Chu is another small village, Nyuri; these two together are usually known as Mago. The Dungma Chu is joined here by the Goshu Chu which comes down from the Tulung La (the main pass into Tibet), and about a mile below the combined streams enter a deep granite gorge which is impassable. There is no cultivation and the people live on the produce of their yaks and sheep eked out by a little 'satu' which they import in exchange for butter and wool. They wear skins and garments of rough wool and hair—hairiness in fact was their chief characteristic; the men were hairy in themselves, and they wore hairy caps with little tails hanging down all round. We put up in a room festooned with pieces of drying yak meat. Bits of yak hung everywhere, we ate yak butter, drank yak milk, slept on yak skins, and were duly rewarded with a bountiful crop of yak fleas. The herdman, a veritable Esau, visited us. He promised us 40 lb. of satu and the help of two men to move our stuff from Lap farther up the Gorjo Chu. He confessed complete ignorance of the valley above Lap. Devoting the next day to seeing the local sights, we walked up the Goshu Chu to a bridge where there was a water prayer wheel, a mill, and some hot springs, with pleasantly warm but rather slimy water. We returned through Nyuri to our Chamber of Horrors, which on closer inspection proved to be worse than I had thought—fleas visibly hopped about, fat white maggots crawled out of the floor, and a deaf mute mowed and gibbered at us from the corner.

When we came to pay for our board and the 40 lb. of satu some confusion arose over annas and tankas. The latter is a Tibetan coin whose value was finally assessed by some hairy professor of economics at 2 annas. Having thus settled our obligations we set off, recrossing the Chera La. Much snow had fallen, was falling, and continued to fall all day. It was a bad march. Wangdi went well but blew like a grampus the whole way; I could not make out whether he was ill or not. I finally decided that he had Cheynes Stokes breathing while on the march—a diagnosis which did nothing to help my problem. Tea in a hut revived us to some extent and we went on to Lap without stopping. There was less snow up here at 14,500 ft. than there was down at Mago, but apart from this our homecoming was cheerless enough. Thundu seemed worse and was in bed, Nukku was ill but moving about; the one groaning and spitting, the other groaning and vomiting. What was to be done? It is easy to be wise now. Obviously what I should have done was to have taken advantage of the presence of the Tembang men at Mago and go down, although it meant giving up all our plans. On the other hand, if we hung on there was a good chance of the fever abating, and if the worst came to the worst we could probably get help from Mago. Hitherto my experience of malaria in Kenya and elsewhere had led me to believe that people seldom died of it, but I had yet to learn of the deadly 'terai' malaria of Assam.

On the 7th I went for a solitary walk up the Gorjo Chu to see what sort of a place we had come to. The weather was behaving abominably; after an hour or two of early morning sunshine the usual snow drizzle set in and continued all day. Two miles above Lap an old moraine spanned the valley except where the river came through. A mile and a half above this the valley bent sharply towards the north, and at the corner was an excellent camp site—a grassy 'maidan', big boulders for shelter, and juniper wood and yak dung for fuel. Round the corner the valley divided, and dimly through the drizzle I could see that the eastern arm held a snow-covered glacier. Coming back along the hillside I saw two herds of 'bharal' and blew some feathers out of a snow pigeon at a range of ten yards.

The following day, the 8th, we started work. Wangdi and the two men who had come over from Mago carried some loads to the proposed Corner Camp site which I had already visited, while I sweated up a hill north of our camp with the plane table to get a 'fix'. A thousand feet higher there was a cairn, evidently built by local shepherds, at which I set up shop and took sights to Gori Chen and two unidentified snow peaks. These were too close together to give good results, and I realised I should have to move to the east to bring myself broadside on to the main range. At half-past eight it was still clear. I pushed on quickly up the ridge hoping to get another 'fix'; but at nine o'clock the wisps of floating vapour coalesced with extraordinary rapidity and in a few minutes everything was hidden.

Though the mountaineer, and much more the surveyor, may revile mist and cloud, how greatly mountains gain by their effects! How their mystery and magnetism is enhanced! In mist the lowest and homeliest hill becomes a scene of adventure. Hillocks appear unexpectedly in the guise of high peaks, and nearby boulders become grim towers looming distantly through cloud. The clouds that are the almost inseparable companions of mountains lend even the best known the mysterious power of attraction of the unknown. Even when we are aware of what lies beyond the veil, the lifting of it never fails to thrill, like the raising of the curtain on the first act of a play which we have longed to see. How much greater then is the thrill when the veil of mist conceals the unknown, the unseen.

Think for a moment of Stanley in the Congo, who for weeks gazed longingly at the solid bank of cloud enveloping the Mountains of the Moon (for he must have suspected what lay behind) until one day: 'I saw a peculiar-shaped cloud of a most beautiful silver colour which assumed the proportions and appearance of a great mountain covered with snow . . . I became for the first time conscious that what I gazed upon was not the image or semblance of a vast mountain, but the solid substance of a real one, its summit covered with snow', or of Lord Dufferin beating up for Jan Mayen island in thick weather, and seeing suddenly, in a rift in the driving scud, between the masts of the ship, the lofty summit of Beerenberg, appearing almost to overhang; or of an experience of our own on those same Mountains of the Moon, when we sat on what we hoped was the summit of Margherita in a sea of fog, which boiled up from some seemingly inexhaustible source, waiting patiently for a glimpse of the neighbouring peak of Alexandra in order to verify our position; and of innumberable dramatic revelations in the Himalaya all producing, according to our hopes, pleasure, dismay, astonishment, fright, but always exhilaration.

The tantalising visions of Gori Chen, the glacier, the more distant peaks, had filled me with impatience and made me fret at the physical weakness which prevented our coming to grips with the problems they would present. Our next day's work was a repetition of the first except that we started earlier and that Nukku turned out to carry the gear for me. This was the first work he had done and was a hopeful sign, but Thundu was the same, moaning, groaning, and eating nothing. We got to 16,000 ft., took some sights on the same peaks, and were then driven down by the mist at half-past nine. I went to bed feeling very cheap, leaving Wangdi and the Mago men to carry more loads to Corner Camp.

I meant to lie at earth next day, but it was such a wonderfully fine morning that I went to a point across the river to do another 'fix'. This was a liberty which the malaria parasites in my blood seemed to resent, and for the next seven days, when fever and headache allowed, I had leisure to reflect on the absence of our quinine and the fearful virulence of the Assam breed of malaria. It is of no interest to read of the symptoms and sufferings of others, so I pass over a grim week and come to the day when the fever departed and I was able to get up, make bread, potter about the camp, and take stock of our position. The two Mago men had gone back, having finished the job of making a food dump at Corner Camp. A herd of yaks had come up and were now grazing in the Gorjo Chu, from which all snow had now gone. Thundu seemed better, but much thinner, while Nukku's condition was puzzling. He would not go to bed, but just sat about not interested in anything, complaining only of pains in the shoulders. Wangdi was as brisk as ever though still on occasions having his midday bout of fever. He was by now getting annoyed with the helplessness of the other two, railing at them frequently, especially at the poor unfortunate Thundu for making such appalling noises and even for allowing his long hair to hang over his face.

Lying alone in my tent racked with fever I had not unnaturally thought of giving up the struggle and of sending to Mago for help, but now that I was up I thought differently—'. . . when the devil was well, devil a monk was he'. It was too early in the game to throw in our hands. If the fever had finally left me, as seemed possible, so it would the others. We had done nothing, and much remained to be done. So I speciously reasoned, or shut my eyes to facts, according to the point of view.

On 18 May, Wangdi and I walked up the dry nallah which entered the main valley from the north. About 3 miles up it came to an end under what I called the Black Cliffs, which we were not strong enough to climb. As we crossed a low col into the next nallah to the east, the mist came down and we returned to camp without having seen anything. During lunch I was amused to observe Wangdi's method of treating his ration of half a mug of pea soup. He took six large chillies, a dozen cloves of garlic, an ounce of salt, and ground them together on a stone to form a paste. This was scraped off into not more than a quarter cupful of water. *Half* the soup was added and then, with an occasional shake of the head and a blink of the eyes, the only indications that he was taking a powerful blister and not bread and milk, this fragrant mess was quickly dealt with. The Sherpas like their sauce piquant.

With steam rising gently from him as a result of this volcanic meal, Wangdi and I discussed plans. Nukku said he was fit enough to carry, so we decided that two of us should go to Corner Camp to explore the head of the Gorjo Chu, leaving Nukku and Thundu to follow in three days' time provided they felt strong enough. Accordingly, the next day, we moved up. We took all morning to get there and I began to realise just how weak we were. Nukku came in an hour behind and my load of 35 lb. felt like 80 lb. There were a lot of yaks about, but seemingly no one in charge of them. We rigged up a tarpaulin in the lee of a boulder for a kitchen, collected yak dung and juniper, and produced a prodigious amount of smoke but little heat. The usual drizzle fell all afternoon.

We made a courageously early start next morning for a station on the south side of the river. I say courageous because a really thick mist hid everything, and we had no good grounds for thinking it would lift. Presently it began to snow. We plodded on to the top of the ridge out of mere cussedness, sat there for some time, and then returned to camp. This fall of snow continued all the next day, but it was so light, and the weather so warm, that it had no effect at all on the appearance of the Gorjo Chu valley, which presented the same bare, brown, rather desolate appearance. Presumably the weather we were experiencing was the effect of the monsoon which, here, at the extemity of its long range, was weak and ineffective.

On the third day the dawn was murky, but the snow had stopped. We went up to the same place and managed to do a rapid 'fix' before the mist overtook us. From all these various stations Gori Chen and several 19,000 and 20,000 ft. peaks were visible; of Kangdu and its satellites to the east there was no sign. We had a fleeting glimpse of the head of the Gorjo Chu, which apparently ended in a snow ridge well to the south of Gori Chen. From this ridge we might be able to look down into the basin at the foot of the mountain, but whether I would be strong enough to get there was becoming doubtful. On the following day, one of our few fine days, I was not well enough to move, but on the day after that, after a poor night, we made a bid for it.

Had the gods been looking down that morning upon good men struggling with adversity they would have been moved either to pity or to laughter. Wangdi was going all right, but I found I was quite unable to get past a boulder (and there were a great many boulders) without sitting on it. Whatever the criteria employed to judge my rate of progression—snails, tortoises, slow-moving glaciers, or the mills of God—it was obvious I was below standard. After an hour of it, finding my pulse rate was over a hundred, we returned to camp and I to bed.

As it was only eight o'clock I sent Wangdi down to Lap, for it was five days since we had left and nothing had been heard of Nukku or Thundu. In the early afternoon he returned in the rain with bad news. Thundu was no better and Nukku, who had helped to carry our loads up, was in a very queer state. According to Wangdi he had failed to recognise him. This was decisive. I had an acute fit of ague when Wangdi returned and was shivering too hard to talk properly, but as soon as this had subsided I gave orders to Wangdi to go down again to arrange for three yaks to come up next day to take our gear from Corner Camp to Lap, and to make inquiries for a yak or yaks to take Nukku and Thundu down. He had reported that there were now two yak-herds living at Lap.

I had been living on hopes and false expectations too long and now had to acknowledge defeat. Whether we should escape even some of the consequences remained to be seen.

CHAPTER FIVE

Retreat

WANGDI returned early next morning alone except for three yaks which he had managed to collect. It was ten o'clock before we started, because owing to the yak's dislike of being handled by Europeans he had to do the loading single-handed. This discriminating beast is handsome, and I can think of no animal which serves its fortunate owner so well in return for so little. Milk and butter, hair from which clothing, rope, or even boots, can be made, and transport, are some of the by-products of this admirable ox, all at a negligible charge for maintenance. From the point of view of economy of upkeep the camel and reindeer vie with the yak. The last seems to exist on grass-flavoured gravel, the other two on thorns and moss respectively; but if one considers both his noble mien and the wide range of real necessities he provides, the supremacy of the yak is undeniable.

I crawled down to Lap in the wake of the yaks. Inside the stone hut Thundu lay in his sleeping bag from which he had apparently not stirred for some days. Wangdi at once removed him bodily to a nearby hut. Nukku lay fully dressed on the floor with his boots in the ashes of an extinct fire. He was unconscious and breathing stertorously. Thundu said he had been like that for the last twenty-four hours. We called in the two yak-herds, an old man and a lad, but for no consideration on earth could we induce the old man to let us have two yaks for the sick men: his reasons were vague but his intentions clear-cut. He went on to tell us that there were neither men nor ponies at Mago. For the time being we seemed to have reached a deadlock. In the afternoon we tackled him again and told him he must send the lad tomorrow to Mago to return with six men, and poles for rigging up litters. To clinch the thing we sent the .22 rifle as a gift for the headman. If this stratagem worked, as we hoped it would, we might expect help in two days' time; if it failed then the outlook was black indeed. I had no great hopes of saving Nukku, Thundu was too weak to stand, and in a few days I should be the same.

Next day the invaluable Wangdi went to Corner Camp to bring down some more food for the expected porters. He returned in the afternoon to find me in the throes of another fit of ague with Nukku dead. This news, though expected, was a shock; the burning question now was whether we should get Thundu down safely.

In the morning, 27 May, we buried Nukku among some large boulders where we built a cairn of stones. The old man was away with his yaks, and since I was so weak we had a struggle to carry him to the place we had chosen. In 1936 on Nanda Devi we had lost a Sherpa who had died at the base camp of some disease, the seeds of which he had had on him before we started and against which we were powerless. As he had never left the base I did not see him, but here the circumstances were different. Nukku had been our intimate companion for nearly two months. Moreover, I knew him well from 1937, when he had shared our life and done our work for several months. Now the responsibility for his death lay heavy upon me.

Malaria is depressing at the best of times, but my dejection that evening was extreme until, very late, the boy returned from Mago with word that some men would come next day. This was one of my bad days when a fresh symptom made its appearance—a feeling of imminent suffocation lasting for an hour or more. My relief when six men and four zos arrived in the evening was great. I had hardly dared to expect so prompt a response, and I felt that the rifle had at last justified its presence. The headman seemed pleased beyond words, and next morning, lying in my sleeping bag at the door of the tent, with shaking hands and throbbing eyes, I had to fire a demonstration shot.

Instead of making a stretcher for Thundu the six men decided to carry him single-handed by turn. They rigged up an Everest carrying frame with a sort of stirrup for his feet, on which he sat, facing forward, with his arms round his bearer's neck. In this way they carried him for long stretches at a time with seemingly little effort. Admittedly he was by now a mere skeleton of a man, but even so it was no mean feat, for he cannot have weighed less than 90 or 100 lb. As I could now only walk downhill, the headman mounted me on a zo which he led himself. The zo, which is a cross between a cow and a yak, is a milder animal in its behaviour towards Europeans. We had a very convincing demonstration of this on the second day's march when the headman tried to mount me on a yellow yak.

The snow on the Tse La had disappeared. The carriers made light of their human load, the zos stepped out, and the only halts we called were for the sake of Thundu, who was so weak that the mere effort of sitting on the carrying frame became exhausting. From the top of the pass I looked back at the stone huts of Lap, now deserted; at the place where we had buried Nukku; at the green grass and black boulders of Corner Camp. Cloud covered the snow ridge which we had failed to reach, and beyond, the dim, ghostly outline of Gori Chen showed through the drifting mists. The summit alone shone clearly, but between us there passed no nod of recognition or farewell. The bond between men and mountain who have met and measured themselves together had not been tied. We had neither trod its glaciers, nor slept on its slopes; its ridges, faces, gullies, meant nothing to us for we had never grappled. After six weeks of futile endeavour Gori Chen remained a mere peak of the Assam Himalaya, a name on the map. I turned and went down the other side.

From Samjung we crossed the Poshing La and once more camped at the hut by the pond. Everything was the same, the mist on top and the thunderstorm which struck us in the evening. Thundu seemed to be standing his journey well, and my cold fits were now merely part of the day's routine. We reached Lagam on the last day of May, our loads and sleeping bags soaked by a heavy storm, and men and animals badly bitten by leeches—another 'trifling sum of misery now added to the foot of our account'. The lush grass surrounding the monastery was so infested with these pests that the animals had to be kept away from it. We gave them a load of maize as compensation. Our old friend the Lama had now an assistant, a sort of female acolyte, who came in the evening to attend to the lamps and to empty the thirty-six little brass bowls of water into two bamboo jars. While this was going on my food was brought to me where I lay in the corner, but before I could begin to eat the woman had begun to pray and I felt constrained to lie still, ignoring the savoury smell of lentil soup and pemmican, until she had done.

The headman of Mago now left us suddenly without a word, taking with him a man and one of the zos. It was of no consequence, however, for our loads were lighter now, and the priestess stepped manfully into the breach.

Tembang seemed to be empty—like London in August, no one of consequence was in Town. We camped behind the 'gompa' and immediately sent for the kit we had left behind. It was brought to us intact. Thundu and I took four tablets each from the forgotten bottle of quinine which had the immediate effect of nipping in the bud my attack of shivers. We paid off the Mago men and their zos, and in their place hired eight porters as no animal transport was available. It was, however, only a short march to Rahung, most of it downhill.

The Digien river was now in flood, flowing full and brown, and we clung thankfully to the cane hoops of the bridge as it swayed above the swirling water. The talkative little headman made us welcome, brought firewood with his own hands, and promised ten porters and a pony for the morrow. I had all the loads ready by 6 a.m. as I hoped to cross the Bomdi La, but it was not to be. The promises made in the evening, prompted by hospitality and arak, were forgotten in the cold light of morning. Eventually the party of six men, three girls, and a pony, straggled off three hours behind schedule. We made heavy weather of it with Thundu, but the track was devilish and consistently steep. I was impatient to get on, and, riding uphill on a pony, more or less at ease, I was tempted to underrate the exertions of those on foot. I always think it must have been either uncommon hardihood, or a sublime sense of their own importance and disregard for anyone else, which allowed the old traders and travellers in tropical Africa to do their 'marching' in litters borne by four or more sweating negroes—possibly many of them had the excuse that they were suffering from malaria.

There was never a chance of getting over the pass. There was no Wangdi to encourage and browbeat with his raucous gibes and threats. That admirable man, who had the makings of a dissipated but dynamic drill sergeant, had fallen out with another of this two-hour fever bouts. The Sherpas can grow little or no face hair, but had Wangdi been able to sport long waxed moustachios he would have closely resembled a sergeant-major I had—a man in whose presence the Battery Commander (myself) became uneasy, subalterns frankly nervous, and other ranks slightly unhinged.

We reached Rupa on 4 June. There was a big 'tamasha' in progress and the headman was ill with fever. We learnt that the road leading over the Bompu La through Doimara over which we had originally travelled was now flooded and consequently we should have to use a roundabout road to the east touching the Miji Aka country. A deputy headman, remarkable for his gross, copper-coloured face, engaged to find porters and two ponies to take us to the first 'tame' Miji Aka village of Jamiri two marches away. With this business, as I hoped, satisfactorily settled we were invited to cast care aside and join the revels. It would be an exaggeration to say that everybody except ourselves was drunk, but the crowd was in that uncritical frame of mind customary in the early stages of drunkenness, and therefore very easily amused. The entertainment provided, if it could be called entertainment, made this outlook quite essential for enjoyment. The high light was a dancing yak act performed by two men; the one in front carrying a yak's head was connected by a pole draped with cloth to his partner, to whom was attached a yak's tail.

In the ring with them, as a sort of sparring partner or clown, was a man wearing a grotesque Tibetan mask. It was his part to do a few steps of Tibetan-style dancing—arms outstretched, slow turn on one foot, hop, and turn again—a manœuvre designed to bring him very frequently into collision with that ignoble caricature of a yak which would then proceed to kick him violently. The patience of actors and audience seemed inexhaustible, ours was insufficiently elastic.

Next morning when we greeted the 'Copper Portent' with whom we had arranged the details of our departure he seemed quite taken aback, as though his suspicions of the presence of strangers in Rupa were suddenly confirmed. Wangdi and I immediately sat down on the steps of his house, like a couple of bailiff's men, until we saw him saddle one pony, order another, and tell off six reluctant porters. We then went back to camp, packed up, and got under way. Thundu was now riding a pony, not because he was any stronger but because of the difficulty of finding sufficient relays of men to carry him. Keeping to the north bank we followed the Tenga river which flowed down an open arid valley of pines and oaks, apparently uninhabited. Our destination was Dahung, where the 'Copper Portent' had assured us we should find good stabling for man and beast, and possibly eggs and maize beer. At about four o'clock our porters, who were showing signs of having had enough, indicated that we had arrived. True there were trees and water, the main ingredients of a camp, but nothing else, and I realised that 'Dahung' was just a joke bought by the unsuspecting stranger. Any place at which the porters chose to stop was apparently 'Dahung', just as wherever the Macgregor sat was the head of the table.

I was not particularly happy about this forced deviation from our old route. I knew very little about the Miji Aka and nothing at all to their advantage, neither did I know how much significance to attach to the prefix 'tame' when applied to those whom we hoped to see on the morrow. I was not anticipating losing my head, for if the Mönba men could trust them so could we, but I feared they might not be quite so ready as the Mönba to provide porters, and now that we were once more in malarial country any delay was dangerous for us.

Next day, 6 June, brought us, particularly myself, many ups and downs. As we left the river to climb up to Jamiri my pony, who had just crossed a side stream, jibbed at a steep bit and stepped over the 'khud'. I rolled off quickly but one foot caught in the stirrup, and the frightened beast, recovering its footing, darted off at speed down the trail we had just climbed dragging me with it. This is a situation in which, so far as I know, there is nothing the 'dragee' can do until someone or something stops the animal. From a dragging parachute one can release oneself by a smart blow on the harness fastening, and the normal stirrup leather detaches itself from the saddle automatically; but native stirrup leathers are not so obliging, although, of course, most of them can be relied upon to break. This one did not. As we sped down the track towards the stream I realised that I should certainly get a ducking and possibly a cracked skull. By now one of the men was pursuing the pony with wild cries down the track with the sole effect of making it go faster.

We took the water with a rush, missed all the worst boulders, and breasted (man and beast) the opposite bank. Luckily this was extremely steep, the pony faltered, and the Mönba caught it. Even before I was released I had determined on walking to Jamiri no matter how weak I might be, so I was unlucky to find when I stood up that the only injury sustained was a bruised thigh.

We came to the Aka village of Jamiri at three o'clock after a long uphill slog. There was no striking difference between these 'tame' Akas and the men I had with me except their very independent attitude. They appeared to live in communal huts of which there were three, each 150–200 ft. long, rectangular, with a grass roof. The men carried a sword like a Burmese dah, and bows and arrows. The last are said to be baited with aconite. In the first years of the British occupation of Assam these Akas were very troublesome, and in 1883 they broke out again. A small expedition under a General Sale Hill was successful in quieting them; since then there has been no serious trouble. According to the Assam *Census Report* they are divided into two clans bearing the very suggestive names of Hazari-Khoas or 'eaters of a thousand hearths', and the Kapah-chors or 'thieves that lurk in the cotton fields'.

Our reception was of the coolest. 'There was no camp site near the village, and we had better go back to the main river from which we had just come, where we should find water and wood. There was none for us here. Moreover, they had no porters or ponies to hire out even if the road to Charduar was passable, which it was not. And, finally it was no use my flourishing the Government "purwana", which asked all whom it might concern to help us with food and transport, because this particular village did not recognise any Government.' The headman who delivered this declaration of independence was a prim, severe little man in a smart Tibetan coatee of yellow silk. Of course, taken as a whole, our party was not calculated to impress. The Mönbas could be written off as potential slaves. Thundu looked like a wasted effigy of Death on the Pale Horse, Wangdi a disreputable Nepali (which in fact he was), and myself one of the poorer 'poor whites'. But when our gorgeous friend tried to put us in our proper place he over-reached himself in asserting in such a very offhand way that he had no truck with any Government. As we found later, he was lying about his status because he was one of the 'tame' Aka chiefs who received a small subsidy from Government. He visited Charduar shortly afterwards and, having the bad luck to find me still there, received a 'rocket' from the Political Officer for his ill manners.

To camp on the site indicated for us, some three miles from the village, was obviously equivalent to putting ourselves in Coventry, so we camped as close to the village as due regard for our health allowed in order to give our nuisance value full play. When we had thus settled in on his doorstep, so to speak, the headman came off his high horse and sent word that we should write in English what we wanted and he would have it sent to Sadeyo, a rajah of a neighbouring village. In the evening this prim little man paid us a swift visit in person to tell us that six porters would be here next day and that he himself might supply the other six at the rate of 6 rupees to Charduar, cash strictly in advance.

Jamiri was most unsavoury, flies abounding. Our policy of letting our nuisance value have full play acted also in reverse like Lend-Lease. By midday the prim rajah and I were paying each other social calls, and having exchanged presents—eggs, a chicken, and a load of wood on his part, and some sugar and a Balaclava helmet on mine—we began pouring libations. Although he had thus mellowed towards us the rajah was careful to point out, as he refilled my bamboo mug, that this condescension was only due to a personal regard for me and the weak condition of our party, and that Sadeyo rajah, who was a creature of the Government and heavily subsidised for it, was the man to whom I should have gone for help in the first place. At this moment a small, stout, but majestic figure appeared in the doorway. What with the dim light of the hut and the maize beer I was not seeing too well and at first thought it to be a reincarnation of Napoleon dressed as a Ghurka officer, but it proved to be Sadeyo himself fully accoutred with hat, revolver, belt, shorts, boots, and puttees. He was voluble but efficient, having brought the porters along with him; and, having cadged a water-bottle which he had seen in my camp, he departed as suddenly as he had come, wisely declining to join in a party which obviously had had a long start. From this I managed to extricate myself before nightfall, taking with me as a parting gift a bushel or so of bamboo shoots.

For one reason or another that was a bad night. Outside the tent there seemed to be more midges in the air than oxygen, and shutting the tent merely meant including the midges and excluding the air; from the men's hut came the most maddening, prolonged singing, which at times reached such a pitch of frenzy that I almost thought the prim little man was inciting his warriors to assert their independence by massacring us on the spot. Malaria and maize beer have a lowering effect on one's morale.

However, dawn came at last, as dawns do, and we got under way by seven o'clock with ten porters, men and girls, six of whom had to carry Thundu. Between Jamiri and the Bhareli river there was a 6,000 ft. pass to cross, and having climbed over that we camped by a side stream short of the Bhareli. The going was bad—a succession of steep, thickly forested valleys. Lush, damp, sunless jungle, with its smell of decaying vegetation, depresses me. A botanist or naturalist might find such a march enthralling, but, for one who is neither, it is just a matter of one damned thing after another—stinging nettles, thorns, beans which produce a painful rash, tree ticks which bite venomously and worst of all leeches. The foliage overhanging the paths, and the paths themselves, are the springboards from which they leap on to the passing traveller; and seeing them weave their little bodies hungrily in mid-air as they scent their prey (if scent is the means by which they work) arouses in me almost as much horror as does a snake—possibly more, because a snake can at least be struck down with a stick or kicked.

The next day's march brought us to the junction of the Bhareli and Sessa rivers, the latter being crossed by a bamboo bridge. Ever since leaving Jamiri there had been much talk of an unfordable, unbridged river, and on the third march we met six rivers in succession. Every time we approached one of these I expected to be held up, but one by one, by bridge or ford, the difficulty was surmounted until I began to think the local men were mistaken. However, as we approached the seventh there was a decidedly menacing murmur of fast-moving water. There was no sign of a bridge, and the experts pronounced it unfordable. I made one or two tentative attempts which soon satisfied me that for once the experts were right. We moved upstream a few hundred yards to where just round the first bend two single strands of cane, one directly above the other about 3 ft. apart, spanned the river. Three of the men forthwith crossed at the double like so many monkeys, hardly troubling to use their hands. It looked so easy that I thought I would try, but there was so much play in the ropes, which were too close together for my comfort, and so much nervous strain, that I barely got over.

It was obviously impossible to take loads across, particularly loads like Thundu, whom it would have been a pity to have lost after having carried him so far. I wondered how the Akas would manage, but they proved fully equal to the occasion. Quickly selecting a tree near the bank, they skilfully felled it, so that it spanned the water. It was rather too high on one side, so they fixed stakes on each end of the tree and ran a handrail of cane across. In a short time the whole party was over. An hour later the last river was behind us, and we camped that night in some grass bandas on a flat above the Bhareli—a favoured picnic place called Balipung, only 20 miles from Charduar.

Capt. Lightfoot had heard of our coming and met us half-way with a car. This was not the least of his kindnesses. Thundu was packed off to hospital where he was found to be suffering from kala-azar, or black fever, as well as malaria, from both of which he made a good recovery. Wangdi and I were taken to the Political Officer's bungalow where we received every kindness and were soon restored to normal by good food and quinine.

So ended my 1939 journeying, and a more unqualified failure has seldom been recorded. Sometimes we climb the wrong mountain, cross the wrong pass, or find ourselves in the wrong valley, but that can be laughed off provided we get somewhere or do something. Here we got nowhere except to a starting point and achieved nothing but a sense of endurance.

It will be seen that the Assam Himalaya are not easy to reach, but neither were Christian's Delectable Mountains, nor is any place that is worth reaching. By this I mean country which is more or less unknown, sparsely or not at all inhabited, inhospitable, difficult to move in, and, of course, mountainous. I admit there are many parts of the Himalaya which do not fulfil all these exacting conditions, but there the magnificence of the mountains covers any deficiencies and still leaves a credit balance.

The malaria difficulty could, I think, be overcome if strict precautions were taken for the first week's marching—that is, everyone under a net before sundown, long trousers instead of shorts, and mepacrine. It would be at least as difficult to supervise Sherpas as British soldiers to ensure that these precautions were carried out, but if they were, parties would be able to reach the mountains unhampered by sickness. Porters will always be difficult to obtain owing to the few villages and the small number of inhabitants. Small parties will therefore be, more than ever, essential. In this group of Himalaya there are nearly twenty peaks over 20,000 ft., none of which has been looked

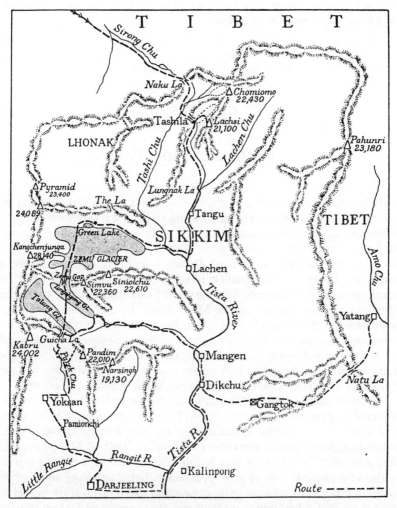

SKETCH MAP OF SIKKIM TO ILLUSTRATE ZEMU GAP
AND LACHSI JOURNEYS

(not to scale)

at closely, much less climbed, and only four of which bear names. To those
who understand, this will perhaps be some measure of our disappointment
and of our eagerness to try again.

CHAPTER SIX

The Zemu Gap—Failure

IF, slightly to amend a remark of Chateaubriand, the mistakes of our nearest
and dearest are not altogether displeasing to us, then, *a fortiori*, the mistakes
of those we do not know must be highly gratifying. Nothing can be more bitter
than the controversies of divines and explorers, and the rivalries of
mountaineers. Of the quarrels of divines I shall say nothing—there are so
many—but I recall the bitterness evoked by the explorers Speke, Burton, and
Grant, over the Nile sources; by Peary and Cook over the North Pole; and by
Whymper and the Italians on the Matterhorn. In the writings of these men,
particularly in the Journals devoted to their exploits, there is often found a
regrettable harshness as they refute or demolish the theories or claims of their
rivals. In the following chapter there is no theology, the exploration and
mountaineering are pitched in a minor key, but the illustration will serve to
explain, if not excuse, an occasional gibe at the mistakes of others.

The small native State of Sikkim in north-east India, bounded on the west
by Nepal and on the north and east by Tibet, has been open to explorers and
mountaineers for nearly a hundred years. Sir Joseph Hooker, the great
botanist-explorer, was at work there in the years 1848–9. Many have followed
him, and after the 1914–18 war hardly a year passed without several small
parties and possibly one large expedition either attempting some of the few
unclimbed peaks or traversing its passes and glaciers. In spite of this activity
there were still a few minor inaccuracies on the map of Sikkim, particularly
with regard to the less frequented glaciers. It is probable that these have now
been corrected, for in 1938 and 1939 the Survey of India was engaged on a
new map of Sikkim. This chapter tells how one or two of these inaccuracies
were detected.

The mountainous part of Sikkim, that is, the regions of snow and ice, is
confined to the eastern and northern borders and the north-west corner. The
giant Kangchenjunga (28,146 ft.) on the Nepal border, with its 12-mile-long
Zemu glacier, is the main attraction. A complete map of the Zemu glacier had
been made by a German party in 1931, but there remained one pass,
supposed to have been crossed but once, whose south side was little known.
This was the Zemu Gap (19,276 ft.), a deep notch on the ridge between Simvu
(22,360 ft.) and the most eastern satellite peak (25,526 ft.) of Kangchenjunga.

The two great advantages of climbing in Sikkim are the accessibility of the mountains and the ready supply of Sherpa porters in Darjeeling. If those in the first flight are engaged, as they usually are, then there are others who are glad enough to earn a few rupees in a less degrading way than by pulling the rickshaws of people too idle to walk. The gambling and drinking habits of the Sherpas provide an ever-present stimulus to work. This may offend the moralist but it helps anyone in search of porters. It is therefore easy to make a short impromptu trip. So in April 1936, having some unexpected time on my hands and wishing to try out some porters for the Nanda Devi expedition, I thought I would cross the Zemu Gap. According to an article in an old number of the *Geographical Journal* which I found by chance in that hospitable place, The Planters' Club, there seemed little to prevent it.

In May 1926 the author of this article had crossed the Guicha La, gone down the Talung and up the Tongshyong glaciers, and had then crossed the Gap to the Zemu glacier and back again—the latter part before breakfast. The main difficulties were encountered on the two glaciers which, owing to stone and ice bombardments, resembled a road near the front line on one of the more unquiet days on the Western Front. Only two other parties had interested themselves in the Zemu Gap. One in 1920 had visited the Talung glacier but had decided against going on by reason of the unpleasantness already referred to; the other in 1925 with Mr N. A. Tombazi, who claimed to have ascended to the Zemu Gap from the south. He had not crossed it.

A photograph taken from the Guicha La suggested that the ridge separating the two dangerous glaciers could be crossed in a direct line between the Guicha La and the Zemu Gap. If this were so there would be no necessity to remain for long under the barrage of stones and ice which apparently played constantly on any party foolish enough to traverse these glaciers. There seemed to be no insuperable difficulties in crossing the Gap itself, so I was tempted to give orders for my mail to be forwarded to Lachen, the village by which I expected to return after a triumphant crossing of the pass. Fortunately, being naturally pessimistic, I gave no such hostage to fortune.

The party, consisting of four Sherpas, two ponies, and myself, left Darjeeling on 1 May bound for a place called Chakung. This plan necessitated a double march, as we wished to avoid sleeping in the hot, malarial valley between. One of the Sherpas, Pasang Kikuli, deserves special mention on account of his magnificent record. Born in 1911 in Sola Khombu in north-west Nepal, the home of most Sherpas, he carried on the three Kangchenjunga expeditions in 1929, 1930 and 1931. In 1933 he reached Camp V on Mount Everest, and was one of the survivors of the terrible Camp 8 on Nanga Parbat in 1934. He stayed with his sahib, Uli Wieland, until the latter's death at Camp 7, and then with three other Sherpas eventually got down badly frost-bitten. In 1936 he was with us on Nanda Devi, where snow-blindness prevented his going high, and he was the only porter to accompany Houston and myself on the crossing of 'Longstaff's Col' on the way back. In 1938 he accompanied Houston and the Americans on the highly successful reconnaissance of K2. A year later, on the same mountain, he and two other

Sherpas perished in a gallant attempt to bring down an American, Dudley Wolfe, marooned at 24,700 ft. He was a great-hearted mountaineer if ever there was one.

From Chakung the ponies returned, leaving us and a local man to shoulder the loads for the next 13-mile stage. Travelling on the beaten track in Sikkim is delightful. The sight of heavily forested valleys contrasting with the green and brown patches of cultivated fields, the well-spaced stages, the comfortable rest-houses, make a pleasing introduction to the sterner work ahead. Most important of all is the fresh food such as hens, milk, butter and eggs which can often be obtained. I like eggs, and on this hilly 13-mile stage had acquired a dozen which I intended eating as soon as we camped. Like Jane Austen's Mr Woodhouse I am of the opinion that 'an egg boiled very soft is not unwholesome', but on this occasion Pasang blotted his copy-book by hard-boiling the lot.

From the Pemayangtse bungalow, reached by doing 5 miles down and then 5 miles up, Yoksam, the last village on our route on the other side of the Rangit valley, seemed to be within shouting distance, but such is the valley-seamed nature of the country that it takes two days' marching to reach it. The last stage to Yoksam is a short one, so short that we arrived at eleven o'clock in the morning. I had hoped to camp beyond it, for camping for the day at that hour of the morning seemed to me to be almost as abandoned as to go to bed in the afternoon, but the Sherpas would not suffer themselves to be torn so rudely and so unnecessarily from their last hold on civilisation and the good things which it meant. At Yoksam the former Lama of the now defunct monastery proved to be one of the most obliging men we had met with in Sikkim. He produced an overpowering brew of 'chang' and a chair, and undertook to find a couple of men to help us with our loads as far as the Parek Chu, the valley below the Guicha La. It can be taken, I think, as a general rule that the nearer they live to mountains the better the men; which may be one of the reasons why in so many mythologies mountains are the home of the gods.

Rising at five next morning I was staggered to find our two local recruits, provided by the ex-Lama, waiting to start. This keenness was no flash in the pan. They proved to be an admirable couple, indifferent to rain and not averse to snow. It rained all day, but low down the Parek Chu we found a 'lean-to' built against an overhanging rock. We were soon drying ourselves in the comfort of a fire. Having had previous experience of Sikkim weather I had brought with me an umbrella from the Darjeeling bazaar. I found it extremely useful, as it kept both rucksack and shoulders dry. Under its shelter and clad only in shirt, shorts, socks and gym shoes, I found that rain, provided it was not cold, became a matter of indifference to me. I found too, odd enough though it may seem, that bare legs and shoes are no bad anti-leech measure. The leeches attach themselves, of course, but they are easily removed long before they have time to settle down to serious drinking. On the other hand, if boots and puttees are worn they are not discovered until the end of the day by which time the blood has almost to be wrung from one's socks.

Next day we reached the grazing alp of Dzongri (13,000 ft.) on a plateau above the Parek Chu valley out of which we had been forced to climb. Scorning the warmth and shelter of the yak-herd's hut, and in spite of a cheerfully persistent drizzle, I obstinately put our camp a quarter-mile beyond it in order to get a view of Pandim (22,010 ft.), a peak just south of the Guicha La which had an added interest in that as yet no one had attempted to climb it. My obstinacy was rewarded when, towards sunset, the mountain drew back its cloud curtain, and revealed first the south ridge with its forbidding defences, then the summit, and finally a section of the long north ridge under which we should have to pass next day. The light was poor, but it was good enough to show why Pandim's summit had enjoyed such a long period of seclusion.

Some 4 in. of snow fell during the night, but the two local men turned up barefoot but smiling for their last march. We dropped down again through rhododendron forest, now a blaze of colour, to the Parek Chu and followed its left bank. Through the lowering clouds bits of the north ridge of Pandim furtively disclosed themselves, as if aware of our intentions. We camped under a rock below the ascent to the Guiocha La, within reach of the last of the juniper bushes.

In the evening we had a clear view of the north ridge of Pandim. The lower end, near the Guicha La, was decorated with formidable gendarmes, but I observed that these could be out-flanked by means of a snow gully, which led to a deep cleft in the ridge above them. This was undeniably long, and even if it were reached at this point I was by no means certain that the remaining two-thirds of the ridge could be climbed. However, the invitation of this conveniently placed gully, just above our camp, though it might be declined could not be ignored. I wrestled with temptation for most of the night and finally gave in. The Zemu Gap could wait for a day. Even if we got no farther, it would be good to get on to the ridge and see what the difficulties were.

I felt as if I were Jorrocks stealing out for a surreptitious by-day in Pinch-me-near-Forest. Nevertheless, we took most of our loads. It would be foolish to reach the ridge, find the going good, and then be unable to camp there in readiness for exploiting success the following day. Kikuli and I could sleep there and the other two could go down. We got off early, I still clutching the umbrella with one hand and an ice-axe with the other. There was a long grind up scree to about 16,500 ft., where the gully narrowed and snow appeared. By keeping well to the side we were able to avoid the snow for another 500 ft., until at length the snow impinged against the steep rock wall and we were driven on to it. The notch must have been still about 500 ft. above us, but through the mist we could make out to the right of it a high gendarme, and to the left a crazy-looking pinnacle which seemed as unstable as a house of cards or a 'serac' on a hot day. The snow in the middle of the gully appeared likely to provide better going, but between us and it was a water-worn runnel of ice, 3 or 4 ft. wide, across which I had to cut steps. The time had come to discard the umbrella, which I forthwith stuck in the snow by the runnel to fall to work cutting steps. Three of the Sherpas were still below, well into the side of the gully, when Pasang and I stepped across the runnel. There was no warning sound, but some instinct made me look up, and there, coming straight for us out of the mist, were half a dozen large boulders. They hit the snow above with a thud and then took the line of the runnel in a series of menacing bounds, some in the runnel itself, some outside. There was nothing to be done, and in a flash the crisis was over. The umbrella disintegrated as a rock hit it, and Kikuli and I remained staring stupidly at one another, rather white about the gills. There was no need for debate; the decision was immediate, silent, unanimous. We recrossed the runnel, cast a thoughtful glance at the place where the unbrella had stood, and went down the gully.

That afternoon I climbed to the Guicha La, whence I saw the Zemu Gap and the intermediate snow saddle between the Talung and Tongshyong glaciers. Even at that distance the steep ice-fall leading up to the Gap and a rock wall crowning it roused misgivings.

Once more we found that time spent in reconnoitring is seldom wasted. When we crossed the Guicha La next morning snow was falling so thickly that we had to steer by a compass bearing I had had the sense to take. There was a fairly steep snow slope down the north side where three of the Sherpas showed themselves to be novices by a good deal of unsteadiness, one of them even parting company with his load. By the time we had reached a grassy shelf a few hundred feet above the Talung glacier the snow had stopped. We spent an hour in crossing to the moraine on the other side, where we found more grass, a little juniper, a herd of bharal, and, most fortunate of all, a pool of water.

The daily fall of snow was becoming a nuisance. Snow fell continuously that night, but the morning broke fine and clear. Weather in the Himalaya that spring was worse than usual. The Mount Everest party led by Mr Hugh Ruttledge had found the upper rocks white with snow on 30 April, and, although the arrival of the monsoon in southern India was not officially reported until 19 May, the weather throughout the month was mild with occasional heavy falls of snow. It was very similar in fact to what we were experiencing, except that in Sikkim snow fell nearly every day.

A weary trudge through deep powder snow brought us to the saddle on the ridge whence a gently sloping field of névé led down to the Tongshyong glacier which we quickly crossed. It is here about half a mile wide. As we steered for the foot of the ice-fall of the small tributary glacier which descends from the Zemu Gap, snow began falling heavily again. The map showed the Zemu Gap as lying at the head of the Tongshyong, but it is in fact half a mile short of the head and has a small glacier of its own at right angles to the main one. There were two ice-falls on this subsidiary glacier. The first was so steep and intricate that we were forced to traverse off to the left and take to the rocks. We camped at about 18,000 ft., nearly level with the top of the ice-fall, taking a lot of time and trouble to find accommodation on a little patch of rock still clear of snow—trouble that was largely wasted because snow fell throughout the night. The Sherpas are masters of the art of digging out or building up rock platforms for tent sites. They turn themselves into human bull-dozers, lying down with their backs against a rock for purchase and their feet firmly wedged against the half-ton rock they mean to shift. A series of back-cracking heaves then does the trick.

We could now take stock of our position. The two stone-throwing glacier-valleys had been crossed without trouble—not so much as a pebble had fallen. Indeed, they were wide and open enough for us to avoid anything but an avalanche on the Kangchenjunga scale. Actually there were no slopes to give birth to such except at the head of the Talung. A thousand feet above us was the Gap, guarded first by the even steeper and more intricate ice-fall, and finally by 100 ft. of ice-wall.

The snow froze on the tents in the night, so next morning, since packing these would be troublesome, I left the men to follow later and pushed on alone to reconnoitre. The snow terrace between the lower and upper ice-falls was so badly crevassed that I was forced to wait on the lip of the first big one until the porters arrived. We roped up and crossed, camping a little higher right at the foot of the upper ice-fall. Shut in as we were between two high rock walls we found the heat and glare so overpowering that it was essential for us to get some food and drink before having a look at this formidable affair. Owing to the nature of the ground and the crevasses there was hardly room even for our two small tents, and we were too nearly under the Simvu slope for comfort. Small trickles of snow, incipient avalanches, kept hissing down, but all came to a respectful halt about 10 yards from the tents. At an occasional louder roar the Sherpas would rush panic-stricken from their tent, so frightening me that I did the same. The Sherpas bore me no ill-will for the Pandim gully incident, but this was trying them too highly. It was obviously no place for a prolonged sojourn.

These alarms ceased about three o'clock, when, feeling stronger, I kicked and cut steps up the ice-fall for about 100 ft. Here a doubtfully flimsy bridge over a large crevasse led to a steep wall of ice which would certainly take a long time to climb, so after casting about vainly for an alternative, I left it for the next day. Although we were loath to give in, defeat seemed imminent, for beyond these obstacles lay the final ice-wall which from below appeared impregnable.

Pasang Kikuli joined in the assault next morning, and together we hacked a big staircase up the 30 ft. of steep ice, a job which took two hours. Above that we were able to kick steps, but there were only a few inches of snow overlying the ice, and we realised that when the sun had done its work the snow covering would not hold. A little higher we came to a horribly frail bridge over a deep crevasse. Moving gently with the utmost circumspection we crossed in safety by crawling. Whether or no this bridge would hold the weight of a man with a load was a nice point which I had already half decided ought not to be settled by experiment. A short snow slope led to yet another bridged crevasse from where we had a good view of the final wall two or three hundred yards away up a gentle snow rise. It was fully as high as we had feared, all iced, and appeared to overhang in places. An icy gully on the Simvu side might have been forced from a camp on the plateau, but it was beyond the strength of our weak party even had we come safely over the two dangerous crevasses.

If the Sherpas had any regrets at leaving the Zemu Gap uncrossed they managed to conceal them. Not a moment was lost in packing up and standing away from the threatening slope of Simvu. We took to the rocks on the north

side of the ice-fall. We had funked this route on the way up—justifiably, too,
as it happened, because in order to get from the rocks to the glacier we had to
'rope down'; that is, to suspend the doubled rope over a convenient rock and
slide down it, hoping that the rope will *not* slip off, and then hoping nearly as
much that when everyone is down, the rope *will* slip off and *not* jam.

The weather thickened as we camped early in the middle of the glacier, for
I wanted to examine the head of the Tongshyong. The Zemu Gap of our
experience differed so widely from the one about which I had read that I was
inclined to believe that a mistake had been made and that the genuine Gap lay
concealed behind some corner near the head of the glacier. But, as I found
that evening, there was no other break in the mighty east-south-east ridge of
Kangchenjunga, and the easy, low col at the head of the Tongshyong
obviously led into the wide bay at the head of the Talung. It occurred to me
that in the thick weather which prevailed when the first alleged crossing had
been made, this, and not the Zemu Gap, was the place which had been
crossed.

There is something eminently satisfactory about a circular tour. It rounds
off the journey and is as satisfying in its way as the complete traverse of a
mountain. We therefore decided to go back down the Talung Chu, a river
valley which joins the main Tista valley route at Mangen. The only Europeans
who had followed it down were Messrs Raeburn and Tobin in 1920. From the
map it seemed about three days' journey—it had taken them eight, but of that
I was not aware or I might have forgone the satisfaction of a circular tour.

It was a glorious morning on the 14th when we walked down the
Tongshyong. The rough surface of the glacier was now covered by a smooth
carpet of frozen snow along which we strolled, enjoying the easiest glacier
walk I have ever had. The Tongshyong was narrower than the Talung and
perhaps stones did fall from its steep containing walls (though we neither saw
nor heard any), but a party that steered a reasonably central course could not
possibly be hit. We had some bother getting down the steep, high, terminal
moraine to the river. I slid—intentionally I think—and the porters roped
down. Having with some trouble crossed to the right bank of the swiftly
flowing Talung Chu we plunged at once into a tangle of dense rhododendron,
where we had a gruelling time. There was no vestige of path but there were
signs that native hunters, probably Lepchas, came here occasionally; we
found a dead buck in a recently set snare and a single log bridge spanning the
river.

A fine night, which we spent round a gigantic fire, was followed by another
glorious morning. By midday, after three hours of heavy going, we were
driven down to the river, which was crossed by a snow bridge. Shortly after
we had to go back, this time by a natural rock bridge. This place was a most
astonishing cleft, barely 3 ft. wide, with the river boiling through the gorge
100 ft. below. A difference of 10 ft. between the take-off and landing sides
made it a fearsome jump.

The third day gave us a ten-hour bush-crawl along the right bank, with
midges, tree ticks, and leeches doing their best to enliven the proceedings.
The tree ticks were in the minority but by far the most troublesome. They

were strategists. When they dropped on one, instead of attaching themselves at once to the first handy bit of skin, they invariably sought out the soft under-belly before burying their heads deep in the flesh.

On the 17th, although we had found a track of sorts, we had another bad day. An hour was spent in roping the loads over a rickety three-span bridge, then the track petered out and the going became atrocious, until at last we spotted another bridge. We crossed this and camped. We had only covered a mile in nine hours.

Next morning we found that by crossing this bridge we had made a false move. The track disappeared and no progress was possible, so we crossed back and picked up a good path which at long length brought us to a new field of maize surrounded by dense forest. There was no one there, but a mile or so farther on we came to a small village where there were a few women. We got nothing out of them, not even curiosity, which was surprising, not to say disappointing; for I had begun to feel that this Talung Chu journey of ours was fast becoming epic. It is mortifying to appear, apparently from nowhere, feeling that you have done something remarkable, to find that the first person you meet, and that a woman, ignores you completely.

The path we now followed had evidently been constructed empirically. It went up and down with the most damnable reiteration and frequently scaled steep rock 'pitches' which were cunningly roped and laddered like a popular Dolomite climb. One particularly fierce place was a bamboo suspension bridge over a 100 ft. drop—'for those free from dizziness only', as Baedeker puts it. Presently we met a man but he, like the women, was dumb and spake not. It would have been interesting to know more precisely where we were, for our dead reckoning must have been wide of the mark. After twisting about high above the valley in a hesitating manner the track suddenly made up its mind and without more ado dived straight down to the river, 2,000 ft. below. Somewhat dazed, we camped there in a field of cardamoms. We were now down to about 4,000 ft., but here there seemed to be fewer pests than in the forest higher up.

If we were anywhere near where we thought, we might expect to emerge at the end of the Talung Chu on the 19th. The track maintained its vagaries and even introduced us to a new method of surmounting steep rock 'pitches' by a single slippery bamboo on a slanting traverse. At the next houses we reached the only woman in residence ran away, but a man stood his ground and even told us where we were. The rest was plain sailing, except for a memorable thousand-foot slog up to Mangen, a small town on the Tista valley route.

On the way back to Darjeeling we called at the Residency, Gangtok. Dressed as I was in torn shirt and shorts, with bare legs and a beard not yet strong enough to conceal the dirt beneath—in short, travel-stained—I was rather surprised that I got past the servants at the door, resplendent in their scarlet and gold livery. And it was unfortunate that there should be a dinner party that night, where, with the Resident's spare trousers hitched up to my armpits (he was a very big man) and his coat sleeves turned up several times, it was difficult to feel really at ease. Contrast, no doubt, is the relish of life. Comfort is only valued after hardship, luxury after squalor, riches after poverty. If experienced in the reverse order the appreciation is, perhaps, less keen; and, I reflected that evening, the transition should not be too violent.

CHAPTER SEVEN

The Zemu Gap—Success

THE earlier interest in the Zemu Gap was provoked by the thought that it might provide a more direct route to Kangchenjunga than did the Tista valley–Zemu glacier route, but, once the south side of the Gap had been seen, this possibility could be ruled out. Any further interest that I took in it was therefore academic, the unprofitable solution of a problem in mountain travel and a desire to tidy up the map. I now doubted very much whether the Gap had ever been crossed and it was therefore more necessary for me to try. From what I had seen, the crossing from the south was not to be undertaken single-handed, but from the north side it might be easier. It might be possible to rope down the ice-wall or one of the flanking rock walls, and there would be no need to run the risk of avalanches by camping on that narrow overhung glacier below the menacing slopes of Simvu.

Accordingly, on the way back from Mount Everest in the summer of 1938, I resolved to devote a fortnight or so to a journey in Sikkim, including if possible a return home by the Zemu Gap and the Guicha La. The monsoon would be in full blast, but in Sikkim there appears to be no pre-eminently 'best' season for mountaineering. Climbs have been undertaken before, during and after the monsoon, even as late as November, and the weather has been uniformly poor.

As is usual with a party returning from Mount Everest, we soon began to break up, like rats leaving the sinking ship. We had seen quite enough of each other for a time, and delays in getting transport were trying the patience of all. The crowning blow fell at Tingkye Dzong, where a box belonging to the eminent mountaineer and geologist, N. E. Odell, was stolen. The box contained valuable geological specimens, and the surprise and chagrin of the thief must have almost equalled the fury of Odell. It was a serious matter from every point of view. The results of several months' work had gone, and, if the thief talked, the Tibetans would learn that we had been collecting stones against their express wishes. They quite rightly object to people going about knocking their rocks to pieces with a small hammer, thus releasing any spirits which may happen to be in them. Of course, the thief would probably be feeling too much of a fool to advertise the fact that he had risked his life, or at any rate the skin on his back, for a box full of stones.

Shipton had already left to do some survey work in the Nyonno Ri, happily brandishing a theodolite instead of an ice-axe; Smythe, sniffing the fleshpots from afar, disappeared over the plain, leaving behind a cloud of dust and small stones; Odell and Lloyd intended returning by a pass called the Choten Nyima La: I was bound for another, the Naku La. Dr Warren alone stuck to the ship, having to look after a porter who had been struck with paralysis while on the mountain.

My relief will therefore be understood when, on the last day of June, leaving Karma Paul, the Tibetan interpreter, to wrestle with transport problems, I escaped with two Sherpas, rejoicing in the knowledge that our progress would depend on our own exertions and not on the whim of a Tibetan official.

In Tibet one marches at will over a seemingly endless expanse of bare, brown, gently undulating plain, steering as often as not by some distant landmark, under a pale blue lucent sky, perhaps lightly flecked with cloud. These conditions contrast strongly with those in Sikkim. There, under a leaden canopy of heavily charged rain clouds, men and beasts follow a roughly paved mule track winding through deep-cut valleys whose high, steep, densely forested sides shut out all but the highest peaks.

The two Sherpas I took with me were Renzing, wild and unruly, but a first-class man and an Everest 'Tiger'; and Lhakpa Tenzing, quieter and with less fire in his belly, but also a 'Tiger'. We succeeded in hiring a pony to carry our extra food, and set out for the Naku La, an 18,000 ft. pass on the main Himalayan range between Tibet and Sikkim. The pass is used by Tibetans who graze their sheep in the Chaka Chu valley on the Sikkim side. The map of the Tibet-Sikkim Himalaya is pleasingly sketchy hereabouts, and it was impossible to identify the group of villages at which we halted for the first night. We were told that from here the pass could be crossed by a long day's march, so we started early, travelling over gravel and sparse grass up the flat Sirong Chu valley. There is a beautiful lake half a mile long and a quarter wide on the Tibetan side, and a smaller one on the Sikkim side. Before one reaches the lake a curious thing is seen. Spanning the valley floor from hill-side to hill-side, a distance of about three-quarters of a mile, is a roughly built, dry stone wall about 4 ft. high and 6 ft. thick at the base. Doubtless it is of Tibetan construction, but when and why it was built I have no notion.

The rise to the pass is so gradual that it is almost imperceptible. A fierce wind blew, and when we reached the grass-covered summit we ran immediately into rain, mist and cloud, which were to be our constant companions throughout the trip. I particularly wanted a view from the top because I had designs on Lachsi, a 21,100 ft. peak lying west of Chomiomo (22,430 ft.). We were completely ignorant of the mountain and its approaches, and I did not know until later that an ascent had been attempted in 1936. According to the map, the valley into which we were looking was bounded by Lachsi on the east, but although the clouds were thick, I could see enough to convince me that no high mountain bounded the valley on that side, but only a low rock ridge.

The descent was as gradual as the climb. After passing a glacier flowing down on our left from Chomiomo we camped with some Tibetan shepherds at a place called Naku, about 4 miles from the top of the pass. To the north-east

a depression on the ridge bounding the valley invited me to cross into the next
nallah, which, I argued, must lie immediately below Lachsi. We crossed this
the next day. A Tibetan volunteered to help us with our loads, which were
still very heavy, since we were carrying a fortnight's food. Going up to the col
we found cairns and learnt that it was known as the Tashi La and was used by
the Sikkimese with their yaks. It leads into the Tashi Chu nallah by a descent
which is exceedingly steep, even for yaks.

Here we had one great stroke of luck. It was the usual cloudy, drizzling day,
but, just as I reached the col, a rift in the clouds disclosed for a bare minute,
immediately opposite across the valley, a peak which I took to be Lachsi. It
appeared very similar to the mountain which we had noticed some months
before on the way into Tibet—a long snow ridge, almost a plateau, crowned
by an unmistakable snow pimple. This momentary glimpse had also revealed
a possible route up; but the Sherpas who reached the col a few minutes later
saw nothing of this, so that next day, when we climbed it, were quite
bewildered. We descended, camped in the moraine trough below the col, and
sent our Tibetan friend home to his sheep.

Starting at 5 a.m. and moving north, we skirted the ice-fall at the head of
the small Tashi Chu glacier and then turned round a half-circle until we were
heading almost south. This intricate manœuvre was designed to land us on the
main ridge, but, when hitherto unseen peaks began to loom up through the
mist on our left, I began to wonder whether we were really on Lachsi. The
snow was very soft until at a height of about 20,000 ft. signs of an irresolute
attempt at freezing appeared. We progressed slowly and the 'pimple'
obstinately refused to show itself. At the same time the so-called plateau
became less like a plateau than ever. it narrowed to a knife-edge, which on
the right fell away in a steep and broken ice-fall, and on the left in a rock
precipice. At last we came to a notch which yesterday I had welcomed as a
landmark. Now a closer view showed that it needed consideration. Lhakpa,
not liking the look of things, decided to stay where he was, but Renzing and I
descended by a steep and tortuous way into the notch and, what is infinitely
more important, succeeded in climbing out the other side. The snow was
good. The pimple, which now appeared, was about 100 ft. high, and with care
we managed to reach the summit by a ridge of very unstable rock covered
with snow. There was just room to stand on top. During the ascent, which had
taken six hours, the increasing warmth of the day had reduced the snow
everywhere to a uniform softness compelling us to take almost as long over
the descent. It was so warm that we even had rain at 20,000 ft.

The first part of our programme thus completed we headed for Tangu on
the main route from Sikkim to Tibet, reaching it on 4 July. A traveller's first
feeling on seeing that the Rest House where he proposes to stop is already
occupied is one of disgust, his second one of curiosity about those whom he
will shortly meet. Mules and other signs of activity near the Tangu Rest
House had warned me that this had happened, but I was not prepared to see
the Nazi flag flying and the members of a large German scientific party led by
a Dr Ernst Schaefer. He was a tough-looking, interesting man who had
travelled much in western China and Tibet, and had written two books about

it. The party was spending several months in Sikkim collecting birds, insects and plants, and doing other scientific work; later, as already related, they 'infiltrated' into Tibet. The party included every breed of scientist known to man: ornithologist, zoologist, entomologist, anthropologist, and many other 'ologists' of whom I had never heard. There was also a photographer whose special subject was Alpine flowers. I think they were genuine enough. They were not a party of those German 'technicians' of whom we were to see and hear so much a year or so later.

Next day we took the Lachen road and then turned up the Zemu glen, camping with some cowherds near Yaktang. Their rough wooden shanty rose like an island out of a sea of mud and was amazingly squalid inside, but we passed a pleasant night with the cowherd, his wife, and some female relations. There were seven of us and a hen in a hut 10 ft. by 10 ft. Our next camp was in a cave about a mile below the glacier snout, which like most caves could be summed up as 'draughts and drips'.

In the morning, through mist and rain, we could see the snout of the glacier only about 500 yards above. There was some very rough going in the trough for about a mile, until the river which we had been following, the Zemu Chu, disappeared under the ice. I was glad to see the last of it; for two days it had been a close and terrifying companion. After crossing another stream, which at that early hour was not very formidable, we reached the old German Base Camp in three hours. Here there was a collection of tins and rubbish which would bear comparison with the collections to be found on any of the more popular beauty spots of England, but here it had the shock of unexpectedness. We should be thankful that Tibetans are such thorough scavengers. Anyone walking up the East Rongbuk glacier past Camps I, II and III, on the way to Mount Everest, would not realise that here there had probably been more tins opened in the last twenty years than anywhere in India. On the Rongbuk there is not a trace of a tin to be seen. The grimness of life at Camp III would be greatly increased if the accumulated debris of seven expeditions was still to be seen.

We pushed on to the Green Lake the same day. In good weather this must be a glorious walk among grass and flowers, with the glittering precipices of Kangchenjunga and the great peaks of the Nepal border in full view. Unfortunately we could see less than a mile ahead. There was a little furze growing here, which the Sherpas used to get a fire going in the lee of a boulder. Lhakpa nursed it as if it were a sick child, not caring how wet he became. From here a cairned track led to the foot of the North-east Spur, the route by which the Germans made their attempts on Kangchenjunga. Before reaching this we took to the glacier again and crossed to the arm which descends from the Zemu Gap. Again we were in luck. This was the only day on which the clouds conceded a view for any length of time. Never at any time did they rise above the 19,000 ft. level, but that was just enough to resolve any doubts we had about our being on the right track. Two glacier arms on our right, one of which I at first thought might be ours, obviously ended under the cliffs of Kangchenjunga, but of this mountain, or of Simvu, or of Siniolchu, or of any other landmark, we saw nothing.

We had started at five o'clock with the intention of tackling the Gap that day, but we did not reach the foot of the approach glacier until eleven. The col, barely discernible under the cloud canopy, looked near enough, but taking into account the time and the weather I decided to wait until the next day. I had, once, decided wisely. Unfortunately our Primus stove, like the Dutchman's anchor, had been left behind, not for the sake of lightening our loads but for the more usual reason of forgetfulness. However, Renzing went back to the foot of the North-east Spur and presently returned with some sort of fuel, so that our camp on the ice was not so cheerless as my carelessness deserved. It is surprising how far up the eastern slopes of Kangchenjunga fuel can be found.

I roused the men at 3.30 next morning and we started making tea in the open in the drizzle of rain. Two hours later this became worse, driving down the glacier from the Gap. Within a quarter of an hour of leaving, on reaching the névé, our expectations were realised—the snow was rotten. At this season, below 20,000 ft., the sun's effect upon snow conditions needs little consideration, for whether you start at midnight or midday the snow will still be soft. It took us four hours to reach the Gap (19,200 ft.) although I suppose we had not more than 2,000 ft. to climb. There were no great difficulties, but the approach was narrow and subject to avalanches from both sides—the remains of two very big ones were seen. As the day drew on the drizzle changed to snow, and a fierce wind from the pass driving this in our faces so obscured our vision that I had to remove my snow-glasses to find a way through the crevasses.

We noticed one thing which I hestitate to mention for fear of reopening old controversies. A single track of footsteps, which in view of the weather conditions could not have been more than two or three days old, led up the glacier as far as the crest of the Zemu Gap and then disappeared on the rocks of the Simvu side. On returning to Darjeeling I made inquiries, but so far as was known no party had been out anywhere near Kangchenjunga. The last known visit to the south side of the Gap was made by John Hunt on 18 November the previous year. Moreover, lunatics are scarce, and who would go 'swanning' about alone on the Zemu glacier?

The last time I had reported having come across strange tracks in the snow (in the upper basin of the Biafo glacier, Sir Martin Conway's Snow Lake) on my return from the Karakoram in 1937, considerable comment had appeared in the correspondence columns of *The Times* from both learned scientists and experienced mountaineers. This correspondence, illuminating but inconclusive, should be read by students. G. K. Chesterton has remarked on the loving care and patience bestowed by the professors on their building up of Pithecanthropus—a bit of skull here, a few teeth there, and a thigh-bone from somewhere else—until at last they produced a detailed drawing, carefully shaded to show that the very hairs of his head were all numbered. How amused he would have been to see the ferocity with which the professors fell upon Homo Nivis Odiosus and tore him (and those who believed in him) limb from limb.

In the present instance there were no tracks like 'soup plates' which, according to fancy, could be conveniently attributed to bears, snow leopards, otters, leaping hares, or gigantic one-legged birds, but plain tracks of large boots. Of course, for this there is only the word of one man, albeit an unexaggerative man of scrupulous veracity. Given the existence of an Abominable Snowman, there is no reason why he should not have picked up a discarded pair of climbing boots at the German Base Camp and put them to their obvious use. We are not to suppose that a Snowman, or an animal if you like, has not wit enough to keep its feet dry if they happen to be the shape that go into boots. These tracks were in fact so real that the Sherpas and I discussed the possibility of one of Schaefer's party having preceded us and crossed the Gap; but whoever or whatever it was had certainly not descended from the crest. I was pleased to recall the friendly hint I had given to the anthropologist of Schaefer's party—an earnest, inquiring man—over a few glasses of Kümmel, encouraging him to spare no pains in solving the problem of Homo Nivis Odiosus, and begging him not to be put off by the zoologist, who would infallibly tell him that any tracks he found were not those of our abominable friend, not even of a Snark or a Boojum, but those of a bear.

To return to the crest of the Zemu Gap where we were now standing, craning our necks to see if those mysterious tracks went down the other side, and if so, which way they went. The weather was too bad and I was too anxious about our descent to start looking for the pair of crampons which Tombazi (see Chapter Six) had reported having left on the rocks on the north side when he ascended to the Gap from the Tongshyong glacier in 1925. Instead we addressed ourselves at once to the problem of getting down.

From our visit in 1936 I knew of the steep ice-wall on the south side, and had taken the precaution of bringing 240 ft. of Alpine line. Even so on first looking over the top I got a shock. There was a wall, over 200 ft. of it, and overhanging sufficiently to prevent one from seeing where one would land. We could not use the rope down this. However, search revealed a very steep and narrow gully descending from the junction of the crest of the pass and the precipitous shoulder of Simvu. Between two runnels of ice was a thin ribbon of snow. It was loose and wet, but with careful handling ('footling' would be better) steps could be made in it. I will not guess at the angle for fear of being called a liar, but it seemed to me that a man with a long nose, standing upright, could have wiped it on the snow. I went down a rope's length and hacked out a platform in the ice for Lhakpa, who followed me. It was so misty below that I was not at all sure whether we could reach the plateau short of the wall on which Pasang and I had gained a footing in 1936. There was a bergschrund at the foot of the wall, but another rope's length sufficed to see me over this.

Having climbed back to the platform where Lhakpa was, I got Renzing, who was still on top, to begin lowering the loads down the ice runnel to our level so that we could drag them on our platform by making a long arm with our ice-axe. Lhakpa was then sent down over the bergschrund, Renzing joined me on the platform, and the load lowering began again. To save time I sent my own load, which was lighter than the others, down the runnel under its own steam. Leaping the 'schrund' it disappeared across the snow into the

mist at the rate of knots. I thought I had seen the last of it, and the probable
loss of sleeping bag, mat, spare clothes, tobacco, camera, and 10 lb. of sugar,
was offset to some extent by the certainty of having no load to carry. The
remaining loads were lowered.

Crossing the little snow plateau we found my load, which had stopped just
short of the next obstacle. This was the upper ice-fall which had given us
trouble in 1936; since then it had altered out of all recognition. A great chasm
more than 100 ft. wide and 100 ft. deep had opened up across the glacier. We
found a place where an 'abseil' of 50 ft. would have done the trick, but the
edge overhung slightly and at the bottom of the chasm was a crevasse into
which there was an even chance of landing. A situation in which one found
oneself dangling at the end of a 50 ft. rope over a crevasse instead of over firm
ground was full of possibilities, but as we had a second rope with us I think
that even that situation would not have been irretrievable. But in such places,
employing rope tactics, one of the difficulties is to make the man above
understand what is wanted. In the gully we had just descended my shouted
instructions to Renzing were lost in the wind.

This overhang was of no use to us so, moving over to the right, I
reconnoitred another route. It started in an unorthodox manner with a 15 ft.
jump, and it was therefore essential to know whether the rest of the route
would 'go' before committing the whole party; we had in fact already burnt
our boats, or at any rate set them alight, by our descent of the gully, for to
climb that with loads on would have been a hazardous performance. The
lower part proved possible. The Sherpas jumped, and down we went. The last
30 ft. to the floor of the chasm was a steep, icy funnel which terminated very
close to another crevasse. I well remember the plaintive cry of the first man,
Lhakpa: 'Do you want to kill me?' on being told to trust the rope. One load
on being shot down did finish in the crevasse, but it stopped on a ledge from
which we fished it up. Having lowered the Sherpas down I cut steps for half
the distance and then, being in a hurry, slid the rest. Having climbed out the
other side I was half afraid there were other surprises in store for us, for the
mist hid everything; but as we went down the ground became easier, and
presently we reached the spot below the ice-fall where we had camped in
1936. It was now hidden by the debris of a colossal avalanche. It can be
assumed that most big avalanches take place after the first heavy monsoon
snowfall when the temperature is rising rapidly; but avalanches are very much
an Act of God, and behave, in spite of our knowledge, in an incalculable way.
Especially is this so in the Himalaya, where they also assume an unimaginable
size and travel unbelievable distances. The only safe rule is to take every
precaution, trust nothing, and expect one day to be caught out.

We reached the Tongshyong glacier at 3 p.m., having taken five and a half
hours to come down from the top, and nine and a half from our camp on the
other side. The crossing of the Gap in the reverse direction with heavy loads
would be extremely difficult, although conditions undoubtedly vary
considerably from year to year. Even so the alleged crossing in 1927, on which
I have already commented, must have been a remarkable feat. The party left
their camp on the Tongshyong at 3 a.m., crossed the Gap, descended to the

1 2 3   (above) Tilman as a schoolboy at Berkhamsted: posing with friends ;
training with the Officer Training Corps c.1914.

4   Tilman (front row – centre left), an officer with B Battery, 161st Brigade, Royal Field
Artillery, somewhere in France, 1916.

5 (above) The North Face of Mt. Kenya showing the Northey Glacier leading to the West Ridge of Batian on the right.

6 (above right) Eric Shipton and Bill Tilman.

7 (right) The peaks of Mt. Kenya, Nelion (left) and Batian, seen from the north-east. The West Ridge is in profile on the right.

8 (above) The Ruwenzori massif, with the summits of Mt. Stanley (left).
9 (below) The road between Masinai and Batiaba, Uganda.

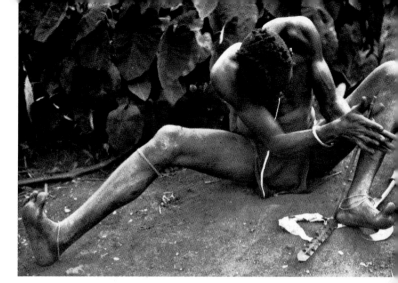

11   12
ages of Africa:
king fire (top); a hut
he Ituri Forest (centre)
oes on the Upper
ngo (bottom).

Views of Nanda Devi:

13 (above) The summit slopes. The route follows the line between the snow slope and the mixed ground on the left.

14 (left) West Peak from the South Glacier. The route follows the obvious diagonal line.

15   The 1936 Nanda Devi team. Tilman (left), W. F. Loomis (US), T. Graham Brown
(UK), Charles Houston (US), Peter Lloyd and N. E. Odell (UK),
Arthur Emmons and H. Adams Carter (US).

16   (right) Nanda Devi from Nanda Kot. The route follows the left profile.

On the Nanda Devi climb:

17 (above) Camp 1, 19,200 ft. with the peaks of the rim of the sanctuary in the background.

18 (left) Resting at the foot of the gully above Camp 4 (22,500 ft.). 'It was no place for a long sojourn without prehensile trousers. There was not enough snow to afford a step, much less a seat.'

19 (top right) In the gully c.23,000 ft. 'We began to search the snow above us for the slightest break in the relentless angle of the slope.'

20 (bottom right) Longstaff's Col and Nanda Kot from near Camp 5.

21 (left) Four members of the seven-man 1935 Everest reconnaissance Expedition: Tilman (left), Edmond Wigram, Dan Bryant and Eric Shipton (leader). During this successful venture, glacier systems on the north side of the mountain were explored and mapped, many passes were reached or crossed and first ascents were made of twenty-six peaks. The party lived mainly 'off the land' – on one occasion these four climbers ate 140 eggs in a day.

22 (below) The snow-plastered final slopes of the North Ridge of Everest in 1938. This view was taken from Camp 6 (27,200 ft.) sited 200 ft. lower and 300 yards to the east

Everest, 1938:

23 (left) Sherpas load-carrying on the western slopes of North Col.

24 (below) Tilman in Camp 4.

25 (right) Frank Smythe at the highest point reached. 'An hour's exhausting work yielded little more than a rope's length of progress . . . we were in obvious danger of being swept off the rocks by a snow avalanche . . . we returned, convinced of the hopelessness of our task.' (Shipton)

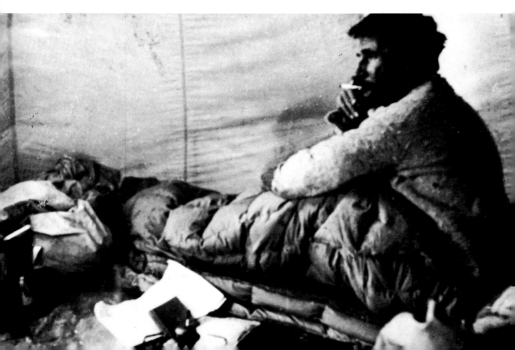

26 (left) Two views of the difficult, south (Tongshyong) side of the Zemu Gap in the Kanchenjunga massif. Tilman made an abortive attempt to climb this side with Pasang Kikuli in 1936 but failed to ascend the final ice wall. They had been hoping to discover a more direct way of reaching the Zemu Glacier from Darjeeling, but the difficulty of the pass rendered this impracticable. Tilman eventually traversed the pass with Renzing and Lhakpa Tensing from the north (Zemu) side in 1938 while returning from the Everest expedition.

Albania, 1944:   27   (top left) Two young partisans;   28 and 29   Tilman with local partisan leaders, Shefket Pezi (lower left) and Islam Radowicke (right), outside the HQ in Shepr.

Belluno, Northern Italy, 1945: 30 (above left) Tilman on his return to the City after the end of hostilities. 31 (above right) Italian partisans. 32 (below) Receiving the Freedom of the City to honour his war exploits with the partisans.

CITTA' DI BELLUNO

La popolazione Bellunese saluta il nuovo concittadino
Maggiore della Reale Artiglieria Inglese

Harold William Tilman da Liverpool

CITY OF BELLUNO

The population of Belluno greet their new citizen
Major Harold William Tilman R. A. of Liverpool England
to whom the freedom of the city is given

Zemu glacier, and returned to camp in time for breakfast at 9 a.m.!

We were getting tired, our loads and we ourselves were wet through, and the thought of finding abundant fuel at the snout of the glacier led us there rather than cross at once to the Talung glacier by the snow-saddle route we had used in 1936. We had had enough snow wallowing for one day; we were in that frame of mind which recoils shudderingly from the mere thought of going uphill again, and we had not yet made up our minds to abandon the original plan of returning by the Talung Chu route. In 1936 that journey had not been easy and now the weather was much worse, but it was the most direct route to Gangtok which I had to visit before going on to Darjeeling. We found some fuel late that evening, but it was the wrong kind of shrub, and nothing would make it burn. In monsoon conditions in Sikkim only wood like juniper or 'chir', full of resin, would have consented to light. We dined austerely on cold water, sugar and satu. The whole, mixed and squashed together in a cake, is palatable. I had just written up my diary, commenting on the really remarkable fact that, although I had gone practically the whole day without snow-glasses, my eyes seemed to have taken no harm, when they began to smart; presently I was in all the agony of snow-blindness. There was little sleep that night either for me or for Lhakpa, whose eyes were also affected. Next morning the pain was less, but I could only bear to look at the ground at my feet. Under the circumstances this was not a great handicap, for only someone blessed with infra-red eyes could have pierced the prevailing mist.

We started off, stumbling in the wake of Renzing, intending to cross the foot of the dividing ridge in order to get on to the Talung glacier. Once there we would make for the Guicha La, for, what with our blindness and the weather, the Talung Chu route was unthinkable. The very few who know that trackless vale of tears will agree that this decision was wise, but it soon became evident that in trying to reach the Talung by the route we had chosen we were extremely foolish. We kept too low, as tired men will, and soon we were fighting a losing battle with rhododendron and other close-growing abominations. After a six-hour struggle, in which we gained about a mile, we found ourselves above the snout of the Talung. As we were unable to get down to it at this point on account of the very high, steep moraine banks which are a feature of the country near the Talung-Tongshyong junction, we had to continue bush-crawling to the right and soon found ourselves spread-eagled on a rocky cliff. By this time we were getting desperate, so using a rhododendron root as a dubious anchor, we lowered the loads and roped down after them. Tired, wet, and cross, we trudged over the glacier to the moraine on the other side and followed it up until five o'clock when we camped. There was plenty of scrub about but none that would burn, and we dined as frugally as before. However, the pain had gone from our eyes, and in spite of having wet sleeping-bags we slept well—he who sleeps, dines.

The mist was as thick as ever next morning when after more satu, sugar and water, we set out to look for the Guicha La. We had been there before, but I feared there would be much 'trial and error' work before we hit it off in the mist. But our luck still held. We had not been going an hour before I spotted a wisp of mist with a decidedly bluish tinge. I dared not suggest that it was smoke for fear of rousing false hopes, but presently the Sherpas, who had probably noticed it long before, announced that it was smoke. In a few minutes we were drinking sheep's milk, and warming ourselves in a matting shelter with some very astonished shepherds camped at the foot of the Guicha La. They had come over the previous day.

Our misadventures were not over yet. We toiled up grass slopes for an unconscionable time until we all agreed we should have reached the pass. Casting about, we hit on a path and eventually reached the pass—but not the one we were aiming for, which must have been nearly a mile to our right. This one was the higher Guicha La at the foot of Pandim. We dropped down to the Parek Chu, seeing the sun for the first time in many days. We draped our sleeping-bags outside our loads to dry, and set off at speed down the valley, bent on reaching Dzongri before nightfall.

The glacier stream, swollen by melting snow and rain, looked formidable so, certain that Dzongri was on its other side and uncertain whether the bridge lower down still existed, we decided to cross while the going was good. On the far side we picked up a half-hearted track down which we proceeded gaily enough in spite of the heavy rain which had begun again. The track became more and more tenuous until finally, in the heart of a thicket, it petered out. Having noticed some sheep and a shepherd's hut on the other bank about a mile back, we decided to return and ask about the bridge, though we feared that by now there would be too much water to recross in safety. Retracing our steps until we were opposite the hut, we plunged into what had become an angry river; we could get no wetter and death by drowning seemed preferable to another night in the open. The hut appeared to be empty except for a heap of blankets, but in response to our shouts the pile of blankets stirred and a boy came to the surface. He was a lad of prompt decision and had evidently at once made up his mind that we were not desirable guests. In reply to our question he answered unhesitatingly that Dzongri was a bare two miles away. We sped away in the rain, hardly stopping to thank him for his glad tidings. A long two miles brought us no farther than the bridge, and for another three we climbed steadily for what I thought must be 10,000 ft. but which was probably only 2,000.

I was well ahead of the Sherpas when, just about dusk, I took up quarters in a muddy, leaking, derelict yak-stable, which seemed to be the only shelter in Dzongri. By hacking bits off the less wet parts of the underside of the roof I managed to get a fire going just as the others arrived. They seemed surprised and a bit disappointed at our poor quarters and meagre fire. The pan was put on for tea, Lhakpa went off to look for juniper, but was back in a minute to tell us that just round the corner was a billet, with a roaring fire. We moved over and spent a luxurious evening in the company of a young yak-herd and half a dozen still younger yaks. In three days more we reached the Tista valley again at a point 18 miles from our destination, Gangtok. The Sherpas were now lagging. Leaving word for them to make their way to Darjeeling, I procured a car the same afternoon and reached Gangtok.

We had climbed a mountain and crossed a pass; been wet, cold, hungry, frightened, and withal happy. Why this should be so I cannot explain, and if the reader is as much at a loss and has caught nothing of the intensity of pleasure we felt, then the writer must be at fault. One more Himalayan season was over. It was time to begin thinking of the next. 'Strenuousness is the immortal path, sloth is the way of death.'

Part 2

WARTIME

CHAPTER EIGHT

Three Climbs in Wartime

IRAQ

IN wartime there are few opportunities for mountaineering. Normally an army avoids mountains as far as possible, and even in a war embracing the whole world it is remarkable how little fighting has taken place amongst them; by which I do not mean just mountainous terrain, where there has been fighting to spare, but mountains of interest to the climber. The Himalaya, in any case, would be given a wide berth by even the most enterprising army; the Caucasus were never really reached; Switzerland has been out of bounds on the last two occasions; while in Norway the campaign was over before the mountaineer, who felt that here at last was his opportunity, had had time to send off his first appeal: 'Sir, I have the honour to forward this my application for transfer, etc., etc.' to whomsoever might be interested or influential.

This business of trying to adapt a war to one's own ends can be overdone. At least such was my own experience in the first two or three years of this war. It is better to lie passive, neither helping nor hindering the current, but drifting with the stream of events as directed, or so one likes to think, by Higher Authority. You may well find yourself in a backwater or spinning round and round in a whirlpool, but if you stick in an oar in an attempt to stem the stream or to explore some interesting-looking creek, anything may happen. After returning from Dunkirk I moved heaven and earth to get myself sent to East Africa, a country about which I knew a good deal. The result was that I found myself in a regiment earmarked for Singapore, of which I knew nothing. I had the very greatest difficulty in extricating myself from this ill-starred unit only twenty-four hours before it embarked. I lay quiet for a long time after that until I was tempted to make some passes at a job in a mountain battery, whereupon I received orders to report forthwith as an instructor at a school of mountain warfare. I escaped being left high and dry on that barren reef by submerging quickly again in the sea of regimental soldiering.

Iraq is not a country which I would recommend to mountaineers; indeed I should hesitate to advise anyone to go there unless, as the Shipping Agents say, 'sufficient inducement offers'. No special inducement was offered to us (a Field Regiment R.A.) to go there in May 1941 except that all expenses were paid. After a diverting voyage up the Persian Gulf in a 35-year-old 'City' boat, which was too slow to keep up with the convoy even though we lent a hand with the stoking, we were cast ashore at Basra, driven 20 miles into the desert, and invited to make ourselves at home. Apart from its heat, the desert outside Basra has some unusual climatic features. The most noteworthy is the violent gale which begins before 8 a.m. and continues with unrelenting fury until late afternoon. It is, of course, accompanied by a great storm of sand, so that it is impossible to do anything between those hours except cower inside a tent until it collapses, and then to continue cowering under the flapping folds until the wind abates.

After a week of this we dug out the half-buried trucks and marched in three stages up the Tigris valley to Mosul to take an inglorious part in the tail end of the Syrian campaign. The march was notable for the mortality rate of the tractors due to overheating by day, and for the number of Arab rifle thieves in the night. Many stories are told of the uncanny skill of Pathan rifle thieves on the North-west Frontier, but I believe that the Arabs of Iraq have little to learn about this difficult and hazardous art. On this march two men with a Bren gun buried it and slept on it, and next morning were facing a charge of 'losing by neglect' one Bren gun. Rifles were taken from men who slept with them stowed in a specially constructed pocket inside the blanket, with the sling wrapped round their wrists. In consequence of this the leaguer after dark was like No-man's Land. Verey lights soared into the sky and bullets zipped across the ground fired both by our own sentries and by the sentries of neighbouring units. It was safer to sleep below ground-level.

Having crossed the Syrian border west of Mosul on the Aleppo desert-track, we speedily reduced two small towns which were still hostile. The guns were laid on the white, red-roofed house of the French Commandant, who was given until eleven o'clock to march out with the garrison. At five minutes to the hour nothing stirred but the Tricolour, still fluttering from the roof. On a little hillock close to the battery, the Commander of the Brigade Group, our Regimental Commander, and 'back-room boys' like myself, waited expectantly; those who had them nonchalantly brandished brightly coloured horse-hair fly whisks. The layer sat at his gun, squinted again through the sights at the distant house, and put his hand on the firing lever. For it was one of those rare and pleasing occasions when in the absence of anything bigger than a machine-gun on the other side, one can come into action in the open in full view of the target to work one's wicked will without fear of retaliation—just as at a practice shoot, in fact, without umpires or safety officers, and instead of dummies in the danger zone with real people and real houses. It was a pity that on this occasion they happened to be French.

At one minute to eleven a cloud of dust appeared in the gateway of the fort, and a small car bearing a white flag shot out of the town and came tearing towards us. It was fortunate, I reflected, that during the pourparlers the synchronisation of watches had not been forgotten. The other town, El Haseke, some miles south, was even more of a disappointment for our fire-eaters. Our fast-moving light column, rumbling across the grassy plain in tactical formation, breathing only fire and slaughter, had barely covered ten miles before word came back that El Haseke had surrendered.

We showed the flag to the Sheiks of the Shammar tribe of Bedouins, ate vast trays of mutton and rice with them and drank little cups of cardamom-flavoured coffee; calmed some frightened Armenian villagers who every moment expected to have their throats cut by the Shammar; soothed the excited Syrians and saw that some sort of civil government was functioning; and then retired to Mosul to dig ourselves in against the arrival of the Germans. The contingency might be remote, but it served as an excuse for the digging which kept us occupied for the rest of our stay in Iraq. The men, unversed in higher strategy, did not appreciate it. We had spent the winter of 1939 digging gunpits on the Belgian frontier and now we were to do the same on the borders of Iraq. I can only remember one occasion when a previously prepared position was occupied, and then we had our guns pointing in the opposite direction to that for which the pits were built—a trifling but irritating circumstance.

Reconnoitring the defences on the border west of Mosul was more amusing than digging them. The architect, the Colonel of a battalion of the Frontier Force Rifles, employed me as his artillery adviser. We made our H.Q. in the buildings of a railway station near Eski Mosul. From this comfortable billet we made extensive surveys of the proposed defences in the Colonel's station wagon, accompanied by a bearer with tiffin basket, an orderly with sun-umbrella, the Colonel's shotgun, and his dog. If a bustard or a pack of sandgrouse was seen, the siting of company localities, battery positions, anti-tank guns, and machine-guns had to wait. After lunch we would forgather on some convenient 'tell', or burial mound, and survey the scene of our labours through closing eyes. To call this part of the world the Syrian desert is a misnomer. At that time of year, early summer, it was like the Sussex Downs; great sweeps of gently rolling country were covered with flowers, iris, anemones, and periwinkles. The climate conformed to the country, for the nights were cool and the days sparkling.

It was an unwelcome change to leave these pleasant uplands for our camp at Mosul between the river and the railway. It is true that there was the Tigris with its attendant strip of green cultivation; but beyond that narrow strip the desert was true desert, arid and stony; the hills were distant, and the heat was severe. Sickness made its appearance. Sandfly fever was the chief complaint from which, I think, the whole regiment suffered at one time or another with the exception of an officer who drank a bottle of whisky a day, and myself, who drank none. The Trade and the Temperance Societies may make what they can of it. There was a little malaria, and jaundice was a prevalent complaint which preferred to attack officers rather than men.

I attributed this invidious distinction to our over-eating and under-working. We certainly lived very well. A Syrian contractor, efficient but of imperfect morals, looked after the mess and the men's canteen. Every Sunday he put on a chicken curry for which guests used to come in from far and wide. It was best eaten with a towel or sweat cloth round the neck. Turkeys were even more plentiful than chickens, for this part of Iraq seems to be the home par excellence of the turkey. The Syrian wished me to go into partnership with him after the war in the turkey export business, but whether this was a tribute to my honesty or my gullibility I never decided. Peaches, apricots, and grapes were cheap and plentiful, as was the local wine, which was thick, sweet, and very strong. For special occasions we imported a superb walnut brandy from a monastery in the hills.

The river was a great boon because, apart from football, excursions to Nineveh or Erbil, or getting drunk in Mosul, there was nothing for the troops to do but watch the Taurus Express go by every other day. Kind-hearted passengers used to fling newspapers on the embankment just above our camp. The Taurus Express, linking two such fabulous cities as Baghdad and Istanbul, seemed to me in wartime the quintessence of romance. I liked to think that most of the passengers were German spies, 'technicians', British secret agents; that every woman was some wicked but glamorous 'Lucy Felucci', and that every man, equally wicked but less glamorous, was known only by a cipher number in the most obscure room of the Foreign Office or the Wilhelmstrasse.

The river was dangerous for poor swimmers, like any other river, and acquired an undeserved reputation. I used to make the whole battery trot down to it for an early morning bathe; some disliked the trot down, more disliked the bathe. The great event was a swimming gala which, appropriately enough, included a race for home-made boats. A boat made from the petrol tank of a Messerschmidt, insubordinately called 'Tilly's Filly', won easily.

For those who preferred to think of the remote past rather than the uncertain and probably distasteful future, there were excursions to the nearby Nineveh or the more distant Erbil. The great earth mounds of Nineveh are just across the river from Mosul, but for the inexpert there is not much to see. Of more interest is the shrine and mosque of Nebi Yunus close by, where there is the spurious tomb of the prophet Jonah. Some pieces of bone, apparently from the sword of a sword-fish, are exhibited as part of the backbone of the famous whale. Archaeologists, it is said, roll their eyes at the mention of Nebi Yunus. It is believed to be built on the site of the palace of Sennacherib but, because of the fanaticism of the Moslems of Nebi Yunus, no excavation can be done. Erbil, the ancient Arbela, is on the Kirkuk road 40 miles east of Mosul. Here the last Darius buried his treasure before the battle in which he and his empire were overthrown by Alexander. The present town is on a great mound which presumably consists of the remains of successive Arbelas from the first foundation thousands of years ago. It is the oldest inhabited city extant.

The winter in northern Iraq is severe. By mid-November the hills to the north and across the river to the east, six to seven thousand feet high, were coated with snow. Around Mosul itself winter brought cold, wind, prolonged rain, and flooded camps. This year just after Christmas there was really bitter weather, when a foot of snow fell and lay for a week. At night it froze hard and the crackling of snow on my tent roof reminded me of better times. The only form of heating we could find for the tents was charcoal braziers. All the cooking in Mosul is done on charcoal, so that when we came into the market the price rocketed from five shillings a sack to a pound. The supply came from the forested hills near the Turkish border north of Mosul, to which my thoughts, stimulated by the snow, now began to turn. An official inquiry into the charcoal business at the source was as good an excuse as any for a week in the mountains.

In Mosul I had met a climbing friend from India who had thoughtfully come to war with his ice-axe, and I was able to borrow that essential implement. Tents were no difficulty, for everyman had his bivouac tent, and the Mosul bazaar supplied 30 ft. of clothes-line for a climbing rope. The lack of suitable boots was more serious, but 'with bread and iron one may get to China'.

In the summer, about 70 miles north of Mosul, there had been a convalescent camp. From the accounts and photographs of those who had been there, I felt sure that in winter something in the nature of real mountaineering could be done there, and that Amadia would be the best centre. With that object in view three of us left Mosul in a 15 cwt. truck in the first week in February. No precise information about the state of the road was available, but we started under the impression that we would be able to reach our destination by truck. Much depended on our doing so, for we had only a week's leave. I had with me my own driver-batman and a bombardier from the 'Q' stores.

Thirty miles from Mosul the plains gave way to the foothills of the tangled ranges of Kurdistan, the home of Kurds, Assyrians, and Armenians; the Kurds are Sunni Moslems, the Assyrians Christians. Amadia was once the headquarters of the Turkish administration and is entirely Moslem, but in the same valley there are many Christian villages. The Christians of these parts have suffered for their beliefs as few others have. They are always subject to oppression, and up to as recently as 1923 were liable to be massacred. In that year several hundred Assyrians of Dohuk and Simmel were murdered by the Iraqi army and the local Kurds.

After leaving the small trading centre of Dohuk the road climbs the Charkevi Dagh range, the last barrier before the Khabur valley in which Amadia lies. For the most part the hills were studded with stunted oaks, but occasionally my eyes were gladdened by clumps of juniper forest, as refreshing as the sighting of land after a long voyage. As we neared the top of the Charkevi, drifts of snow appeared on the road. One by one these were rushed until at last the inevitable happened and we found ourselves stuck up to the axles in snow. A road gang helped us to dig ourselves out and told us that half a mile on the road was blocked. Beyond this, for the remaining 15 miles to Amadia, there were 3 ft. of snow. These men, lithe keen-faced Assyrians, looked as though they should have been carrying rifles rather then long-handled shovels. They were dressed in baggy trousers of coarse grey wool with a thin green or purple stripe. Round the waist they wore the voluminous cotton cummerbund, said to contain seven yards of cloth, and on their heads untidy grey turbans. One or two had sheepskin jackets, others army greatcoats, which from their appearance must have been relics of the 1914–18 war.

We selected a camp site by the road and turned the truck round with difficulty. Leaving the men to dig a site for the tents, I went off to a village above the road of which we had caught a glimpse. This proved to be a Christian village with a tiny stone church and half a dozen flat-roofed houses. I asked the black-bearded priest for two mules to carry our stuff to Amadia. He promised his assistance and begged us to sleep in the village.

Next morning, instead of following the road which winds round the southern slopes of the wide Khabur valley, we struck down into the valley with our mules and across to the northern side. After a tiring march we camped about 4 miles short of Amadia in a spot which had few attractions other than its proximity to the shapely snow and rock peak on which I had had my eyes all day. Snow lay everywhere, and one place was as good as another. Camping in snow, and using snow for cooking, was a new pastime to my two gunners, who were not at all enthusiastic until we made friends with some nearby Assyrians, who brought us loads of wood and promised chickens and eggs.

In the morning, leaving the men to recover from the long march, to which they were unused, I climbed the peak. It was about 6,500 ft. high and of almost Alpine standard. When later on I took the men up they were extremely steady and did very well until the spectacular summit ridge was reached, which they promptly decided would be, in the language of Baedeker, 'fatiguing and not repaying'. Our two remaining days were devoted to a long snow walk towards the Turkish border and to visiting Amadia. I have never seen a town so situated. It is built upon the summit of a great knoll whose limestone sides are so smoothly precipitous that they appear to have been quarried. A long winding staircase, cut in the living rock, leads up through an arched guard-house to the town, which is further defended by a wall built upon the edge of the cliff. Within the walls, the mean, narrow streets and squalid houses form a town altogether unworthy of the strange and imposing pedestal on which it has been built.

After our return to Mosul the regiment moved from the river to Qaiyara where there are a number of oil wells. The crude oil, which we were allowed to draw freely in buckets, was used both for fuel for cooking and for surfacing the roads in the camp. Digging was given up for the time being. Instead we carried out exercises in the desert to the west which, at this time of year, early spring, was as pleasant a place to drive about in as one could wish. A smooth surface of young green grass ran for mile after mile, broken only by small and infrequent wadis, a rare burial mound, or the tents and herds of some wandering bedouin.

Fifty miles out in the desert, untenanted except for the goats of the bedouin, were the ruins of the Parthian city of Hatra—Al Hadhr as the Arabs call it. Here, to my mind, is something far more astonishing than the earth mounds of Nineveh. An immensely thick wall encloses an area of perhaps half a square mile within which are ruined houses and streets, and in the centre a massive stone building of two stories known as the Palace of the Sun. A dark barrel-vault connects two great halls, on the wall of which are sculptured heads, partly defaced by stones from the slings of Arab urchins. On the perfectly cut ashlar can be seen the private marks of the masons. To see the remains of this once powerful fortress rising so incongruously from the surrounding wilderness lends forcible emphasis to the contrast between the Iraq of the past and that of the present. To support the numerous inhabitants of such a fortress, the desert in the vicinity must then have been in a high state of cultivation. It was an important place in the second century A.D., an outpost of the Parthian Empire. Two Roman Emperors, Trajan in A.D. 116 and Severus in A.D. 178, besieged the city, but failed to take it. It was eventually sacked, and afterwards abandoned, by the Sassanian king Sapor seventy years later.

Still moving southwards the regiment was next halted at El Fata where the oil pipe-line from Kirkuk crosses the Tigris on its way to the Palestine coast. This must be one of the hottest places of a hot country. At this point the Tigris breaks through the Jebel Hamrin range, and the barren rock ridges on both sides of the river radiate heat like a hot-plate. Sandy, stony desert hugs the river. Here the desert has come into its own, and though the river flows broad, strong and deep, it is powerless to nourish on its sterile banks the hardiest of trees or even one vestige of greenery.

Sandstorms occurred daily and no vehicle could move without creating a local sandstorm of its own. Here, every day, we dug fiercely against time, constructing an all-round defensive position on each bank; for, by now, Higher Authority had announced a date by which all these positions were to be ready. We were not the first who had dug and suffered at El Fata. The place was honeycombed with trenches dug by the Turks when they took up a defensive position here towards the close of the 1914–18 war. These old trenches were the home of innumerable scorpions, small snakes, giant centipedes, and giant spiders, all of which seemed to transfer themselves immediately to the holes we had dug for our tents. We had learnt by experience that the plan of digging down four or five feet before erecting tents not only gave more headroom but made for warmth in winter and coolness in summer.

The only relaxation we had from digging was a 48-hour exercise in the desert to accustom us to move in desert formation and live on a pint of water a day. A month later we were doing this in the Western Desert in earnest, where the heat was admittedly of no consequence, but where there was no time limit to the exercise. On this occasion we struck an uncommonly bad spell with the wind blowing in the same direction as that in which we were moving, with results similar to those of a following wind in the Red Sea. Before the exercise was well started the water ration had to be doubled, and later, as more heat casualties occurred, all restrictions on drinking had to be removed. Finally the whole Brigade had to halt, facing into the wind, to wait for evening, as few of the engines could run for any length of time without boiling.

PERSIA

On the eve of our departure from El Fata a stroke of luck came my way when the Brigadier took me with him on a tour of the Persian defences. There, too, some unfortunates of what was then called the 9th Army had been busy throughout the winter altering the Persian landscape. Their lot, however, had fallen to them in a more pleasant place for both climate and scenery than had ours. A hasty glance at our proposed route on the map showed me that near one of our stages, Kermanshah, there was a 10,000 ft. peak called Bisitun, so I determined, if it was possible, to tarry there awhile. The Brigadier, who knew on which leg I halted, was quite agreeable. He, and another major who was coming, were keen fishermen, and they had heard of a river near Kermanshah which, whatever might be its merits as a defensive line, was excellent for trout.

There is no bridge across the Tigris between Baghdad and Mosul. At El Fata it is crossed by a light transporter bridge, built by the oil companies, which takes single trucks, but our Sappers supplemented this by a cable ferry like the 'bacs' of the Congo basin. In such ferries a pontoon, attached to a pulley running along the cable, is driven across by the action of the current. Having crossed the river, we drove for two hours over the desert to Kirkuk, the centre of the oil industry and itself a large producing centre. A few miles from Kirkuk, in a small hollow in the desert, is the reputed site of the 'burning, fiery furnace' which was heated seven times for the benefit of Shadrach, Meshach and Abed-nego; here the gas, which escapes from the oil below, burns with a perpetual, bluish lambent flame.

We spent the night in a dry river bed south of Kirkuk, and next morning drove happily along the wrong road for some 70 miles. When such mistakes occur the responsibility lies with the senior officer but the blame automatically falls on the junior, whether he happens to be driving, reading the map, or merely sleeping in the back. It was not until we reached the Persian frontier beyond Kanaqin, where the only formality was the signing of a book, that the constraint occasioned by this untoward happening began to wear off. After staying so long in Iraq we were not disposed to be hypercritical, but nevertheless our first impressions of Iran were far from favourable. The custom-house was a terrible rococo affair, but the greatest eyesore were the men, who were one and all dressed in shoddy European suits and cloth caps. I believe the late Shah was responsible for this dismal uniformity, who not only decreed that European clothes should be worn, but himself, through his agents, sold them to his unlucky subjects. Thus attired, the people looked so incongruous that, for me, even the nobility of the Persian background was qualified—the wide flat valleys, filled with fruit trees and fields of corn; and the great, sweeping sparsely wooded hills, transmuted by a soft, clear atmosphere reminiscent of Kashmir.

From the frontier the road climbs steadily to the foot of the Paitak Pass (5,300 ft.), the gateway through the Zagros mountains to the Iranian plateau beyond. The road up to the pass is steep, loose, and has many hairpin bends. We camped that night near the top and reached Kermanshah next day. As we approached the town from the south we looked straight at the lofty, serrated ridge of Bisitun, the black rock face slashed with the white of snow gullies, the whole rugged mass rising abruptly from the green plain beyond Kermanshah. The town itself, which is modern, commercial, and tinny, holds nothing of historic interest, but a few miles out where the main road meets the mountain barrier and turns east, are the grottoes and rock carvings of Tak i Bostan. The place was a pleasure retreat of the Sassanian kings. The grottoes and carvings are cut on the face of a limestone cliff from whose foot a mighty jet of water gushes into an artificial rock basin fringed with trees. One noble old 'chenar' tree looks as though it must be almost contemporary with the carvings. Of these there are several, the principal being a colossal figure of Chosroes (A.D. 400) in armour mounted on a horse. Twelve miles along the road to the east, on the rocks of Bisitun itself, are other carvings commemorating the life of Darius.

We sampled some cheese and wine in a fly-blown hotel whose name, the Bristol, had aroused false hopes, and then drove out to the local military H.Q. which was sited not far from the deep, azure pool of Tak i Bostan. As if that in itself was not enough, their tents were pitched right under a magnificent face of rock, while up a narrow side valley we caught a fascinating glimpse of peak after peak receding into the wild highlands of Kurdistan. They had been several months in that delightful spot, surrounded by some of the noblest works of God and man, and seemed surprised when we failed to express sympathy with their hard lot. The Brigadier left next day to examine the defences of his trout stream, leaving me, with an officer from the H.Q., to examine the defences of Bisitun.

The mountain consists of a hog's-back rock ridge, broken by a number of towers, and running for several miles in an east-to-west line. A deep notch high up on the Tak i Bostan end of the ridge seemed the obvious jumping-off place for a complete traverse of the mountain, which was the ambitious project I had in mind. It would involve sleeping on top, finishing the traverse on the second day, and 'jumping a lorry' on the main road at the eastern end to get back to Kermanshah in time.

By means of a narrow gorge between the west end of the mountain and the cliffs above Tak i Bostan we penetrated to the back, or north side of Bisitun, where grass and shrub covered the steep slopes stretching up to a scree gully below the notch. A convenient sheep track led us to some sheep folds high up on these slopes before leaving us to find our own way to the scree. Although we were carrying only light loads, food for the night and a blanket, my companion soon began to show signs of distress. Before the scree was reached he decided to turn back. About midday I reached the notch where serious climbing began. The rock was sound and I had taken the precaution of bringing rubber shoes. The towers presented the main interest on a seemingly endless ridge; many of these would not yield to a frontal attack and had to be turned from the south, as the north side is precipitous. It was four o'clock by the time I reached the foot of what I hoped was the final peak. After several unsuccessful attempts to climb it direct I had to go down 500 ft. to find an easier way. As I stood on its summit it seemed to me that another tower half a mile away challenged our superiority, but I had had anough for one day, and so descending a few hundred feet I bivouacked by a patch of snow, lit a fire from a few scarce twigs, and dined off water, chapatties, cheese and chocolate.

There is no more statisfying ending to a climb than to spend the night on the mountain, preferably on the top. The bond between man and mountain, forged in a day-long struggle, never seems so strong as when at its close you seek the meagre shelter of some rocky overhang near the summit with which you have been striving all day to get on terms. But usually this happy consummation is not possible—the weather, the site, the ability to carry even the most modest necessities, conspire to prevent it. But if it be possible, and we spurn the delights of tea, beer, baths, and a warm bed, in favour of cold stones and hard fare, we may remind ourselves, as we lie shivering, that 'abstinence from low pleasures is the only means of meriting or obtaining the higher'. To protest, as we often do, that our pleasures are derived simply from being on the mountain and not from reaching the top, and then, having inadvertently, as it were, arrived on the summit, to hasten down after the briefest of halts, is surely to give ourselves the lie.

Such may have been my reflections as I lay alone on Bisitun watching the shadows creep down the slopes and then stretch across the valley to mingle with the golden haze still lingering on the distant hills. With a companion it would have been perfect. Society has not yet condemned the man who sleeps out alone, but it regards the activities of the solitary climber and the solitary drinker with distaste. The one is unsafe, the other unsocial, and both are likely to lead those who indulge in them into difficulties. A man who habitually climbs alone for preference is liable to be misunderstood. The state of mind of men like Maurice Wilson who died when attempting to climb Mount Everest alone, and the young American, E. F. Farmer, who lost his life similarly on Kangchenjunga, must be regarded with suspicion, and as a confirmation of a part at least of Dr Johnson's dictum, that the solitary mortal is certainly luxurious, probably superstitious, and possibly mad.

In such cases, the disaster, if there is one, involves only the responsible person, unless it happens that a search party has to go out to find the remains; while the rash but orthodox climber involves others besides himself if he comes to grief. The practice of climbing alone teaches self-reliance and caution, though the critic may cavil at the paradox of learning caution while performing an admittedly incautious act. But, from my own experience, it is true that one is far more cautious when alone, even too cautious. No normal person would, I think, climb alone from choice; it is usually the absence of a suitable companion which drives one to solitary climbing and afterwards to its justification: and in wartime the opportune occasion was more frequent than the man. Inaction in the face of fleeting opportunity is a crime, whereas climbing alone rather than not at all is but a venial impropriety.

I was up at five next morning and by seven had reached what I thought was the higher peak. Now, of course, it looked the lower. Without instruments it is often impossible to say which of two points on a ridge is the higher. You can go backwards and forwards from one to the other and still be in doubt. I did not propose doing this. I did not, in fact, propose continuing the traverse. From the point I had now reached its completion might take almost another day. I had no food left and not a great deal of energy so, with an uneasy feeling of having left undone something which I ought to have done, I turned to go. I took a direct line to the road down the south face, which was a mistake. I had forgotten, or I had never noticed, that for a thousand feet above the road there was a long rampart of steep cliffs. Taking the first gully which offered, I was soon brought to a stand by impossible water-worn slabs. I tried the next three or four successive gullies to the west but met with no more success, and it was two o'clock before I got off the mountain and on to the road. The lorry drivers must have been taking their siesta. I trudged the whole length in the hot afternoon sun, buoyed up by the thought of the cold, blue pool of Tak i Bostan.

Here one more was added to my already long but exclusive list of memorable bathes. To qualify, the first essential is for the bather to be really hot and tired. Then, if not sea-water, the water must be clear, deep, and cool (or otherwise have some unusual compensating feature), so that as it closes over one's head the whole body seems to absorb its clean, refreshing goodness. To make this clear, a bathe in the Dead Sea, for example, would not be refreshing but might qualify as unusual. Lastly, and this is important, one must be stark naked, with no clinging costume to impair the unity of body and water.

These exacting conditions were fulfilled on several occasions: in the Atlantic off Kribi on the West Coast after a cycle journey in the Congo; a deep pool in the Indus during a hot march; under the spray of a 100 ft. waterfall in Kashmir where Shipton and I danced wantonly for a full quarter hour; the first dip in the Mediterranean after a month's marching and fighting in the desert; in a glacier pool amongst young icebergs (very memorable but short-lived) during a hot climb in the Dauphiné; and in the lake at Habbaniya where at all times one might enjoy the 'cool silver shock of the plunge in a pool's living water'.

When we returned to Iraq at the end of May the regiment had moved to Habbaniya, the R.A.F. station west of Baghdad. The battle in the Libyan desert was approaching its disastrous climax of 8 June, when we lost two or three hundred tanks, and soon afterwards Tobruk. Losses in 25 pr. batteries, either overrun or cut off in 'boxes' (the origin of the 'hedgehogs' of the Russian front) were so serious that almost every day field regiments were leaving the 9th Army for the desert. Seven days after quitting Habbaniya we joined an Indian Infantry Brigade near Mersa Matruh over 1,000 miles away. In two days we had crossed the Syrian desert, the Jordan, and Palestine. After a much needed halt of one day on the coast for rest and maintenance, we carried on southwards through the Sinai desert to the Canal, jammed in a stream of reinforcements moving down from Syria. We moved on to Cairo and thence westwards along the coast road, all the way jostling against a double-banked stream of traffic escaping from the advancing Germans—administrative units, R.A.F. ground staffs, mobile cinemas, and all the 'cankers of a calm world and a long peace' in the back areas.

There are no mountains in the western desert. There is scarcely a hill until the Green Belt west of Derna is reached, unless one counts Himeimat, a curious excrescence on the edge of the Qattara Depression where we had an observation post in the early days of July before the Germans took it. In the desert the eyes of the mountaineer acquire a troubled look, searching for something that is not there. Stale, flat and unprofitable indeed seems a world which is smooth, wrinkleless, and uninteresting as a death-mask, spacious as the sea but as empty, where no distant line of hills speaks of some yet more distant soaring range, 'a greyer portion of the infinite sky itself . . . permanent above the world'.

In the desert the first six months of 1942 were the heyday of 'Jock' columns, small columns formed as a rule of a battery of 25 pr. guns for hitting power and a troop of 2 pr. anti-tank guns and a battalion or company of infantry to protect them. They were named after their inventor the late Brig. 'Jock' Campbell, a Gunner V.C. In the confusion of the retreat to El Alamein after the fall of Tobruk, such *ad hoc* formations were used extensively with doubtful wisdom or effect to delay the enemy until the El Alamein line was prepared.

Two days after we joined the Infantry Brigade my battery was detached to form such a column, and found itself 'swanning' about in the desert west of the undefended minefield which ran from Mersa Matruh to Siwa Oasis. We had with us a platoon of Punjabi infantry, a troop of 2 pr. guns, and orders to stop 'at all costs' an approaching enemy tank column. As hitherto we had only done this sort of thing against imaginary tanks we moved around in some trepidation, scanning every moving vehicle or cloud of dust with nervous expectancy. The first shots fired came as something of an anti-climax. Although there was a thin screen of armoured cars a few miles to the west between us and the enemy, whenever we halted we invariably brought the guns into action ready to fire. During one of these halts, a vehicle, apparently a British 2 pr. *portée* (a gun carried on a 3-ton lorry), was seen approaching. An officer drove out to exchange news and promptly had his truck (an armoured O.P.) holed by the 2 pr. The whole battery of eight guns incontinently opened up, but the stranger escaped untouched. Our difficulty was that the Germans had captured so many of our vehicles that we could never quite believe what we saw.

Greatly to our relief we got permission by wireless to retire behind the minefield for the night, but we were given to understand that from that position there must be no retreat. The minefield was undefended except for odd columns like our own, each fighting its own battle in complete ignorance of what was happening to its flanks. Next afternoon our observation patrol was driven in and we were attacked by artillery and some thirty tanks, which stood off and shot at us from 'hull down' positions. After three hours' fighting we suffered forty casualties. All our guns were still firing, but so were the enemy's, and it was impossible to see whether we had inflicted any damage or not. It seemed probable that we were on the way to joining the many other batteries which had been overrun or otherwise extinguished. However, at the last minute, as the sun went down and the tanks might be expected to begin to close in, reprieve came in the form of permission to withdraw. We did this successfully under cover of our own smoke screen. We had saved all the guns and it was, therefore, all the more galling to lose one of them during the subsequent night march when it parted company with its trailer. The surprise and chagrin of the sergeant of the gun when, at the first halt, he discovered there was nothing behind his tractor, would in other circumstances have been funny. The other battery of the regiment, some miles north of us, was overrun by German infantry in British lorries and lost four guns.

The next serious engagement took place two days later on 28 June at Fuka after the fall of Mersa Matruh; but this time the whole of our Brigade Group was involved in an effort to stop the advance. The Germans, following their usual practice of attacking towards dusk with the sun behind them, speedily overran the position. Luckily for us the value and scarcity of 25 pr. guns had by now been fully realised by whoever was directing the storm in that corner of the battlefield. The guns were to be saved, and when the enemy tanks were about 500 yards away we received orders to pull out. The whole of the Infantry Brigade and our own Regimental H.Q. were put 'in the bag'.

We went into the 'box' position of Abu Duweis in the extreme south, and marched out again next day when it was discovered that the water supply could easily be cut. From 1 July, for the next fortnight, the battery was again the nucleus of a 'Jock' column supported by a company of the West Yorks. Alarms and excursions at all hours of the day and night, retreats and advances, shelling and being shelled, with on the whole never a dull moment, was the order of our existence. One can laugh now, but at the time the laughter was a bit hollow. I remember driving up to within two hundred yards of a tank, in response to a beckoning figure on the turret, before spotting its black cross; and at another time approaching on *foot* a ridge which we had intended using as an observation post and hearing an enemy vehicle coming up the other side, obviously with the same intention; and I recall how we lay in close leaguer on a dark night watching an enemy column pass a few hundred yards away.

There is no doubt that if a good word can be said for any form of warfare then the war in the Desert, as in the days of small columns, had much to recommend it. There were no long periods of boredom and waiting and no long periods of being harassed in static positions. Provided one had a little experience, a lot of luck, and kept wide awake, then it was possible to have plenty of shooting without being shot at too much in return. Moreover, in those days the 8th Army was small, most of its units were known to one another, and all felt like members of a family; so that when we were having a bad time, or in retreat, there was, as there always should be with good troops, a more comradely helpful spirit abroad than the 'devil take the hindmost' air of a successful advance.

At no time, to descend to a more material plane, did the battery ever live so well as during the days on column. There was no interfering H.Q. to blunt the edge of initiative, to ask silly questions, and to demand irritating, tell-tale returns. Wandering about as we did in a more or less trackless waste, here one minute and gone the next, it may seem odd that we fed so well, or that we were able to draw adequate supplies of petrol, water and ammunition; but so it was, and the Supply services of the Indian Division with whom we served were always able to meet our requirements once we had established contact. We were blessed in having a battery captain without a conscience, a man of small body but Falstaffian mind, who scoured the desert for supply points and overdrew freely from each. It was very easy, because no one really knew where or what units were operating. We no longer wondered whether we had enough milk or sugar for tea with each meal. The amount we drank was limited solely by the amount of water available, and every halt which seemed likely to last longer than twenty minutes was the signal to 'brew up'. The spare vehicles which we had somehow acquired in the course of the retreat were used for fetching water, and the only time we went short was when one of these mistook west for east and was picked up by the enemy.

All good things come to an end. By mid-July the El Alamein line was becoming firmly established, and the days of small mobile columns were over for good. We realised that our free-booting life had ended when we dug ourselves in on Ruweisat Ridge and connected ourselves by telephone to various inquisitive and interfering headquarters from division downwards. Once more life became real and earnest. Rations were counted, ammunition was counted, and when we were not harassing or being harassed by the enemy we were pulled out to train for the mobile warfare we had so recently and reluctantly concluded. Only once, immediately after the break-through in early November, did we come near to recapturing that 'first fine careless rapture'. But our share in the pursuit was shortlived, and we spent a bleak, cheerless winter at El Adem, near Tobruk, clearing the old battlefield of Knightsbridge. In the course of this at least sixty or seventy of our 25 pr. captured that summer were salvaged and made serviceable.

In February we made another long forced march to take part in the battles of Mareth, the Gabes Gap, and the Wadi Akarit, until at length we were detached to support the 19th French Corps in the final stages of the North African campaign.

Tunis and Zaghouan

We took over positions from a unit of our 1st Army. It was pleasing to be treated with the deference they thought due to men of the 8th Army but, since solid pudding is better than empty praise, it was even more gratifying to be given the run of their canteen—to buy real matches that lighted instead of Monkey or Crocodile brands whose heads flew off before they were struck; to smoke English cigarettes instead of the notorious 'V''s; and to eat English chocolate instead of the mottled desiccated substitute from Palestine. We really felt we had at last shaken ourselves clear of the East—both Middle and Near.

The French Corps had little mechanical transport. Their artillery was horse-drawn and their infantry relied on mules, but in the heavily wooded hills of the Djebel Mansour, where they were now fighting, animals were of more use than motors. The infantry of the division on our front consisted of battalions of the Foreign Legion, of Tirailleurs Marocains and Algériens, and of Goums. In the division on our left there were also Senegalese. The Foreign Legion came up to my expectations; they looked tough, lived simply, and observed remarkable discipline. I visited a battalion in the line and was surprised to find that, whenever possible, men sprang up and saluted; a great number of them seemed to be Spaniards. For lunch the officers had coarse bread, dates, and wine—a simple satisfying diet which was, in my opinion, preferable to the white bread, tinned stews, jam and margarine of our army, besides being healthier, cheaper, and no trouble to prepare.

The Goums were irregular Arab troops, mostly recruited from a tribe called the Shaamba, who are hereditary enemies of the Touaregs. They draw pay, but find their own food and clothing—a system which possibly accounts for their informal appearance and their predatory habits. 'Find' is the right word. Their officers and N.C.O.'s, whose job must be no sinecure, were French. These troops were not often employed in set battle pieces, but were held in leash and turned loose in the event of a break-through—'Cry havoc and let slip the Goums' was possibly the Corps Commander's order when he thought the situation ripe for exploitation. Whether it was true or not I cannot say, but it was common talk that for a prisoner they received 100 francs and for an ear 25 francs. An ear is an ear, whether German, Italian, or British, and 25 francs is 25 francs, so one had to exercise more than ordinary care when operating with Goums.

The attack on the Djebel Mansour went according to plan and resulted in an advance by the whole Corps to a line south of Pont du Fahs, where we occupied as usual the flat plain and the Germans the high ridge. It was difficult enough to find gun positions which were not in view from this ridge, but behind it towered the rugged limestone massif of Zaghouan, nearly 4,000 ft. high, which dominated the country far and wide. The French put in another very gallant but ineffective attack against the ridge and the foothills of Zaghouan, but it was not until the Germans withdrew, as a result of pressure by the 1st Army on the left, that we advanced beyond Pont du Fahs to come into action in what was to be our last position in the African campaign.

As we moved along the straight road which led through Depienne to Tunis, the wide, flat, cultivated plain on either hand seemed uncommonly devoid of cover. At last we spotted a winding shallow wadi, deep enough to conceal the guns, if not to hide their flash. We dived into it like rabbits into a burrow, dispersed the vehicles, and returned to the road to await the coming of the guns. Their arrival was the signal for considerable shell-fire, probably directed from O.P.'s on the lower slopes of Zaghouan, which now frowned at us on our right flank. So long as we remained here in action any movement of vehicles in or out of the wadi was discouraged by both sides. The wadi soon became uncomfortably crowded, for we were not the only ones to covet the shelter of this natural trench, so that when a shell did fall fairly inside someone usually got hit. Meantime the French on our right were trying to force their way along the foot of the mountain to the small town of Zaghouan, but for the last two days there had been little indication of any progress.

However, in conjunction with the general allied assault, another attack was put in beyond Depienne, and as early as ten o'clock on the morning of 12 May, it was clear that the enemy was going back. Thin columns of smoke from burning vehicles and mushroom-shaped clouds from exploding ammunition dumps could be seen behind his lines. At dawn the regiment had fired a barrage in support of a battalion of the Foreign Legion, but now the battle had rolled on and, as yet, no orders had come for us to advance.

At last, towards midday, came the welcome signal 'Prepare to advance'. Skirting Depienne, as the road was mined, we soon crossed the Zaghouan-Tunis road and ascended the two hills that the French had taken earlier in the day. A couple of long Russian 5 cm. anti-tank guns, some weapon pits and a machine gun or two, marked the first enemy defences. There was no one about, dead or living, but a mile or two farther on the scene was lively enough. From three Valentine tanks, part of the small tank force used by the French in their attack, smoke was ascending cheerfully, while the crews stood around discussing the phenomenon. A stream of Senegalese infantry with pack mules was moving up. Below, in a narrow valley, were three abandoned batteries, one of captured 25 pr. and two of 10.5 cm.'s. The guns had been destroyed, and their vehicles were still smouldering. Strewn around was the usual litter of clothing, blankets, ammunition, rifles, food, equipment, letters and newspapers. The Senegalese loitered hopefully on passing these riches, but the French N.C.O.'s would stand no nonsense. A short burst from a Tommy gun was directed at the feet of the loiterers as a hint to keep moving. Across the valley a white flag was being waved anxiously.

Reports from our forward armoured O.P. indicated that all resistance had ceased except in Zaghouan itself. The French wanted us to push a troop forward to deal with it, but this was unnecessary as it was within range of all our sixteen guns from where we were. But as surrender was in the air it seemed a pity to fire needlessly on those pleasant white walls lying at the foot of the mountain.

We dropped our trails more or less where we stood. My choice of site for Regimental H.Q. was possibly influenced by the presence of two German field kitchens, one with its copper full of a stew ready for dishing up, the other containing a slightly overdone rice pudding. By late evening the Germans in Zaghouan had come to heel, but the French Commander mistrusted them, and insisted on our remaining at a half-hour's notice. Naturally, since coming into those parts from the 8th Army front near the coast I had had my eye on Zaghouan, the only mountain I had seen since Bisitun. Many long broken limestone ridges help to form a striking mass which, on the north and west sides, rises abruptly from the Tunis plain. It seemed to be a case of now or never; we were only 3 miles away; tomorrow we might be anywhere.

One of the battery commanders, who was full of enterprise though not a mountaineer, was of the same opinion. Promising to be back soon after dawn, we got the C.O.'s permission to absent ourselves for the night. A well-graded track, or even road, appeared to lead to a white building perched jauntily on the face not 1,000 ft. below the main ridge. George said we would take his Jeep, and suggested starting at midnight. I said we would start at nine, one of the only two sensible decisions we made that night. The other was to take the German equivalent of a Verey light pistol. The big idea behind this was to have a Brock's benefit on the summit to celebrate the victory. Even while we discussed ways and means, coloured signal smoke was going up from all directions. This was customary in the desert after a successful action. The Germans were equipped on a lavish scale with all manner of light signals which our men delighted to fire off when they got hold of them. I was soon equipped with a captured pistol and a supply of coloured signals.

At 9 p.m. the Jeep proved to be a non-starter, and obviously the 15 cwt. truck we had to use would only take us to the foot. To uphold my principles I pointed out that this was far more satisfactory than being driven almost to the top. George was more honest. He heartily regretted the absence of the Jeep.

I was rather worried about mines, for the French were less experienced and less particular about removing these than the sappers of the 8th Army; but we got safely to the main road and soon passed through Zaghouan behind a stream of captured lorries full of Germans. A mile beyond, following a road which appeared to lead round the mountain, we met some Goums. They had with them an enormous Boche who was not unnaturally apprehensive of the green turbans and bandit-like accoutrements of his captors. Our appeal to their French N.C.O. was immediately successful. His patrol had just crossed the mountain and he would put us on the track. A few hundred yards on we parked our truck while the N.C.O. pointed out a rough mule track leading upward into the gloom of the woods at the foot of the slope. 'You can't go wrong', or words to that effect. 'Montez toujours, toujours montez', was his parting admonition. The aptness of his words impressed me, so we decided to adopt them as our watchword for the night.

At 11 p.m. we started climbing. At hour later the moon went down, and the bridle path lost its usefulness, for it disappeared over a col. This was evidently the route by which the Goums had crossed from the south to the north side of the mountain. Another well-marked track led off to the right, but it was impossible to tell whether it trended up or down. George, whose mind seemed to run tourist-like on tracks and roads, thought it would lead us by 'une pente insensible' to the summit, and I was weak-minded enough to consent to try it. After a good fifteen minutes at a cracking pace, for we were going downhill, even George admitted that we were not abiding by our watchword. Back we went to the col, and this time struck boldly up the slope.

We soon found there was some difference in moving on a path and moving on an unknown boulder-strewn hillside in the dark. Presently the slope narrowed to a ridge whence sharp rocky teeth loomed up vaguely against the black sky. It pleased us to think we were now on the summit ridge, but from what I could remember of that, having only seen it from some distance away in daylight, I had misgivings. However, as always in such cases, when one feels the country is not at all it should be, we could hope for much from time and chance. The east side of our ridge now began to fall away sheer. Keeping as far from danger as possible we groped our way along until brought up short by a chasm of unknown width and depth. The firing of a success signal was perhaps premature, nevertheless a red Verey light soared into the air disclosing, some 20 ft. below us, a knife-edge ridge, the only link with the opposite side of the chasm. Such a questionable place at such an hour in the morning called for consideration and another light. Suitably enough this one was green. The revolting colour it lent to the surrounding rock and my companion's face, gazing curiously into the depths, tipped the scale in favour of retreat.

The turning of this obstacle cost us some loss of height and several more cartridges. Some of these broke into pleasing clusters of stars, but these were not of much value as pathfinders. I have since learnt all about German light signals. By a simple system you can tell by touch, in the dark, the various colours and types. A white flare has the edge of the cartridge base half milled, green is smooth, red is fully milled. The 'Sternbundel', a white rocket bursting into stars, has six studs on the top of the cartridge. The 'Fallschirm', or parachute flare (which would have been just the thing for us), has a parachute in relief on the top. There is also a 'Pfeifpatrone', or whistling flare, which has a point on the top. Unluckily we had none of these. A shriek of dismay from the light as it hovered over the chasm would have been an artistic touch.

This gap or cut-off was the first and worst of several others, but using our light pistol freely, we reached the highest point of the ridge. It was 4 a.m. now and the sky was perceptibly lighter. Across a valley we could see the outline of the summit ridge, and the two familiar rock towers at the top. We used the last of our lights finding a way down into the valley, and then we wearily climbed a steep slope to the foot of the final tower. Up this a mild scramble led to a wooden beacon marking the top. A tricolour flag was fluttering proudly in the dawn wind, and at the foot of the beacon lay an unexploded 75 mm. shell. There was no Boche O.P. on the top; most of these were on the lower ridges, but evidently some French gunner had felt it incumbent on him to drop a round on the top. As a gunner this interested me, for to land a shell on such a place is extremely difficult.

We lay on the top exhausted by the night's work. I ate some 'Knackebrot', the German ration biscuit, each packet of which carried a slip of paper eulogising the properties of the biscuit and beginning with the rhetorical question 'Kamerad, kennst du Knackebrot?' It is, in my opinion, very good, much better than our own. George was past eating, even if he had shared my passion for Knackebrot, which he did not. Away to the east some battery fired fitfully for a time and then stopped—the last shots of the African campaign. I should like to be able to add that far to the south the pine forests of the Djebel Mansour, which we and the French had cleared so gallantly a week ago, lay dark and sombre, that eastwards the sea threw back the rays of the rising sun, and that to the north the Tunisian plains stretched like a carpet of green and gold to the black olive groves and white walls of distant Carthage; but unluckily a blanket of cloud hid everything.

The rest is mere disillusionment. From below the tower fifteen minutes' walking took us to the road we had seen from below. Our 15 cwt. truck would almost certainly have made the grade. An hour's zigzagging down another mule track brought us to the truck, which we found had been pillaged unmercifully by the Goums. The driver, not unexpectedly perhaps, had chosen to sleep during the night, and roving bands of Goums, who had already found numerous abandoned enemy vehicles, had acted on the wise and plausible assumption that ours was merely one more. One might say of the Goums, as Stonewall Jackson said of his Texans: 'The hens have to roost mighty high when the Texans are about.'

CHAPTER NINE

Albania

Their habits are predatory—all are armed.   Byron

IT may be an odd view, but I think one drawback to the army is that promotion is almost inevitable. No one is allowed to remain where he is; once having set foot on the slippery slope of promotion he must either go up or down. That is possibly why so many good men refuse to accept a stripe, and prefer to remain in a position of important permanence at the bottom. In the Artillery the command of a battery is the best that life affords. It is a post a right-minded gunner would wish to hold for ever; once beyond that he feels that it is a case of 'farewell the tranquil mind, farewell content'. Even at the head of a battery he still has both feet on the ground, in close contact with his men and the seamy side of war; he is still on the right side of the gulf which separates those who plan from those who act, and which is crossed immediately he becomes part of a Headquarters—even the modest headquarters of a regiment. From the throne to the scaffold is a short step; short and equally decided is the transition to Second-in-Command of a regiment—the ultimate end of the senior Battery Commander. Though the appointment carries with it an extra 6d. a day, it is the equivalent of the Chiltern Hundreds so far as any active responsibility is concerned. It is a stagnant pool, from which in the fulness of time and chance he may be fished up to command a regiment himself, but the unlucky or unworthy may float there for long enough gathering seaweed and barnacles. Having drawn my 6d. a day in such an uncongenial post for several months I was prompted to answer an advertisement in General Routine Orders, which, in the Army, corresponds to the Agony Column of *The Times*. Volunteers were wanted for Special Service of a kind which involved almost complete independence. Better to reign in Hell than serve in Heaven, I thought, as I wrote out my application. Various qualifications were essential, or at least desirable, but unlike the alluring posts offered in the advertisements of civil life, no capital was required.

So it came about that one moonlight night in August 1943, after a month's training, I found myself flying over the Mediterranean bound for Albania in company with a sapper sergeant and a corporal wireless operator. My known predilection for mountains had possibly accounted for my being sent to Albania—reputedly a mountainous country. We counted ourselves fortunate in having been dispatched so promptly, but even so we feared there would be little for us to do but dissuade the Albanians from massacring the helpless Italians, and to arrange for the transport of prisoners back to Italy. Italy was already on its knees and appeared likely to throw in the towel at any moment.

There was already one British mission in Albania. This had moved up from Greece in the previous May, and we were to be dropped to them before proceeding to our own particular area. Two other independent missions were also in our aircraft. We had an uneventful flight, but if there is any charm in flying at night, which I doubt, it is quite spoilt if you know that presently you will have literally to take a leap in the dark. However, the pilot of the Halifax found the signal fires with a precision which was admirable or disgusting according to one's feelings at the time. At the energetic prompting of an efficient dispatcher we dropped through the large hole in the floor and,

GENERAL MAP OF ALBANIA

shortly after, we had all landed safely but rather wide of the target. We must, I think, have been dropped at over 2,000 ft. and consequently drifted too much. The usual height for dropping is from 600 to 800 ft., but in hilly country at night there is no doubt a strong tendency for the pilot, unless he is supremely confident, to maintain a liberal safety margin.

This mission to which we were dropped, consisted of a major and a captain. They had been playing a lone hand in Albania for three months and were, I think, as pleased to see us as we were to arrive. We had a warm reception, and having walked from the dropping ground to their village headquarters, we sat down to fried eggs and sweet champagne at three in the morning. My principal feeling was one of intense satisfaction at having at length got back to Europe, even though it was enemy-occupied, after so long in the wilderness. I could almost have hugged the ground.

We spent a few days there organising the mule transport to take us to our respective areas, and acquiring some very necessary knowledge of the situation. If it is true that 'happy is the nation that has no history', then Albania must be one of the unhappiest. Her history is an unbroken record of invasion, oppression, and wrong by the Turk, Greek, Austrian, Serbian, Bulgarian, and German. Few countries can have been so ravaged and so subjected to oppression at the hands of its stronger neighbours, and yet have retained its will for independence unbroken as did the Albanians for 500 years, from the time when Skenderbeg, their great national hero, first made headway against the Turk. After the 1914–18 war, after various interested countries had been forced to relinquish their claims. Albania was declared an independent Republic. The first President was Zog, a landowner and politician, who in 1922 was proclaimed King. Mussolini had long had an eye on Albania—there are small deposits of oil and chrome ore there—and in the years before the war had by means of loans acquired a considerable hold. In Holy Week of 1939 he presented Zog with an ultimatum which, if accepted, would have made Albania an Italian colony. The ultimatum was rejected. On Good Friday the Italians invaded the country and Zog fled to England.

The country can be divided socially and physically into northern, central, and southern Albania. In the north, which is wild, mountainous, and therefore the most backward, feudalism is blended with a clan organisation, and the Roman Catholics outnumber the Moslems. Central Albania is more open and less mountainous; the great families are less powerful, and most of the land is in the hands of small farmers with a leavening of country squires. Roman Catholics are few, and there are more Moslems than Orthodox Christians. As Tirana, the capital, is in central Albania, it is here that communications are the most developed; but there are no railways[1] anywhere in Albania and not many motor-roads. South Albania is mountainous also, but the mountains follow a simple plan. Two wide open valleys running from south-east to north-west provide an easy through route, and since the frontier

---

1 The fact that there were no railways in Albania was not so widely known as it might have been; for Base were in the habit of sending us explosive charges designed specially for blowing them up.

between Greece and Albania is not naturally difficult for travellers, the south is open to Greek influence; this may be one reason why the people there are the most progressive, the most educated, and the most democratic. Here also the Moslems outnumber the Christians. For Albania as a whole the proportions are 70% Orthodox (not the Greek Orthodox Church, for the Albanian Christians have their own head). But in Albania religious tolerance is the rule and nationality comes before religion. As Byron observed, 'The Greeks hardly regard them as Christians or the Turks as Moslems.' One reason for this is that, except in the central coastal plains, where there are some fanatics, the majority of Moslems belong to the Bektashi sect, or reformed Moslems, which is a philosophy rather than a religion, whose members neither observe the Moslem fasts nor abstain from strong drink. Albanian is an Indo-European language of unknown origin. The vocabulary, in which there are many Latin words, is largely borrowed. There are two different dialects, spoken by the Ghegs of north and the Tosks of the south, the dividing line being the Skumbi river south of Tirana. As with all other languages I was dismayed by its difficulty, but more so than usual.

At the time of the Italian invasion, when King Zog fled and left the country to its fate, the Albanians, in the absence of any leader or rallying point, offered little resistance to the invader. But after the initial shock of surprise had worn off, a resistance movement began to take shape, at the instigation, as in most of the invaded countries, of a few Communists. This became known as the L.N.C. or 'Levizja Nacional Clirimtare'—National Liberation Movement—and embraced all classes, all political opinions, all religions, and a good three-quarters of the people of south Albania. It identified itself with the Allies against Fascism and Nazism, and had for its first objective the freeing of Albania from Italians and Germans, and for its second the establishing of a 'free, independent, democratic Albania'. For these aims they were prepared to sacrifice everything. Unhappily, as in other Balkan countries, one such single-minded movement was not enough. There were others who looked beyond the immediate struggle, who, it could be argued, paid more regard to the material welfare of Albania. The principal rival party to the L.N.C. was the Balli Kombetar, or National Front, which regarded the Greeks and Yugo-Slavs as the real enemies and preferred, therefore, to husband its resources until the war was over. Under an outward show of resistance they were prepared to temporise with the Axis powers, and were not willing to incur suffering by an unnecessary display of zeal in a cause which would probably triumph without the aid of Albania. If it did not triumph so much the better for them, who would then be in a position to crush their rivals. There was a third group, of little importance in 1943 but becoming more prominent later, which comprised supporters of the absent King Zog. They too were chiefly concerned with party, and were not prepared to antagonise the Germans to please the Allies. Both these latter parties took Mr Facing-both-ways as their model. They were ready to help us if it could be done without embroiling themselves with the Germans, and they would co-operate with the Germans up to a point short of offending us. Unfortunately our official policy, the guiding principle of which was to avoid the appearance of taking sides in local politics, enabled them to do this, and both received our support without doing anything to earn it.

In August of that year there was suspicion but no open hostility between the two major groups, while Abas Kupi, who later became leader of the Zoggists, was still a member of the L.N.C. It was obvious, however, that their differences were irreconcilable and must soon become wider. Meanwhile, the British Government, anxious to remain neutral in these local squabbles and to assist anyone who professed to be willing to kill Germans or Italians, proposed having British liaison officers with all parties with the laudable intention of persuading them to sink their differences and to unite in the common cause. It was the peculiar tragedy of Albania that this well-meaning policy was persisted in after it had become clear to most observers that these differences were fundamental, and even when only one of the parties was fighting and suffering while the other two were either actively hostile or feebly neutral.

In the week I spent with the mission at Stylle, near Korca, it became evident to me that the L.N.C. alone had war aims similar to our own, and were ready to go to all lengths to attain them. Accordingly I elected to go to the Gjinokastre area which promised to become the centre of the L.N.C. movement. The small mule train necessary to carry our wireless stores and kits was provided by some nearby Vlachs. These interesting semi-nomadic people, who are widely distributed over the Balkans, call themselves Romani and speak a langauge akin to Roumanian. They are muleteers by nature, horse-copers by intuition, and live the life of shepherds, travelling in the spring with vast flocks of sheep to the high uplands, where they pass the summer, and then in the autumn returning to their scattered settlements in southern Albania and the Greek Epirus. Showing no interest in politics or war, they seem to be the one unchanging, untroubled race in the Balkans which knows enough to meddle only with its own affairs and to let the great world go by.

Our cross-country journey took three days. It was pleasant to stroll along behind our sleek, active little mules through the sun-drenched countryside, stopping perhaps at a village where we were elaborately entertained, or perhaps with some Vlachs who pressed on us maize bread and bowls of 'kos', similar to the Bulgarian 'yoghourt'. In a village the entertainment always began with 'meze'—a sort of grace before meat consisting usually of soft white cheese and 'raki', which is the fiery brandy they distil from grape juice, plums mulberrries, or even figs, often flavoured with aniseed. This was followed, after a formal interval, by eggs, mutton, pastry dishes of various kinds, and concluded with thick sweet Turkish coffee. For a few leks we bought luscious figs and bunches of grapes, and once we were made free of a tree laden with the largest mulberrries I have ever seen—from this orgy the three of us emerged stained from head to foot a rich and royal purple.

There was no sign of the war until we reached the town of Permet; but of past wars there were many, for in this troubled country there are few places free from scars. The village of Frasheri, for example, which we passed had been ravaged by the Greeks in 1914 in company with 150 other Albanian villages; and on the highest mountains one would find stone sangars and heaps of spent cartridges fired by the Greeks in the campaign against the Italians. Permet itself had suffered in that campaign, and had recently been burnt again by the Italians as a reprisal for some partisan action. It was now garrisoned by Italians who occupied newly built barracks.

The town lies in the Vjose valley on the motor-road from Jannina in Greece to Berat. In addition to this there is the road from Jannina to Korca; another to Gjinokastre, Tepeleni, and Valona; and a coast road from Saranda to Valona. There are but two short east-west roads; one linking Tepeleni with the Permet road, and one linking Saranda with Gjinokastre. This scarcity of motor-roads made Southern Albania an almost ideal country for partisan warfare. Enemy garrisons were confined to towns on the roads, while the country in between was more or less under partisan control; and the necessary strengthening of garrisons and the collecting of mule transport were ample warning signs that a drive through partisan territory was in preparation. The partisans would have been even more favoured had there been extensive forest or thick scrub, but most of the south is singularly bare of trees. There are patches of oak, pine, and beech forest between Korca and Frasheri, but eastwards the forest gradually thins out to stunted oak scrub, so that west of Vjose one finds a country of high bare ridges where wood of any sort is of almost famine scarcity.

In order to avoid the Permet garrison, we crossed the road and forded the river about a mile above the town. From the west bank a steep stony path zigzags up to the 6,000 ft. pass over the Nemercke range into the upland valley of Zagori. Dawn overtook us still below the pass. We halted for a moment to look down upon the fertile flats on the banks of the Vjose, the blackened skeleton of Permet half-hidden among cypress trees, and the blatantly unscathed Italian barracks inside their barbed-wire perimeter.

On the pass we had to give an account of ourselves to the partisan band or 'cheta' on guard there. With one exception they seemed suspicious of our *bona fides*. The exception was a voluble little man, not unlike Charlie Chaplin, who had once owned a restaurant in Tirana, and who now attached himself to us, unbidden, in the role of chef to the mission. Though not unmindful of his own wages and trade perquisites, he filled this post very satisfactorily for three or four months. His pastry was ethereal, his soups substantial; and the mission at Shepr, where we lived, earned a well-deserved reputation for good fare. His long and successful reign came to a sudden end with the discovery in his house of various bits of parachute silk. For this he was condemned to be shot. In saving him, which I did with difficulty, I acted from purely altruistic motives, for it was unfortunately impossible to re-employ him.

The village of Shepr where we established ourselves consisted of about one hundred houses. It lay on the eastern slope of the wide and rather barren valley of Zagori, between the long, level, almost unbroken ridges of Nemercke and Lunxheries which rise to over 6,000 ft. The floor of the valley is about 3,000 ft. above the sea. Some 15 miles to the south is the Greek frontier, and a few of the villages south of Shepr have a Greek population.

The Greeks are in the habit of making extravagant claims to most of southern Albania, including Gjinokastre, Korca, and Valona, but it appeared to me that a very slight adjustment of the present frontier or a small transfer of population is the most they can fairly ask.

About 5 miles south of Shepr the Lunxheries mountains are cut by a wild and difficult gorge, by which a paved mule track leads down to the Dhrino valley and Gjinokastre, about six hours' march away. The people of Zagori are mainly Orthodox Christians, and most villages enjoy the blessing of a venerable time-mellowed stone church of a uniform pattern, with an arched cloister on one side, and a high tower of which the upper part and the belfry are built in the form of three open arches, one above the other. The houses are of stone with stone roofs and are enclosed by a high wall. Large double wooden doors under a tiled porch lead into the flagged courtyard and the stables, which usually occupy the ground floor of the house. Stone stairs lead to the living rooms above. The old alluvial fan on which Shepr stood had been built up into terraced fields where wheat and maize were grown in rotation, while in the village itself were many fruitful terraced vineyards and orchards. However dirty the narrow alleyways between the high walls might be, there was no dirt inside the houses, and over the whole village lay an air of pride, modest well-being, and content.

We hired an empty house for one gold sovereign a month, and there awaited the arrival of the partisan command—the Shtab—which was then located at a village called Kuc, south of Valona, two days' march from Shepr. The whole area, from the Greek border north to Valona, and east as far as Frasheri, was called the 1re Zone. The commander was Islam Radowicke, a middle-aged, competent, cautious soldier, liked and respected by all, but no Communist. His political commissar, for they were organised on the Russian model, was Badri Spahiu, a man younger than Islam, and a fiery patriot and Communist. Both were ex-officers of the Italian-trained Albanian army. Badri's house in Gjinokastre had already been burnt and his wife and child forced to lead an unsettled precarious life between various villages. He was able and tireless, and spoke forcibly and persuasively, using a wealth of quiet gesture. Albanians, like Irishmen, seem to have a natural genius for fighting and generalship. Most of them have carried a rifle from their youth up, and until fairly recent times the national pastimes of brigandage and blood-feuds necessarily made the survivors cunning in the use of ground and cover. They served as valued mercenaries and janissaries with the Turks, from whose ranks came Skenderbeg, the Albanian Alexander, Taut Gaiola, the great Pasha of Constantinople, and Mehemet Ali of Egypt. We see them serving under the miserable Ferdinand of Naples, and against him in Sicily, where both before and after the arrival of Garibaldi and his Thousand the Albanian colony played a part fully in keeping with Byron's estimate of their race, 'faithful in peril, indefatigable in service'.

At this early stage the partisan movement was weak. Apart from the arming and equipping of the 1st Brigade by the mission then near Korca, nothing had been done. Nearly every man had a rifle, captured, stolen, or inherited, which might be of Italian, German, Greek, Russian, Austrian, or French origin; but except for a few Italian light machine-guns there were no automatic weapons. The riflemen wore broad leather belts supported by cross straps in which they could carry 150–200 rounds. Almost as serious as the lack of automatics was the shortage of boots. Normally Albanians wear very stout hand-made shoes with slightly turned-up toes which slip easily on and off, or a sandal with a rubber-tyred sole. Now there were neither the leather, the tyres, or the cobblers to turn out footwear in the required quantities. In the 1re Zone there were about 3,000 poorly-armed men organised in five groups—Berat, Mesoplik, Kurvelesh, Malakastra, and Zagori—and in addition to the 'active' battalions, there were reserve battalions which only turned out in the event of a levy *en masse*. The 1st Brigade of Korca was the forerunner of some dozen mobile brigades which were recruited from the active battalions as arms and ammunition became available. Just before I left the country in May 1944 I attended the inauguration ceremony of the 8th Brigade, by which time the L.N.C. forces of southern Albania were believed to comprise nearly 20,000 men, most of them well armed, organised as a Division under a General Staff.

Even in those early days I was impressed by the camaraderie and *esprit de corps* of the various battalions and 'chetas', the easy-going relations between men and leaders, and the severity of the discipline. For immorality, theft, looting, or even failing to put into the common pool what had been captured from the enemy, the penalty was death. On one occasion five boys of Shepr who had found and sold some drugs, which they had picked up near the dropping ground long after they had been dropped, were sentenced to be shot. Only their youth and the strenuous pleading of every family in the village saved them. And one afternoon, just before I left, three men were tried in Shepr, two for immorality and one for stealing cigarette papers from a comrade. The British officer who happened to arrive that day to relieve me had to step over the bodies lying in a lane by the church where they had been shot. He reached our house perceptibly shaken, wondering among what sort of cut-throats he had fallen. Military offences were punished by disarming and dismissal—a disgrace worse than death—and such was the feeling of dedication to a noble cause that they were willing to accept this Draconian code.

To show their boundless admiration for the Russian army, and to distinguish them from the Balli Kombetar (or Balli as we called them), the partisans of the L.N.C. wore a red star in their caps. Otherwise they looked like any other Albanians—perhaps a trifle more travel-stained. They seldom shaved but, on the other hand, they did not grow beards. Later we were able to clothe most of them in battle-dress, but for the time being the townsmen worse something 'off the peg' and the peasants their rough natural woollen homespun, with trousers like badly cut Jodhpurs. A few had German uniforms, more had Italian, and after the Italian collapse the appearance of partisans in white naval rig with straw hats added a touch of originality to a far from uniform body. The unalterable and obligatory form of salutation was 'Death to Fascists', to which the reply was 'Liberty to the People', or in Albanian 'Vdekje Fashizmit—Liri Popullit'. This rigid formula helped to smell out anyone of Balli tendencies, whose own particular slogan was 'Death to the Traitors', by which they meant the L.N.C.

The partisans had little to occupy them when not on patrol. They sat about endlessly but animatedly discussing the war, politics, or the next meal, smoking hand-rolled cigarettes, and singing. Their songs, which were all about partisans, were melancholy, tuneful, and pleasing. When in particularly good heart they danced. This always took the form of a ring dance in which a file of men, of any length, imitated the slow steps and actions of a leader who flourished a handkerchief and crooned an improvised topical catch which the chorus emphasised at the appropriate place. If any women joined in they formed a separate ring. I enjoyed watching the comical steps and actions of the leaders of these dances.

There were a number of young girls with the partisans, some working as clerks or interpreters, some in the ranks. The arms which they carried were symbolic, for their job in action was to tend the wounded. Those who were clerks led a busy life, for, as I discovered later with the Italian partisans, the amount of paper circulated would not have discredited a real army. A duplicating machine which I procured for them considerably augmented the ammunition supply for this war of words. Having so much time on their hands the partisans, I thought, might well have benefited the country and improved their already good relations with the villagers by helping in the fields. But they left all the ploughing and the fetching of wood and water to their wives, sisters and mothers; for, like most amateur soldiers, they considered that fighting alone was consistent with dignity. In Albania the women's place is fully on a level with the men's, and they earn it by doing most, if not all, of the work.

CHAPTER TEN

The Italians Collapse, the Germans Arrive

I first saw the partisans in action in a night attack on Libohov, a small town on the opposite side of the Dhrino valley to Gjinokastre. A garrison of fifty Italians lived there in the Citadel, and it was the home of many prominent Balli. My part in the action was to prevent the arrival of reinforcements from Gjinokastre by mining the earth road which connects Libohov with the main road, but from what I had heard of the Italians in Albania, the last thing which the garrison of Gjinokastre would be likely to do was to stir from the barracks after dark.

We found Islam Radowicke with two or three hundred partisans lying concealed on a hot afternoon in the wooded bed of the river which cuts through the gorge from Zagori to the Dhrino valley. The strictest precautions to avoid observation from the air were enforced. This was, of course, sound practice, but the Italian Air Force had done little to deserve the exaggerated respect shown to it by partisans. One bomb had been dropped on Shepr, and the effects of it were still felt. I remember how puzzled I was on the morning of our arrival, when the only man in sight, to whom I wanted to speak, persisted in cowering flat in a maize field. The hum of an aeroplane a good 10 miles off was responsible for his odd behaviour. But aeroplanes could not be entirely discounted. The mission at Stylle told us how on one occasion an Italian plane had followed one of ours over their dropping ground and off-loaded a bomb on to the signal fires, to the great surprise of all concerned. The Germans frequently used an aeroplane during their drives, and my successor at Shepr, who was living outside the village in tents, had his camp bombed. Lt. Col. Leake, who was on a visit from our H.Q. in Italy at the time, was killed there.

At dusk, after a meal of bread and cheese, the men filed out of the river bed for the three hours' march to Libohov. In spite of the secrecy imposed prior to this night attack, someone had warned the Italians who were waiting for us inside their fort. Their morale was known to be low, and perhaps the partisans thought that if sufficient noise was made the walls of the Citadel might oblige

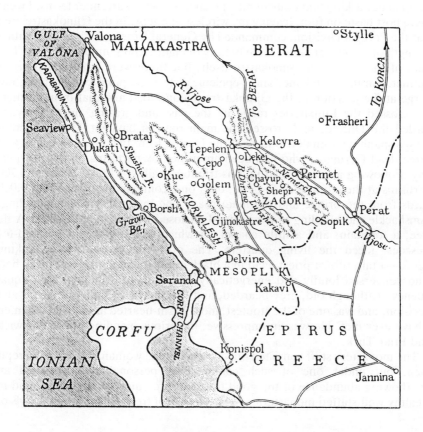

like those of Jericho. A hot fire was opened with all the rifles and the few machine-guns available, to which the Italians replied with machine-guns and mortars. The darkness was intense, but with so much stuff flying about some of us who were not behind stone walls were bound to be hit. Six of the partisans were killed. The bugle sounded a charge, the attackers closed in through the town towards the fortress, set alight the houses of the most-hated Balli, and withdrew in good order before dawn. It was a bold but quite futile effort.

A grim scene was enacted next morning in the little village of Labove on the way home. Under the mellow red brick walls of an old Byzantine church, one of the partisans who had died of wounds was buried. Badri delivered a funeral harangue. As he finished, a trembling wretch was led to the open grave and almost without warning shot to death by the partisans standing round. He was a spy captured in Libohov during the night.

After this abortive action Radowicke returned to Kuc and Badri to a place called Cepo, 6 miles down the Dhrino valley from Gjinokastre, where a subsidiary headquarters was established. On 8 September, preceded by only twenty-four hours' warning, there came the news of the Italian collapse, and orders for me to get from them all the arms I could by fair means or foul—even purchase was allowed. Having dispatched a letter to the Italian commander asking him to meet me at Cepo to discuss surrender terms, I went there post haste on foot, leaving my wireless at Shepr. In the Gjinokastre area was the Perugia Division, commanded by General Ernesto Chiminello, with a strength of 5,000 men and a mule battery of eight 75 mm. mountain guns. The bulk of these were at Gjinokastre itself, but there were small garrisons at Permet, Saranda, Delvine, and Tepeleni, a strategic point commanding the gorge at the junction of the Gjinokastre-Valona road and that from Permet.

I crossed the Lunxheries range by the pass and grazing alp of Chayup, forded the Dhrino, and crossed the main road in daylight. On a concrete bridge spanning a small tributary of the Dhrino were two German trucks and three dead Germans, who had been ambushed by partisans on the previous day. Following an earth road up this tributary valley, I found Badri and 200 partisans at the monastery of Cepo, built on a commanding spur about 3,000 yards from the bridge and the main road. The monastery was a rambling, ramshackle old building in a courtyard enclosed by a high stone wall. A fig tree, a fountain, and a little chapel, in which were some old uncared-for frescoes, faced the living quarters. The presiding genius was a striking figure—a tall, robust priest, clad in a black cassock and a high stiff black hat, who conversed loudly and energetically in Greek or Albanian with equal fluency. Although old, grey-bearded, and spectacled he radiated vigour and decision, and was one of the stoutest, most warm-hearted and hospitable men I have ever met. He was an impressive, imperious blending of Mr Pickwick and Friar Tuck.

The monastery staff consisted only of an old mad woman and a few decrepit men, but under one of such commanding personality it provided an overflowing abundance of the good things of life equal to anything found in wealthy well-staffed monasteries—great hunks of fresh wheat bread, bowls of white liquescent cheese, honey from the hundred hives lining the south wall, figs as big as pears, grapes, wine, raki. Fortunately the Albanians take no breakfast—they say their stomachs are too coated with chalk to function properly at that early hour—so we could face with perfect equanimity the rich oily stew served up twice a day in an enamel bowl the size of a baby's bath.

General Chiminello proved elusive. He failed to attend a meeting we arranged halfway between Gjinokastre and Cepo, having been frightened, he said, by the presence of a Balli patrol on the road. Meanwhile the leaders of the Baeli Kombetar were in touch with him demanding his surrender to them in the name of the Provisional Albanian Government of Tirana. At length our patience was exhausted and on the 14th we all marched by night towards Gjinokastre. The partisans, whose numbers had swollen to 500, took up positions in a ravine about 1,000 yards from the northern perimeter of the barracks, and Badri and I with a small escort climbed up to the fortified outpost ridge and passed through the wire under a white flag. From the ridge, which was strongly held, we looked down on the fine modern barracks, the vehicles and guns neatly parked. Our mouths watered, like Blücher's at the sight of London. The company holding the ridge were bewildered but friendly. They conducted us to the General's office, which was situated on the main road. We were afraid of the arrival at any time of Germans from Jannina or Valona, in fact some German trucks had stopped at the barracks the previous day, so the first request I made of the General was to take us somewhere where we could talk without fear of being surprised. He was a tall, thin, weak-looking man. With him were five of his colonels. They were all very smart, in shiny black riding boots and much beribboned uniforms. In a distant corner of the barracks Badri, who like many Albanians spoke Italian fluently, opened negotiations.

It had been reported that a small German force was attacking the Italian garrison at Tepeleni, so we proposed to the General three courses: to join us in attacking these Germans, to hand over everything to us as representing the Allies, or to burn everything. His counter-proposal was that he should be allowed to march his whole force to the port of Saranda where, when transport to Italy had been arranged, he would surrender all he had. He said that he had received no orders, that he was not in touch with Rome, that his men would certainly not fight the Germans, and that he would not consider handing over any weapons until he was safely at the coast. To receive the arms at Saranda did not suit us. Here at Gjinokastre, where men were available, we could quickly disperse and hide all the material, for time was the all-important factor. It was strange that the Germans had not already come. Badri assured me that the Saranda road would be blocked by partisans, and as we could stop any move in the direction of Valona, we told the General he must make up his mind by five o'clock that evening, although it was obvious to all that if he refused we could not impose our views. I threatened to have his barracks bombed, Badri swore at them in Italian, and the colonels raved about their military honour. The party broke up in a temper and we repaired to the outpost company to await the issue. They sent up lunch for us, and while we ate, Shefket, one of Badri's trusted henchmen, took on one side the company commander who had privately intimated that he was ready to 'sell the pass'. This was treachery, and I was not sure that the Italian could be trusted to carry out his part of the bargain or that we would not have to fight the rest of the garrison afterwards. Down below the Italians appeared to be packing up and at five o'clock came a terse note from the General: 'I will give up my arms to nobody.'

Feeling rather foolish, we left, and we had not got back to our lines before heavy firing broke out on the main road. For reasons that were obscure the company on the rige opened up in our direction with all they had, while the mountain battery started plastering some empty fields across the river. The partisans held their fire and presently the Italians calmed down. Badri agreed with me that an attack on the garrison would be too expensive, but we hoped that they would move out, when we should be better able to deal with them. To hurry them up we arranged to cut off their water supply, which was piped down to the barracks from the town above, and the same night I returned hot-foot to Shepr to report progress. When I got back at dawn on the 16th I found the worst had happened. Finding the water cut off, the thirsty Italians, after burning what they could not carry, had marched in the night, and had reached Saranda unhindered. Elsewhere, after burning their equipment, the garrisons of Permet and Kelcyra had surrendered, and the partisans had taken and were holding Tepeleni.

Instead of at once following the Perugia Division to Saranda, which was a long two days' march for the partisans, Badri arranged for a somewhat premature triumphal entry of Gjinokastre. The town, the capital of the Province, had a population of over 10,000. It is a lovely old place, straggling terrace-wise over the steep slopes of three spurs or buttresses of the high barren mountains which bound the Dhrino valley on the west. Led by Badri on a white charger, recently captured from the Italians, the partisans filed slowly up the narrow cobbled streets between old-fashioned houses, stone-arched doorways, trellises of vines, minarets, and cypresses. The people were wildly excited, casting bouquets of flowers, and embracing long-lost relatives and friends in the ranks of the procession. At length we reached the massive walls of the citadel. This was built in 1808 by the notorious Ali Pasha, the cruel Lion of Jannina, and completely dominates the town. The great crowd which had gathered in the sun-baked square outside the walls of the gloomy fortress now gave themselves up to an afternoon of undiluted oratory. First the mayor, then Badri, then myself, faced the delighted crowd, and after that anyone who felt he had something in him demanding utterance. One of the L.N.C. representatives from Zagori, a spectacled student called Shemsi, embarked on a long harangue which appeared to be nothing but an all-embracing Ernulphus' curse directed against the Balli Kombetar. A Balli leader, Bahri Omari (for the rupture between the parties was not yet final), was standing next to me fanning himself with his Homburg hat, as much to cool his rising indignation as to mitigate the hot blast reflected from the blazing white square. Hemmed in as he was by partisans and L.N.C. adherents, his position was delicate, but he stood his ground stoutly enough and even attempted to raise his voice against some of the more outrageous accusations. At this point, fearing trouble, I begged Badri to silence the exuberant Shemsi. More certain help, however, was at hand. The appearance of an ancient and solitary biplane sailing sedately through the sky far to the south, dispersed the crowd in disorder and brought the celebrations to a timely, if undignified, end.

We dined and slept that night in one of Gjinokastre's oldest houses. Most of these are two- or three-storeyed buildings with projecting wings and a balcony between. The ground-floor windows are small and barred, those on the second floor are high and latticed. Above them the broad eaves are supported by wooden struts projecting from the wall. The stone floors and stone walls of the ground-floor rooms make them delightfully cool and dim, and the austerity of the stone is relieved by brightly painted fireplaces and by red and blue pointing between the stones of the floor. Upstairs the wooden ceilings are carved or painted in red, green, or yellow designs, and adorned with an abundance of crude stars and crescents. We dined in Albanian fashion from a common dish of 'pillau' placed in the centre.

In the morning I set off for the Greek frontier in a war-weary Italian truck with six partisans and 70 lb. of explosive. As the road from the north was barred by partisans at Tepeleni, we thought that if we could blow the bridge near Kakavi on the road to Jannina, we might delay the Germans sufficiently to save some of the booty we expected to get at Saranda. Badri and his men were already *en route* for the port. Between Gjinokastre and Kakavi on the Greek border the road runs through flat open country, and is more or less invulnerable to sabotage. There were three bridges spanning mere dry river beds which formed no obstacles, but a mile or so beyond the border we had been told of a more promising place where the road crossed a deep ravine. We trundled along the dusty road, half expecting to run into a German column, crossed the Greek frontier, and reached the unguarded bridge without incident. It appeared to be a recent replacement of one destroyed in the Greek-Italian campaign, and consisted of three massive concrete piers supporting a wooden roadway. The piers were 6 ft. thick, but the builder had thoughtfully provided holes in them for demolition charges. With my six partisans acting as a covering party I hastily rammed 35 lb. of powerful explosive into each of two piers and connected the charges with a length of detonating fuse. Just as all was ready some Greeks from the nearby village appeared, took in the situation at a glance, and launched an indignant protest on behalf of the doomed bridge. It was of no particular value to them, they said, but if the Germans found the bridge blown they would certainly burn the nearest village, which happened to be theirs. I quite saw their point, but war is war. Lighting the safety fuse, I told them to run, and set them the example myself. A few minutes later there was a satisfactory roar and bits of bridge shot high into the air. When the last piece had fallen I ran back to survey the work of my 'prentice hand with the modest pride becoming to an amateur in crime. The bridge had 'had it in a big way', but the ravine was not so difficult to cross as I had hoped, and it was clear that a diversion could be quickly effected.

We returned to Gjinokastre, burning a small wooden bridge for good measure on the way. I made another forced march to Shepr to report to Base, returned almost without stopping to Gjinokastre, and from there reached Saranda by car on the 22nd. It is about 40 miles away over bleak uplands.

Saranda is a small town almost opposite the northern tip of Corfu which is only about 10 miles distant. This small, modern, dusty and indefensible town lay on the shore of a deep and sheltered bay. Steamers could lie out about 300 yards from a wooden jetty on which, however, there were no cranes.

Chiminello and his staff were installed in an office building on the water front. Badri had already seen them, and since neither side chose to offer recriminations for recent past events, they were on good terms with each other. Moreover, the Italians were jubilant, for 2,000 had embarked in an Italian ship the previous night. Chiminello said he was now in touch with Ambrosio, the Italian Chief of Staff at Rome, who had ordered them to retain their rifles. We agreed to this and, in return, the General agreed to defend the town if the Germans came—a promise which I felt sure would not be fulfilled by the thoroughly demoralised men waiting impatiently to be taken home. Meanwhile the handing over of vehicles and mules, of which there were 300 belonging to the mountain battery, had begun, and the partisans worked furiously to remove to Kuc and Cepo as much of the stores, arms and ammunition as they could handle.

While this went on I made a quick journey on foot to Konispol to see what was happening there. This is a small town on the Greek border 25 miles south of Saranda to which it is linked by a motor-road. I was pleased to note that a blown bridge had stopped all traffic, and that the unbridged, fast-flowing river looked likely to present a more formidable obstacle than our ravine at Kakavi. I was surprised to hear afterwards that the Germans had reached Saranda by that route. The few partisans at Konispol were jumpy. They explained their fears by taking me to a high hill whence we looked down upon a small jetty on the Greek side of the frontier where, through glasses, I could see a large number of naked Huns sporting in the sea. Across the narrow Corfu Channel columns of smoke were rising from a town which the Germans had been intermittently bombing during the day.

On our return we forsook the road for a footpath which, winding through low hilly malarious country, past dirty, fever-stricken villages, eventually brought us out near the mouth of the narrow Vutrinto channel which links the long lagoon of that name with the sea. Hard by were the ruins of Buthrotum, a very ancient Greek settlement, and before the war a centre of archaeological research. It was dark when we pushed through the last reeds bordering the channel. We hailed the ferryman, who at length grudgingly consented to take us across to his hut, where we dined off fat juicy mullet while a boat was being prepared to take us up the lagoon. All night we pulled quietly over the black glassy water under silent wooded hills, until with the dawn wind puckering the calm surface, now growing pallid before the oncoming day, we landed at a little jetty at the northern end.

A German reconnaissance plane making a dawn patrol passed overhead, and when we topped the rocky neck of land separating us from Saranda bay, I was amazed to see a steamer lying peacefully at anchor a few hundred yards from the town. I went straight to the General's office and heard his tale of woe. only a few more men had got away, and the ship lying there, a rusty Italian tramp of about 3,000 tons, had fouled her cable and was unable to move. The crew had deserted her, wisely, I thought, in view of that German 'recce' plane. As we talked inside the room, idly regarding through the open doors of the balcony the lifeless ship, we were startled by the familiar sounds of a diving plane, and the whistle of falling bombs. The ship disappeared in a cloud of smoke and spray, and when this had subsided I saw that I was alone and that the ship was undamaged. I went to the house where we were stopping, which was not quite so close to the harbour, but found it empty. Saranda was deserted. At intervals throughout the day six Stukas returned five times to the attack, dived low, released their bombs, and flew off for more. From this target practice the ship sustained one hit which set her on fire and she eventually sank at five in the evening. It was a pity, I thought, that so few partisans had stayed to watch such a pitiful performance.

I never saw General Chiminello or his officers again. When the bombing started, all the Italians, realising that Saranda's brief day as a port of embarkation was over, fled north to Porto Palermo. I heard later, and believe it to be true, that the Germans found them there and shot the General and 150 of his officers. The remnants of the Perugia Division I was to see once more living on berries in the woods near Kuc. Leaving the partisans to deal as they could wish with the enormous booty they now had, I walked once more to Shepr and back again to Gjinokastre on 29 September. There seemed to be an air of gloomy expectation over the town which I was at a loss to understand. The Germans had been so long in coming that I thought they must have decided to abandon Albania; but this morning it was rumoured that Konispol and Saranda were occupied and that a large column was even then on its way from Jannina to Gjinokastre. At eleven o'clock I left for Cepo and at midday the head of the column arrived.

At Cepo there was more definite news, most of it bad. The Germans had entered Saranda two days after I had left, where they had found large quantities of stores, mainly grain and petrol, which the partisans had not had time to remove. From there they had advanced up the coast road, and were now attacking the H.Q. and depot at Kuc in the Shushice valley south of Valona where Radowicke was stationed. Coming up the road to the monastery I had seen, at the foot of the spur, a big dump of grain, rice, 40-gallon petrol drums, some trucks, and two 40 mm. anti-tank guns. It was probable, however, that the Germans were unaware of the importance Cepo had thus acquired. The Tepeleni position astride the main road a few miles north of Cepo was strongly held. It was Badri's intention to fight the Germans there and to 'lie doggo' at Cepo, but as a precautionary measure some 200 partisans were occupying a long horseshoe-shaped position on the low hills commanding the approach to the monastery.

Having been told that a bridge in the gorge south of Tepeleni had been prepared for blowing, Badri and I went down by car to see it. It was a concrete arched bridge which carried the road over a small nallah with steep cliffs on one side and the Dhrino on the other. These cliffs, at the foot of which the road is cut, made it very vulnerable to attack by explosives; but two months later the heavy winter rains closed it far more effectively than we could have ever done by bringing down a large landslide. This bridge had been well prepared for blowing by the Italians, who had sunk five timber-lined holes 4 ft. square and 6 ft. deep in the crown of the arches. The partisans had already laid their charges of Italian blasting powder and had filled the holes to the brim with earth and stones. Unluckily the man in charge, who knew nothing of the fine art of destruction or of the use of detonating fuse, had fused each charge separately with safety fuse. This meant that the charges would go off at different times, thus losing much of their effect, or that the explosion of the first might perhaps dislodge or break the fuses of the others before they had acted. It was too late to dig out the holes and connect up with detonating fuse. The anticipated failure occurred next day. Only two of the charges went off, blowing a small hole in the middle of the road and a bit out of one side.

On the morning of 1 October, I watched the long-expected German column drive past. From the monastery spur several miles of the white ribbon of road were in sight before it disappeared round a corner just short of the bridge about to be blown. Headed by motor-cyclists and staff cars, sixty troop-carrying vehicles and two 115 mm. guns crossed the bridge at the bottom of the Cepo valley—where they halted to inspect the three dead men and the ambushed trucks—and parked themselves in a wood 2 miles beyond. The troops disappeared round the corner on foot and a distant rumble announced the partial blowing of the bridge. Battle was joined. We were merely distant spectators. Only the bursting of shells on the heights across the Dhrino, and the burning of villages high up on both sides of the valley on the second day, told us that the attack was making headway. A small cluster of houses at the foot of our valley was wantonly burnt by men from the vehicle park. Although they were a bare 500 yards from our outposts, the partisans held their fire. It is possible to write calmly enough about burning villages, but when we actually see men at work setting fire to one peaceful, familiar little homestead after another, the rising flames, the roofs falling in, and the labour and loving care of years dissolving irretrievably in a few minutes, it is impossible not to experience a hot wave of dismay, revulsion and hate. To watch fires caused by bombing or shelling is bad enough, but guns and planes seem impersonal and their effects do not rouse the same intense feeling.

Couriers kept arriving at our H.Q. in the monastery at all hours. In the little room in which we ate and slept, a sea of confusion eddied round the stalwart figure of the 'Papa', who unmoved as a rock, served our meals with the same regularity as before. At night he slept fully clothed, his hat on his head and a handkerchief over his face, oblivious of comings or goings, or the ceaseless clatter of a typewriter.

On the 4th we heard that Kuc and its depot had been abandoned, and from the silence that reigned over the distant Tepeleni gorge we concluded that the Germans had at last broken through. But worse was to come. On the evening of that day a mule train with about 150 men appeared from the direction of Gjinokastre and suddenly halted on the bridge where the road to the monastery turned off. Were they going to bivouac there for the night or were they after our dump? We breathed more freely when they started to move on but, having crossed the bridge, they turned off the road up a narrow valley which would lead them right underneath one of our outposts. Regular troops might have contained themselves, but for irregulars the target was altogether too tempting. It was impossible to send any orders there in time, and a few minutes later the crackle of rifle fire warned us that our precious dump was now in jeopardy. I have never understood what intentions those Germans had, but from the unconcerned way in which they marched into that narrow defile I am sure they had no knowledge of our presence. Had the partisans who opened the ball been in sufficient force, or well-enough armed, to have made a clean job of the ambush, all might have been well. As it was, a few men and mules were hit, the rest promptly scattered in the scrub, and under cover of the gathering dusk began to fight back. Signal lights soared up, and the ripping sound of the fast-firing German machine-gun showed us with what we had to deal. One could not but admire the speed with which they recovered from what must have been a very painful shock.

The battle so unluckily begun continued for two days. In the morning the Germans, who had withdrawn to a position near the bridge, were reinforced from Gjinokastre. On the 6th twelve troop-carriers and two 115 mm. guns arrived from the north. Although the partisans fought well, the ultimate issue was not in doubt. Our two 40 mm. anti-tank guns, to which as a gunner I attached myself, firing from some scrub on the face of the spur, made the main road impassable. A truck which foolishly stopped near the bridge was hit at a range of 3,000 yards and set alight. The guns were, of course, soon spotted and neutralised by the fire of a heavy mortar firing from behind cover. One of them received a direct hit. While the fight went on those men who could be spared laboured to clear the monastery and the dump of arms and to hide what they could in the bush. The difficulty of feeding men in the firing-line, 1,000 yards or more from the monastery, made a long resistance unlikely. Everything had to be carried by hand and nothing hot could be provided for them.

When the two guns began shelling the monastery and its approaches Badri gave the order for retreat. The dump was set alight and the partisans started to steal away, covered by the fire of a few machine-guns. All tracks converged on the monastery, where the shelling seemed likely to start a panic among tired men unaccustomed to that kind of warfare. Badri and Shefket cursed the fugitives into shame and some kind of order, while the 'Papa', armed with a gigantic umbrella, showed the most soldierly bearing of any and beat into submission anyone who attempted to argue. He, who was shortly to see the monastery to which he was devoted go up in senseless flames, was the most to be pitied; he would, I think, have preferred us all to stand there and die. I was ashamed to look him in the face.

We retreated up the valley towards the barren Kurvalesh hills while the Germans followed slowly, burning every village in sight. Badri's plan was to reorganise before crossing the Dhrino back to Zagori. I was anxious to return to Shepr, so I started out alone that night. Skirting high above the Cepo valley

I dropped down into the Dhrino valley in the dark, where I found a house with a light burning. The occupants were, with difficulty, persuaded to open and with more difficulty to give me a guide for the crossing of the river. No doubt they thought I was a German or a Balli.

Thus in October, with winter at hand, the bright prospects of the partisans and their supporters had faded. They had lost most of the recently gained arms and equipment, two of their strong-holds had been overrun and burnt, and the burning of ten villages at the beginning of winter had severely shaken the morale of the population upon whose support the partisans depended for food and shelter. In addition, their break with the Balli Kombetar was now almost complete; from criticism, recrimination, and suspicion, they were about to pass to open war. The L.N.C. declared that their plans were betrayed to the enemy by Balli spies, that no Balli had yet fired a shot for the liberation of the country, and that now they must make up their minds to fight the enemy or the L.N.C. But in spite of these setbacks their organisation throughout the south had been growing stronger, and that of the Balli Kombetar weaker. Whether they wished it or no the Balli were forced for their own preservation to proceed from covert to overt co-operation with the Germans.

CHAPTER ELEVEN

Winter

DURING September and October, arms clothing and boots for the partisans had been arriving at the rate of three or four plane loads a month. The pilots were always able to find the dropping ground in the Zagori valley about 2 miles from Shepr. It was a heartening sight to see a big four-engined Halifax roar down its load, do a tight turn without troubling to gain height, and come back for its second run. As the plane turned the navigation lights on the wings seemed almost to brush the hillside. In my subsequent experience I never met any squadron which approached the standard of that one operating from Derna in the autumn of 1943. One night we had three planes over the target at the same time, their headlights full on to avoid colliding. The valley looked like Croydon on a busy night, and I wondered what the Germans in Gjinokastre thought of it. Between sorties life at Shepr became almost indecently dull and placid. My sergeant and corporal had our establishment well organised and were on excellent terms with the villagers. From a prosperous trader, whose morals were not severe, who had irons in many fires, and whose black-market activities would, I feared, end one day in front of a firing party, we bought amongst other things six mules. They were to carry our equipment when the Germans obliged us to run; in the meantime we used them for carrying wood to the dropping ground and stores away from it. We ate our three good meals a day, ciphered signals, visited neighbouring villages, showed the partisans how to use explosives, and argued more or less amiably with various people who came to see us. The main points on which they desired to be enlightened were, when were the British going to invade the Balkans, why we continued to support the Balli and the Zoggists, and why the Albanian broadcasts of the B.B.C. never denounced these two organisations by name and carefully refrained from naming the L.N.C. For many months all actions in Albania were referred to as having been carried out by 'patriots' which, of course, might mean anyone. To none of these questions, except the first, was it easy to find a convincing answer.

From this comfortable cabbage-like existence I had frequently and gladly to depart on longer journeys, travelling fast, living hard, and always returning with increased zest to the master-pieces of Cesio our cook. The first of these sorties was provoked by the burning out of the condenser of our wireless set. The corporal went off to the nearest mission in Greece for help, while I went to a mission of ours near Valona to send a signal. On this and on subsequent journeys I took with me one partisan, dispensing with the escort which the partisans deemed necessary and liked so much to provide; for to travel with an escort was to double the time taken and to multiply many times the difficulties of food and shelter at the villages on our route. For our safety I relied on speed, and the good sense, native caution and craft of Mehmet my partisan guide. He came from the Korca area, but soon got to know all the tracks and by-paths of our zone perfectly. He was uncannily clever in the dark and could follow the faintest of paths on the blackest of nights. He was intelligent, active, stout-hearted, cheerful, good at driving a bargain, a good mixer, and a good walker. Most Albanians are not good walkers. They are for ever stopping, either to have a chat, a smoke, a drink of water, or a rest. On the limestone mountains of Albania the rain sinks down (leaving the upper parts bone dry) to gush out in innumerable springs near the valley floor. In summer it is quite impossible to get an Albanian past one of these springs. They are great water connoisseurs, and will distinguish between the excellence of one village and another solely by its water. But even between one spring and the next, and usually the distance is not great, you will often hear from the perspiring rear-guard a plaintive cry of 'Avash, Avash'; for which a free translation would be, 'For God's sake, stop', I say 'perspiring' advisedly because they liked to wear all the clothes they possessed all the time. However hot the day or steep the hill they never shed a garment. While I would be going along coolly and comfortably in nothing but a pair of shorts, they would be wearing two or three sweaters and a pair of thick homespun trousers. No wonder they were thirsty souls. Through his long association with me, during which he complained of loss of weight, Mehmet acquired more sense—in this respect, at least, if not in others—but I don't think I saw him with his shirt off more than once. I believe he thought it indelicate.

We crossed the Chayup pass in the dark, where the Vlachs were preparing for their winter trek to the coast, and where we had a running fight with one of

their savage white dogs—our hard-flung stones he just tried to catch, so that
Mehmet was reduced to using his Sten, fortunately without fatal results.
These dogs are said to be descended from wolves and they seem unable to
forget it. We forded the Dhrino, crossed the road, and headed for Cepo.
Amongst the black shadows cast by the cypresses, the moonlight played on
the blackened shell of the silent monastery. No burly 'Papa' welcomed the
wayfarer. The vines were cut down, the bees were gone, and the body of the
old mad woman lay buried in the courtyard. The little church stood alone
untouched and untended amid the ruins.

  Our first halt was at Golem, one of the highest and poorest villages of
southern Albania set in the middle of the barren uplands of Kurvalesh. It was
as yet unburnt. The inhabitants were Moslem and, until recent times, could
look back with pride upon a long and successful record of brigandage. If there
were no partisans in a village Mehmet would go to the headman, who either
took us in himself or sought out for us the best accommodation. We would
leave our boots in the passage outside the living room (this sensible and
labour-saving custom is facilitated by the type of shoes Albanians wear), and
our host would seat us in the place of honour on sheepskin rugs on each side
of the fire-place. The wood fire would be heaped up and a bottle of raki
produced, while the women prepared food. Before eating, our host or one of
the women would bring basin and ewer and pour water over our hands. Then
the low round table was brought in, the bowl of food, and a hunk of bread and
a spoon for each man. Everyone except the women squatted down, seized a
spoon, bared his right arm, and then devil take the hindmost. To sup with the
devil requires a long spoon, but for me it was equally necessary when supping
with Albanians. With a short body and not long arms, unable when squatting
to tuck my legs neatly under me, I started with a heavy handicap. That I was
not holding my own was so apparent that they usually conceded me a small
private bowl. When the big bowl was emptied we threw our spoons into it, the
bread was swept up, the table carried out, and we went back to our rugs.

> We cleansed our beards of the mutton grease,
> We lay on our mats and were filled with peace.

For simplicity, economy of utensils, labour, and washing up, much can be said
for the Albanian way of serving a meal.

  From Golem we crossed another pass and dropped down to the Kuc valley
where the partisans still had their H.Q. in a farmhouse. In the town itself
there was not a single house with a roof—burnt-out trucks, burnt rifles and
guns, littered the streets. Passing down the Shushice valley through the woods
of Kalarat we met hundreds, or even thousands, of semi-starved Italians who
lay about listlessly in improvised shelters. They were ultimately dispersed by
the L.N.C. amongst various villages, where they were fed in return for work.
In my opinion, for thus maintaining alive, at no small sacrifice to themselves,
the men to whom they owed the invasion of their country and the destruction
of their homes, the Albanians acquired great merit. Acts of magnanimity
amongst nations, especially those of the Balkans, are so rare that this example
of returning good for evil deserves remembrance.

At Brataj, 15 miles south of Valona, we came upon an unfinished motor-road. Brataj was occupied by partisans, but the next two villages were strongholds of the Balli who looked at us with curiosity and suspicion as we passed through. To all enquiries Mehmet's reply that I was a German officer greatly facilitated our passage and threw some light on the changing attitude of that party. We finally ran the mission to earth in a leaky hut on the summit of the high ridge which separated the Shushice valley from the sea. In an area where sympathies were so mixed their position was unenviable; after doing his utmost to work with both parties, according to instructions, the officer concerned eventually elected to champion the cause of the Balli. This had unfortunate results for everybody. He established a sea base in some caves on the rocky coast of the Karabarun peninsula, known to us later as Seaview, where in time a good many tons of arms and ammunition were landed. As in the meantime the Balli had become so flagrantly unfriendly, the distribution of these arms to them was banned; but since they held all the land approaches to Seaview, the arms could not be issued to the L.N.C. So they lay there uselessly until in the end the base was betrayed to the Germans, who stepped in and took the lot.

With the coming of winter weather the supply of arms sent by air became extremely meagre. In November it rained every day and on the 9th of that month the first snow fell. Nevertheless, in accord with the exhortations of the B.B.C. broadcasts to augment the resistance movement, the forces of the L.N.C. steadily grew larger. By December five mobile brigades were in being, and if they were to be maintained increased supplies were essential. We, therefore, made efforts to establish a sea base in territory controlled by partisans.

From their point of view the most suitable place was Grava Bay, just south of Panermo Point. From here there was a track leading inland to Kuc, which could be used for the rapid distribution of stores.

Accordingly, Mehmet and I set out on another long journey, first to Seaview to consult a naval officer who had been sent there to assist with sea sorties, and then to Grava Bay to reconnoitre. As the Dhrino was now in flood we took a different route. After crossing Chayup we traversed the hillside high above the river by a path which led to a big iron bridge near Tepeleni. We stopped at the village of Lekei where we were entertained by the very militant priest of the church, who was one of the many Albanians who had been to America and spoke very fair English. Finding his congregations becoming less, he had exchanged the Bible for a rifle and now marched in the ranks of the partisans.

The bridge above Tepeleni was a fine steel girder structure upon which I should very much have liked to have tried my hand. But it was the only link between Gjinokastre and Kelcyra where there was a large grain market upon which Gjinokastre and many other places depended for food. At that time Kelcyra was in the hands of the Balli. When they banned the export of grain, as they presently did, the people of Gjinokastre experienced a lean time until Kelcyra was finally taken by the partisans in the spring. Avoiding Tepeleni, where there was a garrison, we marched for two days through wild, sparsely inhabited country until we again reached Brataj. There we found the 1st Brigade whose inauguration parade I had watched in August near Korca. A state of war now existed between the Balli and the L.N.C., and the 1st Brigade had been sent there to gain control of the country with an eye to opening the way to the arms and ammunition accumulated at Seaview. The commander of the brigade, Mehmet Schio, an able soldier and an ardent Communist, was not pleased when he heard where we were going. He doubted if we should get through the Balli village of Dukati where we had to go to obtain a guide to Seaview, but at the same time he gave no hint of his own intentions regarding that village. He expressed the greatest disgust at our policy of backing both parties, and gave me a personal message for the officer at Seaview that he, Mehmet Schio, would not be responsible for what happened if the 1st Brigade ever got there.

He himself talked at length but he was far outdone by a young woman on the Brigade staff. Her manners were offhand, her appearance was a 'check to loose behaviour', and she poured out an incessant stream of parrot-like propaganda until after midnight. There was only one bed in the room the brigade staff occupied, and I made no bones about accepting when they offered it to me. The woman slept under it.

At dawn next morning Mehmet and I stole silently away without as much as a 'Goodbye' to avoid reawakening that terrible tongue. We crossed the Lungara range by a narrow pass, whence we caught a glimpse of the Adriatic and the barely discernible Italian coast, and then zigzagged steeply down through a forest of oak and pine to Dukati. Before entering the village Mehmet was careful to remove the red star from his cap. The houses of Dukati straggled along the bank of a deep, dry ravine. In 1930 it had been shattered by an earthquake, but I was not aware of this at the time, and we did not notice any evidence of the disaster in the well-built houses. We were in no mind for close observation for the nature of our reception engrossed our thoughts. The place made little impression on me, and I confess I was surprised when I read how Edward Lear the landscape painter had painted Dukati in words in 1852: 'Shut out as it stood by iron walls of mountains, surrounded by sternest features of savage scenery, rock and chasm, precipice and torrent, a more fearful prospect and more chilling to the very blood I never beheld.'

As a British liaison officer I was politely received, though there were black looks when they heard with whom I was working. The English-speaking Balli leader, dressed in 'plus-fours', gave us lunch in the inn and was perfectly frank about his attitude. The village was in easy reach of the main coast road and neither he nor anyone else there had the slightest intention of doing anything to provoke the Germans. They were willing to help us clandestinely, but to be openly hostile to the Germans, like the L.N.C., was absurd. Their only ambition was to keep themselves alive and their homes unburnt until the war ended, when they naïvely hoped for the coming of what they called a British 'political' mission to settle their differences with the L.N.C. or 'Communists', as they preferred; and, of course, since the Germans opposed Communism, it was natural if occasionally they gave them a hand against the L.N.C.

After lunch they found us a guide, for they were in close touch with the officer at Seaview, and an escort to see us safely over the coast road. We had then to face a strenuous climb over the 5,000 ft. bare limestone ridge which still separated us from the sea. As we reached the crest the sun was sinking behind the far-off southern Apennines. As the leaden pallor of evening crept slowly across the face of the Adriatic, behind us, to the east, the snow-clad summit of Tomorres still glowed opalescent in the dying rays. Five thousand feet below, where the sea broke gently on a rock-bound coast, our guide vaguely indicated the direction of the caves and left us for a shepherd's camp. There was no path, so down over rough coral-like rock we sped in a race against darkness. We found the troglodyte mission, discussed our business, and left early next morning for Brataj.

A disinterested listener in the cave that night might have thought that representatives of the Balli and the L.N.C. in British uniform were telling each other a few home truths. Most liaison officers must have found that after living and fighting with people for some time that they become partisans in the real sense—blind followers of party or cause. The ideal liaison officer, I suppose, would not be subject to this fault; but ideal officers are rare, and no doubt for this reason the views of those in the field were heavily discounted by the dispassionate Olympians at Base. In this account I have tried hard to be objective, but, like Boswell's Mr Edwards who 'tried to be a philosopher but found cheerfulness always breaking in', I have found it difficult to exclude a preference for men who fought on the same side as ourselves.

On top of the ridge next morning we ran into rain and drizzle so thick that we got temporarily separated. Half-way down the other side when we had emerged from this we anxiously scanned the road for signs of movement. There was no traffic but we were alarmed by sounds of battle apparently from the direction of Dukati. When some frightened villagers whom we met on the road told us that it had been attacked that morning by the 1st Brigade, we struck straight up the hillside in order to skirt it on the south. We came out on a ridge some 1,500 ft. above the village and sat down for a bite of bread. Below were groups of armed Balli, and moving along the hills to the east we saw long files of partisans. A light mortar was in action against the village and machine-guns were stuttering. Although we had not exposed ourselves unduly the partisans had spotted us. A shell from a 40 mm. landed on the slopes below and the next round burst on the ridge to our left. We backed hastily away and continued up the reverse slope, where we were at once seen by the Balli who proceeded to spray us with a machine-gun. We were too tired for any more detours so we pushed on recklessly over bare grass slopes, hoping to get within speaking distance of the partisans before they shot us down at long range. Suddenly a shout rang out and we found ourselves covered by a machine-gun and several rifles 100 yards off. In spite of his parched throat and some excusable nervousness Mehmet waxed loud, eloquent and convincing. We were not known to them personally, but they sent us under escort to Mehmet Schio with whom we had few recriminatory words for not having warned us more explicitly of his intentions. Presumably, as we were going through Dukati, he had thought it better to say nothing.

Before we parted I strongly advised him to go himself to Seaview rather than to take his whole brigade there. At present there seemed little chance of this happening. The battle was not going well, and as we sat there in the rain and gathering dusk, eating freshly killed Dukati mutton, we heard the familiar quick burst of a German machine-gun. The garrison at Logara Pass had come to the aid of Dukati.

From Kuc we went down to the coast at Grava Bay. Towards evening, for it was advisable not to advertise our presence, we walked down a rocky valley and emerged on the narrow strip of fertile coastal plain. In a passing snow squall we walked through groves of olives and orange trees, laden with golden fruit, and came out upon the coast road and the sea. After scrambling down two or three hundred feet of rock we found a sandy beach, hidden from view except from the white houses of Borsh, a mile to the south. Although it was almost dark and looked like snowing again, I felt that a report on the beach would not be complete without a bathe. I found it steep-to, with a bottom of small shingle—an ideal place for landing craft.

It was not until May that we received anything at Grava Bay. For the partisans the sea base became synonymous with the Greek Kalends, or pie in the sky. When they grumbled about the little they received by air, I cheered them by glowing pictures of what a sea base would mean once it was working—tons of ammunition, thousands of boots, telephones, wireless sets, printing presses, or anything they fancied. But, in the opinion of the Navy, Grava Bay lay open to the prevailing south wind and accordingly was undeservedly damned. Stores continued to pile up at Seaview and little interest was shown in any other place. In January I did manage to arrange for a three-day stand-by period but, having gone there with a wireless set, the first signal we received was that no boat was available.

Travelling as we usually did without a wireless set and living mostly on maize bread and cheese, I was always in a desperate hurry to get back to Shepr. I was always anxious to know if any sorties had been received, how many we were likely to get the next month, and whether or no there were any signs of our policy of equal treatment for all belligerents, no matter which side they were on, undergoing a change. About this time Base were still asking us for concrete evidence of Balli collaboration with the enemy.

On our return one very unwelcome signal contained news of the wounding and capture of the head of the British mission to Albania, Brigadier Davies, who had only recently arrived with a large staff. After being on the run for several days he was wounded and taken prisoner and the staff dispersed. His senior staff officer, who then became head of the mission, escaped to Abas Kupi, the Zoggist, but he died subsequently of the effects of frostbite contracted while escaping. The loss of Brigadier Davies, an officer of sufficiently high rank to influence policy, who in the short time he was in the country had come to the same conclusions as myself, had a serious and lasting effect.

There was another signal which seemed to contain the seed of trouble—not so much because it introduced a feminine element, but because it threatened to disturb the placid regime of winter at Shepr. A party of ten American nurses and twenty orderlies who had made a forced landing near Berat were reported on their way to Shepr for evacuation by sea. They had been flying from Sicily to Taranto in a Douglas and found themselves over Yugo-Slavia where they were shot at. Having run out of petrol over Albania, they had the good fortune to crash-land near Berat on the only flat surface for a good many miles around. They reached Shepr in charge of a British Officer, the nurses in good heart and looks, the orderlies—big, stalwart men—tired, bedraggled, and depressed. We started them off for Seaview but they failed to get past Dukati where fighting was still in progress.

The next idea was to have them picked up from the airfield at Gjinokastre, where at the moment there were no Germans. They took up a position of readiness in a village a few miles from the airfield, but no sooner had the detailed arrangements for the pick-up been made than some enemy troops arrived in Gjinokastre. However, the Germans might go, and since no aircraft were to be sent until asked for, they waited. I went over to visit them; and much to my surprise, for I knew the Germans were still there, as I was crossing the Lunxheries I saw eighteen Lightnings sweeping down the valley and a Wellington followed by two Douglases coming in as though to land. When I reached the village I heard what happened. Apparently the officer in charge of the operation in Italy had got tired of keeping two squadrons standing by and had sent a signal that morning to say they were coming. The British officer took his long-suffering party down and lay up near the airfield, but since there were a couple of armoured cars on the main road just across the river, he rightly refused to give the signal for the planes to land, in spite of the hysterical pleading of his flock. A subsequent attempt to get away by sea was successful. Thus after two months or more of painful wandering, for the most part patiently borne, they landed in Italy and were made much of.

CHAPTER TWELVE

The Tide Turns

WITH the turn of the year the weather became more severe. All the passes and high mountain paths became snow-bound so that avoiding action became difficult. Partisan activity was slight, for it was necessary to balance very carefully the value of any action against the consequences which might follow it. Bad as it was to have your village burnt in summer, in winter it was many times worse. On the other hand, the Germans, who were aware of the partisans' difficulties, increased their activities. Having broken up the H.Q. mission they turned their attention to the mission near Korca, where there were also several officers who had come out to join Brigadier Davies.

On 19 January all these arrived at Shepr, having been driven out with the loss of all their kit. Replacements for this were dropped almost the next night. It is pleasant to recall that missions in Albania were very well cared for by Base; almost too well, in fact, for one of the L.N.C. leaders, Tashko, at one time Albanian minister at New York, gave me a severe lecture on our shortcomings, of which one was the undue proportion of mission stores in aircraft loads. At the time I was pressing for ammunition, of which there was always a shortage, and boots for a new 6th Brigade about to be formed, so that the arrival of a plane with nothing but mission stores caused me some embarrassment.

The Permet pass was still open, and on the 24th I walked over it to attend the first parade of this new brigade. I found Radowicke, Badri, and the other leaders there all very preoccupied. Garman armoured cars had attacked Kelcyra, from which the partisans had momentarily driven the Balli, and troop concentrations were reported from Gjinokastre and Perat on the Greek border south of Permet. Perat, where there was an important and heavily guarded bridge, lies at the junction of the road to Korca and the road to Permet. The ceremony was cancelled and we returned to Shepr to find these ill-tidings confirmed. A mixed force of Germans and Balli had already crossed the frontier at Dhrimades, at the southern end of Zagori, where fighting was in progress; another had left Gjinokastre for Zagori; and the bridge at Lekei was guarded. All pointed to a concerted drive against the partisans and mission in Shepr, and the only escape route left open was that over the Permet bridge to the east, which was already threatened from north to south. The rain which fell steadily throughout the 26th augmented the gloom hanging over Shepr. The villagers, rightly anticipating the worst, busied themselves hiding their valuables, but still found time for casting reproachful looks at us the authors of their impending misery. That contingency for which for so long we had fed six mules having at last arisen, the mules were not available, having gone to Kelcyra to fetch grain. Most of our kit could therefore be written off, but we hid the wireless, batteries, charging engine, and some food, in a nearby nallah. The other officers, who had spent a happy day lavishly re-equipping themselves, now had to relinquish all and set off for Permet, while I rang up Badri on our local telephone to ask what we should do. He advised leaving with all speed as he could not guarantee holding on to Permet for another day. In spite of the weather I was tempted to lie up in the hills until the gathering storm had spent itself, but decided that the wiser course was to stick to the partisans and the other mission.

We left that night in a snowstorm to the sound of machine-gun fire from lower down the Zagori valley. Although we had started late we soon ran into the tail of the long column of fugitives struggling in the deep snowdrift at the top of the pass. Partisans, wounded men, refugees, mules, and donkeys, plodded dejectedly through the snow. The Permet side of the pass is much steeper. The snow on the track had been beaten into ice, so that our pace became a crawl. We fell in behind a stretcher party. It was questionable who most deserved sympathy, the partisan with a broken leg or the sweating bearers striving in inky darkness to keep their footing on that stony ice-bound path. Our torch helped them a little and, thanks to the drive and determination of the Albanian doctor looking after him, the wounded man was got down before dawn.

Except for a small party which remained for observation, Permet was abandoned that day by the partisans, who crossed the Vjose and took up positions in the scrub-covered hills to the east. There they were reinforced by two mountain guns from the 1st Brigade, manned entirely by Italians who had thrown in their lot with the partisans. The Germans mistimed their advance from Kelcyra and Perat so that the trap closed too late. It was not until the morning of 28 January that the smoke of burning villages on both sides of the river near Permet announced its capture. Taking us with them, the L.N.C. staff rather unnecessarily retreated as far as Frasheri. For although desultory fighting took place on the east bank, and a plane came over to bomb some villages, the Germans made no serious attempt to follow us. After three days at Frasheri monastery I was allowed to depart for Shepr, which I did, leaving the partisans to reorganise.

At Permet no one could tell us what had happened at Shepr, but it seemed extravagant to hope that it was unburnt. Since the village is not visible from the pass, our anxiety remained until we were almost there. Only five houses had been burnt and no one had been shot, but an army of Bashi Bazouks could not have plundered and ransacked the place more efficiently. Everything movable had gone, as had all the animals, which were used to carry away the swag. For this, the Balli who followed the Germans like jackals, led by a man called Ismael Golem, were mainly responsible. Other villages had not escaped so lightly. The small town of Sopik at the south end of Zagori had been completely gutted by fire, as had many villages at the north end, around Permet, and on the other side of Lunxheries. At a place called Hormove, thirty-five old men had been shot in reprisal for an ambush carried out some time before, in which a German patrol had been wiped out near the Lekei bridge.

All our mules and kit had gone, but the vital wireless equipment which we had hidden was intact. Many others have remarked how frequently it happens in war that at moments of crisis the signals one receives are entirely irrelevant or quite infuriating, or both. One expects to be maltreated by one's enemies, but now that the L.N.C. had received a knock-down blow, had had a number of their villages burnt, had seen the Balli everywhere revengefully triumphant, we received a rude kick on their behalf from our friends. On the reopening of communication the first signal to come in conveyed the considered opinion that the partisan brigades were expensive to maintain, militarily useless, and politically objectionable.

Thanks to the weather, supplies by air were so infrequent that the possibilities of using Grava Bay were again canvassed. An officer to assist me in running a sea base was landed at Seaview, but the disturbed state of the country prevented our meeting. He was unable to get past Dukati with his wireless equipment, and we were turned back by the presence of Germans in the Kuc area. This was one of our worst journeys. Bands of Balli were moving about freely, so that a village which was safe one day might be occupied by them the next. Golem was in a state of extreme misery. There were 3 ft. of snow on the ground and the few remaining inhabitants were on the border of starvation. Some houses had been burnt and all had been looted. We could get no news of Kuc there, so we crossed a high snow pass to the even more miserable village of Progonat, where, either through fear or changing sympathies, we met with an indifferent reception. We were not thrown out but, on the other hand, no one would take us in. Cold and wet, we tried one house after another until at last we imposed ourselves almost by force on an elderly couple. Mehmet stuck his foot in the door to prevent them shutting it, while behind it man and wife almost came to blows with each other on the question of whether we should be admitted or not.

Unable to get any further towards Kuc, we re-crossed the pass next morning in one of the severest blizzards I have ever encountered. We were accompanied by some young, thinly clad partisans who, I thought, would never get over alive. The gusts on top were so fierce that it was only possible to move in lulls. Poor and desolate though Golem might be, we could always depend on a warm welcome there. They freely burnt their scanty firewood to thaw us out, and offered us their maize bread. But now that food was scarce in consequence of so much having been burnt, we seldom accepted it.

We had one more adventure before we got back. We were ascending a path from the Dhrino to one of the Lunxheries villages in dense mist. We had heard vague rumours of Balli activity in the Lunxheries, so that when we were loudly challenged by a figure with a rifle, vaguely visible through the mist about 30 yards away, we were considerably startled. Both our Marlin automatics were slung and any attempt to use them would have invited a shot. It was a ticklish problem for Mehmet to solve. If they were Balli and he confessed who we were we should get shot, while if they were partisans and he did *not* say who we were we should likewise be shot. A tense staccato dialogue, which I could not follow, ensued; with Mehmet apparently sparring for time and a clue as to who they might be. The tension gradually relaxed. We walked forward, rather dry-mouthed, to be welcomed by the partisan patrol leader.

A heavy new fall of snow took place in March. Three feet of snow covered the dropping ground, where on several occasions we were nearly caught out by having the wood for the signal fires buried or by it being too sodden to burn when needed. If a sortie was expected we would tramp out there at dusk with sheepskin coats and a supply of tea and 'raki'. As the partisans were mostly poorly clad, we left them behind with instructions to come out if the plane came. As soon as this was heard the fires were blown into a blaze, signals exchanged, and then, if the plane was for us, the pilot started his run. Along with the loads on parachutes there were usually a number of free bundles of great-coats, battle-dress, blankets. The partisans (and we too for that matter) were a bit nervous about these, for they came down unheralded with a most vicious thud. Occasionally a parachute would fail to open and a big iron container weighing a couple of hundred pounds would half bury itself in the ground. One night a container full of mines, which were 'unarmed', but with the detonators for 'arming' them included in a separate box, landed harmlessly a few yards from where we were standing gazing expectantly upwards. When all the loads had been dropped as many as possible were brought in, and then we bedded down in the snow on a parachute and slept till dawn.

At the end of March a more serious attempt to use Grava Bay was made. There were several bodies from other missions waiting to be evacuated, but we also hoped to receive stores. Our large party from Shepr reached Sterre, a village near Borsh, on the 23rd where we met my officer from Seaview who had at last got through himself, but still had not been able to bring his wireless set. However, a stand-by period from the 24th to 31st had been arranged beforehand. The citadel of Borsh was found to be occupied by Balli, so we moved round to the next valley to the north, where we took up residence in one room of a house in the little village of Khudesi. Fifty local partisans were detailed as escort and beach party.

For seven successive nights we fell in at dusk and walked for two hours down to the seashore where we sat until one the following morning. The partisans picketed the surrounding area, while we took it in turns to sit upon a look-out rock, 30 ft. above the water, solemnly flashing a signal with a hand torch at frequent intervals. The weather was cold, but for most of the time conditions were very favourable with good visibility and an almost flat calm. For the first few nights we rather enjoyed sitting there, the Adriatic murmuring gently at our feet, while we watched a thin crescent moon disappearing behind the black hills above and strained our ears for the sound of an approaching boat. We were in a happy state of expectancy—I felt like a smuggler waiting for a cargo.

But happy expectancy cannot be sustained indefinitely and patience is a virtue easily fatigued by exercise. On the march back in the small hours of the morning, with hopes unfulfilled, such happiness quickly evaporated. We had purposely chosen a period of little moon, lights were not permissible on the march, and the boulders which littered the track had the peculiar quality of merging invisibly into the background. As we stumbled sleepily up the hill to Khudesi, which we usually reached as dawn was breaking, only the thought of the jorum of tea we should presently brew sustained our flagging energy. After that was drunk we slept till midday, had a meal, and slept again until it was time to get ready for the next performance.

On the fourth night an incipient carbuncle on my foot became so painful that I had to ride down on a mule. The partisans became more and more discouraged, and increasingly nervous of the possibility that one fine night we should be surprised. It certainly seemed not unlikely that our strange antics had been observed or reported, so no one was sorry when the curtain was rung down on the seventh and last performance. It was none too soon. We left Khudesi on the very appropriate morning of April Fool's Day, pursued by a German patrol from Himara, where curiosity about our doings had at last been aroused. We heard later that a boat came over on the night of 1 April, having been delayed until then by bad weather off the Italian coast. We had at least learnt that it was essential to have wireless with us, and that unless the partisans could occupy Borsh and securely hold a strip of the neighbouring coast, a sea base would have a short and precarious life.

In April, as the snow melted, activity on both sides increased. The Germans and Balli in occupation of Gjinokastre did their utmost by threats and starvation to bring the populace to their way of thinking. Ismael Golem alternately harangued and cut off supplies. 'Renounce the L.N.C.,' he proclaimed, 'urge your sons, brothers, husbands, to come back from the mountains, and all will be well.' Since no grain was being sent now from Kelcyra, we blew the road between it and Tepeleni. We also started laying mines on the road south from Gjinokastre by which the German garrison brought supplies from their base at Jannina. I attended the first mine-laying exploit in the capacity of safety officer and umpire. It was chiefly remarkable for the smallness of the bag and as a demonstration of how unlucky a man must be to get a hit at night. About three in the morning a large ten-ton lorry came along and was duly wrecked, whereupon our machine-gun party, carefully posted in a ruin 50 yards away, opened up. The gun, which was Italian, was on its best behaviour that night. For nearly five minutes by the clock the night was rendered hideous, and then, in a silence that could be felt, three trembling figures emerged unscratched from underneath the lorry—a German N.C.O. and two Balli. The lorry was empty.

In addition to our harassing by night, the R.A.F.were now making the roads unsafe by day. We also projected an attack on Gjinokastre with air support; for the suffering of the people was having an adverse effect on the partisans, many of whose families were there. We calculated that, if attacked, the Balli would withdraw inside the Citadel, a move which could only be prevented by some well-timed bombing. A plan was made and approved, but after repeated postponements we were advised that no bombers were available. The partisans concentrated for the attack were drawn off by a German drive in the Konispol area. By a stroke of luck a Spitfire sweep, happening to coincide with this drive, wrought great havoc amongst the transport—a success which offset our failure to secure the bombers, for the partisans wrongly attributed it to our foresight. Perhaps, like the fly on the wheel, the partisans thought they were responsible for the greater part of the dust raised by the Allied forces in the war effort, but when they heard daily of the thousands of sorties flown in Italy, and saw twenty planes immediately set aside for the evacuation of the American nurses, they felt neglected.

By May most of the snow had gone. Unrestricted freedom of movement, the *sine qua non* of guerilla warfare, was once more restored. The 5th Brigade, commanded by Shefket Peze, an old friend of mine of Cepo days, having occupied Borsh, seized a strip of the coast from Panormo Point for several miles south, and blew up the road at many points. My assistant, Lieut. Newell, was dispatched to Grava Bay with a wireless set, and the L.N.C. staff was asked to assemble a thousand mules in the neighbourhood. In view of the destitute state of the country this seemed a tall order but, acting with great energy, they succeeded admirably.

Before the landing of stores on a large scale took place, a small craft came over bringing with it my relief. Although I had been ten months in the country I was by no means tired of it, but I was tired of the anomalous position in which liaison officers were placed. The Balli, having been given so much rope, were now out of favour both with ourselves and the Germans, but their place had been taken by Abas Kupi, the Zoggist leader, on whom patience and money, and the services of the senior B.L.O., were now being spent to goad him and his few thousand followers into activity on our side. He might, of course, have re-joined the L.N.C., but that would have suited nobody but them.

On 18 May, having handed over to my successor at Shepr, I said farewell to Radowicke and other leaders. On the 20th I joined Newell and the others who were waiting to be evacuated in a farmhouse not far from the shore. At midnight on the 22nd a great army of men and mules assembled on the beach. In quick response to our signals a light flashed once far out to sea. We waited tensely expectant, until suddenly the open maw of a tank-landing craft loomed out of the dark heading straight for us. As her keel gently took the shingle she looked like some great sea monster coming ashore. Some minutes elapsed before the partisans recovered sufficiently from their astonishment to go on board. Then things moved quickly. An endless stream of excited men leapt up one side of the ramp, rushed to the stern where the loads were stacked, seized one and doubled back down the other side. In thirty minutes thirty tons of stores, neatly packed in 40 lb. loads, were ashore, and by dawn the beach was clear. As the last load came off, we bodies embarked. The escorting Italian destroyer which lay off shore was picked up, and together we chugged slowly over the calm water while the hills of Albania faded away between sea and sky.

For my part I returned convinced that our policy of giving moral, financial, and material support to the L.N.C. was just and expedient. Unhappily the goodwill thus earned and deserved was offset by the dislike we incurred for supporting the other two parties. At first all were treated equally, but even after two of the three parties had shown themselves to be useless and untrustworthy, we continued to sustain them morally by sending them missions, by refusing to denounce them by name, and by making only obscure references to the deeds and sacrifices of the L.N.C. The result of this ambiguous policy was that the honesty of our intentions was doubted and that not one of the parties trusted us. In view of our alliance with Russia a plain man could not conceive that it was the taint of Communism which precluded our giving undivided support to the L.N.C. By helping the one party we might offend a large number of Albanians and put them in a difficult position after the war, but having once encouraged the resistance movement we were obliged to befriend those who resisted and no one else. Whether it was over-sensibility or ignorance which moulded our policy I cannot tell. Nevertheless, I was startled by two incidents which came to my notice the day we reached Bari, which seemed to show that if the facts were known they were not understood. At the time I left Albania the L.N.C. were holding an important conference at Permet to state their war aims and to elect a provisional government.[1] The Albanian broadcast put out by us at the time naturally

1 This government was accorded recognition by the British Government in November 1945.

referred to this, but saw fit to deplore the fact that no representatives from the other two parties had been invited to attend. And on 23 May there appeared in the papers a report of an answer to a question in the House about Albania in which the Deputy Prime Minister stated that 'all parties in Albania were fighting the Germans and that we were endeavouring to bring them together', the first part of which was very wide of the truth.

The L.N.C. had their faults. For one thing they hoped to form the governmnt of the country after the war. Their declared aim was for a free, democratic, independent Albania, and they were convinced that they alone could realise these aims.This familiar formula has been used elsewhere without too much regard for its meaning, and it remains to be seen how the L.N.C. interpret it. Yet the fact remains that the partisans of the L.N.C. fought, suffered and died for these professed aims and by so doing helped us., The resolution they showed through many months of hardship, danger and disappointment, the will to win, their faith in themselves and in their cause, all seemed to me to establish their claim to leadership and to manifest that in them lay the best hope for Albania's future.

CHAPTER THIRTEEN

Arrival in North Italy

IT was my good fortune to spend the winter of 1944–5 in the mountains of north-east Italy, ostensibly with a view to the better prosecution of the partisan war, but in reality with the hope of seeing mountains more satisfying than those of southern Albania. After two abortive attempts we were dropped by parachute ('infiltrated' in official jargon) at the end of August.

Much had to be endured before this happy release took place. To some of us, that summer spent hanging about in southern Italy waiting to be used, seemed very like the previous August when we had suffered a lot of unnecessary anxiety as to whether there would be anything for us to do in Albania when we got there. Now that the Gothic Line had been broken and the Allied armies were at the threshold of the Po Valley, it really seemed hardly worth our while going in for the few remaining weeks, or even days, during which the enemy might yet retain his foothold in Italy. In my own case this impatience could partly be attributed to the call of the mountains; and in Ross, my second, perhaps to the spirit of vandalism innate in many of us, especially in the young—the desire to blow something to bits; for he had not been with partisans before and was probably suffering from a sense of frustration. The other two members of the party, who were Italians, were no doubt anxious to strike a blow for their country.

However, in the last week of August, the operation known as 'Beriwind' (humorists immediately rechristened us 'Bellywind') in which we were concerned was definitely 'on'. Besides myself there were three others. Ross, a young gunner captain who, when the war began, was studying medicine at Cambridge; Marini, who might be described as an elderly naval man except that, unlike Gilbert's elderly naval man, he was far from weedy and long but, on the contrary, short and very rotund; having been a wireless operator in Italian submarines for twelve years he was so accustomed to a sedentary life that I had some qualms as to his fitness for the work in hand; and lastly Gatti, the interpreter, who was an ex-officer of Alpini from Trento, with a short but varied career. During the early years of the war he had been, for an Alpini, in

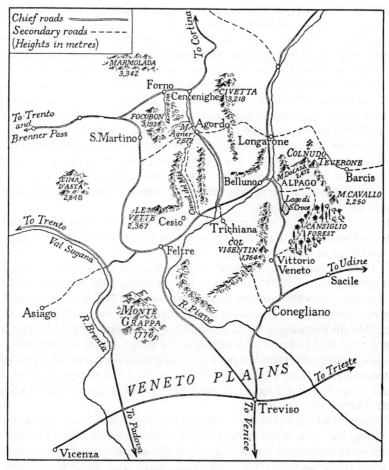

SKETCH MAP OF N. ITALY TO ILLUSTRATE
BELLUNO AREA

Railways and many secondary roads are not shown

the seemingly anomalous position of subaltern in the Italian Camel Corps, somewhere on the south-west border of Tripoli. Having come back to Italy, he was caught by the Germans at the time of the Italian surrender and put in a train bound for Gorizia but, since he was a man of resource, he jumped off and made his way to Rome, where he joined the Allied Army, serving for a time as interpreter with the Long Range Desert Group. He was not long and weedy but emphatically lean, with features so clean-cut as almost to resemble the 'hatchet-faced' men of American detective stories. He spoke excellent English and presumably impeccable Italian.

On a southern Italian airfield at dusk on 26 August our small party, strapped up in Sidcot suits and parachutes, might have been seen moving stiffly towards its appointed plane, a Douglas. We had already concluded a brief and tepid colloquy with the pilot, discussing such matters as our favourite dropping height, whether we preferred going before or after our kit, and signals. As the principal actor in the midnight drama soon to be enacted, we felt the pilot was not as interested in us as he might have been. No doubt he had his own worries, or perhaps he was more accustomed to dropping bombs, which need no consulting, than bodies. We groped our way to the forward end of the plane and subsided uncomfortably on to the piled-up loads. The plane roared down the runway, the lights were turned out, and we settled down in the dark to three hours' gloomy anticipation, chewing hard. At midnight the pilot reported that he was over the target but could see no signals. The moon was three-quarters full, and as we looked down from the door, roads and houses stood out plainly; altogether too many of them, we thought, to be anything like our more secluded target area. As the pilot turned the plane for home, relief at not having to jump was tempered with the thought that it would all have to be done over again.

On the 28th a different plane made the attempt. This time we felt more at home and watched with interest the lights of Trieste appear on the starboard side and those of Venice to port. As I stood idly by the door, peering into the void, I was startled to see several orange-coloured lights wink angrily at us from apparently just outside the door. Then a search-light shot up from below and I realised that the winking lights were bursting flak. Sorrows shared are sorrows halved, so I immediately communicated the intelligence to the others Marini fortunately failed to understand. He only heard about it when we got back, and suffered such retrospective pangs that he almost refused to try again. Shortly after this the pilot sent word back that we were approaching the target area. Taking advantage of my seniority I had already decided that I should jump first, for I never derived any encouragement from waiting to watch others go before me.

We stumbled back to the door, hitched the 'static lines' of our parachutes to the 'strong bar', put in the safety pin and tested it turned round and tested it several more times, and finally begged for the assurance of the next man that we were really secured. The four Yugo-Slavs who were responsible for throwing the loads out after we had gone were quite incapable of dispatching bodies. We had to do that ourselves. As I stood in the door, holding hard to either side and glaring fixidly at the red warning light, waiting for it to change to green, time passed unnoticed. I began to wonder if I had gone suddenly colour-blind, incapable of distinguishing green from red, while Ross, in a moment of aberration, suggested I should jump and hope for the best. Fortunately there is a limit to the time for which one can remain in a state of high tension. The spring began to unwind. We began to exchange disparaging remarks about the pilot, who at last sent to tell us that he could not find the target and was going home. Never was word more gratefully received. We had been standing at the door for an hour.

Our third attempt took place on the last day of August. This time there were nine bodies in the plane, another mission having had orders to go. Again I took first place, the leader of the other mission offering to dispatch me. A good dispatcher is most useful. A determined roar of 'Action Stations' pulls everyone together, and a still louder and more determined roar of 'No. 1 Go' compels the first victim, however reluctant, to leap into the void in a more or less correct position. So it was on this occasion. Word came that we were 'running up', but there was no need for me to concentrate so intensely on the warning light. Red turned to green and simultaneously, with a stentorian 'Go' still ringing in my ears, out I went.

There is a verse in that pathetic lament 'Nothing' which, to my mind, aptly expresses the act of stepping out of a plane in mid air:

> Nothing to breathe but air,
> Quick as a flash, 'tis gone.
> Nowhere to fall but off,
> Nowhere to stand but on.

After the first wild and whirling moment, when you sense the grateful tug of the harness, the first emotion is one of satisfaction, not unmingled with surprise, that the thing has actually worked once more. Then you feel you would like to shout with exultation and pride in being such a clever fellow as to float there so delightfully in the moonlight; you wish you could float there for ever. But this pride and exultation does not last. A glance at the smoke of the signal fires below seems to indicate a strong ground wind. You try to remember which way you ought to face and reach up for the rigging lines to make a turn. The ground seems to be rushing towards you. You realise there is no time to do a turn. Remember at the last minute to keep your feet and knees together, and then ——. If all goes well you land like a piece of clumsy thistledown, roll gently on one side, and recapture that feeling of exultation you had when you first became air-borne. But all parachute descents do not end so happily. You may acquire an uncontrollable pendulum motion, or other factors quite beyond control, such as the speed of wind or the nature of the landing ground, may lead to minor accidents.

So it was on this occasion. I was swinging pendulum-wise and on landing went over like a ninepin, striking a rock with the base of my spine with no ordinary violence—a blow which even the packet of two million paper lire stowed away in the seat of my Sidcot suit failed to mitigate. Ross landed in a tree from which he had to be cut down, Gatti was all right, and Marini sprained his ankle. All of us landed wide of target. Worse was to follow. Mist and cloud swept over the fires, and though we could still hear the plane circling we could not see it, and no doubt the pilot would be unable to see the target. Accompanied by the reception committee, and feeling some concern about the absence of the other five and more concern about the loss of our kit, we made our way to a nearby hut, where we had hot milk. A few minutes later the missing five walked in to report that the pilot had only had time to drop them before the target was obscured. The plane had now gone home, taking all our stores with it. This was upsetting, but we imagined that another plane would be sent in the course of the next few nights. As luck would have it, four months were to elapse before the next successful 'drop'.

The place where we had landed was the Alto-piano d'Asiago, a broad heavily wooded plateau between the Brenta and upper Adige valleys, overlooking the plains north of Vicenza. Ever since the Italian surrender in September 1943 the bolder spirits of northern Italy, eager to atone for the long years of willing slavery under Fascist rule, and burning to show once and for all where their sympathies lay, had been organising themselves into resistance groups—clandestinely in the cities, town, and villages of the plains, and more openly in the mountain regions. From east of Udine, where they were in touch with Tito's Slavs of Gorizia, round to the French border in the west, there were ill-armed, inexperienced, but eager and determined bands of men. In the late summer of 1944 hopes ran high. Large stretches of country in the more mountainous area were completely controlled by partisans, the Allies seemed likely to break into the plains beyond the Po at any moment, and as yet neither Germans nor Fascists had had either the time or the men to devote much attention to the increasing attacks on their communications.

For our part we had already dropped a large number of Italian agents, recruited from our side of the lines, to send back information about the strength of the various groups and to organise the reception of supplies. British liaison officers were now being sent in to act, as their name implies, as a direct link between the partisan leaders and the Allied army, to encourage and train bands in the use of arms, explosives and incendiary devices, to arrange for their supply, and generally to hearten the whole resistance movement and discourage political differences. Organisation and command were the responsibilities of the partisans themselves.

There were already two widely separated British missions in north-east Italy when we arrived to bridge the gap between them, one of them being that of Major Wilkinson who received us. He was unfortunately killed in an ambush in the following March. My mission was allotted to a formation called the Nino Nannetti Division, then operating in a large area stretching from Monte Grappa to Vittorio Veneto in the south, and from Monte Marmolada across to Cortina in the north, that is to say, a large slice of the Dolomites, the foothills to the south of them, and the upper Piave valley.

In view of the shortly expected break-through on the Italian front and the retreat of the Germans it was essential, we thought, for us to make contact with the Nannetti Division as as soon as possible. For in these operations the partisans would be required to play an important part by blowing up bridges and roads and generally harassing the retreating enemy. Unfortunately our wireless set had gone back with the plane and, until one was dropped, which we hoped would be in the course of the next night or two, we could be of little use to either the partisans or the Army. Marini, the operator, was unable to walk and I was unable to stand—for an 'actual necessity', as the French put it, I had to crawl away into the forest on hands and knees. We therefore sent Ross and Gatti off on 2 September to find Divisional H.Q., trusting that by the time a set arrived we should be able to follow.

Major Wilkinson and a band of some 200 partisans were living in rough shelters made from parachutes in the middle of a pine forest. The smell of the pines and the air, for we were about 5,000 ft. up set my blood tingling. On 2 September I walked 50 yards, the day after that 300 yards, and on the 4th I managed to reach a hillock half a mile away, from where I could look down to the chequer-board fields and poplars of the Veneto and see to the east the massive rounded hump of Monte Grappa. As our missing stores had not yet arrived, Wilkinson, knowing I was impatient to be off, lent me a spare wireless set and battery, and another Italian operator in place of the injured Marini. This was the last I saw of the elderly naval man. I heard later that some time during the winter he had crawled out of his 'bunker' or foxhole straight into the arms of some waiting Germans. He was said to have proved a first-class operator but quite unable to walk. As I had expected, his twelve years' submarine service had deprived him of the use of his legs. The operator who came in his place deserves a few words of introduction. He rejoiced in the name of Pallino. He was young, and his service in the Italian Air Force had not only failed to quell his natural exuberance, but had instilled in him a violent dislike of control of any sort. He was a gifted operator. With the most amateurish aerial, which the experts would view with derision, he would in a few moments make contact with Base several hundred miles away, and pass and receive messages singularly free from corruptions. But his other virtues he hid under a bushel. He was idle, insubordinate, temperamental, mindful of his own comfort, and extremely touchy if any of his shortcomings were pointed out to him. He was like a desert sore, always there, always irritating, and quite incurable. Many times we sighed for Marini. Many times we were on the point of having Pallino shot. But good operators were irreplaceable, and when he was working, pounding out messages with frozen fingers by the light of a guttering candle, we forgave him all; indeed we almost loved him. But when he had finished his schedule and started crooning, probably the 'Internationale', for he was an ardent Communist, murder would again raise its snaky head.

On the night of 5 September Pallino and I set off to join Ross and Gatti. The speed of our journey was a striking tribute to the good organisation of the partisans and to the control which they exercised over the country at that time. Accompanied by a small escort armed with Stens and Berettas (the Italian sub-machine-gun) our truck shot through Asiago in the middle of the night, and early in the morning we were delivered safely to an outlying company of the brigade. The next night they took us to a village overlooking the Brenta valley. Here we met another escort who was responsible for getting us safely over the main road and railway down in the valley, the only place where there was any chance of meeting a German patrol. The clatter we made descending a steep, loose, stony path roused all the dogs in the neighbourhood, but in the valley all was as quiet as the grave. Having crossed the river in a boat we began to grind up the slopes of Monte Grappa, a journey which engaged all our energies for the rest of the night. Monte Grappa was the scene of fierce fighting in 1917 and 1918. Parts of the summit are as much pitted with shell holes as the most hotly contested ground on the old Western Front.

In an 'albergo' near the summit we found the mission who had dropped with us already installed and holding a conference of partisan leaders. Monte Grappa was in the Nannetti Divisional area, but was occupied by a motley collection of partisans from various formations and of various political hues. The inevitable lack of cohesion probably had a good deal to do with the debacle which took place a fortnight later when the Germans attacked in strength and completely broke them up. Commanding as it did the Brenta and Piave valley routes, Monte Grappa was of great tactical importance, and the Germans saw to it that no partisans remained there.

After another all-night march we joined Ross and Gatti, who were temporarily held up in the village of Cesio in the Piave valley. They were occupying the best villa in the company of one of our Italian agents, a man of infinite resource and sagacity who had fought in the Spanish war. He disdained secrecy, and trusted to forged documents and a good 'cover' story which seemed to enable him to go where he wanted and get what he wanted. Although the owner of the villa, who had the misfortune to be wealthy, was suspected of having Fascist tendencies, the villa was later burnt by the Fascists, presumably because it had harboured the agent and ourselves. To be neutral in civil war is to be damned. One side helps itself at your expense, and the other side either shoots you or burns your house for having helped its opponents.

Several times in the months to come we were to live in the vicinity of Cesio or to pass through it furtively at night, for the personality and energy of one man had made it a focal point of partisan activity. This excellent man, Orestes by name, was always a present help in time of trouble. He was an old soldier of the previous war, a man of decided opinions, in politics a democrat, a loud and indefatigable talker, and withal he was extremely deaf. He ran a small squad of half a dozen local men, whom he called his 'boys', who did odd sabotage jobs. He also helped the regular partisan formations living in the hills by organising their supplies. This type of partisan, who lived peacefully in his village by day and became an active partisan at night or as occasion warranted, belonged to the organisation known as G.A.P. (Gruppo Azione Patriotico). Almost every town and village of northern Italy had its own small G.A.P. squad, and very bold and keen partisans many of them were. Orestes was a builder by trade, and one of the best types of Italian artisans. He had a wife and several children, who were later turned out in the street by the Fascists and their house burnt. Around Cesio, Orestes was something of an oracle. Men hung on his words. With a hideous white-peaked cap on his head, and a thick stubble on his chin, he loved to talk of General Alexander and of what orders he, the General, had sent to Orestes. Every telling point, and there were many, was delivered with a characteristic gesture of smiting the hollow of the right arm with the left hand, and with the exclamation of 'Ostia'!

A cloak of fictitious secrecy hung round us while we were in Cesio, for I think everyone knew what we were. When darkness fell we were taken round to the 'Albergo' to drink with the local patriots, and the priest, who was also a staunch patriot, entertained us to a bottle of wine. With the priest's permission we had already climbed the church tower to obtain a view of the Piave and the villages on the south side through which our route lay. Like most of those in the villages of the Piave, the church had a very lofty tower in which the bells had been hung by no less a man than Orestes himself. Many of these towers are built separate from the parent church. The valley hereabouts is wide, hot, fertile and beautiful; full of vines, apples, pears, peaches, mulberries, walnuts, maize and wheat. One of the severest penalties of our furtive existence was that we seldom saw the charming pastoral scenes of that lovely country by day. Sometimes, like a belated fox making for its earth, we might be surprised by dawn while still on the move, wandering through country lanes under shady chestnuts, through orchards and field paths, by trellised vines, plucking the red grapes still wet with dew.

By 8 September Orestes' arrangements for taking us across the Piave were complete. Flying patrols, supplied by girls on bicycles, were put out along the road as far as the main Feltre-Belluno highway. Towards dusk we piled into a sort of butcher's van. Three of us were concealed in the back, while I with my uniform hidden by an an old raincoat sat in front with Orestes. We crossed the highway without incident, and found our escort waiting for us on the bank of the river. Even at that time of year there was a lot of water, but, as it flows in several channels in a wide stony bed, it was just fordable. As we were not allowed to wade we crossed on the shoulders of the escort. By midnight we had reached Trichiana, where we were received in a large country house by an English-speaking Italian lady, known to us subsequently as 'Giuliana', or sometimes as the 'Countess'. She and her two brothers were active patriots, and were always very kind to us.

Here we got bad news. Nannetti H.Q. were then in Cansiglio Forest on the east side of the Vittorio Veneto-Belluno highway. In this ideal partisan country there were said to be some 3,000 men. They were, of course, indifferently armed, had few machine-guns, and little experience. There were in addition three brigades, of perhaps 500 men each, in the country to the west of the highway and to the south of the Piave. Couriers from these were now coming in to report the beginning of a big 'rastrallamento' (literally 'combing') against the partisans in Cansiglio. They had had no communication from Divisional H.Q., which had been dispersed, and they were unable to get us across the road even supposing we still wished to go. Conflicting reports continued to come in all day, but the upshot was that we finally decided to join the Gramsci Brigade, then located in the mountains to the north-west of Cesio, and there await news of Divisional H.Q. The local leaders assured us that this was where H.Q. would 'rendezvous' if they had been dispersed. Accordingly we recrossed the Piave that night, passed once more through the sleeping village of Cesio, this time in real secrecy, and next afternoon joined the Gramsci Brigade on Le Vette. Our experiences on Le Vette and the dispersal and flight of the Gramsci Brigade, in which we were willing participants, deserve a chapter to themselves.

CHAPTER FOURTEEN

With the Gramsci Brigade

LE Vette is a high grassy plateau (c. 7,000 ft.). To the north it presents a long cliff face of rotten rock, which can only be climbed by one difficult path, while on the other sides there are only four possible lines of approach. The top is a large saucer-like depression divided into two parts by a high grass ridge running between the northern and southern rims. Except for a few boulders it is bare of trees, scrub or anything that might give cover. At first sight its scant and easily defended approaches would seem to make it an ideal partisan stronghold. They merely give to it a pleasing but entirely false sense of security. The approaches are of necessity the exits, and if these are closed all freedom of manœuvre, the *sine qua non* of partisan warfare, is at an end.

As we plodded slowly up the last steep zigzags of the mule track we were suddenly challenged by an obvious Englishman dressed in the shabby nondescript clothes of a partisan. He proved to be an escaped prisoner-of-war and this was the block-post guarding the main approach to Le Vette. Inside a tin-roofed shed were ten other Englishmen, all escaped prisoners-of-war, who had thrown in their lot with the Gramsci Brigade. They formed a small detachment of their own known by the honourable title of the 'Churchill Company'. Of the many British prisoners who had escaped at the time of the Italian Armistice, some had been recaptured, many were living with Italian families, a few had escaped through Yugo-Slavia, and a few had joined the partisans.

Naturally they were surprised and pleased to see us, and questioned us closely, particularly as to the probable duration of the war, for they were undecided whether they should or whether they should not try to get through to our lines. Our advice was to stay. We argued that even if the expected break-through did not succeed and a German withdrawal did not take place, the battle was almost certain to become more fluid, and escaping through the lines then would be a simpler matter than now.

The block-post was connected by telephone line to Brigade H.Q., about ten minutes' walk away. Our arrival was reported and permission obtained for us to pass through. Suspicious or highly improbable arrivals, such as we were, were always detained at the post until their *bona fides* had been established.

Spies and informers abounded, and if discovered met with no mercy. It was astonishing how many there were. They were even found in the ranks of the partisans and no one not personally known could be trusted. The systematic elimination of spies and informers in towns and village went on all the time, and information was forcibly extracted from them before they were shot.

There were about 300 partisans in Le Vette. A very numerous H.Q. staff was living in a long, stone, tin-roofed cow-shed (a 'malga' as it is called) at Pietena. A battalion called Zancanaro lived in another 'malga' in the other half of the basin beyond the ridge; and the Battisti Battalion lay two or three miles to the east guarding the approach on that side. The Nannetti Division itself, its brigades and battalions, were all named after either heroes of the Risorgimento, such as Mazzini, Bixio, Pisacane, Cairoli; or patriots, mostly Communists, who had bitterly opposed Fascism in the twenties, or had fought and died in the Spanish Civil War on the losing side. Nino Nannetti and Gramsci, for example, were two such patriots. Later on battalions, or even brigades, were named after well-known partisans who had been killed in action or who had been executed in the present struggle.

The Nannetti Division was what was known as a Garibaldi formation. These Garibaldi units were raised and organised in the first place by the Communists who, in Italy, as in Yugo-Slavia, Albania, and perhaps Greece, were the backbone of the resistance movement. There was, in my opinion, no doubt that the Garibaldi formations were the most effective. They were better organised, better led, and attracted a more ardent and more determined type of recruit than the so-called independent brigades or the brigades sponsored by other political parties. The practice of forming brigades on a political basis was, of course, deplorable. But until someone could be found strong enough to lead and control the whole resistance movement, and until the Communist Party relinquished control of the Garibaldi formations, such a basis was presumably unavoidable. Later all formations, irrespective of political colour, were embodied in the Corpo Volontario Della Liberta, or C.V.L., under the control of the military branch of the Central Milan Committee of the C.L.N. or Comitato di Liberazione Nazionale.

Most of the Garibaldi leaders were Communists; some of long standing and of conviction, others more recent converts whose interests were politic rather than political, who had embraced the faith for the sake of peace and quietness and to avoid the barrage of political harangues to which they would otherwise be subject. The rank and file, or 'garibaldini' as they were called, were more mixed. Among them would be found the fanatic, the enthusiast, the lukewarm, the indifferent, and the politically independent, who had become 'garibaldini' merely because they were the most numerous and the best organised. At this time the whole of our area with one small exception was 'Garibaldi'. Later two independent brigades were formed, but they were not of much importance.

The 'garibaldini' liked to wear red scarves, as much presumably on account of the red-shirts of Garibaldi's Thousand as of any Communist association—and when possible a grey long-peaked cap, like a French kepi but softer, with a red star in front. Below that anything was permissible, nay welcome; scraps of

German, Italian and British uniforms of Italian policemen, firemen, sailors, customs officials, forest guards, or carabinieri; and, of course, every conceivable kind of civilian rig. Many were ex-Alpini and wore the dashing Alpini hat of their regiments. Alpini beards were always fashionable, until they became too dangerous, as a man with a beard was *ipso facto* a partisan or brigand according to one's point of view. I never saw the clenched-fist salute given by the partisans of the mountains, though I believe it was common enough in the plains. A normal salute was used and the invariable greeting on meeting, or on entering a room or leaving, was 'Morte ai Fascisti' (or Fascismo) with the reply 'Liberta ai Popoli'.

Every H.Q. down to that of a battalion had its Political Commissar who was particularly responsible for relations between partisans and the civilian population, for the maintenance of morale, and for political instruction. He worked in the closest contact with the Commandant and all orders were invariably signed by both. In the Gramsci Brigade the 'ora politica' was strictly observed. This was a daily set period when the Commander or Commissar addressed the men on questions of discipline, organisation, interior economy, or politics, and when any man could get up and raise any question, not excluding the behaviour of his leaders. Later it fell in abeyance either because of the reduction in numbers, or because of the weakening of political interest in the face of the increasingly critical situation of winter. A few Russians, escaped prisoners-of-war, who were on Le Vette with the brigade (one was a Company Commander), took particular care that there were no absentees during the 'ora politica'. They seemed efficient soldiers, these Russians, who took life seriously. There was nothing funny about them except their names— Borlikoff, Orloff, Shuvoff, etc.

Discipline was fairly good but nothing like so rigid as that maintained in similar formations in Albania, where minor thefts, drunkenness, or immorality, were alike punished with death. Discipline in a spontaneously formed, free body of men is a delicate and difficult problem. If the men are highly imbued with a sense of dedication to a sacred cause, then extremely severe rules may be made without much fear of having them broken and without the correspondingly severe penalty having to be enforced; but in the case of a more mixed and less highly principled body, the eyes of those in authority must be frequently shut to all but serious military offences. Much then depends on the strength of personality of the commander. Things were certainly more lax in Italy. Even control of stores received on a dropping ground, an elementary and fundamental matter, was not always satisfactory. I knew of only two instances of partisans being shot, one for drunkenness when out on patrol, and one for repeatedly taking food from civilians by force for his own use. For disobedience or neglect of duty a man might be tied to a tree for a few hours, or in more serious cases dismissed.

Bruno, the Commander of the brigade, was a man of strong personality, repected and liked by his men. He was an ex-officer of artillery but, having served only with anti-aircraft units, he had no experience of infantry tactics or of fighting. His brigade was well organised and well disciplined, and the arms, such as they were, well cared for. They were extremely keen to fight—'Give us arms and ammunition' was the daily burthen of their song. This theme became more insistent as one blank night followed another, and as indications of an impending 'rastrallamento' became stronger. But in spite of our fervid signals, couched in language which became ruder as time went on, nothing came except our signal stores and kit which were eventually dropped at Monte Grappa, where they were either stolen, or lost in the 'rastrallamento'.

That Pietena was not impossible to find was shown when an American plane came over to drop two Italian agents. The ground was most unsuitable for bodies, but having been told to receive them we lit the signal fires. About midnight a Liberator flew over high, circled once, and disappeared. Nothing was seen to drop. However, at dawn a strange and rather haggard figure, wearing a Sidcot suit, appeared and asked if we had seen his companion. Search parties were sent out. They found the unfortunate man suspended head downwards over a cliff. He was not seriously damaged, but we took no credit for that.

Although the partisans were surprised and disgusted at our inability to help, we remained good friends. I think they attributed our failure to incompetence rather than to unwillingness, and in this, of course, they were quite right. The more ardent Communists among them liked to believe that their politics were responsible for this apparently deliberate withholding of arms, and short of a plane-load of Bren guns falling at their feet, or better still on their thick skulls, the theory was difficult to kill no matter how strongly we might protest that so long as they were willing to fight they might be anarchists for all we or our employers cared. In spite of our shortcomings they accepted us as one of themselves. They supplied bedding, for we still had nothing but the clothes we wore, toilet kit, bowl and spoon; they saw that we got our cigarette and tobacco ration, and even supplied a tame Fascist, whom they had not yet shot, to bring our meals from the kitchen, where food for all was cooked in a vast copper cauldron. We fed very well. We began the day with a bowl of *ersatz* coffee and a roll—the small Italian loaf of about 100 grammes of good coarse wholemeal; at midday a bowl of broth with meat or 'pasta', or sometimes 'pasta asciutta', and another loaf; for supper a bowl of minestrone, that is, thick vegetable soup with beans, another loaf and perhaps a bit of cheese—uncompromisingly Italian but satisfying.

Beyond ciphering and deciphering messages, visiting the battalions, and getting to know the geography of Le Vette, there was nothing much for us to do. On 17 September, taking advantage of the presence of the Commissar of the Pisacane Brigade who was about to return, Gatti and I made a quick trip to Forno, south of Monte Marmolada where this brigade was stationed. It was a journey remarkable for the variety of transport employed, and is worth describing very briefly to show the ease with which one moved about at that time compared with the difficulty we experienced later.

Upon reaching the valley head below the Battisti Battalion post, we took a mule trap to road-head represented by a blown-up bridge. There we embarked in a long, lean, black car driven by a partisan who professed to be a racing motorist. Two beady eyes peering out of a mass of auburn beard and hair were all I could see of his face. In the gathering dusk, without lights or brakes, along narrow winding secondary roads, we careered at something like 40 m.p.h. For a hundred yards or so we had to traverse the main Belluno highway before turning on to another side road, and when we caught sight of the lights of a German truck behind us, the speedometer needle appeared to revolve completely in front of my frightened eyes. Our mad career was happily cut short by the necessity of observing the curfew restrictions imposed at eight o'clock, after which hour no civilian cars were allowed on the road.

We pulled up with two flat tyres to spend the night in a hayloft. A closed van belonging to the T.O.D.T. organisation was waiting for us next morning. T.O.D.T. was the civilian labour corps nominally working for the Germans but with the least display of zeal consonant with safety. In delightful contrast with the Grand Prix affair of the previous night, we tooled sedately up the Canal dell Mis, stopping a few miles short of Agordo on the main road, where there was a German garrison. Here the plan was to find the local head of the T.O.D.T., a man in league with the partisans, whose presence in the front seat might, they thought, ensure our passing the German block-posts unchallenged; the Commissar, Gatti, and I were to sit in the back, presumably with our fingers crossed. Although it would save us a long walk, the plan was not one which I liked. In fact, I was seldom more relieved in my life than when we heard that this useful official could not be found. It was then one o'clock, so hiding the van in a wood we set off on our feet. Agordo, with its streets full of Germans, whom we could see walking about, was successfully avoided, and a pass, the Forcella Cesurette (6,000 ft.), crossed. From there I caught a glimpse of a tiny glacier high up on the Pala di S. Martino which gave me a thrill out of all proportion to its size. Eight hours later we limped into Forno. The Commander of the Pisacane Brigade came in next morning to discuss arrangements for dropping grounds, and I handed over a substantial sum of lire as an earnest of our intentions. Tall, lithe, dark and good-looking, with pistols sticking out of every pocket, he looked like a Naples bravo. Carlo was in fact a Neapolitan, which was strange, because there is no love lost between northern and southern Italians; but by his many bold actions he had earned the command of the brigade and the respect of all. One of these actions was a daylight raid on the Belluno gaol where, mainly by bluff, he had released a number of partisans. He later commanded the Belluno G.A.P. and carried out some quiet but effective work with a silent pistol we had got for him. He was an exponent of the 'cloak and dagger' school, wore strikingly different clothes each day, and never slept twice in the same place.

The situation at Pietena when we returned on the 20th was unchanged, except for the weather which was becoming colder. The pond in which we washed wore a film of ice in the morning and on the 28th snow fell all day. Pietena would be untenable during the winter, but Bruno, wishing to hang on as long as possible, proceeded to have the draughty 'malga' well lined with hay. His decision was determined by the lack of arms and by the ever-present possibility of their arrival. But it was now becoming a question of which would arrive first, the arms, winter, or the Germans; and the odds were heavily on the last. It was evidently the enemy intention to clear up the whole of the Piave valley. They had already dealt with the Cansiglio area and the Monte

Grappa, and on the 29th our turn came. In the meantime we had our first contact with the Nannetti Division in the form of a flying visit from Filippo their Commander. He promised to return in a few days to take us to their new headquarters, but on his way up on the 29th he ran into the Germans, who were attacking us, was shot at, lost all the division's secret files, including the locations and signals of all dropping grounds, and disappears from history.

About five o'clock on the evening of 29 September we were startled by a distant burst of machine-gun fire. The Churchill Company block-post reported that a German patrol had attacked the post and the store in the valley some 2,000 ft. below. The store was in flames. The long-expected 'rastrallamento' was evidently about to begin. The commanders of the Zancanaro and Battisti Battalions arrived to attend a council of war, bringing with them news of German movement below their posts. Bruno, who was something of a fire-eater, had only one thought, or plan—to fight to the last man and the last round.

'The camel driver has his thoughts and the camel he has his', was the reflection that crossed my mind on hearing these ominous words. I had heard them before, but never in connection with partisan warfare, for here the loss of ground or positions should mean nothing. The function of the partisans was to remain intact as a fighting force, constituting by their mere existence and by occasional pinpricks, a constant threat, to meet which the enemy must hold in readiness troops which could be more usefully employed elsewhere. The only value of Pietena was as a dropping ground. But it was neither a good one, nor was it the only one, and winter would soon force us to abandon it. As yet nothing had been dropped there and we could give no guarantee that anything would be dropped in the future. We pointed out these objections—but to no purpose. The honour of the Gramsci Brigade was at stake; the rout of the partisans on Monte Grappa must be avenged: sentiments which were received with acclamation by an easily swayed, uninstructed audience. I might have gone on to point out that the best of partisans cannot hope to hold even the strongest position for long against trained troops with mortars, machine-guns, unlimited ammunition, inter-communications, and the power if need be to reinforce; that the ammunition available was 300 rounds per L.M.G. and 30 per rifle; that there was food for only a few days with no hope of getting more; and that partisan morale can best be served by inflicting casualties and suffering none in return.

These warnings went unheeded. Perhaps they lost their force in the interpretation, or perhaps were attributed to our pusillanimity. Indeed Bruno suggested the mission should withdraw that night before it was too late, but this eminently sensible plan was rejected. It was a question of what interpretation would be put upon our action if we agreed. Would they take the commonsense military view that the safety of the mission with its wireless set and all the possibilities of future supplies which this implied, should not be hazarded uselessly, or would they think that we were running away? Not that this should have mattered much to me, for in common with the rest of the British Army I had spent much of the war running away in order to fight again; but it might adversely affect the future by impairing what little influence we had. On Bruno's assurance that he would not only see that the mission got away but that the brigade would also emerge from the crisis intact, we decided to await the event. In face of the fact that the four known exits were already in process of being blocked, his plan for effecting this was not very obvious. We hopefully assumed that there were other routes unknown to us and went to bed.

Developments in the morning were slow. The only news of fighting was from the Zancanaro Battalion on the west, and by noon it was clear that this was where the attack was being pressed, and that on the other approaches the enemy were merely in the nature of 'stops' to prevent the game breaking back. The majority of the Battisti Battalion were brought over to Pietena to reinforce the northern rim and the ridge dividing the basin, on which machine-gun posts had been prepared some time before. Some official visitors from below, who had been caught out by the promptness with which the exits had been blocked, tried to get out by the difficult track down the north face. They came back later with the news that that too was blocked by patrols.

There were at least fifty partisans hanging about round the H.Q. 'malga': the H.Q. staff, clerks, cooks, couriers, intendants, and the other idlers who commonly collect round a H.Q., those whom the Army call rather unkindly the 'unemployed men'. There were also stragglers from Battisti who had come down to try to find out what was happening. They were not the only ones seeking enlightenment. News was scarce, and in no very easy frame of mind we kicked our heels in the customarily depressing atmosphere of those left out of battle. Bruno still radiated confidence, but early in the afternoon he went up to the dividing ridge from which there already came sounds of firing. Shortly after this he sent orders to remove everything and everybody to the top of Duodieci, a rocky broken summit on the rim just above the north end of the dividing ridge. Legs of beef, sacks of bread and beans, cooking pots, typewriters, were hoisted on to men's backs and carried away in a manner that one could not help thinking was only half-hearted. Preparations for a last stand on Duodieci at this early stage was surely a counsel of despair and that must mean the battle was not going well.

Leaving Ross and Pallino at Pietena with orders to have our few belongings ready to move, Gatti and I went up to find Bruno. The climb of nearly 500 ft. to the ridge took us about twenty minutes. On our side of it, the lee side, most of the stuff removed from Pietena had been dumped, and only a few of the more obedient were still struggling up the rocky slopes of Duodieci with their loads. The crest of the ridge was under mortar fire. Seizing our opportunity we ran over the top and found Bruno in a covered machine-gun pit on the forward slope very busy with an old French machine-gun which would only fire a couple of rounds at a time before jamming. Through the slit I could see that the Zancanaro 'malga' was already in German hands. Where the mule track crossed the western rim, 2,500 yards away, the mortar which was now busy with our position could be seen firing. More Germans were advancing unconcernedly across the basin toward our ridge, while another party of a hundred or more had just begun moving along the crest of the rim towards Duodieci. All partisans had withdrawn to the dividing ridge.

Bruno, with the light of battle in his eyes, paid little attention to my question of what he proposed doing. My suggestion that at this moment he ought not to be fiddling with a machine-gun, and that in any case to fire that ancient and obdurate weapon at men over 2,000 yards away was a waste of effort, fell on deaf ears. In the moments he grudgingly spared from his struggle with that miserable piece, we wrangled uselessly while mortar bombs burst more or less harmlessly about the position. Three partisans had so far been wounded. The Germans, I imagine, were unscathed. Most of the partisans in the vicinity, except Bruno, looked decidedly and, I thought, justifiably, scared. At length Bruno agreed to withdraw at dusk and promised to send out orders to that effect. Whether this had been his intention all along I cannot say. Perhaps the speed with which the Germans got to the Zancanaro 'malga' had surprised him, but as we had waited so long it was sensible to wait until dusk before retiring.

We left Bruno with his machine-gun and went back to Pietena to warn the others of the new plan. It was then about 7 p.m., just about sunset. Whether 'our brows, like to a title-leaf, foretold the nature of a tragic volume', or whether it was the few words we exchanged together, I cannot tell. The effect of our arrival, however, was immediately harmful. A lot of shouting broke out amongst the H.Q. company, and some Battisti who had wandered down from their post to the rim, and a 'sauve qui peut' seemed imminent. At the same moment men were seen streaming away along the northern rim from the direction of Duodieci. That was decisive. The time had come for us to fend for ourselves. We picked up a blanket each, put the 6-volt battery on a mule, and Ross shouldered the suitcase containing the wireless set. I went off to see if the Churchill Company had received any orders to retire—for it seemed likely that they would be forgotten in the confusion—while the whole mob straggled off towards the Battisti track. They had not gone far before figures appeared silhouetted against the evening sky on the southern rim. Spurts of flame ran along the ridge and tracer bullets began zipping over the heads of the fugitives or thudding against the rocks. Although the Germans were at least 1,500 yards away they made good practice in the failing light, and so frightened the mules that we lost our battery. When it was dark we halted and Bruno came up. He handed over the conduct of the withdrawal, an unenviable task, to his second-in-command, saying that he would wait to see what the Germans did.

The track to Battisti followed the north rim just below the crest, and at about eleven o'clock when we were within about a mile of the Battisti 'malga', a patrol was sent ahead to estimate the chance of passing the block-post unseen, or of attacking it. There was a lot of snow about and for an hour the fugitive mob, for we were little better, sat about on stones waiting dejectedly for the verdict. When it came it was the expected, 'None'. More talk broke out, but this time it was conducted in fearful whispers. The plan favoured by the majority was to try to cross a valley to the south, though it was known that it was picketed by the enemy.

Burdened as we were with a wireless set which we could not afford to lose, I did not fancy the idea of running the gauntlet in this valley, so I suggested to the others an alternative plan of lying low on the north face of Le Vette until the enemy got tired of looking for partisans. We might even find a way down, but at the worst the Germans were not likely to remain up there for more than a couple of days. This plan they agreed to. The Churchill Company, in a body, asked to come with us, and the Italian cook from Pietena, who was a friend of ours, offered to carry the wireless set. This made a party of sixteen (and others would have attached themselves had they been allowed) instead of the four of five I should have preferred. We left the path, shook off some would-be adherents, and struck straight up to the crest, carelessly leaving our tracks in a patch of snow close to the path. As we gained the crest we saw below us the fires of the enemy pickets in the valley the partisans hoped to cross.

We began a descent of the first likely looking gully on the far side, the first few hundred feet of which consisted of steep frozen scree and patches of snow. Soon we were brought to a standstill by the gully falling away abruptly, so we scratched out a platform of sorts and turned in—that is to say, lay down. We had one blanket apiece and no food; moreover, we were 7,000 ft. up and it was late September. I entertained a slight hope of being able to force a way down, but a search made next day showed this to be difficult for a small, strong party of climbers and quite impossible for a party such as ours. We were a very weak party for mountaineering, even on Le Vette.

A cautious look over the top of the gully at dawn revealed groups of Germans on the track below evidently engaged in the search for the no doubt numerous Brer Rabbits who, like us, were 'laying low and saying nuffin'. They were three or four hundred yards away, and to my imagination, quickened by a night's fast, they seemed to be discussing the marks we had made in the snow as we left the track. I tiptoed carefully down the gully and warned the others. The first hour of a day of continuous apprehension was the worst. After that it became obvious that the party I had seen was not coming to inspect the north face, but for all that we breathed more freely when dusk fell.

That night the wind rose. By dawn a blizzard was blowing from the north, the one quarter from which we had no protection. It blew all day, but wretched though our situation was, the faint sound of automatic fire, borne to our ears against the gale, persuaded us to stick it out for yet another night.

By the end of the third day we had to move whether or no. No one had eaten for seventy-two hours, some had frozen feet, and all were stiff with cold. The start was not auspicious. Having gone to the top of the gully at dusk to reconnoitre I was recalled by wild cries from below. Since for three days no one had dared to raise his voice above a whisper, it seemed something important must have happened—perhaps they had found some food. In fact, one of the ex-prisoners-of-war had slipped. I found him lying dazed with a severe gash in his head, on a ledge 60 ft. below our 'gîte' on the lip of a straight drop of a like distance. His hands were lacerated too, but securing him to the tail of my coat, I eventually dragged him to the top of the gully where the remainder were now waiting. We had lost much time, and what with having frozen feet, and limbs so stiff that for many walking was a matter of difficulty, my plan of finding a safe way out along the crest of the rim had to be abandoned in favour of following the track. With every step we took our confidence increased. We met no one and by daybreak we were lying in a wood staring with longing intensity at a farm below. One of the Englishmen who knew the place went down, the signal for 'all clear' was given, and soon we were enjoying our first meal since lunch on the day of the attack. The Germans had left the day before, having first burnt all the 'malgas' and a few farms in the valley suspected of being sympathetic towards the partisans.

CHAPTER TWENTY-SEVEN

The Nino Nannetti Division

ALTHOUGH they had escaped with comparatively slight loss from the trap into which faulty tactics had led them, the Gramsci Brigade, which was regarded as the best in the division, ceased to exist. It was reorganised in skeleton form during the winter, but it did not become effective as a fighting force until the following spring. The whole division was now in a critical state. A new H.Q. had yet to be organised, the partisans at Cansiglio, Monte Grappa, Pietena, and those on the south side of the Piave, had been dispersed; and the comparative ease with which this disastrous disruption had been brought about had gravely shaken the confidence of the population in the partisans and of the partisans themselves. Many 'malgas' and houses had been burnt and some partisans hanged. It was said that they had been strung up on meat-hooks inserted under the chin, but so many atrocity stories were in circulation that unless proof in the form of a photograph were available we reserved judgement. For instance, it was strenuously asserted that Gianna, a young and very pretty girl courier, having been caught at Pietena, had met a terrible fate. She had been tied to a wire cable-way used for bringing wood down the mountain and sent hurtling down it like a faggot and had been smashed to pulp at the bottom. Happily, however, in May, after the surrender, Gianna stopped us on the road and we had the satisfaction of giving her a cigarette. But even without the horror stories there was enough killing and burning to lower everyone's morale, and the widely expresed dissatisfaction was directed at the H.Q. and leaders generally because of the obviously faulty tactics employed.

One of the first of the critics to express his views in the most vehement way was our friend Orestes. When we reached the valley we sent for him to give us a picture of the general situation and to find us a hide-out until our next move was decided. With much arm slapping and many 'Ostia's', he inveighed unceasingly against the stupidity which had resulted in the rout of the brigade which he had done so much to help. His contempt for so-called guerilla leaders who allowed their men to sit on top of a mountain until they were surrounded was boundless. He himself was as crafty as a fox in war or politics. In politics his heart might sometimes get the better of his head, but his mature experience would never have allowed this to happen in action. When night fell he took us to a hay-loft on the hill behind Cesio. There were several houses on fire in the valley that night, his own amongst them, which added fresh fuel to his anger.

We remained there for three nights while various partisan leaders from far and wide came in for discussions. One of these was Hugo, the Divisional Commissar, who shortly afterwards resigned. He was a cheerful, pleasant man, with the appearance of a prosperous gentleman farmer, but was in reality, as we were told by one of his non-admirers, a professional revolutionary, having taken a degree in that difficult art in Russia. Like so many of the partisan leaders, he had served a long term of imprisonment in the early days of Fascism. These men who had thus proved their early and rooted antipathy to Fascism had considerable ascendancy over their fellows. Another of them was Boretti, a Bologna Communist, who took Hugo's place for a short time; he had done his twelve years, and his health had suffered for it. There were many Bolognese among the partisans in the Belluno area. They seem to have the same reputation in Italy as Scotsmen have abroad. You may go anywhere in Italy but will always find yourself forestalled by a Bolognese running whatever there may be to run.

Deluca hailed from Bologna, too, and was one of the original organisers of the Nannetti Division. He was a Communist and a successful business man who was said to have done very well in the fur trade. He used his business as his 'cover' when bicycling through northern Italy on partisan affairs, as he continued to do untiringly until the war ended. He always carried with him as corroborative detail a couple of moth-eaten marten skins to give 'artistic verisimilitude to an otherwise bald and unconvincing narrative'. The production of the necessary forged documents to cover those who had to play a double game was an essential and highly successful branch of the C.L.N. organisation. Either the Germans were pretty 'dumb' or skilled forgers were common. Deluca was an able, active and influential man, and the greatest help to the mission and the partisan cause; among his many accomplishments were the ability to skin, dress, and cook anything that walked. His spiced kid, spitted and roasted, was perfection.

The present situation found the Germans very much in the ascendant, with the people increasingly fearful and less sympathetic or even hostile to the partisan movement. The loss of arms and equipment, food dumps, and shelter (through the burning of so many 'malgas'), demanded a new policy of small mobile groups and a period of quiet in which to build up a new organisation and to try to obtain supplies.

As there was by now too much coming and going in our vicinity, we moved very secretly to a small hamlet east of Cesio, where we lay hidden in a farm for a week awaiting the arrival of the new commander of the Nannetti Division. Though we were comfortable the strict confinement was irksome. Ross and I shared a double bed with sheets, but we were not obiged to remain in this all day. The wireless could only be worked with an indoor aerial. One morning the sound of firing in S. Giustina, a village 2 miles away, alarmed us all so that we packed and moved into a small wood a short distance from the farm. Anxiety turned to fright when a battery of 88 mm. began firing from the road below into the hills above our wood. This activity proved to be a two-day exercise of which the Germans had omitted to give notice to the civilians, either through malice aforethought or through forgetfulness. The nervousness of the civilians at this time was extreme. We slept in the wood to ease the minds of our hosts and in consequence enjoyed two suppers, one from the farm and one from a woman who found us lurking in the wood and who no doubt mistook us for escaping prisoners. It consisted of a magnificent minestrone, cream cheese, peaches, and unfermented grape juice.

At last, Milo, the new Divisional Commander, having arrived, we set out for Cansiglio forest where Divisional H.Q. was again to be set up. Milo was an ex-officer of infantry and a recent convert to Communism. He was an able man, talked well, knew his business, and ultimately made the Nannetti Division one of the best partisan formations in northern Italy.

Travelling as usual by night, we crossed a 300-yard-long bridge over the Cordevole river, fortunately meeting no one, and then gained the south side of the Piave by another bridge. We stopped the day with one of the brigades (Tollot), and next night crossed the Vittorio Veneto-Belluno highway to a small 'malga' on the edge of the Cansiglio forest, above Vittorio Veneto.

We lived with about fifteen men of the H.Q. staff and a floating population of visitors from outlying brigades, civilians, members of the C.L.N. (Committee of National Liberation), couriers from nearby brigades, and from committees and formations as far away as Padova. The courier service was maintained by girls who found it a simple matter to cycle about the country without being stopped or searched. Although it was a risky job, we heard of only one who came to grief. The 'malga' consisted of a hay-loft in which all, men and women, slept, and a small kitchen in which we all ate. The room below was the quarters of four cows who stayed with us until they were sent down for the winter. We regretted their going, as much for the loss of their milk as for the absence of the sweet-scented warmth their presence gave to our dormitory above.

Besides the Commissar, Vice-Commander, Chief of Staff, clerks, intendant, cook, there were one or two odd-job men such as a guide for the forest and a mule-man who went down daily for supplies. The guide was an unbelievably dirty, shock-headed, uncouth youth who appeared to have only recently given up living in the trees. We called him 'Tarzan' or the 'Animal Man'. He played a mouth organ excruciatingly and was responsible for some classic remarks. Of these perhaps the best was when he was detailed to take down a battery for recharging. The weight rather staggered him, and he wanted to know 'if it weighed so much when discharged, what the devil would it weigh charged?' The mule-man, who did more work than anyone else, was a cheerful soul with a Rabelaisian wit and a loud laugh which in his case did not 'bespeak the vacant mind'. A sinister appearance earned him the title of 'the Second Murderer'.

Another character not 'on the strength' was the bird-man, who was in appearance rather like the wrens he spent his time catching. The owners of these 'malgas' on the outskirts of the forest eke out the slender income from their cattle by the netting of small birds, mostly wrens and finches, which they sell for the table. The trap was an elaborate affair of a 12 ft. high, small-meshed net, hung on poles surrounding a circular space of about 15 yards across. Some twenty live decoy birds in cages were put down and the trapper, armed with a number of throwing sticks, took station in a big camouflaged tower just outside the net. When the decoys had attracted sufficient birds inside the enclosure, the man threw one of his sticks high into the air. The whistling sound it made, not unlike the rush of a stooping hawk, so frightened the birds inside that they flew straight into the net. A day's catch might be anything up to a hundred. In peace-time they are sold in the markets of the plains, but we ate most of those caught by our bird-man. They are either fried or cooked in a thick stew and are eaten whole, bones, head and beak. Helped down with 'polenta' or maize cake, the staple dish in poorer households that cannot afford wheaten bread, they make a crackly, tasty mouthful.

Although the 'malga' was not much more than an hour's march away from the nearest Fascist garrison, H.Q. were absolved from finding its own guards by the presence of partisans in neighbouring 'malgas'. The nearest of these was the so-called 'Tiger' Battalion which had just come up for a rest after a month of action in the plains. The Tiger himself was a terrific figure with a bronze bushy beard, two automatic pistols, ten bombs, a knife, and a large Alsation dog. He later increased his bomb load to the round dozen by having a special waistcoat built to his own design. Another battalion (Nievo) of about thirty men lived in a 'malga' up in the forest, about an hour and a half's journey from us, which was at first the site of our dropping ground. During October and November six attempts were made to send us stores, but all failed either because of bad weather or bad navigation. The system used to advise us whether or not to expect a plane was simple and worked well. It consisted in short Italian phrases (known as 'cracks') supplied by us and broadcast by the B.B.C on the Italian news at 4.30 p.m., 6.30 p.m., 8.30 p.m., and 10.30 p.m. One phrase was 'negative', meaning no plane need be expected, and the other 'positive', which meant we must stand-by. For example, 'Polenta e Grappa' might be the 'negative' and 'il Maggiore senza barba' the 'positive' phrase. Our arrival at this place, to await the coming of planes of which we had been advised, soon became a time-worn jest and was usually the occasion for the consumption of the battalion's reserve supply of 'grappa', a fiery white brandy similar to the raki of Albania or the arak of India which is much in demand in winter, and in summer too, for that matter. There was also a pleasant, sweeter, darker, thicker type made from plums, called Grappa de Pruna, similar to the Slivovitch of Yugo-Slavia; but that was for pleasure, whereas the ordinary grappa was for use—the bread of life, not the cake. What the partisans, or we, would have done without this bottled lightning I hesitate to say. The higher criticism of various marks exercised our minds during many weary hours; in moments of despair or jubilation it was our unfailing solace, and for heat or cold, dryness or thirst, fullness or fasting, it was an unfailing remedy.

On the last day of October Milo, Gatti and I went down to a house on the outskirts of Vittorio Veneto to meet the local Committee of National Liberation. To any civilian we met on the way Gatti and I posed as German prisoners, an easy pretence as there was a general ignorance of foreign uniforms. At an 'albergo' we stopped to confer with the engineer in charge of the electric-power system for the Veneto region, concerning our 'anti-scorch' policy, and the sort of sabotage the partisans might effect without doing irreparable damage to the plant or without inflicting too great hardship on the populace for too long. Towns such as Venice depended entirely on electricity for light and cooking. The little charcoal that was being made was used solely in gas-driven vehicles. As a rule 'albergos' were better avoided. They were the favourite hunting-grounds of Germans who came both for pleasure and for business. The 'business' consisted of the rounding up of young men either as suspects or as recruits to swell the ranks of the TODT organisation, or for work in Germany, or for enlistment in the local Alpine Polizei. Churches on Sundays, or when there were 'festas', were also favourite targets for raids of this type. Being near Vittorio Veneto we were no longer in Germany but in Republican Italy. The Province of Belluno to the north had been annexed to the Reich and was administered and policed by Germans, while Treviso Province, in which we now were, was run by the Fascists, so that Germans were not very numerous. The conditions were much less dangerous for the partisans, who held the Fascists in supreme contempt.

The Committee of six was in conclave when we arrived. It comprised one representative from each of the political parties—from left to right, Communist, Socialist, Action, Christian Democrat, Liberal— and an independent chairman. Shortly after this meeting the chairman was arrested and languished for many months in gaol in Venice. He was a remarkable figure—a professor—with a very soft voice, small beard, and delicate features. Both his legs were paralysed, and he sat with a little machine in front of him rolling and smoking endless cigarettes. The atmosphere of this secret meeting, with the passwords, pistols, and the suave, soft-spoken, paralysed chairman, was the very essence of romantic story; while they deliberated my fancy strayed to the sinister forms of Prof. Moriarty, Long John Silver, and the paralysed Couthon of the Committee of Public Safety.

At the latter end of October, gales of wind and rain heralded the coming of winter, forcing upon us all the consideration of how best to meet it. Hope of an allied advance was no longer entertained. General Alexander in a broadcast to the partisans had already stressed the wisdom of reducing their numbers, and had urged them to hibernate and husband their resources for the spring campaign, while our H.Q. had warned us, perhaps unnecessarily, that the R.A.F. would only be able to send a few sorties during the coming winter. This, indeed, was a glimpse of the obvious, for we had already been in the field nine weeks without receiving so much as a pair of socks or a spare shirt, and we were to pass yet another eight before this happy event occurred. We became halting disciples of Socrates, striving to accept the master's dictum that to 'want nothing is divine, to want as little as possible is the nearest approach to the divine'.

Early in November Deluca came, bringing with him one of the Regional Committee from Padova, which was the C.V.L. committee responsible for partisan affairs in the whole of the Veneto region. This was Ascanio, a Communist of long standing, who had suffered imprisonment for his beliefs. On leaving Cansiglio on this occasion his assistant was arrested near Belluno and subsequently hanged. This had repercussions, as had most arrests, for the Germans had ways of making their victims talk. Ascanio was himself arrested and remained in daily expectation of death until rescued in the last days of April by the patriots of Padova. He was a man who impressed me with his ability, patience, commonsense and sincerity.

Lying in the hay, the door firmly shut, with rain sweeping incessantly across the little clearing in which the 'malga' lay, the leaders discussed winter plans for the best part of two days. The fortunes of the partisans were at a low ebb. They had received no help from us, their abettors, and now they were faced with the problem of maintaining themselves during the difficult winter months. Warm clothing, food and shelter, were as urgently needed as arms. We were asked to guarantee enough winter clothing for 500 men, but this was, of course, impossible. Before this conference there had been some talk in H.Q. of dispersing or even of retreating to Yugo-Slavia. Ascanio asked us what we proposed to do, and we could only say that we intended to stay as long as there were any partisans with whom to work. He was quick to squash any idea of withdrawal. It was finally decided to reduce numbers to a minimum, to keep only the strongest and trustiest men in the mountains, to build alternative huts in the forest, and to procure as much warm clothing as possible locally. The organisation of Division and Brigades would have to be adapted to present needs and with a view to rapid expansion when weather and the state of the war justified it. In practice this meant that only about sixty men remained in Cansiglio and a similar number west of the highway. North of the Piave, where conditions were more difficult, a new division, known as the Belluno Division, had been formed, comprising Gramsci, Pisacane, and three other brigades. The British officer who had dropped with us, and who had lost all his wireless equipment on Monte Grappa, had since joined me, and I decided that as soon as a second wireless set arrived, Ross and I would go to the Belluno Division, leaving him with the Nannetti.

On 10 November the first snow fell at Cansiglio. Snow had already fallen on the mountains to the north, and in my opinion the draping of the Dolomites in a mantle of snow was a notable improvement. In late summer they seemed to me altogether too stark and ragged to delight for long even such a mountain-starved eye as mine. Snow softened their jagged outlines, toned down the angry colouring, and dispelled the atmosphere of fierce aridity which, in summer, had forced upon me unwelcome comparisons with those terrible bare carcases of mountains seen along the shores of the Red Sea. But aesthetically pleasing though the snow may have been, from the point of view of a partisan it was everything that was evil. The once friendly mountains turned hostile overnight, shelter became a necessity instead of a luxury, movement became difficult or impossible, and tracks were an open book betraying all who made them.

The snow brought a brief spell of fine, sunny weather. The southern edge of our little glade became a 'belvedere' where we could sit and gaze at the ordered, civilised expanse of plain at our feet, melting in the distance into the lagoons of the Adriatic coast, where the spires of Venice showed like a mirage, partaking of neither sea nor land. Away to the east the snow-covered Julian Alps swept in an unbroken arc to meet the warm brown of the Istrian hills beyond Trieste. Far above, the vapour trails of four-engined bombers stretched out towards Austria in ever-lengthening wedges, while above these the fighters drew graceful curves in faint single strokes. Perhaps a burst of flak or the rumble of bombs would draw everyone with a rush to this vantage point to watch with satisfaction a cloud of smoke ascending from some train attacked by fighter-bombers.

It was on such a morning that our interest in attacks on trains was diverted to the more pressing interest of an attack on ourselves, of which the first intimation was a burst of 20 mm. fire obviously aimed at our positions. Soon we could see the enemy deploying on the slopes 1,000 ft. below us, and the men of the Manara Battalion running to occupy their posts on a spur commanding the track. We packed up ready to move, hid the surplus stores, and an excellent bean soup simmering on the fire was prodigally poured away. Then we thought the Manara men had halted the attack, the stores were brought back, and another lunch was prepared. Finally, bullets started whipping over our heads as we lay watching on our belvedere, and we hid everything once more before hurrying away to a higher 'malga'. In the evening we returned to find several 'malgas' burning, but our own intact. Three men had been killed and the leader of the Manara Battalion, a fine partisan, gravely wounded.

Our alternative barracks, hidden high up in the forest, were now ready, but Milo was loath to move into them until compelled. The Manara Battalion, having had its home burnt, had withdrawn, leaving no one between Divisional H.Q. and the enemy. That night snow fell heavily, and next morning there was rain. Milo, having decided to hang on for another day, was still in bed when firing broke out in the direction of the 'Tiger' Battalion. Sacks of bread, beans, macaroni, were hastily hidden in the dripping bushes, and the heavily laden procession set out again in the snow and sleet for the Nievo Battalion 'malga'. We had stopped to rest before crossing the main mule track up to the forest known as the 'Patriarchal track', when a prolonged burst of automatic fire, not 200 yards away, shattered the silence of the forest. We thought it was a Hun patrol on the track which was firing random bursts into the bush, the tactics they usually employed when carrying out a 'rastrallamento' in thick country. A few days later, however, when we were discussing the day's events with the Nievo Battalion, they themselves claimed to have fired the burst at an enemy patrol and to have killed three. When all was quiet we crossed the track and reached the Nievo 'malga' only to find it abandoned. Trudging through a foot and a half of snow had made us so wet that we decided to stay for the night. We had our reserve rations (every man now carried bread, salami, sugar, and pasta for six days), sundry bottles of 'grappa' were found in the pockets of our rucksacks, and we spent a cheery evening.

More snow fell during the night and all paths were obliterated. Led by Tarzan, the procession stole stealthily through the silent forest like a party of mourners going to a wake. A large sooty cauldron dangled from a pole carried by Ross and myself, the Second Murderer carefully balanced on his shoulder a straw-covered 'grey hen' of grappa, while the necks and corks protruding from coat pockets and rucksacks showed that there was still plenty of corn in Egypt. We approached our new home in a roundabout way, very conscious that in our wake we had left damning evidence of the passage of a small army. There were two log cabins about 100 yards apart in the middle of a magnificent straight-growing beech forest. The larger had two tiers of bunks to take about twenty, the other formed the kitchen and mess room. Water came from a pond 300 yards away. This was now snow-covered, but later in the winter was covered with a foot of ice, for we were over 4,000 ft. up and Cansiglio Forest is a notoriously cold place. Half a mile to the west and 500 ft. below was the house of the Forest Guard situated on the motor-road leading to the Plain of Cansiglio and to Alpago and Belluno. We worked all afternoon clearing a track to the pond and doing what we could to efface our tracks of the morning.

Some time before I had arranged by signal a meeting with the next mission to the east at a place called Barcis in the Val Cellina. Any escaped prisoners-of-war or forced-landed airmen we collected for evacuation to Yugo-Slavia had to go via Barcis, which was on the other side of the Passo di Cavallo, two days' march away. As, in addition to keeping our appointment, I was anxious to see if the pass was still open, Gatti and I left on 19 November, taking with us all we possessed, for it was unwise to leave anything in case of a 'rastrallamento'. At some higher 'malgas', now occupied by the men of Nievo and Manara, we picked up two guides and began a hard day's work breaking trail in soft snow. The close of the short winter afternoon found us on the other side of the pass, but in some doubt as to the whereabouts of the partisans with whom we were to spend the night. Our shouts and shots met with no response. We dosed the guide and Gatti, who were showing signs of collapse, heavily and unwisely with grappa, and struggled on. Two hours later we made contact. The guide was now helpless and Gatti little better. The first partisan I met was extremely suspicious. He thrust a Sten into my stomach, searched me, and finally took away my pistol; but with these trifling formalities over I was allowed to go to their hut to send out help for the others and to get food and drink ready. When the two stragglers were brought in they had to be carried straight to bed, drunk with exhaustion and grappa.

Next morning, when we were but a short way from the hut, the partisan commander who was guiding us pointed with satisfaction to a patch of blood-stained snow marking the grave of a spy they had shot the day before. By the way he eyed me I think he still inclined to the belief that if everyone had their deserts I should be lying there too. Having introduced ourselves to another battalion of the Osoppo Brigade, living in a charcoal-burner's hut, we left our kit and went down into the Val Cellina to Barcis, where every house but the inn had been burnt. My opposite number did not arrive, and as I had another appointment with an American mission in the contrary direction, we hurried back. All was quiet at the barracks, where we found a welcome addition to the English-speaking community in three American airmen who had been shot down. We made several attempts to send them to Yugo-Slavia for evacuation, but all failed owing either to snow or to enemy activity. When the war ended they were still at Cansiglio, along with some twenty more who had been brought in by the partisans. By then we had a landing strip on the Plain of Cansiglio, and had made arrangements for their removal by air.

On the night of 22 November Ross and I set off with the Commissar of the Division bound for the Tollot Brigade, stationed west of the Vittorio Veneto-Belluno highway, to meet an American officer who had recently dropped there. We hoped that he would be able to make good the needs of the partisans in that area. We crossed the road at midnight about a mile from a German block-post, and addressed ourselves to the steep climb to the high ground west of the road. Hardened though we were to night marches, we again experienced the deadly weariness that attacks one in the small hours. Our vitality required replenishing—mine had nearly all ebbed away—so we called a halt at a house known to the Commissar. The women in Italy never grudged being roused at two or three in the morning to attend to the wants of spent partisans. Here the mother and a laughing comely daughter, who were alone in the house, bustled about, lit a fire, and soon had us sitting comfortably toasting our feet, eating roast chestnuts and drinking red wine. The chestnuts were roasted to such perfection in a sort of warming pan that the skins fell away at a touch, and the wine had the rich earthy tang of the local 'Clintot'. One of the nicest features of the houses in these parts is the fireplaces. This is a 6 ft. by 6 ft. stone dais, about 1½ ft. high, surrounded on three sides by a wooden bench. Sometimes it occupies a corner of the room, and sometimes it is built in an alcove projecting from the room. The fuel is faggots of small dry twigs which blaze gloriously, while a huge hanging chimney, with a mouth as big as the dais, takes care of the smoke. From the chimney dangles an iron chain and hook for cooking pots. If a tavern chair be the throne of human felicity, commend me to one of these noble fireplaces with a bottle of wine on the hob and a plate of roast chestnuts by my side.

When we gained the ridge at dawn we were greeted by the sound of firing. Our hearts sank. If there were a 'rastrallamento' in progress our journey here would be in vain. However, at Tollot Brigade H.Q. all was quiet; we were told that the neighbouring Mazzini Brigade was engaged near the San Boldo Pass. Tollot was not inclined to worry about the troubles of others, having enough on hand at the moment with the turning of two large pigs into salami. After witnessing this display of single-minded devotion, it was distressing for us to hear that two days later they were themselves attacked and all the salami captured.

Having seen the American officer, Deluca, and other leaders we returned to Cansiglio. The great question there was how, with the number of men available, twenty or less, we could best ensure our safety. The nearest battalion was 2 miles further from the road than we were, and this road was used daily by German trucks either going through to Alpago, where there were garrisons, or engaging in the transport of wood. On some days there were as many as twelve of these loading the timber which was being felled a bare quarter mile from our barracks. We made a practice of sending out two standing patrols before dawn. These were relieved every two hours until eleven o'clock, when we considered the danger over for the day. Patrolling was bitterly cold work, especially the dawn patrol; but volunteers for that were never lacking because they were allowed a grappa ration. These patrols covered all the likely lines of approach. Merely by listening we could usually tell what was going on for some miles around, for in the still cold air of the forest sound carried amazingly. On one occasion, during an attack on the Nievo Battalion, we heard the shouted orders of their commander and thought they came from some Fascist patrol about to attack us. We imagined the place reasonably secure against surprise, but early in January, after our mission had left, a party of Germans in snow-suits approached unseen and unheard from an unlikely direction. Had they held their fire they might have captured Nannetti Division H.Q. lock, stock, and barrel, but they opened up at 300 yards range, giving the alarm to everybody and hitting no one. Except for a spare wireless set and some reserve food which were buried, everything was lost and both barracks were burnt. Without doubt this must have been the work of a spy well informed about the locality and the dispositions of the patrols.

Another security measure required everyone to pack and be ready to move by seven o'clock. The enforcement of this wholesome rule demanded more discipline than the partisans possessed. At that hour it was barely light and very cold, and I have seldom met anyone so reluctant to get out of bed, even in milder conditions, as the Divisional Staff—there might not have been an enemy within 100 miles of them. If at nine o'clock, when I came back from the kitchen, my cry of 'Waky, Waky' met with their unfailing response 'yet a little sleep, a little slumber, a little folding of the hands to sleep', I immediately lit the stove which smoked abominably. The acrid fumes soon penetrated to the top tier of bunks where Milo and the higher ranks slept, who would seldom hold out for long after that. The mission occupied a modest portion of the lower tier, where we lay cheek by jowl in comparative comfort except for the disturbing presence immediately above of the Second Murderer, who snored. As Mr Bulstrode remarked: The society of a grampus delights nobody and offends me.' The presence of so many more or less unwashed bodies in close proximity, inevitably occasioned the usual troubles. We longed for a change of clothing.

Patrols, ciphering, chopping wood, fetching water and hay for 'Giulietta' the mule, and visiting the battalions kept us occupied. At night there were often stores and recharged batteries to be brought up from the Forest Guard house, which was used as a sort of entrepôt by us at night and by the Germans during the day. Since our move into the barracks the dropping ground had been changed to the new Nievo Battalion location. Our luck, however, remained the same. On 2 December two planes dropped their loads, including our wireless stores and three months' mail, to a Fascist garrison 10 miles from Cansiglio. This tragedy naturally disgusted the partisans. Visitors from the plains described to them with a wealth of loving detail how the Fascists were smoking English cigarettes and eating English chocolate, while they busied themselves stripping and reassembling handsome new Bren guns and Stens for use against the partisans. We were angry and depressed, refusing to believe such a fantastic story until a signal told us it was only too true. But, in spite of this deplorable record of failure, we remained good friends. That we were in the same destitute condition and that we shared equally their guards, patrols, and fatigues, were possibly points in our favour. We could offer no plausible explanation for this unbroken failure, for the partisans found it difficult to believe that the R.A.F., in whom they had such confidence, could be so incompetent.

During Christmas week we enjoyed a spell of exceptionally good weather—fine days and clear cold nights. Preparations for Christmas were in full swing, and for our part we hoped to make the partisans the sort of present we had been waiting for for nearly 4 months—a good load of arms and stores. A few scraggy hares and hens, quantities of wine, brandy, and grappa, were brought up; the wife of the head forester baked prodigious cakes; but no plane was signalled. Christmas Day opened promisingly with a generous tot of 'zabaglione' (a sort of flip made from cognac and egg) for breakfast. For dinner we had a very special *pasticcio di maccheroni, ricotta del Cansiglio,* chicken *alla Bolognese* (the cook hailed from Bologna), and several hunks of delightfully soggy creamy cake. The usual toasts were drunk and speeches made; and then Ross, Gatti, and the more educated members of the Divisional Staff, excluding, that is, Tarzan, the Second Murderer, and myself, began a long and exciting discussion on 'What is Art?'

All things come to those who know how to wait. On Boxing Day the great event occurred. Two planes were signalled, and off we went at dusk through the deep snow to light the signal fires. When all available partisans, excluding those needed for patrols and guards, were standing by, we had about fifty men to handle the expected five tons of stores. We sat round the fires, as we had done so many times, in a mood of cynical expectancy trying hard to think of something fresh that might go wrong. This time there was no mistake. The leading plane (we heard later the crew was Polish) was over us almost as soon as we heard it. It flew straight on to the target and dropped its load within 200 yards of the fires. The other followed and then we got to work. Some Christmas comforts, including several bottles of inferior whisky which had been scattered promiscuously among the various loads, were soon discovered by the partisans, but in spite of this handicap we had nearly everything hidden by three o'clock. One body, a wireless operator for the other mission, dropped wide of the fires but made a comfortable landing in deep snow. Perhaps he had been priming himself with what Jorrocks called 'jumping powder', or perhaps the men who retrieved him from his snow bed had been administering our whisky as a restorative, but when I first saw him, he too, like a few of the partisans, was not quite sure whether he was in Jericho or Jerusalem.

We slept by the fires until dawn, when the search for missing packages was continued. The patrols reported that all was quiet below. No inquisitive Huns or Fascists from Alpago or Vittorio put in an appearance, though they must have been aware that a 'drop' had taken place. And then, as if to emphasise what none of us had ever doubted, that 'drops' were to be 'like angel's visits few and far between', we recorded another failure two nights later. A plane was signalled. We sat round the fires until midnight, singing songs of expectation and listening to a plane, which may or may not have been ours, circling questingly in the distance, and then trooped sorrowfully home through the snow to bed.

Our mission at last was free to depart for the Belluno Division whom we feared would by now be in despair. We had done little enough for the Nannetti Division, and for the last three months of 1944 they had achieved little themselves except to keep a few enemy troops preoccupied on their account. The insecurity of the partisan's position and our inability to supply their urgent needs had imposed almost complete inactivity. This state is always demoralising, and upsets partisans much more than it does regular troops, who have routine duties and training programmes to keep them up to the mark. Nevertheless, their keenness was undiminished and had withstood the drastic reorganisation, the impact of winter, and much disappointment. In many respects they were stronger. Experience in living and fighting in winter conditions had been gained, and they had learnt how to allow the storm of a 'rastrallamento' to blow itself out more or less harmlessly. We left the Nannetti Division in good heart, fully assured that when better times came the little we had sown would bear good fruit.

CHAPTER SIXTEEN

The Belluno Division

I must confess that when I decided to leave the Nannetti Division to the other mission, I was aware that north of the Piave we should be nearer the Dolomites. Living in a forest in winter has its own particular charm. Perhaps this can be best appreciated when you are one of 'the hunted', for the feeling of security it gives compensates for the absence of sunlight and the monotonous and limited outlook. But after some weeks in Cansiglio the sense of confinement became oppressive, and I greeted a clearing in the forest with the delight that a townsman greets an open space, free from bricks and mortar, in the heart of a town.

Though we left Cansiglio on 29 December we did not establish contact with the Belluno Division until 9 January 1945. The Tollot Brigade, located south of the Piave, was being harried by the Germans, who had posted numerous small garrisons throughout the area. Their communications with the north bank of the river were therefore interrupted. We lived for a week with the

Brigade Commander in the company of other birds of passge—a Frenchman, who was subsequently shot, a Yugo-Slav, two Poles, and a Russian. This was no happy band of brothers. The Poles hated the Russian, and, being in opposite political camps, concealed any love they may have had for each other; the Frenchman disliked the Italians and the Italians distrusted him; while the Yugo-Slav despised everyone, including ourselves, except the Russian.

We once more met Deluca, who was now accompanied by a Major Abba, the recently appointed Zone Commander, whose function was to control and co-ordinate the two Garibaldi Divisions and the two or three non-Garibaldi Brigades in the Belluno Zone. They pressed for a mission to be allotted to Zone H.Q., but I thought this was premature as at that time H.Q. consisted of Abba and Deluca, who were living nomadic lives on bicycles, 'travelling', as they said, 'in furs'. Moreover, it was of the first importance that we should join the Belluno Division, who had been so neglected, and supply them with arms before they became disgusted with us.

We finally crossed the Piave on the night of the 7th and marched across country to the foothills west of Belluno where we slept in a cowshed. The presence of thirty cows made blankets superfluous. Our only adventure was when a German cyclist patrol passed close by us. In our anxiety we took it to be a patrol, but it may equally have been some men with late passes returning from the Belluno cinema. A heavy snow-fall next day, and the nervousness of the 'padrone' and his family at the dangerous guests secreted in their cowshed, kept us indoors during the day; but at night we moved on to another cowshed near the village of Bolzano where we at last met Franco, the Divisional Commander. Conditions here were very different. The partisans lived for the most part in the villages as civilians, sleeping out in caves and holes. Their activity was confined to the cleaning up of spies and informers, of which there had been a great many. The Belluno G.A.P. under Carlo, formerly Commander of the Pisacane Brigade, was engaged in Belluno itself in eliminating prominent Fascists. Bolzano was only a couple of miles from Belluno where a large garrison and S.S. Headquarters were stationed, but so far it had escaped their attentions, and people were intensely loyal to the partisans. Though it was desirable to arrange a drop somewhere near Divisional H.Q., we did not think it expedient in view of the close proximity of Belluno. There would be the risk of losing anything dropped, and in the event of a 'rastrallamento' there could be no refuge in the snow-covered mountains. Also, if Bolzano were compromised, the whole divisional organisation would be disrupted. We therefore decided to find a dropping ground near Forno, where sorties could be received in comparative security. There would be obvious difficulties about the subsequent distribution of stores, but Franco thought that might be managed by civilian trucks.

The Fratelli Fenti Brigade, who occupied the Forno area, had to be warned of our intentions. Until they were ready for us we were to live in the strictest seclusion. Accordingly, the same night, our kit was loaded on to a sledge drawn by two oxen and we started for what was called 'the cave'. At the entrance to a narrow valley we left the sledge, shouldered our rucksacks, and began one of the most perilous night walks I have ever indulged in. Along the precipitous valley side a sketchy path, deep in powder snow, pursued its tortuous way, around trees, past jutting boulders, and across frozen gullies. 'He who stands upon a slippery place makes nice of no vile hold to stay him up.' We clutched with bare hands at branches, brambles, and glazed rocks, until our fingers froze and the sweat of fright and effort dripped from our faces. At midnight we reached a high cliff which overhung slightly. Under two of the best overhangs the partisans had rigged up a kitchen and sleeping quarters with the help of Italian bivouac sheets. It was a wild spot. The stream, frozen into silence, lay some 500 ft. below, its opposite bank rising abruptly to the rock and snow of Monte Serva 5,000 ft. above. Beyond our bivouac the cliff was split by a frightful chasm whose smooth walls, at their base only a few yards apart, also met 100 ft. above. By daylight it was a strange place, by night an eerie one; and much more so when we found that it served as an execution ground for spies.

Here, with three partisans, we lived for three weeks like hermits. Sometimes, growing weary, like that profane monk of Algeria, 'we gave a yell and jumped out of our cell.' In other words, we left our camp to spend a evening in the hamlet of Gioz with the family of Burrasco, one of our fellow hermits; but the perilous path, which had always to be traversed at night, was a powerful deterrent to too frequent breaches of security. On those rare occasions then, having reached the road-head, Burrasco would borrow a sledge from the nearest farm and the three of us would pile in, with him in front as pilot. As 'burrasco' is Italian for 'storm', it was a suitable *nom de guerre*, for he was of a vehement, headlong nature, and he urged the willing sledge accordingly. He was an ex-Alpini soldier of dashing appearance and manner, great among women, and great in war too. Later he was severely wounded in the chest, and when we saw him again in Belluno after the surrender he was but a shadow of his former swashbuckling self. This mile run through the cold night air down the winding smooth-surfaced track to Gioz was, to say the least of it, stimulating. We spent the evening in a small kitchen, usually crowded to capacity with partisans, while Burrasco's mother, a delightful, homely, stout women, plied us with food and drink. Her younger son, a nice-looking lad, was an active partisan too, but was not known to be one. He was thus able to go into Belluno to buy stores and to arrange for forged documents when needed. Once he went into the hospital there to commiserate with a prominent Fascist who was lying at death's door as the result of a murderous attack by Carlo's amateur assassins.

Pulling the loaded sledge back was less exhilarating, and by the time we had done that and overcome the 'via pericolosa', we were sobriety itself no matter what our condition when we set out.

One other diversion I had was to climb Monte Serva (c. 7,000 ft.). It took me about seven hours and, although it was not a difficult matter, even in winter, it had the salutary effect of astonishing the natives—even 'The Storm' was impressed. There was a bitter wind on the summit ridge where I had to cut a few steps with an axe borrowed from Burrasco, who thus had a vicarious interest in the climb. Like most easily accessible mountains, Monte Serva had not escaped the enormous wooden cross with which the Italian priest loves to decorate any handy summit.

Our departure was delayed by the necessity of organising escorts and stopping places for the four-night journey to Forno. This was not so simple a matter, because beyond Agordo we had to use the main road. After one false start we set out on 30 January, stopping the first night in a house at the entrance of the Canal del Mis, which was then the H.Q. of the Pisacane Brigade. Their commander was killed the same day by an S.S. patrol on the road near Bolzano. We took with us as divisional representative, Carduci, a very fine type of partisan. We met him first on Pietena, where we admired his activity and liked his ways. He was most unfortunately killed on the last day when attacking an armoured car near Belluno with hand grenades.

The Canal del Mis must be one of the deepest and narrowest rock defiles in the Dolomites. Nevertheless, it is traversed by a motor-road. In some places it is hewn out between the limestone wall and the torrent; in others the rock is tunnelled. The number of excellent roads cutting through the Dolomites in all directions always astonished us. First thoughts would suggest that this was ideal country for partisan warfare;) in practice the number of roads was a serious menace. The Dolomites do not run in ranges like the Alps, but are formed of half a dozen isolated groups of mountains separated by deep, narrow, flattish valleys. They are thus extremely accessible—I am not thinking of the tops—and sitting in a car one can almost touch the living rock at their bases. Though this is literally true for the Canal del Mis, elsewhere, perhaps, it is an exaggeration; but in better-known places than the Mis valley, Agordo or San Martino for example, the great carved, fluted, many-hued rock faces, two or three thousand feet in height, stand so close to and rise so cleanly from the valley that they have not that quality of aloofness that the big mountain ranges possess.

We were fortunate in that we met no patrols in the Mis, for even on foot it is often not easy to get off the road. There was considerable evidence that the Germans were busily engaged in making emplacements and dug-outs for a defensive line. In one of the long rock galleries we passed a concrete-mixing machine which our escort obligingly promised to throw off the road into the river on their way back. At dawn we reached the village of Rivamonte where we stopped in a wooden house of alarming cleanliness, owned by a very active old lady who was a pillar of the local resistance movement. Her wireless set, the only one left in the village, daily attracted a large crowd to listen to the news. After the straw bunks, hay-lofts, cowsheds, and rock shelters which had been our portion for so long, one needed assurance and a certain indifference to the impression left behind to make use of the beds and sheets provided.

From there we descended into the Agordo valley, striking the main highway just above the town where there was a garrison and a flood-lit power station. These places were heavily guarded. At night low-power searchlights swept the vicinity searching for saboteurs. At midnight we stopped at an 'albergo' facing the main road. Instead of merely having 'one for the road' and pushing on as we expected, we were astonished to find that we were to pass the next day there. From an upper window, discreetly curtained, we had the pleasure of watching staff cars, fatigue parties, and civilian lorries pass along the road beneath us. At the sight of these novelties we experienced all the sensations of a 'hick', who, with the straw still in his hair, had just arrived in town, and the rarer pleasures of a spy observing his enemy at close quarters. One or two cars stopped at our inn, and then our pleasure stopped too. We even worked a very successful wireless schedule with an aerial in the loft while the Germans made merry on the floor below.

The final stage to Forno was tricky. We had to follow the main road for 65 miles to Cencenighe before turning off on to a secondary road. Here we had to elude a garrison and a searchlight. We started the night badly by meeting a truck unexpectedly—an incident which cost me a piece of the seat of my trousers, which was torn away as we leapt off the road down the revetment. Our entrance to Cencenighe resembled a rehearsal for the 'Dance of the Gnomes' by a nervous and very third-rate caste. In single file we tiptoed over a bridge past a lighted house, while the producer of our ballet, the leader, with muted voice and gestures of terrifying intensity, imposed the silence we were only too anxious to give. Having turned the corner of the house we had to plough our way through 3 ft. of soft snow lying on the wooded slope on the outskirts of the town. Whenever the searchlight of the power station turned its inquisitive beam in our direction, which it did frequently, we dropped like one man. Carduci, who wore a very hairy coat and who was of very short stature, would often disappear altogether in the snow, to reappear a moment later looking like a small, angry bear, emerging prematurely from hibernation. An hour or more of this very hard labour brought us, still undiscovered, to the far end of the town where, so deep was the snow, we only found we were walking on the cemetery wall by tumbling off it into the cemetery. Another detour over a high spur was needed to avoid the barracks, and then we more or less fell down a steep slope on to the Forno road. There the usual cowshed was waiting for us, but we only stayed long enough to compose ourselves with grappa before putting the loads on to a sledge and beginning the last stage up the Val di Gares. The Val di Gares is a charming little valley which runs south from Forno for 5 miles to terminate in an imposing rock cirque below the Altipiano delle Pale di San Martino. Up on the Altipiano are the peaks of the San Martino group, which rise to 10,000 ft. The valley floor is nowhere more than half a mile wide, and both sides rise steeply to seven or eight thousand feet. A more difficult target could hardly be found. In the first place it was not easy to pick up and, secondly, a plane could not come down to obtain the necessary accuracy of aim. If the drop was inaccurate, the amount of snow and the nature of the country would prevent the recovery of the loads. For the dropping ground we chose an open space, clear of pines, about 3 miles up from Forno, and arranged with Base to use delay-action parachutes. If this were done the plane could fly high enough to clear all the nearby peaks, say seven to eight thousand feet above the floor of the valley, and at the same time ensure that the parachutes did not open until only a few hundred feet above the ground. We had had no experience of these, but it was that or nothing.

While awaiting the event we lived in a little wooden cabin, cunningly built under a rock overhang, 1,000 ft. above the valley. Two partisans came up daily from Forno with supplies, using skis up the sleigh track as far as the dropping ground. Most of the Forno men were good on skis, the Brigade Commander, Della Nera, being very expert. As perhaps was only natural, the men from these high valleys seemed more virile and tougher than any we had yet met. In marching, carrying loads, or digging snow, they were eager and enduring.

The first plane came up on the night of 13 February, ten days after our arrival. In order to maintain secrecy we had made no preparations on the dropping ground, so, in the few hours between the warning signal and the expected time of arrival, we had to work hard. Signal fires had to be sited, the holes dug, and several sledge loads of wood brought up. The men worked with a will, shovelling away the snow with their long-handled shovels until they reached the earth 3 ft. below. The wood arrived, small fires were lit, and we settled down to wait in no easy frame of mind. Would the plane find us, hidden away as we were in this deep valley? And would the delay-action parachutes work? These were the questions we repeatedly asked ourselves. At last there came the welcome cry of 'Rumore'. Sure enough it was a plane. The partisans had provided as a signal lamp the giant headlight of a truck. With this young searchlight Pallino got to work, almost beside himself with excitement when he got an answering flick from the plane. Seemingly miles high, it made repeated wide turns until we almost thought he was not going to 'drop'; and then, with the sound of rushing wind, there suddenly appeared floating above the fires a beautiful array of parachutes and containers. It was a first-class shot at a very awkward target. The partisans worked fiercely, up to their waists in snow, and by dawn everything had been sledged down to Forno and hidden. Four nights later two more planes made almost equally successful drops to the great delight of all concerned.

Having thus received fairly substantial quantities of arms and explosives, we were now anxious to get back to the Belluno area to see that they were used to the best advantage. Moreover, as the weather in February had been so extremely fine and warm, the snow was now fast disappearing from the southern slopes, and it seemed probable that by March we should be able to find a dropping ground that was more accessible. Having advised Divisional H.Q. of this we had to wait for ten days while arrangements were being made for our return. During this time I amused myself on the ridge above the hut. With the aid of a pair of snow-shoes I could move fairly freely, and presently I discovered a long gully which proved to be the key to the climbing of Cimon della Stia and the other bumps on the main ridge in spite of the existing snow conditions. This had been swept by an avalanche which had left behind it a bed of hard snow in which I had to kick or cut steps with an axe lent me by Della Nera. So pleasing was this gully and so greatly did it facilitate movement, that I even entertained ideas of climbing the Mulaz or Focobon itself, but after a narrow escape from being taken for a ride on an avalanche my ardour cooled. I was alone on these occasions, for Ross, although young, strong, and in full possession of his faculties, mental and physical, was strangely unappreciative of the mountains which surrounded us. At times this indifference verged on hostility, and only the presence of Huns in the valley could persuade him to forsake it for the mountains. Perhaps his attitude towards climbing might be likened to that of the Johannesburg Jew towards shooting lions. Of him it is related that when asked by some keen big-game shot why he never hunted lions, he replied that he saw no reason to as he had not lost any.

The rapid disappearance of the snow enabled us to return to Rivamonte by the Cesurette Pass (c. 5,000 ft.) which led into the Val di San Lucano, thereby avoiding the main road. Walking down this valley the mountaineer has eyes for nothing but the magnificent tower of Monte Agner on one side and the gaunt yellowish cliffs of the Pale di San Lucano on the other. As the sun sank behind the pass, an endless variation of colour and form played upon these two mighty bastions. The yellows turned to a warm terra-cotta, to grey, and then to black, as the shadow of some isolated tower, hitherto invisible against the face, was cast upon the parent mass behind. It is one of the beauties of the Dolomites, some compensation for the absence of the glory of glacier and snow, that the rocks reflect with a warmth and richness of their own the most delicate variations of the sky.

At Rivamonte, which we reached on 1 March, we met unexpected difficulties. The Canal del Mis was now constantly patrolled, the passes were not yet open, and the sole means of communication with the Belluno area was the main Agordo road. A bus service was still running from Agordo, by means of which the girl couriers kept us in touch with Divisional H.Q. whom we kept advised of our plans. One of the reasons for this enemy activity was that, on the night of our arrival in Rivamonte, all telegraph and telephone lines in the Zone had been cut by partisans and some 30 miles of wire totally removed.

We spent a week in Rivamonte in strict confinement, for Germans from Agordo visited the village frequently on foraging expeditions. Having been advised that two attempts to send our escort through the Mis valley had failed, we fell to discussing other means of getting down. The suggestion of going by bus or truck dressed as civilians was vetoed 'nemine contradicente'. Because of my beard and the intrinsic slovenliness of a well-worn British battledress, I was assured frequently that if I kept my mouth shut I could pass as an Italian labourer—a wood-cutter. Of Ross I was doubtful. He spoke Italian well, but though no one would suspect him of looking very English, his appearance might arouse curiosity as to what country he did profess to belong. Gatti, who was frequently mistaken for an Englishman by his own countrymen, had fortunately gone on a week's leave to his home in Trento. Pallino had not to be considered because he had already assumed civilian clothes, and had more or less dissociated himself from us except when working his wireless set. It was our opinion that if we were caught wearing uniform, there was only a likelihood of our being shot, whereas if we dressed as civilians there could be no doubt at all as to what would happen. In discussing this hypothetical question the partisans may have thought we were unduly sensitive about our own safety, but Ross and I took the view that it would be a mistake to give the Germans the chance of resolving these doubts for us merely to get to Belluno quickly. The 'upshot was that they arranged to take us in a wood-truck, concealed under the wood. We sketched out the general idea; the details were left to their undoubted ingenuity.

The first attempt on the night of 3 March failed owing to the big ten-ton lorry stalling on the icy road up to the village. We could have gone down to it, but we should have had to do without the essential shroud of wood which was lying in Rivamonte waiting to be loaded. On the 8th a smaller truck arrived in the village before dark. The civilian driver was extremely nervous on account of the compromising freight he was to carry, for whatever happened to us the Germans would show no mercy to him. At dusk we went to the loaded truck waiting for us outside the village. They had built a lidless, open-ended coffin, big enough to hold two bodies and a few rucksacks. This had been laid upside down on the floor and then covered with two or three tons of wood. When the side of the lorry was let down we were able to insinuate ourselves, head-foremost lying on our backs, into the coffin. The raising of the side was the equivalent, so to speak, of screwing down the lid. Thus we were driven boldly, but at a suitable hearse-like pace, down the Agordo-Belluno highway past several German block-posts. At these the lorry was stopped and the driver's papers inspected, while the beam of a torch shone cursorily over the innocent load of wood. But no one suspected the presence of the nigger, or niggers, in the woodpile. A good example, I think, of 'exfiltration'.

At a point in the Piave valley an escort had been arranged to meet the truck to help us quickly off the road with our loads. When the truck stopped and noises indicated that the side was about to be let down, we, of course, had no notion as to where we were or who was about to exhume the bodies. Someone laid hold of my feet and dragged me out, and Ross followed in a cascade of rucksacks and Marlin automatics. A figure, which I now recognised as the driver, told us in Italian to 'scram', and off the lorry went. The headlights of several cars coming along the road not far away explained the driver's haste to be gone. With a muttered word of thanks and a handshake we followed his example, staggering away with the loads to the cover of a nearby cemetery. Coffins and everything associated with them seemed unavoidable that night. We were at the rendezvous all right, but though we waited and whistled cautiously for some time no one came. We gave it up and pushed on alone to Bolzano where we were challenged and nearly shot by our impulsive friend 'Thunderstorm'.

With winter now behind and the expectation of great events not far ahead, the partisans were more confident. Divisional H.Q. was now living in a small farmhouse up the hill above Gioz. A new policy of 'bunkers'—or 'boonkers' as the Italians called them—had been instituted on a hint from Regional Command. This consisted of a system of cleverly concealed dug-outs, individual or collective, in which everyone slept or went to ground in the event of a 'rastrallamento'. It was a dodge which had been worked very successfully during the difficult winter months on the plains. The one we dug at H.Q. was a good example. In front of the farmhouse was a small terraced field, with a dry-stone supporting wall about 6 ft. high. A hole 12ft. by 12ft. by 6 ft. deep was dug in the field near the terrace wall, the inside was lined with boards, and a timber roof added, leaving about 4 ft. headroom inside. On top of this the earth was replaced, the field was levelled, and potatoes planted. A small passage-way was made in the dry wall, so built that by replacing two or three big stones at the entrance the wall appeared unbroken. Every night we moved ourselves and our belongings into this, being careful to leave no trace in the farmhouse of our occupation. We were thereupon sealed in by the son of the old man who lived in the farm, and unsealed the next morning by the same hand if all was quiet. While we were there the perfection of the deception was never put to the test. Personally I should have been afraid of a dog scenting us and starting to scratch up the potato field.

The day we returned, the Chief of Staff of the division, a young ex-officer of Alpini who rejoiced in the *nom de guerre* 'Radiosa Aurora'—Shining Dawn— had brought off a highly successful coup, in the shape of a booby-trap, with some of the explosive devices we had got for them. On the Belluno rifle range he had erected two targets representing Hitler, with the adjuration 'Shoot Straight', and had decorated the butts with 'black' propaganda which had been sent us. One target was harmless, under the other he placed a few pounds of explosive and a pressure switch. The party which visited the range next morning for firing practice happened to be a large one with several officers and N.C.O.'s. Such, apparently, was the indignation of the officers, that instead of ordering the men to pull down the offending targets they did it themselves—with fatal consequences. Four officers and N.C.O.'s were killed and many injured. However, the German officers of the Belluno S.S. were notorious for ruthlessness. Ten prisoners from the gaol, partisans and political suspects, were promptly taken up to the rifle range and hanged there on trees. Four more were hanged in the public square of Belluno a few days later as a reprisal for the shooting of a prominent Fascist by the Belluno G.A.P. At or about this time a total of thirty partisans were thus executed in the Belluno area.

A large proportion of the arms and explosives had been brought down from Forno in safety by the same simple expedient of concealing them under loads of wood. Nevertheless, much more was needed if the plans made for blocking all the roads in the Zone were to be effective, and if the Belluno Division were to be armed to the same extent as Nannetti. Since we left Cansiglio, the ball having been set rolling, planes came frequently. The Nannetti Division had had about forty consignments and was better off for automatic weapons than British or German troops. In view of the urgency, and of the fact that owing to the disappearance of the snow, movement was becoming possible, we decided to arrange for 'drops' near Bolzano, and also further down the Piave valley where our old friends of the Gramsci Brigade were again coming to life.

Meantime Abba and Deluca came to see us and once more raised the question of a mission for Zone H.Q. which was now established and functioning at Alpago, about midway between the two divisions. After some discussion I decided to go myself, leaving Ross to look after the Belluno Division. Since he could talk Italian fairly fluently I could take Gatti with a clear conscience. Another wireless operator was needed, so we arranged for one to be dropped at Cansiglio to which there was now almost a daily, or rather nightly, service of planes.

Much as I liked Abba and Deluca, and confident as I was in their judgement, and in the advisability of having a mission with Zone H.Q. which would have an important part to play when the Allies reached the Piave or when the Germans attempted to withdraw, I was loath to leave the division— the more so as we now had some arms and explosives to use. Though to a less degree, it is the same with partisans as it is in the army, the higher the formation the more it loses touch with realities—a loss which no amount of visiting can replace. However true it may be that a looker-on sees most of the game, I have not yet outgrown the preference for being in the thick of it rather than being relegated to a seat in the grandstand, which is how the headquarters of a formation appears to me. The unreality and disparity of war as experienced at a remote headquarters and in a fighting unit must fill anyone there with a sense of uneasiness, and may well sicken one who grudges the pleasures and wishes to share the pains of the men who have to march and fight. In war personal preference is seldom consulted, but no doubt most of those who have the invidious and onerous task of directing a battle or organising victory would prefer a post of less responsibility, more fellowship, and more danger.

CHAPTER SEVENTEEN

At Zone H.Q.—The Liberation of Belluno

OUR new Italian operator was reported as ready to drop by 22 March. That night Gatti and I walked over to Alpago, escorted by some of Carlo's boys of Belluno G.A.P. They were likely-looking lads and beguiled the journey with stories of their 'gangster' exploits in the streets of Belluno. Italians are excellent raconteurs, telling stories in the way that children love to have them told with a minute attention to detail and a wealth of appropriate gesture and sound effects. Gangster life and stories of 'rastrallamenti' lend themselves to this graphic method of description—no rifle is fired without the corresponding 'pom', no automatic comes into play without a prolonged 'b–r–r–r–r', while the hand grenades explode with a violence almost as alarming as the real thing. Most of them are natural orators, masters of debate, or at the least accomplished talkers, who can express as much with their hands as with their mouths, demolishing an opponent or charming their listeners with a perfectly timed wave of the arm or shrug of the shoulders.

We forded the Piave a mile above Belluno, the town which we had so often seen but never entered, the town whose liberation would be for the partisans the sign and seal of their final triumph. It had already borne with fortitude the Austrian occupation of 1917 and 1918, and was now suffering with undaunted hope and indomitable spirit a longer and more terrifying ordeal.

At a time of year when one would expect to find rivers in flood, I was surprised that on this occasion the Piave was not more than a foot deep. The reason was that the long dam at Soverzene was closed and most of the water was flowing down the 5 miles of canal to the Lago di San Croce, where there are the largest hydro-electric installations in Italy. The fall of 1,050 ft. is distributed over five power stations with a total horse-power, capacity of 300,000. It was assumed that the Germans before leaving Italy would do their utmost to wreck all power stations. One of the main tasks of the partisans, in conjunction with the officials of the Electric Companies, was to prevent this; but when it came to the point the Germans had neither the time nor the will to attempt any destruction anywhere.

We found Zone H.Q. established in a small farmhouse at the southern extremity of the Alpago district. This is an extensive area of rich, hilly farmland north of the Cansiglio forest and east of the San Croce lake. On the east and north it is hemmed in by an unbroken mountain wall beginning at Monte Cavallo, above the pass of that name, and ending with Monte Dolada which dominates the Piave valley at the point where it makes its right-angled bend north. The peaks on this long chain rise to seven or eight thousand feet, but are not true Dolomites. Our cottage was grandly situated 3,000 ft. up, overlooking all the villages of Alpago. A stream which had its source on the slopes of Col Nudo (c. 8,000 ft.) ran immediately below us, and on the far side its steep banks merged quickly into the steeper cliffs of Teverone, a more graceful but slightly lower peak than Col Nudo. To our north only a narrow belt of silver birch separated us from the long 7,000 ft. ridge of Monte Dolada.

We had intended going straight on to Cansiglio to pick up the new operator, but we were held up for two days by reports of a 'rastrallamento' there. Meanwhile we made the acquaintance of the Zone H.Q. staff. In addition to Abba and Deluca there was Sergio, the Chief of Staff, an ex-Colonel of Alpini artillery; Rudi, who was one of the first, if not the first, to organise the resistance movement in Belluno where he was a bank manager; he was by politics a Socialist, was well known and respected, and formed an invaluable link between partisan H.Q. and the Committee of Liberation. He was nominated for and later elected as the first post-war Mayor of Belluno. There was also Toni, a clerk from Rudi's bank; Azeglio, a solicitor from Venice who acted as Intelligence Officer, and finally Attilio Tissi who worked mainly with the Committee of Liberation which met almost daily in the nearby village of Plois. He was a celebrated Italian rock-climber who gave his name to the 'Via Tissi', an excessively difficult route on Monte Agner. His most famous climb was on Civetta. This was what the Italians call a 'sesto grado', a climb of the most extreme severity (or 'the limit of human possibility'), entailing possibly fifteen hours of climbing on a 3,000 ft. rock face with a liberal use of 'pitons' to overcome the overhangs which seem essential features of a 'sesto grado'.

On the night of the 25th, accompanied by Abba, we walked to Nannetti Division H.Q. which had now returned to its original locality on the edge of the forest above Vittorio Veneto. When we arrived it was actually down below in the plain, living in some perfectly concealed 'bunkers' near a village, while a 'rastrallamento' was in progress near the old dropping ground. This was but a half-hearted affair, for Nannetti were now very strong. A short time before they had ambushed and wiped out a party of seventy of the Black Brigade of the Fascist Republican Army. These men had just arrived from Venice, and were sent up the Cansiglio motor-road under the mistaken impression that the partisans were no longer a force to be reckoned with. Twenty were killed in the first volley, the rest captured and subsequently shot. This may seem cruel, but there was really no alternative. The guarding and the feeding of prisoners were extremely difficult, but, in spite of this, Zone H.Q. had set up a prisoner-of-war cage for a limited number. They actually succeeded in exchanging a few German prisoners for partisans, but there was no market for Fascists.

It was interesting to see all our old friends again, particularly in the happier conditions that now prevailed—vastly increased numbers with adequate arms and equipment, and, above all, no more snow. Most of them wore battle-dress and all were of high morale. Three separate dropping grounds were in use, the road leading to Cansiglio was mined, and a landing strip for evacuating airmen who had made forced landings was being prepared on the Cansiglio plain. Small actions agiainst the road and railways in the plains were carried out almost nightly.

It was not until a few nights later that our new wireless operator, Nicola, arrived. He was more amenable to discipline than Pallino, but not in the same class as a wireless operator. He frequently failed to make contact, and the deciphering of his messages, filling in the blanks and adjusting the corrupt parts of the text, was a fine exercise in imaginative writing. Fortunately traffic was not heavy and what there was, was less important than when we were with division when he had sorties to worry about. But even 'top priority' signals, which at first sight are of stupendous gravity and urgency, will in time answer themselves.

The staff of Zone H.Q. was fully occupied. In addition to maintaining close liaison with the civil side of the movment through the C.L.N. and the general supervision of affairs in the Zone, they dealt with higher appointments, discipline, and the boundaries of brigade areas. These last were sometimes troublesome, because there were now three independent brigades directly under command of Zone who had to be kept in step with the Garibaldi formations. Political jealousies were a fruitful source of headaches for Zone H.Q. For example, a good but over-zealous battalion commander of one of the independent brigades caught and hanged a woman spy out of hand, whereupon the Communist party, professing to be grievously shocked at such brutality, demanded the offender's instant trial as a war criminal. The Intelligence branch at H.Q., as well as collating information received from the two divisions, had its own agents, one of whom was a sergeant-major in the S.S. at Belluno. Contact was maintained with divisions by a daily courier service of girls on bicycles, and less frequently with Regional Command at Padova which also sent round its own inspector once a month. Funds were received from the Central Committee at Milan through Padova and re-allocated to divisions and independent brigades. For the two divisions only general directives were issued and the plans co-ordinated. Each division had already made and submitted its own plan of action in the case of an enemy withdrawal or collapse. Zone H.Q. had no partisans for its own protection, but relied on early warnings of impending trouble and fleetness of foot. A very elaborate 'bunker' was under construction and had just been finished when the war ended.

My duties, therefore, partook of the nature of those of a *Maître d'Hotel*, who has to be on view but who seldom does anything so vulgar as work. As a matter of fact even this was not always necessary, so I went methodically to work climbing all the peaks within striking distance. In addition to those already mentioned there were Capel Grande, Monte Messer, and Monte Venal, all about 8,000 ft. None were real Dolomites, yet in late March, when still carrying much snow in good condition, they afforded a lot of fun. Each could be climbed in the course of a long morning, and from most of them our H.Q. cottage could be seen, an advantage in the case of an alarm. Teverone was the most attractive. On the south-west face, which got little sun, there was the better part of 2,000 ft. of snow for kicking or step-cutting, and on the rock summit ridge there were two easy but pleasing pitches that one took *à cheval*.

These jaunts were of necessity solitary. For although the partisans lived among the mountains, sang beautiful songs about them, and liked hearing themselves called mountaineers (with or without the usual epithet 'hardy'), they would nevertheless have been dumbfounded at the thought of climbing one. Tissi was too busy, and in any case these could not be of much interest to one of 'sesto grado' calibre. On an Easter Monday expedition to Col Nudo, however, I had company.

As usual I started out alone. The Zone Commander Abba, lying on his back in the sun, unblushingly declared he was too busy; Gatti, with praiseworthy frankness, thought it was too far—admittedly there were 5,000 ft. to climb. At this time of year there was no grass or hay on the higher slopes, and I was therefore surprised to see two people on a converging track obviously bound for the mountain. Before reachiing the snow, I saw above me two others inspecting me through a pair of field-glasses. When I reached them I found they were carrying small rucksacks, a liberal assortment of hand grenades, a Sten, and a Mauser rifle. Kowing that the partisans were allergic to mountains I wondered who they were. Had total war been declared on the chamois? Was it the Easter Meet of the Alpago Alpine Club? Or had they merely come up to cool their heads in the snow after the festivity of Easter Sunday? For, as Michael Finsbury remarked of another solemn occasion, the Italian 'festa' is 'serious business and requires a great deal of drink'. But whatever might be their errand, clothed as I was in nothing but a pair of trousers and carrying nothing more dangerous than an ice-axe, the advantage and the first move lay with them.

The very few Italian words I have are seldom understood by those to whom they are addressed, nevertheless we exchanged the usual question. They claimed to be partisans, but I left them to guess what I was and uncommonly hard they must have found it. It was necessary to be cautious. Spies were still common, and the Germans had recently begun experiments with gangs of what were called 'contrabanditi', namely Germans or Fascists going about in small parties disguised as partisans. This was not, by the way, a difficult disguise to assume. Whiskers, an Alpini beard, or at any rate some hair on the face, and a total lack of uniformity of dress, were the prime essentials. Trust no one was, therefore, the watchword: 'I am suspect, thou art suspect, he is suspect.'

They were bound for the Valbona pass which led into the Barcis valley to the east. My route to Col Nudo actually traversed the pass, which is a high one, but when I started they moved off in the direction of another and lower col. The veteran of the party had been represented to me as a guide, and though their route did not look promising, I assumed they they knew what they were about.

From the pass some 1,200 ft. of snow led almost directly to the summit. In spite of the hot sun the snow remained in good enough condition to climb without using the snow-shoes I had brought. 'Fatiguing but repaying' was how Baedeker might have described it. To the north was the tangled forest of Dolomite peaks, rejoicing gloriously in the bright colouring of a spring day and the scanty remnants of their winter mantle; to the south lay the green and peaceful plains, with the merest hint of the Adriatic beyond. Some fighter-bombers roaring up the Piave valley struck a note of discord. On leaving the summit I found the snow in excellent condition for a sitting glissade. I must have come down that 1,200 ft. to the pass in less than a minute. In parentheses, and for the benefit of the serious student of military equipment, I may remark that the battle-dress made in America withstood this sort of fair wear and tear better than the British makes, which by 1945 were little more than shoddy.

As I slowed up just above the pass I heard voices. There on an opposing pinnacle above the pass, to which there was obviously no descent, I beheld the four travellers wistfully regarding the haven where they would be. To tell them they were on the wrong road was merely another glimpse of the obvious, but no sooner had I begun to impart this piece of gratuitous information than they turned and fled. I too went down.

A few days later I heard their story at second hand, for they were, in fact, partisans from a neighbouring village. They had set out on their lawful occasions to cross the Valbona Pass, as they had said, but my appearance (I mean my appearance on the scene) had so staggered them that in order to part company as quickly as possible they were driven from their course and to the attempt of a very forlorn hope. The panic which had seized them had evidently had a shattering effect on the guide's judgement; but whether they had taken me for an S.S. Obersturmführer or merely a late survival of the now almost extinct Abominable Snowman Dolomiticus, I was unable to discover.

The final Allied offensive opened slowly. The Germans contested every inch of ground and no spectacular advance was made in the opening phases. It had always been my opinion that if the Germans stood and fought where they were, with the bridgeless Po behind them, and were beaten, they would never be able to get away. They were short of transport and petrol, and they no longer had sufficient troops to keep their lines of retreat open in the face of attack by partisans. This view was a great solace to Zone H.Q. who ruefully contemplated the Piave valley becoming a battlefield with themselves in an uncomfortable position in the German front line.

The Germans did not crack until the third week of April when an American column breaking through raced ahead to capture Verona, the vital communication centre for the Brenner route. We heard of this on the night of the 26th on the Italian news broadcast at 10.30 p.m., whereupon Zone H.Q. sent orders to the two divisions to start blocking the roads in their areas. The following morning we moved to a small village called Arsie, from where we had good observation over the two main high-ways—one from Vittorio Veneto crossing the Piave at the bridge of Ponte Nelli Alpi and then going northwards up the Piave valley, and the other route from Belluno which joined the first beyond the bridge. It was unlucky that the break-through coincided with a break in the weather, which from now until the end remained wet and misty.

On the first day we counted some fifty vehicles on the road, which was patrolled by an armoured car, but by the 29th all traffic from Vittorio Veneto had ceased. In front of the Nannetti Division was a vast accumulation of transport which had been halted south of the town and which was now under attack from the partisans and from the few fighter-bombers able to fly. Traffic was still passing northwards from Belluno. One source of this flow was the Piave valley route south of Feltre, which a Brigade of Nannetti in whose area it was had failed to block. In their eagerness to reach the two whose liberation meant so much to them, there was a tendency among the partisans north and south of the river to attack the Germans in and around Belluno instead of concentrating on the traffic on the road.

By the 30th all small garrisons south of the Piave had withdrawn or surrendered, but Belluno was full of Germans, who still controlled the road on the north bank. Our H.Q. had now moved down to an inn close to the main road, only about half a mile from the Ponte Nelli Alpi bridge, and Abba and Deluca were in contact with the German General in Belluno, trying to persuade him to surrender. The rest of us were just sitting down to some food when a report came in that some Germans were preparing to blow the bridge. The bridge was of no use to the Germans, the road having been blocked long since beyond Vittorio, but it was of great value to the 8th Army, a small column of which was already at Treviso. Gatti and I, with a partisan, hurried off to the bridge to find all quiet. The only signs of life were a few Italian refugees returning from Austria. At this point the Piave flows through a narrow rock gorge bridged by a single steel and concrete arch supporting the roadway below. Underneath the roadway, close to the water, was a small footbridge for inspection purposes which was reached by some twenty stone steps cut in the rock of the north bank of the gorge. Wishing to make quite sure that no demolition charges had been laid we crossed the bridge. I climbed over a little iron gate and began descending the steps in order to have a good look at the abutments. I had got about halfway down when a machine-gun opened up from the south side with vindictive accuracy. Bullets flattened themselves on the steps, and the acrid smell of stone dust filled the air. To run up the steps, fall over the gate, and lie down behind the wall bordering the road, was a matter of seconds. Gatti and the partisan were already behind the wall, the latter, with his hat hoisted on his rifle, shouting at the top of his voice. We only needed a German truck to come down from the Belluno road to see what was happening to complete the tableau. At last the gentleman with the machine-gun, assuming that we were all dead or suspecting that he had been too hasty, took his finger off the trigger. Gatti and I prudently remained prone, but the partisan bravely stood up and continued addressing his remarks to a hedgerow about 300 yards from the bridge. The machine-gun crew then stood up and the commander came down to survey the damage. He was full of apologies when he found out who we were, but I could only compliment him on his good shooting and vigilance.

The same afternoon, 30 April, we got in touch with Vittorio Veneto by telephone. A column consisting of one squadron of the 27th Lancers and a motorised company of the Rifle Brigade had just arrived. I suggested that they should move up that night to block the Belluno-Longarone road along which traffic was still escaping. This was now the only road on which traffic was moving northwards, and even this was blocked beyond Longarone. The reply was indefinite as the colonel commanding the column was at Treviso and would have to be consulted before action could be taken.

We waited by the roadside until midnight when, as no column had come, Deluca took me to Vittorio on a captured German motor-bike. The major in command of the column said he had now got orders to establish a road-block north of Ponte Nelli Alpi and would start at 05.30.

By then Deluca had discarded the motor-bike in favour of a small car (he was an energetic 'snapper-up of unconsidered trifles') and in this we went on ahead of the column as far as the bridge, where we met Abba. He had just returned from another meeting with the Germans in Belluno, who were apparently in no mind for surrendering to the partisans, but who, he thought, would readily surrender to the British. The column arrived and Deluca and I in our tiny Fiat took a less prominent place behind the very large armoured car leading the column. At the 'T' junction where the Vittorio road met the road from Belluno, we ran head-on into a long stream of German transport coming from Belluno. The armoured car opened fire with its Browning and the Germans leapt out of their trucks, not knowing whether to put up their hands or to run. Most of them ran, while the armoured car continued to spray the road and the neighbouring fields, and to pick off the individual trucks with its 2 pr. They got such satisfaction out of it that they found it hard to stop, but after a few thousand rounds had been fired silence reigned once more and the badly frightened Germans began to crawl out of the ditches like beetles after a thunderstorm.

Marshalling the prisoners and collecting their arms was a difficult job for such a small force. The infantry, who were in the rear of the column, were a long time in arriving, and as far as one could see the enemy transport stretched in an almost unbroken line back to Belluno about 3 miles away. The vehicles, motor and horse-drawn, were loaded to the axle with men, food and loot. A gigantic petrol bowser was full, not of petrol, but of cigarettes.

Most of the Germans cringed, making no bones about handing over their pistols and automatics, and begging to be allowed to take their personal kit out of the trucks. The back seats of our car and of Abba's were already pile high with Luger pistols. But further along the road we ran into trouble. At a small cross-roads where there were a few houses, the leading armoured car stopped. I had heard a single shot, which might have been from a pistol, but I thought no more of it. An 88 mm. gun had been abandoned in the middle of the road, and I busied myself getting some civilians to help to push it off the road. This done I climbed up on to the armoured car for a word with the squadron leader, and was shocked to find him sitting dead on his seat, killed instantaneously with a bullet through the heart. There were a lot of German officers about, some of whom turned truculent, refusing to give up their pistols to the partisans. I suspected the shot may have been fired by one of these from inside a house when the squadron leader was standing up in his turret.

Another armoured car came up to take the lead and off we went again, Deluca and I smoking quite good German cigars. We were now not more than 2 miles from Belluno. Half a mile further on, as we were approaching another lot of transport, a hand grenade was thrown at the leading car and heavy firing broke out. Deluca and I leapt out of our car and made a dive for the roadside, where, cigar in hand, we lay like the centipede 'distracted in a ditch considering how to run'. Meanwhile, those in the armoured car, not liking the look of things, decided to retire. They backed on to our little Fiat, mauled it, and then went off down the road with it wrapped drunkenly round their rear towing hook. Deprived of our transport, alone in an unfriendly world, Deluca and I turned tail and legged it down the ditch back to the houses where there was the 88 mm.; the Germans meanwhile, having manned a 20 mm. Breda in the middle of the road, fired indiscriminately in all directions. There were several abandoned cars about. We managed to start one and so escaped down the road to where the armoured cars had halted. The affair now took on the proportions of a battle. The Germans advanced and remanned the 88 mm., which we had foolishly neglected to destroy, and so forced the armoured cars to retire still further. The Rifle Brigade took up a defensive position covering the 'T' junction, and a battery of 25 prs., which had arrived from Vittorio, went into action south of the river. The Colonel commanding the column was also now on the spot and made his H.Q. at the inn by the 'T' junction where a portentous array of vehicles soon assembled—armoured cars. White Scout cars, jeeps, and Bren carriers. As luck would have it, this was the first fine day. The R.A.F. were out in force and had already put in some good work on the enemy transport near Belluno, from which several columns of black smoke were now ascending. It was painfully obvious that in the confused situation the concentration at the 'T' junction was the sort of target that would not be given the benefit of any doubt, and sure enough, in spite of recognition strips and coloured smoke signals, it was presently attacked. One man was killed, two or three wounded, and six of the precious vehicles set on fire.

In the afternoon the Germans developed an infantry attack to open the road. There was an excellent observation post for our guns from the roof of the 'albergo' where the H.Q. were located, and the attack petered out under the accurate artillery fire of the Essex Yeomanry battery. The Germans then sent in a flag of truce. That night 4,000 of them surrendered, and by eleven o'clock next morning, 2 May, the stubborn remnant in Belluno had laid down their arms.

That morning three of us went on another of Deluco's motor-cycles into Belluno, for so long the goal of our ambition. I should like to report that we were wrenched from the cycle by an enthusiastic crowd, borne shoulder-high to the Piazza del Duomo, and there crowned with laurel wreathes to the prolonged and deafening 'Viva's' of the assembled multitude. We were too soon for that. The streets were nearly empty, most of the people wisely remaining indoors until the situation cleared. The few we met smiled happily. In the Piazza some partisans were proudly guarding an ever-growing mob of bewildered Germans, and in the Prefettura, a beautiful fifteenth-century building with arcaded windows from which hung an enormous Italian flag, the Committee of Liberation the newly elected Prefect, the head of the Administration (our friend Tissi), and Rudi the new Mayor, were already making headway against a sea of troubles.

There we shall leave them. The rejoicing came later when the citizens of Belluno showed in full measure their pride in their partisans and their gratitude to us. But before that happy day there was a miserable interregnum of weeks of weary waiting until the tens of thousands of Germans, who had been trapped by the partisans in the Belluno Zone, and had laid down their arms, were at last deprived of them; when the camps of armed and slightly arrogant 'Tedeschi' with their looted Italian vehicles, horses, and food, were broken up; and when the partisans had attended their last parade.

It is only justice to the partisans that a considered opinion of their worth should be given, for in a few liberated countries, and to a lesser degree in Italy, the misguided actions of some have tarnished the reputation of the whole resistance movement. It is, I imagine, generally agreed that the speed and totality of the German collapse in Italy was in no small measure due to the partisans. In the last week of the war they occupied Milan, Genoa, Turin and other towns without waiting for the arrival of the Allies. They blocked all the roads to the north-east so that tens of thousands of Germans struggling to escape to Austria had to surrender where they stood. Had they done nothing else, the time, the trouble and the lives given by the Allies to augment the resistance movement were amply repaid. But this was not all. For eighteen months the movement had been a running sore in the side of the Germans and Fascists, and in addition had sent out invaluable intelligence, sustained many thousands of our prisoners, and helped hundreds of airmen to escape.

Owing mainly to the excellent Italian road system the occupying and holding of large tracts of country as was done in Yugo-Slavia, and to a certain extent in Albania, was never possible. The partisans themselves were slow to discover this; not in fact until after September 1944 when the Germans found the partisans just where they wanted them—in large concentrations—and were able to do with them pretty much as they pleased, did they alter their tactics. Militarily the faults of the partisans were due to lack of experience and not of the will to fight—experience of any kind of fighting was lacking in most cases, and few of the leaders, only some of whom had been in the army, had experience of guerrilla warfare. In September they were thinking in terms of fixed positions instead of hit-and-run tactics; nor did they realise that in fulfilling that mistaken role the lack of training, the lack of any weapons other than personal arms or of any means of communication other than runner, and their isolation which inevitably exposed them to encirclement, all precluded a successful defence.

The quality of brigades and battalions was very uneven. Naturally in an irregular, improvised army, without training or tradition, nearly everything depends on individual leaders. In some units the care of weapons was excellent, in others bad. Some men were brave to the point of recklessness, others the reverse. They were often unduly elated or correspondingly depressed. Like our own men, but with more excuse and more opportunity, they believed every rumour. They grossly exaggerated their own losses and those of the enemy, especially the latter. No 'rastrallamento' was ever carried out by less than several thousand Germans who invariably incurred losses which ran into hundreds. Many of the leaders even were subject to this fault and would unthinkingly pass on unlikely or obviously untrue reports.

But when I recall these trivial faults, by no means peculiar to them, I recall too the conditions in which they served which were peculiar to them alone. An Italian who became a partisan had to suffer greater hardships and run greater risks than those incurred by regular troops. Capture almost invariably meant death, with the probability of being tortured first and hanged afterwards. If they were badly wounded their chances of getting away were slim, while for those who did get away medical care was rough and ready. A successful action usually meant reprisals during which friends or relatives might be shot, hanged, or at the best imprisoned, their houses and villages burnt. Food was monotonous, clothing was insufficient, boots bad, cleanliness nearly impossible. They could have no pay, leave, amusements or mail from home; the only newspapers they saw were Fascist; there were no canteens, cigarettes and tobacco were either scanty or unobtainable. There was no organised training or even sufficient work to counteract the long weeks of waiting and inactivity. In short, everything that makes life tolerable for the regular soldier, that sustains his morale in quiet times and in battle gives him a reasonable chance of survival, was absent from the life of the partisan. Nor was this all. There were no periods of rest for the partisans. They lived under the constant strain of surprise, betrayal or attack; the G.A.P. who lived in villages never dared to sleep in houses. And most serious of all, perhaps, were the political fears and jealousies, existing even in their own formations, and the suspicion that for them the end of the war might only be the beginning of fresh political strife.

It is with all this in mind that the partisans must be judged. With no Garibaldi to inspire them with his dauntless and unquenchable spirit the men of northern Italy took the course that he would have taken on the terms he himself had offered to their forebears: 'I offer neither pay, nor quarters, no provisions: I offer hunger, thirst, forced marches, battles, and death.' Such were the terms on which they served. That they held together indissolubly during the hard winter months, and were able and willing to give of their best when the time came, is some measure of their determination, self-sacrifice, patriotism, and of their rekindled ardour for the cause of freedom.

EVEREST 1938

Everest 1938

First published by Cambridge University Press, 1948

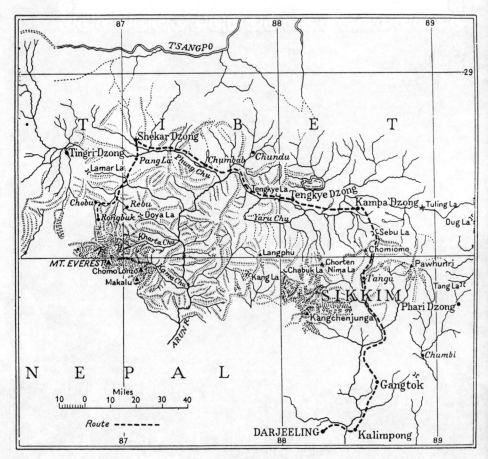

The route to Rongbuk

Contents

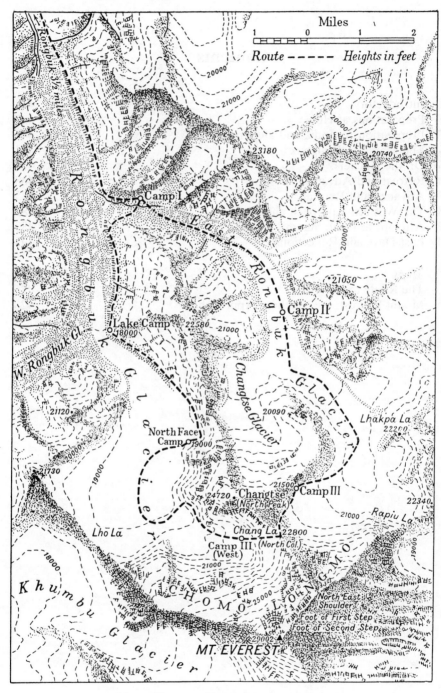

Mount Everest, the northern approaches

CHAPTER ONE

Introductory

'The sight of a horse makes the wayfarer lame.'   Bengali Proverb

THE last book written about Mount Everest by Mr Ruttledge, the leader of the 1933 and 1936 expeditions, was aptly named *The Unfinished Adventure*. This present account should be read merely as yet another chapter in this adventure story, possibly one of those duller chapters from which even the best of adventure stories are not always free. In the twenty-five years which have elapsed since the first expedition went out the story has lost the gloss of novelty. The approach march and the establishing of camps have become almost a matter of routine which with luck and judgement should be devoid of incident. Misfortunes and hair-breadth escapes, suffering and hardship, are the making of an adventure story, but from all such a well-found expedition blessed with a fair share of luck should be exempt. Here I have no hardships to bemoan, no disasters to recount, and no tragedies to regret.

Some day, no doubt, someone will have the enviable task of adding the last chapter, in which the mountain is climbed, and writing 'Finis'. That book, we may hope, will be the last about Mount Everest, for we already have five official accounts, besides a few unofficial, and no one can tell how many more will be written before the epic is complete. Apart from reasons of continuity in the record of this unfinished adventure, the story of the fifth abortive attempt to climb the mountain is only worth relating because a fairly drastic change was made in the methods used. That is to say we broke away from the traditional grand scale upon which all previous expeditions had been organized, and to that extent the story has novelty. But we made no change in the route taken or the tactics employed on the mountain, which are the outcome of the judgement and hard-won experience of some of the best mountaineers of recent times, whose achievements are a guide and an inspiration to all who follow where they led.

It is difficult to measure that margin in terms of additional effort (it may be greater than we think) but, in view of the apparently narrow margin by which two of the earlier expeditions failed, it may seem presumptuous to imagine that any change of organization should be needed. So before recounting our experiences of 1938 I feel it is due to those who sponsored the expedition, the friends who backed it, and to the many mountaineers interested who may sympathize with some of the views here expressed, to attempt some explanation. The expeditions of 1924 and 1933 seemed to come so near to success that few if any thought of questioning the soundness of the methods employed, at least for the getting of someone to the top of the mountain; for long before then mountaineers had begun to dislike the excessive publicity which was a direct consequence of the scale of the expeditions and the large amount of money needed to pay for them. But after 1933 criticism began to be heard—Mr E. E. Shipton was possibly one of the first to doubt that in mountaineering the great and the good are necessarily the same—and the unfortunate experiences of 1936 when, through no fault of those concerned, but little was accomplished, had the salutary effect of rousing doubts in others. What had happened once might happen again. For financial reasons, if for no others, it seemed the time had come to give less expensive methods a trial.

Although our expedition of 1938 was the seventh to visit the mountain it was only the fifth to attempt the ascent. The first, and in many ways the most interesting, expedition was the reconnaissance of 1921 during which, of course, no attempt was made on the summit. Until 1921 no European had been within 90 miles of the mountain and the first party had to find the best approach and then a likely route to the top. Both these difficult tasks and much additional work were successfully accomplished at a cost of about £5,000—a figure which is not unreasonable considering the complete lack of previous experience, the time spent in the field, and the amount and importance of the work done. But the first attempt on the summit which took place the following year cost more than twice as much, and set standards in numbers, equipment, and cost, which until 1938 were equalled or even exceeded by all subsequent expeditions excluding only that most interesting and significant expedition of 1935 which was again a reconnaissance.

Late in 1934 the Tibetan Government unexpectedly announced that they would allow us to send an expedition in each of the following years, 1935 and 1936. Time was short, for in those days the gestation period for a full-blown expedition was, suitably enough, like that of a whale or an elephant, about two years; but so that the benefit of the surprising gift of the extra year should not be lost, Mr Shipton was hastily appointed to organize and lead a small, light expedition in 1935. Their main task was to try out new men and equipment for the full-scale attempt the following year; other tasks were the examining of snow conditions on the mountain during the monsoon and the survey of glaciers north and east of the mountain. At a cost of only £1,500 a large area of country and the North Face of the mountain were surveyed, and twenty-six peaks of over 20,000 ft. were climbed. In the course of these operations the North Col (Camp IV) was occupied, and it became plain that, had conditions warranted and had a few more tents been available, then a serious attack on the summit could well have been launched. This should have opened everyone's eyes, especially as the expedition had been sent out so that its lessons might be of use to the all-out attempt of the following year. But this example of what could be done with a moderate expenditure was ignored and the expedition of 1936 saw no diminution in scale, either of men or of money. Twelve Europeans, including two doctors, a wireless expert, over a hundred porters, three hundred transport animals, and some £10,000 were employed, and the North Col was the highest point reached.

It is not easy to see either the origin of or the reasons for these unwieldy caravans organized on the lines of a small military expedition rather than a mountaineering party. Were it not that the pioneering days of Himalayan climbing were past one might find a parallel in the earliest days of mountaineering in the Alps, when numbers were considered a source of strength and not the weakness they usually are. For de Saussure's ascent of Mont Blanc in 1787 the party numbered twenty. The elaborately organized expedition of the Duke of the Abruzzi to the Karakoram in 1909[1] was the original Himalayan expedition in the grand style, but before and since that time many private parties had climbed and explored with a minimum of fuss and expense—notably those of Mummery, Conway, Longstaff, Kellas, Meade, to mention a few.[2] Of course the means must be proportioned to the end; there is a difference between rushing a moderate-sized peak and besieging one of the Himalayan giants, but any additional means we think we need for the more formidable task ought to be taken reluctantly and after the severest scrutiny. Anything beyond what is needed for efficiency and safety is worse than useless. In 1905 Dr Longstaff and the two Brocherel brothers, with no tent and one piece of chocolate, very nearly climbed Gurla Mandhata, a peak in Tibet north of Garhwal, 25,355 ft. high, a practical illustration of the application of that important mountaineering principle, the economy of force—an imperfect example, perhaps, because one might argue that with a tent and two pieces of chocolate they might have succeeded. But away with such pedantic, ungracious quibbles. Did not Mummery, who more than any one embodied the spirit of mountaineering, write: '. . . the essence of the sport lies, not in ascending a peak, but in struggling with and over-coming difficulties'?

Though all mountaineers will agree with Mummery, it is no use concealing the fact that most of us do earnestly wish to reach the top of any peak we attempt and are disappointed if we fail: especially with Mount Everest parties where the desire to reach the top is supreme. No one would choose to go there merely for a mountaineering holiday. It is not easy therefore to criticize men for taking every means which they consider will increase the chances of success. It is a matter of degree, and on any expedition, even the most serious, the tendency to take two of everything, 'just to be on the safe side', needs to be firmly suppressed, for a point is soon reached when multiplication of these precautions, either in men or equipment, defeats its purpose.

Owing to the frequency of Alpine huts the longest climb in the Alps requires no more equipment than can be carried on the climber's back; while for numbers, although two are adequate and move fastest, three are no doubt safer. Any additional members usually lessen the combined efficiency of the party. In the Himalaya the peaks are twice as high and the climber has to provide his own hut. The climbing of a peak of, say 21,000 ft., will require a tent of some sort to be taken up to at least 17,000 ft. From a camp at this height a peak of 23,000 ft. has been climbed (Trisul by Dr Longstaff), but most people would prefer to have a second tent at some intermediate point from which to start the final climb. Obviously for higher peaks more

1 270 persons (12 Europeans) and 95 baggage animals crossed the Zoji La.

2 The Norwegians, C. W. Rubenson and Monrad Aas, who nearly climbed Kabru (24,002 ft.) in 1907, must not be omitted.

intermediate camps are required and it becomes necessary to employ porters
to carry and provision them. These porters will mean other porters to carry up
their tents and provisions, and so it grows snowball fashion until in extreme
cases like that of Mount Everest you have to find food and accommodation
for at least fifteen men at 23,000 ft. in order to put two climbers in the highest
camp at 27,000 ft.

It should be clear that the fewer men to be maintained at each camp and the
less food and equipment they need, the easier and safer it is for all concerned.
I am not advocating skimping and doing without for the sake of wishing to
appear tough, ascetic, sadistic, or masochistic, but for the reason that no party
should burden itself with a man or a load more than is necessary to do the job.
If this principle be accepted and applied all along the line from the highest
camp to the starting-point—London—the more likely will the expedition be
economical and efficient, in short a small light expedition. The unattainable
ideal to be kept in mind is two or three men carrying their food with them as
in the Alps. How far this can be done has not been discovered—probably not
very far—and there is the complication of supporting parties which though
desirable are perhaps not essential. If the highest party is unable to get down
on account of bad weather, the party below is not likely to be able to get up to
help them—as happened on Masherbrum in 1938. Support or not, the
importance of not being caught short of food in the highest camp is obvious.

Between the two wars many small private parties, refusing to be frightened
by the portentous standard set by the Everest expeditions and strenuously
maintained by German and French expeditions,[1] accomplished much in the
Himalaya, demonstrating that for peaks up to 24,000 ft. nothing more was
needed, and thus keeping alive the earlier simple tradition of mountaineering
with which the big expedition is incompatible. This was readily accepted, but
the question of whether for the highest peaks the grand-scale expedition
was either necessary, efficient, or expedient, was debatable. Everyone
recognized that an extra four or five thousand feet in height necessitated more
camps and more porters, and although Nanda Devi (25,660 ft.) had been
climbed practically without the help of porters it was admitted that similar
methods would not work on Everest—the difference of 3,500 ft. in height
between the two mountains is no adequate measure of the difference in
degree of accessibility of the two summits. But if the provision of two more
camps entails more equipment and more porters, it need not entail a small
army with its transport officers, doctors, wireless officers, and an army's
disregard for superfluity.

Then if the big expedition is unnecessary, is it efficient? In view of what was
accomplished by the four expeditions up to 1933 it would be impertinent to
say they were inefficient, but I believe the same men could have done as

1 International Expedition to Kanghcenjunga, 1930: Europeans, 13; porters, 300. German
expedition to Nanga Parbat, 1934: Europeans, 14; porters, 600. French expedition to the
Karakoram, 1936: Europeans, 11; porters, 500. In these foreign expeditions of which the above
are fair samples the climbing party usually numbered eight or nine, the balance being scientists,
doctors, photographers, secretaries (in one case), and British liaison officers to run the porter
corps.

much, perhaps more, at a quarter of the cost, using methods more in keeping with mountaineering tradition. It is possible to argue that with less impedimenta to shift, fewer porters to convoy, and fewer passengers to carry, the strength of the climbing parties when it came to the last push would have been greater than it was. Theoretically the extra efficiency of the large party consists in having a reserve of climbers to take the place of those put out of action by sickness or frost-bite. Of the first four attempts of 1922, 1924, 1933 and 1936, the numbers taking part were thirteen, twelve, sixteen and twelve respectively. From these have to be deducted the supernumeraries such as non-climbing leader, base doctor, transport officers, wireless expert, leaving an effective strength of eight, eight, ten and eight. In 1938 there were seven of us. But we were all climbers and we carried only one-fifth of the gear and spent only a fifth of the money of previous expeditions. The actual number of climbers taking part does not define the 'big' or the 'small' party, and on this point there is not much in it between the advocates of either. As the best number to take part in the final climb is two, and as the odds against favourable conditions continuing long enough to allow of more than one attempt are high, provision for two attempts is all we need consider. Two parties of two and two spare men, six in all, should therefore be enough. A party of eight has a reserve strength of 100% which should satisfy the most cautious. Most expeditions have had the benefit of a nucleus of three or four men whose ability to go high had already been proved. But if a party was not so fortunate in this respect, as might well be, then allowance would have to be made for a possible failure to acclimatize. The same would apply to the porters, for owing to the war and the lapse of time very few if any of the old 'Tigers' will be available.

With experienced porters such as we had the necessary convoy duties could be done comfortably by six or seven Europeans. Indeed, there is more to be feared from underwork than from overwork on these expeditions. Far too many off-days are forced upon a party and much time is spent lying about in sleeping-bags. Mr Shipton, who has taken part in two of the large expeditions, has remarked that there is sometimes a grave risk of contracting bed sores. I am sure many other climbers will bear me out that the common effect of too many off-days is a feeling of deadly lethargy. The risk of serious illness developing is not great and is over-emphasized. The party are fit men when they start and presumably able to take care of themselves. Coughs, colds, and sore throats seem to be inseparable from a journey across Tibet in the early spring, but their effects are not very grave. Indeed, it seems better to face the possibility of serious illness than the certainty of having useless mouths to feed and men falling over one another for lack of work.

A method is expedient if it tends to promote a proposed object. Whether the methods of these earlier expeditions were the best for the climbing of the mountain is a matter of opinion—I have tried to show that they were not, insomuch as they were wasteful and cumbersome—but I think there is no doubt whatever that they were not those best calculated either to preserve the well-being and goodwill of the peoples of those countries through which the route of the expedition lay or to maintain the best interests of mountaineering. The first point was raised in several letters to *The Times* in 1936 of which I quote from two, written by men[1] with Himalayan experience:

Apart from obvious cumbersomeness and expense, the huge expedition suffers from other serious objections. The first lies in the demoralizing effect which those visitations have on the people of the villages, by upsetting their scale of economic values. The arrival of an army of porters led by Sahibs apparently possessing boundless wealth and wasting valuable material along the route, makes a most corrupting impression. I was conscious of this when staying at the charming village of Lachen in North Sikkim through which several large expeditions, have passed. The occurrence of theft in the later Everest expeditions, so out of keeping with the Tibetan character, is probably another case in point. It would be a tragedy if the visits of climbers to the Himalayas were to destroy one of its greatest charms—namely the honest character of the inhabitants and their splendid culture.

And in another letter:

In discussing the demerits of large expeditions a point not yet touched on is the unbalancing effect of the passage of a large transport column on the economic life of the country through which it passes. The part of Tibet traversed by the Mount Everest expeditions is by Tibetan standards and in comparison with the northern deserts fairly fertile. But actually only just enough barley is grown or can be grown to pay taxes and to carry the population through the winter and spring. The flocks of sheep and yaks are just as large as the grazing will permit. When an Everest expedition comes with 300 animals and a horde of hungry porters, reserves of food are broken into and sold: while grass which should have fed Tibetan ponies goes into the stomachs of the visiting yaks. It is true that good silver, British Indian rupees, are given in exchange. But, as a headman remarked to us in 1935 just after receiving Rs. 200, what good will that silver do? It cannot buy more corn where there is no surplus, nor will it fertilize the pastures. But it will quite certainly cause the neighbouring headman to be jealous, and enduring quarrels may be started. Where the balance between production and consumption is already precarious and where there are no reserves to draw upon the effect of a large expedition is materially disastrous.

There is certainly something in this; though the people along the line of march who receive good money for services rendered, who 'win' a number of useful articles of various kinds, and who also have their ailments attended to gratis, might take a less gloomy view. The Tibetans are shrewd people and will not exchange food for money unless they see their advantage in it, much less if it spells starvation. Anyhow, the Indian Government is alive to this danger and now only one of what are euphemistically described as 'major expeditions' is allowed to operate in any particular area at a given time. And if the interests of the local inhabitants suffer from the large expedition so do the strangers who come after, who find the market for goods and services in a very inflated state.

Whether we climb mountains for exercise, love of scenery, love of adventeure, or because we cannot help it, every genuine mountaineer must shudder involuntarily when he sees anything about mountains in newspapers. As Mr Jorrocks, who consistently refused to be weighed, used to say, when asked to mount the scales, 'his weight was altogether 'twixt him and his 'oss',

1 Marco Pallis; Michael Spender (killed in an accident May 1945).

so is mountaineering altogether a private affair between the man and his mountain; the lack of privacy is disagreeable and particularly so if, as usually happens, the newspaper gets hold of the wrong mountain wrongly spelt, adds or deducts several thousand of feet to or from its height, and describes what the wrong man with his name wrongly spelt did not do on it. Most human activities, especially the more foolish, are regarded nowadays as news, so there is perhaps the less reason to expect mountaineering to be an exception; nevertheless, it is indisputable that it is the big expedition that has occasioned this news value, the reason, of course being that to finance them recourse must be had to the newspapers. No one bothers about climbers at home or in the Alps unless they fall, or in the Himalayas unless some newspaper is paying for the story. Thanks to this publicity the interest taken in Everest expeditions is now world-wide; news about them is published whether authentic or not, whether paid for or not; it is therefore very difficult, quixotic in fact, to refuse an offer for the story when a refusal will make not a jot of difference to the sum total of publicity.

The effect of this on the climbers taking part, and on mountaineers generally, should be taken into account. It is considered an honour to be asked to join a Mount Everest expedition; but, human nature being what it is, the exaggerated glamour which now surrounds an expedition of this sort has made the competition for a place even keener, so that much canvassing takes place before the final selection and much heart-burning after. The chosen party finds itself burdened with unnecessary responsibilities; responsibilities to a committee, to a newspaper, or even to the nation as the 'pick of young British manhood', as one unfortunate party was described. A feeling that the eyes of England are upon you may be very bracing before a battle but is not conducive to sound mountaineering.

Finally, it was publicity which engendered a competitive spirit individually and nationally. I think it is true that the big German expeditions received financial as well as moral backing from their governments and certainly the Tibetans themselves are convinced that we are sent to climb Everest at the bidding of our Government to enhance national prestige. One result of this is that mountains tend to become national preserves and the Indian Government has thrust on them the thankless task of deciding whether a party from one nation should be allowed to attempt a mountain that has already been visited by that of another. A question which might easily be settled by a little consideration and co-operation amongst the climbers themselves. The evils are there for all to see, but how or whether they can be abated is less obvious. Probably the phase is only a passing one, born of an age of advertisement. Many mountaineers fervently hope that the big mountains like Everest, Kangchenjunga, K2, and Nanga Parbat, will be climbed soon so that Himalayan climbing may regain the more normal atmosphere of Alpine climbing and cease to be a mere striving for height records. Whether these mountains are climbed or not, smaller expeditions are a step in the right direction which should make even parties attempting the very highest peaks less subservient to publicity than heretofore, if not quite independent of it. Much will have been gained by that. For men living in India there should be no financial difficulty; but in the nature of things most young climbers in England are not in a position to pay their full share of expenses of a Himalayan expedition; although, be it noted, two men did find it possible to spend five months in the Himalaya at a cost of £143 each, including passage money both ways. With the money that has been spent in trying to climb Everest a fund could have been endowed, the income from which would have more than sufficed to send a party annually to attempt some Himalayan climb. However, such a fund might have done more harm than good; a man who is bent on getting to the Himalaya will find ways and means.

Books, though they endure a little longer, are a less baneful form of publicity than newspaper articles because few read them. 'No man but a blockhead', says Dr Johnson, 'ever wrote except for money', a remark which is quite true of the writers of Mount Everest books who wrote in the first place to defray the expenses and who must now write to preserve the continuity of the story. Unlike the desert and the sea, mountains have not yet found a writer worthy of them. Perhaps those who could have written in a way that would live have felt about books and publicity as Mallory felt. In his contribution to the 1922 expedition book, which was a hint of his ability in this respect, he makes an eloquent but unavailing plea for silence: 'Hereafter, of contemporary exploits the less we know the better; our heritage of discovery among mountains is rich enough; too little remains to be discovered. The story of a new ascent should now be regarded as a corrupting communication calculated to promote the glory of Man, or perhaps only of individual men, at the expense of the mountains themselves.'

But we protest too much; for at bottom does it matter what is written about that 'considerable protuberance' Mount Everest or any lesser mountain? Let man conquer (revolting word) this, that, or the other, and write volumes about having done so, nothing he does or says will tame the sea or diminish the glory of the hills. The sea, immense and romantic though it is, is a commercial highway; the desert, with toil and money, can be made to blossom; but the mountains, thank heaven, are a sanctuary apart. None of our tricks can change them, nor can they change that man who looks at them for their beauty, loves them for the way they infect and quicken his spirits, and climbs them for his fun. 'If there are no famous hills, then nothing need be said, but since there are they must be visited.'

But though the mountains cannot change, our approach to them may; and if in this chapter, and the last, the note of criticism and protest appears faintly querulous it must be attributed to a perhaps presumptuous jealousy for all that mountaineering and mountaineering tradition stands for. Mountains mean so much to so many, as sources of comfort and serenity, as builders of health and character, and as strong bonds of friendship between men of all kinds, that any tendency to diminish their might, majesty and power, should be resented and resisted. Well was it said, 'Resist the beginnings', and therefore these protests have been written in the hope that promoters of Himalayan expeditions will think twice about the use of innovations designed to soften the rigours of the game or lessen the supremacy of the mountains. Of the many strange tricks that man plays before high heaven that would be one of the strangest, one which if it did not make angels weep would strike moralists dumb, if our efforts to subdue the mightiest range and the highest mountain of all should be the means of losing us our mountain heritage. There will be small danger of this happening if we do not treat our highest mountains too seriously, the attaining of their summits as the only end, and an attempt upon them as 'man's expression of his higher self'—whatever that may mean. When our forerunners were busy discovering the Alps, as we are now discovering the Himalaya, I feel sure they did not look upon themselves as so many bearded and be-whiskered embodiments of man's unconquerable spirit striving to attain the highest. In German accounts of Himalayan climbing between the wars one came upon this high-falutin' attitude, and occasionally in reading of Mount Everest one detected a portentous note, as in a dispatch from the front. As soon as we begin to talk or write thus about men and mountains we should remind ourselves of a remark of Chesterton, that cheerful apostle of common sense and paradox: 'Physical nature must be enjoyed not worshipped. Stars and mountains must not be taken seriously.' Which I take to mean that we may enjoy our mountains and love what we enjoy, keeping our passion for them this side of idolatry, but that mountaineers and astronomers committing their follies shall be viewed by others with the indulgence customary towards foreigners, dons, and the eccentricities of genius, and by themselves with only the very mildest esteem.

CHAPTER TWO

Preparations at Home

'What creates great difficulty in the profession of the commander of armies is the necessity of feeding so many men and animals. If he allows himself to be guided by the commissaries he will never stir, and all his expeditions will fail.' Napoleon

THE unfortunate experience which befell the 1936 expedition converted many to the idea of smaller, less expensive, expeditions—above all less expensive. Not that a small expedition would have fared any better in that year, but the defeat would have been less resounding. Here was an expedition on which no expense had been spared, organized and equipped in a way which was thought would ensure success, turned back by unfavourable conditions at only 23,000 ft. What had happened once might happen again; and now that it had been shown that there might very well be no story worth selling, the large sum required for a similarly elaborate expedition would in future be less easily found. When, therefore, it was known that the Tibetan authorities would permit another attempt in 1938, by general consent the expedition was organized on a more modest scale. The Tibetan authorities have been very indulgent towards us in the past and we must hope for a continuance of their goodwill in the future; but the obtaining of permission to go to Mount Everest is still one of the major difficulties in the way of climbing the mountain. I venture to think that had it lain in a more accessible part of the Himalaya and had more frequent attempts been possible it would have been climbed before now. I have been told by one who should know, that so sacrosanct do they regard Mount Everest that asking the authorities at Lhasa for permission to climb it is like asking the Dean and Chapter for permission to climb Westminster Abbey. That may be so, but it is certainly not the impression one gets from the people who live almost under the shadow of the mountain—the people who, one might expect, would be the most sensitive to any hint of sacrilege. I mean the people of Rongbuk, particularly the abbot of the Rongbuk monastery who has seen all the expeditions pass and who welcomed us in a most friendly way, doing all in his power to assist us. Of course, it may be said, he is so serenely confident of the mountain's power to defend and, if need be, avenge herself, that he just treats us with the innate courtesy and friendliness common to Tibetans. Gathering information through an interpreter is unsatisfactory, but so far as we could understand, the monastery is not a very ancient foundation: founded and built, in fact, largely by the present abbot who is now a very old man. Nor could we discover whether it was built on its present site for the sake of proximity to the mountain or for some other mythological association.

Permission having been given, the Mount Everest Committee appointed a leader and gave him, as is usual, a free hand. It was with some diffidence that I accepted this responsible post, for amongst those whom I proposed to invite were men with a greater mountaineering experience than mine and particularly more experience of Everest. But I took comfort from the thought that with men like E. E. Shipton, F. S. Smythe, and N. E. Odell amongst the party, it would be my part to sit listening with becoming gravity to their words of wisdom, waking up occasionally to give an approving nod. In fact I should have a sinecure, as should be the case with the leader of any well-balanced climbing party. And so it was so far as making decisions on the mountain went, most of which were imposed on us, willy-nilly, by the weather.

A party of seven was finally made up, of whom only one was not a first choice. It was unfortunate that neither L. R. Wager nor J. L. Longland, who had done so well in 1933, was available. Where men have had Himalayan experience selection is not as difficult as it might be; a man who has been high before can be counted upon to go high again, and the more often he has been high and the more recently the better he is likely to go. The number of those who do not acclimatize well to height seems to be very much smaller than those who do, but in taking a man who has never climbed outside the Alps there is the risk that he will not acclimatize; so that if men are available who have proved themselves capable of going high, and are otherwise suitable, then the making of an experiment would not be easily justified. Enough is now known about the technical difficulties of the mountain to show that as well as being able to acclimatize well a man must be a good all-round mountaineer; not necessarily brilliant on rocks or ice, but at home on both and capable of looking after others as well as himself on difficult ground. There was no mystical value about the number seven; when all are climbers it represents a high margin of safety against casualties. It is possible to hold the view that any number more than one constitutes a large party, but it is more the amount of baggage and porters to carry it, than the number of Europeans, which earns the epithet 'large'. In this sense our party was small, though possibly not so small as it could have been. We hope that the number seven would form a homogeneous party, small enough to move rapidly, and large enough to split up into two or more parties if necessary.

The names and qualifications of the members were as follows: E. E. Shipton (aged thirty) had climbed in the Alps, Africa (Mounts Kenya, Kilimanjaro and Ruwenzori), and had been six times to the Himalaya, on three occasions leading his own party. On Everest in 1933 he reached 27,500 ft., led the reconnaissance of 1935, and was there again in 1936. In 1937 he took a small party to the Karakoram Himalaya where it explored and mapped a large area of difficult glaciated country in uninhabited regions destitute of supplies. The work done received the approval of the Surveyor-General of India, Brigadier C. G. Lewis, to whose sympathy Himalayan climbers owe much. As Shipton and I had climbed much together our views on the composition and methods of Himalayan expeditions were the same; he was to take my place if the necessity arose.

The record of F. S. Smythe (aged thirty-seven) is well known. He had had great Alpine and Himalayan experience, having been five times to India, first in 1930 with the International expedition to Kangchenjunga, then to Kamet (25,447 ft.) which his party climbed, and in 1933 and 1936 to Everest. In 1937 he had been in Garhwal with Oliver and had climbed seven peaks including the difficult Mana peak (23, 860 ft.).

N. E. Odell was in the front rank of mountaineers with long and varied experience in the Alps, the Rockies, the Polar regions, and the Himalaya. His efforts on Everest in 1924 in support of Mallory and Irvine are well known, and it has always been a matter for regret that he did not have a place in one of the climbing parties. In 1936 he climbed Nanda Devi (25,660 ft.) when he seemed so much fitter than the rest of us that I considered his age (forty-seven) to be immaterial. The years between twenty-five and thirty-five have been laid down as the best for high-altitude climbing, but as in most things much depends on the man. The average age of this party worked out at thirty-six.

Dr C. B. M. Warren (aged thirty-two) was a doctor as well as being a mountaineer with considerable Alpine and Himalayan experience. He was climbing in Garhwal with Marco Pallis in 1933, and on Everest in 1935 and 1936. He had devoted much time to the study of the use of oxygen and had carried out some practical tests in the Alps, and in 1935 and 1936 he collected physiological data. He was in charge of our oxygen apparatus.

Peter Lloyd (aged thirty) had had much Alpine experience and was first-rate on rock and ice. In 1936 on Nanda Devi he carried a load to the high bivouac at 23,500 ft. proving himself capable of dealing with difficult rock at that height. As a chemist he was able to help Warren with the oxygen.

Capt. P. R. Oliver[1] (aged thirty-two) of Coke's Rifles climbed Trisul (23,400 ft.) in 1933 with one porter. This was the second ascent, the first being by Longstaff and the two Brocherels in 1907 when the party climbed from a bivouac at 17,600 ft. to the top and back in one day. In 1936 Oliver was with the Everest party and in 1937 in Garhwal with Smythe. He was therefore another member of the party with the benefit of recent acclimatization.

For my part I had climbed in the Alps, Africa, and the Himalaya, which I first visited in 1934 with Shipton when we explored the Nanda Devi basin. In 1935 I had accompanied Shipton's reconnaissance party to Everest when E. H. L. Wigram[2] and I had degenerated into mere peak-baggers, collecting seventeen all over 20,000 ft. In 1936 I had been with the Anglo-American party to Nanda Devi, which we climbed, and with Shipton again in 1937 to the Karakoram Himalaya. The obtaining of the necessary leave of absence by some members of the party was not easily arranged and in some cases involved sacrifices.

The personnel having been chosen it remained to collect the material. After the 1936 expedition, Shipton had drawn up estimates of equipment for an attempt on Everest by a small party and to these we adhered closely. The final cost was very near the estimated cost and on the right side, £2,300 against £2,500. The equipment had been ordered in the spring of 1937 before he and I had left for the Karakoram, so that on our return from there in the autumn there remained but the food to be bought and the oxygen question to be decided. The sole innovation in the matter of equipment was that we took only essentials and not too many of those. Three very good types of tents have now been evolved from bitter experience so that many of the discomforts suffered by earlier parties are things of the past. It cannot be pointed out too often that each party draws on the experience and profits by the example of its predecessors—we, of course, benefited most. The types of sleeping-bags, warm clothing, and wind-proof suits, as now used will not easily be improved upon, but the search for the ideal boots and gloves for high climbing still goes on. Thanks to the interest shown by the makers, a Primus stove that burns well at extreme altitude had already been evolved, but this year, at the suggestion of Mr P. J. H. Unna,[3] an improved form of pump-plunger was fitted which made pumping at great heights very much less laborious—a dozen strokes sufficing instead of possibly a hundred. We had to be careful not to fit these altered pumps to the stoves used at lower levels because the extra pressure they gave might have resulted in an explosion.

For the unscientific it might be worth while noting the alteration in atmospheric conditions during an ascent and its consequence:

Atmospheric pressure and consequently barometer readings fall. Air expands as it rises and therefore cools; each cubic foot of air weighs less and therefore contains a smaller weight of oxygen, the proportion between nitrogen and oxygen remaining the same. The quantity of air available for intercepting the sun's rays and for preventing

1 Killed in action in Burma, 1945, commanding a battalion of the 13th Frontier Force Rifles.
2 Killed, climbing in Wales, 1945.
3 Mr Unna, in his role of helpful scientist, appears in a more baleful light in the final chapter.

radiation from the earth becomes less thereby speeding up evaporation. The following consequences ensue: warmer clothing becomes necessary not only on account of lower temperatures but also because anoxaemia or oxygen lack reduces vitality. Better tents are needed to reduce radiation; it becomes more difficult to strike matches; to keep candles alight; and for fuel to burn. Cooking becomes more difficult and slower; the lower boiling point and greater cold acting together make it more difficult to keep drinks hot. Strong sunlight may cause snow-blindness and with rapid evaporation may cause sunburn; rapid evaporation causes increased thirst. Reduced external pressure entails a relatively higher internal pressure in enclosed vessels, therefore corked bottles break more easily and cans of liquid tend to leak. Rubber perishes more easily on account of the cold.

All these effects are noticeable in the Alps but are intensified and of more importance on higher mountains.

The question of food does not present any great difficulty until heights of 22,000 ft. or more are reached, if a few simple rules are borne in mind. The technique of travelling light which Shipton and I employ on our own expeditions does not mean that we deliberately starve ourselves or our porters. It does not and should not imply inadequate or indifferent food. As we once lived perforce for a few days on tree mushrooms and bamboo shoots there is a general impression that this is our normal diet, eked out with liberal doses of fresh air, on which, thanks to a yogi-like training, we thrive and expect every one else to do likewise. Nothing could be farther from the truth. Like Dr Johnson, we mind our bellies very strenuously: 'for I look upon it', he said, 'that he who will not mind his belly will scarcely mind anything else.' The more restricted a ration is the more need is there for careful thought in its selection. For normal men a ration of 2 lb. a day is ample (I have kept Sherpas happy for two or three weeks on 1½ lb.) and the whole art lies in getting the most value for weight.

On Polar expeditions where conditions are more severe, the work as hard and the period more prolonged, the sledging ration varies from 25 to 33 oz. and it is usually far simpler and apparently more unappetizing than the food eaten on Himalayan expeditons. The difference is that the men are hungry. Watkins wrote of his 1930 expedition in Greenland: 'We soon found that these rations (39 oz.) were more than enough for men travelling between 20 and 30 miles a day at low temperatures at a height of about 8,000 ft., and towards the end of our time in Greenland we reduced the rations by about one-third, so that the total amount eaten by one man in a day was 23.6 oz. This was found ample for all normal winter sledging work. On all future expeditions I would keep the rations per man per day under 1½ lb.' Martin Lindsay, on the other hand, wrote: 'We found ourselves ravenously hungry on 26 oz. a day . . . Were this journey (the crossing of the Greenland ice-cap) to be done again I should increase the ration to 32 oz.' If 2 lb. a day is adequate for that sort of journey it is more than enough for Himalayan expeditions. In 1938 we had food in abundance. The supply of candles may have been short, but we were never reduced to eating them.

On the weight of 2 lb. a day estimates are based, and consequently foods which contain the greatest value for weight should be chosen. Jam, for example, is hardly worth taking; the only useful part of it is the sugar so that a 1 lb. tin of jam, which probably weighs 1 lb. 3 oz. gross, will contain only 10 oz. of actual food. From a quarter to a fifth of the weight of all tinned food is provided by the tin, but perhaps even more powerful arguments against its use are cost, lack of freshness, presence of preservatives and sameness. After a fortnight or so of a diet of tinned food all taste the same—sardines or ham, salmon or spaghetti. Fresh food is always to be preferred to tinned food and as much as possible should be made of whatever local supplies there may be in order to save transport and money. The proportions of food to be taken can be allocated roughly to 30% protein, 10% fats, and 60% carbohydrates, dividing the last item into half sugar and half cereals. Simple foods are better than processed foods—nobody but the maker knows what has gone into a packet or a tin. Coarse local flour is cheaper and better than white flour, unpolished rice than polished, sugar from a local mill (*jaggery* in India, *gur* in Africa) than white refined sugar. This last is almost as good to eat as home-made fudge, but there is so much moisture in it that the main sugar supply must be white sugar. Of this ½ lb. per man per day is not too much to allow; this 1938 expedition is the only one on which I have not run short of sugar.

Transport to Everest is so simple and is now such a cut-and-dried affair that considerations of weight have not to be so rigorously regarded as in difficult journeys—there is nothing like having to carry or pull your own loads (sledging in the Arctic, for example) for teaching sense in this respect. Consequently we did ourselves pretty well. Our diet included much that was not really necessary; much which (as the sage in *Rasselas* says of marriage) was rather to be permitted than approved. The principles followed in its selection were simplicity and the avoidance as far as possible of tins. There is no rule without an exception, and in this instance it was the welcome present of a case of tinned tongue; an offer of a case of champagne from the same donor[1] I was short-sighted or hard-hearted enough to refuse and have experienced twinges of regret ever since. It only occurred to me later, when faced like Moses with the murmurings of his people, that the presence of this would in every sense have cut the ground from under the feet of the Sybarites.

The aggregate result of my selection was not so simple as it would have been for a private party but was far too simple for some of us. We took plenty of bacon, ham, cheese, butter and pemmican. Eggs we knew could sometimes be obtained on the march, and by eggs I mean half a dozen or more each— fewer are not much good, but for use on the mountain we had 600 eggs preserved in water-glass, so that every morning we had the Englishman's breakfast fetish of bacon and eggs, even on the North Col. As far up the glacier as Camp III (21,500 ft.) we ate normal food like meat, potatoes, vegetables, rice and lentils; the meat consisted of either freshly killed sheep or yak meat, or failing that dried meat which is a staple commodity in Tibet. For two or three rupees one can buy a whole dried sheep's carcass and this is rather better eaten raw than cooked. That we were able to eat food like this was due mainly to our having a pressure-cooker without which cooking at these heights is almost impossible owing to the low temperatures at which

1 Mr R. W. Lloyd, Hon. Treasurer of the Mount Everest Committee.

water boils. At 20,000 ft. the temperature of boiling water is only 180° F. instead of 212° F. With the help of dried yeast we made very excellent bread and scones from the coarse local flour—very unlike the white, flaccid, spongy stuff sold[1] as bread in this country, the product of self-raising starch and chemicals. This meagre diet, which might be all very well for ascetics, was eked out with additional items such as milk, porridge, jam, honey, dried fruits, sweets, chocolate, sugar, glucose, dripping, biscuits and soups. Nevertheless, some of us were mightily relieved to find at Rongbuk large quantities of stores left behind by the 1936 party, and considered that this windfall, consisting mostly of nourishing food like jam, pickles, and liver extract (of which there were several cases), alone saved the party from starvation.

It is at heights above 22,000 or 23,000 ft. that the problem what to eat becomes acute, more especially if a week or more has to be spent at such heights. This admission may please the 'caviare and quails in aspic' school of thought, but the fact is that so far it has been found impossible to eat enough of any kind of food in those conditions— even the supposedly tempting foods out of tins or bottles for which the shelves of the high-class grocers have been pretty well ransacked. Owing to its weight the pressure-cooker has to be left behind so that cooking, apart from frying or merely heating things, becomes impossible. One is therefore driven back upon preserved and processed foods out of tins and jars, and the disinclination to eat anything which is already making itself felt thus becomes even stronger. Eating is then a distasteful duty rather than a pleasure, but whether food eaten under such circumstances is of any benefit is a question for physiologists. It is the absence of hunger which makes the problem of Everest so different from that in the Arctic where the sledging ration, within the necessary limits of weight, has only to be designed to maintain the bodily heat and energy of hard-working men. There, concentrated foods rich in fat are the solution which any dietician can work out, and there such foods can be eaten with gusto; but a way of maintaining the heat and energy of equally hard-working men who are not hungry, and to whom the thought of food is nauseating, is less easily found. If you do succeed in getting outside a richly concentrated food like pemmican a great effort of will is required to keep it down—absolute quiescence in a prone position and a little sugar are useful aids. Without wishing to boast I think the feat of eating a large mugful of pemmican soup at 27,200 ft. performed by Lloyd and myself, is unparalleled in the annals of Himalayan climbing and an example of what can be done by dogged greed. For greed consists in eating when you have no desire to eat which is exactly the case anywhere above Camp IV. Of two equal candidates for a place in the party it might pay to take the greediest, forbearing his disgusting idiosyncrasy at low levels for the sake of his capacity at these great heights, and the quantity of sugar consumed either neat or in tea makes up something of the deficiency suffered in other respects. All the same a straight meal of sugar or glucose hardly gives one the comfortable sensation of having dined. The loss of weight and consequent weakness which

---

1 'Which used to be sold' would be more correct though the present article is just an anaemic and less attractive to look at.

follows a stay at high altitude is probably due as much to lack of food as to the effort expended. I think more use could be made of eggs. They are not very difficult to carry and can be easily cooked in a variety of ways or eaten raw. Sardines, dried bananas, pickled beef, kippers, cream cheese and fruit cake, are some other suggestions, made, be it noted, at Camp III, and not at Camp VI where they would have to be eaten. The fact is that lying in a sleeping-bag doing nothing is, at those heights, so pleasant that some show of resolution is required even to begin the simplest preparations for eating, particularly when these entail the search for food amongst the bedding, spare clothes, boots, rope, stove, candles, cameras, saucepans, and snow littering the tent floor.

Whether to take oxygen or no was an open question which was finally decided in the affirmative for the rather cowardly reason that if we encountered perfect conditions on the last two thousand feet and were brought to a standstill purely through oxygen lack, not only might a great chance have been lost but we should look uncommonly foolish. My present view of the very unsatisfactory nature of even a successful oxygen attempt is recorded in a later chapter, but at that time I mistakenly felt that half a loaf would be better than no bread. Moreover, Warren, who had been trying out a new type of apparatus in the Alps, was very enthusiastic about its possibilities, although I gathered that the opinions of those with whom he had been climbing were more qualified. Some oxygen and some kind of breathing apparatus had to be taken anyhow for medical use in case of frost-bite or pneumonia.

Messrs Siebe Gorman have always taken a great interest in our oxygen apparatus, and this year they spared no pains in fulfilling our requirements at very short notice. These consisted of two of what we called the 'closed' type, and two of the simpler, old-fashioned 'open' type. In the first, to which Warren and most other experts, pinned their faith, pure oxygen is breathed through a mask covering the mouth and nose, the carbon dioxide in the expired breath being absorbed by soda-lime carried in a container fitted above the oxygen cylinder. Although only four hours' supply of oxygen is carried, the whole thing weighs 35 lb., but the smaller supply of oxygen is compensated for, first by the fact that less oxygen is used than in the 'open' type because none is wasted, and secondly it has the effect of providing the wearer with the atmospheric conditions of sea-level, and even gives him a little additional 'kick' into the bargain, so that he should move quicker and thus need less oxygen to complete the climb. We were told of a fireman who, wearing the apparatus, ran for four miles and then carried a man up a ladder, but who failed dismally in attempting the same feat without the apparatus. Inspired by this anecdote I took one of this type to the Lake District and rushed violently up a steep place wearing the apparatus but not carrying a man. From Stockley Bridge up Grain Hill to the Esk Hause path took 45 minutes, and from the path to climb Central Gully on Great End another 25 minutes. Next day over the same track, carrying the apparatus but not wearing the mask, the first part took five minutes less; in the Gully where there was climbing instead of walking the difference was more marked. There was ice and snow in the Gully and the mask hindered while the oxygen did not help. Such tests at anything but high altitudes are of no value, but I felt then that the bad effect of wearing a mask when undergoing great exertion would not easily be obviated.

Professor G. I. Finch, who had had practical experience of using oxygen on Everest itself, held strong views about the unsuitability of this type and the simplicity, lightness and greater comfort of the 'open' type. At his urgent advice I had two of these made. They carry half as much oxygen again, weigh 10 lb. less, and there is no mask; the oxygen is supplied through a tube to the mouth, and air, such as it is at that height, is breathed in through the nose. The difference in weight is accounted for by the absence of soda-lime and a simpler mechanism, which is of course, less liable to go wrong.

It was with a similar type that Finch's party made their great effort in 1922 when they reached the highest point then attained—27,230 ft.—which was about 200 ft. higher and nearer the summit in lateral distance than the non-oxygen party reached. Moreover, Finch's party was not well acclimatized, having spent only five days no higher than 21,000 ft.; it was a weak party, for Finch himself was the only experienced mountaineer; and judging from the times given they appear to have been slightly the faster party of the two. Both parties suffered slight frost-bite and both on coming down appeared equally exhausted. There is no doubt that oxygen will greatly assist those who wish to go high before they are properly acclimatized, a process which involves time and trouble. Indeed, it is arguable that the benefit of acclimatization attained by living at about 23,000 ft. for a few days is more than offset by the loss in strength, and it was Finch's idea that the mountain should be 'rushed' by an oxygen party which had not had its strength sapped away by too much acclimatization. But even this 1922 evidence, which is the best we have, is inconclusive. The party was moving on easy ground where it was not considered necessary to rope, and higher up, where the climbing is far more difficult, the oxygen apparatus might be more of a hindrance than a help. Of Mallory's experience with it in 1924 we shall never know, while Odell in the same year found he went as well without as with oxygen.

Before shifting the scene to India I must deal with the financial arrangements. We budgeted for a cost of something like a quarter of previous expeditions—£2,500[1] as against £10,000—and more than enough to cover the estimate was subscribed by generous friends and by members of the party themselves. I asked members to do this because I thought that if each of us had a small financial interest there would be more incentive to economize. It also seems to me to be the proper thing; an expedition to Mount Everest may not be every one's idea of a climbing holiday, for which no one could object to paying something, but it is a great privilege for which many would sacrifice more than money.

We had sufficient money to do without newspaper support, and at first we thought of doing without because there was general agreement amongst mountaineers that publicity concerning Everest had increased, was increasing, and ought to be diminished. But some of our subscribers quite rightly hoped to be paid back; and since the mountain is now a matter of

1 Actual amount spent £2,360.

world-wide interest it is almost essential to have some official news channel, for otherwise the Press in general will and does see to it that there is no lack of unofficial news. We made arrangements with *The Times*, who treated us generously. This was satisfactory from our point of view in that there was no obligation upon the leader to send back long messages while actually at work upon the mountain, but it was a matter of regret on our part that through an unfortunate incident *The Times* had good reason to complain of our treatment of them. In the forlorn hope of damping down our news value we intended to send as little news back as possible and then only important news. What was sent, therefore, was scanty but sufficient to keep informed those who prefer a straightforward statement to surmise, sensation, and ballyhoo.

CHAPTER THREE

Preparations in India and Departure

'We're clear o' the pine and the oak-scrub,
We're out on the rocks an' the snow...'   Kipling

SHIPTON and I reached Kalimpong on 14 February, a fortnight in advance of the rest of the party, where we were very kindly received by Mr and Mrs Odling. Two old friends, Angtharkay and Kusang Namgyal, were already installed there undergoing a course of instruction in cookery—the long white aprons they affected gave them a most comical air. Not that Angtharkay wanted very much instruction in the sort of cooking we should expect of him; his stews and curries had always been masterpieces, and, like most natives of India, he could, of course, turn out rice to perfection. To students of recent Himalayan literature his character must be already familiar. This year he added the duties of cooking for seven of us to his usual jobs of bossing up the porters, bestowing valuable advice and encouragement upon his employers, and carrying a heavier load farther and higher than any one else if called upon to do so; in fact, a sort of Jeeves, Admirable Crichton, and Napoleon rolled into one, but taking himself less seriously than any of those redoubtable men. Kusang I had not seen for four years, but had no difficulty in recognizing him in spite of the apron and the fact that he was not crooning the mournful dirge of two notes and three words which I shall always associate with him. He seemed to be less carefree than in those far-off days; I think he had married. We had to take him out of his apron next day to send him off to buy food in Solu Khumbu, and to arrange for it to be brought to Rongbuk by thirty Sherpa porters on 7 April or thereabouts, all of which he did with great faithfulness.

Karma Paul, the zealous and energetic interpreter and general factotum, whose sixth Everest expedition this was, had already met us at railhead on the way to Kalimpong and had taken charge of us. Everything seemed to be either done or in hand except the actual climbing of the mountain. Next day he and I went over to Darjeeling to select porters, armed with a list drawn up by Shipton and myself, or perhaps more correctly, by Angtharkay. No one who was not vouched for by him stood very much chance of being selected. This was not so unfair as it may sound. There was no nepotism, but all were either friends of Angtharkay or their characters were well known to him. As Lord Fisher used to say: 'Favouritism is the secret of efficiency'; and there is some justification for confidence in the friends of a man who sets such a high standard for himself. Nor is it likely that a man would stretch a point in favour of a friend whose failure would be likely to throw more work upon himself.

Besides picking twelve porters for ourselves we had to choose twenty for three other parties coming to the Himalaya later. After this was done there seemed to be no good experienced men left. One, Nursang, who had accompanied several German expeditions as head-man, was collecting porters for Nanga Parbat, and was having some difficulty in persuading men with the memory of so many dead comrades fresh in their minds, to go again to that unlucky mountain. Nursang's forcible appeals reminded one of the exhortation of Frederick the Great to his wavering troops: 'Come on you unmentionable offscourings of scoundrels. Do you want to live for ever?'

The old hands amongst our lot were Pasang Bhotia with whom I had travelled in 1934, when with Angtharkay and Kusang Numgyal he was the third of an incomparable trio; and also in 1935, the occasion when he had combined business with pleasure by marrying a good-looking buxom Tibetan girl on the way back from Everest—the girl has since died, but the fate in store for poor Pasang himself was even more unkind.[1] Then there was Rinsing, who is a grand chap once he gets above, not the snow-line, but the beer-line—that is beyond the reach of villages and liquid temptation; Lhakpa Tsering, who has the manners and appearance of an Apache, but does more work than several others put together; Tensing, young, keen, strong, and very likeable; and Nukku,[2] bovine but tireless. At Smythe's earnest request we also took Ongdi Nurbu and Nurbu Bhotia. Ongdi is in a class only with Angtharkay; of a character that makes him the natural leader of the other porters who delight to call him Aschang or Uncle. Besides being a tower of strength in any caravan he is an exceptionally capable mountaineer, but is handicapped by a susceptibility to pneumonia which he has now had twice on Everest; but if he contracts it easily he manages to throw it off with still greater ease.

A telegram from the railway which read: 'Expedition bits dispatched by forty up train', advised us of the imminent arrival of our stores and not that which it might reasonably have led us to hope or expect. The young mountain of bales and boxes of all shapes and sizes which was presently to be seen covering the floor of a godown, made for me a depressing sight—more

1 He was struck with paralysis on returning from Camp VI, and although he recovered the use of his limbs some weeks later, he would probably never be able to climb again.
2 This was the Nukku who died of cerebral malaria when with me in the Assam Himalaya the following year.

depressing still perhaps had one been a Sikkim mule or a Tibetan donkey—but with the help of Karma Paul and the Sherpas it was soon divided into loads of more or less suitable size and weight. I had brought out some particularly strong gunny bags which took the bulk of the stuff and stood the journey sufficiently well. The lightest box that will hold 80 lb., itself weighs about 10 lb., so that for every eight useful loads there is one additional load of almost useless boxwood. A box is just as easily stolen bodily as a bag (Odell will confirm this) and not much more difficult to break into by a determined thief. There was only one attempt at pilfering on the march; and the only serious loss on the way up occurred when we were beyond Rongbuk, when there were with us in camp only Sherpas.

On the march back a box of fossils and stones of scientific interest, highly prized by Odell, was taken from outside his tent where it was playing the part of anchor for one of the guy ropes. The thief no doubt mistook it for coin (the box was very heavy) and whatever amusement one felt at the thought of the chagrin awaiting the thief, had to be severely repressed out of respect for Odell's cold fury. It was a serious matter any way one looked at it. The results of several months' work had gone, and if the thief talked, as he might, for sorrows shared are sorrows halved, the Tibetan officials might learn we had been collecting stones against their express orders. They quite rightly object to any one knocking their rocks to bits with a hammer, thus releasing any malign spirits which may happen to be in them. We could only pray that the thief's professional pride would restrain him from advertising the fact that he had risked his life or the skin of his back for a box of pebbles.

It seemed that fifty mules would be sufficient to carry the stuff, but with the arrival of the oxygen, most inconveniently packed, the number rose to fifty-five and later had to be increased. The transport of the oxygen outfit is always a source of worry to those concerned, but perhaps no worse than that of the kerosene oil. The cylinders have to be closely watched for leaks, the tins of soda-lime have to be protected in boxes, and the apparatus itself, whether packed in a vast coffin shored round with sweaters and socks, or carried on the back of a trustworthy porter, always seems to develop some defect. Suitable containers for kerosene are not easily found:[1] I spent much time and cracked one of Odell's geological hammers in keeping the leakage of ours within reasonable bounds. After every march screw-tops had to be tightened up or leaks soldered.

Meantime, the Sherpas had to be sent to the hospital for treatment for worms. One was found to have boils and had to be left behind altogether, and Rinsing and Pasang developed some other complaint—I think the local beer must have been bad—which necessitated their following us later with Smythe. A second visit had to be made to Darjeeling to draw money (3,000 silver rupees and 5,000 in paper); oil drums had to be tested for leaks and mostly rejected; sugar (880 lb.), rice, atta, vegetables, candles and matches, presents for Tibetans, cooking and eating utensils for ourselves and the Sherpas, had all to be purchased. Regardless of expense, every European was given a plate

1 The 'jerrycan' will solve this problem.

in addition to a mug, and there were even dish-cloths for wiping them. Altogether there was sufficient to do, especially as Shipton had retired into confinement for the speedier delivery of a book which he had carelessly omitted to finish before leaving home.

The rest of the party, except Smythe, who followed later, arrived on the last day of the month and were immediately handed a little list which Shipton and I had thoughtfully drawn up for guidance in deciding what to bring. I have no doubt it was read with the tolerant interest bestowed on such things. Although the mules were to leave before dawn next day all was ready in time—even Odell, whose baggage I received in the godown at 8 o'clock that night. It was a pleasure to see he had not forgotten his glacier drill.[1]

The mules were not quite the first of us to get away. Two days earlier I had sent off a very redoubtable advance courier in the form of Purba Tensing. He was to act as mail runner for us, as he had done before, but meantime he had gone to Shekar Dzong armed with a wad of rupee notes to buy tsampa. Besides many others, Purba has three qualifications which Montaigne considered necessary for a good servant: 'That he should be faithful, ugly and fierce.' He is an Eastern Tibetan; a big man with an air of amiable ferocity, carries a long Tibetan knife, walks or rides great distances with equal facility, and is a whole-hearted believer in small light expeditions. He travels alone and carries nothing at all. The last glimpse I had of him was cantering swiftly through the Kalimpong bazaar bound for Shekar 200 miles away, and if he was carrying any luggage it must have been concealed about his person. We met again at Guru, in Tibet, three weeks later, when he very apologetically asked me for some more money to defray travelling expenses. To show that he was exercising due economy and that the claim was not unwarranted or inflated, as claims for travelling expenses sometimes are, he added that on the last march to Guru from Shekar he had been obliged to boil his shirt in order to make a cup of tea. An infusion of shirt might look like tea—might even taste like it—for Tibetan tea is not as ours.

The mules were to reach Gangtok on 3 March where the loads would be taken over by Lachen muleteers who were to accompany us as far as the first march into Tibet. Last-minute purchases and presents of vegetables from well-meaning friends had resulted in raising our mule requirements to sixty— a number which almost justified the question of the reporter of an Indian newspaper: 'When does the expeditionary force start?' It suggested, too, that a little more ruthless 'scrapping and bagging' would not have oeen amiss. Another question which I thought pleasing, addressed to me by an otherwise intelligent man, was: 'And is Mr Smythe a climber, too?'

We ourselves left by car on 3 March to reach Gangtok at 2 o'clock that afternoon. The road was very greasy after a night of heavy rain. Even at this early stage the weather was arousing comment; owing to heavy clouds we had scarcely seen the mountains during our fortnight at Kalimpong. Mr B. J. Gould,[2] the Political Officer, who had already shown us many kindnesses— amongst others he had made our Sikkim transport arrangements—added to

1 Vide *The Ascent of Nanda Devi*, chap. XII.
2 Now Sir Basil Gould, C.M.G., C.I.E.

our indebtedness by having the Residency opened for us in his absence. Here the Maharajah's sister, the wife of the Bhutanese Prime Minister, very charmingly acted as hostess in Mr Gould's absence. There was much to be done and little time to do it in, for that night at the Palace we had to attend a dinner which H.H. the Maharajah was very kindly giving for us. The loads had to be checked; kerosene tins, already leaking, soldered or re-washered; the Gangtok mule-men to be paid off and the Lachen men given an advance; all before a perfunctory wash—the last—and a battle with a boiled shirt. Some careful planning had to be done in the matter of dinner kit. As we did not want to dress every night on the mountain, or even on the march, we packed our things next morning in two communal suit-cases and returned them to Kalimpong. There was one slight hitch which only became manifest next August when I was dressing for dinner at Government House in Shillong, when I discovered that my shoes were about three sizes too small. The mountaineer in India, particularly the member of a large expedition, must firmly suppress any latent tendency he may have to go native or even to slovenliness. Once in Darjeeling I was obliged to borrow a suit of Karma Paul's as my own was condemned as unsuitable for a luncheon party; and on another occasion to wear my host's evening clothes which hung about me like a 'giant's robe upon a dwarfish thief'.

Most of the European residents of Gangtok had been invited by H.H. so that it was quite a large party which sat down to dinner that night. Speeches were made, and to me fell the task of replying on behalf of the others to the good wishes expressed by our host. Observing how faithfully they were dealing with the magnificent dinner provided, I remarked that my comrades had all the appearance of men who had either just undergone a long fast or were about to undergo one—a thought which had possibly occurred to others besides myself; and in view of the slightly less luxurious diet in store I ventured to remind them of what I thought was a not inappropriate saying of Thoreau, that great apostle of the simple life who practised in the American woods what he preached in his book, *Walden*: 'Most of the luxuries and many of the so-called comforts of life, are not only not indispensable, but positive hindrances to the *elevation* of mankind.'

Our sixty mules left at 9.30 o'clock next morning, but our departure was postponed to a more civilized hour, namely after lunch, which enabled us to complete our postal arrangements and write final letters. The Maharajah and a large gathering gave us a hearty send-off from the Residency, but before we were allowed to depart much film was wasted on an uncommonly sheepish-looking group doing its best to pass for intrepid mountaineers. Even at this eleventh hour kind friends interposed between us and too sudden an introduction to hardship by carrying us in cars to the extreme limit of the road just below the Penlong La. From here the remaining eight miles to Dikchu is all downhill so that we were able to complete the first stage of a 300-mile journey without unduly exhausting ourselves.

On Everest expeditions an unfortunate tradition has grown up that the Sherpas carry nothing until the mountain is reached. It is in strict accord with the principle of the conservation of energy, but I cannot think that the carrying of 25 or 30 lb. for three weeks would have any seriously debilitating effect upon men who habitually carry twice as much for as many months. This time I gave the twelve Sherpas a mule between them to carry some food like rice and lentils, which are not obtainable in Tibet, and cooking gear, but their own kits they were expected to carry themselves. It was a pleasant surprise, therefore, when I found them insisting on carrying our light rucksacks containing odds and ends; I thought it showed praiseworthy keeness until I found they had distributed their own kits amongst the mules in order to carry our sacks which were very much lighter. We had encountered the same trouble in 1935, when an effort to save transport costs by making the Sherpas carry loads resulted in a strike. The tradition has now spread beyond the confines of an Everest expedition, and it is wise to discount the Sherpas as a carrying force so long as any other transport is available. They either put their loads on the already sufficiently laden animals or hire animals on their own account and present you with the bill. The evil of large expeditions is thus made acutely manifest to those who follow; and not only in this way, but because they set standards of work and pay which are not always fair to the employer, and which generally spoil the market for goods and services for all time. Anyone who goes to Askole, for instance, in the Karakoram, and offers the usual rate of Rs. 1 per day is regarded as either a skinflint or a 'poor white' because a large expedition which went there before the war paid their porters Rs. 2. We ourselves, at a place in Tibet, were regarded as cads, or at any rate not quite gentlemen, because the tip we gave to the servants of a house in which we had been entertained was thought small; as indeed it was in comparison with what had been given in the same place on previous occasions.

Over the first few days of any march it is wise to draw a veil. The things that have been forgotten are gradually remembered, and the whole organization creaks and groans like your own joints. You wonder if man was really intended to walk, whether motoring after all is not his natural mode of progression, and whether the call of the open road is as insistent as you yourself thought or as the poets of that school sing. Nothing much happened. It rained; but the Sikkim marches are mercifully so short that generally we managed to avoid it. At Mangen, at what corresponds to the local coffee-stall, we had the usual 'elevenses' of sweet tea in a glass, soup, curried eggs, and pork pies made from the lean hyena-like pigs rooting about in the dirt outside. At Singhik we drank *marwa*, the local beer, with our supper. Six great bamboo jorums about a foot high, in which the beer is served, give the table a falsely convivial air, for the contents are 99% millet and 1% beer which is laboriously sucked up warm through a bamboo tube. I found a frog on the table that evening and was curious to know from whose beer-jug it had come.

On the march before Lachen a landslip temporarily dislocated the traffic. It was a small slip but the smallest is serious where the narrow mule-track is carved out of the face of a precipice. After some repairs had been done we got the whole mule train safely over, but just beyond, one of the mules carrying fodder, shied and stepped off the path, to be instantly killed in a sheer fall of 200 ft. to the Tista river below. The owner, a poor woman, who had to be compensated for the loss, was most distressed. We were very relieved to know that none of our baggage was lost, but we persuaded Tensing, Warren's servant, to break the tragic news to his master that the mule carrying all his kit had gone over the 'khud'. Wretchedly bad actor though he was, Tensing managed to convince his master that the worst had happened; but we were disappointed of our jest because Warren, instead of acting in the expected fashion, beating his head against a stone or tearing his hair, expressed no more concern than he might have done at the loss of a pocket handkerchief.

At Lachen we heard rumours that the road was blocked with snow. Inquiries about the state of the road had of course been made before we left but no definite information had been forthcoming. Leaving the party to rest after its labours, Shipton and I took horses and rode up towards Tangu some 13 miles away. Within half a mile of Lachen snowdrifts were met, and six miles this side of Tangu the snow lay everywhere two feet deep. A narrow track had been shovelled up which we rode until we met a gang of forty men at work on it. Theses had been sent up by the Sikkim Road engineer in accordance with the wishes of the Maharajah that we should receive every assistance. The men expected to clear a track through to the Tangu bungalow by next day but they told us that snow lay deep for another 10 miles beyond. It would evidently be a long job, so next day Lloyd and I went up to the bungalow to superintend the work while the rest of the party remained at Lachen.

Tangu has earned an evil reputation by reason of the exaggerated effect its moderate altitude of 12,000 ft. has on most people, not even excepting seasoned mountaineers. On our arrival I was suffering from a splitting headache and Lloyd laid all before him; nor were we very much better the following morning, Lloyd losing his breakfast. The others, when they arrived five days later, were less troubled, but Smythe told me that when he came through later he too vomited. I have not found any other place of similar altitude in the Himalaya which has this effect upon those coming up to it for the first time. A suggestion has been made that it is due to its great humidity.

Accompanied by the road foreman we walked up the road next day for six miles which seemed like sixteen. There was a couple of feet of snow almost the whole way and for several miles beyond, but on the way home when we met the road-gang already two miles out from Tangu, we thought the job would soon be finished. In spite of their primitive implements they shifted a surprising amount of snow. A fresh fall of snow next day tempered our optimism, and on the 12th, the day the mules had been ordered up, snow began falling at 7 o'clock and continued most of the day. I hoped the mules would turn back, but at 4 o'clock they duly arrived, their loads covered with snow. There was nothing for it but to off-load and send them back to Lachen; for now there was no prospect of the track being open for some days and there was nothing here for them to eat.

It was exasperating for the men to have all their work to do over again, snow and wind having completely filled in the trench they had dug. During the next few days this happened repeatedly. The Tangu bungalow is comfortable enough so that we might have sat there waiting patiently for better weather were it not that we had engaged to pay the mule-men half rates for every day we were delayed. We amused ourselves exhorting the road-men, walking up the nearby hills, and stalking a herd of bharal. The mule contractor lent us our only weapon—an old, cross-eyed carbine which needed humouring—and with it some twenty rounds of ammunition. Oliver, representing the Army, fired seven ineffective shots; a feat which evoked murmurs of 'Thank God, we have a Navy'. Shipton also made no impression on the long-suffering herd and it was left to Angtharkay to bring one down with the last remaining round.

On the 14th the road-men were driven down early by a blizzard. This was bad enough, but they had also finished all the food they had brought up, so in desperation we ordered up the mules for the 16th and persuaded twenty of the road-gang to stay and see the mules through to the next camp, Gayokang. The morning of that day dawned bright after a windy night. Fine weather seemed to have set in at last and the men were much cheered by the sight of birds flying north—tiny white wedges high up against the cold blue sky. In the morning some of us climbed a hill of about 16,000 ft. whence we got a magnificent view of Kangchenjunga and Tent Peak. The reckless rapidity of our descent by means of sitting glissades over a mixture of snow, grass, and stones, considerably astonished the natives.

The mules arrived that evening and at last on the 17th we made a start. The pine forest which at Lachen takes the place of the tropical rain forest, comes in its turn to an end at Tangu. Silver birch, rhododendrons, and juniper bushes, struggle on for a bit higher up the road until these too cease, the grass withers, and soon only a few thinly scattered hardy Alpines are left to fight it out with the stone and gravel wastes. The track was in fair condition, but at the eighth mile we encountered an undug drift which delayed us for half an hour. Here we dismissed the road-men, for as the road climbed the snow gradually grew less until at Gayokang the only remaining traces of winter were some large sheets of ice. The reason for this seeming paradox is that north of Tangu the climate becomes more Tibetan in character. The north-west wind which blows in Tibet for the greater part of the year drives back the moisture-laden winds from the south. Little snow falls, and wind and evaporation between them account for its rapid disappearance. One wondered whence the snow-clad peaks right and left of our bare, brown valley—Kangchenjau, Chomiomo, Lachsi—received all their snow.

The mule bells jangle merrily as the beasts hurry through the stony defile which they well know marks the approach to Gayokang and the end of one day's journey. Round the corner are the smoky hovels; mean and dirty enough in truth, but bright and friendly when viewed against the cold and desolate slopes sweeping up to the northern skyline. Men and beasts crowd in. The mules are picketed under the walls, kicking and squealing, while the men run down the lines putting on the nose-bags containing a woefully small feed of barley. As dusk falls the men disappear into the flat-roofed huts to cook their meal over the yak-dung fires. With the night comes wind and snow.

CHAPTER FOUR

The March to Rongbuk

'For if everyone were warm and well fed, we should lose the satisfaction of admiring the
fortitude with which certain conditions of men bear cold and hunger'.   Mr Pecksniff

An efficient mule train is one of the most satisfactory means of transport. Mules travel as fast as a man can walk so there is no need for the baggage to leave hours in advance of its owners in order to complete the march in reasonable time. They carry their 160 lb. effortlessly; and knowing what is required of them seem intent on completing the day's stage with as little fuss and delay as possible; whereas donkeys, bullocks, or yaks, wander about snatching mouthfuls of grass, stop, and even lie down, unless constantly driven. Moreover, mules have not that air of patient suffering which yaks, ponies and especially donkeys, assume when travelling under a load—an air which, if the loads happen to be mine, awakens in me a feeling of acute discomfort. A man under a load never arouses this feeling of pity, because men, unlike animals, will not and cannot be driven to carry too much or too far. If they do it at all they do it voluntarily, and stop long before that state of exhaustion is reached which sometimes causes animals to drop dead in their tracks.

These Lachen mules of ours were well up to their job—fine, upstanding animals with clean legs, neat feet, smooth shiny coats, and a general air of breeding. They come from the northern part of Tibet. In Southern Tibet the donkeys are little bigger than St Bernard dogs; so small that no pony could very well mate with them, and so melancholy is their appearance and so hard their lot that it is difficult to imagine they should ever wish to procreate their species. The mule-men, too, on the trade routes between India and Tibet, understand their job and take a pride in their animals which they deck with collars of bells adorned with bright scarlet tassels of yak hair, or scarlet wool tufts, and decorative brow-bands. The drivers wear homespun natural coloured trousers, stuffed into high, red felt boots secured at the knee with brightly coloured garters, and an easy-fitting coat of the same material reaching to the knees. The sleeves of this are long and loose, but the right arm is nearly always kept out of the sleeve which therefore hangs empty. The coat is secured round the waist so that the upper part forms a capacious sort of kangaroo's pouch in which are stored pipe, tobacco, snuff-box, purse, a piece of dried meat, and probably some *tsampa* in a skin bag. A knife, which more often resembles a short sword, is slung at the waist, and a short-handled whip carried in the right hand or stuck into the top of the boot, completes the outfit.

We did not stir until 9 o'clock when the sun had warmed men and mules after a night of bitter cold. After some of the mules had come down with prodigious thumps they picked their way more carefully round the sheets of ice which partly covered the flats at the foot of the long final rise to the Sebu La. As we mounted the bare brown slopes, the wind gained force until on the top (c. 17,000 ft.) it was blowing with the peculiarly cold, unrelenting ferocity of Tibetan wind. The sun had long disappeared behind the scurrying clouds when we passed the cairns marking the summit and began the long easy descent with bowed heads and averted faces. This, I thought, is the kind of weather we must expect in Tibet so early in the year, and the fact that I was wearing shorts lent poignancy to the thought. As we hurried down to Guru, intent on finding shelter, we passed large herds of yaks and sheep grazing happily on gravel, contentedly oblivious of any wind, while the herdsman stood about equally regardless of the piercing blast. The inhabitants of Tibet are tough. For our part, not being so tough, we sought food and warmth in the dark interior of the headman's house, pitching our tents in the lee of the compound wall.

As evening drew on the absence of Odell began to cause uneasiness to those who had not travelled with him before, and who were consequently unaware of the long detours and longer halts which were sometimes imposed on him by his devotion to science. Accustomed though I was to his vagaries, and perhaps not as sympathetic as I should have been towards their cause, the alarm of the others infected even me. Search parties were about to set out when the wanderer cast up. Instead of telling us, as well he might, of the discovery of some intensely interesting rocks which had necessitated prolonged examination, he frankly confessed to having lost his way. Such frankness was worthy of belief, but the Sherpas were sceptical, and unkindly suggested that the afternoon had been spent at a neighbouring nunnery or *ani-gompa*, as they are called. Henceforth he was known to them as the 'Gompa La Sahib', for it was in the direction of that place he had strayed. When, as not infrequently happened, he again took the wrong path, their advice to him about the right one was always accompanied by the assurance that there were no nunneries in that direction.

After this rude welcome into Tibet, next day's march to Kampa Dzong was done in wonderfully clear, calm, cloudless weather. Close on our left Chomiomo and many other peaks sparkled in the sun; farther lay Kangchenjunga and his satellites; while a hundred miles to our left front Everest and Makalu drew all eyes. Nor was this benignant day to be the one exception. Our gloomy forebodings about the rough passage we were likely to have on the way to Rongbuk were falsified by a more or less unbroken succession of sunny days. The wind seldom became violent before noon, but after that it was unpleasant. At Kampa Dzong a furious blast drove the pole through aspices of two bell tents, an occurrence which the Sherpas considered extremely funny. The local weather experts assured us that these comparatively genial conditions were unusual for March, but Shipton thought they were not very different from those experienced in 1933. As in our case, the 1922 and 1933 expeditions encountered bad weather on first crossing into

Tibet, but thereafter enjoyed fine but cold weather. In 1924 and 1936 conditions seem to have been definitely milder. General Bruce, comparing 1924 with 1922 speaks of an 'infinitely milder climate', and Mr Ruttledge in 1936 calls the weather 'comparatively warm'; but no useful conclusions can be drawn from this because in the first case the monsoon was later than usual and in the other much earlier.

Two days were spent at Kampa Dzong, the last resting-place of Dr Kellas who died there in 1921. A very remarkable sight is the old fort imposingly situated on the summit of a high yellow rock which on two sides falls away sheer. On another side a long fortified wall runs from the fort to the foot of the rock to give the garrison access to a well. This wall runs across some slabs which in angle and smoothness are not unlike the rocks on the upper part of Everest, though less steep. On these we scrambled about, hopefully wearing the oxygen apparatus whose weight made it difficult to walk up the easy slope with any confidence. Rope tied round the boots to cover the nails helped. Smythe had brought out a specially made pair of *scarpetti* which he hoped to use on the upper rocks of the mountain; but, alas, these devices we were never to try.

Three memorable things at Kampa were a dinner of blood-and-rice sausages from a freshly killed sheep, long arguments about the zodiacal light, of which at night there were most brilliant displays, and a highly successful stratagem on the part of the Sherpas. With very long faces they complained that they had eaten all the food brought with them, that owing to bad crops food in Tibet was very dear, and that a special food allowance of two annas a day until Rongbuk was reached, and an immediate advance of Rs. 3 a man, were an imperative necessity. I fell in with this very plausible request only to find that its immediate result was an uproariously successful 'blind'.

When we started again on the 22nd it was amidst the usual indescribable confusion following upon a change of transport. A scratch assortment of ponies, bullocks, zos (a cross between a cow and a yak), and donkeys, took the place of the efficient mule team. There was not a single yak, because, we were told, an epidemic the previous year had reduced the yak population of the district from seventy to seven. There were almost as many owners as animals and of course, each fought strenuously for the lightest and handiest loads for his own animal, and to avoid being left with the heavier and more unwieldy loads. With energetic voice and gesture Karma Paul gradually produced order out of chaos and at length the whole caravan had straggled off with the exception of one donkey which very wisely refused to carry any load at all. For this the headman's own pony had to be impressed.

We all walked on the march up; not because we liked walking but because it was warmer and in some ways less tiring. A good Tibetan pony can amble fast and comfortably for a long time but only if the rider has mastered the correct aids which are by no means the same as those used in the *haute école*. A bad Tibetan pony is worse than no pony at all, as, in addition to the primary discomfort, there is the added danger of a fall; for one sits perched high over the animal's head (they are all very short in the rein), on top of a doubled sleeping-bag tied insecurely to the saddle, which in turn is girthed still more insecurely to the horse. The stirrups are seldom wide enough to admit a European boot, and the leathers are so short that you have to ride like Tod Sloan, which is particularly fatiguing for long periods at walking pace. The art lies in balance, and though a climber can balance on his feet it does not follow that he can balance on his seat.

At Tengkye Dzong another two days were spent camped by a placid lake whose waters lapped the walls and almost surrounded the village. Even at this early stage Oliver had a cold and Warren a sore throat. The Dzongpen was very friendly and entertained us to several meals of macaroni, stew, radishes, so-called mushrooms, which were really fresh-water weed, and Chinese sauce. Later he tried to teach us Chinese dominoes—a very difficult game which our poor brains, even had they not been dulled by bowls of macaroni and beakers of local brandy, would have had trouble in mastering. Next day we received him officially, a ceremony for which Karma Paul insisted on our washing, and for which Angtharkay got himself up like a bird of paradise in sky-blue coat and scarlet trousers. We produced our passport and some presents before settling down to a long haggle over the rates to be paid for the fresh animals which were to carry for us from here. Owing to rigid custom it is impossible to have one lot of animals to carry right through to Rongbuk; changes have to be made in passing from the jurisdiction of one headman to that of another. On this occasion the Church, represented by the genial but shrewd-looking abbot of a nearby monastery, took a leading part in the negotiations and drove an unconscionably hard bargain.

As the next march from Tengkye is a long one, involving the crossing of two high passes (c. 16,000 ft.), our new transport did not get in until dark. On the way up to the pass we caught magnificent views of the Tsomo Tretung lake, its deep blue expanse ringed with warm yellow hills. Most of the Europeans usually arrived in camp long before the slow-moving transport and passed the time until its arrival lamenting its slowness and drowning dull care in Tibetan tea or beer. A few Sherpas were detailed to accompany the baggage and I usually stayed behind myself, more as a matter of form than for anything I could do in the way of hastening them or preventing pilfering. We lost a pair of boots, and one night an unsuccessful attempt was made to remove a load bodily, but that was all. The animals were never off-loaded during a march; the men would sit by the roadside to drink 'chang', which they carried in a skin, from wooden bowls, while the beasts picked up a few mouthfuls of gravel and weeds. At night if there was no gravel and weed but only gravel, the animals would be given a few wisps of wiry hay (imported, one presumes, from India), the yaks receiving a ball of *tsampa* about the size of a child's football. *Tsampa*, of course, was also the men's supper, which simplified the cooking, and having eaten it they stretched themselves luxuriously on their spacious bed—the ground—alongside an extinct fire (fuel is scarce), sheltered by the wide canopy of the sky. There is a Tibetan proverb which says that he who knows how to go about it can live comfortably even in hell, and certainly the inhabitants of that country, human or animal, will not fail in that respect for want of practice.

Following down the valley of the Chiblung Chu we reached Jikyop, or 'The

Place of Fear'. It lies in a narrow gorge flanked by steep sand-hills, and is said to have been a favourite place for bandits until the little fort, which is its only building, was built. No wind-tunnel constructed by man could more efficiently produce concentrated gales than his shallow gorge. We left the redoubtable Purba Tensing here, for it was the half-way point at which he would hand over and receive mail from the two men who were to carry it to and from Sikkim. He was content to work alone, but the Sikkim men had insisted on working in pairs.

On emerging from the gorge the track fords a shallow river, which was frozen up, and then crosses a dreary waste of sand dunes before turning up the comparatively green valley of the Phung Chu. By the first river is a hot spring, so hot that it was five minutes by the watch before I was able to get in up to the neck. Numerous little worms, however, swimming about in it, seemed to find the heat very tolerable. After being thus parboiled we found the crossing of the thin ice of the river in bare feet an interesting contrast. The transport animals, especially the poor little donkeys with their small feet, made heavy weather of it in the soft sand; two of them foundered and one of them died. Trangso Chumbab, where we slept that night, is merely a caravanserai; there is no village. Once again we changed transport so that the buildings were crowded with a double number of men and animals. After supper a hue and cry was raised by Lhakpa Tsering who had spotted a man making off with a load which he had taken from the dump in the courtyard and carried over the flat roof of the room where the Sherpas were sitting. The man escaped, but the load was recovered, and for the rest of the night the Sherpas took up their quarters on top of the baggage. According to Karma Paul this was a notorious place for thieves, but he omitted to mention it until the fact was self-evident.

Owing to the fresh transport, the third change between Tengkye Dzong and Shekar Dzong, we did not leave until 9 o'clock with our fifty-five donkeys, one pony, and two zos. Half an hour later, the wind got up and continued strongly throughout the day so that when I got in with the transport at 5.30 o'clock I was glad to join the rest of the party crouching miserably behind a stone wall which was the only shelter available. On this march we passed five very big chortens each about 30 ft. square, built up in steps like the Pyramids to a height of about 20 ft. Four were placed at the corners to form a square, and one in the middle. Karma Paul's explanation was that they are prisons for the spirits of witches. Every witch in Tibet has to pay a fee of Rs. 10 to the church so that her evil spirit may be exorcized and shut up in these chortens and the witch rendered harmless.

This Phung Chu valley was remarkable for the unusual feature of scrub growing in the river-bed and for the number of ruins and deserted villages. In these parts of Tibet it is rare to find any growth worthy of the name of brushwood or scrub except the willow groves which have been planted and cared for by man; on very favoured slopes juniper may sometimes be seen. Owing to the dry climate, walls of sun-dried brick or *pisé*, of which most are made, last for a very long time even if unprotected by a roof, and it was therefore difficult to come to any conclusion about the age of the numerous ruined buildings and chortens. On one of these we found an interesting burnt tile and an earthenware cup of a different type from those now in use locally. The commonest cause of a deserted village is the failure of the water supply on which the irrigation of the fields depends. The source is often merely an old snow-bed high up in some gully into which little sunlight penetrates, and consequently its duration is very uncertain.

On 31 March we reached Shekar Dzong where we camped in the willow grove belonging to one of the two Dzongpens. The district of Shekar is a large one divided into north and south with a Dzongpen for each, and the town, which is the headquarters of the district, is as remarkable as it is important. Village, monastery, and fort, in that order are built one above the other on a steep rock which rises for nearly a thousand feet straight from the wide, flat valley floor. 'Hill of Shining Glass' is the Tibetan name for it; a name which is by no means inappropriate when the place is viewed from a distance on a sunny day, for the rock has a peculiarly lucent appearance and all the buildings except the fort are whitewashed. The fort, perched on the very summit, is disused and is falling into decay. As there is no water there its greatest value must have been as a watch-tower, but now no one ever visits it except the monk who daily climbs to the topmost wall to burn juniper, the Tibetan's incense. We climbed up there in order to have a look at the mountain, but the day was dull and visibility poor. Descending from the fort by a new route which brought me out on the roofs of the village I was attacked by two dogs and scarcely succeeded in withdrawing unscathed behind a brisk covering fire of stones. To meet a dog in Tibet is to be attacked, but fortunately there is never any lack of stones to repel these attacks.

Besides allowing us to camp in his willow grove and giving us a hundred eggs, a couple of dried sheep, and six bags of *tsampa*, the Dzongpen invited us to spend the day with him. There is something spacious about Tibetan hospitality in keeping with the spaciousness of that vast country. You arrive at your host's house before lunch and remain there eating and drinking—mostly drinking—until after dinner without any perceptible pause. Feeble folk, like the coneys, that we were, we begged for a short break between the afternoon and evening session; so when lunch had come to a rather premature conclusion at 4 o'clock, we retired to our tents for a rest before facing the music again at 6 o'clock. One of the principal features of a Tibetan feast is the 'chang' girl, or girls, whose job it is to see that the guests drink up and that their cups are always full to the brim of 'chang' or Tibetan beer. This drink, which is pleasant and not very strong—it has been likened to slightly alcoholic barley water—is found in seemingly unlimited supply in most Tibetan households, rich or poor. It is brewed from barley which is the staple crop of Tibet, and I believe half the annual barley crop, or it may be two-thirds, is consumed as beer, the remainder being eaten as *tsampa*. Some travellers who have recorded their dislike of *tsampa* (of whom I am not one) may think it a pity that the whole crop is not turned into beer, and since the best medical opinion says that alcohol is food, no harm would be done. But at the evening session of the feast in question the drinking of this innocuous 'chang' was superseded all too quickly by that of 'arak', a spirit distilled from the 'chang', and of course bearing a very strong resemblance to hooch or bootlegger's whisky. Moreover, it was drunk from larger cups which the 'chang' girls were equally assiduous in filling. The Governor of North Carolina would have had no cause to remonstrate with his fellow Governor of the South, that profound thinker—there was no time at all between drinks. In order to make time we took advantage of a Tibetan drinking custom by which, if the guest chooses, he may challenge the 'chang' girl to sing a song which she is then obliged to do before refilling his cup. Unluckily there was a footnote to this sensible custom of which we were not aware, which is that the challenge having been accepted and the song sung, the guest is then obliged to drain the cup at one draught. So we were hoist by our own petard. The songs sung were all improvised. That in response to Odell's challenge likened him to the reincarnation of a god; Warren was told that the women of the household were not in immediate need of his services—while that to the address of Karma Paul was unprintable. It was late when we got back to our tents amongst the willows, where for some reason or other best known to themselves, the Sherpas insisted on taking off our boots for us before we went to bed.

Smythe caught us up here next day, thereby escaping this sandbag. He had with him Pasang and Rinsing whom we had left behind sick, and also Ongdi and Nurbu with whom he had travelled the previous year. This brought our strength of Darjeeling men up to sixteen, while one more Sherpa who was wandering about loose in Tibet, also attached himself to us here. On 3 April we crossed the Pang La (17,000 ft.), obtaining a remarkable panoramic view of Everest and the neighbouring giants from the summit. There seemed to be a sprinkling of fresh snow on the North Face.

Our camp at Tashidzom in another willow grove was one of the pleasantest of the whole march. A surrounding stone wall kept the inquisitive villagers at a respectful distance; and in the absence of the usual afternoon wind, we could lie about on the grass, basking in the rays of the declining sun, watching Angtharkay cooking our supper, or soldering leaking oil drums. In fact, every prospect pleased, but man, as usual, was vile; for presently there was a hubbub in the kitchen tent and a wretched, beggarly, half-naked old man was dragged out still clutching the bag of sugar which he had been trying to steal. He was forthwith lashed to a tree while Angtharkay, thoughtfully putting some knots in a length of rope, suggested charitably that considering the subject's age and infirmity one hundred stripes might be almost sufficient to meet the case. The headman, whose servant the thief was, happened to be in the camp and flung himself at my feet begging for mercy as earnestly as if his own back were in peril. I was quite ready to let the man off, for he was already frightened out of his wits, but unfortunately I had just inflicted a heavy fine on two of the Sherpas who had stayed behind in Shekar dead drunk and had only caught us up that day; while Angtharkay, like Thwackum, was for doing justice and leaving mercy to heaven. However, we finally handed the man over to his master who promised to punish him.

On 6 April we reached Rongbuk, ten days earlier than the earliest of previous expeditions. In view of the awful warning of 1936 we had taken the precaution of being on the spot in good time; those with an over-keen sense of humour will appreciate the fact that after all this forethought, we were to be caught out by still stranger behaviour on the part of the weather.

CHAPTER FIVE

On the Glacier

'And now there came both mist and snow, and it grew wondrous cold.'   Coleridge

COMPARATIVELY mild though the conditions on the march had been, wind and dust had taken their usual toll; all, except Shipton, Smythe and myself, had sore throats, coughs, or colds. At Rongbuk, Warren's sore throat had developed into influenza, while Shipton took to his bed with some stomach trouble. If the facts are investigated I think it will be found that we suffered no more from these kinds of ailments than other Everest expeditions. Coughs, colds and sore throats, accompanied sometimes by loss of voice, are a nuisance; a bad sore throat might prove to be a serious handicap on the final climb as it was to Somervell on the occasion of his great ascent with Norton to 28,000 ft. in 1924. But by the time we got on to the mountain itself at the end of May, most of us had recovered, while in some cases a loss of voice might be considered a positive gain for the party as a whole. Influenza, if that was the disease which attacked three of us, is more serious because it produces marked weakness; but as neither this nor the other complaints are preventable or even curable by the combined skill of the medical profession under the comparatively mild conditions of an English winter their occurrence on Everest expeditions is not really very startling.

Critics of the small light expedition like to atttribute any illness of the members to their inadequate unscientific diet. Personally, I incline to the belief of the food reformers that much of our modern ill-health is due to faulty feeding—to the almost complete absence of fresh, natural food in the average man's diet in favour of preserved, processed, denaturalized food. But the effects of unbalanced faulty diet are long term—general ill-health is the result of months or years of wrong feeding—and it is ridiculous to blame our diet for the coughs, colds, sore throats and influenza which afflicted us at this early stage, a mere three weeks away from the plentiful food of Sikkim. Three weeks on bread and water would hardly have had this effect; indeed, it is well known, or should be well known, that coughs and colds are one result of over-eating, especially of starches and sugars.

I am not one of those who decry the mountain as unimpressive, shapeless, or even ugly—what some mountaineers rudely call a cow peak. Seen from Rongbuk it looms up magnificently, filling the head of the valley. The final pyramid, with or without its streaming banner, is a glorious thing; the face looks what it is—steep; and the two great ridges seen now in profile would make any mountaineer's heart leap. Were it 20,000 ft. lower it would still command respect and incite admiration.

When we arrived, the mountain was of course black, the snow having been blown off the upper part by the winter winds; so too, and this was unexpected, was the North Peak, 5,000 ft. lower, which in the numerous photographs that have been taken of it seldom appears as anything but a snow peak. A wind, which from the rapidity of movement of the cloud banner might be estimated at something like force 8, was still blowing up there. Down at Rongbuk there was not much wind.

Next day Kusang and Sonam Tensing came over from Sola Khombu with men and food, as arranged: forty-five Sherpas, and 1,300 lb. of rice, atta, kodo and potatoes. As 7 April was the appointed date for meeting us this was good staff work, but we had asked for only thirty men. We took them all on, however, and after a day devoted to ceremony at the monastery began moving loads up to the old Base Camp. Solu Khumbu is the district in Nepal from which most of our Sherpas come, and, except for a few who have settled in Darjeeling, they return there when an expedition is over. It is not very far away from the south side of Everest, but the journey to Rongbuk over the 19,000 ft. pass, the Nangpa La, takes about a week. Later in the season even women and children cross this pass; relatives of some of our men, for instance, came over in June to see them and to pay their respects to the abbot of Rongbuk whose fame as a very holy man is widespread. The pass is therefore an easy one; but I was told that no animal is ever brought across it because the guardian spirit of the pass takes the form of a horse and any other four-footed animal which presumes to cross is instantly struck dead.

The abbot, who is now an old man, and seldom moves from his seat of audience behind a trellis-work grille, seemed pleased to see us all again. He gave us a large meal, his blessing, and some advice. An earth tremor had been felt there in February which was thought might in some way have affected the mountain; we were warned to be careful, especially Lloyd, who in spite of his superior beard was considered too young for such an adventure. We had the pleasure of watching our macaroni being made by the grimy but accomplished hands of the monastery cook before it was served to us in bowls with meat and sauces. Our bowls were replenished so many times before we finally laid our chopsticks on top of them as a sign of repletion, that I felt constrained to ask the abbot, who sat watching with pleased amusement, what the punishment was for greed in the next world. To which he made the answer that the greedy receive their punishment in this world, and very quickly. Our present to the monastery was a very fine altar cloth, and the Sherpas gave rupees (provided by us) which were offered stuck upright in a bowl of uncooked rice with a piece of sugar on top.

On 9 April we made our first carry, taking 57 loads to the old Base Camp where we left two men. There was much ice about. On the way back it snowed and blew hard—conditions which, attending our first move in the game, were regarded by the Sherpas as of evil omen. They betook themselves to a very holy man who lives alone in the severest simplicity in a small house close to the camp four miles above Rongbuk. His serene and cheerful countenance filled me with wonder. Each man listened with reverently bowed head to the few words said to him and received with manifest joy some large, repulsive-looking brown pills. The march from Rongbuk to the old Base Camp takes but an hour and a half, but it was with the greatest difficulty that the men were persuaded, against all precedent, to make two carries on the next day. This completed our first move, and by 5 o'clock on the 10th we were all installed there except Warren whom we had left with Karma Paul in a house adjoining the monastery. The previous night there had been a violent storm with zero temperatures resulting in the North Peak turning white. Everest itself remained black, either because less snow fell up there or because the wind blew harder.

Our porter corps was now twice as large as the thirty we had anticipated. We had neither tents nor clothing for so many and since we were in no hurry now to reach the mountain—for owing to the prevailing cold it seemed unlikely that anything could be done until May—we decided to dismiss some. So after making two carries to Camp I, we picked out fifteen of the Sola Khombu men and sent thirty home, thus leaving us with a total Sherpa strength of thirty-one. Sorting out the sheep from the goats was largely guesswork; only two or three were old hands whom we knew, and for the rest we had only appearances to go by which in the case of Sherpas is not always a reliable guide; nor was the advice offered by their friends amongst our Darjeeling men entirely disinterested. All were pathetically eager to stay. The thirty who were dismissed with a gratuity consoled themselves further by taking with them five of our thirty precious pairs of porters' boots—a serious and unexpected loss, for with only Sherpas in the camp I had imagined that precautions against theft might be relaxed. By borrowing spare boots from the Europeans some of the shortage was made good, but three of our thirty-one porters never had anything except their Tibetan boots and consequently were unable to go any higher than Camp III.

Partly as a result of this boot shortage a regrettable incident has to be recorded. As Angkarma, who was Odell's servant, had been speechless with laryngitis for the previous fortnight and did not look robust, it was thought kinder to send him home and retain someone who was more likely to go high. With this idea in mind it became essential to have the boots which had been issued to Angkarma at Kalimpong, which were now of far more importance than he was. But with these the owner very resolutely declined to part. A scene ensued in which Angkarma lay on the ground, making what noise a person in his condition could, but managing to name in a hoarse whisper such a stiff price for the boots that he easily won the day and we got neither the boots nor a better porter.

The next day, 13 April, we occupied Camp I. We took with us all we should require for a month's stay on the mountain, and maintained neither lines of communication nor any base except Rongbuk where Karma Paul remained with the rest of the stores. I spent a long afternoon issuing kit to the fifteen new men, and Primus stoves, oil, and cigarettes to all. From now on cooking for the whole party had to be done on stoves.

Someone had to go without boots, and since Sonam Tensing was mainly responsible for recruiting the Solu Khumbu men, amongst whom there were apparently some thieves, I made him one of the scapegoats. In any case it is usually a waste of money giving kit to the 'Foreign Sportsman' (the name he went by among us) because he has a habit of wearing his own clothes throughout the campaign and retaining ours for subsequent sale or barter. I remember in 1937, when we last travelled together, he favoured a natty double-breasted grey summer suiting with very nice thick white stockings worn outside the trousers, while in 1938 I never saw him in anything but the clothes he came in from Solu Khumbu which kept him just as warm as our elaborate sweaters and wind-proofs. His attitude to clothes was thus very different from when he began his mountaineering career in 1935 and first earned the sobriquet of the 'Foreign Sportsman'. He joined us then at Camp II on this same glacier, having blown in unasked and unheralded from heaven knows where. We admired his enterprise, so we took him on and gave him a complete rig-out which he never discarded until Darjeeling was reached some months later. In July or August, miles from any snow, he would be seen equipped as the complete mountaineer in wind-proofs, gloves, puttees, snow-glasses, Balaclava helmet, as though about to face some terrific blizzard. He is a good and likeable porter with many attractive features, but amongst them I would not put the deep bass voice with which he croons endless Buddhist chants. The patience shown by his comrades in bearing with not only these, but also with his faculty for evading camp chores and a not unwise regard for his own comfort, led us to suppose him an unfrocked monk.

Oliver and I accompanied the first relay of loads to Camp II which was reached in four hours on a fine, cloudless, almost windless day; that is to say windless so far as we were concerned, but the banner streaming from the top of the mountain showed only too clearly what was happening there. Now that we had thirty-one men, of whom—owing to camp duties—only twenty-nine were usually available for carrying, four relays were necessary for every move of camp.

There seemed to be a disgusting amount of stuff to shift. No one could have accused us of lightness or mobility. The slogan 'No damned science', if raised at all, had evidently not been heard by Odell. We had amongst our scientific equipment our old friend the glacier drill and a machine which, in return for the slight trouble of winding up, recorded the relative humidity. The results were so unexpectedly various that one concluded the thing was only guessing. Then we had batteries of thermometers, and they were all needed; for in order to register impressively low temperatures they have to be whirled joyfully at the end of a piece of string, and, naturally a lot of them flew away. Our library, too, was a weighty affair. Shipton had the longest novel that had been published in recent years, Warren a 2,000-page work on Physiology. Odell may or may not have had a book on Geology, but he himself daily wrote the equivalent in what he humorously called his field notes. Oliver, no doubt, had Clausewitz on the Art of War and Lloyd a text-book on Inorganic Chemistry, but I had carelessly omitted to bring either a standard work on Mountaineering, Mrs Beeton, or the Chemistry of Food. Moreover, I had to use all my persuasive art to induce Angtharkay to leave at Rongbuk a great bread-making oven, though he well knew we should seldom have any fire for baking and though he had often watched me turn out perfectly good bread from an ordinary 'degchi' or cooking pot. One of the troubles of having a real cook is that he always wants a great quantity of impedimenta. If you curtail it and then curse him for any shortcomings he can always retort that it is your own fault for having thrown out some particular implement or ingredient. But there was never any trouble in this respect from Angtharkay, for whom cooking was a diverting side-line, and who could manage on very little and manage uncommonly well. So long as camp cooks have not got the five-course-dinner complex, from which all Indian cooks suffer, and content themselves with one simple dish such as they themselves would eat, then one can be sure of having a square meal.

On Good Friday we gave the men an off-day with the result that their stoves, filled in the morning, were empty before evening. Owing to leakage and prodigal usage, oil was a constant source of worry; but having managed to buy eight gallons, left there in 1936, from the monastery, we finally finished up with several gallons in hand. The rest of us lay about, played chess, or read the less technical portion of our curiously assorted library. This included *Gone With the Wind* (Shipton), *Seventeenth Century Verse* (Oliver), *Montaigne's Essays* (Warren), *Don Quixote* (self), *Adam Bede* (Lloyd), *Martin Chuzzlewit* (Smythe), *Stones of Venice* (Odell), and a few others. Warren, who rejoined us that day, besides his weighty tome on Physiology—in which there were several funny anecdotes if one took the trouble to look—had with him a yet weightier volume on the singularly inappropriate subject of Tropical Diseases. Perhaps he wished to be prepared for all possibilities, or, since the temperatures were around zero, he found it a vicarious source of heat and thus supplied the answer to Bolingbroke's question:

> O, who can hold a fire in his hand,
> By thinking on the frosty Caucasus?
> Or wallow naked in December snow,
> By thinking on fantastic summer's heat?

Camp II was occupied on 18 April. It was in the glacier trough on the 1936 site, but of that camp there was scarcely a trace. No one walking up the East Rongbuk glacier would dream that there in the last twenty years more tins had been opened and more rubbish dumped than in any comparable area in India. It is, indeed, fortunate for us that the Tibetans are such thorough scavengers; the camps on the glacier would be even grimmer than they are if the accumulated debris of all the past expeditions still lay there. Returning through Sikkim this year I happened to visit the base camp on the Zemu glacier used by the Germans for their *two* attempts on Kangchenjunga; the amount of rubbish strewn about was reminiscent of the day after a Bank Holiday at one of England's more popular beauty spots.

Immediately on arrival at Camp II I went to bed with an attack of influenza following hard upon the preliminary warning of a sore throat. One carry was made to the old Camp III situated just on the corner where the glacier bends round towards the North Col, and then we sent all but three of the men down to Rongbuk where they could have a day's rest before returning with some more loads. The thermometer was now recording temperatures of 46° and 47° of frost at night. On the 22nd I felt strong enough to go down to Rongbuk, but before I went we held a discussion about plans; or rather the others discussed while I listened, for since going sick I had completely lost my voice. Whether the others noticed any departure from the normal I cannot say. The decision reached was that, after having a look at the North Col slopes, Shipton and Smythe were to retire to the Kharta valley while the rest of the party were to go up to the Col, and, if conditions warranted, proceed with the establishing of camps on the mountain. Both Shipton and Smythe, who had had most experience, were emphatic that the best time to attempt the mountain was the end of May or the beginning of June—that is just before the onset of a normal monsoon if there is such a thing in these parts. They were strongly averse to making an earlier attempt. As they were considered our most likely pair it was decided to reserve them for this main attempt. Meantime, we others would have a look at the North Col and decide whether conditions allowed of commencing operations on the mountain. Shipton and Smythe were not to wait for our report but were to proceed direct to Kharta from Camp III and there fatten up for the kill.

Accompanied by the 'Foreign Sportsman' I went down to Rongbuk in one march, passing on the way the porters who had that day begun their return journey. I put up with Karma Paul in his quarters by the monastery gate, and after a strong dose of hot 'arak' and butter at bedtime felt very much better by next day, which we passed playing piquet with satisfactory financial results to myself. I was told that the porters had also dosed themselves liberally with 'arak' when they were down, but not medicinally. Karma Paul's servant, Pensho, cooked for us. He was quite black with smoke from his cooking operations and had completely lost his voice although he had never been above Rongbuk. This versatile lad grooms and rides racing ponies in Darjeeling in ordinary life—sometimes for Karma Paul, who himself is a bit of a racing man. Pensho, by the way, has his name tattooed on his forearm very large and legibly.

On the 25th we went back to Camp II in one jump, the 'Foreign Sportsman' doing a man's job by carrying up about 80 lb. Twenty porters were there, six of them sick, but none wanted to go down, so next day we all went up to Camp III where the rest of the party now were. On leaving the moraine trough for the open glacier we were upon bare, slippery ice; but powder snow, collected thinly in cracks and hollows, allowed us to progress skidding about or having to nick steps. Only Pasang was in Camp III; the others could be seen half-way up to the North Col whence they presently returned. They reported that there was much ice on the slopes, which had obliged them to cut steps as far as they had gone, but that the route would probably 'go' all right to the top; they also reported that it was extremely cold—a fact which I had already discovered for myself without leaving camp. The whole party were now, 26 April, at Camp III with a month's supplies, and the question was what to do next.

In view of the prevailing wind and cold the general opinion was against proceeding with the establishment of the higher camps at present. None of the party, except Shipton, was at this time free from some minor ailment. Oliver's cold had become chronic, Odell had a cough, Smythe a sore throat, Lloyd and Warren colds, while I was merely convalescent. For these ailments drugs are of no more use on Everest than they are anywhere else; the only remedy is to go down. In accordance with the original plan, Shipton, Smythe, Oliver, and nine porters, started for the Kharta valley on the 27th. The rest of us intended waiting for a bit, partly to see whether the weather would become any warmer, but principally in the hope of receiving a mail which we thought might arrive on 1 May. But extremely low temperatures, combined with inactivity, were having no good effect on us either physically or mentally, so on 29 April we too set out for Kharta with thirteen porters.

On account of its low altitude (11,000 ft.) the Kharta valley was the place where we should most quickly throw off our manifold infirmities. The only alternatives to this move were to stay and carry on with the attack or to go down to Rongbuk, or Camp I, which would have been nearer to the mountain but less beneficial to health—Rongbuk is dusty, dirty, and 16,500 ft. above the sea. Before we left England, General Norton had advisedly warned me against the danger of committing the party to an early attempt with the possible result of putting most of us out of action with frost-bite. In 1924 his own party had suffered severely from cold weather early in May even at Camp III; twice they had to retreat down the glacier with the result that when favourable conditions at last arrived the party were worn out with the battering they had received. So severe were conditions this year at Camp III at the end of April that frost-bite was not so much a possibility as a certainty for any one on or above the North Col. Had we decided upon going to Rongbuk in order to be nearer the mountain nothing would have been gained. The cold and the wind continued unabated for the next six days and then on 5th May snow fell heavily and continued to fall daily for the next week. After this the mountain was never in climbable condition. That lull, on which all depends, between the dropping of the north-west wind with accompanying milder weather and the first heavy monsoon snowfall never occurred. I think it is true to say that at no time this year was the climbing of the mountain ever within the bounds of possibility.

In a letter expressing his best wishes for our success a candid friend warned me that whatever befell I was not to put too much blame on the weather. Such a caution might be more widely applied. How ready many of us are to find in the weather a handy and uncomplaining scapegoat for our less successful enterprises, our ill-health, or low spirits. Dr Johnson, that arch-enemy of cant, had a hearty contempt for the man who permitted the weather to affect his spirits or his work. 'The author who thinks himself weather-bound', he declared, 'will find, with a little help from hellebore, that he is only idle or exhausted.' A weather-bound mountaineer is more common and more likely to prove a genuine case for sympathy than a weather-bound author, but if we search our hearts we may have to confess to having on occasions made the weather a pretext when in fact we were idle or exhausted, or to cover up our irresolution, unfitness, or lack of judgement or skill. Nevertheless, I think it is generally admitted that the weather factor and the condition of the mountain is of greater consequence on Everest than on other mountains. At least all mountaineers now recognize the overwhelming importance of it; but I sometimes wonder whether the layman may not think that just as a bold sailor takes the weather as it comes, refusing to be cowed by it and only running for shelter in the last extremity, so a sufficient show of resolution on our part might overcome our difficulties. But the mountaineer, obedient to his code and aware of his limitations, must be allowed to judge what is possible and what is not, what risks he can justifiably take, nor must he rely very much on luck to retrieve his mistakes. Where the prize is so great he is not likely to err on the side of caution, but we should not forget that mountaineering, even on Everest, is not war but a form of amusement whose saner devotees are not willing to be killed rather than accept defeat.

The morning of the 29th, when we abandoned Camp III, was very cold indeed, as I quickly found when standing about making up loads for the journey to Kharta. We expected to be away about a fortnight, returning to Camp III by the middle of May. We left behind nine Sherpas, who, after spending a week at Rongbuk, were to return and carry the camp to the new Camp III site about 500 yards higher up the glacier. Looking up at the mountain, seemingly in perfect condition for climbing, it was impossible not to feel some misgivings at turning our backs on it and marching away. But even here, at 21,500 ft., with no wind blowing to speak of, the cold was sufficiently intimidating to banish all regrets. The fact that we never again saw the mountain black inclines one to curse one's pusillanimity for missed chances; but it is only necessary to recall that a month later, when conditions had changed so much that the heat at Camp III was positively enervating, at 27,000 ft. the cold was barely tolerable. There is no question that at this time no man could have climbed on the mountain and lived.

CHAPTER SIX

Retreat and Advance

'I'll go, said I, to the woods.'   Coppard

THE route by which we retreated from the East Rongbuk glacier to the Kharta valley was that used by the party which first set foot on the mountain. In the early stages of their exploration of the Rongbuk glacier in July 1921 Mallory and Bullock realized that the two great ridges descending from Everest to the north-west and south-east were not practicable routes to the summit; apart from their great length, and whatever difficulties there might be higher up, neither of them was easily reached. There remained the north ridge, which unlike the other two did offer some hope of approach by means of the comparatively low col joining the north ridge to the North Peak. The western side of this col, which came to be known as the North Col, was examined but discarded as being unsuitable for laden porters. The eastern side remained hidden, and although an exploration of the East Rongbuk glacier was to be undertaken, Mallory and Bullock did not suspect that it would lead to the North Col; they thought the glacier draining from that side of the col must flow away to the east and south; for the quantity of water in the stream which issued from the snout of the East Rongbuk glacier hardly seemed great enough if that glacier had its source at the foot of Mount Everest itself. Their exploration of the East Rongbuk glacier which would have cleared up the topographical puzzle, but at the same time might have deprived the party of much of the interesting work accomplished later, was deferred. The time allotted to it had to be devoted to the retaking of a number of important survey photographs which previously had proved failures, and the opportunity never recurred.[1]

The party abandoned the Rongbuk glacier and moved round to the Kharta district to examine the eastern approaches to the mountain. One glacier, the Kangshung, brought them under Makalu and the south side of the great north-east ridge; but at length Mallory, Bullock and Morshead, climbing a col at the head of the Kharta glacier, looked across a wide glacier floor leading directly to the North Col. They were on the Lhakpa La (22,500 ft.), and the glacier below them was, of course, the upper extremity of the East Rongbuk. Running eastwards from the North Peak was a ridge which hitherto they had imagined formed the head wall of that glacier, but now it was seen to be merely a buttress round which the glacier swept in an almost right-angled bend. In September, from their base in the Kharta valley, they attacked the mountain from a camp on the Lhakpa La itself. In view of the condition of the party at the end of a long and strenuous season, the inexperience of the porters, the state of the snow, and the weather, the fact that they reached even the North Col is suitable evidence of their strength and determination.

During this year's attempt we discussed the future possibility of using the Kharta valley as a base. Its principal advantages are: a shortening of the approach march by about four days by cutting out Shekar Dzong; very much pleasanter living conditions at the base compared with those at Rongbuk; more easily obtainable food and fuel; and a local porter supply. There is no question that Rongbuk is not a pleasant place in April, May, or even any other time. It is cold, dusty, and as dirty as might be expected from the presence in a confined space of two or three hundred permanent residents with no notions at all of sanitation. Our tents are pitched on the only patch of grass; for the rest it is stones and rocks with never a tree and scarcely a flower.

1 Col. Oliver Wheeler, however, who was working on a photographic survey detached from the others, went far enough up the East Rongbuk glacier to hazard the guess that its source was beneath the slopes of the North Col, but this hint did not reach Mallory and Bullock until they had transferred their attentions to the Kharta valley side.

All food and firewood have to be brought from the nearest village a day's march away, and there is no labour available locally. Yet it is my belief that these disadvantages, which are not slight, are offset by the shortness and ease of the approach to the mountain. Having to cross an obstacle such as the 22,500 ft. Lhakpa La on every journey to or from Camp III would be a serious consideration; the Kharta side of the pass is steep, while there are many crevasses on the upper part of the Kharta glacier. Therefore, men could not travel alone; parties would have to be roped; bad weather or heavy snowfalls, which on the old route can be almost ignored, would on this route be regarded with concern; and the difficulty of getting down sick or injured men would be greatly increased. Two other points for consideration are, first whether or not the Tibetans would raise any objection, and secondly the fact that the North Face of the mountain is not visible from the Kharta side. No doubt special permission to alter our route and to base ourselves on Kharta instead of Rongbuk would have to be sought, for when the Tibetan authorities grant a passport they lay down a route and expect us to follow it. What effect if any arises from a party's having the mountain ever before its eyes I cannot say. Like most things in life one probably gets used to it, and it would be unwise to suggest that there is any effect, lest in the interests of science some future party finds itself saddled with a psychologist to study the question. But it is valuable in other ways to have the mountain always in view. I regretted later that Karma Paul was not given the job of taking a photo of the mountain at the same hour every day of our stay; such a record of the changes in snow conditions on the face would be interesting and informative, as would be meteorological records which could also be kept by whoever was left at Rongbuk. No active member of the party can take regular four-hourly observations.

Odell, Warren, Lloyd, myself and thirteen porters left at 10.30 o'clock on 29 April. Heading straight across the glacier on slippery grey-blue ice we had on our right the foot of the north-east ridge where it runs down to the Rapiu La. Odell and I were behind so that as we approached the eastern bank of the glacier we could see the others beginning the climb to the pass moving in single file up the crest of a rock spur of which the flank was sheeted in ice. Suddenly a figure, which I recognized as Warren, slid down the ice. We hurried forwards as fast as we could on the slippery surface, but before we reached him he had come to an abrupt halt among some rocks after sliding about 100 ft. I was relieved to see him sit up. No serious damage had been done but he was severely bruised and shaken. He had great difficulty in going on, but accompanied by Odell managed to do so slowly. What had happened was, that when following the rocks lying just above the ice-slope, he had stepped on a stone which was not frozen to the underlying ice and which consequently slid away.

We struggled upwards in a very cold wind. I seemed to be going very badly, but took comfort from the thought that no one else seemed much better. At 2 o'clock we reached the top where we were relieved to see the large steps cut by the other party down the eastern side still intact. The slope was ice but the porters tackled it confidently in spite of their heavy loads. It was too cold to linger, but as I turned my back on the mountain to begin the descent the chief impression I took with me was the unpleasant appearance of the north-east arête and the amount of cloud away over Sikkim to the south-east. The glacier was not slippery ice like the East Rongbuk but afforded good going on hard rough snow. We walked rapidly down it, admiring on our right the beautifully fluted snow ridge between us and the head of the Kangshung glacier, beyond which, over a low saddle, we watched the clouds forming and dissolving upon the black precipices of Makalu. There was but little wind this side, and the fact that the glacier surface was snow and not bare ice suggests there never is enough wind to sweep the snow off.

We continued the march next morning down the left-hand moraine. After going for two hours we reached the snout of the glacier and from there followed the excellent hard highway provided by the frozen river. Warren, stiff and sore from his fall, had much difficulty in walking, so for the last mile or so he was carried perched on the broad shoulders of Nukku. We were now entering a more genial climate; grass and plants, only recently freed from their snow-covering, were beginning to show green promise of fresh growth. On 1 May we camped close to the first village, having already passed the yaks moving up to higher pastures. A recurrence of my influenza began here; but, expecting to come across Shipton's party, we pushed on down the valley to camp at length in a delightful grass meadow by the side of a big 'chorten'. Juniper wood abounded. The attractiveness of the place and my sickness made me disinclined to move next day, so here we stayed while Lloyd and Warren went on down the valley, crossed the Kharta Chu to the south side, and found the camp of the other party tucked away in a wood overlooking the Arun gorge. We joined them next day, 4 May, when I had to take to my bed with a bad cough, a worse cold, stiff legs, and a temperature.

We moved the tents out of the wood into a broad meadow sheltered on two sides by forests of birch, juniper and rhododendron. On one side of our tents a little tarn reflected the sky while on the other side, barely fifty yards away, the ground fell sheer for nearly a thousand feet to the bed of the Arun river, the roar of whose waters came faintly to our ears. Yaks grazed in the meadow, the rhododendron was in bud, birds sang, the pale green shoots of the birch were beginning to show; only an Eskimo could have regretted the ice and snow of Camp III. There was no village near us, but the Kharta Chu down which we had come is a fertile valley with many prosperous looking villages each one with its monastery, so we sent out daily foraging parties who brought back sheep, flour and eggs, although at that time of year food was scarce and consequently dear. Moreover, since leaving Rongbuk the rate of exchange had moved against us in the mysterious way exchange rates have, and now we received only 25 Tibetan 'tankas' instead of 30 for our rupees. This movement was more unaccountable than those which take place on the international market; for there, however the rate may vary from time to time, it does not vary from place to place—a pound is worth the same paltry number of dollars in Boston as in New York. To the ordinary man the only fixed point in the shifting phantasy of exchange rates is that they are usually unfavourable to him.

The Arun gorge, at the head of which we were camped, is only one of several great gorges carved out by rivers in the Himalayan ranges. It is, however, a peculiarly striking example when seen by the traveller from the Tibetan side; for he is already familiar with the sluggish meanderings of the river, apparently so easily diverted from its course by slight barriers, and has stared amazed at the seemingly impenetrable front of the gigantic barrier which it at last pierces. It is another instance of a phenomenon frequently observed: namely the proximity of deep gorges to high peaks, for the rivers often cross the range near its highest points. The Arun gorge is within 10 miles of Makalu and 20 miles of Everest; the gorge of the river Gori, in Garhwal, within 12 miles of Nanda Devi. Other instances are Namcha Barwa and the Tsangpo gorge; and Nanga Parba whose foot is almost washed by the Indus. The principal branch of the Arun in Tibet is the Phung Chu, which drains the whole area stretching westwards for 200 miles from the point where our route enters Tibet, and northwards to the watershed of the Tsangpo or Brahmaputra—from the Sebu La, near Tangu, to Gosainthan, a 26,000 ft. peak nearly 80 miles west of Everest. It forms the principal tributary of the Kosi river of Nepal which in turn flows into the Ganges. How these great gorges came into being is a fruitful source of geological speculation and controversy. Several theories have been evolved to account for the phenomenon of a river flowing directly across a great mountain chain, the two most favoured being either the 'cutting-back' by the river, or the antecedence of the river to the mountains, with the maintenance of its original course as the mountains were raised. The parallel question of the antecedence of hens and eggs inevitably suggests itself to the irreverent.

Though our meadow was sheltered by steep wooded slopes and the tents themselves pitched in the lee of a clump of trees, yet it was one of the windiest of spots; a constant blast swept up the gorge like steam from a safety valve. On our third day there the wind brought with it clouds and rain, which fell as snow on the heights overlooking the gorge. Clouds also formed away to the north, but overhead was a patch of blue sky where two opposite wind currents battled for mastery. It was at this time, had we known it, that snow was falling heavily on the mountain, but we flattered ourselves that the unsettled weather we were experiencing was only what might be expected when the moisture-laden airs of the plains, drawn up through the funnel of the gorge, met the cold winds of Tibet.

Nobody was very active during the six days spent here. The more energetic went for short walks, the most favoured being to a point of vantage on the very lip of the gorge where you could sit on a rock with your feet dangling over the water a thousand feet below. Those with a mathematical turn of mind exercised it by hurling stones into the river and estimating the height from the time they took to reach the water. A track carved out of the cliff on the opposite side aroused such interest that we made plans for going down the gorge and home through Nepal, knowing very well that we never should. I remained for the whole time on my back except for tottering a few yards on the last day to see that my legs were still functioning—a sort of training walk preparatory to the march back. So did Smythe, but for a different reason; for his belief is that a rest should be a rest and that only essentially unavoidable movements such as lifting a cup or reaching out a hand for food should be undertaken. A pleasant custom was started of dining together at night round a huge fire lit in the midst of the clump of trees. Interminable arguments on serious subjects were carried on, but sometimes snatches of livelier conversation were wafted to me on the breeze as I lay in my tent. Thus:

'. . . but since there is an entire absence of lacustrine deposits . . .'
'. . . good, but do you know the one about the young man of Baroda?'
'. . . I thought the Turner pictures frightful.'
'. . .brought Peacock instead of Montaigne. Old Montaigne is delightfully bawdy but Peacock's cleverer and his descriptions of food are grand.'
'Food, my God! Mutton every day since Gangtok . . .'
'. . . and suddenly a tall Frenchman with a green face and a thermometer suspended round his neck was sick on the floor of the hut.'
'. . . have you heard the story of Simpson the strong guy? . . .'
'. . . lucky to get all that stuff at Rongbuk. Bath Olivers, Pumpernickel, pickled onions . . .'
'. . . probably metamorphosed rock with . . .'
'. . . never bothers about lunch—thinks it sissy. . .'
'. . . The Rembrandts gave me the willies . . .'
'. . . saw me putting a hunk of bread and cheese in my pocket for lunch and offered me a tiffin coolie to carry it . . .'
'. . . Did the Meije and got back to Grenoble by . . .'
'. . . ah well, I said we should starve. Don't eat all the jam, it's all we've got . . .'
'. . . by taking levels to the river terraces . . .'
'. . . four different kinds of marmalade in '36 . . .'
'. . . write my field-notes up by the light of half an inch of candle. Good night.'

On 10 May five of us left to return by the Doya La to Rongbuk; this way was an easier way than the Lhakpa La and I hoped to get a pony to ride. We left behind Shipton and Smythe who were to return by the Lhakpa La and meet us at Camp III on the 20th. Shipton had a sore throat which proved to be the beginning of a mild attack of influenza. Our first march was a short one of about five miles to a village at the foot of the Chongphu valley which leads to the Doya La. I felt weak and was bothered by spasms of coughing, but unfortunately I was unable to hire a pony; we were told that everything on four legs had gone away to take part in some mysterious 'races'. However, we bought sixty eggs and a sheep which were more useful. The Sherpas have a curious dislike of slaughtering a sheep. They love meat, especially the messier bits of the stomach; they enjoy slicing off chickens' heads, cutting up a dead sheep, cleaning the intestines, removing the brains, but they jib at the actual killing of the animal. If no one else will oblige they cast lots amongst themselves, while the loser is usually so upset that he bungles the job and makes two or three half-hearted blows with the kukri instead of one, before severing the beast's head. No doubt if we had to slaughter our own meat there would be many more vegetarians than there are.

Our valley was very pleasant; the stream which bubbled down it was so clear, and brown, and merry, that it reminded me of some Lakeland beck. No great glacier feeds it; its source is a lake which in turn draws its water, not directly, from a small glacier. I think no glacier-fed stream can appear friendly as other streams do. It is neither good to drink, pleasant to bathe in, nor easy to cross; over it hangs the dank smell of a grave dug in clay, and it has the cold, grim, forbidding air of its parent. We were too early to see many flowers, but later on this valley is full of roses, clematis, and primulas; for on this side of the Doya La the climate is very much damper than on the north. Only the children remained in the villages to take any interest in our passage; all men and women were out in the fields busy sowing barley and guiding the water from the furrow on to the sown plots.

We crossed the Doya La (17,000 ft.) on 12 May, a dull day with a threat of snow in the air. Odell and I, who mistook several likely-looking depressions for the real pass, steered a rather erratic course, but we caught up Warren and the porters below the true pass and spent two hours and a half very pleasantly, brewing tea. To be more accurate, brewing one small cup of tea; for so exiguous was the fuel supply that it took all that time to boil the water. We were so long about it that Lloyd and Oliver, who had also visited a false pass, came back to look for us thinking we had made camp. There was snow on the way up and more on the north side of the pass which we crossed in a snowstorm. On the top Odell took advantage of the excellent light afforded by the mist and falling snow to take a round of photos of topographical or, perhaps, meteorological interest. An hour's swift run down brought us to a wood where we camped.

And so next day to Chodzong where we joined the road from Tashidzom which we had traversed in April on the way up. Here we heard news that Purba Tensing had just gone through with the mail and were put into a fever by the thought that Karma Paul, ignorant of our whereabouts, might send it straight up the glacier. Hard though one might strive to persuade oneself that it was just as cold now as in April, there was no denying that the weather was positively mild. The glimpse of the mountain which we caught as we moved off next morning on the way to Rongbuk confirmed our worst fears. It was perfectly white, and from the summit a plume of cloud trailed lazily from the south-east to the north-west carrying to us an unmistakable message. I did my best to convince myself and the others that it was not Everest that we were looking at but some other mountain. Those amongst us who habitually took a gloomy view were certain the monsoon had begun, but we only voiced this fear for the pleasure of hearing it scoffed at by those with more robust minds. It was still early in the season and the hope that the north-west wind would re-establish itself and clear the mountain was not unreasonably entertained by all. It seemed a reasonable hope then; but it was no light dusting of snow at which we were looking but a heavy coating which grew daily thicker.

At Rongbuk we heard from Karma Paul what had happened. How on 5 May snow had fallen and continued to fall daily for the next week. In his diary for 5 May he writes: 'The mountain is as white as anything . . .' We found our mail, devoted a day to reading it, and on the 16th started once more for the mountain.

CHAPTER SEVEN

Advance and Retreat

Hoping for the future, tormented by the present.

AT Camp I there was a lively exchange of news when we met Ongdi and his men whom we had left behind. They had just returned from up the glacier where they had been busy shifting Camp III to the higher site. They reported a foot or more of snow on the glacier. It was calm and mild as we moved up this time, and when we reached Camp III on 18 May we realized how drastically conditions had changed; a foot of snow covered both the ice of the glacier and the rocks of the moraine, while water was found lying about in pools ready to hand whereas before we had been obliged to melt ice. For some reason or other—we preferred to put it down to the heat—we all found the 500 yards going up the moraine to the new camp site particularly trying. I checked the stores and found we had now accumulated sufficient food for five weeks.

Very early next morning clouds began pouring up from the south over the Rapiu La bringing in their train snow which fell intermittently throughout the morning. This was not encouraging, but Odell and Oliver went a short way up the North Col slopes to find the snow in good condition. Lloyd and Warren spent the day trying unsuccessfully to mend one of the 'closed' type oxygen apparatus which had gone wrong, while I offered advice from the depths of my sleeping-bag where I lay with limbs which ached as though they had been racked. This, I thought, heralded another attack of influenza, but nothing came of it. Lloyd was not feeling well and in his case influenza developed the next day, 20 May, so that he was unable to accompany us when four of us and four Sherpas began the task of making the route up to the North Col. The temperature that night was 1°F.

As at first we had intended taking laden porters with us, Oliver went off early with two men to kick steps, leaving us to follow an hour later escorting the porters. After prolonged discussion we decided that it would be wiser to leave them until the route was nearer completion, so Odell, Warren, myself and two Sherpas, started rather late. The route we chose was a fairly central one in preference to a slightly easier line more to the right which, however, involved a very long traverse across the place where Shipton and Wyn Harris had nearly been avalanched in 1936. Half-way up there was a rather critical place where we had to cross the line of fire of a threatening ice cliff from which a mass of big blocks had already fallen; and for a time we were in a sort of funnel which was rather too well adapted to act as an avalanche chute had one been started from above. Actually, we never had any trouble at all here, but on this first morning, right at the foot of the slope, we late-comers were reminded of the advantages of an earlier start by the fall of several large blocks of ice just to our left.

The snow was good and the climbing so easy that Oliver did not call upon those behind to take any share in the work until within about 300 ft. of the top. There the slope steepened abruptly and broke into ice cliffs; in consequence we were forced to traverse to the left for about a hundred yards before the slope eased and allowed the route to be finished by a direct climb to the top. The snow on the traverse was steep, loose, and soft. A rope would obviously have to be fixed here for the laden porters, so Oliver wisely waited for the rest of us to come up before embarking on it with his two Sherpas, who were carrying one end of a 300 ft. line for fixing, and some long wooden snow pitons like cricket stumps. They had not proceeded far before they became bunched together with the result that the snow at once avalanched. The leading man, who was a Sherpa, was beyond the cleavage, which was about two feet deep, and the light line which we were paying out to him got mixed up in their own climbing rope so that we easily held them before they had been carried far down. They climbed back to where we were sitting, on a snow boss, which made a convenient and safe stance at the beginning of the traverse. Then, having thus 'tried it on the dog', Odell and I, secured and doubly secured by many ropes, took over the task of cutting and stamping out a continuous track in the steep snow. The first part of the route at least had now been made safe.

Oliver's party were sufficiently safeguarded to prevent any serious consequences arising out of this avalanche which at the time none of us regarded very seriously. I did not report it, but there was a leakage of news somewhere and later I was disgusted to find the popular Press had got wind of it and had related the story with their usual happy accuracy. Glaciologists will be interested to know that the party had been 'caught by the tail of the glacier', and meteorologists that they were 'nearly carried away by the monsoon', both these nasty mishaps taking place on the 'North Column'. But it would be ungenerous to withhold praise where praise is due; a less pedantically accurate Press than ours might have wiped out the whole party on the snout of the glacier.

It was such a hot, sweltering day, and at that height the flogging away of the snow was such exhausting work, that by 3 o'clock, although we had not accomplished a great deal we were of the opinion that it was time to stop. The making of mere steps was not enough. Three or four feet of snow had to be scooped out of the slope to allow room for the body, and a continuous track wide enough for both feet stamped out. We put in pegs to secure the rope as far as we had gone, and then gave the word for retreat. Back at camp at 4 o'clock we found Shipton and Smythe who had re-crossed the Lhakpa La very early that morning on account of the very bad snow conditions on that side. They had watched our performance with interest, not untinged with anxiety, and were glad to see us coming down. Shipton brought a cold back with him, but the party as a whole were now much less troubled with coughs, colds and throats than they had been in April; of course, in view of the change in the weather, this was only to be expected.

At 5 o'clock that evening a snowstorm began which went on for several hours. Until far into the night avalanches could be heard roaring down off the north-east ridge of the mountain opposite, and from the North Peak at our backs. This fall of snow, and the hot muggy morning which followed, gave us something to think about. It was certain that the slopes would be unsafe for two or three days, and with the coming of the north-west wind, which we confidently hoped would presently begin blowing to clear the snow off the mountain, the formation of wind-slab snow might make them dangerous for an indefinite period. This is a snow formation due to wind-driven snow, fallen or falling, being deposited on lee slopes; it is very liable to avalanche and difficult to detect. The avalanche in which Shipton and Wyn Harris were nearly involved in 1936 was thought to be of this type. The uncertain behaviour of the snow on these slopes in other years, once milder weather had set in, was a menacing thought never far from our minds. There was the 1922 disaster when seven porters lost their lives, the narrow escape of 1936, and the more unaccountable happening of 1935, when for no easily ascertainable reason a great avalanche broke away almost across the whole slope. Of this Shipton wrote: 'We were brought up short at the brink of a sudden cut-off which stretched for several hundred yards in either direction. This indicated that an enormous avalanche had recently broken away largely along the line of our ascending tracks. In fact the whole face of the slope had peeled off to a depth of six feet. Very little new snow had been deposited on the slopes and this cannot have had any appreciable effect on the stability of the old snow which we had unanimously agreed seemed perfectly sound.' All that we did know for certain was that we knew very little at all of how the snow on these slopes would behave from day to day.

In these circumstances our thoughts began to turn to the route up the western side of the North Col, which had been warmly recommended by the 1936 party as a useful alternative route if monsoon conditions rendered the east side dangerous as is usually the case. In June that year they had examined the slope from close underneath it, but had thought its ascent inadvisable. However, they considered it definitely safer from avalanche dangers, especially from those arising from the presence of wind-slab. This may well be, but the angle is uniformly steep, and its surface, unlike that of the eastern side, which is broken up by crevasses and ledges, is a straight slope which is liable to avalanche at any place. As the upshot of a long discussion on 21 May, we decided that Shipton and Smythe should go round, and, if they succeeded in getting on to the Col, should make an attempt. They were to have the use of all the available porters for two days, after which thirteeen would return and go up from this side with us if conditions allowed. The plan was not ideal; it would take a week to execute and the contemplated division left both parties numerically weak in porters. But it did promise that one or other party would reach the North Col.

A windy night, followed by a fine cold morning which gave promise of better weather, made us drop the plan for the moment. Uncertainty whether the western side would 'go', or whether it was any less dangerous than this side, made us reluctant to commit ourselves to it yet. On the 23rd there was no wind. High cirrus clouds were drifting from the north-west, but clouds again began to appear very early over the Rapiu La to the south-east. Lloyd was now in bed with influenza and would have to go down when strong enough to walk. Shipton, Smythe, Oliver and myself, went half-way up to the Col and found the condition of the snow good enough to warrant another start; so on the 24th all of us, except Lloyd who went down to recuperate, made the ascent to the Col with twenty-six porters. Shipton and Smythe, starting soon after 6 o'clock, had finished the remainder of the traverse and were on the top by 9.30 o'clock. Odell and Oliver followed half an hour later, so that when Warren and I arrived with the porters at the beginning of the traverse, soon after 10 o'clock, most of the rope required was fixed ready for use. Warren led the porters while I followed behind nursing a fresh infirmity—a pain in the ribs which for the remainder of the campaign so adversely affected three of the unavoidable functions of the human body on Mount Everest, that breathing became uncomfortable, coughing painful, and sneezing agonizing.

So nervous were we about the traverse that at first we sent the men over one by one, but as confidence increased we put five on a rope. The traverse finished along the underlip of a crevasse beyond which there was a very steep snow slope, broken half-way up by another crevasse, leading to the crest of the Col 200 ft. above. This was made safe with ropes which the porters used to haul themselves and their heavy loads. For a heavily laden man the crevasse in the middle was a formidable obstacle, so there Odell spent a busy hour shoving lustily on the behind of each man as he strove to bridge it with his legs. Nearly two hours were spent in climbing the last 300 ft. We dumped the loads about 50 yards north of the spot where we reached the crest, on the site of the 1936 camp. Of this the only indication was the apex of a pyramid tent just showing through the snow. The men burrowed down into it for six or seven feet but all they retrieved for their labour was a rubber mat. We descended on five long ropes and were back at Camp III by 3 o'clock.

Next day Smythe and I went up again with fifteen porters. The importance of an early start had been made so manifest the day before that we left early and reached the dump on the Col by 10 o'clock. The heat was oppressive and the air around us still as we lay outside the tent in which the loads were dumped, dejectedly regarding the snow-covered mountain. Norton's Traverse was white; the snow beneath us deep and soft; on either side, from the Lho La and the Rapiu La, clouds billowed up; and over towards Sikkim a sea of turbulent white cloud lay between us and the distant summit of Kangchenjunga just appearing above it. Even so we were not entirely convinced that the monsoon had begun; like a man marrying for the second time, hope was indeed triumphing over experience. Nevertheless, that feeble spark of hope was very near to extinction. At present there was too much snow on the mountain for an attempt to be made, and with the absence of wind and the presence of occasional fresh falls the snow was increasing instead of diminishing.

Upon our return to Camp III more discussion took place when it was decided that Shipton and Smythe should go down to Rongbuk until the mountain was clearer, and that we others should occupy the North Col in order to examine the snow conditions higher up. It was just possible things were not so bad as they looked. We were still reluctant to commit ourselves to the west side route, but meanwhile there was no sense in keeping more men than necessary at Camp III. No one could say if the conditions ever would change for the better; but it would be as well to find out what the snow was really like higher up, and at any rate the weather was favourable in so far as that it was warm and windless enough to make high climbing possible.

Although we knew well, from the experience of earlier parties, that there was little likelihood of a successful climb being made in such conditions, not one of us would have been content to come away without putting that knowledge once more to the test.

Nothing was done next day, except that I, fired by the reports of some of the others who had been to the Rapiu La the previous day, walked over there to enjoy the view down into the Kangshung valley. By starting early enough to reach the pass by 7 o'clock I was barely in time. Already clouds filled the valley to the foot of Chomo Lonzo, while half an hour later the black stone-covered glacier far below was submerged, and the first waves of the rising tide of mist were breaking on the crest where we stood. Like the Lho La on the west side of Everest, the rise to the Rapiu La from the north is very gentle and the fall on the south side terrifically abrupt. By descending a short way on a rope held by Lhakpa Tsering from above I could see something of the fluted, snow-covered south side of the north-east ridge.

At 1 o'clock that day the sun temperature was 117°F. and the air temperature 33°F. A heavy and prolonged fall of snow that afternoon and evening made us revert to our earlier plan; so when Shipton and Smythe started for Rongbuk next day, the 27th, they took with them fourteen porters, intending to return, when they did, by the west side. After lunch Oliver and I walked up to the foot of the North Col slopes; whether it was the lunch or the heat, or the customary effect of an off-day, we felt particularly lethargic. We were disgusted to find that the snow on the moraine and on the glacier was now becoming very rotten, but after a very cursory inspection of the snow at the foot we decided that we would go up next day. I fear we were becoming callous or fatalistic about the avalanche danger, which nevertheless we were never able to forget; but as it turned out events justified this attitude, for after the affair of the 20th nothing ever happened or ever looked like happening. We were particularly careful to avoid the slopes after fresh snow had fallen, but there was always the possibility of a repetition of the 1935 avalanche to keep us on tenterhooks.

The thermometer fell to 10°F. that night. Next morning Odell and Oliver left at 6.30 o'clock, and Warren and I followed about 8 o'clock with thirteen porters. A stifling mist hung over the snow slopes from which the sun beat up in our faces as though from a desert of sand. We always found ourselves afflicted with a terrible thirst on the trips to the North Col, whereas above we found no real discomfort. Thermos flasks were always in great request by the time the snow boss below the traverse was reached. The heat, and its possible effect on the snow, induced us to treat this with the utmost respect. We crossed it one by one, securing each man on a rope over the worst bit. We were up soon after midday and proceeded to pitch the dome tent which we had now brought up from Camp III. It comprised two loads of 40 lb., but it was worth having up because all the Europeans could live in it together in comfort. Eight men were sent down in charge of Angtharkay with orders to come up next day with more loads if no snow fell. That afternoon, however, it snowed until 8 o'clock at night. Brewing tea took 40 minutes, but it was satisfactory to find the stoves burning well and the specially fitted pumps, which we were using for the first time, very effective. On the 29th we lay at earth. Nearly a foot of snow had fallen overnight and there was wind and more snow that afternoon. There could be little doubt left now that the monsoon was definitely established—had been probably for the last three weeks. Conversation in the tent was of nothing but sardines and tinned fruit; the atmosphere seemed almost defeatist. It was surprising to be told that the temperature in the tent fell that night to 17°F; judging from the state of the snow the outside temperature must have been hardly as low. I was out early on the morning of the 30th to rouse the Sherpas who usually take longer to regain full consciousness than most people owing to the overpoweringly poisonous atmosphere which they love to encourage inside their tents by sealing up any crevices suspected of letting in dangerously fresh air. Having broken a pricker in their Primus stove in an endeavour to expedite matters, and set a guard to watch and report any signs of movement down at Camp III—we did not want them to come up—I returned to the tent to brew a handsome dish of scrambled eggs; what the Sherpas expressively call 'rumble-tumble'. Upon this we all became pretty active and by 8 o'clock were in a sufficiently robust frame of mind to contemplate the notion of starting with something approaching Christian resignation. It was then that the look-out reported Angtharkay's party moving up the glacier from Camp III, some 1,500 ft. below us and a mile or more distant. However, a prolonged bellow from all hands on the Col was heard by them, interpreted correctly, and acted upon with almost indecent haste. They returned to camp.

Of our party, Oliver was to examine from the end of a long rope the state of the snow on the western side, while the rest of us went up the north ridge in the direction of Camp V as far as our enthusiasm or energy would carry us. The snow was knee-deep as we steered a careful course amongst the crevasses at the foot of the ridge, and began plodding up the easy slope. Warren tried out the 'closed' type apparatus with unlooked-for results. Instead of making him skip upon the mountains like a young ram it seemed bent, first on bringing him to a standstill, and then on suffocating him. He did not wear it very long. Whether there was something wrong with the works or whether there is something inherently vicious about the design has yet to be discovered. Its fellow was already definitely broken but this one appeared to be functioning correctly.

In front we had the tireless Tensing to make things easy for us until we came to a steeper slope where the snow seemed very insecurely poised. Here I went on ahead, bringing up Tensing with the help of another rope which Odell had been carrying, for I had to go on for two rope-lengths before finding a secure stance. Then as we could not get this rope back to Odell he waited there for Warren and Oliver while I pushed on slowly with Tensing. At 1 o'clock we were still on the long snow-bed which permanently covers the lower part of the north ridge to a height of nearly 25,000 ft. We were just below the bulge where the angle eases off, at a height of about 24,500 ft., and there we sat down feeling remarkably little inclination to go on. Tensing complained that his feet were cold—they had probably got wet. But it was a pleasant day—I myself wore neither wind-proofs nor gloves—and though most of the country below was hidden by a veil the clouds themselves formed a wonderful and constantly changing picture. Oliver was coming on from below, but I signalled him to stop, for we had seen enough to realize that little would be gained by occupying Camp V in those conditions. We went down; and that evening, when more snow fell, decided to abandon Camp IV for the present. A change for the better might come sometime, but even if no change came I was eager to return to give the upper part of the mountain a trial.

As we were anxious to start early next morning while the snow was in good condition, we decided, rather unwisely, as it proved, to postpone breakfast until we got down to Camp III. In mountaineering, as in war, it seldom pays to defer a meal if an opportunity for eating offers; at the best the next opportunity may be long in coming, at the worst it may never come again. A suggestion that two of us should go down by the west side to acquire first-hand knowledge of the route, and possibly to meet Shipton's party, was coldly received on account of Oliver's adverse report on the state of the snow there. We struck the dome tent before leaving to prevent it blowing away, but left the pyramid and the small Meade tents standing with the stores piled inside. The descent took longer than expected. At first the snow was good, but on the lower half the thinness and looseness of the snow, with the presence of ice beneath, imposed the necessity for much step-cutting and of constant vigilance to prevent the porters taking liberties, as those without much ice experience are apt to do. We were feeling pretty limp when we got back to Camp III about noon, not alone from hunger but also from heat. Snow began falling at 1 o'clock and continued until 5 o'clock. The joy occasioned by the arrival of the mail which might have helped one to forget the weather was offset for me by the news that Rs. 800 had been stolen from the cash-box at Rongbuk.

CHAPTER EIGHT

The Western Approach and Defeat

'The attempt and not the deed confounds us.'   Shakespeare, *Macbeth*, II. ii. 12.

A distinct change in the weather occurred on 1 June. The morning was dull and by midday the sky was covered with low clouds driven swiftly before a strong west wind. Taking only our bedding and some tents we walked down to Camp I where we expected to meet the others or at any rate to hear news of them. Amongst the ice pinnacles bordering the glacier trough the warm weather had wrought great changes; everywhere water ran or formed in deep pools. Close to Camp I the glacier stream, which before ran silently under a deep covering of frozen snow, was now a grey flood crossable only at certain places. A Sherpa, whom we had sent on ahead, reached the camp in time to find some of Shipton's porters engaged in relaying loads up to Lake Camp where his party now was. A chit having been sent up telling them to wait, Oliver and I next morning walked up to discuss plans.

A glance at the map will show that Lake Camp is only about 1½ miles from Camp I; the approach to it is across the East Rongbuk valley, below the glacier snout, and then up the moraine shelf on the right bank of the main Rongbuk glacier. Camp I is as good a camp as one could expect at 18,000 ft., but Lake Camp is better. Of course there is no fuel, but it is warm and sheltered, for it lies tucked away between a high moraine bank and the bounding wall of the valley; a stream of clear water meanders through a grassy lawn to empty itself into a little lake which is pleasant to look at if not to bathe in. Because of the sheltering slopes the morning sun reaches it rather late in the day, a disadvantage which is offset by the fact that it is open to the sun until a late hour in the afternoon. No one, I imagine, who visits this camp is likely to grow tired of looking at grass, for as the shadow of a great rock and water in a thirsty land so is grass to the sojourner among ice. But should he do so he has only to climb the moraine bank to see Everest with its stupendous north-west ridge sweeping down to the Lho La, the fascinating pinnacles of the main Rongbuk glacier, and the striking group of mountains, Pumori and the Lingtren group, lying between the West Rongbuk and the upper main Rongbuk glacier.

Shipton, Smythe and Lloyd, who had now recovered, were on their way up to the west side of the Col; but having heard that we had come down became uncertain what to do and were toying with the idea of making an excursion up the West Rongbuk glacier. However, this change in the weather kindled fresh hope in us all. By stepping a few yards from the camp we could see the north face of the mountain, and, through breaks in the flying scud, snow being whirled off it in the most encouraging manner. If this continued we might yet

482

accomplish something, but while the wind promised to clear the mountain it also threatened to form wind-slab snow on the east or lee side of the Col. Bowing to Smythe's repeated warnings, we decided to abandon that side altogether and to concentrate on an approach from the west. I attached myself to Shipton's party in order to make up two climbing parties of two, and we brought up our porter strength to seventeen by sending for two good men from Camp I. The remaining fourteen porters were left to bring down some necessary loads from Camp III, and then, with the three Europeans, were to follow up as quickly as possible.

The wind having blown for 48 hours dropped on the 3rd, a very fine, almost cloudless day, with very little wind at all except high up. The march to the next camp is a rough one; at first over moraine boulders and later along a trough on the right bank of the glacier. The camp is close to the point where the short glacier leading to the west side of the Col joins the main glacier. Tents were pitched on the glacier itself, the coolness of the ice being tempered by the layer of stones which covered it. Some debris left by the 1936 expedition, including a wireless aerial, still lay about—evidently the Tibetans have not yet heard of this departure from the usual route. This place was called North Face Camp but perhaps Corner Camp would be a better name. It was so mild that afternoon that we sat about on the moraine boulders talking until after 5 o'clock; the ancient philosophers sat on stone seats expounding their systems, and no doubt our topics—the absurd height of Mount Everest and the evils of processed foods—were so congenial that we too were indifferent to comfort.

Some snow fell in the night, and the morning was cloudy when we left at 9.30 o'clock. Turning the corner we proceeded, roped, up the glacier, steering a course close to the slopes of the North Peak above us on our left. The snow was good. The clear view we had of the north-west ridge of the mountain again impressed us with the difficulty a party would have in setting foot on it. When we had made about a mile up the glacier an icefall compelled us to bear to the left still closer under the North Peak, but as we changed direction mist came down to obscure the route and at the same time we noticed a lone figure hurrying after us up the glacier. The figure proved to be Lhakpa Tsering, who, as he had not been able to join us yesterday, was now coming straight through from Lake Camp. Leaving some men here whom he could join on the rope, for there were a number of crevasses about, we pushed on through the mist with eyes and ears cocked for anything which might fall from the North Peak so unpleasantly close above us.

By now the snow was rapidly deteriorating, but, as the many big crevasses were adequately bridged, soon after 1 o'clock saw us camped in the middle of the wide snow shelf above the icefall, two or three hundred yards from the foot of the slope leading to the Col. On account of possible avalanches it was advisable to keep as far away as possible from the snow-slopes surrounding us on three sides. The height of this West Side Camp must be about the same as that of Camp II, about 21,500 ft. The afternoon was fine and hot; on the Col snow was still being blown about, and the rocks of the Yellow Band looked deceptively free from snow. The outlook, in fact, was encouraging.

We breakfasted at 5 o'clock and left at 7 o'clock on a bitter cold morning, already chilled to the bone by the inevitable waiting for loads to be adjusted and frozen ropes disentangled. The sky had a curiously dull glassy look against which, to the west, the beautiful Pumori (the 'Daughter Peak' of Mallory) appeared flat as if painted on grey cloth. Smythe and Lloyd went ahead to make the track, the rest of us following on three ropes. As we made our way to the foot of the slope the most phlegmatic might have remarked on the fact that we were walking over the debris cone of the father and mother of all avalanches, the tip of which reached nearly to the camp. This had apparently fallen a few days before—possibly on the day on which I had suggested two of us should descend this way from the Col. One result of this fall was that the first five hundred feet of our route now lay up bare ice, thus entailing much hard work for the leaders step-cutting; and in order to reach snow which was still in place, and which at that early hour, if our pious hopes were fulfilled, might possibly remain in place, a long traverse had to be cut across the ice, in crossing which it was impossible adequately to safeguard the porters. Two of us were roped to the porters, but this was done in the hope of inspiring confidence and not in the expectation of checking a slip. All that one could do really was to urge caution and pray that no slip occurred. Having reached the snow we were faced with about 800 ft. of steep slope; but the snow was of doubtful integrity and of a consistency that gave us plenty of hard work. The appearance of the sun over the Col, warned us of the need for haste, so we pressed on with all the speed we could muster. When we reached the top at 11 o'clock the sun, feeble though it was, had been on the slope for an hour and from its effect on the snow I felt it was high time for us to be off it. It was fortunate that the sun that morning was but a pale reflection of its usual self, for it peered wanly through the glassy sky surrounded by a double halo. Surprisingly enough no abnormal weather followed these alarming portents. Some snow had accumulated round the tents which we had abandoned on 30 May, but nothing had blown away. We re-pitched the dome tent, and four Europeans and sixteen Sherpas (one was left behind sick) were once more in occupation of Camp IV.

6 June dawned fine. As one of the porters had gone sick we had only fifteen available for load carrying, but this was just sufficient if they carried between 25 and 30 lb. Some time was spent making up loads which had to contain all that was required for Camps V and VI; that is to say, tents for two Europeans and seven Sherpas at Camp V, and for two Europeans at Camp VI; sleeping-bags and food for three days for two Europeans and seven Sherpas at Camp V, and sleeping-bags and three days' food for two Europeans at Camp VI. We took two pyramid tents to Camp V. They make heavy and awkward loads but would enable a party to sit out any bad weather in reasonable comfort; a similar type is used in the Arctic where their great advantage is that the four poles have merely to be brought together to enable the tent to be placed on a sledge ready for travelling. Pitching is equally quick and simple, but this is not possible when the tent has to be carried by a man, for then the poles have to be taken out and disjointed.

We finally got away at 10 o'clock to make good progress up board-hard snow. A week ago we had sunk to our knees in the snow of this north ridge, but now it was so hard that a strong kick was needed to make a nick for the edge of the boot. The question of the behaviour of snow at high altitudes is difficult. For example, this hard snow extending up to 25,000 ft. gave us some reason to expect fair snow conditions higher up, but above Camp VI it was loose and soft and apparently quite unaffected by the wind. A variety of factors have to be considered besides the mere force and direction of the wind which may of course vary greatly in different places and at different heights. Mr Seligman, who is an authority on Alpine snow conditions, believes that if some evaporation of snow cannot take place no packing can occur. That is to say, the wind must be dry. Further, the lower the temperature the less easily does snow evaporate so that it is possible that above a certain height temperatures are too low for any evaporation to take place.

Lloyd was wearing the 'open' type oxygen apparatus in which he went well once he had mastered the technique of breathing. Not that he climbed any faster, but perhaps he did so more easily. The hard snow-bed which afforded such excellent going comes to an end at something below 25,000 ft. Here there is a momentary easing of the slope where a party can sit comfortably while it summons up the little energy remaining for the next 800 ft. of mixed scree, rock and snow. Above this two of the men, who were feeling the height, struggled on for only another 100 ft. before giving in altogether. They had to be left where they were together with their loads. Tensing was going very strong, but none of the others seemed at all happy. When still some 300 ft. below the site for Camp V (25,800 ft.) a sudden snowstorm sapped their resolution so much that there was talk of dumping the loads and going down. By now Smythe and Lloyd were nearly up; they must have wondered what Shipton, myself, and the porters, were doing, strung out over the ridge in various attitudes of despair and dejection hurling remarks at one another. In the end better feelings prevailed. All struggled on, and by 4 o'clock reached the fairly commodious snow platform of the Camp V site.

Unluckily one of the two abandoned loads was the second pyramid tent. Consequently, the sole accommodation for two Europeans and seven porters was a small Meade tent (later to go to Camp VI) for the former, and one pyramid which at best would take five Sherpas. The prospect of sleeping seven in a tent made to hold four was bleak, but that of going down and returning next day was worse. Lloyd and I started down with six porters at 4.15 o'clock, but we had not gone far before shouts floated down to us from above. I could not understand what was said, but apparently it was a request to us to bring up the other tent which had been dumped six or seven hundred feet below. The only possible reply to this was the Sherpa equivalent for 'Sez you'; for I do not think that any of our party, had they been willing, were capable of doing it. We carried on, picked up the two sick men, and continued the descent very slowly; for the men were too tired to be hurried and called frequently and successfully for halts by the simple expedient of sitting down. The snow, too, was now very soft. Looking back at one of these halting places I saw, descending from Camp V, two men whom our Sherpas recognized as Pasang and Tensing coming down to retrieve the abandoned loads. To descend and ascend with loads another seven hundred feet, on top of the toil they had already endured, was a remarkable example of unwearying strength and vitality gallantly and unselfishly applied. We reached Camp IV at 6.15 o'clock, pleased at having at length established Camp V. For my part I was very hopeful that something might yet be done. The last entry in my diary for that day runs: 'Frank and Eric going well—think they may do it', which showed how little I knew.

Camp V was established on 6 June; the party's activities in the following days may best be told in Shipton's own words:

On 7 June a heavy wind was blowing from the east; this prevented our advance up the ridge. The weather, however, had been fine for a week, and as there had been a lot of wind we hoped that the snow would be coming off the mountain. The following day was calm and fine. We started at 8 o'clock. The whole party was fit and full of hope that we were going to be granted a chance for an attempt at the summit, which had been denied us for so long. The upper part of the mountain was very white. It had always been presumed that when it presented such an appearance there was little chance of success. But no one had ever climbed far above the North Col during the monsoon, and this idea had been founded on pure conjecture. Conditions on the ridge as far up as Camp V had led us to hope that with the recent fine weather and cold winds the snow on the upper slabs might have consolidated; for now it was clear that at this time of year (on account of the increased humidity) no amount of sun and wind would remove it.

We had not gone far before we found that our hopes were vain. The rocks were deeply covered in snow, which, unlike that below Camp V, showed no tendency to consolidate and was as soft and powdery as it had been when it had fallen about ten days before. The ridge which in 1933 had not caused us the slightest trouble now demanded a lot of very hard work. It was almost unbelievable that such a change could take place on such simple ground. There was one small step that both Smythe and I failed to climb, and we wasted a considerable time making a way round it. It was hard work, too, for the porters, and our progress was lamentably slow. It was 1 o'clock before we reached the site of Norton's and Somervell's old camp at 26,800 ft. The porters worked splendidly and without any complaint. They were determined to put us in the very best position possible from which to make our attempt, and would not listen to any suggestion that they might have difficulty in getting back before nightfall. Previously it has always been rather a question of driving these men to extreme altitudes; now the position was almost reversed. I do not think future expeditions need worry about the establishing of their higher camps provided they choose the best men. Pasang was not well and his comrades went back to help him with his load more than once. Ongdi, too, showed signs of great exhaustion.

At the top of the north-east ridge, we reached at 4.15 o'clock, a gentle scree slope below the Yellow Band. Here we pitched our tent at an altitude of 27,200 ft. I have never seen the Sherpas so tired, and they must have had a hard struggle to get back to Camp V before dark.

The weather was fine, and the sunset over hundreds of miles of monsoon clouds far below was magnificent. But all we wanted to do was to lie quietly down in the drowsy condition which seems to be a permanent state at great altitudes. It was a big effort to cook and eat any supper, and all we could manage that night was a cup of cocoa and a little glucose. I had brought a small book with me against the possibility of a sleepless night. But the meaning of the words kept becoming confused with a half-dream, as when one is reading in bed late at night before going to sleep.

We started cooking breakfast at 3.50 o'clock, and started before the sun had reached the slabs of the Yellow Band. But we were surprised to find the cold was intense. Very soon we had lost all feeling in hands and feet, and it was obvious we were in serious danger of frost-bite. We returned to the tent and waited until the sun had arrived, and then made a second start. Norton's route below the Yellow Band was quite out of the question for there was an enormous deposit of snow on the gently sloping ground. Also conditions in the couloir were obviously hopeless. Our plan was to try to make a diagonal traverse up to the ridge which we hoped to reach just before the First Step. At best it was a forlorn hope, for the ridge in any condition must be a tough obstacle, and it now looked really villainous. The only chance lay in the remote possibility that some unexpected effect of wind and sun at these little-explored altitudes had produced firm snow on the steep slabs and on the ridge.

We started flogging our way up the steep ground, through powder snow, into which we sank up to our hips. An hour's exhausting work yielded little more than a rope's length of progress, even on the easy beginning on the slabs. We went on until, on the steeper ground, we were in obvious danger of being swept off the rocks by a snow avalanche. Then we returned, completely convinced of the hopelessness of the task. It was bitterly disappointing, as we were both far fitter at these altitudes than we had been in 1933, and the glittering summit looked tauntingly near.

There can be no doubt that one day someone will reach the top of Everest, and probably he will reach it quite easily, but to do so he must have good conditions and fine weather, a combination which we now realize is much more rare than had been supposed by the pioneers on the mountain. It is difficult to give the layman much idea of the actual physical difficulties of the last 2,000 ft. of Everest. The Alpine mountaineer can visualize them when he is told that the slabs which we are trying to climb are very similar to those on the Tiefenmatten face of the Matterhorn, and he will know that though these slabs are easy enough when clear of ice and snow they can be desperately difficult when covered in deep powder snow. He should also remember that a climber on the upper part of Everest is like a sick man climbing in a dream.

So much for the first attempt made this year, if indeed attempt is the right word; for neither of the parties which started out from Camp VI this year was under any illusions regarding the possibility of reaching the summit. A more accurate description of the final stages of this year's expedition would be that a brief inspection of the conditions above Camp VI satisfied both parties that reaching the summit was then an impossibility. And, as Shipton says, this was the more disappointing because both he and Smythe were feeling strong enough to justify some confidence in the result had conditions been favourable. This point needs stressing in view of the argument sometimes brought forward that small party methods impose too much strain on those taking part.

CHAPTER NINE

Attempt to Reach Summit Ridge

How pitiable is he who cannot excuse himself.

DOWN at Camp IV on 7 June we were almost as inactive as the party at Camp V—but with less reason, for here there was no wind and the day was fine. The temperature at night outside the tent had been 5° F. We rose late, and after a leisurely breakfast Lloyd put on the 'closed' type oxygen apparatus and started to walk towards the foot of the north ridge. I watched with interest and soon saw that all was not well. When he was about 200 yards from camp he sat down, took it off, and came back. The feelings of suffocation which he experienced were exactly similar to Warren's. I put the thing on for myself for a few minutes and executed a light fandango in the snow with such remarkable feelings of sprightliness that I resolved to give it a proper trial. I regret to say that this resolution, like so many others made at high altitudes, was not kept; but there is no reason to believe that my experience would have differed from that of Warren or Lloyd who had both given that apparatus a fair trial. They could find no mechanical defects at the time, but whatever faults may have since been detected, and whether or no they can be remedied, I think the most obvious lesson to be learnt is that the only trials and experiments of any value at all are those carried out by mountaineers themselves at heights of over 23,000 ft., but not necessarily on Mount Everest.

We were up very early on 8 June in order to take three sick men down to the West Side Camp; they were not exactly sick but were incapable of acclimatizing sufficiently to go higher. Therefore they were better out of the way. As Lloyd and I had to return it was important to start early in order to have safe snow conditions on the way back. The men's own sleeping-bags were down at the West Side Camp; for use on the Col we had a common stock of high-altitude sleeping-bags for every one which were of course much warmer than the ordinary bags. When these three worthies heard that no sleeping-bags were to be taken down they became recalcitrant and refused to go, but as it was too early in the morning, and too cold, for argument, we tied them on to the rope and started off. We were fortunate that the temperature during the night had fallen to 5° F., consequently the snow was in such excellent condition—firm but not too hard—that we descended the snow slope in half an hour. While I belayed the party so far as any satisfactory belay was possible on the ice, Lloyd recut the steps across the traverse. Once across that we left the men to look after themselves for the short and safe remaining distance down to the tent left there, while we returned to the Col reaching it at 9 o'clock. Although the sun had not yet touched the slopes, the crust which had supported us going down now began to break under our feet. For the rest of the day a mist which enveloped the Col prevented us from seeing what the Camp V party were doing.

Next day, 9 June, saw us moving up to Camp V in accordance with a prearranged programme. We took with us six porters lightly laden with a little extra food and five oxygen cylinders. Lloyd again wore the 'open' oxygen apparatus while I was without. Thus we constituted rather a hybrid party but such a party might function quite well for an attempt on the summit. The reason that I was without was not solely one of high principles or an intolerant scorn for the use of oxygen apparatus, but because if we were to use it all the way, as Lloyd intended, then there would not be enough cylinders to supply the two of us.

As we began the ascent of the north ridge we saw the rear party—Odell, Warren, Oliver—accompanied by two Sherpas coming up from West Side Camp. They had crossed the traverse, but as we could not afford the time to wait and exchange news we continued on our way. A little later we met the seven men coming down from Camp V, very tired; their names were: Ongdi Nurbu ('Ashang'), Pasang Bhotia, Rinsing, Tensing, Lhakpa Tsering, Da Tsering, Lobsang. About this time Shipton and Smythe must have been leaving Camp VI, so altogether the mountain presented such a scene of activity that morning that it reminded one of Snowdon on a Bank Holiday. On reaching the top of the snow slope one of our men, whose cough was troubling him, dropped out, but the rest of us reached Camp V at 3 o'clock almost simultaneously with the arrival of Shipton and Smythe from above. Their report of conditions up there effectually quenched any hopes we may have entertained of reaching the summit. A valuable plan was to investigate the possibilities of the north-east or summit ridge, and, if we could reach it, to have a look especially at the Second Step. In any case, with such snow conditions, the ridge was undoubtedly a safer place than the slabs.

After some tea and talk they went down, taking with them three of our porters. Kusang Namgyal and Phur Tempa stayed with us; the former needed no prompting, electing to stay as of right and privilege, but some persuasion was required before one of the other four volunteered. It is of course a matter for wonder, no less than thankfulness, how much these men will do and how far they will go with, one imagines, few of the incentives which act as a spur to us. There is, as Shipton remarks in the passage I have quoted, no longer any need to drive them to go high if care is taken to pick only the best. It was not always thus. Amongst other factors which have brought about this change, and to which we are chiefly indebted, are the care, sympathy and mountaineering skill, with which the porters of earlier Everest expeditions have been handled. The value of the confidence which a leader and his party now derive from the knowledge that the porters will carry a camp as high as need be cannot be over-estimated.

We slept little if at all that night. We were warm enough, in spite of having only the tent floor between our sleeping-bags and the snow, but from sunset until four in the morning it blew so hard that the noise made by the flapping of the double-skinned pyramid tent kept us awake. The night temperature was

$-1°$ F. We got away soon after 8 o'clock with Kusang and Phur Tempa carrying between them two oxygen cylinders and the little extra kit and food we needed. Camp VI was already provisioned and equipped with sleeping gear. With snow lying everywhere the climbing for the first thousand feet was not easy, and the tracks of the first party had for the most part been filled by the wind. Lloyd went ahead making the track while I followed roped to the two porters. Although it was naturally harder work making the route, Lloyd reached the camp some half an hour before us, and, by the time we arrived, had re-erected the small Meade tent which the others had struck for the sake of safety. As was to be expected the higher we went the more benefit he felt from the oxygen. On the other hand, I was roped to the two laden porters, and though at this distance of time I like to think I was accommodating my pace to theirs I should not like to have to take my oath upon it. For the short distance we went next day he again went better than I did, but perhaps under the circumstances that is not such a valuable testimonial for the oxygen apparatus as it might seem. It is conceivable that a better man, or a man who had had less sickness during the previous month, might have gone as well as or better than Lloyd, who, it must be remembered, was carrying a load of 25 lb. I am inclined to think that any benefit likely to be obtained from the use of oxygen is cancelled by the weight of the apparatus. But this may not always be the case—a very much lighter apparatus is probably only a matter of time. It is well known that the effect of great altitudes is to sap not only the powers of the body but also of the mind. To say that the resolution of every man who goes high is thereby weakened to some extent would be too sweeping, but the will, or even the urge, to ascend and to overcome the difficulties standing in his way, which is the instinctive feeling of every mountaineer, is less strong than at lower levels. What I did rather hope and expect, therefore, was that the revivifying effect of oxygen might be sufficient to overcome this disquieting tendency, and that a few whiffs of oxygen would boost Lloyd up those rocks which next day so easily defeated us—and of course would enable him to pull me up too. But, as will be seen, there was no such effect; oxygenated and unoxygenated man acquiesced tamely in defeat.

Shortly before reaching the 1924 camp site (26,800 ft.) we untied the rope as here there was little likelihood of a slip having any serious consequences; but it was needed again on the smooth slabs just below the tent, which a covering of snow made very awkward indeed. At the top of these slabs the angle eased off, and a gentle slope of small scree, almost free from snow, continued for nearly a hundred yards up to the foot of a steep rock wall. For thirty or forty feet this wall was very steep—steep enough that is to necessitate the use of the hands—until the angle eased off where broken slabby rock led to the north-east shoulder (27,500 ft.) and the summit ridge, about 300 ft. above our camp. Fifty yards to the left (east) of the scree patch the north ridge fell away steeply to the big snow couloir which has its origin almost directly below the shoulder. On the right (west) at the same level a wide bed of snow ran up to the foot of the heavily snow-covered rocks of the Yellow Band, the wide band of light-coloured rock running almost horizontally across the face of the mountain. The whole face looked steeper and more formidable than I had imagined. We had placed Camp VI two or three hundred yards to the east of and about 200 ft. below the 1933 camp site owing to the impossibility of getting there. Ours was less advantageously placed for making an attempt, but otherwise it is probably the best site on the mountain; reasonably flat, and, even at this time, free from snow except for a little hard patch close to the tent from which we drew our supply for cooking.

We were all up by 12.30 o'clock. Having sent the men down we collected snow for cooking and turned in, for the wind was already rising. It blew all afternoon and continued for most of the night, so that again we slept little. For supper that evening we each had the best part of a pint mug of hot pemmican soup which we swallowed with equanimity if not with gusto; nor did I think it was this, and not the wind, which accounted for the rather miserable sleepless night which followed. To drink a cup of pemmican soup is very well, and to do it at that height is indeed a triumph of mind over matter; but the whole cupful does not amount to more than 4 oz. of food. This was probably more than half of our total food intake for that day which again was only a quarter of the amount considered necessary for men doing hard work. Pemmican and sugar have high calorific values—the former the highest of any food—but to provide the requisite number of calories, supposing only these two foods were taken, one would have to consume ½ lb. of pemmican followed by 1 lb. of sugar which would at any rate help to keep it down. Perhaps this could be accomplished easily enough in the course of a day; but how many pounds of caviare, quails in aspic, chicken essence, sweet biscuits, jam, dried fruit, tinned fruit, pickles, and other things beloved of those who believe this high-altitude food problem could be solved by the tempting of the appetite, would be required to do the same? In many counsellors there may be wisdom, but in many foods there is neither sense, nourishment, nor digestibility. There are several foods still to be tried out, but I believe the fact will have to be faced that at these altitudes it is impossible to eat very much and that one will have to be satisfied with eating as much as one can of some food of high value, even if not very palatable, rather than pecking at kickshaws. In spite of having been inhaling oxygen for most of the day Lloyd had no more appetite than I had, but perhaps he ought to have taken alternate sucks at his mug of pemmican and his tube of oxygen. Proverbially difficult though it is to blow and swallow at the same time, no doubt in the near future some genius will produce an apparatus which will make possible the assimilation of oxygen and food simultaneously.

We rose early on the 11th; not so much because we were panting to be off, like hounds straining at the leash, but because being up would be less wretched than trying to sleep. To say that we rose conveys a wrong impression; we did nothing so violent, but merely gave up the pretence of trying to sleep by assuming a slightly less recumbent position. Then one of us had to take a more extreme step—sitting up, and reaching out for the stove; and for the saucepan full of snow, waiting in readiness at the other end of the tent. Once the stove was lit an irrevocable step had been taken, for it had to be tended. But once lit it burnt well considering that it was labouring under the same difficulty as ourselves, anoxaemia—not so well, however, that one could afford to leave it to its own devices and pretend to go to sleep again. Occasionally it would splutter, which was the signal for going out altogether, or for a long tongue of flame to lick the roof of the tent playfully—an emergency calling for some deft work with a pricker and a match until it was burning normally again. In the course of half an hour or so the lifting of the saucepan lid reveals no merrily bubbling water, but a murky pool of slush or half-melted snow, its surface coated with the remains of last night's pemmican. Feelings of impatience for a hot drink and thankfulness for further respite in bed are mingled equally. If patience is bitter, its fruit is sweet. Presently the water bubbles feebly and breakfast is served—a mug of tea, not completely valueless as it contains a good quarter pound of sugar, a few biscuits, and possibly a fig. None of us has been able to face porridge above Camp III, nor is there time for making both porridge and tea.

By morning the gale of the night had died away, but it was not until 8 o'clock that we considered it warm enough to make a start. (All times given, by the way, are relative and not absolute. It was 8 o'clock by my watch, but by the sun it might have been 7 or 9 o'clock.) While waiting we dressed by putting on wind-proofs, and boots which had been kept more or less unfrozen in our sleeping-bags. The sun was still below the ridge but the morning was fine and calm except for what appeared to be a gentle zephyr from the west. In reality it may have been blowing hard for I suppose if the atmospheric pressure is only one-third of normal, wind strength is also reduced. On our arrival the previous afternoon I cannot say that the rock wall which we proposed climbing as the most direct way to the summit ridge had made a very good impression. Like boxers confidently announcing their victory on the eve of a fight we told each other it would 'go', comforting ourselves privately with the thought that rocks sometimes look worse than closer acquaintance proved them to be. But now, in the cold light of morning, as they looked still less prepossessing we decided not to waste time but to turn the wall on the right where it merged into the easier angle of the face, and where a shallow depression filled with snow led diagonally upwards to the summit ridge. As we moved slowly up the scree towards the right-hand end of the wall I kept changing my axe from one hand to the other thinking it was that which was making them so cold. But before we had been going ten minutes they were numb and I then began to realize that the gentle zephyr from the west was about the coldest blast of animosity I had ever encountered. I mentioned the state of my hands to Lloyd who replied that his feet were feeling very much the same. We returned to the tent to wait until it was warmer.

We made a second brew of tea and started again about 10 o'clock by which time the sun had cleared the ridge, although it was not blazing with the extraordinary effulgence we should have welcomed. In fact at these heights the only power which the sun seems capable of exerting is that of producing snow-blindness. It was still very cold, but bearable. We skirted the snow lying piled at the foot of the wall and took a few steps along our proposed route, where Lloyd, who was in front, sank thigh-deep into the snow. I believe it was somewhere about there that Shipton and Smythe had tried. Without more ado we returned to the rocks. There seemed to be three or four possible ways up, but first we tried my favoured line of which Lloyd did not think very highly. It was one of those places which look so easy but which, through an absence of anything to lay hold of, is not. I did not get very far. A similar place was tried with like result and then we moved off to the left to see if there was any way round. This brought us to the extreme edge of the north ridge where it drops steeply to the gully coming down from the north-east shoulder. There was no way for us there. Retracing our steps along the foot of the wall Lloyd had a shot at my place which he now thought was our best chance; but he too failed. It was not really difficult; at least looking back at it now from the security of an armchair, that is my impression, but the smooth, outward-sloping rocks, covered in part by snow, very easily withstood our half-hearted efforts. I then started up another place which I think would have 'gone', although the first step did require a 'shoulder'. Very inopportunely, while I was examining this our last hope, there was a hail from below and we saw Angtharkay, presently to be followed by Nukku, topping the slabs just below the tent. I had left word for him to come up with the oxygen load abandoned by the porter who had failed to reach Camp V with us. We wanted to have a word with him, and of course to go down to the tent was a direct invitation to go down altogether—a course which I am sorry to say was followed without any demur.

It will be a lasting regret that we never even reached the summit ridge, but I think the information we would have brought back had we reached it would have been mostly of negative value. From the point we were trying to reach close to the north-east shoulder, the Second Step is about 1,200 yd. distant; the summit itself is a mile away, and 1,500 ft. higher. The ridge, on which there was plenty of snow, did not look easy, while the Second Step looked really formidable; so much so that the only chance seemed to lie in the possibility of making a turning movement on the south face, which of course we could not see. The only reason for preferring the ridge route to Norton's Traverse would seem to be when there is snow about; but since under such conditions the ridge itself is not easily attainable little remains to be said for it as an alternative route.

We descended to Camp V in a storm of snow and wind which made the finding of the best route a matter of difficulty. Kusang and Phur Tempa were still in residence. After some tea and an hour's rest we started again at 4 o'clock for the Col. The Sherpas were roped together, while we went ahead making a track for them down the snow; but they went so slowly that we had constantly to wait for them. The storm had blown itself out and the evening was now calm and fine, so near the bottom we pushed on ahead leaving them to follow at their leisure. Amongst the crevasses at the foot of the ridge, where the storm had obliterated all old tracks, we had a discussion, about the right route, which threatened to be interminable until Lloyd settled the matter, or at any rate pointed out the wrong route, by falling into one; thus bringing an inglorious day to its appropriate conclusion. As we were unroped at the time, this slight mishap will possibly evoke neither surprise nor sympathy. In response to my inquiries a muffled cry from below assured me that he was unhurt and had not fallen very far; but as nothing could be done until the porters arrived with the rope, I had to leave the victim down there for a good ten minutes—possibly penitent, certainly cold. It should never happen, but if one does fall into a crevasse in free unfettered fashion (I speak from experience), as one does if the rope is not being worn, it is a question which feeling predominates—surprise, fear, or disgust at having been such an ass. I could see the Sherpas up the ridge and they could see me, but they neither heard my shouts nor took any notice of my gesticulations except to sit down once again and ponder at this new form of madness. At length one of them, who was possibly a better arithmetician than the others, must have totted up the number of Europeans who had left Camp V that afternoon and discovered that there was one short. Down they came, and Lloyd was hauled out none the worse.

Only Odell, Oliver and seven porters remained at Camp IV as the others had gone down that morning by the old route to Camp III. Warren was obliged to go too in order to look after Ongdi who on his return from Camp VI had suddenly developed pneumonia; at least the symptoms pointed to pneumonia, but his recovery was so speedy that it may not have been. They went down by the old route because for a sick man that was the easier. Another Camp VI man, Pasang Bhotia, was lying there alone in a tent, sick. The first report was that he had gone mad for he was unable to articulate, but it soon became clear that his right side was completely paralysed and he was therefore incapable of movement. They had attempted to take him down that morning, but two sick men in one party were too many. The other Sherpas seemed rather to wish to shun him than to assist him in his piteous plight; he could neither dress himself, put on his boots, feed himself, talk, get out of his tent, nor even out of his sleeping-bag. They regarded this misfortune as a judgement, either on him or on the whole party, for supplicating too perfunctorily the gods of the mountain.

With this sick man on our hands, with some anxiety about the safeness of the descent, and since there was now no hope of climbing the mountain and the weather was not improving, we decided on the prudent course of going down. Oliver was keen to go to Camp VI, more for the sake of treading classic ground than for any good he could do. I sympathized, and was sorry to disappoint him, for dull indeed must be the man whose imagination does not quicken at the thought of treading that ground which in its short history of sixteen years has been the scene of so much high, even tragic endeavour. A well-known passage of Dr Johnson comes to mind, though it seems almost impertinent to quote it in connexion with what is after all only a series of attempts to climb a high mountain:

To abstract the mind from all local emotion would be impossible if it were endeavoured, and would be foolish if it were possible. Whatever withdraws us from the power of our senses, whatever makes the past, the distant, or the future predominate over the present, advances us in dignity of thinking beings. Far from me and from my friends be such frigid philosophy as may conduct us indifferent and unmoved over any ground which has been dignified by wisdom, bravery, or virtue. That man is little to be envied whose patriotism would not gain force upon the plain of Marathon or whose piety would not grow warmer among the ruins of Iona.

CHAPTER TEN

Last Days and Reflections

'I cannot imagine any place less suitable to choose than the high mountains,
wherein to display the mastery of mankind.'   Julius Kugy

On 12 June, therefore, taking as much as we could carry, we went down by the old route. There was a traverse to be crossed on either side, but that on the western route was across ice which made the lowering of a helpless man impossible. I kept back three good men, Angtharkay, Kusang and Nukku, to help with Pasang, whose rescue, as he lay there impassive on the snow, unable to crawl, much less stand, seemed likely to prove an exacting task. The first two of these, with Pasang himself, had in 1934 comprised the happiest, friendliest, and staunchest trio with whom I have ever travelled, so it was therefore the more startling when, after some futile attempts to construct a stretcher from tent poles, they calmly suggested leaving him where he was. As they saw it, the mountain claimed a victim, and if we cheated it of Pasang then some other member of the party would be taken; for choice one of those who had taken pains to bilk the mountain of its due. My indignant splutterings were probably incoherent, but the dullest-witted must have quickly grasped the fact that the suggestion was unacceptable. Taking it in turns they carried him pick-a-back through the soft snow along the crest of the Col to the point where our fixed ropes descended. There we treated him as we did our loads, tying a bow-line round the unfortunate man's chest and lowering him down to the beginning of the traverse. Crossing this was not so simple, but Nukku, who is very strong, hung on to the fixed rope with one hand, and dragged Pasang along by the feet with the other while I supported his body with another rope from above. For the rest of the way we lowered him rope's length by rope's length, dragging him where the slope was not steep enough for him to slide down by his own weight. In this fashion by midday we reached the glacier where the rest of the party were waiting. By shouting from the Col, Angtharkay had persuaded two men to come up from Camp III to help. It is to be feared poor Pasang had had a very rough passage, for his clothes were of course sopping wet, and he was half dead with cold. Now, however, he could be seated on an ice-axe which the Sherpas carried in turns by a head-strap and we soon had him in bed at Camp III.

Shipton and Smythe were waiting there, the former having now almost lost his voice since his trip up the mountain. Among the porters, Tensing too had lost his voice, but Ongdi was much better and well on the road to recovery thanks to Warren's care and the oxygen. I remember we had a heated argument that afternoon, lying about in the sun, on the ethics of the use of oxygen for other than medicinal purposes. Next day we went down to Camp I. There was some trouble getting men to take their turns carrying Pasang until the job was organized systematically and a roster devised by which each man carried him for five minutes at a time. It was a heart-breaking job that anybody would have been glad to shirk. The glacier stream was by now high, but fortunately a snow bridge was still just standing above camp. Although we reached Rongbuk on the 14th we had to stay there until the 20th waiting for the small amount of transport necessary for ourselves and our belongings. After a rest the Sherpas were employed in bringing down what they could of the stuff still lying at Camp III and West Side Camp. Most of this was left in the keeping of the monastery as it is seldom worth the cost of bringing back for the use of some problematical future expedition. Whatever is on the mountain is best left there; for it is not worth risking men's lives for the sake of tents and sleeping-bags, valuable though these are.

We discussed the question of waiting or returning in the autumn, but the discussion was largely academic as only Shipton and myself were available and as far as I was concerned there was a great deal to be done in winding up the affairs of the expedition. It might have been possible to go back to India and return later, but for such a step the approval of the Tibetan authorities would be necessary. The general opinion was that the chances of finding favourable conditions in October or November are extremely remote. The fact is not known, but assuming that winds strong and dry enough to remove the snow from the upper rocks are then blowing, there is no reason to expect any such lull as there is before the approach of the monsoon. Moreover, the wind and cold would be increasing rather than diminishing; the days becoming shorter; and, perhaps most significant, the north face receiving less and less sun. Length of daylight and warmth are both vital factors in the final climb, and Smythe's opinion is that unless there is sun on the face climbing is impossible on account of the cold.

Before leaving I wished to improve our relations with the steward of the monastery. As a result of the theft of money which took place while we were on the mountain, these were at present slightly strained. The steward had put at our disposal a room in the courtyard in which we had placed our surplus stores, including one of our cash-boxes, containing Rs. 800, enclosed inside another box. Few knew it was there, but to anyone who knew what to look for the theft presented little difficulty, so that one morning Karma Paul discovered the box broken open and the cash-box missing. He naturally complained at once to the monastery, but unfortunately gave them to understand that in his opinion the thief was one of themselves—a charge which made the steward justifiably angry. However, for a small fee, a great ceremony called 'kangso' was held in which, I gather, the thief is solemnly abjured to return the stolen goods or suffer penalties. It is a sort of comprehensive cursing or excommunication—readers of *Tristram Shandy* will remember the appalling Ernulplus' curse recited by Dr Slop while Uncle Toby whistled 'Lilliburlero'. Equally terrific was this Rongbuk cursing, for a day or two later Karma Paul found the broken cash-box lying outside his tent with half the missing money. Why only half the money was returned I fail to understand, unless the thief reasoned as many people do when going through the Customs, that the declaring of only a few of the dutiable articles carried will at the same time satisfy their consciences and the curiosity of the officials. After accepting the offer of a room in which to store our things it was tactless, to say the least of it, to place the responsibility for our loss upon the monastery officials; but having assured the steward, verbally and in writing, that our interpreter's suspicions were unworthy of him and were certainly not shared by me, good feeling was restored.

The abbot invited the whole party to a meal, adding a special request that we should be merry. Although we had throughout enjoyed a sufficiency of plain wholesome food we were naturally hungry after our recent exertions and the business of eating was taken so seriously that it was not until after the seventh, or possibly eighth, bowl of macaroni stew that we remembered our host's injunction. The abbot himself dropped a hint by saying he had heard that we occasionally sang and would we mind obliging now. In fact we were not a very musical party that year and seldom gave tongue unless warmed by 'chang', but as nothing of that kind is allowed in the monastery we had to do our best in cold blood, and, which was worse, on full stomachs. Moreover, Shipton had just lost his voice and mine had not yet fully returned. By request our first number was a hymn. That was easy. I forget what it was; possibly that old favourite: 'No matter where it leads me, the downward path for me.' But then we were asked to put the mystic formula or invocation 'Om Mane Padme Hum' into lyric form. With a little adaptation we found it went very well to the tune of 'God Save the King', and we received many encores.

When our audience—a large concourse of monks and Sherpas—had suffered sufficiently for politeness, we turned to conversation which took the form of question and answer conducted through the medium of Karma Paul the interpreter. First of all we had to disabuse the minds of our hosts that expeditions to climb Mount Everest are undertaken at the instigation of and assisted by the British Government for the sake of national prestige. We assured them that this was not so and explained that Mount Everest, supreme though it was, was not the only mountain we tried to climb; that we belonged to a small but select cult who regarded a Himalayan expedition as a means of acquiring merit, beneficial to soul and body, and equivalent to entering a monastery except that the period of renunciation was short and that such admirable macaroni stew as was served in monasteries was seldom available.

Odell, who as a member of the 1924 expedition was particularly interested, then asked who had destroyed the big cairn erected at the Base Camp in memory of those who had died on the mountain that year. The abbot disclaimed all responsibility on the part of the monastery and suggested that the culprits were the 'Abominable Snowmen'. This reply staggered me, for though I had an open mind on the matter I was not prepared to hear it treated so lightheartedly in that of all places. I was shocked to think that this apparently jesting reply, accompanied as it was by a chuckle from the abbot and a loud laugh from the assembled monks, indicated a disbelief in the existence of the 'Abominable Snowman'. Such an answer in such a place, if not intended seriously, was flat blasphemy. I was soon reassured. Tibetans, like others whose beliefs are steadfast and have never been questioned, are able to treat their most sacrosanct beliefs with a frank gaiety which the outsider would deem profane. Further questioning showed clearly that no jest was intended, and we were told that at least five of these strange creatures lived up near the snout of the glacier and were often heard at night. Indeed, on one occasion some monks actually saw them. Terror-stricken, they fled to the monastery where they lay unconscious for several days—a misfortune which the sceptics among us attributed to the unwise exertion of running at high altitudes. Later we were taken over the monastery where we watched an artist painting a 'thank-ka' (temple banner) while his assistant ground a white stone into powder for paint, and finally we were conducted into the innermost shrines including that reserved for the devotions of the abbot himself. In one of these was a large lump of greenish-black rock, probably crystalline, measuring about 18 in. cube and weighing perhaps ½ cwt. On its smooth flat surface was the very clear impression of a large human foot. It was said to have been found in the vicinity of Camp I and was evidently regarded with some awe. The imprint appeared to be genuine enough and the fact that the stone was kept in one of the innermost shrines and not exposed to the admiration of the vulgar seemed to rule out the likelihood of its having been carved by hand.

Now Odell, who was with me, is a geologist of some standing, so with my childlike faith in the omniscience of scientists I turned confidently to him for the answer to the enigma. How, when, and where, did the stone receive this remarkable impress, and who made it? The Oracle was dumb and spake not. Not so much as a few technical words about the stone itself, about igneous rock intrusive in calc-gneisses, cretaceous eocene limestones, or compressed synclines caught up in folded Jurassic schists, and the rest of the jargon with which the geological pundit baffles and dumbfounds the humble inquirer. Not even the usual tantalizing ambiguous couplet beloved of Oracles which I myself could have supplied at a pinch had I been asked, as for example:

> Whoever trod upon this stone,
> Was a thing of flesh and bone,
> If you will any further know,
> The secret's hidden in the snow.

Having been found in the moraine near Camp I the stone must have been brought down by the glacier and deposited there at some very distant date. We know for a fact that no Tibetans ever traverse the glaciers, least of all the Rongbuk which leads nowhere and which owing to its proximity to Mount Everest they regard with special awe, and we are driven to associating this footprint in some way with people whose habitat is above the snow-line, in other words the 'Abominable Snowmen'. But I will not press the argument. A scientific friend (for I am not without them) points out that the footprint was probably fossilized and may have been made at a recent date in the geological time scale—the middle tertiary—when the northern part of the Himalaya and most of Tibet were covered by a great sea, called by geologists the 'Tethys Sea', in which deposition of sediment had continued for ages. And there the matter must rest until some future visitor to Rongbuk shall tell us whether the stone in question is crystalline or sedimentary. In the Himalaya any strange footprint inevitably gives rise to a certain train of thought, and this print is one of the strangest. Since the subject is one of interest to scientists, and since no book on Mount Everest is complete without appendixes, I have collected all the available evidence, old and new, and relegated it to the decent obscurity of Appendix B[1].

As his leave was up Oliver left ahead of us on the 17th. On the 20th the rest of us began the march back—impatient of delay, disappointed at what had been accomplished, but satisfied that the expedition had not been without its lessons. Of these I think the most important was to show that a small expedition, of seven or even fewer, costing less than £2,500, has as good a chance of climbing the mountain as one of a dozen members costing £10,000 or more. Expense, of course, is not an absolute criterion. But we live in a commercial age and as a measure of relative efficiency, when the accomplishment has been very nearly equal, it is a fair yardstick. This modest claim that such an expedition stands at least an equal chance will be substantiated by members of the party who agreed that the methods employed were sound; but I like to think that enough was done to convince all who are interested in these matters. At any rate mountaineers will not dispute that such methods, if they can be employed, are preferable and more in accord with mountaineering tradition and practice. In spite of very unfavourable conditions two parties of two—a third could have been sent up had conditions warranted—were put in position to make a bid for the summit. Nor were these men weak or worn out through overwork and rough living. No hardships had to be endured through inadequate equipment or insufficient food. The coughs, colds, sore throats and influenza which troubled us also troubled those expeditions equipped and fed in a comparatively luxurious way regardless of expense. As Mr Shipton says of the attempt by Mr Smythe and himself: 'It was bitterly disappointing, for we were both far fitter at these altitudes than we had been in 1933, and the glittering summit looked tauntingly near.' And again, in a discussion at the Royal Geographical Society[1] subsequent to the expedition he said: 'As regards the health of the expedition, I am convinced that the party kept far fitter than in 1933, when two members were confined to their beds with 'flu for a fortnight, one other was sent to Kharta with bronchitis, another was incapacitated for months with a gastric ulcer, and we all suffered more or less severely from laryngitis, colds, etc. No party has ever been at full strength on Everest.'

Of course the organization was not perfect. Some thought that the process of rigorous economy had been carried too far, others that it had not gone far enough. Unanimity in the matter of food, for example, is no more to be expected among seven members of an expedition than it is among seven members of a family. Some grumbles were heard, but more can be heard in the dining saloon in any passenger ship where the choice of food is as bewildering to the mind as its assimilation is to the stomach. Those who have experienced or read about the large expedition (whose members are often free of any financial concern in it) have a different scale of values from those who have not. The necessity of one man becomes the luxury of another, but

1 *Geographical Journal*, 1938, pp. 490–98.

with a little give and take a suitable compromise can generally be reached. For instance, if a man expects to have a choice of three or four kinds of marmalade for breakfast it is a disagreeable surprise to find none at all. The important thing is to keep firmly in mind the essentials, and then to make a few, very few, concessions to human frailty; not, as is often done, to include in the expedition stores everything which might conceivably at some time be wanted by somebody—a process which is often undeservedly called thorough organization. The French Revolutionary armies, destitute of most things needful and with twisted hay-ropes for boots, might justifiably think or even hint that their equipment was in some respects deficient; but the Convention Representative with the army (the Political Commissar of those days) was deaf to complaints of that sort and met them with the laconic remark: 'With steel and bread one may get to China.' I do not mean to suggest that with pemmican and an ice-axe one can get to the top of Everest, but a touch of this spirit is not amiss in the organizer of any expedition and will form a wholesome corrective to any tendency to over-equipping and over-feeding. Mr R. L. G. Irving maintains this view: 'And do we destroy nothing by using all this mass of men and material to conquer Everest?' he asks; Mallory, after a catalogue extending to some forty lines of the various items in the vast collection of stores and equipment carried across Tibet, concludes: 'When I call to mind the whole begoggled crowd moving with slow determination over the snow and up the mountain slopes, and with such remarkable persistence bearing up the formidable loads; when after the lapse of months I envisage the whole prodigious evidence of this vast intention, how can I help rejoicing in the yet undimmed splendour, the undiminished glory, the unconquered supremacy of Mount Everest?' And what mountaineer would not agree with Mallory if the mountain is only to be won by the skilful use of material carried to the nth power? Mr Irving adds: 'Everest will be conquered by just the very thing in which the present age excels, the skill to use the material things that nature has provided.' Let us hope he will be proved wrong; the 1938 expedition will have served a useful purpose if it has done nothing more than show that this need not be so.

Apart from unnecessary elaboration of food and equipment there are, amongst the material resources now used in Himalayan mountaineering, more baleful things, like aeroplanes, wireless, and oxygen apparatus. For some years past aeroplanes have been used in Alaska for carrying men and stores to a base, and enabling a reconnaissance to be made in a few hours instead of a whole season, the time required by older methods of transport. There, the great distances, the shortness of the season, and the absence of any porters, are at least reasons if not excuses for using a method which takes account solely of the end to be attained—the rapid subjugation of some peak. It is akin to the use of cars and lorries by shooting safaris in Africa; at first they were actually used for shooting from because it was so much easier to approach the game; but as public opinion was sufficiently strong to stop this they are now merely used to convey the party to its ground, and to make sure that the members derive neither enjoyment nor benefit from their short excursion into the wilds. In 1938 an aeroplane was used in the Himalaya to drop loads near camps on Nanga Parbat. The success may not have been great but the technique will soon be improved; indeed, I can safely say has been improved, for during the war the dropping of supplies to inaccessible places, even by night or in mist, was brought to a high state of perfection. Doubtless some of our most progressive thinkers are already toying with the idea of dropping men as well somewhere near the summit. As a dropping ground the north face of Everest leaves something to be desired, but I can imagine it being done on a mountain like Nanga Parbat with some degree of safety. Still, it will probably be found safer and quicker to climb there in the end, and if we must move with the time then we must give up mountaineering, or at least cease calling what we do mountaineering, for when such adventitious aids are used that it certainly is not. If our end is just to plant a man on top of the mountain then I suppose any means are justified, but if our end is mountaineering in the true sense then we should stick to the rules. All's fair in war and the habit of talking of the assault and conquest of a peak may lead us to think that the same holds good for mountaineering and that mountains are foes to be subdued rather than friends to be won. There is a good case for dropping bombs on civilians because so very few of them can be described as inoffensive, but mountains can claim the rights of 'open towns' and our self-respect should restrain us from dropping on them tents, tins, or possibly men.

Then with regard to wireless it may be thought that a foolish prejudice against it by one holding old-fashioned views robbed the party of a possible chance through their ignorance of weather changes. Such was not the case; nor, I think, will it be for some time. Mountains, particulary the big Himalayan peaks, make their own weather, and at present the wireless forecasts are based on weather conditions prevailing hundreds of miles away from the Himalaya. Dr Sen, of the Indian Meteorological Department, thinks that even with the meagre information at present available it should be possible by February of any year to foresee any exceptional acceleration or retardation of the advance of the monsoon. Such information would of course be useful, but Everest is a special case. It is not possible to wait until February to decide whether an expedition will take place or not. If permission is received for a particular year the expedition must go that year, and if it knows that the monsoon will probably be early then it merely knows that its chances are greatly diminished, for the weather will probably be too cold to do anything beforehand. But this is rather different from the expectation of basing climbing plans upon weather forecasts when actually on the mountain. A German party on Nanga Parbat in the same year had wireless and were defeated by the weather at 23,800 ft.; an American party without wireless, climbing on the difficult and less well-known peak of K 2 only 120 miles away, reached a height of 26,000 ft. in perfect weather.

Knowledge of the onset and progress of the monsoon is of interest but it is not enough. The phenomena known as 'western disturbances' seem to be what usually upset the apple cart. If a succession of these are encountered from early May onward then the attempt can be written off, be the monsoon early or late. On 30 April 1936 and on 5 May 1938 one such storm turned the mountain white and in neither year was it ever again in climbable condition.

One has only to read Mr Ruttledge's account of what happened in 1936 to realize how useless are weather forecasts to the leader. On 30 April, three weeks before the schedule date for establishing the North Col Camp, they received wireless warning of the approach of a 'western disturbance', and with remarkable punctuality it began to snow at 3 p.m. the same afternoon. Naturally, this snowfall did not cause them to alter their plan; it has been the opinion of every expedition that in early May the cold is too severe for high climbing, and in any case the damage was already done. From all previous experience, they expected this early snow to be blown off before the onset of the monsoon and this expectation was disappointed, as ours was.

To take our own case; supposing in the last days of April we had been warned of the approach of bad weather I do not think we would have altered our plans. The cold at Camp III was a convincing deterrent to going any higher and we would have gambled on the very reasonable chance of there being enough wind to clear the mountain before the arrival of the monsoon at the beginning of June. The leader would have been given the invidious choice of having some of his party disabled, perhaps permanently, through frost-bite in a desperate attempt to forestall the weather, or of ignoring the forecast and being subsequently reviled for his unheeding contempt of science. Even if some omniscient being at the other end had informed us by wireless that 'western disturbances' would follow in rapid succession until the beginning of the monsoon proper (which was what happened), we should certainly have been well informed but quite unable to do anything about it except perhaps pack up. The long-range forecasts of the probable date of the monsoon appearing, which Dr Sen considers possible, are not really of such importance as a forecast of the weather in the pre-monsoon period, the month of May. And I doubt if this is possible even if we submit to the stipulated establishing of a meteorological station with its transmitting set in the vicinity of the mountain. With the mass of weather data available in Europe can anyone tell us, for example, what sort of a season we shall have in the Alps? Will July or August be the best month? How much easier it would be to arrange our climbing holidays if they could. No, mountaineering, like farming, sailing, and all our most interesting activities, is a chancy business ruled largely by the weather which we take as it comes as philosophically as we can; unless or until we make an idol of 'success' and stake too much upon it in money or material to submit to the ordinary rules, when we wish to become like Hamlet's politician 'one that would circumvent God'.

The recent war has introduced us to wireless receiving sets which can be slung from the shoulder like a water-bottle and which weigh very little more. Although by doing so the party lose one outstanding advantage of being in Tibet, should they wish to have their thoughts and feelings harrowed by listening daily to the news I see no reason why one of these should not be taken, particularly as the volume is such that no one need be compelled to listen. If such sets were to be used for receiving weather forecasts from Calcutta special arrangements would have to be made with the Indian Meteorological Department and an Indian broadcasting station, and if such arrangements could be made for the reception of forecasts on one of these pocket sets weighing 5 or 6 lb., well and good. The forecasts would be of interest if not of use, and would at any rate excite great degrees of what Hazlitt called the great springs of life—Hope and Fear—and so prevent the emotional faculties of the party from becoming dulled. But whatever value there may or may not be in weather forecasts, I believe there is no justification for the taking of a big set with batteries and engine such as was used in 1933 and 1936. It is costly, difficult to carry, and involves the addition of one or possibly two mouths to feed; while if it is to be used for sending messages on the progress of the expedition, the leader, in order to justify its presence, has to betake himself ardently to journalism.

Very small sets for short-range talking as well as receiving are also available now. Their weight, though small, is appreciable, and above the North Col every pound counts. It is easy to imagine circumstances in which they would be useful, but none in which they would be indispensable. In my opinion they would not be worth their weight.

An expedition that sells itself to a newspaper is liable to find itself saddled with a wireless set as a result. Nearly every one admires and upholds a free, uncontrolled and uncontrollable Press, throwing the searching beam of publicity into obscure corners and generally taking care that the State receives no hurt; but when the fierce beam lights upon the mountains, the people climbing them, or better still falling off them, then our admiration is apt to be withheld. The Press, with some honourable exceptions, has no soul to be saved or body to be kicked, and neither violent protest, savage scorn, nor corrosive sarcasm, will turn it or its minions from what is mistakenly conceived to be the path of duty. All this was acknowledged and regretted in more temperate but sufficiently plain language by one of the few responsible Dailies left. A leading article declared that: 'The standard of intelligence, taste, and accuracy of the Press today is admittedly not what it was 30 or 40 years ago. This may be merely a reflection of lower standards on the part of the public which the Press itself has done its best to lower. Either way the responsibility cannot be escaped.' The evil is there and we can do nothing about it; only time, the great healer, will diminish or worsen it.

Whether an expedition makes an agreement for the sole rights of the story with one particular newspaper or not, every newspaper will join in the hunt. If no agreement at all were made, the position would be worse, for there would be no untainted source to which the serious inquirer could turn for reliable information. Possibly if the contract were made with some news agency, which would supply news to all newspapers there would be no obligation upon any paper to regale its readers with sensational and distorted accounts. Such an arrangement might even mitigate the persecution of relatives of members, another unpleasant aspect of publicity at present as common as it is deplorable. At any hour of the day or night relatives may be rung up and asked to provide news or comment on its absence. The slamming down of the receiver before a word has been said will not prevent the appearance next morning of some fatuous remarks wrongly attributed to the victim, whose cup of bitterness is still to be filled by a tart reminder from the man on the spot that nothing must be said to the Press.

Something more was learnt about the use of oxygen and the apparatus itself. Opinion amongst the party as to the ethics of using oxygen was about evenly divided; few thought that in its present stage of development it was of much value. My own opinion is that the mountain could and should be climbed without, and I think there is a cogent reason for not climbing it at all rather than climb it with the help of oxygen. It is only fair to say that many men of far greater authority to speak for mountaineering tradition and the ethics of climbing take an opposite view to mine. The late J. P. Farrar, for example, who in 1917 to 1919 was President of the Alpine Club, and from 1920 to 1926 Editor of the *Alpine Journal*, stated in a review of the 1922 expedition that 'this objective, the conquest of the mountain, must be kept steadily in view, and its attainment be attempted . . . with *every available resource*'. This is the conclusion of an article largely devoted to the oxygen problem in which he answered the question 'Would it be unsportsmanlike?' by saying: 'Yet Everest is to be allowed to clothe itself with air containing a far less proportion of oxygen than is needed for the development of the full powers of man, and the mountaineer who attempts to make good the deficit is held to create conditions so artificial that they can never become legitimate mountaineering.' This seems to me equivalent to saying that since Everest allows itself to add several thousand feet to its stature beyond that of any ordinary mountain we can make good the deficiency of our climbing powers by using a man-lifting kite; or since some particular rock face assumes an unwarranted degree of steepness we will therefore drive in a few pegs. The views of a representative body of mountaineers have never been taken, but, ethics apart, my feeling and my principal reason for opposing it, is that a successful oxygen climb would only inspire a determined wish to repeat the climb unaided. There would be no finality about it and we might see, always assuming the consent of the Tibetan authorities, another long-drawn-out series of attempts such as we have already had. Man's competitive instincts are fortunately not easily tamed; until the South Pole was reached rivalry was intense, but once it was reached honour was satisfied. Mountaineers are never content until a mountain has been climbed by every possible route, but since there are probably no alternative routes on Everest I feel sure that if it were climbed with the help of oxygen there would be for mountaineers an instinctive urge to climb it again without. The plausible argument that it is better to climb the mountain with oxygen rather than not at all is therefore unsound. And it is rank materialism unless we assume charitably that those who think thus believe that the mountain will never be climbed without oxygen, and hope, as we do, that once it is climbed the striving for height records, the publicity, the national rivalry which was a feature of the thirties, will then cease and that the Himalaya will become the playground they should be. Mountaineering is analogous to sailing, and there is not much merit to be acquired by sailing with the help of an auxiliary engine. If man wishes gratuitously to fight nature, not for existence or the means of existence but for fun, or at the worst self-aggrandizement, it should be done with natural weapons. Obscure though some of them may be, the reasons which urge men to climb mountains are good enough reasons for wishing to climb the highest mountain of all, provided it is done in the normal way of mountaineering by a private party responsible only to themselves. The various other reasons which have been adduced in the past, such as demonstrating man's 'unconquerable spirit', or increasing our knowledge of man's capacity, should not persuade us to alter our methods, especially when by so doing we stultify the reasons themselves. I take it that when a man has to start inhaling oxygen his spirit has already been conquered by the mountain and the limit of his capacity has been very clearly defined. Even the hard-worked but astonishingly powerful reason, the advancement of science, has been brought to bear. As the late Sir Francis Younghusband wrote in an introduction to *Mount Everest: The Reconnaissance*: 'No scientific man, no physiologist or physician, can now say for certain whether or not a human body can reach a height of 29,000 ft. We know that in an aeroplane he can be carried up to a much greater height. But we do not know whether he can climb on his own feet to such an altitude. That knowledge of men's capacity can only be acquired by practical experiment in the field.' I do not know whether it is so, but if the scientists are interested in their cold-blooded way in a man's behaviour at 29,000 ft.— whether he dies a quick or a lingering death, for example—then another unanswerable objection to the use of oxygen presents itself, for the means defeats the purpose. Far be it from me, or from any mountaineer, to balk our scientists. But they want to have it both ways. The physiologist may be genuinely interested in a man's capacity at great heights, but other of his fellow scientists are more interested in equipping a man with some device that will overcome natural difficulties. And, as modern developments show, it is an engaging but fatal characteristic of scientists that once presented with a material problem of this kind they set about the solution with a single-minded devotion that excludes any other considerations whatsoever, be they ethical, humane, or merely of common sense. This fanatical approach to a problem is pleasantly illustrated in the following statement made in 1922 by one who is a mountaineer as well as a scientist:[1] 'If this year's expedition is not successful, some enthusiastic millionaire may yet provide a liquid oxygen generating plant near the mountain which will reduce the ascent of Everest to a question of £. s. d.' Thus the frenzy of the scientist readily extinguishes the common sense of the mountaineer and raises a very ugly head indeed. As the Spanish proverb says: 'Science is madness if good sense does not cure it.' The point about liquid oxygen is, I believe, that it would be much more portable, but owing to its rapid evaporation it would have to be manufactured on the spot.

In reply to any ethical objections that one may raise the oxygen enthusiast merely points significantly to one's clothes, well-nailed boots, snow-glasses, or ice-axe, all of which he considers sufficiently artificial to condone the use of yet another artificial aid, namely oxygen. And it is a difficult argument to refute. An appeal to common sense merely invites the retort that it is precisely that to which he is making this appeal. 'Why', he asks, 'jib at using oxygen? If your oxygen could be provided in the form of pills you would use it quick enough, just as some of you use pills to make you sleep.' Well, perhaps one would. Oxygen pills, one hopes, would not weigh 25 lb. But it will be time

1 Mr P. J. H. Unna.

to decide that knotty point when the pills are forthcoming; meanwhile, if we are being illogical, which I doubt, let us continue being so; for we are an illogical people and mountaineering is an illogical form of amusement which most of us are content to have as it is. It is a case of the pot calling the kettle black. The gas school contend that it is very doubtful if the mountain can be climbed without oxygen. But they hasten to assure us that even with the aid of oxygen it will be sufficiently difficult; that all the difficulties, physical and mental, will not be thereby abolished, or even greatly diminished. Possibly not; in the opinion of some they will be increased, but here they are themselves illogical; for the point is that with a little more scientific research and applied ingenuity they hope and expect to produce the perfect apparatus which will go nearly all the way towards abolishing fatigue, breathlessness, cold, the benumbing mental effects of high altitudes:[1] in fact the very foes with which the mountaineer takes pleasure in grappling, and those without which Everest, in particular, would not be the very redoubtable mountain it is. Possibly those who take a different view on the use of oxygen and aeroplanes as accessories to Himalayan mountaineering will say that on these matters instead of doing a little unaccustomed thinking I have been content to consult merely my feelings. Even if this were so, and I admit that thinking is an unusual and difficult exercise for me, my views are not on that account worthless. We have not to go far from England or far back in history to see the effects of using reason alone and neglecting to consult human feelings. A far greater authority, the author, editor and educationalist, Mr George Sampson, has laid down: 'Reason looks well on paper: but in reality we have scanty grounds for assuming that reason is a better guide to life than feeling.'

But reverting from theory to practice I can fairly say that on this year's showing the advantages conferred by using oxygen did not outweigh the disadvantages attending its use—difficulties related to the weight itself, to the unbalancing effect of that weight on steep ground, and the number of extra porters required to carry up cylinders. The unbalancing effect will become really serious on the crucial part of the climb—Norton's Traverse, the Couloir and the final pyramid.

Oxygen apparatus, wireless sets, or aeroplanes, are not the sort of things one expects or delights to find with a mountaineering party, of which the keynote should be simplicity. No lover of mountains would care to come upon such things (a liquid oxygen plant for example) lurking obscenely at the foot of the 'Delectable Mountains' of his dreams; but since the Himalayan giants, Nanga Parbat, Kangchenjunga, K 2 and Everest, have repulsed all attempts upon them man seems more and more inclined to resort to scientific aids in order to force success and to reassert his superiority over nature. Since fair means are ineffective we begin to think out foul means, and treat a mountaineering problem as a scientific problem, or what the Americans would call a problem in logistics—how to get a man by any means to the top.

1 As long ago as 1922, before anyone had shown what could be done without oxygen, Professor Dreyer, who, with G. I. Finch and P. J. H. Unna, took a principal part in developing the idea of using oxygen, confidently expected 'that the artificial supply of oxygen will make the climbers as physically fit as they would be at some altitude between sea level and 15,000 ft.'

As every expedition has learnt, the most important factor in climbing Everest is the weather and conditions near the summit. Without favourable conditions, no matter what auxiliary aids are employed, the mountain will never be climbed, and with them it will probably be climbed unaided. In 1938 we found that even after the monsoon had deposited a generous layer of snow on the mountain it was possible to reach a height of twenty-seven thousand odd feet, but no higher. This was merely a reaffirmation of what had been categorically stated by Norton in 1924 and by Smythe in 1933—that snow on the upper rocks is fatal to success. The climbing of many mountains after snow has fallen (when a few days have elapsed) is easier, but near the summit of Everest snow behaves in a different way and appears never to consolidate. That it does not is obvious, for otherwise the upper rocks would not be entirely devoid of snow in the early spring as they always are. In 1938 there appeared from below to be less snow on the upper rocks than there actually was; but though I think we realized that what snow there was was quite enough to damn us, some of us went up with the lurking belief, or at any rate hope, that we should find the snow hard; that this incontrovertible theory was wrong, that the snow behaved in the normal way and that it was merely the wind which was abnormal, blowing in the winter with sufficiently searching ferocity to tear off a layer of several feet of hard frozen snow; but alas:

> The heart of man has long been sore and long is like to be
> That two and two will still make four and neither five nor three.

We found the snow as loose and powdery as on the day it fell, with no sign at all of consolidation or of adhesion to the rock beneath, thus forming a fatal barrier. In such conditions the enormous effort involved in moving at all, the correspondingly slow rate of progress, and the danger from avalanching snow, are insurmountable difficulties. At that height, prolonged siege tactics, methodically clearing away the snow, are not to be thought of; and if they were, the avalanche danger still remains. If in order to be sure of finding the summit clear of snow the party makes its attempt too early it is met with the equally fatal and more cruel impediments of wind and cold, which, of course, become more severe as the climber ascends, who in turn becomes less able to withstand their effects owing to oxygen lack.

The approach by the west side of the North Col has already been discussed. Perhaps if the old route had behaved as we expected, and as it often does, treating us to an exhibition of 'frightfulness', we might have been more enthusiastic about the alternative route. Before monsoon conditions are established the old route is safe and nothing is gained by using the slightly longer approach; even after the onset of the monsoon, except in conditions considered certain to result in the formation of wind-slab on the east side, I should hesitate about using the other. The only really large avalanche we saw that year fell from the west side and there were spells of strong westerly winds blowing snow over the North Col and depositing it on the east side which should have resulted in the formation of wind-slab but which apparently did not. Uniform regular slopes such as on the west side are, I should think, more prone to avalanche than broken, crevassed slopes. On the other hand the east side is steeper. But in the present state of our knowledge Himalayan avalanches are as unpredictable as they are vast, and though one's judgement will probably be faulty it is at least satisfactory to have two alternative lines of advance and retreat upon which to exercise it.

In conclusion I should like to record my gratitude to the Mount Everest Committee who placed their confidence in us; to the friends known and unknown who generously subscribed; and to all members of the party, European and Sherpa, who did so much. Of the future little can be said. No one who has been high on the mountain, though very aware of the appalling difficulties, affirms that it is impossible to climb it given the right conditions— no snow on the upper rocks and a sufficiently warm, windless day. Such conditions occurred in 1924 and 1933, and will no doubt occur again. The job is taking longer than anyone expected, but it is not impossible, or at least it is in accord with Nansen's definition of that word. That great man and great explorer defined the 'difficult' as that which can be done at once, and the 'impossible' as that which may take a little longer. The climbing of Everest is evidently one of his 'impossibles' which is taking a little longer.

No doubt more attempts will be made but after the bitter disappointments of 1936 and 1938 it is clear that the odds against meeting perfect or even favourable conditions on any one particular visit are longer than was thought. If future expeditions were to be carried out on the lines indicated in 1938, there should be no great difficulty in financing more frequent expeditions. The ideal to aim at would be a consecutive series of three, four or five attempts. But we should make up our minds whether they are to be mountaineering or scientific expeditions, not a combination of the two, both for the sake of not diminishing the sufficiently scanty chances of success and for maintaining the true tradition of mountaineering. If the scientists really wish to carry out high-altitude tests in the field they could not make a worse choice of laboratory than Everest. For political reasons it is extremely inaccessible and the opportunity granted by the weather for climbing high upon it is fleeting. Moreover, there are two other mountains less than a thousand feet lower to which they could go every year were they so minded with no one to say them nay.

I am not asking that access to mountains should be denied to scientists, or that anyone found upon a mountain making scientific observations should be forthwith abolished more or less painlessly according to the purity of his motives. In that case we should soon have to regret the demise of many of our most ardent mountaineers, the Alpine Club would be decimated, and to the long list of martyrs in the cause of science we should have to add the familiar names of de Saussure, Tyndall, even Whymper himself, whose adventures with a mercury barometer in the High Andes are the comedy after the tragedy of the Matterhorn. No, I merely ask that mountaineering and science should be kept distinct, in particular that the problem of climbing Mount Everest, like any other mountain, should be left to mountaineers to solve, and that those actively engaged in solving it should not be expected to enter what Goethe calls the charnel-house of science. For it is only on the biggest mountains that we have to be on our guard against the encroachment of science. Without the aid of any formal rules, climbing at home and in the Alps is much as it was (except of course in standards) when first begun, and the earliest traditions of the Alpine Club are common to all and upheld by all; and this because the droves of mountaineers with a scientific bent, and the mountaineering scientists, while enjoying themselves in company with their less gifted brethren, and at the same time wielding geological hammers, swinging thermometers, or boiling them, have studiously refrained from suggesting any mechanical or scientific aids to lessen the ardours of their studious pleasure. Admittedly some provocation was lacking—there was no mountain high enough to tax their lung power—but it goes to show that a scientist with a feeling for mountains is not so utterly forsaken as one without, that his humanity is not yet extinguished, and that a powerful tradition may still be respected. May it ever be so, and may the provocation offered by the problem of Mount Everest be firmly withstood.

Whatever we may propose with regard to Mount Everest it is the Tibetans who dispose. We are under an increasing debt to the authorities of Lhasa for their goodwill; for permitting men whose motives, if not suspect, are at any rate incomprehensible, to visit their wonderful mountain—not only permit them to visit it but afford them powerful help and kindly hospitality. Their friendliness in the past encourages us still to hope. Meantime let us count our blessings—I mean those thousands of peaks, climbed and unclimbed, of every size, shape and order of difficulty, where each of us may find our own unattainable Mount Everest. And may those of us who have tried and failed be forgiven if we ask ourselves the question put by Stevenson: 'Is there anything in life so disenchanting as attainment?'

TWO MOUNTAINS AND A RIVER

Two Mountains
and a River

First published by Cambridge University Press, 1949

Contents

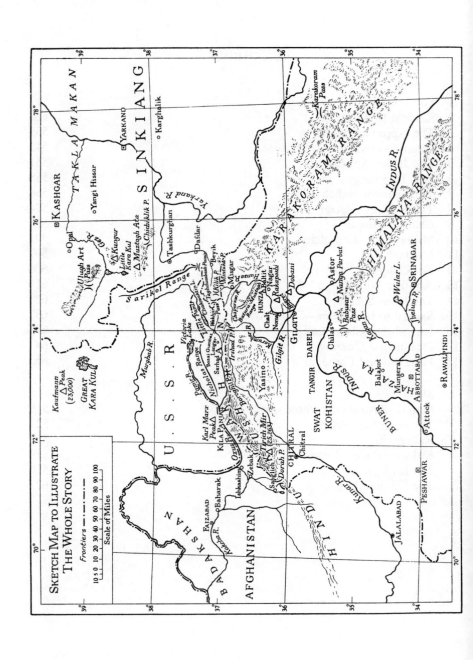

SKETCH MAP TO ILLUSTRATE
THE WHOLE STORY

Frontiers ·—··—··—

Scale of Miles

10 5 0 10 20 30 40 50 60 70 80 90 100

TAKLA MAKAN

SINKIANG

KASHGAR

⊡ YARKAND

○ Karghalik

Opal

Yangi Hissar

Ulugh Art Pass

Kungur
Little Kara Kul

Mustagh Ata
Chichiklik P.

Beyik

Tashkurghan

Dafdar

Sarikol Range

Yarkand R.

Kaufmann Peak

GREAT KARA KUL Peak (23,000)

Murghab R.

Victoria Lake

PAMIR

Nicholas Range

Pamir Range

Sarhad

Langar

P A M I R

Karl Marx Peak

KILA PANJA

Zebak

Ishkashim

Lutkho R.

Dorah P.

Trich Mir (25,263)

Yasino

Gilgit R.

GILGIT

Chalt

Nomal

HUNZA

Nagar

Baltit
Aliabad

Misgar

Rakaposhi

Dobani

KARAKORAM RANGE

Karakoram Pass

Indus R.

HIMALAYA RANGE

Astor

Nanga Parbat

Babusar Pass

Wular L.

⊡ SRINAGAR

Jhelum R.

CHITRAL

Chitral

Kunar R.

SWAT

TANGIR DAREL

KOHISTAN

Chilas

Indus R.

BUNER

Balakot

Munsera

HAZARA

ABBOTTABAD

Attock

⊡ RAWALPINDI

HINDU KUSH

FAIZABAD

Baharak

Kokcha R.

B A D A K S H A N

AFGHANISTAN

Kunar R.

PESHAWAR

JALALABAD

U. S. S. R.

Oxus R.

CHAPTER ONE

Food and Equipment

THE worst part of a war, as many of us are beginning to realize, is the end. For the majority war can be at worst an inconvenience and may even be advantageous; but just as vice and indulgence often result in disease and poverty, war has after-effects no less dreadful. And we are the less prepared to withstand the shock of these effects because while war is in progress our political prophets, amateur and professional feel it their duty to keep up our spirits with words of present hope and, more particularly, future comfort—pie in the sky, in fact. In the late war, though careless talk, as it was called, about military matters was almost indictable, anyone was free to indulge in careless talk about the new and better world which would emerge refined, as they put it, from the crucible of war. And both those old enough to know better and those young enough to think more cheerfully availed themselves of this licence.

For many, therefore, life became even more earnest, almost a crusade; they returned from the war resolved to better not only themselves but their unfortunate fellows. Not all, however, were taken in by this talk of a new heaven and a new earth. Some had heard it before during an earlier and better war and were therefore sceptical, while others although not content were prepared to put up with the old. These, the minority, feeling that standing still was better than progress in the wrong direction, and mindful of the words of Ecclesiasticus, 'be not over busy in thy superfluous works', and who were too old, perhaps, to change or too stupid to see the need of change—these, instead of looking about for a new role, made what pathetic haste they could to pick up the broken threads of their pre-war lives. Among these modern Bourbons, so to speak, I counted myself, and my survey of the war-shattered world in the autumn of 1945 was directed naturally to the Himalaya, to the ways and means of getting there, and to the chances of finding like-minded survivors with the same extravagant ideas. So loud was the din raised by the planners of the new world that it was hardly possible for me to avoid absorbing something of the spirit of the times, so that I did feel some slight uneasiness at attempting to do once more what I wanted to do. But I argued as Falstaff did about stealing, it was my vocation.

Just as after the first war, when one took stock, shame mingled with satisfaction at finding oneself still alive. One felt a bit like the Ancient Mariner; so many better men, a few of them friends, were dead:

> And a thousand thousand slimy things
> Lived on; and so did I.

But casualties were not solely responsible for the absence of like-minded companions. Though interest in mountaineering and exploration was, or seemed to be, greater than ever, I could find no one who was either brazen enough to turn his back on the promised land or who was not indispensable to a planned economy. Still, if one is bent on travel or exploration rather than on mountaineering, provided one has the strength of will or the prudence to resist the challenge of the higher peaks, it is practicable to wander in the Himalaya without other companions than Sherpas. In 1946 I would gladly have done this but there were more serious hindrances to be overcome.

In 1946 England could be compared to the married state—those who were out (most of the Services) wishing frantically to get in, while many who were in wished as much to get out and found it devilish hard. For a few months in the beginning of 1946 I fluttered about like a bird in a cage beating my head vainly against the bars of shipping offices which had no ships, stores which had no equipment, and export and currency regulations which would not yield. My reward in the end was but one short flutter to Switzerland, official negligence or short-sighted planning having temporarily left that door of the cage open.

Early in 1947, as would-be travellers will remember, there was a kind of false dawn before darkness descended again; the bonds were slightly eased while fresh knots were being tied, and the Continental traveller having been given enough rope duly hanged himself. Travel at home and abroad became easier that spring and summer, and Mr Bevin's generous vision of a world of visa-less travel had in one or two countries been realized. Shipping firms when asked for a passage no longer laughed sardonically, but deigned to accept £70 in return for a single comfortless passage to Bombay under more or less military discipline in a 'dry' trooper; equipment of a kind could be ordered and even obtained if several month's grace was given; if it was to be taken abroad no coupons were needed, while pemmican, as I belatedly discovered, was not rationed. By 1947 great numbers of V.I.P.'s, the chief obstacle to private travel, had been redistributed or recalled, either to gratify some distant fragment of the dumb herd with their presence or to leave it to bemoan their loss, so that at length the ordinary man by cunning, luck, or impudence, stood some chance of having his wants attended to.

By 1947 my modest arrangements for a journey to one of the less well-known parts of the Karakoram were all but complete—passage booked, equipment ordered, and three Sherpa porters engaged. The Survey of India had promised to arrange for a surveyor to accompany me, for in this utilitarian age it is more than ever necessary to have some scientific or quasi-scientific purpose—to assume a virtue though you have it not. If one wants to go to the North Pole to collect cosmic dust, to the bottom of the sea for globigerina ooze, or to Patagonia to count the number of albinos, money and every facility are readily available. But an aimless wanderer is not pleasing to the mandarins. The only hitch in my arrangements was that permission to go through Kashmir had not yet been received from the authorities at Srinagar.

The porters had been engaged through our old friend and companion of many expeditions, Angtharkay, who had now blossomed out as a transport agent in Darjeeling, fertilized no doubt by the numbers of Americans and

British who had visited Darjeeling and Sikkim during the war. Through him ponies, porters, cooks, and anything else needful could be obtained, but unluckily neither he himself nor any porter that I knew was available this year. Many were engaged, some were absent, and, according to Angtharkay's report, drink and the devil had done for the rest; for the Sherpa is not a perfect specimen of economic man—what he gets he spends, usually on drink or gambling. To this rule Angtharkay is an exception, but then as his record shows he has many other qualities not usually found in Sherpas. This year he and twenty other Sherpas were going to Sikkim and eastern Nepal with a large party, the members of which had not to disguise themselves as scientists for they were the thing itself. The flora, fauna, entomology, morphology, and geology of Sikkim having been exhaustively examined, there was left only the snow, and this they were going to measure.

In February while waiting impatiently for the expected permission from the Kashmir Durbar, I received an invitation to join two experienced Swiss mountaineers, Hans Gyr and Robert Kappler, who were going to the Himalaya under the aegis of the 'Schweizerische Stiftung für ausseralpine Forschungen' or 'Swiss Foundation for Mountain Exploration'. This Foundation is a private affair—quite independent of the government—whose purpose is to encourage, organize, and assist the dispatch of mountaineering expeditions to any part of the world. It has financed one expedition in the past, and is in a position to finance others, but naturally prefers that such expeditions should be financially independent. It is primarily concerned with mountaineering rather than scientific exploration. An expedition under the patronage of the Foundation is expected to concede the copyright of all photographs, articles, or books which are the result of the expedition's work to the Foundation. Naturally this arrangement would do little towards meeting the expenses incurred, but the Foundation is fortunate in having wealthy backers. In 1939 it was financially responsible for a very successful expedition to the Garhwal Himalaya. This year under its auspices one expedition went to Garhwal, and ours, for which we paid, to the Gilgit region with the ambitious project of an attempt upon Rakaposhi (25,550 ft.). One criticism I have of the Foundation, and it is shared by my two Swiss companions, is that it has a weakness for publicity, especially for advance publicity. Quite apart from the ethics of mountaineering it is bad policy. It is a rash marksman who calls his shots, announces which particular coco-nut he is shying at—the wise man keeps his own counsel. So when going to the Himalaya it is foolish to broadcast one's intentions, for after the event it is not easy to describe an unsuccessful attempt on a mountain as a mere reconnaissance.

Having received this tempting invitation before my own arrangements were completely cut-and-dried I was in a quandary; whether to accept and thereby give up my own plans or to refuse and then possibly find that I had lost both opportunities. When presented with the choice of two evils one usually finds that one gets both. To have to choose between two proffered benefits is less frequent and more difficult; one never can have both and whichever one chooses there will always be a lingering regret after the other. To have one's cake and eat it, or to ride two horses (both with equal chances) in the Derby, are well-known examples of this particular vanity of human wishes.

In this instance, though the side-issues were many, the choice was roughly between mountain exploration and mountaineering on the grand scale, between something which might be of use by enlarging in a minute degree the sum of geographical knowledge and something which would be perfectly useless to anyone including the people who did it. A choice, too, between care-free licence and responsibility, for in the one there would be only myself and the Sherpas to consult and please, while in the other, as the only climber with Himalayan experience, I would be responsible for anything that might happen, good or bad. Mountaineering and mountain exploration are very much alike and in the course of an expedition the one frequently merges into the other. They might be compared to an omelette and scrambled eggs, the ingredients are precisely the same, one is perhaps a higher form of art than the other, and it frequently happens that what was meant to be an omelette turns out to be scrambled eggs and vice versa. To explore mountains one must climb and to climb an unknown mountain one must first explore. Perhaps the essential difference is that in mountain exploration strenuousness, hardship, and peril, can be increased or decreased at will, whereas in high climbing these present pains and retrospective pleasures are unavoidable. Their degree and intensity varies with the height and difficulty of the chosen mountain, but such things are then implicit in the enterprise and cannot be lessened or avoided without giving up.

Since a bird in the hand is worth two elsewhere my decision was made easier by the lack of any reply from Kashmir. Having delayed as long as politeness permitted I settled my doubts by accepting the Swiss invitation, which was no sooner done than permission arrived from Kashmir. By this time, late February, my friends had collected nearly all the equipment and food needed and I was asked to go to Zürich to cast an eye over it.

Without immodesty British mountaineers can, I think, claim to have had as much or more experience of high-altitude climbing than any others; I was therefore surprised to find that in the most important matter of tents our experience had not been taken into account. The 'Meade' pattern tent (R.G.S. *Hints to Travellers* prefers the name 'Whymper') with a zip-fastener or a 'sleeve' door has stood the test of several Mt Everest expeditions and many others. For severe conditions of wind, cold, snow (not rain), it is hard to beat, and for simplicity, strength, lightness, is unsurpassed. But in Zürich they seemed not to have heard of it and had taken for their model a tent of French design, shaped like a coffin but of less simple construction than that article and far less easy to get into. One of the virtues of the 'Meade' pattern tent is its simplicity and its willing obedience and docility when being put up with cold hands in a high wind, whereas this Swiss tent by reason of having a fly and a sort of boudoir or ante-room at one end was unnecessarily complicated and difficult to erect or take down. The door fastenings, too, were not likely to be proof against driven snow, which will penetrate anything, even cloth if not tightly woven. For the good reason of economy the porters' tents, which are just as important as those for Europeans, had been borrowed from the

Swiss army, but they were quite unsuited for our purpose. The material was thick and heavy, the poles were long, heavy, unjointed alpenstocks, while there was a door at either end secured only with buttons; one door in a tent is an unfortunate necessity, two are a disaster. Hannibal, I should say, or at any rate Napoleon, had probably used similar tents on their expeditions. For these I substituted a 'Logan' tent for the porters and took also three of my own 'Meade' tents. The 'Logan' tent, which I had first used on Nandi Devi, was a pattern designed and developed in Alaska, but it was not unknown in India for I read in *Hints to Travellers* that it was used by a Survey of India party in the Pamirs as early as 1913. Weighing only half as much again as the 'Meade', it holds four instead of two and is in many other ways as good.

It was impossible to quarrel with the sleeping-bags which were of real eider-down, so hard to come by now in this country, and were very warm and light. The rubber mats, which are used for insulation under the sleeping-bag, were thicker, lighter, and spongier than ours. This of course, is all to the good, but as their edges had been left unsealed they had also the absorptive capacity of a sponge which was all to the bad. The other items were all good and there was little to criticize except the variety and the quantity. Nothing had been forgotten except the great doctrine of 'the Minimum', taught and practised by one or two Himalayan pundits, but at Zürich regarded hardly at all, certainly not as inspired revelation not lightly to be departed from. The doctrine of 'the Minimum is implicit in the name and is simply the logical expansion of the precept (which, by the way, is a Spanish proverb) that 'a straw is heavy on a long journey'. As I count myself one of these pundits, this was as great a shock to me as it has been to other prophets who have found their teaching ignored. Greater men, on less provocation, might have shaken the dust of Zürich from off their feet, but on the expedition I was in that embarrassing position of guest, or at least paying guest, in which it is not easy to set about one's host's furniture, throwing an armchair or an occasional table out of the window on the slender grounds of superfluity. However, I effected some trifling reductions, guaranteed to prejudice neither our comfort nor our cumbersomeness, and resigned myself sorrowfully to totting up the weights of the many packages—a list whose contents occupied some dozen sheets of quarto paper. It is a good working rule that an expedition that cannot organize itself on an ordinary sheet of notepaper, or, if all members are thorough-paced 'scrappers and baggers', on the back of an old envelope, is bound to suffer from the effects of too much organization. That I had applied the axe very tentatively was evident when we reached India, when at Karachi, Abbottabad, and Gilgit, we left behind us a tell-tale line of dumps.

Crampons and skis were to be taken, though personally I have never had occasion in the Himalaya to use either. The crampons were made of some specially light alloy with ten short spikes. I suppose such things will always justify their awkward prickly presence as an insurance against the possiblity of having to climb a long steep slope of very hard snow or a short piece of ice on the final bid for the summit. Anywhere below that level steps will always have to be cut to safeguard the porters who are not likely to have had the experience necessary for the use of crampons.

The use of skis for mountaineering in the Himalaya is a debatable point. They have been used on high mountains, I believe, only on two occasions. First on Kamet (25,447 ft.) in 1931 by Mr R. L. Holdsworth (an expert skier) whose use of them is alluded to in the *Himalayan Journal* (vol. IV) as follows: 'The use of ski by Holdsworth was fully justified. As far as Meade's Col (23,500 ft.) he was able to use them throughout the whole route with the exception of the rock face between Camps 3 and 4, and by ski-ing at 23,500 ft. he must surely have created a record for high altitude ski-ing. Furthermore, on the descent he was able to take his frost-bitten feet in one day from Camp 3 to the base, whereas others similarly affected, but not so fortunate, were compelled to drag them down in two long and tiring marches.' It will be noted that this benedictory paragraph while saying 'the use of ski was fully justified', says nothing of whether the carrying of them from Ranikhet to the mountain, a journey which took twenty-seven days, was also fully justified. In Mr Smythe's account of the expedition in the *Alpine Journal* (vol. XLIII), although the unregretted absence of raquettes is mentioned, there is no reference to skis except in the bald chronological summary at the end of the article. One cannot help feeling that if Mr Smythe had been impressed by the possibilities of skis for high mountaineering he would have remarked on it.

They were used again in 1934 in the Karakoram Himalaya by André Roch, a noted Swiss mountaineer who accompanied Professor Dyhrenfurth and his international cinema-mountaineering party. In their ascent of Baltoro-Kangri, or the Golden Throne (*c.* 23,500 ft.), he and his two companions used skis part of the way, and of this Roch remarks: 'Thanks to skis it took us only two and a half hours to reach a point which three days previously had been reached by our companions in five hours.' In conversation André Roch told me that at such heights it is impossible to use any other turn than a 'Kick-turn', as 'Stem' turns or 'Christianias' are too exhausting. But this is of small moment for, contrary to expectation, it is in ascending not descending that skis might be of value in the Himalaya. Provided the slopes of the mountain are not too steep and that one has confidence that they will be used and enough energy to carry such an awkward burden to the starting point, they should be taken.

In 1934 when Mr Shipton and I were in Garhwal, we did a high-level traverse from Badrinath across the watershed to Gangotri over the névé of several glaciers where we encountered snow conditions in which skis would undoubtedly have kept us somewhere near the surface instead of two or three feet below it; but then our three porters were also indispensable members of the party and more time would have been lost in teaching them how to shuffle on skis, and of course in digging them out when they fell, than was wasted by floundering along on our feet. In the Karakoram, too, in 1937 when we were crossing the Snow Lake at the head of the Hispar and Biafo glaciers, skis would have added to our pleasure and enabled us to cover more ground; but for many weeks before that the carrying of them would most certainly have detracted from our pleasure and obliged us to cover less ground. But both these instances happened in mountain exploration, when one is necessarily accompanied by several porters, as distinct from high mountaineering. Such conditions could be met, I think, by an invention of Mr Seligman's (author of *Snow Structure and Ski Fields*) which anyone can use without previous instruction. What he calls his 'racket-ski' is about 40 in. long and 5 in. broad, wider in front than behind, which helps it to rise to the surface at each step. Owing to their shortness and weight, which is only 5 lb., they can be carried easily on the back. They appear to be well worth a trial.

However, having seen some photographs of Rakaposhi I was confident that I for one, being no skier, would not be using them—not even Mr Seligman's— and I did my best to dissuade Gyr and Kappeler, who are both experts, from taking them. In this I not only failed but was persuaded in my turn to address myself seriously to the ski-ing business, for in Switzerland it is a business in every sense of the word. In that country, I imagine, a mountaineer who cannot ski is regarded with pity or with even something more derogatory. In a class apart from the votaries of the 'downhill only' school, are the ski-mountaineers who practice their difficult art not only in winter but in midsummer as well. Late in June 1946 I was the only ski-less mountaineer in the Bétemps hut where a ski club were holding a meet. From there they would climb the Lyskamm on skis, or all but the last few hundred feet of Monte Rosa, and then whistle down to the hut in some twenty minutes.

In vain I protested the inability of old dogs to learn new tricks—to Davos of all places I had to go to be put through the mill. Before this I had worn rather than used skis for a few hours in the winter of 1945 in the Dolomites, where I had reason to envy the partisans of Forno, a small village south of Mt Marmolada, who seldom wore anything else. To see them hurtling down slopes, dodging in and out of trees, in the middle of the night, while they collected the fruits of a widely scattered 'drop', was instructive and humiliating. In fact in winter snow three or four feet deep the valuable loads scattered over a wide area by errant parachutes would not have been recovered at all but for these men on skis.

The skiers at Davos were quite different from these, though they were no less skilful. To one accustomed in the main to unspoilt mountains the intrusion of commerce so high up their slopes subdued and desecrated with funiculars and ski lifts, the cafés with blaring wireless, and the ascending herd of over-dressed women and men, breathing cigarette smoke into each others' faces in the train, was very depressing. Though, in fairness, I must admit that the sight of some of this same crowd descending in what seemed to me to be one suicidal swoop was no less encouraging and exhilarating. To Gyr and Kappeler, whose minds, no doubt, were casting forward to the execution of linked 'Christianias' on the slopes of Rakaposhi, the sight of their future companion's antics must have been equally depressing. Whilst I committed all the known mistakes and a few I had thought out for myself, they would circle round with encouraging cries. To a distant observer they must have appeared like hawks striking at a heron with a broken wing. The skis were duly taken to India, but as I have explained, skis in the Himalaya are no more indispensable than skates, and by the time Gilgit was reached my companions had seen enough to reconcile them to the truth of this. We had carried them far enough.

We were all fitted with specially made boots with the new type of moulded rubber sole which is becoming popular in Switzerland; many Swiss climbers, amateur and professional, seem inclined to change from nailed soles to rubber. Our boots were very stoutly made, perhaps unduly so, for my own size 'nines' weighed nearly 6 lb. They took longer than usual to break in and the 'expedition' boots became one of our stock jests. I coined the aphorism that an extra pound on the feet is twenty pounds on the back, which though it may not be scientifically correct is a measure of how these boots felt to me. Nevertheless, leather is not wool and it is difficult to have warmth and strength without weight and on the whole these are the most essential qualities. A light pair of boots would be knocked to pieces in a couple of months. I think the rubber sole is very suitable for the Himalaya. With no iron in the boot the chances of cold feet and frost-bite should be lessened, while for boulder-hopping, which occupies most of one's time, they are supreme. They grip well on ice or snow, and though I thought they did not bite quite so well as nails when kicking steps in hard snow, this impression may have been a result of my own diminishing leg power. As regards their use in this country, except for the sake of hotel carpets, I should say that they are unnecessary and possibly a menace, since our rock is so often wet and greasy. One item of equipment new to me was a canvas boot cover reaching well up the ankle which, if well fitted, obviates the use of ankle puttees and keeps the boot dry even in wet snow, a benefit of the greatest value in the Himalaya.

Formerly travel was undertaken to broaden the mind or to acquire culture, but nowadays many people go in search of food. I would not admit that this was our prime motive, but we took a keen interest in the matter as every member of an expedition should. In the exercise of this franchise there is seldom any slackness. Even the mountaineering mystics whom we sometimes read or read of, though they may not like to mention food, are certain to think of it. In 1947 the collection of enough food was, of course, impossible without the granting of special facilities, and it was consoling to find that the Swiss Government, which I had always regarded as a model of unobtrusive sense and efficiency, behaved in this matter much as any other government. Having with reluctance granted a permit for food for four men for five months, at the very last minute it occurred to some official with more perspicuity than his fellows that the loss of this amount might be detrimental to the four million odd Swiss who were not going on an expedition. Peremptory orders were therefore given that all our meat, all the butter, and half the cheese must be left behind. Fortunately our own food officials, with far more reason to be difficult than the Swiss, played up nobly and granted an export licence for enough butter and cheese to make good the loss. I also increased the amount of pemmican ordered. So many people ask what pemmican is that I might explain that it is a Red Indian ('Cree') word for dried buffalo or caribou meat prepared so as to contain the greatest amount of nourishment in a compact form. As made by them it consisted of the lean parts of meat, dried in the sun, pounded or shredded and mixed into a paste with melted fat in the form of a cake. It appears to keep indefinitely, has a high protein and fat content, and is expensive; it is the standard Arctic sledging ration, eked out with biscuit and chocolate. It is not the same thing as 'biltong', the sun-dried meat prepared by the Boers, or 'boucanned' meat from which the word 'buccaneer' comes. In the seventeenth century the island of Hispaniola (Santo Domingo) was the home of great herds of wild cattle which the natives used to hunt. The meat was dried in the sun without salt and cured in the smoke of a green wood fire. The adventurers who used to provision at Hispaniola learnt from the natives the art of 'boucanning'.

Today we complain of lack of variety in our food but on Rakaposhi I could have borne with less variety and more solid simplicity. Many travellers, the Swiss among them, believe in the advantages of a highly organized system of food-boxes. In a generous but futile endeavour to please all tastes a little of everything—and the quantities are of necessity small—is put up in 50 lb. boxes, one of which is supposed to feed so many men so many days. Each box is neatly stencilled, with a list of the contents and the dose to be taken pasted inside the lid; and in severe cases of organization the date and place where any particular box will be eaten is also laid down. The amount of each item being so small, the tins, jars, cartons are the more numerous so that in a 50 lb. box there is only about 30 lb. of food. Naturally, too, the most desirable things are soon spotted, so that by the end of a week one is left with a number of rifled boxes, like so many honeycombs from which the honey has been extracted and about as interesting. Not one of us ever contemplated, much less tried, living on a box for the stipulated number of days. It was the sort of experiment I should not care to see tried—even on a rat. The compilers of such boxes are like the compilers of anthologies, assuming seemingly that no one really knows what he likes, or that at high altitudes the mind is too sluggish to select and the body too feeble to pile the fruit of one's selection into a rucksack.

The Swiss were remarkable for their devotion to a food beverage with the sinister name of 'Ovosport'. They ate it dry, they drank it neat, and they even committed the solecism of mixing it with their tea. I always mistrust these food beverages which claim, amongst many other things, to quench thirst and satisfy hunger at the same time, for I submit that it is no more possible to do this than it is to blow and swallow at the same time. One eats soup and no one pretends he is thereby quenching his thirst; one drinks beer and no one but the brewer claims that he has therefore dined. Besides 'Ovosport' and other beverages of that type, without which health, strength, or even sleep are hardly to be expected, we had all the usual aids to comfort and well-being. In each box there were no less than twenty different species of food and over forty varieties, though since there was a whiff of the laboratory about some of them it would be more correct to speak of forty chemical combinations. As usual all failed of their effect; the Swiss had complaints ranging from boils to knee, stomach, and eye troubles; Secord, who will be introduced presently, suffered from a consumptive cough; while I had mountaineer's foot—inability at times to put one in front of the other.

Having thus equipped and provisioned the party I must shift the scene to India where our times of arrival were 'staggered'. I reached Karachi by air on 1 May, the Swiss a week later, and Secord on 6 June.

CHAPTER TWO

Karachi to Abbottabad

AT Karachi I found that the Swiss consignment of stores had already arrived. Under a guard provided by the 'Stiftung' to prevent pilfering *en route*, it had been taken by road to Genoa and there shipped. 'Every writer of travels', I have read, 'should consider that, like all other authors, he undertakes, either to instruct or please, or to mingle pleasure with instruction'; for the benefit therefore of readers as ignorant as myself, I pass on what I learnt while we were discussing this question of shipment, namely that during the late war Switzerland maintained a merchant fleet and a port. The port was a quay and warehouse at Genoa from which coastal vessels plied to other Mediterranean ports. My share of our stores came in two ships, one of which arrived a day later than myself while the other was delayed at Bombay. This hitch was to cause us some trouble. Already the breeze of anxiety was playing around the brow of expectation, as it was to do frequently during the next three weeks.

Rakaposhi lies in the extreme north-west corner of India (now Pakistan) in what was until recently the Gilgit Agency. This comprised the petty states of Hunza, Nagar, Ishkuman, Yasin, Gilgit, Ghizar, Darel, and the Chilas republic, all of which were administered by a British Political Agent with headquarters at Gilgit. Gilgit itself was actually a 'wazirat' of Kashmir from whom the Indian Government leased it in 1935, although the Agency itself was established in 1889. These small states acknowledged the suzerainty of Kashmir but were never part of its territory. In August 1947 when the Gilgit Agency was hurriedly handed over to Kashmir, the Kashmir Durbar sent its own representative to Gilgit. This unfortunate, being a Hindu, was *persona non grata* and by the end of October was accordingly put in prison for his own safety. The states refused to be subject to Kashmir and declared their adhesion to Pakistan.

The usual route to Gilgit goes from Srinagar in Kashmir over the Burzil pass (13,900 ft.); another, about the same distance, avoids Kashmir and goes from Abbottabad by the Kagan valley and the Babusar pass (13,000 ft.). Both these passes are closed in winter for ordinary traffic but open about the same time in the spring in late May or early June. (The Gilgit mail-runners continue to cross the Burzil throughout the winter.) Col. R. N. Bacon, then Political Agent, Gilgit, had advised us to come by the Kagan valley route so that Abbottabad, which is railhead, was to be our starting-point. Coming out in the plane I had met as fellow-passenger Col. R. C. F. Schomberg, an old and very experienced Central Asian traveller, who having time after time begun his expeditions from Srinagar was concerned to find we were proposing to start from Abbottabad. There was no place like Srinagar for assembling and starting an expedition, for there, as he put it, 'you could buy anything from a set of false teeth to an ice-axe'.

However, having announced our route to the authorities we could not now change, so to Abbottabad I went on 8 May by train, along with twenty-four packages. To get this disgusting amount of stuff on a passenger train requires much local knowledge, and the Swiss firm Messrs Volkart Bros. readily put their ample stock of this commodity at my disposal. Arrangements had

The Approach March

already been made for our four Sherpas, who were at Darjeeling at the other extremity of India, to meet me in Abbottabad on the 9th. As I had waited a few days in vain for my missing shipment I was already late, and the breeze of anxiety which had begun to play about me at Karachi, increased in strength and was presently to rise to gale force on account of these Sherpas.

Before I attempt to unravel and explain another complication in which we had landed ourselves, I must introduce the fourth member of our party, Mr Campbell H. Secord, who was, I think, in some ways responsible for it. As we shall see later he had been on Rakaposhi, or at least a ridge of it, in 1938, and as a pioneer, so to speak, had strong claims for inclusion in any attempt upon the mountain. Although he was working in a Government office his time was not his own, so that it was not until Gilgit was reached that we knew for sure that he would be coming. This important piece of news was brought by Secord himself.

To get to Abbottabad from Karachi one changes at Rawalpindi whence one goes on either by train or bus. Col. Schomberg had given me the name of a friend of his at Rawalpindi, a Maj. C. W. M. Young who is a keen traveller and an expert user of a cine-camera. Quite by chance, for I am not usually so long-headed, I had wired him of my arrival and given his name to Volkart. On Rawalpindi station at about 9 o'clock at night, as I alighted to look after my twenty-four packages, Maj. Young met me and handed me a telegram from the Government of India offering to fly[1] us and our kit to Gilgit for a consideration. So considerable was this consideration that I decided to stop the night, if not longer, at Rawalpindi to think it over.

Very early in our acquaintanceship the Swiss had been canvassing the idea of having ourselves and our kit flown to Gilgit. Our kit, by the way, would have to have been 'dropped' since the Gilgit airfield can receive only small planes with a load of about seven passengers. It was thought, however, that the R.A.F. in India might welcome such an opportunity for an exercise, so negotiations, were opened by the 'Stiftung' with the Government of India through the usual channels. Secord, who at that time was toying with the idea of joining us, took up the flying project with enthusiasm, and since he had been in the R.A.F. during the war, where he had made some valuable acquaintances, he hoped he could pull wires to some purpose. After receiving an official reply to our application in rather discouraging terms we heard no more about it, and I mistakenly thought that the project had happily been consigned to limbo. But as the Chinese proverb says: 'Beware what you ask lest it be granted.'

The chief reason for this air-mindedness, of which I heartily disapproved, was the sound one that communal trouble at Abbottabad and in the Hazara district—then a very disturbed area—through which we had to travel, might prevent us starting at all. In addition the Swiss were anxious to save time, in particular Kappeler who regarded every day not spent in climbing as a day wasted. Perhaps such an uncouth method of approaching a mountain can be justified in a place like Alaska where the mountains are more inaccessible, the season shorter, and where the party itself has to hump or sledge the gear. In the Himalaya I think the approach by air is a mistake. In the first place no one who wants to do a lot of climbing should go to the Himalaya where he will do very little. Secondly, the time spent on the approach march, be it only a week or as much as three weeks, is in my opinion time well spent. It may well be the only enjoyable part of the trip. One's body gets a chance to accustom itself to strange conditions and to acquire a little fitness: one gets to know one's companions and porters under conditions where the worst can be faced with manly resignation, whereas if some maddening habit or peculiarity was suddenly sprung on one when lying cheek-by-jowl in a tent with snow falling

1 In two planes—the bodies in an 'Anson' and the kit in a 'Dakota'.

outside, the result might be manslaughter; and the porters in their turn have time to become familiar with tents and gear generally so that the place of everything is known and pitching and striking camp has become mere routine long before the mountain is reached.

And last, though I believe it should be put first, there is our old friend the 'thin end of the wedge'. I have quoted elsewhere the Bengali proverb that 'the sight of a horse makes the traveller lame', and I have some fear that the sight of an aeroplane might make the mountaineer think. To see an aeroplane accomplishing in four hours a journey which will take him nearly three weeks of toil and sweat is bound to give rise to thought—some of it subversive; whether the time so spent can be justified in the face of heaven and, perhaps, his family or employer; whether (unless he is a Fascist reactionary) it is not his duty to spare the oppressed coolies staggering along behind him their tribute of toil and sweat which his longer purse commands; or, still more to the point, whether it is not his duty to spare himself a little toil and sweat—a proposition which, of course, strikes at the very root of a mountaineer's religion. Such a picture is not entirely fanciful, and I have urged at length elsewhere[1] the case against the use of the aeroplane by Himalayan expeditions. 'Resist the beginnings' is a well-tried maxim. The farther away from mountains we can keep aeroplanes the better; a sentiment with which even pilots will not quarrel, and which, I hope, even those mountaineers whose pleasure it is to keep abreast or well ahead of the times will echo.

It did not take me as long to make up my mind as I had expected. By the time Young and I had dealt with a large rump steak and a beer—in India even in the hot weather one must be uncompromisingly British—I had decided to refuse the offer without waiting to consult the Swiss. Perhaps I feared that Kappeler's eagerness to reach the mountains might overcome any desire for economy. Another beer encouraged a new train of thought—why not combine speed and economy by doing away with the 'Anson' which was to take our party of seven, and drop the bodies as well as the kit from the 'Dakota'? Any recalcitrance on the part of the Sherpas or the Swiss could be easily overcome if I had a good 'dispatcher' in the plane with me. On the other hand, what would my friends think of this *volte-face* after what I had said and written about dropping things on mountains; and above all, would the idea be as pleasing to the Swiss as it was to me, heated by rump steak and beer? After another bottle, alcoholic remorse set in. The cost of hiring the 'Dakota' alone would be the equivalent of one man's share of the whole cost of the expedition, the R.A.F. would probably insist on some preliminary practice in jumping during which someone might hurt himself, and in the end one of the Sherpas would get tangled up in the tail as he quitted the plane. This reminded me of the Sherpas. What were they doing whilst their unpunctual and heartless employer sat carousing in Rawalpindi? Sleeping under a bush in the garden of the dak-bungalow at Abbottabad seemed to be the answer to that. We finished our beer and sent telegrams to all possible sources of information at that place. Four men, I thought, with pronounced Mongolian features, one or two possibly with pigtails, should be conspicuous

1 *Everest*, 1938.

enough in this part of India; only later did I discover that Abbottabad was the station for a brigade of Gurkhas with many camp followers who were not in uniform, so that Mongolian features were perhaps the commonest of any, and that none of our Sherpas had pigtails.

Needless to say the replies to these telegrams were all negative and I naturally assumed that our men had not yet arrived. Indeed, this was the obvious explanation considering their long cross-country journey and the crowded trains, for at that time India was like an ant's nest into which someone had poked a stick. I therefore decided to wait for them at Rawalpindi where for the next few days I cycled to the station several times a day to meet all the likely incoming trains and to peer into every third class compartment—even into those reserved for women, for I knew the Sherpas to be men of resource. I recollected having gone through this sort of performance before, twice before in fact, at Sealdah station, Calcutta, and again on one hot dark night at Bareilly. Readers of Mr Shipton's *Nanda Devi* may remember our frantic and futile search of a train, our rushing back to our own train which was on the point of leaving, and our finding the missing Sherpas already safely ensconced eating oranges. Anyone who has seen a third class compartment on an Indian train will appreciate the task I had set myself. The usual description of sardines in a tin is pitifully inadequate because there the inmates are dead and lie in orderly tiers; a tin full of maggots gives a better idea of such a compartment because there, there is life and movement and all the vigorous competition which life implies as individuals fight their way to the surface to breathe. I became a familiar figure to the station staff and an object of curiosity to the *habitués* of Rawalpindi platform. All Indian platforms have a semi-resident population comprising the sellers of tea, the ice vendor (blocks of ice are his stock in trade, not ices), the fruit, curry, mineral water, and betel-nut merchants; the odd fakirs dossing down more or less permanently on the platform, and the sweepers who for a small consideration will raise a dust-storm in one's compartment from the dust which before was lying thickly but inoffensively on the seats, the floor, and one's belongings. For such as these my repeated visits and my harassed face became the cause of kind inquiries about my missing wife: from where was she coming; why was she travelling third class; and why had I left her behind?

On the 15th Gyr was due to arrive, the unlucky Kappeler having been left at Karachi to collect and bring forward my delayed shipment of stores about which I was beginning to feel not only worried but guilty. It was a nice thing if a representative of the Island race, a resident, too, of a great sea-port, was unable to ensure the arrival in time of a few paltry bales. What an ass I had been not to insist on their being shipped with the rest direct to Karachi instead of allowing them to go on a ship calling first at Bombay where anything might happen and apparently was happening. By this time I was heartily sick of Rawalpindi station and its curious denizens, so I decided to move on to Abbottabad to allow the Sherpas to look for us for a change. So on the 16th we went there by bus and took up our quarters in a very indifferent dak-bungalow. Once again all inquiries about the Sherpas drew blank, while a wire to Darjeeling asking if they had started brought the reply that they had left on the 4th—now, indeed, the brow of expectation was being blown upon.

Next evening as we were standing outside the Post Office, I was accosted by an unmistakable Sherpa who proved to be Angdawa their 'sirdar' or leader. 'How long had they been there?' 'Six days'. 'Where were they living?' 'At the Palace Hotel.' A twinge of anxiety on behalf of the expedition accounts mingled with my relief. Four men for a week at the Palace Hotel, the best in Abbottabad, would cost us a pretty penny; but my fears were needless, for the bill, I think, was Rs. 3. They must have slept under a bush in the garden after all.

Having introduced ourselves to the Deputy Commissioner, Mr B. O. St John, we were invited to take up our residence in the comparatively luxurious quarters of the Circuit House bungalow which besides being secluded had an ample veranda for our boxes and an empty garage in which the Sherpas could be locked at night. The Deputy Commissioner was having an anxious time and many sleepless nights. During the few days of our stay there were unruly slogan-shouting processions by day, and burnings in the Hindu bazaar and of outlying Hindu temples by night, while occasional bomb explosions added to the general uproar. The Moslem theory about these fires was that they were started by the Hindu traders themselves, who having first insured their stock set it alight and were thus free to depart unencumbered to collect the insurance money at the other end.

Abbottabad is a hill station 4,000 ft. above sea-level, about sixty miles from Rawalpindi. It is the headquarters of the Hazara district and is named after its founder Sir James Abbott who was responsible for the settling of that wild district after its annexation to the Punjab. He was Commissioner at Abbottabad from 1847 to 1854, but before that, he had been the first Englishman to visit Khiva on the Amu Darya in Uzbekstan. The only feature of interest at Abbottabad is a rock inscription of Asoka near by which I am ashamed to say we did not visit. But mindful of my mentor's remark about mingling instruction with pleasure I might remind readers that Asoka (c. 247 B.C.) was the great Buddhist emperor who was largely responsible for the spread of that religion. His empire included all India, Nepal, Kashmir, the Swat valley, Afghanistan up to the Hindu Kush, Sind, and Baluchistan, that is an area rather larger than British India. Instead of interesting ourselves in archaeology we made the usual last minute purchases in the bazaar or what was left of it, walked the surrounding hills where pine trees gave us a zest for joys to come, and even visited Munsera by car in order to see the Black Mountain and some snow on a distant range. The Hazara district is like a tongue protruding from the N.W.F.P. for 120 miles in a north-easterly direction. It is bounded on the east by Kashmir, on the north by the outer Himalaya which separate it from Chilas, and on the west by a mountainous region occupied by the independent unadministered hill tribes of Kohistan, the Black Mountain, and others. It is not mountainous on a true Himalayan scale. On the Kashmir side of the Kagan valley, of which Hazara largely consists, the highest peak is Mali Ka Parbat 17,360 ft., while on the Indus side there is nothing higher than 15,000 ft.

To calculate the number of mules required for an expedition is not so simple as one might think. Sometimes, if the mules have to be brought from some distant place the calculation must be done with precision, for a mule too many or even a mule only half laden, engaged at Rs. 6 a day is apt to give one a sharp pang every time one looks at it. It is simple enough to weigh all the loads and divide the total by 160, at the rate of two maunds of 80 lb. each per mule, but the loads, even to the last moment, are what an arithmetician would call a 'variable', and there is often some local custom which decrees that each mule must carry only 1½ maunds (120 lb.); or, as was the case betwen Chilas and Gilgit, 2½ maunds (200 lb.). An experienced man, an Angtharkay, for example, will take one look at a veritable tumulus of assorted loads and say at once so many mules—and, lo, it is so. The inexperienced will take paper and pencil and a spring balance, and when the mule train moves off he will be astonished to find two or three of his loads are still on the ground. On the whole it pays to err on the right side. The mule-men will grumble in no uncertain voice if their mules are overloaded, while any spare mule can always be handed over to anyone rash enough to ride.

Our mules were to meet us at Balakot a place forty miles away near the junction of the Kunhar river, which flows down the Kagan valley, and the Jhelum, to which we were to take the loads by bus. We chartered a bus for this journey and, having ordered the mules, tentatively fixed the 22nd as sailing day. We only wanted a wire now from Kappeler giving his expected time of arrival, but before this came we received two others both of which rudely ruffled the placidity of life at the Circuit House. The first reopened the question of flying, which I thought had been settled, by advising us that 'the cost would be reconsidered'. This gave it a new and insidious gloss, for I suspected that the words might be interpreted as 'nothing at all', our descent on Gilgit having been in all probability arranged to take place under cover of a R.A.F. exercise. The eager Kappeler was happily elsewhere at this critical moment. Gyr, I found, was now lukewarm about flying, while I myself was positively cold. Moreover, our transport was now arranged, an advance had been paid, and we were to start in three days. To this offer we therefore returned a polite but firm refusal on the grounds that it was now too late.

The other wire came from Kappeler and although it called for no such bold decision caused me personally much more worry. It was to say that my Bombay argosy had at last arrived at Karachi but that one package of the seven was missing. This, I suppose, was not really surprising since the ship instead of discharging at Bombay and coming to Karachi to load according to schedule, had decided to reload first at Bombay. All these seven packages were vital, not to me alone although one contained my personal kit, but to the expedition, for they contained the 'Meade' tents, the 'Logan' tent for the porters, porters' boots, sleeping-bags, and windproofs, and all our pemmican, and which bale contained what I had no idea. The firm that packed them had not provided any list of the contents of each bale and no bale had any mark of identification except my initials. All that could be done was to wire Kappeler that every package was necessary and that he must sit in Karachi until the tally was complete or until his patience was exhausted.

The next news was from Young at Rawalpindi to say that he had fished the long-suffering Kappeler out of a train and that he had with him all seven packages. This came at lunch on the 21st. Our start was arranged for dawn next day for by now we were chafing to be off. Regardless of economy or Kappeler's feelings, for he and Young were both cine-camera enthusiasts and would have much to discuss, we hired a large car and sent it off with Gyr to Rawalpindi to collect the wanderer and the precious baggage. They were back that evening at dusk, Kappeler full of lurid tales of his experiences in the holds of the hell-ship *Historian* (for that was her name and by now that was what I thought of her), of the babus, stevedores, Customs' officials, and ship's officers, whom he had bullied and cajoled, of his despair and final triumph when he himself had lit on the missing bale lurking obscenely in some foetid corner of the hold, its sketchy markings obliterated with coal dust. I plied him with beer.

Far into the night Kappeler and ourselves did battle amidst a sea of boxes and bales in a way reminiscent of the scenes that must have been staged in the *Historian's* hold, though now the stage, the Circuit House, was cleaner and probably not so warm. There was a lot of damage to wrestle with and many momentous decisions to be taken; whether we needed one shirt or two, two pairs of pants, three, or none at all; whether Gilgit should be gratified by our lounge suits or insulted with mere khaki. The despised and rejected had to be packed and transferred to the Commissioner's godown, fresh loads had to be made up and more weighing had to be done, the porters fitted with boots and issued with sleeping-bags, windproofs, and warm clothing—enough in fact to keep us up till midnight, and we were billed to start at 4 a.m.

With unusual forethought we had loaded the bus before calling it a night and turning in; but what avails forethought in the face of sloth? The driver, having carefully removed himself out of our reach overnight, returned only at 5 a.m., his head and face enveloped in shawls against the air of that unwholesome hour. We were off at last on our sixteen-day trek—nor were we mocked by the hum of any distant aeroplane.

CHAPTER THREE

The Approach March

WITHOUT wishing to be thought a self-righteous zealot I confess that I still find a dawn start fascinating. Heaven knows, during the war-years, there were enough of these to surfeit most people, while seamen or farmhands, for example, and thousands of workers going to work or coming off night-shift in winter, have every reason to view the very early morning with an indifference bordering on aversion. But the words 'start at dawn', which sometimes used to crop up in 'Orders' despite their unmilitary vagueness, invariably gave me a thrill of expectation. Possibly 'start' is the key-word rather than 'dawn', for it implies a move, an adventure, or at least a full day ahead of one.

Some writers of exotic stories would have us believe that east of Suez dawn is too abrupt to be enjoyed as we enjoy the lingering beauty of an English summer dawn. There they liken it to the drawing of a blind or even the switching on of a light, one minute it is black night the next it is full day. I have always found the several stages of an Eastern dawn long enough to savour fully each transformation. First, the stealthy transition from darkness to half-light, when mountains surprisingly resolve themselves into nearby trees and trees into clumps of grass, while the western sky momentarily darkens in contrast to the heightening pallor of the east; and then full light when the landscape falls into shape like the pieces of a puzzle; and at last the sun himself to dispel the lingering mists and to banish mystery and romance with his keen shaft of reality.

I have never forgotten a verse in a poem of the First World War although I have forgotten the author. His description of an Eastern dawn, or to be exact a Middle-Eastern, perhaps appealed more strongly because it was obviously written by a man who had served in a smart battery of Horse or Field Artillery:

> How when we went down Sparta way,
> To sandy Sparta, long ere dawn
> Horses were harnessed, rations drawn,
> Equipment polished sparkling bright
> And breakfast swallowed ere the light
> Of Eastern heavens had turned to white.
> Dogs barked, last farewells were said.

The misery, ill temper, and mistimed facetiousness of very early Alpine starts are forgotten and forgiven with the first hint of dawn, bringing with it a lessening of strain and restoring the mastery to eyes and feet. A new unimagined scene unfolds, affording the satisfaction of height gained and hours stolen from time. The renewal of well-being and kindly feeling which we had temporarily lost is partly attributable to our rewon ability to see and move freely on strange or difficult ground; but even when walking down a familiar street in the most commonplace surroundings the thrill of dawn can still be experienced, and possibly this is owing to our feeling that while others sleep we are the sole witness of the pageant of a new day, as if we were alone upon a newborn earth. De Quincey delighted in the silence and peace of early summer morning because—'Man is not yet abroad'.

However, when driving along a hill-road in an Indian lorry, dawn and the full glare of the day cannot come too quickly. The scales are already sufficiently weighted in favour of a violent death without the added perils of the half-light. On our journey from Munsera we found the road only third rate and provided with enough hidden corners to keep one on tenterhooks even in broad daylight. No on who is in the habit of driving from the passenger's seat should undertake this section unless he is blindfold. But in the end we dropped down through the pines to the valley of the Kunhar without mishap and pulled up at Balakot rest-house.

The Deputy Commissioner of Hazara, in the midst of the prevailing unrest, had found time to deal with the additional worry of having us and our Sherpas passing through the district. One of his junior officials, a 'thesildar' who knew the people of the Kagan valley and who spoke good English, had been detailed to accompany us as far as the Babusar pass, and a local rajah had been asked to provide an escort. The peaceful looking valley with its well-kept mule track, where people were too busy with their fields to notice us, did not seem the place to warrant an escort, but in the hills to the west there is unadministered territory from where, perhaps, trouble might be expected. It was possible, too, that the presence of our Sherpas might excite the Moslems of the valley. They are not Hindu, but are if anything Buddhists. Such a distinction would not, however, have been recognized by a Moslem, at that particular time, for just as all cats are grey in the dark so anyone with a brown face who was not obviously a Moslem must be a Hindu and consequently anathema.

Our conductor, the escort of a dozen men headed by the local rajah, and the mules, were awaiting our arrival. The rest house had been opened and breakfast prepared, so thither we adjourned leaving the muleteers and the Sherpas to wrangle over the loads. Just as letters will answer themselves if left quite alone, so at such moments if one avoids the scene of action for a sufficiently long time things will quite likely straighten themselves out. Our first sight of the escort suggested that it was in our honour rather than in our defence. Their most advanced weapon was an old single-barrel shot-gun while the rest defied classification. But at least there were no bows and arrows. However, Kappeler judged them sufficiently picturesque to expend an alarming amount of film.

On Bacon's principle that 'it is pleasant to see a battle from a distant hill', I lingered over breakfast as long as possible watching with one eye the scene of semi-activity in the compound. At the end of an hour five mules had been loaded, but as the march was to be short—the first day's march cannot well be too short—there was no cause for allowing angry passions to interfere with digestion. Patience, according to Buddhists is the greatest prayer. At last the loading was complete, though not before I had been compelled to accept one more mule, for my estimate though mathematically correct did not satisfy the mule contractor. In this case the 'variable responsible for error was the presence among the mules of one or two dwarfs, but rather than wait to have them changed or to see them wilt under a full load I agreed to one more.

The mules filed out of the compound, the escort fell in, we were bidden to fall in behind, and off we went. We felt it unfortunate that the rajah took his escort duties so seriously. Except Kappeler, who was permitted to go ahead for cinema duty, we were not allowed to stray in front or very far behind, and the rajah was never really satisfied unless he had us all under his eye, bodyguard in front and we marching dutifully behind.

This year, as will appear, I was to have my fill of armed men. I do not dislike them as such in their proper place but I do dislike them in the

Himalaya or in any out-of-the-way place where one goes in the expectation of solitude. If there are to be any people at all let them be 'the thing itself— unaccommodated man', not interlopers bearing arms or wearing uniforms who serve but to shatter the carefully fostered illusion that one has at last strayed beyond the last frontier. These sentiments are, of course, inapplicable to our harmless escort so thoughtfully provided and so kindly meant; nevertheless, without them my felicity would have been perfect. Just as so slight a thing as the wearing of a bathing dress detracts from the perfection of an otherwise perfect bathe, so the slight feeling of constraint marred the perfection of this long-looked-for return to marching and camping in the kindly valleys of the outer Himalaya. Still I felt uncommonly happy at trekking once more behind a string of mules with their bright headbands, gaudy red wool tassels, and jingling bells, over a road and country new to me with the promise of sixteen such days ahead. I felt I could go on like this for ever, that life had little better to offer than to march day after day in an unknown country to an unattainable goal.

Perhaps only a seeker after the Way who has attained those lofty realms where mind and thought are divorced from bodily feeling can hope to remain insensible to freshness or fatigue, hunger or satiety, cold or heat. The morning was well advanced and it was uncommonly hot, so that my thoughts underwent a gradual change. Far from wishing the march to go on for ever I did not care how soon it would be over. I did not care if it was my last. My companions evidently felt the same. They looked about feverishly for water and when we reached a stream one could sense the tremendous struggle between desire and prudence; for, no doubt, like most new-comers to India they had been warned that dysentry and death lurk in every river. Certainly on this day we cut a poor figure and qualified for inclusion among Carlyle's 'gluttonous race of Jutes and Angles lumbering about in pot-bellied equanimity; not dreaming of heroic toil and silence and endurance, such as leads to the high places of this Universe.'

We all have our theories about drinking on the march. I have always found it better in every way to abstain, which is not difficult if one is fit; for, as the Arabs say of the husbands of the talkative, 'great is their reward hereafter'. If one is not fit then a pebble in the mouth is a help provided that it is not swallowed. Others who should know adopt what appears to be the commonsense view and hold that the best way of dealing with thirst is to satisfy it; but I believe that it is not possible to do this while on the march, when one drink merely increases the desire for another, and that with thirst as with every other craving, 'to deny early and inflexibly is the only art of checking the importunity of desire'. On this occasion our self-denial was not severely tried, for Ahmed Sultan the thesildar, who was our cicerone, had arranged for a wayside halt where we were hospitably regaled with tea and maize bread, with a puff or two at a hubble-bubble for those who could use it. Maize bread is pleasant enough, once in a way, but its presence as a staple article of diet usually indicates a poor country where the peasants cannot afford to grow a much lower-yielding cereal like wheat. In Hazara, where land is scarce, it is the staple food as only the bigger landowners can afford to grow wheat. Owing to the dry climate the maize is a short-stemmed variety. At 3 o'clock, hot, footsore, weary, we reached the Kuwai bungalow at a height of 5,000 ft. Tea was ready and those who had denied themselves on the march reaped the full, exquisitely grateful reward of their abstinence. Below the bungalow there runs a small stream where I soon found a waterfall under which I could stand. I seemed to absorb as much fluid through the skin as I had done previously through the mouth. So great was my longing for this bathe that had the stream been more ample and its surroundings more gracious it would have qualified for a place in my list of 'memorable bathes'.

Kuwai was remarkable for the complete absence of flies, mosquitoes, ants, and similar noxious creatures. We dined outside in comfort. There were no flying beetles or moths to immolate themselves on the lamp or to drown themselves in the soup, and at night we slept outside on the ground without having to pick ants out of our hair or centipedes from under the pillow. When the mountain is reached 'sleeping out' loses its attraction, but on the approach march through the hot valleys I find it a great joy. As a prelude to sleep, reading in bed though good, is not to be compared to listening to the restless mules, to the distant bark of a jackal, or to the wind in the pines. And while the fire glows red at one's feet one can watch the Great Bear take shape as one by one its stars rise over some black, jagged ridge, while Scorpion peers faintly over the mists of the southern plains.

There are eight stages along the Kagan valley to the Babusar pass, the exit from the valley over the Himalayan range at its head. Most of them are short or very short. This arrangement seems to be the most satisfactory, as no day is too short for the lazy or tired man and no day too long for the lusty or impatient, who, if he wishes, can do two or even three of these stages. But in a place like the Indus valley, for example, or the Karakoram pass route, where one must do twenty or more miles before finding shelter, grass, or even water, it is a case of 'Pike's Peak or bust' for all alike. Of course, if one is riding, the length of a stage is really only of concern to one's mount, but with a view to undergoing a 'hardening' process we made a point of walking all the way. It seems that in walking our standards, or at least mine, are far below those of the early mountaineers. Though I cannot trace the passage, I remember reading of a friend of Whymper's who was about to join him in the Alps, apologizing in advance for bringing with him a young companion who through having been recently ill could not be expected to do more than fifty miles a day. I once walked forty-five miles myself, but I look on that as one of my more sensational adventures—as a man might who had once swum the Channel.

Our second march was more enjoyable than the first, perhaps because we were in a fitter state to enjoy it but probably because it was blessedly short. We left at 7 a.m. and were in by noon—a long enough time, too, for the enjoyment of scenery however fine. The track lay high on the left bank. Below us was the river running now over shallows in green and white foam, now swirling in pools of the deepest blue. Beyond the forest swept up to the snow and rocks of Raggan Pajji and to the gentler summit of Musa ka Musallak (13,378 ft.), the Praying Carpet of Moses. Snow lends grandeur to the lowest and mildest mountain as a bearskin gives stature and fierceness to a Guardsman; in full summer when these mountains are stripped of their winter finery the valley must lose much of its Alpine character. The forests which grow freely on both sides of the Kunhar are worked for their timber which is floated down river to the Jhelum. Deodar cedar, blue pine and chir(*Pinus longifolia*), silver fir and Himalayan spruce, of which the last two are most common, are all used. On to-day's march we had our 'elevenses' at a timber contractor's logging camp where they were getting the felled timber down to the river which, as the snow melted, would soon reach its full height.

At Mahandri, twenty-five miles from Balakot, we were plagued with flies, while Kappeler in spite of his self-imposed water discipline had a bout of stomach trouble. Next morning we regretted our late breakfast when we found we had to eat yet another at a village half-way on the eleven-mile stage to Kagan, for the lambadars, or headmen, were always eager to offer hospitality and help. Travelling under official patronage may involve constraint but it does ensure comfort and freedom from minor worries. At Kagan, at the far end of the gorge, our rajah friend and his escort left us, their place being taken by another local rajah with his retainers.

The new rajah was less of a martinet than his predecessor and his escort was smaller. March discipline was relaxed and our march to Naran, nearly 8,000 ft. up, was the most pleasant we had had, for we were now getting high enough to be always cool. Naran was even more favoured than Kagan for arable land. There were many fields of dwarf maize, buckwheat, and barley, and water-meadows where the grass was rich and the flowers numerous; even I who am no botanist could recognize and welcome the blue and purple violets, light blue forget-me-nots, great white peonies, pink mallows, and yellow primulas. On this march we crossed our first snow-bed and the snow on the slopes of the valley appeared to come well below 14,000 ft., two facts which made our proposed crossing of the Babusar problematical— particularly as we heard a fresh account of its condition every day. We had been told at Balakot that there was no snow, at Kagan the road was reported blocked, and to-day we had met two lithe, picturesque looking heathens, who turned out to be Kohistanis, who assured us that the pass was open, for they had just crossed it. Still, as we were the first mule train of the year I was not confident; for snow upon which a man may easily walk may not support a laden mule.

Another difficulty presented itself. Apparently the flooring of the bridges on this route is dismantled in winter and stored; perhaps to safeguard it from the elements, perhaps to prevent it becoming an addition to the wood pile of some indolent villager; and now we had overtaken the road gang which was busy putting the road in order for the summer. From Naran we had boldly proposed doing a double march to Burawai, thereby cutting out a halt at Battakundi, but the road foreman objected to this because there were still two bridges this side of Burawai which had yet to be reassembled. With a little pressing he promised to make the two bridges ready for us and in return we graciously consented to take our day off at Burawai while he and his men laboured on the road beyond. This road foreman was admirable. He was a little shrunken Hindu of great spirit—foreman of a gang of Moslems in a Moslem country—and he drove his gang as if they were so many untouchables and he a high-caste Brahmin. No doubt when Pakistan became independent he lost his job, and possibly his life too.

We had another pleasant march to Battakundi. The road, still in woods and still on the left bank, followed close by the river which here flows peacefully in a wide bed, eddying quietly round rocky headlands and small islands all with their stand of sombre pine or fir. The thesildar promised us a dish of fish from one of these quiet reaches but the fish thought otherwise. 'The camel driver has his thoughts and the camel he has his', as the Arabs say. The bungalow, where we halted only for lunch, occupies the finest site imaginable on a grassy spur overlooking the river. In the distance were slopes of bare grass which now began to oust the forest, and on our right we looked up a side nallah to the magnificently jagged wall of the 16,000 ft. Dabuka. During the eight remaining miles to Burawai the scene becomes wilder, the trees scantier, but the flowers more numerous than ever. We caught up the road gang, who had just put one bridge in order, and waited half an hour while they floored another over a side stream just short of the bungalow.

We were at about 10,000 ft. here, the weather was windy and unsettled so we slept inside for the first time since Balakot. Our day of rest which was cloudy, windy, and wet, we devoted to climbing a 13,000 ft. hill nearby in order to try out the 'expedition' boots. During the march each wore whatever he favoured. Gyr tried 'chaplis', the universal Frontier wear, and soon discarded them as I think do most sensible people. Since they act as a trap for stones and gravel and provide no support for the ankles, I cannot conceive why anyone should commend them, much less wear them. On a hillside, for which they are supposed to be the footwear *par excellence*, there is the further disadvantage that the foot, especially the heel, is seldom inside and overlaps the 'chapli' thereby becoming bruised and cut. Most natives wear them in the hills, though as often as not one sees them being carried, but since natives are quite at home with nothing on their feet and have never known what it is to wear boots, they can hardly be expected to realize the disadvantages. I favour plimsolls (the American 'sneaker') for the sake of their lightness on the feet or in the load, but their quality nowadays is not what it used to be. My first pair were finished before we reached Gilgit and my third pair did not carry me beyond Kashgar. On this 13,000 ft. peak of ours we encountered grass, gravel, rock and snow. We found that the rubber soles gripped well everywhere, but the boots themselves were damnably heavy and so stiff that our ankles were all chafed.

We were met here by a Chilasi with a letter from Capt. Hamilton, the Assistant Political Agent, Chilas, telling us that a party of Scouts would meet us below the pass and that a fresh lot of mules would be ready for us at Chilas. The next stage was to Besal from where after a conference with the road foreman we planned to cross the pass without the usual halt at Gittidas. Whereupon the foreman armed his men with long-handled shovels and hurried them on to clear the numerous drifts reported to him by the Chilasi.

Besal is 10,700 ft. up. Pines and birch in their turn, had given up the struggle for existence, and even the hardy juniper bush was but rarely seen. The bungalow, too, as if in keeping with the barrenness of the land was bare of door or of windows—defects which caused our thesildar to mutter darkly about thievish Kohistanis. Close to the bungalow was a large circular platform of stones about six feet high; with a stone staircase, on top of which was a tomb, the whole beflagged with tattered bits of cloth mounted on long poles. The story was that this was the tomb of a very holy man who had come to Besal to pass the winter in solitary meditation, bringing with him as fuel for the long winter months one piece of wood. Not only had this provided the saint with fire throughout the winter, but when spring came there was still enough left to plant in the ground. Here it presently took root, sprouted, and in due time flourished into a noble tree. All this had happened within the memory of living man, but when we asked the thesildar where was the tree he replied that some sacrilegious pagan had cut it down and burnt it. Nevertheless, none of our men neglected to say prayers at the shrine of this holy man, and the thesildar was obviously stretching a point when he permitted us to mount the platform with our shoes on.

Forewarned of troublesome snow-drifts ahead we arranged to start at 5 o'clock, and by getting up myself to indulge in some indiscriminate kicking and cursing of sleeping forms we achieved a 6 o'clock start. For some such occasion as this I had with me a Swiss pocket alarm-watch—a gift from the 'Stiftung'. This went well as a watch but after giving me one or two successful calls it ceased to function as an alarm. Some two miles beyond Besal is the mountain lake of Lulu Star which Kappeler with abundant energy had already visited the evening before for photography. This morning as we skirted its eastern shore he had further opportunity to catch the glories of snow and rock reflected in its passive blue waters.

We now began to find that all the side nallahs and re-entrants were drifted up in earnest, and the nearer we drew to Gittidas (11,860 ft.) the wider the drifts became. I cursed our late start, the mule drivers regretted it; for though a man could still walk on the surface the snow had softened so rapidly that the mules broke through at every step to plunge and flounder belly-deep. Here occurred our only serious loss, but since it more concerned our friends than ourselves we bore it with unexampled fortitude. We were carrying a case of whisky to our friends at Gilgit as a token of gratitude for benefits to come. The mule carrying it—evidently a Moslem mule with scant respect for this kind of white man's burden—in lurching himself violently clear of a drift, unshipped the whole load, and the case bounded off down the 'khud'. There was a merry sound of tinkling fragments, the eager nipping air became balmy with the gentle fragrance of whisky, and we realized that all was over and that our friends had sustained a very serious misfortune indeed.

Two miles away the wide pastures of Gittidas and the bungalow came in sight. It seemed to be occupied and presently lithe figures began running towards us. They were the Scouts from Chilas who had seen the plight of our mules. They threw down their packs and rifles and set to work with a will. Their lieutenant did not confine himself, as do so many officers, to the mere directing and encouraging of his men but worked himself harder than any of them, hauling at head collars, heaving on tails, carrying forward and readjusting fallen loads, and acting generally as a human bulldozer.

Under this welcome and compelling impact drivers and mules took fresh heart and in a short time we arrived at Gittidas where we dismissed with thanks our rajah, took the thesildar's photo and dismissed him also with thanks. Neither he nor the rajah would hear of any present, which was as well since I was armed only with presents for the Mirs of Hunza and Nagar. Once clear of Gittidas we found no more snow this side of the pass. Four miles away on a bare stony hillside, we could see the saddle and the cairn marking the summit. We reached this at 2 p.m. and should have seen, but did not, the mighty snow massif of Nanga Parbat 35 miles to the east, the giant before whom the peaks of our Kagan valley trip must bow their diminished heads, and far to the north, dominating all the Hunza peaks, the graceful Rakaposhi herself. There was no reason to linger. The Himalaya had been crossed, though there was little in our surroundings to impress the fact upon us, for between Nanga Parbat and the Indus fifty miles west of us, the Great Himalyan range droops, dwindles, and terminates for good. Nanga Parbat itself is an abnormality, for it does not lie on the main axis of the range but on a great buttress pushed out to the north, while in height it towers far above the main range itself. Another unusual feature of the Himalaya west of the Sutlej is that they are not pierced by rivers as are the Himalaya of Garhwal, Nepal and Sikkim. The only way over them is by passes such as the Babusar, and the Burzil and Zoji in Kashmir.

On the north side there was still some snow, but a few hundred feet down it ended and there we found Capt. Hamilton awaiting us with an ample lunch already spread. By 4 p.m. we were down to 10,000 ft. again and close to Babusar village where we found the A.P.A.'s summer bungalow, the barracks for a company of Scouts, and a polo ground. We were played in by the drum and pipe[1] band which any place of any pretensions in the Gilgit Agency maintains to welcome and later speed the guest, and to provide the essential musical accompaniment to polo matches. The match arranged in our honour was delayed by a thunderstorm during which we ate quantities of jam and scones in Hamilton's bungalow. The rain then ceasing and his cook and bearer, who were playing in one of the teams, having washed up, he donned white breeches, boots, and helmet, and we all walked across to the ground to begin the game.

As the reader will have guessed, polo in those parts is a democratic game. It is also the national game from Chilas up to Astor, throughout the Agency, and throughout Chitral too; and since it has often been described I need not waste many words on it. Essentially it is a game with few or no rules either as to ponies, players, or the size and shape of the ground. In these vertical valleys horizontal space is scarce and valuable so the ground is usually a long narrow strip, some 200 by 40 yards, with a low stone wall bounding the two longer sides. These walls have a dual purpose—as a stand for the spectators and as a cushion for the ball and the players. The space between the walls is

---

1 According to Conway the reed-pipe is like a bag-pipe chanter. It has a scale of nine notes of the same intervals as the chanter except that the three upper notes are flat.

usually grassy, sometimes stony, but seldom level. The six players of either side, not uniformly attired, on ponies not uniformly equipped, take up some sort of loose formation; the band strikes up, the less placid ponies prance and dance, the ball is thrown in by some distinguished guest (on this occasion myself) seated under a covered stand opposite the half-way line, and the game begins. Literally it is fast and furious. Hard riding, harder hitting, and no quarter given or asked, are its characteristics. When a goal is scored they change ends and the man who scored has the honour of what is called the 'tambok'; that is to say he gallops full belt up the field carrying the ball in one hand and when in mid-field opposite the distinguished visitors he throws the ball into the air and clouts it (if he can) towards the goal. Experts seldom miss the ball from the 'tambok' and quite frequently score a goal. There are no 'chukkas', but there is an interval at half-time, play each way lasting, I think, half an hour. I have seen only one or two of the more civilized polo games played on a vast acreage of ground, but as a spectacle I do not think it compares with the intimate wall game, with the squalling pipes, ponies and players in one constant mêlée, and the cheers and jeers of the crowd squatting on the wall on the very fringe of the battle. It sounds dangerous, and to me it looked dangerous, but Hamilton emerged unscathed from this long hour of peril and, as he wiped mud and sweat from his face, assured me that accidents were almost unknown. On the other hand, when I was at Kashgar, Mr Shipton told me that twice attempts had been made to start the game there but that on each occasion a man had been killed in the first few minutes. Anyhow I concluded that like Prince Hal's duel with Hotspur, 'you shall find no boy's play here, I can tell you'.

CHAPTER FOUR

Gilgit—Arrival and Departure

FROM Babusar bungalow to Chilas is twenty-four miles, but the march is not so formidable as might be thought for it is downhill all the way. From a height of 10,000 ft. the track drops steadily and steeply to 4,000 ft. On this side of the watershed conditions are reversed; forest or vegetation becomes scantier as one descends, until near the bottom of the Indus valley it ceases altogether. On this day's march we stopped short of the starkest aridity, for Chilas lies on a spur well above the main valley and is watered by a fine stream; indeed, in the garden of the A.P.A.'s bungalow the vegetation is almost tropically lush and various—giant blue gums and clumps of bamboo, mulberry and apricot trees heavy with fruit, walnut trees and edible pines. A warm shady oasis haunted by long-tailed paradise fly-catchers, hoopoes, golden orioles, and king-fishers from the nearby stream.

We were in by 4 p.m. and were soon reclining in long chairs screened by wire-netting against mosquitoes, eating without discrimination chocolate cake, mulberries, and apricots. Though our descent had been rapid the mules were not long in following. Last to arrive was Ningma, one of the Sherpas, who had been foolhardy enough to wear the 'expedition' boots. These boots preyed on my mind as their weight did on my feet; so much so that I sent a wire to Abbottabad for the porter's boots I had brought with me from England.

From below the junction of the Astor river with the Indus down to Jalkot on the Swat border the people are grouped in small communities inhabiting one or more nallahs, each community forming a separate republic. They constitute the area known as the Chilas subdivision of the Gilgit Agency and are administered by the A.P.A. stationed at Chilas village where there are also a fort and troops. Chilas was conquered by Kashmir in 1851, but when the British Agency was established at Gilgit in 1889 it was included as the Chilas subdivision. In 1892 a British mission was attacked by Chilasis and this led to the occupation of the country and the appointment of a Political Officer at Chilas. This appointment was, I imagine, an enviable one; Hamilton's only complaint being the number of murder cases, the result of blood-feuds, which came up for trial. There is, however, a close season for murder when game like ibex, markhor, and red bear would be in season, and in addition there is trout fishing and polo. Right up to the time the British left India for good the life of a British official in the remoter parts was similar to that enjoyed by officials everywhere fifty years before. He was not tied to his office by ever increasing paper work, but was free to wander at will throughout his district, getting to know the people, learning where the shoe pinched, and amusing himself incidentally with rod and gun.

In accord with this well-tried method of administration Hamilton was able to accompany us to Gilgit, so that our march assumed even more the character of an officially conducted tour. Beyond getting myself from one stage to another I had no responsibilities. We paid off our Hazara muleteers and left at 6 a.m. next morning with a fresh lot of mules and ponies, the mules now carrying 200 lb., the ponies 160 lb. The Indus valley stages are long; moreover they are hot. The river lies at only 3,000 ft., the air is dry, the sky cloudless, and the sun correspondingly fierce, so that the wayfarer trapped between the stark rock walls of the gorge is grilled like a herring suspended in a Dutch oven. The northern wall of the valley collects the heat and reflects it back to the opposing wall on the south bank. Trees which might afford a refuge from the sun or even grass upon which the eyes could find relief from the glare, are to be found only where man has tapped the life-giving water of some infrequent side nallah. Such places seldom fail to arouse admiration and astonishment—admiration for those who first had the enterprise and skill to make their homes on such an unpromising and uncompromising slag heap, and astonishment that water skilfully applied could overcome even that hideous sterility.

We marched on a stony track high above the river and instead of doing the brutal twenty-three-mile stage to Jalipur halted for the night at Gunar where there is a Government farm. The principal crops are lucerne for fodder, and wheat, and while Hamilton went off on his tour of inspection we went down to the river. The slow-moving dark brown canal which we had seen from the height of our stony track proved to be a fast and turgid river of great volume. Though it did not look inviting, not to bathe in the Indus would be an affront. But so fast and frigid was the water that all that could be done was to allow one's numbed body to be swept down for a short way and then scramble out and burrow a scoop in the hot sand of the beach. Though it was not what I would call a 'memorable bathe', yet it gave great satisfaction to bathe in so mighty a stream and to fancy that the water supporting one had come from the distant Mansarowar in Tibet or perhaps the great Baltoro glacier.

We dined in a mulberry grove off a savoury pilau in the strangest conditions. Almost as we took our places under a venerable mulberry, darkness having just begun, a violent thunderstorm with wind, dust, and a sprinkling of rain struck us. Men will go through fire and water on occasion for various reasons. In this case it was for the pilau. Like Lear we defied the storm. 'Rumble thy bellyful. Spit fire. Spout rain'—we might have declaimed—'but we *will* have our pilau.' So we put on our coats, turned up our collars, clung to the table with one hand and shovelled in rice with the other.

Having only to do the six miles which we had left undone the day before, we reached Jalipur at 9 a.m. and breakfasted there. The bungalow was sited on a bluff round the foot of which the turbulent brown flood swept angrily. Upstream was a bay where it ran more calmly and here I tried my hand at washing the black sand for gold. Just across the river were the ramshackle huts of a family of gold-washers, but my choice of site was evidently poor for not the faintest trace of 'colour' in the pan rewarded my efforts. In the Indus in Baltistan gold-washing is an industry of some importance. So it is near Gilgit, particularly in the Bagrot nallah south of Rakaposhi which is said to be rich, and in many of the rivers of Hunza and Nagar. The usual time is in winter when the river is low; some families do nothing else, but they are driven to it by poverty and can only make a bare living.

This widely scattered gold must be brought from some reef or reefs which, one would think, it would be worth someone's while to seek. I have been interested in gold (and who is not) since my Kenya days when I spent six enjoyable and exciting months in vain efforts to find it. Prospecting, like many other attractive ways of making a living or near-living, is not the quiet, ruminative, ambulatory occupation of former days, when one went off into the 'blue' with a donkey-load of supplies, rifle, pick, shovel, dolly, and pan, chose a nice camp site near a stream and roamed the surrounding hills until the supplies ran out or one struck a Bonanza reef. Nowadays, I understand, sleek scientists consult their geological maps, are flown or driven to the chosen area, where, by peering into a box of tricks or listening through ear-phones they inform themselves or their employers with more or less accuracy what minerals there are several thousand feet below them.

From Jalipur to Thelichi is a very dry eighteen miles. Travelling in country like that of the Indus valley is best done at night or after a very early start. We were away by 4 a.m. in bright moonlight thus cheating, for a time at least, the crude hot day of its power to weary and dazzle. There is no better light to march by than that of a kindly moon—a quarter moon will serve—which, while revealing clearly enough the stones and pitfalls in the immediate path, hides discreetly the distant landmarks, cheating them, too, of their power to tease us with the slowness of our approach. By moonlight, too, is the best time to view, if one must, the bare bony nudity of our earth as disclosed by the Indus valley,[1] when the livid rock is transformed into black opacity, the hot sand into cool silvery greyness, and the dark river glistens.

We reached the Rakhiot bridge in time for a haversack breakfast. The Rakhiot nallah, the time-honoured approach to Nanga Parbat, joins the Indus at this point, where it flows in a narrow gorge, spanned by an iron suspension bridge. On the stone supporting pillar of the bridge are carved the names of the seven German mountaineers who with nine Sherpas were buried in the avalanche that swept over their Camp IV on Nanga Parbat in 1937. Far away, framed in the dark cleft of the Rakhiot nallah we could see the mountain itself glimmering white and high. From now on we were seldom without a snow mountain in view to which we could lift our eager eyes from the barreness on either hand. As we climbed out of the gorge on the right bank and the valley began to swing northwards, the whole vast face of Nanga Parbat came into sight, while at the third mile from Thelichi we had our first glimpse of Rakaposhi. There was no mistaking it. There was the high snow plateau on the western side which we had seen in the photographs, and there, too, was the graceful final pyramid to which the plateau served as a plinth. From the plateau to the summit alone was visible, and there seemed nothing there to arouse misgivings.

A similar early start on 3 June brought us to Jaglot[2] bungalow by 7 a.m. Here the A.P.A. from Gilgit (Mr Paul Mainprice) had arranged for us another polo match. Both he and Hamilton played, but we did not. I would not advise any mountaineer friend of mine to play anywhere, least of all on this ground at Jaglot where the background or sight-screen to one goal is formed by the fluted ice and snow faces of Nanga Parbat while directly behind the other is the less majestic but equally distracting Dobani (20,126 ft.), an outlier of the Rakaposhi range. After polo came breakfast, and after breakfast a display of dancing to the same drum and pipe band which had recently been setting the polo ponies prancing. The dances are done by one or sometimes two men or boys. But here is no prancing. Violence and speed have no place, a slow graceful movement is the rule, more use being made of the arms, the body, and the head, than the feet, while the natural grace of the performer is helped by the flow of the long sleeves and skirts of his 'choga'. The dancer comes into the ring, gravely salutes the company, and then turns towards the band with whom he seems to be in close communion throughout the dance. When done the company is again saluted.

After this we all took horse and instead of following the valley to Parri, our next stop, we went up the side valley of the Sai stream with the hope of the noble prospect of Rakaposhi which is sometimes obtained when coming back

1 'Mere crumpled Sahara', is Conway's apt description.
2 Not to be confused with Jaglot village at the foot of Rakaposhi.

over the ridge between this nallah and the Gilgit river. Just above Jaglot the
Indus valley strikes off to the east and the Gilgit river joins it from the north.
We were disappointed of our promised view by cloud, but it was a pleasant
ride in which Kappeler, who had never been on a horse in his life,
distinguished himself by staying on throughout. He did more. Unlike Captain
Miserrimus Doleful who 'sat a horse with ease and grace until it began to
move', he cut a very creditable equestrian figure even at a sharp canter. Parri
is on the Gilgit river in which we must bathe to pay our footing. This river,
like all the others at this time of year, was flowing fast, and the water was
thick and discoloured. In winter when they shrink they become blue and
limpid, and are then what all rivers should be, lovely to look at and friendly to
swim in. A few years ago the P.A. Gilgit (Major Galbraith) and his wife were
drowned in this river when their collapsible boat hit a rock and sank.

On 4 June we completed our final stage to Gilgit. We now experienced the
truth of a proverb I have already quoted that 'the sight of a horse makes the
traveller lame', for having now three horses, provided by Mainprice, at our
disposal it seemed ungrateful not to use them. Moreover, having once tasted
the joys of swift motion, effortless travel, the rush of cool air on our brows,
the sparing of legs and feet, and the unnecessary saving of time, none of us
was reluctant to taste them again. Between Parri and Gilgit, a matter of
nineteen miles, the road is very suitable for riding, so much so that we
covered it in little more than three hours. We drew rein but twice to peer
hopefully up the Bagrot and Dainyor nallahs on the opposite side of the
valley, condemning the first as being remote from our mountain and the
second as being a too repulsive line of approach. But of that more presently.
We received the kindest of welcomes from Col. and Mrs Bacon at the
Residency where I was to lodge.

Gilgit a township lies in the middle of what is for this broken country a large
tract of flat easily irrigated land on the right bank of the Gilgit river near the
junction of that and the Hunza river. In the whole of the Himalayan region I
can think of no other township so surrounded by mountains. Within a radius
of sixty-five miles there are eleven peaks from 18,000 to 20,000 ft., seven from
20,500 to 22,000 ft., six from 22,000 to 24,000 ft., and eight from 24,000 to
26,600 ft. In a country so inimical to agriculture it is therefore, I suppose, a
valuable prize, but compared with Kashmir, for example, one might well
dismiss it as:

> . . . a little patch of ground
> That hath in it no profit but the name.
> To pay five ducats, five, I would not farm it.

Nevertheless, many have considered it worth fighting for. In the first half of
last century neighbouring rajahs quarrelled over it and there were five dynastic
revolutions. In 1842 Sikh troops entered Gilgit and installed a garrison there.
Then it was taken by the Hunza rajah and retaken by Dogra troops. Ten years
later this Dogra garrison was annihilated and in 1860 Kashmir troops once
more recovered it. In 1889, as we have seen, the British Government, acting
as the suzerain power of Kashmir, established an Agency there in order to
forestall any possible Russian advance.

Buddhist rock carvings—there is a good example at the mouth of a nallah two miles up river from Gilgit—suggest that this region was once the seat of a Buddhist dynasty, but nothing more is known of this and for centuries the people have been Mahomedans, either Shiahs or Maulais (followers of the Aga Khan). They are Aryans, and ethnologists call them Dards of Dardistan. They themselves would probably say that they were Shins living in Shinaka and speaking Shina. They are a likable people though not so virile or so hard-working as their neighbours of Hunza and Yasin. Passing from a Gilgit village to a Hunza village one sees at once how much more skill and labour has been applied to the building and upkeep of terrace walls, water channels ('kuls'), and houses, and the consequently better state of the fields and crops. But superficially all these people, Gilgitis, Hunzas, Nagars, even Chitralis, look very much alike to the stranger. Their dress is a long woollen homespun coat reaching to the knees, pyjama-like trousers of the same stuff, untanned skin boots ('pabbus'), and the distinctive white or brown wool cap which consists of a bag half a yard long which is rolled up outwards at the edge until it fits the head. Those who are better off usually wear a 'choga' which is a loose coat-like dressing gown, embroidered, and with long sleeves. It is worn flung over the shoulders with the sleeves hanging empty. This garment is more commonly worn in Chitral, and in Afghanistan the 'chapkan', as they call it there, is almost universal. The dislike of putting one's arms inside sleeves is not merely a habit of the lazy East, but is common in Albania and in Italy.

The little township of Gilgit (4,800 ft.) is attractive, well planted with trees, the fields and houses pleasantly intermingled, and the stone walls of the fields are bright with sorrel. Unlike most Indian stations there is a blessed absence of corrugated iron, so useful but so ugly. This is not unexpected when one considers the distance and the awkward mule-load such sheets would make. Barracks for the Gilgit Scouts, bazaar, hospital, court, and some half-dozen houses for European officials make up the sum of buildings. Only when a caravan arrives from Kashgar does the bazaar show much life. About six of these a year come down from distant Kashgar, bringing with them principally felt 'numdahs' and salt. One arrived when we were there and with it were two delightful Swedish missionaries who had been obliged to quit their Kashgar mission on account of Moslem prejudice.

Having arrived on the 4th we decided to leave on the 8th, so we had little leisure. Reorganizing the loads, arranging transport, and buying all the necessary stores, kept me busy; while the kindness of our friends would not allow us early nights, for upon each night of our stay we had an engagement to fulfil. In spite of our mishap with the whisky there seemed to be enough to drink, and when the imported article ran out there were local resources to fall back on. A small amount of wine, rough as a rasp, comes down from Hunza for friends of the Mir, while one or two of the residents had manfully attempted the distillation of apricot and peach brandy; indeed, if alcoholic content is any criterion, success had been achieved, for some we sampled was mere bottled lightning. Bottled mulberry juice in large quantities was available for those who did not wish to char their insides, or might be taken as a lenitive by those who had already done so. Gilgit and fine fruit are synonymous terms. Were I going again I should pay more attention to making my arrival coincide with the fruit season, and should this happen to be the best time for climbing the mountain—well, so much the worse for the mountain. But only the apricots were ripe, and they I found palled after a few days gluttony. The mulberries—large as bantams' eggs—the peaches, apples, and pears were not ready.

Any spare time I had was spent either in the swimming pool, or in whittling away odd slices of rubber and leather from my 'expedition' boots to reduce their weight—a futile proceeding prompted by the same futile hope with which a drowning man clutches a straw. Still, I was face to face with the fact that our start was imminent, that in a matter of days I should have to drag this weighty handicap up many thousands of feet, and that no amount of apricots or apricot brandy would make the task any lighter. It was also high time to decide finally on a plan of campaign.

Rakaposhi lies about twenty-five miles to the north of Gilgit on the east side of the Hunza river.[1] According to the report of the Karakoram Conference, which was held in the winter of 1936 with the object of clarifying the range-names of the Karakoram, Rakaposhi lies on the Rakaposhi range and is the outstanding peak of what is called the Rakaposhi group. It is the only peak of the group which has been triangulated and its height is 25,550 ft. The naming of Himalayan peaks is always a matter of difficulty. Either the regions round the mountain are uninhabited or the natives are too uninterested to name individual peaks. If a peak happens to be so awe-inspiring as to demand christening them those living on another side might give it a different name, so that the early and possibly ignorant traveller is given two names both of which he probably takes down wrongly. There is thus still scope for originality on the part of the later travellers, but in due time one name becomes generally accepted and later appears on a map. This is the signal for interested linguists or ethnologists to step in and practise their science by suggesting alternative spellings or interpretations of the name. Monographs have been written on the correct spelling of Kangchenjunga, while the Tibetan name for Mt Everest, Chomo Lungma, the spelling of which also occasioned a number of quarrels, has been given a great variety of meanings. Similar confusion surrounds the name Rakaposhi—its meaning and even its original language. 'Devil's Tail', the first meaning ascribed to it, has long been exploded; more probable is 'Raka's View-point', Raka being a mythological character who once climbed the mountain with a strong party of fairies; but Conway's interpretation is much less poetic, for he was told that it meant 'like the white matter exuding from a boil'—Raka, perhaps was subject to boils. But the Hunza and Nagar people, who live closest of anyone to the mountain, settle the matter by calling it Dumani which means 'Necklace of Pearls' or 'Necklace of Clouds'. However, the Karakoram Conference plumped for 'Rakaposhi' (refraining from any attempt at elucidation) with the proviso that the Hunza name 'Dumani' should also be retained or at least not quite forgotten.

Fortunately for the reader the mountain is almost without history. Lord

1 See sketch map on p. 553.

Conway (then W. M. Conway) explored the Bagrot nallah in what was for Himalayan climbing the almost prehistoric year of 1892. In his book *Karakoram Himalayas* he describes how his party climbed the ridge between the Bagrot and Dainyor nallahs and looked down on to the Dainyor glacier 'and up to the highest point of Rakaposhi on our right. We noticed that the great, though from here strangely insignificant-looking mountain, could be ascended by the arête which is a long gentle snow crest apparently corniced. The only difficulty is to get on to it, for the wall leading to it was entirely avalanche-swept from end to end.' It is not very clear to which arête he refers, but it is probably the south-west. The mountain is not heard of again until 1938 when Messrs Campbell H. Secord and J. M. K. Vyvyan explored the approach by the Jaglot nallah. They climbed a peak at the western extremity of the north-west ridge which in their account (*Himalayan Journal*, vol. XI) is given as 22,500 ft, but which from our experience I should say is not more than 20,000 ft. From here their advance was stopped by a steep drop of 700 ft. to the ridge and by the unpromising aspect of the long icy knife-edge stretch of ridge which followed. It is not very clear why so little interest should have been shown in so noble a mountain, why such a high and glittering prize seen by so many travellers and so easily reached should not have been snatched at before. At first I attributed this neglect to the 'eight thousand metre' fetish which beset nearly all Continental climbers in the 1930's, when any mountain which failed to reach this lofty standard was despised; but now having seen the mountain myself I think there were sounder reasons for its immunity from attack. Even at this comparatively late hour in its history Himalayan climbing is still in that rude, happy, and despicable stage when no one looks for a hard way up a peak if there is an easy one, when there is no need for the aspirant to glory sternly to ask himself whether or no his chosen objective is difficult enough to test his skill, courage, and luck, but whether it is easy enough to offer a chance of his climbing it. And, of course, the higher the mountain the easier it must be to offer him that chance.

On this fairly slender basis of fact and with the uncertain help of some photographs we had to make our plan. At first it seemed that the soundest method would be to reconnoitre every side of the mountain beginning with the Bagrot nallah, then over into the Dainyor by way of Conway's saddle, from there round to the Jaglot nallah, finishing possibly with the north face. On the march in, this idea was modified. In the first place it would take a long time, although until we came to reconnoitre the Jaglot approaches none of us fully realized quite how long so wide a reconnaissance would have taken. To split up into two parties of two (or two and one since we did not yet know whether Secord would come) would not have been satisfactory because the Swiss had no Himalayan experience and we had no common standard, so that to compare and settle the respective merits of routes recommended by either party would not have been easy. Moreover, our time was short. I had arranged to leave for Kashgar by the end of July, when Secord's time, too, would be up, and if we were to reconnoitre three widely separated nallahs and possibly the long northern face there would be little enough time left for the climb itself.

On the march between Parri and Gilgit we were impressed by the distance between the Bagrot nallah and the summit, while the Dainyor nallah, in giving us a brief but horrifying glimpse of little else than ice and rock-walls, also gave us good reason why it should be ignored. As for the north side, Secord had seen that and had written it off as too steep—a view which the photographs confirmed. So by the time we reached Gilgit we had practically decided to gamble on finding some way up from the Jaglot nallah. According to Thucydides, 'it is a habit of mankind to entrust to careless hope what they long for, and to use sovereign reason to thrust aside what they do not fancy', and though we did, perhaps, overmuch entrust ourselves to careless hope in the matter of the Jaglot nallah and readily thrust aside the alternatives which we did not fancy, we happened, I think, to choose or guess rightly.

Meantime, on 6 June, returning to the Residency from shopping in the bazaar, I stumbled over a vast, strange rucksack on the veranda and concluded at once that Secord had come. He had left London the previous Sunday and here he was in Gilgit on the Friday. He may have been lucky or he may have had even more influential friends in the R.A.F. than we knew; for that morning Col. Bacon had gone by air to a conference in Srinagar, and whether the plane which brought one and took away the other had been arranged for Secord's particular behoof or for the Resident's was a point which, with its implications of relative importance, I should hesitate to decide.

Having been told of our plan Secord concurred heartily since he was more confident than we were that the Jaglot nallah offered not only the best but our sole chance. There remained, therefore, only the job of finding the necessary porters to carry two months' supplies to the head of the nallah. Col. Bacon himself had already begun negotiating by telephone with the Mirs of Hunza and Nagar for a dozen likely men, but the Mirs, anxious to do their best for their subjects, had stuck out for a rate of Rs. 3 a day and food. As this was the rate we were paying our Sherpas, serving a thousand miles from their homes and doing more than merely carrying loads, I thought it too much, so that when the Commandant of the Gilgit Scouts told me that some of his men were keen to accompany us and that he was willing they should, I jumped at the offer. Volunteers were called for, and almost all responded to the call. From them we picked fifteen, who, in the short time showed great powers of marching and load-carrying and a ready cheerful obedience. These local levies of the Gilgit Scouts, smart on parade and with a very military bearing, are organized in platoons on a tribal or territorial basis—a Hunza platoon, Nagar, Gilgit, Yasin, and so forth. Of these we were told the Hunza platoon was the pick. It seems a pity that such a fine well-trained body of men should not have been given the chance of proving their fighting worth during the late war. I think they would have given a good account of themselves and I am sure the peace of Gilgit would not have been broken in their absence.

So at last we were ready; loads made up, mules for the first day's march to Nomal engaged, and the last heart-rending decisions—two sweaters or three, Shakespeare or Charles Reade—irrevocably taken. Our last party was attended and our last farewell said at midnight against what some hoped and others feared would be a 3 o'clock start.

CHAPTER FIVE

The Jaglot Approaches

THE seventeen-mile stretch of road between Gilgit and Nomal is in local opinion the worst stage in the Indus valley. The road is in many places buried in sand and there is no oasis of greenery or even a solitary tree to break the monotony of sterility. The only water is at one point where the road approaches the river. In summer, at the height of the melt, these big rivers have the colour, consistency, and temperature of pea-soup which has been burnt and then iced, but the local people drink it with avidity. Just as some prefer a wine with plenty of body, so I noticed Hunza men purposely avoiding rills of clear water in favour of the thick river water. The hot dry march in front of us was therefore one very good reason for such an early start, and through the devotion of Mrs Bacon's servants, who got up to give us breakfast, we were spared 'the heaviest stone which melancholy can throw at a man', which, according to Fuller, is to learn that there is no breakfast. But although we were all on our marks by 4 a.m. three of the mules had wisely absented themselves, so that it was not until an hour later that we got away with five donkeys as substitutes.

However, except for the air-borne member, the party was now fitter, and with the help of a bathe (where there was no temptation to drink) we made lighter of the march than we had expected. For the last three miles the road winds through the pleasant rice and wheat fields of Nomal, for the bungalow is placed at the far end of the village. It seems to be part of the natural perversity of inanimate objects like bungalows that they invariably place themselves at the most inconvenient end of a village or on the highest ground available. For a week or so we were to be accompanied by Mr Mainprice, whom we had already met on our way to Gilgit, who had a matter to discuss with the elders of Jaglot village. He caught us up at Nomal late that night along with Gyr who had chosen this inopportune moment to have an outbreak of boils which had had to be treated at the Gilgit hospital.

At Nomal the mules returned, for on the next march the Hunza river had to be crossed by a rope bridge; all loads therefore had to be made up into man-loads. We determined to be off at 5 a.m., and so we should have been had my pocket alarm-watch been working. Some fortunate people will guarantee to be awake at a given hour, and so can I but only by dint of lying awake most of the night. If you wish to rise at four, for example, you simply think hard of the figure four and tap the forehead four times repeatedly to advise whatever there is inside of your intentions; but this unseen mentor often seems to be unable to count, and having woken you up at 1, 2 and 3 o'clock, without any activity resulting on your part, gives up in disgust and allows you to have your sleep out undisturbed. So it was at Nomal, but as we were sleeping outside we sensed the coming of dawn so that our start was but an hour later than intended.

Two miles from Nomal we left the main Hunza road to cross the river by the rope bridge—one of those contraptions which has struck fear into the hearts of many travellers and which has in consequence been often described. Our natural inquiries as to its condition received the usual assurance that it was very rotten, not having been repaired in the memory of man. I have yet to hear of one of these bridges breaking or even, which seems the more likely event, of anyone falling off. On this particular bridge there was the usual deep sag in the middle, the usual thick cables far too thick for a real 'Thank God' handhold, and the usual grey flood surging angrily below. I have never tried, but I have been told that if you incautiously allow the eyes to rest on the water too long the bridge begins to sail rapidly up stream. Then anything may happen—either complete catastrophe or more likely the victim is paralysed, like a rabbit by a stoat, and clings on helplessly until rescued. The Swiss crossed without hesitation although such bridges were outside their experience. Not so the Sherpas, who cut poor figures, all except Phurba having to have their loads carried over, while the sirdar Angdawa had to be carried by one of the Scouts.

Some eight or nine miles above the bridge the track strikes up the hillside away from the river, and after a steep climb of several hundred feet debouches quite suddenly upon grass meadows and fields of ripening wheat where channels of water were bubbling merrily downwards. A mile further up the nallah were the willows and apricot trees marking Jaglot village (8,000 ft.) and beyond the glorious but deceitfully foreshortened Rakaposhi. We reached the village by noon expecting that after lunch the march would be resumed. I was not so sure, for I knew of old the symptoms indicative of 'thus far and no farther', and true enough both Scouts and Nomal coolies declared that for their first day they had had enough. None of us, I imagine, regretted the wasted but blissful afternoon spent lying on the grass in the shade by the apricots, the fruit of which one might with a little trouble catch as it fell; least of all Gyr who was not at all well because of his boils. I had leisure to discover what had been left behind—medicines was one item—and still worse what we had forgotten to leave behind—a useless mess-tent, for example. This halt gave us the opportunity of making bread and scones, and having once shown Angdawa, who doubled the role of cook and sirdar, we seldom went without bread in the lower camps. Chapatties are good enough in their way, but I pride myself on supplying bread whenever possible. With 'atta', dried yeast, the ordinary aluminium 'degchi', and a wood fire, it needs no great conjuror to turn out a loaf in a short time; a much better loaf, too, in my opinion, than that which we eat at home, not unfairly describable as 'a deleterious paste mixed up with chalk, alum, and bone-ashes, insipid to the taste and destructive to the constitution'. Thus Smollett describes the bread of his day and if in place of 'bone-ashes' we read 'calcium and other fortifiers' the description is still pretty accurate. Nevertheless, it seems likely that since successive generations have put up with such bread for 200 years they will go on putting up with it to the end of time or until their constitutions break down altogether.

The next day's march involved a steady climb of about 4,000 ft. The lambadar of Jaglot accompanied us to show the way, bringing with him the princely gift of two sheep for which we had to pay. Mainprice remained behind to look at the crops and to harangue the elders who were not seeing eye to eye with him in the matter of a new water furrow ('kul') for irrigating some

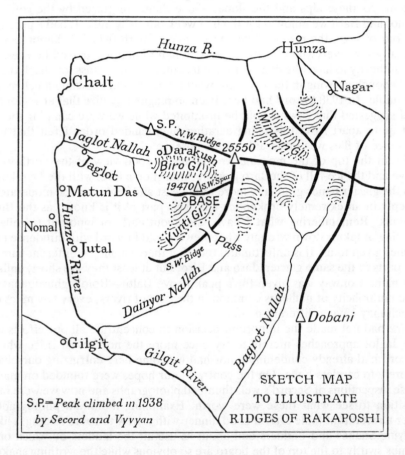

SKETCH MAP
TO ILLUSTRATE
RIDGES OF RAKAPOSHI

S.P.=*Peak climbed in 1938 by Secord and Vyvyan*

land in the main valley on which Mainprice was eager to see some Hunza folk settled. The Hunzas, who are far and away the best agriculturalists of these parts, suffer from a shortage of land. This new 'kul' was to be taken from the Jaglot stream in which there seemed to be water to spare, but the Jaglot elders were properly jealous of their water supply.

A thousand feet above Jaglot is the last permanent habitation, the small hamlet of Barit. Beyond that we mounted steadily through pines until at about 11,000 ft. we left these behind and emerged on to the high lateral moraine of the Jaro glacier. At this point the Jaglot nallah divides; the arm in which this glacier lies runs up between the north-west ridge and the south-west spur of Rakaposhi, while the other is contained between the south-west spur and the south-west ridge. We followed the right-hand moraine of the Jaro Gamuk ('gamuk' means glacier) until at about 12,000 ft. we quitted the moraine for the ablation valley between moraine and mountain side where there are two grassy alps, a lower and an upper. The upper alp called Darakush is the better of the two and had been Secord's camp site in 1938, but today, since the Scouts with their heavy loads were lagging behind, we camped in the lower at 3 p.m. As these alps and the slopes above them are grazed by the cows of Jaglot and Barit we enjoyed for the first week our daily milk. It had a peculiar flavour of sage, the result of the beasts eating a herb (which I cannot name) which grows everywhere in these parts. When Mainprice arrived he exerted his authority to have the cows confined to a diet of sweet grass, of which there was enough growing in the two alps, whereupon the milk became much more palatable. In 1938 Secord had here been so plagued by flies that at Jaglot he had suggested that cows should be prohibited while we were camping there; but quite apart from this being a rather high-handed order I felt that the presence of flies was preferable to the absence of milk.

From the top of the moraine we had had a good view of the north-west ridge and the ice-fall of the Jaro glacier. Almost on a level with the Darakush alp the glacier bends gradually more to the east and begins to rise moderately steeply in an extremely broken ice-fall. This part of it is known as the Biro Gamuk. Remembering what I have said about early or ignorant travellers hearing or taking down wrongly what they are told I record with diffidence the names given to us. It is unfortunate, too, that there should be different names for parts of the same glacier, Jaro and Biro, but at least they are short, unlike the name Conway was given for a peak above Baltit—Boiohaghurduanasir. The multiplicity of names is common in the case of rivers, every few miles of which may have a different name.

We had not made the important decision to concentrate all our efforts on the Jaglot approaches merely to try once more the north-west ridge which Secord had already condemned; nor had we come here entrusting ourselves entirely to careless hope. On the contrary, our hopes were founded on many close inspections of Secord's well-thumbed photographs and now we were in a position to see what these were worth. Examining mountain photographs over a restaurant table after a good dinner with a view to route-finding is like playing Snakes and Ladders and about as useful; the ladders by which one climbs swiftly to the top of the board are so obvious while the writhing snakes of Pride, Anger, and Covetousness which compel one to start afresh are readily overlooked. Secord had condemned his ridge on account of the difficulties at its beginning, and I must admit that here the photograph did not flatter it. The south-west spur, which is inaccessible from the Biro side, did not look any more promising, but the ice-fall on the other hand, appeared in a photograph almost inviting. It was upon this then that our hope mainly rested. True the upper part was hidden, for our scientists (bless them) have not yet invented a camera which can see round corners, and most of the visible portion was endangered by the ice-walls and hanging glaciers which menaced it from both sides. But in the absence of anything better our hearts had warmed to this route in spite of such deterrents to affection. We argued that the worst of ice-falls must yield to time and patience and that by sticking diligently to a middle course in the traditional British way we might find safety. Both these theories were subsequently found to have flaws.

Having now had the ground in question in view for the best part of an afternoon I confess our hopes were a little dashed. But the length and exposure of both the north-west ridge and the south-west spur gave the ice-fall route added attraction, although even at such a distance we could see how broken it was and how little, if any, appeared to be completely free from danger from above. In the Himalaya, avalanches and the discharge of seracs are often on a grand scale and will unexpectedly sweep across large areas of even flattish ground. Still, the ice-fall route would at least be more sheltered from bad weather than the ridges. The climbing there, however, slow and intricate, would be neither difficult nor dangerous for our inexperienced Sherpas, and 3,000 or 4,000 ft. up there was a convenient rock 'island' which might serve as a base. We determined to try it.

The mention of weather recalls to me that by now we had complaints to make on this score. When Secord was here in July 1938 he enjoyed a month of hot cloudless weather, tormented only by flies, and I had been firmly of the opinion that in Gilgit rain was almost unknown. In the few days we were there the weather had been neither hot, cloudless, nor settled, and though we were assured by the residents—as one always is—that such conditions had never been known before, the fact remained that they existed then. Up in the mountains we might expect worse and in this expectation at least we were not disappointed. Our first day was cloudy with much wind higher up; in the evening it rained, and early next morning there was a heavy thunderstorm.

The Scouts were sent back to Jaglot for the rest of the loads while we climbed over the moraine, dropped down to the glacier, and started up it to see what we could make of the ice-fall. It proved to be a good deal more broken than Secord's camera had thought, and after 500 ft. we were brought to a stand. Disregarding our avowed intention of steering a safe middle course we made wide casts right and left but without success; seracs, ice-cliffs and crevasses running criss-cross in all directions completely baffled us. This was all the more annoying and unreasonable since the angle of slope was less than thirty degrees. In thoughtful mood we returned to camp were we devoted the rest of the day to moving it to the higher and more favoured site at Darakush.

A better base camp in every respect but one I have yet to see—a flat roomy carpet of short grass, through which a stream meanders, surrounded and sheltered by birch trees interspersed with great boulders, a few of which afford dry and ready bivouacs. And the alp is so situated that while reclining on the grass one may look out from this perfect setting to the summit itself, to the long flat north-west ridge, to the broken heavily-corniced south-west spur, and beyond the foot of this to a fascinating cirque of rock and ice precipice at the termination of the south-west ridge.

The one serious drawback to this camp is its lack of height, for it is somewhere between 12,000 and 13,000 ft. On most big mountains one can usually achieve a flying start from a base at 17,000 or 18,000 ft. to which the local porters can carry without difficulty, but to attain even this modest height on Rakaposhi usually involved some serious climbing. All the valleys here are exceptionally low, taking their cue from the Hunza river into which they drain. To the north and west, where it almost washes the foot of Rakaposhi, the river runs at a level of only 6,000 or 7,000 ft., and the northern slopes of the mountain drop from 25,000 ft. to this level in less than seven miles. Still, this is an imperfect world and we were too content with our surroundings at Darakush to worry much about the lack of height. We sat about outside that evening watching a herd of ibex at the foot of the north-west ridge, while a wan and watery sun fitfully lit the highest snows. Rain fell most of the night.

We were not quite finished with the ice-fall. While one party tried to find a way round by the right bank, I took Phurba with the intention of making a very high and wide detour on the slopes of the south-west spur. Mainprice, with his rifle, accompanied the first party intent on murdering an ibex; while Gyr, who was still convalescent, had chosen that moment for a quiet stroll along the top of the moraine clad in a dazzling white suit of windproofs. When after a careful stalk Mainprice gained his point he was chagrined but not surprised to find that the ibex had taken the hint.

Phurba and I had a successful day. After climbing for a thousand feet up loose rock and steep grass we crossed a wide bay of snow and dropped down again to the ice-fall which at the edge here was much less broken. Stones fell intermittently from a black cliff on our right and obviously the snow bay was sometimes swept by avalanches, but otherwise the route seemed safe. At 2 p.m. we reached the rock 'island' at about 16,000 ft. This rock refuge in the ice-sea lay close to the edge of the ice-fall which out in the middle was proportionately more contorted and convulsed than below. Even if it was possible further progress would be slow and difficult, nor could we yet see what lay round the corner a thousand or more feet higher where the glacier bends south to articulate with the south-west ridge. While we were climbing we had seen a large avalanche pour down from a big snow-field on the slopes of the north-west ridge and out on to the lower part of the ice-fall, and when we returned to Darakush at 4 p.m. we heard how the other party had come well within its fell whiff and wind. They, too, had seen an avalanche fall into our snow-bay after we had crossed and were in consequence less enthusiastic than they might have been over our having reached the 'island'. Owing to ibex and avalanches they had not gone far up, but anyway their route was unpromising since to reach the 'island' they would have had to cross the ice-fall.

Sitting over our curry and rice that night, lamenting the saddle of ibex that might have been and cursing Gyr for its absence, we faced the facts and came to the reluctant conclusion that the 'corridor' route, as we called it, had not been fairly presented in the photographs and that it had better be left alone. 'Corridor' was an apt name; it was narrow, it undoubtedly led somewhere, and like other corridors, the Polish for example, it was subject to interference from either side.

I have never made a proper study of mountain photographs. Perhaps if I had I should not have received so many unpleasant surprises as I did on Rakaposhi. On the other hand, it may have been sound instinct which made me regard such photographs rather cursorily, for there is no doubt that they conceal as much as they tell and that as guides to route-finding they are unreliable. I am not blaming the camera; the human eye is no less fallible. Slopes which appear innocuous from below are found by experience to be horrifyingly steep, while others which when viewed *en face* look like vertical walls turn out to be veritable belvederes. On Rakaposhi these illusions were frequent. In one instance, even a slope viewed in profile—a view which admits no deceit—appeared far less steep than we, having climbed it, knew it to be. No doubt my scientific friends have an explanation for this as they have for everything, but in the end most of us are content to believe what we see.

Having thus rejected the 'corridor' route we had but three shots left in the locker and one of these we expected to be a misfire. While the 'corridor' had been falling into disfavour some of us had been casting rather wild despairing glances over our left shoulders at the north-west ridge where the searching eye of faith thought it could see a way of gaining the ridge at a point well on the summit side of Secord's difficulties. He, it will be recalled, was stopped by the steep drop from the peak at the west end of the ridge and by the long knife-edge section below it. We could see that the great snow-field—almost a hanging glacier—from which yesterday's avalanche had fallen to so alarm the 'corridor' party, swept down unbroken from the crest of the ridge at a point half a mile on the summit side of the knife-edge section. It was guarded on the near side by ice-cliffs, but if we could reach it and if the angle did not prove to be quite so sharp as it appeared, then there seemed a very fair chance of reaching the ridge at a most advantageous point. For the ridge was certainly the shortest and most direct way to the plinth or plateau on which the summit pyramid stands. Except for one harmless-looking rock step and one snow cupola, which could be turned, it was apparently devoid of difficulty.

There were undoubtedly a lot of 'ifs', and Secord for one had little faith, so before wasting time there we decided to look at the other arm of the Jaglot nallah where there were two unexplored possibilities, the south-west ridge and the south-west spur. Again it rained all night and we started late for our day excursion round the foot of the south-west spur. We crossed the dry ice of the Biro opposite our camp and walked down a pleasant valley of grass, birch trees, and clumps of wild roses, lying between the left-hand moraine and the slopes of the spur. We turned the corner and climbed a long boulder-strewn slope to the moraine of the Manogar glacier. The splayed-out foot of the south-west spur must be nearly two miles in length and at the upper end of it the Manogar glacier is joined by another branch, the Kunti glacier. This lies between the south-west spur and its parent south-west ridge, and from the junction with the Manogar to the head is not more than three miles. The upper part of Manogar flows in almost the opposite direction to the Kunti. It arises in the great rock cirque at the curving tail of the south-west ridge and then sweeps down towards the foot of the south-west spur. But as Byron said: 'Damn description, it is always disgusting.

Our interest lay up the Kunti so we walked out on to the glacier well beyond the foot of the spur. There was no ice-fall to block our view and we could see it sloped gradually upwards to its termination under an extremely steep and broken wall below the junction of ridge and spur. Two miles up the glacier the snow-slopes of the south-west ridge to our right looked as if they might afford a way to the crest. The upper part of the ridge leading to the great plateau seemed very broken, but we thought it had possibilities. Accordingly the next move was to bring a light camp round for a thorough reconnaissance.

Next day, 14 June, we moved round with two Sherpas and six Scouts to carry the loads. Instead of going out on to the glacier as before we climbed the broken moraine on the right bank, keeping close under the cliffs of the spur. As we toiled up a thunderstorm broke, bringing with it rain, hail, and then snow, so we were obliged to camp sooner than intended at the first available trickle of water. The height was about 13,000 ft.

After lunch we continued in knee-deep snow up the glacier to within half a mile of its termination, and the more we saw of the south-west ridge the less we liked it. The slopes leading to it, which from a distance had looked attractively easy, now looked steep and difficult. There was much argument about their angle; some thought it not more that 45°, others a great deal more, but whatever it was the ridge itself was not sufficiently encouraging to induce us to go and find out. Turning our backs on this we searched the slopes of the spur and here at any rate there seemed a ready access by way of a snow gully not very far from camp. From Darakush we had had a good view of this ridge in profile, and from photographs we knew it abounded with pitfalls, but as it seemed to be the only accessible ridge we decided to give it a trial. We walked slowly back down the glacier in snow showers and sunshine, our sense of indecision only slightly alleviated.

CHAPTER SIX

The Two Ridges

ONCE more snow fell that night so, instead of climbing the gully, we made a short excursion to the great cirque, partly to see if a low rock col leading to the Matun Das nallah south of the Jaglot could be crossed, and partly to get a view of our south-west spur. On this upper part of the Manogar glacier we had to climb an ice-fall to reach the cirque, beneath which we presently stood, gazing up respectfully at the grim grey slabs shot with streaks of yellow rock and festooned with long glistening slivers of ice. From a closer view-point the col looked difficult (later Secord and Kappeler were repulsed by it), but we had a clear view of our spur and beyond it to the summit. At the point where the spur bends sharply at the head of the Kunti glacier to articulate with the main south-west ridge there is a high snow-dome, guarded near the top by an ice-wall below which a steep crevassed snow-slope falls away to a low gap. This feature became known to us as the Monk's Head and was evidently a major obstacle.

That evening at supper I introduced the Swiss to pemmican soup by way of warning of what they might expect higher up. There were no delighted cries, no hearty lip-smacking appreciation. In fact of Gyr one might have said that he:

> Sighed, as he chewed the unaccustomed food:
> 'It may be wholesome but it is not good.'

The refrain 'snow fell all night' is becoming a rather monotonous dirge, but once again the fact must be recorded. Leaving the others to ponder over pemmican and the weather I walked round to Darakush to arrange for the remaining loads to be brought up. Angdawa had been left there with Angtingit, our fourth Sherpa, who had some kind of fever, together with the Scouts in charge of their Subadar. The latter were now due to return, so as we had at last made up our minds to explore the south-west spur we had to move our base camp before they went. Mainprice having already gone back, taking with him his rifle, the Subadar had beseeched me to get him one; for the ibex by now had forgotten a few days ago and were again grazing in provocative proximity. On his strolls the Subadar had been tantalized by the sight of so much fresh meat walking about, and he had no doubt often exclaimed as the old Boer did: 'God, what things a man sees who goes out without a gun.' Believing that he knew something of the game and that he would not blaze away indiscriminately, I had sent a Scout back to Gilgit with a chit asking for a rifle. It is worth noting that the man did the double journey within two days.

When I arrived at Darakush I was told the Subadar was up the hill after the ibex and while I was devouring fried eggs and chapatties I heard a shot. 'Good', I thought, 'he's got one'. But to my horror this was immediately followed by four more in rapid succession and after a brief interval another two. I blushed for the Subadar, and for myself at having let such a miscreant loose upon the hill, for it was clear he had not killed with his first shot and had tried to mend matters by the grievous sin of firing away at the running herd. That this had happened I heard next day when he came up with the Scouts and proudly presented us with the leg of a diminutive buck. One undersized animal killed and three wounded was the tally, but my Hindustani was not fluent enough to paint the enormity of his crime.

By the time the Scouts arrived we had moved our camp up 200 or 300 ft. to some grass off which the snow had recently melted. Unlike Darakush this camp was neither silvan nor pastoral, but it had the advantage in height by nearly a thousand feet. For wood we used to send the Sherpas down to the foot of the spur where some gnarled juniper bushes grew on the cliffs above. Having settled in here with all our stores and gratefully dismissed the Scouts with a reward, we were ready to launch a fresh blow; but the unsettled weather and the amount of snow which had recently fallen admonished us not to launch it too violently.

On the 17th we set off for the gully. Quitting the moraine above the camp the way led up a broad fan of soft snow through which we ploughed until we reached the rocks at the foot. To the top there must have been 2000 ft. of snow-filled gully, the lower half of it very soft and deep; nor was there any escape from the snow to the rocks on either side, for they were too steep and rotten. The gully itself was much steeper than we had bargained for. Once more our judgement had been confounded by experience. Good judgement is, perhaps, the most valuable of all mountaineering assets, and whether our own was deficient or not we took comfort from a dictum of Dr T. G. Longstaff, an old Himalayan traveller and now President of the Alpine Club, who declared that in the Himalaya one must first rub one's nose in a place before being able to say whether or no it will go.

We reached the crest of the ridge in five hours from camp. Later journeys only took four hours, but to-day we had the exhausting work of treading out steps. Kappeler seemed to be going well, Gyr and I slow and steady, but Secord was obviously suffering from a too sudden transition from office desk to mountain. A notch at the top of the gully made a convenient camp site, roomy and flat enough to permit the digging of platforms for several small tents. On one side a big rock gendarme forbade any movement along the ridge in that direction, while on the summit side a snow-slope rose steeply for a thousand feet, blocking out any further view of the ridge. We judged the height to be something over 17,000 ft. That day there was not much to be seen, but later we enjoyed many noble prospects from our eyrie.

The gate now seemed open, or at any rate the latch was off, but instead of rushing at it like bulls we took a day off. A plan had to be made and loads arranged to conform to it. We decided to put a camp at the notch with tents for ourselves and two Sherpas, and stores and oil for a week. From there we would push another camp as far as we could along the ridge from which two of us could explore further—as far as the Monk's Head we hoped. The morning of our off day was delightfully fine and sunny, so much so that Secord, who has a salamander's passion for the sun, exposed almost every inch of an extremely long body to it. By evening wind and hail had driven us to crouch once more in our stone 'sangar'.

When we went up next day everyone carried loads, the two Sherpas, Ningma and Phurba, had about 40 lb. each and ourselves 25 lb. The steps of the previous day were a great help so that in spite of our loads we reached the notch in 4½ hours. With 'Bernina' shovels we dug platforms for two small tents and the Logan, and having pitched these we went down. Another carry the following day with food and personal kit was done in four hours with only one short halt at the foot of the gully. We kept Phurba and Angtingit with us and sent Angdawa and Ningma down with instuctions to do another carry next day. It was obvious that neither Phurba nor Angtingit had ever camped on snow before, for I had to put a Primus stove together for them and show them how it worked. Although this was but one day off Midsummer Day and although the camp was at no great height, no snow was melting on the rocks so that to get water we had to use the stoves. We had with us as well two shiny black squares of light oil-cloth which given enough sun and enough time would collect sufficient heat to melt snow; but such a source of supply is pretty meagre. Secord was out twice in the night crying loudly for water, perhaps in the hope that the black cloth squares also functioned by moonlight.

So far the Sherpas have not had much notice. Angdawa, the sirdar, was reliable and efficient either as headman, porter, or cook, and he could also interpret fairly successfully between two people speaking different languages neither of which he knew. Angtingit, bovine, cheerful, tremendously strong, with the chest of a gorilla and with a facial resemblance to one of the more refined, was afflicted on and off with sickness and finished up in hospital. Phurba, young, shy, but anxious to please, was the most typical-looking Sherpa of them all and the most likable; while Ningma, with the appearance of a slightly battered veteran, was unluckily without a veteran's experience— at least not in mountaineering, though by his looks he had had much experience of life. He was afflicted with a smoker's cough, but in spite of my reiterated advice to abstain (which he probably thought was not disinterested) he always clamoured the loudest for his cigarette ration. He was the weakest member of a not very strong quartet, and as the emptiest barrel so he resounded the most. They all did their work, but they had little or no experience of climbing and seemed somewhat averse to enlarging the little they had. Their war-time experiences, either in some labour corps or with English and American service people touring Sikkim, seemed to have opened their eyes, particularly Angdawa's to the main chance; whereas, before the war one had the impression that the pleasure and success of an expedition were of far more importance to the Sherpas than the reward. But that is a criticism which, perhaps, few of us can escape; for Darjeeling, or even remoter Solah Kombu, is no more immune to the shrivelling economic blast than anywhere else, and to thrive in times like the present greed must become greedier and generous carelessness must e'en sharpen its wits.

A glorious sunny evening on which we stood around outside watching the shadows lengthen across the face of Nanga Parbat far away to the south, gave no hint of the weather to come. Morning broke cold and dull with a rasping wind from the east; no one seemed eager to leave his tent and no Sherpa appeared with kind inquiries about breakfast. Since the stomach carried the feet I got up and heated and broached a large tin of sausages, but by the time we had eaten them there was no sign of improvement in the weather. Loath to give up we started unladen up the snow slope hoping to see something of the ridge higher up. We climbed through steep and deep snow with occasional patches of rock showing through until after an hour's climbing the angle of slope began to ease off. We were near the top of the ridge at a point marked on the map as 19,470 ft., but by now mist and sleet were driving across reducing visibility to a few yards. There was no obstinate contest of disagreeable virtues. With one consent we turned to hurry down to the notch whence, in order to save kerosene, we retired to the base. On the way down we met Angdawa and Ningma coming up with loads and a parcel of mail, dried apricots, and tobacco from Gilgit. All the dried apricots of these parts are good, but these were a special sort with the kernel of the nut wrapped in the dried fruit, a present from the Mir of Hunza. Down below a thunderstorm raged, and when it had passed we made bread, chewed apricots, smoked, and felt better.

In the Alps where time is usually of the first importance it is difficult to sit still during a spell of unsettled weather, but in the Himalaya where time is measured in months rather than in weeks there is no reason for impatient activity and every excuse for complete idleness. Instead of lying at earth as we should have done, we kept on carrying loads to the notch, so that when we reoccupied the camp we had there enough stores to mount a full scale attempt, although we had yet no idea whether the route would really go. The weather was behaving very oddly. I have never experienced so many thunderstorms in the Himalaya where I have always regarded them as rarities. On a fine morning the Swiss, two Sherpas and myself, made another carry. We found that the snow in the gully had avalanched, obliterating all our steps, not only those in the gully but also those right down to the bottom of the fan. While it was agreeable to learn that this had taken place in our absence we had the less pleasing thought that next time we might not be so fortunate. In the afternoon there was more snow and thunder—an odd mixture—so next day we stayed at home to give the snow time to settle.

An idle hour could always be spent in a treasure hunt in the food boxes where something might have been overlooked, or another more careful translation (by Secord) of the German on some strange packet might rouse fresh hope or at lest stimulate curiosity. One of the more disquieting aspects of the American way of life has been taken up by the Swiss. What are called cake, pudding, or pancake 'mixtures' are put up in packets (no doubt sterilized) in some hygienic food factory, so that all the modern housewife need do is to apply water and fire.[1] For supper that evening we tried a pancake 'mixture' with a thick dressing of dried banana flakes to ease it down. It was not a dish to be eaten on one's knees, and the banana flakes, I thought, closely resembled glacier sludge.

On the 24th all, less Ningma who was sick, went up to the notch with more food and a load of wood. We cleared the snow off the tents, dug out the buried stores, and squared up generally. The weather was very different from that of a week ago; summer seemed to have set in at last and 300 ft. down the gully we found a trickle of water. What lovely and memorable pictures were painted for us that evening while the setting sun crowned the distant Nanga Parbat with a halo of bright gold and drew dark indigo shadows upon the white cliffs; while the tangle of snow-peaks to the west, too lowly to be crowned, stood out cold and sombre above the turquoise haze of their valleys. Just as from some Cumberland crag we search for distant Snowdon or Snaefell, so here, not content with Nanga Parbat, we saw or thought we saw Tirich Mir 150 miles away in Chitral.

June 25th was another fine day and a critical one. Our plan was still to push a two-man camp along the ridge, so when we started at 8.30 a.m. the Sherpas,

[1] The self-heating tins which we met with occasionally during the war will save even that, for she will merely have to apply her cigarette end to the tin.

Phurba and Angtingit, were carrying about 30 lb. each and ourselves 15 lb. The snow was in good condition and in two hours we had reached what we took to be the point marked on the map as 19,470 ft. though no amount of tapping could persuade our altimeters to confirm this. We had two of these instruments and their readings agreed like brothers, but they seemed to feel the effects of altitude less than we did and usually lagged behind by a thousand feet or so. From this point the ridge stretched away almost horizontally. It was heavily corniced and in the distance it seemed to terminate in a horn overhanging space like a question mark. We climbed on two ropes with a Sherpa in the middle of each. Gyr, who was now leading my rope and apparently allowing ample margin for the cornice, suddenly broke through it with his outside foot and a large chunk of ridge disappeared. I was thankful to see that even without much help from his second he was able to retain his *status quo* and his equanimity.

As we drew nearer the question mark assumed a more questioning shape, reminding me somehow of a rhino horn viewed from a flank—such as would qualify for inclusion in Rowland Ward's *Records of Big Game*. With one accord we dumped our loads. By midday we had reached the foot of the horn to find it guarded by a spacious crevasse bridged in only one place, on the very crest of the ridge. There we had lunch—'a full belly and then to business', as the Duke of Wellington used to say before battle.

It seemed to be my turn to lead, at least no one else pressed his claim, and having crossed the bridge (a frail link, I thought) I was able to appreciate the full beauty of the route. The northern side of the horn consisted entirely of vast cornice curling out over space on our left, while the convex side was so arranged that if one took too high a line one would fall through, and if too low then one would equally obviously fall off. On the passage of the horn itself there was no question of kicking steps, the snow was so deep and soft that I had to shovel with both arms and with great labour carve out a sort of communication trench. Some mild protests on my part were drowned in cries of encouragement from behind. At last the concavity straightened itself out and having rounded the horn I stepped on to the gap beyond it, a move which brought into view the startling drop on the north side which previously had been hidden. Ahead, along 200 ft. of loose knife-edge rock covered with snow, the ridge ran up to the tip of another gendarme. Phurba, who was behind me, having taken a quick look into the abyss and to the knife-edge along which we should have to balance, remarked sensibly enough that he was going back. I was not prepared to argue for I thought he had quite a strong case, so we did some juggling with the rope in order to detach the two Sherpas and sent them back to the crevasse in charge of Kappeler. While this was being done I looked back and noticed that a section of my communication trench had disappeared; however, no one can have been on it at the time or his absence would have occasioned remark. When the rock had been cleared of snow the knife-edge presented no difficulty and presently we were all assembled on the tip of the gendarme thoughtfully contemplating the steep drop to the gap and the Monk's Head still nearly a mile away. The height, I imagine, was about 20,000 ft.

I was already convinced, and all the others agreed, that as a route this was no go, so after an interval for photography we started for home which we reached at 4.30 p.m. Angdawa and Ningma had come up with more tents and wood; Ningma went back, but since we intended going down next day Angdawa stayed to help with the loads in spite of having no sleeping-bag. Having slept on the problem I was still of the same mind, but Secord broached the idea that we should make an attempt by this route without the Sherpas. His main argument was that it was our last chance, a cogent reason but in my opinion not good enough to justify using an unsound route. As an incident in a climb it was very well, but it was a dangerous route over which to have to make several journeys carrying loads. Yesterday's conditions had been ideal but with bad weather or after fresh snow it would be unpleasant in the extreme; moreover, the way beyond was doubtful, particularly up the Monk's Head, and even when we were over that difficulty we were still a very long way from the upper and easier part of the mountain. Nor did I think we were a strong enough party to do our own load-carrying. True, on Nanda Devi we had carried our own loads, but there were seven of us and the route was neither so difficult nor so exposed as this one. Altogether I thought the chances of success too slim to justify the attempt. After a long discussion we agreed to go down. It was a hard decision—especially for me. The risks were theoretical, while turning our backs on them was an irrevocable fact for which I should be largely responsible. Having had most experience I was credited— by no means of necessity rightly—with the best judgement so that my opinion would have most influence. I must play the oracle, but here no oracular vagueness or ambiguity would do. The answer must be 'yea' or 'nay' and, unlike oracles, I was involved in my own decision.

By this time it was late and once more Ningma was coughing and blowing his way up the last few steps out of the gully. He reported falling stones and the exposure of more ice as the result of avalanches and melting snow. We resolved to take only one bite at the cherry by carrying everything down with us, so every one set to work making up loads as gigantic as each thought he could cope with. Gyr and I contented ourselves with a modest 50 lb., Secord had 60 lb.; Kappeler had 80 lb. tied up like a bundle of washing in the cover of his sleeping-bag; the Sherpas in the neighbourhood of 100 lb. each, except Angtingit who took well over that. A 10 lb. tin of pemmy which no one had room for was thrown down the gully to find its own way home. In the upper part all went well, but the lower half was so icy that in one place the loads had to be lowered for 300 ft. This took time. In such places loads stick and have to be freed, bodies fail to stick and have to be stopped. See Ningma, for example, who:

> . . . from the mountain top
> Pleased with the slippery surface swift descends,

and has to be stopped and fielded with some difficulty, not once but twice.

Two successive fine days had led us to believe that fine weather had set in, but that night a tempest raged, snow fell heavily, and in the morning was still falling. That, however, was no consolation for defeat, and over our 'basins of nice smooth gruel, thin. but not too thin', we faced each other pretty blankly.

Gyr and I still had some hopes of the 'short-cut' to the north-west ridge, so we packed up and started for Darakush. The others remained with the intention of exploring a pass over the south-west ridge to the Dainyor nallah which in our reduced circumstances we thought should now be looked at.

Having descended as far as the foot of the moraine I discovered we had no matches, for which Angtingit, only a semi-willing victim, had to be sent back. It was raining hard at Darakush where we found a snug bivouac, tolerably free from drips, under a big boulder. Angdawa and Angtingit, who knew a thing or two, wisely slept under the boulder, generously allowing Gyr and me to spread ourselves in their spacious Logan. Like other high altitude tents, the Logan is not good in rain; but this one, a relic of Nanda Devi, was unnecessarily bad by reason of having the guys secured to the tent by a toggle inside the fabric. Where the guy passed through the fabric to the toggle, there rain passed too, so that during the night Gyr and I had to coil up smaller and smaller against the spreading flood until by morning we appeared like two small half-tide rocks.

By 10 o'clock next morning the rain had let up a bit when Gyr and I started up the long scree slope, now snow-covered, leading to a wide bay at the bottom of the north-west ridge. From the upper corner of this bay it looked as though there might be a way of reaching the great snow slope which, starting from the crest of the ridge well on the summit side of Secord's knife-edge, fell steeply to within a few hundred feet of the Biro ice-fall. It was in crossing a gully below this snow slope that one of the 'corridor' reconnaissance parties had been nearly caught by an avalanche. The snow slope could not be reached from directly below and its near flank was guarded by ice-cliffs, but from the bay there seemed to be possibilities of reaching it by climbing a small tributary glacier. If this snow-slope could be reached and climbed we should land ourselves at an advanced and advantageous point on the ridge, which appeared, both to eye and camera, to be shorter and easier than the south-west spur. A harmless looking rock-step and a snow-dome seemed the worst difficulties.

After two hours' slogging we reached the mouth of the bay and sat down on a boulder for lunch. 'He that sits on a stone is twice glad.' It was not long before we got up to go whereupon Gyr found that what he rightly called his 'glare glasses' had been left behind like the Dutchman's anchor. There was in fact a remarkable absence of glare, but at these heights without glasses one can achieve snow-blindness on the dullest days, so he was forced to retire. I pushed on through very soft snow into the bay which proved to be a rock cirque cleft by several gullies. I traversed under the steep rock-wall, in some places climbing the rock to avoid waist-deep patches of snow, and in time reached the upper corner where a shallow gully, almost a ledge, led to the upper part of the small tributary glacier which descends from the big snow-slope. About 500 ft. up I found a convenient but far from permanent site for a tent under a large overhanging serac, whence by cutting steps down its outside edge one could reach the glacier about twenty feet below. Since this glacier was attainable there seemed every chance of our reaching the snow-slope and finally the ridge.

After allowing a day for the snow to settle (we were still too impatient) Gyr and I went up to camp at the serac. From the very start at the mouth of the bay the route impressed itself most unfavourably upon our two Sherpas. Miniature avalanches and a few very respectable ones hissed down the several gullies from the slopes of the ridge with alarming frequency. We reached the serac without mishap and pitched the tent. The two Sherpas started down and we heard later that Angtingit had come unstuck on the shelf and had finished up well out in the middle of the bay, for which unlucky incident our route received (in this case unjustly) another black mark. Before pitching the tent I had cut down to the glacier with the intention of camping higher, but as the glacier surface was bare ice which would involve more step-cutting we decided to content ourselves where we were. In the evening, which was fine, we improved the steps and Gyr reconnoitred a way out from our *gîte* by the rock-wall above the shelf.

In the morning we woke to find a foot of snow and a thick mist. There was nothing for it but to go down. By this time the others had arrived and they, too, had had adventures. They had climbed to the top of the col on the south-west ridge and were confident that we could descend the other side, but the Matun Das col which they had also tried had foiled them by a rope's length. They had pressed the attack until dark and until Kappeler, who was leading, had come off and nearly demolished the expectant Secord.

On 2 July Gyr and I tried again. Our two Sherpas had the air of unwilling martyrs in a not very worthy cause, and I must say they had good reason for their dejection. Before we reached the bay the debris of a large avalanche slid gently to rest at our feet, while in the bay still others fell before and behind us with even more distressing frequency than before. There was at least one of some weight which roared down from another gully right at the foot of our own. In order to camp in a safer place and to avoid the short icy descent to the glacier we tried to break out of our shallow gully by the rock-wall on our left. It was too steep and the Sherpas refused, so we went on to the serac wher Gyr repeated his climb of the wall to see if we could haul up the loads and the Sherpas. It was no good, and in the end we both had to 'abseil' down a short icy funnel to the ice-cave under the serac. The Sherpas, having watched these manœuvres with concern, then departed.

Next morning when Gyr and I dropped down on to the little tributary glacier by the steps already cut we were blessed with a fine day, just as we had been on the one critical day on the south-west spur. Although the snow had peeled off, leaving the glacier bare, the slope was so gradual that we mounted rapidly, having only to nick a few steps. Wishing to get off the ice on to snow we left the glacier and steered a course for some cliffs. Under these there was plenty of snow of a kind soft enough and deep enough for a water buffalo to wallow in. In order to climb out of this morass Gyr led directly up the cliff and after steep climbing gained footing on a rock and snow-rib. The little glacier was now far below and the big snow-slope less readily attainable, for the ice-cliffs guarding it ran up unbroken to meet our rib some 2,000 ft. above. Like boxers side-stepping to avoid trouble we had overdone it and stepped right out of the ring. It takes a strong mind to throw away height laboriously gained, so instead of descending to the glacier and a sure route we trusted ourselves to luck and the rib. For the rib itself beckoned us upwards and beyond its junction with the ice-cliff a snow-scoop led directly to the ridge. The climb which followed was arduous and at times, I thought, perilous. Having followed our rib to the bitter end, I eventually found myself with one shoulder wedged against the ice-cliff, which was about thirty feet high, grubbing away in soft snow lying on ice in an endeavour to reach the scoop beyond. Owing to the underlying ice neither of us was secure. We started to discuss retreat, in fact we had already begun to move down, when looking back we noticed a rock island sticking out of the ice not far from the foot of the ice-cliff. To go down now would waste the whole day so we determined to try it. The passage across the bare ice was awkward, but Gyr reached the rock safely and led on up to the foot of the scoop. Here the snow became thinner and thinner. Below lay hard blue ice and to break out of the scoop on to the snow slope, or to follow it to the top, would entail long and arduous step-cutting. Having already said so much about eyes, cameras, and their ideas of angles, I will not attempt to estimate the angle of the slope out of the scoop, but it was of daunting steepness. We went down 200 or 300 ft., found a break in the ice-cliff which we had overlooked, gained the big snow-slope, and at 2 o'clock sat down for lunch a hundred feet below the crest of the ridge, wondering why we had not seen the break before.

Having eaten we dragged ourselves to the ridge for by now we were both pretty tired. We thought the ridge at this point was something over 20,000 ft. The 'serac' camp we estimated to be 15,000 ft. and having left it at 6 a.m. we had been climbing steadily and steeply for seven hours. Our situation was very grand. Over the curling cornices of the south-west spur we looked to the ice-fluted ridge beyond, and over that far away to the white flashing pyramid of Haramosh (24,270 ft.) and the massive Dobani (20,126 ft.). On the north side the Hunza valley lay spread at our feet, or rather 13,000 ft. below them, so far below that fields, villages, and barren earth blended into one brown smudge. But of more moment was the view eastwards along the ridge. A quarter of a mile away, what had seemed from below to be but a harmless rock-step now took shape as a formidable gendarme. We were too tired to visit it, but we were close enough to see that for porters it would be a serious obstacle; if our minds needed making up, this new trouble was decisive, although I think we had already tacitly decided that this route, too, was no go. Try as one might there was no ignoring the fact that at the start the avalanche danger was considerable, and though our difficult line of ascent would not be repeated the alternative line up the snow-slope was not a route by which we could bring up porters. That evening we descended it direct and found it devilish steep, the snow uncertain, and in places ready to avalanche.

We reached the tent at 6 p.m. to be greeted by a brisk discharge of snow cataracts into the cirque and by the strident roar of a more formidable avalanche from the offending gully. We packed up, listening uneasily to these monitory voices, whose message seemed to be that of a familiar hymn:

> Lo, it is not yours to say
> When to march and when to rest.

We waited till dark, for that night there was a full moon. Unluckily it chose to rise immediately behind Rakaposhi and so far as we were concerned it need not have troubled to rise at all. As another hymn goes, 'the night is black, the feet are slack', but we stumbled down in safety, carrying all the gear, and were met by the Sherpas with lights half-way down the long scree slope. And so to Darakush to meet our companions and to extinguish their last hope.

CHAPTER SEVEN

The Dainyor Nallah

As Gyr and I wolfed a late supper we all sat by a big fire discussing plans. Since it is a poor plan which admits no modifications, ours on the whole must have been good, for they were repeatedly frustrated and had to be just as repeatedly revised. Though Secord and Kappeler were disappointed by our gloomy report they were hardly surprised, for Angdawa's account of the 'via dolorosa' to the 'serac' camp had lost nothing in the telling. The possibilities of the Jaglot nallah having been exhausted, the next best thing seemed to be a descent into the Dainyor nallah by the new pass to see if there was any possible route there. Not that we should be certain to attempt the mountain again if there was, for it was now 4 July, a week would be needed to take the stores round, and Secord and I were due to leave by the end of the month. Were we to discover a very promising route, then a struggle between duty and pleasure might occur.

While waiting for coolies from Jaglot to bring the stores down from the Kunti camp we had a day of rest. It was very hot and cloudless. Secord's friends the flies were out in full force in spite of the fact that the cows had long since left. For the future I made a resolve not to begin climbing until assured by a plague of flies that summer had really come.

On the 5th we walked up the Manogar with two Sherpas and camped by the last of the wood. The col we were to cross was reported to be 'not very easy', so we sent the Sherpas back and went on ourselves carrying three days' food. We took no tents except for a very light one of Secord's weighing 6 lb. Having crossed the foot of the Kunti glacier we climbed a wide snow-fan which gradually narrowed to a couloir. A hundred feet or so below the short rock-pitch which led to the summit of the col our leader became involved in some step-cutting. Until then we had been comfortably kicking our way up in good hard snow. This unwelcome change of tactics gave rise to a warm argument between two schools of thought—the rock limpets and the snow hogs—as to whether, since the ice appeared to continue to the foot of the rock-pitch, it would not be better to take to the rock-wall of the couloir at once. The point at issue was settled by Gyr, who, taking a giant stride into the centre of the narrow couloir, triumphantly thrust his axe into *snow* and began *kicking* a large step; much in the same way that Johnson refuted Bishop Berkeley's proof of the non-existence of matter by kicking with mighty force a large stone, exclaiming with equal force: 'I refute it *thus*.' Whereupon Kappeler and I on the second rope ungraciously moved up past them, leaving the rock limpet to detach himself as best he could from the rocks to which he was already clinging.

The short rock-pitch to the top was very enjoyable. It was not difficult and the rock was of sound granite, a regrettably rare occurence in the Himalaya. We had been climbing for four hours and we put the height at 15,000 ft. It might well have been 16,000 ft. but our candid friends the altimeters refused to believe that it was a foot more than 14,000 ft. On the other side of the col (or pass as we were now entitled to call it) only a few feet away, the rock reverted to the Himalayan average of rottenness. Like burglars descending a creaking staircase, we picked our way down a treacherous little gullly to emerge presently on a snow-field where we had lunch. It was not easy to decide whether the snow-field was the remnant of a glacier or the embryo of one, but it did not extend far and soon we began plunging down boulders, scree, and finally grass, to fetch up at a little alp and a hut situated on a shelf above the Dainyor glacier. Opposite to us on the other side of the glacier was another col. This we took to be Conway's Uchubagan col which he had climbed from the Bagrot nallah and which had given him his glimpse of Rakaposhi.

The south ridge of Rakaposhi on which this col lies was clearly of no use to us, for between the col and the mountain lay a high and difficult peak. At the head of the Dainyor glacier, between the south and south-west ridges, was a very long, steep, and dangerous-looking snow-slope, while coming down from the south-west ridge was a re-entrant into which we could not properly see. But we knew what that ridge was like, so we soon came to the conclusion that there was nothing here for us.

We followed a path leading down the valley and presently, a few miles down, we found ourselves in delightful needle-carpeted pine forest. As I was steaming along in front looking for fresh water by which to camp I heard an agonized cry, or possibly a Swiss oath, from behind. Gyr had slipped and sprained an ankle—an accident to which even mountaineers are not immune if careless, tired, or in a devil of a hurry. Thus, our camp site was determined, and it happened not to be a bad one, under a friendly canopy of pines with just enough water for our needs. It was good to have found an eligible camp, but more important was whether we should be able to leave it, for Gyr's ankle had by now puffed up to an alarming size. After some tea I walked on down the path to see where we had got to. Half a mile on the forest petered out at the tip of an ancient moraine strewn with boulders. Here there was a clear view down the valley, and here, picking a sparse living from between the boulders, was a herd of goats tended by two men. One was dumb and the other half-witted, but both successfully 'registered' what I took to be astonishment. Very frequently one finds that the village goats are herded by a man with some such affliction, and I often wonder whether it is that which marks them out for the office or whether the affliction is the result of their long communion with goats. Rational conversation with a dumb man or a half-wit is at all times difficult, but more so when there is no common language. But my dumb friend seemed very much 'all there' and I gathered from him that there was a short way back to Matum Das up a big nallah which I could see coming in from the north two or three miles down.

The weather considerately allowed us a good night's sleep and time to start the fire before heavy rain set in to quench it. Painful though Gyr's ankle must have been, it was a great relief to find that he could get a boot on and hobble. Below the old moraine were many abandoned fields and presently we came to the first dwelling where we got a lot of milk but very little information; while at the first village a mile or so on the people were very off-hand indeed, and would give us neither one nor the other. This village was situated at the junction in the nallah I had seen the day before and the Dainyor. To follow the Dainyor stream down to the main valley below Gilgit and then back up to Jaglot would be a long way, and we had already vaguely learnt that there was a short-cut to Matun Das, the village below Jaglot close by the rope bridge.

If a short-cut existed it must lie up this nallah, but the head of it was out of sight and we knew from the map and the lie of the land that to reach Matun Das that way we should have to cross some very high ground indeed. From this village we could see another path which struck straight up the hillside, evidently heading for the Hunza valley somewhere on the other side but not in the direction of Matun Das. Should we play for safety by taking this, or be bold and with only one day's food left go up the unseen nallah and trust to luck? Secord was not in favour of either. 'No matter where it lead me, the downward path for me', was his view as he pointed down the Dainyor. Questions of food and funk decided it, as they often do, and in the midday heat we began the plod up bare, waterless, seemingly interminable slopes. Having gained some height we could see at the head of the nallah a deep notch of rock and snow and above it a nice looking peak of some 19,000 ft. The notch looked crossable, but to cross it would have meant another day and a hungry one.

Having had a dry lunch under a tree which had a sad, drooping air, as if it had taken root there one day inadvertently and regretted it ever since, we at last reached a saddle on the ridge some 3,000 ft. above the village. On the other side was a wide nallah which would obviously take us in quick time to Jutal (the village below Matun Das), and to water as well, from the lack of which we were all beginning to feel a bit peevish. Secord, having fallen in once with our whims and having sweated for it, was resolved not to do so again. Like a thirst-maddened horse scenting water from afar, he shot down the 'khud' in a cloud of dust and small stones. We other three were in a pig-headed mood. Having gained 3000 ft. of height at the cost of a prodigious thirst we were bent on making some use of it, regardless of the fact that sooner or later we should have to drop to the main valley. But we scorned to 'bummel' along it and if there was no short-cut direct to Matun Das, then we would make one. The fact that the track we had followed so far continued in the direction of the fast-disappearing Secord counted for nothing, for a faint broken scar along the bare stony hillside at our level suggested that in Buddhist times or some earlier era there had been a high-level route to Matun Das.

Secord, rightly suspecting that our need might be greater than his, had generously left us the bulk of the remaining food, so that Gyr in spite of his damaged ankle was not unwilling to cast in his lot with the high-level party. Off we went through brambles, briars, boulders, casting about for traces of a path and more anxiously for signs of water. There was not a hint of this, but we came upon some fine thick rhubarb. Some was sucked on the spot and some taken for supper. By four o'clock we had reached a rock-shoulder where the tenuous path ended for good. Ahead was a deep nallah and we strained our ears vainly listening for the sound of water. High above some snow-beds still lingered on—there must be water somewhere—so off we went again on a high traverse only to become spread-eagled on some cliffs. Secord, we reflected, must by now have finished his last cup of tea and would be reaching for his pipe. Hunger makes men bold, thirst makes them foolhardy. Recklessly we plunged down a horrible loose gully—Gyr twisting his ankle once more in his haste—by means of which, just before dark, we reached the nallah bed, water, and some old withered junipers.

It was a queer place for a camp. To sleep we had to hollow out coffin-like scoops in the loose rock, to fetch wood we had to climb up, and to draw water we had to climb down. Only immediately opposite our bivouac was there any way out on the opposing side. Upstream and down the rock-walls leant over the narrow bed where the water dashed unquietly from rock to rock and from one cascade to another. Lying on our stone shelves at the bottom of this stone crevasse we looked up to a ribbon of steel-blue sky across which the stars sailed slowly like lights on a dark river.

At dawn we woke to a clap of thunder. Hastily blowing up the fire we turned the remnant of our flour into chapatties and as the storm broke we ate them as we crouched under the overhanging wall of the gorge. When the rain was over we crossed the river and climbed out of this friendly nallah to continue traversing over rocky slopes which appeared to have been ploughed by some giant hand into ridge and furrow. At 10 o'clock we came to a grass shoulder beyond which was a deep valley and a path. We had had our bellyful of traversing this trackless hillside. Obstinate pride gave way to sweet reasonableness and we took the path which must lead, as we well knew, only to Jutal.

Having so far refused to yield an inch of the height we had gained so laboriously yesterday we had now about 7000 ft. to descend pretty abruptly, but we found some scree-slopes which allowed us to make such short work of this long plunge into the Hunza valley that we arrived at Jutal by midday. We retain kindly memories of Jutal where the villagers fed the chastened wanderers on eggs and delicious bread which tasted like well-leavened bannocks. Later in the day the lambadar conducted us to the outskirts of his village, past the inevitable polo ground, and there dismissed us to follow the track by the left bank of the river to Matun Das and Jaglot. Early in the march we encountered two characteristic features of this country—a blinding sand-storm whipped up from the sand-banks of the river, and a fine example of a 'parri', a well-known word here indicating a precipice across which the path is taken. Sometimes it is made by hewing out the rock, sometimes by supporting the path on a stone revetment, and sometimes, in extreme cases, by supporting it on wooden brackets driven into the wall of the precipice which may be either of rock or boulder-clay. On this particular 'parri' the path is dangerously narrow so that transport animals cannot use it.

Instead of climbing up to Matun Das, which lies on a shelf 200 or 300 ft. above the river, we slunk past below in the extravagant hope that Secord, whom we suspected would be there gorging fruit, might believe we had reached Jaglot by an even shorter cut than we had hoped. This over-careful regard for saving face cost us the rest and refreshment we might have had. By 7 o'clock we were at the foot of the steep climb out of the main valley and we gained the open fields above in time to see Rakaposhi aglow with the rays of a sun which for us had already set. The north-west ridge looked to be an easy walk, while the Monk's Head, I thought, leered at us scornfully. The Sherpas were there with all our stores and, having eaten an omelette of Himalayan grandeur prepared by Angdawa, we lay down to sleep under the apricots.

After a morning's haggling we settled our account for coolies, mutton, and milk, and started for Matun Das, bathing on the way in a 'kul'. These main 'kuls' are two or three feet deep, several feet wide, and sometimes several miles long. There is a famous one—the Berber—at Baltit, the capital of Hunza, which is six miles long. Once a year they are cleaned out and the fine alluvial deposit is used to enrich the fields.

Matun Das, outside the borders of Hunza proper, is a Hunza colony, as the well-terraced fields, the orchards, and the well-kept 'kuls' bear witness. We found Secord there in company with our friend Mainprice who was on his way to Jaglot to strike the first blow in the construction of his new 'kul', the opposition of the Jaglot elders having at last been overcome. They were reclining more or less gracefully in an orchard surrounded by trays of peaches, figs, apricots, and apples, both looking. I thought, understandably pale. Small boys re-appeared frequently with more trays and baskets, received their few annas, and departed for fresh supplies. In the end these imports had to be summarily stopped, more in the interests of our stomachs than our pockets.

Once more we were faced with the necessity of making a plan, and I began to have a sneaking admiration for our professional planners who make such things with less trouble than we should take to strike a match. It was now 10 July, we had about a fortnight left, and our first thought was to visit the Bagrot nallah to round off the reconnaissance of the mountain which we had failed to climb. One objections to this was that if we went the shortest way by the left bank of the Hunza river we should pass within a stone's throw of Gilgit on the opposite bank. This we thought would be carrying austerity too far and might even be considered discourteous to the residents. A graver objection was that if we should discover later that we ought to have gone there in the first place rather than to Jaglot, then our consequent regret and remorse would be too poignant to bear. Moreover, the Bagrot nallah was not new ground and ever since our first glance at our map (Survey of India, ¼ in., Sheet 42L) we had been tantalized by the presence of a long white strip of glacier marked 'unexplored'. About half this map-sheet is unsurveyed, the dividing line being roughly the Batura-Muztagh range which runs in a north-westerly direction from Baltit until it meets the Hindu Kush on the Hunza-Wakhan border. The triangular tract north of this range, between it and the Hindu Kush and west of the Hunza river, had been surveyed pretty thoroughly by the Dutch Visser-Hooft expedition of 1925 and the Montagnier expedition of 1927, both of which had had the assistance of Indian surveyors lent by the Survey of India. South of the range, as far as the Gilgit river, the country is not only unsurveyed but is in a few places still unexplored, so that the map is for the most part more or less intelligent guess-work.

Whether an unexplored portion should be left a clean white blank on the map or whether it should be drawn in, in speculative fashion, fitting as best it may into the contiguous surveyed area is a nice point. Like a great many of us, some explorers wish to eat their cake and have it. They enjoy the thrill and claim the credit of traversing new country and at the same time are ungrateful enough to complain of the inadequacy of the map. The genuine explorer would prefer, I think, to have with him a Snark-hunter's map—a complete and absolute blank—upon which he could first exercise his own talent for intelligent guess-work and then later by experience discover his own mistakes. On the part of the map in question the guessing had already been done for us and its results, merely by being published, had acquired a sufficiently authoritative air to induce us, foolishly perhaps, to base our plan upon them. On any but the most modern maps of mountainous country—and in the Himalaya there are now many such, thanks to the Survey of India and private exploration—one expects the detail to be wrong or vague, but takes for granted that the general lie of the land is as represented.

Referring to the map it will be seen that the Bola Das river, entering the Hunza river near Chalt from the north, has its origin in two big glaciers near a place called Toltar. The eastern branch, the Baltar, we found had been visited by Col. R. F. C. Schomberg who had also seen the first few miles of the larger northern branch, but no one had been to the head of this, which, according to the draughtsman, extended for more than 15 miles between the Batura-Muztagh range on the east and another rather queer-looking range to the west. West again of this was the Karumbar river and reality. Though it did not, it should have occurred to us at the time that there really was not much room for a glacier of this size and another mountain range between the Batura-Muztagh range and the Karumbar valley. Anyhow we accepted the draughtsman's dream, guess, or fancy at its face value and laid our plans accordingly. Having allowed ourselves seven days to reach the northern end of the unexplored glacier, perhaps climbing an easy peak on the way, we should cross a pass (which we should no doubt find) leading either to the Koz Yaz or Yashkuk Yaz glaciers. We preferred the former but we would not be too particular. Both these glaciers we knew to be as drawn on the map, for they had been surveyed by the Visser-Hooft party. But if by some mischance there was no pass to either, then we should have to break out over the western wall of the Karumbar valley. That was all right so far as it went; but we were no dithering amateurs planning a Sunday School treat for one afternoon. We were engaged in long-term planning, according to the best modern practice, and so having crossed the pass, say, to the Koz Yaz glacier, the party would then crack a bottle of 'Ovosport', shake hands, and disintegrate. Secord would bend his weary steps westwards to Chitral via the Chillinji pass and many others which were no concern of ours; I, having accompanied the Swiss down the Chapursan valley as far as Misgar, would head happily northwards, once more free from care; and the Swiss would turn southwards from Misgar, pay their respects to the Mirs of Hunza and Nagar, and continue with whatever they might have a mind to. But as the Spanish proverb has it: 'He that shuffles does not always cut.'

Since Secord had first to have permission to go out through Chitral and since I had some things to collect for my Kashgar trip, we were obliged to return to Gilgit before setting forth on this new venture. The thought of having to do twice more the seventeen miles between Nomal and Gilgit was sufficient to modify any transports of joy we might have felt at the prospect of a few days in Gilgit with our friends. We had not been out long enough or fared hard enough to have any overpowering longing for the flesh-pots, but on the other hand it would be churlish to refuse the hospitality that would certainly be offered. 'When they bring you the heifer be ready with the rope', were the words of advice most frequently uttered by Sancho Panza.

We recrossed the bridge to Nomal, Angdawa once more having to be carried, and left there again at noon on a blistering hot day. We had already sent off a courier to announce our coming and at Nomal we mounted Kappeler, who had a stiff knee, on a 'Rosinante' of a pony, and sent him off as a second herald, having some doubt about the energy or willingness of the first. We advised Kappeler to spare neither man nor beast; but although the foot party started some time later we soon caught him up and in the end arrived in Gilgit dirty, hot, shaggy, and unannounced.

CHAPTER EIGHT

The Kukuay Glacier

CHALT, our starting-point, is the next stage beyond Nomal. The distance is only 15 miles, but for many of these the track lies over sand or loose pebbles. On either hand are bare rock-walls and once the sun tops these the traveller has no relief from its concentrated power until he reaches Chalt. Good judges of misery, amateurs with a taste for suffering, would hardly know to which stage to award the palm—Gilgit to Nomal or Nomal to Chalt. This straggling village occupies the alluvial fans deposited by the Chaprot and Bola Das nallahs and its fort once commanded the routes of Hunza and Nagar. Thus Chalt and its fort became at one time a bone of contention between the petty states of Hunza and Nagar as well as between these states and the Kashmir garrison at Gilgit. In 1891 when British authority had to be asserted over the Mirs of Hunza and Nagar because of their defiant attitude towards the British Agent, Chalt was the advanced base for the troops whose formidable task was to storm the strong position of Nilt a few miles up stream on the opposite bank.

As usual the bungalow was at the farthest and highest point of the fan. We arrived at midday in a gale of wind to find awaiting us the thesildar from Gilgit whom Col. Bacon had kindly sent to help us in our negotiations for coolies. In addition to this Col. Bacon had advised the Mir of Hunza that we should shortly be coming down the Chapursan valley, which is in his territory, and had asked him to send someone up there to assure the people that the coming invaders were neither Afghan nor Russian. Presently the local rajah arrived with a gift of fruit. We arranged transport rates with him and then we settled down to serious business with the lambadar. The lambadar of a village is the man who makes or mars the getting of coolies or ponies, while the chowkidar is equally powerful in the matter of food and quarters. I never quite got the hang of local government. I suppose there was in reality only one 'King of Brentford', but when it came to distributing largesse we found there were seldom less than five lambadars and more than one chowkidar.

The lambadar of Chalt, a spare, oldish, dignified man was much-travelled, having made the journey to Kashgar several times. Wishing to enlarge the bounds of his experience he made us the welcome offer of his company, but that evening he and the thesildar had a slight tiff during which I feared we should lose the services of this valuable ally and that the ally himself would lose his life. It seemed that ponies could only be used for the first seven miles up the Bola Das whence we should need ten coolies to carry for us up the glacier. Some sample 60 lb. loads had been made up, around which there gathered an interested circle of idlers, critics, and prospective carriers all eyeing the loads rather lugubriously. The lambadar agreed with them that 60 lb. was too much; the thesildar, acting for us, thought otherwise. A weight-lifting contest began, one party handling the loads as a professional on the stage handles a 200 lb. lift, the veins starting out on their foreheads as they grunted and heaved, while our party, represented by the Sherpas, flipped them about contemptuously like men stacking bricks. We seemed to be getting nowhere, until the thesildar, his rage suddenly kindling, clutched with both hands a 60 lb. bag of atta and hurled it violently at the semi-venerable lambadar, sending him reeling to the ground. Since the lambadar was not killed and since soon after he was even able to stand, everyone agreed that 60 lb. had been proved by demonstration to be a very fair load.

Two or three miles up the Bola Das nallah is the village of Budelas. We were standing in a field buying flour, idly viewing the sullen clouds to the east, when suddenly above the cloud a small white triangle, faint but harder than a cloud, took shape—it was the summit of Rakaposhi. The clouds began slowly to dissolve upon the face of the superb pyramid and its plinth of ice, the north-west ridge rose above them like a white whale breaking surface, and the grandest view of the mountain we had yet seen burst upon us—one from which we found it was hard to turn away. The north-west ridge was to us three-quarters on; we should have preferred it square on so that Secord's peak, the knife-edge section, the point reached by Gyr and me, and the gendarme beyond, could have been identified more easily. A few miles on we came to some hot springs, where the coolies took over the loads and our forceful friend the thesildar bade us farewell. His semi-venerable victim, armed with a mighty staff, now took his place as guide and counsellor.

Water from the hot spring having been led into a rough stone tank and the plug, in the form of clods of earth, having been inserted, the bath filled itself and the distinguished visitors bathed. We then moved on up the narrowing valley, crossed the Daintar nallah, and finished the march to Bar with a delightfully easy and pleasant walk alongside a 'kul' several hundred feet above the river. The people of Bar seemed marvellously ill-favoured, but were eager to see us and ready to supply us. I was amused and sorry to see the precaution taken by a little old man who guided us through the village, running ahead to warn any approaching women of the invasion of infidel males. Those who were about at once scurried off the track to hide in the crops, or else pulled a 'lungi' over their face. If women are more curious than men, which I doubt, then Moslem women must suffer agonies from its enforced repression. Think of what a sight they had to deny themselves now, one which would not (though it did) pass that way again. An uncommonly long European, a short young European gentleman, a black-bearded professor-like European, a grizzled veteran, and four strange smooth-faced, slit-eyed, coloured gentlemen.

At Bar some shuffling of our coolie team took place, some Chalt men went back while Bar men took their places. Two recruits also joined us here—Robinson Crusoe and Man Friday—who said they had been some way up our glacier after ibex and proposed now to show us the way and to keep us in meat. Crusoe was the embodiment of unquenchable optimism, as indeed he had to be to hunt ibex with his primitive firelock—a long gas-pipe innocent of sights with a couple of wooden prongs like the business-end of a hay-fork mounted on the barrel as a rest. The firing mechanism was a length of fuse wound round the butt, its lighted end held poised above the pan by a clip; on pressing the trigger this descended with decorum on to the primed pan and in due course a large round bullet proceeded up the barrel to speed gravely on its deadly mission. Man Friday carried this weighty antiquity, Crusoe the accessories, which were slung round his person in little skin bags—powder, flint and steel, tinder, wadding, and ramrod.

Four miles beyond Bar is another small hamlet—the last outpost of civilization—above which, on the old terminal moraine of the glacier, the track becomes sketchy and the going bad in the extreme. We reached the junction of the two glaciers at 1 o'clock. The eastern branch which originates under two 25,000 ft. peaks on the Batura-Muztagh range was called by the locals Baltar, while our unexplored glacier, which from here bore away slightly north of west, was known as the Kukuay. That day's destination was the sheepfold of Burjukush three miles away on the south side of the glacier, but owing to the rough going and the consequent slowness of the coolies it was always doubtful as to whether we should make it. However, the promise of a sheep persuaded them at least to try. Just short of Burjukush a glacier stream, the Aldarkush, comes in from the south. When we reached it in late evening it was in full spate, but Crusoe, our guide, having climbed a hill and gazed long at the turbulent flood, beckoned us on. There was no sign of a bridge, but presently Crusoe began stripping his nether garments and we realized the bridge was of a peculiar kind—an Irish bridge—for most of the water was going over it instead of under. Here both Crusoe and Man Friday worked their passage by standing for minutes at a time in the icy torrent helping Sherpas and coolies across and sometimes carrying their loads. The shepherds and their charges were in residence. After due haggling two sheep were slaughtered and everyone turned in happy, except perhaps myself who in the role of Moses overheard the murmuring of his people at the length of their first march into the wilderness and their avowed intention of making the next very short.

From the old moraine bank between alp and glacier we could see that two miles up another glacier (the Sat Marau, or Seven Ibex—which a shikari had once killed there) swept down from the west in a wild jumble of ice, and that beyond this the Kukuay took a more promising northerly course. Around the bend, and still on our side, there was a fine birch spinney, probably the last, the obvious place for our next camp, provided the thoughts of camel and camel-drivers would agree. We made a late start at 8 o'clock and the pace set, which was not even a brisk crawl, suggested that so far at least these thoughts were totally at variance. No effort was made to take the decisive step down to the glacier; instead we shunned it as though it were a quicksand, creeping through the jungle of trees and bushes growing in the ablation valley behind the old moraine, until it became clear that no such drastic step was in view but that the intention was to camp on the moraine well short of the bend. Having first won over to our point of view the lambadar and Crusoe we called a conference of coolies and persuaded them by a mixture of imprecation and cajolery to commit themselves to the glacier. Once we were there, the elements came to our help, for it began to drizzle and since there were huts at the spinney everyone got a move on.

We were now out in the middle of an ice-sea, or more correctly a sea of stones, for the Kukuay bears down on its surface great quantities of stone and debris deposited by either the numerous tributary glaciers from the west or by the mightly cliffs of the Batura peaks on the east. An exceedingly rough sea it was—a maze of waves and troughs. At one place where a mass of white marble debris lay, the waves seemed to be breaking in foam on some reef. For five hours we threaded our way in and out of the hollows of this tumbled surface, for there was neither lateral nor medial moraine, nor any grassy ablation valley to ease our progress. Having landed at last on the western shore we climbed steeply to our camp among the birches, a place whose name we were told was also Darakush. The trees surrounded a clear unrippled tarn

TWO MOUNTAINS AND A RIVER

in whose water the reflected peaks vied in beauty with the peaks themselves. Astonishment is a salutary emotion and the Kukuay glacier administered it to us in large doses. From the snout its course had been a little north of west, it had then swung to the north, and now it appeared to be coming from a point well to the east of north. The draughtsman's dream which had been committed to paper now became for us a nightmare where we talked of nothing but courses steered and distance run in order to arrive at some sort of dead reckoning. One thing was clear—that we were a long way from the Koz Yaz glacier, and that to bring us within striking distance of it the Kukuay glacier would have to mend its ways and behave as the draughtsman had expected.

Crusoe and Friday were now bidden to bestir themselves and fulfil their office. They therefore arranged a crack-of-dawn start for themselves in order to catch the ibex asleep, for this, I should say, was the only way by which they could get within killing distance. They would then meet us (bringing home the bacon, we hoped) at another alp called Little Darakush. This was four miles up on the far side of another big tributary glacier and it was the bourne beyond which no traveller had yet gone. There would be grass but no birch trees. We reached it in two hours of glacier-walking over a rather better surface. It proved to be a very pleasant grass flat tucked in between the old moraine and some cliffs, the home of choughs and ravens. Dwarf willow, whose dead branches made excellent firewood, grew profusely on the moraine, while under the cliff wild rhubarb flourished as though in a hot-bed; blue and yellow violets and golden columbine graced the sward, but the only water in this alpine garden was that obtained from a snow-bed which still lingered in the cool shadow of the cliff. The height, we thought, was 12,500 ft.

As we approached this place we had noticed away up on our left an easy-looking snow col of moderate height at the upper end of this big tributary glacier which the locals called Djuriti Gah. We had made a careful note of this as a possible way of escape to the Karumbar in case the Kukuay played us false as seemed now not unlikely. After lunch we climbed to a vantage point and saw not far ahead a long stretch of dry clean ice which promised fast easy travelling, while beyond the glacier curled round a high rock cape on a more northerly course. This raised our hopes. We had now covered about twelve miles up the glacier and had it followed more or less the expected course we should now have been within a few miles of its termination and the divide between it and the Chapursan glacier system. Instead of this it had described almost a semi-circle and the dry debris-free ice seemed to indicate that the end was not far off, but that end could not be where we hoped.

Spurred on by curiosity we dropped down to glacier level, found an intricate way on to it by a corridor of black, dirty ice, reached the clean, smooth surface beyond, and went on at our best speed. After about a mile and a half we reached and rounded the cape, but there the greater part of our hopes died. Four or five miles away a great snow cirque marked, without room for mistake, the beginning and for us the end of the Kukuay. Far up in the high north-east corner of the cirque a dwindling arm of the glacier curved out of sight and our prospects of crossing the cirque seemed to depend on what there

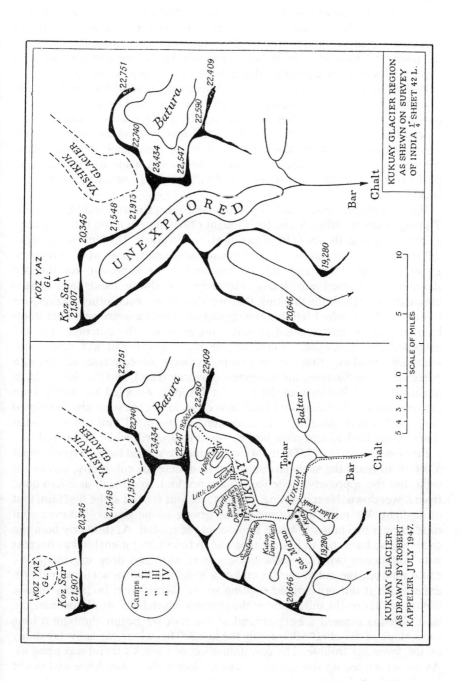

KUKUAY GLACIER REGION
AS SHEWN ON SURVEY
OF INDIA 1" SHEET 42 L.
¼

KUKUAY GLACIER
AS DRAWN BY ROBERT
KAPPELER JULY 1947.

SCALE OF MILES

was round the corner. If there was a col it must be high, the approach by an ice-fall looked difficult, and what lay beyond was anybody's guess. Most of us thought that the answer would prove to be the Yashkuk glacier, but we had an uneasy feeling that it might just as well be the Batura, for we had already identified (or so we thought) the big 23,434 ft. peak on the main Batura range. Subdued and sorrowful we walked back to camp where our sorrows were slightly alleviated by a gigantic rhubarb pie of Angdawa's baking.

Having dumped one load of atta in favour of a load of firewood, for our journey up the glacier had taken less than the estimated time, we started on our last march with the men of Chalt and Bar. It was a hot cloudless day, indeed the weather so far had been so good that we doubted our wisdom in leaving Rakaposhi. Below the rock-cape was a meagre supply of wood, but as we were anxious to get the most out of the coolies while we had them we pushed on for another half-hour and finally pitched our camp on the last rocks.

We paid off the coolies and tipped the lambadar, Crusoe, and Man Friday. Tipping is always difficult and the thought of having given too little is almost as hard to bear as the thought of having given too much. This time it was more difficult than usual because the coolies had earned more than what I proposed giving to their elders and betters, for neither the lambadar nor the two shikaris had carried any loads. However, we shook hands and parted amicably enough, little thinking that we should see each other again—one reason, perhaps, why I felt that the tipping need not be overdone. One stout-hearted man of Bar decided to stay with us to see the outcome. He had proposed this hazardous course at the start, but I had not paid much attention, thinking that his complete inability to converse either with ourselves or the Sherpas, the roughness of glacier travel, and the sight of large quantities of ice and snow at the end of it would have cooled his ardour when the time came. The rigour and loneliness of his future life were kindly pointed out, but his determination was unshaken. So we fitted him out with what spare things we had and took him on—and well worth while he proved.

From our camp (c. 14,000 ft.) we estimated we should have to climb about 5,000 ft. to reach the snow cirque. Even from here the col, if any, was out of sight, but the approach by the ice-fall did not look so difficult as it had done from lower down. Next morning, the 21st, we four started at the first faint hint of daylight. We made good time up the dry ice of the glacier, but even so it took us over two hours to reach the foot of the ice-fall. At this early hour the snow was so hard that in places steps had to be cut, but it enabled us to cross with confidence two frail snow bridges over wide and deep crevasses. We could now see the col at the far end of a wide and flat snow corridor. From underneath it did not appear inviting so we discarded it in favour of one slightly higher on the north side of the corridor which here ran almost east and west. Having crossed a bergschrund at the foot we began climbing a long snow-slope of about 60° where only the last 200 ft., where the snow lay thinly on ice, gave any trouble. The consummation of a week's travel was upon us. As we scrambled up the summit rocks to decide the issue, hope and doubt were equally balanced.

TWO MOUNTAINS AND A RIVER 581

What we saw on the other side was satisfactory only because of its decisiveness. Sometimes on reaching a col which one hopes to cross the worst is not revealed until one is more than half-way down, when the dislike of going back is only matched by the dislike of going on. But here an impossibly steep drop at our feet left us in no doubt at all, so that the prudent had not to incur the suspicion of timidity by objecting to a route which the boldest dared not commend. Had there been a chance of going down, the fact that the glacier so far below was undoubtedly the Batura might have dissuaded us from the attempt, though to travel in the wrong direction is probably preferable to retracing one's steps. It was now clear that we were not north of the big 23,434 ft. peak as we had thought, but were probably between the two 22,000 ft. peaks to the south of it and barely ten miles north of the junction of the Kukuay and Baltar glaciers. Glaciers are sometimes as erratic as men, and only when both behave in a normal way do they become dull. I was never more disappointed in my life than by the perfectly normal behaviour of the 'Cornice' glacier, near the junction of the Hispar and Biafo glaciers, of which the account of earlier explorers[1] (whom I dearly wished to believe) had led me to hope that it was unique among glaciers in that it had no outlet, being entirely surrounded by mountains.

Looking down on to the wide bay with several arms at the head of the Batura, the biggest glacier in this region, we could see more than one exit to the north, but neither to the right nor to the left of our col was there any way of reaching them; the only way out of the impasse was to go back. Moving one at a time we stepped gingerly down the first 200 ft. where the midday sun was rapidly clearing the thin snow support from the steps we had cut coming up. Then in deeper, safer snow we plunged swiftly to the bergschrund. Gyr continued his plunging a shade too long and fell in. It was not very deep so that he was able to climb out the other side. I decided to jump, but foolishly neglected to learn from Gyr what the landing was like I lit on ice, slipped, and hit the ground a hearty smack with the back of my head. At first I thought my thick skull had suffered no harm, but by the time we had reached the top of the ice-fall headache and vomiting had set in. In my condition the descent of the ice-fall, the crossing of the lightly bridged crevasses, more dangerous now by the softening snow, and the long trudge back, made our return a slow and dreary business. Two Sherpas came out to carry me the last half-mile and when we reached camp at 4 p.m. I turned in and slept solidly till 6 o'clock next morning.

I woke more or less cured and breakfasted heartily on the very fine supper I had missed the night before—a spaghetti and another of Angdawa's rhubarb pies. Our last shot in the locker was the low easy col to the west which we had noticed on the way up and which we little doubted would lead us to the Karumbar valley. Except that it would take more time this route would be no less satisfactory or interesting than the other. We could continue up the Karumbar to the Chillinji pass whence Secord could turn west for Chitral, while we others crossed the pass and went down the Chapursan to meet the Mir of Hunza's man who by this time would probably be a little tired of

1 Mr and Mrs Bullock-Workman.

waiting for us. By going this way we might also clear up the mystery of the unexplored gap between the heads of the Kukuay and the Koz Yaz glaciers. Accordingly we packed up and went down to Little Darakush. Neither Kappeler nor Angtingit were well so, while two of us remained to help with the loads, Secord pushed on to see if there was any suitable camp up the tributary glacier. He found that, though the grass shelf of Little Darakush continued round the corner for some way, except on the glacier itself there was nowhere any water. He had gone nearly to the foot of the ice-fall and reported that the col looked quite near but that the ice-fall might prove troublesome. That afternoon there was a halo round the sun, but its evil promise was not fulfilled until twenty-four hours later, when there was a fierce thunderstorm.

The reconnaissance party left at 5 o'clock next morning. In one hour we reached the foot of the ice-fall, which was short but steep and quite the blackest and ugliest I have ever seen. The best line seemed to be on our right, where the ice met the rock-wall. Both were so black that it was difficult to say where the ice ended and the rock began. Despite its repulsive aspect Secord and I advanced light-heartedly to the assault and had hardly taken the first few tentative steps up a rock-scoop overhung by a wall of ice when a stone the size of a football whistled down, missing my head by inches and catching Secord fair and square on the forearm. At first we feared it might be broken but, although this did not prove to be the case, he had to be escorted back to camp by Kappeler.

Gyr and I then crossed to the other side. There was a corridor between ice and rock but it was from our point of view a hopeless chasm, difficult to get into and impossible to get out of, and made even more repellent by water streaming into it from the rocks. We then went back to the middle, where the fall of a succession of seracs had flattened out a sort of roadway. Up this we made rapid but fearful progress. The ice was unbelievably rotten and we tacked from side to side seeking but failing to avoid the poised and weighty threat of many tottering seracs. I used to smile at the accounts of very early mountaineers, whose guides imposed on them strict silence when passing close to seracs lest some careless but violent 'Damn' might suffice to bring down a serac on top of the whole party; but I confess it was in complete silence and with bated breath that I passed within range of these leering towers of soft, dripping, honey-combed ice. We were through the worst and the slope had begun to ease as we approached the plateau above the ice-fall. The crevasses became more uniform, more clean-cut, wider and deeper. Success seemed assured when suddenly we were confronted by a series of monster cracks which split the ice from side to side, from one rock-wall to the other. Through, round, or over them, there was no way.

As we retreated, losing our way several times in the labyrinth of cracks, cliffs, and pinnacles, we worked over to the rocks above the the scene of the first mishap. There was a way there all right, but it could only be reached by means of the rock-scoop under the cliff from which stones were now falling frequently as the heat of the sun released them from their ice-bed. Perhaps, if the nights had been cold enough this route might have been used, but it would have been a black business in every way and now with three sick men in the party it was not to be thought of.

Our defeat was complete. There seemed to be no way now of saving anything from the wreck of our hopes. Time was running short, so that even if all the party had been fit neither Secord nor myself could have remained looking for another way over to the Karumbar. Before this was discovered we might easily have found ourselves as far south as the known route by the Daintar nallah below Bar. Our time had not been wasted, however. We had explored the Kukuay from snout to source and it was our misfortune that in so doing we had dissolved our own dreams as well as the draughtsman's. The foundations of our airy castle had collapsed. That dream bubble was pricked, and it was time to acknowledge that 'things are what they are and the consequences will be what they will be', of which the most unpleasant for us was the long dreary march back down the glacier without the buoyancy of novelty and hope which had animated us on the way up. Neither was there any balm for our hurts in the thought of our far from impresssive return to Chalt, nor in the remembrance of the Mir's patient emissary watching and wondering at some high alp in the Chapursan.

Painful ordeals of any kind, from a visit to the dentist to a wedding reception, cannot be too soon over. We determined that our sufferings would at any rate be brief, so that two days to Chalt was all we allowed ourselves. We started at 8 a.m. and except for a halt of two hours walked all day until 6 p.m., steering a direct course across the big bend of the glacier for the sheepfold at Aldarkush. All of it was exasperatingly rough going, but although we were clear of the glacier by 5 p.m. we went on until we camped a mile below its junction with the Baltar. We had another casualty when Gyr slipped and cut his hand badly on a stone.

On the 25th we set out for Chalt. Since Angtingit was now unable to carry and travelled slowly even without a load we sent him off early. The rest of us had not been going long before we met him walking back towards us looking even more glum than his sickness would warrant. He reported that the swollen river had overflowed a short piece of the track and that there was no way round. There was certainly no way over, for the river was now in roaring spate and it looked as if we should have to go back to the glacier snout to cross and then find a way down the other side. However, beyond a wide talus of mud and stone, the result of a landslide, there was a steep cliff of hard mud and rock mixed, traversed by a sloping narrow ledge. Beyond this, if we could cross and descend again, was dry land and the track. The man of Bar and I climbed up to and across the traverse and found a way down at the other end, the Bar man leading and hacking steps in the mud with a borrowed ice-axe. It was an exposed place and it was no consolation to know that if one did come off one would only fall into the river. The crossing of the talus was even more perilous, for stones and boulders were shooting down this frequently and rapidly. We carried the loads over, with both eyes on the slope above as a batsman stealing a run watches the fielder. Not one of the Sherpas would take his load across the traverse, but the man of Bar performed prodigies of work and sure-footedness in carrying every load himself.

This caused some delay, but by midday we were eating our lunch at Bar, whence, having hired three coolies to help, we made a push for Chalt. Robinson Crusoe, hearing of our arrival and then of our departure, pursued us almost to the hot springs to offer hospitality, but we were firm and pressed on. Our bathe was welcome, for these springs are reputed to cure all ills and at least three of our party stood in need of their healing waters. At Budelas our mad career was checked for a while by the irresistible desire to gaze long and wonderingly at Rakaposhi. This time it was bright with the glories of a setting sun; but in a short time sky, snow, and shadow mingled, and the spell broke. We reached Chalt as night fell, and for two hours our Sherpas and coolies dribbled in one by one.

That night at Chalt was our last together. Very early next morning Secord departed on his thirty-two-mile march to Gilgit where, as we heard, he duly arrived, dead from the feet up but still standing; and a little later, accompanied appropriately enough by one donkey, I left for Misgar and the north.

Though it was the last night, no bottles were cracked (perhaps the 'Ovosport' had run out) and no speeches either of farewell or of recrimination made. Nevertheless, as I lay out under the stars, 'chewing the cud of sweet and bitter fancy', I paid a silent tribute to these companions with whom the adventure had originated, who had shared equally and uncomplainingly both the worries of preparation, the more bearable physical troubles of realization, and in the end the keen disappointment of failure. In particular they had submitted to a certain amount of dictation which was often unexplained or, by reason of language difficulties, inexplicable. On many occasions they had had good reason to exclaim with Omar:

> What, without asking, hither hurried whence?
> And, without asking, whither hurried hence?
> Another and another cup to drown
> The memory of this impertinence.

German or French have I none. My English is neither clear nor pure, yet in spite of, or because, perhaps, of these language barriers, harsh words, though they may have been thought, were seldom uttered. Climbing parties of mixed nationalities are not always harmonious, and tempers are more tried by defeat than by success, but possibly the reason that our party had been so happy was that Swiss and English are as near in outlook as different nations can expect to be. Above all, our respective attitudes to mountains and mountaineering are pretty much the same.

As for our crushing defeat by Rakaposhi, while not wishing to diminish the part played by the mountain in bringing this about, I think our chief mistake was in attempting the climb too early in the season. This was largely my fault for having arranged to leave for Kashgar in July. To devote less than two months to a big unknown mountain is bordering on disrespect, and if the mountain be a Rakaposhi then two objectives in one season are too much. Whether either of our two routes would be easier later in the year is unlikely, but they would undoubtedly be less dangerous. Though July's weather was by no means perfect it was better than that of June. Later still there would, of course, be less snow to avalanche and perhaps the cornices would be less formidable.

Our ignoring of other ways and our gamble on the Jaglot approach seems to have been justified, for in August the Swiss had a look at the north side and the Bagrot nallah and in their opinion our approach, such as it was, was the best—probably the only one worth trying. Had we carried out our first plan of reconnoitring every side we should have got nowhere. In the Himalaya it seems to be almost impossible to tell whether a given route will go without trying it, and to do this on a high mountain is prodigal of time. Judgement I repeat, is, perhaps, the greatest mountaineering asset of all, and though our difficulty in judging routes may have reflected on ourselves, it nevertheless confirmed the truth of Dr Longstaff's dictum which I have already quoted, that in the Himalaya the only certain proof of a route is to try it.

Whether our judgement in abandoning the two routes we did try was also at fault I cannot tell. Who shall draw the line between prudence and pusillanimity. Prudence, as Dr Johnson tells us, 'Quenches that ardour of enterprise by which everything is done that can claim praise or admiration, and represses that generous temerity which often fails and often succeeds.' To which I shall only add that in mountaineering one man's prudence is another man's poison.

CHAPTER NINE

Chalt to Misgar

FOR many people distant places have a peculiar form of magnetism which grows as the distance increases. I am thus attracted, and besides its remoteness there is for me a strange thrill in the mere sound of Chinese Turkestan, situated as it is in the heart of Central Asia where place-names like Kashgar, Yarkand, Urumchi, awaken half-forgotten memories of Marco Polo and the old Silk Road linking Peking and Samarkand; of Turkomans and Kirghiz; of rich camel caravans and mud-walled caravanserais. There, too, are the Takla Makan desert, the grave alike of great rivers and of cities of an ancient civilization, and the Pamirs, the so-called Roof the World, that strange barren region where the three Empires of Great Britain, Russia, and China once met.

Many travellers have succumbed to the lure of Chinese Turkestan or Sinkiang as it is now known: Shaw, Dalgliesh (murdered near Yarkand), Bower, Forsyth, Hayward (murdered in Chitral), Trotter, Dauvergne, in the last century, and in more recent times Younghusband, Sven Hedin, and the late Sir Aurel Stein, who did more than anyone to increase our knowledge of Central Asia. These men, more especially the earlier travellers, had danger to face and real difficulties to overcome, for owing to the extreme lawlessness which prevailed they travelled as often as not in peril of their lives. But at the end of the last century and the beginning of this the heyday of Central Asia travel dawned. By then order had been established and any man, even one who was neither a scientist nor an official, could wander alone and unarmed, except for a passport, facing nothing more serious than the ordinary hardships of travel. Now, however, the pendulum has swung to the other extreme. Hardship and peril are to seek, but law and order have between them generated official obstruction and any would-be traveller must first overleap its wellnigh impassable barrier.

Ever since it was established (1890) the British Consulate at Kashgar has been a refuge, a home, and a base for travellers in Sinkiang, and sometime ago the present (1947) Consul, Mr E. E. Shipton, had invited me to join him in a climbing holiday. The project was one of many months' standing, but although we live enmeshed like flies in a cobweb world of plans—mostly on a five-year basis—all plans, particularly those of individuals, become of necessity more and more tentative. Fresh circumstances, some new regulation, civil commotion, or rumours of war, cause them to be recast or scrapped almost as soon as made, so that it was with relief and surprise that I found myself actually on the point of starting out for Kashgar; the more so since Sinkiang, isolated though it is, has been in recent years in the same state of nervous effervescence as the rest of the world. Even while we were on Rakaposhi I had read in a paper of disturbances there.

Very early in our acquaintance, the Sherpas had made it clear that none of them had the wish or the intention to go with me. I attributed this either to their dislike of me or to their fear of the fatal attraction of Kashgar, for a Sherpa who had gone there with Mr Shipton in 1941 had never returned, but had settled, married (or contracted a liaison), and prospered. I was therefore alone for the first part of my journey to Misgar, the last post on the British side of the border, where I was to meet a man sent down by Shipton. Having hastily packed a few things, seen Secord start, admonished the Sherpas to behave themselves, and said good-bye, I took the road with my donkey. The road passes through Budelas and then follows the right bank of the Hunza river to its source near the Mintaka pass. Travellers are few, but I met a Punjabi who had strayed rather far from his parish, and to him I was able to give a note for the Swiss asking them to send on a climbing rope which I had forgotten. At Maiun, opposite Nilt, I changed my slow-moving donkey for a coolie. We were in Hunza proper now and I noticed at once how much more obliging, business-like, and tractable the people were than those around Gilgit. Many of the men were ex-soldiers of the Indian Army and if one of them was about I was always well served.

That night we slept at Hini in a dusty shack which was the school by day and the rest-house by night. Hini is a big village which suffers from water shortage, and had it not been for the unusual rain this summer the crops would have been in a poor way. As all the villages depend on irrigation, rain, if it comes at all in summer, is not often welcomed, for in June the apricots will be spread to dry, in July the lucerne will be cut, and in August the wheat will be ripe. Provided the water supply comes from a substantial glacier the farmer, and even his children's children, may face the future with confidence, but should it come merely from high snow-beds which must be replenished every winter, then these people are as completely at the mercy of the weather as farmers elsewhere. The feelings of these water-starved Hinians must have been daily harrowed by the sight of two enormous streams pouring down from the Minapin glacier to waste their goodness on the fields of the despised and hated Nagars just across the river.

In Hunza territory there is a system by which coolies must be changed every few miles. Whether the change takes an hour as it sometimes does, or much less, such delay is maddening to anyone in a hurry. But no one should hurry in the East—that no man hurries except when catching flies is a proverb with a far wider application than Egypt its home, and Kipling, too, has some advice for the would-be hustler:

And the end of the fight is a tombstone white with the name of the late deceased,
And the epitaph drear: 'A fool lies here who tried to hustle the East.'

The time taken to change coolies depends on whether the lambadar of the village is within easy reach, how far his voice carries, and whether or no his selected victim is within earshot. Between Hini and Baltit, the capital of Hunza and the Mir's residence, I had three of these changes to make. A few miles from Baltit the road meets and follows the great Berber 'kul' alongside which one walks in the comforting assurance that water will not flow uphill. This, the one day which I wanted to be fine, was not; lowering clouds obscured the Minapin glacier and shut out the whole northern face of Rakaposhi which I had hoped so much to see. On the way I met a brother of the Mir bound for Gilgit; the Mir himself was away in Srinagar, but all arrangements for my comfort had been made at the guest-house in the Palace grounds.

On the other side of the river is Nagar territory. The capital, Nagar, lies about five miles up the Nagar river from its junction with the Hunza river just below Baltit. Though they are such close neighbours and though they seem to come of the same stock and to speak a similar language the people of the two states have never been on good terms. The Hunza are Maulais, followers of the Aga Khan, while the Nagar are Shiahs. On one occasion only have the two states agreed and that was in 1891 when a British force was obliged to occupy both states in order to enforce a more rigid observance of their agreement to forego their old custom of raiding on the Karakoram trade route between Leh and Yarkand. The then Mir of Hunza fled to Sinkiang and Muhammad Nazim Khan, his half-brother, reigned in his stead until his death in 1938. His autobiography is one of the books to be seen in the guest-house. There has long been a vague connexion between Hunza, or Kanjut as the Chinese call it, and Chinese Turkestan. The Mir claims the Taghdumbash Pamir north of the Hindu Kush and now exercises grazing rights there for which he pays an annual but nominal tribute of gold dust to the Chinese.

The exceptional health, vitality, and cheerfulness of the Hunza, and their superiority in these respects over their neighbours, has long been recognized by all who have had anything to do with with them except, of course, by those aforesaid neighbours. It has been made a matter for study and for speculation and has been variously attributed either to the climatic conditions or to merely their way of life and mode of cultivation. One theory is that since they live on the northern slopes of the valley they enjoy more sun, but those who have lived among and have had opportunities of studying the Hunza maintain that their almost perfect health is owing principally to their food and above all to the way such food is grown. Sir Robert McCarrison, C.I.E., a nutrition expert with long experience of India, who lived as a doctor among the Hunza; Dr G. T. Wrench, who also lived with them and wrote about them in a book, *The Wheel of Health*; and Mrs Lorimer, who made a study of their languages (see *Language Hunting in the Karakoram*), while living with them are in agreement on this matter and lay particular stress on the 'wholeness' of their system of agriculture—every scrap of vegetable matter, all organic waste that comes from the soil is put back in the form of compost. Of them and their system of terrace cultivation Dr L. J. Picton has written in *Thoughts on Feeding*: 'Somehow their life, seemingly hard and austere, has endowed these people with a happiness I forbear to overstate. They have achieved engineering without mathematics, morality without moralizing, agriculture without chemistry, health without medicine, sufficiency without trade. In the harsh and unpromising surroundings of the Hunza, mastery of the art of life has been engendered by an unremitting agriculture.' Their diet consists of wheat bread (I can testify to its deliciousness), a little milk and its products, vegetables, lentils, mulberries, and in particular their great stand-by, apricots. These are their only source of sugar, and the stones of the apricot are ground to extract the oil which is their one illuminant. The dried fruit is their principal winter provision. While one is willing to concede that this way of living will go most of the way towards ensuring health and vitality, it does not explain their superiority in these respects over their neighbours, whose diet and method of agriculture are substantially the same. None of these neighbouring peoples has been or is likely to be picked out as the embodiment of perfect health and well-being. Perhaps the more robust character and industry of the Hunza is accounted for by the poverty of their country, which in the three great needs of arable land, water, and wood, is less well off than any of the neighbouring territories. As well as in manliness and husbandry they excel as craftsmen. As carpenters, masons, ironsmiths, builders of roads, bridges, or flumes, they are superior to their neighbours; even their home-spun cloth is a better article. It rather looks as though in spite of the similarity of appearance, habits, and language they and the Nagar do come of a different racial stock. Col. R. C. F. Schomberg, who knows as much about the people of these parts as anyone, thinks that the Nagar is a mixture of Balti, Gilgiti, and, later, Dogra blood, and is quite distinct from that of Hunza. The Hunza themselves claim to have come originally from Badakshan, and the theory that they are descendants of some of Alexander the Great's soldiers is, I suppose, no more far-fetched than some theories of racial descent.

A few miles from Baltit, on a cliff overhanging the Hunza river, is the village and castle of Altit—once the northern limit of Hunza territory. At the present time the state extends as far as the Hindu Kush, although not all the intervening villages are occupied by Hunza folk for many Wakhis from Wakhan, in Afghanistan, have settled there. From Altit the track narrows and deteriorates as well it might, for the valley of the Hunza river now becomes an almost continuous gorge, cut on a scale to daunt the most resolute builder. To Gulmit, a stage of twenty-two miles, every mile of a devilish loose, rough, up-and-down track lies in a uniformly stark and barren cañon. Sometimes, when the water is low, it drops to the river-bed to take advantage of a brief stretch of sand or gravel flat. Other times it climbs dizzily to cross some perpendicular precipice by means of ingeniously constructed galleries. Before and behind, the traveller's view is limited to the short livid-grey reach of water between one frequent bend and another, and on either hand by leaden cliffs or long sombre slopes of scree. The sense of confinement induced by the long passage through the gorge is only momentarily relieved by glimpses of the bright fields of Gulmit, happily situated on a wide, sunny, well-watered alluvial fan where every available scrap of land boasted either the fresh green lucerne, yellowing wheat, or pink-white buckwheat.

From Gulmit to Pasu is but nine miles and though to the traveller the tedium of the gorge may be relieved, its savageness is enhanced by the entrance of two glaciers, the Ghulkin and the Pasu, which the track skirts. Near the snout of the former I estimated the moraine to be nearly 500 ft. high. Immediately beyond and within a mile of the ice of the Pasu is the village of the same name. It is a Wakhi village and is reputed to grow the finest apples in the country. I tasted them and was disappointed, but I met with a new bread made with fat in it which is excellent to eat and keeps well.

Above Pasu the track crosses the great Batura glacier, the head of which, twenty-five miles to the west, we had looked down upon nine days before. It took me nearly an hour to cross the ice, which flows down almost to the water of the Hunza river. Like most Himalayan glaciers it is at present slowly retreating; in 1930 the snout actually reached the river. This year when I crossed the track was easy, but naturally it varies from year to year, so that animals have often to make a wide detour round the snout or, in former years, to cross the river and back again. Just before reaching the glacier one notices, on the other side of the river, the forbidding entrance to the Shingshal gorge, up which lies a difficult route to the upper Yarkand valley and the Leh-Yarkand road. This was one of the routes favoured by Hunza raiders, especially in winter when the shrunken state of the river allowed the use of the river-bed as a road.

The next village beyond the Batura glacier is Khaibar, thirteen miles from Pasu. It was the rule at these villages, as it is in most out-of-the-way places which happen to lie on a trade route, for the incoming traveller to become the centre of a news-hungry circle of inquirers. Julius Caesar remarked of the Gauls: 'It is a habit of theirs to stop travellers and inquire whatsoever each of them may have heard or known about any sort of matter; the common people beset the passing trader, demanding to hear from what regions he came, what things he got acquainted with there'. And so it was 2,000 years later at Pasu where, as I ate my eggs and bread, I was asked to make known whatsoever news and views I had. It is at any rate a pleasing change to have news that is not common to all and to have people listen with respect to one's callow views on world affairs; and as such things are acceptable, to give them in full measure is but a slight return to make for hospitality received. While this time-honoured custom was being observed two men carrying loads joined the circle. I thought the loads looked familiar, and presently I discovered they were the two I had dispatched to Misgar from Gilgit. They had been taken up the Chapursan nallah to meet us, but as we had not arrived they were now on their way back to Gilgit.

In the afternoon I went on the remaining five miles to Malkhun accompanied by one coolie, one donkey, and one madman, to carry my new and heavy acquisitions. It was a comparatively pleasant march. The gorge began slightly to relent, the road became easier, the vista wider, the scenery a shade milder, and, as one who considers himself a rugged mountaineer, unappalled by the most savage rock scenery so long as he is safe at its foot, I'm ashamed to say I felt it a relief. We are in the habit of smiling at the childish fears and fancies of eighteenth-century writers when they came upon a mountain scene. The matter-of-fact Defoe, for instance, who writes of the 'high and formidable Hills of Cumberland with a kind of unhospitable Terror in them', and of Westmorland as 'the wildest, most barren, and Frightful of any that I have passed over'— I cannot help wondering what he would have written and how many capital letters he would have employed to describe three or four days' imprisonment in the Hunza gorge. I confess that by the time I began to emerge, the wild intractable savagery of the scene had become overpowering and depressing.

Malkhun is a very small village. Instead of the usual large audience there were but two men and a boy to watch the stranger eat his evening meal of eggs, bread, 'lassi' or curds, and a vegetable of the spinach variety very nicely cooked in butter by the lambadar's wife. Here, as in every village I had passed, they asked earnestly for quinine which, as malaria is unknown, they must eat as a sweet—hard men with acrid tastes as befits their inexorably harsh home. The gorge had relented, but only for a moment. Above Malkun it became nearly as morose and inhuman as before, but now an otherwise stern scene was gladdened by the river, which lost its livid glacier-fed complexion to become a cheerful sparkling blue, while here and there a handsome heliotrope weed (called, I was told, 'phobshing') brightened the bleak monotony of rock and rubble slopes.

Misgar, which I reached on the afternoon of 31 July, is on a wide sunny shelf lying well above the river. Despite the height of 10,000 ft. wheat grows well. I pitched my tent in a field by the Post Office, the last link in the telegraph line to Gilgit, where I was soon discovered by Naiad Shah, the Hunza man whom Shipton had sent from Tashkurghan to meet me. He was a wiry little man, lame in one foot, with the sad earnest inquiring expression of a Cairn terrier which, indeed, he closely resembled. He told me he spoke four languages besides his own, Burishaski, which is that spoken in Hunza, Nagar, and Yasin, and which is without affinity to any other. Turki, Persian, Wakhi, and Hindustani, were his other four, but it seemed to me that at times he was not quite clear which of the five he was using.

Shipton, who employs a number of Hunza servants in the Consulate, has his own theory about this much admired race. While admitting in full their qualities of industry, keenness, enterprise, willingness, cheerfulness, and loyalty, he considers this altogether admirable make-up is marred by a lack of intelligence, *nous*, or gumption—that in the day-to-day business of life they display a sort of bucolic 'dumbness' comparable to that of the good people of Haddenham who built a shed over their village pond to keep the ducks dry, or the shrewd folk of Steeple Bumpstead who rejected a proposal for a second windmill on the grounds that there was barely enough wind for the first. Although my experience of them is small I would not go the whole way with him in this, but I must say that in the short time he was with me Naiad Shah did his best to convince me that Shipton was right. Much of his apparent stupidity may have been owing to language difficulties, for if one asked him how far it was to the next halt he might reply that he had some in his saddle-bags. But it does not argue much intelligence to pack eggs in the bedding and leave them there. Still he looked after me with great faithfulness, and since he was well known and liked all along the road his presence was enough to ensure every available comfort for man and beast.

After breakfasting with the Kashmiri telegraph clerk, a Hindu alone amongst Moslems, Naiad Shah loaded our baggage pony, mounted or rather climbed from a rock on to his own flea-bitten sorrel, and off we went. His mounting difficulties were owing to his lame foot and to the capacious saddle-bags which stuck out far enough on either side to make any mounting in the orthodox way impossible. The gorge embraced us once more though now less fiercely, and soon, in the narrowest part of the defile, we passed the fort at Kalam Darchi occupied by a platoon of Gilgit Scouts, the last outpost of British India. On this day, 1 August, the Gilgit Agency was being handed over to the Kashmir State and, although British rule had ended, the Subadar in charge of the fort appeared to be in no hurry to haul down for the last time his Union Jack.

CHAPTER TEN

Misgar to Tashkurghan

THE Hunza river, now little more than a beck, here ran in a wide, deep stony valley. We halted for the night at Murkushi in a setting of grass and birch trees. All around us were snow mountains, and so I was shaken by the sight of two very fat camels contentedly grazing, as unexpected a sight as polar bears in a desert. Later I was frequently to see camels against a background of snow mountains, but so close in one's mind is the association of camels with hot sandy deserts that the apparent incongruity was always striking. These camels are the two-humped Bactrian type with shorter legs and more massive body than the dromedary; great shaggy ruffs of hair on thighs and neck added to their ponderous appearance, so very different from the bald, scraggy beasts one sees dragging carts in Karachi. These two had strayed from a herd belonging to the Mir of Hunza which was grazing up the Kilik nallah. And I was delighted to see them, for though we had reached a pretty remote part of India and turned our backs on the last British outpost, the magic of Central Asia had not yet begun to work. True, Naiad Shah was from across the border, but he was a Hunza man and looked it, about whom there was not a vestige of glamour or mystery.

Murkushi is the starting-point for either the Kilik or the Mintaka passes, which are not many miles apart and are of about the same height, 15,500 ft. In winter the Mintaka is said to carry less snow. The ascent to this pass is gradual except for the last few hundred feet, when the track quits the moraine of a very fine, active-looking glacier to climb a low rounded ridge to the north. Though the ascent is easy the track is for the most part made of boulders. I remarked on this to Naiad Shah, who assured me that on the other side things were better, and left me with the impression that not only did the boulders end on the top but that a grazier's paradise began. That we had already left one region for another was apparent by the character of the low ridge ahead of us, so different from the opposite containing wall of the glacier, where a high rampart of rock buttresses, snow gullies, and tumbled ice-falls, culminated in a noble 21,000 ft. peak—a fitting sentinel for the last north-western bastion of the Karakoram. And so when the pass is crossed, though there is nothing to warn the traveller that he has reached a political boundary, the most myopic could not fail to realize that he had crossed a geological and climatic boundary. In place of the deep-cut valley of the south, filled with rivers of crevassed, wrinkled, grey ice and flanked by high jagged peaks, there are now smooth rounded hills, whose higher summits are crowned with white unblemished slabs of ice, spilling over for a short way into the upper part of wide shallow valleys to end abruptly on the dark scree.

We had some way to go down the northern slope before Naiad Shah's rash promise was fulfilled. I did not count them, but I estimated that for every hundred boulders on the north side there were ninety-nine on this, but by the time we reached the valley-floor the track had indeed become one on which one could walk, trot, or canter with ease and safety. The valley had all the appearance of some high Welsh valley, but on a vast scale. There was no tree, no bush, no lowly shrub to break the sweeping expanse of scree and brown earth. Grass there was, but the blades were so sparsely scattered that even at this time of high summer one's eyes received but the vaguest impression of anything green. This was Naiad Shah's grazier's paradise, but the beasts which live on it—the yaks, camels, sheep, goats—seem to prefer it that way. They love to fossick about on a heap of gravel for rare tufts of grass in the hopeful energetic way of a down-at-heel miner fossicking the tailings of an old mine for specks of gold. Put a yak down in a lush water-meadow up to his knees in grass and he would not know what to do with it. In a short time you would, I think, find him out on the road snuffling happily over a heap of road metal where, if it had been there long enough, a few spare weeds might have struggled into existence. Yaks and camels, both beasts of prodigious strength and size, are a lesson in what dogged persevering browsing can do for one even on the most meagre diet.

Such was my impression, but in reality the grass of the Pamir valleys, though coarse and yellow, is rich and succulent enough to be famous throughout Central Asia. Horses thrive on it. Marco Polo remarks of the Taghdumbash Pamir that it is 'clothed with the finest pasture in the world; insomuch that a lean beast will fatten to your heart's content in ten days'. There are eight of these so-called Pamirs which are merely high shallow valleys, lying at a height of between 10,000 and 15,000 ft., and rounded mountains, some of which carry perpetual snow. Their characteristics are treeless desolation, meandering streams, peaty bottoms, and shallow lakes. The meaning and origin of the word 'Pamir' has been, and perhaps still is, a rich field for conjecture which I am happily not qualified to explore.

The Taghdumbash Pamir lies along the Chinese-Russian frontier from the Wakhjir pass northwards where it merges into the Sarikol range. Below it on the Chinese side lies the spacious valley of the Tashkhurgan river. This country along the western border of Sinkiang is known as Sarikol, the principal town of which is Tashkurghan. In recent years it has been a disturbed area owing to the incursions of trouble-makers from the Russian side of the border.

It had been a long day. We had started at 6 a.m. and did not reach the first habitation at Mintaka Karaul until 7 p.m. Here our valley was joined by another coming down from three important passes, the Kilik, the Wakhjir leading to Wakhan, and the Tigurmansu by which there is a way to Kizil Robat in Soviet Turkestan, and at this strategic point there was a mud-walled Chinese fort. The fort was then unoccupied, but hard by were three 'yorts', the circular felt tents of the nomads, at which we were well received by the Tajik owners. These people are semi-nomads who are found mainly in Sarikol. Their mode of life seemed very similar to that of the Kirghiz. The only way I could tell whether my hosts were Kirghiz or Tajik was by the fireplace which in a Tajik 'yort' is a round clay affair about two feet high, whereas the Kirghiz use an open fire. The traveller who has studied books of Central Asian travel will be already aware that the two most important features in the landscape are yaks and yorts, but should he ask to ride on the one or sleep in the other he will be disappointed, for neither seem to be known by those names. 'Ak-oi' is the name of the Kirghiz round dwellings, or 'aoul' for a collection of them, while 'koshgau' is the most generally understood word for *Peophagus grunniens*. However, being far from pedantic I shall continue to speak of yaks and yorts, both easy, pronounceable words with a strong Asiatic flavour.

The yort consists of a circular framework of willow sticks about five feet high and fifteen feet diameter, covered first with a reed mat and then with felt. On top of this, curving willow rods support the felt roof, in the centre of which a hole about five feet across serves the dual purpose of window and chimney. At night or in bad weather felts are drawn across this hole by a rope on the outside. In the better yorts the felts are decorated outside with bright patterns and tufts of coloured wool and are secured inside with wide bands of embroidered loose-woven cloth. Carpets, cushions, and pillows are neatly stacked round one-half of the inside wall while a mat partition in one corner screens off the larder and dairy. Here they keep meat and milk, and the enormous copper pans and other utensils for turning the milk into butter and 'joghrat'. Three yaks can carry a yort and its furniture.

'Joghrat' is Wood's (the famous explorer of the Oxus sources) spelling for the curdled milk of the nomads, which seems to be the same word and the same stuff as the Bulgarian 'yoghourt'. The Albanian 'Kos' and the Afghan 'Mos' is the same thing. This is the food popularly supposed to be responsible for the extreme longevity of many Bulgars and Turks. In those countries centenarians are two a penny and they attribute their health and length of life to their earnest devotion to 'yoghourt', just as our more infrequent centenarians attribute their success to either beer or total abstinence. In a few restaurants in London a jar of 'yoghourt' the size of a large tea-cup can be bought for ninepence, but in a yort a bowl of the stuff the size of a wash-basin is put down in front of the guest or odd caller to keep him quiet until tea is brewed. In appearance it resembles junket, and it can be swallowed in the same easy absent-minded way, but its taste is sharp and sightly acid. If there are three or four wooden spoons at work the bowl is soon emptied and it is then replaced by a larger one. I had my own spoon, but in many yorts there seemed to be only one with which each man took a mouthful and then passed it to his neighbour. Sipping is not quite the word, but unlike port there are no rules for dealing with 'yoghourt', the spoon can be passed either way.

Naiad Shah and I stretched ourselves luxuriously on felt rugs, propped and cushioned with pillows, while between us a bowl that had just been dredged of 'yoghourt' was replaced by a large copper teapot. The Tajik men and boys sat or squatted, smoking our cigarettes and peering at us out of little pig-eyes from under their great hairy caps. The Tajik women worked. Obviously mutton was to be the main supper dish, but I took more interest in another which was in preparation. A lump of dough was rolled out to the shape of a very thin disk three feet across on a bit of flat board less than half that size. Under less skilled hands a lot of the earth floor and a quantity of carpet would have adhered to the dough long before it had reached the desired acreage. The thin disk was then smeared liberally with clotted cream, cut into strips, and the whole wound up into a round flat loaf which was then baked. The result was a pastry of angelic flakiness, saturated but not sodden with cream, which oozed gratefully from the corners of the mouth as the flakes melted in it. It was a rich meal.

> We cleansed our beards of the mutton grease,
> We lay on our mats and were filled with peace.

And as we did so a youth played a three-stringed fiddle in one corner, Naiad Shah related the latest lies from Misgar, our host spread his mat to pray on one side of us, while on the other our hostess bared her breasts to feed her youngest baby. I felt I had been made free of Central Asia.

We rode on down the valley in an easterly direction with the Taghdumbash Pamir on our left until we saw the dust of an approaching cavalcade. This proved to be the 'beg' or headman from Beyik who had come to welcome us, and he was presently followed by the Tajik commander of the police post with an armed escort. The Beyik post watches the road to the Beyik pass to Russian territory a day's march away, but this pass like all the others between Sinkiang and Russia is now closed. Politeness obliged us to drink tea at the small fort where only something far more compelling would have persuaded us to stay. The police quarters, doorless and windowless, lined the inside walls, on top of which stood a sentry sourly eyeing the blank uninspiring landscape. The commandant's room, as sparsely furnished as a hermit's cell, smelt like a slum or a disused dug-out. A piece of fish skewered to one wall and a mutton bone to the other were the only concession to interior decoration. The walls of the fort positively oozed 'cafard' and although this small force of Tajik police had only been in residence nine months one would have guessed from their moss-grown appearance that the period had been much longer. No formalities were required, but I felt that already the free air of the Pamirs was slightly tainted with officialdom and I wondered what kind of reception we should receive from the first real Chinese official whom we were due to meet next day at Dafdar.

Seven miles down from Beyik the valley bends north and is joined by the valley of the Oprang river from the south. At the junction there is a small settlement where barley is grown despite the height of nearly 12,000 ft. The serious obstacle presented by the Oprang had to be overcome with the help of two men from the settlement who came to our assistance with a horse as high as a camel in order to keep our loads out of the water. While the men thawed their frozen legs we ate barley bread fresh from the oven. The flat cake, leavened with sour dough from the previous baking and sprinkled with milk on one side and water on the other is slapped on to the clay wall of the fire-place which has been well hotted up with yak dung fuel. When baked it peels readily off the wall.

Our next halt was at the long straggling Wakhi colony of Dafdar on a flat by the river where fields of wheat and barley extend for several miles. Water for irrigation is led from springs seeping out between the flat and the foot of the slope. Most of the square flat-roofed mud houses were unoccupied, as their owners stay with their herds until the autumn when the crops are ripe. Outside each house was a little clump of willows, the first trees I had seen in Sinkiang. We quartered outselves in a yort on the outskirts where we were soon visited by the Chinese lieutenant and an interpreter from the fort about a mile away. He was the conventional-looking Chinaman of the young student type, complete with horn-rimmed spectacles, full of affability and politeness. A mark of politeness which nowadays is often overlooked, especially by those whose minds run on forms and questionnaires and by enthusiastic amateurs of general statistical information, is to refrain from asking personal questions. The lieutenant asked nothing, not even for my passport, but he did threaten to post a sentry over the yort and its valuable occupant and also to see that the occupant had a hot bath at the fort in the morning.

Both threats were carried out. At the fort I found the whole platoon of about thirty men had been turned into stokers and boilermen, and I had no option but to get into the long narrow tin coffin which seemed to be one of the few pieces of barrack furniture allowed in the Chinese army. The lieutenant's room was as austerely furnished as the Tajik policeman's—table, chairs, bed—bare of books, papers, or pictures, not even a pin-up girl or a piece of fish to brighten the mud walls. I felt sorry for this youth from Chunking shut up here in control of thirty men as devoid of occupation as himself. He had no interest in shooting, climbing, or even travelling, which are three of the more obvious diversions the country can offer. These troops had newly arrived from China proper, where no doubt they had had experience of war and judging by their looks they had not quite got over it. In a town, well-turned-out soldiers with nothing to do grate on the senses only slightly less than do slovenly ones, but in a wild, barely inhabited landscape any soldier at all is an eyesore; particularly when, as here, having neither parades nor training to attend, he sees the sun rise with no other hope than that he will fill his belly before it sets.

Between Dafdar and Tashkurghan there are two hateful stages across stone and gravel plains whose almost complete sterility is only broken by a small patch of sweet short grass at Taghlak Gumbaz. A 'gumbaz' is of very common occurrence in Sinkiang and Wakhan. It is a tomb or a monument to commemorate the name of some holy man, made generally of mud brick, or clay and gravel, and shaped like a bee-hive which has outgrown its strength. It is set on a low square foundation in which a single door, never more than three feet high, seems built mainly to discourage entrance; but I imagine that a 'gumbaz' is intended to shelter travellers who thus will be reminded of their benefactor whose name it commemorates.

On this occasion we were not obliged to make use of its rather sepulchral interior, for close by there was an unoccupied yort. We reached it early in the afternoon, and the wretched horses, according to the custom of the country, were then tied up short with their heads in a position of constraint instead of being turned loose to drink and graze. There they remained until sundown, when they were freed. This system of horse-mastership is wrong according to our ideas, but all—Kirghiz, Tajik, Turkoman, and Chinese—affirm that it is harmful to horses to allow them to eat or drink immediately after a journey. In spite of my protests Naiad Shah strongly supported this heresy. One reason he gave was that, apart from ill-effects, a horse so treated is sure to graze all night instead of wasting his time in sleep. Nor will these people allow their horses to drink on the march, though sometimes when crossing streams it is as much as they can do to urge the thristy beasts across.

Between this 'gumbaz' and Tashkurghan, in what is now perfect desert, many traces of old abandoned fields can be seen. According to Sir Aurel Stein, these were once watered by an ancient canal known as 'Farhad's

Canal', parts of which are still visible along the hillside. For hours a white blur in the distance across the river shimmered unchangingly in the heat haze, seeming to defy our approach. That, I concluded, must be Tashkurghan, the ancient capital of Sarikol. Far beyond it, very faint and dimly white in the loess[1] haze, rose a great dome—Muztagh Ata.

CHAPTER ELEVEN

Muztagh Ata

In a tent in the garden of the Postal Superintendent (a Hunza man) I found the Consul and his wife. They were on an extended tour and had arrived the previous evening. In most countries I associate consuls with long flights of stairs at the top of which is an office with a locked door and a small printed card bearing the legend 'Consulate of Utopia—Office hours, Saturdays only, 10–12', and it struck me that in Kashgar a consul must be an even rarer bird of passage. The answer is, however, that here the British Consul being no mere parochial stamper of passports is expected to travel about and, like the sun, to shed his beneficent rays over the whole of Kashgaria. Tashkurghan, the capital of Sarikol, is also a receiving and dispatching centre on the mail route to India and is therefore important enough to deserve official attention. If then by any chance his return journey were to lie in the direction of Muztagh Ata the Chinese of all people would be the last to demur; for did not Confucius say: 'The wise find pleasure in waters, the virtuous in mountains': and again the epigrams of Chang Ch'ao tell us: 'If there are no famous hills then nothing need be said, but since there are, they must be visited.'

In former days Tashkurghan must have been a town of some importance, for it lies on one of the two ancient routes from China to Western Asia and the Persian Gulf. Two very great travellers, Marco Polo and the Chinese Buddhist pilgrim Hsuan-tsang (c. A.D. 600) must have visited it. Nowadays it is only of secondary importance, for the bulk of what trade there is with India goes by the Leh route. A lifeless bazaar, some serais usually empty, the modern Chinese fort and magistracy, and the ruins of the walled town of earlier days, are all it can boast. But its proximity to the Russian frontier, across which there is a pass less then twenty miles south-west of the town, make it of some interest to the Chinese, who have installed a small garrison. In 1946 the local 'nationalists', with assistance from over the border, took and held Tashkurghan for some time.

1 A very fine porous yellowish loam. Loess deposits are remarkable for their capacity to retain vertical walls in the banks of streams. Such wall are characteristics of the scenery around Kashgar.

Before we could start for Muztagh Ata the duties of hospitality had to be discharged. The Amban and the officers of the garrison invited us to lunch and, since we were in haste to be off, the Consul insisted that they should give us our revenge by dining with us the same day. The Chinese custom of multiplying the courses of a meal almost to infinity is well known, and though the resources of Tashkurghan did not give our hosts the scope they would have wished they did their best and we had to deal seriatim with the following: by way of limbering up there was tea with brandy butter in it, cake and apples; then meat patties, meat balls, fried eggs and radishes, roast mutton, liver, duck, local fish, soup, and rice, the last being the accepted way of delivering the *coup de grâce* at these feasts. Chopsticks, knives, spoons, forks, and fingers, were all brought into play according to the toughness of the opposition, and the whole was eased down with 'kumiss', fermented mare's milk—colourless, slightly alcoholic, sour, and reminiscent of cider. The uncultured yahoo when he gives a feast (and I prefer it his way) merely increases the amount of the ordinary meal. Instead of a few scraggy bones, one or two sheep are dished up, instead of a bowl of rice or pilau, a bucket of it; but civilized people like the Romans, the Chinese, and to a lesser extent ourselves, like to measure their social status by the number and variety of the courses, which I consider a barbaric habit, destructive to the stomach and inimical to good cooking.

One of the principal difficulties in entertaining a posse of Chinese officials (Mrs Shipton had fourteen to cope with) is to get them inside the room. Questions of precedence lead to what threatens to be an interminable contest of polite diffidence until it is cut short by the pressure from behind of those whose claims are too lowly to be worth disputing and whose hunger is too sharp to be any longer denied. The posse surges forward, and when the less nimble have picked themselves up from the floor the contest is renewed over the question of seating. It was a pretty motley assortment that eventually got themselves sat down—one which was difficult to weld into a convivial whole, aided though it was by Russian brandy and Shipton's manful sallies into the uncharted intricacies of Chinese, of which he had enough to excite my admiration and to fascinate the Chinese. Most Chinese are abstemious to a fault. Only the Amban and a man who claimed to have accompanied Sir Aurel Stein on some of his journeys (in the capacity of coolie I judged from his appearance) willingly submitted themselves to the mellowing influence of the brandy.

Next morning, 8 August, we got off at the surprisingly early hour of 9.30, accompanied by two camels carrying the baggage and a Mongolian horde to speed us on our way—the Amban himself, all the officers, and Sir Aurel Stein's coolie, whom I only recognized with difficulty, as he was now wearing a Homburg hat, silver-rimmed sun goggles, and knickerbockers, looking like a great explorer in his own right. At the first village the cavalcade dismounted and after a long bout of grinning and handshaking the Lesser Horde took its departure and we headed for the north.

At this point the Tashkurghan river is deflected eastwards and a low ridge, pierced by the narrow gorge of the Tagharma river, separates its wide valley

from the even more extensive Tagharma plain. This extends to the north for
about twelve miles, until it meets another ridge upon which lies the Ulugh
Rabat pass (14,000 ft.). The pass leads into another almost equally wide
valley running north between the Sarikol range on the west and the Muztagh
Ata and Kungur groups to the east. The Tagharma plain abounds in villages
and cultivation, while the higher valley beyond is the happy home of many
Kirghiz, their herds and their flocks.

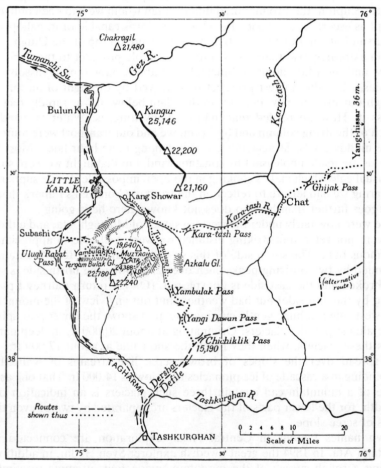

Map for the Kashgar Journey

Emerging from the bare yellow rock gorge we were delighted by the sight of
the green Tagharma vale, its scattered villages, the tall poplars, the browsing
herds, and waving wheat-fields. Our guides, vaguely aware that the consular
mind was intent on mountains, took us too far to the east in the direction of
the most southerly foothills of the Muztagh Ata group, until we finally came
to rest in a village at the foot of a nallah, which undoubtedly led directly to the

heart of the mountains. With some difficulty we resisted the insistent invitation of this interesting unknown nallah, and next morning we sheered away to the north-west in the direction of the Ulugh Rabat pass. The transport—ponies now instead of camels—passed us going at the rate of knots and Naiad Shah was instructed to tell the men to halt for the night at a grazing ground this side of the pass. But he apparently failed to select from his repertoire the correct language in which to give the order, for when we reached the place—all of us fully ripe for stopping—there was no sign of the ponies. Shipton, the two mounted infantrymen whom we had been obliged to accept as escort, and anyone else whose beast was capable of it, galloped off in pursuit but without success. By 7 p.m. we were on top of the Ulugh Rabat and in extremely bad tempers. There was a noble prospect to the dark plain below and the white dome of Muztagh Ata above, now rapidly dissolving in the dusk. But the noblest prospect is improved by the sight of an inn, and though our inn was now in sight on the plain below, it was rapidly receding across it. How we reviled that man of many tongues. Water arrested the march of the flying column and by 8 p.m. we and our transport were united by some muddy pools. Stragglers were still coming in an hour later. Most high uplands are made unpleasant by constant wind, but that night we were spared the usual gale which makes cooking in the open impossible. While supper was preparing we had leisure to reflect on the truth of Cromwell's remark that 'no man goes further than he who does not know where he is going'.

We were now fairly under the western slopes of Muztagh Ata, and although we were not yet within striking distance we were well able to appreciate its enormous bulk. The south side of this so-called 'Father of Ice Mountains' is defended by two outlying peaks each over 22,000 ft.; the north side is steep and broken and the east side is unexplored. (On my return journey I passed round by the east side, but bad weather shut out any view of the mountain.) The west side is a huge gently curving sweep of snow, the lower part split by three almost parallel glaciers. Originating at about 20,000 ft. in deep narrow clefts these glaciers, when they reach the snow line at about 17,000 ft., spill and spread over the slopes of brown scree like streams of white lava, descending in a cascade of ice pinnacles to as low as 14,000 ft. That one aspect alone of a mountain can contain three such glaciers is an indication of its breadth, for the lower parts of the glaciers are separated by two or even three miles of scree slope.

Two names famous in Central Asian exploration are connected with Muztagh Ata. In 1894 the great Swedish explorer Sven Hedin, in addition to making a rough survey of the mountain, made four attempts to climb it. Rough survey is the word, for he ascribed to it a height of 25,600 ft., and 'the unchallenged pre-eminence over the peaks which cluster round, which is proved by its name "Father of Ice Mountains"'. The Kungur group, less than twenty-five miles north-east, he either ignored or else did not see, for the unaided eye can appreciate that one at least of its peaks is higher than Muztagh Ata. As for the name, the story is that the reply to the question about its name was simply 'Muztagh, Ata' or 'Ice Mountain, O Father'. In 1900 the late Sir Aurel Stein made a survey of the Sarikol valley and his surveyor, Ram Singh of the Indian Survey, carried out the triangulation of the Muztagh Ata and Kungur groups, discovering that the highest peak of Kungur is 25,146 ft. against 24,388 ft. for Muztagh Ata.

Having studied both the ground and Sven Hedin's account of his attempts we decided that the best line of approach was that between the two largest of these western glaciers, the Yam Bulak and the Tergam Bulak. Some Kirghiz yorts were reported to be in a valley north of the Yam Bulak glacier about two hours away and there we thought we would have our base. In these parts of Sinkiang yorts exert a powerful attraction which the wise traveller should on no account resist. Such a thought never occurred to us for a moment—we merely crawled from one yort to the next, drinking tea, eating yoghourt, and studying nomadic life, though we ourselves were much more nomadic than our hosts, whose lives seemed to be remarkably static, even sedentary. Since travellers are rare they are usually welcome; food, fire, and shelter are automatically put at their disposal by the kindly Kirghiz.

When we reached the little valley under the slopes of the mountain where we had proposed harbouring, we were disturbed to find only one yort. All the families but one had just moved down to Subashi a few miles away and the principal place of the Sarikol plain. The remaining one, too, was about to go but they readily postponed their departure when they heard that Mrs Shipton would be alone for a few days while we were on the mountain. In the afternoon we sorted out food for our expedition and in the evening we walked up towards the Yam Bulak glacier to reconnoitre a route for the morrow. On the moraine two herds of what looked like wild goats were playing about.

Sven Hedin was a great explorer, but he made no claim to be a mountaineer. As he therefore had no false pride to maintain he made full use of the local aids to progress in his attempts on the mountain. Of the four his most successful was the second, when, carried on the back of a yak, he claimed to have reached a height of 20,600 ft. As he justly observes, the secret of freedom from the troubles of altitude (a secret which so far has eluded research) 'is the avoidance of bodily exertion'.

He employed yaks for all his attempts and from his free use of them on the mountain we may deduce several things; the absence of any technical difficulties on the west side, at any rate for a great part of the way up; the absence of man-power in Sinkiang, where no Turki who can afford an ass and no Kirghiz who owns a yak or a pony ever walks, much less carries anything; and finally the all-round supremacy of yaks over donkeys, mules, horses, camels, or even elephants, though Hannibal might dispute the last. As a load-carrier the yak's powers are well known, but his virtues as a hack are unrecognized. Although Central Asia is the ancestral home of the horse, one may travel there a long time without becoming aware of it, or if already aware of it one may conclude that he has remained at home too long. No doubt there are some good horses, but the locals very wisely keep them for themselves, mounting the innocent stranger on their sorriest screws, so that if it should happen to fall down with him no harm is done except, perhaps, to the stranger.

A good riding yak is much to be preferred to the sort of beast one is commonly invited to put one's leg over. He will do his three miles an hour without the incessant kicking and flogging which is essential in keeping the local jade up to the bit (the yak, by the way, has no bit, only a rope through the nose), while his short legs and quick step give the rider the comfortable if illusory impression that he is covering the ground at a great rate. On going uphill there is no need for the rider to dismount to spare his yak. On going downhill there is no need for him to dismount to spare his own neck, for the yak takes everything as it comes, uphill or downhill, rough or smooth. In fording rivers, despite those short legs, he is as steady as a rock, for his great weight keeps him well anchored to the bottom. And, of course, at heights of 16,000 ft. or more, when the horse like the rest of us is beginning to suffer from the effects of height, the yak is just beginning to feel at home; he may blow like a grampus but his tremendous girth ensures that there is plenty of air in the bellows. And finally, if the snow is reached, he is sent ahead to break a trail for the floundering men and horses behind him; and should his fortunate rider need a pair of sun glasses all he has to do is to turn round and yank a length of hair from his copious tail.[1]

Profiting by Sven Hedin's example Shipton and I determined that though we ourselves might condescend to walk we should have a yak to carry our camp to the snow-line at about 17,000 ft. Not wishing to retract much of what I have just written I must assume that our yak was the exception that proves the rule, or that like all other mountaineers yaks have their off days. He was, indeed, a total failure.

With stores for six days three of us started on 11 August accompanied by a Sherpa (Gyalgen, a former Everest porter and one of Shipton's servants), a Turki lad, a yak and his driver. The weather since we left Tashkurghan had been cloudy and unsettled, but this day was fine, calm, and sunny. Having rounded the snout of the Yam Bulak glacier, three or four miles from the yort, we took the long easy scree slope lying between that glacier and the Tergam Bulak to the south of it. Unencumbered ourselves, confident in our yak's prowess, we climbed comfortably to about 16,000 ft., where we sat down to await the arrival of the yak and the rest of the party. Time passed, our confidence waned. Nothing could be heard, nothing seen, for the slope, from the bottom almost to top, being as convexly regular as a schoolroom globe, limited our horizon to less than a hundred yards. Reluctantly we started down to investigate and presently came upon Gyalgen, the Turki, and the yak driver, staggering up under heavy loads. Of the yak, the party's main hope and king-pin, there was no sign. He had very sensibly struck and sat down at the very first hint of what was expected of him. The driver, too, thought no more of mountaineering than did his charge. Groaning and moaning on account of his splitting headache, and fearful of the certain death that awaited us if we proceeded, he had to be sent down at once, pursued by sounds of desultory ill-will. The rest of us struggled on with the loads, marvelling how much better they did these things in Sven Hedin's time.

Shipton, discarding chivalry in favour of the principle of economy of force,

1 A few black hairs stretched across the eyes, while allowing one to see, are semi-effective against glare.

had allowed his wife to relieve him of a sleeping-bag and a cork mattress. There was apparently more in marriage than I had yet realized, but now it was too late to repair the omission and I had to bear my own burden. We plodded on for another thousand feet and camped at 3 p.m. just below the first snow at about 17,000 ft. From here Mrs Shipton and the Turki lad went down, leaving Gyalgen, myself, and her grateful but unfeeling husband to finish the job.

That evening we did a short reconnaissance. Just above our tent, scree gave place to snow, or rather ice, for the snow had melted from the lowest 200 or 300 ft. of underlying ice. The slope, however, was gentle, so that with care one could walk without nicking steps. Higher up was a short ice-fall which could be turned, beyond that a long stretch of crevassed snow-slope, and beyond that again unbroken slopes extending to the summit dome. Most of this, except for the actual summit whose exact whereabouts we could not locate, we had already seen from below. Our safe and methodical plan was to have a camp at about 20,000 ft. and another at 22,000 ft. from which no matter how moderately we rated ourselves, we ought to have no great difficulty in crawling to the top.

Next day we started, Shipton and I carrying very modest loads and Gyalgen rather an immodest one. The ice-fall was soon overcome by an outflanking movement, and having threaded our way through the worst of the crevassed section we camped at 3 p.m. in a snow hollow, crediting ourselves with a rise of 3,000 ft. The snow was in really excellent condition, everything was going to be too easy. This gratuitous supposition and Gyalgen's faltering under his too heavy load had already caused an alteration in a perfectly sound plan. Assuming that the snow, so good here, could be no worse higher up and might well be better, we agreed to cut out the intermediate camp at 22,000 ft. and to take only one bite at the cherry—an agreement which I, aware of my advancing years and limited high-climbing powers, had no right to make. We arrived at this pregnant decision during a halt on the way up from Camp 1, while we were pondering over ways of easing Gyalgen's burden, neither of us having the indelicacy to suggest taking some of it upon ourselves. Since this new plan meant that we should, if all went well, spend only one more night on the mountain some of the food (we had four days' supply) could be dumped. But Shipton's liberal ideas of dumping and his ruthless whittling down to a bare one day's supply led to a sharp debate. Although I may have had private misgivings about our only needing one day's food I had already agreed to the change of plan and there was little I could urge against this wholesale sacrifice beyond the desirability of keeping an ample reserve. Possibly the fact that nothing from my own load was dumped made me the more reluctant to see so much left behind.

As I had been on Rakaposhi only two months before, I expected to be better acclimatized than I proved to be; but there, though we had been twice to 20,000 ft. we had never slept higher than 17,000 ft. That night I had a violent headache and in the morning felt no more like climbing four feet than the four thousand odd which we had cheerfully set ourselves. Still it had to be done—one day being our self-allotted span— so at 6 a.m. we got under way.

Though not a breath of wind stirred in our hollow, it was noticeably cold in the bleak and pallid dawn. Merely by fumbling with buttons after some necessary business outside my thumbs and forefingers were so chilled that they never felt right for the rest of the day. Well down as we were on the west side of this considerable protuberance on the earth's sphere— almost another sphere in itself—the sun would be long in reaching us. The more reason therefore for pressing rapidly onwards and upwards to meet it, so off we went over the good hard snow. For a thousand feet we climbed rapidly and hopefully, and then conditions suddenly became worse. The snow assumed that vile consistency which necessitates one's stamping with all one's might once, twice, or even three times to ensure that the step will not give way the moment it is stood upon. Worse still, a wind started to blow. Its force seemed negligible—in the unlikely event of our wearing straw hats I doubt if we should have had to hold them on—but nevertheless it cut to the bone. The exertion of stamping steps contributed nothing to our warmth, nor did the sun when it at length reached us, so that even at this early stage the effects of these conditions became serious. Shipton was overcome by a fit of rigor and lay shaking in the snow, while we sat by shivering with a violence only a little less.

On we plodded up that vast tilted snow-field, seeing no other mountains either to north or south by which to measure our progress. Though we moved slowly we moved continuously, for it was too cold to sit and rest and eat. As early as 1 o'clock we had the impression of arriving somewhere, but two hours later all we could say was that that impression was no weaker. Still we thought the end must be very near. We reckoned we had climbed a thousand feet in the first hour when the snow was good, and having been climbing steadily since then for eight hours we argued that most of the remaining three thousand odd feet were below us. Whenever we dared to look up our eyes met the same unbroken snow horizon, maintaining its unconquerably rigid distance of two or three hundred feet. And now the long hours of cold, fatigue, and deferred hope began to tell.

Some while before this my contribution to step-kicking had become of small account and presently Gyalgen, too, found himself unable to take his turn. Shipton had still a little left in him, so that we agreed to struggle on for another half-hour until 3.30 p.m. when, if there was still no firm indication of the summit, we would give up and try again another day. Quite early in the afternoon I had suggested going back so that next day we should have the advantage of a great many ready-made steps; but this had been overruled on the ground that tomorrow the steps might no longer be there. This was true enough because, when we did come to go down, we had trouble even to find the steps, so completely had the driving snow filled them.

After a generous half-hour's extra play in this hard-fought game between the mountain and ourselves a decision in our favour seemed as far off as ever. For me the delusion of the summit being at hand had long become stale, stimulating despair rather than hope. I feared that even if we reached a point from which the summit could be seen we should find it at the wrong end of a long flat ridge, for the perversity of inanimate objects is always a factor to be reckoned with. By this time we were all pretty well on our knees. Had the summit been in sight and our remaining task measurable, some hidden reserves of strength might have been found, but there was still nothing to be seen beyond the next hundred feet or so of snow. To persevere one must have hope, and this, which had been pretty severely tried, had now perished, worn out by too long deferment.

If we allowed only two hours to get down there was still time enough to struggle on for another hour could we but force our bodies onwards. But before the clock had time to impose its decision on us we gave up. Perhaps we were weak-minded—in fact, we damned ourselves heartily later—but our wisest actions are sometimes those for which we are not fully responsible and the sequel showed that we did well to go down. Exclusive of halts for vomiting by Shipton the descent did take about two hours. Our up-coming tracks were by now obliterated, so that the finding of the way through the crevassed area was less easy than it had before been. After dark we could not have found it.

Back in the tent an unpleasant discovery awaited us. All the toes on one of Shipton's feet were frost-bitten. They were dead white that evening and black the next morning. The tips of both my big toes were slightly touched and went black, but came painfully back to life 48 hours later. I was wearing the 'expedition' boots with the heavy moulded rubber soles and Shipton a pair of the heavily nailed porters' boots which I had brought out for Rakaposhi and which he maintained had got wet the previous day so that they had ice inside them before we started. Gyalgen, who was wearing lightly nailed boots, came to no harm. As a purely speculative consolation it may not amount to much, but there is little doubt that had we persevered for another hour the damage would have been much more serious. Success would have been a very considerable consolation, but it would only have been gained at a high cost. Failure with frost-bite thrown in was a tough bullet to chew.

The condition of Shipton's foot was, of course, decisive—we had to go down—but in point of fact not one of us was fit to try again next day or even for several days. The effort had taken more out of us than we realized and a week later I still found it more than usually trying to walk uphill at all.

Whether the top of the mountain is a long flat ridge or whether, as seems more likely, it is a flattish dome we still do not know. Shipton is of the opinion that we were on the summit dome and not more than a hundred feet below the top. An inexcusable assumption of the probable snow conditions, over-confidence in our powers, and the unexpected cold, had proved our undoing, and of these, only of the last had we any right to complain. In early June on the North Col of Everest one would not experience such cold. Here it was mid-August, and though Muztagh Ata is in Lat. 38° and Everest is 10° further south one would not expect that to make so much difference. We live and learn, and big mountains are stern teachers.

CHAPTER TWELVE

To Kashgar

CUSTOM ordained and self-respect demanded that in the morning we should talk of taking the camp higher. Nevertheless, having packed up, we turned our backs to the mountain and went down, finding that not altogether easy. We reached the foot at 1 p.m. where we dumped the loads and hobbled dejectedly back to the yort. My toes were beginning to tingle, Shipton's were numb and blistered. The Kirghiz had their own remedy for frost-bite—a nasty mixture of soot and butter—but there was really nothing to be done except to apply clean dressings, get back to Kashgar, and await the event.

We moved down to Subashi, where there is a considerable 'aoul' (a village of yorts) and also a Chinese post. Kirghiz and Chinese both contended for the possession of the bodies, so that before we escaped to a large and clean yort we were obliged to drink tea and lunch with both. From there we loitered onwards across this pleasant plain, past browsing camels and yaks, while ahead of us towered the great Kungur ridge with its glaciers tumbling down to the plain like so many waterfalls. In due course we came to the Little Kara Kul—a sapphire gem set in green and gold—and camped by its quiet waters, now gently ruffled by the wind, now calmly reflecting that 'sunny pleasure-dome with caves of ice' from which we had so recently been turned away.

Little Kara Kul is a fine sheet of water, but it is less than half the size of the better known Great Kara Kul over on the Russian side of the Sarikol range which is some twelve miles in length. Little Kara Kul is a lake formed by a moraine of one of the Kungur glaciers of a former era. It drains to the north to the Bulun Kul by a passage cut through the moraine.

Bulun Kul, which was our next stage, lies in one of the windiest defiles imaginable, comparable as a natural wind-tunnel to the Jikyop gorge through which one passes on the way to Everest. The rocky western slopes of the defile are covered for several hundred feet up by great sand dunes, which from a distance we mistook for snow. The ferocious blast which met us explained how the sand had got up there, but we did not solve the puzzle of where it had come from until next day when the track led us for several miles over a dry lake-bed of salt-encrusted sand.

At Bulun Kul there was the usual squalid dreary police post with its equally squalid garrison. This seemed more apathetic and miserable than the usual run of garrisons, for its commander had died the previous day as the result of a bursting rifle. The bolt had blown back and penetrated the forehead. A messenger had brought a confused account of this accident to us at Subashi where he had come to ask Mrs Shipton for some medicine suitable for a man

with a headache. Some headache! A few days before she had had to treat a
Kirghiz with half his fingers blown off and his face mottled with powder blast
as the result of a similar accident. 'Ah me, what perils do environ, the man
who meddles with cold iron'—especially when it is old and of unreliable
make. This explains, I think, why our escort was so loath to take potshots at
geese or duck when the chance offered. They said that ammunition was scarce
and strictly checked, but I should think the fear of a bursting rifle was the
chief deterrent.

Either the searching and incessant wind of Bulan Kul, or maybe the
Chinese garrison, had stripped the local Kirghiz of most of their wealth and
with it had gone their hospitable nature. Having taken shelter from the blast
in a dirty and draughty yort where we crouched by a feeble fire for an hour
without the offer of a drop of milk or a spoonful of yoghourt, we slunk away
to our tents only to have them presently levelled to the ground by gusts of gale
force.

By morning the wind had dropped and we cantered happily away from that
sandy seat of misery across the wide salt plain. The river meanders through
this dry lake-bed until at the north end it plunges suddenly into the Gez defile.
This is the shortest road to Kashgar, but in summer when the rivers are up it is
not possible to go through with animals. We therefore turned left-handed up
the Tumanchi Su, another glorious vale, dotted with 'aouls' and fat with great
flocks of sheep and herds of yaks and camels. Anxious to give the Kirghiz the
opportunity of retrieving their good name and to erase the bitter memories of
the night we repaired to the nearest yort. We were not disappointed. Having
drunk tea, we lay on rugs, ladling in yoghourt, and gazing through the open
door across the plain to the two splendid 22,000 ft. peaks of Chakragil on the
north side of the Gez defile. With mingled pleasure and mortification, for
these peaks were to have been our objective after Muztagh Ata, we followed
our route to the top and in imagination saw below us the pine-clad valleys of
the eastern slopes. It is one of the curiosities of Kashgaria that whereas on the
Sarikol side of these Chakragil mountains not a stick grows, the eastern
valleys are heavily timbered.

Our next day's march up the narrowing Tumanchi Su valley was the most
unashamed yort crawl we had so far achieved. A short half-hour after starting
we were climbing unreluctantly from our mounts by the smart whitey-grey,
opulent-looking yort of the local 'Beg'—the 'big shot' as I very wittily used to
call these wealthy patriarchs. Tea, bread, and cream were put before us—
such cream as was not to be drowned in tea, nor was any bread required to
assist in the swallowing of large quantities of it. The tea that is drunk in the
course of a persevering and extended yort crawl, such as ours, not to mention
that which is drunk in camp, is as varied in colour, constitution, and taste as
the bottled pain-killers on a chemist's shelves. The only common factor is that
none of it much resembles tea. It may be hot water stained by the tea-pot, hot
water in which the loess haze has settled, hot milk into which a used tea-leaf
has inadvertently strayed, hot milk with an infusion of willow bark, hot water
with a dash of curry powder, or merely very badly made tea. The usual
ingredient for making tea, it will be gathered, is scarce among the Kirghiz so

that it is wise to travel with half a sack of cheap tea—a mixture of tea dust and loess dust—and to confer the doubtful blessing of a double handful of it in return for any benefits received.

We pulled up at our fifth and last group of yorts early in the afternoon, though at the head of the valley there were two more 'aouls' in sight which the purists of the party thought ought not to have been neglected. However, the cup of pleasure should not be drained at one gulp. We should have to pass them tomorrow, and today had much to arrange, for the next march included, or should have included, the crossing of the Ulugh Art—a pass of 16,600 ft.— and our final departure from the friendly Kirghiz of Sarikol. Sven Hedin had crossed this pass in the reverse direction and on the descent to this side had had his horse killed by a fall; he devotes several pages to a description of it and calls it 'a perilous pass, the worst I have ever crossed in any part of Asia'.

The Leh-Yarkand trade route over the Karakoram crosses several high passes, two of which are over 18,000 ft., and although horses are the principal means of transport their mortality is dreadful. For high passes the yak is much to be preferred, but here, we were told, none was available. To our inexpert eyes there seemed to be quite a few suitable yaks grunting about, but these were either in calf or in milk so that when we started we had, in addition to Shipton's black horse (on loan) and Mrs Shipton's languid chestnut mare, five ponies and three donkeys. We were aware we should have a long day, but no one could tell us how long. On the usual routes the accepted measure for distance is the 'pao t'ai', the Chinese 'mile-stone' which is actually about 2½ miles, but the impossibility of getting a rough estimate of distance or even of time from a Kirghiz or a Turki is extraordinary. 'Very far' or 'near' is as much as they will commit themselves to, which may mean anything from one to fifty miles. A bow-shot or a biscuit-toss, even in the absence of bows or biscuits, are fairly definite ideas, but in Sinkiang a 'day's march' conveys no more information than a 'day's run' in a car where much depends on the car and the driver's ideas. A man alone riding a horse with his baggage under him may do fifty miles in a day, while a string of baggage ponies will not do much more than twenty. Nor could the pony men tell us anything about the route which they must have known well enough—whether there was anywhere to camp this side of the pass, or whether, once committed, it was a case of all or nothing. To make things more difficult, our linguist Naiad Shah had retired to Tashkurghan, his stock having slumped since the Ulugh Rabat episode, and Gyalgen's Turki, though fluent, seemed lacking in precision.

Having crossed a low ridge, whence we had a view of Kaufmann Peak[1] (23,000 ft.) a hundred miles away west of the Great Kara Kul, we found ourselves in the wide stony bed of the Ulugh Art river. The water had all disappeared under the stones to emerge lower down and there was no grass to refresh the animals during the midday halt. In the afternoon, as we climbed the slopes on the north side of the valley, we passed a 'gumbaz' and a bit of grass, but we were so intent on the pass that no one suggested that we should spend the night there. The crossing of two glacier streams cost us some delay, the path became rougher, and four miniature passes intervened, so that it was

1 Now called 'Lenin Peak'.

not until 6 o'clock that we stood at the foot of the pass itself, regarding with dismay the track zig-zagging steeply upwards for nearly a thousand feet. To be confronted by this at the end of a long hungry march was too much, but we could not stay where we were. On our right lay the ice-stream of the Ulugh glacier, descending from insignificant hills of 17,000 ft. and surprising us by its size, while on our left great cliffs of green and purple rock looked like the scene of a mountaineer's nightmare. A grey glacier pool, in which small icebergs jostled, offered us water, but not a blade of grass, a stick of wood, or a handful of dry dung were to be had. There was nothing for it but to go on. But when we in front had got about half-way up we began to have serious doubts about our transport. Every few steps horses and donkeys were stopping and it was only with increasing difficulty that they were urged on again. It would be dark before they were up. None of us knew how bad the descent might be, so we turned tail and spent a cold hungry night by the glacier pool. The animals ate nothing whatever, for though we offered half a sack of rice none of the drivers would consider giving it to their beasts.

However reliable the transport and easy the road there is often reason to regret having left the baggage train to fend for itself. To get separated from one's baggage is a mistake usually avoidable, often committed, and always regretted. On this occasion it was, I think, the biting cold of the early morning which persuaded the three of us to push on ahead of our transport. We climbed the pass before 8 o'clock, sat on its broad gravel summit until driven off by a cruel wind, and then descended a thousand feet by an equally steep rough path. When last seen the transport had just started up the lower slopes. We sat with our eyes glued to the pass playing at 'Sister Anne'. By 11 o'clock the only signs of life we had seen were some figures which mysteriously appeared and disappeared by the summit cairn. Had the caravan been attacked by bandits and were these their scouts watching us? It seemed a far-fetched explanation, but we could think of nothing better which might account for their taking four hours to climb a thousand feet.

With disgraceful slowness—the after-effects of Muztagh Ata—I climbed back to the cairn, taking the fanciful precaution of not approaching it directly from the path. There was no one there, but some of the baggage lay piled. On the other side I met Gyalgen and two Kirghiz lads carrying up loads, driving the three donkeys and the unladen chestnut mare, Lydia Languish, in front of them. The disaster had been pretty complete and these were the sole remnants of our caravan. Shipton's black horse had dropped dead soon after starting, breaking the stock of his gun as it fell, and the Kirghiz had taken back their three sick and sorry animals lest they too should follow his untimely example. Lydia Languish was too exhausted to carry anything, but the gallant little donkeys still had their loads. In the course of the afternoon we collected everything by a wretchedly inadequate patch of grass at the foot of the pass. The last to come in was a Turki lad bearing the skin of the black horse which he was taking back to Kashgar to satisfy his master that the horse was in fact dead and had not been sold or lost.

Next day with everyone carrying a load or a parcel of some sort we made about seven miles down a vile barren valley where even a yak or a camel would have been hard put to it to find nourishment. Gylgen disappeared up a side nallah to some yorts to get help, and returned the following morning alone driving six yaks and eight calves. The owners, who no doubt mistook him for a Chinese soldier, were too frightened either to stop him or to come with him. Before he got back we had had a scene with the two Kirghiz boys who had first tried to bolt and then wept, but upon the arrival of the yaks they cheered up and helped to load them. In Northern Tibet there are wild yaks and I think we can claim to have discovered that they exist also in Sinkiang. These behaved like wild steers. Each in turn bucked its load off and then galloped grunting up the nallah. Finally, we started with two of the more placid, followed by four woolly calves and our three donkeys which were still strong enough to carry though this was their third day without a proper feed. That morning we had made large numbers of 'chapatties' for them.

That evening our transport troubles were solved, for we reached a small Turki village at the foot of the valley where we managed to hire two camels for the long stretch of desert to Opal Bazaar. Here was grass in abundance, but almost before the wretched donkeys had got used to the sight of it they were whisked away by the two Kirghiz boys who hurried off up the valley without even waiting to be paid. In order to make an early start the next morning the camels were brought to our camp and tethered for the night. Our precaution was in some ways unfortunate, for one of them proceeded to make night hideous by roaring for her calf left behind in the village. A camel mourning for its young makes a noise very like a fog-horn blown at regular intervals.

At the mouth of the valley the river loses itself beneath its stony mile-wide bed not to reappear again until near Opal, the intervening tract of thirty miles being a sand and gravel plain utterly devoid of water or life. Opal is a large fertile village situated some thirty miles west of Kashgar on a plateau of rich loess soil. To an observer on the desert it appears as if it were placed upon a hill and its groves of tall poplars so strengthen the illusion that one wonders how water reached it at all. On entering the oasis one has the impression of landing on a tropical island[1] after a long sea voyage, so bewilderingly sudden is the transition from dreary waste to rich fields of lucerne, maize, and melons, and brimming channels of brick-red water. We were all very tired, but although the bazaar was five miles further on we straggled towards it against an out-flowing tide of donkeys, stopping often by the way to eat melons from the fields. Long after dark we reached the noisy, thronging, lamplit bazaar. The house of the 'big shot' which we automatically sought was deserted, but we soon had our legs under a table in the house of his deputy. Having eaten as much bread, melon, and grapes, as we could hold, not without some grumbling at the lean fare, we went to bed and at midnight were awakened to eat the dinner for which these were but the hors d'oeuvre.

A messenger, we were assured, who would ride like the wind, had been dispatched almost as soon as we arrived, so that we fully expected a lorry to come for us next morning. We sat all that day in the high, bare, mosque-like room, brushing off flies and visitors, while each successive meal betrayed a

1 The Chinese for oasis is 'lu chow' = green island.

fall in the standard of living. That fish and guests stink after three days and must be thrown out was evidently a saying not unknown to our host who seemed preparing to act on it betimes. Towards midnight the truck arrived, and we learnt that the swift, hard-riding messenger had left that morning at 7 o'clock on a donkey.

Opal is like a reef thrown out from the great Kashgar oasis—a few short desert inroads are crossed and soon forgotten when one enters what appears to be one vast garden stretching unbroken in every direction, lavishly watered and carefully tended. Kashgar is, perhaps, the largest of a string of great oases which lie round the periphery of the Takla Makan desert. The simplest way of grasping the geography of Sinkiang as a whole is to think in terms of desert, oasis, mountain. The heart and by the far the largest part of the country is the Takla Makan desert itself, 600 miles long from east to west and 300 miles across. Except for the narrower eastern end which forms the Kansu corridor—the link between China and its westernmost province—this desert is surrounded by snow mountains which are also roughly the boundaries of Sinkiang. On the north are the Tien Shan; to the west Chakragil, Kungur, Muztagh Ata, and Sarikol; and to the south the Karakoram and the Kun Lun. Between snow mountains and desert lies this comparatively narrow strip of rich land, which owes its fertility entirely to the many rivers which hurry through it in the course of their short life from their birthplace among the high snows and glaciers to their death and burial in the thirsty desert. No river ever leaves Sinkiang.

In the middle of Kashgar, like a quiet inner oasis, is the British Consulate where within the high walls of the compound there broods a Sabbath calm, free from the rude turmoil of the city. In a place whose motor vehicles could be counted on one hand one might think that turmoil would be far to seek, or that the easy-going medieval way of life in Kashgar would be incapable of creating much stir; but when a sufficiency of Turkis, their asses, their oxen, their camels, their men-servants and their maid-servants, gather together on a market day it is surprising how like it can be to Oxford Street during the New Year Sales. True it is that there are a lot of flies, that the street is littered with melon rind instead of bus tickets, that the equally dense traffic consists mainly of donkeys, and that the smell is something other but no more offensive than that of petrol fumes, but there is the same sense of infectious haste and false urgency.

Bazaars and markets are always interesting and sometimes attractive, especially if one has a profound admiration for food in the raw and in vast quantity, and here in Kashgar the narrow streets are every day adorned with the same horticultural splendour as the inside of a church at a Harvest Festival. If bread is the staff of life, to the Turkoman melons are life itself, and here they are in prodigious quantity and variety—green and golden spheres, sliced half-moons of cream and scarlet—major planets among a galaxy of peaches, nectarines, apricots, rosy deceitful pomegranates, and white and purple grapes. Against this rich back-cloth are set piles of more homely massive onions, mountains of grated onion, stately leeks, radishes as big as turnips, pyramids of eggs, hills of rice, and towers of bread. There was

TWO MOUNTAINS AND A RIVER

really little else but food, raw and cooked, to be seen. The odd junk shop seemed to apologize for its unbeautiful, unwanted presence; no jeweller's wares challenged the coruscating fruit; no craftsmen plied their trade save in the obscurity of a back street where they could not impede the great business of life, the buying, selling, and eating of so much wholesome 'belly-timber'. A delightful scene, even to a stern ascetic moralist; for who, having seen even once the full tide of life in Kashgar bazaar, would not feel his confidence in the human race restored, or would not, in the words of the hymn, fail to 'ponder anew what the Almighty can do' even with a people not remarkable for diligence.

I visited this stirring scene but once and even then I hurried through very early in the day while there was still room to squeeze between the donkeys without being beaten to the ground by their maunds of melons. Nor, with one exception, did I visit any shrines, mosques, Chinese temples, or celebrated antiquities, where I could presumably count on being alone. The exception was a climbing archaeological expedition to what Sir Aurel Stein calls the 'Öch Mirwan'—three caves or 'cellas' with the painted head of a Buddha, carved out of a solid cliff of loess situated in the bed of the Artush river two miles beyond the northern end of the Kashgar oasis. The caves were half-way up, or down, the 100 ft. high vertical cliff, so that to reach them it was necessary to 'abseil' down with the rope anchored to a wooden stake driven into the top of the cliff; then to affect a lodgement in the cave by drawing oneself in with the feet; and, having satisfied one's archaeological lust, to continue the 'abseil' to the bottom. As Shipton was *hors de combat* I was the victim required to make a Roman holiday for a small party of visitors we had brought out to watch proceedings from below. Although my grace and agility may not have impressed them, I feel sure that the possibilities of the situation did. I was amazed by the extraordinary preservation of this relic of a distant age carved in such a seemingly insubstantial medium as a cliff of loess.

This, I'm afraid, was the sum of our meagre tribute laid on the altar of learning. As Dr Johnson says: 'if love of ease surmounted our desire for knowledge, the offence has not the invidiousness of singularity', and so pleasant was it at Chini Bagh, the Consulate, dissecting melons, critically fingering peaches, and thinking of the busy world outside that it was distasteful to sally out even in response to calls of hospitality.

In Kashgar the Consul must undertake the duties which hospitality requires with all seriousness, so that anyone staying at the Consulate is drawn willy-nilly into the whirlpool. My first call—Shipton on crutches was absolved—was to the Russian Consulate for lunch. The Consul was a pleasant man with an original sense of humour, which, I should think, most Russian officials must develop, even if unconsciously. The English-speaking interpreter was a flaxen-haired, pink and white young man, but even with his willing assistance I did not penetrate very far behind the Iron Curtain. I made a point of asking about this piece of stage furniture and was chagrined to find that neither of them had the slightest idea what it meant or what it implied.

The Russian and British Consulates in Kashgar—the only two of the kind—are like the ends of a see-saw, each has its ups and downs. From 1934 to 1942 the Russians were up. They had everything their own way and the Chinese Governor in their pocket, but in 1942 when they were in serious difficulties the Chinese reasserted themselves. Since then the Russian end of the see-saw has stayed down, much to our advantage. Although communications with Russia as compared with India are short and easy, all traffic, whether goods or mail, is at present (1948) suspended. As the Consul lugubriously explained to me, after sitting secluded for three months doing nothing beyond maintaining correct but distant relations with the Chinese, he spends a day or two of activity making up and dispatching the consular mail and then relapses into hibernation until the next Quarter Day. Having in accordance with tradition consumed a sufficiency of brandy, vodka, and champagne, I stumbled from behind the Iron Curtain not much wiser than before.

My next duty was to attend the Chinese celebration of 'V.J. Day' held on an open field near the New City six miles east of Old Kashgar. The Chinese as colonists of the 'New Dominion', as it is called, keep even more to themselves than do we in our tropical colonies though, perhaps, with less reason. They are not content to segregate themselves in one part of the town, but usually build a new settlement exclusively for themselves a few miles away. As they take little or no part in either business or in agriculture the Chinese population consists almost entirely of civil officials and the army. In spite of disasters and expulsions the Chinese have for many centuries clung tenaciously to their 'New Dominion'. This is all the more remarkable because of the enormous distance from China proper—a distance of 4000 miles. Even today travelling by lorry it is a matter of months rather than weeks. Since the first century B.C. Chinese power in Sinkiang has ebbed and flowed. Their last expulsion was in 1862 when the Dungans (Chinese Mahomedans) rebelled and drove them out. Yakub Beg, a man of great ability, whose government was recognized by both Britain and Russia, ruled in Kashgar until 1877 when a Chinese army recaptured their ancient dominion. The march of an army through 4000 miles of country upon which it was not possible to live, was accomplished by sending in advance troops who sowed cereals and vegetables in each oasis to be reaped in due course by the main body.

To drive through the Old City to the New in the consular truck was a moving experience for everyone. For none of the men, women, children, asses, or camels of these parts has any road sense (and why should they?) and assume, wrongly in this case, that the driver of a truck will either stop his vehicle or swerve out of the way, or that if he does not the resulting collision will be no more serious than that of two dawdling donkeys. It was refreshing to see such complete contempt for a mechanical vehicle, but one felt sorry for the victims.

The guests assembled on a raised pavilion, decorated with flags and the fly-blown portraits of the Allied leaders, to drink tea and eat melon seeds until all was ready. Opposite the pavilion were drawn up a long line of cavalry, some infantry who seemed to feel their lowly position, some school-children, and a band. The ceremony consisted mainly of speeches in Chinese followed by a Turki translation and the repulsive shouting of slogans by the children and the troops in response to the ranting of a cheer-leader. The whole show was both

amateurish and boring, and I inferred from the expression on the face of the
Russian Consul, who arrived last in the uniform of a Bohemian admiral, that
they did these things better in Moscow.

That night there was an official dinner on the grand scale which excited
ripples of similar hospitality by officials of diminishing rank as though a stone
had been cast into a quiet pond. Whether there were ten, twenty, or thirty
courses at these banquets there was not as much variety as one would expect,
for at least half of them were of meat served up in slightly different forms of
vapidity. At Tashkurghan, some ten weeks' journey from the sea, our hosts
had apologized for the absence of the usual delicacies, but here where it was
only a matter of nine weeks there were the seaweeds and sea-fruits beloved of
the Chinese—if sea-fruit is a permissible term for sea-slugs. The Chinese, like
Peacock's Mr Jenkinson, though no anatomists, have concluded that man is
omnivorous and on that conclusion they act.

From descriptions of Chinese feasts and from the competitive targets they
set themselves in the number of courses, one might conclude that food played
a paramount part. That is not so. Drinking is what is expected, particularly on
the part of the guests, and this is done in the polite ceremonious fashion of the
eighteenth and nineteenth centuries. There must be no quiet private sipping
or swigging, but you must select your victim, raise your glass, and challenge
him to 'bottoms up' for which the Chinese formula was what sounded to me
like 'gambay'—at least if an ejaculation something similar to this is
accompanied by the waving of your glass as you stand up your intentions are
readily understood. Very rarely the chosen victim may not like your face or
your manner, or more rarely still might think he had had enough, in which
case the password is 'mambay' and there is then no obligation on either side to
drain the glass. This formula should only be used *in extremis*, for a too
frequent recurrence to it is considered bad form. The glasses were very small
and contained, if one was lucky, nothing more deleterious than Russian
brandy, so that even if one was struck by a salvo of 'gambays' after each
course no great harm was done.

After one of these decorous orgies I was invited to the 'Russian Club'
where a Chinese opera was being performed. The 'Club' is a fine large hall,
holding possibly a thousand, with a big stage and its own lighting plant. It was
put up by the Russians in the days when their influence was at its height. It is
the only place of its kind in Kashgar and therefore the only place for any
entertainment—the Russians occasionally show films, the Chinese use it for
plays, operas, dancing, and meetings—so that it forms a constant and
unmistakable piece of Russian propaganda.

Since I am an unenlightened Yahoo in the matter of music and opera I am
not qualified to write a criticism of the Chinese opera or music drama for
which we arrived, most fortunately, only in time for the last act. Not that my
ignorance of music or of Chinese would be any handicap, because of the first
there was none, and as for the second whether an opera is sung in English,
Chinese, or Italian, is all one to me so far as hearing and understanding goes.
However, even I could comprehend the gestures and postures—not that they
were indecent—and the grace of movement of even the lesser lights who took

the parts of maids or messengers was fascinating to watch. The whole action took place round a sort of 'Punch and Judy' box stuck bang in the middle of the enormous stage. Behind it, where the puppets should have been, stood people who may have been prompters, stage managers, scene-shifters, or merely friends of the principals. Anyone, it appeared, was at liberty to stroll on from the wings to pass the time of day with the actors when they were not busy. The singing was the really excruciating part of the performance because it was all done in a high, forced falsetto, which the orchestra accompanied or not just as the spirit moved them, punctuating and emphasizing the declamatory passages with gongs, cymbals, castanets, drums, and other percussion instruments at what each individual musician thought was an opportune moment. When the singing reached a pitch too high even for their accustomed ears they simply turned on the heat and extinguished it in a blast of cacophonous sound. A packed audience of Chinese soldiers and Turkis listened to all this in ominous silence with which I heartily agreed.

The stage was then cleared for a display of Turki dancing which was spirited and graceful but too long drawn out. As Swift says: 'there seems to be no part of knowledge in fewer hands than that of discerning when to have done.' This apparently was also the opinion of my Turki host, the Assistant Secretary. Inflamed to a moderate degree by the barrage of 'gambays' to which in his capacity of host he had been subjected, he felt that the shortest way of bringing the show to an end was to occupy the stage himself. Having lit a cigarette and donned a maroon-coloured gown he mounted the stage and brought down the house with an admirable and not very unsteady display of grace and agility.

Three weeks soon passed, but it would be a mistake to suppose that they were passed in a round of banquets. Apart from those by which Mrs Shipton took her revenge there were only these few and a luncheon given by the Indian trading community. This, which was entirely devoted to simple but strenuous gastronomy, was more in line—no drink, no idle chat, but a sustained and savage assault upon successive platters of pilau,[1] shirt-sleeves rolled up and towels round our necks

For the most part I remained in the semi-monastic seclusion of Chini Bagh, walking in the garden and tasting the fruits thereof, and trying not to hear the daily argument between Shipton and another guest. The serpent in this garden was a journalist busy priming himself with the politics of Sinkiang with a view to unleashing them on an unsuspecting American public. Even with some striking examples of nourishment before him he was unable to disabuse his mind of the idea that the people of Kashgar were starving oppressed serfs; for instead of talking to the starving serfs at work on their bounteous crops, or getting himself crushed by a cart-load of melons in the teeming bazaar, he adopted at second or third hand the views of disgruntled politicians. He was distressed by the absence of any attempt to improve the Turki education, culture, or amenities—so different from the attention bestowed on such matters across the border—and he seemed not to agree with Mark Twain concerning the application of these things to the so-called backward races,

1 The Chinese word for pilau is 'chua' = 'rice that is grabbed with the hand'.

that 'soap and education are not so sudden as a massacre but they are more deadly in the long run'. Like other progressive thinkers and fervid reformers—from our own bluff monster King Hal down to the disciples of Marx—he was not particular about the means used, but unlike them he was not really confident that the end was good. Such a fatal combination of views would not matter if unexpressed, but these roaming American journalists are well paid for their views even though these are sometimes half-baked. 'Does the wild ass bray when he hath grass?' was a question asked by Job, to which the answer seems to be that nowadays he very frequently does.

CHAPTER THIRTEEN

Another Way Home

No conscientious traveller turns homewards on the route by which he came if a reasonable alternative offers itself. I shall not try to define the saving word 'reasonable', but if this premise is granted then my curious choice of route for the return journey will be at least understood if not condoned.

Between Kashgar and Tashkurghan there are several routes to choose from: our own Ulugh Art route; the usual route by the Chichiklik pass; that by the Gez defile, and a variation of this by the interesting Bel Art pass which joins the Gez route from the north. Mr C. P. Skrine has an attractive description of the Bel Art in his book *Chinese Central Asia*, and had it not been that there was some doubt as to whether there was not still too much water in the Gez river I should have gone that way. As it was I chose a rather devious route of my own invention. Travelling by the Kara-tash pass to the north-east side of Muztagh Ata I would cross two little-known passes to the east of that mountain, the Tur-bulung and the Yangi Dawan, and then join the usual route at the Chichiklik 'maidan'. Apart from the opportunity of seeing the eastern side of Muztagh Ata I was drawn to this route by the absence of any red dotted line marking a known route over the Tur-bulung and by the fact that the name of the pass itself had an interrogation mark after it.

So far so good. From Tashkurghan to Gilgit, however, alternative routes are hard to find, for the only two obvious ways are those by the Mintaka or the Kilik passes, which hardly differ and which are both well known. But the conscientious traveller need not despair. If he casts his net wide enough some less obvious ways can be dragged in. There was one to be found by making a wide sweep to the east by the Oprang river and back into Hunza by the Shingshal gorge; but if wide sweeps had to be made there was a more attractive one for me to the west over the Wakhjir pass and then back into the extreme north-west corner of Hunza territory by either the Irshad or the Khora Bhort pass and down to Gilgit by the Karumbar nallah. The particular attraction of this route was that I should see not only the source of the Oxus and the Hindu Kush, but also the mountains north and west of our 'unexplored' glacier and so possibly get some idea of what lay in the wide gap between the head of the glacier and the Chillinji pass, a problem which we had expected to clear up in July.

It did, of course, occur to me that going by this route I should have to cross not only the Wakhjir pass and the great Central Asian water-parting, but also the frontier of Afghanistan of which Wakhan is part, and that in the present sorry scheme of things frontiers are apt to be more difficult than passes. But I argued that Wakhan is a pretty remote part of Afghanistan where it was unlikely that I should meet any Afghan officials, that any Wakhis I had so far come across had seemed kind accommodating folk, and that by nipping smartly back into India from the vicinity of Bozai Gumbaz by the Irshad or Khora Bhort I should almost certainly avoid being caught up in the spider's web of passports, visas, and inquisitive officials. For it was unfortunately true that I had no Afghan visa nor any chance of obtaining one, but by going without I should merely be anticipating Mr Bevin's express wish for visa-less travel. In any case, if the worst happened, as usual much could be hoped for from time and chance.

At Tashkurghan I intended picking up our old friend Naiad Shah, for Wakhi was one of his five languages, which had, I hoped, been learnt more recently and perhaps less imperfectly than his Hindustani. I had found him faithful, helpful, stupid, and anxious to look after my interests without neglecting his own. He liked to travel with a few copper teapots and some rolls of cloth stowed away in his capacious saddle-bags with which he drove pretty hard bargains with the simple Kirghiz. But I also had a volunteer to go with me from Kashgar—a Turki from the considerable colony of gardeners and servants of all kinds which has thrived and multiplied exceedingly in the course of a few generations within the walls of the Consulate compound. It had occurred to him that it was his filial duty to look up his old father who was vaguely reported to keep a shop somewhere between Gilgit and Srinagar, and hearing that I was going that way he had thought that since he had no passport it would simplify matters if he travelled with me. I was not in a position myself to be particular about a trifle like that. Indeed, I was rather astonished that in remote Central Asia such sinister tokens of civilization should be expected from those whom we sweepingly classify as 'natives'. The world was evidently a grimmer place and had progressed more rapidly than I had thought. It was explained to Usuf that I might not be going by the most direct route to Gilgit and Srinagar, but his ideas of geography were scattered and whether I went by Timbuktoo or Baghdad was all one to him so long as he could travel in the 'reserved' occupation of sahib's servant and so long as we eventually fetched up in Kashmir.

Yusuf had his own white pony of which he was very proud and very fond, but he had unfortunately no language but his own which was of no use at all to me. He carried bedding, and grain for the pony, and like Naiad Shah he had capacious saddle-bags which were crammed with goods for bartering on the road. The Eastern traveller seems to hold that a journey should not only be free of cost but also that it should show a profit—as witness the high proportion of travellers on Indian railways who neglect the formality of purchasing a ticket, and the profit a few of them make by robbing the paying passengers. I had my own baggage which amounted to a light pony-load for which I intended to hire transport from stage to stage. This obvious arrangement was, as it happened, a very foolish one, as it gave too many hostages to fortune; but I had not the spare cash to lay out on a pony for which in Kashgar I should have had to pay through the nose.

For the seventy miles from Kashgar to Ighiz Yar I got what was almost but not quite literally a flying start in the Consulate truck, costing the lives of a donkey, two dogs, and several hens. Yusuf who had gone ahead with the ponies met me there. We breakfasted in the dark before setting out early on 14 September with the outward-bound mail ponies with which we travelled until we turned off to the west up the Ghijak Sus. It was one of the thickest days I had seen, the sun peering wanly through a white fog of loess dust. We had a long climb the next day over the 13,000 ft. Ghijak pass before dropping to the narrow Kara-tash valley. As travelling companions we had a mob of yaks and donkeys one of which provided us, and even its Kirghiz owner, with a good laugh. Donkeys, as soon as they are off-loaded, love to have a roll; they usually stick half-way with their legs in the air without completing the roll. At the midday halt one of them started performing on a steep slope and was amazed to find that he not only completed the roll with ease, but continued rolling with increasing speed until brought up with a terrible thump by a dry water-course.

We halted for the night at Chat where there was a mixture of yorts, mud-walled houses, and so many 'gumbaz' that the place looked like a stack-yard. The people seemed to be Kirghiz and Turki hybrids, unable to make up their minds whether to live in a yort or a house, with the usual deplorable results consequent upon indecision. When we crossed the valley and continued to the west up the long, winding Kara-tash nallah we soon found ourselves in real Kirghiz country. It was a very long march so that it was not until dusk that we reached the last yorts below the Kara-tash pass at a height of about 15,000 ft. They were tucked away on a shelf of grass out of sight from the track and had it not been for the acrid smell of their yak-dung fires we should have missed them. Here we found good entertainment notwithstanding the presence of a large party of Turki grain merchants and their donkeys. It was bitterly cold although early September and I found it difficult to believe these folk who assured us that they lived there all the winter.

The Kara-tash pass is 16,388 ft. high, only slightly lower than the Ulugh Art, but neither of our ponies found the crossing difficult. There was some snow, but except for the boulder-strewn summit it is an easy pass for animals. Behind us a thick bank of loess haze reached up almost to the level of the pass where a fierce gale was driving it back, while to the west lowering rain clouds hung about the eastern face of Muztagh Ata which I had wished so much to see. We descended easily to the Ik-bel valley below, where on the far side of the river there were a couple of yorts. Filling the valley head, a broad stream of unsullied ice flowed gently downwards from a low ridge to the south. I was tempted to embark on it, for it led in our direction, but hampered as we were with ponies it would have been a chancey business. We joined the grain merchants while they brewed tea, crouching round a fire in the bitter wind, and then pushed on to the junction of the valley with that of the Tur-bulung. Here I had expected to find yorts where I could get some information about the Tur-bulung pass, but there was no one there and so we went on until nightfall compelled us to camp at the first grass.

Three hours further down we came to an 'aoul' (Kang Showar) and took up our quarters in a yort where there happened to be a scolding wife, a brawling husband, and a crying baby. The disadvantages of life in a yort were unmistakable. The Tur-bulung, we were told, was only fit for yaks, our ponies would have to go round by Subashi; but Yusuf, who so far had always ridden on top of his own baggage, volunteered to come with me provided he could have a yak to ride. Like any other Turki he was not much good on his feet and he had suffered from headache when crossing the Kara-tash.

We started back up the valley next day, Yusuf on one yak and our reduced amount of kit and a Kirghiz on another. The weather seemed set on balking me of one object of my journey, for it was a wretched day of low cloud and falling snow. However, the Tur-bulung valley itself was interesting enough for it contained a big glacier of the normal Himalayan type—debris-strewn, dirty, wrinkled—so different from the white, unblemished slabs of ice which are plastered on the west side of Muztagh Ata and on the slopes of Kungur. When level with the snout of this glacier our track turned away from the main valley to follow the Tur-bulung stream which here cuts its way down through a gorge from a hanging valley a thousand feet above. This upland valley was a wide, peaty bottom of coarse brown grass, like a typical Pamir valley. We were pressed to stop at one of the cleanest yorts I have ever seen, by a cheerful, bustling woman who lived there alone with a child; but it was too far from the pass, so having gratefully drunk tea and eaten maize bread and cream we pushed on to an 'aoul' of some dozen yorts at the head of the valley. We reached it at dusk—a dreary spot surrounded by bleak snow-covered hills and guarded by a pack of savage yellow dogs. I was bidden to mount a yak before approaching, and no one dared dismount before their owners had driven them off.

It snowed heavily throughout the night, but a cheerful banjo-playing youth assured us he would see us over the pass and down to the Chichiklik 'maidan' in spite of all. After a snow-fall the response to reveille in a yort is amazingly prompt, for as soon as the cord of the felt covering the smoke-hole is pulled preparatory to lighting the fire, a small avalanche is released to overwhelm the occupants. When we started we could see nothing, not even the track, but the guide led on unerringly through low rounded hills until we realized we were on the pass, unmarked even by a pile of stones. It is, I imagine, something over 16,000 ft. and could be crossed by lightly laden ponies when clear of snow. We halted a thousand feet down the other side to give our yak some weeds and gravel before beginning the climb to the second pass, the

Yangi Dawan, 16,100 ft. We reached this about 2 p.m. and looking down we could see the great plain of Chichiklik across the far end of which lay the main route to Tashkurghan. It was comparatively clear of snow, but though we looked long and hard neither yort nor yak could we see.

All travellers from Sarikol to Kashgar or Yarkand who pass south of the Muztagh Ata range must traverse the Chichiklik 'maidan'. It lies at over 14,500 ft. and is in such an exposed position that only for a very short time in the year is it free from bitter winds and heavy snowfalls. Sir Aurel Stein discovered in the middle of the plain the ancient ruins of a hospice or serai. This had been mentioned by the Chinese Buddhist pilgrim Hsuan-tsang who described the Chichiklik as a 'region where icy storms rage. The ground, impregnated with salt, produces no crops, there are no trees and nothing but wretched herbs. Even at the time of the great heat the wind and snow continue. Merchant caravans in coming and going suffer severely in these difficult and dangerous spots.' According to Hsuan-tsang a great company of merchants and followers had once perished here, whereupon a saintly person of Tashkurghan, with the aid of the riches lost by this doomed caravan, built and endowed the hospice for the benefit of future travellers.

We descended to the plain and crossed it, with the ruins of this hospice away to our left, wondering at its emptiness and by no means relishing the prospect of a night out in such an inhospitable waste. A man with some donkeys was moving along the road and from him we learnt of the existence of a yort. Late in the evening we found it tucked away in a snow-filled hollow of the hills on the western edge of the plain. A very miserable place it was too; but any clothes will fit a naked man, and on the Chichiklik 'maidan' in September any roof is better than none. The family of the yort seemed to be trying to live like Kirghiz without the essential stock which alone enables the Kirghiz to exist. Their sole livestock were six sheep, and they seemed to eke out a precarious existence by sheltering (though not feeding) rare travellers like ourselves who had failed to make the usual stage. Though I am all for preserving undisfigured the beauties of the natural scene, I thought that here was a good case for a modest advertisement. Had we not by chance met the donkey-man we should have spent a perishing cold night and they would have been so much the worse off.

Poverty by no means always implies dirt though it often goes with a large family. Here there was a large and a very dirty family, and though a well populated head is held to be the sign of a generous mind I took what few precautions I could to avoid that distinction. From the 'maidan' the road climbed for some miles before beginning its plunge through the Dershat gorge to the Tashkurghan valley. It was another day of cold wind and sleet which chilled us to the bone before we could enter the sheltering wall of the gorge— a loathsome, waterless, bone-yard of a place, littered with the dried bodies and bare skeletons of donkeys, ponies, and camels. The ascent to the Chichiklik from this side is nearly 5000 ft. There is no water, and the track is such as to break the heart of the stoutest beast. Most of the donkeys of Sinkiang must die in harness, laying their bones by the side of some such cruel road as this.

Just before we reached the 12,000 ft. level we ran into fine weather. White fleecy clouds cast their racing black shadows over the yellowing fields of the Tagharma vale, while the river which a month ago ran brown and turgid now flashed clear and blue. Nearing the first village nine miles out from Tashkurghan, we were surprised to see the ponies coming out to meet us—a neat piece of staff work for which the pony-men must be given the credit. Not knowing much about the route I had told them we should be four days in crossing, but when they reached this village and heard that the Tur-bulung was only three days journey they had off-loaded and brought the ponies back to meet us. We joined them at the serai where the loads had been dumped and enjoyed the finest mutton I have ever tasted.

We had a day's rest at Tashkurghan while Naiad Shah fettled up himself and his pony for the Wakhan trip. As I was no longer under the aegis of the Consul in person I was at once humiliated and relieved by the absence of any offers of hospitality. The magistrate and a few Chinese officers waited on me, but the meeting was short and cool, their former deference being nicely readjusted to meet my new circumstances and my slightly more travel-stained appearance. There was some uncalled for inquisitiveness about Yusuf's passport, or his lack of one, and passes for the returning pony-men had to be obtained. I felt that I might as well be in Europe.

At the Taghlak Gumbaz, the first stage out, the yort had been removed so that this time we were obliged to cook inside the monument. Any feelings we may have had that we were desecrating the tomb were easily suppressed. At Dafdar we enjoyed excellent fare in the house to which our former friends of the yort had now removed against the approach of winter. Reaping was almost over, threshing the winnowing were in full swing, and there was the genial air of prosperity and abundance usually attendant upon harvest time. The inside of a mud-walled house is, however, not nearly so pleasant as that of a yort. There is no light at all except when the door is open, while instead of lying luxuriously on the floor round the fire one must sit primly on the hard clay platform which serves as both bed and seat.

At Beyik I was surprised and displeased to find that the former Chinese post had been withdrawn and that a detachment of soldiers had been moved up to Mintaka Karaul. I had some fear that when the Chinese saw us heading for the Wakhjir instead of the Mintaka pass they might try to stop us. There were only two yorts here, one occupied by Tajiks the other by Kirghiz. We stopped at the latter, and an excellent, lively, good-humoured woman who ruled the roost made us one of the flaky pastry, cream-smeared loaves for supper. Even in a yort punctilious ceremony is observed, and it was amusing to see our heterogeneous assembly—Kirghiz, Hunza, Turkoman, Englishman—gather preparatory to eating while our host went the rounds with a long-spouted ewer as each in turn held out his hands to wash. One dried them by the simple expedient of crossing the arms, squeezing the hands under the opposite armpits, and then withdrawing them swiftly to wipe off the moisture. When we had finished, at a signal from the reverend Naiad Shah, we raised our hands in a supplicatory attitude and then brought them down as though stroking the beard, muttering the appropriate grace.

Between Beyik and Mintaku Karaul, Naiad Shah took us a short way up a side nallah to visit the yort of a Hunza woman who had married a Kirghiz with whom he hoped to do some trade. We timed our arrival well. She had just finished baking so we gorged ourselves on hot fresh bread and firm, fresh yoghourt. The road from Tashkurghan to Mintaka is I think, the finest stretch of 'yoghourt' road in the country. Here it is solid enough to be eaten only with a spoon, whereas up north it is altogether a thinner brew usually of what cooks call a 'pouring consistency'.

As if to remind me that life had its rubs and was not all yoghourt and skittles, I came an imperial cropper that afternoon as I was trying to cross a stream by leaping from boulder to boulder. One of my rubber-soled 'expedition' boots slipped and ice-axe, wrist-watch, and a tin of tobacco went to the bottom. They were all recovered, but Naiad Shah, knowing my fondness for water, thought I had done it on purpose; nor did I trouble to undeceive him.

We marched past the Chinese post, telling them merely that we should look in later, and went on to the yorts a mile or so up the Mintaka valley. These people knew Naiad Shah well and readily agreed to provide a yak for my baggage and a guide to take us over the Wakhjir. The carcass of a sheep which had recently been slaughtered was produced and the whole party fell to work stripping it bare. I have seldom met anyone, not excepting meat-starved Kavirondos, so avid for meat as the Kirghiz. Men, women, and toothless infants gnaw away at bones like so many dogs.

As we wished to proceed up the Wakhjir valley there was no escaping the Chinese post, so positioned as to command views up both valleys. One could make a short-cut a mile or two away from the post, but it was no more possible to leave the Mintaka route and head for the Wakhjir without attracting attention than it would be to do a strip-tease act unobserved in Hyde Park. To call on the officer at the post seemed to be the boldest and the best. In order to counter any objections on his part I armed Naiad Shah with a bottle of Russian brandy I had with me, which he was told on no account to produce unless the Chinese began raising difficulties. Frankness and goodfellowship must be the approach to this far-flung Celestial.

Our start was delayed. The ponies had strayed up the hill, while Naiad Shah was dodging from yort to yort busy picking up unconsidered trifles, a bit of meat here, a skinful of yoghourt there—the latter was tied to his saddle where it gurgled musically. It was 10 o'clock before we reached the post where we were told that the commanding officer was still in bed. It seemed a pity to waken him so we began to unfold our plans in a casual way to a subordinate of unknown rank. He seemed a bit surprised. No objections were even hinted at. The only condition was that a Chinese soldier would have to accompany us for the first day to ward off the attacks of Russian Kirghiz. I was therefore surprised and annoyed when Naiad Shah before I could stop him produced the bottle with a flourish from under his coat and handed it to the astonished Chinaman with the air of a prince bestowing a princely gift—as indeed it was. Gratifying as it must be to the one party there is nothing so annoying to the other as having made an unnecessary bribe, particularly when the bribe in question might have been put to a hundred better uses. One at any rate I thought of, even as the Chinaman accepted the precious gift with disgusting indifference.

Before the commanding officer could be awakened to see what Santa Claus Naiad Shah had brought, and possibly to make inquiries about our plans, I got the party mounted and rode off. An hour later, looking back, I saw a small cloud of dust. Presently the thud of hoofs could be heard and we were overtaken by our armed escort of one. As it is irksome to the Chinese cavalryman to move on the wide open spaces of Sinkiang at anything less than a gallop, soon our modest pace exhausted his patience and off he went. I had half-feared that this annihilator of space might be the bearer of orders for our return, but to my relief he brought nothing, not even thanks for our costly mistake. At last, I thought with complacence, we were clear of soldiers and frontier posts. There were none on the Wakhjir pass and certainly none on the Irshad. On the Wakhan Pamir we should, no doubt, meet friendly Kirghiz, and perhaps at Bozai Gumbaz a few rude tillers of the soil who would gladly speed us on our way and ask no questions. Life seemed very good.

CHAPTER FOURTEEN

The Oxus Source

THE Wakhjir is a fine open valley, comparatively rich in grass. Nevertheless, it was then uninhabited—at least neither Kirghiz nor Chinese knew of anyone living there. Its position is isolated and close to the Russian frontier and in the past it had attracted the attention of raiders who used to enter by way of the Tigurman Su pass. At the foot of the nallah which leads to this pass we stopped for lunch. I bathed in a clear deep pool and found that the midday sun even at the end of September was still hot enough to dry one. A little beyond on the other side of the valley is the Kilik nallah and the path leading to the pass of that name. A deserted Chinese fort stands at the entrance.

The horns of *Ovis poli*, the great mountain sheep, lie scattered thickly in the upper Wakhjir. These sheep range over a wide area in Central Asia, but the Pamirs are their favourite haunt. A head was first brought to Europe by Wood, the first Englishman to explore the Oxus, and the beast was so named in compliment to Marco Polo's original description. In Sarakul there are many cairns of *Ovis poli* heads which have been collected and stacked by the Kirghiz, just as in other days their ancestors under Gengiz Khan liked to build mounds and pyramids of the skulls of their enemies.

Naiad Shah had promised that that night we should sleep at a 'gumbaz', but the sun sank, the valley narrowed, and the little glacier of Khush Bel came into view without any sign of it. Instead we had to pitch our tents in a hollow while there was still light by which to gather fuel, and even as we did so we saw to our astonishment a couple of Kirghiz on yaks apparently bent on the same errand. Their yorts, they said, were five miles further on. They had arrived there two days before from the direction of Bozai Gumbaz and the Chakmaktin Lake, a region they were now quitting in fear of raiders from the Russian side. On a clear moonlit night we sat by the fire until driven to bed by the cold. In the night the weather changed. We woke to a dull snowy morning with snow on the ground, so, foregoing our breakfasts, we set off hot-foot for the yorts, passing Naiad Shah's 'gumbaz' on the way. Triumphantly he pointed this out to me, for he thought, quite rightly as it happened, that on the previous evening I had not believed him.

There were three yorts, or more correctly the walls of three. Their roofs had not yet been put on because the owners were in transit, bound for lower down the valley. Snow drifted through the open roof while men, women, and children huddled down under the walls to shelter from the wind. They were in much better plight than refugees usually are, having with them all their goods and chattels and a house to put them in. Outside stood their yaks and their horses, busy scraping away the snow in search of grass. Emigrants would be a better description of them, for they intended leaving Wakhan for good and settling in Chinese territory. Their yaks seemed to me bigger and more powerful than any I had seen—some might have rivalled the Durham ox itself.

After food and talk we learnt that a party of men and five yaks were returning to Bozai Gumbaz to fetch the remainder of their goods. We therefore shifted our loads to these, sent the Mintaka man home, and started for the Wakhjir. The pass is only just over 16,000 ft. but I found it perishing cold in spite of wearing a 'poshteen'—a sheep-skin coat—on top of my windproofs. Descending a valley on our right, from what we were told was the Kara Jilga pass, were streams of laden yaks, ponies, and sheep. Thirty families were said to be moving out of the enclave east of the Chakmaktin Lake with the intention of settling in Chinese territory. I wondered if they, too, had passports.

The ascent to the pass is gradual, finally flattening out to a broad saddle just below the summit containing a considerable lake about half a mile long and 200 or 300 yards across. From it the Wakhjir river flows to the east. Overlooking the pass on the south is a fine snow mountain of over 19,000 ft.— the eastern extremity of the Hindu Kush. As we descended into Wakhan the clouds melted, the sun came out and far below we saw the thin blue ribbon of the infant Oxus winding through a wide shingle bed, edged in places with grass the colour of old gold, and flanked on the north by the smooth, brown slopes of the Wakhan Pamir and on the south by the bold snow-covered Hindu Kush. Sheltered behind a 'gumbaz' built on a grass shelf near the foot of the pass I sat and gazed wonderingly at the snout of a large glacier two or three miles upstream whence from a black ice-cave emerged the new-born Oxus. Here the river is called the Ab-i-Wakhan.

The question of the true source of the Oxus once aroused as much interest and controversy as did the problem of the Nile sources. Perhaps even more, because which of the upper confluents of the Oxus was the parent stream was of political importance, for it was that stream that was to mark the boundary between Russia and Afghanistan. Where there are several confluents with fairly equal pretensions the first discoverer of each naturally presses the claims of his to be the true and only source. Explorers are sensitive about their discoveries and should these affect the location of international boundaries then controversy may be long and bitter.

Wood's great joureny of 1838 and his discovery of the lake to which he gave the name Victoria (see Wood's *Journey to the Source of the Oxus*) was thought to have settled the matter, and the Pamir river issuing from that lake was held to be the true parent stream. It was upon this geographical basis that the Boundary Agreement of 1872 with Russia was made. The next claimant was the not very significant stream which joins the Ab-i-Wakhan, twenty-five miles below its glacier source. This stream, the Little Pamir, rises in hills near the western end of the Chakmaktin lake. To add to the confusion this same lake is the true source of the Murghab or Ak-su which, emerging from the eastern end of the lake, describes a great loop north round the Pamirs in Russian territory and enters the Oxus in the big bend a hundred miles north of Ishkashim. For many years this was held to be the main river by reason of its greater length and volume compared with that of the Ab-i-Wakhan. The difference in length, if anything at all, is but a few miles, and the volume varies with the season. Both points were disputed very strongly by Lord Curzon who in 1894 crossed the Wakhjir, visited the ice-cave giving birth to the river, and followed it downwards as far as Sarhad. His exhaustive description and discussion of the rival claims from every possible angle appeared in the *Geographical Journal* for July, August, and September 1896. The question is now of purely academic interest. My opinion is worth little, but to my mind, speaking as a mountaineer, the only fit and proper birthplace for this mighty river of most ancient fame is the ice-cave in the glacier at the eastern extremity of the Hindu Kush, at the innermost heart of Central Asia. For it is a river whose waters, to use Lord Curzon's words, 'tell of forgotten peoples and secrets of unknown lands, and are believed to have rocked the cradle of our race'.

We passed some more Kirghiz families on their way over the Wakhjir, and then having reached the valley we turned upstream to some yorts tucked away between moraine and river bank not more than a mile or so from the glacier source. Though the Kirghiz with whom we were travelling were friendly enough, we fell into such poor hands here that I wondered which of them was truly representative of the Kirghiz of Wakhan. There were only two yorts—a large and a small. We naturally went to the first, but our reception was so cool that we were obliged to resort to the smaller where the sole occupant turned out to be an orphan girl about fourteen years old. All we got was a little milk which we eked out with the hard lumps of 'karut' which the Kirghiz had brought with them. One sees balls of this stuff being dried on racks outside most yorts. It is made from the surplus yoghourt and it looks and tastes like solidified sawdust with a faintly bitter suspicion of cheese. Much of it is sold in

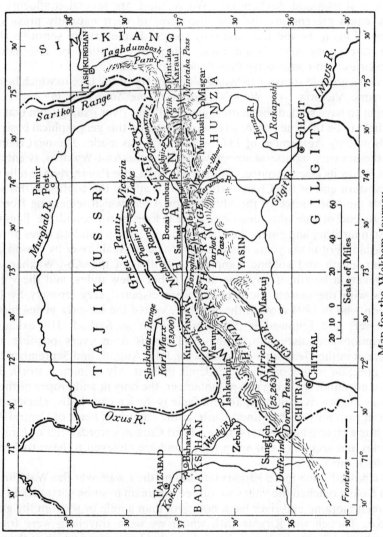

Map for the Wakham Journey

Kashgar where it is used for flavouring soups, while the Kirghiz take it on a journey as a haversack ration.

We made a short march of only eight miles next day to some yorts on the south bank of the river where the Kama Su nallah joins it. There is a pass leading from here over the Hindu Kush to Misgar and I was tempted to try it in case my assumption about the absence of officials in Wakhan proved to be ill-founded. My information was that it was already blocked by winter snow, but in point of fact I could not face a repetition of the journey between Misgar and Gilgit, particularly as by going that way I should miss seeing the country near the Chillinji pass in which I was more interested. There is a lot of peat in the Ab-i-Wakhan valley hereabouts and that night we had a glorious peat fire in the yort. Naiad Shah got on very well with these people; his saddle-bags were opened and trade begun with the headman—an intelligent man who proved to be a bit of a mechanic. He had a complete set of tools and mended a broken pin on my watch in a workmanlike way. From him we began to hear the first mutterings about our uncertain future—the difficulty of the Irshad pass and the Afghan spies at Bozai Gumbaz. Such talk, I think, infected Naiad Shah who probably now began to evolve a private plan for himself in case mine miscarried. Neither he nor Yusuf, I'm afraid, was a lover of variety; neither cared at all how often he followed the beaten track.

For the seventeen miles to Bozai Gumbaz the track follows the right bank of the river where for the first few miles there is abundance of grass, brown and withering now before the onset of autumn. On the south bank the snow on the slopes of the Hindu Kush came down to below 14,000 ft. Apart from one small homestead where an attempt was being made to grow barley there were no habitations; the two villages marked on the map did not appear to exist and their names were not known. Some stacks of peat drying on the south bank suggested that possibly there were more people about in summer. At the present time, however, there were more 'gumbaz' than people, for I counted at least a dozen of these queer conical mud cupolas, built on a low square foundation, between the foot of the Wakhjir pass and Bozai Gumbaz. Here, on the wide grass and gravel plain between the Little Pamir river and the Ab-i-Wakhan, at the junction of two important routes, there is nothing whatever but a cluster of these 'gumbaz'. They are apparently of no antiquity and according to Lord Curzon are the tomb and memorial of one Bozai, a local chief who was killed in a fight with Hunza raiders about 1850.

From the vicinity of the pass we had been accompanied by a young Kirghiz mounted on a good-looking horse which he shared with one whom I took to be some sort of dependent, for the young man had about him an air of authority. We discovered that he was the son of the local chieftain whose 'aoul' was on the slopes across the Little Pamir river about three miles from Bozai Gumbaz. For a chief's son he was not an imposing figure; he was short-sighted and wore dark glasses which, I thought, would do little to alleviate this particular affliction. His chief claim to admiration was his very fine round velvet hat trimmed with fox fur. At first he had seemed rather stand-offish, but now he became quite affable and assured us that he would see to it that we got yaks for our journey over either the Irshad or Khora Bhort pass.

Two or three miles above its junction with the Ab-i-Wakhan we forded the Little Pamir river which was muddy and meandering—not to be compared either in beauty or volume to the blue, rushing Ab-i-Wakhan. The valley itself is wide and flat and stretches a great way until finally it is shut in by mountains far to the east, so that I could understand how travellers coming up the river might well mistake this branch for the main valley. Indeed, this is the obvious and most direct way to Tashkurghan. It is a route which is open at all seasons, and in former days when travellers had not to consider international boundaries in their choice of route it was no doubt more frequented than the Wakhjir route.

Having climbed for two or three miles up rough grass slopes we came to the chief's 'aoul' and were ushered into an empty yort reserved apparently for guests. By the grazing herds dotted all over the landscape I concluded the the chief was a man of substance, spacious in the possession of yaks. The son brought tea and a bowl of cream and Naiad Shah once again opened the question of hiring yaks in the hope of clinching the matter there and then. To our disgust he said that he must first ask his father. Father was out, counting his flocks and herds I presumed. When he did arrive he was not at all the sort of patriarch I had hoped to see. He was short and stout with a bluff John Bull air which agreed ill with his cunning blood-shot pig eyes.

He was obdurate from the start. He would not hear of our going by such an irregular route. We must go to Sarhad forty miles away to report to the Afghan official who would then send us out by the usual route over the Boroghil pass. We pointed out that while we should be charmed to meet the Afghan, to go to Sarhad would cause us serious inconvenience and loss of time, and that since no one yet knew we were here no one need ever know which way we had gone. Neither argument nor entreaty had the least effect. On the Irshad pass side of his head he was stone deaf. Should the Afghan official hear of our going out by the back door, as he assuredly would, he, the local authority, would be held responsible and would suffer penalties. I tried another tack and chaffed him about the thirty Kirghiz families, his neighbours for whom he was probably responsible, who were now entering Chinese territory without permission; but he heartily approved of that incursion on the grounds that humanity knows no frontiers. When asked why they were moving he replied cryptically that Kirghiz, Chinese, and English were all brothers. The relationship was not flattering, but I took his point.

I went to bed in very ill humour, still hoping that in the morning he would prove more accommodating, or that Naiad Shah would show more spirit or suggest some way of conciliating this Tartar. So far he had merely acquiesced in everything said, having already made up his mind that he, for one, was going back by the Wakhjir. I discovered later that he had bartered some cloth at the last yort for twelve seers of butter which he had arranged to pick up on the way back. Every man is supposed to have his price, but it did not occur to me to try to bribe Father, for paper money would have had no attractions for one whose real wealth was probably immense, and although a camera or a watch might have tempted him I did not think the occasion called for such a sacrifice. After all it was only forty miles to Sarhad, and when the Afghan there had got over his surprise and, possibly, delight at meeting strangers, he would probably be glad enough to get rid of us by the shortest route. Even from the Boroghil route we could still traverse back on the other side of the Hindu Kush to the Chillinji pass with the loss of no more than a few days. However, the time for bribery had gone, for according to Naiad Shah this 'unconversable horse-belching Tartar' had already queered his pitch and mine by sending a swift messenger to Sarhad with news of the English invasion.

In the morning Father was no more agreeable. We sat talking about this and that amicably enough, while he admired my camera and looked into the film window expecting to see a picture, but when we returned to the question of routes 'Sarhad' was all he could say. Finally I gave in, and rather grudgingly and with some delay he found us one yak out of his many hundreds. To Naiad Shah I gave his wages and a very perfunctory blessing, for I thought, possibly wrongly, that he had shown neither zeal nor skill in playing an admittedly weak hand. All the indignation and vindictiveness that I felt for Father as the blighter of my cherished hopes, fell, as it usually does in these cases, on the luckless interpreter. All this argument about routes had passed over Yusuf's head. He took no part and seemed not to mind Naiad Shah's desertion, for his confidence in the sanctity of his 'reserved' occupation of sahib's servant seemed still unshaken.

We rode down to the junction and joined the track which follows the right bank of the river to Sarhad. Almost immediately below the junction the combined streams enter a gorge which continues with but one intermission to Sarhad nearly forty miles away. On the one bank bands of green and vermillion rock and on the other slopes of snow made the scene weird and wild. Two or three miles down on a rock knoll above the river is a 'gumbaz' of roughly hewn stone. This is Karwan Balasi which Sir Aurel Stein identified as the 'Hall of the Red Buddha' mentioned in the account of the successful expedition of the Chinese general, Kao Hsien Chi, against a Tibetan army in Yasin in the year A.D. 747. This remarkable man marched three columns from Sinkiang by different routes, concentrated them at Sarhad, crossed the Boroghil and the Darkot (15,400 ft.) passes in the face of strong opposition, and led his victorious force down through Yasin to Gilgit.

At this point I noticed on the south side of the river the track which leads to the Kirghiz 'aoul' of Baikra and thence in one day to the Irshad or Khora Bhort pass. I halted our small party and sat down to think things out. Naiad Shah's example infected me; like him I began to wonder whether we had not seen enough of Wakhan and this appeared to be our last chance of getting out. But how? The yak driver had his orders which he dared not disobey, and if I abandoned the yak and my kit, within an hour the driver would be telling his story to Father who would be quite capable of having us stopped. From this it followed inexorably that the driver must be rendered incapable of movement or somehow eliminated, and I had got as far as pondering the questionable wisdom of this step and whether Yusuf would be either a willing or a useful accomplice in crimes of violence, when a party of men and yaks appeared coming up the gorge. As the omens were evidently unpropitious, with a troubled mind I gave the order to go on.

Some ten miles down, the barrenness of the gorge is interrupted by an extensive grass 'maidan'. Here yaks were grazing and at the far end was a small Tajik settlement. We rode up to it, for now I had a vague hope that by taking advantage of a full moon we might persuade them to help us to do a moonlight flit to Baikra and thence across the border. But there were too many people about for any private conversation; there were several mounted Kirghiz visitors and a number of newly arrived Tajik settlers busy building a stone house.

From this point the gorge closed in relentlessly. 'Beyond Hyde Park', said Sir Fopling Flutter, 'all is desert', and beyond here all is gorge on a violent and stupendous scale. By dark, when we had made good fifteen of the forty miles to Sarhad which I was bent on reaching next day in order to put our fortunes quickly to the test, we reached Langar where there is a 'gumbaz'. We went inside to cook. At 2 a.m. of a bright moonlight night we started again. Gorges and deserts are best traversed by night, and when day broke, except for a graceful snow spire on the south side, nothing was revealed that would not better have remained hidden in the soft obscurity of moonlight.

The track lay a thousand feet above the river, but some twelve miles from Langar we were obliged to descend to river-level to cross the Dara Jilga coming down from the Nicholas range to the north. The ford, a dangerous one full of boulders, was taken by the yak without a stumble, but Yusuf's nag which I was riding came down twice, nearly drowning himself and his rider. Yusuf wisely went round by a footbridge. Having laboriously regained the height we had lost, we had breakfast. It was 9 a.m., more than half the journey had been done, but now the mountains were drawing in closer and steeper about the river, forcing the path farther away and ever higher, until at last it left the river altogether to cross a great projecting spur by the high Daliz pass.

The pass was steep and deep in snow, both yak and pony were by now tired and lagging, and near the top when I was well ahead and alone, I met two men on foot—a dirty, unsavoury pair, one of whom seemed to be wearing some semblance of a uniform. Their manners were no better than their appearance. They shouted at me truculently and unintelligibly, so I waved them airily in the direction of my followers and passed on. This would not do. They came after me shouting still louder at which I turned round. One of them bawled out questioningly 'Russi?' To which I, not caring much what they might think, made a gesture indicative of assent. The effect was all that I could have wished. Without a word they turned and went on their way.

On the other side where the track begins to drop steeply down a stony gully, I sat down to wait for the others whom to my disgust I saw were now accompanied by the two low comedians. The passportless Yusuf, hearing already the clank of chains, informed me in his most mournful tones that they were two policemen who had been sent to look for us. The word 'police' seems to be current in these parts and it had an unwelcome sound. Not that I felt a criminal, but in the last month or so I had seen something of Central Asiatic police and soldiers and had not liked what I had seen. A slovenly uniform and a rifle of antique European make are their stock in trade. Having done so much, Authority then considers it has done enough—that it has in fact provided for them handsomely—which is perfectly correct. For, armed with the power which such things confer, their possessors need take little thought for the morrow what they shall eat or what they shall drink, for any Kirghiz, Turki, or Wakhi, who is not in uniform must provide. The police at Sarhad proved to be true to this dirty, parasitic type—a queer mixture of buffoonery and brutality.

At Sarhad the Oxus burst from the gorge and, rejoicing in its freedom, spreads in meandering streams over a wide flat stony valley. The valley-floor is in fact all river-bed so that the cultivated land lies on the lower slopes of the hills where small streams fed from the snows above can be used to irrigate the fields. Wheat, a beardless barley, beans and peas, are grown, and since the height is over 10,000 ft. it follows that the valley must be a regular sun-trap. Even so in early October many of the crops were not yet harvested. On the north side, where all the cultivation lies, there are some half-dozen widely scattered villages of mud and stone houses each with its inevitable patch of white poplar saplings. Opposite on the south side a wide green valley leads gently to a broad gap flanked by a noble array of snow mountains—the Boroghil pass, the high road to India.

Lying thus on the route from India and on that from Badakshan by the Oxus valley, Sarhad is of some importance, for it is the last place at which east-bound travellers can obtain grain before crossing the Pamirs and reaching the oases of Sinkiang. In accordance with this importance the Afghans have here a frontier post of police and soldiers under a 'sirdar' whose duty and pleasure it is to obstruct all travellers, however important or however insignificant, and whether they are provided with credentials or not. In 1890 Mr and Mrs Littledale (the first and probably the only English lady to visit the Pamirs) were detained for twelve days, and four years later Lord Curzon, who was a guest of the Amir who had himself warned the post of his guest's coming, would have been detained, too, as a Russian spy had not his party been in superior numbers to the Afghans. He reported the too zealous 'sirdar' to the Amir and the sequel he relates as follows: 'The Amir instituted inquiries and the reply of the now frightened "sirdar" was really so ingenious as to extort my reluctant admiration. "He was still awaiting", he said, "the arrival of the great English lord sahib, whose coming had been announced by His Majesty the Amir, and who would no doubt appear in uniform with an escort of a thousand men. In the meantime two of the lord sahib's servants (i.e. Curzon and his companion Lennard) had already passed through with an insignificant following. He himself would continue diligently to await the great lord". I heard afterwards that this polite intention on the part of the sirdar had been frustrated by an imperative summons to Kabul; but what may have since transpired I do not know.'

CHAPTER FIFTEEN

Sarhad to Ishkashim—Open Arrest

THOUGH the tempo of change nowadays is everywhere rapid, in the East change is traditionally slower. As it had been the custom to detain travellers at Sarhad fifty years ago then assuredly they would be detained today. But I was not to know that. Had I been aware how strait was the way, how fine the mesh, I should certainly have withdrawn discreetly with Naiad Shah by way of the Wakhjir; but as it was I marched more or less blithely, though very tired, to my fate. The first house we came to was the police barracks which promptly emitted a noisy crowd of seedy, undersized ruffians (at Sarhad there are more police than inhabitants) eager to congratulate our captors and to inspect the captives, for so I suspected we had now become. The Afghan commander's house, to which we had to go, was a mile or so further on. The inhabitants were too busy with their threshing and winnowing to care about us, but the police alone were numerous enough to play the part of the crowd at what might have been the triumph of one of the less successful of the Roman Consuls, whose poor best was one disconsolate shaggy barbarian and his smooth but still more disconsolate slave.

Presently the 'sirdar', whom I took to be a Pathan, appeared clad in a smartly cut grey greatcoat with brass buttons. He spoke only Pushtu so neither he, nor Yusuf, nor I, had any pleasantries to exchange. He gave us one cold look, the word 'Ingreze' was spoken by someone, either in extenuation or reproach, and he strode away to his house. He was a tall dignified-looking chap with hook nose and severe eyes—a stern path-of-duty man, I felt—who in his subsequent rare appearances outside stalked gravely round, a blue turban on his head and a flowing 'chapkan' flung loosely over his shoulders. He looked somewhat like a young but earnest bird-of-prey whose dignity was only slightly impaired by the squalor of his cage, which was a mud and stone hovel, distinguishable from the others by the presence of window frames, one covered with nothing and the other with paper. This house also did duty as an office, to which there came a surprising number of callers at all hours of the day. Behind was another hovel which served as ~hen and guard-room combined where the police on duty waited patiently empird-of-prey's calls for tea or for a crime to be committed. I pitched my over ~le and a guard was immediately posted.

Hindustani and ~ling as I was breakfasting at the tent door in the sun the 'sirdar' leisurely survey of his domain, and then stalked gravely ~rs. One of his myrmidons had a few words of vile this unsatisfactory medium I was given to understand

632

that we must remain here until orders for our release or disposal had come from the Commissar (ominous word) at Ishkashim. Hastily scanning my map, which came to an end eighty miles west of Sarhad, I could find no trace of Ishkashim until in the margin in small lettering I read: 'Ishkashim 30 m.' My heart sank. The distance alone, coupled with the presence of a 'Commissar', boded no good. As Mrs Elton remarked of Birmingham: 'One had not great hopes from Ishkashim, there was something direful about the sound of it.' And how long would I have to wait for this permission? Four days, they said, and a messenger had already left. It seemed little enough for a journey of over a hundred miles each way and I wondered whether a messenger had really gone or whether this was merely a conventional opening calling for a bid. But the aspect of the bird-of-prey was not encouraging in that respect.

We were quite ready for a day off, so the first day of our captivity passed away pleasantly enough as I lay in the sun reading and smoking. Ignorant of how seriously our captors regarded their prize I began to look about for a mountain to climb; if four days must be spent here they might be well spent, but on this side was nothing but slag heaps and scree slopes, all the climb-worthy mountains were on the other side of the river and to reach them I would need transport and a camp. I thought I might become a ticket-of-leave man by asking the 'sirdar' for a few days leave to explore the surrounding country, which, since (as I learnt later) I was regarded as a dangerous spy, was an assumption not unlike that of the boy who having murdered his parents asked to be acquitted on the grounds that he was an orphan.

Next morning the bird-of-prey again stepped over to my tent for his morning cigarette, this time alone. I was ready for him, and began playing ostentatiously with a spare watch I had with me. When this evoked no sign of interest I was reduced to making vulgar movements of thumb and fingers suggestive of the passing of money. He was not agreeably impressed by this, for he sent for his Hindustani scholar and asked sharply what I meant. I quickly changed the subject, for he was either that *rara avis* an incorruptible official, or else he really had sent word to his superior at Ishkashim and was no longer a free agent. All these people, I thought (Father had done the same) act too impetuously and are too eager to divest themselves of responsibility, thus depriving themselves of the possibility of hearing something to their advantage.

After this rebuff I went for a walk to cool off, but I had not gone a hundred yards before a couple of police were in pursuit clutching at me. Who did I think I was to go wandering about Wakhan like this? High words passed, and to prevent being dragged back I staged a sit down strike which had the effect of making one of them go back for instructions. I was allowed to make a restricted tour of the village accompanied by a guard.

About midday on the third day I was greatly surprised by hearing that a messenger from Ishkashim had just arrived. It seemed hardly possible, but so it was. However, nothing (except the journey) was to be done in hurry and an hour passed before the bird-of-prey flapped his way slowly and solemnly to my tent. I had some misgivings as to the purport of the message, but hope was uppermost. I rose and greeted the 'sirdar', trying hard to suppress a smile of satisfaction at our impending release and succeding quite easily when I learnt that the Boroghil was not for us, but that we were to go to Ishkashim and thence, if we were lucky, out of Chitral. This was bad news. Even if we were allowed to go out by Chitral we should be still farther from Gilgit where there was my kit and two months' mail, but I feared even more that the same gambit would be played again. I saw ourselves passing through the whole hierarchy of Afghan officials, each curious to see English spy, each afraid to let us go, until finally we reached the fountain-head at Kabul, heaven alone knew how many week's journey away. I was concerned for poor Yusuf who had to get himself and his pony to Srinagar and back to Kashgar before the passes closed, and more nearly for myself since tobacco and sugar were running short. There was no help for it. A fat donkey was provided for my kit and after the coolest of farewells off we went in charge of the inevitable escort of two blackguards on one pony.

However uncertain our future I rejoiced to be once more on the move and on a route both historic and unusual. Although the upper Oxus valleys have been visited by many, few Europeans and possibly no Englishman have followed the valley as far as Ishkashim since Wood made his famous journey to Victoria Lake a hundred years ago. A great many travellers have seen the valley above Sarhad and a few have been down to Kila Panja where the Pamir river from Victoria Lake joins the main stream. In 1873 Col. Gordon's party of the Forsyth Mission to Kashgar went down to Kila Panja where they were stopped, but a native surveyor, travelling under the obscure generic title of the 'Munshi', went on to do a remarkable journey, following the river for a hundred miles byond Ishkashim, before returning to India via Kabul. The 'Mirza' was another of these nameless explorers who were sent out by the Indian Survey Department in the latter half of the last century to unravel geographical problems in remote trans-frontier regions inaccessible to Europeans. In 1868–69 the 'Mirza' made a route-survey from Faizabad to Ishkashim, thence up the Oxus to the Chakmaktin lake and across the Pamirs to Kashgar, finally returning to India by Yarkand and the Karakoram pass. The most noted of these 'pundits', as they were called, were two men from Milam in Garhwal, Nain Singh and Kishen Singh, or 'A-K', to give him his more famous name, both of whom explored extensively in Tibet in the 1860's and 1870's.

We forded the river to the south side without difficulty and stopped for the night at a little hamlet by some wonderfully clear springs some ten miles from Sarhad. It became bitterly cold as soon as the sun disappeared. Beyond bawling their loudest when they wanted us to stop or go on our escort, of whom only one had a rifle, was not overbearing, though the armed man never let me out of his sight, sticking closer than a brother. At night, curiously enough, he assumed that no sane man would think of running away. I was allowed to sleep in the tent while they and Yusuf took up snugger and dirtier quarters in some house. Undesirable though their company was in such strange and interesting surroundings, it meant that I could cast aside dull care and leave them, the agents of the Afghan government whose guest I was, to worry about food, shelter, and transport for my kit if not for myself. And I must say they did it well—ponies, milk, and good mutton never failed us—but the entire cost fell upon the unfortunate inhabitants.

We travelled twenty-one miles next day to the village of Baba Tangi through a narrow but pleasing valley whose monotonous brown slopes would suddenly become aflame with the bright copper of a patch of dwarf willow. Near Baba Tangi, a large village, the river flows through a rocky gorge narrow enough to be bridged by a few logs. Like all the villages of the upper Oxus it lies on the flank of an alluvial fan, but unlike most of the rivers which feed these fans this one descends abruptly from a nearby glacier above which rises a very noble mountain of some 20,000 ft. Although we were not allowed by our escort to talk to anyone, I tried without success to learn the name of this Hindu Kush peak.

Early in the afternoon though it was, I should not have minded stopping here if only to worship metaphorically at the foot of this fine mountain, but the escort, desirous of emulating the speed of the Sarhad courier, talked of pushing on to Kila Panja twenty miles away. Two miles farther on they thought better of it and pulled up at a very squalid village, vowing that there was no other within reach. As usual a sheep was slaughtered and poor and dirty though this place was its mutton was superbly succulent. As I ate I thought of Manning's description of Phari Dzong, that notoriously dirty Tibetan town on the road to Everest: 'Dirt, dust, grease, smoke, misery, but good mutton.'

Next morning after only two hour's marching I was not in the least surprised to come upon a much more pleasing village where we could have stopped, but it would have needed more than a trifle like that to disturb the calm, placid, unruffled impudence of our two ruffians. They laughed it off shamelessly, not even feigning to be astonished at the existence of this village. The road now left the river to climb steeply for a thousand feet before descending gradually to meet the river again at its junction with the Pamir river. Yet another thousand feet above the track smooth glacier-polished slabs of red granite glistened in the sun. At the junction we met a standing patrol of two soldiers which was apparently posted here to watch the river, at this point the Afghan-Russian frontier. Here the river-bed is some two miles wide with willow jungle, sand-banks, and islands, while the water flows in several easily forded channels between the numerous sand-banks.

The Pamir river, coming down from the Great Pamir and Victoria Lake, appeared sightly less in volume than the Ab-i-Wakhan and the valley did not have the appearance of being the main valley. At the Bozai Gumbaz junction I had thought that a traveller might be in doubt as to which valley was the main one, but here it seemed that there was little room for mistake. Wood himself when faced with this question, having to make up his mind which of the two valleys to follow, wrote: 'To my eye the stream of Sarhad (Ab-i-Wakhan) appeared the larger, but the Wakhanis held a different opinion.' As Lord Curzon tartly observes: 'Had he followed his eye instead of his guides the true source of the Oxus might have been determined half a century earlier and the two governments of Great Britain and Russia might have been spared the long controversy over the ignorant agreement.'

While the men-of-war chatted with our escort I added one more to my list of memorable bathes and afforded them fresh matter for conversation. In summer the river spreads over the whole bed and here, beside the track, the receding water had left behind it a series of very deep, clear blue pools. A rock ten feet high was my springboard from which more than once I revelled in 'the cool silver shock of the plunge in a pool's living water'. A few miles below the junction is Kila Panja, a big wide-spreading village with an old castle and a more modern mud-walled fort in the usual Asiatic style covering nearly two acres of ground. But of much more interest was the view across the river to Russia where I was astonished to see a lorry travelling along a road and followed a little later by another with a huge trailer. What appeared to be the continuation of this road could be seen as a faint straight trace along the hillside up the valley of the Pamir which, above the junction, rises fairly sharply.

If the sight of a horse makes the traveller lame, what must a lorry do? I was a little put out to find that civilization[1] had penetrated to the upper Oxus, but I should not have scorned the offer of a lift to Ishkashim had its blessings embraced both banks of that river. On the Russian side there were two or three small villages each with an imposing-looking white building which I imagined must be the H.Q. of the local O.G.P.U.—or possibly the jail or hospital, two necessary adjustments adjuncts in the advance of civilization.

In the night a furious gale blew which left behind it a thick pall of dust haze hanging low over the valley. On the other bank trucks were astir early and even at night the citizens over there seemed to gad about. Lying in my tent I frequently heard the 'revving' of an engine in low gear, and it was a mortifying reflexion to think that which ever way I travelled on my side of the river, several weeks of marching would elapse before I should be able to avail myself of a lorry.

A few miles lower down we crossed two vast gravel fans. The fan is a sort of convex delta formed by the deposit of stones, gravel, and sand brought down by the torrent rushing through a narrow ravine. From its apex at the mouth of the ravine the surface of the broadly convex cone of debris is scored with water channels spread out like the ribs of a fan, so that the crossing of a large one is a troublesome busines. One mounts steadily over the loose, rough surface, crossing one shallow water course after the other, expecting every minute to arrive at the summit of the slope, only to be disappointed as new sections of the cone intervene until at last the central rib is reached and the process is repeated down the other side. Cultivation is usually found tucked away between the edge of the fan and the hillside adjacent to the ravine. Between the nallahs and their respective fans, which may be five or ten miles apart, there are, of course, no villages. The intervening space may be either arid, stony waste or salt flats with a strong growth of wiry grass. There are many signs of old moraines and in the river at one place there was a high island which was probably part of an old moraine cut off by the river.

Having crossed these we marched for a brief space alongside the river, now confined in a narrow channel barely fifty yards across, while the motor road

1 'Transportation is Civilization.' Vide Kipling's *With the Night Mail.*

ran close along the other bank. At midday while we were changing ponies a storm of wind and dust developed and raged for two hours. This cleared the air, the sun came out, and as I looked back I could see the great snow mountain, marked on our maps as 23,000 ft., a few miles north-west of Kila Panja on the Russian side in the Shakhdara range. In a report on Russian post-war climbing activity it is stated that in 1946 a party climbed this, the highest peak of the Shakhdara range, to which they attributed a height of 7,000 metres, and gave the name of 'Karl Marx'. The giving of personal names to mountains is usually a mistake. Fame is often ephemeral, the mountain is always the same. Perhaps the patron saint of revolutionary communism is worthy of commemoration, and I can think of several ways in which it might be done, but a more unfitting memorial than a great mountain to a malignant little man it would be hard to imagine.

That night at Pigish I pitched my tent in an apricot orchard. These were the first fruit trees I had seen in Wakhan, for we were now for the first time below 9,000 ft., but the trees were poor and stunted. Pigish lies so close under a spur of the Hindu Kush that the October sun does not reach it until 9 o'clock. Only at this comparatively late hour did we feel it warm enough to start. The next village was even worse off, for at 10 o'clock when we rode through it was still in shadow, the grass white with frost and ice on the water furrows. Here the fields of short-stemmed wheat, less than a foot high, were still unreaped. In most villages, however, threshing was in full swing with mixed teams of six, eight, or even ten bullocks and donkeys tramping in a circle on the threshing-floor from dawn till dusk. The man or boy, who walks behind driving them round, carries a large wicker spoon in which to catch the droppings.

Beyond Warup where we halted for lunch the motor-road and the penitential way ran for some miles within 200 yards of each other, separated only by the river which in one place, from bank to bank, was barely forty yards across. It was an easy place to bridge, but there was, of course, none as there seems to be no intercourse whatever between the peoples on either side. It seems a pity that so unnatural a boundary as a river should be adopted as a frontier since the people of a valley are essentially a unit. A watershed is the obvious frontier, and heaven knows there are enough of them in these parts. If the Hindu Kush had to be ruled out as bringing two mighty opposites into actual contact there was the Shakhdara range and its continuation the Great Pamir.

I had already counted ten lorries that day, but here where the two roads ran side by side we met none. I was not sorry since it might have worried the Russians had they seen a Wakhi walking along dressed in khaki shorts and carrying an ice-axe. Ten lorries a day may not seem to be an extravagant use of transport, but I would have been interested to learn what they carried, for superficially the Russian side appeared more poverty-stricken than the Wakhan. The villages were fewer and smaller. The arable land, too, was less extensive, as in general the Oxus hugs the north side of the valley. Moreover, the side nallahs on which cultivation depends were deep-cut, short, and less generous, for there are few glaciers on that side and the mountains wore their snow covering with an air of unusualness. On the south side the nallahs are longer, and up them one could sometimes catch glimpses of true snow-mountains, upon which the snow lay with the assurance of eternity, untouched by time or season. To see these fine mountains almost hidden from the sight of man, unnamed, never visited, seemed a prodigal waste of beauty; their sole, unconscious purpose was to provide water enough to grow wheat to keep, perhaps, 500 Wakhi families rather unnecessarily alive.

We camped six miles beyond Warup. It was now 10 October, we had left Sarhad on the 5th, and according to my map which terminated here, Ishkashim was still twenty-four miles away. For the last two days we had been told that it was 'nazdik', which in India, as I well knew, is an elastic term meaning anything from a hundred yards to five miles; but in Wakhan I found its elasticity boundless, or at any rate stretching to fifty miles, which the Sarhad courier, no doubt, would regard as a short day. At three in the afternoon we reached a large and very delightful village on a fertile flat watered by a laughing amber torrent; there were many tall poplars and shady willows, while on a cliff overlooking brook and village was a sort of grotto decorated with flags which served as a mosque. I made sure this was Ishkashim though I could see nothing which looked worthy to house a Commissar or his satellites. I began making anxious inquiries for I was in a feverish and, as it turned out, a foolish haste to meet this gentleman upon whom our immediate future seemed largely to depend. But our escort advised me to relax since Ishkashim was still someway off.

CHAPTER SIXTEEN

Ishkashim—Close Arrest

ISHKASHIM lies two or three miles back from the Oxus and at this point the river begins its great bend to the north. To reach it from this village of Qazi Deh, where we now were, the road crosses an intervening shoulder before descending to the wide Ishkashim valley formed by a stream which comes down from Shad Ishtragh, a 19,000 ft. peak on the Chitral border about fifteen miles away. Ishkashim marks the eastern extremity of Badakshan and the beginning of Wakhan of which it is the administrative centre. On one side of the stream is the small village whose extensive terraced fields fall away to the Oxus, while on the other is the official quarter—'Whitehall'—comprising the usual mud-walled fort and barracks and the unpretentious private residence of the Commissar where all business is transacted.

We reached the village at 5 o'clock. There was not the bazaar which I had expected the principal place of Wakhan might possess, and all the people were out in the fields cutting and carrying the harvest. Our escort halted at the stream to button their collars and tidy themselves so that their presence would be slightly less displeasing to the Commissar, whom they seemed to hold in considerable respect. Neither Yusuf nor I troubled to preen our draggled feathers or even to wash, a formality which I had observed as recently as three days ago when I had bathed at Kila Panja; travel-stained, hard-used, poor but honest men who had once known better days, and now worthy of compassion, seemed to be our best line.

A sentry with some pretension to smartness stood at the gate of the high-walled compound of the Commissar's house. Nearby was gathered a small crowd of idlers, petitioners, and the tethered horses of visitors. We were told brusquely to wait, but after a bit I was led into the compound through a small garden surrounded by flower-beds and the veranda of the living-quarters, and then into another walled garden with more flower-beds, in the middle of which was an oval cemented dais about three feet high on which some half-dozen Afghans squatted on carpets. Mindful of the Chinese precept, 'When you bow, bow low', I paid my ample respects, whereupon I was invited to climb up on to the dais. Tea was being served in very small cups, a hubble-bubble was being passed round, while a packet of American cigarettes lay on the carpet. I filled my own pipe from my last tin and generously offered the Commissar a cigarette from my last packet. I had no difficulty in picking him out. He was a short, thick-set man about 35 years old, wearing a blue turban and a handsome embroidered white 'chapkan' which failed to conceal a Napoleonic paunch. His full features, too, were not unlike Napoleon's, had that great man affected a Hitler moustache.

Whether this was a garden party, a reception committee assembled on my behalf, or an official conference, I could not tell. Conversation between us was practically impossible, and had it been possible I could think of no topic which would be suited to or explanatory of my presence at this gathering, whether it was a garden party or, as seemed more probable, a court martial. Willing to please I produced my passport, half hoping that one of the many visa stamps it contained might be mistaken for an Afghan one. It was examined curiously but it failed to produce any general expression of respect or benevolence, and when it finally reached a scowling sour-faced man, whom I was presently to discover was the Chief of Police, he began comparing the photograph with its purported original then sitting opposite to him smoking a pipe. As became his office his suspicions were at once aroused. This was not surprising considering that I was now wearing a beard, that the photograph had been taken before the war, and that he was looking at it upside down. Bacon tells us that there is nothing makes a man suspect much, more than to know little. This man, I was to find, was a most dangerous combination of abysmal ignorance and instantaneous deductive power.

The atmosphere engendered by a party seated on a cement dais at 6 o'clock of an October evening in Wakhan cannot be warm, but when the Chief of Police began drawing attention to the invidious comparisons he was making it became perceptibly cooler. Yusuf was now introduced, but since he had no passport at all and no one could understand Turki his appearance gratified nobody except, perhaps, the Grand Inquisitor. To him we were already a couple of rather amateurish spies upon whom his deductive talents, though they might be exercised, could hardly be sharpened. An uncouth individual who was suspected of talking Hindustani was then summoned. He talked in a fast screech, so fast as to be hardly understandable even had it been in English, but I caught a word here and there and through him tried to convey to the court that though we were bound for Gilgit and had been obliged by the Commissar to come so far out of our way, we bore no malice and would be content with Chitral—at which they seemed amused. This mangler of Hindustani was in reality a soldier, as I think they all were, but he was in mufti and appeared to act as scullion and purveyor of the Commissar's hubble-bubble in his spare time. Most of the men, I found, only wore uniform when on duty, either to save wear and tear or because there were not enough to go round.

The sun had by now sunk. The Commissar rose, turned to the west, spread his carpet, and began his evening prayer. One or two of the more devout fell in behind him to follow suit while the rest continued to smoke and chat. This done the Commissar stood up and delivered a long harangue in a stern military manner directed mainly at the Grand Inquisitor. This, as we soon learnt, was our sentence and his orders, but I was yet unaware of this and when the meeting broke up I walked out through the compound and began to look about for a place where I could pitch my tent. The Chief of Police who was behind motioned me on. I followed him into another walled compound a little way off, lined on one side with a series of small rooms. It was dirty, and some lime strewn over an excavation in the middle was unpleasantly suggestive of wholesale executions and mass graves. It was not at all the sort of place I should have chosen for a camp site, but that was not the idea. At the door of one of these cells, for so they were, the Chief of Police suddenly turned on me and thrust both hands into the pockets of my windproof. I started to hand him off but I soon found a couple of soldiers, one in front and one behind, threatening me with fixed bayonets. Having gone through the upper pockets he signed to me to take off my trousers. This I refused to do. Someone then suggested it would be better done indoors so we were bundled into one of the rooms followed by the policeman and a couple of assistants.

This mud-walled room, although only about ten feet square, was not without amenities. There were a couple of chairs and half the earth floor was covered with a carpet. Yusuf and I were put on the chairs while the search party ranged themselves opposite on the carpet. All our kit—the two pony loads—was brought in and thrown on the floor between us; but before starting on this I had still to be properly 'frisked'. Accordingly I handed over my windproof trousers. These were of double thickness so the ends were slit and a search made for sewn-in papers. At last the stage was set for the big scene. My rucksack and kit-bag were unceremoniously up-ended and a pyramid of miscellaneous articles rose in front of the Grand Inquisitor. His scowl rested lovingly on this wealth of material—each piece a clue in some grotesque chain of reasoning—and he metaphorically rubbed his hands at the happy chance which had provided him with a long night's work of inquisitiveness. As for me I was well-nigh gibbering with the indignation I was unable to express at this

Seven illustrations of
the Anglo/Swiss Rakaposhi
Expedition, 1947:

33 (top) Some members of
the party: Hans Gyr (left),
Angdawa, Angtingit, Phurba
and Robert Kappeler.

34 Tilman relaxing during
the approach march.

35 (bottom) The polo
ground in Babusar.
'In these vertical valleys,
horizontal space is scarce
so the ground is usually a
long narrow strip (200yds
× 40yds) with a low stone
wall bounding the two
longer sides.'

36 (top) Approaching the site of Base Camp on the Kunti Glacier.

37 (centre) The Camp on the South West Ridge of Rakaposhi.

38 (bottom) On the r[...] between the Kukuay a[...] Batura glaciers.

39 The western slopes of Rakaposhi (25,550ft.) with the Biro Glacier in the foreground. The South West Ridge is on the right, the obvious rounded snow peak being the Monk's Head. The final part of the North West Ridge comes in on the left. This valley was the expedition's proposed 'corridor' route to the peak, but after reconnaissance it was considered too dangerous. Tilman and Phurba pushed a route up the glacier to the avalanche-threatened snow basin (centre right), but then judged that further progress towards the Monk's Head would be unwise. A route to the ridge was eventually found from the Kunti Glacier to the south (right), but the attempt failed at the Monk's Head. This proved to be the eventual ascent-route, but there were three further attempts before the mountain was finally climbed in 1958 by Mike Banks and Tom Patey. *Photo: Mike Banks*

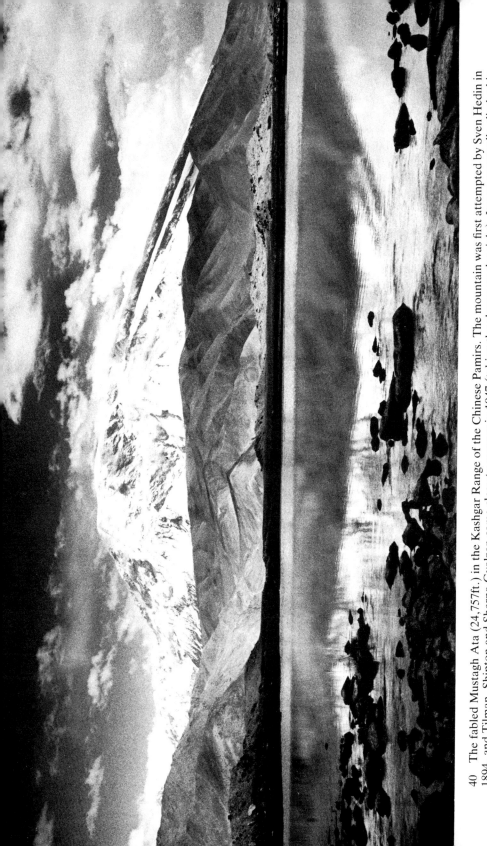

40 The fabled Mustagh Ata (24,757ft.) in the Kashgar Range of the Chinese Pamirs. The mountain was first attempted by Sven Hedin in 1894, and Tilman, Shipton and Sherpa Gyalzen came close to success in 1947 (taking the slopes on the right). It was eventually climbed in 1956 by a Sino-Soviet expedition. *Photo: John Cleare*

41 A Kasak yort – the ubiquitous dwelling of the nomadic peoples of Central Asia. 'The yort consists of a circular framework of willow sticks . . . covered first with a reed mat and then with felt. On top of this, curving willow rods support the felt roof, in the centre of which a hole about five feet across serves the dual purpose of window and chimney . . . three yaks can carry a yort and its furniture.'

42 The Dodge mail truck at Suchow. 'The driver leans nonchalantly against the cab; his assistant, in well-cut trousers, is on the left and in between is the postmaster.'

43 Kazaks in Urumchi. 'Contrary to rule this particular pair of centaurs have dismounted.'

44 The main street, Urumchi. The pony drawing the shandrydan is harnessed in Russian fashion.

45 Schokalsky Peak (c.15,000ft.), in the Bogdo Ola group of the Tien Shan.

48 (above) Travel in Central Asia. 'In the distance, tucked away at the foot
of pine-clad slopes we saw some yorts for which we made at full speed like
homing pigeons. The baggage train (seen here) had to approach more sedately.
Hill Billy, heavily armed, brings up the rear.'

46 and 47 (opposite page) Two views of Bodgo Ola from the East Ridge.
The lower picture clearly shows the principal summits of the group, from right
to left, East (the highest), Centre and West, above the upper basin of
the Chigo Glacier

49   Langtang Lirung (23,769ft.), the main peak of the Langtang Himal seen from Paldor in the Ganesh Himal. *Photo: John Cleare*

50 (below left) 'Tabet from the south. Tilman and Lloyd climbed the mountain from the east (right).'

51 (below right top) 'Our camp on the roof of the fort at Rasua Garhi.' 52 (bottom right) Tilman and Lloyd crossed into Tibet briefly during their Langtang explorations but were soon detected by 'a stout, affable official, in Homberg hat and dark spectacles, sent expressly for the purpose of reminding us that we were on the wrong side of the Lende Khola'. Tensing, on the left, appears embarrassed as Tilman records the event.

53 A view up the Langsisa (East Langtang) Glacier to Dorje Lakpa (22,930ft.). Bhuadda is the peak on the right. *Photo: John Cleare*

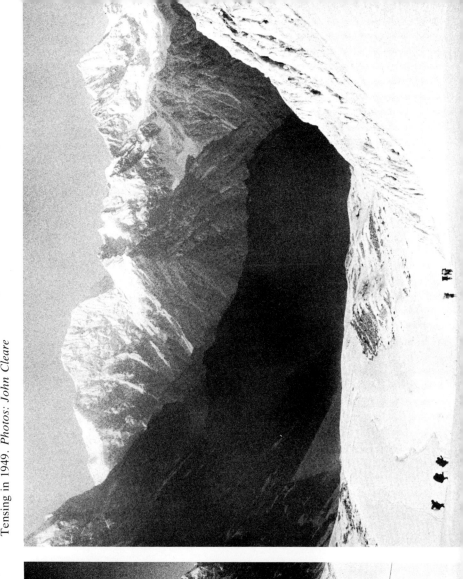

54 and 55 The north slopes of the pass to the east of Fluted Peak (left). The peaks north of the Langtang Glacier are seen in the right-hand photo – Shalbachum (left) and probably Kyunka Ri (right) – divided by cols that may have been those reached by Tilman and Tensing in 1949. *Photos: John Cleare*

56 57 and 58 (left)
Photographs taken
during the attempt
on Annapurna 4 in
1950. The lowest
picture shows
Annapurna 2 on
the left.

59 (above) Members of the Anglo-American group that reconnoitred the Khumbu approaches to Everest in 1950, seen at Thyangboche Monastery: 'Mrs Cowles is on the left; in front is Mr Oscar Houston, draped with the recently presented ceremonial scarf and charm locket; Dr Charles Houston is standing behind the excessively gross lama, and Anderson Bakewell is on the right.'

60 (right) 'The young abbot could hardly be expected to mingle with the mob seen in the previous picture. Here he is seated in state with his tea equipage, bell, and all the tools of his trade. Above the throne hang three temple banners. The picture was taken by Mrs E. S. Cowles.'

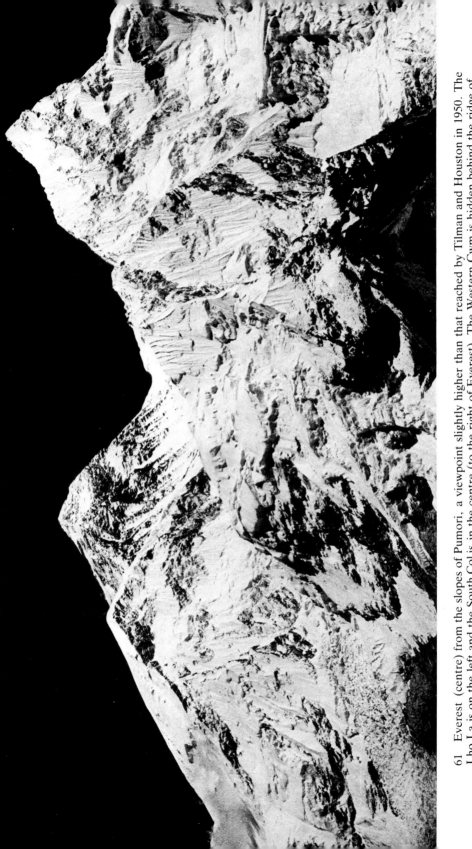

61 Everest (centre) from the slopes of Pumori, a viewpoint slightly higher than that reached by Tilman and Houston in 1950. The Lho La is on the left and the South Col is in the centre (to the right of Everest). The Western Cwm is hidden behind the ridge of Nuptse (right). The view from this position, combined with pre-war studies of the Western Cwm from the Lho La, left the tantalizing question of the difficulty of the slopes leading to the South Col from the Western Cwm unanswered, until Shipton's party got a better

high-handed business and the rough treatment bestowed on my precious possessions.

One assistant, having first satisfied his own curiosity, handed each article to his superior, while the other, armed with paper and pen, made an inventory. Pieces of clothing were scrutinized, felt, and thrown in one corner without comment, but I was fiercely challenged to explain by demonstration the significance of a silk scarf and a hair-brush. Then they found the money, of which I had a considerable amount in single rupee notes and coin and Chinese paper dollars—the latter of no great intrinsic value but useful for spills. All had to be laboriously counted, note by note, anna by anna, so that by the time that was done my indignation had cooled and I had taken to making sarcastic suggestions which, though they were not understood, were not liked. Then came a packet of 'Bromo'. This baffled them, but that too was counted leaf by leaf until at length arithmetic failed and I helpfully supplied the answer as printed on the packet. Camera and films, of which I had about twenty exposed and a few unexposed, excited less joy than I had feared. They wanted to open a few of the films to see what was inside, but I managed to express such convincing consternation that they surprisingly desisted. then came the find of the evening—a photo-electric exposure-meter. The Grand Inquisitor's eyes fairly sparkled with satisfaction. 'Telegram' he almost yelled in his excitement, meaning apparently that it was some cunning wireless gadget for sending messages, and a soldier was immediately dispatched with it to the Commissar. Solid 'Meta' fuel puzzled them, but after I had failed to persuade them to eat some I had to demonstrate its use by lighting it. Maps, photographs, books, excited almost as much interest as the 'telegram' and each was carefully examined every way up but the right one. The double bottom of my kit-bag was slit open, every seam of my sleeping-bag felt, and finally the tent turned inside out. It would have puzzled a conjuror to conceal anything from these hawks. Nevertheless, when the search was finished the Grand Inquisitor coolly asked me where were my pistol and binoculars.

Yusuf's gear was then overhauled and I was surprised at the oddities my companion in misery saw fit to carry, most of it presumably for trade—many embroidered Turki caps, copper teapots, a pair of new riding boots, yards of cloth, atta, a bag of bread hard as rock, some 'kurut', and numerous little packages of queer-looking powders, pills, bark, whose use the Afghans seemed to comprehend perfectly. It was now getting on for 11 p.m. The search had lasted for some four hours, so that I rejoiced to see a large tray of food brought in. 'All sorrows are alleviated by eating bread', but here we had a very rich mutton stew and a large bowl of yoghourt which they called 'mos'. Yusuf, overwhelmed by this last turn in our misfortunes, was now sobbing quietly to himself and would not eat. Loud challenges and slapping of butts outside heralded the arrival of the Commissar and the return of my exposure-meter which he now handed back. I had already noticed a single wire mounted on poplar poles near the Commissar's house, and it was the telephone operator, the local expert on Western gadgets, who had been asked to decide the significance of the exposure-meter. I learnt later that this line was connected to Faizabad 100 miles north-west.

The Commissar gravely surveyed my belongings littering the floor like the wares of a junk shop, and while the Inquisitor handed him everything which he considered compromising or dangerous, such as maps, compass, books, diaries, papers, passport, photos, pencils, my pocket-knife and ice-axe and Yusuf's sheath-knife, I was bidden to pack the rest. This gave me the opportunity of spiriting away the camera and films. The only light came from a cracked 'Dietz' lantern, so that it would have been equally easy for the Inquisitor or his assistants to spirit away a few rupees, but as far as I could tell not an anna stuck to their fingers. Before leaving us to digest our sorrows they told us that there were two sentries by the door and that if we wanted to go outside during the night we must knock on the door which was unlocked—failure to do this would have fatal results.

Next day, except for two soldier servants who brought our meals from the Commissar's own mess, no one came near us. The food bore out the promise of the Commissar's paunch. He was no ascetic. He liked rich food and plenty of it, and a capable cook saw that he got it. For breakfast we had bread, fresh butter, a plateful of sugar in lieu of jam, and pale scented tea. For lunch and supper the changes were rung, not too frequently, on spicy pilaus, rich stews, fish from the Oxus, and always a liberal helping of yoghourt as a corrective. Yusuf did not fare quite so well for his meals were brought from the guard-room.

Even so between these welcome gastronomic landmarks there were many long hours to contemplate the helpless degradation of captivity, our complete subjection to the will of this taciturn, suspicious Commissar and his armed blackguards outside, and our problematic future. There was nothing to read and nothing to do except stare through the open door at the officious sentry outside who stared back at us. The guards, who lived within the compound, carried out their sanitary duties under the compound wall and thither we had to go but always attended by the sentry who all the time stood over us. How I came to hate him.

Yusuf was in a poor way. As well as having collapsed morally he now had fever and spent the day huddled out of sight under his 'poshteen', groaning, sighing deeply, and occasionally poking his head out to spit. As a companion in misery he was an unqualified success and I began to eye him with almost as much loathing as I did the sentries. It has long been remarked that we hate those whom we have wronged more than those who have wronged us, and though I might think I had not done Yusuf any harm it was quite clear that I had not done him any good. He had trusted himself blindly to me and for that he was now languishing as a suspected spy in an Afghan jail, 400 miles from his home, further from his destination than when he started, sick without medicine, and his horse (which he regarded with the affection Sancho bestowed on his ass 'Dapple') tethered outside uncared for, at the mercy of the first Afghan horse-thief who should come along. Instead of travelling respectably and respected under the aegis of a sahib who, he thought, would no doubt be received everywhere with deference, he was lying in a mud cell, watched by an armed man, in company with the same sahib who was himself being treated with as much respect as a Kashgar donkey-boy.

Whenever the servants brought a meal I asked to see the Commissar, for my uncertainty as to his intentions was my chief worry, so after breakfast the following day, as this request was still ignored, I determined upon a hunger-strike. It was the only weapon I had; it had been used effectively by many more distinguished prisoners, and though their denial of their prison fare undoubtedly called for less strength of mind than I should have to exercise to deny myself pilau, mutton, and yoghourt, I felt sufficient sullen dogged resentment against the Commissar to throw his food in his face if I got the chance.

At lunch time then, instead of starting up with shameless eagerness I just lay still, averting my eyes from savoury temptation and calmly waving it away. At first they thought I must be ill, then they asked if there was anything wrong with the food, and when I had made them understand that I was resolved not to eat any more of the Commissar's food until I had seen him, their consternation and concern were most gratifying. The sentry came in to see what was the matter, followed shortly by the whole of the guard—about a dozen of them—who quite filled the room as they expostulated excitedly. Word of this ominous turn on the part of the worm was sent to the Commissar and the answer came back that he would see me after I had finished lunch. This was no good. Another messenger went and returned to say the Commissar was a busy man but that he would see me some time. I steeled myself for at least another forty-eight hours' fasting, for he did not seem to me a man sensitive to the suffering of others, and meanwhile I made some tea from our own small store on a Primus stove since I was more anxious to mortify the Commissar than myself. But within half an hour an orderly came to say that he would see me at once, and forthwith I was conducted to the house, into the first garden where the living quarters were.

The Commissar was indeed a busy man. Surrounded by a few choice friends, my particular enemy the Chief of Police among them, he was reclining on a divan smoking a hookah, killing time with a pack of cards. The Chief of Police occupied himself mending a mandoline and occasionally bent his powerful mind to helping the Commissar cheat at Patience, while the Secretary read aloud a thundering leader from the 'Kabul Clarion'. Presently they started a round of Afghan 'Nap' in which I joined.

They were friendly enough and it was an amusing afternoon. But it was one from which I got little satisfaction. A few puffs at the hookah (not an easy smoke for a beginner) and a bland promise that we must remain at least five days or until orders came for our disposal was the sum total. This, I thought, meant just what I had feared—Kabul, and five days more confinement before we even set out for a place which for all I knew might be a month's journey away. Before I was conducted back to our cell the Commissar gave me the pack of cards—greasy, thumbed, torn. I remember it still. The two of clubs was missing and the queen of spades had lost her head, but I think that that pack saved me losing mine. I am no card player, but now I played Patience from morning until it was too dark to see, and when the servants brought the meals we used to have a quick whist drive. The Afghans, by the way, deal and play in the opposite direction to us. Apart from this reason-saving concession our treatment was as rigorous as ever. Except for necessity we could not stir from the cell, and once when I tried to sit on the doorstep in the sun—for it was cold inside—a fierce altercation with the sentry ensued. He ended it in his own favour by loading and cocking his rifle. Yusuf implored me to come in and at this I did so, for I never knew quite how far one could go with these uncouth Yahoos.

There was an unexpected and pleasing development next day. About 10 a.m., comparatively early for the Commissar, I was summoned once more to the garden where I found him sitting at a table drinking tea in company with a young smiling, shifty-looking man, dressed in an elegant 'chapkan', who addressed me first in fluent Hindustani and then startled me by switching suddenly to very good English. He was a man of many tonuges, and of guile, too, as I later found. He tried several more of them on me, including Russian, but, of course, got no response; and I soon discovered that he had been sent for by the Commissar for a purpose which presently appeared. After asking me what I thought he was and receiving the correct reply—an Afghan army officer (for it was a safe bet that most educated Afghans were that)—he acknowledged with a smirk of satisfaction that he was a lieutenant. I was told later that he was below commissioned rank, and from some financial transactions I had with him subsequently I formed the opinion that he should have been below any rank at all.

Having drunk tea we got down to business. The Commissar produced a formidable wad of paper, the sheets of which he folded down the middle lengthwise. On one side he wrote a question in Persian, to which, when it had been translated by the shifty scholar, I had to write the answer in English and sign it. The questions were ingenious and cunningly devised to bring out all my past history and background, and since I had nothing to conceal I began giving it them. However, as soon as they learnt I had been in the army during the war they had something to work on and I began to see that in their eyes a British officer in Wakhan was *ipso facto* a spy. So, while telling the truth, I deemed it advisable to suppress one or two facts, such as, for instance, that long ago until I had thought better of it I had been a professional soldier. This involved me in writing a treatise on the selection and promotion of British officers in war-time, the status of reserve officers, and kindred subjects. Nor did it seem necessasry to tell everything about the last war, for in their vivid imaginations the word 'parachutist' would have at once conjured up visions of furtive but dare-devil activity in hostile country. This was by no means my cup of tea, but the knowledge would have made them suspect the more that I was now following my old vocation in their country. A long morning's work only whetted the Commissar's thirst for knowledge and he had hardly approached the main question of why I was in what he was pleased to think was the very important strategic frontier district of Wakhan. I was warned to attend at the same time next day.

All criminals know, or should know, that it is most unwise to volunteer either information or opinions, or even to make any remarks except, perhaps, about the weather, in the presence of one's accusers. Before we continued this game of 'Consequences' there was some chat about the late war and its politics from which I gathered that the Commissar was soaked in Russian propaganda. He repeated the familiar point that the Russians had suffered fifteen million casualties, the British Empire half a million, *ergo* the Russians had fought and won the war almost unaided. My answer, that it merely showed bad tactics and generalship and a reckless disregard for human life, was not well received. The recent attainment of independence by Indian and Pakistan was then referred to, and not wishing to waste an opportunity of showing him how foolish his suspicions were, I airily remarked that however great the importance of the Wakhan frontier may have been to the British before, it was of less than none now that we had left India for good. Ten hours later, when I was still being examined, a garbled version of this was to recoil on my own head.

It was naturally difficult to convince two such men that I had come to Wakhan simply and solely for my own pleasure. Many of these Afghan officers had had their military education in Turkey and it is, I think, a Turkish proverb which says that all travel is a foretaste of hell. That anyone should wish to see the source of the Oxus or the Hindu Kush was to them the flimsiest of pretexts. Having been posted here willy-nilly so far from the delights of Kabul the Commissar was determined not to go any farther—I doubt if he ever left his compound; and the shifty scholar reluctantly confessed that once he had been obliged to go as far as Kila Panja; so that to ask them to believe that I travelled purely for the sake of travelling was too much.

Where, when, and why, therefore, had I first conceived the idea of coming to Wakhan? Had I left England with that intention? Where had I been and what had I done since arriving in India? And what had I seen in Wakhan that was of military or political importance? To answer the last was, I thought, extremely simple, and at the risk of offending the *amour propre* of the Commissar, the governor of that important territory, I replied that while I was extremely ignorant of such matters and no more a judge of military and political questions than they would be of beer, I could answer in one word—nothing. Finally, my maps—why did I have a map showing part of Wakhan? And the possession of this, I found, was thought to be as incriminating for me as the possession of a jemmy would be to a man accused of loitering with intent. It was useless to point out that the map in question showed also parts of India, China, and Russia, for they seemed to think that since they had no map of Wakhan and did not know that one existed, I must have obtained it from some very secret source and that whoever compiled it had no right to include the strategically important Wakhan.

The session continued all day, with a break for lunch, until 11 o'clock at night, by which time we were sitting on rugs in the Commissar's house eating apples and pears after an uncommonly good dinner. While I wrote the Commissar played Patience, but his mind was evidently on his next question rather than the game, for we had frequently to point out opportunities of moving a card which he had overlooked. Occasionally, he executed a few soulful strophes on the mandoline. There were two other breaks while he said his prayers, first at sundown and then again after supper. In almost the final question my voluntary remark of the morning was turned in exactly the opposite sense and used against me, for the Commissar seemed to have more than an inkling of trial procedure as carried out at Moscow, the last syllable of which, by the way, he always pronounced to rhyme with the domestic animal. If I thought, the question ran, that Wakhan was of no military importance why had I said that morning that it was of great importance to the British. The shifty scholar would not admit having mistranslated and since the Commissar insisted on having an answer I merely wrote that it was a waste of time answering stupid questions. All three of us were getting tired of playing 'Consequences', but I imagine the Commissar was compiling this precious document more for the benefit of his superiors at Kabul than for his own pleasure and wished to impress them with his acumen and thoroughness. Before leaving them I asked for some assurance that we should start for Chitral on the fifth day as promised, to which he assented with the saving remark, 'Insh Allah'.

On returning to the cell I found Yusuf had been removed elsewhere in order to prevent any collusion prior to his cross-examination. The pseudo-lieutenant could speak Turki too; and we later met several officers who were able to converse a little with Yusuf with the help of the Turkish they had picked up when attending military schools in Turkey. In the afternoon Yusuf rejoined me, his examination, of course, having produced nothing, and with him came Ghulam Moxd, our shifty interpreter. He was becoming quite affectionate towards me and the mere fact that he spoke English was enough to make me grateful to him. He now assured me that the 'Chief' as they called the Commissar (who was in fact a Colonel in the army) would send us off next day to Chitral by way of the Sanglich valley which, he said, was three or four days' journey away. I would be well advised to have some Afghan money for the journey, and since the Afghan rupee (the 'Afghani') was the equivalent of an Indian rupee the exchange was simple. Whereupon I changed twenty rupees with him and also relieved him of a nice 'chapkan' he had brought to sell, the price of which, he said, was eighty 'Afghanis'. For this I handed over eighty Indian rupees.

Bright and early next morning he came with a final quittance for me to sign by which I acknowledged the return of all my money, papers, and belongings. I had not got back any maps, papers, or diaries yet, but an escort would conduct us as far as the frontier and there hand them over. This sounded reasonable and I was too pleased at the thought of getting away to haggle over terms. The Commissar, looking me straight in the face and solemnly shaking hands on it, had assured me that he was satisfied of my innocent motives and that he would see we got to Chitral. Ghulam, too, protested that the Chief was a man of his word and that everything would be done as he said. Yusuf and I had had our loads ready since dawn, Yusuf having donned his new riding boots for the occasion and thrown the old pair away. But as the morning wore on and nothing happened our mood quickly passed from impatience to desperate hope, and by afternoon had reached utter despondency.

At last at 5 o'clock, when we had given up hope and when the first gusts of a brewing dust-storm were shaking the tall poplars, we were summoned to the

Commissar's compound. The escort of four soldiers was waiting. All four were dressed regardless of expense in uniform, with greatcoats and belts, and armed with rifles and bayonets. The Commissar had ready a sealed package containing my papers, which he delivered to the senior soldier together with a long harangue. Ghulam, as if deeply impressed with the Commissar's benevolence and my exceptional good fortune, explained that the gist of this was that we were no longer to be treated as prisoners, that the escort was merely a safe conduct, Badakshan being a wild country, where the inhabitants were totally opposed to strangers. My papers, pocket-knife, and ice-axe, now in possession of the escort, would all be handed back at the frontier, and I dwelt with fond anticipation upon the delightful ceremony presently to be conducted on some high pass, near some Afghan boundary stone on which I should spit, while the bodyguard, saluting respectfully, would lay our belongings reverently at our feet and bid us a long farewell.

The dust cut short our mutual expressions of esteem, regret, and farewell. I shook them warmly and almost gratefully by the hand, little realizing that both were liars and one a swindler.

CHAPTER SEVENTEEN

Destination Unknown

FROM Ishkashim the track at once began climbing gradually in a south-westerly direction to a low pass (the Sardab), with the telephone line running alongside it. We had not gone half a mile in the gathering gloom of the dust-storm before I learnt that, instead of being safely escorted, we were being closely guarded, for when I attempted to take a short-cut across a bend in the track I was immediately driven back with threats and imprecations. The soldier in charge of our party, who had stayed behind to collect a horse, now rode up carrying my documents tied up in a blanket. It occurred to me that I ought to have checked these before leaving. Apart from my diaries, which I valued, I was concerned about my passport, for without it I should look uncommonly foolish on my arrival in India. I therefore asked to be allowed to see the papers. When this was refused with a snarl I signified that either I would not go on until I was satisfied or else that I would go back. The whole escort immediately clustered round, shouting and pushing, whereupon I had recourse to my Sarhad tactics of a sit-down strike. But these soldiers were of sterner stuff than the police. The three on foot whipped out their bayonets while the man on the horse, not wishing to inconvenience himself, cocked his rifle. I got up and went on, reviling them loudly but uselessly, for I had not the courage to push provocation to extremes, in order to find out how far they would go. My friend the Commissar might even have hoped for some such outcome, and I could well imagine his official report of the regrettable incident: 'The Commissar regrets that the Englishman was unfortunately shot while resisting his escort.'

This was a bad start to a bad journey. By nightfall, having lost the man with the baggage pony, we were stumbling about the narrow ways of a village on the other side of the pass. Having pushed our way into several courtyards we were at length led into a narrow whitewashed room, which with its thick walls and niches reminded me of a private chapel. It was lit by resinous slips of willow about two feet long placed horizontally in holes in the wall. An hour later the baggage turned up, the door was locked, and our four blackguards made themselves comfortable alongside us. To show my dislike of their company I turned in without joining in their meal, but I found they were not so sensitive to slights on their hospitality as was the Commissar.

It was a sparkling, frosty autumn morning, the blue smoke from the stirring villages curling lazily in the still air, as once more we took to the road and headed south-west down an open grassy valley—such a morning that for a time I forgot my resentment against the four chattering hooligans behind me. In two days, or at most three, we should be rid of them and their likes for good. Freed now from any control, they had exerted the authority conferred by their uniforms and rifles to procure themselves mounts. One rode on top of my baggage while the other two rode double. Badakshan is a country of horses—few people walk—and its horses are much sought after both in Gilgit and in Chitral for polo. Yusuf was always pressing me to ride his nag, partly out of kindness and partly because for prudence sake he had long since given out that the horse was mine. But with his new boots and his continuing fever he was in no shape for walking.

After six or seven miles the valley debouched on to wide flats where its small stream joined a fine, fast-flowing river coming down from higher mountains away to the south. I felt sure that up that river lay the way to our pass into Chitral, and it was therefore with surprise and some disappointment that at the junction we turned off to follow the combined streams into a gorge running west. Apart from some superb rock scenery this gorge and the road through it were as wearisome and as long as most. Except for a small village close to the entrance there was nothing until we reached another (Tirguran) eleven miles farther down. I was troubled by the direction of the gorge, which tended to edge away rather north of west. It was easy enough to tell our general direction, but I had no map and not the shadow of an idea about the geography of Afghanistan. Kabul, I thought vaguely, must lie to the west and Chitral to the south. Any course therefore that was not south of west would be unlikely to lead to Chitral, unless the boundary shot out to the north in the erratic and unexpected way that boundaries sometimes do.

We had covered about twenty-three miles before we stopped at the rest-house of Tirguran. In Badakshan all villages have these square single rooms. There is a raised earth platform for sleeping running round the walls, and in the middle of the floor is a circular fireplace sunk in the ground. The merits of this type of fireplace are that no one can see it and only about two people can get near enough to appreciate it. Even the boiling of a pot is a difficult operation—only possible by first kindling a great conflagration and then making use of the resulting ashes. At these places all travellers are welcome and as our party was of transcendent interest 'House Full' notices were up very soon after our arrival. The soldiers were regarded with a respectful attention which, though perhaps deemed necessary in the interests of prudence, was unworthy of honest peasants who bestowed it, quite unmerited by the recipients, and sickening to an observer such as myself. I was beginning to hate the sight of a uniform. At the social evenings in these rest-houses our senior soldier was listened to with deference and the wag of the party with sycophantic applause; and although any attempt at conversation between us and the villagers was strictly forbidden, there was, of course, no embargo on their discussing us.

It was not until 11 o'clock that we got our relay of ponies, so we started off going as fast as I could walk to make up for lost time. We had another twenty-two mile march to do before reaching what our mendacious guard informed us would be Sanglich, at the foot of the pass to Chitral. We crossed the river (here the Warduj, later the Kokcha) to the left bank by a bridge over a narrow cleft, and twelve miles on halted to change ponies at a pleasant village (Sufian), where the persistent walls of the gorge at length began to give ground. I had been troubled yesterday by our line of march but today I began to feel more than anxious. At every twist of the gorge—and there were many—I hoped and expected to see the river break back southwards. Indeed, it seemed eager to do this, but round each corner there was always some spiteful buttress of rock to thrust it farther away, so that from west our direction became north-west, and then for the last ten miles due north. We walked wearily up the last fan to where the so-called Sanglich (in reality Chakaran) stood in its russet and vermilion-leaved apricot orchards. Night fell, the stars of the Plough appeared one by one, until the Pointers confirmed too surely our unpromising course and shattered a wild hope I had that the sun had somehow gone astray.

Besides a supper of bread and a thin 'goulash', in the morning the rest-house provided tea and bread to speed the wayfarers on their road. This came in waves like a flowing tide. The first intimation that the tide was making would be the arrival of the headman himself carrying a copper-pot of tea and some flat round loaves; a few minutes later another greybeard[1] would totter in with similar contribution; then a boy with his and a trayful of small China bowls, then more and more until the whole place was awash with bowls, and teapots, and bread. Anyone could join this tea-fight. In addition to the *bona fide* travellers and those who brought the breakfast, most of the village elders and certainly all the village idlers muscled in on this gratuitous pipe-opener and broke the back of the morning with tea and chat. It was a pleasant and inexpensive custom, for no one minded what he drank so long as it was hot.

Sunday 19 October was the great day when, according to the fiction assiduously sustained by our guards, we should reach the frontier, so that when a mile below Chakaran the river swung abruptly round to the west my

1 'Greybeard' is a misnomer in the East, where grey beards are usually dyed red with henna.

hopes revived. Evidently, I thought, there was no pass to cross. Lower down, perhaps, the river itself would become the frontier. Some twelve miles farther on, when I saw a bridge and on the south side a broad road which disappeared into another valley running due south, I became quite excited. My annoyance and disappointment were therefore all the keener when we held steadily to our course along the north bank of the river, leaving the bridge behind us. So far we had marched at a great pace without a halt, for I was buoyed up with the eager hope, but having passed the bridge and the valley leading south I sat down sullenly to eat some bread. This occasioned another scene with the senior soldier who, while the others went on, remained with me as he always did, his confounded horse almost treading on my heels. He raved, pointed his rifle, and finally cocked it. My already parched mouth became dryer with tension, but I munched away, sneered at him, and went on.

The two valleys having joined, their combined rivers (now the Kokcha) flowed north-west again through a fertile plain, where on our side were a fort, barracks, and parade ground, with a large village almost hidden in the trees. Was this the frontier town with Chitral across the river? As I have admitted, my notions of the geography hereabouts were childish. I had a suspicion that the Hindu Kush must intervene somewhere, but on the other hand by the Kabul river, I knew, one could reach India without climbing a pass. But so persuaded was I that Chitral was our destination and so hateful the prospect of any other, that no hypothesis was too wild and no supposition too flimsy for me to clutch at.

As we reached the outskirts, our road met another coming from the barracks and at the corner stood a party of young men headed by a familiar figure in an elegant white 'chapkan'. It was Ghulam Moxd, the shifty scholar.

'How the devil did you get here, Ghulam?'

'Oh, by riding. Major, we have both been deceived.'

'How's that? Aren't we going to Chitral after all?'

'Oh yes, you will go to Chitral. But the Chief has deceived us both.'

'Well, when shall we get there?'

'Oh, perhaps this evening. I have brought my friends. They want to see the Englishman who is my friend. But the Chief has deceived us both.'

'Well, I don't understand you. Damn you and your friends. I'm in a hurry to get to Chitral and can't stop. Good-bye.'

And with that I rudely left them to hurry on by a shady, dusty road, through a well-stocked bazaar where I greedily eyed piles of melons and apples, and then down to a bridge over another river flowing in from the east. On the other side of this our guard took us into a court-yard opening on to a neat bungalow, in front of which was a small terrace and a veranda. We were left in charge of a dignified looking man with a black spade-beard, who seated us on the terrace and brought tea and fruit, while the guard departed in search of fresh horses. Presently another man, whom I took to be the village school-master, joined us. He was dressed in European fashion, and though the afternoon sun beat warmly into this walled garden he wore a buttoned-up overcoat, black woollen gloves, and a black Astrakhan hat. They had evidently been forewarned, for when we questioned them as best we could we learnt that if we were lucky enough to obtain fresh horses then Chitral might be reached that night. Ghulam's reiterated refrain became even more worrying and inexplicable. Had the Commissar bilked me of my papers and passport?

Against all the rules imposed by our guard they told us that this place was Baharak. On the map it is marked as 'Khairabad' but that name is unknown locally. Mr Evert Barger, historian and archaeologist, who in the course of an expedition to northern Afghanistan in 1938 rode here from Faizabad, asserts that some ruins he found at the north end of the Baharak plain mark the site of the ancient capital of Badakshan. In a paper in the *Geographical Journal*, May 1939, the reading of which, by the way, made me feel that I had traversed Wakhan with unseeing eyes, Mr Barger argues that, contrary to accepted opinion, this southern branch of the old Silk Route which followed the Oxus valley through Wakhan was nearly as important as the northern one going from Termez on the middle Oxus, north of the Pamirs and between the Alai and Trans-Alai mountains to Kashgar. 'Wakhan', he wrote, 'is known to be full of fortifications, buildings, and caves which Sir Aurel Stein believed to be of Sassanid date, and among which he also found traces of Buddhist worship. No site in Wakhan has yet been excavated and in a sense it has never been explored. The route through Wakhan has always followed the southern bank of the Oxus, for the floor of the valley is broader there, and the chief settlements lie on the Afghan side. Sir Aurel Stein and Olufsen have explored the Russian bank, but, so far as I am aware, no record exists of any traveller who has been on the Afghan side of lower Wakhan since Wood made his famous journey to the sources of the Oxus a hundred years ago. Excavation of some of the ancient sites in Wakhan must be perhaps the most important single item on any agenda of archaeological work in Central Asia . . .'

For once the guards seemed to have met their match; by the time they had stolen horses, or brow-beaten their owners into lending them, it was too late to start. Accustomed to soldiers living in the barracks, the people of Baharak either had a more just appreciation of their status than had the up-country hicks, or else they knew better how to out-bluster them. While our hooligans were considering this unwonted show of spirit by the civilian rabbit, a slim, wiry man with grey goatee beard, fierce hooked nose, and shrewd but rather grey eyes rode into the courtyard. He rode on top of a couple of bushels of apples and was followed by a servant sitting upon two more. Having washed ceremonially in the water channel which ran along the terrace, he first exhorted the company and then fell to praying. No one responded—neither Spade-beard, the Schoolmaster, the hooligans, Yusuf, his servant, nor myself—so when he had done he stood up and delivered, *ex cathedra*, what I believed and hoped was a severe homily on the neglect of religious duty. In extenuation I might have told him that four at least of the company were already damned and that no amount of prayer, I hoped, would save them from burning in hell fire. Whether he was the owner of the villa, an itinerant fruit broker, or a prophet sated with locusts and wild honey, I never discovered. But it was all one, for he behaved as though he had bought the place.

The whole company, including ourselves and an officer and his servant who had ridden in at dusk, took supper in the villa, seated in a long row against one wall with the the Prophet in the place of honour on the extreme right and myself in the place of dishonour on the extreme left. Having dealt with the mutton stew and having seen the tea begin circulating, Spade-beard produced a lamp and began a mysterious game. Concealed about his person were several bundles of folded pieces of paper which he proceeded to unfold one by one and read, commenting occasionally on what he read to the company at large. Whether they were ballot papers, begging letters, testimonials to his stewardship (for that I thought he must be), or the blackmailing letters of a 'poison-pen', is a problem which I shall never solve. The Prophet grew restless and when Spade-beard reached for yet another bundle, he indicated by standing up to pray that he for one had had enough. Calmly and methodically Spade-beard continued unfolding papers, rudely ignoring this strong hint, but the Soldier and the Schoolmaster obediently ranged themselves in echelon behind the Prophet, while the rest of the company signified their respect for his foibles by ceasing to chatter. That done, all except the Schoolmaster made their beds where they sat. But in the corner by me was a real bed about two feet high to which the Schoolmaster strode with a resolute air like a man going to his fate. He took one stride on to it, stood up while he replaced his black gloves with a pair of white ones, and then lay down.

We left early next morning, without a blessing from the Prophet, but encouraged by a speech in English from the Schoolmaster which he had evidently been thinking up in the long night watches—'Chitral one'— meaning, we supposed, one day's march to Chitral, thus dutifully doing his little best to support this elaborate hoax.

At the northern end of the Baharak plain there is a small village and a serai, Pa-i-Shahr (at the foot of the town), which is close to the site of the ancient city discovered by Mr Barger. From Baharak the road was wide, having evidently been recently constructed with a view to motor traffic, but below Pa-i-Shahr, road and river plunge into a narrow gorge. Here, the new road has been hewn out of a solid rock face—a considerable feat of engineering, for it is wide enough to take a Jeep or possibly bigger trucks. The gorge persists for 18 barren miles with only one small half-way village, where there is a serai and a few tea-shops. We took tea here, and from this point onwards the road was alive with donkey traffic, most of it returning empty in our direction. Evidently there was a biggish town ahead, but what it was I neither knew nor cared. We were still going north-west and in spite of the Schoolmaster's reassuring words I had at last concluded that we were bound for Kabul. An ominous sign was the telegraph line which still dogged us and which I grew to hate almost as much as I did our guard.

At length the walls of the gorge began to recede, leaving space for terraced fields, orchards, and houses to cluster in a narrow strip on either bank. At 3 o'clock we were on the outskirts of a town. We passed an ancient stone bridge and entered a bustling bazaar to be finally shepherded by our guard under an open archway leading into a compound. The first thing I noticed was a lorry and at once I guessed we were in Faizabad; for had not the shifty Scholar informed me with pride that from Faizabad there was a motor-road to Kabul?

CHAPTER EIGHTEEN

Faizabad and Freedom

So we had been led up the garden path after all and the meaning of Ghulam's incantation at Baharak was clear; though why he, one of the parties to the deceit, should have taken the trouble to ride ahead to confess and couple himself with me as one of the deceived I cannot imagine. It had been a well-wrought stratagem in which I could see no sense except, perhaps, as a rather cruel jest. But I admired the thoroughness with which the plots had been sustained and the way in which outsiders had entered into the spirit of the thing; for in our intercourse with the guards and in theirs with the hundreds of people we had encountered on the journey, I had not once heard the word 'Faizabad'. The talk had always been of Chitral—although we were heading in precisely the opposite direction. Which merely goes to show that all Afghans are experienced, industrious, and quite often picturesque liars.

Faizabad, the present capital of Badakshan including the district of Wakhan, has seen much worse days. In 1821 it was completely destroyed by Murad Beg, an Uzbek chieftain of superior talent and predatory habits—a man after the style of Sikander Beg the Albanian hero of Mehmed Ali of Egypt, but handicapped by a meaner and less known sphere of action than theirs. Having wiped out the town he removed the inhabitants to his capital at Kunduz a hundred miles to the west. In 1838 Wood visited him there and found it a wretched, unhealthy place built in a swamp. From there Wood proceeded to the desolate Faizabad and, having seen the ruined houses and wasted orchards of this far more eligible site, felt constrained to remark: 'It was impossible to behold the desolation of so fair a scene without commiserating the unfortunate inhabitants and execrating the tyrant, or without shuddering to think that one man should have the power to work so much mischief.' Though Murad Beg worked on a small canvas he seems to have wrought some notable mischief in his time, but our more recent practitioners in this line would quickly exhaust a Wood's powers of shuddering. Later the Uzbeks were expelled and under Abdur Rahman (1867) Faizabad regained its former status. Now it is a considerable trading centre and the cantonment for northern Afghanistan. Situated as it is in a narrow valley, it can never at any time have supported a large population so that it probably owes its importance to its position on the Kokcha river where routes from the Oxus, Khanabad, and Wakhan converge. In 1937 a motor-road to Khanabad, 135 miles away, and Kabul, was opened.

After a short wait we were taken through another and busier bazaar to the cantonment and administrative offices on a hill half a mile from the town.

Unlike the Commissar's these were real government offices equipped with doubtfully efficient telephones, dry ink-stands, and nibless pens—but for the absence of empty tea-cups one might have been in Whitehall. We were set down in the Governor's office (by no means ornate or even comfortable) and presently a frightening bark from the sentry at the door announced the arrival of the Governor. He was in khaki uniform with Sam Browne belt, breeches, gaiters, and spurs with chains, things which I had not seen since 1915 when I had had to clean them. He was a general, or perhaps a brigadier, grave and stout as becomes that high contemplative rank, but with a dry sense of humour, a quizzical expression, and eyes that sometimes twinkled. Evidently he had been advised of our coming, for without much questioning he dismissed us to our new place of confinement in a back alley off the bazaar.

The General's own house was one side of the alley, his kitchen and servants' quarters in a compound on the other. The cook and his assistant were cleared out to sleep on a veranda while we were put in their room. This was only a little larger than the Ishkashim cell and no less sparsely furnished. Here we had to stay under the eyes of a sentry—unarmed I was thankful to see—but we were allowed to walk in the compound or to sit on a bench by the kitchen door. There were no sanitary arrangements, so that we had to go out into the highways and by-ways attended always by the sentry. Apart from that we had few complaints. Our meals, which were probably the same as his, came direct from the General's kitchen, and I was delighted to find that he appreciated good food as much as the Commissar and took a lively interest in what went on in his kitchen. Very early in the morning one would find him, unshaven and wrapped in a 'chapkan', nosing around seeing what was toward. His eldest son was sick and had been seconded for duty as messing officer to the General's family, a nearby officers' mess, and now to ourselves. He was a model messing officer. He was always present to see our meals dished out, to wish us 'buon appetito', and to receive our praise. If we wanted anything from the bazaar, he would have it brought for us. He was only the second man I had come across in Afghanistan who could speak Hindustani fluently, so that in the nine dismal days we spent here we became good friends. All that we bought from the bazaar were some shoes for Yusuf's nag, some local soap and tobacco, which for all the good they were might well have been interchangeable, and a flannel shirt for myself which cost 50 Afghanis. My original shirt was not only in rags but was also fit food for the incinerator. In eating and scratching, we are told, everything is in the beginning. I had begun scratching at Ishkashim, I was still scratching at Faizabad—and with good reason. Even my new shirt went over to the enemy and that, too, had to be burnt at Chitral.

The programme proved to be much as I had feared. We must await the receipt of a telegram from Kabul which, according to the General, would take three or four days. We therefore settled down to wait with what hope or patience we could muster. Yusuf, now sunk again in profoundest gloom, retired under his 'poshteen', coming to the surface occasionally to ask me how far I thought it was to Kashmir. He now had the idea that we should do better to go to Kabul by bus, and when I pointed out that horses were not allowed on buses, airily suggested that the nag should be consigned to the care of some reliable Afghan to take to Srinagar by road. For my part I borrowed a pack of cards (only two were missing) from the cook's mate and played Patience grimly and unceasingly.

The only other diversion was watching what went on in the kitchen. The making of bread I found particularly fascinating. Every day the cook's mate had to turn out a couple of dozen loaves, or rather flat oval pieces nearly two feet long. Having made the dough and left it to rise he fired the oven. This had been built beneath the floor. It was about three feet deep and shaped like the inside of a jug, with the mouth a good deal narrower than the base. When the bottom of the oven was a glowing inferno of ashes the baker, having first wet his hand and forearm to prevent singeing, thrust his arm deep inside to plaster a piece of the slack dough on to the concave sloping side, running his hand up its length as he withdrew it. The bread acquired its long shape on the way in and it was this last stroking action which left the four characteristic deep furrows in the finished bread. Very rarely a piece failed to stick and became a total loss, the others swelled up, were baked, and peeled off in a matter of minutes.

We had arrived on the Monday and by Friday we learnt that not only had no telegram arrived but also that the Mahomedan festival of 'Id' began that day and that all business, including the dispatch of telegrams, would be suspended for four days. Everyone took a holiday except the cooks, whose work redoubled for the General was giving a lunch to all the Faizabad notabilities. He himself was early on the scene of action and having first submitted himself to the barber he spent an anxious morning in the kitchen, dealing out advice, encouragement, and occasionally abuse, and dispatching a stream of runners armed with a few copper coins to buy pennyworths of chillies, carrots, milk, tomatoes, or to hire mincing machines and crockery. When all was ready the General himself dished up, and before going to his guests brought Yusuf and me some of the choicer dishes with his own hands. A rich pilau was, of course, the solid core of a meal embellished with half a dozen spiced vegetable dishes and followed by a pudding, 'fit', as Heine said, 'for a glass case'.

The following day was the big day. It started off with gun-fire from the fort, followed later by a second salvo which was the signal to assemble for prayer. Meanwhile, a couple of sheep had been slaughtered in aid of the General's staff and coloured hard-boiled eggs, sweets, and fruit were distributed to all and sundry, including the poor captives. Yusuf, on my strong recommendation, obtained permission to attend prayers. The Imam must have been a more powerful spell-binder than the Prophet of Baharak, for Yusuf appeared to have undergone a religious revival; from then on he prayed puntiliously five times a day, obtaining thereby solace and a fair amount of occupation; for at times he seemed to forget that he was on his knees and would spend whole minutes gazing reproachfully at me, the source of all his woes, or at the blank wall. I found his devout frame of mind (in which I could not partake) and his reproachful stare so disconcerting that in my games of Patience I very frequently overlooked the moving of a vital card.

On the Sunday a Sabbath calm reigned, although the fires of hospitality were still smouldering. Hosts of well-wishers came to salute the General and had to sit down to tea, fruit, and sweets. One began to feel sorry for the General lest his entertainment allowance should prove inadequate. Since, however, nothing stronger than tea was drunk it seemed likely that no great harm could come either to his pocket or to his guests. On Monday the smouldering fires blazed up once more. This time tables and chairs were set on the veranda adjoining our room, the battery of brass samovars in the compound was stoked up, and the whole day devoted to a desperate orgy of tea-drinking. The flow of visitors slackened not at all until towards evening, when the General and a few of the more obstinate guests settled down to chess. I was invited to play and it was not through any tact on my part that the General demolished me in a comparatively short time.

At supper that evening his son came in to ask how many ponies we needed for our journey to Chitral. Great was our relief and joy. I shook him rather unnecessarily by the hand while Yusuf once more spread his prayer carpet. A telegram ordering our release had come, but unfortunately there was a catch in it. I learnt next morning at the General's office that all my papers, less the passport, were to be sent to the Foreign Office at Kabul. Several hours were spent in an effort to save my diaries, but in the end, after taking a receipt, I was obliged to go without them. Before leaving I changed some more money with the General's son, during which I learnt that an Indian rupee was worth five Afghanis. The shifty scholar had therefore received the equivalent of 500 Afghanis for twenty and a 'chapkan' worth eighty. The General's son indignantly denied Ghulam's claim to officer's rank, but whether it was a fact or whether he did it merely for the sake of the honour of Afghan officers I do not know. The General smiled at this successful deal in foreign exchange, but reached for the telephone and asked for a trunk call to Ishkashim—perhaps Ghulam eventually learnt something to his disadvantage.

And so we began to retrace our weary steps—not quite as far as Ishkashim but to Zebak within a day's march of it. Now we were attended only by a solitary young soldier armed with a stick. This was reassuring to us, but it had its inconveniences in that a stick was less efficacious than a rifle for persuading villagers to provide food and transport. What they thought when they saw us returning—except that we were a damned nuisance—I cannot tell. Perhaps they accounted me a sort of Flying Dutchman doomed to fly backwards and forwards through Wakhan to the end of time, like a doomed soul rejected by heaven and hell and not really wanted on earth.

Of all the exasperating marches I have ever experienced this was the worst. Transport was hard to come by and harder still to keep, for our young soldier was no match either for bearded headman or for the impudent beardless donkey-boys. We reached Baharak only by marching half the night, but the worst march was that through the last part of the Warduj gorge to the junction of the Ishkashim road and the valley leading south to Chitral. For this long stage we had but two unwilling donkeys driven by two still more unwilling urchins, with whom we had distressing and undignified scenes at each village in our efforts to force them onwards to the next. At the little village near the mouth of the gorge, fortune smiled on us and we found in the headman (a Pathan, I think) a man and brother, who gave us food without our asking, fresh donkeys, and a little 'lean, old, chapped, bald, shot of a man' who, when it came to driving them, was a human dynamo.

On the morning of the fifth day we reached Zebak at the foot of the Sanglich valley, a prosperous-looking village surrounded by apricot orchards and walnut trees still bearing their foliage of brown, copper, and gold. It is bigger than Ishkashim and has a Commissar, too, who detained us for two hours while we answered his stupid questions. In spite of the soldier with us he was not satisfied, and rang up Faizabad before allowing us to proceed.

The telegraph line ends here, so now lest someone at Kabul took it into his head to stop us I decided to get as far as I could as quickly as possible. By 3 o'clock we had reached Isitich, ten miles short of Sanglich village. The usual crowd gathered round us; but this time without waiting for the soldier to utter a half-hearted apologetic request for a fresh baggage pony I pulled out a 20 Afghani note. That did the trick. I handed over an earnest of ten and within five minutes we had changed loads and were off again. At Sanglich, which we reached at dark, we found an Afghan post in charge of an officer to whom our soldier handed a note from the General. It was a potent talisman, for this handsome, swashbuckling captain in well-cut great-coat and peaked cap was at once all over us, paying us polite attentions until late at night, and then coming back early in the morning with breakfast and a promise of transport.

This promise was not so easily fulfilled. It seemed that the good people of Sanglich, aware of what might be expected of them, had taken steps to have their animals either out of the way or in use. Unluckily for the owner, the nag which I had hired yesterday foolishly stuck its head out of a stable. The captain saw it and before the poor beast knew what was happening it was being loaded by half a dozen soldiers. The owner put up a spirited resistance—the horse was lame, he was sick, his wife was dying—but his clamour went unheeded. Across the Dorah pass he must go with his horse or suffer penalties. The captain posed for a photograph, begged me earnestly to say nothing of any part of my stay in his country which had not been to my liking, shook me warmly by the hand and wished me good luck.

The young soldier now returned and his place was taken by a very short blackguard, whose duty it was to accompany me to Chitral in order to obtain an official receipt for the body. That he had the misfortune to be dressed as an Afghan soldier was possibly not his fault, but it damned him in my eyes. Still he had his points. Instead of bawling at me when he wanted me to stop, turn, or go on, he whistled gently like a poacher to his dog. He could walk as the others could not, and since he wanted to get back he walked fast. The Dorah pass, just under 15,000 ft., is the easiest pass over the Hindu Kush between Badakshan and Chitral, and is about fifty-five miles from Chitral town itself. The route is much used by Afghan traders and horse-dealers.

When we left Sanglich it was a fine morning but so cold that the water furrows were all frozen. Seven miles farther on the valley forks and we turned up the left-hand branch where half a mile up we came to the last Afghan outpost, an indescribably dirty hovel in which three unkempt Afghan soldiers blended harmoniously with the squalor as they dozed away their time. To me such a post was now a familiar sight and one upon which I looked for the last time without a shadow of regret. By midday we were near the foot of the pass with a great deal of steep climbing in front of us. The path follows the shore of a mile-long lake of deepest blue, the Hauz-i-Dorah or Lake Dufferin, which is surrounded on three sides by some impressively glaciated though not very high mountains. We turned away on to steep grass and rubble slopes up which we laboured for the next three hours. Either because of the forced marches of the last few days or because of a cough I had now acquired I found it trying. Yusuf and the 'short blackguard' seemed much less distressed than I was, but could go no faster, as their pace was governed by the horses they were leading. Snow began falling as we crossed the wide drift-strewn plain just below the summit.

I made for the cairn and gazed down unbelievingly into Chitral. Were we really free or was there some other surprise in wait? The one side appeared as bleak, inhospitable, and uncharitable, as I knew the other to be—a tangle of trivial peaks, rock ridges, and deep scored valleys. My satisfaction was immense, shorn though the scene was of all the adjuncts I had wished for. There was no Afghan boundary stone marked out for ceremonial desecration, no diaries (alas!) to be laid at my feet, and if the 'short blackguard' felt any inclination to salute, he managed to suppress it.

Yusuf, though disappointed to find no tangible evidence that we were on the threshold of the great British raj, gaily mounted his nag, now ribby, wayworn, and lean, and begged me to take his photograph. For the last two days he had been visibly perking up, and his religious zeal, I was sorry to note, had diminished. If his religion was a sheet anchor to be used only in storm, he was casting it off much too soon. Had he but known it he was not nearly out of the wood and his cup of sorrow not nearly full. The war in Kashmir, which we first heard of next day, prevented his going there, where, in fact, he had never any reason to go, for he was presently to learn from a Turkoman trader in Chitral that his poor old father was not in Kashmir at all, but Lhasa. Finally, though we had just passed a month with the wicked without suffering the loss of a hair, the very first night at Chitral they stripped the clothes—a valuable saddle-cloth—from the back of his nag. Thus, his mission unaccomplished and his filial duty unfulfilled, he had to return alone by a weary and devious way through Gilgit back to Kashgar, getting himself nearly drowned in a river (as I heard later) on the way.

But the bleak prospects were fortunately hidden and there on the Dorah pass I think he forgave me. As I, I suppose, must forgive the Afghans, particularly those who stand most in need of forgiveness, the Commissar, the Shifty Scholar, and the entire garrison of Ishkashim; but to the General, whose attentions shone like a good deed in a naughty world, I give not forgiveness but grateful thanks. For if one lives in a buffer state one must, I suppose, act like a buffer and repel everything, from individuals to army corps. And who are the Afghans that they should have heard of a brave new world of visa-less travel to which I, one of the early exponents, had fallen a sacrifice? Still, since the Afghans and the British have been neighbours now for a good many years, even fighting occasionally as these will, their behaviour on the whole was, I thought, unneighbourly; for, as the Chinese proverb says, 'when a neighbour is in your garden inattention is the truest politeness.'

For me it had been a season conspicuously lacking in success. Every enterprise had either failed or led me into trouble. But man is born to trouble, and failure is such a common occurrence in men's affairs that most of us have at our finger's ends some trite but nevertheless true sayings calculated to lessen the sting of defeat and to turn adversity to our advantage. Seneca, I think, has asserted that to escape misfortune is to want instruction, and that to live in ease is to live in ignorance; and as I turned to go down into Chitral, tired, lousy, and bereft of my diaries, I felt that the year had at any rate been rich in instruction.

CHINA TO CHITRAL

China to Chitral

First published by Cambridge University Press, 1951

Contents

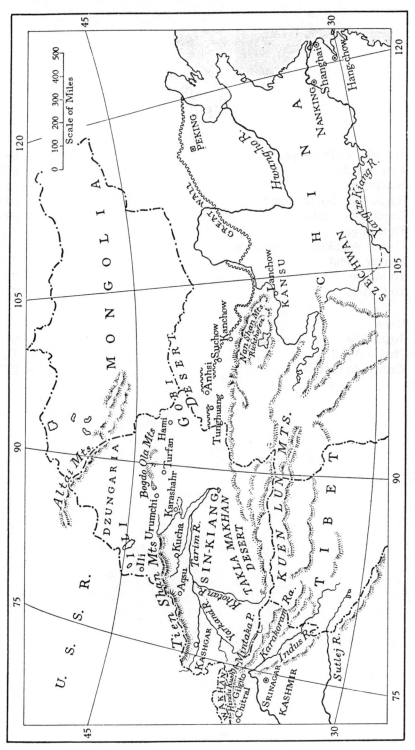

GENERAL MAP. SHANGHAI–CHITRAL

CHAPTER ONE

Traveller or Passenger?

'BETTER fifty years of Europe than a cycle of Cathay' is a sentiment that might well be endorsed by a man who has seen no more of China than, say, Shanghai. But within the borders of Cathay is Chinese Turkestan, and for my part, having seen only a little of that fascinating country in 1947, I did not mind how soon or how often I saw it again. There can be no part of Asia, or indeed of any continent, which exerts a more powerful attraction on either the mountaineer, the geographer, the archaeologist, or any man who travels merely 'for to admire an' for to see'.

In the first place its very remoteness forms a deadly lure for the ambitious traveller. Some of the peaks and valleys of the Himalaya are also remote, but their appeal is mainly to the mountaineer. In time even he may become satiated with rocks, snow, and glaciers, and when he reluctantly or, perhaps, gladly descends to grass, forest, and villages, he finds with few exceptions that the villages are only the slightly squalid homes of a cheerful but uninteresting people without history, arts, or even trade. I have had many happy and amusing hours and enjoyed much hospitality in Himalayan villages and I think that, although one must be grateful to and respect those contented, hard-working, penurious folk, their villages are not one of the main attractions. They are merely incidents on the route, depots for the recruiting of porters, sources of food, or perhaps places where beer is brewed.

In Chinese Turkestan, or Sinkiang, the lures are many. Where else is there such a startling and satisfying mixture of desert and mountain, of Moslem and Buddhist, of settled folk and nomad? where the bread and melons of the one are rivalled by the cream, yoghourt, and kumis of the other; and all these found in a country of historic fame, a country which itself has undergone but little change and which was once the link between the great civilizations of China on the one hand, and of India, Persia, or even Europe, on the other. There are spacious deserts elsewhere; some also holding the buried secrets of past civilizations; but nowhere else is there such a desert fringed with rich and teeming oases, shut in on three sides by vast snow ranges whose glacier streams nourish the oases and upon whose slopes yaks and camels graze side by side; where in their felt yorts Kirghiz and Kazak live much as they did in the days of Genghis Khan, except that now they no longer take a hand in the devastation of Europe.

Just as it is a good thing to have a friend at court, so it is good to have a friend in a remote country, especially when it is hedged about with political barriers under which the meek must crawl. In 1948 my friend Mr E. E.

Shipton, in the post of Consul General, Kashgar, was still spreading his beneficent rays over Kashgaria, touching sometimes distant Dzungaria, or at least Urumchi which lies on its outskirts. Within easy reach of this place Urumchi, the capital of Sinkiang, there is a mountain called Bogdo Ola upon which Shipton had long meditated assault, and it was in order to aid and abet him in this attempt that in May of that year I turned up at Shanghai.

To reach Central Asia by way of Shanghai may seem a Chestertonian approach, reminiscent of 'the night we went to Birmingham by way of Beachy Head'; but by sinking one's pride and opening one's purse wide enough to take advantage of air travel, such an indirect approach takes no longer than the ordinary routes. From England the usual way to Sinkiang is from India, either through Kashmir to Leh and thence over the Karakoram Pass (19,000 ft.), or through Gilgit and over the Mintaka Pass (15,000 ft.), both of which routes, particularly the first, are hard on man and beast. I am not averse to hard travel, in fact in retrospect I like it, but in 1948 owing to the Kashmir dispute the first was impossible and the second doubtful. Moreover, both these routes lead to Kashgar, while Urumchi, to which Shipton had already gone, is a thousand miles further east.

Instead of saying I travelled to Shanghai by air I should prefer to say I was carried there; for it seems to me time to draw a hard and fast line between travellers and passengers before the word 'traveller' loses its romantic flavour. A journey of many thousands of miles by air and bus, such as that which I undertook to Urumchi, without the least physical effort on my part and with a despicably small increase of knowledge as a result, can hardly be called travelling. To my mind two distinguishing marks of a traveller are that he exerts himself and that he moves slowly. Indeed, this must be so by definition; for to travel is defined as to pass from point to point in a *deliberate* and systematic manner; while the qualification that he must exert himself was recognized by those most potent, grave, and reverend signiors who drew up our admirable licensing laws, when they defined the *bona fide* traveller (with whom we are concerned) as one entited to call for refreshment on Sunday at public houses by having *walked* three miles.

The Chinese saying that the further one travels the less one knows must have been prescient of the air age. Nothing could be truer of air travel. It is about 10,000 miles from London to Shanghai, a journey which had it been done by sea in a small boat, overland on foot, or even by car, would have provided an education in itself, a bottomless fund of anecdote, and perhaps a final eradication of that tormenting desire for travel. Whereas when it is done by air the traveller is poorer in pocket and no richer in experience. Nor is his appetite for travel satisfied; it is merely whetted. Places like Singapore, Bangkok, and Hong Kong, which were just names to me when I started, were still names when I was dumped at Shanghai, but which now kindled in me a dangerous spark of interest.

I realized at once that I should have visited Shanghai many years earlier—a surmise which probably holds good for most parts of the inhabited globe—before the first world war perhaps, when Englishmen and even Europeans still had 'face', and when the presence of numerous 'old China hands' made even the longest bar in the world a desirable goal. But in 1948 Shanghai seemed to me a place that one could hardly leave too quickly. I suppose it was not unnatural, but there were a great many Chinese, far too many, all of them apparently in the streets at once, in cars, in pedi-cabs, and a multitude on foot.

Despite the teaching of Taoism the Chinese, at any rate in private life, are active, bustling people with an eye firmly fixed on the main chance. Not for them, 'the business of Tao which is one of day by day dealing with less and less until you arrive at inaction'. On the contrary, all of them appeared to be in trade and all those who were not serving in one or other army, tilling rice or drowning in a Yangtze flood, had assembled in Shanghai to ply their vocations. There were not enough shops or even barrows for the five million inhabitants of Shanghai, but there was plenty of pavement which could be used as business premises. Thus anyone not actually buying or selling had to walk in the street among the cars, pedi-cabs, and foot people, all of necessity going the same pace. Fruit sellers predominated; bananas were in season; and judging by the number of cast-off skins most of the five million seemed to be in favour of eating more fruit. In short, the impressions I took away were of too much noise, dirt, heat and a population badly in need of decimation— either by planning or by some less subtle means.

But to return to my thesis. The distinction between a traveller and a passenger is that the one uses travel as an end in itself while the other is merely carried as a means to an end. If I seem to disparage air travel, which is a very handy means of transport, it is partly to excuse my ignorance of China. For though I may now talk of having travelled in China, indeed even of having crossed it—being hurtled half-way in the course of one day by air and hurtled the remainder in twelve days by lorry—I am yet no sinologue. The true traveller, as I have said, must move by his own exertions, while the passenger is moved swiftly by machinery. My distinction is not a hole-proof definition, for I can conceive of circumstances in which the passenger moves so slowly as to have time to look about him, thereby qualifying as a traveller. In which category the occupants of a Chinese-controlled bus must be placed is hard to say, for, although they do not move so very slowly, there are other factors which come into play.

Consider for a moment a bus which I boarded in Nanking. The mere boarding of it was a bold step which few of the class derogatively described as 'passengers' would have taken, for I knew neither Chinese nor where I wanted to go. Nanking is like Euclid's definition of a line—length without breadth—for it consists of a street six miles long. The hotel in which I stayed—truthfully describable as quaint and old-world—was at one extremity and I had to get myself and a suit-case to the other. Buses ran frequently and mostly under their own power, so that I concede that once inside one was technically speaking a passenger. But to get in called for some personal effort, in fact for the utmost violence, and no less was needed to get out.

Those tiresome people who constantly remind us that a pint pot holds only a pint never can have seen a Nanking bus. There, private enterprise had free play. There were no trammelling by-laws; and evidently the conductor had a large personal stake in the success of his bus; for there was no nonsense about standing room for eight only. The capacity of the bus was limited only by the amount of compression a passenger could sustain, and yet live. And in the event, hardly by that, because the step, the bonnet, and any excrescence to which a human foot could adhere took a share of the payload. To insert oneself in the door like the thin end of a wedge was difficult, but it was enough. Fellow combatants, like so many mauls, drove one right home, and having thus become merged among China's struggling millions one lost all volition. As in a pail full of maggots there is a constant seethe—the backwash of those entering and leaving—and just as fresh maggots are constantly coming to the top, so I found myself in a short time at the driver's end of the bus. There was a door there, too, through which I was immediately pressed, and although we had come only a couple of blocks I decided to walk the rest.

Before reaching Urumchi in Chinese Turkestan where I hoped to become once more a traveller, I had first to fly to Lanchow in North China on the Hwang-ho (Yellow River) and then to suffer 12 days in a post-bus. Once a fortnight a plane did the 1,200-mile hop from Shanghai to Lanchow in a day. I had difficulty in getting a seat in it, for the Chinese seemed to be over-addicted to air travel. I suppose if one has had much experience of road and rail travel in China, this is what one is apt to become. The advantage of soaring safely over the heads of war-lords and beyond reach of bandits is worth paying for. But it struck me that flying was remarkably cheap. The price of other things seemed to keep well abreast or even ahead of the rapidly falling exchange, but one could fly to Nanking for the price of a tin of tobacco.

The war-time transport plane, fitted with iron bucket-seats as became the iron-hard seats of the military gentlemen who had formerly used them, left Shanghai at 8 a.m., landed at Hankow, and reached Lanchow that evening. It was the same plane in which an American possessed of much money and considerable hope, had been recently scouring western China in search of a mountain higher than Mt. Everest. No doubt on the China-Tibet border there are many unmeasured peaks, indeed parts of the maps of those regions are still largely conjectural, but most of it has been traversed by explorers who, had they noticed such a considerable protuberance as a 30,000 ft. mountain, would certainly have drawn attention to it. On this occasion no mountains higher than 20,000 to 21,000 ft. were seen.

The American pilot was assisted by a Chinese co-pilot whose duties were nominal, part of them being no doubt to save face. He could fly the thing when it was airborne, but, according to the American, he was no great hand at anything else; and since what goes up must at last come down it was a relief to see that this essential ending was left to the pilot. After flying for some time in cloud, through which one occasionally glimpsed hideously eroded, reddish hills, we touched down. I heaved my accustomed sigh of relief:

> So between the starry dome
> And the floor of plain and seas,
> I have never felt at home
> Never really been at ease.

Lanchow-fu, to give it its full name, is the capital of Kansu province. It lies on the right bank of the Hwang-ho at an altitude of 5,000 ft. The river is bridged here and it is as a bridge-point on the chief overland approach to China from the West that Lanchow owes its importance from very early times. When I learnt that the nearest railhead was in western Honan 25 days' journey away, I felt that the C.N.A.C. (Chinese National Air Corporation) had earned every penny of the fare.

Lanchow was the army headquarters of what was called the 'North-West' which included Sinkiang. The commander was General Chang Chi-chung, a man prominent in the peace negotiations after the revolt of the three northern districts of Sinkiang—Ili, Chuguchak, Altai—in 1944, when, having killed or driven out the Chinese troops and civilians, the rebels proclaimed a Republic of East Turkestan. These three districts, half of whose inhabitants are Kazaks, lie to the north of the Tien Shan range and form the wealthiest part of Sinkiang. They produce a surplus of grain, upon which Urumchi is dependent for food, and also oil, gold, wolfram, and coal. Peace terms were negotiated by the General, who became Chairman of a Provincial Coalition Government, but they were never implemented. After more trouble in 1947 a Turki was appointed Chairman and Chang Chi-chung became commander of the 'North-West'. But Chinese troops were still excluded from the Ili district, the Chinese had lost all control over it, and in 1948 it was well on the way to becoming another of the Soviet Asiatic Republics.

However, Chinese writ still ran in Urumchi and the rest of Sinkiang, and the name of the General, to whom I had a letter of introduction, was potent enough there. He was a man who looked a very fit forty, though I believe he was nearer sixty years old, and he had a charming wife who had spent several years in England. He gave me a *laissez-passer* for Sinkiang and a dinner of eight dishes, all as new to me as the steamed bread and the Russian chocolate with which we finished. Another powerful ally was the secretary of the China Inland Mission, a Mr Walker, through whom I obtained a seat in the post-bus to Urumchi for a modest 28 million dollars. The Lanchow mission ran a very active hospital situated on the other side of the river.

The town is as nondescript a place as I have seen. All I remember of it is a steam-roller. I stopped my rickshaw to have a look at this *rara avis* whose name, I think, was Hercules. How Hercules had got himself there from the coast is a question to which I still devote much thought. The Hwang-ho, known sometimes as China's Sorrow, is not a traffic artery, a Chinese railway could surely not accommodate him; had Hercules therefore chugged his way patiently from the coast? If so, it was surely an example of patient progress and dogged perseverance as worthy of an epic poem as the advance of the Chinese army to the re-conquest of Sinkiang in 1877; when, owing to supply difficulties, an advance guard had first to plant crops and reap them before the hungry horde behind could make its next forward spring.

The post-bus service seemed to retain something of the efficiency and panache of the old courier service, which, where it ran from Sian-fu in Shensi to Kashgar, was the longest in the world. The drivers of the big 5-ton Dodge truck had the lofty, swaggering airs affected, we are told, by the drivers of the old flash coaches. They were the aristocrats of the road, such as it was. Our driver would stroll up at the last minute smoking a cigarette which he would throw disdainfully to the admiring onlookers before donning a magnificent pair of white leather gauntlets. He would touch nothing but the driving wheel and that only with gloves. If anything went wrong, he would dismount to stretch his legs, leaving his two assistants to maltreat the engine and get themselves dirty. Off duty, however, he unbent. We changed driver and crew several times, but I never met one too superior to eat with his mechanics or even with me, and to do them justice they usually paid their bills and mine too. As became mail drivers they did themselves as well as the inns of the road would afford, drank when they could, and played Mah-jong and cards for what looked like great sums of money. Mah-jong, by the way, as played in the inns of the Kansu corridor road by the lorry fraternity has little resemblance to the laborious, stately wall-building we know. It is played at unnerving pace, the tiles being picked up and banged down with the speed and clatter of a machine gun.

The driver's freedom with his money, while in character with these brothers of the road, could probably be well afforded. Besides his pay there were, I imagine, some trifling perquisites, for in addition to mails the truck carried goods and passengers, who sat comfortably but precariously on top of the load. All, that is, except myself who had the place of honour and discomfort, on the box, as it were. It was cooler on top of the luggage and one could stretch out and sleep. I noticed, however, that no passengers presented themselves at the official starting-point where they would presumably have had to buy a ticket. But on the outskirts of the town we usually found waiting for us a small group who had no doubt come to some private arrangement with the driver the previous night. En route we would be frequently 'thumbed' and the driver could pick out instinctively the paying and non-paying 'thumbers'.

When I was not a guest of the driver, which happened only at the midday halt, I found the food question fraught with difficulty and anxiety. Before embarking on this lone journey I had carefully written down phonetically five or six essential words—words, I mean, for food—but there is a wide gulf between the writing and speaking of a foreign tongue and after a few discouraging essays I gave up trying to bridge it. Fortunately, in China there are no ridiculous hygienic regulations for the sale of food, puzzling to the buyer and a hindrance to the seller. It is displayed openly and conveniently in the street, neither behind glass windows, under glass cases, nor, worst of all, in cellophane wrappers. All I had to do therefore was to point to or seize what I wanted and flourish some notes; and the stall-keeper, mistaking me for a wealthy deaf-mute, complied with alacrity. Still, I like to get value for money, even Chinese paper money, and at first it was difficult to know whether to tender 10,000 dollars or half a million for a piece of bread. If the man was honest, and most of them were, one found oneself either with a derisory portion or with more than one could carry away.

This method, of course, restricted one to al fresco feeding; good enough in its way, but there were times when I wanted to get my legs under a table and to probe more deeply into the mysteries of Chinese food. As befits a civilized race the Chinese regard food with commendable gravity and have some unusual ideas about what may be eaten and how it should be cooked. It was quite maddening therefore, for me to see and smell these bizarre and possibly pleasing dishes in preparation and not to be able to ask for them. As the only barbarian then on view I was everywhere a conspicuous figure and was therefore followed generally by a small crowd. If I went into an eating-house, the crowd came too to watch the fun. In a place where the cooking and eating go on in the same room it should be easy to get what one wants, but watched by a hundred eyes I found the process too embarrassing. If, on the other hand, I managed to sneak in unobserved and sat down expectantly at the first table, I found myself either ignored or subjected to a volley of uncouth sound. No one had the nous to plank down in front of me something edible. Perhaps they thought, not unreasonably, that I had merely come to study the habits of the flies.

When hunger did eventually drive me to confront these obstacles to the eating of a square meal I found 'a trifling sum of misery new added to the foot of my account'. For when the guest at a Chinese eating-house finally lays down his tooth-pick with a sigh, pays his bill, and quits the table, the waiter in a strident bawl announces to the remaining clients the amount of the bill and the size of the proffered tip. The shades of meaning which can be expressed by the voice, even when uttering some bald figures, are no less numerous than the inferences suggested by a restaurant bill. Until custom has made him brazen, the fear that he has been publicly tried and found guilty of either extravagance or meanness, gluttony or crapulence, will in turn cross the mind of the replete but unhappy guest as he bolts for the door. I suppose this is done so that the owner of the 'joint', ensconced behind a pile of rice, can jot down the amount taken by his various waiters. Obviously it saves labour and book-keeping, and since publicity or the fear of publicity is a powerful monitor, the system is one worth the attention of a Minister of Food in any Welfare State.

The road crossed the river, quitted it, and climbed to a 10,000 ft. pass where snow still lingered on the hills above. At this season the river was rising, fast-flowing, and of a dirty yellow colour (hence the name Yellow River) owing to the quantity of yellow loess soil carried down in suspension. The Yellow Sea into which the great river flows is presumably so called on account of its discoloration by river water. The hills of north-west China consists for the most part of thick deposits of loess which, according to Prof. Albrecht Penck (*Geog. Journ.,* vol. 76), were derived from mud brought by the Hwang-ho from Central Asia during the Ice Age. The loess is being constantly eroded by rivers to form numerous gorges and the yellow soil is then carried to the plains whence it is again swept up by the wind and redeposited elsewhere. The loess haze to which this process gives rise is most marked in west Sinkiang where more often than not visibility is limited to a few miles only. This haziness occurs on even perfectly still days so that one might almost believe the loess dust to be so fine and impalpable as to be equally at home in the air or on the ground.

Von Richthofen was the first to recognize loess as an aeolian deposit. He made a series of remarkable journeys in China in the 1870's, and we were presently to catch sight of that part of the Nan Shan range between Kanchow and Suchow which has been named after him. We reached Kanchow the second night about 320 miles out. At many points we had passed close to the still impressive remains of the Great Wall on the north side of the road, and Kanchow was a typical Chinese walled town. The Chinese have a sublime faith in walls, even to this day. Apart from the Great Wall, their earliest architectural monument still above ground, cities and towns must be surrounded by walls. In China, no wall no town is axiomatic. At all the towns that I passed sentries paced these walls, the guards had their quarters in them, and at night the great wooden gates in the massive arched gateways were solemnly shut. These town walls are solid; a core of earth and stone covered with unburnt brick, 20–30 ft. high, and wide enough on top for a cart to be driven.

Walls are considered efficacious not only against the outer barbarians—Mongolian hordes and such like—but also against evilly disposed devils. A few feet inside the entrance to a Chinese compound there is often built a piece of wall[1] rather longer than the width of the entrance, so that anyone entering the compound has to make two right-angled turns. Such a device is quite devil-proof, for devils move only in straight lines. It is said, and I like to believe it, that the strongest objection to the building of the first railways in China was on the grounds that such remarkably long, straight lines would facilitate the movement of devils. I noticed these walls mostly in the compounds of government buildings which are rightly held to be more devil-ridden than any others.

Kanchow was a place of life and colour where the modern bazaar street was happily obscured by the neighbouring old-style houses, willow trees, and temples, of which the principal is the Hall of the Sleeping Buddha which for size almost rivalled the famous one at Bangkok. The Buddha is 120 ft. long and 40 ft. high, constructed of hollow clay, painted and lacquered. Whatever the old houses may have been like inside they looked delightful from without, with their curly projecting roofs of warm glazed tiles and elaborately carved eaves and supporting brackets. I have heard a theory that the curling concave roofs of Chinese buildings derive from the shape of Mongol tents. But the normal Mongol tent is the yort with a sensibly convex roof, the sagging ridge-pole type of tent being used only when on the move. Moreover, Chinese culture is quite alien to Mongolian; nor is it easy to see why the Chinese, who were building pagodas hundreds of years before the rise of the Mongolian Empire, should have been indebted to those wide-spreading, hard-riding ruffians for any architectural ideas except perhaps that of a stout wall for keeping them out. Such obscure, insoluble questions, however, are best left to sinolgoists for whom they provide a smouldering slag-heap of conjecture and controversy, which is ever ready to blaze anew at the wind of some fresh archaeological find.

1 These walls are known as 'pi-hsia-ch'iang' or 'avoidance of uncanny influence wall' (Lattimore).

CHAPTER TWO

To Urumchi

To Suchow in three days was good going. We had averaged 150 miles a day until a halt here of four days spoilt our average and checked my rising admiration for the Chinese Postal Service. However, a stay of four days at 'The Spring of Wine', as Suchow is known, should have sounded gratefully in the ears of anyone but an anchorite; but the poetical extravagance of Chinese place-names was for me already suspect and the drab appearance of the town did nothing to allay that suspicion.

Having been rebuilt on a new site after the destruction of the old town during the Tungan (Chinese Moslem) rebellion of 1860, it lacked the old houses, temples, and trees of a place like Kanchow which had successfully resisted the rebels. The rebuilding had evidently been in the hands of a barbarian town planner, for it was laid out in the convenient but dull criss-cross style. 'The Spring of Wine', which is outside the present walls, proved to be as pleasant as its name. I found it a large walled garden, so informal as to be almost a wilderness, with reed-filled ponds and melancholy willows, moss-grown temples, grottos, and paths, all surrounding a stone basin in which a limpid spring was bubbling. In a shady arbour by the spring were stone seats where one could sit and drink tea.

Marco Polo once passed through Suchow; as had Benedict Goez, the lay Jesuit traveller, 'who had sought Cathay and found heaven'. Leaving the court of Akbar in 1603 Benedict Goez went by the upper Oxus and over the Pamirs to Yarkand and Khotan, and finally to Suchow where in 1607, after being detained for 16 months, he died of disease and privation just as aid reached him. Marco Polo dismisses Suchow in half a page and wastes little more on Kanchow where he spent a whole year. But a first journey, like a first ascent, needs no embellishment; the thing either speaks for itself or there is so much to be told that there is neither room nor need for digression. Subsequent travellers, on the contrary, to make amends for any lack of novelty must needs digress often at the risk of losing their reader's attention; just as the climber on a hackneyed crag seeks for novelty at more serious hazard.

When the driver dropped me and my kit in the Post Office compound and advised me to 'scram', I was at a loss. The best of prospects is improved by an inn, but here was neither prospect nor inn. I looked at one and recoiled in dismay at the thought of spending four nights there—an example of 'the initiate fear which wants hard use' and which was later to be got at the inns of Hami and other places. Very reluctantly I billeted myself upon two American ladies of the C.I.M. who kindly took me in, although their house, which was being rebuilt, was all at sixes and sevens.

According to Stevenson, a taste for general information, not promptly checked, had sapped Uncle Joseph's manhood. Air and bus travel were sapping mine; hoping to restore it I tramped the uninteresting, flat countryside where I could walk abroad without becoming a public portent. Shod in climbing boots I walked far and fast, taking my lunch of steamed bread with meagre date-filling off the last barrow-boy's pitch without the city wall. Poor anaemic stuff it was, too, not to be compared with the rough Turki bread obtainable further west. That the confines of China were not far off was evident, for Tibetans were occasionally to be seen in the streets, and the black tents of nomads with their yaks and camels outside the walls.

Although Urumchi was still 700 miles away I managed to speak by telephone with Mr Paxton the American Consul with whom Shipton would be staying. A long-distance telephone call always impresses me as something of an achievement both by myself and by Alexander Graham Bell, and this last feat pleased and astonished me. There is no reason, of course, why the noise a Chinese makes should not be as acceptable to a telephone instrument as any of the more recognized forms of speech; but I am still puzzled as to how telegrams are handled in a language that has no alphabet.

A compulsory visit to the police station in accordance with the Suchow immigration by-laws led to my meeting a young student who had some English. He asked me to dine and I gladly accepted, for restaurants had no terror for me when accompanied by an *habitué*. We went to the upstairs room of a place chosen with some care. It had not struck me before, but there were degrees of dirtiness in the restaurant world of Kansu and my companion was more fastidious than I. It would not have been in Dr Johnson's opinion a dinner to *ask* a man to. It consisted of spaghetti laced with bean sauce or red pepper according to choice, which is the common eating-house dish called 'kua mien'. The equipment is equally simple, a bowl, a saucer for the sauce, chopsticks; and to wipe the latter in case they had not been washed, the proprietor provided, regardless of expense, two bits of paper. Fans could be borrowed gratis and one could spit on the floor if one wished—Liberty Hall, in fact. To finish we had what sounded to me like 'champagne' tea which implied the most expensive kind. It was heavily flavoured and since the ordinary tea was not flavoured at all, in future I always asked for 'champagne'.

The bus did not leave until the fifth day, but partially made up for lost time with a run of 170 miles to Anhsi. At a place called Chia-yu-Kuan (Barrier of the Pleasant Valley) just west of Suchow the road passes through the remains of the western extremity of the Great Wall. This was the western limit of the old Middle Kingdom, China 'Within the Wall'. The wall here is of puddled clay about 12 ft. thick and 20 ft. high. The late Sir Aurel Stein has shown that west of Suchow there were in fact two walls. One dating from the second century B.C. continued westwards to Tunhuang beyond Anhsi; its purpose being to protect the narrow line of oases strung along the foot of the Nan Shan (the South Mountains) which were indispensable as a means of commercial and political advance into Central Asia. The second wall, of far more recent construction, was built for the opposite purpose, to close the Central Asian route at a time when China was on the defensive.

In the early afternoon we reached Yu-men-hsien, the 'Town of the Jade Gate'. We remained here until 6 p.m. to avoid the heat of the desert lying between us and Anhsi. This section of desert, by the way provided the best running of the day. In two fat, fascinating volumes, *Ruins of Desert Cathay*, Sir Aurel Stein describes how he found the ruins of the west wall of Tunhuang and how having first dug up a reference to 'Jade Gate', at length located the actual fort in the neighbourhood of Tunhuang:

> Among our first finds [he writes] was a label evidently once tied to a bag, referring to a hundred bronze arrow-heads and naming a certain company of 'Yu-men'. So at last I had found the name of that famous Jade Gate which I had thought from the first was to be located somewhere along this westernmost part of the 'limes'. Again and again in the course of subsequent excavations I felt grateful for the *amor scribendi* which seems to have prompted these ancient 'military Babus'—like those whom one now meets in queer corners of the fortified posts scattered along the Indian North-West Frontier— to beguile their ennui and demonstrate their own importance by a constant flow of reports, store statements, and other documents so familiar to soldiering men in most regions.

And later goes on:

> The thinnest layer of gravel sufficed to preserve in absolute freshness even such perishable objects as shreds of clothing, wooden tablets, arrow-shafts, straw, and chips. Whatever objects had once passed under this protection were practically safe in a soil which had seen but extremely scanty rainfall for the last two thousand years, was far removed from any chance of irrigation or other interference by human agency, and had suffered on its flat surface but rarely even from wind erosion. Often a mere scraping with my boot-heel sufficed to disclose where the detachments holding the posts had been accustomed to throw their refuse. With all the reports, statements, and enquiries which a fully developed and, no doubt, scribe-ridden military organization had kept moving along this chain of border watch-stations for more than two thousand years, was it wonderful that I soon grew accustomed to picking up records of the time of Christ or before, almost on the surface?

We did not reach Anhsi, the 'West-protecting', until late at night and though we left again at 5 a.m. it was no hardship for me who had to pass the short night on the Post Office counter. Nor would the tourist have missed anything, for crumbling city walls and one wide dilapidated street made up the sum total of Anhsi. And here I must enter a protest at the mutability of Chinese place-names, attributable sometimes to change of government and sometimes to change of mind on the part of scholars. How is one to travel to the right place or even write about it when Anhsi may be Ngan-hsi or Anhsichow; Kanchow equally Chang-yeh; and Suchow Chin-chu'an? Most flagrant of all is Peiping for what most of us go on calling Peking. This was one of the far-reaching reforms carried out in 1928 when the Nationalist armies took the place and transferred the capital to Nanking. Nor was this the only change made. Practically every street in Shanghai, and there are a good many, was renamed, but the old names had been in use so long that to this day a street map is provided with a key showing the original names. This itch to efface old memories is a habit that has derived, with many other bad habits, from the French Revolution. It is high time some public-spirited man called a meeting of prospective revolutionaries and persuaded them to pass a Self-Denying Ordinance that whatever other violent changes they might have in view, all place-names, especially those of mountains, should be sacrosanct.

Anhsi was formerly important as the junction of two great routes to the West, south and north respectively of the Tarim basin. And it was by the control of the Tarim basin through the occupation of Sinkiang that China kept open this essential road. The old road, which we had followed as far as Anhsi, passed along the southern edge of the Lop Nor and Takla Makhan desert (both part of the Tarim basin) to Khotan, Yarkand, Kashgar, and thence either north of the Pamirs or south through Wakhan to Bokhara and Samarkand. In Marco Polo's day this route had almost been abandoned in favour of one which struck north-west from Anhsi across a part of the Gobi desert to Hami and thence along the north side of the Tarim basin to Kashgar. This last is the present motor-road, but recently there was some talk of making the old southern route practicable for lorries.

The missionary authors of *Through Jade Gate and Central Asia* who have vividly described the Gobi desert do well to lament the gradual ousting of the camel caravan by motor transport—a process which, beginning in the thirties, has accelerated rapidly during the war. Poets see what others miss. It is all very well for Kipling to write of Romance bringing up the nine-fifteen, but to my prosaic mind a truck is a vehicle fatal to Romance. The more wild and lonely the environment, the more incongruous and romance-shattering is the presence of a truck; although the desert may hold something of the grandeur and terror of the sea, in the desert these qualities are more easily dissipated by mechanical transport. The desert may have moods, but it never can assume the aggressive violence of the sea, which can so easily reduce machinery to scrap-iron and impotence. True, trucks often break down in the desert— 'It is but machinery, Sahib,' as an apologetic Indian driver reminded me—but these misfortunes cannot be ascribed to its wrath. Nor if they break down are they in any danger of foundering or driving ashore. On the whole, I think that Romance in travel is inseparable from an element of risk:

> My mistress still the open road
> and the bright eyes of danger.

Perhaps too early and heavy a breakfast of bread gave rise to this melancholy train of thought as we chugged slowly away from Anhsi across the desert, where the scene was indeed favourable for Romance if only the smell of petrol could have been excluded. The mind might spread its melancholy freely as the desert which on our right hand stretched to the bitter Mongolian steppes, and on our left to the thirsty sand of the Lop Nor; for the sun had not yet risen to redeem a little the harsh unfriendliness of this gravel wilderness in which the ragged outline of jet-black hills appeared like islands rising from a sombre sea. That deserts are rarely sandy was a fact which impressed itself upon me during the late war when we careered across the Syrian and Sinai deserts in a matter of days, and then for six months rolled backwards and forwards, rather less light-heartedly, across the desert of Libya, where gravel is the rule and pockets of sand the exception. Nor need they be flat; the scorched and scarred mountains on either side of the Red Sea at once come to mind, and here in the Gobi we often had to wind through defiles between low rocky hills.

We left Kansu and entered Sinkiang at a place in mid-desert, Hsinghsingsia, where we stopped the night. It was full of police and soldiers in marching order, more powerful dissipators of Romance even than trucks. I slept at the Post Office where I had lunched in a pretty lordly way with the driver and other high officials. It was brought to us from some no doubt squalid inn and I noticed that a fantastic amount of paper was handed over in exchange. In the middle of the Gobi one must expect to pay for one's pleasure. But one might have hoped that in a country of harsh facts, where man existed only on sufferance, so remote from treasuries and banks, that the man-made mystery of exchange rates would have been unknown. Nevertheless, for reasons best known perhaps to some bland financial wizard fanning himself at Hong Kong, the Sinkiang dollar or 'kuchen' was worth five Chinese dollars. Thus, since the money was the same, until one got used to multiplying or dividing by five one was constantly being cheated or detected in a cheat.

We left early, fresh and fasting. The road climbed to a pass and then began dropping steadily to a flat plain of gravel and hard clay where the heat began to increase noticeably. Having broken our fast in the company of some soldiers at a Chinese post we drove rapidly westwards at the foot of the distant snow-covered Karlik Tagh until in the late afternoon we reached the prosperous oasis of Hami. As there was some doubt about when we should go on, I had to find quarters. At the third inn I tried, either from curiosity or pity, they took me in.

Much has been written about the inns of China and Sinkiang, little of it to their credit. It should be remembered, however, that those who write about these inns were never expected to stay in them. They are meant for travellers whose wants are conspicuously few, whose luggage consists of a little tobacco or opium, and who do not regard the presence of a few bugs (a weak point in these inns) as an indictable offence. They are part and parcel of the country.

The 'Inn of the Overlapping Teeth' at which I stopped was happily named because it was only a sleeping inn. That is to say you were given a mud room or cell and nothing else. In my cell I seem to remember a table, but as there was never anything put upon it, not even an aspidistra, it was purely symbolic. The bed was the usual raised earth dais with a fire-place underneath for heating in winter; very naturally the bed had become the ancestral home of not a few bugs. A little sweeping and watering to lay the dust and one's bed is made; and should one be addicted to washing then there is a well in one corner of the serai. 'Simplify, simplify', as Thoreau constantly urged.

The traveller or the reader of travel books who reaches Hami will find the matter of place-names becoming even more troublesome. Now in addition to the Chinese name with all its variants, there is a Turki name also with scholarly variations. Hami is the Chinese name, Kumul or Qomul the Turki.

Marco Polo in his swift way discussed Camul, as he calls it, in three paragraphs devoted largely to the people and their manners, which a traveller might condone but which a moralist must certainly condemn:

They are a people who take things very easily, for they mind nothing but playing and singing, and dancing and enjoying themselves . . . And it is the truth that if a foreigner comes to the house of one of these people to lodge the host is delighted, and desires his wife to put herself entirely at the guest's disposal, while he himself gets out of the way. The guest may stay and enjoy the wife's society as long as he likes while the husband has no shame in the matter, but indeed considers it an honour. And all the men of his province are made wittols of by their wives in this manner. The wives themselves are fair and wanton.

Hami has always been important to the Chinese as a commercial centre and as a base for the frequent reconquests of Sinkiang which they have been obliged to undertake. Early in the seventeenth century Hami came under the Moslem Khan or Prince of Kashgar, and until recently it was nominally a political entity ruled by a Khan of its own just as Khiva and Bokhara once were. The Chinese recovered it in 1720, lost it during the Moslem rebellion of 1865, and recovered it again in 1873. There are now three towns—the Chinese walled town containing barracks and government offices, a modern hybrid bazaar, and the old walled city of Kumul of narrow alley-ways containing the palace of the Khan.

Having put through another call to Urumchi to report progress, and having had a hair-cut (70,000 kuchen), I took once more to walking—the alternative to lying in my cell brushing away flies and curious visitors. But I found the country ill-suited to walking for pleasure. No matter which direction one took, sooner rather than later one struck a dry, flat, gravelly plain without landmarks or objectives of any kind. Mounted upon a horse is the way to enjoy this sort of country, and then only if the horse is a free-moving, generous beast and not the usual dull hireling fobbed off upon strangers. Until it gets bored a horse is inspired rather than depressed by an unbroken expanse of flat gravel. Wild ancestral memories of boundless freedom take possession of it, giving great satisfaction to the rider in whom speed of movement foster the false impression that presently he will see something new.

As there was still no activity at the Post Office, another day had to be spent in aimless wandering. Not quite aimless, however, for on my way out of the town I visited the tombs of the Hami princes which with their high domes of green glazed tiles and blue and white tiled walls were well worth seeing. As usual I took a lunch of bread with me. Without a chaperon I preferred to avoid the rubs and forgo the delights of eating in the town, for having poked about the bazaar pretty thoroughly I had become almost a national figure and now avoided it whenever possible. In Hami, as everywhere else, there is nothing funnier than a foreigner. I noticed that ice was on sale which, from its worn, dirty appearance, might well have been a relic of the Ice Age, but which is, I suppose, gathered in winter and stored in ice-houses.

A great deal of rice is grown, also grapes, and the melons for which Hami is famous. They used to be sent to the Imperial Court at Peking. Such a journey must have taken the ordinary caravan about three months, so perhaps the melon began its honourable journey as a seedling in a pot of Hami soil and finished it fully ripe for the Imperial stomach. Or ripe melons might have gone by relays of couriers, for in his book *High Tartary* Lattimore speaks of Bara-kul ponies (Bara-kul is a lake north-west of Hami) which can do 100 miles a day; or, perhaps, dried melons were sent, for in the intense summer heat of this region melons can be dried before they rot. In my opinion these melons were not worth so much trouble. Although luscious enough, they were not the equals of the best Kashgar—the 'beshak shirin', for example, which is a yellowy-green Cantaloupe of exquisite flavour.

When I went round to the Post Office that evening and interrupted a brisk Mah-jong session I learnt that we would go that night. In summer the lorry drivers do as much night driving as they can owing to the heat which becomes ever fiercer until the Turfan Depression is reached and passed. We left at 11 p.m. and stopped 40 miles on to sleep on the road. By 6 a.m. we were off again and twelve hours later had reached Chiktam nearly 200 miles from Hami. The road clung to the foothills of the Karlik Tagh which are an easterly extension of the Bogdo Ola, separated from it by a narrow gap through which there is a pass to the north. Having climbed nearly to the gap at a height of about 4,000 ft. the road turned south-west away from the mountains and ran down to the plains. All this is even more desert-like country than the Gobi, and there are even fewer posts and wells.

We carried on till 11 p.m., slept a few hours, and finished the remaining 40 miles to Turfan before 6 a.m. Of Turfan, which looked interesting, I was not allowed to see much, for after some delicious hot bread and tea with the postmaster we were off again at 8 a.m. One Turfan peculiarity which I had already noticed on the way was the long lines of spoil from the wells of the 'karez'.

This underground system of irrigation practised by the Turkis of the Turfan Depression is unknown to the Chinese who in any case do not occupy themselves with agriculture in Sinkiang. They come to this Chinese colony not as settlers, but as soldiers, officials, or traders. The 'karez' was introduced from Persia in the eighteenth century. It consists of a series of wells tapping an underground flow of water. The furthest well is sunk until water is reached and then a series of wells of diminishing depth (owing to the slope of the ground) are dug at intervals of about 10 yards. An underground tunnel is then driven to connect the whole series so that the water finally emerges at ground level beyond the last well. The wells facilitate the digging of the tunnel and the cleaning of it. All the people of Turfan are not dependent on 'karez' water, for water is also obtained from streams that drain from the southern glaciers of Bogdo Ola—streams which, having disappeared under the gravel plain at the foot of the mountain, reappear from the red sandstone hills bordering the depression on the north.

Turfan town is about 250 ft. above sea level, while the lowest point in the Depression, some 30 miles south is 426 ft. below sea level. Outside the basin the ground rises rapidly to 2,500 ft. The soil is loess which, except in the lowest parts where it is saline, is extremely fertile wherever water can be brought. Rice, cotton, wheat, grapes, melons, and vegetables of all kinds grow to perfection. The piles of prime fruit and vegetables displayed in the mat-shaded bazaar gladdened the heart; but even for the sake of eating its produce I should not wish to live in Turfan, except in winter. Besides shading their streets with mats, trellises, and vines, the people employ whole fleets of donkeys for the carriage of water which is flung lavishly over floors, walls, and streets to mitigate the parching heat. By nine of a morning the busy streets fall silent and the shady market-place is abandoned to flies and sleeping donkeys.

The long gruelling climb out of the Depression up the steep gravel glacis in the heat of the day sorely tried our labouring engine which threatened constantly to boil over. Still climbing, we entered a gorge with a dry river-bed; then a few willow thickets appeared, bits of grass; and soon without quite realizing how the trick had been peformed we found we were winding along the verdant banks of a laughing river. The gorge opened, and as though crossing a pass we debouched upon a green plain. On our right the grass soon yielded to another great gravel glacis scored with dry water-courses, and above the glacis rose the steep ramparts of Bogdo Ola, castellated with ice and snow. At a good inn at Davanchin (Dawan Ch'eng, the City of the Pass) some 30 miles from Urumchi, I ate for the last time with the crew of the lorry. From the upstairs room I watched the clouds form and dissolve about the great mountain which, I thought, looked decidely hostile.

We drove on, the now cloud-hidden mountain far on our right and on our left a broad, blue, reed-fringed lake without visible inlet or outlet; I was elated both with the glimpse of the noble mountain I had come so far to see and by the long-looked-for meeting in this distant country with an old tried friend. The journey had been long and more tiring than it should have been: for I had been from the start a passenger and not a traveller, with neither animals to care for nor porters to cajole.

At last, 10 miles from Urumchi, I saw a familiar truck and by it a familiar figure. Two familiar figures, in fact, for Mr Shipton had with him his Sherpa servant Lakhpa who had been with us in our disastrous attempt upon Muztagh Ata the previous year. Ready hands took charge of my scanty luggage, and as the Dodge trundled onwards towards the now setting sun the gratitude I felt was only tempered by the regret that the old ways of travel had been almost extinguished by the truck and its kind.

CHAPTER THREE

Bogdo Ola

URUMCHI is a fine outlandish name for a town, a name whose richness and raffish promise makes the Chinese name of Tiwha sound thin and prim. That celebrated list of places at which Uncle Joseph settled his imaginary recipient of £80 a year when he lectured to the Working Men's Institute, Isle of Dogs, on how to live on that amount, would, I think, have rolled more richly from the tongue had Urumchi replaced, say, Brighton: 'London, Paris, Bagdad, Spitzbergen, Bussorah, Heligoland, the Scilly Isles, *Urumchi*, Cincinnati, and Nijni Novgorod.' My feeling that it belied its promise of rollicking iniquity might have been unjust, but I only spent a few days there—many more are needed before one should pass judgment on such a place. And who can say what went on behind the high walls of the Russian Consulate, for example; in the Chinese yamen of the new town; or, above all, behind the massive façade of the Central Bank of China, which was of the expensive, solid, confidence-inspiring type of architecture, an incongruous building to see rising amid a huddle of unburnt brick and corrugated iron.

The American Consulate, where Shipton and I were grateful guests, had neither the aloof mysterious air of Russia nor the opulent magnificence of the Bank. The Americans had established their Consulate only during the last war (1943), whereas the Russians were almost coeval with the resumption of power by the Chinese in Sinkiang in the latter part of the last century. Hence they had not had the time to buy or build something more worthy of the present inheritors of the White Man's Burden—at any rate of his financial burden. The Consulate buildings were in a side-street on the outskirts, and hard by was the four-roomed establishment destined for the British Consul and his family then on their way from Shanghai. This is a lodging well suited to a representative of the New Poor when they at last give up their ideas on keeping up appearances.

But whatever the American Consulate may have looked from outside, there was a great amount of activity and hospitality inside. Seldom less than a dozen people took breakfast there. In addition to the staff and a fellow-consul like Shipton, who without straining the imagination could be said to be there on business, there were myself, who by no stretch of imagination had any business at all, two or three American officials and visitors, and above all American journalists. The latter were always coming and going, relentlessly interviewing, and persistently acquiring information with which to rear edifices of theory upon the shifting sands of Central Asian politics. The great question then (by now resolved) was whether the revolted province of Ili would return to the Chinese fold or whether it would remain under the increasing Russian influence.

We gave ourselves three days to put our affairs in order—to pay our respects to Chinese officials, to pack, and to collect food for our three weeks' excursion to Bogdo Ola. Mrs Paxton, the wife of the American Consul, gave us the run of her overflowing store, and although we may have tried to sustain a undeserved reputation for austerity there is little doubt that we failed. I, at any rate, seldom make the vulgar mistake of not taking enough, if it is enough only of unvarnished belly-timber such as flour or rice; which is, no doubt, what the Chinese sage had in mind when he affirmed that a well-filled stomach is indeed the great thing—all else is luxury. Nearly all climbers would agree with the first part of this proposition, but might with to make reservations about the second. I say nearly all because I have in mind one of the early climbers of Mont Blanc who advised a friend with similar ambitions that 'provisions are of no use, all that is wanted is an umbrella and a scent bottle'.

The food of an expedition is governed largely by questions of transport and since in most serious expeditions transport is likely to be difficult it should be taken as a general rule that the food should be austerely simple—bare necessities, in fact, like flour and sugar which require no other packing than a sack. Hence it is a seductive, convincing, and possibly sound argument—one that I find myself using too often—that the only good reason for cutting out all the luxuries and most of the comforts of life is the difficulty of transport. If, the argument goes, the expedition is not likely to encounter these difficulties—the English of which is that you will not have to carry any load yourself—then there is no very urgent call to practise austerity. Let yaks grunt, porters sweat, and donkeys quiver at the knees, but let there be enough luxuries in the way of butter, jam, cheese, marmalade etc. to help down the humdrum necessities of flour and rice. After all—applying theory to practice—Bogdo Ola was a mere 30 miles by lorry road, whence ponies would carry our belongings easily to the foot of the mountain, so why quibble over a few glass jars of pea-nut butter (the glass weighing considerably more than the contents) or whether to take five or six 2-lb. tins of marmalade? If it is true, as Dr Johnson observed, that abstinence is not a virtue in itself but only the groundwork of a virtue, it is a thing the high-souled man can afford to ignore.

Urumchi lies athwart all roads to the east or to the west, on which account, alone, I imagine, is it the capital, for any other merits are not easily discernible. Roads lead to China either north or south of the Bogdo Ola group; a road leads to Outer Mongolia, another to Russia by Ili or by Chuguchak, and there is the road to Kashgar south of the Tien Shan. As befits a capital it is thus a commercial centre and a focal point for travellers and their tales; some of which are authentic, but the majority are merely rumours of a most lurid kind. Although the important Ili road had long been closed on account of the revolt, the Turki bazaar was still a lively place, much livelier than the Chinese shopping centre in the new town—the Chinese city proper—where a lot of American and European fountain-pens, watches, torches, and so on were for sale at fancy prices.

Besides poking about in the bazaar, looking at jade cups and ornamented whips and speculating on the queer vegetables and spices on offer—for wheresoever any particular herb grows there lives the ass who is to eat it—we spent much time bathing in a newly constructed reservoir five miles out, or vainly trying to get a shot at the duck and geese which occasionally visited it. So pleasant was this lake that I even used to trot out there before breakfast, partly to fettle up and partly to exorcise the combined effects of American and Chinese hospitality. Apart from the constant knife-and-fork play at the Consulate and an occasional chopstick match against the Chinese, the American Military Attaché and his wife, who were also visitors, liked to have informal snack parties at odd hours—a purée of red chilli spread on biscuits, grapes, raw paprika, Turki bread, and peaches, all of which needed to be assuaged with the local rice brandy or Russian vodka. It might be thought that using a weapon as ineffective-looking as a chopstick, would prevent anything more than polite pecking, but with a little practice it is surprising how much one can rake, claw, or shovel in. The postmaster, who was from Canton, gave us a dinner of Cantonese food which in China is regarded as *hors concours*. Fried oysters on lettuce perhaps qualified as a 'dish to be eaten on one's knees'; but the custom of drinking tea before dinner and brandy throughout is, like marriage, rather to be permitted than approved.

But enough, something too much, of these low pleasures; especially when one may see, as we did, on leaving the house of a morning, a far-off tower of ice and snow, severe in outline, but warm and friendly in the rising sun. Having loaded the truck overnight we left early on 10 July for Fukang some 40 miles away. The climbing party consisted of four: Shipton and myself, the perhaps slightly blunted spearhead of the attack; Lakhpa, a Sherpa, who was Shipton's major domo, factotum, and knowledgable adviser in mundane affairs; and a Hunza man whose name other than that of 'Hill Billy' by which we knew him has escaped me.

Lakhpa had been with Shipton or me on several Himalayan journeys, notably on Everest in 1938 when he had carried to Camp VI, and afterwards on the return home he had accompanied me over the Zemu Gap. He had gone to Kashgar in 1940 when Shipton did his first spell there as Consul. He had taken very readily to life in Kashgar, and through his zeal for his master's affairs and his own he had now acquired an influential position among the menial staff of the Conuslate, a Turki wife, and a great belly. The Chinese saying that no honest official has fat subordinates carries, in this case, the doctrine of collective responsibility too far. Anyway, what mattered was not Lakhpa's honesty but his obesity which we feared might now prevent his carrying our loads. The Hunza man was one of the Kashgar mail couriers on the Kashgar-Tashkurgan run. He looked cheerful, tough, keen, and had come perhaps under the mistaken impression that he was on holiday. He was not much given to idle chat, but that may have been because we had no common language.

Fukang is on the north road to Hami and the east which lies along the edge of the Zungarian plain and the foothills of Bogdo Ola. Not far from Urumchi there are some coal measures where open-cast mining is carried on in a desultory way. At Fukang we expected to find ponies ready to take us the same day as far as the lake of Tien Shih (Heavenly Pool), but the enthusiastic promises made to us at Urumchi had not yet been translated into action at Fukang. We must take the truck on as far as we could and hope that ponies would be sent up that evening. By noon we had reached the end of the rough road well among the foothills, and from there we manhandled the loads to a pleasant camp by water and willows and settled down to await our transport.

At dark they arrived, and with them, in a jeep, Greeson of the American Consulate accompanied by their White Russian mechanic. Both were heavily armed, for ever since his recent arrival in Urumchi it had been Greeson's devouring and as yet unsatisfied ambition to slay something, no matter what. Having been in the American Marines during the war he should have had enough of shooting and being shot at, but his eyes still lit up at the sight of a firearm, and to achieve his ambition no journey was too far and no labour too great. I think I felt much the same on first going to East Africa, but there one's blood lust could soon be sated whereas around Urumchi I saw no way of doing this short of manslaughter.

From here the road climbed more steeply through bald or scrub-covered hills which little prepared us for the startling beauty of the country immediately ahead. After topping a sort of pass (6,000 ft.) we saw below us a great sheet of deepest sapphire water, hemmed around by dark green pines, except on our side where a terrace of short grass dropped steeply to the water. Across the lake and above the pines shone the splendour of the new mountain world that we had come to seek.

In this glorious spot there is a Kazak village, and a monastery inhabited by Chinese Taoist monks; but to neither, picturesque and congruous though they no doubt were, did we pay any regard. Obviously the first thing to be done was to leap into that heavenly water—'the swimmer into cleanness plunging'—and the next secure the boat, of which we had heard, for our passage across the lake. As became a Marine, Greeson charged himself with this task and he soon had a large, cranky, flat-bottomed craft in perceptible motion. It was more than half full of water and when that had been baled out it filled up again rapidly. As a cargo boat it was useless so the ponies had to go round. We, however, who were not to be easily baulked of a day on the water, gaily embarked, stripped to the waist, and plied the oar—both oars, to be exact, but one was broken. More than an hour passed before we could sing the hymn

> Now the labourer's task is o'er,
> Now upon the farther shore
> Lands the voyager at last:

and I shall not be rating our oarsmanship too highly if I say that this lovely lake of Tien Shih is a mile long. Anyhow, we had beaten the ponies; and when, in concern at their long absence, we walked back to look for them and saw the nature of the track we understood why.

A little beyond the lake the wide valley we were following divided and a valley of almost equal size came in on our left. We had no guide, but our map seemed to show the route going up the left-hand valley. Shipton, whose judgment in these matters is usually better than mine was certain the way lay straight on. The two streams seemed much of a size and neither looked like glacier water, although Shipton was equally certain that his stream drained the main Grachimailo glacier which he had seen from a distant hill on a previous visit. We took the left-hand valley which proved to be correct. A glance at the map will show how Shipton was deceived. Looking at the glacier

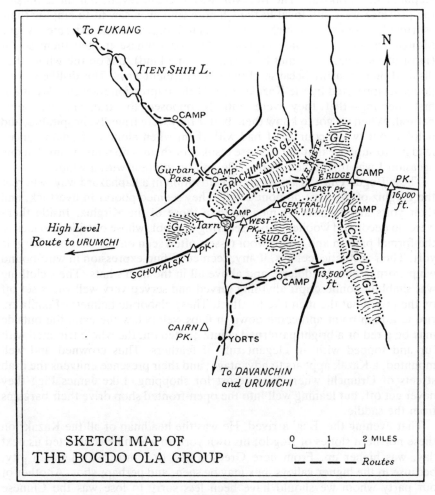

BOGDO OLA

from a distance no one would suspect that at its western end it drains *south* through a narrow gap between the main mountain and the Schokalsky peak, and that both our streams are cut off from the glacier by a low ridge not more than 12,000 ft. high.

The path now rose steeply until at about 8,000 ft. we came to some Kazak yorts pitched on a steep grass shoulder where we camped. The Kazak are nomads or semi-nomads very like the Kirghiz of Kashgaria of whom they are a branch; but the intricacies of relationship between Kirghiz, Kazak, Cossack, Mongol, Tatar, the identity of the Great, the Middle, and the Lesser hordes, and such like, are conundrums only for students. There are said to be half a million Kazaks in north-east Sinkiang and about three million in the Soviet Republic of Kazakstan. The Ili revolt was a Kazak revolt, but those outside the province were still loyal to the Chinese who even saw fit to employ them as irregular troops in the bickering always in progress on the extremely vague Mongolian border. It was surprising that the Chinese trusted them so far (most of the Kazaks we met had arms of some kind): but on the whole they disliked them heartily because of their independent ways. This dislike was no doubt reciprocated by the Kazaks, so that the impression they gave us at our first meeting—that they were entirely opposed to strangers—was only natural. When we got to know them better they were friendly, hospitable, and helpful; but two encounters I had with them when alone and unannounced lead me to suppose that the Chinese dislike for them is no mere whim. On one occasion I was threatened with a rifle and on another with a whip.

These Bogdo Ola Kazaks do some cultivation in a haphazard way, whereas the Kirghiz of the west do none at all. They seemed poorer in livestock, and their yorts and furnishings meaner than those of the Kirghiz. Inside there were no decorated woollen bands securing the roof, whose outside also lacked the formal pattern and bright wool tassels often seen on the roof of a Kirghiz yort. Their aesthetic feelings, if any, seemed to find expression in wire-bound whips, ornamented saddlery, and above all in the men's hats. Their clothing was shabbily nondescript; anything served and served very well when set off by the proud hat the men like to affect. These elaborate helmets of lambskin rise to a high point and come down in flaps well below the ears; the outside may be a red or a bright patterned chintz quilted on, the whole trimmed with fur and topped with an elegant tuft of feathers. Thus crowned and well mounted, a Kazak appears to advantage; and their presence enlivens the drab streets of Urumchi where they resort for shopping. Like James Pigg they never get off, but leaning well into the open-fronted shop drive their bargains from the saddle.

That evening the 'Beg' arrived. He was the headman of all the Kazaks on these northern slopes of Bogdo; his own yort, to which he conducted us next day, was higher up. From here Greeson had to return; which was a pity, because in the higher valleys ibex may be seen, and perhaps shot. Another of our party whom we should have been less sorry to lose was the Chinese policeman (mounted) who in spite of our protests had been detailed to accompany us. Whether the Kazaks helped us on account of his presence or in spite of it was not clear, but we hoped that conditions higher up would overcome the scruples he had at leaving us.

The Beg's yort was in keeping with his position. Though perhaps not as fine as that of a Kirghiz Beg, it was well enough; the milk pans were impressively large—two or three feet across—and we had no criticism to make of the quality of the yoghourt. Lying on rugs in this spacious yort, sipping thin, slightly sour 'kumis' and sucking in spoonfuls of yoghourt, we felt much at ease. Unfortuately it was not yet midday, too early even by Himalayan standards to call it a day. 'Stretched on the rack of a too easy chair', we experienced some stirring of conscience and against our better judgment and against the inclination of everyone else we pushed on.

Owing perhaps to our going so slowly or to the drowsiness induced by 'kumis', the familiar transition from juniper to grass, from grass to gravel, boulders, and finally snow, passed almost unnoticed. That we were getting high impressed itself upon us by the growing unwillingness of our followers, the yaks, the ponies, the guide, and especially the policeman. It began to rain and blow. We crossed the ridge at about 12,000 ft. and saw dimly below us a big, dry glacier, the Grachimailo. Thunder boomed. The rain turned to hail and then snow, so we hastily pitched camp on the first convenient bit of scree a few hundred feet down the other side. The men departed unreluctantly with their yaks and ponies, the policeman with very little persuasion followed them, and we four were left to contemplate what I thought a distasteful scene.

Our welcome to Bogdo Ola had been rude. Snow continued falling intermittently and the little of the mountain we were able to see gave us no pleasure. The main massif of Bogdo is a ridge two miles long crowned by three upstanding peaks, the West, Central, and East, the last being the highest by several hundred feet. Apart from steep buttresses descending from the peaks the north face is a wall; both extremities of the ridge are cut off pretty abruptly, and there is no easy passage along the top from one peak to the next. That is to say that if one wanted to climb the highest peak, as of course we did, there was no getting at it from either of the other peaks or from the ridge between. It had to be climbed direct or not at all.

Between our camp and the mountain flowed the Grachimailo glacier, our camp lying opposite the west end of the ridge. Looking up the glacier and across it to the East peak we could see the profile of a steep rock arête descending from the peak. It looked attractively short, exciting, and formidable and we decided that our first move must be to have a closer look at it. Merzbacher's map (the survey was done by his assistant Groeber)[1] credits the East peak with a height of 6,512 metres or 21,350 ft. To our weak minds such a height in such a northerly latitude—about that of N. Italy—seemed quite excessive. We preferred the results found by a Swedish geological party, which had mapped the region in 1932, which allotted to the East peak the more manageable height of 18,000 ft. We had learnt to our cost the previous year on Muztagh Ata that latitude makes a big difference in temperatures and snow conditions on high mountains; for in August we had experienced there much colder conditions than we had ever done in the Eastern Himalaya at similar heights. It disturbed us to see that so far our two altimeters agreed closely with the heights on Merzbacher's map; but, as will appear, we have reason to believe that his heights for the three summits are 1,000 metres too much. I have since had Merzbacher's and Groeber's account translated, from which it appears that the heights of the places he went to at the base of the

[1] Dr Gottfried Merzbacher, an Austrian explorer who travelled in Central Asia 1903–4.

mountain were calculated from carefully controlled barometer and hypsometer readings, while the heights of the peaks were ascertained by theodolite readings from a measured base at Urumchi. The technical details will be found in a note at the end of the chapter.

The Grachimailo glacier up which we walked next morning afforded excellent going, at first on a surface of flat stones and then on clean, dry ice. It is a unique glacier in my experience, for it drains in two opposite directions. It is a sort of saddle-shaped glacier, the upper eastern part draining to the north by a valley parallel to that by which we had come, while the stream from the lower western half flows south through a deep cleft between the West peak and the Schokalsky peak (c. 15,000 ft.). Our modest objective was a snow col on a low ridge running north from the foot of the East Peak; and we toiled up the long easy névé slope towards it with our thoughts and eyes fixed on our goal and on the arête descending from it. Although we advanced but slowly, the aspect of the arête must have been continually altering, for it was curious how rapidly hope and fear, confidence and despair, succeeded each other. At first sight the arête had inspired admiration rather than apprehension. Its spare outline and simple directness appealed strongly to a climber's better and bolder instincts. But, as Dr Johnson says, 'there are charms made only for distant admiration—no spectacle is nobler than a blaze': as we drew nearer, the clean outline appeared to be marred by at least one abrupt step, while the general steepness aroused misgivings. There was no need to make any immediate decision as climbing was not possible until the recent snow had disappeared from the rocks.

On the far side of our col (c. 13,700 ft.) another glacier flowed from the bay between the arête and an eastwards extension of the main mountain, but this we could not well see on account of mist. There was some talk of descending to this glacier to have a closer look at this east ridge as a possible way up to the peak, but the silence which met this suggestion proved fatal. Unlike travelling in an aeroplane, when one crosses a col it is a case of what goes down must come up again; so this one-sided discussion ended by our climbing a short way northwards from the col. The slight gain in height we achieved would have given us a better view of the arête had not gathering cloud and mist shut it out. As we turned for home the storm broke.

Sleet, hail, and thunder continued for the rest of the day. 'Better is the end of a thing than the beginning thereof', said the Preacher, and most mountaineers will cordially agree. They begin their day early to the accompaniment of broken bootlaces, a hasty meal, cold, darkness, and a rock-strewn path; and end it—a pious hope—by returning to a hut or a dry tent, a hot meal, or even a fire. Even if, as in the Himalaya it frequently happens, the return is to a wet sleeping bag in a dripping tent pitched on snow, there is nothing more delightful, except the reality, than the anticipation of lying in that wet bag grasping a pint mug of hot sweet tea in one hand, a spoon for the shovelling in of 'satu' in the other.

These delightful anticipations were not to be realized. Our leaking tent was by no means the only domestic calamity to be faced when we got home wet through. Given reasonable weather, with the wood we had brought, we should have been able to cook on a fire under the partly imaginary cover of a boulder. But the weather was most unreasonable, and Lakhpa, who like most Sherpas can perform prodigies of open-air cookery with wet wood in the rain, had now fallen sick. Hill Billy, slowly learning the routine of camp, was a comparative greenhorn and pretty useless. To call a man who spent his life travelling as a mail courier a greenhorn may seem severe; but most native travellers expect to find a house of some sort at night or at any rate a dry cave. If there is nothing at all, then they just don't travel that way. If by ill-luck they happen to find themselves spending a night out in conditions in which a fire and cooking are difficult, instead of persevering they fold themselves in whatever rags they have and sleep. Who sleeps, sups.

We were not so apt to take things lying down. Greed, or a spirited defiance of adverse conditions, compelled us to have a meal and a hot one at that. We must use the Primus, though it seemed wrong to use it with a load of wood lying by—a sentiment with which the Primus seemed to agree. Flames licked the roof of the tent singeing our hair on the way; pricker after pricker was bent, broken, and discarded; bonfires of matches and pints of methylated spirit were burnt in the priming pan, and the oil changed and rechanged to little purpose. Very soon the inside of the tent was a murky hell of soot, snow, mud, lit frequently by lurid imprecations.

At last we did coax the stove into giving us a hot meal and settled down in our wet sleeping bags to smoke and face the future—a mental exercise which by a curious association of ideas has become the last thing any of us cares to do. That Lakhpa would have to go down and that the Primus must be made to behave better in future were our first conclusions. But now that the arête was for the present out of the question, what were we to do next? The better to answer this question I reached for the map and failed to find it. Seeing me vainly groping Shipton began to grope in his kit, too; but this valuable aid to mountain navigation had been left behind, like the Dutchman's anchor, at the Kazak yorts.

He who knows not whither to go is in no hurry to move. The day broke fine and had we been in the habit of washing or shaving we should have made a leisurely toilet. We began, however, by moving camp to a larger boulder which promised more shelter for the fire. Then the policeman came up with a skinful of yoghourt and having attended to that we saw him off together with our sick man Lakhpa. In the afternoon we explored a route to the south. Crossing the snout of the glacier we dropped down the high terminal moraine to a desolate tarn still half covered with ice, putting up a couple of Brahminy duck from the water. On the shore we found pony tracks which we followed till we came upon a rough track and cairns on the lip of a big drop; for on leaving the lake the water tumbles over a rock shelf several hundred feet. At the foot of this the valley opened on to wide grass slopes and old river terraces. There were no trees, nor could we detect any signs of life.

We had seen enough to know that we could get ponies down the valley for we were already thinking of a move to the south, and in particular to the Chigo glacier to the south of the East peak. How far we should have to go down before being able to take animals across the ridge between we did not know, so before committing ourselves we went to have a look at the east ridge.

Next day (15 July) was fine. In two hours we reached the snow col, descended on the other side, and climbed an ice-fall to the glacier bay at the foot of the East peak. Fifteen hundred feet above us the ridge ran almost horizontally until it reared up to merge into the steep eastern buttress of the peak. The ridge looked possible and the buttress slightly less daunting than the arête; but on this side the approach to the ridge was guarded by hanging seracs so that the using of this route seemed to depend on our finding a way on to it from the south.

The assessing of risks of this kind is always difficult. Many factors have to be considered: the state of the snow or ice, night temperatures, how soon the sun will strike the offending seracs, how long the party will be directly under them, and whether any accompanying porters would think the mountain worth the risk. Most porters would, I think, offer only half-hearted approval. According to sound mountaineering practice risks of this kind should be avoided, and neglect of this rule is quickly followed by censure. On the other hand, by risking nothing, nothing can be gained. Most of us, no doubt, err on the side of caution. As Dr Johnson remarks: 'It can indeed raise no wonder that temerity has been generally censured; for it is one of the vices with which few can be charged, and which therefore great numbers are ready to condemn.'

Merzbacher's heights

The altitude of each camp site was taken by readings of three Bohne's barometers of 10 cm. diameter every evening at 8 p.m. and every morning at 6 a.m. Observations were also taken with an Assman's aspiration-psychrometer and a minimum and maximum thermometer. These readings were controlled through observations of boiling-point thermometers which were made en route every other day. Besides this, at stations of several days' occupation they were checked by a diagram obtained from the Naudet barograph. During the march we used an aneroid barometer and at specially important points took boiling-point thermometer readings.

As there were no basic stations sufficiently near for the reduction of the barometer to sea level, the barometrical recordings taken during three days before leaving Urumchi were used as a check. For this period a correct mean height of the barometer was ascertained by using the observations made by Strokowsky over a period of three years in Urumchi. These calculations showed Urumchi to be 912 metres above sea level. The trustworthiness of the altitudes of the points climbed was further augmented by two control barometers kept at the main camp.

To ascertain the height and position of the peaks of the central group by means of trigonometry, a base of 791 metres was measured at Urumchi on a site 23 metres above the town on the west side. The instruments used were a Hildebrand theodolite and an invar tape which had been verified by

Guilleaume in Paris. The calculations have been carried out at the Geodetic Institute in Munich. An accuracy of plus or minus 30 metres is claimed for the altitudes of the East peak, 6,512 metres (21,164 ft.); Centre peak, 6,501 metres (21,125 ft.); West peak, 6,397 metres (20,787 ft.).

CHAPTER FOUR

Bogdo Ola: South Side

HAVING dithered for three days, we now had to make a plan. Although the fine weather of the previous day had removed some of the new snow from the arête, its appearance still daunted us. The shock we had received by our first view would, we had assured ourselves, be lessened by a few days of exercise and acclimatization. We had had our exercise, we had had the arête under constant survey, and yet we shied at the notion of trying it except as a last resort.

We had a long discussion. There was the whole of the south side to look at, where unexplored and therefore comforting possibilities might lie. Shipton thought we should go there at once, since we had already wasted a lot of time. His opinion was that of Moses on another occasion: 'Ye have compassed this mountain long enough: turn you *southward*.' I was not so sure. Although the mountain is by no means vast—were it not for the uncrossable barrier of the east ridge one could walk round it in two short days—I felt that if we went south we should not return; and that before going we ought to rub our noses against the rocks of the arête if only to assure ourselves it was as bad as it looked.

At the subsequent enquiry held to decide whether our failure was owing to lack of competence, courage, judgement, or of all three, Shipton maintained that we should have done better to have made a wide preliminary reconnaissance of the mountain from all sides. Whereas I held the opinion that in the Himalaya a strategic reconnaissance of this kind is nearly useless because so few routes can be confidently approved or discarded without actual trial. Only a close reconnaissance is worth making, and unless the preliminary reconnaissance is very swift there is seldom time for both, and never time to give two routes a thorough trial. I think this is certainly true of a big mountain, even when two or three months are available; but, of course, much more can be learnt about a lesser mountain like Bogdo even in three weeks which was all we had at our disposal.

In the end, contrary to a well-tried maxim, we preferred the unknown evil and went south in the expectation of finding a route less exacting than the arête. We had sent for animals, but as we did not expect them till late I went on alone to reconnoitre. Having reached the cairns at the top of the big descent I at once noticed two or three flocks of sheep grazing up the valley.

The knowledge that one is descending into an inhabited valley is usually welcome both to Europeans and their followers, implying, as it does, meat, milk, shelter, and possibly transport. Our Kazak followers were no doubt already aware of the fact, but for Shipton's benefit I scratched the glad tidings on a rock and sped on. At the bottom some horses were grazing, but the shepherd were still far away when I turned up the first likely-looking valley to the east.

This is the valley into which the small Sud glacier between the West and Central peaks flows. The ridge at the head of the valley is thrown off from the Central peak but here it was quite low, without snow, and could be easily crossed. I went up to it by a loose scree slope and looked down on to the Chigo glacier which was the haven where we would be. I judged that the ridge (c. 13,500 ft.) could be climbed by yaks, which was a big point. If we could have our loads carried up I was almost confident that neither of us would flinch from carrying them down the other side. True, we should have to bring them back, but by then they would be much lighter. On this flying reconnaissance of mine I thought I had made an even more important discovery in the form of a likely-looking route to our peak. But my whereabouts were not so clear to me then as I imagined, clouds were down to about 16,000 ft., and I could not be sure. We found later that this peak up which I saw a way was only a 'false' peak and one a long way from the true East peak.

As it was now about 2 p.m. I hurried back to the main valley concerned to know whether the rest of the party had come down and gone on. Some Kazak women I met gathering dung merely looked surly; there was no sign of anyone having passed, nor any sign of movement up the valley. I started back and presently met a shepherd towing a sick sheep, accompanied by a nasty-looking blackguard with a rifle. We had nothing to say, but I was sociable and sat patiently smoking a pipe while they looked through the wrong end of my field-glasses and handled my ice-axe. Presently the armed gentleman indicated that he would like my shirt, so I got up to go. It wasn't a very good shirt, but it was the only one I had.

Being worried about the absence of the others I put on all steam up the valley and up the steep ascent to the cairns. Nearing them I heard a shout which I thought must be Shipton, but looking round I discovered the armed blackguard hot in pursuit either of me or my shirt. As I was near the top and he well down I had a good start; and a Kazak is better on a horse than on his feet. However, he was game. He topped the rise as I was approaching the lake several hundred yards away. But when I started climbing the moraine I saw he had sat down—not, I think in order to draw a bead but merely to draw breath. Ammunition, no doubt, was scarce.

I reached camp at 5 p.m. to find them just loading up and presently we got under way. With baggage animals the direct route was out of the question, so we had to fetch a long circuit which finally brought us to the lake from the other direction. There was a faint track, but it was hard to hold to it amongst the rocks. Several times animals fell and several times we had to go back to try a fresh line. It is astonishing how much ponies, and even yaks, dislike boulder-strewn track or hillside. Holding the beast's headrope one picks out what one thinks is an easy line and steps confidently over or between rocks only to find that the obstinate animal will have nothing to do with the carefully chosen way. At 7 p.m. we settled down for the night on the grassy margin of the tarn between two massive boulders. It was a good camp, and was heartily welcome to me, for I had had a long day.

Our animals picked their way gingerly down the steep zigzag path to the valley from where we turned up the Sud glacier nallah and camped by the last grass at about 11,300 ft. On the way our pony men had made friends with the shepherds and later the son of the local Beg rode up to our camp with a present of yoghourt. We had this for supper mixed with *purée* of chilli to smarten it. Some foolish people—and, I'm afraid, most women—judge a dish by its colour, recoiling in disgust from peas, for example, or sprouts which have not been turned to a bright emerald with an almost lethal dose of soda. I feel sure that such misguided folk, although they probably would not have liked the taste of our dish, would certainly have applauded its artistic colour— the off-white of the yoghourt delicately marbled with salmon-pink veins of the *purée* oozing from a great blood-red gout in the centre.

Before taking a camp over the ridge we had to make sure that there was a way on to the east ridge of the mountain from the Chigo glacier. We told the Kazaks that we should probably want a couple of yaks to go as far as the ridge; meantime we held on to our original transport in order to remain strategically 'in balance'. The col on the ridge proved to be higher than I had imagined when I first climbed it, and the drop to the Chigo correspondingly long. There were but few stretches of 'runnable' scree, which in one way was a comfort. Obviously if one has to descend and re-ascend 1,500 ft. of scree, as we had, the more exhilaration one has from scree-running on the way down, the more exasperating will be the plod up the same shifting surface. We crossed to the east side of the Chigo, which is a fine broad glacier, and sought for a vantage point from which to view the peak and the east ridge.

There was fortunately no doubt about our ability to climb the easy snow slope which led from the head of the glacier to a nick on the east ridge; but as our eyes travelled along the ridge to the peak we began to wonder. Certainly, when seen from this side, the ridge looked longer, narrower, and altogether less adapted to the passage of a laden party. As for the peak itself, writhing mists prevented our seeing it steadily and seeing it whole. A short piece of snow rib momentarily seen would fill us with confidence, until a hole torn in the swirling vapour would reveal the rib springing out of nothing or ending in a horrid black cut-off. Obviously two camps would be needed—one at the nick and a second as far as possible on the further side of a deep gap.

We had much to ponder as we trudged homewards. The rolling, slow, rhythmic plod up scree, hands in pockets or folded behind the back, is conducive to deep cogitation. Perhaps it was on some such slope that these sublime lines occurred to Joseph Cottle:

> How steep, how painful the ascent:
> It needs the evidence of close deduction
> To know that ever I shall gain the top.

On our return, Hill Billy, who had accompanied us on this walk, took to his bed. It was no doubt an unjust thought, but it did cross our minds that this sudden collapse had been brought on by the revolting aspect of the east ridge and the peak upon which we meditated assault. But he need not have had any cause for alarm either on his own behalf or on ours, for at that time temerity was the last vice with which we could be charged. Without assistance of any kind we were momentarily tethered, but as the next two days were wet and windy we were content to potter. We climbed a rock gully in pursuit of ram chikot—a very noble bird for the table—and paid a visit to the nearest yorts for tea and chat. They now agreed to let us have two yaks, and upon returning to camp we found Lakhpa had turned up. Prospects looked brighter, but so uncertain were we of the wisdom of this coming move that we now regretted our offhand rejection of the arête.

Hill Billy was left in charge while the three of us with two yaks and their driver started for the ridge at the head of the valley. At times we doubted if the animals would make it. The final bit was steep and loose and their feet were badly cut. However, by midday we were all on top. Here we left the yaks to browse a bit of gravel while we four bipeds went down with the loads. After brewing some tea at the bottom we sent the yak man back and continued up the glacier to a camp (c. 13,000 ft.) on some rocks at the foot of the snow slope. The Primus was at its tricks again and the three of us had to occupy a two-man tent; nevertheless, we had a fair night.

July 22 was a fine, hot day which proved to be the hardest we yet had. The lower part of the slope turned out to be of rough ice upon which one felt very insecure without nick or rudimentary step to stand up on. Without a load one might have walked up it easily, but we soon found that with an unwieldy 40 lb. load on one's back it was extremely hard to use an axe, so that the leading man had to carve out a small stance for his load, cut ahead for a rope's length, and then come back for it. Thus occupied, I debated, without settling to my own satisfaction, whether we were caught in a bottle-neck or in a vicious circle. Without loads there was no need for steps while with loads they were needed but could not be cut. The process was varied by the leading man hauling up all three loads, but it was no quicker and was not good for the loads.

Lakhpa made heavy weather of it. He was fat and he had not properly recovered from his recent illness, so at 3 p.m. we sent him down, hoping but not believing that he might have time to recross the ridge and get back to Hill Billy before dark. With three loads to handle Shipton and I struggled on till 5 p.m. when I for one was quite willing to stop. Even then we were not clear of the ice, for there were still another hundred feet or so. However it was pretty soft ice in which we soon carved out a platform for the tent.

Next morning, carrying half-loads and treading hard snow, we soon finished the climb to the ridge and returned for the rest. By midday we had everything up and the tent and ropes spread out to dry on a great rock that projected through the snow, as the previous day's manœuvres had thoroughly soaked them. On this brilliant morning, climbing easily on firm snow, and not overladen, we had leisure to look about us; and the higher we got the more we became convinced that we had made a mistake. We could see now that the section of the ridge between our camp and the mountain was no fit place along which to carry a camp. It was long, knife-edged, and in places heavily corniced. Moreover, the final cimb of nearly 3,000 ft., where the ridge stood up on end and leant against the peak, seemed to bristle with climbing problems well above the low standard of difficulty we had set ourselves.

Although we were thus almost reconciled to defeat before we had even completed the carry to the ridge, we had the resolution neither to cut our losses and go down forthwith nor to persevere in an apparently hopeless attempt. But had we gone down there and then we should have lost much. Defeat had its compensations, for the site of our camp was very grand; had we come up merely to enjoy the airy position and the view we had not done amiss. To the north side of our ridge, where the tent hung upon the very lip of space, the eye could range freely to the black and gold wastes of the desert; from the tent door the slender, glistening ridge stretched away to a hidden gap whence it leapt up to merge with the precipitous rock and ice of the east face of the peak; while to the south, beyond the broad white ribbon of the Chigo glacier, the tawny Asian landscape seemed as infinite as the pale sky.

That night a violent wind blew. Our tent had been used on Everest in 1938 so that considering its age and the fury of the gusts our surprise that it held was equalled only by our gratitude. The night was clear and cold, stars blinked calmly, but even under this benign sky without any fierce accompaniment of thunder, lightning, or driving snow, the roar of the wind was terrifying. Against the walls of the abyss below the winds seemed to beat as if imprisoned, gyrating and bellowing in a swiftly rising crescendo of sound until at last they sprang out and burst over the ridge with a savage howl, plucking wildly at our frail shelter. The fabric flapped madly, the poles to which we clung groaned and bent, as the spent gust sobbed and moaned away across the snow. In the ensuing lull we lay with wan smiles and questioning eyes listening for the faint rumble which would herald the next onslaught. Prepared for the worst, we lay in our bags clothed in wind-proofs, helmets, and mitts, with boots ready to hand.

It cannot be laid down as a general rule for all high camps that joy cometh with the morning. The dawn may well be worse than the night, because there is no longer any excuse for lying still. Should one decide to continue lying, there is still the Primus to be lit. On this occasion, however, the rule held. Towards dawn the wind died and the dawn itself promised well. Without any debate or much compunction we turned our backs to the mountain and began climbing along the ridge in the opposite direction. The ridge seemed to continue for miles culminating at last in a snow peak very nearly as high as the main mountain. This was out of our reach, but we picked on an intermediate bump as our target for the day. It made a good snow ridge climb, with a bit of ice here and there, a cornice to add interest, until we at last achieved our modest summit. All this, too, in those conditions which are so desirable but, in the Himalaya, so rare—hard snow underfoot, and a warm sun overhead. What more could a mountaineer want than to climb easily along the bright crest of this high, untrodden ridge, where glittering slopes fell away on either hand to smooth snow bays; and to the wrinkled glaciers from which flowed rivers that must presently perish in the hot sands of Asia.

Is it, by the way, a sign of decadence, senility, or merely sanity thus to couple ease with enjoyment? I like to think it is sanity; for though on a difficult mountain one may experience many moments of 'fearful joy', the keenest pleasures of difficulty and danger are for most of us largely retrospective. Nevertheless, when, having achieved the summit of our modest ambition, we turned and allowed our eyes to dwell upon the sterner delights of the East peak we felt, like Macbeth, 'To be thus is nothing'. Our felicity was far from perfect; and this is perhaps one of the wholesome merits of mountaineering that there is nearly always some other mountain or route at hand to modify the raptures of the climber's success, prick his self-satisfaction, and fire his ambitions.

The height of this 'incident' on the ridge was about 16,550 ft. and our camp something over 15,000 ft. It was from these heights, which our altimeter gave and which our map confirmed, that we concluded that the East peak could not be much higher than 18,000 ft.

We were back in camp by 4 p.m., and so grand was our eyrie that we were in no hurry to quit. We expended much film in an attempt to record the light and shade cast on the snow by the sinking sun; and my confident assertion that the results would, as usual, be undistinguished led to a dispute about mountain photography and the difference, if any, between a competent and a beautiful photograph. Owing to our lack of theoretical knowledge the discussion assumed a personal aspect, slightly vitiated by the absence of any examples of our respective masterpieces. I think we were both prepared to waive the claim to ever having taken a beautiful photograph, but my declaration that I could not remember either of us having ever produced a competent one was hotly disputed by Shipton.

At this interesting point we were interrupted by a violent blast of wind, the precursor of another anxious night. With that prompt energy and decision which hitherto, when it was a question of going up, we had entirely lacked, we packed up and started down, carrying everything. When we came to the icy part we began to lower the loads rope's length by rope's length, until when near the bottom Shipton's impatience got the better of his judgment. We were not so near the bottom as all that. Our bulging rucksacks, cartwheeling and bounding madly, did stop at last, badly split, soaked in paraffin, and the lighter by the loss of several pounds of sugar. We retrieved them and carried them up to the old camp site in the dark. The Primus once again refused to burn so we supped drily on a crust of bread in profound silence. The ruck-sack episode seemed a likely topic for conversation, but it was one upon which only a very determined philosopher could have embarked dispassionately.

In the morning we carried everything down to some wood we had dumped at the bottom of the long scree slope and there we had breakfast. Leaving the tent to be brought up later we climbed to the ridge and got down to camp soon after 2 p.m. Hill Billy, who had now recovered, was dispatched for the tent while I set about making bread. Lakhpa had swapped his 'chapkan'—a quilted gown, once maroon, now black with age—for a sheep, so that night we did ourselves well; better, in fact, than either of us felt we deserved.

The question now was what to do with our four remaining days. We had neither the time, paraffin, nor the inclination to go back and have a closer look at the north-east arête, whose summary condemnation we more and more regretted. There was the Schokalsky peak for which we just had time, or a lower but attractive looking isolated pinnacle above the yorts. We tossed up, and this Cairn peak, as we christened it, won.

Leaving the yorts at 5.30 a.m. we halted for breakfast on a snow shoulder just below what small difficulties the climb offered. And then, with Hill Billy tied inescapably between us, we mastered a short piece of ice and reached the top by easy rocks. Here Hill Billy built an immense cairn while we admired the tranquillity and subdued colours of a vast Asian landscape. It was an exceptional day, very fine, still, and warm; and an exceptional view-point. Besides the long south face of Bogdo immediately behind us and another group of snow pinnacles further east, fifty or a hundred miles to the west rose peak upon peak of the great Tien Shan. Far below us the grass of a treeless valley dwindled away and died, swallowed up in the grey, gravel glacis beyond which, 20 miles away, lay the Urumchi road and the pale, reed-fringed Ainak lake. From this lake, according to local tradition, spring the fierce Turfan winds, one of which, no doubt, had tried to blow us off our ridge. 'All this wind', complained a dweller in the Turfan Depression, 'comes from a little lake on the way to Urumchi. There is an iron gate in the lake and it is only half-shut, if any one could shut it, the wind would stop.'[1]

Thus ended our first grapple with Bogdo Ola in which we had displayed little judgment and not much energy. We took horse next morning and after six hours bumping and jogging across the dismal gravel plain against a hot wind reached a small village by the lake. Although there was a telephone line, there was no telephone, so we spent the night in an inn and in the morning boarded the first Urumchi-bound lorry. We were back in time for breakfast at the Consulate where we met a warm welcome and many fresh faces.

CHAPTER FIVE

Bogdo Ola Again

IN theory we should have started next day for Kashgar by truck; but, as the driver might well have said; 'Alas, Sahib, it is but machinery.' The truck had been ailing before we left and the three weeks it had since spent in a Chinese workshop had quite undermined its constitution. The week of waiting that followed was trying enough for us. Every day some new ailment was discovered and towards the end the workshop closed down to allow the Turki

1 Huntington's *Pulse of Asia*.

and Tungan (Chinese Moslem) workmen to take part in the Moslem festival of Id.

It happened, too, to be a week of hot, cloudless weather and our ill-humour mounted daily as we watched the mountain and its north-east arête become more and more in good climbing condition. This touched a sore spot, for we had come back disgusted with ourselves for our lack of judgment and the pusillanimity which had stayed us. Except that they were strictly private, our talks concerning the conduct of the recent expedition resembled what is said to go on at conferences of Soviet officials, where each in turn methodically and ruthlessly examines his own shortcomings and consecrates himself afresh to mental and moral re-armament.

Since this was our frame of mind, it is not surprising that on the following Saturday afternoon we might have been seen throwing our belongings into an American truck about to start for the Sud glacier. The immediate impulse for this step came from the Pathan driver of our truck who had walked into the compound after lunch carrying a newly cracked piston which he thought we might like to see. How the American truck came to be standing by all ready to go, almost as if waiting to catch us as we reeled under this last and heaviest blow, needs some explanation. The fact that we had been at the yorts, within a few hours of a glacier the one day and in Urumchi the next, had made a strong impression at the Consulate. Always eager to promote interest in mountains we had pointed out that provided a truck was driven across the gravel glacis to the foot of the valley the journey to the yorts could be done in one day. This verdict clinched the matter so far as Greeson our former companion was concerned; all that remained was to obtain leave. In Urumchi, for the greater part of the year, the American passion for ice is catered for by an ice-house. In August, however, this was empty; so at our instigation Greeson suggested filling it from the Sud glacier. A *modus operandi* was quickly sketched out and the Consul persuaded into allowing him to make a trial trip. Speed was the essence of the thing, and since he had command this was likely to be forthcoming.

Greeson rejoiced to be reinforced by us at the last moment, for in spite of our explanations his ideas of the geography of the place or even of the appearance of a glacier were a bit scattered. And not only our reputation but his chance of any future mountain holidays depended on his bringing back a substantial load of ice. Besides us two, Hill Billy and Lakhpa, there were the White Russian mechanic and his wife, an American girl visitor and an American journalist. All these piled into a jeep and a 2-ton six-wheeler which already held an amount of gear in keeping with the urgency and importance of the expedition—arms, of course, in great quantity and variety, food and drink to correspond, tents and bedding, and an assortment of iron implements for carving up the glacier. These ranged from felling axes, bill hooks, pick-axes and crow-bars to cross-cut saws. It was a pity we had neither explosives nor a glacier drill.

It was late afternoon before the convoy left the main road and began bumping slowly over the long gravel slope towards the foothills. Here the presence of parties of gazelle delayed progress, for Greeson seldom let us get past them without stopping for a shot. That this was done more by way of a salute than with malicious intent the gazelle seemed to recognize as they waited patiently until the fusillade subsided before bounding happily away. By nightfall we had reached the mouth of the valley. The truck could go no further, so here, where there were trees and where the stream had not yet disappeared under the gravel, we off-loaded our curious cargo and camped.

Overnight the weather broke, but this did not deter the eager Greeson who, accompanied by the mechanic who spoke Turki and Chinese, left for the yorts while the rest of us still slept. That they had found them was shown by the arrival in the afternoon of three camels. There were also a couple of ponies which we rode turn and turn about, for it was a steep grind up to the yorts which we did not reach until eight o'clock. The Beg was away, but his yort was crammed to capacity. Besides his family, his son's family, and eight of us, a couple of Tungans turned up. They were on business, for it seemed they owned most of the sheep and goats which by now—milking time—were creating an uproar outside. The Kazaks told us too that for the most part they were merely the custodians of the yaks, ponies, and camels strewn up and down the valley.

The Tungans are the Mohammedans of China who observe most of the tenets of Islam. Their origin is obscure, but their more recent history is written ineradicably in blood; for they have rebelled fiercely and frequently against the Chinese both in Sinkiang and Kansu. Ruined towns and abandoned fields testify to the bitterness of these revolts and of their quelling. The Tungan is noted for commercial ability and enterprise as well as for his surly independence, which combines the business instincts of a Chinese with the aggressiveness of a fanatical Moslem. It is not surprising that he is disliked equally by his more easy-going Turki neighbours and by his Chinese masters.

In addition to preparing a meal, making bread, nursing babies, and milking goats, the women made tea for the men, who had more important things to do or at least to talk about. In the absence of father the Beg's son did the honours—served the tea, led the prayers, and from time to time executed a strophe or two on a one-stringed instrument. The young man had a good deal on his hands; his Tungan visitors no doubt wanted an account of their sheep, we wanted transport, while Greeson, having relegated the getting of ice to its proper place in the scheme of things, wanted his company on a proposed ibex *battue* early next morning. This suggestion seemed unwelcome to our host, either out of regard for the ibex or for his duties as flock-master to the Tungans; but a few swift words from his bustling young wife settled the matter. 'A wife's counsel is bad, but he who will not take it is mad.'

The weather had worsened considerably by next morning when the rest of us assembled for a late breakfast at which we calmly assessed the certain discomfort of the hunters who were long since upon the hill; for, as Mr Pecksniff rightly observed, 'if everyone were warm and well fed, we should lose the satisfaction of admiring the fortitude with which others bear cold and hunger'. According to plan the truck with its load of ice should have returned to Urumchi that day, but it was midday before Greeson turned up, wet through, without any trophy, but still cheerful, and two o'clock before the ice-cutting party started. In two hours we had reached the snout of the Sud glacier, having with us five yaks which were able to come very nearly to the ice. Each man chose his weapon and began a violent assault upon the watery, singularly impure ice of the glacier. The difficulty was to get chunks large enough to remain unmelted during the journey back. Even when one had got a good working face the stuff came away in bits instead of blocks, so that a piece of more than 10 lb. weight was a great prize. Filling the sacks was precious cold work, but soon all ten were filled, wrapped in straw to keep the ice cool, and loaded on the yaks.

By dusk we were back in triumph at the yorts where we had to spend another night, which was neither fair on the ice, the Kazaks, nor the American Consul. None of us, however, took this to heart, least of all the Kazaks who no doubt hoped that we were but the first of many equally rich parties of ice collectors. With the aid of some bottles of rice wine we made quite a night of it. We had few songs in common, but each nationality did its untuneful worst. An extravagant dance by the White Russian mechanic inflamed Hill Billy to pirouette economically as they do in Hunza; and impelled one of the Kazak women (several months gone) to a merry and slightly unseemly dance popular in the high Altai.

The morning broke cold, wet, and windy. Shipton and I had long given up any hope of climbing the north-east arête—that prize, if it ever had been within our reach, was now snatched away. But we could at least go and look at it, so we seized upon two yaks and started up the valley, leaving the ice merchants to shift for themselves. We camped that evening by the tarn above the rock shelf near the foot of the Grachimailo glacier.

On another cold, windy morning we set out to reach if possible the high snow col at the foot of the arête, leaving the camp standing. Some six inches of snow now covered the dry ice of the glacier and the rocks of the ridge we had to climb. Below on our left lay the approach to the low snow col we had crossed on the earlier trip, and on our right between us and the mountain itself was a steep narrow ice-fall. The ridge of loose rock which we were climbing terminated in a high gendarme overlooking the col we hoped to reach. It was a day of sunshine and storm, of wind squalls and scurries of sleet, and after climbing steadily for over three hours we were till several hundred feet below the col. But we were high enough to see sufficiently well the lower rocks of the north-east arête only two or three hundred yards away across the ice-fall. They were now well plastered with snow which was not likely to clear for several days, if at all, at this time of year. At this height and in this latitude I should doubt if much melting goes on after August. For what it was worth—for our judgment throughout the expedition had been palpably at fault—we recorded our opinion that the East peak might be climbed by this route by a strong party. It is less hazardous to suggest that it is not likely to be climbed by another way.

The possibility that the Beg and his long-suffering family had by now seen enough of us may or may not have occurred to us; but anyway we decided to return to Urumchi by a new high-level route. The spine of high ground from which Bogdo Ola rises like a dorsal fin descends gradually to the vicinity of

Urumchi and then rises again further west where it merges into the main Tien Shan. In theory, having got on to the spinal ridge one could walk along it almost to the town, but in practice ridges are seldom so accommodating. Usually a ridge proves to be so broken that one must traverse below it, thereby crossing gullies innumerable or even whole valleys.

So it happened on this occasion. Having first outflanked the big Schokalsky peak we had to descend into and climb out of no less than four valleys. We were carrying our own loads, Shipton had sprained an ankle, and Lakhpa was not well, so that four times we were sorely tempted to forgo the anticipated pleasure of a ridge walk and to descend the valley in search of yorts and transport. In fact in two of the valleys we came upon yorts, and as the only fit man in the party it was my self-imposed and thankless task to steer my companions past them. In another valley we saw a herd of ibex grazing the lush grass like so many cattle. Ibex, like yaks, usually like their grass sparse and in fairly inaccessible places. We camped in the fourth valley where horses and camels were grazing but where the yorts, happily, were some way down. As we were still well above the tree-line we had to boil the tea on a yak dung fire, a process which took an hour. Dry yak dung makes an excellent fire with a pungent-smelling smoke not unpleasant in small doses or at a distance, but wet dung, like green wood, is merely a hissing and an abomination.

Having cleared this valley we did at last attain the axis ridge to the west of the last snow peak. It was broad and smooth, and though we enjoyed our promenade for but a short time, the efforts we had made to reach it were well repaid. We experienced again the pleasure we had had on the Cairn peak. Normally the eye's range is so circumscribed that it seems to take peculiar pleasure in mere distance. Here hundreds of miles of Asia lay spread on either hand. There was nothing particularly to catch the eye, unless it was the Ainak lake, the only vivid piece of pattern and colour in a vast carpet of indefinite forms and subdued tones of opal, indigo, and old gold.

For five miles we proceeded thus easily, learning once more that it is not necessary to balance along a knife-edge ridge to feel the exhilaration of a vision of boundless space and breadth. Ahead the ridge grew less and less accommodating until, not far from Urumchi (which we could see), it plunged into a tangle of rocky hills and nallahs. On Lakhpa's earnest recommendation we committed our bodies to the depths of the first easy-looking valley to the north. In the upper part there was water, for which we were by then thankful, and at 9,000 ft. the pines began, but it was rough going to the first yorts, which we came upon suddenly, pitched in a pleasant glade. We failed to impress the Kazaks with either our importance or our weariness. They gave us yoghourt but no horses. In order to explain ourselves we said we were walking to Urumchi for fun, to which the Kazaks coolly replied that in that case we might as well prolong our fun by walking for two more days until we reached Urumchi.

At the next yorts we met with the same treatment. It was late evening, Shipton and Lakhpa were both very willing to stop, but since we needed ponies to make sure of reaching Urumchi next day we determined to push on. What looked like a wheat field lower down the valley acted as a lure. Knowing the ways of these streams we might have foreseen that like the others the one we were following would presently dive underneath the gravel. At about eight o'clock I reached the field well ahead of the rest when I was immediately accosted by two mounted Kazaks who first threatened me with a whip and then tried to ride me down. While I was parrying the attack with an ice-axe the others arrived and Lakhpa explained who we were. When they told us that there was no water for three miles my companions were for making a dry night of it, but in the end we agreed to go on until night-fall. Once more well in the van I met another Kazak, the first kindly one I ever did meet when alone. We must dine and sleep with him at his yort hard by; so while we waited for the others I helped myself to the skin-bag of yoghourt attached to his saddle. No doubt it had been dangling there all day so it was thoroughly well churned.

By ten o'clock we had reached the yorts where we dined on bread and milk and slept in the open. Choosing a bed in the dark was difficult. It was essential to get well beyond the attentions of a multitude of sheep and goats and the clear space upon which we eventually bedded down turned out to be the main track. Early in the morning a party of Kazaks thundered along it, their horses neatly avoiding our bodies. Here we got three horses for the 18 miles' ride to Urumchi. The Kazak who came with us rode double with me most of the way. Probably he could have gone on for ever sitting a horse's hindquarters but I found I could not, so I finished the last few miles on foot.

We arrived in time for a late lunch to find the usual number of itinerant Press correspondents who again impressed us with their ardour in the pursuit of knowledge. One hoped, though hardly expected, that their findings would be read with equal ardour. References to the ice expedition, we noted, were avoided. That the party had been further delayed on the way home had not told in their favour, and although no less than 850 lb. of ice had been weighed in, the quality met with criticism. While admirable for preserving tired fish or for applying to the heads of delirious patients, it was found to be a trifle too gritty for the ices and iced drinks with which Americans like to refrigerate their stomachs.

Our truck was now ready for the road, but we had one or two serious engagements to fight on the Chinese food front before we were able to disengage in tolerably good order, our heads aching but unbowed, to begin the journey of a thousand miles to Kashgar.

Although I can hardly read without a tear the sublime descriptions of eating and drinking by such master hands as Dickens, Surtees, and, best of all, Peacock, there are no doubt many readers who, like Mr Woodhouse, love to have the cloth laid but are rather sorry to see anything put upon it. A description by any feebler hand of what is put upon the cloth may merely disgust, and is almost certain to sicken should the feeble hand attempt to describe what the Chinese put upon their cloth, where indeed it is often true to say, 'There's death in the pot'. It is curious and, I think, true that few readers will flinch at what is considered the more polite pastime of drinking, and none at all at references to love-making. In these respects readers are like Captain Wattle who was all for love and a little for the bottle.

The night before we left the Mayor of Urumchi gave us a farewell dinner party. Although upon these feasts the Chinese love to expend a deal of anxious thought, great gastronomic skill, and wads of paper money, it is not too much to say—and it is a very strong statement—that drinking plays almost as serious a part as eating. This, of course, is only as it should be, and the guest can only regret that the materials are such that they would be better poured into the sink than down the throat. He can, however, comfort himself with Sancho's reflection that 'cursed bad wine is better than Holy water'. But the Chinese value politeness even more than we do, and as the politeness they value most on these occasions rests chiefly in the guest refusing nothing, he had better save his honour by staying away should he feel that such a meal is likely to be a too severe trial.

I have read of a British consul who would attend these Chinese functions and sit through them in perfect silence neither eating nor drinking. Whether such a practice is regarded as a piece of sturdy British independence, abstemiousness worthy of a saint, or merely resolute and studied offensiveness, it is a feat rather to be admired than imitated. Certainly on this occasion this was Shipton's view, who made a point of taking things as they came and not infrequently taking them once again. Nor was I behind-hand in doing our host honour, so that in the end the example of Confucius, who stopped drinking just short of mental confusion, was forgotten.

CHAPTER SIX

To Kashgar

THE truck in which we made this journey has already been the subject of some derogatory remarks but, in justice, it deserves honourable mention, for it was the sole survivor of the two 30-cwt. Fords which Sir Eric Teichman drove from Peking to Kashgar in the autumn of 1935. Even at that not very distant date, motoring in these parts was in the pioneer stage, so that such a journey reflected much credit on the truck and on its occupants. Since those days, the truck had been constantly in use, seldom on metalled roads, and had been to Urumchi and back more than once. During the war the road to China across the desert and through the Kansu corridor had received some attention to facilitate the trickling flow of Russian aid to China, and at the same time the Kashgar road had been re-aligned and in places re-made. Nothing had been done to this road since, and now its pot-holes and corrugations were to give this veteran truck yet one more shattering experience.

The driving throughout was shared by Shipton and the Pathan driver Mir Hamza. Out of what I took to be consideration for my nerves or mistrust of them I was allowed to enjoy the purgatory of the spare seat in the cab. Mir

Hamza was a fine figure of a Pathan, tall, lithe, bearded, rather temperamental, and addicted to enterprises of a most private kind. When we reached Kashgar, he found that his wife had been thrown into prison on a charge of opium smuggling; and it was as difficult for the court as it was for us to believe in the husband's protested ignorance of the ways of the viper he had so long nourished in his bosom. It was an episode embarrassing both to him and to his employer, and one which it was extremely difficult to laugh off.

He was a good but careless driver—in fact completely carefree so far as anyone else on the road was concerned—a hard-hitting mechanic, not without some intimate knowledge of his own vehicle. He had with him a Turki assistant, a fellow Moslem, but as meek and insignificant as he himself was proud and overbearing. He only performed the onerous but menial duties of filling up with water and petrol, but his life was made a burden to him by the Pathan. Between them, however, they could change a tyre with noteworthy élan.

The Kashgar road follows the Turfan road as far as Davanchin before branching west to Toksun. Beyond Toksun the road enters the Subashi gorge (where it becomes mixed up with and indistinguishable from the river bed) through which it climbs for the best part of 3,000 ft. to the Argai Bulaq pass. One gorge is very like another. They vary only in depth, narrowness, and starkness; but a pedestrian is much more likely to be overwhelmed and oppressed by them than is the motorist whose passage is brief and whose mind is absorbed by the perils and difficulties which such a road provides. In this Subashi gorge, however, there was little danger of meeting oncoming traffic and none at all of going off the road to hurtle to death in the river below; for the road remained in that safest of places, the bottom, so that one drove among the sands and boulders of a perfectly dry river-bed. After halting at dark, we could find no water with which to brew tea, and we were by no means sorry to start again at 3 a.m.; when a waning moon had transformed the rather dreary rock trench into a sculptured cloister etched with silver and ebony.

I walked most of the way up to the pass; and such was the nature of the road that there was little danger of being overhauled. We dropped down from the pass through strangely chromatic hills of ochre and black to Kumush, where there is little else but a spring. Here we broke our fast and our thirst. Thus fortified, we embarked upon the hundred-odd miles to Karashahr where we were to spend the night at the Chinese yamen. Even if I could remember the scenery I should hesitate to describe it; for a mountaineer must agree with Ruskin that mountains are the beginning and the end of all scenery. Here the mountains were far off, and even if one takes a less exclusive view of what constitutes scenery it is difficult for anyone, who is not a Doughty or a Lawrence, to say anything fervid, or even kind, about desert or near-desert.

Whether a passenger as distinct from a traveller has any call to be interested in the passing scene is questionable. The driver of a vehicle certainly has not and by choosing that mode of travel his passengers have clearly indicated that their interest begins only at the destination, and the way there is a tedious interlude best passed in sleep. I have not often experienced it but I imagine that sitting in a cinema is much the same as a journey by car, in that both are as it were negative experiences. One looks at the screen or out of the window (on both of which it is probably raining) to an unfamiliar scene with which one has no concern. The scenery or the story unfolds rather rapidly, carrying one by places at which one might wish to pause, if only for elucidation, and lingering or stopping at those which can hardly be passed too quickly. As the journey or the film comes to an end the senses begin to function again, and all that has passed might never have been. The eyes have seen but the brain has wisely refused to receive an impression too blurred to be accurate, too inconsequent for reason, and happily too slight to be recalled.

As we approached Karashahr we found that haze shut out any view of the great Bagrash Kul. From this lake comes a fine carp-like fish, while on its shores are bred the famous Karashahr ponies, the breed to which, according to Lattimore, we should look rather than to the Badakshan for the true Macedonian strain. We ate the fish of Bagrash Kul that night, but on this journey, alas, we were more concerned with broken springs, worn-out tyres and petrol, than with the points of some Bucephalus.

The river which flows through the town rises in the Yulduz valley of the Tien Shan and flows into the lake. It was the finest river I had yet seen, wide, deep, fast-flowing, and of a clear steely blue colour; and yet in a short distance this living, dashing torrent dwindles to a trickle and dies in the sand, an end which awaits all the rivers of Kashgaria. But for few of them is this a matter of regret; except in winter most of them are some absurd colour—brown, red, yellow—wherein no really edible fish will live and no fastidious man will care to bathe.

As became passengers, we were hell-bent for Kashgar and had no time to waste on Karashahr, the Black City, with its mushrooms and melons, its ponies and fish, and bazaars where Kazak, Tungan, and Turki jostle and chaffer. We arrived late and we left early for Kucha, 180 miles distant. Beyond the pleasant oasis of Korla there are a hundred miles of semi-desert. It is not true desert, for the soil is loess and supports occasional wild poplars and tamarisks. The latter, growing out of huge mounds of earth from 15 to 50 ft. high, are characteristic of this country, and according to Huntingdon, indicate climatic changes:

. . . one finds the tamarisk mound in every stage of development from one foot high with a vigorous growth of bushes, to sixty feet high with nothing but huge knarled trunks, dead for hundreds of years. On flood-plains from which the water has been diverted for four or five years half the tamarisks are usually dead. In later stages still more die, and only those with very deep roots persist. Then the wind begins to dissect the plain, carrying away the finer materials and heaping up the coarser grains of sand in the protected spots where living bushes check its force. Thus mounds are formed and their height is increased by aeolian erosion at the base and aeolian deposition at the top. The depth to which erosion can proceed is limited by the level of underground water, and the deposition by the amount of sand available from surrounding areas. The actual size of mounds depends partly on the length of time since the water was withdrawn. I should say that mounds fifty to sixty feet high must be nearly two thousand years old . . .

We stopped some 17 miles short of Kucha, an ancient and celebrated town, one of Turkestan's Six Cities, where the girls are reputed to be 'all like flowers'. This failure, however, did not deter us from rising again at 3 a.m. for the third morning running to cover an equally long distance to Aqsu. However much one dislikes motor travel, I should dislike travelling this road by any other means, unless perhaps in a faster car or on some winged steed 'fretting to roam the desert'. A few weeks in a horse-drawn cart, for example, would soon pall, even though the road is enlivened by tamarisk mounds. But from Bai, which is about half-way, we saw some real scenery—the Tien Shan. There had been a gale in the night which had swept the sky clear of loess dust and far to the north above the dun plain rose the silvery slopes and white towers upon which a mountainer can never look without a sudden urge of joy. Whether we could see Khan Tengri (23,620 ft.) the highest of the Tien Shan we could not say. Khan Tengri has long been accepted as the highest, but our Russian friends have bedevilled this as they have done so much else by asserting that they have discovered a higher.

Whether the following account, from a Russian source, of this discovery is correct or not, it is interesting for its refreshingly immodest style. Nevertheless, the survey of the Tien Shan by Merzbacher in 1904, was fairly thorough, and the discovery of a mountain 1,500ft. higher than Khan Tengri only about 10 miles away is remarkable to say the least. The following report made by V. Ratsek, a member of the 1946 Tien Shan expedition, may be of interest:

The knot of mountains lying due east of the Soviet Tien Shan have for a long time attracted the attention of explorers. Here, surmounting passes hidden beyond the clouds, by-passing roaring rivers and gigantic glaciers, went expeditions whose work tore asunder the veil which hitherto had kept the secret of Nature concealed from Science. Until recent years the current opinion was that Khan Tengri, the principal summit of the Tien Shan, was the highest peak in Russia. The alpinists conquering the Sary-Jas range observed in the south-east only clouds covering the peaks of the Kokshal Tau [Khan Tengri lies here]. Thick banks of cloud perpetually lay on snow-covered ledges. Travellers considered the mists over the Kokshal Tau as a regular phenomenon. Members of the 1940 expedition, however, managed to get a glimpse of the summits of the range from the Sary-Jas pass. These peaks clearly surpassed the Khan Tengri in altitude which, however, could not be finally determined as the explorers did not have the necessary precise geodetic instruments; neither had they the benefit of the important preparatory exploration of the Military Topographic Department carried out in 1943. Surveys made by that expedition ascertained that about 16 kms. south of the Khan Tengri on the upper regions of the Zvezdochka glacier there towers another gigantic pear-shaped ice wall. This peak of 7,440 metres (24,180 ft.) is not only the principal summit of the Kokshal Tau but is the highest point of the whole Tien Shan. The Khan Tengri 6,995 m. (22,730 ft.) hitherto regarded as the highest of sky-piercing mountains should thus stand aside and give up its right to pre-eminence. The 7,440 m. peak discovered in 1943 is the principal summit and not the Khan Tengri. This summit was discovered and its height determined in the phase of our patriotic war when our victory over the enemy was a foregone conclusion. That is why this gigantic summit, the second in altitude in the U.S.S.R., should serve as a monument to our great victories and bear the proud name of Victory Peak.

One feels sorry for Khan Tengri thus triumphantly diminished to the greater glory of Soviet topographers who have also lopped it of a thousand feet. According to 'Burrard and Hayden' its height is 23,620 ft. which V. Ratsek reduces to 22,730 ft. The highest peak in the U.S.S.R., to which this new Victory Peak (Pik Pobedy) comes second, is what the Russians call Stalin Peak, 24,590 ft., climbed by M. Abalakov in 1933; the large party, of which he was one, approached the peak by way of the Fedchenko glacier, 48 miles long, the longest in Asia. This peak, listed by Burrard and Hayden as Garmo, is in the Trans Alai at the junction of 'Peter the Great Range' and that of the 'Academy of Sciences'; thus, judging by this name, in the U.S.S.R. mountaineering and science are honourably married and not in illicit liaison as they are with us.

In the article from which the above is an extract there is a lively account of the post-war activities of Soviet 'Alpinists'—scaling cloud-splitting summits, planting the Red Flag in what have unfortunately proved to be not inaccessible places, and generally tearing asunder Nature's veil for the benefit of Soviet science. In fact they have been doing a great deal more high mountaineering than we have, even if they have done it to a jarringly loud accompaniment. Nature by now must be getting used to having her veil torn, and will, no doubt, continue to smile, or sometimes frown, upon the scientists busy in what Goethe called their charnel-house.

We reached Aqsu at 7 p.m. on the fourth day out from Urumchi. There we spent a whole day, a break which we had well earned, but it proved to be of such social activity that I found it almost as benumbing as counting tamarisk mounds. At Aqsu there is a large garrison and we spent our time at the barracks as guests of the Brigade Commander who was a friend of Shipton's. On the first evening we dined in the Mess in simple, soldierly fashion. We enjoyed the meal, but our hosts apologized for it, and threatened at the same time to treat us to a European dinner before we left. My heart sank. There is nothing so dangerous as a cook who meddles with foreign affairs; and this threat, which was amply fulfilled, hung over me all next day as we grappled with our successive gastronomic problems. The company at Mess was remarkable for its preponderance of generals and colonels who themselves were remarkable for their youth—Chinese subalterns, one imagines, very properly take their meals in the nursery. The whole atmosphere partook of that youthful fervour which the Kuomintang has long since outgrown. Smoking, drinking, and the use of imported luxuries were frowned upon or even forbidden, and the walls were hung with elevating texts. Moral re-armament was, rather belatedly, in full swing.

The Chinese are not great hands at breakfast. This is perhaps not surprising for most of their favourite foods would greatly astonish a dormant stomach. However, that did not prevent their sitting us down in front of a great bowl of rice and seeing that we ate it. Too soon after that the scene shifted to a pleasant villa on the outskirts of the town where we immediately began lunch with a General Li and his wife. General Li, as the commander of the garrison, was a man to whom the rules of moral re-armament either did not or could not apply. Austerity is all very well, as the General profoundly remarked, but it does not suit everybody. It was not one of those long drawn-out affairs of many courses beloved of Chinese officials, but there were a great many good things put on the table at once amongst which one could browse and experiment like a bee passing from flower to flower in search of the true nectar. Perhaps if I had to award the palm it would be to the bamboo shoots stewed in syrup, though the less exotic mince dumplings with a good dollop of soya bean sauce were not far behind. We finished with a famous blend of Hangchow tea with chrysanthemum petals floating in it—perhaps the 'Precious Thunder Tea' we read of in Marco Polo. The flavour was so delicate as to be imperceptible.

This luncheon party was a sort of training meet for the real business of the day. This was a garden party given by a Turki who was in official jargon the Administrative Superintendent—in unofficial jargon the 'big cheese'. This had little in common with the tepid, top-hatted ordeal that an English garden party appears to be.True it took place outside, but the only evidence of a garden was a tired zinnia and a rampant vine, under which the guests were firmly seated instead of being allowed to stroll about to meet and avoid friends. Though the vine was a magnificent wide-spreading thing like Jack's beanstalk, laden with grapes, it could hardly be expected to cast its ample shade over the whole multitude. The host, a loose Falstaffian figure in flowing robes, sat with a few exalted guests, like the Chinese generals and ourselves, behind a long table in the grateful dappled shade; beyond the table, at a respectful distance and on the earth, squatted the remainder of Aqsu in tight circles of which the outer rows basked or sweated in a pitiless sun. There is nothing easier to bear than the discomfort of others; indeed, this was a refinement that gave us added pleasure as we sipped our tea and cracked our melon seeds in coolest ease.

When we arrived the company was being entertained, or more correctly entertaining itself; but those at the high table might partake of tea, melon seeds, and conversation in order to mitigate the ordeal. It is, perhaps, true, that few amateur entertainments need be given undivided attention, but this was well worth watching. No man and very few girls showed any reluctance when called upon to do a turn. They could all dance and sing, gracefully and pleasingly, but rather too incessantly, either in groups or singly. There was a man, a hunchback, who laughed—a performance which nowadays, as one can well understand, is heard only on gramophone records—and finally Aqsu's woman delegate to the Urumchi assembly of Collective Wisdom, home for a visit to her constituency, was called upon for a dance. She performed very capably but concluded with a short and powerful appeal to patriotic fervour.

All the Aqsu girls were graceful and many of them comely. Even those with more unfortunate faces looked well enough with their black hair falling in long plaits adorned with black silk tassels, embroidered velvet caps perched jauntily on their heads, many-hued satin waistcoats, and equally vivid skirts. Beside these birds of paradise the men, some in seedy European suits, looked commonplace, but they danced and sang with no less grace. They moved stiffly but with much graceful arm-work to a band of two guitars and a tambourine; when each dancer considered he had done enough he took station opposite some fellow guest and danced there until the victim obliged by taking the floor.

Meantime at the high table more serious matters were being attended to. From pecking at melon seeds—a despicable chicken-feed, in my opinion—we had progressed to green and purple grapes, the bloom still on them, piled high on brass trays; water melons—messy and flavourless; real melons—food for angels; apricots, and roseate, fleshy peaches. Then came great discs of hot, rich-golden Turki bread into which I sunk my teeth pretty freely, defying the threatened European dinner and unaware that this was merely the harbinger of the coming storm. Greed struggled with dismay when a sumptuous platter of pastry and mutton was planked down in front of me with the intimation that there was plenty more where that came from. Here was no child's play, no finicking chop-stick work, no knife-and-fork cut-and-thrust, but a bitter hand-to-mouth struggle. I set to work manfully. The pastry was crisp and melting, the meat fell juicily from the bone at a touch, but no sooner had greed triumphed without much difficulty over dismay than our brigadier gave the signal to go. How I hated that austere man. Usually I am of the opinion of Mr Woodhouse that the sooner every party breaks up the better, but on this occasion I was never so reluctant to leave in all my life—to have snatched from me that 'rich and gigantic vision of the higher gluttony'.

We had warned our generous Chinese host that we must take the road again that evening, but they were not to be denied the pleasure of confronting us with a European dinner as a mark of their esteem and as a salutary warning to themselves. Apart from the Garrison Commander's lunch and my short but severe onslaught on the mutton and pastry we had been pecking at some trifle or other most of the afternoon. But there was no escape. At five o'clock we had not only to eat but appear to enjoy eating a slightly distorted version of a European meal which might have been intended either for breakfast or dinner, but which was in fact a mixture of both. The hors d'œuvre were in their rightful but always unnecessary place, as were the fish, meat and game which remorselessly followed; but then we were startled and very nearly subdued by bacon and eggs, slightly cheered by the appearance of pancakes, staggered afresh by soup, dumbfounded by hard-boiled eggs, and palsied by an ice.

We left at 6.30 p.m. and at 9 p.m. we camped. Beyond Aqsu all is desert; and that night as I lay upon its slightly heaving surface a Chinese general in an embroidered cap danced across it eating chysanthemum petals with a wooden spoon.

After another long day in which we covered about 180 miles we had to spend yet another night on the road some 50 miles short of Kashgar. An average speed of more than 10 m.p.h. on this Urumchi-Kashgar road is good going. Evidently, after the road had been re-aligned and drained under the spur of war, it had been handed over to Providence for care and maintenance; this is an arrangement that works well on surprisingly few occasions, but is the easiest to make for a road through uninhabited country. A solution satisfactory to everybody except to the troops would have been to remove them from the towns where they were kicking their heels to employment on the road; but the 'brutal soldiery' seldom appreciate what is good for them, and, except in war-time, must be handled carefully.

The country through which the road runs is not completely uninhabited. Gazelle thrive in spite of the rifle fire to which they are subjected from passing lorries. Mir Hamza, by luck or marksmanship, slew two which had foolishly lingered within 200 yards of the road. He dropped them dead with two shots, a feat which reminded me of that friend of mine in East Africa who killed two elephants with one shot. The first beast, feeding on the edge of a steep-sided donga or wadi (we are momentarily in Africa), on being hit, fell and broke the back of the second which was feeding in the dry river-bed below.

Next morning our hard-used truck, festooned with haunches of venison and the Consul's flag, delivered us safely at Chini Bagh in time for a second breakfast. Chini Bagh, the residence of British consuls since 1890 and a port of call for Central Asian travellers both distinguished and undistinguished, was now nearing its end as such. It was to be handed over to representatives of Pakistan and India and Shipton awaited only the arrival of the newly appointed Indian Consul before hauling down the Union Jack and quitting Kashgar for good.

CHAPTER SEVEN

Chakar Aghil Reconnaissance

THE motives which had impelled us to transfer ourselves so swiftly from Urumchi to Kashgar were mixed. As Shipton had been absent for more than two months from his office it seemed just possible that a letter or even a telegram requiring an answer might be waiting for him, while my chief concern was the advancing season (it was now September) and the need to act quickly if we were to attempt another climb.

In spite of this urgency I spent a week at the Consulate wrapped in sensual but perfectly proper delights, 'till languor suffering on the rack of bliss, confess that man was never meant for this'. The only exercise we took was a ride of some ten to twelve miles before breakfast and as this seldom took more than an hour it was fairly violent exercise, at any rate for the horse. Since my visit of the previous year and the death of Shipton's borrowed steed on the Ulugh Art pass he had acquired one of his own. This bright bay was no 'pampered jade of Asia', at least not in that brief early hour when we pounded out of the town along the red, dusty road scattering the incoming tide of donkeys, splashed through the shallow river like speed-boats, and charged along the country lanes and through the narrow alleys of outlying villages. Like Jorrocks, neither of us was afraid of the pace so long as there was no leaping.

This picture of flying hooves and wind-tossed manes had to be slightly modified if one was not mounted on the fiery bay. My mount had to be chosen from the stable of post-horses used for carrying the mails from Kashgar to Tashkurghan. As I learnt later, when I did the same journey mounted on one, these stocky animals could amble along all day under a load with a man sitting on top without noticing it; but they were not the fleetest of their kind. Though they may have been bred on the high Pamir amongst the Kirghiz, they could never have swept across Asia and half Europe as did their ancestors with the Golden Horde, and had they made the attempt they would certainly have arrived too late for the capture and sack of Budapest. They lacked spirit, they were immune to the contagion of speed which is enough to set most horses alight and will sometimes make even a donkey cut capers. The few that were

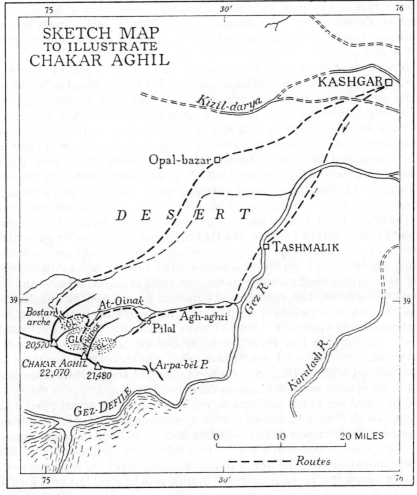

CHAKAR AGHIL

not immune and gallantly strove to match the flying bay were so crippled by their efforts that I was never allowed to ride the same horse twice.

The doctor, who was also vice-consul, having held the fort for so long, was in need of a change and he therefore decided to come with me on a reconnaissance of Chakar Aghil, a 22,000 ft. mountain upon which Shipton and I had had our eyes for some time. In fact it had figured upon our programme of the previous year, but our plans had been upset by the Muztagh Ata episode. The day before we started we lunched at the Russian consulate as we had in 1947. I calculated in the interim that M. Bikmozin had done four days' work, for the business consequent on the receipt and dispatch of the Russian mail was a quarterly affair. This quite ample interval was owing to the broken bridges on the Andijan motor road which the Chinese authorities preferred should remain broken. A truck, I gathered, could do the journey, but as it had to be hoisted bodily across rivers three months' preparation and thought were none too much. I suggested to M. Bikmozin that he should use an amphibian truck to which he replied with his own particular brand of humour that such a vehicle svoured too much of militarism for so civil a man as a Russian consul to use.

Nevertheless he was neither sinking under the fatigue of this brisk correspondence nor comatose with boredom. For he was about to be relieved from what he no doubt thought the living death of Kashgar and was accordingly sprightly, congratulating Shipton on his approaching release and at the same time condoling with him at the demise of the British consulate. Our entertainment differed in no way from the first occasion except that this time I suspected the vodka of being watered, for I drank a great many glasses without beneficial effect of any kind. A straw shows which way the wind blows, but whether this frugality indicated the coming economic collapse of Russia or treachery on the part of M. Bikmozin's butler I could not decide.

The doctor and I went by truck to the road end on the bank of the Gez river some 25 miles west of Kashgar. Mir Hamza, whose wife was still a guest of the police, drove vindictively, giving the donkey traffic even shorter shrift than usual. On emerging from the mountains where it runs through a difficult defile the river spreads itself over several hundred yards of gravel and sand and thus becomes fordable. The mount I had borrowed for the passage foundered in mid-river where it sank belly-deep in sand, depositing me in the water. Our destination was Tashmalik, about 15 miles away at the edge of the foothills where our baggage had already gone by bullock cart. The doctor rode a borrowed horse—what J.J. would have called 'a hugly beast' if ever there was one—while I walked. The sight of a horse is said to make the traveller lame, but in my opinion much depends on the horse. I am a little nice in the matter and provided the way is neither long nor across absolute desert I find it less trying to walk than to be carried at walking pace on the kind of nag commonly allotted to the borrower or hirer of horse-flesh. In walking one soon attains a soothing state of non-self, a sort of Buddhist trance, impossible to a rider whose mount, sensing the rider's condition, either takes the wrong way or in its turn adopts the Taoist principle of dealing with less and less until it finally arrives at inaction.

Strolling thus through poplar-shaded lanes or across short sun-bleached stretches of desert we arrived towards evening at the oasis of Tashmalik and made our way to the house of the Beg. The Beg, or headman, of a large oasis like Tashmalik is a considerable figure, whose household is likely to be run on lines agreeable to his dignity and with whom it is therefore desirable to lodge. The doctor had already had some professional dealings with the Beg's son so we dumped our gear on a veranda in his courtyard and sat there in happy expectancy. We sat for so long on the carpet of hope smoking the pipe of expectancy that I began to fear that the doctor's professional attention to the son had had ill or even fatal effect, but at last some slaves arrived bearing tea, a plentiful supply of melons, and apologies for the Beg's absence, and at ten o'clock expectation was fully realized with the serving of a rich pilau—'chau fan', as the Chinese call it, 'rice that is grabbed with the hands'.

In these regions food is provided freely, but transport either grudgingly or not at all. It was late in the morning before we were mobile. The animals reluctantly given were to accompany us only to the next village three miles away where we were assured we should easily find transport to take us to the mountains. After two hours of pleading, wrangling, and some show of violence on the part of the Beg's man who came with us, we got away from there with two woe-begone ponies and a donkey. This gallant little beast had the task of leading the two horses over the Gez river which had to be crossed again by a less easy ford than the first. If by some unhappy chance a murrain were to carry off the donkey population of Sinkiang, the whole economy of the country would be at an end. Without them the women, the greybeards, indeed, most of the manhood, would be anchored to their homes; upon them depends all the day-to-day carrying of wood and water for the people of the oases, while upon the extended journeys of the traders it is the ass which leads the long string of camels and which shows the way across rivers to animals twice as big as itself. For these services the only rubbing they get is with an oak towel and the only food chaff into which a grain or two of barley may have inadvertently strayed.

By a good track we followed the left bank of the river. The foothills were now close at hand, but still gave no hint of the mighty Kungur range rising just behind them. Towards 7 o'clock we reached the junction of the Oitagh Jilga, a river fed by the glaciers of Chakar Aghil. The camping ground lay on the other side and at this hour of the day the river was well up. Having had much experience of fords I find that my preparations for crossing them take an increasingly long time—the unlacing of boots and securing them round the neck, the rolling up or removal of shorts and the emptying of pockets—and I have an uneasy feeling that this deliberation is in the hope that someone else will be ready to take the water first. Unluckily on this occasion it was the inexperienced doctor who was ready first and who before I could stop him stepped light-heartedly into the flood and was at once in difficulties. Having no visible means of support, that is without ice-axe or stick, his legs crumpled under him, the boots which he was carrying were let go, and after being unceremoniously rolled over two or three times he crawled out on the further shore considerably battered and with the loss of those useful articles. But it's an ill wind that blows nobody good; I found I had left behind all my socks except for a thin pair I wore with rubbers, and to fill the gap thus left in my climbing boots I was now able to borrow from the doctor, whose 'chaplis'—the only footwear he had left—required none.

Our route now became more exciting. The warm red rock and the eroded yellow loess walls of our new valley were terribly gaunt, but high above them was the dark green of pines and faint behind them floated a white mass, detached as a cloud, which could be no other than Chakar Aghil. Some seven miles on, after climbing to a sort of hanging valley, we came to the golden wheat-fields, square mud houses, peach trees and poplars of Agh Aghzi. Still higher the valley forks, the left branch descending from the Arpa Bel pass (13,000 ft.) and the glaciers draping the north-east side of Chakar Aghil, and the right branch, the At Oinak, draining the glacier system to the north-west. It was the watershed between these two systems, the north ridge of Chakar Aghil, which we wished to see. In a previous visit Shipton had been up towards the Arpa Bel from which side the north ridge of the mountain appeared inaccessible, so that by going up the At Oinak we hoped to find a way on to the ridge from the north-west.

Half a mile above the junction, up the left branch, is the village of Pilal where we camped. It was not much out of our way, for near the village is a bridge and the track to the At Oinak. Pilal village is graced by a noble plane tree which put the reedy poplars to shame. Most of its inhabitants were up at their summer grazings where they live in yorts like Kirghiz, though they themselves are 'Taghliks' or mountain-dwelling Turkis. Its height is about 7,000 ft. I climbed another thousand feet to where some stunted juniper grew. From here I could see up the valley the first of the pines and the wrinkled snout of a great glacier, but the clouds were low, the weather thick, and promising to become worse.

Having crossed the main stream by the bridge we followed a rapidly deteriorating track up the narrowing valley of the At Oinak. Apart from some camels grazing by the river there was no sign of life. A few miles up, the track quitted what had now become a gorge to turn unexpectedly up a side nallah of insignificant size. It seemed to lead nowhere, but presently the track climbed abruptly out of it to land us upon a wide plateau of short grass well above the gorge. In the distance, tucked away at the foot of pine-clad slopes, we saw some yorts for which we made at full speed like homing pigeons. Whether it is seen at the end of a long day or at the beginning of one, a yort is the traveller's lode-stone. If it occurs in the middle of a march, as here, then it is a temptation to stop and I for one am not overfond of resisting temptation. The inhabitants were true Kirghiz whom we trusted were as pleased to see us as we were to see them. Anyhow we made ourselves at home, graciously accepted tea, and set the women to work making bread. Once they had got over the suspicion that we were tax collectors the neighbours began dribbling in, and when the doctor's profession had been bruited about 'House Full' notices had to be put up.

We were now at about 9,000 ft. but cut off by trees from any view up the valley. Above the yorts on the north side was a high bare ridge which looked a likely view-point and as it was advisable to see something before making a plan for the next day I decided to climb it. The day was still young, and the doctor, having seen the last of his patients, wanted to come with me. As he had only chaplis for his feet I did not encourage him, but he was determined to come. This stout leather sandal with thick, nailed sole is the footwear *par excellence* of the North-West frontier, where there are undoubtedly hills which chapli-shod tribesmen undoubtedly climb—and pretty nimbly, too, I gather. But on other hills, or on unpractised feet, the chapli is a form of foot-gear which neither I nor any wearer I have seen could or would use for long. This heretical view was amply confirmed that afternoon at the expense of the doctor. Having cut his feet and bruised his ankles by the stones and brambles on the way up, he found that as soon as the slope steepened his heels were more often out than in. When crossing difficult places he had to take them off, for there is no guarantee or even likelihood that one's foot will remain in the same place as the chapli.

I made matters worse by picking a direct but very bad route up steep unstable rock and across hard gravel slides where one had to scrape steps. But I had to retreat in some fear for the safety of my companion. However, by 5 o'clock we reached the ridge at about 13,000 ft., the determined doctor with lacerated feet and socks, and with the supreme footwear for hillmen dangling from his waist. Although the clouds were down to 14,000 ft. we saw something of value; below us lay a glacier-filled valley, the right moraine of the glacier being flanked by wide grass flats on which grazed yaks and scattered sheep.

The next day was the last we could spare for reconnaissance, so that it behoved me to get as far up this glacier as I could. The doctor's feet, very nearly beyond repair, urgently required his own professional attention, so I went alone. The cloud which for the last few days had covered the mountains and which had no doubt deposited much snow had now lifted, so I started early in anxious haste to get as high as I could before they closed down again. A mile up, the valley divided again and at the point of junction the snouts of two glaciers converged. The path turned up the left-hand valley climbing to the moraine of the glacier flowing in from the north upon which we had looked the previous evening. Just round the corner were two yorts. I passed these unnoticed and sped across the grass flats below the moraine.

A couple of miles of good flat going brought me level with the foot of the first ice-fall where the glacier tumbled over a steep step. From a shale shoulder above the step, at about 12,000 ft., I paused to take stock. The glacier, very crevassed and broken, extended more gently upwards and then divided into three great bays of névé. The bay in which I was interested lay out of sight round a corner to the left so I started traversing upwards across steep shale slopes thereby cutting off a good slice of the corner. Above me on the left was an extraordinary peak of perpendicular faces and right-angled cut-offs which I called the Geometry peak. Beyond the corner, between the glacier and the shale slopes, a snow slope lying at an easy angle afforded excellent going until at a height of 14,000 ft., having come far enough, I sat down on a rock to puzzle things out. An unexpected sight, even though unwelcome, may have charm. Indeed, that eminent critic Mr Gall decided that in the laying out of pleasure grounds unexpectedness and beauty were equally necessary ingredients, although, as someone unkindly pointed out, the charm of the unexpected cannot be exerted more than once. Here I had expected to find the scene dominated by Chakar Aghil, but whoever had laid out this pleasure ground had taken pains to disguise that notable peak. A magnificent ridge of snow and ice stretched in a great half-circle around the glacier head and its several bays. It ran almost horizontally at about 19,000 ft. except where it shot up to two peaks of over 21,000 ft. neither of which looked in the least like Chakar Aghil. Moreover, they were too far west to be visible from the Oitagh valley as Chakar Aghil had been. Up in the corner of the left-hand bay the snow upon which I stood appeared to continue unbroken until it met the extremity of the cirque, and some way west of the point of junction was a rather insignificant snow bump. The sky was curiously dead, the light too feeble to cast shadows, so that it was impossible to say whether the bump stood on the cirque or stood back from it. Anyhow it could hardly be Chakar Aghil. And where on earth was that considerable protuberance of 22,000 ft.? If it was the first outstanding peak westwards along the cirque, then it would be the devil of a long climb, especially if we had first to traverse the bump. Certain of nothing except that what must be the north ridge could be reached, I went down.

On the way back, from the village Pilal, we had a view of Chakar Aghil which was quite the best we had had and which increased my bewilderment. It looked like nothing I had seen from the north-west side, so although my report of the mountain's elusiveness might make Shipton laugh it would hardly encourage him to come and climb it. We camped at Agh Aghzi under some willows in a garden whose owner took pleasure in giving. Eggs we might expect, but he pressed upon us melons brought all the way from Tashmalik. It is too cold for them at Aghzi, but the donkeys which take to Tashmalik charcoal burnt in the higher valleys return with loads of melons.

We met with another example of Turki kindness when early next morning we rode down to the Oitagh Jilga ford. A party of traders were breakfasting there, one of whom at once started up and ran across to us with a plate of sliced melon and bread. While most Central Asian travellers have something disparaging to say of the Turki character, few fail to remark on their kindly disposition, a quality which a casual traveller will instantly discover and appreciate, while his other virtues and vices go unsung or unrebuked because unnoticed. Fortunately unanimity of opinion is still fairly rare in the present world and one well-known Central Asian traveller, Col. Schomberg, feels obliged to record that 'the Turki will never entertain anyone unless compelled . . . There are exceptions, but, generally, in a land where food is particularly cheap and abundant, true hospitality is as rare as true morality.' Ellsworth Huntington, in his *Pulse of Asia*, lists the Turki's qualities as follows: among the good 'are gentleness, good temper, hospitality, courtesy, patience, contentment, democracy, religious tolerance, and industry; among the bad are timidity, dishonesty, stupidity, provincialism, childishness, lack of initiative, lack of curiosity, indifference to suffering, and immorality'. But

Burke long ago pointed out the difficulty of drawing up an indictment against a whole people, and so, I think, the traveller had best refrain from generalizing about the moral qualities of a whole people, but content himself with heartily damning or praising those of the individuals he meets.

As if to point this moral we were presently able to acquit some Turkis at any rate of that lack of initiative which Ellsworth Huntington charitably ascribed to them all. At Tashmalik we changed transport for the last time, leaving that pleasant oasis with two horses (both lame) and a donkey. Sitting by the bank of the Gez ford was a gang of semi-naked loafers who from time to time could turn an honest penny by giving a hand to bullock carts which frequently got into trouble in mid-stream. In crossing a wide ford local knowledge is everything, and these worthies very obligingly volunteered detailed sailing directions which, when followed, quickly sunk us in the deepest part of the river. Whereupon, the horse having lain down and the donkey floating away, the loafers with a whoop of joy dashed to our assistance, carried the stuff across, and reaped the reward of their enterprise.

The faithful Mir Hamza who was waiting for us quickly drove us back to the Consulate. He seemed more cheerful, for he was once more enjoying the society of his wife, justice having been tempered with mercy or with something more tangible.

CHAPTER EIGHT

Chakar Aghil

THE less successful a mission the more reason there is to wrap its lame conclusions in a cloud of verbiage. My report on the chances of climbing Chakar Aghil by the north ridge was neither lucid nor conclusive, in fact, as we have seen, I was not at all sure I had been looking at the right mountain.

Having cleared a space at Shipton's office table by sweeping to the floor piles of those dreary, cheap brown paper files affected by Indian Government offices, we sat down to sketch on the backs of official telegrams our representative ideas of the Chakar Aghil massif, its ridges, glaciers, and valleys. The map of the region is content with indicating roughly some high ground. Shipton therefore based his map on what he thought he would have seen on his previous visit if the mountain had not been in the way, while I drew what I actually had seen on a day when the mountain wasn't there. Shipton's, I think, was the more credible. This was to be expected as it was in accord with the latest philosophic teaching whereby the evidence of one's eyes is of little value compared with the results of pure reason and higher mathematics. Anyhow, from our combined efforts it rather looked as though the mountain had no west side, or that if it had the glacier there had no outlet. But I hastened to point out, as we picked up, perhaps unnecessarily, the files, that conclusions which are drawn logically from unsound premises must of necessity be erroneous. We decided to have a go.

Two days later, 11 September, we loaded the truck and started once more for Tashmalik. Instead of Lakhpa we took his brother, Gyalgen. He was without Lakhpa's great belly, but also lacked his experience, intelligence, and drive. That, of course, is a negative description, and since Lakhpa's intelligence was of no mean order it would be truer to say that his brother had none at all. In addition we took a long, lean, cadaverous Kirghiz of grave aspect. Had his fine features and habitually grave expression been set off by a well-trimmed beard instead of a few straggling wisps he would have resembled my notion of a Spanish Don. On several occasions the Don had been out with Shipton on some biggish hills after *Ovis poli* and had so astonished him by the speed with which he moved up, down, or across difficult ground that he, Shipton, concluded that upon Chakar Aghil the don would hardly draw short breath.

We reached Tashmalik that same evening where the Beg put as bright a face on the matter as he could. Three visits from me in ten days were a little hard. But having a full-blown Consul on his hands instead of a mere Vice- he bestirred himself over the transport to such purpose that we got away pretty early. Before leaving, we climbed to the flat roof of the house whence we had a grand view of our mountain. The day before we left Kashgar there had been a prolonged and violent storm of wind and dust which had swept the sky so effectively that even at that great distance the snow upon the mountain fairly sparkled. The north ridge, which we could see well, looked a likely route, but why this outstanding summit had not been visible from the west side was still unexplained.

Crossing the Oitagh Jilga in the early afternoon we pushed on to Agh Aghzi where we camped in the same willow-hung field. And on the third day, sternly ignoring the proffered entertainment at the first yorts, we rounded the corner and took up our quarters at the two rather mean yorts close by the glacier. There are not many towns in Asia, or Europe either for that matter, so pleasant as Kashgar, and there are fewer still from which within three days one can reach the foot of a 22,000 ft. mountain. Gilgit is one and Chitral another; both very pleasant, but hardly towns in the sense that Kashgar is. This two-yort valley, we were told, is the Kichik Chi. There is no timber, only a little juniper bush, but with the long wall of 'eagle-baffling mountains' at the head and the wide grassy maidan at its foot it is a valley in which men might well live a hard life and yet exult in living.

True to the principle of the economy of force we took a pony to the far end of the maidan and as far up the shale slope at the side of the ice-fall as we could. The applications of this principle is one that the wise mountaineer fully understands, especially in the Himalaya where, unlike the Alps, opportunities for practising it readily present themselves. In short there is nearly always some man or brute beast to carry one's load. And since at the moment of writing I have not to practise what I preach, I may safely deplore that this should be so. As long as such reliable porters as Sherpas are available there cannot be the compelling incentive of necessity, which otherwise would before now have obliged the mountaineer to improve his own carrying power by studying the technique of load-carrying; and to lighten his equipment, both by the use of new materials and by elimination of much that is still held to be necessary. It might urge him to consider, for example, the use of snow holes instead of tents, so that it should become normal practice for peaks up to, say, 23,000 ft., to be climbed without porters, whose cost in wages and clothing is a severe drain on the resources of small parties. (On the north-east spur of Kangchenjunga in 1929 the Bavarians used an ice-cave at 21,600 ft. and thought it warmer than a tent.)

From the earliest day of Himalayan travel and mountaineering porters have of necessity been employed to reach the mountains or to cross passes, but their use for carrying camps up a mountain is a comparatively recent innovation. General Bruce first thought that Gurkhas might be useful in this respect; and in 1894, in order to test them, Conway climbed with two Gurkhas in the Alps. In 1895 Mummery and his two Gurkhas were killed while crossing a pass on the north-east side of Nanga Parbat. Nevertheless, before the first world war the usual practice for Himalayan mountaineers was to take Alpine guides. In 1905 Longstaff with the Brocherel brothers (Italian guides) reached a height of 24,000 ft. on Gurla Mandhata (25,350 ft.) when, by the way, they camped at 23,000 ft. in a snow-hole; and in 1907, accompanied by the Brocherels and a Gurkha, he climbed Trisul (23,360 ft.) from a camp at 17,500 ft., so that on the actual climb the party carried nothing at all. However, after the first attempt on Everest in 1922 the capabilities of the Sherpa porter became fully realized. Their employment in putting camps high on a mountain saved a great deal of sweat, and, as compared with Alpine guides, a great deal of money. Since then their use has become normal practice both on the great mountains where they are really needed as well as on the lesser where they might be dispensed with. Thus, in my opinion, their discovery and use may have led to the abandoning of earlier, simpler, and harder methods, and thus to slowing down the progress of Himalayan climbing in general.

If any such stern line of reasoning presented itself it was very quickly suppressed as we dejectedly acknowledged that our pony could be taken no further and that our backs could no longer escape their share of the load. Traversing across the shale slope carrying loads would have been so laborious that we stuck to the glacier trough where the way lay partly on dirty, black ice, partly on moraine, and in one place up a river of mud sliding slowly down the underlying ice. Although it is often the best way and sometimes the only way up a steep glacier, this trough where the ice of a glacier rubs against the mountain is always extremely rough and has a dismal air of dank decay from which one is always glad to escape. When we reached the corner and came to the foot of the same snow slope which I had struck higher up we found that the snow of a week ago had gone, leaving bare a bed of old, dirty semi-ice. We climbed easily up this and at four o'clock pitched the tents at my highest point. Our altimeter made this 14,400 ft. and a hypsometer reading gave 13,600 ft. All the snow had gone, so that we lay warmly on gravel, and this disappearance of the fresh snow combined with the brightness of the day gave to everything a different aspect. My continuous snow slope to the ridge was found to be broken by an intervening glacier, and my contemptible snow bump, which we now saw stood well back from the cirque, was no other than the distant and very noble summit of Chakar Aghil.

The discovery of this inconvenient break in the snow slope gave me some uneasiness, for the principal inducement which I had held out to Shipton to come had been this supposedly certain way to the north ridge. That evening I went up another 800 ft. and satisfied myself that the route would still go. At 6 p.m. a sharp fall of temperature to below freezing-point augured well for the morrow.

With our sad experience on Muztagh Ata the previous year still fresh in our minds we were in no doubt as to the necessity of having two camps, one at 17,000 ft. and the other at 20,000 ft. For this we should have a total load of about 100 lb. to carry. For some reason, about which I am not yet clear, this calculation was based upon a decision to take only one tent and therefore only one porter. Had we taken both tents and both porters our individual loads would certainly have been no more, probably a little less. But we make so many stupid mistakes in the course of an expedition, a climb, or from day to day, that unless the consequences are painful to pocket, person, or pride, our reasons for making them are seldom analysed. Should, however, an attempted analysis fail to disclose the wherefore, then one may at any rate congratulate oneself on not being reason's servile slave. If we had a reason for our odd decision, it was, perhaps, because boots, bedding, or warm clothing were insufficient for both Gyalgen and the Kirghiz. Anyhow, the fiat went forth that only one victim was required and unhappily the lot fell on the Don.

Shrinking from the ugly thought of having to assume our full burdens so early in the day we roped in Gyalgen, so that when we started he and the Don carried the bulk of the stuff between them. The route went very neatly. Our slope quickly narrowed to a ridge which took us up to the intervening glacier at the one point at which it could be reached. Immediately to our right it tumbled in a steep ice-fall to the main glacier bay below, and to our left rose a high rock wall. Having got on to the glacier by an ice bridge we walked across to a broken ice-wall on the far side up which we climbed with only a little step-cutting. This move landed us fairly on a smooth unbroken slope running easily up to the foot of the north ridge. Here we divided the loads more or less equally amongst the three of us and sent Gyalgen down with instructions to go to the yorts taking with him the spare tent.

Up to this point a slow slug would have had no difficulty in keeping up with our two porters, particularly the Kirghiz. We attributed this to their loads and refrained from comment, which must always come ungracefuly from the unladen man. When we started again, the Kirghiz had no more weight on his back but he soon began to lag. The slope was easy and uncrevassed, there was no need for the rope, so we plodded on while the Don dropped further and further behind;

> And slow howe'er my marches be,
> I shall at last sit down by thee.

One began to doubt it.

Towards evening we reached a snug snow hollow, a hundred feet or so below the crest of the ridge, where we decided to camp, the height being about 17,000 ft. Dumping our loads we went down several hundred feet to the Don who by now had almost ceased to struggle, and relieving him of his load we got him up to the tent. He seemed to be very ill, spitting, coughing, groaning incessantly, and refusing all food. We ourselves had a very curious dish of Vienna sausages which were sizzling hot at one end and frozen at the other—a striking example of the non-conductivity of sausages in high altitudes. It is an original way of serving them which I cannot recommend.

Few indeed are those high camps where the inmates at one time or another are not 'acquainted with sad misery, as the tann'd galley-slave is with his oar'; and the misery is particularly poignant when one sleeps, as we did, three in a two-man tent. It blew hard in the night which I spent cold and restless, to wake, or rather sit up at last, with a fierce headache. Shipton, who is usually more at home in high places than elsewhere, greeted the unwelcome dawn with some muttered comparison between the worth of the game and the candle, while the cadaverous Kirghiz was in a thoroughly poor way. He had eaten nothing and had spent the night only semi-recumbent, moaning and spitting, until he at length became a total wreck.

The implications of this were obvious. Even if we were sufficiently callous to leave him there alone we could not go on because we had only the one tent. Brought up in comfortable homes and with a background of more or less comfortable mountaineering neither of us proposed going on to sleep in a snow-hole at 20,000 ft.; or of attempting the climb from where we were; or, perhaps best of all, leaving the Don in a snow-hole. By no means this last, for the unhappy man now alarmed us by beginning to spit blood. There was no question but that we must take him down; and since Gyalgen had removed the other tent ours must go down too. In short Chakar Aghil had beaten us.

A cold but fine, sunny morning served to deepen our chagrin, but before packing up we climbed to the ridge and a little way along it for the sake of photography. This ridge in no way resembled that of Bogdo Ola; on its comfortably broad back we could see no great obstacles between us and the distant summit. The long cirque or semi-circular ridge, whose gigantic scale we could now appreciate, filled the whole western horizon like the flood-lit façade of some giant's palace as the rising sun kindled its rock buttresses to a warm glow and its two high bastions to pyramids of fire. On the east our ridge overhung a broad snow plateau upon which the slanting rays of the sun etched an intricate pattern among the seams and terraces of the crevasses. Many thousands of feet below lay the Oitagh valley, still in cold shadow, where a grey glacier crept down to the sombre pines.

We had now to rid ourselves of our sorrowing incubus who was wellnigh helpless. Most of the descent he accomplished in a sitting position held by the rope, and when we reached the little glacier where such effortless progress was not possible he was just able to stand up and stagger. At the 14,000 ft. camp site we put up the tent and left him with some food for a recovery squad to bring in; while we, a little too readily perhaps, responded to the call of the fleshpots at the yorts.

The case of this Kirghiz was so striking and the results so lamentable that at Kashgar we had him medically examined. For what it was worth, for in Kashgar such an examination could be only superficial, it showed him to be in normal health. Yet here was a man who had lived his life at about 10,000 ft., who danced like a flame upon his own mountains provided they were not much higher, and yet collapsed completely at 17,000 ft. In 1947 another Kirghiz, who in the course of a brief morning climbed to about 16,500 ft. on Muztagh Ata, also became ill—severely ill judging by his groans—but he was not, like our Don, a picked man who had shown a superlative aptitude for running up and down hills. Two men are not a fair sample, but one is tempted to conclude that mere living at 10,000 ft., as most Kirghiz do, does not increase the body's toleration to greater heights.

While Gyalgen went up to retrieve the Kirghiz Shipton and I turned our hands to 'shikar'. That is to say, Shipton carried a gun and I acted presumably as the 'tiffin coolie' without whom the thing is on a pretty low plane. Our quarry was the ram chikor, a big, fat, juicy, partridge-like bird, marked like the small chikor, but because he lives on or near the snow-line has much more white about him. We poked about, gradually gaining height, until we saw some ram chikor planing down to settle on a ridge above us. The birds generally feed uphill so our object was to get on to the ridge below them and stalk them until either we got a shot or they took fright and zoomed off the ridge. Pursued in this way the ram chikor is a very sporting bird; for although you have every intention of shooting him on the floor you have to climb hard and fast for your one shot and are not likely to get another. This lot led us a rare dance up the ridge and finally took off with their number still complete.

The Kirghiz came down that evening, looking a little wan but otherwise well. Gyalgen informed us that he had taken an even graver view of his own condition than we had, for after we had left him in the tent he had occupied himself drawing up his will. The feeling of remorse we experienced upon hearing this pathetic tale almost extinguished the disappointment to which his failure had contributed. But that evening the weather broke, much snow fell in the night, so after all we might not have got up Chakar Aghil.

Thus disappointed of our peak we indulged in a little mild exploration by returning over a new route. The local 'bojang', having now heard of our presence, carried us off to his yorts further up the At Oinak where he gave us a meal and also guides and ponies for the crossing of the Bostan Arche pass. The head of this glacier valley is enclosed by the western end of the cirque and the 20,500 ft. peak of Kara Boktor which is one of its two bastions. North of this peak the ridge droops and dwindles until it is easily crossed by the 13,000 ft. pass. Having topped this and taken our inevitable snack at a yort on the far side, we rode down a pleasant wooded valley to Yelche Moinak. But the pleasantness of these mountain valleys does not extend far down. Very soon the grass and the pines give way to bald, parched, eroded hills, the river as if in disgust buries itself in the gravel, and instead of kindly Kirghiz spacious in the possession of yaks, we find a few miserable bastard Kirghiz, gipsies rather than true nomads, with herds of goats which thrive in the wilderness they have helped to make.

At Yelche Moinak we joined the route by which we had descended in such crippled fashion from the Ulugh Art pass in 1947,[1] and two longish rides brought us back to Kashgar. I see that on the last day we covered the 33 miles to Kashgar in five hours, so that either I rode, as J.J. would say, uncommon galvanizingly, or else I drew a better mount than usually fell to my lot.

Owing to the impending departure of the twin pillars of Kashgar society, the British and Russian consuls, an epidemic of dining broke out. As rulers of Sinkiang the Chinese may not have deliberately set themselves the task—the proper duty of a Colonial power—of making two blades of grass grow in place of one, but they have at least encouraged agriculture by consuming large quantities of produce. The Foreign Secretary struck first, and at his banquet, as was most fitting, the lion and the bear grazed amicably side by side. Glorious as they may be in feasting, the Chinese, as I have hinted, are not backward in drinking. The way in which successive bumpers (of a pitiless size) were downed on this occasion did something to restore one's confidence in the human race, but even so the pace was not hot enough for our mild-mannered host who introduced various quickening devices.

One of these was almost too simple for a sober man to appreciate but fortunately there was not one present. It consisted in the rapid circulation of a flow of match-boxes with a lighted match stuck in them and whosoever held the box when the match expired had to drain his glass. Provided the guests entered into the spirit of the thing a match could be made to expire in the hands of any half-hearted drinker with gratifying frequency. A noisier, more intellectual, and more effective method—for everyone might take part at once—was the stone, scissors, paper game, in which the opponents fling out their hands simultaneously to express one of the three symbols, the winner either wrapping up his opponent's stone, blunting his scissors, or cutting his paper. It is easy to play and not really necessary to explain. Even more noisy was the game in which the players in quick succession extend a certain number of fingers and guess at the combined total. It is no game for the inexperienced if the penalty exacted by the man who guesses right is the drinking of a glass of rice brandy. I had last seen this played in Italy (without the brandy) where the partisans took particular pleasure in it because Mussolini had formally banned the playing of it in albergos and other places where they sing. They played it with enormous speed and gusto, banging the knuckles hard on the table and shouting each time they showed their hands, which was just about as fast as one could count. After a long session the knuckles of the players hands would be bruised and swollen.

The dinner given by the G.O.C. Kashgar was a remarkably good one thanks to the absence of anything found in the sea and, in my opinion, mistakenly removed from it by the Chinese. One could therefore deal more or less faithfully with each dish on its merits, secure in the knowledge that no sea-slugs, shark-fin, traveller fish tripe, or seaweed soup, lurked obscenely in the bowl. One of the first-named I still carry about as a charm against bee stings or sea-sickness until an opportunity occurs for planting it for the benefit

---

1 Crossing the Ulugh Art in 1947 Shipton's horse died, Mrs Shipton's was weary unto death, and the hired baggage ponies deserted. Three starving donkeys formed our train.

of some geological friend in search of a trilobite which it much resembles. Departure from established custom, as our host regretfully explained, was owing to a recent memorandum circulated by the Central Government who, taking a leaf from the book of our own mandarins, severely discouraged luxury in high places. The curious ideas held by the Chinese on what constitutes 'food' naturally does nothing to limit their ideas when dealing with more ordinary fare. On this occasion we had, for example, oxtail soup served in a half-melon, some fried meat with cheese, and stewed pears stuffed with rice.

The Foreign Office and the Army having done their worst, we had little to fear from the Law, Civil Administration, Public Works, or even the Post Office. But by the time the epidemic had run its course the loess haze had, as it were, settled upon our complexions. 'You see', as the eminent Dr Swizzle used to say, 'it's all done by eating. Most people dig their grave with their teeth.' However, on the march home on which I had now to start there was to be little opportunity for that.

CHAPTER NINE

To Misgar

By the end of September it was clear that as the incoming Indian consul would not soon arrive Shipton would have to leave before adjudicating upon the division of Chini Bagh into two equal halves for the respective Consulates of India and Pakistan—a delicate task which might well have baffled Solomon. He decided to delay his departure until mid-October and to proceed to India as quickly as possible. I, on the other hand, wanted leisure to deviate slightly from the direct route and so left ten days in advance. We expected to meet at Chitral. I have a rooted objection to following the beaten track, but because my deviations of the previous year had led me into trouble, this year I intended waiting until I was on the Indian side of the Mintaka pass before making any wide cast. Owing to the Kashmir dispute, the route which I should have liked to have taken was not possible.

In the absence of anyone in Kashgar anxious to see the world, and having no follower of my own, I arranged to travel with the mail runners. For the five-day stage to Tashkurghan the mails are carried on the ponies whose paces I had already tried and found wanting; but our friend Hill Billy, the Hunza lad, whose turn it was to go this trip, undertook to see me well mounted.

We had 43 miles to do the first day to Yangi Hissar, so at the morbid hour of 2 a.m. I crept out of the Consulate to be hoisted with my two rucksacks and a bag of fodder on what might have been for all I knew a camel. I soon discovered that travelling with the mail was to be no picnic for I sat shivering in shorts and 'chapkan', balanced high on the load with my legs dangling free, high on the beast's shoulder. The succeeding six hours of jogging and walking would have been unbroken had not my horse stumbled in the dark and saved me the trouble of dismounting by pitching me off. Breakfast-time had long passed when presently we turned in to a wayside house, dismounted stiffly, and without staying to count the cost treated ourselves to a mealie cob—one each, that is to say.

Hill Billy's companion, evidently the senior of the half-section, was a little wizened, grey-bearded man—a Wakhi, I think—whose meagre frame was

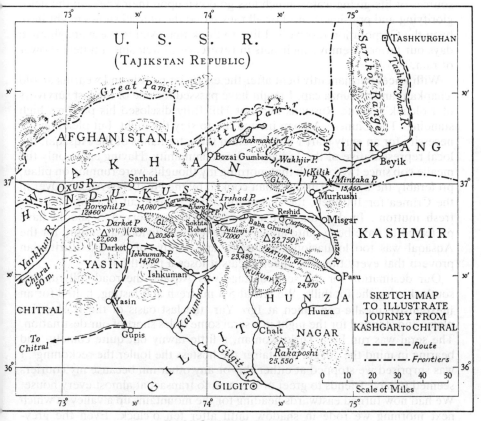

KASHGAR TO CHITRAL

eminently in keeping with a ration of one mealie cob and whose stern ascetic expression hinted that no one should want or expect more. As for the horses they knew better than even to look as though they knew what food was. Since our stomachs would have regarded any long pause for digestion as derisory, we soon climbed on and took the road. When accomplishing this ungraceful act I was always reminded of the withering scorn with which the commander of a Horse Artillery battery, dissatisfied with their drill, instead of giving the order 'Mount', adjured his drivers to 'Climb up you ruddy monkeys'. In the absence of anyone to give him a friendly hoist, the would-be rider manœuvres the beast alongside some bank or boulder and jumps for it, hoping the animal will be in the same place when he comes down.

We went on without a stop for another six hours to reach Yangi Hissar about four o'clock. The country was flat, sometimes with rich fields sometimes with wilderness, but on our right hand, austerely aloof, the Kungur range shone clearly. Seeing that their subsistence, their very being, is bound up with these mountains it is surprising how successfully the Turkis ignore them. I never saw them bestow even a passing glance upon these sources of life-giving water, much less go down upon their knees in the fields glorifying and praising them. For all they cared the eternal snows might have been the Corporation reservoir. I like to think that even in these enlightened days our farmers remove their hats in reverence to welcome a timely shower of rain.

With knees permanently bent after the excruciating ride and wearing an old 'chapkan' and a Hunza cap, I might have passsed for one of the last survivors of Kolchak's White Russians had not Hill Billy disclosed his patron's high standing. The Chinese Amban invited me to stay the night, but pleading the necessity for an early start I put myself in the safer hands of the Aqsaqal, the local representative of the Indian trading community. Having eaten only the mealie cob since two o'clock that morning my thoughts were running on pilau, preferably the kind of Turkish pilau cooked by the great chef Alexis Soyer in the Crimea for 100 men, the recipe for which begins 'cut or chop 50 lb. of fresh mutton'. In due time an adequate meal was served. I should have preferred to have been quite alone to give it my undivided attention, for the Aqsaqal was too loquacious—ignorant, apparently, of the old Ruritanian proverb that every time the sheep bleats it loses a mouthful.

Our destination for the second stage was Aqsala, the road still running south skirting the foothills. We left at 5 a.m. fresh and fasting, halted for an inexpensive mealie-cob lunch at Igiz Yar, the last oasis of the Kashgarian plain, and stopped for the night in a serai some miles short of our destination. The serai was run by a Turki woman, a little tawny but quite comely, and bearing in mind the adage, 'the fairer the hostess the fouler the reckoning', I was surprised we stopped at either this or any other inn because my couriers seemed to have friends to greet or business to transact at almost every house. We had now turned eastwards heading for the mountains up a valley in which next morning we rode in shadow until after ten o'clock. Even the grey-bearded Wakhi, who disliked walking, had to get off occasionally to keep warm. Now that we had passed beyond cultivation there was no point in dismounting in search of mealie cobs, we therefore carried on without food or drink until we halted for the night at a couple of yorts. I did not mind this, for I should hardly regard a mealie cob as an adequate reason for getting off a bicycle let alone a horse, and when riding there is really no need for food, at least not for the rider.

In this narrow sunless valley my two stalwarts found it too cold even for them to make an early start. We had some lost ground to make up if we were to reach Tashkurghan next day, but after a late start and with two passes to cross there seemed little chance of doing so. Although it was already late when we dropped down from the Tari Art (13,340 ft.) to the Karatash valley at Toilebelung, where there was a serai and a Chinese post, we did not stop. Scorning the serai and grimacing at the soldiers we entered the mouth of the Tangitar gorge in which just before dark we were received at a miserable hovel with a hearty welcome. Without counting dogs, calves, and lambs, there were already fifteen inside so three more made little difference. The women added a little more water to an already watery stew, Hill Billy disclosed a hidden reserve of mealie cobs, and I contributed a cigarette. Nearly all fifteen, including the children, had a pull at it and all were extremely grateful.

When we started not very early on the fifth day I hardly expected that we should reach Tashkurghan for it was still nearly 40 miles away on the other side of the Chichiklik pass (15,400 ft.). For several miles the boulders in the river-bed of the gorge, which was, of course, the track, kept the ponies to a walk. Soon after midday we emerged upon the great glass plateau, the Chichiklik maidan, and bumped across it at a good pace in the teeth of a shrivelling blast—a feature of this region upon which many travellers from Hsuan Tsang (A.D. 624) downwards have remarked. In 1947, a month earlier, we had crossed it one dull evening with snow on the ground when there was slightly less cold than we now experienced at midday under a brilliant sun. Beyond the maidan the road climbs gently to the pass and then drops rapidly for 5,000 ft. through a cruel gorge strewn with the skeletons and mummified bodies of donkeys. A dead donkey is a forlorn object but one which his living brother very sensibly, I suppose, meets with indifference. Nevertheless, I personally felt that this goodly fellowship of death would have looked better had the skeletons of one or two of their owners been stretched alongside their animals.

Once we had quitted this horrible nallah we had good going upon which the tireless beasts jogged rapidly towards the green Tagharma vale, while away to the north the mighty dome of the Muztagh Ata flushed in the setting sun. At length, as darkness fell, we reached the poplars and the stone tower of Tashkurghan, the empty bazaar and the deserted serais of this seedy capital of Sarikol. I reckoned that in five days the horses had covered about 150 miles, carrying a man as well as a load, on a ration which can safely be described as meagre. In the strength of horses such as this the psalmist might well have taken pleasure.

It is all very well to speak of the capital of Sarikol, but one must not expect too much from a village 10,000 ft. up, which happens to be the largest one in a poor, straggling, inclement district. No part of Sarikol is lower than this, and most of it is much higher, comprising as it does the eastern edge of the Pamirs, the valley of the Tashkurghan river and the Tagharma valley, both of which descend to Tashkurghan. Kirghiz inhabit the Pamirs and Tajiks the valleys where they grow barley. It is a place of great antiquity, but one suspects that even the ancients, superior as they no doubt were to their descendants, could have done little with such a place. Anyhow no trace remains of the stupa built, according to the Chinese pilgrim Hsuan Tsang, by Asoka (264 B.C.), nor of the convent built in honour of a Buddhist monk of Taxila in the Punjab who preached to the Sarikolis. Neither does Marco Polo tell us anything of what it was like in his day (c. 1270), for he leaps in his headlong way from the upper Oxus to Kashgar in what he calls 'forty good days', pausing only to revile the idolaters met with on the way who were 'in truth an evil race'. Even Col. Yule, Marco's thorough and pious editor, who has elucidated much, can add nothing to this, nor tell us whether or not Marco passed through Tashkurghan. It is very rare, but it happens occasionally, that a traveller's tale is too succinct.

From Tashkurghan to Misgar on the Indian side of the Mintaka pass the mail bags are carried on donkeys, one of which I hired for my kit. After a day's rest Hill Billy and the ponies started back for Kashgar, and our party of three donkeys, two Hunza men, and myself headed south. Certainly, as the ponies stepped proudly out of the gate and we shambled after them I felt I had taken a step down in the world, but from Isgar onwards I should have to fall lower and begin carrying a load myself. Just before we left my rage had kindled against these two donkey drivers by reason of their refusal to accept payment for my donkey in Sinkiang dollars, and since the number of rupees offered for them by the Shylocks of the bazaar was quite ridiculous I ceremonially burnt the ten million I had left—a haughty gesture which fell disappointingly flat.

The two stages to Dafdar, 34 miles away, are not kind to the man on foot; whichever side of the river is taken, the way lies over a featureless gravel plain. When going southwards the traveller has not even the inspiration of the kingly Muztagh Ata to which to lift his eyes for now it lies directly behind hm. Beyond Dafdar the man on foot may take heart, he has done with deserts and gravel plains and is entering the region where, if he has good lungs, he is on more than equal terms with a horse. After crossing the Oprang river, which was not now the obstacle it is in high summer, the Taghdumbash Pamir closes in upon the valley, and a river of clear cobalt blue, dashing over a white pebble bed, becomes an intimate and cheerful companion by the roadway. I noticed that the number of Kirghiz yorts had greatly increased since I passed this way in 1947; then there had been only a few clustered round Beyik, but now there were many on both banks of the river. No doubt they belonged to some of the thirty families whose vanguard I had met in 1947 crossing the Wakhjir pass.

At Mintaka Karaul, beyond Beyik, I met the chief of these people living, as befitted him, in the most princely and spacious yort I had yet seen. The rugs, the highly ornamented saddlery, and the pile of brightly coloured boxes against the wall, testified that the owner was a man of substance. He was very friendly and very well-informed. He had heard of and regretted the departure of the British Consul from Kashgar, and he spat at the mention of the Russians who were apparently the reason for the migration of his tribe from their grazing grounds near the Chakmaktin lake in Wakhan. Although he spoke no English he could read the names of places on my map, and seemingly was familiar with all the country from Wakhan to the Murghab. He was eager to talk; but, naturally, he understood quite as well as I did that an empty stomach has no ears. When his women had placed in front of me a large wooden bowl of thick cream and a suitable acreage of flat, fresh loaves, I gave him what attention I could spare.

On 11 October we started early from a yort at Lupgaz which is the last habitation on the Chinese side of the Mintaka pass. No doubt we should have fared better at the chief's yort, but our resting places were usually dictated by the necessities of trade of which the mail couriers privately did a good deal, picking up wool, skins, and numdahs at all kinds of out-of-the-way places. The unfortunate donkeys' loads had increased, were increasing, and no doubt ought to have been diminished, but the only diminution was in their pace. I welcomed this because, though I generally dislike donkeys as baggage animals on account of their despicably slow pace, up to Beyik it had been as much as I could do to keep up with our three flyers. Donkey driving is an art in which a stout cudgel and a strong arm are of less avail than knowledge of the appropriate cries and the skill to utter them. Stevenson found that the application of a wand with an eighth of an inch of pin to Modestine's mouse-coloured rump had a very galvanizing effect, and the fat Turki, sitting astride his donkey, indifferently uses the point of his knife.

Just beyond Lupgaz we found the unwelcome innovation of a Chinese check post where they turned all my kit on to the road. No one, least of all the Chinese soldiers, knew what they were looking for, but the search occupied one of their many idle hours and gave them a lot of fun. Apart from the inconvenience, it is humiliating to have one's belongings exposed to public view on an Asiatic highway, where the contents of even a rucksack must look shamefully superfluous in the eyes of men who travel further and no less comfortably with nothing whatever. It is impossible, we are told, to do any act not in itself morally wrong for the last time without feelings of regret. There may have been a slight moral taint about my last dealings with Chinese soldiers and customs officials—for I had in my pocket a piece of jade which I intended keeping there—but I experienced slight regret and certainly no remorse as I looked upon them for probably the last time. Their presence accorded ill with my notion of the fitness of things. In this bleak but noble landscape with which the Kirghiz and his yaks were quite in harmony, the occupants of this post—disreputable and slightly insolent—struck a jarring note. Since mountain ranges are so often frontiers it is unreasonable, I suppose, to expect that the passes should not be guarded, but along the frontiers of the Himalaya and the Hindu Kush it is only people like the Chinese and the Afghans who have the childish notion that the only way to guard a pass is to sit upon it. Whatever goes up into the mountains must soon come down, so that it is sensible, cheaper, and more agreeable to the parties concerned, if the frontier guards wait at the bottom for this to happen, leaving the mountains themselves free of their discordant presence so that the felicity of mountaineeers and travellers may be more perfect.

In shorts and shirt-sleeves, for it was a calm sunny day, and rejoicing to think that on the far side there were neither soldiers nor officials, I continued the way to the Mintaka pass (15,450 ft.). The delay occasioned by this kit inspection could not be made up by rattling down the other side, for baggage animals, particularly donkeys, pick their way down with cautious, stilted steps, at even slower pace than they go up. At the foot of the Mintaka pass there are some rather snug caves occupied in summer by goatherds. They had gone down by now, but I went to the caves where I lit a fire assuming we should stop there, but the donkeys held resolutely on their way to Murkushi which we reached long after dark. It is a place well suited to benighted travellers. Water is hard by and fuel even nearer to hand, for the camp is pitched upon a thick seam of dry goat dung, the deposit of ages. It can be dug up in bricks like peat. But it is an even better fuel, and burns with hardly any smoke.

When we reached Misgar next day it was time for me to quit the beaten track which I had followed quite far enough. Misgar, at the end of a telegraph line, is ten stages from Gilgit, whence roads go either to Abbottabad by the Babusar pass and Kagan Valley (about 15 days), or to Chitral in about 10 days. Instead of going to Chitral by Gilgit it would be a little shorter in theory and in practice certainly much more amusing to strike cross country by way of the Chapursan nallah, the Chillinji pass (17,000 ft.), the Karumbar pass, and thence by the Yarkhun valley to Chitral. This route, which follows pretty closely the south side of the Hindu Kush, would be of particular interest for me because in the previous year we had intended to traverse a part of it but had failed.

The Hunza men of Misgar professed ignorance of the route, but provided a man and a donkey to come with me as far as Reshid the principal village of the Chapursan valley where I was assured I should find a guide. This assurance was hardly justified. When we reached Reshid I had to draw many maps in the dust of the headman's veranda, where I had settled for the night, before he had even an inkling of what I wanted to do. At last one or two of the audience of the pavement artists' graphic work grasped the key to these problem pictures and began bawling out the names of places on the itinerary, very few of which figured on my map. However, the headman promised that two volunteers, or, if necessary, conscripts would be found, meantime I might go on to the head of the valley with a pony and await the event at the local Mecca, the tomb of Baba Ghundi.

CHAPTER TEN

To Chitral

THE Chapursan is a fine open valley inhabited by Wakhis from Wakhan. Despite the great elevation of over 10,000 ft., they grow wheat, any surplus being taken by Kirghiz who reach the valley from Wakhan by the Irshad pass (16,060 ft.). The floor of the valley is flat and easily irrigated, but a hundred years ago much of it was devastated by a great flood which covered the fertile land with a thick deposit of clay and boulders. Above Reshid the valley is still littered with high mounds of this stuff like great ant-heaps. The flood was presumably caused by the formation of a glacier dam like that which dammed the Shuok river in 1929 when a lake 1000 yd. broad and 25 ft. deep accumulated. This burst on the morning of 15 August, with a noise 'like a cannon-shot'. Two days later at Patab Pul, the bridge below the great 'knee-bend' of the Indus 300 miles away, the river rose 45 ft. Loss of life and damage to property were remarkably little.

At Yashkuk, where we had to ford the deep stream of the Yashkuk glacier, there is a pleasant oasis of grass and thorn trees. We met there a company of some twenty pilgrims, men, women, and children, who had been to pay their respects at the shrine of Baba Ghundi. The tradition is that when this prophet found, as is customary, that he was without honour in his own country, he took a short way with dissenters by wiping out the whole valley with the aid of this memorable flood, an apostolic knock which earned him implicit respect and obedience for the rest of his life and utmost veneration after his death. Pilgrims from Wakhan and even Gilgit visit the shrine, and the Mir of Hunza, who has a rest-house in the vicinity, takes a personal interest in its upkeep.

The shrine itself, which according to Schomberg,[1] does not contain the saint's remains, is a small tomb of mud and stone covered with a wooden roof, enclosed by a high stone wall. At a gate in the wall is a huge pile of old ibex horns and within is a perfect forest of poles adorned with white flags and yaks' tails, the offerings of pilgrims. The caretaker of the shrine also looks after some of the Mir's more worldly interests in the form of a herd of yaks and a flock of sheep. Some barley is grown, and this, when I was there, was being removed from holes in the ground and spread out to dry.

I began to think I might have to return to Reshid, having been pushed off here perhaps by the headman merely for the sake of peace and quiet, so I kept the pony until next morning when at ten o'clock the chosen victims arrived, clamouring for bread. Grudgingly I doled out some atta, having brought with me only 30 lb. which would have to do for the three of us until we reached the first habitations in the Yarkhun valley. Besides this I had some tea and sugar but nothing else, not even a tent or a Primus stove. The Wakhis having fed and invoked the protection of the saint, we shouldered our burdens, crossed the river, and proceeded up the north bank accompanied by two mounted Kirghiz. These had spent the night at Baba Ghundi in religious meditation alleviated by opium, and at the Ishad nallah, a few miles up, they turned off for the pass to Wakhan. I sent with them my respects to 'Father', the Kirghiz chief on the other side, who in 1947 had prevented me from crossing back into India by that pass. Indeed this upper Chapursan had other objects of wistful interest for me. We passed on the south side the white rampart of the Kukuay-Batura watershed, and the Yashkuk and Koz Yaz glaciers descending from it, down either of which we should, in 1947, have been delighted to come had the topography only accorded more with our ideas and less with reality.

1 R. C. F. Schomberg, *Between Oxus and Indus.*

The red rock conglomerate walls of the valley drew together for a brief space into a gorge to open out again upon the grass and boulder covered moraine of the Chillinji glacier. Here, at a spot known as Buattar, is a sheepfold and a cave under a great rock in which we spent the night.

According to my altimeter which registered only 13,000 ft. we were faced with a longish climb to the pass. My two heroes seemed aware of this, but by no means dismayed; indeed, they talked boldly of reaching Sokhta Robat several miles up the Karumbar valley on the other side of the pass. Accordingly we broke camp at 2 a.m. A waning moon shed enough light to have shown us the path had there been one, but the men seemed to know very well what they were about. Instead of making for the glacier they struck straight up the hillside by a route which presently became a rock-climb. At first light we began a downward traverse to the glacier, now some way below and just beginning to emerge from the uncertain gloom; and when the first rays of sun struck fire from tall peaks guarding the pass the glacier still lay cold and grey, the ice of its surface-water crackling underfoot.

The easy slope of névé upon which we presently embarked looked so short that I allowed but half an hour for the ascent; but two hours later the rigidly distant snow horizon still mocked my longing eyes. Far behind were the two black specks of my companions, whose eyes, I imagined, would be fixed on the same goal with less longing and some despair. Though they were not carrying much more and had also the benefit of my laborious track, they made heavy weather of it. They were suffering in milder form the pangs of the cadaverous Kirghiz on Chakar Aghil and with no more reason, for they too had lived all their lives at over 10,000 ft. This not only puzzled but grieved me because I had counted on them to break a trail for my own wavering steps. It was even more puzzling to find that there should be any need for breaking a trail after a cold night in the middle of October and after a long spell of fine sunny weather.

Alas! the fine spell of weather had ended. As I topped the last rise I was greeted by a cold wind driving before it menacing clouds which already hung low upon the tangle of peaks to the west of the Karumbar valley. The rising wind cutting short the lamentations of my men, addressed principally to me as the author of their misery, we hastened down 6,000 ft. of scree slopes to whatever shelter the Karumbar valley might afford. We made for a nallah on our right which appeared the easiest approach to the main valley. It was an unhappy choice, there was no hint of a path amongst the boulders and birch scrub of the stream bed along which we had to fight a way for the best part of an hour. At last we emerged on to a sandy flat in the main valley where I was pleased to find a very faintly marked track and a cave. It was raining by now. There was no longer any talk of Sokhta Robat, indeed from the 'misere' sung by the two Wakhis I gathered that if ever they left the cave it would be to go down the Karumbar valley and not up.

The one whose headache was least severe began searching for a flat stone upon which he mixed into a dough and shaped into the semblance of a thick chapattie the flour I gave him. Upon this we dined, reserving a little of the bread for breakfast, and after they had made a second brew of tea from my used tea leaves I gave them a cigarette. This cheered them up, and I enlarged upon the number of rupees they would have earned by the time we reached Chitral. They now confessed that they had never been beyond this point, but they agreed to go on until we came upon some habitation. They would then be free to return. Money is the only argument such men understand. I had not seen much of Wakhis, but I soon realized that nothing could be got by appealing to that which they did not have—a liking for mild adventure, curiosity to see what was in the next valley, or shame at the thought of turning back.

When we woke to a dull, windy morning we saw that new snow had fallen down to about 14,000 ft. Having forded the river we picked up a faint track which we followed for five miles of good, flat going to Sokhta Robat which is a name and nothing more. A little grass, dwarf willow and silver birch, and the fire-blackened stones of someone's camp, alone marked the spot. Across the river a fairly well-defined track zigzagged up steep slopes to the Khora Bort, another pass into Wakhan. Our track hugged the south side of the valley until we lost it in an ablation valley between the valley wall and a high moraine from which we looked down upon the Chashboi glacier. The Karumbar valley has no glacier of its own, but at this point it is completely filled by the ice of the Chashboi, which emerges from a comparatively short and narrow lateral valley, spreads like spilt tar over the wide floor of the Karumbar, laps up against the opposing north wall, and then turns and flows grandly down the valley to the east. The mountain which produces all this ice must be well worth looking at, unluckily the weather was now so thick that we never saw it.

The glacier had to be crossed, so we dropped down into the trough where on a patch of mud I picked up the tracks of a pony and then lost them. The Wakhis were not good trackers, so I threaded a way through the stony labyrinth on the flank of the glacier and launched boldly out on to the smoother ice surface beyond. By reason of its size and its crevasses the Chashboi is a very considerable obstacle, and although I had proof that ponies had been taken across it I was glad we were not so encumbered. It was enough to have two half-willing Wakhis who, like most natives of the Himalaya (Sherpas are an exception), have a singular distaste for walking over ice or snow—a reluctance which is not wholly accounted for by their usually dilapidated footwear. My two men were no worse off in this respect than most, and each had with him a few square inches of goatskin with which in the evening he made good the losses of the day. They were the usual high, soft-skinned boots which are not much good for anything except riding. It is singular that I have never seen anyone wearing a new pair of these boots, just as one seldom sees a man with a new pair of home-spun trousers or a coat. The women still weave cloth, but some curious economic law, similar perhaps to that which prevails nearer home, denies their menfolk the benefit of their industry.

We spent two hours on the ice before putting this great barrier behind us—an obstacle, which, I hoped, would make the Wakhis think twice before turning back. Before us lay a broad, upland valley with nothing but the 14,000 ft. Karumbar pass at its head. Towards evening a drizzling rain set in which made us careful in the selection of a rock by which to sleep. Eventually we found one which after a little digging with the ice-axe afforded some protection. The height was about 12,500 ft. and from my map, which was on a scale of only 16 miles to the inch, I thought we must be six or seven miles from the pass.

In the night the rain turned to snow which, eddying around our rock, covered us all as with a shroud. This, I thought, will finish it. Nevertheless, we coaxed a fire of sorts with the wet heath, ate the remains of last night's bread, and started. On the north side of the valley, to which we had now crossed, we picked up a track which, thanks to the three or four inches of new snow, stood out clearly. Nothing showed at one's feet, but by looking well ahead the faint trace became visible. This discovery had a very heartening effect on all; for though a contempt for tracks is to be encouraged as a sign of an independent mind there are times when such independence proves very expensive. I was no less relieved than the Wakhis; by now the valley had become so wide as to be an open moor where mist and sleet extinguished all landmarks.

But as we slowly gained height the snow increased in depth until it was knee-deep. This not only made walking difficult, but quite obliterated the friendly trace. In these new conditions the Wakhi's morale, which had never been high, sank at once. Upon this trackless waste of snow, cut by a shrewd wind, they sat down and wept; 'We shall all die', was the burthen of their lament. Our case was not quite as bad as that; with a couple of Sherpas one might have struggled on or waited for better weather, but with these men there was nothing to be done. I made several wide casts in the hope of recovering the track and when these failed the Wakhis insisted on retreat. Bowing to fate, an act of homage to which I was now accustomed, I gave the word.

Before recrossing the Chashboi, which we reached that same evening, we picked up a line of guiding marks. They were not quite cairns, but to practised eyes a couple of stones or even a single stone placed on a boulder are sufficient indication. Following these up we took to the ice at what must be the usual crossing place. Since the ice-crossing was shorter, this maybe the best route for ponies, but it landed us too soon in the trough on the other side for we had to make a very rough passage down it. Next morning as we were approaching the big bend near the Chillinji caves we fell in with a party of Kirghiz and four yaks. They had crossed the Khora Bort the previous day and were on their way down the Karumbar to Ishkuman to barter butter and wool for grain.

Instead of recrossing the Chillinji pass my best way now was down to Ishkuman whither the Wakhis consented to come. The path down the Karumbar nallah is one of the roughest and most difficult of these parts and is little used; in summer, owing to the unfordable river and the steepness of the rock walls, it is virtually impassable. Thirty years ago no less than four glaciers, descending from the Kukuay watershed to the east, pushed their ice right down to the river, one of them, the Karumbar, abutting against the rocks on the west bank. In 1916 Dr Longstaff found the first of these, the Chillinji, and the second below it, the Wargot, just touching the water; in 1905 the Wargot is said to have formed a dam which, when it broke, caused flooding as far down the river as Gilgit. When we passed, both these glaciers stopped well short of the water, while the Karumbar, under which in 1916 the river had tunnelled a way, now stopped short by a hundred yards.

We spent the night at a place called Buk Buk where there were a hut, a field, and two Wakhis. Judging by the expression of consternation on the faces of these two, the story to which they were now compelled to listen lost nothing in the telling. A survivor of the retreat from Moscow could hardly have made more of the length of the way, the depth of the snow, and the severity of the weather. To hear these Wakhis talking one might think they had no teeth, but I discovered that it was the curious effect of talking with a quid of tobacco in either cheek. The linguist of my party, that is the one who spoke a little Hindustani, usually tried to be rude to me, in which, with his mouth full of tobacco, he usually succeeded. I never much cared for either of them but as porters their one great point was that they carried nothing whatever of their own.

In the rather forlorn hope of reaching Imit, the chief village and the residence of the rajah of Ishkuman, we started very early next morning. Before sun-up we had had to ford the main river twice as well as a small but fast side stream. The last crossing of the main river was so long and deep that by the time I crawled out I was almost whimpering with cold. Below Bhort, where there was an interesting-looking glacier, the track improved, but we did not reach Imit until next morning. The rajah, who had already heard of our arrival in his valley, sent one of his brothers to escort me in. The brothers of the rajahs of the Gilgit Agency, who are, of course, much more numerous than the rajahs themselves, have always been a difficulty. According to one's point of view, a ruling caste which cannot find jobs for its male relatives is no less worthy of sympathy than a government which cannot find jobs for the boys. Without land of his own to make or mar, the only other opening in these parts for a member of this caste—a 'gushpur'—is polo; this is proper enough, for it is a manly occupation and one which unlike many others does not interfere with other people's business. But with the best will in the world it cannot be made an all-time job.

I enjoyed a day's rest as a guest of the rajah. He did not know me, and my travel-stained appearance can hardly have been a satisfactory introduction, but he made me welcome on the grounds that I was an Englishman. Whatever the British may have done or left undone in the past, it is something to know that in these remote regions an Englishman is sure to meet with a very warm welcome.

Hoping to save something from the wreck of my plan I decided that instead of following the valley down to Gilgit I would cross the Ishkuman pass to Darkot whence by going north over the Darkot pass I might still reach the head of the Yarkhun valley. Much more snow than I expected had fallen on the Ishkuman pass (14,750 ft.), and since it was newly fallen winter snow it was powdery. In summer, I was told, a strong man could go to Darkot and back in a day; it took us 2½ days to get there, and at the end of the second day my three Ishkuman men were so exhausted that they would not even bestir themselves to make bread; an extraordinary state of languor which was perhaps more indicative of the badness of the coolies than that of the road.

Darkot village, 9,000 ft. up, lies at the foot of the Darkot pass (15,380 ft.) to the north of which is Chitral. The pass lies on the southern and higher branch of the Hindu Kush, separated from the lower and altogether milder northern range by the valley of the Yarkhun. Close on either side of the Darkot rise peaks of 21,000 and 22,000 ft. whereas, some 10 miles north, the main range can be crossed at just over 12,000 ft. by the Boroghil pass, within 20 miles of which there are no high mountains at all. A road for wheeled vehicles could be easily made over the Boroghil were there any place on either side of it to which a wheeled vehicle could profitably go.

Both these passes are interesting on account of the discoveries made by Sir Aurel Stein in connection with them. In A.D. 747 a Chinese general led a force of 10,000 men from Kashgar across the Pamirs to concentrate them at Sarahad on the Oxus on the Wakhan side of the Boroghil. His object was to oust the Tibetans who were threatening the Chinese hold on the Tarim basin (the 'Western Kingdoms') in conjunction with their allies, the Arabs, who were advancing up the Oxus valley. After carrying the positions held by the Tibetans defending the Boroghil the Chinese forced the pass, crossed the Darkot pass unopposed, and proceeded down the valley to Yasin and Gilgit. To this one can only add that the presence of a Tibetan army on the Boroghil was hardly less remarkable than the success of the Chinese in driving them off. I suppose it is no more strange than that Japanese should be found fighting in Burma or Germans in North Africa, but it is a striking commentary on the vicissitudes of nations and a queer illustration of geo-politics that Arabs and Tibetans in alliance should be at grips with Chinese upon the barren mountains of Wakhan.

With the experience of the Ishkuman pass fresh in my mind I decided that the Darkot pass, 1000 ft. higher, should not be attempted, and that I must at last resign myself to a more usual route. And I was the more resigned—in fact eager to do it— on account of a talk I had had with two traders from Gilgit who soon after our arrival had joined the throng of idlers and travellers in the headman's house. When I had left Kashgar the situation in Berlin had looked ticklish enough, so I was half prepared to believe these worthies when, after retailing the more important news of the bombing of Gilgit, they casually added that for the last 10 days Pakistan, as they put it, with her allies Great Britain and America, was at war with Russia.

There was no time to be lost. Modern wars are such long drawn out affairs that it would not be easy to arrive too late to take part, yet it would never do to commit such a solecism. In a terrible stew, hot-foot and resolved to march double stages, I set out for Gupis and the beaten track which I could no longer shun. A day later, I learnt that a more or less deep peace still brooded over Europe, Africa, and Asia. In seven more days, on 4 November, I reached Chitral 35 days out from Kashgar.

NEPAL HIMALAYA

Nepal Himalaya

First published by Cambridge University Press, 1952

Contents

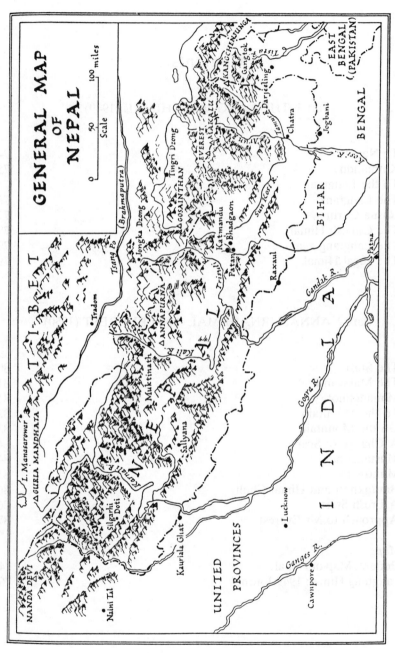

General map of Nepal

Part 1

THE LANGTANG HIMAL (1949)

CHAPTER ONE

To Nepal

THERE can be no other country so rich in mountains as Nepal. This narrow strip of territory, lying between Sikkim and Garhwal, occupies 500 miles of India's northern border; and since this border coincides roughly with the 1,500-mile-long Himalayan chain, it follows that approximately a third of this vast range lies within or upon the confines of Nepal. Moreover, besides being numerous, the peaks of the Nepal Himalaya are outstandingly high. Apart from Everest and Kangchenjunga and their two 27,000 ft. satellites, there are six peaks over 26,000 ft., fourteen over 25,000 ft., and a host of what might be called slightly stunted giants of 20,000 ft. and upwards, which cannot be enumerated because they are not all shown on existing maps.

In trying to grasp the general lay-out of this mountain region it is convenient to divide it into three parts, represented—from west to east—by the basins of the Karnali, the Gandak, and the Kosi. These three important rivers, some of whose tributaries rise in Tibet north of the Himalaya, all flow into the Ganges. The Karnali drains the mountains of western Nepal between Api (23,339 ft.), near the Garhwal border, and Dhaulagiri (26,795 ft.); the basin of the Gandak occupies central Nepal between the Annapurna Himal and the Langtang Himal; and the Kosi drains the mountains of eastern Nepal from Gosainthan (26,291 ft.) to Kangchenjunga. It should be understood that, except for Everest and those peaks on the Nepal-Sikkim border, most of which (except Kangchenjunga) have been climbed, this enormous field has remained untouched, unapproached, almost unseen, until this year (1949) when the first slight scratch was made.

Nepal is an independent kingdom. Like Tibet it has always sought isolation and has secured it by excluding foreigners, of whom the most undesirable were white men. A man fortunate enough to have been admitted into Nepal is expected to be able to explain on general grounds the motives behind this invidious policy and, on personal grounds, the reason for such an unaccountable exception. But now that the advantages of the Western way of life are becoming every day less obvious no explanation should be needed. Wise men traditionally come from the East, and it is probable that to them the West and its ways were suspect long before we ourselves began to have doubts. Anyhow, for the rulers of countries like Nepal and Tibet, whose polity until very recent days was medieval feudalism, the wise and natural course was to exclude foreigners and their advanced ideas. And the poverty and remoteness of those countries made such a policy practicable. A hundred years ago the rulers of China and Japan regarded foreign devils with as much distrust and aversion, but unfortunately for them their countries had sea-coasts and ports; and, unlike Tibet and Nepal, promised to become markets which no nation that lived by trade could afford to ignore.

The Nepalese, who number about five millions, are mostly Hindus. Consequently it has been suggested that the Brahmins have been the most fervent advocates of an exclusive policy. It does not seem logical, because a thin trickle of European visitors has long been admitted to the *sanctum sanctorum* of the Katmandu valley, whereas in remote parts, where Hinduism sits lightly or merges into Buddhism as the northern border is approached, the ban has been most rigid. A simple explanation is that the early rulers of Nepal, themselves independent and warlike, having established their sway over a turbulent people, naturally wished to remain masters in their own house. With the example of India at hand, these rulers, not without reason apprehensive and suspicious of the British, concluded that the best way of remaining in power was to have as little as possible to do with Europeans. And since this avowed policy was approved and respected by the Indian Government, it could be strictly maintained.

Writing in 1928 Perceval Landon (*Nepal*, 2 vols.) estimated that only some 120 English and ten other Europeans had been permitted to enter the Katmandu valley; while from the time of Brian Hodgson (British Resident from 1833 to 1843) onwards not even the British Resident has been allowed to set foot outside the valley. Since 1928 the number of visitors to Katmandu must have increased considerably but the mesh is still fine. However, in 1948 a party of Indian scientists had been allowed to investigate the upper basin of the Kosi river in eastern Nepal where they climbed to the Nangpa La, a 19,000 ft. pass west of Everest; and in the winter of 1948–9 an American party led by Dr Dillon Ripley was busy collecting birds in the foothills of central and eastern Nepal.

Thus encouraged, at the end of 1948 the British Ambassador at Katmandu (Sir George Falconer) sought permission for a climbing party to visit the Nepal Himalaya; and the Prime Minister, when he understood that the project had the blessing of the President of a small band of harmless eccentrics who had no other axe to grind than an ice-axe, readily consented. There were, however, conditions attached. Instead of going as we hoped to the vicinity of Gauri Sankar (23,440 ft.), whence we could also have had a look at the south side of Everest, we were to confine ourselves to the Langtang Himal; and instead of merely gambolling upon the mountains we had to undertake some serious scientific work. Science, of course, is no laughing matter, but I use the word serious advisedly so that there may be no mistake.

Except for the Nepal side of Kangchenjunga, which Hooker, Freshfield, and Dyhrenfurth's party had visited, the Nepal Himalaya is unknown to Europeans. No one part was less interesting or exciting for us than another; but the second of these conditions meant not only a change in the composition of the party but a change, almost a *volte-face*, on the part of a leader who had hitherto refused to mingle art with science. To be too stiff in opinion is a grave fault; a man should be sure of more than his principles before deciding never to break them. Benedick, when he swore he would die a bachelor, did not expect to live until he was married; and just as the great Henry once deemed Paris worth a Mass, so I thought a glimpse of the Nepal Himalaya worth the swallowing of a strong prejudice.

The party finally consisted of four; two scientists, or embryo scientists and two very mature climbers. Botany and geology were two obvious fields in which all that a first visit demanded were the collecting of specimens and the noting of data—tasks more suited to the embryo than to the full-blown professor. A botanist was quickly forthcoming in Mr O. Polunin, a master at Charterhouse, who was acceptable to the British Museum for whom most of the collecting was to be done. Blotting-paper and a love of flowers is not enough for the disciple of Linnaeus. Finding a geologist gave some trouble. The number of them who do anything so vulgar as battering the living rock in the field is extraordinarily minute. As weathering agents they can be dismissed. I worked steadily through a list of twenty of the older practitioners, none of whom seemed eager to pluck his rusting hammer from the wall to strike a blow for his faith. Nor would they detail a subordinate for the job. Research, setting and answering examination papers, kept the whole geological strata of England firmly *in situ*. A very willing victim was at last found in J. S. Scott, and his University, St Andrews, came to our aid with a handsome grant.

Having no wish to be bound too tightly to the wheel of science Mr Peter Lloyd, who was my fellow climber, and myself were prepared to pay for our own amusement. There was little difficulty in raising what money was needed for the others; for I have remarked elsewhere upon the readiness of some learned bodies to support and encourage minor enterprises of this sort, provided that among those who go upon them are men able and willing, as our Russian friend put it,[1] to tear a few more rents in Nature's veil. Breathing this rarefied air of high purpose must have gone to my head. Encouraged by the impreciseness of the map of our area, I found myself suggesting to Lloyd that we, or rather he, should undertake to improve it. This would be of benefit to future mountaineers, and would put all four members of our party on the same high intellectual plane. Lloyd, to whom theodolites were strange but who was familiar with much more recondite instruments, welcomed the idea.

Nepal is usually referred to as 'unknown'. Possibly the reader has already mistakenly inferred that the whole country, including the Nepal Himalaya, is

1 See *China to Chitral*

unexplored, whereas there are maps of the whole country on a ¼-in. scale. One of these pleasing traits of the Westerner or Paleface is to assume that what is not known to him cannot be known to anyone. 'Unexplored' country means country unexplored by him, rather in the grand manner of Mrs Elton who had never been to Box Hill and talked ardently of conducting an exploring party there. Unknown Nepal must have become thoroughly well-known to the fourteen Indian surveyors (European officers of the Indian Survey Department were excluded) who in three seasons, 1924–27, surveyed the whole 55,000 sq. miles from the 'terai' along the Indian border to the Himalaya. Even before this, Nepal must have been tolerably familiar to its inhabitants, and some of the remote valleys were made known to the outside world by a few of the devoted 'pundit' explorers sent out by the Survey of India. 'M.H.', for example, who in 1885 travelled up the valley of the Dudh Kosi west of Everest to Tingri in Tibet, whence he returned to India by Kyerong and the Trisuli valley, thus traversing Nepal twice; while in 1873 Hari Ram, another Indian explorer, followed the valley of the Kali river to Tradom in Tibet. Two Jesuit missionaries are also believed to have returned from Shigatse in Tibet to Katmandu in 1629, probably by Nyenam, but unfortunately they left no record of their journey. Moreover, the various British Residents of Katmandu from 1802 onwards have collected from native sources a mass of information—in particular, Hodgson, who for ten years made it his principal task. He never moved out of the valley, but he knew fairly accurately, for example, the drainage system of the Gandak river and much of the natural history of the country. In short, Nepal is by no means *terra incognita*, but it is true to say that it is the largest inhabited country still unexplored by Europeans.

The area we were to visit had thus been surveyed (of which more hereafter), but a glance at the relevant map sheet (71 H ¼ in.) showed a tract of country immediately north of the Langtang Himal in Tibet that bore the magic word 'unsurveyed'; this was the more interesting because in it lay Gosainthan (26,291 ft.) some ten miles north of the main Himalayan crest-line. Tibet was out of bounds but it occurred to me that by lugging a photo-theodolite up to several points on the frontier ridge we might with luck get enough data for the mapping of this stretch of country of which not even the drainage system was known. Gosainthan probably lies on the watershed between the Trisuli Gandak and the Kosi system, but the ¼ in. map shows an intervening ridge to the west of the mountain, the whole of which is thus made to lie in the Kosi basin.

Gosainthan (Place of the Saint), is the Sanskrit for the peak the Tibetans call Shisha Pangma [now Xixabangma]. Kailas and Gurla Mandhata are two other Sanskrit names for very famous mountains, both in Tibet, given by Hindu pilgrims visiting the sacred shrines in the vicinity of the peak. With the spread of Buddhism the same places became the goals of Buddhist pilgrims who gave the peaks Tibetan names. Kailas (22,028 ft.) lying to the north of Lake Manasarowar was Siva's paradise, and still is the resort of Hindu pilgrims who walk right round the mountain prostrating themselves as they go, a journey which under these arduous conditions takes three weeks. No

Hindu pilgrim visits Gosainthan; were it not for the evidence of the name it would be difficult to believe they had even seen it. They do, however, visit in large numbers the sacred lake of Gosainkund situated high on a long southerly spur of the Langtang Himal on the east side of the Trisuli valley. Possibly some confusion exists between this lake and the mountain; for in the Nepalese map published in Landon's *Nepal*, the frontier is so drawn as to include the mountain, implying that it is of importance to Hindus.

It is not often possible to visit the Himalaya at the best time. West of the central Himalaya there is probably not much to choose between any of the summer months, but in the eastern Himalaya from the end of June to the end of September the prevalence of monsoon conditions is a serious handicap to climbing and to comfort. Comfort must not be expected by folks that go a-pleasuring, but the first consideration would persuade the mountaineer, if he could, to climb in May and June, to lie at earth during July and August, and to return refreshed in October for a final fling. For those who visit the Himalaya for less serious reasons the weather is of less account, the only exception being the surveyor for whom weather is all important. In order to see the first flowers a botanist should be in the field by early May, remain throughout the summer (having much trouble drying his specimens) for successively later ones, and stay until the end of October when most of the seeds have ripened. Generally such nice considerations of the ideal time have to be omitted; the party goes out when it can and returns when it must, which in our case was late May and early September respectively. Thus only our geologist could view with indifference our arrival in the field only a week or two before the expected breaking of the monsoon.

It did not take long to collect the necessary stores and equipment, to sketch a rough plan, an even rougher estimate of cost, and to arrange for the assembly of the motley party in Katmandu towards the end of May. Lloyd and I, coming from opposite directions, met in Calcutta, while the other two travelled via Bombay. The four Sherpas I had engaged met us safely in Calcutta, in spite of the fact that in coming from Darjeeling they had had to pass from India to Pakistan and then back again to India.

Travelling north across the great flat alluvial plain of Bengal and Bihar, where for hundreds of miles a man may lift his eyes no higher than a mango tree, is a salutary but fortunately short-lived experience for a mountaineer. In 24 hours, after a steamer voyage across the Ganges, when we were nearly separated from our nineteen bulky packages, we reached Raxaul near the frontier of India and Nepal. From here a narrow-gauge railway, opened in 1927, runs to Amlekhganj, the railhead twenty-nine miles away. Shortly after crossing the frontier at Birgunj the line enters the terai. This is a peculiar strip of jungle, twelve to twenty miles wide, stretching more or less continuously along the whole southern border. The thin gravel soil is of little use for cultivation, but the terai is of value on account of its flourishing growth of sal trees, which are in great demand for railway sleepers; it is also a big-game reserve, where tiger, panther, the one-horned Indian rhino (found also in Assam), wild elephant, wild buffalo, and smaller game abound. In the cold weather, H.H. the Maharajah and members of the ruling family, many of whom are keen shikaris, organize shoots to which privileged guests are sometimes invited. The renowned Jang Bahadur, Prime Minister from 1846 to his death in 1877, the most illustrious of a distinguished line, one who is now an almost legendary character, was a very mighty hunter. Before he had settled himself firmly in the saddle, he hunted his numerous enemies as vindictively and as effectively as later he did the tigers of the terai. He became his country's greatest benefactor, and proved a very staunch friend to Britain in the critical years of the Mutiny.

Another curious denizen of the terai at one time was Nana Sahib, the leader of the Indian Mutiny, who after his final defeat at Tantia topi fled across the Nepal frontier and took refuge in the terai. He opened negotiations with Jang Bahadur, who, refusing either to shelter him or to give him up, yet managed to acquire at a quite moderate price the Nana's principal jewel—the Naulahka, an unrivalled necklace of pearls, diamonds and emeralds. The circumstances of the Nana's death, or even the time and place, are still a mystery; but he was reported to have died in 1859 which, if he remained in the terai, is very probable. For six months of the year it is an unhealthy, indeed, a lethal place, where anyone who spends a night unprotected is almost sure to contract the deadly local form of malaria called 'awal'. Deadly malaria is not a monopoly of the Nepal terai. The belt of country between the Himalayan foothills and the plain of India is unhealthy everywhere from central India eastwards. In 1939, after one night in the Assam terai, three Sherpas and myself all contracted different forms of malaria, all of which were serious and one fatal.

From Amlekhganj the journey is continued by car or lorry, and the dejected traveller soon perceives from the frightful grinding of gears, that the world is not so flat as he had feared. In the journey of twenty-seven miles to road-head at Bhimpedi (3650 ft.) the road rises a hundred feet in every mile. This country of the Siwalik foothills is well wooded and well watered, but sparsely inhabited and probably fever-ridden. The Siwalik is a remarkable range; though never rising above 5000 ft. it stretches almost unbroken, parallel to the Himalaya, from the Brahmaputra to the Indus. The ancient Aryans called it, very appropriately, 'the edge of the roof of Siva's Himalayan abode'.

The motor-road passes under the crest of the Siwaliks by a tunnel 300 yd. long; the old road crossed by the Churia pass, which is a place of some military interest. In the Nepalese war of 1816 a British column 13,000 strong under General Ochterlony, advancing on Katmandu, outflanked the defended pass by means of a goat-track to the west, thus turning the main Gurkha position based on the fortress of Makwanpur. Two higher passes and much difficult country still lay between Ochterlony's force and their objective, while the Gurkha army was still intact, but the Nepalese, fearful for the hitherto inviolate Katmandu valley, made terms. Ochterlony, from whom the suggestion must have come with double force, was the first to suggest, during this very war, that Gurkha troops should be enlisted in the Indian Army.

Beyond the Siwalik range the road enters and ascends the valley of the Rapti, on the north side of which forest-clad hills rise to over 8,000 ft. The motor-road ends at the head of the valley at Bhimpedi, a straggling corrugated-iron bazaar. We turned off two miles short of this to the ropeway station, Dhusing. The electrically driven ropeway, opened in 1925, is fourteen miles long and rises to a height of 4,500 ft. above Dhusing; each sling carries about 5 cwt. and travels at four and a half miles an hour. The mountaineer who allows himself and his load to be hauled uphill attached to the endless rope of a ski-lift should feel a slight sense of guilt, much as an anchorite would who changed his hair shirt for a silk one; but in consigning our nineteen packages to the care of this invaluable machine we experienced nothing but relief. At much less cost than the hire of coolies and with no worry on our part, the baggage would be in Katmandu before we arrived. The ropeway can deliver fifty or sixty tons a day, the equivalent of 1,500 coolies working for two days. The goods shed was overflowing with bags of grain, salt and general merchandise, waiting to go up; but since very little comes down these imports must be paid for by 'invisible' exports of which the major one, no doubt, is Gurkha soldier.

Having arranged this matter we drove on to Bhimpedi where we were decanted at three o'clock of a hot afternoon at the foot of a formidable hill quite devoid, so far as one could see, of anything in the nature of a lift. True the pylons of the ropeway could be seen marching up in giant strides, but on that no passengers are carried. So far, thanks to the admirable arrangements made by the Nepalese authorities and the British embassy, no effort, physical or mental, had been required of us until now, when for the next eighteen miles we had to put foot to ground. Even that we might have spared ourselves had we wished, H.H. the Maharajah having sent two ponies for us.

Between Bhimpedi and Thankot in the valley itself there are two passes, the Sisagarhi (6,225 ft.) and the Chandragiri (7,700 ft.). A night is spent at a rest-house below the first pass whence the journey to Thankot can be done in six or seven hours. Our early arrival on the pass having gone unrewarded—for on a clear day the Himalaya can be seen—we dropped 2,500 ft. to a valley across which the ropeway swings in one enormous span of 1,300 yd. Crossing the clear rippling Kuli, a tributary stream of the sacred Bagmati river which alone drains the Katmandu valley, we continued up an open valley to Chitlong at the foot of the steep rise to the Chandragiri, where, in company with the coolie traffic, we paused to brace ourselves for the serious business of the day. As the ropeway cannot deal with very heavy or bulky loads there is the opportunity for coolies to prove the superiority of man over machine by dealing with things like brass cannons and motor cars, for which there seemed to be a steady demand in the valley.

A team of thirty coolies handled a brass cannon easily, almost running in fact, while seventy, or perhaps ninety, if it is a Rolls Royce, are needed for a car. Two long poles which project well fore and aft are lashed under the car as it stands. To these wooden shoulder pieces are attached, each of which is supported by two men, one each side of the pole. On level ground this works well, but the Chandragiri pass is steep, particularly so on the Katmandu side, and a load carried thus on a thirty-degree slope must set up some curious stresses. We met several car-carrying parties but the coolies each time were taking a rest, of which, no doubt, they need a lot.

As he looks from the Chandragiri pass upon the fair and spacious valley below, the most jaded traveller must feel his imagination stirred by its secluded position, its turbulent past, and by the mystery and sanctity attending this most ancient shrine of Hindu and Buddhist tradition, with its temples and stupas of Asoka, sacred groves and burning ghats. Even the traveller who views it upon a cloudy day, without seeing the sublime background of the Himalaya which are the source of these religious traditions, cannot but be charmed by the pattern of green and yellow fields, the terra-cotta houses, the gleaming white palaces and the dark roofs of the city, the whole ringed with gentle, wooded hills. Since almost the whole valley, only some twenty by fifteen miles, is in view, he may well say he is looking at Nepal: for to those who live outside the valley this is Nepal. And in a sense it is true enough; for in this small arena has been enacted and recorded in brick, wood, and stone, nearly all the ancient and modern history of what we call Nepal; and within it is concentrated nearly half a million people and nearly all the power, art, prosperity, commerce—in short everything appertaining to the life of the country.

Pursued and finally overtaken by a thunderstorm we reached Thankot during the afternoon, where we were picked up by the waiting embassy car and transported, in some luxury, the remaining nine miles to Katmandu.

CHAPTER TWO

Katmandu

ARRIVING on 24 May we planned to leave on the 29th provided the Bombay party joined us in time. Had there been less to attend to we might have spent four very tranquil days, for at Katmandu tranquility is the key-note. This was not so a hundred years ago, when intrigue and faction were the rule; when incidents like the throwing of Jang Bahadur down a well, his shooting of his uncle, and the imprisonment and suicide of a Prime Minister, were but mild preludes to the scene in the Kot courtyard when anything from fifty to five hundred notables and officials were massacred. Perhaps it was these scenes as described by Laurence Oliphant (*Journey to Katmandu*, 1850) and particularly that of a royal review which 'surpassed even the wildest notions of our highly civilized community' which gave Kipling a hint:

> And the wildest dreams of Kew are the facts of Katmandu,
> And the crimes of Clapham chaste in Martaban.

But times have changed. Now the uninhibited life of surburbia might astonish the natives of Katmandu where propriety is the rule, and where landaus, visiting cards and formality set the tone.

Our baggage having been collected from the ropeway station had now to be made up into man-loads for the journey up the Trisuli valley where animal transport, we were told, was not used. It is only a matter of seven or eight days to the Langtang by a well-used trade route about which, however, little or no information could be had. The question of whether we could buy food at Langtang had to be resolved, for obviously if we had to carry all the atta and rice we needed for three and a half months many more coolies must be engaged. Maize, and not much of that, was thought to be all we might obtain, so we compromised by taking food for a month and after that, if the worst happened, we could send back for more. There are few places in the Himalaya where the food arrangements can be left in such a conveniently fluid state; where having once arrived at one's base the question of sending back for anything is worth considering. Apparently this trip was to be another example of one 'with no transport difficulties', where each item in each load has not to be jealously weighed and where comfort has not to be sacrificed to mobility.

The rules of haggling having been sufficiently observed, we contracted with a coolie agent for forty men to go to Rasua Garhi and to find their own food. Dealing with one man who will make himself responsible for all, instead of forty, is probably more satisfactory from the point of view of the traveller and the contractor than it is from that of the coolies. It may cost a little more, but the saving of trouble is as worth buying as silence. The coolie agent—known as the 'baria naik'—receives a lump sum, half at the start and half later, but how much of this is received by the men is another matter, one which, we may hope, is attended to by that device known to economists as 'the price mechanism'. Apart from the ropeway, coolie transport is used everywhere, so that it is an organized business; it would probably be quite impossible to collect men except through such an agent, whom the traveller is free either to respect as an essential cog in the machine or to abuse as a parasite according to his political views.

This difficult business was managed with the advice and help of Col. R. R. Proud, First Secretary to the Embassy, in whose house we were staying. Besides this kindness he arranged our official visits, modified the size of the escort which the goodwill of H.H. the Maharajah would have wished larger, lent us cars for sightseeing and an orderly to see fair play in our dealings in the bazaar. Were it not for the restriction on movement outside the valley, there could hardly be a more pleasant place for a British official than Katmandu, provided he has other than social interests. Our host had plenty of these, among them an interest in mountains, but it must have been galling for him to think that even had he been free his official position would have prevented his accompanying us.

After the heavy thunderstorm of the previous day our second evening was so clear that Col. Proud took us—rather too quickly we thought—up one of the local hills for a view of the Himalaya. We went by car to the foot of the hill at Baleji where, surrounded by woods, there is a water-garden of green lawns and grey stone tanks in which monster black and green carp ogle the visitors for food. From the tanks the water is led to a long castellated wall below the terrace through which it flows by twenty carved and vermilion-painted dragon spouts. Submerged in another tank is a stone carving of Narain (Brahma the Creator) on a bed of snakes, the face alone, wreathed with cobra heads, showing above the water. This submerged symbol of Vishnu is supposed to be a replica of that which the worshippers of Shiva see in the sacred lake of Gosainkund. I offer the legend with some diffidence because, in my opinion, Hindu mythology is too much addicted to what Fowler calls 'elegant variation'—the attentive reader will have noticed that four names have already been used for the same god. But as these legends usually lead sooner or later to the Himalaya they must be respected.

When three hundred and thirty million gods—very early officials or planners of some kind, one fears—churned the ocean in search of the water of immortality, they stirred up a poison which threatened to destroy the world. In this extremity their only resource was a petition, a monster bearing three hundred and thirty million signatures, which they presented to Mahadeo. Upon receiving this strong hint the god obligingly drank the poison. The poison burning his throat blue, he acquired thereby yet another name—Nila Khanta or Blue Neck—and a raging thirst. In order to cool off he repaired at once to the Himalaya, but aware of the futility of eating snow to quench thirst, he struck his trident against a rock from which three streams immediately burst forth. In their waters he enjoyed what must have been a memorable bathe; and so exquisite did he find the icy water flowing round his head that he has remained there to this day; the waters meanwhile gathering themselves to form what is now the Gosainkund lake. The peak Nilkhanta (21,640 ft.), a strikingly beautiful and still unclimbed peak in Garhwal, is named after the god.

Climbing through the forest above Baleji, where we disturbed some barking deer, we reached an open glade just before the sun went down. From the Ganesh Himal to somewhere in the region of Everest, a hundred miles of snow mountains sparkled in its last rays. Several of the groups which the Nepalese call Himal—the Ganesh, Langtang, Jugal, and the Rowaling Himal—could be identified; but the only *peaks* we could be sure of were Langtang Lirung (23,771 ft.), the highest of the Langtang group, and Gauri Sankar (23,440ft.) in the Rolwaling. Everest, had it been clear, would have appeared as an inconspicuous bump just to the east of Gauri Sankar, a peak which has often been mistaken for the monarch itself. The identification of very distant peaks is a harmless and fascinating amusement so long as the results are not taken seriously—a proviso that is borne out by the Everest-Gauri Sankar controversy which will bear retelling.

The triangulation of the Everest region from stations in the plains was completed in 1850, and two years later, when the results had been worked out, that peak was found to be the highest then known. In 1855, as no local name for it could be found, Sir Andrew Waugh, the Surveyor General, suggested the name of 'Everest' after Sir George Everest who was his predecessor at the time when the triangulations were made. Hodgson, then Resident at Katmandu, who besides being a great naturalist was also a learned philologist, affirmed that the mountain had a local name,

Devadhunga, which he had apparently come across in Nepalese literature. Although he had seen neither Devadhunga, which nowhere existed, nor Everest, he stuck to his point, and assured Sir Andrew Waugh that if he (Waugh) would give him the bearing and distance of any Nepal peak, he (Hodgson) would tell him the name of it. In the same year Hermann de Schlagintweit, brother of Adolph who was later murdered in Kashgar, made observations of the newly discovered peak from two directions, Sikkim and Nepal, with the unluckiest results. From Sikkim he observed and drew a panorama of Makalu, which obscured Everest, and from the 7,000 ft. Kaulia hill in Nepal (a few miles west of where we sat) he mistook the prominent Gauri Sankar for the insignificant-looking Everest. However, his observations and drawings were sufficiently accurate for the Survey of India to show by calculations the error he had made. In 1859 a committee decided from the available evidence that the two mountains were not the same; and this was later confirmed by Capt. Wood who, from observations made from Kaulia, proved that the two mountains were thirty-six miles apart.

The Embassy grounds, known to the natives as the 'Lines', are a mile from the centre of Katmandu. On the left on the way in, behind a high brick wall of great length, lies the palace of the King of Nepal; one of several similar buildings which are palaces in very fact as well as name. The Singha Darbar, the residence of the Prime Minister, is a vast white colonnaded palace, fronted by a formal garden, carriage drives and wrought-iron gates under a white arched gateway. The homes of other Ranas, the Commander-in-Chief (who is head of civil, not military affairs), the Senior Commanding General, and General Kaiser, G.B.E., lately Nepalese Ambassador in London, are on a correspondingly spacious scale. The centre of the town is the wide, tree-bordered, grass 'maidan' which is used as a parade ground. On one side are modern office buildings, the Chaudra College, and a clock-tower, and on the other the old and new bazaars and the old town. The whole town is lit by electric light from two hydro-electric stations.

The narrow streets of the old bazaar are lined with two-storied house of brick and wood. The lower parts of these form open shops, interspersed with shrines, idols and brass grotesques, around which surges a flood of warm humanity. Fortunately, unlike the Kashgar market, the flood carries with it no scurrying droves of donkeys to overwhelm the idle onlooker who can, therefore, stand and admire a scene less imposing than the palaces but far more rewarding. Helped by Tensing, a Sherpa who doubled the role of cook and headman, we bought a glorious miscellany of soap (largely symbolic), nests of aluminium cooking pots, chillies, enamel pint mugs, candles, tea, paraffin, ghee, umbrellas, lentils, 'ghums' (mats for protecting loads), sugar, matches, cheap cigarettes, spices, onions, atta and rice. In addition to six maunds (480 lb.) of rice, which took a long time to weigh and bag, we wanted two of 'satu' or parched barley flour. This commodity was unknown to the Newars of Katmandu but Tensing buttonholed a passing youth in the maroon gown of a lama who directed him to a place where Tibetan tastes were catered for.

Having done all this we went on to the bank to collect 2,500 silver Nepali rupees (a load in itself), pausing on the way to admire the oasis of comparative quiet of the Darbar square of the old town. Here are the old wooden pagoda-roofed house from which Katmandu takes its name, the five-stored Taleju temple overlooking the Kot of sinister memory, and an horrific four-armed figure of Kala Bhaibar, painted black, yellow and vermilion, flourishing a great sword in the attitude of a pantomime dame at bay with a poker.

Nowhere in the valley is there a place without either temples or shrines. As Kirkpatrick, one of the earliest writers on Nepal, said: 'There are nearly as many temples as houses, and as many idols as inhabitants, there not being a fountain, a river, or a hill within its limits that is not consecrated to one or other of the Hindu or Buddhist deities.' But the concentrated essence of religious art is to be found in the Darbar squares which the Newar craftsmen delighted to embellish with the finest conceptions of their artists; and the richest squares are those of the two neighbouring towns of Bhatgaon and Patan, the ancient Newar capitals. In 1768 the Gurkhas completed their conquest of the valley by the taking and sacking of Patan, from which the town seems never to have recovered. Except for the Darbar square there broods over it an air of melancholy decay. But dilapidation and decay are thought by some to be essential to picturesque beauty, and here they do enhance the charm of the gloomy, narrow, deserted lanes, overhung with half-timbered balconied houses; especially when adorned, as we saw them, with great banners of green cloth fresh from the dyer's vat. In the square there is nothing, except perhaps the telephone wires, that is not a delight to behold; but all the sculpture and carving, down to intricate detail, is symbolic, and unless one understands the religious significance of these symbols the emotions which such art should excite is apt to be extinguished by curiosity. Instead of marvelling at the delicate carving or the airy grace of the pagoda roof, one is willingly amused by the endless repetition of elephants, peacocks, fish, rats, lions, snakes, mythical monsters and all-in wrestlers.

To give some idea of these architectural wonders, the following description of Bhatgaon from *Picturesque Nepal* (Percy Brown), conveys something of the enthusiasm of a man who understands Indian art:

At a cross street a shrine comes into view, with crimson draperies, bright brass entrance, glittering metal pinnacle, painted woodwork, brackets of caryatid deities bristling with arms, and a large bronze bell supported by rampant dragons. From this one passes through winding streets of old wood and brick houses, each displaying some different form of ornate carving in window or doorway, and each placed at an apparently fortuitous angle. Gradually the buildings become larger and more important and the decoration more profuse. Then a whole street of overhanging balconies and wooden colonnades comes into view, with doorways crowned by heavily carved tympanums of deities and devils, and lattice windows with peacocks cunningly carved posing in the centres, until we suddenly debouch into the main square and are confronted with the culminating effect of the combined arts of the Newars, probably the most entrancingly picturesque city scene in Nepal. Around a rambling open space of flagged pavement, temples are irregularly grouped on terraced plinths, their pagoda roofs of red tiles and golden finials climbing into the blue sky. Some of these are approached by flights of steps, flanked by stone statues of humans in elaborate costumes, elephants, horses, and rhinos, gaily caparisoned and heavily chained to their pedestals, and monstrous fauna of the nether world.

In Bhatgaon is a doorway of brick and embossed copper gilt which Percy Brown calls 'the richest piece of art work in the whole kingdom . . . placed like a jewel flashing innumerable facets in the handsome setting of its surroundings'.

For their spiritual needs, which I was sorry to see were not very urgent, the Sherpas had to go to one of the two famous Buddhist temples of Bodhnath and Shambu-nath. Although it stands upon no eminence Bodhnath is one of the most conspicuous objects of the valley. Surrounded by the houses and maize fields of Bodhnath, there rises from a square plinth a huge white 'stupa', in shape like an umbrella; on top is a lofty spire with a square base on each face of which is painted in crimson and black a pair of eyes, and between them a nose indicated by a '?'. In the vicinity of Bodhnath, or indeed from much farther away, there is no escape from the impassive, questioning gaze of those strange eyes. I suppose even a Buddhist who lived always in their sight might become indifferent to their mild reproach; a supposition which only an enquiry into the morals of the people of Bodhnath might decide. To a stranger they were powerful monitors, bearing an injunction more poignant than the *memento mori* of a grinning skull.

The base of the stupa is ringed with prayer wheels and a stone-flagged ambulatory round which the pilgrim walks, turning the wheels as he goes. In a building close by is a small 'gompa' in which the contents—the painted Buddhas, the banners, books, lamps and frescoed walls—seem mean and tawdry, quite out of keeping with the glory of the stupa and the fame of Bodhnath as a place of pilgrimage. We saw hardly anyone, but in the winter months I believe numbers of Tibetans, both lamas and laity, make their way there.

Although at Shambu-nath a smaller but similar stupa, with the same grave, all-seeing eyes, occupies a commanding position, its effect is less striking. The eyes are too far above the earth-bound mortals of the valley, so that their searching admonitory gaze is directed to the four quarters in vain. I felt I could live in the village at the foot of Shambu-nath and sin at ease. The temple stands a mile west of Katmandu on a wooded hill which is climbed by several hundreds of stone steps. The whole hill, the temple itself, and the neighbouring houses of its attendants, are the home and playground of a far too numerous colony of Rhesus monkeys, which pay even less attention than their human brothers to the unspoken question of those eyes. Instead of studying the medley of architecture, I stood fascinated by the antics of these amusing but disgusting beasts as they clambered upon and defiled the deities, and played hide-and-seek among the prayer wheels. As a climber I could only regret that if we are descended from apes, monkeys, chimpanzees, gorillas, or a blend of all four, we have not inherited their prehensile toes. I stood spellbound by the ease with which they climbed the holdless walls of the adjacent houses to poke their long arms through the carefully barred windows reaching for anything within. Living in one of these houses must be an everlasting nightmare, what with the eyes of the stupa just about level with the upper window, the sad, unblinking eyes of some damned monkey on the sill outside, and the hairy arms groping within.

In Nepal, Hinduism and Buddhism mingle and overlap; the Newar architects and craftsmen have been inspired by both, just as they have been by the art of China as well as India. In most of the temples Hinduism, Buddhism and Lamaism are represented, and in them the devotee of each will find his favourite image. Landon thus describes the surrounding of the Shambu-nath stupa:

A multitude of smaller shrines, of guardian beasts, of chaityas, of sacred pillars crowned with images of divinities, peacocks or sarduls, of representations of the holy footmark, fill up the rest of the sacred compound. To the west of the stupa stands a building wherein Buddhist priests tend and keep alive a sacred flame. Between are pillars crowned with exquisite gilt bronze work, and between these again are a couple of statues of which the southern is perhaps the finest piece of work ever achieved by those masters of bronze modelling, the Newars. It represents Tara, and is a reminder to the Tibetan visitor of the Nepalese woman to whom he owes the introduction of Buddhism into his country in the seventh century. Adjoining the temple of the flame is the shrine of Sitala, the dreaded goddess of smallpox. Sitala is a Hindu goddess, but Buddhists—just to make quite sure—bend the knee to her as reverently as do the followers of Vishnu or Shiva.

What with the monkeys, the squad of sweepers for whom their habits occasioned constant employment, a couple of shops, and a constant trickle of visitors, there was more liveliness at Shambu-nath than at any of the other temples. Liveliness may not be natural to the precincts of a temple, but it is better than neglect. Shambu-nath is popular because it caters for all religious tastes; it is beautiful to see, and from it great beauty can be seen. There is a variety of images for the devotee, and from its height the visitor may look down upon a glorious prospect of rich vale and meandering river. It is also close to Katmandu, which we must now leave. Having completed our preparations we might cease from viewing temples carved by man to go in search of those natural temples of rock and ice.

CHAPTER THREE

To the Langtang

THE gang that shuffled out of the Legation compound on 29 May was at least formidable in numbers. Besides four Europeans, four Sherpas, and forty coolies, there were Lieut. S. B. Malla with two orderlies, and a smart havildar with two sepoys. The military bearing of the escort so far redeemed our slovenliness that we might almost be said to have *marched* out of the compound. Gratifying as this might be, I regarded the presence of our spruce escort with some misgiving, having always a great horror of the addition of *bouches inutiles* to an expedition—of men, that is to say, who do not or will not carry loads. Such misgivings were needless. Both the lieutenant and the havildar proved their worth, without whom we should have had much difficulty and delay in our negotiations with the local people for food and transport.

Even so the party was not complete. At Bombay, Polunin had engaged a Goan, Toni Mathos, a bird-skinner, who had acted in that capacity to Dr Dillon Ripley's party the previous winter. He had been left behind to bring on a stick-gun, a small-bore gun for collecting disguised as a walking stick, which the Bombay police had removed from Polunin's care; the weapon having created some despondency among the police who regarded it as precisely the sort of thing that no good assassin would care to be without. Polunin had also a 410-bore gun, but its ammunition was packed with that of the confiscated stick-gun. The collecting of birds, upon which the British Museum set great store, was therefore more or less at a standstill until mid-August when the gun and ammunition, after a lot of trouble, at last reached us.

Of the eight stages which the baria naik allowed for the journey hardly one figured on the map; we were therefore in his hands, but a fixed sum for the round trip having been agreed upon, the coolies were not likely to waste time. The road took us past the Baleji water-garden and out of the valley over the Sheopuri Lekh to Kaulia where we camped. ('Lekh' is the word used for a ridge or range without permanent snow.) It was warm work dragging our unaccustomed legs up the Sheopuri ridge, and we suffered all the pains of a first march. But those philosophers who assure the wretched that there is always someone who is worse off were quite right, for I would not have cared to change places with any of the labourers at work in the terraced fields. In the absence of ploughs and oxen they stretched their own backs against the stubborn glebe with an implement which would dismay the most stout-hearted digger. The handle is about 2ft. long, and the blade, lying parallel to and a few inches from it, is almost as long, so that as the digger strikes, his head almost touches the ground. On these less fruitful hills outside the valley everything is done by hand, from breaking the soil to threshing and grinding the corn. Nor are animals much used in the valley, where the land is too rich to spare for grazing.

Kaulia is the hill from which Wood and Schlagintweith had made their observations, whence next morning we too enjoyed, lying in our sleeping-bags in a field, a noble prospect of peaks. From this cool lodging at 6,000 ft. we had now to plunge nearly 4,000 ft. to the valley of the Trisuli, which is here only 2,500 ft. above the sea. Instead of camping on the hill at Nawakot, the principal village of this part, we stuck to the valley. At Nawakot in 1792 the treaty of peace was signed between the defeated Gurkhas and the pursuing Chinese army which was then only two days' march from the capital. The Gurkhas had brought upon themselves this Chinese avalanche by their invasion of Tibet two years before and by the looting of Tashi-lhumpo. Provided they got their plunder away, this bold foray, 260 miles beyond the border, must have richly rewarded the raiders; for even to-day the great monastery at Tashi-lhumpo near Shigatse is reputedly crammed with jewels and precious metals. The head of the monastery, the Tashi Lama, is second only to the Dalai Lama.

In India in May, only 2,000 ft. up, a march can be devilish hot. The first river we met, the Likhu, was shallow and warm—for it is not snow-fed—thus long before we reached it my hopes centred upon the Trisuli as the river for a bathe. The more I thought of it the faster I went, gradually attaining such state of simmering exhaustion that a plunge into a warm and weedy duck-pond would have been exquisite enough to rank as a memorable bathe. At last the path met the river, surging swift, swollen, and turbid, between rocky banks— a river with which in cold blood one would prefer to have nothing to do. But just as any clothes will fit a naked man, so any water is welcome to an over-heated man provided it does not drown him. The nearest bank was mere cliff, so hurrying across the suspension bridge I turned down the other bank at full speed until at a respectful distance from the village, I stripped and plunged in. Mahadeo himself could scarcely have given such a gasp of ecstasy as the icy water closed over his head. But here there was no reclining; for having been swept helplessly down for an exhilarating minute one was glad to scramble out on to the sun-warmed rocks. Scott soon joined me, and presently the small boys of the village came along to put our timid coasting to shame by launching themselves boldly across this dangerous-looking river.

We camped in a big mango tope on the right bank of the river, some way from the bazaar but not far enough away to throw off the sight-seers. In the evening great numbers assembled round our camp, attracted less by us than by the witticisms of a wench whom I christened Trisuli Trixie, who being slightly tipsy had maintained a brisk exchange of ribaldry with the Sherpas from the moment of our arrival. But to understand all is to forgive all, and once we had sampled some of the 'raksi' which had set her alight, we forgave her from the bottom of our hearts. For the first and last time we put up our mosquito nets, less to baffle the mosquitoes, perhaps, than to protect us from Trixie. Both Europeans and Sherpas had already been taking 'Paludrin' which is not only a cure but also a preventative of malaria. In mosquito or leech-ridden country it is customary and convenient to assume that the coolies (for they are many) are either beneath the aid of science or too pachydermatous to need it.

We were astir early but dallied in the bazaar buying snacks for the road until the unwelcome rays of the sun flooded the valley. Thus warned we hurried off over the bridge, where Trixie was waiting to say farewell, sober enough to recognize us but not sober enough to cross. For two or three miles we walked easily along a terrace a little above the river. This was too pleasant to last. In my experience a Himalayan track is seldom content to follow the bank, but is always busy either climbing to escape the river or rushing down to it in order to avoid some impassable cliff. Our terrace soon petered out, and upon crossing the small Betravati stream we were faced with the choice of going high at once or climbing to the valley bottom little longer. The Betravati stream is said to have been the scene of a vigorous action in the war of 1792 when the Gurkha rearguard cut the chains of a suspension bridge and precipitated a great many non-swimming Chinese into the river. An open debate determined for us the question of high road or low; and when in obedience to an almost unanimous vote we embarked up a 2,000 ft. climb in the heat of the day, I concluded that such grave decisions should not be left to the many-headed. Pursued by the perspiring havildar, who seldom let me out of his sight, I pushed on up the steep waterless track until we reached a small village and a gigantic pipal tree. As we sat in the grateful shade, reflecting upon the vicissitudes of life and the sweating coolies, we agreed that they would never get past this tree. I doubted if they would get so far, for in the cool of the morning along the pleasant stretch by the river they had sat down under every tree—and there were a great many—trees, too, which were far less umbrageous than this. However, soon after four o'clock they began trickling (le mot juste) in, dropped their loads as if they bore them some ill-will, and made a bee-line for the meagre water supply.

We were astir even earlier next morning, roused by a brisk thunderstorm from our untented beds under the pipal canopy. The track maintained its height at a couple of thousand feet above the river only by dint of striking an average, for its course resembled the line traced on a barograph in very unsettled weather. We camped outside a mean village of five houses under a great rock overhang. The shadow of a great rock, either in a thirsty land or a wet land, is the refuge of many travellers and its vicinity is consequently filthy. But a rock roof is better than a pipal tree, however gigantic or luxurious, and the dried goat dung with which the place is carpeted makes for soft lying.

We had a lucky meeting here with a Sherpa and his wife who were pleased to see our Sherpas and to hear the latest gossip from Solu Khumbu, their common home on the Nepal side of the Everest region. Driving a couple of donkeys they were on a trading venture to Kyerong, a day's march over the border to Tibet, a road they knew well. According to them atta and rice were procurable a few marches farther on, and when the man, who seemed a keen hand, offered to collect whatever we needed, I closed with him by giving a firm order for ten maunds of atta, rice, and satu, for delivery in July.

The track behaved more sedately next morning until it suddenly dropped by a staircase of stone steps nearly a thousand feet into the Trisuli nullah. This was not the main river but a small tributary descending from the Gosainkund lakes, the same sacred stream which the trident (trisul) of Mahadeo had released from its rock prison. A track, well marked with 'chortens' and 'mani' walls, leads up to Gosainkund which is sacred to Buddhists as well as Hindus. The main river, which I shall continue to call the Trisuli, rises sixty miles beyond the Tibet border within fifteen miles of the valley of the Tsangpo. Of the seven tributaries of the Gandak, of which the Trisuli is one of the biggest, four have cut through the Himalaya, while two, the Trisuli and the Kali, drain the trough beyond the Ladakh range in Tibet. Several other Nepal rivers, notably the Karnali in the west and the Arun in the east, cut through the main range in deep gorges. The Trisuli gorge is no mean cleft; a few miles south of the Tibet border, where the river crosses the main Himalayan axis, the bed of the gorge is less than 6,000 ft. above sea-level, yet only six miles east lies the 23,771 ft. peak of Langtang Lirung. (Overleaf are some figures for Himalayan gorges.)

River Gorge	Height of bed near axis	Width between peaks
Kali Gandak	5,000 ft.	12 miles at 24,000 ft.
Trisuli Gandak	6,000 ft.	16 miles at 19,000 ft.
Arun	6,000 ft.	14 miles at 16,000 ft.

River	Height of bed	Mountain	Distance	Fall per mile peak to river bed
Kali	5,000 ft.	Dhaulagiri 26,795 ft.	4 miles	5,449 ft.
Hunza	6,000 ft.	Rakaposhi 25,550 ft.	9 miles	2,172 ft.
Indus	4,000 ft.	Nanga Parbat 26,620 ft.	14 miles	1,616 ft.
Trisuli	6,000 ft.	Langtang Lirung 23,771 ft.	8 miles	2,200 ft.

The above comparative tables of heights and widths of the principal Himalayan gorges are taken from *Himalaya Mountains* by Burrard and Hayden.

Our bathe in a clear green pool of the sacred stream fed by the Gosainkund lake afforded so great joy that we willingly renounced the merit, to earn which one must surely suffer pain. On other accounts, too, this was a red-letter day. Polunin began his botanical collection and his activity reminded me that I, too, had a purpose in life. Hitherto I had always contrived to suppress my ardour for science, but on this occasion a friend, an amateur of beetles, had entrusted me with the task of collecting some. They were to be all of one species—'meligethes'—of which I had been given a rough description—small, black, shiny beggars— but having a poor memory for faces I decided to make sure by sweeping every beetle I met, regardless of age, sex, or species, into what I called my battery of Belsen chambers, small test-tubes impregnated with amyl acetate. This insistence on one species, without limit as to numbers, was a little puzzling to a man who hitherto had not given beetles the thought which, possibly, they deserved. Perhaps they were for swops? On the beetle exchange a man with a few hundred 'meligethese' would have the whip-hand of rival collectors who had dissipated their energies by striving for a little of everything. Still a collection of hundreds of small fellows, all as like as two pins and all clad in sober hues, could hardly delight they eye. Such an assembly, I thought, would be the brighter for the company of some of their more flashy relatives of which happily there was no lack—gorgeously striped, spotted, barred, tricked out in colours more striking than mellow, after the style of an American tie.

Having toiled up from the valley of the little Trisuli we camped in a wheat stubble at the village of Bhragu. This early harvest of wheat, which must have been sown the previous autumn, reassured us about our food supplies. Bhragu village consisted of a few two-storied wooden houses, with some crude carving round the doors and windows, and roofs of rough shingles, roughly put on and held down with stones. The family live on the top floor where a balcony serves as a pleasant day lounge, while the ground floor is used for stables and stores. The people are Tamangs; at least this name, pretty widely and indifferently applied, seemed to satisfy our lieutenant's ethnological curiosity. They are more Hindu than Buddhist; but since leaving Trisuli bazar we had begun to see 'mani' walls and 'chortens' in the vicinity of villages, and the farther north we went, the more numerous they became. At the next village of Syabrubensi, at the junction of the Langtang Khola and the Trisuli, we saw the first 'gompa'.

Having so little information about the resources of the country, our plan had been to make our headquarters at Thangiet on the west side of the valley which the map showed to be the largest cultivated area of the region. However, our food problem had now been solved by the Sherpa corn chandler who, at the same time, had painted a charming picture of the idyllic life we might lead at Langtang village, two marches up the Langtang Khola, where food, including butter and beer, abounded, and where tough men and strong women would be eager to carry our loads. This welcome and surprising news, the village being over 11,000 ft., decided us to make our base there. Neither the baria naik nor the coolies objected to this change of plan, and meantime the garrison commander at the frontier post of Rasua Garhi, to whom we ought to pay our earliest respects, would have to wait.

On crossing the Langtang Khola by a suspension bridge just above its junction with the Trisuli, we regarded the river with interest. As the melting increased, the glacier-fed rivers were rising fast, and to the raging, brown flood of the Trisuli the Langtang added an impressive volume of equally turbid water. At Syabrubensi near the junction, barely 5,000 ft. above sea-level, we stopped to ask about the road. This small village, with scarcely any fields, seemed to live by what it could fleece from travellers—which, I thought, would be very little judging by what they had to offer and the kind of traveller who passed through. It is a dull place, like the other villages on this rather dull trade route where neither mule-trains with jingling bells and scarlet wool-tufted harness, nor tea-houses where the picturesque muleteers forgather, are met. Possibly in winter the road is lively with Tibetans and their mules, but in summer it is thronged only with sweating coolies trudging south with loads of salt. This is obtained, in exchange for rice, from a salt lake at a place called Chang, a day's march beyond Kyerong. At Rasua Garhi they told us some 5,000 man-loads pass through yearly. Wool, of course, is the most valuable Tibetan export, most of which passes down the Chumbi valley to Kalimpong. According to Sir Charles Bell the trade of that one route equals that of all the other Tibetan trade routes from Assam to Kashmir.

The track traverses high above the lower Langtang Khola to the village of Khangjung where we camped alongside a small, poor monastery. In these parts the monasteries are very different from the important, thriving establishments, often very wealthy, of Tibet. The single-roomed building, usually dilapidated and seldom open, is merely a receptacle where, on a kind of altar, are kept two or three Bodhisats of painted or gilded clay and some unlit butter lamps; a few dingy temple banners, masks, and a drum, hang from the roof, and some some wood-bound volumes, thick with dust, complete the religious furnishing. So dark is the interior that the wall frescoes can hardly be seen, while those on the verandah walls are partially destroyed by weather. But where they are intact, especially if they are old, the spirited pictures of fierce and terrible deities, saints, demons, or the Wheel of Life, look like the work of pious, vigorous and skilful hands. These are done by no local artists; they have been and still are painted by lamas from Tibet, who thus earn money to support them on their pilgrimages to Katmandu or even to the Buddhist shrines of India.

Whether he was a lama or merely a caretaker, the man in charge of these places, with few exceptions, neglected the duties of both. Except at infrequent festivals, the tolling of a bell at dawn and dusk satisfied the demands of religious ceremony, while leaking roofs and peeling wall frescoes testified to the lack of regard for the fabric. The monastery doors remained shut for weeks together so that the villagers, and indeed the lama himself, with less excuse than Falstaff, must have been in danger of forgetting what the inside of a church was made of. Few readers will have escaped hearing the tragic monologue of how Mad Carew, spurred on by his Colonel's daughter, stole a superb emerald from 'the one-eyed yellow idol to the north of Katmandu'. But such being the mournful state of the monasteries to-day north of Katmandu we looked in vain for idols with gleaming emeralds in their eyes.

Syarpagaon, the next village, was the last of the lowland villages, where they have few cattle but lots of goats, and where maize is grown in tiny terraced fields. At Langtang village, 3,000 ft. higher, we were to find a different economy. From Syarpagaon the track plunged down to the river bank into gloomy rain forest. Among many strange trees the familiar oaks, maples and firs themselves looked exotic, festooned as they were with lichen, moss, ferns and orchids. The steeper south bank had a dense stand of bamboos. Judging from the vegetation we thought that the lateral valleys received more rain than the north and south trough of the main Trisuli.

From mixed forest we passed to pure pine and then to grassy glades surrounded with roses, pink and white cotoneaster, and orange berberis. The valley opened out but its high and steep sides shut out the snow mountains lying immediately above. Then the low, brown roofs of Langtang came in sight and, having reached the first of the three hamlets, we climbed to the gampa to introduce ourselves to the spiritual and temporal head of the Langtang community. The man who combined the role of lama and headman was about fifty years old with close-cropped iron-grey hair; from his slightly foxy appearance one judged him to be a priest qualified for this world as well as the next. He showed more astonishment than delight at our arrival—which I readily excused on account of the hungry half-hundred trailing behind us whom he rightly feared would require feeding. He brightened up when he heard that the coolies would be here for only one night and conducted us forthwith to a camping ground near the main village.

The barai naik with his flock next morning departed unobtrusively for Katmandu where they would collect the balance of their pay. No farewells were said and no gratuity seemed to be expected. It had certainly been an easy approach march. The track was no worse than any other hill-country track and the coolies had shown themselves docile and willing. They had neither grumbled nor cadged. Cigarettes and baksheesh, if thought of, had not once been mentioned.

CHAPTER FOUR

The Langtang

THE upper Langtang is a fine, open valley, rich in flowers and grass, and flanked by great mountains. It is a grazier's paradise. At 11,000 ft. one might expect to find a few rough shelters occupied only in the summer, but at Langtang there is a settlement of some thirty families rich in cows, yaks and sheep. These are, besides, like young Osric, spacious in the possession of dirt; for their fields are no mere pocket-handkerchief terraces clinging to the hillside but flat stone-walled fields of an acre or more growing wheat, buckwheat, potatoes, turnips, and a tall, strong-growing beardless barley called 'kuru'.

The grazing extends from the valley bottom to the slopes above and far up the moraines and ablation valleys of both the main and the tributary glaciers; and dotted about are rich alps with stone shelters, called 'kharka', where the herdsmen live and make the butter. Considerable quantities of this are exported to Tibet. In the Langtang gompa I saw 25 man-loads of butter sewn up in skins which a lama had bought for his monastery at Kyerong, and which, he told me, represented a year's supply. Besides being drunk in innumerable cups of tea, butter plays an important part in religious ceremony. In well-run monasteries butter lamps burn continually before the images and at certain festivals pounds of butter are moulded into elaborate decorations for the altars. I noticed the Langtang lama placing a dab of it on people's heads as a blessing, while a little is always placed on the edge of the cup or plate offered to a guest.

The valley has religious traditions. Like many out-of-the-way places it was originally the home of the gods, those happy beings, to whom, with their ready means of locomotion, remoteness was of little account. But at a more recent date the beauties of the valley were revealed to mortals in a way reminiscent of that other story—'Saul he went to look for donkeys, and, by God, he found a kingdom'. In this case the missing animal was, of course, a yak which its owner, a very holy man, tracked up the Langtang. The spoor was not difficult to follow, for at Syabrubensi and at Syarpagaon the beast left on a rock the imprint of a foot which is visible to this day. The lama caught his yak at a place called Langsisa, seven or eight miles above Langtang village where, having fulfilled its appointed task, it promptly died. The lama, with less regard for sentiment than for money's worth unfeelingly skinned it and spread the skin on a rock to dry; but the yak had the last laugh; for the skin stuck and remains there to this day, as a big reddish-coloured rock at Langsisa plainly testifies.

Near Langsisa there are two other rocks of greater note. A couple of miles up a valley to the east, standing some hundreds of feet above the glacier, are two big rock gendarmes which are said to represent two Buddhist saints, Shakya Muni and Guru Rumbruche. Tibetan lamas come as far as Langsisa to worship them. Since the etymology of many English place-names is still, as it were, anybody's guess, I have little hesitation in offering the following

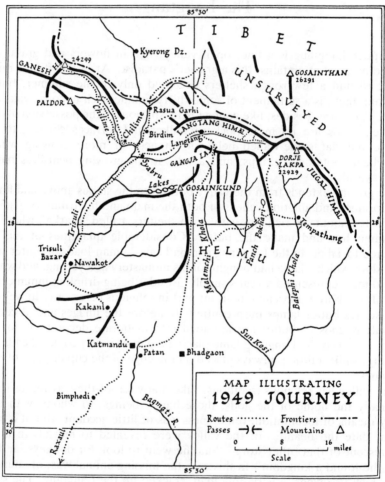

Map to illustrate 1949 journey

derivations. 'Lang' is Tibetan for cow or yak, 'tang', or more correctly 'dhang', means to follow. Langsisa means the place where the yak died.

A valley with such tradition is, of course, a sanctuary; within it no animal may be slaughtered. According to the lieutenant, the observance of this ban on slaughter, which dated back for hundreds of years, had been neglected and the present headman, Nima Lama, took it upon himself to visit Katmandu to have the matter put right. The original decree, having been looked up and verified, was formally confirmed, and the fine for any breach of the rule was fixed at Rs. 100. Our wish to shoot small birds for specimens had to be met by the issue of a special licence; but apart from two sheep thoughtfully slaughtered for us by a bear of non-Buddhist tendencies, we had no meat while in the valley.

The people of Langtang are very like Tibetans, engagingly cheery, tough and dirty; but they have sufficient regard for appearances to wash their faces occasionally and were scrupulous to remove those lice which strayed to the *outside* of their garments. They themselves say their ancestry was a mixture of Tibetans from around Kyerong and Tamangs from Helmu—the district to the south of the valley. They now call themselves Lama-Tamang. (It should be noted that 'lama' is the name for a class of Gurungs, one of the Nepal tribes from which many of the so-called Gurkhas are drawn.) They conversed very readily with our Sherpas in what was presumably some sort of Tibetan dialect. According to Tensing their speech is like that of the people of Lachen in north Sikkim.

We had arrived on 5 June, and since the monsoon might be expected to break at any time we immediately began the survey of the middle valley so that we could have fixed points to work from when we reached the frontier ridge at the head of the valley. The triangulated peak of Langtang Lirung, only two miles to the north, could not be seen from the village, and a tiny triangle of white, sometimes visible over the rock wall behind our camp, might or might not have been the tip of a 21,500 ft. peak to the west of it. Accordingly we started next day with six Langtang men carrying three weeks' food, leaving behind Polunin and the escort. With him we also left a Sherpa, a lad called Phutarkay who had been with me on Rakaposhi two years before, who as well as looking after his master had already learnt to press and handle specimens. On the march few strange plants escaped his keen eyes.

Tensing, who combined the roles of sirdar and cook, was widely travelled and an experienced mountaineer whom I had last met on Everest in 1938 when he carried a load to Camp VI. Having spent the war years with an officer of the Chitral Scouts he had further enlarged his mountaineering and ski-ing experience. Since then he had been to Lhasa with an Italian Tibetan scholar, for whom he had purchased whole libraries—he told me they had brought away forty maunds of books. Tensing, who gets on with everyone and handles the local people well, has a charming smile, great steadiness on a mountain, and a deft hand for omelettes which he turns out nicely sloppy but firm. With paragons such as this one can afford to be blind to minor faults. Neither of the others, Da Namgyal and Angtharkay, had had any experience, but the former soon learnt what was expected of him either in camp or on a mountain. Angtharkay, who is not to be confused with his well-known namesake, who is probably the best Sherpa porter ever known, was a little old for the job and a little 'dumb'. In fact I suspected that he had not long come down from his tree. He came to us with a pigtail which I was sorry to see him remove, but it had to make way for the heavy Balaclava helmet which he wore even in the hottest valleys. I have a liking for men with pigtails because the first three Sherpas with whom I ever travelled all wore their hair long and were all first-rate men. Nowadays, among the Sherpas, long hair and pigtails are out-moded, but not long ago they indicated a good type of unsophisticated man who had not been spoilt by long residence outside Nepal. Angtharkay, unsophisticated enough for anyone, unfortunately lacked mother-wit. He had the air of an earnest buffoon which neither the striped heliotrope pyjama trousers he wore one day, nor the long woollen pants he affected the next, did anything to diminish.

Half a mile above Langtang was another hamlet with large fields of wheat and kuru, still very green, a big chorten, and the longest mani wall I have ever seen—nearly three hundred yards of it. These walls or 'mendongs', which are seven or eight feet high, must be passed on the left. On each side are flat stones with carved Buddhas or religious texts for the benefit of passers-by on either hand; and the equally well-worn paths on both sides of the wall show that the rule is observed. In the main Trisuli valley Buddhism, or at any rate the observance of this particular tenet, seemed to be weakening, for one of the paths round each mani wall tended to fall into disuse. In Timure village, only a day's march from the Tibetan border, some abandoned scoffer had had the hardihood to carry his miserable maize field right up to a mendong, thus abolishing the path on one side.

Having crossed a stream issuing from the snout of the Lirung glacier we camped a short four miles up from Langtang village. The grass flat, white with anemones, where we camped, lay tucked under the juniper-covered moraine of the glacier. Hard by were the gompa of Kyangjin Ghyang, some stone huts and turnip fields, and beyond a wide meadow stretched for a mile or more up the north side of the valley. The Lirung peak, from which the glacier came, and several others, overlooked it, but across the river the south containing wall was comparatively low. It can be crossed by the Gangja La (19,000 ft.) over which lies a direct route to the Helmu district and thence to Katmandu. On that side, the north-facing slope, birch trees and rhododendrons maintained a gallant struggle against the height which, by altimeter, was 13,500 ft.

Naturally, for two of us the Lirung peak had a powerful appeal. At Katmandu we had admired its graceful lines with longing eyes. It had looked eminently climbable then, as indeed most mountains do when looked at from far off, but now we were forced to admit that its south side, defended by a great cirque, was quite impregnable. However, at the moment, climbing took second place. Neither of us was ready for serious work. Indeed, as the result of some months spent in Australia, Lloyd had become a little gross, a fault which an insufficiently arduous approach march had done nothing to rectify. Moreover, in our cautious eyes, not one of the few Langtang peaks we had seen invited immediate assault, and in new country the urge to explore is hardly to be withstood. Around a corner of the valley a few miles up, the whole Langtang glacier system waited to be unravelled, and at its head lay the untrodden frontier ridge and the unknown country beyond. During the monsoon, we hoped, we might still climb, but the survey work must be done now or never. Our first three weeks, which were moderately fine, proved to be the only fine weeks we were to have.

We spent nearly a week at this gompa camp. Lloyd wished to occupy stations on both sides of the valley before moving up, while I had made the exciting discovery of a way on to what we took to be the frontier ridge to the north. Having walked up the left moraine of the Lirung glacier, Tensing and I turned right-handed up steep grass and gravel slopes until we came to a sort of glacier shelf lying along the foot of the ridge upon which Lirung and its neighbouring 22,000 ft. peak stood. We judged the lowest point to be under

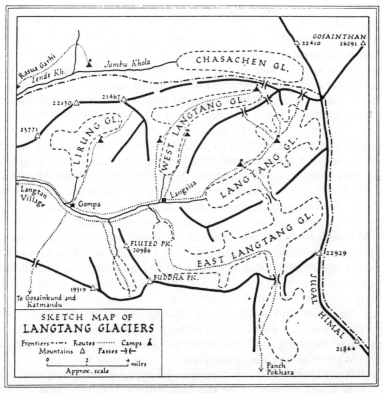

3 Langtang glaciers

20,000 ft, A little tarn at the foot of the ice offered a convenient and tempting camp site at about 17,000 ft. Going back we made a wide detour over a bleak upland valley of more gravel than grass, where we found a scented cream and mauve primula (*P. macrophylla*) already in flower though old snow still lay about. On the way we took in a great rounded bump of over 17,000 ft., its grass summit incongruously crowned with long bamboo poles and tattered prayer flags.

On the assumption that this ridge would prove to be the frontier ridge upon which we should have a most valuable station, we stocked the tarn camp and occupied it, intending to spend a full week. Early next morning, having gained the glacier shelf, we plodded eastwards on good hard snow to a point below the most accessible part of the ridge. Warned by gathering clouds, Lloyd decided to get busy while he could, so at about 19,000 ft. he put up the machine, as he called the theodolite, and began taking rounds of angles and photographing the fine confusion of peaks and valleys spreading eastward. Meanwhile Tensing and I pushed on up good snow to the ridge and traversed along it to a small summit. Having expected to see much from here, we were proportionately cast down at seeing so little. Another ridge, the frontier and the watershed, intervened to the north, and between the two lay a high glacier bay from which the ice curled over like a breaking wave before falling abruptly to some hidden arm of the Langtang glacier below. To the north-east, behind a tangle of peaks, rose a lump of a mountain with a long, flattish summit and a western face of more rock than snow. We thought it neither high nor distant enough to be Gosainthan which, according to the map, was over twelve miles away. It so happened that we never saw this mountain again, but Lloyd's survey data show that it was, in fact, Gosainthan.

Under a threatening sky we trudged back to camp through snow which was already soft and wet. A night of rain fulfilled the threat of morning and when we turned out at 4 a.m. it was still falling. Since the frontier ridge could not be reached there was no point in staying, but before going down we wanted to put the theodolite on the small summit reached the day before. What with the drizzle and the waterlogged snow Lloyd soon turned back, leaving Tensing and me to struggle obstinately and rather aimlessly towards a notch in the ridge. Although the snow was too wet for them, a pair of snowshoes I had with me seemed to make for easier progress. Later I wore them a lot and tried to convince myself that those behind, who had no such aids, benefited from the huge steps I made. Having reached the rocks below the notch and found them very loose we contented ourselves with collecting a few inexpensive rock presents for Scott and a couple of hibernating moths for myself. As a lepidopterous insect a moth has something in common with beetles, and I thought that anything that contrived to live at 19,000 ft. deserved an honourable place in any insect museum.

On returning from this damp excursion I went on to Langtang to check the food, where I was astonished by the swift growth resulting from the recent rain—by the many new flowers, the masses of white erica which had suddenly blossomed, and the dwarf rhododendron whose resinous fragrance filled the air. Kyangjin, too, had suddenly come to life. The long bamboo poles of the gompa and the roofs of the now occupied stone huts carried small flags of red and yellow, and the long, grass flat was thick with yaks and horses. Kyangjin is the first stage on the summer grazing itinerary which the yaks graze down before moving successively higher with the advance of summer, the sheep following humbly in their wake eating what is left. The horses roamed at will. They, we were told, were the property of the Government—the reason, perhaps, for their moderate condition.

Our friend Nima Lama had come up, bringing with him an adequate supply of beer, the better to fumigate the gompa and to confront and exorcise any evilly disposed spirits which might have occupied it during the winter months. Tensing had a private chat with Nima Lama, obtaining from him some confidential information which he unhesitatingly passed on to me. Having warned him on no account to let the sahibs know of it, Nima had told him that there was a pass into Tibet at the head of the valley. Neither he nor any living man had seen it, much less used it, for it had been closed at the time of the second Nepal–Tibet war (1854)—whether by man's edict or by some natural cataclysm was not made clear. It is difficult to imagine any shorter or easier way to Tibet than that by the Trisuli valley, but the oldest inhabitant well remembered people coming by the pass, bringing their yaks with them. Now I admire the yak, but his reputation for crossing passes, like that of Himalayan climbers, is apt to be enhanced by time and distance. Still, some weight must be accorded to tradition, and we resumed our journey to the valley head much encouraged by the story of this ancient pass.

We started with a scratch team, two men, three women and a boy, on a fine sunny day. The Langtang has not only the austere beauty of ice mountains accentuated by the friendly smile of flowery meadows alive with cattle—but it has the charm of reticence and the witchery of the unexpected—a quality which Mr Milestone considered more desirable in a garden landscape than the beautiful or the picturesque. A gentle but continuous bend tantalizes its admirers, draws them on impatiently to see beyond the next corner, maintaining for them the thrill of discovery almost to the end. So far we had seen no more than two miles up the valley where the bend began, a place marked by a magnificent peak which we soon acknowledged to be the loveliest gem of the valley. On account of the snow fluting traced like the ribs of a fan upon its western face we called it the Fluted Peak. It is a few feet under 21,000 ft., but it stands alone, smiling down upon the valley with a face of glistening purity framed between clean-cut snow ridges of slender symmetry.

As we drew past, fresh vistas of higher but less graceful mountains opened before us. But close at hand, stretching across the floor of the valley—still wide and green—lay a vast moraine, some 500 ft. high, the piled debris of a great glacier descending from the west. The narrowest of gorges, cut by the river draining the main Langtang glacier beyond, alone separated the toe of the moraine from the eastern wall of the valley. Beyond this barrier lay Langsisa, which we should easily have reached the first day. In our haste to see round corners we outran the porters, missed the path which went by the gorge, and charged straight at the giant moraine. While we were scurrying about on top of this eyesore looking vainly for water and a camp site, the porters sat calmly below in a pleasant meadow where presently we were obliged to join them.

Next day Lloyd explored this west glacier, while Tensing and I went to Langsisa and straight on up the main valley. Neither of us got anywhere near the heads of our respective glaciers, both of which seemed to terminate without undue abruptness at the frontier ridge. On returning I found the lieutenant had brought up our Sherpa corn merchant, with whom we did some hard bargaining. In the end I advanced Rs. 100, receiving as security his necklage of large corals. I would not have given 6d. for it, but Tensing assured me it was worth Rs. 200. Anyhow the owner evidently set considerable store by it and not very much on my honesty. He wanted to have it sealed up so that there could be no juggling with the corals.

Three of us, three Sherpas, and two Langtang men, carrying 400 lb. (twelve days' supplies), now moved up the main valley. In an hour we reached Langsisa, a rich meadow on the river bank where there is a stone shelter. Hard by are three inscribed stones set in the ground whence pilgrims make their obeisance to the two saints. The ice of the big east glacier flows down almost to the river on the opposite side, and a couple of miles up the two rock gendarmes or saints stand out prominently. To these our Langtang men at once paid their respects by going down on their knees, along with two Tibetan lamas who had come for the same purpose. Beyond Langsisa the track grew rougher and steeper. We walked for five hours up the right bank, sometimes on moraine and sometimes in the ablation valley below, the tumbled stone and ice of the main Langtang glacier lying on our right. Polunin came part of the way to collect a very lovely primula we had noticed the previous day—a pale blue, scented, bell-shaped flower, five, seven or even nine on the one stem. It was *P. Wollastonii* which Wollaston had first found when, as members of the Everest reconnaissance party of 1921, he and Morshead were travelling in the vicinity of Nyenam. This village lies over the Tibet border about twenty miles east of where we were.

On leaving this camp we were forced on to the glacier up which, in a sort of trough, we made a short but very rough march to a little tarn tucked away behind the moraine of a side glacier. We were still not within striking distance of the frontier ridge but the two local men would go no farther. Up to and a little beyond the last camp we had followed a track which might well be accounted for as a grazing track; but down in the glacier trough I found traces of what might have been its continuation, indicated by stones placed on top of boulders. As there was no grass farther on, this ancient track, if track it was, may have led to a pass. The existence of a pass at the head of the Langtang is thus supported by a track as well as tradition—the keys, or rather the only clues we have, to another Himalayan enigma, the Abominable Snowman.

For the next day we had a full programme. While the Sherpas moved the camp to the head of the glacier, Lloyd and I, carrying the machine, attempted to reach the most westerly of three cols. This precision instrument which, by the way, used plates and had no shutter, made an awkward load. As it was essential to beat the clouds, which usually came over between 9 and 10 a.m., by seven o'clock we had covered the remaining mile or so of level glacier and had begun to climb. From an upper snow shelf which we reached at 10 o'clock, the low rock ridge marking the col looked close enough. But it was noon before I got there, while Lloyd, who was still carrying too much weight, sank by the way. Excited though I was, my plodding steps could not be hurried, and when at last I looked over the top to the glacier below, its surface seemed to wrinkle in a derisive smile. The col was not on the frontier ridge and the glacier below was none other than the west Langtang whose high, ugly snout we had rounded on the way to Langsisa. The altimeter registered

20,700 ft., a height which I could easily credit. Unhappily that was the instrument's last coherent message. A knock which it got on the way back, besides shattering the glass, must have affected it internally. Never again did it speak a true word. Instead, with little or no provocation, it would often shoot to heights undreamt of in our philosophy, heights which we could only have attained by means of a balloon.

This was not the only misfortune. When, after a long and fruitless day, we reached the appointed camp—a shelf above the glacier—there were no tents. To save themselves trouble the Sherpas had camped on the glacier, thereby compelling us to lie on devilish knobbly stones with ice underneath instead of on warm, soft gravel. Scott's altimeter, which had not yet met the inevitable fate of all such instruments, made our height 18,000 ft. Rather surprisingly, rice cooked well, and we slept warm in only one sleeping-bag.

There were yet two cols to visit. Unless the curling west glacier was longer than the main trunk, which was unlikely, the easternmost col must be on the frontier ridge. In order to ensure reaching it in good time we took a light camp to some rocks at the foot of the snow slope, the height being about 19,000 ft. We spent a poor night and overslept ourselves, for it was warm even in only one sleeping bag and we were both excited. The view from any col, a mountain window opening upon a fresh scene, holds an expectant thrill; how much keener is expectancy if that view promises to reveal unsurveyed country and perhaps a 26,000 ft. mountain.

Aided by this flying start of a thousand feet, on better snow, and with Tensing making light of the 30 lb. theodolite, we reached the col by 7.30 of a fine morning. It proved to be a false col. Nearly a mile away and at the same height lay the true col, and in between was a snow hollow which drained by a sort of backdoor into a tiny branch of the Langtang glacier. On each side of the true col rose high peaks of the order of 22,000 ft. Lloyd remained with the machine on the false col to get a fix from known peaks, while Tensing and I sped on across the still hard snow. Now was our big moment, the moment for which I had been, as Pepys says, in child ever since leaving Katmandu. Our survey plans depended on what we saw and to our disgust we did not see very much. Below us a big glacier flowed westwards, across it lay a knot of mountains, part of a range which stretched north-west into Tibet, effectually blocking our view to the east. We could not even see the junction of this range with the Himalayan crest-line a mile or so to the east of our col, but since there was no hint of the great mountain elsewhere, we surmised that Gosainthan lay just about the point of junction. The key move for the solution of the problem was a descent to the glacier on the Tibetan side, thus violating the frontier. We had no scruples on that score, having persuaded ourselves, with commonsense rather than logic, that no trespass would be committed provided we remained within the uninhabited glacier region.

> He that is robbed, not wanting what is stol'n,
> Let him not know 't and he's not robb'd at all.

But it was too steep. Even had we had with us that earlier and better strain of yak, habitual crossers of traditional passes, I do not think we could have taken a camp over that col.

After collecting some spiders and rock fragments we returned to the high camp. We had still to visit the third col which lay between the other two and looked slightly higher. With perhaps as much luck as skill we climbed in dense mist by an intricate corridor, reaching the foot of the final pitch as the mist dissolved. We knew pretty well what to expect this time, and sure enough we looked once more upon the west glacier and beyond it to a mass of undistinguished-looking Tibetan peaks. We had now done our duty. Certainly, for Lloyd, our visits to the three cols held little pleasure, taken up, as they were, with the twiddling of screws, booking of angles, changing plates, all of it having to be done against time. I, on the other hand, once I had recovered from the successive disappointments, had merely to sit munching biscuits while Tensing scrabbled in rock crevices for victims for my Belsen chambers.

Since there was no reaching the unsurveyed territory on the Tibetan side, our survey work had to be confined to the Langtang itself. Nor was this merely painting the lily; for the existing ¼-in. maps published by the Survey of India in 1931 are good only so far as they go. Good enough, that is, to destroy any illusions one might have of being an explorer, all the main peaks having been triangulated and the general run of the main valleys indicated. But the detailed topography of the mountain regions is either not shown or is largely guesswork, thus the glaciers often provided charming surprises and the cols unexpected and puzzling vistas.

The station on this col was the last for some time. Next day, 22 June, when we began moving down, expecting to complete several stations on the way, the weather broke. Monsoon conditions of mist, rain, with rarely any sunshine, established themselves and prevailed almost unbroken for the rest of our stay.

On the way down Tensing and I crossed the main glacier to take a one-night camp up a tributary glacier to the east. The eastern side of the Langtang glacier is a very high wall of mountains unbroken except by this one glacier. Having crossed a high pass at its head, and having gone some way down the other side, we recognized below us the east branch of the Langtang which, after making an abrupt bend close to the two rock images, follows a course almost parallel to the main glacier. Beyond it we noticed yet another col leading southeast, a discovery of which we made good use later when we tried to reach the Jugal Himal. In a sanctuary one would expect to see game, but in this valley alone did we see any—three wary tahr, the rufous, shaggy Himalayan goat. At much lower altitudes we had occasionally seen a small deer which we took to be a musk deer, and on one occasion we had assumed without any strict enquiry the presence of some kindly disposed bears. Apart from that we saw no game, not even a marmot.

Twice, once at sunset and again at dawn, we carried the theodolite to the top of the 500 ft. moraine which in better weather would have made an excellent station, and then in disgust we went straight down to Langtang village. On this stroll, the more pleasant because it was all downhill, we met with a fresh crop of flowers, most of them, like Mr Pyecroft's lilac, 'stinkin' their blossomin' little hearts out'. Besides the tall cream primulas, nearly 2 ft.

high, there were little ground orchids of a delicate pink, bronze bell-shaped fritillaries, copper-coloured lilies, and great hairy yellow poppies. Lurking behind a bush of white briar, clutching a catapult, was a dark, hungry-looking figure, wearing, by way of dazzle camouflage, an American shirt. It was bird-skinner Toni who, with more zeal than sense, had left Bombay without waiting for the release of either stick-gun or ammunition.

CHAPTER FIVE

Rasua Garhi

WE had now to transfer ourselves and our baggage to the frontier post of Rasua Garhi, whence we hoped to reach the north side of Langtang Lirung and possibly to climb it. At this point the Nepalese have pushed their frontier to the north of the Himalaya to the Lende Khola, a river which joins the Trisuli at Rasua. No doubt it flows from the glacier upon which we had looked down from the col. Thus there was a small strip of country between the Langtang Himal and the river which, politically, we were free to explore. In the event, physical difficulties curtailed this freedom.

We were to move with twenty-four coolies on the 29th, but on the appointed morning, apart from the imposing array of loads laid out by the Sherpas, there was little sign of departure. Men, women and children would stroll up, regard the waiting loads with some distaste, hoist one or two tentatively, and then stroll back to the village for breakfast. To keep a dog and bark oneself is foolish. We had a shrill pack—the havildar, the sepoys and the Sherpas—yet I waited fussily until all the loads were safely away and then discovered that no one remained to carry the one upon which I was sitting, my personal kit. That the majority of our porters were women would surprise no one who had studied life in the Langtang. In addition to their household work the women do the digging, the weeding, carry much to the fields and harvest the crop. Except for a few who are up the hill tending the cattle, the men sit about and weave mats. In a more perfect world, no doubt, they will just sit.

These mats are in constant demand, and they could hardly be woven more deftly even by fairer hands. Every household has a number of these big, close-woven mats, easily portable, with which a shelter can be rigged in a matter of minutes. They carry half a dozen up to a kharka and with the aid of a few forked sticks and a ridge pole build a tunnel-like shelter some 10 ft. wide and 5 ft. high, closing the ends of the tunnel with a rough stone wall. If the mats are laid singly the shelter is almost weatherproof, when placed double it is perfectly so. Whenever we camped at a village, a mat kitchen for ourselves and one for the sepoys was quickly run up.

In spite of a late and long-drawn-out start—a matter of two hours between the head and the tail—all made Syarpagaon that evening. A note in my game-book reminds me that it was such a grand day for beetles that the extremely mournful appearance of a heavy bag of little black beggars had to be offset by the inclusion of a scarlet tick. Instead of descending to Syabrubensi, we continued to contour some 2,000 ft. above the river to the village of Birdim. As it was raining hard the headman invited us to use the gompa, which was in comparatively good order and remarkable for its wind-driven prayer wheels and a bell of very lovely tone. The fact that we were sometimes accommodated in gompas or on their verandahs did not wholly account for the regret one felt at their common neglect. On general grounds the neglect of any place where men once worshipped is to be regretted, but the realist, I suppose, before allowing himself to be much perturbed, would want to know what kind of worship went on in these gompas. No doubt it was never a very exalted kind—by no means pure Buddhism, but a superstitious animism mainly concerned with the propitiation of a hierarchy of malign and terrible demons, over which, nevertheless, from wall, altar, and banner, the placid eye of the Master presides. However, a belief in demons and the pains of hell is better than nothing. Just as one beats the saddle so that the ass may ponder, so imaginary terror is a harmless and efficacious preceptor; and the weakening of even such a belief as this (as the neglect of the gompas implies) is to be deplored if there is nothing to take its place.

We were invited to the headman's house where his family lived together in one spacious upper room furnished with shelves, cupboards, chests, and a raised dais for a comprehensive bed. On a stone hearth in the middle was the fire from which the smoke of juniper wood had coloured ceiling and rafters to a highly polished black, so bright and so clean to touch that one first thought it had been coated with black enamel. A traveller came in to borrow the family's stone hand-mill to grind some barley for a meal. In half an hour's hard work he turned out less than 2 lb. of uncommonly coarse flour; but few villagers are without water-mills, so that in one respect they are less backward than the Romans were.

From Birdim the track dropped to join the main road in the valley near the biggish village of Timure. This is the village where some land-hungry heathen has planted and fenced his maize right alongside a row of five noble and ancient chortens, so that the south-bound traveller must pass them, willy-nilly, on the unlucky side. In villages in the valley bottom, where the climate is warm, maize is the main crop, and even rice can be grown. Timure lies barely 6,000 ft. above sea-level. Having passed another village at the mouth of the Gatte Khola, a large tributary crossed by a suspension bridge, we reached Rasua Garhi lying in the narrowest and deepest part of the gorge. There was no village to speak of and the alert-looking militia-men who met us led us at once within a substantial stone fort, its wall embrasured for cannon and loopholed for rifles. The fort had been squeezed in between the Trisuli river and one rock wall of the gorge. Fifty yards to the front ran the Lende Khola, little if any less in violence or volume than the Langtang Khola, and nowhere to be crossed except by a bridge.

The fort, they said, was about a hundred years old, built probably about the time of the second Nepal–Tibet war (1854). The ostensible *casus belli* was the maltreatment of Nepalese traders in Lhasa, but the Nepalese, then ruled by the redoubtable Jung Bahadur, were in fact planning to retake the mountainous territory south of Kyerong and Kuti (Nyenam) which the Chinese had annexed to Tibet after the first war in 1792. Acting with his usual vigour, Jung Bahadur sent two forces against these places, both of which were taken. At Kyerong there was no opposition and, after Kuti had been lost and re-captured, negotiations were opened. By a peace treaty made in 1856 the Gurkha troops withdrew to the present boundary.

Having pitched our brightly coloured tents on the green-sward inside the walls we were conducted by the stout babu-like commander out through the gate and down to the Lende to admire the wooden cantilever bridge, half of which is maintained by Nepal and half by Tibet. A glance up the Nepal side of the river, where steep rock slabs thickly clad in a curious mixture of pine and bamboo running up for a thousand feet, served to chill our hopes. The Tibetan side, where there is a path, is much more gentle. By the bridge stood a stone slab inscribed with Chinese characters which no one present even pretended to be able to read. Nor do I think we should have learned from it anything useful, the number of 'li', for example, to Kyerong. More probably the industrious mason had bent his talents to imparting to travellers one or more of those sublime and immortal glimpses of the obvious which the Chinese relish so much: 'Every road leads in two directions', perhaps, or 'When struck by a thunderbolt it is superfluous to consult the Book of Dates as to the meaning of the omen'.

Apart from this stone there was nothing, not even an empty sentry-box, to denote that one had crossed a frontier. And this absence of any hint of might, majesty, dominion or power, is in accord with Tibetan genius which up to very recent years has managed to maintain its privacy behind quite imaginary barriers. Of course, should one happen to intrude, sooner rather than later one is seen off, not by an armed guard but by some stout affable official in Homburg hat and dark spectacles. Along the southern frontier of Tibet, from Assam to Kashmir, there are many passes and river gateways but nowhere are there any guards. This passive policy seems to have been clearly implied in one of the articles of the treaty which put an end to the war of 1854, in which, *inter alia*, it lays down that 'Tibet being merely a country of Monasteries of Lamas and a place for recitation of prayers and practice of religious austerities, if any foreign country attacks, Gorkha will afford such assistance and protection as it can'.

It has been amply demonstrated that there is now no part of the earth so wild, remote or unprofitable, that it is unlikely to become the scene of alarms and excursions. Nevertheless, I felt sorry for the commander of these nimble little militiamen in their neat blue uniforms, for it seemed that his prospects of advancing in his profession through some feat of arms were pretty slender. The garrison, in its boredom, must have welcomed the diversion we afforded. Five thousand man-loads of salt spread over the whole year cannot be a very absorbing spectacle, and since there are no customs' exactions, the men of the garrison have not the usual solace of frontier posts of making themselves a nuisance to travellers. Trade is blessedly free. We ourselves imported by the hand of our Sherpa corn merchant some quite drinkable raksi from Kyerong and paid no duty.

Local opinion affirmed that there was no way along the Nepal side of the Lende Khola and our eyes told us that on this occasion local opinion was probably right. There was, however, a path leading to a high grazing alp known as Dudh Khund, which lay vaguely in the required direction. Dudh Khund, or Milk Lake, is a common descriptive name for a lake whose water is opaque or any colour but white. We decided to visit the Milk Lake. Four of the Langtang squad stayed with us, but the majority went on to Kyerong. Owing either to trade or to a common origin there is a close association between Langtang and Kyerong.

By preparing overnight the necessary loads for a fortnight's absence we did a quick turn round. With an additional four local men we left the following morning, having sent on word to a village above Timure that a guide would be wanted. At Timure we quitted the valley to strike in a brutally direct manner up the pine-clad hillside. In the three days to the lake this uncompromising track continued as it had begun, seldom conceding anything to weakness by making a zigzag.

At the hamlet of Kedet at about 8,000 ft. we had to wait for our guide who had regarded the message, perhaps not unnaturally, as a rather crude leg-pull. While he accustomed his ideas to unwelcome reality and the knowledge that his hour had struck, we refreshed ourselves with charred potatoes and beer which, from its colour, one concluded had been drawn from the Milk Lake. At length all was ready and, after some more hard going, we camped at an abandoned monastery at about 10,000 ft. The last two days in the main valley had been bright, but from now until our premature return a week later we hardly saw the sun. At Rasua, however, it continued fine, thus confirming our impression that, for some reason, the main valley received less rain than the tributary valleys. Probably it is a question of altitude rather than the lie of the land. At this time we considered the monsoon to be extremely heavy, while at Katmandu they had begun to talk of it failing.

Leeches now began, literally, to intrude upon our attention. They, too, seemed to vary in numbers with the altitude. In the main valley there were none, above Kedet a few stragglers or harbingers of the coming storm, and then ever-increasing numbers which reached their maximum at 11,000 and 12,000 ft. But height is only one factor; later in the year we met them elsewhere at much lower altitudes in yet greater numbers.

An account in the *Journal of the Bombay Natural History Society* by Mr B. E. Smythies of a journey from Katmandu to the Gangja La along a part of the pilgrim track to Gosainkund, which, as a forest officer, he had been allowed to make, had filled me with foreboding. At one place he had had to put up a mosquito net to ward off leeches at night. At Calcutta I had made some enquiries as to whether a war which had seen the invention of atomic bombs and self-heating soups had not also given birth to something of more general benefit such as a leech repellent. My surmise was correct. The back-room boys had taken time off from nuclear fission to scribble the required formula. Dimethylphthalate or DMP the stuff was called. In Calcutta there was none to be had. Either it had not been a success or some War Disposals Board had sold it as toothpaste. I learnt, however, that an anti-mosquito preparation called 'Squitofax' contained a small quantity of the right venom, and sure enough a little smeared round the top of the boots or ankle puttees did discourage leeches from exploring higher. Paraffin, brine, or dry salt rubbed in, are no less effective, and are likely to be on hand in the most casually equipped expedition. With a moderate infestation, the wearing of boots with sewn-in tongues, ankle puttees and trousers, is good protection, as the leeches can be either flicked off individually when they begin climbing one's legs, or left to amuse or choke themselves in the eyelets of one's boots. Sometimes one or two unusually gifted or agile creatures manage to penetrate the defences to enjoy a well-earned drink without the blood donor's knowledge. The local men used to provide us with little bamboo sticks for brushing off leeches; for in picking or flicking them off with the fingers one is apt to be so flurried by their clinging ways as to flick them on to the back of the man in front.

The great majority of leeches get in on the ground floor, that is, by way of the boots. Half of these may be so small or so emaciated, perhaps no bigger than threads, that they are unable to aspire higher. But the robust fellows, one or two inches long, black, brown, or yellow, soon satisfy themselves that there is no nutriment in leather and advance with great rapidity up the trousers, making for the soft under-belly. If they are in strength, thirty, forty, or fifty of them, all climbing at once, then there is nothing for it but to halt, take off one's rucksack, and set to work to get rid of them with both hands or with the stick, a process which may have to be repeated every two or three hundred yards until clear of the badly infested area. Before moving on after these mopping-up operations the wise man has a good look at his rucksack; if any leeches are left lurking there they have a very easy covered approach to the back of one's neck. On the way back in September we passed through one or two really badly infested places, so bad that it might have been worth while soaking one's trousers in paraffin or brine. Whether the smell of the one or the hygroscopic effect of the other would be more insupportable than leeches is questionable. Walking along a leech-infested path one is usually fully occupied with home affairs, but it was interesting to note how the weight of the attack upon different men varied. The Europeans were easily the most acquisitive, and if one of us suffered more leech bites than another, it could be attributed to carelessness or to walking alone with nobody behind to give warning of an impending stab in the back. The Sherpas seemed to have less trouble keeping themselves free, seldom arriving in camp with a tell-tale trickle of blood or blood-soaked socks. As they were usually carrying salt and paraffin they may have made free use of it, but the fact that even their boots seemed to attract fewer leeches than mine annoyed me. In such matters there is much to be said for equality of misery. They, however, were far excelled by the local men who, in some miraculous way, remained more or less unscathed in spite of their bare feet and legs. I hesitate to say whether they possess some inherent immunity or whether they achieved it by extreme deftness in placing their feet and avoiding contact with the hundreds of menacing, weaving heads, stretching out hungrily from every stone, twig, or blade of grass.

From Gompaling the path mounted as abruptly and unswervingly upright as ever, until at last it landed us by a cairn on a sort of promontory. Not far away on the mist-wreathed hillside we saw a stone shelter and some cows. This place they called Nyangsusa, the place of the 'nyang' or tahr, and its height cannot have been much below 13,000 ft. Having got there about midday and having drunk a great deal of milk, pressed on us by the Sherpas as a sort of sedative, we were told that there was no question of going on. In this matter of camping, the regular staff, like the Sherpas, do as they are told. If there are only two or three local men in the party their views can be safely ignored, but if they outnumber the Sherpas then they will probably decide where the party is to camp. They may be cajoled with extraordinary eloquence or sometimes bribed to go on; but no ordinary bribe will do because it is no use offering an extra day's pay for a double march when they can earn the same by doing it in two easy stages. We had therefore to settle down to eighteen hours upon our backs. A wet fog discouraged sightseeing; it was not good beetling weather; and only Polunin found occupation in a meadow where pink and crimson anemones, orange potentilla, and tall white primulas, all but hid the grass. Thick carpets of moss covering the boulders testified to the wetness of this place, but we had not yet plumbed the profoundest depths of humidity.

We began the final climb to the Dudh lakes (there was an upper and a lower) on a dull morning after a wet night. But soon the sulky clouds slowly drew apart revealing a rain-washed, livid, spacious landscape, and in the distance, above a more solid bank of cloud, rose four high peaks. They were the Ganesh Himal, one of which, a great snowy dome, seemed to invite a closer aquaintance. To the north the Trisuli valley lay clear for several miles beyond Rasua to the neighbourhood of Kyerong, which the guide, without much fear of contradiction, declared he could see. It took time to persuade him that the lower lake which we presently reached, though a lovely place for a picnic, was not our goal, and then the party settled down to heavy collar work up a long scree slope. The faint path landed us, without much obvious purpose, at the foot of a gully which looked too rough and steep even for goats. Encouraged by a diminutive but undeniable cairn the Sherpas led the spreadeagled field up 500 ft. to a sort of pass at about 16,000 ft. In the clammy mist we could see nothing from this vantage point beyond the ill-defined path at our feet. Passing over a desolate but calm sea of flat slabs, the path began descending to a grass shoulder at the foot of which lay the lake, some two acres in extent and of a cloudy green. Its opacity showed that the water came from a glacier which, we judged by the height, could not be far away. Indeed, we soon learnt that it was near from the characteristic sounds, which reminded me of how the discoverers of Jan Mayen island, in similarly thick weather, had found the land by ear rather than by eye.

There were no sheep about, nor had any been there for some time, but under some big boulders were the shelters once used by the shepherds. As to our whereabouts we had no clue, except that the water of the lake drained north-westwards, probably into the Lende Khola. But at sundown, with dramatic suddenness, the clouds vanished. One moment we looked across the forlorn lake to a grey void, the next to a mountain which to our astonished gaze seemed about to topple into the lake. In *Letters from High Latitudes* Lord Dufferin describes an even more startling revelation—that of the summit of Beerenberg on Jan Mayen seen from the deck of the *Foam*; 'the solid roof of grey suddenly split asunder, and I beheld through the gap thousands of feet overhead, as if suspended in the crystal sky—a cone of illuminated snow. There at last was the long sought for mountain actually tumbling down upon our heads.' Our vision gave us more astonishment than delight, for this was undoubtedly the 21,500 ft. peak well to the west of Langtang Lirung. At least we now knew where we were, and it was a long way from the northern slopes of Lirung. Not caring much for the look of this peak we decided to ignore it, flattering ourselves that we were after bigger game. Nevertheless, there was no ignoring a long, spiny ridge which it thrust out to the north and which somehow we must cross.

Scott was not well, Polunin had plenty to occupy him, so Lloyd and I decided to go on with three Sherpas and five Langtang men, the local guides having reached the uttermost bourn of their knowledge. We could carry enough food for an absence of ten days. A wet night delayed our start—the tents having to be dried a little—but the clouds remained high enough for us to see that a crossing of the spiny ridge must be sought for lower down. Though much might be hoped for from time and chance, yet we heartily grudged having to throw away any hard-earned height, well knowing that we could not throw away much before becoming involved in a bush-crawl. The chief incentive for attempting a shot in the dark such as this Dudh Khund trip lay in the fact that at 14,000 ft. vegetation ceases and movement becomes easier.

In the expectation of having not to descend very far, and resolute against doing so, we set off light-heartedly down an old grass-covered moraine by the side of the lake stream, our enemy the ridge on the other. Height, like money, is slowly won and quickly lost; no miser could have viewed with more anguish his dwindling hoard of gold than did we our rapidly diminishing height. After going for half an hour, during which we must have dropped 1,500 ft., we called a halt while Lloyd and I crossed the stream to prospect a possible route across the ridge. Apart from finding some lovely blue poppies (*Meconopsis horridula*), we wasted our time. The route proved too 'thin' for laden men, so we returned and continued the descent. From grass to a strong growth of dwarf rhododendron was but a short transition, and soon we began grappling with their full-sized relatives, backed by assorted juniper, bamboo and thorn.

Wingate, of Burma fame, used to tell his chindits never to report jungle as impenetrable without first penetrating it; and for men with cutting weapons and strong arms there should be no such thing as the 'impenetrable jungle' in which travellers frequently find themselves. But before demonstrating practically the truth of this one ought to be clear about the distance to be penetrated and convinced that the effort is worthwhile. In our case we were sure of neither, and even if our followers agreed to try we had neither time nor energy to spare to hack out a trail for three or four days. While Lloyd and I, sitting on a boulder in a stream—the only space free from jungle—discussed this, one of the local men volunteered the information that the north side of the Langtang might be reached by marching for one day up the Tibetan side of the Lende Khola and crossing back into Nepal by a bridge of whose existence he knew. Lamenting that he had not mentioned it before we had left Rasua Garhi we decided to cut our losses. In three rain-soaked hours, the measure of our rash descent, we climbed back to the lake.

Although this decision was probably wise, our losses proved to be irretrievable. Three days later we found that the bridge in question had been washed away, with the result that we were obliged to spend a second day on the north side of the river on the way to another bridge farther upstream. Delay, as it has often done before, proved fatal to our hopes. The arrival in our camp of a stout, affable official, in Homburg hat and dark spectacles sent expressly for the purpose, reminded us that we were on the wrong side of the Lende Khola.

CHAPTER SIX

The Ganesh Himal

THUS foiled we turned westwards to the Ganesh Himal; Lloyd and I still in pursuit of a peak we could climb—for none of the Langtang peaks seemed in that category—and the others, who all the time had been busy after their kind, in search of fresh ground. So far the uniformity of the rock and the absence of any fossils had failed to please our geologist. Fossils, of course, are desirable finds which even a layman can recognize. But if every bit of rock held a tell-tale fossil, geology would be little better than stamp-collecting—a pastime at the mercy of any fool with a magnifying glass—instead of a highly speculative science interpreting earth history in its own melodious but difficult language.

After a day's rest to give Scott a chance to recover from a bout of dysentery (for which he was being treated without aggravating effect with pomegranate bark), and to write letters of apology to Kyerong, we set off down the valley. (Happily the incident at the close of the previous chapter, upon which one would hardly wish to dwell, had no political repercussions.) Short of Syabrubensi we crossed the Trisuli by a wooden cantilever bridge, climbed over a spur, and entered the valley of the Chilime. This river, the sole drainage for the eastern side of the Ganesh Himal, was much smaller than either the Langtang or the Lende Khola; while Thangiet, which had loomed so important on the map, comprised three small, dirty, decaying villages inhabited incongruously by Newars. Obviously we would get no porters there, so, late though it was, we pushed on to Chilime. Inhabited by Tamangs, this village seemed more prosperous but no more salubrious. Sitting in a drizzle in a muddy rice stubble I paid off all but three of our local coolies, while the lieutenant harangued the astonished headman on the subject of mat shelters and the necessity for speed in erecting them.

Leaving Scott temporarily in the care of the escort, together with Toni who needed more catapult practice, we started next day (13 July) with ten coolies carrying three weeks' food. We had the usual difficulty in getting clear of the village, the seven Chilime coolies having to fettle themselves up, admonish their wives, and eat their breakfasts. Poor specimens of *homo sapiens* they were, too, as we presently found, weak in the legs and not very strong in their heads. A few miles up the valley we crossed the river to the right bank where, rather to our surprise, the track abandoned the valley altogether. We had little confidence in the Chilime men as guides. They could give us only the vaguest information about camp sites; invariably there was nothing, or nothing better, anywhere beyond where we had halted to make the enquiry. They seemed stunned with the magnitude of their task or with remorse at leaving their families. The camp site at which we finally stopped quite early in the afternoon proved to be the most dismal imaginable; a quagmire in a clearing, tenanted for the most part with giant stinging-nettles, horse-flies, and gloomy oaks dripping with moss, and carrying on their branches whole gardens of ferns. That night it rained too hard and too persistently for our tents which before this had begun to drip on less provocation. We found that a gas-cape draped over one end allowed the inmate to focus the drips on one spot. A high-altitude single-fly tent cannot be completely rain-proof, but it should withstand a lot of rain provided care is taken not to touch the inside of the fabric. A piece of advice, to a man in a small tent, like advising a man on a tight-rope not to fall off.

The drizzle which continued all day was of little consequence because the forest already ran with water; the path was a stream, the trees dripped, and every bamboo one touched shook down a shower. However, this damp misery expedited the march. Instead of halting every few minutes for a chat and a smoke, the coolies stopped only when forced to by the stress of their loads. The gurgle and splash of water everywhere nearly brought us into collision with two black bears who were fighting or playing in the bed of a stream about twenty yards away and failed to hear us. Considering their terrifying snarls and the hearty clouts they administered to each other, one could not help wishing to remain unnoticed by such rough customers. But suddenly they took alarm and crashed off, evidently more frightened than we were.

At the time we three were well ahead of the porters, who were too far behind even to hear the noise made by the beasts as they cleared off. Nevertheless a circumstantial account was soon current throughout the district of how the old 'gazebo' (me) had beaten off with his ice-axe the attacks of two of the biggest, blackest and most ferocious bears ever seen.

Thus easily are reputations acquired among a simple people. Had I become resident in the Langtang, devoting my time to talking about bears I had met and carefully avoiding meeting any others, I should no doubt have become the greatest living authority, the man who killed bears with his naked hands. This black Himalayan bear (*Ursus Tibetanus*, I hope and believe) is our carnivorous, sheep-slaughtering friend of the Langtang. But meat is probably a luxury for him. Like ourselves, he makes do on bamboo shoots, wheat, maize and millet in their season. In standing crops one sees a little 'machan' built for the safety and convenience of the bear-scarer. According to all accounts the black bear's sight and hearing are good, and he is very savage, whereas the two we met were deaf, blind and very timid. But it would never do to presume on the truth of our casual observations.

That afternoon we won clear of the obscene forest and camped at a kharka where there was the usual long mat-roofed shelter like an elongated Nissen hut. We fared very well on milk and the eggs and honey we had brought from below. This honey, dark brown and of a pleasingly original flavour, was so thin that it could be eaten only with a spoon, a fault at which few could cavil.

The next march, which took us into the upper part of the main valley, was long and trying. it rained all the previous night and forbore to let up during the day. But this was customary in the Ganesh Himal which receives more than its fair share of monsoon—or so it seemed to us who lived and moved in a world of mist and drizzle, the sun extinguished apparently for good. Nor did the path improve. One could sympathize with its pioneers whose simple plan had been to climb as quickly as possible until clear of the slime, nettles, bears, horse-flies, leeches, sodden firewood, fern-festooned trees and dripping bamboos, and then to enjoy an easy ridge walk until the opportunity for descending to the grass of the upper Chilime presented itself. The ridge, when attained, was not so easy as all that, for the sharp spines of several lateral ridges had to be crossed like so many miniature passes, and it was so high that even in summer it held beds of old snow.

We began the day with a long and brutal grind up to the ridge, where we waited long in the rain while the suffering coolies reluctantly crawled up in their own good time. The last to arrive, a man of resource, put on such a convincing act of agony and imminent dissolution that he deceived us all and reaped the reward of cunning by being sent back. His loss and the subsequent reorganization left us to carry our own big rucksacks which at any rate served to keep our backs dry. Luckily some of the ghums brought from Katmandu remained serviceable enough to protect the loads of atta and satu which are speedily ruined by wet. These ghums or mats, bent length-wise and worn over the head like a roof, keep man and load dry.

Late in the afternoon, when the field was strung out over several miles of an arduous course, the leaders came to the last and steepest of climbs to the highest of the miniature passes. We did not know if it was the last, but obviously it was the last the porters would face provided they got so far. On an unknown track, a steep climb coming at the end of a long march will make most coolies cry 'capevi'; if, under such circumstances, one decides to push on one must be prepared to do without some of the loads. Happily, the track now took a decided turn downhill, at first over boulders and scree, then over kindly grass, until out of the mist below came the welcome bleating of sheep. After following a small but turbulent glacier stream for a short way we came at last to a lush meadow alive with sheep and goats, and, in my opinion, vastly imporved by the presence of several mat shelters. Warding off the attacks of savage dogs with stones, we made for the nearest shelter, pushed aside the mat door and unceremoniously squeezed our dripping bodies round the fire.

The shepherds plied us with cheese, tasting like dried milk that had somehow got wet, and cheered us with the news that eight days previously they had enjoyed a fine day. When the porters began dribbling in we pitched our tents and retired to wet sleeping-bags. In Nepal the absence of roomy accommodation such as yorts provide is a great drawback, for the mat shelter is too like a miniature railway tunnel, including the smoke. It is too low to stand upright, there is not much room round the fire, and the outer darkness beyond the fire is taken up with utensils or lambs and young yaks. Two porters who failed to turn up spent their night under a rock on the cold hillside—a misfortune we bore with fortitude since the loads held none of our immediate wants except the dried yeast. If possible we always liked to make bread. When this was not possible I preferred the kind made by the Sherpas— what I called Solu Khumbu bread—to the poor chapatties a hillman usually makes. All that the Sherpas do is to mix flour and water to a dropping consistency and to pour it on to a hot iron plate. Bread so made, light and full of holes, is more digestible than chapatties when made by the average Sherpa who has not the art of turning out the delicious, wafer-thin chapattie of the expert. Another popular bread in India is the 'paratta' which is merely a chapattie thrown into boiling fat, where it immediately blows itself out into a hollow and delightfully crisp biscuit. A Sherpa's heavy-handed version of a chapattie upon being thrown into boiling fat merely sucks up the hot fat and blows itself out when inside the stomach of the man foolish enough to eat it.

Travellers in regions of stubborn mist should not be impatient. To an even greater degree, those shy, reluctant, provoking ways in which a sinuous glacier valley gives up its secrets, will have to be suffered or perhaps enjoyed. In the morning we were permitted to see a little more than our immediate surroundings. Up towards the ridge by which we had come lay a small glacier which we guessed descended from a modest 19,451 ft. mountain named Paldor. Westwards lay a much bigger glacier, and beyond it a wonderful great mountain whose long and spiky summit ridge at once removed it from the category of climbable peaks. In the Himalaya a peak with a name, unless it is a very giant, is not common, so we decided to go in search of Paldor whose name at any rate gave it some significance. Accordingly Lloyd and I with Tensing and Da Namgyal set off with a two-day camp.

A kindly moraine took us directly up until we could step easily on to the dry ice of the lower glacier which we presently forsook for a big cone of hard avalanche snow. Before entering the gully from which this had poured down, we broke out onto the rocks on one side in order to put a camp on a ledge a few hundred feet higher. We reckoned we were about 17,000 ft., high enough to bring Paldor within reach. Rain soon drove us to our tents, but later the weather cleared enough to allow us to see another thousand feet of our route. Starting at 6 a.m. on a cloudy morning we traversed back to the glacier, crossed it, and climbed a long snow slope to a plateau from where at last we saw our mountain. Having gained a ridge, steep on both sides but not difficult, we had only to follow it to the summit. As we mounted the snow became worse. Just below the summit my axe went in to the head without finding any hard snow to bite on. By 9.30 we were on top. In better weather we should have had a rewarding view, for Paldor is a southern outlier of the Ganesh group and from it we should have seen down the Trisuli valley to the plains. Its prominence when viewed from the south accounted no doubt for its having a name. On the descent the snow resembled porridge, but we soon sank the long slope by first starting an avalanche and glissading down the hard snow in its wake. Having packed up we went down in mist and drizzle to the sheepfold, well pleased with the success of this modest sortie.

Although there had been no sun all day and although he had worn his glasses most of the time, Tensing had a sharp attack of snow-blindness as a result of this excursion. Lloyd and I went up to look at the big glacier to the west in order to assure ourselves it held no surprises like the Langtang. Having crossed the river by a natural rock bridge at another kharka, we walked along the top of a high and very regular moraine until we could see the ice-fall marking the termination of the glacier. Scott joined us that evening bringing with him 150 eggs, a pumpkin, chillies, and a wooden jorum of Tibetan arak. These wooden jorums are thick and hold less than the eye imagines or the rude mountaineer requires. We were relieved therefore to hear that he disliked the stuff.

With nothing more to be done from this camp we moved the whole outfit to another valley. The track crossed the river below the kharka where a great boulder leant over leaving a gap of only a few feet to be bridged. It then turned down-stream, obviously heading for the junction of the two valleys. With one accord we four, who were in the van, followed it, but after ambling pleasantly downhill for a mile I became uneasy about the porters. Returning hotfoot to the bridge I learnt from a shepherd that they had gone straight up the hillside, and presently, in a break in the mist, I spotted them. The other three, enjoying too much the novelty of going downhill, had a sterner chase and a sharper lesson.

Having topped the intervening ridge we dropped a couple of thousand feet to the second and bigger valley and camped in some deserted stone huts by the river. Their stone walls and flagged floors lay open to the sky, but the poles and the wood slabs or shingles for the roof were neatly stacked inside. All we needed were the poles, for we had with us two big ground-sheets (18 ft. x 12 ft.) of very light material which had proved invaluable throughout our journey. With these we made a snug billet, big enough for the whole party, which allowed us to have one fire for cooking and another where we could sit and where Polunin could dry his plants. If it was not ecstasy it was undoubtedly comfort we enjoyed that night sitting round the fire, drinking the last arak in order to subdue or mollify a curious meal of rice and fungi, while outside the rain hissed down and the river roared.

Shortly after our arrival we had a visit from the owners of the huts, who were then living on the other side of the river grazing their yaks. They were Tibetans from Paimanesa, a place a few miles north of Rasua, whence there is a direct path over a pass to the upper Chilime valley. Believing they were in Tibet they regarded us as trespassers. We, however, knew that they were, for the frontier lies north of the main range at this point and coincides with it again a few miles to the west at the big Ganesh peak of 24,299 ft. This peak, which we suspected to be the snowy dome we had seen from near the Dudh Kund lake, had so far eluded us.

At dawn next morning, as if in answer to our prayer, the sight of a great mountain completely filling the head of the valley surprised and delighted us. So perfect were its proportions that at first glance it did not look its full height, but a bearing to it convinced us that it was indeed the highest of the Ganesh group, one which might be called Ganesh mountain. The south-west ridge, if it could be attained, seemed to offer a straightforward way to the summit of this 'snowy pleasure dome'. In spite of the arak Lloyd had stomach trouble, so Polunin and I set off up a valley which bid fair to rival the large richness of the Langtang. Extensive meadows lay on both banks of the river up to the point where it issued from the glacier, and beyond that a wide and grassy ablation valley rose in a series of four long steps.

The abundance of new flowers—a delicate bluebell-shaped codonopsis, purple aconite, crimson and cream louseworts—had persuaded Polunin to stop long before we came to a lake nestling below the moraine at about 16,000 ft. A half mile above the lake the moraine ran out in rock and scree, down which I hurried to the glacier. The mountain, now wreathed in cloud, lay across the glacier which swept out of sight round a buttress at the foot of the south ridge. Making fast going on smooth dry ice I pushed on up the middle until the whole glacier bay came into view—a cirque made up of four monstrously steep and broken ice-falls. Two of these ice cataracts flowed down from the Ganesh peak and two from Pabil (23,361 ft.) which lay to the south-west. There seemed to be no other way on to Ganesh but by the buttress which was separated from the easy south-west ridge by the whole breadth of two ice-falls. Of these only the lower thousand feet of dirty, broken ice could be seen, dropping apparently out of the cloud layer above. On the glacier at the foot of each lay the piled debris of fallen seracs and between them ran a line of black crags. On such a dismal scene, like a dirty, dismantled stage with the curtain only half raised, I was ready to turn my back.

An omelette of six eggs, bread, honey and cake restored the body, but my mind was still haunted by the gloom of that sepulchral cirque, so fearfully savage and black. Yet next day Lloyd and I camped by the Green Lake, as it was called. The name Yang-tso is Tibetan, and as one might expect the water has a bright green hue owing to the quantity of algae growing in it. On our way to the lake the mountain had remained surprisingly clear so that by the time we reached it we had examined and rejected the routes above the buttress, the only weak point in its well-defended lower parts. In the afternoon we discovered that the south-west ridge sprang from a very high col from which one of the tumbled ice torrents descended. The rocks to one side of this seemed a possible route but to reach them we should have to climb some ice-worn slabs immediately under the rotting face of the ice-fall. Back we went down the valley, like that Duke of York who marched his men to the top of a hill and marched them down again.

Meantime Polunin was having a lot of fun with his flowers, being compelled to hang the whole of the billet with drying racks. Scott had turned his attention to a new game, taking rubbings of glacier ice to determine the crystallization at various depths. We must return soon to the Langtang where Lloyd had to tie up the loose ends of the survey, but before leaving I determined to have a final look at the ice-fall which I felt we had not thoroughly examined. For the third time Tensing and I went up, reaching the cirque, six miles up and several thousands of feet higher by 10.30. Climbing over the debris of ice-blocks to the cliffs of the cirque we sat close under them for safety's sake while we examined the ugly decaying wall of ice a hundred yards away. The ice had either retreated or a chunk had calved off, leaving a narrow passage of ice-worn slabs from which, a few hundred feet up, the rocks to the left of the ice-fall could be gained. The ice-fall was far too steep and broken to be climbable. Leaving Tensing, I went up close to the ice to satisfy myself that the slabs could be climbed, or what was equally important, whether they could be climbed in safety. Small fragments of ice whizzing viciously by seemed to hint that they could not. Moreover, a mass of debris showed that seracs had recently broken away from the wall, while the neighbouring cataract, flowing down from Pabil, sent down a frequent discharge of ice blocks.

The greatest drawback to climbing in monsoon conditions, greater even than the bad visibility, is the high temperature. After the monsoon began in June I doubt if it froze on more than one or two nights even at a height of 19,000 ft. The height of this place was about 17,000 ft., but had the nights been really cold one might have climbed under this wall in perfect safety. To weigh the risks attendant upon climbing such a place is a difficult part of the mountaineer's job. Such risks are not easy to assess, especially if there is a very desirable prize to be snatched at the cost of a short exposure to them. If a man refuses to take risks there is nothing to show that he has done right, while if they are taken the proof that he has done wrong may be too conclusive. Had we been able to climb this ticklish place swiftly without loads, or better still without porters, one might not have hesitated, but now prudence or funk prevailed. I regretted the absence of Lloyd who had gone crystal-gazing with Scott, nor was it any use trying to put the onus on Tensing who merely eyed the place lugubriously and said: 'As the Sahib wishes.' Long afterwards I used to lie awake at night tormented by mocking visions of this snowy dome.

We returned by a new route on the long ridge bounding the north side of the main Chilime valley, three of the Tibetans coming with us as carriers and guides. They assured us we should do it in two days, as in fact we did, but had their memories of the route been fresher I feel sure they would have allowed twice that time. No one goes so far or so fast as the man who does not know where he is going. As usual the morning was wet, but it passed pleasantly enough on a gentle ascent where we were refreshed both by many showers and by the sight of new flowers, among them a sort of clover of an intense gentian-like blue. By the time we had crossed two lesser ridges and landed fairly on the main ridge, it was drawing towards three o'clock, high time to ask the guides where they proposed to stop. Whereupon they told us of a pleasant kharka, crawling with yaks, close to a lake to which presently we should begin to descend. The path thought differently. It began to ascend, becoming every moment rougher and more difficult to follow. No one seemed to have used it for many years and when we heard a dog barking in the mist far below I made sure we were wrong.

By now the guides were at the tail of the column a mile back, but the Sherpas assured us we were still on a path and indeed we had now little choice but to follow the woodless and waterless ridge to which we were committed. At six o'clock we came to a deserted kharka where there was not a trace of water, so we pushed on in the gathering gloom of dusk. The mist had gone. Far to the north above the deep indigo of the valleys, already dark in shadow, the pale summits of scores of Tibetan peaks stood out against a leaden sky. Away beyond the black chasm of the Trisuli gorge we saw for the first time the northern slopes of Langtang Lirung. Just before dark we came to another abandoned kharka and again we could find neither wood nor water, essentials which no traveller in Nepal would expect ever to be scarce. Not much relishing the prospect of a thirsty night Lloyd and I, with commendable spirit, launched ourselves down a neighbouring gully, quite determined to go down till we found water and hardly expecting to have to climb back. Having that in mind we descended rapidly with careless abandon. I may have gone down two thousand feet, or perhaps only one, when a faint bellow from above informed me that the coolies refused to follow. Argument was impossible at that range and I remained needlessly puzzled by the recalcitrance of the coolies who, in fact, knew where the water was and had found it. Dragging myself wearily upwards in the dark, full of angry conjecture, I had within me 'a speech of fire that fain would blaze' until at the top the news that water had been found doused it.

Throughout the night it rained cheerfully and we breakfasted in the open in a fine drizzle. Sipping hot tea I regarded with perfect equanimity, almost with satisfaction, the damp, huddled heap of Tibetans who had led us such a long dance along a waterless ridge. Presently the rain stopped, the sun came out. Secure now in the knowledge of where we were going, we enjoyed to the full a long downhill march through all the variegated regions of heath, rhododendron, bamboo, tall silver fir, until we emerged in the yellowing wheat-fields of the Chilime valley.

CHAPTER SEVEN

The Langtang Again

WHENEVER we returned to our base the lieutenant, a most able quartermaster, generally had something good for us to eat. This time he had procured some mangoes from Trisuli bazaar and some locally grown rice, an upland variety of a reddish colour. With the help of twenty-one Chilime coolies of both sexes, many goitrous, and all exceeding poor and beggarly, we moved to Syabrubensi at the junction of the Langtang Khola. From there we sent the havildar and the escort back to Katmandu with some spare loads, and with a diminished party climbed again to Syarpagaon. In spite of their goitres the coolies went well.

We reached Langtang village on 1 August to find it more or less empty, the people having gone to the upper gompa near the snout of the Lirung glacier for a religious festival. With some difficulty we got together a team of five boys and so were able to move on next day. Polunin and his entourage stayed behind to cope with a fresh flush of flowers—notably a delphinium of a right royal blue, a deep purple trumpet-shaped cyananthus, a giant thistle with a head of pink flowers, yellow violets and forget-me-nots. On the way up we met the Langtang people coming down, reeking so abominably of beer that they seemed less like religious celebrants than belated revellers. The weather had momentarily improved. The gloomy permanence of the cloud canopy was broken by a succession of several clear mornings which gave Lloyd a welcome chance to complete the survey. Leaving him thus engaged at Langsisa, Scott and I with two Sherpas and a local man set out to visit the col at the head of the west Langtang glacier which we had already looked down upon from the head of the main glacier.

In order to take advantage of the bend we followed the left bank of the glacier, but when the moraine petered out we were forced away from the glacier up steep scree. What with fatigue and falling rain we were in no mood to be nice about a choice of camp site; so we stopped in a gully at the first available water, a horrible place, with one tent pitched perforce 50 ft. above the other and both on cramped platforms. Angtharkay, who was no fairy on his feet, brought our food down from the upper tent where they had a fire and with it a young avalanche of stones—a contingency we had provided for by placing our tent under the lee of a boulder.

From a distant glimpse I had of the col on a reconnaissance made that evening I decided to reach it without making another camp. We therefore started before daylight, crossed the dry glacier, and climbed a huge avalanche cone on the other side. By sun-up we had begun the long, almost level snow trudge to the col, passing on our right the two cols from which we had looked down to this glacier two months before. Then it had been all dry ice, whereas now there were two or three feet of snow of that trying kind with a hard crust which sometimes supported the feet and sometimes didn't. Whether it is better to try to remain on top of snow like this by treading delicately, or to break the crust purposefully at each step to secure a solid foundation, depends upon whether one is in front or behind. Those behind naturally prefer the leader to stamp manfully at each step. On this occasion, having snowshoes on, I trod like a cat, hopefully ignoring such preferences until a series of violent tugs on the rope indicated that one or both of my followers had sunk waist-deep. Having climbed the low rock ridge upon which the col lay we looked once more into Tibet, to the broad, grey band of the Chasuchen glacier 2,000 ft. below. The height of this col was 19,500 ft. Tensing agreed that a camp could not be carried down. We might have got down without loads, but our plan was to spend a week there with the machine in order to fix the position of Gosainthan. Since that questionable glimpse of a big mountain from the first station we had seen neither it nor any likely rival. When we came to return, no problems in technique suggested themselves. Whether one stamped or not the snow offered no resistance; snowshoes were worse than useless, for at each step a great fid of wet snow remained on the shoe to be lifted. We spent another night at the same camp, too tired to mind its vertical lay-out or its noisiness. As a sort of second to the thunderous bass occasioned by Angtharkay's earth-shaking footsteps, there was a continuous roar, swelling and diminishing, caused by the cataracts of mingled rock and snow pouring down the gullies of the mountain across the glacier.

In the course of our walk back to Langsisa, from a new and more hopeful angle I tried to assess the chances of grasping a long-coveted prize, the Fluted Peak. The moraine down which we strode was worth studying too. Besides great numbers of blue and yellow poppies, gorgeous cyananthus, and the blue codonopsis we had met in the Ganesh Himal, there was a very beautiful dusty blue flower with a ravishing scent; it was a dwarf, hairy delphinium (*D. brunonianum*). According to Tensing its dried flowers are a preventative or at any rate a discourager of lice. The Langtang people used it for this purpose, but obviously did not use enough.

Two days later the whole party met again at the upper gompa, Kyangjin Ghyang. Only ten days remained before Lloyd and Scott had to start for home, time enough perhaps to snatch victory from defeat. For while it was a comfort to reflect that our mountaineering activities would be veiled under the more respectable cloak of science, there was no concealing from ourselves that as a climbing holiday it had been a failure. That is to say climbing of a more advance kind than the snow-plodding, boulder-hopping, and scree-scrambling which the Himalaya impose on their votaries as a daily task. For most expeditions this sort of hard labour, along with bouts of load carrying, becomes the accustomed background. A background sombre enough at times, in all conscience, so that if when in camp one is obliged to read Dostoyevski (as I was) one begins to think that only a writer of the Russian school of resignation and pity could successfully limn its darkest shadows. But it is not as bad as that. I would not wish anyone to believe that because such arduous day-to-day exertions are passed over more or less in silence the Himalayan climber is therefore a man of ape-like strength and agility, with an immense capacity for breathing rarefied air, drinking melted snow or raw spirit, and eating fungi and bamboo shoots. True, on occasions he must live hard or exert himself to the point of exhaustion, necessarily when at grips with a big peak; but for the most part his condition is one of ease bordering upon comfort; he suffers from heat rather than from cold, from muscular atrophy rather than nervous exhaustion; and for a variety of reasons—the weather, the worsening snow, the porters' fatigue— his days are usually short. Thus he spends more time on his back than on his feet. His occupational disease is bedsores, and a box of books his most cherished load.

The weather's brief respite had ended. It was as unpropitious as it could be, with whole days of mist and drizzle, when Lloyd and I decided to have a go at the Fluted Peak. Nothing else offered. Our project for spending a week on the Chasuchen glacier on the Tibetan side had fallen through, and there was no other peak more desirable or so apparently climbable as the Fluted Peak. Accordingly, on 10 August, with three Sherpas and two Langtang men, we crossed the river by a bridge and turned up the left bank. The grazing on this side, which is almost as good as the other, is apparently reserved for sheep and goats brought from outside the valley. One large flock, we were told, belonged to a member of the Rana family, and another to the villages near Chilime. Having reached a point opposite the big moraine of the west Langtang glacier we turned eastwards up a side nallah and camped at a kharka not far below the snout of a fair-sized glacier.

In the wretched prevailing weather the shelter of a mat hut was not to be lightly forsaken. Moreover, he who knows not whither to go is in no hurry to move, and we were uncertain of the whereabouts of our peak, having seen nothing of it for several days. We spent the morning on the high terminal moraine peering into the misty void across the glacier. There was less mist up the glacier where we could see the col at its head nearly two miles away; and where I was sure there must be a biggish peak—probably the Fluted Peak—to account for the glacier. Lloyd did not agree. Nevertheless, on my confident advice we decided to put a camp on a rock island below the col. In the extravagant hope of 'doing a station' Lloyd left early with the machine to climb a hill behind the kharka, and later the rest of us struck camp and began moving up the glacier. About a mile up, happening at one of our too numerous halts to look back, I saw behind us, almost opposite the kharka, the top of the Fluted Peak glimmering high and white. The clearing lasted but a minute. Before even the critical 'step' on our chosen ridge, which we were anxious to see, had emerged, the clouds rolled down. Feeling a little foolish I sent the men across the glacier, in a direction almost opposite to our original line of march, to find a camp, while I loitered behind to pick up Lloyd to whom this welcome vision might not have been revealed. However, he had noted both the peak and our sudden right about turn, upon which he generously refrained from comment.

The Sherpas had found a pleasant oasis for the camp in the ablation valley, where against a convenient boulder they had rigged up a penthouse roof with the big groundsheet. Under this they slept and we ate, for it was very much drier than our tent. Next day the Langtang men went down while the three Sherpas came with us to carry a light camp up the mountain. After a couple of thousand feet of easy going we reached the first snow. The lower part of this south-west ridge is like a wedge with a base, some 400 yards wide, represented by a hanging glacier which converges to a point a thousand feet higher up. From the point the slender ice ridge lies back in a level step before springing up to the summit cone. On the extreme left-hand edge of the wedge where we first attacked it the ice had disappeared, exposing a narrow ledge of steep, loose rock with ice on one side and a precipitous drop on the other. As we climbed it grew steeper, and to avoid a particularly steep or loose bit of rock we had sometimes to move out on to the ice which was covered with a layer of wet unstable snow. We roped up and climbed very close together, for the slightest false step threatened to bring half the ridge in ruins about our ears. None of us liked it, least of all the Sherpas, especially when Lloyd, who was climbing ahead unroped, sent a large rock slithering down the ice just to one side of them. While Lloyd went on a little we called a halt, and when he reported no improvement and no place for a tent we retreated a short way, put up the tent, and sent the Sherpas down with instruction to return in a couple of days.

Climbing on a shattered ridge like this, which is a fair sample of most Himalayan ridges, one finds it difficult to resist the conclusion that were it not for the snow and ice the Himalaya would long ago have assumed the low rounded forms of British hills. When the snow goes there is nothing to stop the loose fragmented rocks of these high narrow ridges finding a more stable resting place in the valley below. Surely the geologist who climbs such a ridge, pondering the age of the mountains the while, and who feels it disintegrating so alarmingly under his possibly clumsy feet, will be inclined to lop a few millions of years from the aeons of his sublime guesses.

At midday snow began falling. Since we were camped at about 19,000 ft. this phenomenon would not have surprised us had it not been the first snowstorm we had experienced throughout the summer. The storm continued during the night, causing the tent roof to sag and leak, the temperature being above freezing-point. But even in a high camp, joy, of a strictly moderate kind, cometh with the morning. We turned out to find 6 in. of snow covering the rocks and a few trial steps taken on the nearby ice showed its snow covering to be as wet and unstable as it had been at midday. Any hope we may have still entertained of climbing the ridge—we had not yet seen the ice-step—was thus extinguished for the moment, so we packed up and departed, leaving the tent standing. We were surprised to find snow lying down to 17,000 ft., but at our oasis the rain, which fell steadily, was merely a trifle colder. Tensing, who had heard our jocund shouts upon the misty mountain, was pathetically trying to bake bread on a fire of green dwarf rhododendron leaves, so we sent the Sherpas back to the kharka for wood and milk and settled down to another twenty hours on our backs. We had spent a like time in a horizontal position the previous day. Apart from the danger of contracting bed-sores, and chilblains, too, which are encouraged by a sedentary life, I was heinously ill-provided for such long stretches upon the rack of idleness. The fact that I had already read *The Brothers Karamazov* and *The Last Chronicles of Barset* three times each is some measure of the wealth of our leisure and the poverty of our combined library.

Having decided to leave the mountain alone for a couple of days while the rocks freed themselves of snow we spent a morning walking up the glacier to the col at its head, more for the sake of something to do than for anything we were likely to see. Except for a short piece of soggy snow at the top we walked on dry ice, and in three hours were on the ridge at about 19,000 ft., peering into the familiar sea of cloud. We had, however, the satisfaction of standing on an important watershed, for the valley to the east drains into the Sun Kosi and not the Trisuli. The Kosi is the third most important of Himalayan rivers with a catchment area of 24,000 sq. miles—exceeded only by the Indus and the Brahmaputra, each of which has a catchment area of somewhere in the neighbourhood of 100,000 sq. miles.

Next day I lay at earth while Lloyd went up very early to the vicinity of our high camp to do a station. He had now more energy and went better than I who, after three not over strenuous months, suffered more and more from what one of the earliest climbers of Mont Blanc described as a 'lassitude which could not be conquered without the aid of liquor'—no less than forty-seven bottles of wine and brandy being required to overcome the lassitude of a party of eleven. When we returned to the attack we moved the high camp across to the other side of the wedge by traversing the rocks under the snout of the hanging glacier—on the face of it an unwise manœuvre, but we moved quickly and kept well clear.

Some snow which fell in the night did not deter us from beginning the climb soon after 5 a.m. On this edge of the hanging glacier a wider band of rock gave us more freedom of choice and the rocks were more stable; only when we had climbed about 500 ft. did the band narrow and finally disappear under the encroaching ice. Here and there rocks still protruded. By using these and by cutting across the intervening ice we reached a steep snow slope below the point where the two sides of the wedge converged. This route, which avoided the ice-step, would, we think, have gone easily in better conditions, but the slope consisted of wet snow lying on ice in which steps would have to be cut, the thick layer of snow having first been cleared away. If similar conditions prevailed for another thousand feet, which was a fair assumption, then the task was too great. We gave up.

The whole party met for the last time at Kyangjin gompa preparatory to the departure of Lloyd and Scott the next day, 20 August. With the assistance of the British High Commissioner's office in Bombay and Delhi the assassin's stickgun had at last reached us. Bird-skinner Toni (whom on account of his voracity I christened Wolfe Tone) could now begin making amends for his two months' idleness. After some wrangling over porters, for no one from Langtang seemed eager to visit his capital city, Lloyd and Scott started for the Gangja La and the direct route to Katmandu. Polunin with Toni went down the valley to spend a few days fossicking in the forest; while with two Sherpas

I went to make a second and more thorough inspection of the col at the head of the West glacier.

Instead of going to Langsisa we stopped at a kharka short of the big moraine with the intention this time of going up the west glacier by the true right bank. The kharka was occupied by herdsmen who were already beginning to move the cattle down from the higher pastures against the approach of the autumn. They told us that in winter two or three feet of snow lie in the valley but that the people remain, most of the men occupying themselves with trade to Kyirong, using sheep for transport. Curiously enough they never seemed to use yaks for carrying. Even when moving up to the higher kharkas the men themselves carried their mats, flour, milking and cooking utensils. In the course of conversation these herdsmen confirmed the existence, or rather the recent presence, of the Abominable Snowman in the Langtang, pointing out to us a cave which had been his favourite haunt. Six years previously these beasts (whose existence is surely no longer a matter for conjecture) had been constant visitors but had apparently migrated elsewhere. The small kind, the size of a child, they called 'chumi', while the big fellow went by the name of 'yilmu'. Since sceptics like to affirm that the tracks made by these creatures are in reality bear tracks, it is worth mentioning that the herdsmen were able to show us some fresh bear tracks. It is noteworthy, too, that although bears were fairly common in the Langtang we saw no tracks on snow, which confirms the natural supposition that it is a rare occurrence for a bear to go above the snow-line. In the absence of rigid proof to the contrary, it is, therefore, safe to assume that if tracks are seen in snow they are not those of a bear.

We came to curse our unlucky choice of route. Though the moraine on the right bank of the glacier was bold and continuous, the long grass and boulders upon its crest constantly invited us to descend either to the glacier or to the ablation valley in search of better going; and having sampled both to return resignedly to the moraine. For most of the day it rained, so that having at last rounded the big bend we were glad enough to creep under a low rock overhang instead of pitching tents. This time, with more confidence than our earlier visit warranted, we took the camp right up to the col. Heavy work it was, too, for the leading man whose 30 lb. load ensured his feet sinking deep into the wet snow whether he trod with the utmost delicacy or stamped hard. We had all had enough by the time we made camp in a snow hollow at the foot of the rocks below the col.

After an unusually cold night, in which snow fell and froze on the tents, we spent a cold half-hour digging out the frozen guys and scraping off the snow preparatory to packing up. Having climbed to the col and dumped the loads, we had soon to acknowledge that our previous impression of the descent on the Tibet side was correct. It had looked difficult then and a closer examination confirmed it. A rib of snow, which early in the season might have taken us down, had turned to ice, and the rocks on either side, which I probed at the end of 120 ft. of rope, were as shifting as the sand. Nor could we see clear to the Chasuchen glacier, as the slope heeled over out of sight. It was a place which we reluctantly decided a laden party had best leave alone.

Wet and defeated we trudged back to our dripping lair. Next day in heavy rain we retreated to the kharka and its store of dry firewood, and thence back to Langtang village. After an absence of nearly a month this appeared quite strange. The waving fields of wheat and kuru had become short stubble, and the remaining fields of ripening buckwheat had turned a bright sorrel. We had long since become acquainted with buckwheat flour which, in my opinion, when merely mixed with water and dropped on to a hot griddle, makes a delicious bread. The bitter tang of the upland variety should appeal to the masculine taste of a mountaineer brought up on glacier sludge and wild rhubarb; while the kind grown at lower altitudes, although free from bitterness, is not insipid. Altogether, it is a wholesome flour, so much lighter than wheat flour that great quantities can be swallowed without the consequences attendant upon cramming the stomach with distressful bread.

Threshing was in full swing, a task laboriously accomplished by hand instead of by the more usual way of driving teams of oxen or asses round a pole fixed in the middle of the threshing floor. Hard and monotonous though the work was, it did not seem to irk the half-dozen men and women standing in two rows each side of a heap of grain swinging their long-bladed flails to a rhythmic chant. Having taken a photograph of the threshing party I had to pay a forfeit, which I did by making a few experimental swipes with the flail. Much practice is needed to bring the blade down, as one must, parallel to the floor without stunning either oneself or one's neighbours.

Only the lieutenant was at Langtang, Polunin having not yet returned from his forest foray. My plan was to find a pass over to the Jugal Himal, the next group of peaks to the east, returning thence to Katmandu where I would meet Polunin about mid-September. Thus, on the point of quitting the Langtang for good, I got the lieutenant to accompany me to inspect the monastery, to say good-bye to the lama, and to make a suitable offering in return for the assistance we had received while in the valley.

It was, in fact, a dry sunny day, but our visit to the lama developed into a very wet morning. First we were shown over the monastery which, as befitted the sanctity of the Langtang, was in excellent preservation and contained some interesting things—among them a library of over two hundred books, long, wood-bound volumes each kept in its own curtained pigeon-hole. An even more treasured possession was a small brass model of a stupa studded with cat's-eyes and turquoises which had been brought from Nyenam (Kuti) by the founder of the monastery. Alongside the usual image of the Buddha reposed another of the first lama, the holy man who had discovered the valley by following his straying yak. Close by were the images of some teriffic demoniacal gods who had to be propitiated with models of leaves and cornucopias covered with butter. These offerings were kept in an alcove below the image and changed annually. A drum, a few tattered and dirty 'thang-kas', twenty-five loads of butter over which our friend Nima Lama and the Tibetan lama from Kyirong were still bargaining, and a stuffed red pheasant, made up the furnishings. Perhaps in the interests of natural science I should have made a bid for the bird which, I thought, looked too bedraggled to be a welcome offering to the pundits of Cromwell Road.

Having done the honours of the gompa Nima Lama asked us to his house where his wife made us welcome with fresh buckwheat cakes and a relish of pounded chillies and salt. Tea, of course, was provided for all, but Nima and I devoted our attention to a wooden bottle of undeniable five-star arak conveniently placed between us. The tea, made in Tibetan fashion with butter, came fresh from the churn, a 3 ft. long piece of bamboo of 9 in. bore which the operator held upright on the floor by means of a thong attached at the base in which she put her foot. The salty relish provoked a thirst which, thanks to Providence and Nima's foresight, we had the means of assuaging. Presently a second bottle replaced the first and the flood of miscellaneous information offered by Nima Lama and interpreted by the lieutenant, who wisely drank tea, seemed to be getting a little turbid; or perhaps the lama was lucid enough but my attention, distracted by the buckwheat cakes, did not strictly correlate the miscellaneous facts—the butter, saints, salt, red pheasants, straying yaks, ancient passes, Abominable Snowmen, bears, and the price of umbrellas in Katmandu. I managed to grasp his fairly lucid exposition of the trade cycle which began by sending butter to Kyirong where it was exchanged pound for pound with salt; the salt then being carried over the Gangja La to Helmu to be exchanged for rice, which rice was taken to Kyirong during the winter, when butter was scarce. But then, I recall, Nima began to relate an anecdote of how he had been the last man to cross the traditional pass in 1854 just before it was closed, accompanied by the now canonized Guru Rumbruche, then a very old man, carrying a load of salted rice done up in butter which they were going to exchange for twenty-five umbrellas at Kyirong. On the pass they met an Abominable Snowman riding the missing yak, which thereupon turned into a red pheasant which Guru Rumbruche shot with a catapult, thus incurring a fine of Rs. 100—and if I cared to pay the fine I could have the pheasant, the very bird I had just been admiring in the gompa.

At this point Mrs Nima Lama removed the arak bottle and reminded her husband that he was due to start for a minor celebration in honour of one Gombu at a sacred rock a day's march up the valley. Preparations for this had been in active progress for a little time; that is to say six long baskets, built for back-packing, were being loaded with a few pitiful parcels of atta and some immense wooden jorums of beer—one half-pennyworth of bread, in fact, to an intolerable deal of sack. In turn the bearers of this precious freight bowed low to present a plateful of grain and a pat of butter to the Rev. Nima Lama, who sat with immense but slightly swaying dignity, and gave each a perfunctory blessing by clapping on their bowed heads three small pieces of butter. Greatly affected by this solemn scene the lieutenant and I bowed too, and withdrew swiftly with unbuttered heads.

CHAPTER EIGHT

The Jugal Himal

THOUGHTS of reaching the Jugal Himal had been in my mind since June, when the col we had glimpsed had dropped a hint of there being a way out to the east. Not only of reaching them but of climbing to a col on the frontier ridge, as we had in the Langtang, whence we might look into Tibet and perhaps pin down the elusive Gosainthan. I took Tensing and Da Namgyal, and two Langtang men volunteered to accompany us as far as Katmandu. These two provided themselves with Tibetan boots and the essential repair kit—needle and thread and spare bits of leather without which the life of such boots on rough going is a matter of days.

Having crossed the river by a bridge near the village we marched up the left bank bound for the east Langtang glacier. A boulder the size of a house afforded our first night's lodging, one side of it sheltering our party and the other a cheery party of men and women who were gathering and drying a bitter root called 'kuchi'. This is used as a febrifuge and fetches Rs. 19 a maund in Katmandu. A glorious evening succeeded by a clear night, and the impression that the river was falling, made me think that the monsoon was over and that we were about to enjoy some lovely autumn weather. An idea which had to be adjusted, for it hardly stopped raining until we reached Katmandu on 16 September.

We had hoped that by now the flowers would be beginning to seed, but there seemed to be a fresh flush. Dark blue and heliotrope carpets of delphiniums and asters covered the grass, and some of the rocks glowed warmly with a coat of bright pink vaccinium. Having traversed round the snout of the east glacier (the Brangbing) opposite Langsisa, we camped at the last grass short of the corner where the rock images of Shakya Muni and Guru Rumbruche stand guard. Upon rounding the corner we were obliged to quit the moraine to launch out on to a wild, tumbled sea of stones until at last we found smoother going on the far side. Late in the afternoon we camped on stones below the smooth ice tongue of a tributary glacier at whose head we hoped to find our pass.

After a coolish night in which a little snow fell we roused out early, but the Langtang men remained huddled under their blankets on a stone shelf they had built for themselves. Since their reluctance to rise was not attributable to the luxury of their couch, it could probably be accounted for by their realization that the Rubicon was at hand. Crossing this pass would bring us a day's march nearer home, but for them it meant a step into the unknown and a long severance from home. With great deliberation they made up their loads, but whether they intended to advance or retreat hung in the balance until a cheering gleam of light thrown by the rising sun upon the mountains opposite turned the scale in our favour. The sprinkling of snow helped us to climb the bare ice of the glacier tongue with a minimum of step-cutting, and the next half-mile of hard snow, sparkling in the early sun, led us easily to the col. From earlier disappointments we knew well that there are two sides to every col, so we pressed eagerly to the top to learn our fate. This time there was no doubt; a hundred feet or so of negotiable rock led to another glacier which, so far as one could tell, for the mist had begun boiling up, held no concealed ice-falls. The footgear of one of the men having already given out, his feet had to be swathed in strips of blanket for the walk down the glacier. After about a mile our glacier joined a bigger glacier near the cirque at its head, and we climbed on to the ancient moraine between the two to survey the scene. In a grass hollow, at a height of about 17,000 ft., lay two small lakes. Overlooking them stood a ruined cairn and close by, stuck upright in the grass, several rusty iron tridents. The Langtang men at once assumed we had reached the Panch Pokhari (Five Lakes), a noted place of pilgrimage of which they had heard; for in their eagerness to believe we were on known ground they readily overlooked the absence of three lakes. The 'trisuli', a name applied to both mountains and rivers of the Himalaya, is the symbol of the Hindu triad. Rarely does one find so high and yet so pleasing a place to camp as upon the banks of these lonely tarns, their still waters reflecting impartially the moods of the sky, and the air fragrant with the superb scent of the blue delphinium. But we did not stay, the aspect of the surrounding mountains discouraging any such plan.

If the roughness of the road they tread counts for righteousness, the pilgrims who once made these lakes their goal acquired much merit. Between them and the distant point where the moraine of the main glacier had to be quitted, lay a long stretch of rough, penitential surface, huge craters and hillocks of stone-covered ice, which, for men from the soft plains, must have been the equivalent of several weeks of hair-shirt wear. In and out of these stony craters we toiled for a long time before the moraine looked tempting enough to induce us to climb it. In the ablation valley beyond, cut off from the desolation of the glacier, we rejoiced in a new and better world of flowers and grass through which we sped in high spirits in a downpour of rain. In a short time we came upon a track and then a kharka with the frame of a shelter still standing. Covering this with the big groundsheet we soon had a fire going.

Early in the morning, before the clouds rolled up, Tensing and I climbed on to the moraine to see where we were. Not far away the glacier terminated and its waters drained south-east into a deep gorge. Beyond we could make out the dark cleft of the main valley, to all appearances an even deeper gorge, where, the rivers still running high, we could count upon meeting all sorts of trouble. Southwards from the kharka a well-defined path apparently followed the ridge lying parallel to the main valley to the Panch Pokhari. We were not long in making up our minds which way to go. Apart from our wish to see the sacred lakes, the path was a temptation which we did not try to resist. If the main valley could not be reached from above, why should we not enter it from below from the nearest village? According to the map there was a village called Tempathang on the east side of the valley close to a bridge; whence, from our experience of the Langtang and the Ganesh, we might expect to find a track to some high alp in the heart of the Jugal Himal.

Accordingly we packed up and began a march which was to last until nightfall. On we went, crossing a succession of small streams and sharp ridges, past many deserted kharkas, until at midday in thick mist we emerged upon a wide down. In the distance we could hear dogs barking. Just as a soldier cannot do wrong by marching towards the sound of the guns, so the traveller in unknown country cannot do better than march towards the sound of dogs, sheep, cattle, or any other token of human habitation. Unfortunately we neglected this rule and in our eagerness to reach the valley took a well-marked path leading downhill through straight-growing juniper trees and bamboo. After dropping very steeply for about a thousand feet, the path, evidently one used by shepherds cutting wood, petered out; and having wasted an hour over this, the first of several attempts to reach the valley, we resumed the march along the proper path in heavy rain.

About two o'clock we came to an occupied kharka where two loud-voiced Tamangs received us with less warmth than we thought our due. Having parted grudgingly with some curds they informed us in a hearty bawl that Panch Pokhari was 'not far away'—ominous words of encouragement, I thought, from men obviously anxious to see our backs. A little later we accosted a half-naked shrimp of a man who surprised us less by giving the same answer than by the extraordinary energy with which he gave it. I have often admired (for a short time at any rate) the loud, virile way in which Frenchmen and other Continentals converse, but these goatherds of the Panch Pokhari ridge seemed to be all descendants of Stentor who, I am told, had the voice of fifty men. At the next kharka, where there was a sodden, fireless hovel, I myself thought to galvanize the listless inmates with a hearty roar. Nobody took any notice except Tensing who was so startled that he hastily offered me a cold potato he had brought from Langtang. Indeed it was time for us to be settling down somewhere for a meal and to pass the night, and had not these men assured us in a powerful bellow that the lakes were now 'quite near' we should have stopped there, miserable though it was.

At dusk my drooping spirits were cheered by the sight of an old moss-grown chorten, and very faintly out of the mist and gathering dark came the bleating of sheep. When Tensing, who was far behind, had caught up I got him to try what he could do in the bellowing line; and upon getting a reply we headed into the mist away from the path, trusting that those behind would hear and act upon this long-range exchange. At last we came to a lake and by it a long matting shelter. Wading through a sea of sheep we went inside. No one got up to offer us a place by the meagre fire and no one offered to mend it until Tensing took the matter into his own hands and threw on an armful of logs. Even the uninvited guest is sometimes critical of his welcome; the shepherds of these parts, I reflected, are merely loud-spoken, churlish skinflints, all cry and little wool. But it has since occurred to me that if a couple of dripping strangers burst in about supper time to claim the best seats by the fire, at the same time heaving on a bucket of coal, my welcome to them might be cool. Yet the fact that both Tensing and I were disappointed by our welcome is a measure of the hospitality expected and nearly always received at the rough, kindly hands of Himalayan peasants and shepherds. Happy the countries where the people are so uncivilized that hospitality is not a virtue but second nature; the better for being accorded spontaneously, without the careful preparations we are often obliged to make when entertaining; the screwing of the host's mind to the requisite sticking-point of geniality—and in due season the long premeditated revenge. Tensing's liberality with their firewood and the number of socks I peeled off made an impression. Perhaps it occurred to them that they might be entertaining angels unawares, so they presently got out their milk and butter and offered it at fully commensurate prices. But after such a long, wet day, seated in front of a blazing fire of which we had now pretty well taken possession, drinking hot tea, we could afford to ignore these little rubs as easily as we could ignore the rain hissing down pitilessly upon the wretched sheep outside.

Unlike the pilgrimage to the Gosainkund lake which is an annual affair, no pilgrims besides ourselves had visited Panch Pokhari that year. There are five shallow lakes and some shelters for the accommodation of pilgrims. These were unroofed, the roofing poles and planks being stacked inside like those of Chilime valley. We resumed our walk along the ridge, having over our left shoulders the high tops of the Jugal Himal—from which we were drawing steadily away—rising grandly above the clouds. Presently we came to an open glade where another path crossed the ridge at right angles. We were now about level with Tempathang which lay immediately below us on our left, so we took this cross track and began plunging down through a thick forest of bamboo and fir. When we had gone too far to think of climbing back, the track divided. Having taken the steepest we were not long in coming to a rough bamboo shelter used by men engaged in cutting and stripping bamboo for weaving mats. It was deserted so we climbed back and tried the other path which, after luring us irretrievably deep into the jungle, ended at a similar hut. However, some embers still smouldered inside and in response to our shouts two men climbed up carrying long bundles, of thin, pliant bamboos. They laughed at our notion of finding a path through the forest to Tempathang—the proper path followed the ridge—but at the mention of money they pricked up their ears and thought there might be something in my proposal that they should carve a way down for us with their kukris. We were too far from Tempathang for that, they said, but for Rs. 3 they would put us on a path on the way to a kharka where we could spend the night. Girding up their loins—that is with their legs bared to the buttock—they shot off through the forest, slashing away bamboos and branches to ease our progress, though in fact it was so steep that we fell or slithered down through any obstructions. In half an hour we emerged on to a muddy track where cattle had recently passed. In a short time, they said, we should reach a kharka. Whereupon, feeling as grateful to them as if we were already there I handed them Rs. 3. Justice should be tempered with doubt. We soon regretted this premature bestowal of their due. We had but to suggest withholding the reward until they had shown us something more reassuring than a miry and infrequently used path, and the clamour that would no doubt have ensued would have taught us how matters stood. Two hours later, having descended a thousand feet to a stream and having climbed a like amount out of it, we were still crawling up an apparently unending slope in heavy rain and gathering darkness. At last we came to the derelict moss-covered remains of a bamboo-cutter's shelter. After a long search we found a spring so we settled there for the night as best we could with soaking loads and bedding. There is no want like the want of a fire, and in a dripping forest, where rain has been falling for several weeks, the chances of satisfying it might seem to be slight. Every dead or fallen branch was, of course, sodden, but where there are bamboos one may always have a fire; for dead bamboo, even though the hollow inside is full of water, will burn. Very soon we had a cheerful blaze, the bamboos popping like pistols as the water inside boiled and the steam burst out.

In the morning, with the rain still falling, we resumed the track which went up and up, until in two hour's time we came out on the ridge and the same well-defined track which we had quitted twenty-four hours earlier. At a kharka a mile on, perhaps that which we were to have reached the previous night, the track at last left the ridge for the valley; and after a steep descent of four or five thousand feet we came to the bridge and the maize fields of Tempathang, a small village inhabited by Sherpas. Tensing and Da Namgyal were, of course, at home and had there been anything worth eating in the village we might have had it. They could give us nothing but green mealie cobs and, what was worse, the information that there was no path up the valley; for their grazing alps had long since been abandoned, the track to them, through long disuse and fallen bridges, being no longer passable.

Having no time to test the truth of this statement, we started back next day with the intention of meeting Polunin who was coming out by the direct route to Katmandu over the Gangja La. Moving westwards across the grain of the country meant our having to cross four deep drainage troughs and their correspondingly high ridges. One night we would be sleeping among fir trees and rhododendrons and the next in a sub-tropical valley where rice, mangoes and even bananas grew. Before reaching the ridge along which lay the path to the Gangja La, we had to part company with one of the Langtang men whose feet had given out. We left him at a Sherpa village where the headman was connected by marriage with our old friend Nima Lama of Langtang with whom he, the headman, had one taste in common—a liking for arak. At the gompa a festival was in progress, indeed judging by the uproar it had been going on for some time. The headman did his best to make up for the unsocial behaviour of a rather strait-laced lama, a man more like a fakir wearing a bun of what looked like tow coiled on top of his head. In his very capable hands we soon absorbed a little of the festival spirit. With the necessary allowance for local conditions the people of these parts act upon the principle:

> There's nought so much the spirit calms
> As rum and true religion.

We waited for the main body at the village of Tharke Ghyang in the Helmu district. It is a big village of some five hundred inhabitants, few of whom can have refrained from putting their heads inside my tent very soon after our arrival. They had, I think, less admiration for its internal arrangements than for my stoicism in supporting the conditions inside. Indeed, after two days of continuous rain, I was compelled to pitch the tent afresh under a roof. This arrangement gave more privacy, but short of posting sentries the headman had no power to restrain their curiosity. He made amends by inviting me to his house where we drank Tibetan tea unwatched by intruders. Like most Helmu women his wife was good-looking and kept house admirably. All her brass or copper pots, pans and utensils—and there were many—gleamed brightly in their allotted places.

I was housed close by the monastery, a building half corrugated iron and half picturesque decay. Under the sound roof reposed the show piece, a prayer wheel of crudely ornamented brass about 10 ft. high and 8 ft. diameter. The walls of the room where this monster revolved were being re-decorated under the direction of a Tibetan lama who drew the designs and supervised their painting by six local artists. Besides the conventional portraits of the Buddha, his disciples, the Wheel of Life, and some domestic scenes which were 'resolutely and offensively coarse', the lama's rampant imagination delighted in hairy monkeys, sea serpents and leopards. He depicted one leopard balancing head downwards on an eight-leaved lotus. The lama thus earned money to help him on his pilgrimage to the Buddhist shrines of India; a devout purpose which I, too, was expected to forward. And I was ready enough to help a man who so well understood the art of travel that he had already passed two years in making a journey which normally takes ten days.

Having joined forces with Polunin's party, we continued down the ridge betwen the Malemchi and Indrawati rivers until near their junction, where we crossed the former by a chain bridge. Such 'ridgeways' are common in these parts where the valley routes, especially in summer, are liable to interruption either from landslides or from the numerous side-streams, few of which are bridged. Immediately after crossing the Malemchi we were confronted by one of these insignificant side-streams in spate. It would have brought us to a full stop but for the timely help of four local men who carried the whole party, even the Langtang men, across on their backs. The next day we crossed the Sheopuri Lekh to enter the Katmandu valley at the north-eastern end by a track which crosses the dam of the Sundari power-station. Silt brought down by the recent flood had put this temporarily out of action. And so on 16 September, strolling through the yellowing rice fields of the valley, we brought our journey to an end.

From the feast of mountains spread before us, Lloyd and I had come more or less empty away—a well-merited rebuke, perhaps, for attempting to prostitute art to science. But there were other reasons, one being that handy scapegoat the weather which can be invoked to conceal our weakness or to prove our indomitable spirit. Although weather conditions during the monsoon are seldom good, up to the present most Himalayan climbing has been undertaken during the summer months. The pre-monsoon period is too short, a month to six weeks at the most. April, or even early May, are too soon to start because the remaining winter snow hinders the approach and increases the avalanche danger, and on big mountains it is too cold. In theory the post-monsoon period is longer, say at a maximum from mid-September to mid-November, but climbing is liable to be brought prematurely to an end by an early fall of winter snow, such as the three-day storm in mid-October 1929 which rendered so hazardous the retreat of the Bavarians from the north-east spur of Kangchenjunga. On three occasions only have big or fairly big mountains been climbed in the autumn. On 20 October 1907 the Norwegians Rubenson and Monrad Aas failed by only 100 ft. to climb Kabru (24,263 ft.); in 1935 the same mountain was climbed by C. R. Cooke and a Sherpa on as late a date as 18 November; and on 5 November 1937 Brig. John Hunt climbed the south-west summit of Nepal Peak (23,500 ft.). Both mountains are in Sikkim where the monsoon is as heavy as it is in Nepal. In recording his climb Brig. Hunt remarked: 'The factors of deep snow (the result of a heavy fall in early October) and high winds affected considerably our efforts at the time, and loom large in my general impressions of our winter visit to the Zemu glacier. Should this heavy precipitation be a regular feature of the late monsoon in this part, and assuming that high winds are normal, then there are serious objections to high ascents at this time of year.' What it amounts to is that seasonal weather is rather less predictable than weather day by day. It is a lottery, and it is better so. If climbing could be done always under a blazing sun, on windless days, on hard snow and warm rock, it would have little merit, and many aspiring spirits would find, like Othello, their occupation gone.

There is much to be said for and against climbing during the monsoon months. Snow precipitation is not as great as might be expected; at high altitudes a heavy fall in October or November may exceed that which falls during the whole monsoon period. At least my own limited experience points that way; had I climbed on Nanga Parbat, which seems to receive some overwhelming summer snowfalls, I might think otherwise. The unreasonable warmth such as we met with certainly precludes the danger of frostbite; on the other hand, it may so increase the danger of falling stones and ice as to deny even the making of an attempt upon certain routes. The extremely poor visibility which hampered us is mostly peculiar to the eastern half of the Himalaya where the monsoon is heaviest. It is a depressing feature. After a succession of blind days one begins to fear that reconnaissance, let alone climbing, is impossible. But all things, including a break in the monsoon, come to him who knows how to wait, thus in attempting to climb unknown mountains time is an important factor. In summer a party should have ample time, whereas before the monsoon it is in a desperate hurry to finish the climb before it breaks. Perfunctory methods are seldom advisable when dealing with mountains, yet—to revert to our attempts—I felt that we were trying to take peaks, so to speak, in our stride. Rather than court it in proper form we preferred to pass on, hoping that some other peak would surrender at sight. When this did not happen and when our time was nearly up, we were obliged to make a more serious, yet a too hasty bid for the Fluted Peak in the worst conditions.

Singleness of purpose is a sound principle. The killing of two birds with one stone, however desirable, is seldom achieved intentionally and never by aiming consciously at both. I am not implying that the presence of the collectors or the strong whiff of science which pervaded the party impaired our aim, but that a lot of luck will be needed if the climbing of a good peak is to be included in the exploration of a large, mountainous area.

Although the mountaineers had thus come hungry away, the bellies of the scientists had been filled with good things. Not that this really applies to field collectors like Polunin and Scott, for with the field collector, as with the honey-bee, it is a case of *sic vos non vobis*. Perhaps the irreverent or the uninstructed will ask, like little Peterkin: 'But what good came of it at last?' And personally, in the role of old Kaspar, I should have to answer: 'Why that I cannot tell.' A similar reply might be made by the field collector himself who, unless he has the time and ability to attend to it himself, may not live to see his collection neatly arranged and ticketed. When specimens are swallowed in the maw of that vast repository of the dead in Cromwell Road, their digestion, for various good reasons, is a properly deliberate affair. Along with thousands of others of their kind from many outlandish parts of the world, Polunin's hardly-won harvest of plants, his butterflies and toads, his slightly ruffled birdskins, must there await their resurrection; their sorting and classifying by expert and critical hands, quick to reject the unworthy or to consign the uncouth specimen to a fiery doom. Severe is the scrutiny of the high priests of science and unblemished must be the offerings laid upon her altars by the neophyte.

As for Scott's rocks, specimens less subject to the vicissitudes of time and chance, a few, after being sawn, polished, and scrutinized under microscopes, may perhaps find an honourable tomb at St Andrews in a glass case, to be looked at, one hopes, by earnest disciples of William Smith on days when it is too wet for golf.

Part 2

ANNAPURNA HIMAL AND EVEREST (1950)

CHAPTER NINE

The Start

THE door to the Nepal Himalaya having been opened I felt it should, if possible, be kept open. So upon paying my farewell respects to H.H. the Maharajah I asked tentatively for permission to go next year (1950) to the Annapurna Himal. Napoleon, on the eve of a campaign, used to place his finger on the map and remark quietly to his awestruck staff that there on such and such a date he would fight a victorious and decisive battle. An intelligent appreciation enabled him to forecast events, to select time and place, and to lay his plans accordingly. Although they are in constant practice, our honourable mandarins seldom plan so precisely as this; and all that I could achieve after the Master's model was to put a finger on the map and suggest hesitatingly to myself that there in 1950—weather and world situation permitting—a campaign of some sort, probably indecisive, ought to take place. 'There' happened to be the Annapurna Himal, because on the map that region seemed to be the most mountainous of a singularly mountainous country.

The Himalayan Committee followed this private approach with a formal application. The favourable reply came so late that little more than a month remained to collect a party and stores and to arrange the necessary passages for April. My intention had been to take a small party such as had previously wandered unobtrusively in the Langtang Himal, collecting plants and birds, battering rocks, amending the existing maps, but attempting no great mountains. Such aims may be thought paltry for a rude and hardy mountaineer but they are aims which, as I have pointed out, facilitate the raising of funds; and are, perhaps, proper enough for a man (like the sage in *Rasselas*) 'whose years have tamed his passions without clouding his reason'.

However, the Himalayan Committee, having in mind the necessity of building up a nucleus of experienced Himalayan climbers such as had existed between the wars, preferred to send a larger party. In the thirties several British parties visited the Himalaya every year, but since the war there have been few. Unsettled conditions and greatly increased costs have been a deterrent. Indeed in recent years too few British climbers have gone even to the Alps, for it is there and not in the Himalaya where technique is learnt and where climbing experience can be quickly gained.

Since 1947 the Swiss have sent four successful parties to the Himalaya, and this year (1950) the French and the Norwegians have re-entered the field and scored great achievements. There is no harm in applying the spur of national rivalry to Himalayan climbing so long as the principles of sound mountaineering are kept steadily in mind. Though it may be desirable, it is exceptional for successful climbing parties to be of mixed nationality, for a party composed of friends who have climbed together before or men who have been brought up in the same climbing traditions is inherently stronger.

In these post-war years life is so real and so earnest, especially for the inmates of a Welfare State, that one hesitates a long time before asking a man to squander money and time on a Himalayan trip. A hollow laugh or a shocked hoist of the eyebrows is the reply one expects and usually gets, according to the man's circumstances and moral outlook. Nevertheless, in a short time I had found five who were free to come and who were reckless or depraved enough to brush aside all impediments. Col. D. G. Lowndes, who had spent most of his life in India with the Garhwal Rifles and had travelled widely in the hills, came as botanist. Major J. O. M. Roberts, M.C., of the 1/ 2nd Gurkhas managed to obtain leave, and since he spoke Gurkhali and had been on several Himalayan trips, including the attempt on Masherbrum (25,660 ft.) in 1938, he was a sound choice. Dr C. H. Evans, as well as being an experienced climber, gave to the party the comforting insurance of medical aid. Honour a physician according to thy need of him, saith the Preacher, but it was not Evans's fault that we needed him most after he had left us. J. H. Emlyn Jones, M.B.E., an experienced Alpine climber, launched a spirited and successful blow at the chains which bound him to a surveyor's office; and to complete the party we had a young New Zealand Rhodes Scholar, W. P. Packard, who had climbed much in New Zealand before becoming a student of geography at University College, Oxford. He, too, was tied by economic and academic chains which were not easily broken. That three of the six names have a Welsh flavour was merely coincidence and not a retort to an all-Scottish party which was then being organized. Lowndes, reasonably enough, disliked being considered a handmaid of science so that, in effect, her sole servant was Packard. Even his allegiance was not complete, for we had a private agreement that he should set foot on at least one mountain. Originally I had hoped that he would undertake some survey work, such work having the merit of producing results which can be understood and which may be of value. But the only light photo-theodolite in England, one which could be carried up a mountain, was earmarked for another expedition, so instead Packard undertook the study of land utilization and soil erosion which were his special subjects. Himalayan villages are so remote that they are not likely to reap any practical benefit from such enquiry; but, perhaps, on that account it will be no less gratifying to our world planners. Even had the theodolite been available our late arrival in the field, coupled with Packard's early departure, would have prevented our using it to much effect in the short time available before the onset of the monsoon; for although the cloud canopy in the Annapurna during the monsoon is neither so dense nor so consistent as in the Langtang, it is bad enough to preclude survey work. There is nothing more baffling for the surveyor than

> Mountains on whose barren breast
> The labouring clouds do often rest.

Apart from snowshoes, which we never used, and packboards, our equipment contained nothing new. In the Annapurna range flattish, névé-covered glaciers, where snowshoes can be used with advantage, proved to be conspicuously absent. The pack-boards were massive structures of the Yukon type, built evidently for professional packers, old timers, 'forty-niners', and such like, men who could 'take it' in every sense. The boards themselves weighed 9 lb. Nevertheless the Sherpas and in time even the local coolies grew fond of them. Provided the canvas back is kept really taut they make a very comfortable load; a lighter type made of plywood should be excellent. Most of us took nailed boots as well as the moulded rubber 'Vibram' type, suggesting that while we wished to move with the times we had not enough confidence in the new to discard the old. For rough walking the 'Vibram' soled boot is more comfortable than the nailed. It is supreme for that everyday Himalayan pastime of boulder-hopping (provided the boulders are dry), and is generally suitable for climbing except on wet rock, wet ice, or fresh snow on rock. It is a matter of taste. Provided one is aware of their limitations and uses care—which, whatever his footgear, a climber must always do, placing his feet circumspectly though not meticulously—they are as good as nailed boots and sometimes better.

The French moralist Vauvenargues remarked that great thoughts come from the stomach. An eighteenth-century French writer is not every man's fireside study—till this minute I had not heard of him—and while we can afford to disregard a Frenchman writing about morals, we cannot when he writes about the stomach. A remark so profound evidently comes from a man of deep insight and robust appetite; and whether true or not there is no doubt about the converse—that great thought should be bestowed on the stomach—especially with a large party, that is a party of more than one, when it becomes necessary to take thought as to what the others shall eat. Of mountaineers in general it cannot be said that:

> Life is with such all beer and skittles,
> They are not difficult to please
> About their victuals.

Or, as the Chinese sage puts it more succinctly, 'a full belly is the great thing; all else is luxury'. Some are prepared to swallow large quantities of the fundamentals, such as bread and rice, provided there is a little something sweet or spicy to assist the swallowing. Others say, give us the luxuries and we will dispense with the necessities, or in other words they like a little bread with their butter and/or jam. Having no great love for austerity I sympathized with them, and since the Annapurna are not so difficult to reach that every extra pound taken becomes a matter of concern, we took luxuries enough and lived uncommonly well.

Perhaps this bald statement, at which some might marvel, should be supported by a few figures. It is a little distasteful to mingle food with figures. I hold strongly with the Albanian proverb, 'When travelling don't reckon the distance and when eating never reckon the amount.' Unhappily such generous advice cannot be followed on an expedition, or, for that matter, under present conditions at home. Apart from solids we took a total of 190 lb. of trimmings—cheese, butter, jams, peanut butter, raisins, chocolate, and dried egg—which for the time spent in the field, 700 man-days, worked out at 3 oz. a day of one or the other. We were fortunate in having genuine Cheddar cheese which I had not smelt since 1939—in glorious and happy contrast with the cheese we took to the Langtang, red plastic bricks, thoughtfully wrapped in cellophane as a warning that they should not be touched. For hard living above the snow-line we had biscuit and pemmican, and enough sugar to allow each man 5 oz. a day throughout the trip. We even brought some sugar back, an event rather to be wondered at than acclaimed. The solid setting for these gastronomic pearls was rice, more or less *ad lib.*, bread, limited by the size of loaf one could bake, and whatever could be picked up locally such as potatoes, lentils, buckwheat, milk, more butter, occasionally meat, very occasional game and beer, which many consider a food. On the whole it strikes me as the conception of a liberal mind, a diet adapted to meet the needs of the fastidious glutton and the voracious epicure. How different from that of the Antarctic traveller who, on his sledge journeys at any rate, lives on biscuit, pemmican, chocolate, butter, cocoa, unalleviated by bread or even rice. Of all who face discomfort for fun or in pursuit of knowledge the Himalayan traveller enjoys the least deprivation and deserves the least sympathy.

Three of the party and all the baggage went to Bombay by sea. Of necessity the sea is much used by an island race, but Mr Woodhouse with whom, except in the matter of gruel, I often agree, once observed that he had long been convinced that the sea was very rarely of use to anybody. It would be unjust perhaps to blame the sea for what was the fault of the ship, for she started late and lost us a week which we could ill afford. As she had originally been billed to sail on Good Friday, I thought this mishap might be only the first of a series of disasters ending with her final disappearance in mid-ocean. But nothing more happened. I went direct to Calcutta by air, ostensibly to pick up the Sherpas and the accursed stick-gun, in reality to avoid the task of seeing rather more than a ton of baggage across India. Lowndes, the seasoned Indian traveller, undertook that and had reason to regret it. Crossing India by train in the month of April is hot work, and our party of four found it hotter than usual owing to their compartment going up in flames somewhere the wrong side of Lucknow. This caused more delay, and the loss of some kit which was borne with equanimity since most of it belonged to Roberts. He met me at Calcutta and together we awaited the others at Raxaul. When they eventually did arrive, they looked like men who had gone through fire and water, as indeed they had. Those of us who were meeting for the first time struggled to conceal their dismay and to put a bright face on the matter.

The party was now complete, our four Sherpas having wisely elected to come direct from Darjeeling to Raxaul without going through the mild hell of a journey to Calcutta. Since partition this journey, formerly a simple one-night affair, involves two crossings of the India–Pakistan frontier with all that that implies. Recently, by linking up various almost unexplored branch lines and arranging a ferry service over the Ganges; the Indian railway authorities have contrived a way round which goes to Siliguri (for Darjeeling) and thence to Assam. This is known as the 'Assam Link', but it is a pretty frail link. It is the sort of journey undertaken only by those in their first youth when the years stretch unendingly ahead; the rest, if they can afford it, save much time and more vexation by going by air.

On 5 May we reached Katmandu where Lady Falconer assumed the burden of looking after four of us at the Embassy, Col. Proud taking the other two to his house. The intervention of the week-end and some trouble in pinning down the coolie contractor prevented our leaving before the 10th, ten days later than I had planned. Even so there was enough to do and much hospitality to be enjoyed in the four days allowed. With the help of Col. Proud we contracted for fifty coolies at Rs. 2.25 (about 3s. 6d.) a day, half-rate for their return unladen, and they to find their own food. Lieut. S. B. Malla, at my request, was again detailed to accompany us, so with his sepoys and our coolies we were about sixty strong.

At the beginning of such a journey one should, of course, be on fire to start, the feet tingling to tread the trail, the back itching for its unaccustomed load, a fierce contempt for motor-cars uppermost in one's mind. Nevertheless we gladly accepted a lift as far as Baleji water garden. Here we sorrowfully took to our feet, remarking with ill-disguised apprehension the length, the height, and the shadelessness of the Sheopuri Lekh over which we must that day go. The coolies whom we had seen out of the compound much earlier in the day, and who should have half finished their task, apparently felt much the same, for they sat smoking under a giant pipal tree whose shade they were loath to quit. Having admonished them without effect we retired to the water garden where we envied the giant carp floating idly in the still pool, and photographed once again the recumbent Narayan on his stone bed of cobras. Two live snakes flickered about his feet, for the statue which should have been mostly submerged was now mostly exposed. Few statues can stand this; the majority, and this one was no exception, are better submerged.

Having thus wasted much time and the best part of the day, we at last straggled off across the flat valley and began the long ascent. After suffering fully as much as we had anticipated we stopped at our old camp site under Kaulia hill where the Sherpas put up our brave array of bright green tents. There was one for each of us—small Meades, big Meades, and a gigantic Whymper tent for the botanist. Scientists, even mere collectors, must have room to work and think, and space for their appliances. Lowndes with his museum boxes neatly arranged as bedside table, dressing table, work table, and party wall, thus occupied a sort of mansion. Around this was a suburb of humbler dwellings, some of which, by reason of their occupant's habits, ranked almost as slums. In contrast with that of Emlyn Jones, who in spite of having a great deal had a place for everything and everything in its place, was my own abode, which resembled a hurrah's nest—everything on top and nothing at hand—the whole generously sprinkled with spent matches and tobacco ash.

Our route diverged from that of 1949 at Trisuli Bazaar where we arrived next day to be welcomed by Trisuli Trixie and the usual crowd. This year we

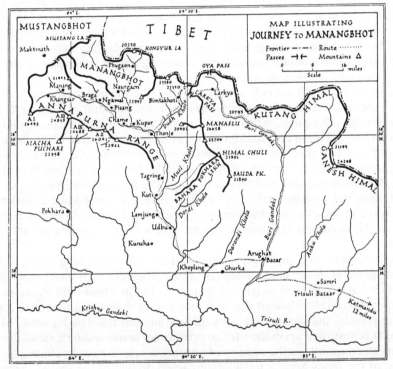

Journey to Manangbhot

were eighteen days earlier, a difference in time reflected in the state of the river which was now lower and almost blue, the melting snow having not yet had time to discolour it. The altitude here is under 2,000 ft. The sultry weather, and the muck-sweat in which we arrived enhanced the delights of leaping into this cool, bright river. Some of the party, however, were already feeling the heat, for they arrived late along with the coolies. These men have their own pace which neither threats nor cajolery can alter. So long as the day's destination is agreed upon before starting—a point upon which opinions will need to be reconciled—it is foolish to worry about the coolies who nine times out of ten will in time cast up. On the other hand the experienced traveller never feels at ease far from his baggage; he wants it in early, especially if there is rain about; and so the prudent man frequently loiters along with the coolies though he well knows that his presence will not hinder them from sitting down any less frequently. Like the Egyptians, their strength is to sit still.

The man who elects to march with Nepalese coolies will find their behaviour unusually exasperating, because in central Nepal the opportunities for sitting down in comfort are too numerous. The proverb that 'he who sits upon a stone is twice glad' is not applicable in warm countries such as Nepal where much time is spent resting upon what are known as 'chautaras'—the coolies' joy and the traveller's bane. In this pleasant land where all loads are carried upon men's backs, where the tracks are rough and steep and the days hot, various pious and public-spirited men—of whom in my opinion there have been too many—perpetuate their names by planting two fast-growing shady trees and building round them a rectangular or sometimes a circular stone dais with a lower parapet as a seat.

These trees, which are believed by natives to be the male and female of the same species, are usually a pipal (*Ficus religiosa*) and a banyan (*Ficus bengalensis*). The pipal, which has a round leaf terminating in a spike, is sacred to both Hindu and Buddhist. It was under a pipal tree at Bodh Gaya, one of the holiest places in the Buddhist world, that Prince Gautama obtained enlightenment and became the Buddha. Hindus hold that Brahma lives at the root, Vishnu in its stem, and Siva at the top. The banyan, which is also sacred to Hindus, has a similar leaf except for the spike and sends down aerial roots. The roots of the chautara banyan are lopped, but Hooker records a banyan tree in the Botanical Gardens, Calcutta, which shaded an area of 300 ft. in diameter.

Both banyan and pipal grow quickly into wide-branching giants under whose grateful shade some dozens of coolies can take their ease, their loads off their backs and their weight off their feet. For in a well-built chautara the parapet is so nicely adjusted that as a man comes to rest against it, like a ship to a quayside, the parapet receives his bottom and the dais his load. Much thought is bestowed upon the site; an open space commanding a view, the top of any steep ascent, or the vicinity of a spring is sure to have its chautara. The name of the pious benefactor is often carved on one of the stones. There is never any lack of them on a much-used track. On long ascents they occur frequently and sometimes they are spaced at such regular intervals that the distance to a place may be reckoned in so many halts of chautaras, for no laden coolie would be so impetuous as to pass one by. This interval is about half-a-mile—a distance which a laden man would cover in perhaps a quarter of an hour, by which time his back is thought to be in need of straightening. There is a Nepali proverb—or if there isn't there should be—that the sight of a chautara makes the coolie's back ache. (Derived, of course, from the oft-quoted Bengali proverb that the sight of a horse makes the traveller lame.)

Such an abundance of wayside impediments added to the normal retarding effect of a 60 lb. load reduce the average speed of a Nepali coolie to 1½ m.p.h., so that few Europeans have the patience to stay with them to keep an eye on their baggage. Until one reaches a mature age, say ninety or more, it is difficult to conform to this pace. Should one insist on being a patient ass and marching (save the mark) with the baggage, the only way to obtain peace of mind is to assume the ass's burden. And then even a modest 40 lb. load makes the coolies' pace too brisk and the distance between Chautaras seem almost interminable.

There is a modified chautara, without any banyan tree, to be seen nearer home—on the Green Park side of Piccadilly. In 1861, at the suggestion of R. A. Slaney, Esq., M.P. for Shrewsbury, the Vestry of St George's, Hanover Square, put up a stone rest 'for the benefit of porters and others carrying burdens'. I have never had the luck to see it being used either by porters or by anyone else; not even by members of the Alpine Club, although their headquarters are not far away and although this same stone is on the direct route across the Green Park to Victoria and the Alps. Such men may be seen carrying heavy rucksacks, but doubtless they are too proud to be seen resting them.

CHAPTER TEN

The Marsyandi

A traveller crossing Nepal from east to west cuts across the grain of the country, for nearly all the rivers flow southwards from the Himalaya to the plains of India. Before dropping into the valley of the Marsyandi which would lead us to the Annapurna Himal, we had to cross two other great drainage troughs, both part of the Sapt Gandaki system, the Trisuli and the Buri Gandaki. The Trisuli now lay behind us but we had several lesser tributary valleys as well as the Buri Gandaki ahead, so that in the first ten days we had a lot of up-and-down work in which we lost rather than gained height. We enjoyed a daily change of climate, camping sometimes in a warm valley below 2,000 ft. and sometimes on cool ridges at 5,000 ft. On the map each day's march looked pitifully short. But in such country there is no monotony. Up to the ridge ahead or down to the next river there is always something to go for and something fresh to see. Let the saddle-sore cyclist caper joyfully across the flat, but for the man on foot, the more broken the country the better. He sees not whither he must go nor whence he has come; neither far enough ahead, nor behind, to modify his cheerful estimate of the distance run or to be done. When on foot

> . . . I do not want to see
> The distant scene; one step enough for me.

But man is a creature of his environment. However reasonable and true such ideas are to a man seated in a chair, they take on a different hue when the same man is 'bummelling' along the tracks of Nepal. Witness the notes made of one march—'up a steep narrow track, like walking in a sewer, 500 stone steps up to Samri—no view—2000 ft. down—hellish steep and rough track—porters slow—no view—no bananas—no raksi'. The broken nature of the country seems to have struck the writer as an offence and the absence of food and drink as a stumbling-block.

In Nepal one can live off the country in a sombre fashion, but it is no place in which to make a gastronomic tour. There are no wayside shops as in Sikkim where one can drink sweet tea or sip maize beer through bamboo tubes; no hospitable villagers who in Tibet dispense buttered tea and blood and buckwheat cakes as a matter of course; no yorts overflowing with cream, yoghourt, and hot barley bread as in Sinkiang; and no apples, pears, peaches, apricots, fresh or dried, such as one stuffs oneself with in Hunza. May, of course, is a bad month for fruit, but outside the valley there is little to be had except bananas and small oranges. Coming back in September we ate a great many of these. Even on a main route such as we were on—to Gurkha, Kuncha and Pokhara—there were no wayside stalls where tea and chapatties might beguile the tedium of the way. Occasionally at some favourable chautara where coolies gathered in great numbers there might be a few women from a nearby village selling rice beer from large wooden jorums. At every likely place we raised the cry of 'dai'[1] but rarely did we obtain this incipient yoghourt, thin and watery but refreshing. Roberts, too, would appeal eloquently, frequently, and often successfully for raksi, a spirit made indifferently from rice, maize, millet, potatoes or pretty well anything that grows. When it was good, which was seldom, we concluded that the ingenuity of man and the bounty of nature had rarely been put to better use.

What with casting about like questing hounds for these finer products of the country, or waiting by chautaras for one of the sepoys to return, usually empty-handed, from a like quest, the day passed quickly. Roberts had long chats with the many Gurkha soldiers either going on leave or returning; the astonishment of a man who came from the same battalion, as one or two of them did, meeting one of his officers so far inside Nepal was extreme. (Hitherto visiting British officers of Gurkha regiments have been confined to the terai or Katmandu itself.) We enjoyed two odd encounters; one with the Sherpa and his wife who had acted for us as corn and rice merchants in the Langtang the previous year; and another with a man who claimed to be Nain Singh, one of the Gurkha N.C.O.'s who had been to Everest with either the 1922 or 1924 party. If he was then he had certainly worn very well.

What cannot be mended must be enjoyed. We accommodated ourselves to the dignified pace of the porters and spent much time standing and staring, foregoing any expectation of seeing them arrive before 3 p.m., more often 5 p.m. Occasionally we saw a few of them before that. During a long

---

1 Dai mixed with gur and water is a good drink. 'Gur' is the unrefined sugar, like fudge, made locally. 'With a lump of gur in one hand and a stone in the other' is a proverbial Pathan expression, descriptive of a diplomatic approach.

midday halt word would go round that the leading coolies had reached the last chautara, whereupon we would hastily organize a sweepstake, the winning ticket bearing the name of the coolie who first hove in sight. Only some six out of the fifty odd were well enough known or considered likely to be in the running. Indeed it was only by coming in very early or damnably late that a man stood out from the ruck. Whoever drew the man known as 'Cheese' was thought to have a winning chance; for 'Cheese' carried a load which, owing to the warm weather, was an incubus which any man would wish to shed as quickly as possible. Any one of the 'Sugars' was a strong favourite, a sugar bag of ½ cwt. making a very compact load.

As well as our own small escort commanded by Lieut. Sher Bahadur Malla we had a local escort for our passage through each district. With one notable exception the men did no service for us personally, but they formed an inexpensive ornament to our train and no doubt assisted our harassed headman of coolies to buy food for his hungry half-hundred. The exception was the escort from District No. 2 West which included a 'shikari'. This man, with the aid of an ancient muzzle loader and a caged 'call' bird, supplied us with a brace of black partridges every day he was with us. Having shot a partridge, he opened its head and gave the brains to the Judas bird as a reward for its betrayal.

The boundary of District No. 2 West is the Buri Gandaki river which we reached on the fifth day, to camp in a mango tope by the river at a place called Arughat Bazar. Except for what we could learn from the map we knew nothing of the Marsyandi route or the Annapurna Himal, and having no agreed plan to which we must adhere we were tempted to strike up the Buri Gandaki where mountains seemed plentiful and were more quickly reached. We began to feel troubled by the length of the approach march and its persistently low level. Here we were, already five days out, still under 2,000 ft., and in five more marches we should be no higher. Whereas by turning up the Buri Gandaki we might gain height at once and finish the march in a week. However, we stuck to our course, which was perhaps as well. Three of the party who later returned down the Buri Gandaki found the going bad, and food and transport scarce.

Next day from a camp (Khanchok) on a ridge at 4,000 ft. we had a clear view of Himal Chuli (25,801 ft.) nearly thirty miles to the north. This mountain did not exactly lie in our path, but with a few limitations we were prepared, like Hamlet's French falconers, to fly at anything we saw. Binoculars and monoculars were trained on its glistening spire, but even at thirty miles, a distance at which most mountains are easily climbable, we had doubts about Himal Chuli. Just to its south lay a beautiful snow peak called Baudha (21,890 ft.) presenting to us an apparently easy ridge; but such was the loftiness of our thoughts at that time that we gave it only a passing glance. Four months later when we were looking for a peak we could climb, Roberts and I regretted this oversight. Neither of us could remember whether Baudha had looked climbable or not.

Upon Baudha's snow slopes and glaciers rises the Darondi Khola in which we enjoyed some of the best bathing of the march. The river flowed through a grassy vale overlooked by a wooded ridge, several thousand feet above, upon the top of which stands the town and temple of Gurkha. It is from rajputs who originally settled at Gurkha that the present reigning family descends; and it was the king of Gurkha and his followers who, in the eighteenth century, overcame all the neighbouring small states, including Katmandu and the valley, and established Gurkha rule over a kingdom a great deal larger than the present Nepal.

Having bathed in and crossed the Chepe Khola, which is another of Baudh's clear and kindly streams, we camped by an aged and stricken pipal tree on a grass plateau high above the Marsyandi. The villages on this plateau were the homes of Brahmans who looked upon us and our horde as little better than outcasts, as of course we were. Roberts knew better than to ask for raksi here; one might as well expect to find fish on trees as alcohol amongst these stern Rechabites, addicted to very plain living and correspondingly high thinking. They grudgingly sold us a small piece of honeycomb containing a little honey and many bees and grubs.

The grubs and the gloomy unsmiling Brahmans reminded me that it was time to begin collecting beetles. Meligethes was still the cry, as well it might be, since out of the 800 beetles which had passed through my Belsen battery the previous summer only three were of that family. One of these, however, had proved to be a new kind, so that instead of my commission as collector being revoked, I had been provided with a bigger battery of tubes and a number of Meligethes specimens. Thus equipped I had no excuse for indiscriminate slaughter, confounding the innocent, such as ladybirds and ticks, with the guilty.

Two days later, after crossing the Marsyandi by a suspension bridge, we parted company with the main Kuncha-Pokhara track and headed north up the west bank of the river. It is smaller than the Trisuli but it was already dark and discoloured owing, we found, to a crumbling hillside higher up and also to the tributary Dudh Khola or Milk river which always ran a dirty white. From Tarpu (2,523 ft.) at the junction of the clear-watered Khudi Khola, which drains the eastern extremity of the Annapurna range, we at last began to gain height with the comforting assurance that on subsequent marches it would not be thrown away.

No sooner had we cleared Tarpu village than Himal Chuli again thrust itself upon our notice, at what seemed fairly close range. It was still some twenty miles distant, but even at that the critical eye of a mountaineer could detect some unmistakable blemishes on its glistening western face. Later in the year Roberts and I were able to confirm by a closer inspection that these unfavourable impressions were justified.

Himal Chuli is not the only great peak on the twenty-five-mile-long ridge of which Baudha is the southern extremity; besides these two there are also an unnamed peak of 25,700 ft., Manaslu (26,668 ft.), and another unnamed peak of 24,150 ft. This huge southerly spur is part of the Great Himalaya range, but is isolated from the Annapurna Himal by the Marsyandi gorge, and from the Ganesh Himal to the east by the Buri Gandaki. In central and western Nepal there are two distinct high crest zones; the Great Himalaya which carries the highest peaks, and farther north, the so-called Ladakh range which, in general, marks the Nepal–Tibet frontier. North of Manaslu and the unnamed 14,150 ft. peak the two crest-zones are in contact, linked by a high ridge over which there is a much-used pass of 17,000 ft. To find a 'Ladakh' range cropping up in Nepal is confusing. Prof. Mason calls the name 'mainly a speculative invention', for the continuity of the Ladakh range so far east has never been proved either geographically or geologically.

When from our camp at Khanchok we first saw Himal Chuli we had also identified the forbidding looking summits of the unnamed 25,700 ft. peak and Manaslu. The precipitous appearance of their eastern faces fronting upon the Buri Gandaki valley as a field of operations. We felt, however, that we had been a little off-hand in writing off a twenty-five-mile-long range on such flimsy grounds; we therefore kept an open mind and were prepared to make a dart in that direction if the opportunity arose.

Beyond Tarpu we entered *terra incognita*; few if any of our coolies and certainly none of the escort had ever been up the Marsyandi. Nevertheless it is a fairly important route where coolies pass constantly, carrying rice up and salt down. Although there was a marked diminution in the number of chautaras our pace did not improve, the roughness of the way obliging the coolies to rest more frequently though less conveniently. Perhaps their absence did not mean that pious and public-spirited men were becoming rare but that they were less rich; beyond Tarpu the country becomes too rugged for any man to wish to add field to field. Tarpu itself seemed to be the home of the last and by no means the least wealthy and public-spirited landowner, a man who has at his own cost built a steel suspension bridge over the Khudi Khola. He it was who sent us a lavish gift of rice, ghi, dal, pepper, turmeric and a plump fowl. We did not see our benefactor, who lived some way off and was ill, but Charles Evans made some return by prescribing for him intuitively and, as we heard later, successfully.

Although the rich rice land ceases at 5,000 ft. cultivation goes on up to 12,000 ft., becoming ever less rewarding and demanding harder labour. As the slopes steepen the need for terraces and the labour of making them becomes greater, and as the height increases the growing season becomes shorter. A chief trouble of those who cultivate the higher, steeper valleys came vividly to our notice on the way to Tagring, the first halt beyond Tarpu. After a long march, when the sight of the village close at hand lent encouragement to the weary, we found we were cut off from it by a great, ugly gash in the hillside scored by a landslide. To cross in safety, while boulders and debris were still slithering down, we had to climb high, thus prolonging an already long march. As is generally the way the camp site was on the far side of the village, and when at last we reached it we sat for an hour in a steady drizzle awaiting the coolies.

Under the stress of these small trials we were feeling a little peevish when a group of village elders came to pay their respects and to ask us, in our wisdom, what they could do to check the landslide. Our troubles seemed shamefully trivial in the face of this major disaster of theirs. Many of their hard-won terraced fields had already been carried away by the landslip which was now threatening to engulf some houses and might in time destroy both fields and village. Could nothing be done to check it, they asked, with complete faith in the scientific resource of the Paleface. Packard, the student of land erosion, had to admit that there was nothing within their means. Only concrete, or vast quantities of fascines and labour beyond their resources, could stop the gradual deepening and widening of the newly formed ravine which would whittle away the hillside until it met solid rock. Many of these big slips quickly stabilize themselves but the Tagring slip proved to be a running sore. Returning along the opposite side of the valley four months later, Roberts and I had our attention again drawn to it by a persistent rumble increasing often to a roar as the constant trickle of mud and boulders suddenly gathered weight and momentum.

Whether it takes place little by little or in one swift calamity soil erosion is generally attributed to man's careless greed, his idleness or neglect. It would not, I think, be fair to blame the people of these valleys on the Himalayan fringe for the frequent landslips which occur there. In turning the steep slopes into fruitful fields they have been neither lazy nor neglectful. Such slopes, of 30° or 40° or more, are laboriously built up in terraces from 10 to 30 ft. wide, whose retaining walls may be from 5 to 15 ft. high, according to the angle of the slope. I have not counted them, but I can well believe there might be a couple of hundred of such hard-won fields on a hillside particularly favoured in soil and aspect whose every foot is put to use. The task of building must be spread over years and their maintenance calls for constant labour over and above that of routine cropping.

One might say that on such hillsides the forest never should have been cleared, in which case the country must be left uninhabited; or that belts of trees should have been planted which would imply first the giving up of their goats by the villagers. It has been pointed out before that but for erosion in the foothills of the Himalaya there would be no fertile Gangetic plain, and similarly no rich Nile delta and no fat Mississippi flood-plain. Yet whatever may be done by man to check erosion in the hills, dwellers in the plains need have little fear that the slow process of erosion so beneficial to them will not go on. Unless perhaps, in the case of interference with the river system on so huge a scale as that of the projected Kosi dam, when all the silt might become imprisoned in the lake above the dam.

Beyond Tagring the valley rapidly becomes a gorge. On the right bank, except for a small pocket of flattish land where there are a few fields and the hovels of their indigent owners, there is neither village nor even camp site. Although the occupants of this place were in the convalescent stages of smallpox we were obliged to camp there. The track, having crossed the river by a bamboo bridge which the rapidly rising river would soon demolish, embarked upon the passage of a series of cliffs. To overcome these the builders of the road had exercised boldness and ingenuity, stringing wooden galleries across the face. Such structures, known as 'parri', are common in the Gilgit region where they are usually stout enough; in the Marsyandi they were pretty frail, particularly the hand-rails which were better left alone or at the most touched rather than grasped. They were seldom wider than a single plank and were reached by a stone staircase or up-ended logs with footholds cut in them. When the river was low many of these cat-walks could be avoided by a little boulder-hopping in the river bed. In the rains the traveller has no choice. He must then mind his step, for the planks are greasy with rain or with spray from the surging river.

Having passed the gorge the track recrossed the river, just below its junction with the Dudh Khola, where there is a village called Thonje. We were now north of the main Himalayan crest-line, and although the altitude was little higher than Tagring the people, the villages and the vegetation had all changed. As a hint of the sterner country above them, severe forests of pine and fir had taken possession of the slopes. Instead of the high-pitched thatch roofs and brick walls of white and terra-cotta, the long, low houses were built of stone with smoke-stained shingle roofs, the lopped tip of a conifer tree tied on one gable end as a charm against leopards, ghosts, bears, Snowmen or tax collectors. At our appearance a number of Tibetan-like men and boys in a variety of queer hats burst into astonished laughter, and we instinctively took refuge in the first house which, sure enough, was a beer shop. I felt we had practically arrived. Such houses and such men, ragged, tough and cheerful, both alike reeking of juniper smoke, speak of high valleys upon the threshold of great mountains.

CHAPTER ELEVEN

Manangbhot

HAVING squandered a few annas on beer, as full of thick sediment as the Dudh Khola, we crossed over to Thonje and camped close to the river. Standing as it does at the junction of two valleys and two well-used routes, Thonje is a key place to which we held what we hoped was a master key. This was a letter of introduction from our rich landowner friend to his son who lived and reigned there. There are a number of smaller villages near enough to Thonje for them to pay some attention to the requests of its headman, so that we were advantageously placed for transport and food. Thus we were able to dispense with the Katmandu men, now out of their element climatically and culturally, and engage local men who could take us up to Manangbhot at the head of the Marsyandi.

We still had an alternative to Manangbhot, and as it would take time to recruit fifty widely scattered volunteers, or to overcome their reluctance to being pressed, we decided to halt four days while a reconnaissance party made a dart up the Dudh Khola valley. Here was a chance to see Manaslu and the neighbouring peaks at close range which no mountaineer could resist. Four of us undertook the reconnaissance while Lowndes and Packard remained with the baggage. As Lowndes's main interest lay in the collecting of palaeo-arctic plants, butterflies and birds, the time had not yet come for him to unfold his blotting-paper or unfurl his butterfly net, for Thonje is only 6,000 ft. above sea-level. It was, however, a suitable example of a lower Himalayan village, so that Packard could open his enquiry into land utilization.

We started after lunch on 23 May, having spent the morning writing letters and arguing with the Katmandu men. Although they begged hard I refused to hand over any cash, they having agreed to receive the balance due to them in Katmandu. If we were to pay our way for the next four months it was necessary to conserve the money we had brought, amounting to Rs. 6000. All of this was in silver, weighing about 100 lb., for the people of these remote parts have old-fashioned ideas about paper money. Thus, whenever I paid out cash, the pangs which a miser suffers in diminishing his irreplaceable hoard were balanced by the satisfaction a traveller has in reducing the weight of his loads.

The track up the Dudh Khola is a well-used salt route. Taking advantage of the dry weather a number of coolies were carrying up rice to exchange for salt at Bimtakhoti at the head of the valley. During the monsoon, when travel becomes unpleasant, the traffic declines, to revive again in September when 'zos' as well as coolies begin bringing salt down to Thonje. The only village in the valley is Tilje, a couple of miles up, where the main track crosses the river by a wooden cantilver bridge. In order to isolate themselves against the prevalent smallpox, the enlightened people of Tilje had closed the bridge with a thorn barrier. Coolie traffic had to use a worse alternative route, but we were armed with a note from the Thonje headman which we presented across the barrier on the point of an ice-axe in the fashion appropriate to 'compromised' persons. This talisman opened the barrier. We passed through the village—one of the dirtiest I have seen—and camped beyond it.

The place of the scattered oaks and maple through which the track wound was soon usurped by silver fir whose dark, stately ranks marched up the ever-steepening valley walls in grave contrast with the merry, foaming river. A bright morning tantalized us with exciting but imperfect glimpses of great mountains until the clouds thickened and made an end. Having camped in a glade at about 9,500 ft. we defied the ensuing drizzle with a noble fire. Leaving the men to follow we set off early next day for Bimtakhoti, passing several cheery parties of coolies still cooking their breakfasts by the rock overhangs under which they had slept. After climbing steeply for 1,000 ft. the track levelled off. From this belvedere we looked over the dark forest to the debris of a glacier below and beyond to the cirque at the foot of Manaslu from which it flowed. On the right two sky-piercing towers of rock and ice struck us with amazement, almost eclipsing by their savage splendour the calm, monumental mass of Manaslu. From a low snow col the long north ridge of the mountain climbed airily over a bump of the order of 25,000 ft., dropped 1,000 ft., and then rose sharply to a snow plateau. On this remote pedestal, lying well back, stood the summit pyramid.

I imagine that a party of mountaineers confronted by a mountain which they think of climbing is not unlike a committee of distinguished Academicians confronted by a picture which they think of hanging. First they have to decide which is the right way up, then, perhaps, what, if anything, it means; whether it is a landscape or a portrait, a mountain or a nightmare; the texture of the paint and whether it is fixed or likely to flake off in avalanches; and finally the danger which they will incur or being thought too bold or too timid. The younger members may possibly see more sense in it than the elder, will interpret it more favourably, and will above all shrink from the suspicion of having old-fashioned ideas. There is thus such wide scope for argument and disagreement that it is remarkable that pictures are ever hung or mountains climbed.

A man looking at a big mountain from a valley has naturally only a worm's-eye view. Thus we had first an acrimonious discussion as to the whereabouts of the actual summit; which was not settled, and would never have been, until by moving on a bit we brought it into view. But so distant, and so fore-shortened was our view of the upper part, that we gave this major consideration the benefit of the doubt, and concentrated our attention on the north ridge whereby lay the only possibility of approach. That the foot of this ridge could be reached by means of a low snow col was about the only point that I could see in its favour; but the dazzling beauty of its immaculate curve spanning the sky, its length, and perhaps its difficulties, together formed a powerful attraction for Emlyn Jones. He must have had an Alpine scale in mind. The ridge might have attracted me, too, had the mountain been only half as high; but to take porters and camps over a long, high, difficult ridge, to descend a thousand feet, to climb again to the plateau (which was probably less of a plateau than it looked), to toil across for a mile or more and then be confronted by the unknown problems of the final pyramid were, in my opinion, tasks beyond our powers.

Anyhow I was loath to pit an untried party against so great a mountain. I still cherished hopes of finding one high enough to test our powers of acclimatization, and yet easy enough to give us a good chance of climbing it. We therefore decided to leave Manaslu and the other peaks of this long southerly spur to better men and to seek our objective in the Annapurna Himal which offered several great and glittering prizes.

Having sent word back to our porters to make camp we pushed on, climbing steadily through forest until the trees ended abruptly halfway up a very large moraine of white granite boulders. The track led up the moraine and then through the mounds and hollows of a wide debris-covered glacier. Here the white ramparts of the Ladakh range, several miles to the north, came into sight, and we halted to examine two of its named peaks, Himlung Himal (23,380 ft.) and Cheo Himal (22,350 ft.), and to try to identify the unnamed peak of 24,150 ft. lying on the ridge connecting the Ladakh range with Manaslu. We failed to do this to our satisfaction, nor did we think either of the two Ladakh peaks were intended for climbing. Beyond the glacier we found ourselves in a pleasant grass flat with a birch-covered slope on one side and the high embankment of the moraine on the other, while below the moraine nestled the few stone houses of Bimtakhoti. Later in the year, as a cripple, I spent ten days at Bimtakhoti; a longer time than its interest really warranted but not long enough for its loveliness to pall. On this first flying visit we were delighted by the bright stream and the purple primulas along its banks, by the pale green of the young birch framing white and crimson rhododendrons, by the mani wall and the browsing sheep, with the shapely Ladakh peaks in front and the mighty Manaslu behind.

After inspecting a store where rice was being weighed and stored against the expected flow of salt—for the passes had been open only a week—we went back to camp in the forest on the far side of the glacier. Thence we did a double march back to Thonje where we found everything in train for the final stage of our journey to Manangbhot. The forty-six coolies necessary for this move assembled and started by instalments. At 11.30 a.m. nine loads—the heaviest, of course—still lay forlornly on the ground; but at last all were claimed and after marching for a short half-hour we overtook the rest of the party having its morning draught at the euphoniously named village of Bagarchap. Evidently the latecomers knew more about the marching habits of their friends than we did.

Beyond Thonje signs of Tibetan culture became common. There the sole manifestation was a big mani wall round which the old women marched morning and evening sprinkling the stones with water. At Bagarchap they had an entrance gateway crowned with three miniature chortens painted black, white and yellow. The houses, though neither huddled together nor built on a cliff like a Tibetan village, had similar flat roofs of rammed earth. A log with steps cut in the shape of a half-moon gave access to the roof, the favoured resort for gossip and for watching the passing scene.

Thence our procession moved off more or less together, three of us remaining behind to urge on stragglers. One whom we presently came upon lying by the path was insensible to urging, breathing stertorously, bubbling at the mouth, apparently in the fatal stage of a fit; but one did not have to be qualified to diagnose the fit as alcoholic. Gyalgen, the Sherpa headman and cook, adminstered a few strong, unavailing kicks and hurried on, anxious, so he said, to get in early to make bread. We three, who did not think as quickly as Gyalgen, had to divide the man's load between us. Thus burdened we went on leaving the body lying by the path, hoping that if a man-eating leopard came along the smell of beer would not put him off his meal. This lad was slightly the less objectionable of two whom Lowndes had unluckily picked out of the Katmandu cohort to remain with him as personal attendants against the time when the Sherpas would be leaping upon the mountains. He did not repeat this offence, but he did worse by wrecking, through curiosity and clumsiness, his master's camera. The other, known as 'Squeaker' on account of a high raucous voice, was a good monkey spoilt. He was idle, cheeky and unreliable, chatterd incessantly, pilfered, and behaved, generally like one of his tailed relatives at Shimbunath. These two stuck to us like burrs. They received less pay than the Sherpas and were equipped only with a warm blanket; but apart from the fact that quietness is worth buying they cost Lowndes the use of his camera and the party a lot of stolen food.

We were now beyond the main Himalayan axis and heading slightly north of west through a forest of oak and sycamore. The little lichen or moss on the trees suggested that in this valley, north of the Annapurna ridge, we would be in the rain shadow and that conditions might be less moist than in the Langtang. The coolies ended better than they had begun, going on until late evening, when we camped by a side stream just short of Thangja, a pleasant village surrounded by fields of young wheat. The next village we came to, in spite of its name of Chāme, vied for filthiness with Tilje. The small gompa was in keeping, neglected outside, dark and dirty inside, furnished with nothing but a tattered temple banner and a thigh-bone horn. At a height of 9,000 ft. the track, carpeted with pine needles, lay through a forest of scattered pines with neither undergrowth nor bamboos. Everything pointed to a tolerably dry climate.

This suspicion, or rather hope, strengthened after the third day's march. Within a mile we crossed the Marsyandi three times by well-built suspension bridges, finishing on the south bank on a broad path running through the pines. Where the forest had been burnt, either purposely or by chance, a strong growth of young trees showed that it was self-regenerating. Looking over to the opposite bank the climbers were astonished by the sight of a clean, unbroken slab of rock, a mile wide and more than a thousand feet high, a landslip having stripped off the shallow overburden. Incautiously we expressed a wish to know what kind of rock this was and were promptly told by our expert. We had no option but humbly to acquiesce in the name supplied, which was I think, argillaceous schist. It seemed as likely as any, and the rock, lying at too easy an angle to offer good climbing, deserved no better. At times one felt like comparing our geologist with the Master of Balliol College, for what he didn't know wasn't knowledge; but such feelings were prompted by envy and envy is a kind of praise.

At last we emerged from the pines and descended to a shallow mere on a wide flat where a few ponies grazed. Grass grew by the shore and by the springs which fed the lake, but beyond, up the valley, the eye met only yellow gravel slopes grudgingly supporting pines and stunted junipers. The landscape had the bare, brown aspect of the North-west Frontier. Wherever water flowed grass and trees flourished, yet it was clear that the rainfall alone was not enough to support vegetation. Lowndes looked glum. Mindful of our dark experiences in the Langtang I rejoiced at these welcome signs, but the appearance of this semi-desert did not please our botanist who had come prepared to be wet but happy amid a wealth of flowers. It was now the end of May and we had seen only a few bronze and white ground orchids, some big white anemones, a small crimson primula, some saxifrage and spiraea, and little else. Meantime we had six large boxes to fill and the farther we went the drier the country appeared. However, Lowndes had plenty to do later. The flower growth proved to be nowhere so abundant as in the Langtang, but above 14,000 ft., where during the monsoon constant cloud lay, he found an ample variety.

While the eyes and thoughts of our botanist dwelt despondently on the barren floor of the valley, the rest of us raised our eyes to the hills. We had already seen the 22,921 ft. peak and something of the north ridge of

Annapurna II beyond—enough in fact to strike it off our diminishing list of possible mountain routes. In the hope of seeing more we camped a little early at a small hamlet where a nallah ran up towards the north face of the mountain. Across the river was Pisang, looking like a Ladakh village with its cream-washed stone walls and flat roofs. Notwithstanding the satisfactory evidence of a dry climate, a steady drizzle continued all afternoon.

Meantime we had begun to make the acquaintance of a few of the denizens of this strange valley. Sher Bahadur, prompted, no doubt, by wishful thinking, had long since aroused expectant curiosity by asserting that we should find it as rich and as well cultivated as the valley of Katmandu. He also told us the people were gypsies and highly sophisticated. We had already had some proof of this in an encounter with three women who addressed us in Hindustani, and a man who demanded 'baksheesh' for allowing himself to be photographed. In the remoter Himalaya it is rare to find a man who speaks this *lingua franca* of the plains; rarer still a woman, who, if she stays at home and works as hard as hill-women must, has neither time nor opportunity for languages. In fact one would suspect a woman who did speak Hindustani of having made a business of entertaining travellers, and of being for business purposes not a very sturdy moralist. However, the people of this Pisang suberb seemed so dirty and ignorant that the women might at once be acquitted of either improvement or impropriety.

30 May, we hoped, would be the last day's march. We sent the men off early so that they would reach Manang or a village near it, while we climbed a few hundred feet above the bed of the nallah in order to see round a corner. By starting first, Roberts reached a viewpoint just before an obstinate cloud sat down on the particular part of the north face which interested us. Belatedly we gazed at a fragment of snow with a mass of cloud lying above it which Roberts assured us concealed the main ridge itself and an easy way on to it. Having sent on the coolies we could not take a camp up the nallah to verify this, and luckily the necessity for so doing never arose. By next day we had discovered that Roberts must have been deceived by extreme foreshortening of the view. Upon this viewpoint stood a chorten crowned by a carved wood symbol, perhaps the perfect eight-leaf lotus, and the problem of the moment was to take a picture of this against a mountain background. Some of us almost stood on our heads to achieve it. In the early days of an expedition everyone suffers from snap-happiness just as a novice with a rifle aches with buck-fever. Regardless of the lighting, the first views of rock, river and hill—'base, common, and popular, such as you may see anywhere in wild, mountainous districts'—are eagerly taken as though the like never would again be seen. Later on, the remaining film is jealously hoarded and one becomes so fastidious about subject and lighting that many good pictures are missed.

On this, their last day, the coolies went with a will. We found them waiting for us at a small hamlet on the north bank of the river where they thought we ought to camp. The fields, the young wheat in them springing green, were irrigated with water from a source in the pines above; and we learnt later that nearly all the crops grown at Manangbhot are irrigated. Before siting our base camp on this apparently suitable spot, we went on a mile to look at the village of Braga. Passing under a massive gateway crowned with a full-size chorten and shaded by a fine old poplar of immense girth, we entered upon a meadow of short grass. This otherwise attractive site was wet in places and completely overlooked by the village set halfway up fantastically eroded cliffs of yellow conglomerate. These strange cliffs, and the houses precariously clinging to them tier by tier, had a truly Tibetan air; which was much enhanced when a horde of barefooted ragamuffins poured down and surrounded us. In a country where flat, arable land is rare not a foot of it can be spared for house sites; villages therefore are built on the nearest waste land, no matter how rocky or how steep; and since labour and material are scarce, the houses are built wall to wall and almost floor to floor, the finished article resembling a picturesque, insanitary medieval castle with the serfs' huts clustered round the walls.

After considering the matter we decided that all the advantages of living at Braga—labour, eggs, beer, and raksi, at hand—were not worth the loss of privacy. We therefore went back and after a little search found a shelf on the hillside among the pines a few hundred feet above the hamlet. A trickle of water ran through it, and some ten miles of the north face of the Annapurna Himal confronted us across the valley. Happy in having wood, water, seclusion, and a noble view, we settled down for the summer at Manangbhot.

CHAPTER TWELVE

To the Mountain

MANANGBHOT is the name of the district which roughly covers the region between the Annapurna Himal and the Tibet border less than twenty miles to the north. The settled part comprises some dozen small villages in the upper Marsyandi valley, and of these Manangbhot (shortened by us to Manang) is the biggest; there are also two villages high up on the tributary Naur Khola which rises in the Ladakh range and joins the Marsyandi below Chāme. In Nepali 'bhotiya' means Tibetan, and 'bhot' is the name for Tibet; Tibetans call their country Bod which in colloquial use is aspirated into Bhot. There are two other districts of Nepal, Mustangbhot at the head of the Kali valley and Chharkabhot still farther to the west, that have the suffix 'bhot'.

The inhabitants of these places, and indeed most of those who dwell along the Nepal–Tibet border, have more affinities with Tibet than with Nepal. They speak a Tibetan dialect, practise a similar corrupt form of Buddhism, and have the same manners, customs and dress. They trade both to the north and to the south. The easiest and shortest routes lie to the south, and food, particularly rice for which they have a great liking, can be got only from Nepal, so that the strongest link lies in that direction. But though they belong to Nepal it is doubtful if the ordinary man at Katmandu would recognize them as fellow subjects or be much flattered by the knowledge that they were. They receive, I imagine, but little attention from the Nepalese authorities and pay them little either in the way of taxes, services or respect. Certainly none of the officials from the nearest administrative centre of Kuncha, who occasionally and reluctantly visited us, had ever been to Manangbhot or knew anything about it. As we now saw, Sher Bahadur's notions of a valley rivalling that of Katmandu were wide of the mark; we had not yet visited Manang itself but we could see that it was only a larger village with rather more cultivation and since it is about 11,500 ft. up, little more could be expected. Yet we found the people a peculiar Himalayan community.

The headmen of these villages, particularly of Manang, were a law unto themselves. In fact the men as a whole had that free and independent air, traditionally ascribed to any hardy mountain race, which we rejoice to find and like to encourage until it begins to conflict with our own needs. The reason, I think, for their strikingly independent ways and for their manners, which were always offhand and sometimes impudent, was that many of them were great traders, spending the winter months in cities like Delhi and Calcutta or as far afield as Rangoon and Singapore. Hence Sher Bahadur's story of their being gypsies and of their wealth, which was in part true. Thus they were familiar with train, boat and even air travel, and with the Paleface and some of his less commendable ways. In these cities, where their strange features, stranger dress, and cheerful smiles are a welcome change from the usual run of mournful hawkers, gloomy fakirs, and whining beggars, they blarney the ignorant, learn how to spoil the Egyptians and to speak Hindustani garnished with American 'cinemese', and return wearing wrist-watches and Army boots without laces. We found no wireless sets in Manangbhot, but a man whom we attempted to photograph retorted by whipping out a camera himself.

On the whole they were not pleased to see us and I was not delighted with them. The traveller to remote parts wishes, indeed expects, to find the natives unsophisticated enough to regard him with the respect which he seldom gets at home. At Manangbhot he will be disappointed. As well as their lack of regard for us they were not at all eager either to sell us food or to provide transport; nor was it surprising that our money held little inducement, for their winter trading ventures seemed lucrative enough for them to devote the summer months to drinking beer and raksi. Thrice happy mortals; or to mangle Goldsmith,

How happy he who crowns in Manangbhot
A month of labour with a drinking bout.

On these forays into civilization their stock-in-trade consists of musk pods, silajit[1], medicinal herbs, semi-precious stones, skins and, I suspect, a great deal of impudence.

These impressions were not all gathered the first day, but we had a quick hint that in Manangbhot we were neither so welcome nor of such consequence as we thought, in the dilatoriness with which the headmen responded to Sher Bahadur's summons and their intimation that no coolies would be available for three days. Each village had several headmen and we had always to deal with representatives from each of several neighbouring villages. The principles of democracy, of one man one vote, and of fair shares for all, were well understood; and no Whitehall mandarin could teach these worthies anything about the technique of dealing with requests from outsiders. If we wanted to buy food or hire labour, each representative had to be consulted and each village had the privilege or the penalty of supplying its quota.

Thus, if we wanted six coolies, Manangbhot, after debate, would send two old crones, Braga and Khangsar one man each, Ngawal a boy and the village idiot, each of whom would arrive at different times or even on different days. Sher Bahadur, native and to the manner born, coped with them patiently, seldom losing his temper. Lowndes, on the other hand, who saw more of them than the rest of us and had more need for the casual employment of coolies and ponies, found them trying, and frequently came to the boil; for discipline and that cheerful, willing obedience to which he had been accustomed are not in the tradition of Manangbhot.

On the whole we got on well enough, and so long as we gave several days' notice of an intended move, or several weeks if we wanted food, we were never thwarted. In fact it occurred to me later that they had treated us very well, since they had good reason for regarding us with an indifference closely bordering on aversion; for Packard, in the name of science, had an insatiable curiosity about their private affairs which marked him down at once as either an official or a tax-collector—both unfamiliar species at Manangbhot and, on that account, all the more suspect. Through Sher Bahadur, who shared the odium, he plied these innocent citizens with questions just as though they were the guilty inmates of some Welfare State—questions about their crops, stock, farming methods, their trade, their wives and children, their health, morals and religion.

---

1 Silajit or 'pathar ka passeo' (meaning 'rock-sweat'). I heard of this mysterious substance from Sher Bahadur who described it as a brown or black treacly fluid which oozes from rock faces; it is collected and sold in Katmandu and India where it is highly prized as a sovereign remedy, and is used, too, in dyeing, printing, and tanning. I never found or saw any, but a fact so strange as a rock exuding a soft substance led me to pursue the enquiry and I ran my quarry to earth in the old India Office Library.

Hamilton in his *Account of the Kingdom of Nepal* (1819) mentions it as a product of Nepal and refers to some he saw in a bat-haunted cave at Hanria Hill in Behar. 'I saw the silajit besmearing the face of the rock where it issued from a crevice in the quartz; the consistency of thin honey, of a dirty earth colour, with a strong disagreeable smell like cow's urine. The whole appearance is disgusting.'

In the *J.B.O.R.S.* 1917, vol. 3, there is a chemical analysis of this Hanria silajit: 'Semi-liquid, dark brown, smell reminiscent of guano, 65 p.c. organic, perhaps the result of water trickling through deposits of bats, also dissolving out some silica and other constituents of the rock.'

This explains the 'black' silajit but there is also a 'white' silajit which is a mineral substance. In *J.A.S.B.* vol. 2, I found an analysis of this but no explanation. It merely described it as '95 p.c. sulphate of alumina, an exudation from the surface of soft rocks'.

A secure base and a sound plan are essential for any striking force. We had found our base and had celebrated our arrival there in a suitable way; liquor, by the way, being the one thing instantly procurable without the approval of a committee of elders. (If Roberts's outsize water-bottle was sent to Braga it came back filled with the right stuff pretty smartly.) In theory we were well placed for striking at any peak on the twenty-five-mile-long Annapurna ridge in front of us, at any one of the scattered peaks behind us, or at those which closed the head of the valley on the west, on the Muktinath range.

At this time we were favoured by clear mornings, and on our second day without moving far from camp, we saw an objective and a possible route to it. The Annapurna Himal[1] consists of a long unbroken ridge. The eastern end marked by a summit of 22,921 ft. and the western end by one of 26,492 ft. known as Annapurna I. (A high ridge, the Muktinath range, links Annapurna I to the Ladakh range and forms the watershed between the upper Kali and the Marsyandi.) Between these two peaks the Annapurna range nowhere falls below 20,000 ft. and on it (from east to west) are Annapurna II (26,041 ft.); Annapurna IV (24,688 ft.); Annapurna III (24,858 ft.); two peaks of 23,000 ft. in close attendance upon A.I, and an outlier to the south called Macha Puchare or the Fishtail (22,958 ft.). Three of the major peaks were in full view from our base, but Annapurna I lies well back and so could not be seen from the Marsyandi valley. This is the great peak which the dash and determination of the French party led by Maurice Herzog overcame on 3 June, three days after our arrival at Manangbhot. We knew, of course, like the rest of the world, that a French party was in the Kali valley bent on climbing Dhaulagiri (26,795 ft.); and we had heard that two of them had been at Manangbhot three weeks before, having crossed a high pass, the Tilicho, to the north of Annapurna I. From this we had concluded correctly that Dhaulagiri had proved too tough a nut and that they were looking for a mountain to climb, probably Annapurna I. Their visit to Manangbhot had also served to reassure them about us; for being needlessly disturbed by rumours amongst their Sherpas that a British party was in the vicinity, they assumed that we should immediately make for the highest peak and possibly race them to the summit. This was flattering but, of course, quite untrue. We had no time to reconnoitre Annapurna I which, according to their account, cannot be climbed from the Manangbhot side.

One of the fascinations of looking at mountains is their knack of changing their appearance when viewed from different places or even in different weather.

> The hills are shadows and they flow
> From form to form and nothing stands,
> They melt like mists; the solid lands
> Like clouds they shape themselves and go.

From this vantage point, what we saw through binoculars and telescopes of the ridge in the neighbourhood of A. II could not easily be reconciled with what we had seen from near Pisang. But in time the pieces fell into place. The first conclusion we drew from the completed puzzle was that Roberts' route to

1 'Anna', we were told, means a 'measure'. 'Purna' means 'heaped-up'.

the ridge was a myth, born of mist, foreshortening, and a heated imagination; and the second that there seemed to be no other way. Only from the broad back of the main ridge west of A. II or of A. IV could either of these peaks be reached, while A. III, bristling with gendarmes and cornices, could not be reached at all. At least that was my first impression.

But after prolonged scrutiny I thought there was a way. Starting from the head of a nallah across the main valley a snow-rib seemed to lead at a moderate angle to a big snow-dome on the ridge almost midway between A. III and A. IV. At about 19,000 ft there was an unmistakably abrupt ice-step which could not be avoided and higher up a similar obstacle. But it was that or nothing. There was no other way on to the main ridge which promised to be a safe highway along whose airy crest a camp might be carried to the foot of A. IV or perhaps even A. II. From the dome to the first peak is nearly two miles at an average height of 22,000 ft., and from there to A. II, at an average height of 24,000 ft., is a like distance. The ridge was therefore no cake-walk, but I was optimistic enough to think that the party could climb. A. IV and that then a strong bid might be made for A. II.

At midday Charles Evans and I ascended the dry, barren hillside above the camp in the hope that from higher up the difficult step would look less uncompromising. On returning we learnt that Emlyn Jones and Roberts, on second thoughts, had withdrawn their courageously direct alternative route, so we decided to have a go at A. IV (with a mental reservation about A. II) by my route without any further ado.

The next day, 1 June, was spent in sorting loads for a three weeks' sojourn on the mountain and the making of five camps. This meant that a total of 700 lb. must be taken up the mountain at the start, that the Europeans must carry their own kits, and that no more than two standing camps could be left. These hard facts modified my hopes. In fact with only four Sherpas, two of whom had not been on a mountain before, and five climbers of unknown strength, a peak so high and so distant as A. II was scarcely an attainable prize. One of the most formidable features of a climb on any mountain is its length. This obvious point is of most consequence in the Himalaya where a long traverse without gaining much height, or worse still a temporary loss of height, reduces the chances of success and increases the risks. The ideal is a steadily rising face or ridge, the steeper the better within reason, where every step is a positive gain and where the time spent on the mountain is at a minimum.

It might be thought that the necessity of carrying one's own load would be a rigid guide in making it up. Most of us managed to finish the job with a load slightly on the wrong side of 30 lb., but Emlyn Jones's remained obstinately at 40 lb. Twenty coolies had been promised for an early start on 2 June; finally, with fifteen, we left just before midday. A few were men but the majority were women and children, one of them not yet weaned. However, the weanling did not have to carry but was carried on top of its mother's load where it was within easy reach of its food. Fortunately the Sabzi Chu nallah was so short that we reckoned two easy marches would bring us to a site for a base near the foot of the rib. We could hardly expect our loads to be carried any higher by what might be called an over-sexed team of coolies.

We followed an easy path through pine forest, crossed the small river by a single-plank bridge over which the women had their loads carried, and camped at about 12,500 ft. by the last firewood—birch, rhododendron and dwarf willow scrub. At Emlyn's suggestion we added to our loads a few bundles of willow wands for marking the route on the mountain.

It may be true that no home is complete without a woman, but it is possible to dispense with them in camp. No doubt our she-coolies were a comfort to the men, but for us they performed no womanly offices. On the march they gave more trouble than the men and they were much slower. Yet anyone who had the courage to comment on their pace was immediately overwhelmed by a flood of complaint and abuse from the whole troupe. That evening a steady drizzle set in, against which the improvised shelters of the coolies were of little avail. To us, lying snug in our tents, it was satisfactory to reflect that 'by observing the miseries of others fortitude is strengthened and the mind brought to a more extensive knowledge of our powers'.

In the morning rain still fell and it was cheering to see that the women were as indifferent to it as the men. Indifference to discomfort is a very essential virtue in one's servants when no comfort can be provided for them. Like the squire of a knight-errant who, according to Sancho, must be sound of body, strong of limb, a silent sufferer of heat and cold, hunger and thirst. They all ate heartily of a breakfast such as only the condemned man, whom one reads of shudderingly, could eat with impunity. A large 'degchi' of meal having been boiled to a semi-stiff state, was parcelled out on flat stones according to the number in the mess. Each man scooped a hole in the top of his young mountain, dropped in a little dried yoghourt to impart a cheesy flavour, added a handful of red pepper, and filled it with hot water. After that I always expected the volcano to erupt, but the man merely took a lump of dough from the base of his mountain, dipped it in the crater of red hot lava, and swallowed it.

The approach to Himalayan mountains is usually by way of a long glacier which may provide either a pleasant promenade or a penitential way. In either event it is an obvious route and sometimes affords a party a flying start for the climb itself from the glacier head at 17,000 or 18,000 ft. A classic example is the head of the East Rongbuk at 21,500 ft. to which height one merely walks. But on the north side of the Annapurna range there are no real glaciers. By this I mean glaciers with big lateral moraines filling several miles of flattish valley; here we found mere ice-falls which petered out on the mountain side at about 15,000 ft. before ever reaching a valley. True, opposite Manang village there is one whose snout touches the Marsyandi, but there the river is adjacent to the mountain and except for the last hundred feet or so this glacier is an ice cataract. From beyond our first camp in the Sabzi Chu valley, which is only about four miles long, we climbed the vast moraine of a glacier of a bygone age. All that remained of it now was a short stretch of living ice which we had to cross at about 16,000 ft. to reach the foot of the rib.

The plod up this moraine took us all the morning. It was pleasant work, however, the sun having come out, as we trod upon short turf, the dwarf rhododendron, now in flower, filling the air with its aromatic scent. The women made heavy weather of it. The day had started badly for one of them who had fallen flat on her back when crossing a small stream. I laughed happily at this (although, I suppose, no gentleman would have done so) until I discovered the clumsy creature was carrying a 56 lb. bag of sugar. Both Gyalgen and I then greeted here on the near shore with some suitable observations, receiving a volley of abuse from the sisterhood in return; but when we opened the bag we found that the packers in Liverpool had done their job so well that no harm had been done.

In a sort of hanging valley, where the slope eased off and where the grass gave way to gravel, we began searching for a camp site. As a dog describes small circles before bedding himself down, so the Sherpas circled round looking for places flat enough for our half-dozen tents without too much digging. At a height of close on 15,000 ft. the last wood was far below, but we had carried enough up to cook with for a few days. Roberts and I, the experienced Himalayan climbers, both had headaches, or at least we were the two who confessed to having them.

Having paid off the coolies and beaten Emlyn Jones for the first and only time at chess, I roused out a carrying party. Four of us and three Sherpas, carrying about 220 lb., set off to make a dump at the foot of the mountain. For about half a mile we followed the bed of a small stream which ran down our shallow valley, then turned right-handed over a moraine and dropped down on to the dry ice of a small glacier on the other side. It was barely half a mile wide, and having crossed it we climbed some scree for a couple of hundred feet and dumped our loads under a boulder. Fatigue, perhaps, prompted our choice, for it was not a sound place for a dump. Higher up were some slabs, the plinth of the mountain, and above them a wide, shallow, snow-filled depression which narrowed gradually to a funnel. Some of the ammunition which a mountain normally throws at one—rocks, ice or snow— would likely be directed by this funnel to the depression and so on to our dump or on to ourselves if we happened to be there. Later a large avalanche did come down, sweeping the depression clear of snow, but by then the dump had been cleared and we were high above it.

We woke to find it snowing gently but firmly and by breakfast time several inches had fallen. At 15,000 ft. we could regard this with equanimity or even welcome it for imposing a day of idleness, but for the French who were that day (4 June) descending from their high camp at Annapurna I the storm had grave consequences. Pa Norbu was sent down to Base to bring up more 'satu' (parched flour), and in the afternoon, the weather brightening, we made another carry. This time we moved the dump to an overhanging ledge at the foot of the slabs.

A sparkling day succeeded the storm, but we decided to give the sun a chance to clear the fresh snow before we moved higher. I went down to Base to have a word with Lowndes, who happened to be out, and to bring back more books and tobacco, neither of which can ever be in too great plenty on a mountain. Sher Bahadur reported that he and Lowndes had had a little brusquerie with the Manang notables who, besides wanting to know the reason for our presence, attributed to it the shortage of rain. This complaint may have been laid before the recent copious fall, but in any case, having with us an official escort, we were minions of Authority to whom all ills are rightly attributable:

> Who makes the quarten loaf and Luddites rise?
> Who fills the butcher's shop with large blue flies?

The snow speeded my passage down, for I glissaded about a thousand feet, and did not hinder my return, since by late afternoon most of it had gone. Having bathed on the way up I was preparing to dry off in the sun when the sight of five vultures, eyeing my naked body with hopeful interest, caused me to dress hurriedly.

A frosty night presaged unfailingly a lovely day. Starting early with another load for the dump we left there at 7.30 to make a carry to Camp I, which we vainly hoped might be somewhere in the vicinity of the ice-step. Nine of us climbed on two long ropes, keeping on the left of the depression to avoid the threat of the funnel. High above glistened a wall of ice, from which fragments might well fall. On this the Sherpas kept their eyes glued, for having nothing whatever of fatalism in their make-up they seem to be even more sensitive than we are to such threats. Out of deference to their views (which are often sound) we made for a gully as far as possible from the funnel, taking the step-kicking in half-hourly spells. A steepening of the gully forced us on to loose rocks, but the Sherpas, carrying 50 lb. against our 25 lb., climbed very steadily and not a stone was disturbed. After more snow plugging we reached by midday a bit of bare scree well below the step. Complete and decisive unanimity of opinion concurred in making this Camp I. We put up a tent, stowed 300 lb. of junk inside and, in order to avoid the rocks went down another gully rather close to the funnel. If, during a climb, nothing falls from where it is expected, there is a tendency to assume that nothing ever will fall; but when descending, of course, less time is spent in the threatened area.

On the following day we five took up residence at Camp I. The Sherpas, who should have joined us the day after with the rest of the loads, were not able to come, one of them having to go down to Base to fetch all the remaining spare axes. In the gully on the way up we had encountered some ice upon which, at almost the first blow, I broke my axe (a new one) at the head. Two days later I broke another on the ice-step. Snapping axes thus, like carrots, does not necessarily imply great vigour in the wielder. A misdirected blow or a faulty shaft is much more likely. Like much else nowadays axes are not what they used to be. The pick bends, the blade chips, or the shaft, as we have seen, comes away in one's hand. A good axe should remain serviceable until it goes into honourable retirement with its owner, provided it comes to no untimely end by being dropped on a mountain or drowned in some fierce river which its owner is attempting to ford.

CHAPTER THIRTEEN

On the Mountain

AT our first camp on the mountain we were rudely greeted by a squall with thunder and some snow. Although the height was only about 18,000 ft. it was very cold, a welcome sign that the warm monsoon current had not yet invaded the Marsyandi valley. Despite the cold, diligent search disclosed a trickle of water which saved us the trouble of melting snow; nevertheless, a supper of biscuit and pemmican reminded us that we were in for a short spell of hard living.

As the biscuits were my choice I had no right to complain, but being now without any teeth to speak of I found them singularly unappetizing. The teeth had been carelessly dropped in the Trisuli river when bathing there the second morning out, and no doubt they were now entering the Bay of Bengal. Such a blow so early in the campaign, by making eating, smoking a pipe, and talking, a little awkward, struck at my morale. Taciturnity can be borne and so far I had managed to smoke and eat, but chewing biscuits was another matter, particularly the brutally hard kind I had foolishly provided. One cannot, of course, foresee every calamity. The biscuits, packed and hermetically sealed in neat 1 lb. tins, were those carried in ship's lifeboats. They were officially approved, as one might easily suppose, by the Board of Trade, for they provide a sufficiency of calories and defy the ravages of weevils and time. And since shipwrecked mariners are either drowned before they have a chance to complain about their rations or so happy at being rescued that they forget, such biscuits are still in use and no official of the Board of Trade has yet been stoned to death with them.

A happy feature of Camp I, and of all our camps except the last, was the early hour at which the sun struck it. So, enjoying that too rare combination of bright sun and hard snow, we began climbing towards the ice-step upon which so much depended. Climbing on two ropes we accomplished 500 ft. in the first forty minutes, which could not be described as storming along but was good enough. Approaching the step our rib narrowed and steepened, and soon we were gazing up anxiously at the wall of ice.

Regard for truth prevents my calling this a vertical wall of ice, but it was near enough and a good 80 ft. high. As we had foreseen it could not be turned, for there were great chasms on either side, so there was nothing for it but to cut bucket steps and fix ropes—a job, we thought, which would take two days. We were relieved to find it no worse and were cheered by the level snow plateau above and by the ease with which the second step of steep ice beyond could be avoided. Before going down we gazed long and earnestly at the final pyramid of Annapurna II which, now that we were closer, looked more difficult. Apart from this and the weak condition of Emlyn Jones, our morning was satisfactory.

Evans, the doctor, was worried about Emlyn Jones, who had come very near to collapse. We tried to persuade him to go down to Base but he thought a day's rest would put him right, for he attributed his weakness to lack of acclimatization, as it might well be. The rest of us went up again to attack the wall. Carving out my third step with some nonchalance, for I was then only 3 ft. from the floor, I broke the second axe, a spare one belonging to Roberts. We found that our ice pitons, which were about a foot long, could not be driven in, so we were forced to use short rock pitons. These held firm only if the pull on them came from directly beneath, a pull from any other direction bringing them out faster than corks. However, one driven in directly above the man cutting steps, gave him some moral support, and crampons added to his confidence.

That afternoon we were joined in Camp I by the Sherpas who reported, with the complacency of a successful prophet of woe, that a large piece of ice-cliff above the funnel had broken off in the night and had poured down over the dump. Besides the remaining loads they brought spare ice-axes and a loaf of bread, thus enabling me to have at least one square meal. As Don Quixote observed, his teeth having been knocked out in an encounter, a mouth without molars is worse than a mill without stones. The others with fully equipped mouths had no complaints, indeed rather liked the biscuits. 'With bread and iron we can get to China', as the French commissar of revolutionary days remarked for the comfort and consideration of an extremely ill-fed, hard-used army. If the bread, as one suspects, was hard bread, a technical term for biscuit, he spoke with more rhetoric than truth.

Thus fortified we returned to the attack on the wall. Taking the Sherpas up we sent them back for a second load while we worked on the steps. A mild cheer greeted Packard as he finished the job with a long and trying lead, his ice training in the New Zealand Alps standing him in good stead. Using a spare axe as an anchor he fixed a 200 ft. rope. With its help I went up and fixed another rope by anchoring it to the shaft of my broken axe. It did not occur to me at the time, but one sees now that this was an act of faith little less than sublime.

All was set for a move to Camp II, and the time had come to make a hard decision about Emlyn Jones whom I thought ought to go down from Camp I so that his escort could get back the same day. However, we finally decided that he should start with us the next day, but that if he went no better on the way to the step he must quit.

At a point half-way to the step he himself solved our perplexity by deciding to go down forthwith. Roberts and Charles Evans, who confided to me that his pulse was almost nil, went with him. Only those who have had to turn back on a big mountain in similar circumstances can understand his bitter disappointment. On reaching the step Packard went up with three Sherpas while Gyalgen and I remained below to handle and tie on the loads. Hauling them on so long a rope, which bit deep into the snow on the lip of the wall, was hard work. It took three hours. When I went up I so disliked the proximity of the proposed camp site to the edge of the cliff that we moved everything a hundred yards further back. Before we had settled in, Evans and Roberts were back at the foot of the steps waiting to be helped up; after which we lifted the fixed ropes and stowed them. There was something of solemn finality about this act of severing our link with earth-bound things; a Caesarian touch of 'iacta alea est'; but we could comfort ourselves with the thought that with bread, rope and an ice-axe we could at least get down.

Useful though it might be to have a fit spare man, the fifth man is like the fifth wheel of a coach. Most convenient is the party of four, as we now were. Two tents are enough; and if these are pitched close together door-to-door it is almost as good as having the party under one roof. (An American climber has designed a tent which is 'zipped' to another one at the door, so making one tent of two.) Thus we could lie at ease and throw biscuits, the jam tin, butter and jokes at each other. As a reward for having overcome the step, we forswore pemmican and regaled ourselves with a tin of self-heating soup which Emlyn Jones had brought out to try. Such tins are too heavy to lump about on a long journey, but for a night's bivouac they do well.

To avoid the second ice-step we traversed to the left for half a mile and then diagonally upwards towards the dome. On the traverse, passing under a lurching serac of horrible frailty, the combined prayers of the party for a temporary suspension of the laws of gravity were offered to whatever mountain deity attends to such matters. The second leg of our course led up a crevassed snow-field backed by cliffs of rock and ice which, as we drew near the dome, merged into a steep unbroken slope. The quality of the snow varied; first good, then deep and soft, and finally thin with ice underneath. In the soft snow, where movement was laborious, we graciously handed the lead to Gyalgen who, in time, landed us triumphantly on a broad snow slope to the west of and below the dome. Gyalgen was an experienced climber (in 1938 he had been on Everest), but except for this flash there seemed little fire left in him. He did no more than was necessary and on one occasion less. The other three, who were steady, reliable lads, took their cue from him, their sirdar, and thus showed less enthusiasm than I had expected for the high places of the Universe. Gyalgen was at his best in the kitchen, and much can be forgiven a man who can be depended upon to produce something eatable very quickly under any conditions. But his manner was not ingratiating, and he had started badly as far as I was concerned by ripping up half a dozen canvas food bags and turning them into a cover for his own sleeping-bag; an act which, under other circumstances, might have earned him a decoration for cool daring and initiative.

After plodding up this gentle slope for a short half-mile we arrived under the lee of the main Annapurna ridge. The first instinct of a mountaineer upon reaching a ridge is to look over the other side, but on this occasion none of us had the energy to do so. We pitched a tent, dumped the loads, and went down. Next day we occupied this camp. Some snow which had fallen during a warm night had obliterated our tracks, and as we all carried loads we found the going very heavy. On this part of the route, particularly on the broad slopes of the ridge, we planted our willow wands, for in descending it was essential to hit off the right line on the steep part below the dome. After drinking pint mugs of sweet tea we mustered energy to crawl to the ridge where we looked out over a sea of cloud pierced by the fang-like summit of Macha Puchare. Away to our left the final pyramid of Annapurna II looked remote as ever and no more attractive. However, one more lift of 2,000 ft. should put us within striking distance of A.IV, to attain which became more and more a desirable first prize instead of merely a consolation for defeat by A.II. My two R.A.F. altimeters showed the height of Camp III to be 20,800 ft; which, as is usually the way, was much lower than we reckoned.

Upon turning out early next morning for photography we found that the sea of cloud to the south had spread northwards and submerged the Marsyandi valley. Only a few white and distant tops remained in sight to remind us of the existence of solid land. This dense and widespread canopy assured us that monsoon conditions were established, but whether the weather would become worse or better, or in what way, was anybody's guess. Of our seven days on the mountain so far three had been fine which, I suppose, is as much as one can expect from mountain weather.

From the camp the broad back of the ridge extended eastwards almost horizontally for some way until it narrowed and mounted steadily to articulate with a shoulder of Annapurna IV at close on 24,000 ft. Its subsequent behaviour had now become of less concern to us, but it appeared to drop a little before rising to the foot of the rocky pyramid of Annapurna II, two miles beyond. Half-way up the rise to the shoulder of Annapurna IV, where a break in the slope intervened, seemed the obvious site for the next camp. In examining the route from below, we had paid only slight attention to this section which we had regarded as little more than a snow trudge. We had done it less than justice. Now the angle seemed high, the ridge narrow, and in its lower part so broken by terraces and crevasses that there might be no through way.

Opinion seemed to be in favour of avoiding this broken section by a descending traverse, regaining the ridge higher up by a steep snow slope. I thought I could see a way through. Not relishing the climb back to the ridge I was bent on clinging to it and insisted on trying, and for once my judgement proved correct. By sticking firmly to the crest of the ridge we worked our way up by an interesting and enjoyable route, skirting crevasses and linking terrace to terrace until the angle lessened and the ridge broadened. On the south side parts of the route were a little exposed for laden men, but in the excellent snow a well-driven axe held like a bower anchor. That day we went no further than a snow boss about 1,000ft. above Camp III. Charles Evans and Packard were going very well. Roberts was labouring a little, while I suffered increasingly from mountaineer's foot—reluctance to put one in front of the other. No sooner had we got down to the level ridge than a blizzard swept over it so furiously that, in the short time required to reach the tents, our outgoing tracks were obliterated. On this part of the route, where they seemed least necessary, our few remaining willow wands had been planted too far apart to be seen in a storm.

By now the amount of food consumed, together with tent, rope and other gear left at Camp II, had reduced our total weight to within the compass of two lifts by the Sherpas alone, each carrying less than 30 lb. On the first carry to Camp IV we arranged the loads so that the three Europeans could stay there until the others moved up next day. In this way one of us could look after the descending Sherpas, a task which I undertook; not because I felt more fitted for it than the others, but less fitted for Camp IV. Indeed, on the climb up I felt so feeble that I plodded disconsolately at the tail-end of a rope, kicking never a step. After a long rest at the boss we struggled on until we came to a snug snow hollow in the lee of an ice-cliff just below the flat bit of ridge which we had marked down for a camp site. The altimeters recorded a height of 22,400 ft. Thus we were camped only 2,200 ft. below the summit of Annapurna IV which, I thought, two at least of the party were fit enough to reach.

In wishing the others good luck I hoped that when we came up the next day they would be coming down from the summit of Annapurna IV. In that happy event we might think of pushing a camp forward along the ridge for at least a reconnaissance of Annapurna II, having now become reconciled to the fact that the party was not equal to doing more. The Sherpas and I started down in thickening mist, the precursor of a blizzard like that of the previous day. Even on a ridge it is fatally easy in thick weather and driving snow to miss the way, to quit the ridge too soon, or to stay on it too long. The broken nature of the lower part of ours made this perhaps even easier; on the other hand the familiar shapes of terraces and crevasses, when they did appear, played the reassuring part of signposts. Although the wide back of the flat ridge below gave ample scope for erratic wandering, the leading man unerringly picked up the occasional faint irregularities—the only traces which the wind-driven snow had left of our tracks. When the tents came in sight I sent the Sherpas on and took a long rest, before creeping home at the best pace a piece of ruined nature could contrive.

When dawn on the 16th broke murky, misty and snowy, inaction seemed the inevitable and most sensible course. For the Camp IV party, straining, one hoped, at the leash, it would be provoking enough, but so far as I was concerned nothing could be better. Musing thus contentedly without wondering overmuch what the Sherpas, who seemed restless, were up to, I was shocked when they began striking my tent. The precept 'not too much zeal' may be very well for disillusioned old men, but zeal in others, however inconvenient, is not lightly to be discouraged. It is too often a transient state of mind, short-lived and possibly non-recurrent. Dissembling any surprise, I rose reluctantly and packed. The wind had dropped and in spite of some desultory snow-fall visibility seemed fair. Zeal was indeed transient; by the time we had reached the foot of the climb little remained. All steps had to be kicked afresh, and Da Namgyal, the best of a mediocre quartette, led through the difficult part. Pa Norbu, having kicked a few steps, cried enough; and Gyalgen, who had to be ordered, led for only a short time with numerous halts. I was incapable of kicking steps, but by ringing the changes on Da Namgyal and Pa Norbu, we crawled slowly up. Snow was still falling gently when we surprised the inmates of Camp IV who were wisely lying at earth.

Morning dawned fine but gusty. Having a bad headache, and having breakfasted like a worn-out libertine on tea and aspirin, I had no intention of moving. Roberts seemed to be feeling much the same, so Evans and Packard set off alone to see what they could do. Just as it is

> . . . Pleasant to gaze at the sailors,
> To gaze without having to sail . . .

so Roberts and I watched the progress of the climbers with the complacency of gods watching the struggles of good men against adversity. They soon crossed the short, flat piece of ridge above the camp and came into sight moving slowly but steadily up the foot of the 1,500 ft. slope towards the shoulder. Meantime the sky began to assume a threatening aspect, and we were disappointed but not surprised to see them turn back after about 2½ hours, when they were still a long way below the shoulder. Soon after 10 a.m. they reached camp in time to escape a storm which rose very quickly to the ferocity of a blizzard. Their report that the slope consisted of hard snow, and that in good weather the summit might be reached, went some way to lightening the mild anxiety occasioned by the wind battering at the tents. Nor could one be over-sanguine when one reviewed the condition of the rest of the party; particularly the Sherpas, who throughout the storm, which towards evening began to relent, lay ominously quiet. It would need more than ordinary bad weather to make the descent hazardous, but obviously we could not afford to stay at Camp IV too long.

The time which the first pair had taken to reach their highest point, perhaps less than half-way to the summit, inclined me to think either that they had gone very slowly or that we over-estimated our height. So far the altimeters had deserved our confidence by their sober behaviour, having more than once surprised the party by their unflattering estimate of our achievements. Anyway, if we were going to take seven or eight hours to reach the top, and if it was the habit of the weather to deteriorate by midday (as on the last three days it had), the earlier we started the better. Accordingly I roused the party for a second attempt at 4 a.m. and got them off by 5 a.m. Gyalgen and Da Namgyal accompanied us. The sun had just risen in a leaden sky, or rather a pale, watery glow showed that it was doing its best, and it was very cold. Treading in deep powder snow, the aftermath of yesterday's storm, we gained the ridge and headed for the foot of the slope a few hundred yards away. On our right lay a vast, cold chasm, with a wrinkled glacier dimly visible below.

We had not been going ten minutes when Roberts complained that the powder snow was freezing his feet. He decided to go back, and, without a word of explanation Gyalgen, too, turned back. No powder snow had been left on the slope. On the contrary the wind had packed the snow so hard that we were obliged to nick steps. The perishing cold, and the sight of Packard in the lead taking five or six blows to nick a step, persuaded me to take over from him but without any noticeable increase in our pace. Meantime, a thin wind accompanied by mist blew steadily across the slope, which was too broad to afford any cover. We struggled up for a few hundred feet, but when the wind showed no sign of dropping, nor the sun of piercing the clouds, we too turned tail. By 6.30 we were back in camp.

For the second time the mountain, or its close ally the weather, had beaten us. As we sat licking our wounds, more precisely restoring circulation to our toes—a long process— we noticed with mixed feelings a gradual mending of the weather. Before midday, when according to our notions deterioration should have set in, the day became more and more delightfully calm, sunny and clear. Packard suggested starting again but no one else thought much of that at so late an hour. Instead we basked in our snow hollow, driven by the heat from our tents, tracing imaginary routes upon distant, majestic Manaslu, and how we might make a real route up a peak overlooking the Naur valley. Of all the mountains displayed, from Manaslu to the Muktinath range, this looked least hostile.

Roberts wanted to go down and, since the spirits of the Sherpas seemed at a low ebb, I thought they had better go too before they caved in. I myself had little expectation of climbing the mountain but I hoped that Evans and Packard might, though the former admitted to feeling less fit. We three, therefore, would make one more attempt, retaining Da Namgyal to keep house for us. Leaving him in camp was, I think, a mistake, for he might have made a second on Packard's rope. Accordingly on 19 June, at a more reasonable hour, but after a poor night owing to increasingly wet sleeping-bags, we three started up while Roberts conducted three Sherpas down to Camp III, taking all the tents except the Logan.

The sun shone bleakly through a veil of high cirrus upon which it had painted, as upon flimsy canvas, an iridescent halo. Climbing even at that height, which was by no means extreme, our pace seemed fully as slow as that of a glacier; unhappily, one feared, without the glacier's inexorability. Having climbed for nearly two hours we paused at a small rock outcrop to take stock and to compare our height with that of Macha Puchare, whose fish-tail seemed to make a rude gesture at us from above a bank of cloud. It is difficult to judge by the eye alone, but the most helpful among us dared not affirm that we were much, if anything, above it; which meant that we had risen only 500 ft. After another hour, during which we gained height quicker owing to the steeper slope, the altimeter put us at a height of 23,400 ft. Packard was going strong, Charles Evans panting a little, while the combined effect of age and altitude threatened momentarily to bring my faltering footsteps to a halt. In fact, my goose was cooked, but I was still strong enough to get down alone. Hoping they would move quicker, I persuaded them to leave me.

At midday the usual snow scurries began, yet with no threat of worse to follow. I still hoped they might do it, for I had last seen them nearing the shoulder. Alas; presently they reappeared coming down and before two o'clock were back in camp. They had climbed beyond the shoulder to an estimated height of 24,000 ft., where our candid friend, the altimeter, which I had urged them to take, registered only 23,800 ft. But Evans had shot his bolt, and Packard, who felt strong enough, was rightly loath to tackle single-handed the last 600 ft. of steep and narrow summit ridge. Thus a fortnight of hard work and high hope ended in deep disappointment.

On this third and final attempt neither adverse weather nor dangerous snow conditions could be made scapegoats for our failure; a failure accounted for only by the more prosaic reason of inability to reach the top. That three out of four picked men should fail at or well below 24,000 ft. was not only disappointing, but a little surprising. The performance of the veteran of the party, with all the advantages of experience, was no better. However well a man in his fifties may go up to 20,000 ft., I have come regretfully to the conclusion, that above that height, so far as climbing goes, he is declining into decrepitude.

CHAPTER FOURTEEN

A Change of Scene

THE descent from our mountain, carried out in swift but orderly stages, can be dismissed briefly. On many Himalayan mountains the descent has proved more arduous and perilous than the ascent, and has consequently provided the better story. One recalls the Germans descending in storm from Kangchenjunga in 1929, and the three who died with their six Sherpas on the retreat from Nanga Parbat in 1934; the benighted British pair on Masherbrum in 1938; and the desperate descent of the frost-bitten French pair from Annapurna I this same June. Such hazardous and sometimes fatal affairs are usually the result of bad weather, an attack pressed too long, or a combination of both. In ordinary circumstances the descent of a big mountain is accomplished in as many days as the ascent took weeks. Climbers and porters are eager, perhaps too eager, to get down; all that is needed is care that the descent does not become an uncontrolled one accomplished in a matter of seconds.

The Logan tent had been considered ample for four Sherpas, but we, who like room, to spread ourselves, expecting to be uncomfortable, were agreeably surprised at passing a reasonable night. Da Namgyal, who lay in the middle curled round the centre pole, did not give us his opinion. The Camp III party were supposed to meet us half-way, but we got down there by eight o'clock of a dull morning to find them asleep. We had no intention of stopping, so we routed them out, rapidly packed up, and went on; of the Sherpas only Da Namgyal seemed alert and helpful, Gyalgen being somewhat morose.

The mist which now enveloped us made welcome the guiding willow wands to direct us to the proper place for the descent of the steep slope below the dome. Upon this more than ordinary care was needed. At the bottom the snow changed markedly for the worse. At this lesser height there had been no freezing, even at night, so that we floundered down to Camp II in typically soft, wet monsoon snow. The same evening we laid out the fixed ropes, anchoring one to the broken axe shaft and the other to a bundle of long pitons, both laid horizontally at a depth of 2 ft. with snow trampled down on top. In the night much snow fell, and we had to dig out the loads before making all ready for lowering. Two hours passed in doing this, and then with a remorseful glance at the friendly ropes which had served us so well, we set off under heavy loads for Camp I. The ropes, of course, had to be left behind after safeguarding the descent of the last man.

Even though we were going downhill this bit exhausted us more than any other; ascending such snow would have been killing work. Constantly the legs and feet of one or other of us became inextricably wedged in the deep, wet snow and had to be patiently dug free. Below Camp I, so great had the changes been, little of the route could be recognized. Large areas of snow had vanished and the descent to the dump lay for the most part on rock. Having picked up there a few odds and ends we set off across the glacier in a drizzle, climbed the moraine, and descended to a kindlier region. Our long sojourn upon ice and snow gave a keen edge to the mere pleasure of treading upon warm earth, where hardy, diminutive plants made some slight show of colour and where small cheerful birds flew about as if in greeting. These sparrows, technically eastern Alpine Accentors, haunt and animate an otherwise bleak and lifeless belt between the last of the grass and the first snow.

As we dropped down to the trees of the Sabzi Chu the changes were less striking, our pleasure, though still great, less intense, and our langour increasingly pronounced. In theory a man coming down from a high mountain should go faster and faster; in practice he becomes slower and more lethargic, and is appalled by the slightest rise. On the short ascent of a few hundred feet to Base camp I found my movements were barely perceptible. A period spent at high levels no doubt affects the heart more or less severely, but fortunately only temporarily, according to the time spent and the age and condition of the sojourner. After a strenuous Alpine holiday the ascent even of a staircase is noticeably fatiguing.

In our absence Lowndes had been making profitable sorties to upper slopes and valleys, for there were not many flowers much below 14,000 ft. Emlyn Jones with Sher Bahadur had visited Muktinath on the Kali side of the Muktinath range. There they had learnt that the French had gone home after suffering injuries, but what mountain they had been on or whether they had climbed it no one could tell them, so vague and ignorant are the local people, about their magnificent mountain environment. Our ascent had been watched through a telescope as far as Camp III, beyond which we had been hidden in the clouds.

As three of the party had to leave by mid-July we had about three weeks left in which to find a mountain and climb it. There was nothing suitable on the Annapurna range and rather than prolong the search for an opponent worthy of our slightly blunted steel, we decided to accept the challenge of the peak which we had marked down as a possible prize from Camp IV. Nevertheless it was a shot in the dark. We had seen nothing but the upper part of the mountain, and in the prevailing conditions of cloud, mist and a little rain, it was unlikely that we would see much more. We gave ourselves three days' rest and the Manangbhot Notables notice of our need for seven coolies. Meantime we learnt that the way to Naurgaon, the village nearest to our mountain, lay over a 17,000 ft. pass to the north, the route up the Naur Khola being longer and quite impassable in summer. The people of Ngawal, a village two miles down the valley, had close relations with Naurgaon so they were comparatively delighted to provide all seven coolies.

Accordingly on 25 June a mixed team of reasonably lusty Ngawalians turned up at midday, an hour which ensured their not having to go any farther than their own village that day. Emlyn Jones came with us, while Roberts, whose feet were still painful, took over the collecting of birds, for which I was very thankful. In the absence of Wolfe Tone, who had been unable to come, we had neither collector nor skinner. The skinning of birds was more of a problem than the collecting. Roberts, after a practical lesson in the anatomy of birds from Charles Evans, entered upon this messy part of the job with diffidence. Sher Bahadur came to the rescue. Having watched Toni practising taxidermy all the previous summer, he now showed his ability to turn out equally good specimens. No doubt Roberts would have seen to it that the museum got the species they wanted, but without Sher Bahadur's help they might have had a little difficulty in recognizing them.

After a pleasingly short march down the left bank of the river amidst stunted pines growing stubbornly on yellowish gravel, we camped near Ngawal, whither our mixed team withdrew to spend a last comfortable night. After climbing about 2,500 ft. we camped at a spring well below the pass. So high above the valley, where more often than not cloud and mist lay, grass and flowers flourished, particularly a tall white primula with bell-shaped flowers and a refreshing scent. Yaks grazed everywhere untended; the kharkas of these upland were unoccupied and consequently we got no milk. We often saw stone huts but they were never inhabited. One wondered why the yaks roamed the hillsides to nobody's benefit but their own.

To reach the pass we had yet 2,000 ft. to climb, mostly over brown scree where we could just discern the faint zigzags of a track. Some unsuspecting ponies which happened to be grazing untended hard by, having been swiftly roped in by the Ngawalians, presently found themselves bound for the pass heavily laden. At 16,000 ft., where the grass fought a losing battle with the gravel, I found a bright mauve primula 18 in. high; and on the north side of the pass at the same height, but on scree, the lovely pale blue delphinium with the ravishing scent which we had found in the Langtang—the plant which the natives use, not wholly successfully, as an insecticide.

The unnamed valley into which we dropped steeply was wide, flat, of typically glacial origin, where now only a meagre vestige of ice remains hanging high above it. A bold, uniform, grass-covered moraine ràn the whole four or five miles to Naurgaon, and strolling along the top as upon a promenade we looked down upon grass flats dotted with grazing yaks. Neither trees nor juniper bushes grew in this high valley, which had an air of rich but unfulfilled promise intensified by numerous abandoned stone shelters, comparatively few yaks, and a solitary flock of sheep.

Naurgaon seemed sufficient unto itself without making much use of this fine valley. Poised high above the Naur river, the village surprised us by its comfortable and prosperous air. The houses, as usual, appeared to grow out of the brown, stony hillside, while below lay terrace upon terrace of young barley of the liveliest green where a swarm of women and children were busy weeding. We camped short of the village by a brook, its grassy bank fragrant with thyme, where the headman soon found us. This man, whose every word confirmed the shiftiness of his eyes, amused me by his anxiety to play down the obvious well-being of his village. Like Justice Shallow, fearing a call was about to be made upon it, he deprecated his goodly heritage: 'Barren, barren, barren; beggars all, beggars all, Sir John.'

'Any eggs?' we enquired, 'or a chicken?' 'No', he replied with a regretful smirk, the lusty crowing of many cocks echoing his words, 'We don't keep fowls in Naurgaon.' 'A sheep or a goat?' 'No', came the answer, almost inaudible amidst the bleating of a large flock wending its way to the village, 'They are all up the valley at a distant kharka.' 'Any milk?' 'Quite unobtainable', he regretted, contemplatively eyeing a nearby hillside thick with yaks and zos. However, he promised to supply seven coolies in place of our Ngawal team, for even his effrontery was not equal to asserting the death, burial or absence, of all the able-bodied when we were surrounded by a milling horde.

The peak we hoped to climb is unnamed on the map but is credited with a height of 22,997 ft.—near enough to 23,000 ft. to satisfy those who were particular about the height of mountains with which they associated. Its local name was Khangguru which merely means 'white snow'—a name so frequently heard in the Nepal Himalaya that strangers might be tempted to believe that some of the mountains were crowned with black snow. Through a cloud vista we caught a brief glimpse of the summit of our peak and of a wide, green nallah, running up to black cliffs, at its foot. Between nallah and summit lay an unshifting bank of cloud behind which any horrors might lurk. However, the nallah hinted at a break in the line of cliffs, and near the bottom we saw some terraced fields where we might have a pleasant camp. It looked close but in between lay a gorge 2,000 ft. deep and our new coolies were no fliers. The team included a child and two old crones. By a display of firmness we exchanged the child for the village idiot; but over the women the headman was adamant, not caring, perhaps, to miss such a promising chance of ridding the village of them for good.

Naurgaon lies close to the beginning of an abrupt 2,000 ft. drop to the river, and upon the very edge, as if defending the approach, is built a stone wall 6 ft. high. Nor is the wall the only sign that the Naur valley may have been the scene of 'unhappy far-off things and battles long ago', for we found the river crossing guarded by a ruined stone tower on the far side. At this point the river flows through a canyon, the merest slit 500 ft. deep and seldom more than 10 yards wide throughout its length of about a mile. We learnt later that Naurgaon was once the capital of a rajah whose territory included Manangbhot; hence these defences across the approach to it by the Naur valley.

Having dropped a great many stones from the bridge, timed their fall, and heard from Packard with becoming humiltiy the answer to a difficult sum, we pushed on downstream to the deserted village. The fields were sown with wheat and buckwheat, and we were told that many of the Naurgaon folk wintered there. Next day, having added some firewood to our loads, we set off up the nallah. It was depressingly misty, the first of a succession of blind days; giant purple poppies and dainty blue corydalis did their best to lighten the drab scene until grass and flowers dried out upon an interminable tongue of gravel. It grew ever steeper as we plodded up shrouded in mist, our horizon bounded on one hand by a gully backed by streaming wet cliffs and on the other by scree and boulders.

Down both gully and scree slope crashed occasional boulders. The mist turned to rain, the tongue obstinately maintained an uncomfortably high angle, and when at length we decided to call it a day we were obliged to dig platforms for the tents. Even for those with tents a more disagreeable and inhospitable spot in which to bed down could hardly have been found. For the coolies there was nothing. The friendly boulder, which in such circumstances at least provides an earnest of shelter, dripped like a gutterless roof and the ground in its lee had the high slope of a roof. Concern for the coolies proved needless, for they had their own ideas about lodgings for the night. No sooner had they straggled in and cast down their loads than they approached, their hands raised palm to palm in supplication, begging to be sent down. With the exception of two stalwarts who elected to stay one more day, I paid them off. Whereupon, with a whoop of joy, they disappeared in the rain.

Light, single-fly tents are moderately weather-proof if they start dry, but when packed wet and pitched wet they will certainly drip. After a wet night we left the tents standing to dry, only to strike them hastily when the drizzle began again. On we went up the tongue, noting with sour satisfaction that no better camp sites offered, until we were stopped by a bed of old avalanche snow, the streaming cliffs over which it had slid looming blackly above. Thus driven out on to the scree we traversed upwards, moving with the best speed we could muster across several deep runnels scoured by falling stones. On the far side, by a stream and a large boulder with a faint suggestion of overhang, we camped. While the Sherpas went back for the remaining loads, three of us followed up the stream until we found a line of weakness in the cliffs where it had carved out a gully. In this we climbed for several hundred feet until we could break out on to easy rocks. Assuming the difficulties were over we built a cairn to mark the route, if the line of least resistance which we were following merits such a description. We had no idea where it went; in such weather, upwards or downwards were the only discernible directions.

Meantime, unless conditions improved we should get no higher. Water oozed up through the floor of the tents, streamed from the walls where the platforms had been sunk, and dripped from the roof, reducing the inmates to sodden misery. Having decided to wait we were rewarded (2 July) with a fine day. A wan sun made sufficient brief appearances to dry everything, and Gyalgen, using the last of the firewood, baked a loaf. Courage was thereby renewed.

By jettisoning fairly severely we were able to carry everything in one shift, Evans and Packard assisting by adding considerably to their own loads. It was a critical day, for the most part blinded by mist. Our reconnaissance had not been pushed far enough. No sooner had we passed the cairn marking its limit than we were confronted by a 15 ft. rock wall topped by some slabs. Success hung in the balance. Using the rope for ourselves and the loads we got by this, and after some anxious moments in the mist, expecting every moment to be stopped, we found the ground became gradually easier. We reached a rock cirque and climbed out of it by an easy but precarious gully of shaky rock. This move landed us on a saddle of warm, dry shale with a glacier and its promise of water just below. At 18,000 ft. we seemed to be in a drier climate. It was still misty but the sun had power to penetrate and we felt that we had at last got our heads above water. Visibility, too, had improved so much that we could now see our route up the glacier to a snow dome, at the foot of the final ridge which we already knew, having seen it from Annapurna. There seemed to be nothing to stop us now unless we met with soft, deep snow such as we had experienced recently at 20,000 ft.

The glacier, seamed with crevasses, many of them concealed, had to be navigated with caution. Beyond it, helped by a long strip of scree laid bare by the sun, we made good progress towards the dome up which we were presently climbing on excellent snow. The others, including Emlyn Jones who seemed to have got over his 19,000 ft. complex, were going well; I was moving with more dignity than ease. We camped at the foot of the final ridge at just below 20,000 ft. The ridge looked steep but apart from a bergschrund about 200 ft. above us and some pale, watery-looking patches which betokened ice, there was apparently nothing to prevent us carrying a light camp to the shoulder at about 21,500 ft. where the summit ridge assumed an easier angle. Encouraged by the perfect snow on which we trod, we thought the peak was in the bag.

At this moment of general benevolence Gyalgen saw fit to announce briefly that the Sherpas had resolved not to touch pemmican. Unlike most European climbers who take it under the perhaps mistaken impression that it is good for them, Sherpas as a rule eat it with the greatest gusto. Evidently there was more behind this than was natural, could philosophy but find it out. Whether they had suddenly and inopportunely discovered religious scruples, or whether they were preparing an excuse for cutting short their stay on the mountain, I never discovered. But it troubled me, much as a workhouse master would be troubled by the refusal of his guests to eat skilly. Not that they were likely to go hungry. We had plenty of satu, sugar and tea, as well as a large bladder of rancid yak fat which they had purchased for themselves at Naurgaon. So powerful was this stuff that it flavoured or contaminated our food as well, merely by its presence in the same load.

With high hopes we set out on 5 July to put a camp as near the shoulder as possible. As far as the bergschrund the snow was perfect, but then the covering grew thinner and thinner until soon we were carving large steps in the underlying ice. Having climbed some 400 ft. in four hours we chose the softest ice we could find and hacked out a platform for the tent. Jones and

Packard had crampons, so on the slim chance that they might complete the climb without having to cut steps, we left them there as a forlorn hope. The appearance of a halo round the sun did not augur well for the attempt next day, while Emlyn Jones's form on A. IV did not afford much assurance that he would go to 23,000 ft. But neither Evans nor I had brought crampons, without which one would be faced with the hopeless task of cutting steps for some 1,500 ft. Wishing them luck we started down with the Sherpas. On the way there were no difficult places, nor was there any place where an ice-axe could be driven in to safeguard a slip.

A fall of snow in the night did not improve the chance of the summit party, and the dull, wintry morning which followed was not the kind one would choose for a long and difficult climb. But then so few are. From the door of our tent, for it was too cold to stay outside, Evans and I had the doubtful pleasure of both seeing and hearing them at work. Wisps of mist hid them intermittently, but we saw enough to know that they would not get far. They were laboriously cutting steps, a task imposed upon them by the steepness and iciness of the slope. Even wearing crampons, they could not descend safely without steps. Having seen them start back from a point about 400 ft. above their camp, we went up with two Sherpas to help them down. In the afternoon we packed up and withdrew down the glacier to the camp on the shale saddle to enjoy the warmth of that pleasant sun-trap. Although it makes softer lying than stones or even shale, no one sleeps on snow a night longer than necessary.

Thus, contrary to expectation and the gloomy forebodings freely announced by the experienced veteran, instead of laboriously having to hew a passage through defences of soft snow, we had been decisively halted on a glacis of bare ice. Forecasting snow conditions in the Himalaya is a task that would puzzle Old Moore.

CHAPTER FIFTEEN

Mustangbhot

On returning to Manang three of the party prepared to depart for home, poor in achievement but rich, one hoped, in memories and in experience. To the armchair philosopher success and miscarriage may be but empty words but the mountaineer, who in his more mellow moments may say the same, cherishes a private belief that success does mean something and he therefore attaches to it no little importance. Some there are who are satisfied with the mere looking at mountains; but to the mountaineer they are a challenge. If he ignores them he loses a little of his self-respect, if he attempts them and fails he suspects himself of incompetence or irresolution. Until age has calmed his passion that mountaineer would need to be endowed with the firmness of a St Anthony who is not inflamed by the sight of virgin peaks, who does not regret opportunities missed and lament desires unfulfilled.

On 16 July Evans, Emlyn Jones and Packard left, with two of the Sherpas, to return by Bimtakhoti and the Buri Gandaki valley. At the height of the monsoon they found this route arduous, the porters unwilling, and food scarce. Packard, who was sailing by a later boat, remained with one Sherpa near Arughat in order to devote a fortnight to studying the agriculture and economy of the lower villages. After a week there he became seriously ill with what was later found to be poliomyelitis; he had to be carried in a litter to Katmandu whence, after receiving every attention at the Embassy, he was sent to Bombay and later home by air. Of all the mischances that may befall a man in the Himalaya this must be the strangest and the most unexpected.

The day after their departure, Roberts being still fully occupied with birds, I started back to Naurgaon, taking with me two Sherpas. On our first visit we had heard something of a pass at the head of the Naur Khola which crossed the Muktinath range to Mustangbhot in the upper basin of the Kali river. This Mustang La, as the pass was called, was reported to be inaccessible during the summer owing to the impossibility of fording the Naur river, but I had set my heart on going there and trusted either to finding or forcing an alternative route along the north side of the offending river. In the matter of routes the local people are sometimes very reticent towards a stranger. It may be that they have a low opinion of a European's ability to traverse them, or think that their routes are not fit for a man of such obvious wealth and importance. Personally I should like to believe that they deliberately conceal their knowledge of remote tracks from higher motives—raiding or smuggling, for example—but in these prosaic times it is unlikely. A more probable reason for reticence is the fear that if the wealthy nincompoop traversing their devious ways gets into trouble, either by breaking a leg or drowning himself, they will get the blame.

We reached Naurgaon over an alternative pass by a most ingenious track which, when one looked back from the valley near Naurgaon, appeared an improbable if not an impossible line. In places one had to resort to using the hands, yet signs that the route had been used by sheep, goats, even yaks, were not wanting. The route followed a series of 'rakes' lying along the foot of reddish cliffs sprinkled with cushions of delicate blue or white aquilegia. Light blue poppies nestled in the crannies, and pale mauve primulas clustered over the wet gravel ledges.

I had threatened the shifty headman of Naurgaon with a second visit and now I had come, armed with a letter written by Sher Bahadur conjuring him in the name of authority to treat me with every consideration, and to send him, Sher Bahadur, an adequate quantity of ghi or butter. The headman, in his valley fastness, could well afford to laugh at notes of this kind whether or not he could read them. He stuffed this one in amongst the village archives, which he kept in his hat, and merely added ghi and butter to the list of what he had not got. Neither from him, nor from more reliable sources, tapped independently by Gyalgen, could we hear any comforting words about the

Mustang La route which starts from Naurgaon. Late September was the earliest at which the river could be forded. We decided to go north to Phugaon, the last village this side of the Tibet border, where an alternative route, if any existed, must start, and where, too, we should be on the north side of the Naur river.

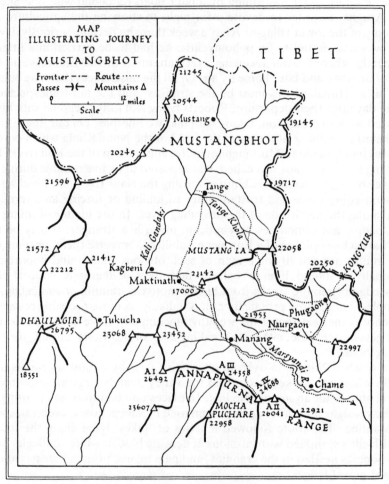

MAP
ILLUSTRATING JOURNEY
TO
MUSTANGBHOT

Frontier —·—   Route ······
Passes →)(←   Mountains Δ

Scale — 12 miles

Journey to Mustangbhot.

Instead of the three coolies asked for, we had to leave with two, and since nowadays Sherpas have rigid ideas about what they should carry when local coolies are included in the party, I carried my own sack. If I expected a startled protest at this piece of bravado on the part of master I was disappointed. Time was when rather than see their employer carry anything on a path—that is when not climbing—Sherpas would cheerfully shoulder 80 or 100 lb.; but nowadays it is fair shares for all—all except the local coolies on whom they pile as much of their own loads as they can.

Once more crossing the bridge over the 500 ft. deep rift we turned up the Naur valley, which presently bore away westwards in the direction of the Muktinath range and the Mustang La. What we could see of it looked bare and inhospitable but by no means impassable. Our route lay northwards up the valley of a river of equal size, the Phu Chu, which rises in a glacier of the Ladakh range. Our camp that night was near an abandoned village, where I estimated there were nearly 100 acres of terraced fields. Judging by the state of the terrace walls they could not have been abandoned for more than a hundred years, though according to our coolies the village had not been occupied within living memory. High above, a small glacier discharged a copious stream from which a long leat had once supplied water to the fields. Possibly its upkeep had proved too great a task for a diminishing population.

The Phu river now entered a series of gorges which were negotiated by means of stairways hewn out of the rock. Having climbed several hundred steps up one of these we had to go through a wooden gate topped with small chortens, and past a red, white and black mani wall. Dropping once more to the river we crossed at a place where it flowed through nothing more than a rock trench. An active man, not necessarily a desperate one, might have jumped it. Here there were several large coloured chortens, and above them a ruined tower high upon a rock pinnacle guarded the defile.

Puzzled by these towers and walls I asked for an explanation from Sher Bahadur who gave me the following story. In early days—that is presumably before the eighteenth century—when Nepal was divided into petty kingdoms, Naurgaon was the capital of a Ghale Gurung Rajah whose territory included Manangbhot and extended to below Thonje. His principal enemy was naturally his nearest neighbour the rajah of Lamjung, a place in the Marsyandi valley below Kudi; and these towers and walls were probably built in the course of a war against him. The Lamjung Rajah was decisively defeated, but subsequently he lured Ghale Rajah, on a pretence of making a peace treaty, to a village called Baman Dande in the Marsyandi valley where he had him and his followers massacred.

Half a mile beyond the gorge, on the west bank, we came to the strange village of Phugaon built on the face and top of a high cliff of boulders and gravel, the eroded remains of a river terrace. At first glance it appears to consist of nothing but narrow, clay threshing floors supported on pillars, underneath which the chaff and grain are stored when winnowing. There are, in fact, some hovels behind these but the best houses are assembled under one roof, and surrounded by a single wall on the summit of the cliff. We had to put our tents on a threshing floor, the only other flat sites being the tiny terraced fields of 'kuru', a barley, already in ear. Phugaon is about 13,500 ft., yet there are more houses and more barley fields 1,000 ft. higher up the hillside. Near the village a river as large as the Phu Chu and equally turbid emerges from the snout of a big glacier, and on the spur between the two rivers stands a small white gompa and a line of thirteen chortens. Such are the austere features of a harsh landscape where hardly a shrub grows, much less a tree; a landscape of yellow cliffs, white granite boulders, and the grey ice of the glacier which had once borne them to the valley.

The headman of Phugaon, who with a straggling beard and a maroon-coloured gown looked like a semi-venerable Chaldean, urged us to drop the Mustang La project, prophesying nothing but woe. If we were bent on seeing passes we could visit the Kongyur La over the Ladakh range two days' march to the north, and he offered a man and a woman to take us there. We accepted this earnest of goodwill but asked him to press the enquiry for men who knew the Mustang La.

With man and wife, who kept us waiting till eleven o'clock, we started on a fine morning for the Kongyur La. The woman went so slowly and rested so often that after half a mile I sent her home; whereupon the man, in spite of his burden being thus increased, went off like a scalded cat, a greater burden having apparently been lifted from his mind. After crossing the river to the gompa the track climbed for 1,500 ft., and then traversed easily across barren slopes of black shale which coloured the occasional stream with the same dismal hue. We camped by a stone hut in company with some Naurgaon men who had just brought a convoy of yaks, sheep and goats over the pass. Some of the animals having foundered on top of the pass, the men themselves had to go back to fetch the loads.

Four of them set off at first light. Interpreting such keenness as an ominous sign boding a long day, we started soon after, leaving our camp standing. Indeed, it proved a hard day which I should have enjoyed more had we been able to see anything. Mist enveloped us at the start, snow fell as we climbed the pass, and a downpour of rain drenched us as we returned. When still well short of a glacier which I could dimly discern was the source of the Phu Chu we turned right-handed up a valley where very soon we came upon the ice of another glacier. Having crossed this we climbed very abruptly above its northern side to a height of nearly 18,000 ft. There was no track. It was a case of every man and animal for himself on a shifting surface of black gravel and mud. The semi-liquid state of the surface, which continued for nearly a thousand feet, showed that underneath lay remnants of ice of the retreating glacier.

At the top of this *route douloureuse* we caught the four early birds and continued in their company on a horizontal traverse over dry scree and boulders with the glacier far below. After two or three miles of this stony wilderness we turned uphill, heading for a gigantic rock curtain which ran diagonally upwards towards some ice-cliffs. The conjunction of these two seemingly impenetrable barriers was swallowed in the mist, but a more unlikely place for a pass could hardly be found. The track climbed steeply close to the foot of the great rock wall from which, I soon realized, stones fell with alarming frequency and appalling velocity. The local talent tackled this section in short, sharp rushes, pausing to draw much-needed breath as they crouched as close as possible to the foot of the cliff; while the foolish flock or the indifferent yak must perforce take its chance of being hit well out in the beaten zone. As we climbed we found that the converging ice-cliff never quite met the rock, the comparative warmth of which served to keep the ice at a respectful distance. Presently we emerged upon a wide snow plateau at about 19,000 ft.

Across this the traffic had worn a foot-deep trench which we followed for half a mile until we came to the bales of wool jettisoned by the last caravan. In thick weather and falling snow there was no point in crossing the plateau to look at the Tibetan side, so that I cannot say what the descent was like. It could scarcely be worse than the ascent, but had we been bound that way we should have been profoundly discouraged by the news that for five marches there were no villages. The way was not littered with skeletons like some central Asian passes I have seen (we found none), but the toil and the hazards of the long ascent before they reach even this comparative oasis of level snow, and the arduous floundering at 19,000 ft. while crossing it, make the pass most cruel for animals. Surely the trader by land who launches himself and his beasts on so perilous a route, as well deserves the proud title of Merchant Adventurer as he who traffics by sea.

On a day of such horrid obscurity it was not easy to place this pass even within three or four miles of a peak of 20,250 ft. shown on the map as standing on the frontier ridge. Over rough going one inevitably overestimates the mileage. Time, or for travellers without watches the telling of beads, must be the only standard of measurement. Nevertheless, I felt convinced that the Ladakh range and consequently the frontier is several miles north of where it is marked on the map, which hereabouts becomes vague and conventional. Rivers and their tributaries are suspiciously like the conventional herring-bone, and the contours have the too-simple curves of a sea serpent. On the Tibetan side the map is a pleasing blank for a space of fifty miles until a large blue line indicates the course of the Tsangpo river. In consequence the goal to which this high and perilous pass leads remains for me only a vague name which varied every time it was uttered—a riddle to be solved by some happy traveller in less troubled and less trammelled times.

Returning to Phugaon we found that the venerable Chaldean had been as good as his word. Under extreme pressure two able-bodied men, whom we assumed were familiar with the Mustang La, had volunteered to share what might be a hungry journey. They took with them five days' food which I hoped would last until we reached some village in the Kali valley. Merlin delivered a harangue, like a priest about to sacrifice, gave us his blessing and a couple of potatoes, expecting, no doubt, to see us back in a few days. According to the map, which in its broader aspects gives a fairly true picture, we had to strike due west across a tributary of the Phu river before launching into the upper Naur valley, where we planned to keep as high as possible along its northern side. I assumed the Naur flowed in a gorge and had a theory that by keeping high enough we should avoid the gorge and find easier going. As Holmes used to tell Watson, it is a capital mistake to theorize before you have data.

Our men did not cast up until eleven o'clock—a delay which enabled us to dry out after the wet Kongyur trip—when we at once embarked upon a 3,000 ft. climb to the ridge barring us from the tributary river. A thousand feet higher we came to the last fields and houses of Phugaon where the men dallied with a Siren, in less classical language, a 'floozie', who sat on a roof combing her wonderfully straight black hair. This danger past we sweated to the top of the ridge on a well-marked path. There it divided, one branch going down to a bridge, as we were told, and the other leading up the valley. Unwilling to sacrifice height so hardly won we took the latter. This led us easily across shale slopes, which though utterly void of vegetation were the home of many 'bharal' (wild sheep). A sharp fall of hail coinciding with our arrival at a spring of water, we camped there and for fuel grubbed up some roots of heath growing in the moist gravel.

The sacrifice of height had been only deferred. We dropped a thousand feet to the river, forded it with the help of the rope, and began another fierce climb which ended in 500 ft. of loose scree. A faint path had accompanied us so long that I began to think we had hit on an alternative route to the pass, until it presently petered out at a place where there was some particularly nourishing gravel for grazing yaks. From the top (c. 17,000 ft.) we expected to see up the Naur valley, so Gyalgen and I made a violent but vain effort to reach it ahead of the gathering mists. The men having arrived and viewed with extreme distaste a brief expanse of gravel and a grey wall, I had to behave as though I knew where we were going; to put into practice my high theory without the least hint or guidance as to how rigidly it could be applied. Well in the lead, I alarmed my followers by taking an even higher line, no doubt giving them reason to think that the idiot in front had no lesser or more sensible goal than the eternal snows. When a line of yellow crags intervened I doubted if our coolies would stand for strict adherence to theory; a theory which no one had expounded to them and which seemed only to drive its advocates ever higher and higher.

After losing some 5,000 ft. by descending to the foot of the crags, we made another mile without further loss until brought to a halt by an enormously deep nallah, guarded by cliffs on the far side and in its upper reaches by a waterfall and a vague hint of ice. No principle or theory could stand in the face of facts like these, reinforced as they were by the sight of a patch of grass and some juniper bushes on the river bank nearly 2,000 ft. below. 'A merciful Providence fashioned us hollow, on purpose that we might our principles swallow', so without demur but with considerable misgiving, I began plunging down the scree to commit the party to the mercies of a low-level route along the river bed.

Other travellers had evidently camped or grazed their animals on that grass by the river, and, although we could not reach it, we were cheered by the sight of a distinct track on the other bank. To our surprise and satisfaction we made good two or three miles among the boulders of the river bed before a series of rock buttresses compelled us to climb high before we could regain the river beyond. Early in the afternoon we came to a point where two rivers of almost equal size joined to form the Naur, one branch descending from the north-west and the other from the north-east. Here was a poser. The path on the other bank, which we still had in view, disappeared after crossing the north-west branch. The Sherpas thought the pass lay up that nallah, the local men were struck dumb. No one had advised them about this critical choice and, as we learnt, they had never been near the pass before. I favoured the north-east branch, not only because any fording would thus be deferred but also because of a hint from the despised map. On the Kali side of the Muktinath range only one of the many nallahs had a name, the Tange Khola, and it seemed more than likely that the way to the Mustang La followed this. Its head lay well to the north-east. But, in fact, the obvious difficulty of fording the river, although its volume had now been reduced by half, left us no choice. We went on up the right-hand branch. Cliffs soon forced us to climb high, and from the vantage point to which we were driven we picked out here and there on the far side of the river an unmistakable track; thus I led on with more confidence until we camped less than a mile below the glacier source of the river. I thought the way to the pass must lie up this glacier, but a walk upstream that evening convinced me that a small side nallah almost opposite our camp held the clue. The constant cloud canopy hovering at the 15,000 ft. level added the charm of uncertainty to the interest of new country, but I had seen enough to realize that the glacier could lead only to a peak of 22,000 ft. at the point of junction of the Muktinath and the Ladakh ranges. Moreover, up the valley there was no sign of the track which apparently petered out on a small grass flat near the entrance to the side nallah, where a few piled stones marked the remains of a stone shelter.

So far up, only half-a-mile from its glacier source, the river was fordable. Having crossed it we searched the flat and the vicinity of the stone shelter for tracks heading up the side nallah. Upon finding nothing our confidence began to ebb. Was it possible the track we had seen led merely to this diminutive grazing ground? Avoiding the stream, which emerged from a gorge, an unlikely line for a track, we climbed the slopes above it, following the natural line a track would have taken. Not the faintest trace rewarded our wide casts. A gash in the hillside caused by a landslip brought us up short, and we sat on the edge of it wondering what to do. For want of anything better I plunged down the loose earth of the slip to the stream-bed below where, to my delight, I found at first some old yak dung and then a faint but definite track in the gravel. At these tidings our coolies, now on their fourth day out becoming a little dubious about their future, brightened instantly and threw off dull care like men who hear the distant summons of a gong.

At a fork of the valley we lost the track, recovered it by a wide cast, and began to skirt a vast slab of white ice which, on the brown shale, appeared detached as a cloud, after the manner of a central Asian glacier. Presently we were standing by a cairn on top of the Mustang La on a broad shale saddle peering into the mist on the Mustang side. Its height is about 18,000 ft. We anticipated an easy run down to some hospitable village in the Tange Khola; foolishly, for it is an almost invariable rule in the Himalaya that a descent to a valley means a great deal of climbing. The valley quickly narrowed to a gorge which the track avoided by climbing back into a small lateral nallah, where we found all the amenities for a camp—fresh water and some scrub.

After hovering briefly over the main valley again the track took fright and sheered off, as well it might from a place that had the appearance of having been the epicentre of repeated earthquakes. In the next lateral nallah we surprised a party of men and women busy gathering and drying wild garlic. They were not local residents but called themselves 'Khumbas' from Tukucha well down the Kali valley; they assured us we should reach the Kali that evening. Having landed us in yet another side valley the track very wisely quitted the Tange and all its deep-cut affluents for a better world. But we went on down, unable to resist the false lure of a large but apparently deserted village on a terrace above the river. On this level shelf, where there were possibly a couple of hundred acres of abandoned fields and scores of ruined houses, the going was so good that we ignored the sinister warning that the absence of any path should have conveyed. Nemesis was at hand. A precipitous gash some 200 ft. deep, cut by a side nallah, yawned suddenly at our feet.

Even if it had promised escape from further trouble, there was no climbing down the vertical gravel walls of either this nallah in front or of the Tange on our left. We must return to the track we had long since quitted or climb 2,000 ft. of scrubby hillside to reach a trickle of water above the lip of this deep trench. It was already late afternoon, so we chose the climb. Men thus frustrated, dashing at it in vehement rage, should have made short work of this paltry ascent; for us, sunk in the languor of sullen resignation, it involved several hours of moody toil. At the top, in addition to water, we found the path from which we had so foolishly strayed.

Dense mist succeeded a night of rain. As usual we began by climbing until the path reached a shoulder where we realized, in spite of the mist, that we were looking across the spacious depths of the Kali valley. Instead of descending at once the path kept well up the hillside in a northerly direction; but we had learnt our lesson and were prepared to follow whithersoever it led, even to Tibet. At intervals we bellowed in unison, like ships advertising their presence in a fog, until at length we were answered by the bleat of a sheep, a welcome sound to weary wayfarers or even to hardy mountaineers whose veneer of hardiness is at last wearing thin. Dogs barked as we approached a black tent and a line of tethered yak calves. Having got some information but nothing else, we pushed on, the path at long length trending downwards. The mist melted, revealing far below the green fields of Tange village, and a line of willows along a flume.

CHAPTER SIXTEEN

Muktinath

THIS little green patch betokening human activity shone like a good deed in a naughty world—a world of shocking sterility, harsh colour and violent shapes. Below 14,000 ft., that is, below the level of the kindly mist, vegetation practically ceases except for a sparse, spiny bush which I am assured, though I find it hard to believe, is a kind of honeysuckle. The plant flourished defiantly on what Cobbett would have called a 'black, spewy gravel', emphasizing by its pervading presence the total absence of other plants of either use or beauty. The Kali river was not in sight. It runs at the bottom of a deep trench as if ashamed of hurrying stealthily by, withholding its life-giving water from so thirsty a landscape. Beyond it, on the western side, lay a similar woodless waste of yellow, grey and black hills—a barren landscape, very rarely refreshed by the green fields of a village to which the water of some side nallah had been cunningly led.

Tange occupied a terrace above the Tange Khola a mile short of its junction with the Kali. The headlong career of this precipitate river drew to an inglorious end meandering over a ridiculously capacious bed for such a pitifully small stream. Its wide gravel bed was sunk between gravel cliffs 200 ft. high scored at regular intervals with gullies. The bright sun on the cliffs and the deep shadows of the gullies gave them the appearance of giant organ pipes. Upon the terrace above these cliffs Tange had ample room to spread, but the houses, as usual, were crammed together. However, they were all on one level and not stacked like a house of cards. Apart from some donkeys, the first I had seen anywhere in Nepal, the village was remarkable for a double row of giant stupas, coloured brick-red, their lower part covered by one big flat roof. The houses with their high battlement of drying firewood, looked even more Tibetan than those of Manangbhot. The height is not much above 11,000 ft. They told us they grew two crops a year—winter wheat or barley, which is cut by June and followed by buckwheat or potatoes.

Tange could give us only essentials like rice, tsampa and buckwheat, a yellowish flour which can be turned very easily and quickly into excellent cakes. Milk or mutton seemed hardly within their scheme of life, though they had some vast herds of goats which presumably lived on honeysuckle. Having exhausted this unfruitful topic and given the Phugaon men the rather one-sided option of staying with us or going back over the pass, I walked down to the Kali river. Its thick waters rolled along a bed similar to that of the Tange, but wider and with higher cliffs. These yellow gravel cliffs have been carved from old river terraces and behind them rise wildly eroded and weirdly coloured hills of slate-blue, cobalt, mauve, chrome and orange, all blending into an inky blue over distant Tibet. It is fascinatingly ugly country, the more fascinating for being so little known. No snowy peaks broke like white waves upon the horizon of this tumbled multi-coloured sea; for across this twenty-mile-wide basin the Ladakh range dwindles to insignificance.

Mustang town or village is some ten miles north of Tange on the west side of the river which is crossed by a ford. The only explorer to visit Mustang and the upper Kali was one Hari Ram, one of the Survey of India native explorers, in 1873.

Lloh Mantang (Mustang) [he reported] is situated in the centre of a plain 11905 ft. above the sea . . . the plain is irrigated by channels. Mustang is enclosed by a wall of white earth and small stones, 6 ft. thick and 14 ft. high, forming a square with a side ¼ mile long, and having an entrance gate to the east. In the centre is the Rajah's palace consisting of 4 storeys, about 40 ft. in height, and the only building to be seen from the outside. In the N.E. corner of the enclosure is a gompa containing copper gilt figures and 250 lamas. There are about 60 other houses, two-storeyed and about 14 ft. in height, forming streets and lanes. Drinking water is brought in by means of a canal, and this overflowing makes the interior slushy; since there is always an accumulation of filth the smell is very offensive. Since no census is taken I cannot say how many people there are but they appeared to be numerous. Besides the residents there are always a number of traders from Tibet and Nepal who either exchange their goods here or take them to Lhasa or Nepal. The trade in salt and grain does not extend very far north. Trade is chiefly carried on by Thaklis, a class of traders of mixed origin, who have the privilege of going to Lhasa and they even go to Calcutta for the purchase of goods. The Rajah, who is a Bhot, collects a revenue from all sources of about 10000 or 12000 Rs a year, out of which he pays 2000 or 3000 yearly to Nepal from the land revenue, and 10% of the taxes levied on goods brought from across the northern frontier to the Lhasa government.

Hari Ram went on to Tradom in the Tsangpo valley but his account is vague, as is the map north of Mustang. The frontier is marked about ten miles north, and the Kali river, indicated by only a dotted line, appears to rise on the Tibetan side. This is very probable because ammonite fossils of the Jurassic Tethys are found along the banks of the Kali in Mustangbhot. I picked up some fragments on the way to Muktinath and found a considerable deposit at Muktinath itself, which, indeed, owes its sanctity to the abundance of these fossils, the sacred 'shaligram' of the Hindus. Hari Ram put the Tibetan frontier at the Photu La (15,000 ft.), a pass two days' march north from Mustang. The pass probably lies on the watershed of the Kali and the streams flowing north to the Tsangpo.

We walked for two days through equally arid country to Muktinath. Our party was augmented by two Sherpas who were returning to Solu Khumbu, the Sherpa district south of Everest. Seven months having elapsed since they had set out on a trading venture to Tibet, it would seem that for the Himalayan business man time is not necessarily money. We followed a broad highway some 3,000 ft. above the Kali; the going, however, was pretty rough, and worn into ruts by the feet of innumerable sheep and goats. We met with many flocks, each numbering several hundred, either carrying rice or grain up to Mustang, the exchange mart, or bringing down salt. From Muktinath the traders go down to the Kali valley to Kagbeni, or lower still to Tukucha at the foot of Dhaulagiri, to pick up their rice. There is another route on the west side of the valley, and if the traffic there is anything like as heavy the combined total must be very great.

Dhaulagiri and its huge ridges dominated that side of the valley, but clouds prevented our identifying with certainty Annapurna I, its fellow portal on the east. Through the twenty-mile-wide gap between these two 26,000 ft. summits the Kali river flows at a height of only 6,000 ft. At this time, the end of July, although the monsoon was in full vigour, Dhaulagiri remained wonderfully free from cloud. I had the impression that north of the Himalayan crest-zone the Kali valley is even drier than the Marsyandi. What bad weather there was seemed to come from the north. On three of the four days we were there heavy thunderstorms gathered in the north to sweep southwards along the crest of the Muktinath range. But no rain fell below a height of 14,000 ft.

The celebrated Hindu pilgrim resort of Muktinath lies at a height of nearly 13,000 ft. at the head of a valley draining westwards from the Muktinath range into the Kali. Well watered by springs and streams it evidently enjoys a comparatively moist climate. Some pines grew in a ravine on its south side— that is, on the north-facing slope where pines and juniper always flourish best—while the slopes above the village were clothed in grass. Although Muktinath is higher than Manangbhot, where the harvest takes place in September, the earlier wheat fields had already been cut and threshing with flails was literally in full swing. We camped near the topmost house of the straggling village where our arrival created no stir. A place to which several thousand pilgrims come every year must be accustomed to strange sights; moreover, within the last two months, it had been visited by two of the French party and by our own Emlyn Jones.

Having collected about 30 lb. weight of fossils from a rich deposit hard by I took the Sherpas to see the sights; or rather they took me, for Muktinath meant much more to them than to one for whom it was merely a name. For the Nepalese, Muktinath ranks with Gosainkund, Pashpati and Ridi, as one of the four great places of Hindu sanctity. According to Sher Bahadur, the name should be Mukti-Narayan, as it appears in old scripts, Narayan being an incarnation of Vishnu to whom the shrine is dedicated. It owes its sanctity to the presence of the thrice-sacred 'shaligram'. This is also found at Ridi and Pashpati much farther down-stream in the same valley of the Kali or 'black' Gandak. Perceval Landon in his *Nepal* says that the stones are regarded as emblems of Narayan or Vishnu and during worship before his shrines they are held in the hand to sanctify the making of a vow. In the temples they are generally contained in a small copper cup, together with some Ganges water and a few leaves of the tulsi plant. In his account of Nepal (*v. supra.*) Hamilton gives the following description of the Muktinath shaligram; but evidently his informant did not make it clear that Muktinath now stands 3,000 ft. above the Kali Gandaki.

On the banks of the Gandaki at Muktinath is a precipice from which the river is supposed to wash the Salagrams or black stones, which are considered by the Hindus as representatives of several of their deities, and which are the most common objects of worship in Bengal where images are scarce. They are of various kinds and accordingly represent different deities. On account of its containing these stones this branch of the river is usually called the Salagrami, and the channel everywhere below Muktinath, until it reaches the plains of India at Sivapur, abounds in these stones. All the Salagrams consist of carbonate of lime and are in general quite black. Most of them are what naturalists call petrifactions and the most common are Ammonites, half embedded in a ball of stone exactly of the same nature as the petrified animal. Others, which are reckoned the most valuable, are balls containing a cavity formed by an Ammonite, that has afterwards decayed and left only its impression. Some balls have no external opening, and yet by rubbing away a portion of one of their sides the hollow wheel (chakra) is discovered. Such Salagrams are reckoned very valuable.

In the deposit which we found at Muktinath itself nearly all the stone balls contained a fossil, but in breaking them open the fossil, too, was usually broken. This deposit occurred in a sort of black shale, smelling faintly of sulphur, which the people dug out for dressing their fields.

The temple and shrine of Narayan at Muktinath does not appear to be ancient. It stands in a sunken stone courtyard surrounded by a stone wall over which flows the sacred spring through 108 metal spouts carved like gargoyles. The spring itself gushes from the foot of a cliff a few hundred feet above the temple. There were no pilgrims other than my two Sherpas. They did the necessary round of the 108 spouts, drinking from each in turn. It was certainly delicious water, what the Spaniards would call 'agua muy rica'—very rich water. The pilgrim, according to Sher Bahadur, having bathed and drunk 108 successive times and performed other ceremonies, takes a vow either to relinquish one of his evil habits or to become a vegetarian.

A far more curious thing than these 108 spouts is to be seen in a nearby Buddhist gompa. For Buddhists, too, journey to Muktinath and thereby acquire merit. As Buddhism spread northwards from India at the time of Asoka, or, as is more likely, when it later declined and approximated to the surrounding Hinduism, the Buddhists put up their own temple at Muktinath and appointed nuns to look after it. The present gompa and the present nuns are both extremely dilapidated, but neither can date from the time of Asoka. The interior of this dark and dingy gompa, into which we were admitted by an old crone, the Sherpas having discarded their boots, is almost devoid of ornament. On a rock ledge at one end sits the usual gilt Buddha with a few butter lamps burning in front of it. But underneath this natural altar are three small curtained openings, in each of which burns a lambent blue flame, presumably of natural gas; through the centre opening flows a small stream and the flame issues from a rock so close to the water as to justify the natives' stories of burning water. The Sherpas prostrated themselves before the Buddha while the old hag held up the curtain over the centre aperture for their edification. They were thus able to examine the flames at their leisure. But my examination of it was perforce perfunctory; for the Sibyl withdrew the curtain only reluctantly and briefly for one who was so obviously far from the Way and who was perhaps not even seeking it. The Sherpas, having finished their oblations, took earth from the floor and filled a bottle with this holiest of water to take back to Darjeeling. When, like an impious Yahoo, I asked them if they were going to sell it, they were genuinely shocked.

We had now to get back to Manangbhot over the Muktinath range which is crossed by a 17,500 ft. pass. This climb of 5,000 ft. nearly broke my heart. Since I was carrying 30 lb. of fossils I might well liken it to the 'severely scientific' ascent of Chimborazo by Whymper with his two Swiss guides the Carrels, when Jean Antoine had to carry his 12 lb. baby, as he called the mercurial barometer. It is an easy and much-used pass. On top there was no view to detain us, so we dropped quickly down to camp in a flowery meadow by the first juniper scrub. Four hours of fast going down this Jargeng Khola, where the vegetation is almost prodigal, brought us to Manang village. In the main part there are about fifty houses built on a terrace overlooking the Marsyandi river. Just across the river and very nearly touching it is the snout of the ice torrent, already mentioned, which comes tumbling down from

Annapurna III. The presence of this ice at the door of the village, so to speak, gives it a stern, almost savage air, which is scarcely merited; strange indeed is the contrast between the ice on one side of the river and the bountiful wheat-fields on the other. In an open space in the middle of the village is a long mani wall crowned with a double bank of prayer wheels, fifty-four each side, which are turned by those who tread the lustral path. Another curious item is the village smithy, the smith and his family being immigrants from lower Nepal. They had lived there for many years, but they appeared just as incongruous in their surroundings as we Europeans.

At the base camp, which we reached on 3 August, only Sher Bahadur was in residence, the two naturalists having gone up the Khangsar nallah, a stream which unites with the Jargeng above Manang village to form the Marsyandi. Of all the small valleys of the Marsyandi basin, Lowndes thought that the Khangsar was not only the richest in flowers but that the people of Khangsar village were the most friendly. Either on account of its botanical treasures or because it was the only valley where milk and butter were to be had, he spent a considerable time there. The base camp had been improved by the installation of a stone-floored sitz bath sunk in an irrigation channel which ran through it. If he had not actually done the building, Lowndes had certainly been its inspiration, for he was much addicted to soap and water, and thought it no ostentation to wash almost every day.

Baking cakes and eating them, collecting some primula seed from the Naurgaon pass, and bathing out of respect for Lowndes, occupied me for five days while waiting for the return of the naturalists and an expected parcel of mail. We had arranged for this to be dispatched at fortnightly intervals to Kudi whence we collected it at highly irregular intervals. This batch gave us our first news of the climbing of Annapurna I on 3 June by the French, a feat of daring, dash and determination, accomplished at heavy cost. The photographs of their route may or may not give a true impression, but from them one would infer that it was a route from which a mountaineer might well shrink without being suspected of timidity.

Before returning to Manang in September to collect seeds, which by then should be ripening, Lowndes wished to examine the flora of the Dudh Khola; and as Roberts had already collected some 170 birds we thought the time had now come to collect a mountain. We therefore agreed to foregather at Bimtakhoti towards the end of August. Meantime I was to go there in advance to search for some peak suited to a party of moderate powers and dwindling ambitions.

CHAPTER SEVENTEEN

Bimtakhoti and Himal Chuli

I quitted Manangbhot for the last time without regret. Annapurna IV, across the valley, was a too-constant reminder of failure; and in spite of a common liking for raksi the natives and ourselves had never got on close terms. They remained content neither to help us much nor to hinder us. On my final departure, I had with me as usual a man, and a goitrous woman of advanced age who had soon to be sent back.

Thonje, as a result of the considerable rainfall which it had received, seemed less attractive. The village was a quagmire of mud, or worse, and flies abounded. But rain or no rain the traffic to Bimtakhoti up the Dudh Khola went on. It consisted mainly of long strings of zos, so that the track up the valley was in a deplorable mess. We camped half-way up at a solitary house, drawn thereto by the smell of beer and meat, for a yak had just been dismembered. The slaughtering of these animals has to be done surreptitiously in a country administered by Hindus, for a yak, in spite of its uncouth appearance, can hardly be refused the protection afforded to cows. Water buffaloes, on the other hand, are not looked upon as cows and are therefore fair game. Strict Buddhists, of course, should not take life of any kind, but Tibetans are meat eaters as, indeed, they must be to prosper in their cold climate. No Sherpas will kill a sheep if he can find someone to do it for him, but he will eat it with gusto, guts, brains and all, even cracking the bones, for the marrow. In Tibet the killing is usually done by butchers, a class who are in a low category, bound for hell anyway; and since the sin of killing for meat is very justly pooled amongst all who partake, the butcher's share is so trifling that his progress thither cannot be much accelerated nor his sojourn there greatly prolonged. According to Sir Charles Bell, if a high lama eats meat he makes a special effort on behalf of the animal slain to ensure that it will be reborn in a higher state. Thus the transaction ends agreeably for both parties.

At Bimtakhoti there was a frequent coming and going of herds of zos and flocks of sheep, to and from either the Larkhya pass or Thonje. The noise of bells was constant as troops of zos, a dozen or so together, plodded past our camp on the short-grass flat. Each animal carried a deep-toned bell, and the leaders of a troop had in addition collars of small bells from which dangled bright scarlet tassels of yak hair. The man in charge of the store, the 'subah', a relative of our rich friend at Kudi, told us that during the short season he weighed in more than 3,000 animal loads. The rate of exchange was sixteen measures of rice for twenty-five of salt; but over the pass at Larkhya, where the Tibetans arrive with their salt, twelve measures of rice are enough to buy twenty-five of salt. According to the subah, what economists call the price mechanism has free play, the exchange rate adjusting itself by the amount of each commodity in sight. But when Roberts visited Larkhya he found all in confusion, the subah having been forced to flee before the wrath of Tibetan salt merchants who accused him of a preference for a planned economy—planned, of course, in his own favour.

Bimtakhoti lies in the shadow of a 200 ft. high moraine thrown up on the true left bank of a glacier descending from the Ladakh range. The path from Thonje crosses this glacier between Bimtakhoti and the snout, which is about a mile below; and the path to Larkhya follows its ablation valley for a couple of miles before turning eastwards to the pass which lies on the ridge joining the Ladakh range to the Manaslu massif. A little above Bimtakhoti this glacier divides into three branches, one descending from Himlung Himal, one from the direction of Cheo Himal, and one from the mountains near the Larkhya pass.

Himlung Himal was one of the peaks I wanted to examine, so we crossed the glacier to the right bank and continued north up the ablation valley of the Himal Chuli branch. There is no cultivation at Bimtakhoti. Apart from one man who spent his time sewing tinsel decorations (bought in Calcutta) on to cheap felt hats, the people, admittedly few, had no occupation other than spectators in life's battle; yet we had the utmost difficulty enlisting even one reluctant volunteer, so that in the end I had to carry my own kit. The weather was as unsuitable for reconnaissance as it could be—we had seen no mountains for some days—and the only source of pleasure lay in the vegetation which was so lush that we were soon soaked. We might as well have been back in the Langtang; for we found here in abundance purple aconite, the delicate blue codonopsis, and a heliotrope delphinium. However, we soon got on to sparse grass and better going across a series of old lake beds until we made camp in the rain not far short of the glacier head. In spite of low cloud we saw enough to rule out the approach to a high col, the only key to Himal Chuli.

On a drizzling morning we crossed this glacier arm and began to climb the ridge separating it from the Cheo Himal glacier. This mountain did not figure on our brief list of possibilities, but I thought we might as well look at it on the way back. Such an abrupt departure from the easy going along the valley floor proved too much for the Bimtakhoti man, who refused to follow. Whereupon the Sherpas divided his load between them and went on with so much ease that I began to wonder what they had been carrying before. On the way up we got separated in the mist, but met again on the descent after some desultory bellowing. The Sherpas annoyed me by having found what appeared to be a better line than mine. Sorrows shared are sorrows halved. When blundering in and out of self-imposed difficulties there is nothing more aggravating than the suspicion that superior judgement has found for one's companions a better way. If roped together one is spared such excruciating thoughts, nor will one's followers quietly submit to being led by ways of which they do not approve. Having reached the glacier we found no obliging ablation valley between mountain and moraine. We had to choose between a hillside of tangled juniper scrub and a loosely flung together causeway of boulders.

We camped on the first flat spot and next day crossed this glacier. A faint track on the far side soon brought us to a half-mile-long lake whose waters, even under a hard, colourless sky, reflected a deep turquoise blue. At the far end of the lake we found ourselves by the junction of the third glacier coming down from the direction of the Larkhya pass. We crossed, scrambled down a vast moraine some 500 ft. high, to come out on the Bimtakhoti track, thus completing a wet, blind, abortive, circular tour of the whole glacier system.

A week remained before the expected arrival of the others, and we had only one more peak to examine; thereafter I intended crossing to Larkhya to see if that valley had any climbable mountains. The peak was that which had puzzled us on our first flying visit; according to the map its 24,000 ft. summit lay immediately above Bimtakhoti about halfway between Manaslu and the Larkhya pass. Without much pause and without asking any local man to put himself out, we crossed the rippling stream of the Bimtakhoti meadow and began climbing through birch woods by a well-worn track leading to a grazing alp. Although this journey was about to prove unlucky for me it is interesting to note that no weasel crossed our path, no solitary magpie hopped menacingly alongside, and no crow croaked thrice. True, I fell into the stream when attempting to cross dryshod, but so did Da Namgyal who got even wetter.

Having won clear of the birch the track mounted straightly and steeply by way of a pleasant grass spur. Mist hung everywhere. When we had made good about 3,000 ft., boulders having taken the place of grass, we decided to camp. Away in the mist in a hollow on our right, we heard the sound of water, but before descending we had to advance a short way along our spur which had now dwindled to a sharp ridge of piled boulders. Hopping from one to another with the carelessness of long use and wont I got out of balance, put a foot back to recover, found nothing, and fell backwards about 15 ft., bouncing on three separate boulders. If one must move after a fall it is better to do it quickly before the body begins to protest. We had to find water, so with the help of the Sherpas I got down to the hollow, and a little later found myself laid stiff on my back where I remained for five days unable even to sit up without help.

Throughout it rained steadily, but the Sherpas kept a fire going and went down twice to Bimtakhoti for more food. When I felt strong enough to be carried we got two men up to take our kit while the Sherpas in turn carried me pick-a-back. I dreaded recrossing that ridge but there was no alternative. I sweated freely, and my injured back winced in anticipation as Gyalgen balanced a precarious way over the boulders, my weight threatening to bring us both down in ruin at every step.

The rest of the party arrived next day, 24 August. There was nothing they could do except sympathize. Time, the great healer, must do its work, so Roberts went over to Larkhya and Lowndes back to Manang, leaving Sher Bahadur to keep me company. As soon as I could rise without help I began to crawl, then to walk, and finally to walk uphill, every day increasing the distance, until on 3 September, when Roberts got back, I climbed to the scene of the accident to collect some flowers. On the Larkhya side, where he had spent an active but fruitless week, Roberts had seen no peaks intended expressly for climbing. Very few Himalayan peaks are so designed. It is a common fault, one which climbers will not cease to lament until the passage of a few thousand centuries mellows their jagged, angular features and smooths away their harshest acerbities. He reported having seen what he thought might be a direct route to the summit plateau of Manaslu, which we discussed with the dispassionate calm of men who have no intention of trying it.

There remained only the 24,000 ft. peak at whose foot I had lain as a cripple for five days without catching so much as a passing glimpse. Still it eluded our gaze from below. Twice we journeyed far out across the stony sea of the glacier by Bimtakhoti and each time a great cloud spread itself obstinately over the mountain. The necessary step of returning to 'Cripple's Camp' was never taken. Neither the weather nor my recent injury gave us much hope and, no doubt, four months in the field had blunted the keen edge of ardour. It is possible, it is certainly so in my own case, that after several months of such a life the body makes a less and less vigorous response to the food, fresh air and exercise it receives. Contrary to expectation the machine begins to run down. Instead of tackling a hill with exuberance, one faces it with premature exhaustion.

We therefore decided to go right down to Kudi, whence we might embark upon an entrancing ridge walk along the Bahara Pokhara Lekh to a sacred lake at the foot of Himal Chuli. We weakly imagined ourselves halfway up this great mountain prospecting a route, but I felt in my heart that serious climbing was over and that this was merely what the Tibetans call 'neko'—a journey undertaken for the purpose of cleansing from sin and sloth. I could not help feeling that Roberts and I stood in great need of it. The thought of going down to 2,000 ft. and then climbing back to 16,000 ft. rather staggered us, but a powerful inducement lay in the expectation of collecting a long overdue mail.

There was little difficulty in finding coolies willing to go down to Thonje, though it is perhaps an ungrateful title for the two comely young women who carried for us. 'Coolie', as it is thus anglicized, is a horrible word; those who use it frequently, as I do, lay themselves open to the suspicion of entertaining a lofty, almost brutal, disdain for their more of less faithful followers, regarding them no more than Falstaff did his fifty tattered prodigals lately come from swine-keeping, who would, however, 'fill a pit as well as better'. Like other men, coolies will sometimes let one down and will always try one's patience, but after reading the accounts of some travellers, one is left wondering whether coolies really are men with souls, whether they have bellies that hunger and feet that feel the cold. I name no names but readers of Himalayan travels will recognize the following extracts: 'difficulty to match them (the coolies) in any jail in India'—'the misery of the night was increased by the moaning and wailing of the coolies from the rocks, where they sought shelter'—'these admonitions failed to impress the coolies, who, in a most critical place, sat down to take the snow out of their boots.' (The Cissies.)

We made one march of it to Thonje, meeting on the way a man with three bags of mail. It was too late to change our plan, in which the mail had had no small part, but the news of the outside world which we now read did not make us regret our decision to start moving down. The three-day journey down the Marsyandi gorge made us understand why it had always been difficult to persuade men to fetch the mail from Kudi. The track, slimy, slippery and half overgrown after months of rain, presented the unwary with many opportunities for misadventure. One had to shuffle very quietly over the narrow planks of the 'parris' which were greasy enough to warrant the strewing of a little sand for those misguided enough to wear rubber-soled boots. A bamboo suspension bridge, frail and rickety, had been put across the river by the smallpox village, but in length, height, sag, decay and all the ingredients of peril, it was outdone by a bridge below Tagring. The landslip there, now in active eruption, was sending down a constant stream of mud and boulders. As no one would attempt to cross this, travellers had to take another route and to cross the Marsyandi at their peril by this aged bridge.

Kudi is merely a place of a few shops selling cloth. In one of these, sitting on his string-bed, and assisted by any passer-by, the postmaster transacts his rare official business. There is no proper village and consequently no headman, so that we had difficulty in replenishing our food and hiring coolies. After spending a blazing hot day in camp by the river, waiting for some maize to be ground into flour, we retraced our steps up stream for a few miles. On the eve of the wettest ten days we had ever experienced, everyone assured us the monsoon was over.

At the junction of the Musi Khola, which comes down from the south side of Manaslu, we quitted the main valley and climbed a thousand feet by a stone staircase to the remarkably neat little village of Usta. The sun was sinking as we pitched our tents in a small square in the middle of the village, the only flat space at hand. Framed between the terra-cotta walls of two houses, the Musi Khola and its pine-clad slopes lay black in the evening shadows. But beyond the trees the rocks glowed warmly, and high over all shone the still sun-gilt face of Manaslu.

Roberts was soon in conversation with ex-soldiers or with men on leave from some Gurkha regiment, of whom there are nearly always a few to be found in these villages. This district, known as No. 3 West, is one of the recruiting areas. He heard news of a former subadar-major who had served with him during the war, who was now tending both his own and the village flocks up in some kharka or ghot on the Bahara Pokhara Lekh. Apart from the pleasure Roberts might have in meeting again a man with whom he had shared some hazardous times, I looked forward confidently to the milk and butter which, I thought, would surely cement this meeting of the old comrades' association.

Two men volunteered to accompany us as guides and porters to this distant ghot. As we toiled up through the forest a sultry morning ended in a thunderstorm which broke over us in copious rain. Trusting to the local weather prophets we had discarded capes and umbrellas at Kudi. Wet and chilled to the bone we were led, not unerringly, among a maze of cattle tracks to what looked like a water buffalo wallow. It was in fact a ghot, where there was a hut. There, on a small island which promised to dry out at low water, we put our tents. It was a most repulsive spot—there seemed nothing for buffaloes to eat but leaves—but we soon drowned our sorrows in successive beakers of hot, rich milk.

Next day we reached the broad back of the lekh where we joined the main track. This was used indiscriminately not only by pilgrims, but also by sheep, cattle, and buffaloes on their way to the high pastures. To our surprise we soon came to what our guides called the Bahara Pokhara, or big lake—a poor thing, more of a pond than a lake, of a dismal pea-green colour, and overhung by dreary rhododendron trees. A small rest house for pilgrims and a shrine showed that sanctity has little to do with beauty, and we were glad of the assurance that there was a bigger and better lake, more worthy of a pilgrimage, much farther away.

We continued up the ridge against a constant trickle of buffaloes and men, carrying their mat shelters, who were vacating the higher grazings, until early rain obliged us to camp at a deserted ghot. Our guides now announced that their food was finished, but Roberts, with a prolonged burst of indignant eloquence, persuaded them to go on for one more day. We should then have to carry the stuff ourselves. After another mile or so along the ridge, whence we beheld a vast prospect of rain-swept hills of indigo blue flecked with white mist, our guides appeared to be at a loss. Instead of sticking to the ridge as they should have done, they were persuaded, like better men have been, to march to the distant bleating of sheep. I must say we were in full sympathy with this move, but it was unfortunate that these sheep must have been grazing in the Musi Khola valley 5,000 or 6,000 ft. below. We were obliged to follow a track which contoured below the ridge and which grew inexorably rougher and apparently more aimless. Our admiration for the pilgrims or for anyone else who used it mounted steadily, but we met neither pilgrims nor sheep. At last we camped in a drizzling mist in a hideously depressing boulder-strewn cwm.

Next day our porters departed, leaving us to shoulder our own burdens. Twice the track cheated our expectations by climbing in a very determined manner to what we expected to be the main ridge, only to drop as far down the other side of what was evidently only a spur. We were quite bewildered when we met a man, a shepherd, who told us the ghot we were looking for was quite near. But he then soured his sweet tidings by adding that he himself was bound for Usta which he expected to reach this evening. Evidently his standard of near and far differed widely from ours, for this was our fourth day from Usta. However, a couple of hours later we heard dogs barking, and through a rift in the mist we caught sight of several mat shelters. Unlike those of the Langtang sheep steadings, these shelters were so small and wretched that we put up our sodden tents to await the coming of the subadar who was up the hill with the sheep. A small, indeterminate man soon arrived. Like the other shepherds he was wrapped in a broad striped blanket, and was a man, one might think, who had never known anything other than a squalid mat hut on a dreary hillside. It was not easy to recognize in him the man of authority, the smart subadar-major, educated and widely travelled. Apart from reminiscences we exchanged very little with him. I gave him some cheroots, but neither milk, butter, nor dai, on which our thoughts had been fastened for some days, were to be had. All the ewes were dry; for their breeding arrangements are such that lambing takes place in the autumn, and at lower levels. In fact the subadar with his barren flocks was himself on the point of departure. We learnt from him that we were on the wrong side of the main ridge, the pilgrim track and the lake to which it leads both lying on the south side.

We spent the next two days in this camp weather-bound. Day and night a fine rain swept the ridge. The great moralist, whom I have frequently had occasion to quote, remarks very justly that 'the misery of man proceeds not from any single crush of overwhelming evil, but from small vexations continually repeated'. The drips inside the tent were the small vexations which by constant repetition occasioned our misery. We did our best to lighten our troubles by smoking cheroots, eating the food thrust at intervals through the tent door, and reading *Captain Slocum* and another book, *Over the Reefs*. The last dealt with the South Sea Islands—sunshine and soft breezes, hula-hula girls and pork—and we could not help feeling that as travellers we had come to the wrong country.

On the morning of 17 September the rain let up for a time and with the help of two of the subadar's men we climbed the ridge, dropped down the other side, and set up our tents on the shore of a very lovely lake, clear, still and deep. With the coarse brown grass of the surrounding fells, the rocks above half-veiled in mist which hid the tell-tale sweep of snow beyond, we might well have been by some Lakeland tarn. But an examination of the shore hard by destroyed this illusion, for built in the shallow water were numerous little cairns, festooned with cords and bits of bamboo, and crowned with maize cobs, lemons, tomatoes, cucumbers, the votive offerings of pilgrims who bathe ceremonially in the shallows. To bathe ceremonially in the lake, which the locals called Memi Pokhara, is reputed to have the most gratifying effect upon those desirous of fertility. Later, when I plunged unceremonially into its deeper parts, I concluded that I was lucky to escape permanent frigidity.

Monal pheasant haunted these lonely shores. The evening of our arrival we put up a covey and one, whose state of mind we could not guess, committed suicide by diving headlong into the lake. In vain the Sherpas hurled stones at the floating corpse, for no one was brave enough to swim for it, but in the morning it drifted to the farther shore and we supped gloriously on roast pheasant.

For three unprofitable days we tramped the brown fells, where aconite and delphinium were still in bloom, climbing to various carefully chosen vantage points where we sat for long hours waiting for chance to lift the veil from the bright face of Himal Chuli. And when at last it came, we were too close under the mountain to experience in full the breath-taking and salutary vision of a 10,000 ft. sweep of snow and ice. Sad, too, that on this side the slender and terrible spire which had so startled us on the march in, splayed out into a wide and characterless face topped by a flat ridge. Perhaps this broad face is for the most part easy, but its lower part is so guarded by ice-falls that it would be a difficult and probably dangerous climb.

On 21 September we were due to leave. A hard white frost at night ushered in a serene morning, and for the first time the placid, green water of the lake mirrored the cloudless, glittering summit of Himal Chuli. Fine weather had come; it was time for us to go.

CHAPTER EIGHTEEN

A Fresh Start

HAD not the day been quite so flawless we might have found the Pilgrim Way as irksome as our other route. But one seemed to tread on air. Clinging mist and grey phantom shapes had vanished and the eye ranged over warm brown fells and blue valleys to far-off, placid, white mountains. That evening from our last camp on the ridge we watched the light fade upon a wide semicircle of familiar shapes from Baudha and Himal Chuli in the east, to Manaslu in the north, and across to the Annapurna and Macha Puchare in the west. But we had now to quit this fair region of high pastures, forgo the clean fragrance of mountain plants, and begin an unwilling descent to the vapid sights and scents of the valleys below.

At Kudi we were joined by Lowndes, Sher Bahadur, and the caravan of specimen boxes, the fruits of several months of hard labour. We celebrated our reunion with a dish of curried frogs assuaged by draughts from Roberts's large water bottle from which we could always drink heartily in the comfortable assurance that it never would contain anything so dangerous as water. I should have liked the frogs better had I not seen them being shaken from wicker traps and then tied together in biliously green slimy bundles, all legs and eyes. But if one professes and practises living on the country one must take the rough with the smooth, rancid yak fat and frogs along with buckwheat cakes and raksi.

Our party then divided, the main body going direct to Katmandu and Roberts to Pokhara, the second city in Nepal, set in a plain almost as large as the valley of Katmandu, containing many large lakes. To me the marches seemed longer and hotter than those of the outgoing journey, and since the paddy through which much of the track lay was still uncut, the fields were still flooded. One was constantly made aware of this fact by being forced off the path into the mud by an oncoming tide of coolies, bowed down under huge bales of cloth. The reason for this seasonal activity in the cloth trade was the approaching festival of Dasahra, the big event of the Nepali year.

Yet even this fatiguing and singularly untriumphant return march was not without its pleasant memories; the bountiful supply of bananas, particularly that king of its kind, the succulent 'malbogue'; the lovely bauhinia trees now a mass of white and mauve star-shaped flowers; and finally a last glimpse of Baudha, seen at sunset, its snow a pale rose and the clouds which ringed the summit glowing like reflected fire.

At Katmandu, where we were lapped in comfort at the Embassy, we did not take long to wind up our affairs. I felt I could safely but perhaps undeservedly murmur; 'Now my weary eyes I close, Leave, ah, leave me, to repose.' But it was not to be. I there met Mr Oscar Houston, father of Dr Charles Houston a companion of Nanda Devi days, who had everything in train for a journey to Solu Khumbu, the district on the Nepal side of Everest and the home of the Sherpas. He invited me to join his party, and a refusal to do so would have seemed ungracious. Moreover the journey would be of supreme interest; apart from viewing the south side of Everest there was the fun to be expected from seeing Sherpas, as it were, in their natural state. Mr Shipton and I had often discussed such an unlikely happening, and here it was offered to me on a plate. In 1949 the Himalayan Committee had asked the Nepal Durbar for permission to send a party to reconnoitre the south side of Everest, but this had been refused and the Langtang Himal. offered in its place.

One or two drawbacks presented themselves forcibly enough to prevent an immediate acceptance. As Dr Charles Houston could not arrive before the end of October, I should have to kick my heels for the best part of a fortnight in Calcutta. Furthermore we had only five weeks to spend on the journey, as both of us had to be back home by mid-December. I had already been 'bummelling' about Nepal for five months, and on this trip there would be a fortnight each way of travel leaving barely a week to spend at the foot of the king of mountains—a time so short that its value could be but small. 'Thus Belial, with words clothed in reason's garb, counselled ignoble ease.' But on the way down to Raxaul Roberts imparted some more bracing and manly thoughts. In fact he called me a fool, and so from Sisaghari I wired acceptance. After all, I thought, if Charles Houston is prepared to fly from New York for the sake of five weeks in the Himalaya, I ought not to grudge waiting a fortnight for the sake of a memorable experience in such good company.

The party met on 29 October at Jogbani, the Indian railway station for Birat Nagar, a short mile away on the Nepal side of the border—a border marked only by a cement boundary pillar. Besides the Houstons, father and son, there were two old friends of theirs, Mrs E. S. Cowles, an American climber of note, and Anderson Bakewell who was then studying at the Jesuit College of St Mary's at Kurseong near Darjeeling. Hitherto I had not regarded a woman as an indispensable part of the equipage of a Himalayan journey but one lives and learns. Anyhow, with a doctor to heal us, a woman to feed us, and a priest to pray for us, I felt we could face the future with some confidence. As the proverb rightly says, Prayer and Provender hinder no man's journey.

Of provender there seemed to be enough. We had eleven scientifically

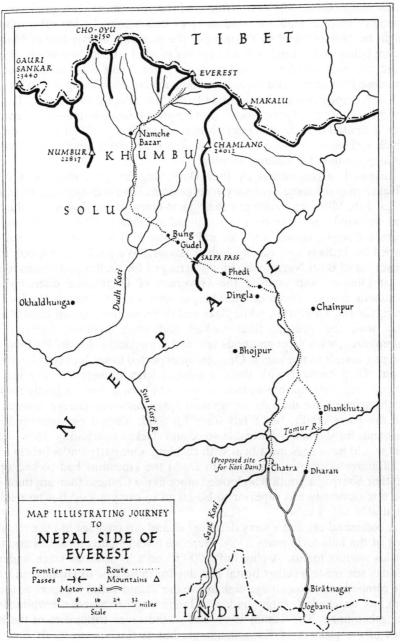

MAP ILLUSTRATING JOURNEY
TO
**NEPAL SIDE OF
EVEREST**

Frontier —·—·— Route ··········
Passes →← Mountains △
Motor road ≈≈

0   8   16   24   32 miles
Scale

Journey to Nepal side of Everest

packed food-boxes, each of which had to be eaten in neither more nor less than four days. The highly organized food-box system of feeding a party, which many respectable and fair-minded travellers mistakenly prefer to more elastic or empiric methods, seldom gives satisfaction. Living off a food-box might be called Ordeal by Planning or the Scientific Martyrdom of Man; the victim being told not only what to eat but in what amount and when. Happily there are still problems, such as space, time, and the human soul, too immense for science; and there are a few subjects, food being one, with which the stereotyped planner's mind had better not attempt to grapple. Thus the optimum contents of a food-box—apparently a simple matter—is too complex for the limited capacity of a man's brain. No one has yet filled a box with food which will satisfy a given number of men for a given number of days with nothing wasted and nothing wanting.

Bakewell, accompanied by four Darjeeling Sherpas, met me a day in advance to make some necessary arrangements. The management of the Birat Nagar Jute Mill very kindly put their guest-house at the disposal of the party and arranged lorry transport to roadhead at Dharan. (Besides the jute mill there are sugar, cotton and rice mills, a saw-mill and a match factory, all owned by Indians and run by Indian labour.) We paid our respects to the Governor of Birat Nagar, who kindly arranged for coolies and ponies to meet us at Dharan, and advised the Governor of Dhankhuta district of our imminent arrival. Three of the Sherpas were our old friends Gyalgen, Da Namgyal and Pa Norbu, while Saki had distinguished himself earlier in the year with the French. Saki looked and often behaved like a genial chimpanzee, with a prognathous jaw and a menacing slouch, his long arms hanging almost to the knees. One almost expected to see him start beating his chest. They brought with them a woman who answered to the name of 'Dicky'. Her relationship to them remained obscure, but we gladly took her on the strength for the sake of her neat appearance and cheery manner. She did the party credit; but I felt sorry for Saki, alleged by some to be her husband, for she had a damnable voice and clacked incessantly. However, he that would have eggs must bear with cackling. Our party undoubtedly had in it an active principle of growth. In Delhi the Houstons had picked up yet another Sherpa, a youth who looked more like a Chinese than anything else. He was obviously too superior to be asked to carry a load but he made an admirable lady's maid.

A command car and a lorry decanted us and our baggage at Dharan, at the foot of the hills forty miles away. Here we found eighteen coolies and three ponies waiting for us. A climb of 2,000 ft. on a loose stony track under the midday sun made a rather brutal first day for those new to Himalayan travel. We camped early at a village high above the Tamur valley whence, as the sun sank, we watched the huge shadow of Jannu lengthen across the white face of Kangchenjunga. The Tamur river, one of the seven tributaries of the Kosi, rises in the glaciers of Kangchenjunga, but at this season its flashing blue waters betrayed no hint of its glacier origin. Having crossed it by a new suspension bridge we began the long climb to Dhankhuta on a broad track thick with coolies bound for Dharan with loads of potatoes.

As one interested in the technique of coolie travel I was struck by the almost complete absence of chautaras; but my early hopes that this might mean fewer halts and quicker travel were soon falsified. As in most parts of Nepal the load was carried in a basket tapering to the base which was strengthened by a wooden strap. The coolie carried a 'T'-shaped stick with a notch in the cross-piece which fitted the wooden strap, so that when a man wished to take the weight off his back he merely slipped the stick under the basket. It was too easy, and perfectly maddening. No one would grudge a man stopping in his tracks to scratch his head or light a cigarette but, marching as they did in close companionable order in single file, every such halt had the effect of stopping everyone else. On a narrow track no one could pass and on a broad track no one wanted to. Nor were these successive checks, caused by the whim or the need of one man, confined to one's own little bunch. If the traffic was dense, several hundreds of coolies would come automatically, and not at all unwillingly, to rest because two friends a mile away had stopped to pass the time of day.

We were all impressed with Dhankhuta—a spotlessly clean little town set on the broad, closely cultivated ridge between the Tamur and Arun valleys. The stone flagged main street is flanked by whitewashed houses with black tiled roofs and wide bracketed eaves; some have open balconies lined with window-boxes. Nearly all these were shops with open fronts in which, however, there was a mystifying absence of anything for sale. All our food had to be purchased through official channels. We were pleased by the school and by the eagerness of masters and boys to speak English, the language in which everything was taught. The tone of the school seemed to be set by a graphic phrase chalked on a nearby Hindu shrine: 'Gather courage, don't be a chicken-hearted fellow.'

We camped in a pine wood (*P. longifolia*) outside the town, and presently the Governor of Dhankhuta paid us a call. He was one of the Rana family, spoke excellent English, and provided us with an escort and an itinerary. Both were needed. Though the people in the remoter parts of Nepal are not opposed to strangers, they are not used to them; and as for the route, it was seldom that shown on the map, which is in need of revision. The usual system is that escort and coolies are changed upon entering another district. The Governor therefore sent a signal to Dingla in No. 4 East on the other side of the Arun, with which he was in touch by wireless, asking for an escort and a fresh lot of coolies to meet us at Kattekaghat, a ferry over the Arun not far from Dingla. Yet another change of escort and coolies would have to be made in No. 3 East or Okhaldhunga in the lower Dudh Kosi valley. Through the miscarriage of the first of these arrangements arose the only trouble we had, and which we overcame only by the staunchness of the jemadar and the Dhankhuta escort.

Neither the jemadar and his escort nor the coolies distinguished themselves on the first march which ended by two Sherpas and myself, who had foolishly gone on to the prearranged village, having to climb back in the dark for nearly 2,000 ft. to where the rest of the party had elected to camp. However, anyone who leaves strange coolies to their own devices on the first march, deserves all he gets. Another disagreeable event for me was the sight of an aeroplane flying south from the Everest region. That mountain was not in view but Makalu and its neighbours stood out against the calm evening sky like a marble frieze. The effect was as though some impious hand had crowned the Hermes of Praxiteles with a bowler hat.

From the broad tableland north of Dhankhuta at an altitude of 5,000 ft., where the scenery reminds one of the dry foothills of Ranikhet, we descended to the Arun valley, to a height of only 1,000 ft. above sea-level. The Arun river cuts a deep gorge east of Makalu (27,790 ft.) and its Tibetan tributaries drain a vast area north of the Himalaya. In one place its head-waters are within ten miles of the Tsangpo. When we met the river it was nearly 200 yards broad, its greeny grey waters flowing through a wide, wooded valley. Whether because of the heat or the unhealthiness of the district there are no villages close to the river, so that the track along its bank lies through almost deserted country.

Nevertheless, at this time of year it affords pleasant marching and camping, and frequent opportunities for bathing and fishing. Charles Houston, a man who does nothing by halves, greedy for a mahseer, had come armed with two rods and a rich assortment of flies, spoons, spinners and other artificial baits. The continent of America, inhabited, we are told, by simple backwoodsmen, the natural dupes of smart foreigners, is apparently the home of equally simple-minded fish. One device we tried, a mere piece of wood painted white, a foot long and prickly with hooks, was, they assured me, an equally deadly lure either for bass in the Bronx river or for sockeye salmon in Alaska. But the mahseer of the Arun, if any there are, knew better.

Bathing in the Arun was rather too sharp a tonic. We enjoyed our most memorable bathe in one of its small tributaries, where the water ran in a long rock trough, deep, clear and blue. Despite the deliberate pace of the march— the coolies averaged 1 m.p.h.—one became so hot and tired that plunging into this enchanting river was exquisite joy. There were fish too, in the pool, and we plied our angle with unremitting zeal and unrewarded patience. On leaving we mounted to a wide terrace, high above the river, where we walked for four miles through glowing fields of sunflowers and under mighty banyans. The ploughman busy with his oxen in a nearby field might have driven his furrow straight by directing his eyes to Makalu, looming magnificently large in the distance like the icy throne of some Hindu deity. The long white wall of Chamlang, rising at one end to 24,000 ft., effectively screened Everest which is seldom visible to travellers approaching from the south.

Having descended from this terrace to the river at Kattekaghat we were ferried across in a dugout canoe. The speed of the current, the fearful list the craft assumed, together with the rising water in which the passengers sat, made the voyage a lively one during which a weak swimmer had ample time for some solemn reflections. As we stepped ashore and stunned the ferryman with a tip—the first paying passengers in the history of the ferry—no fresh escort saluted us and no fresh team of coolies stood by to appraise the weight of the loads they would have to carry. Dingla, which our track avoided, lay several thousand feet above the river. A sepoy we had sent there brought word back late that evening that the escort and coolies had gone to meet us at another ferry two marches down stream.

Here then was the seed of trouble which grew to give the caravan master some anxious moments. Either by waiting, or by going up to Dingla, the mistake might equally well have been put right, but our time was so short that we wanted to avoid delay at all costs. The jemadar who, of course, was now trespassing, agreed to come on with his men, while the coolies consented to go as far as Phedi, a village two marches on. Thus we postponed the day of reckoning and went on trusting to time and chance—either to being overtaken by the Dingla boys or to picking up a fresh lot of coolies at Phedi. From there we had to strike westwards to the Dudh Kosi, crossing several ridges between 10,000 and 11,000 ft. high which our Dharan coolies would be loath to tackle.

For the most part the track to Phedi followed the course of a cheerful, flashing stream, the Irkhua Khola. The stream is now marked in red on our maps, for in it Charles Houston caught our one and only fish. For reasons which defy conjecture, a bearded carp of rather less than ½ lb. in weight took one of his flies. We were still talking of this when we reached Phedi where our transport troubles came to a head. Three coolies had already departed, nine more were due to go, and here neither coolies nor rice were to be had. All hands were busy with the rice harvest which had just begun. Like many others who have trusted to careless hope and to something turning up, we had now to pay the penalty—the loss of time while someone went back to Dingla with news of our distressed circumstances. Too late we deplored the impatience which had landed us improperly escorted in a strange district; for the jemadar and the Dhankhuta escort cut no ice at all with the headman of Phedi. They were mere interlopers like ourselves.

Hitherto I had regarded these men as more ornamental than useful and the jemadar as a cheerful, incompetent, slightly shifty, ass. His unproductive bickering with the Phedi headman did nothing to lessen this view. But that night as I was gloomily turning in, the jemadar, heralded by a strong wave of raksi, thrust his head into my tent to announce that in spite of all we would march next day. He had accomplished the miracle of persuading four of the escort of five to carry loads; an old man and two of his grandchildren, too weak for the harvest, had offered to carry three more; several of the Dharan men agreed to follow us to the world's end and anything that remained over could be dumped. These bold hopes were no alcoholic dream. In the morning grandfather turned up with his infants, the despised escort manfully made up full loads, and only the Sherpas continued to 'work to rule'. These five, six if Dicky was included, who were in the enviable position of emigrants returning to the old country free of cost and on full pay, could have solved half our problem without unduly distressing themselves by doubling their own paltry loads. They were in fact carrying nothing but their own kit and some souvenirs with which to astonish their stay-at-home cousins, but it was not until Charles Houston and I had shouldered what remained that they were shamed into adding something to their loads. On a mountain the better Darjeeling Sherpas will not spare themselves, but they now regard themselves as a *corps d'élite* from whom coolie work should not be expected.

Above Phedi there is an 11,000 ft. pass, the Salpa Banjang. Once over this we should enter yet another district, Okhaldhunga or No. 3 East, where we should no doubt have more trouble over coolies and food. Only when we reached the Dudh Kosi valley and the Sherpas district of Khumba might we fairly expect to leave care behind. How just this expectation was we quickly had proof. As we climbed to a camp below the pass, while I anxiously marked the progress of grandad and the escort in their unaccustomed role, we met three genuine Sherpas on their way to Phedi with salt. They were men of decision who knew a good thing when they saw it. They hurried down to Phedi, rid themselves of their loads, and rejoined us the same evening. These three men, whom we called 'The Three Musketeers', always marched, ate, and slept together. They were sterling characters, dependable and solid as rocks, who worked for us with a will and cheered us by their company all the way up and back again to the plains. The escort showed no sign of flinching from their undertaking, so grandad and the children were sent tottering back to Phedi, and we went on and over the pass with renewed confidence.

Some neglected mani walls on the way up prepared us for the big chorten which crowned the pass. Like alpine flowers these emblems of Buddhism are found only above a certain level. Descending through spruce forest to a small Sherpa village, where, contrary to some not disinterested advice, we refused to stop, we traversed a high waterless hillside covered with tall ilex to the Gurkha (Rai) village of Gudel at about 7,000 ft. The presence of either Sherpa or other Tibetan-like people is governed by height rather than by locality. Their villages are seldom found below 8,000 ft. while those of the Gurkha people are not seen above 7,000 ft. At Gudel they would have no truck with us, so that lack of food for both escort and coolies now threatened to halt our uncertain progress. Our recent access of confidence was further undermined by the appalling prospect of the next stage, from our camp on the rice stubbles of Gudel across an appallingly deep valley to Bung, and thence to another pass over the ridge beyond. Bung looked to be within spitting distance, yet the map affirmed and the eye agreed that we should have to descend some 3,000 ft. and climb a like amount to reach it. Profound emotion may find vent in verse as well as in oaths; despair as well as joy may rouse latent, unsuspected poetical powers. Thus at Gudel, uninspired by liquor, for there was none, some memorable lines were spoken:

> For dreadfulness nought can excel
> The prospect of Bung from Gudel;
> And words die away on the tongue
> When we look back at Gudel from Bung.

The village of Bung, a name which appeals to a music-hall mind, provoked another outburst on the return journey because its abundant well of good raksi, on which we were relying, had dried up.

> Hope thirstily rested on Bung
> So richly redolent of rum;
> But when we got there
> The cupboard was bare,
> Sapristi. No raksi. No chang.

(To disarm the hypercritical I might say that the 'a' in chang, a Tibetan word for beer, is pronounced like a short 'u'.)

The neat houses and terraced fields of Bung, apparently rich in promise, covered several thousand feet of hillside. In Nether Bung they grew bananas and rice, in Upper Bung oranges and wheat. A sepoy had gone on to collect rice but on arrival the whole party scattered in search of provender like hounds drawing a cover. For ourselves we acquired nothing but a goat, worth about Rs. 5, for Rs. 12, having been asked Rs. 20. In order to secure the rice we had to curtail the march and make a late start. Next morning the jemadar, with bloodshot eyes and husky voice, as became one who had attended an overnight harvest thanksgiving, led the rice procession up to our camp in swaying triumph. Thus heartened the party went with a will over the Shipki La (c. 10,000 ft.) and dropped 3,000 ft. to a camp above the Irkhua Khola. Both this stream and that which so drastically divides Gudel from Bung are tributaries of the Dudh Kosi, but we had still another ridge to cross before reaching that valley.

However, we were now in country which our Sherpa followers knew and where we were welcome for their sake. At Panga, a village of stone houses and shingle roofs, a fat, smiling cobbler sat in the sun sewing bright coloured Tibetan felt boots, closely watched by a little Lhasa terrier. The Sherpas disappeared at once into the largest house in quest of beer where, like Brer Bull-frog, they had every right to sing:

> Ingle-go-jang, my joy, my joy.
> I'm right at home, my joy,

for this village was within the borders of Khumbu. On that account we, too, might rejoice and be thankful, but the escort and the Dharan coolies, who by this time had the air of martyrs suffering in a doubtful cause, might wonder what had persuaded them to stray from their warm rice lands into such high, benighted country.

For a day and a half we followed a rough track lying 3,000 ft. above the Dudh Kosi, across two spurs of distressing height, until we dropped slowly to the large village of Chaunrikharka. The village boasts a graceful stupa of great age, but a more surprising exhibit was that of a rain gauge. It had been installed in 1948 by Dr Bannerjee of the Indian Meteorological Survey, who had also left a snow and rain gauge at Namche Bazar. We were shown the records which appeared to be correctly kept. Having descended to the river we crossed by a wooden cantilever bridge and camped; just above was the village of Gumila, the home of our Three Musketeers, who at once brought us eggs and buckwheat flour. I introduced my companions to Himalayan buckwheat cakes, which I consider not only superb in their own right but perfect for conveying large quantities of butter to the mouth. They did not think buckwheat cakes the equal of my bread which they always referred to as 'foot-bread', having noticed that after bread-making my boots were usually covered with flour. As I explained, I did not use my feet for kneading, at least not with boots on, but in baking, or indeed any cooking when empiric methods are used, some of the raw material is inevitably left adhering to the person of the cook if not to the walls and ceiling of his environment.

On 14 November we reached Namche Bazar. The track crossed and recrossed the clear, blue river, here hurrying along like a mountain torrent, by wooden cantilever bridges which in no case had to span more than twenty yards. For a river which drains what is perhaps the grandest thirty miles of the Himalaya it is surprisingly small—a stretch including, besides the Everest group, Cho Oyu (26,750 ft.), Gyachung Khang (25,910 ft.), Ngojumba Khang (25,720 ft.), and a host of lesser peaks. At this season, of course, the snows were not melting, but from the water marks on boulders we guessed the summer rise to be not more than four feet. Near the river upon any big boulder which presented a fair, smooth surface, lama sculptors of long ago had chiselled sacred texts in deeply incised characters. Some which had recently been recarved showed up in black and white relief, but most were worn flat and were black with age. Had the original sculptor but added a date we might have had some hint as to the rate at which the river carves out its bed.

At the junction of the Bhote Kosi nallah, up which lies the road to Nangpa La (19,050 ft.), Tingri Dzong, and Rongbuk, our track quitted the deep gorge of the river. As we climbed the 1,500 ft. to the village the path became wider and the going easier, and presently we were met by a Nepali official (a Gurung) and the Sherpa headman with a string of ponies. Since our first camp in the Arun valley none of the track had been suitable for riding. We were welcomed to the village by an inquisitive but friendly crowd. Namche Bazar, of course, has never ranked as a 'forbidden city'. It is far from being a city, and it has remained unvisited not because of any very serious difficulties in the way, but because no one has thought it worth the trouble of overcoming them. Nevertheless, it had for long been my humble Mecca. As we rode in I shared in imagination a little of the satisfaction of Burton, or of Manning when he reached Lhasa.

CHAPTER NINETEEN

Approach to Mt. Everest

NAMCHE Bazar lies at about 11,000 ft. on the ridge between the Dudh Kosi and the Bhote Kosi, facing westwards across the valley to the peak of Kwangde (20,320 ft.). Unlike the Manangbhot villages where all are huddled together, the houses are detached as if the owners were men of substance. There are about thirty of these whitewashed, two-storied houses, with low-pitched shingle roofs. The ground floor serves as stables and stores, while above is the one long living room, with an open fire and clay stove against one wall, wooden shelves for fine copper ware and cheap china on another, and large trellised window frames set with five or six small panes of glass. To find glass in a Himalayan private house, fourteen days' march from civilization, is a little remarkable.

The extent of cultivation seemed small for the number of people. I imagine that more food is imported and paid for by the trade in salt and rice which the Sherpas carry on between lower Nepal and Tingri in Tibet over the 19,000 ft. Nangpa La. But there are other villages within a few miles of Namche where the acreage of cultivation is much greater in proportion to the number of houses. Kuru (a barley), buckwheat and potatoes are the crops; wheat is grown in the lower villages like Chaunrikharka and Gumila.

We went at once to our allotted house, and when the crowd had ebbed sufficiently to leave space, the tents were pitched alongside. The women accorded Gyalgen precedence at the fireplace and the headman took strong measures against the more persistent sightseers. A few privileged intruders were allowed to remain. These were mostly former porters, vouched for by their Himalayan Club service books and numerous carefully cherished 'chits' and photographs. They were considered to be sufficiently well disciplined to refrain from laughing at our strange ways and stranger faces. After a meal, fearing rightly that neither beer nor raksi was going to be offered, we went for a walk; partly for privacy—for the Americans were a little dismayed by the attentions of the crowd—and partly in the hope of seeing something of the great mountain which was now less than twenty miles away.

A morning sky freckled with high cirrus clouds had foretold accurately a break in the weather. Low clouds were driving up from the south, and when we had climbed a hill to bring the Lhotse-Nuptse ridge into view, the upper part, over which we should have seen the top of Everest, was obscured. Even in clear weather, however, only the summit is seen. The mountain, in spite of its bulk and height, still eludes the eye of the traveller approaching from the south; who, having outflanked and passed the high white wall of Chamlang, finds himself confronted by a black and higher wall. This is the three-mile-long rock ridge linking Lhotse (27,890 ft.), or South Peak, to Nuptse (25,680 ft.), the West Peak. The south face of this ridge is too steep to hold snow. Behind it lies the West Cwm, the deep cleft which separates it from the west ridge of Everest itself.

Although my companions were in ecstasies over Namche Bazar and its friendly people, they were anxious to quit it at once and shrank from staying another night. Charles Houston and I, at any rate, had not time to waste if we were to see anything of the mountain in the six days available. We were due back at Jogbani on 6 December and had therefore to leave Namche by 21 November. Thus it was arranged that he and I should start early next morning for Thyangboche and beyond, while the others would follow later and stop at Thyangboche, where there is a monastery of whose beauty and sanctity we had already heard much.

We were astir in pursuit of these plans and were not to be turned from them by a lowering morning with snow falling briskly. Gyalgen was in his element, chaffing the women, haranguing the men, engaging recruits for the glacier party, and cooking for us a very handsome breakfast—hot buckwheat cakes and eggs, tsampa porridge and fresh milk. With mingled feelings, greed predominating over sorrow, I noticed that their hygienic principles prevented my friends from drinking milk from such dubious sources. Only a timely exclamation of horror vetoed the proposal that it should be boiled, thus rendering it innocuous, and at the same time tasteless. After a few days of intimate life at the monastery where it was obvious that dirt, disease and death lurked pleasantly in every pot and in every corner of the room, they overcame these scruples and took to milk like cats. All except Mr Houston, senior, who was made of sterner stuff, who looked upon raw milk as more inimical to health than raw brandy and much less pleasant to take.

The glacier party had with them Da Namgyal, Saki, a Musketeer and Danu a raw recruit. Although a mere lad Danu was said to be a brother of the redoubtable Angtharkay, who had begun his climbing career in 1933; be that as it may, he certainly behaved like an Angtharkay. Short, barrel-like and solemn, he moved about in camp with the portentous tread of a bishop or a muscle-bound all-in wrestler, his hands resting lightly on an incipient stomach. But in action he carried more and went twice as fast as anyone else besides doing the work of three men in camp. He had a passion for building immense camp fires, nothing less than a holocaust satisfied him. Long before daybreak one would imagine that the sun had risen untimely, but it was only Danu rekindling the overnight bonfire, so that we could breakfast round it in comfort at first light.

A well-engineered track on which ponies can be ridden leads to Thyangboche. After traversing high it descends gradually to the Dudh Kosi which it crosses just below its junction with the Imja Khola. This river comes down from Everest, from the north-east, while the Dudh Kosi descends from the north where it rises in the glaciers of the Cho Oyu group. The track then climbs equally gradually to the monastery (c. 12,000 ft.), a group of white buildings built on a grassy saddle commanding views up the Dudh Kosi, west to Kwangde, south to the fantastic snow spires of Kangtega, and east to the Lhotse-Nuptse ridge which fills the whole valley. The summit of Everest shows not very prominently over the top of this ridge, but the monks call the whole massif Chomo Lungma. It would be difficult to imagine, much more find, a finer site for worship or for contemplation. Lamas may laugh at our love for climbing mountains, but undoubtedly they themselves take great delight in looking at them. Like Christian monks they seemed to be equally lovers of the picturesque and of good living; on which two counts they have the approval of at any rate one mountaineer.

That morning we saw nothing of this noble prospect. It was snowing steadily, and the monastery yaks scuffled hungrily in the snow. The monks were a little taken aback when we walked boldly into the precincts followed by a crowd grinning urchins or sucking lamas. However, they placed a couple of braziers in front of us, and when we heard that the rear party had been sighted we decided to lunch with them before going on to Pangboche, the next village up the Imja Khola.

At this news the interest and excitement of the lamas rose perceptibly. They realized that Charles Houston and I were merely an indifferent curtain-raiser to the coming pageant. When the newcomers rode into the courtyard below, one felt that, had they known how, the lamas would have cheered. Mrs Cowles, of course, stole the show, and soon had them all, urchins and lamas alike, eating out of her hand; nor could they fail to be impressed with Mr Houston's benign dignity—not unlike that of the old abbot of Rongbuk himself—or with Andy Bakewell's bearded gravity and manly bearing— especially as he was wearing shorts. Thyangboche is a very small counterpart of Rongbuk monastery on the Tibetan side of the mountain, not a quarter of its size and having only a handful of monks. Yet its abbot, a shy smiling youth, of reputedly great spiritual power, is held in little less reverence, and its situation is incomparably more beautiful and less austere. It is much less austere inside, too, for they produced a beaker of raksi for our lunch, and when we returned a few days later we found they had the pleasant custom of fortifying their guests with a snorter before breakfast.

Having seen our friends established in an empty house we had no qualms— none, that is, on their behalf—about leaving them in such congenial surroundings. On a fine day it is an entrancing walk from the monastery to the Imja Khola bridge; through open woods of hoary twisted juniper and of glistening silver birch, whose golden leaves were still clinging to branches hung with streamers of pale green lichen. We strolled along, past a little whitewashed hamlet, when suddenly a bend in the path brought into view the white, foaming river and beyond it a massive rock shoulder, like the grey roof of a church, from which sprang the preposterous snow spire of some unnamed, unmeasured peak. The trees ended at the river. As is generally the way, the south-facing side of the valley was bare and bore an abundant crop of stones. Few stretches of the rocky track were without mani walls and chortens, and every convenient boulder had inscribed on it a religious text. Having been warned of sickness at the next village, Pangboche, we camped in a field on the outskirts where there was an empty hut for the men. A dense mist followed the heavy snowfall.

But the storm's malice was spent; after a cold night the morning broke bright and clear. Pangboche, which has few houses and a great many fields, is the last inhabited village. At Dingboche, a few miles up, there are a number of fields but no one lives there in winter. As we walked over flats of coarse brown grass by the river, we had in front of us the long Lhotse-Nuptse rock face with the massive black pyramid of Everest showing above it. One was impressed not so much by its height, for it looked rather squat, but by the suggestion it held of the immensity of its unseen mass. Three miles up, when the valley divided, we took the northern branch; the other continues eastwards, drains the south side of Lhotse, and terminates in a bay a little way south and east of the peak. Makalu, twenty miles away, beyond the head of this valley, bulked big enough, for most of it was in view, yet it was white and shapely and had not the menace of this black fragment of mountain so high above us.[1]

The first two miles of our northern valley consisted of broad, brown pastures dotted with stone huts and grazing yaks. One group of huts is called

1 According to a map constructed from air photographs by the late E. A. Reeves, Instructor of Survey at the R.G.S., Pethangtse (the east peak), like Makalu, lies in the basin of the Arun river.

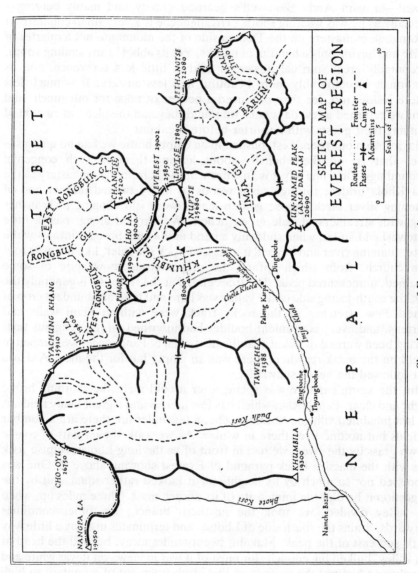

Sketch-map of Everest region

Pheriche and the uppermost, where we camped, Phalong Karpa. All the living huts were securely locked for the winter but we made ourselves comfortable in one which was used as a hay barn. That afternoon we climbed to about 17,000 ft. on the ridge which descends south-west from Nuptse to the fork in the main valley. The glaciers of the eastern branch seemed of no great size and terminated well above the fields of Dingboche, which we now looked down upon. On this bright afternoon with hardly a cloud in sight, we beheld a vast panorama of mountains; from Lhotse, Pethangtse and Makalu in the east, south to Chamlang and Kangtega, west to Taweche, and north to Cho Oyu and Gyachung Khang. In this galaxy, which included a host of unnamed peaks, neither the lesser nor the greater seemed designed for the use of climbers.

At 14,000 ft. at this time of year, mid-November, the nights were bitter. Only a few juniper bushes thrived, yet on returning from this excursion we found Danu Prometheus tending a glorious blaze of sizable logs. Frost soon stilled the murmur of the stream, only the faint note of a bell on some restless yak broke the deep silence. As we sat in the secure circle of the fire, our backs to the stone wall of the hut, the talk turned naturally to the Abominable Snowman. As one might expect they are found in these parts in numbers, especially around Namche Bazar in the depths of winter when the cold drives them lower. Danu affirmed that the previous year, a friend of his named Lakhpa Tensing had had his face so badly mauled by one, on the Nangpa La, that he died. By running downhill, which is, of course, the only way a man can run at these heights, one can usually get away from these creatures whose long hair, falling over their eyes, hampers them; but the unfortunate Lakhpa had apparently tripped and lying half stunned by the fall became an easy prey.

Just above Phalong Karpa is the high terminal moraine of the Khumbu glacier which comes down from the north-east, from Pumori, the Lho La and the West Cwm. The main valley, also glacier-filled, continues northwards towards the head of the West Rongbuk. They told us of a pass, now disused, at the head of this valley, but I think perhaps they were confusing it with the so-called 'Nup La' which leads from the West Rongbuk into the next valley westwards, the Dudh Kosi. I can find no account of it, but I believe this 'Nup La' was actually crossed by Mr Hazard (of the 1924 expedition) and a Gurkha surveyor. They camped just on the west side of it and then returned. We turned up the Khumbu valley where we found good going in a warm, grassy ablation valley where gentians were still in flower. As we advanced we brought into view first Pumori, and then the Lho La and the North Peak beyond it. After going for four hours we camped by a little lake beyond the grass almost in the shadow of Nuptse. Our height was about 16,500 ft.

Our afternoon walk towards the foot of the Lho La, whence we hoped to see up the West Cwm, was very rough. Driven from the friendly ablation valley, now filled with boulders, we took the moraine, and finally sought easier going on the glacier itself. Expecting every moment to round some corner and look up the Cwm, we were baffled by the apparent continuity of the rock and snow wall linking Nuptse with the west ridge of Everest which rises abruptly from the Lho La. Before turning for home and when still a mile from the foot of the

Lho La, I struck out across the glacier but still failed to see any break. Some trick of lighting must have concealed it, for we saw it readily enough next morning before we were half way across the glacier. It is, however, the merest slit, not more than three hundred yards across, filled by a broken ice-fall which falls steeply to the Khumbu glacier almost at the foot of the Lho La.

As we had only one day left, we thought that, instead of trying to enter the Cwm, our best chance of seeing both its head and the south ridge of the mountain would be from some vantage point on the west side of the glacier. Accordingly we sent the men down to Phalong Karpa, crossed the glacier, and climbed a subsidiary feature of about 18,000 ft. to the south of Pumori. The glacier is about a mile wide and only some five in length. Its upper part is pinnacled, like the East Rongbuk glacier, though the ice pinnacles are neither so high nor so continuous. One reason for this comparatively slight glaciation—for it is only half the length of any one of the three Rongbuk glaciers—is that the southern glaciers start and finish respectively nearly 2,000 ft. lower than the northern. The south aspect, too, is warmer, and the temperatures must be appreciably raised by the great expanse of bare rock on the south faces of Everest and Lhotse which are too steep to hold snow.

As we hurried across the glacier under a hard sky that seemed to hold possibilities of evil, we glanced now at the weather and now at the great mountain as bit by bit the terrific sweep of black rock rose above the West Cwm. So anxious were we to gain our point before any clouds appeared that we forced the pace—if pace it could be called—unwisely; for Houston, who had left New York barely three weeks before, found 18,000 ft. quite high enough.

In spite of our height and our distance from it—about seven miles—we could not see the high col between Everest and Lhotse of which the lowest point is 25,850 ft. A shoulder of Nuptse cut across the south ridge of the mountain, hiding the whole length of the West Cwm and this col at its head. We could see at most the upper 3,000 ft. of the south ridge which looked so steep that we dismissed at once any idea of there being a route, even supposing the col could be reached.

From the map, we appeared to be due west of the south ridge and were thus seeing it in profile. On that assumption it seemed to be a waste of time discussing the possibility of reaching it; but I now think we were not looking at its true edge but merely a buttress protruding from the south-west face. For photographs of this high Lhotse-Everest profile, taken during the monsoon from the east by the 1921 reconnaissance party, show a snow-covered slope rising from the col at a much less frightening angle. They also show the east side of the col to be unclimbable. Whether snow lies permanently on the south ridge, and what, at that great height is its consistency, are additional problems. Yet with these pictures in mind, and despite our impressions from the west, one cannot write off the south side as impossible until the approach from the head of the West Cwm to this remarkably airy col has been seen. (It is a pity that the name Lho La, or South Col, has been appropriated by the col at the foot of the west ridge; but there is perhaps no need to find a name for this true south col, 6,000 ft. higher than the false, until it has been reached.)

The West Cwm has been looked at several times from the Lho La. We saw it from there in 1935 and Mr Shipton secured a photograph of it. All that this shows is a short stretch of level snow above the ice-fall, the head of the Cwm being well out of sight behind the west ride. It is a trench confined within two more or less precipitous walls, and it somehow seems unlikely that there will be a convenient snow ramp leading from the level floor at, possibly, 21,000 ft. to the col at 25,850 ft. Moreover, a trench overhung by these two tremendous walls might easily become a grave for any party which pitched its camp there.

On the whole, whatever one may think of the last 3,000 ft. of the south ridge, looked at either from the east or from the west, in my opinion, the chances are against there being any way of reaching it. Of the final 1,000 ft., the crux of the whole matter, we have unfortunately no experience. Certainly they cannot be assumed to be easy.

At great heights a route must be easy to be possible, not only because of the extra exertion needed to overcome difficult places but also because of the time so lost. Even in the early days of the 1921 reconnaissance Mallory was aware of this when he dismissed the west ridge as a possible route: 'If ever the mountain were to be climbed,' he wrote, 'the way would not lie along the length of any of its colossal ridges. Progress could only be made along comparatively easy ground. . .' Mallory, too, had looked into the West Cwm from the Lho La and even from that restricted view drew some conclusions. He and Bullock had hoped to reach the West Cwm from the Rongbuk glacier, but were stopped by the 1,500 ft. drop to the Khumbu glacier. He wrote: 'It was not a very likely chance that the gap between Everest and the South peak (Lhotse) could be reached from the west. From what we have seen I do not much fancy it would be possible, even if one could get up the glacier' (i.e. up the ice-fall of the West Cwm glacier). Although the weather did not worsen, it remained unkind for photography.

Under a dull, hard sky, with neither sunlight nor shadow playing about its huge faces and ridges, the mountain compelled admiration only by its immensity. Mountains without snow and ice are shorn of the greater part of their splendour, and it is not always realized that in its most familiar aspect Everest is a rock mountain. Above 25,000 ft., from the north-east ridge round to the south, no permanent snow lies except in a few gullies and on odd ledges; and so accustomed are we to associate snow and ice with great height that the fact is not easy to appreciate.

The upper part of the climbing route and what looked like the Second Step were visible, but Camp VI and the route to it from the North Col were hidden by the north-west shoulder which from here appeared to be a mountain in its own right, with two snow ridges framing a face of rock banded with fluted snow. It was surprising to see the climbing route in perfect condition, free from snow, barely two months after the end of the monsoon. We still have a lot to learn about Everest. It is not yet known how soon after the monsoon the upper rocks are cleared of snow. It has been generally believed that the snow was swept away by gales in late winter, but if this rapid clearing is caused by evaporation towards the end and immediately after the monsoon, then a favourable month for an attempt might be October when the weather is more settled and when there would be no ever-present threat of an untimely 'Western Disturbance' or an early monsoon applying the closure. On the other hand, this rapid clearing may be affected by October gales which would, of course, preclude any attempt at that time. So far as we could tell there was not much wind when we were there in late November, but even if the weather then is generally fine, the intense cold and the shortening days would be deadly disadvantages for high climbing.

We descended from our little hummock and returned to Phalong Karpa by the true right side of the Khumbu glacier. From what we had seen we were convinced that the south ridge offered little hope, but of course we had not seen enough. We had not seen the true south ridge, neither had we seen the Lhotse-Everest col nor the approach to it from the West Cwm, and until this has been seen one cannot rule out the possibility of there being a route to the summit by the south ridge.[1] From the head of the West Cwm to the South Col must be nearly 5,000 ft.; from the head of the East Rongbuk glacier to the North Col is less than half that and yet it is as steep a place as anyone would like to have to climb with laden porters. One cannot help feeling that the tendency to greater steepness on the south side of the mountain will hold good, and that there will not be any convenient ramp by which the South col will be attainable.

Next morning 'Chimpanzee' Saki went down and very nearly out with malaria, so that for the first mile or two he had to be carried. The medicine chest, a very comprehensive one, had been left at Thyangboche, but I happened to have in my pocket a few Paludrin tablets which worked like a charm. He probably lost the first dose by vomiting, but after the second he began rapidly to perk up and reached Thyangboche on his own feet.

Our friends there had taken to a monastic life with the greatest readiness. Our introduction to it consisted of a large bowl of unexceptionable dai for supper. True we were wakened at 4 a.m. by the din of horns and the clash of cymbals, but we were not expected to rouse out for prayer or meditation, or indeed to do anything beyond reaching for a wooden jorum thoughtfully left in readiness. In this, of course, lurked what we called 'lama's milk', which was raksi flavoured with cloves.

The jemadar, the escort and the Dharan men, all of them blue with cold, were waiting to take us down, but first we had to tour the monastery and to receive the blessing of the young abbot. This ceremony resembled a school prize giving, the abbot, in the role of dumb but distinguished visitor, distributing the prizes handed to him by the business-like secretary. As we sheepishly filed past the dais where the young abbot, attired in full canonicals and a tall cone-shaped hat, sat enthroned, with his cup, copper teapot, silver 'dorje' and all the tools of his trade, so to speak, in front of him, we bowed our heads while he draped our necks with the ceremonial scarf and a small silk talisman, at the same time handing us a paper of formidable pills. The talisman consisted of a tightly folded paper of writing and pictures combined, sealed and neatly bound with red, white, blue, purple and black threads. In

1 Since the above was written a party has been sent out (September 1951) to discover whether the upper part of the mountain can be reached from the West Cwm.

the end curiosity overcame my reluctance to slice open and so destroy this miniature work of art. The monastery possesses a library of 500 wood-bound books each in its own curtained pigeon-hole. Among its rich furnishings are a gilt, life-size image of the late abbot of Rongbuk monastery and some very beautiful religious paintings, temple banners or 'Tang-ka'.

Our return journey was remarkable for the size of our retinue. We had thus no transport worries. If we wanted to lengthen our marches all we did was to transfer a few more of our followers to the pay-roll and so lighten the loads of the rest. Whether they expected to be paid or whether they merely hungered after the privilege of travelling in such distinguished company, a great many Sherpas, men and women, decided to accompany us to Darjeeling if they could raise the money for a ticket. Danu, of course, came, kindling young forest fires all the way. He attached himself to me, and by always having my tent up and bedding out long before any other loads had cast up, gave occasion for some pointed remarks. Another good companion and worker was Sonam Tensing, who is better kown in Himalayan circles as the Foreign Sportsman, a familiar figure on a number of expeditions which we had made together in the thirties. Having always returned to his village after each expedition and never resided long in Darjeeling, he seemed quite unspoilt, a visible token of which being the pigtail he still wore. With a voice as deep as of yore, he still crooned what I imagined were prayers, going on sometimes for nearly half an hour without stopping—perhaps the Buddhist prayer known as 'Clearing of Obstruction from the Path', which should be a favourite one for wayfarers.

We met with no obstructions at all and only a few slight rubs to mar our felicity. Of these, apart from a few affectionate lice which I shared with Danu until I broke him of the habit of carrying his spare clothes in my rucksack, the most embarrassing was our meeting with a large escort from Okhaldhunga which had been chasing us for nearly a fortnight. It was a case of hail and farewell, for we were on the verge of leaving their district when they caught us up. It was hard to know whom their superior would blame most, us or them, but as we were not going to Okhaldhunga it hardly mattered. We solved the difficulty with a carefully worded note to him and a small cash bonus to them. Our jemadar never got over this. Perhaps he feared this diminution of the prize fund might affect his own prospects, for he never stopped talking of the folly of rewarding men for work they had not done.

To our sorrow we met with further evidence of the long if slightly inefficient arm of Okhaldhunga officialdom, stretching out this time to the detriment of our friends of Bung. It seemed that while food grains like rice might be turned into beer, the law drew the line at turning them into spirits. Accordingly a few publicans and sinners, some of Bung's most prominent citizens, had been hauled off to Okhaldhunga to answer for it. Having drunk prematurely a bottle of genuine brandy which had been earmarked for celebrating Thanksgiving Day, we were with difficulty trying to accumulate a stock of the local fire-water; a problem not unlike those set in arithmetic papers concerned with the filling of leaking tanks. With confidence well grounded on experience we had looked forward to remedying any deficiency at Bung, and now, of course, the sources of the spring were dry. The lament on this theme, which will not bear repeating, has already been given.

Nevertheless, in the Arun valley on 30 November, the pilgrims had their Thanksgiving Dinner—table decorations by Mrs Cowles, heating and lighting by Danu, solid fare by Gyalgen, fruit cake by Himal Bill, and bottled lightning from the jemadar's private cellar. For my part I gave thanks for past Himalayan seasons, few without their missed opportunities and frustrated hopes, but all of them good, and of which this, I thought, should be the last. The best attainable should be good enough for any man, but the mountaineer who finds his best gradually sinking is not satisfied. In an Early English poem attributed to one Beowulf we are told:

> Harder should be the spirit, the heart all the bolder,
> Courage the greater, as the strength grows less.

If a man feels he is failing to achieve this stern standard he should perhaps withdraw from a field of such high endeavour as the Himalaya.

APPENDICES

APPENDICES

A Note on Tilman as a Writer

by Jim Perrin

'In the criticism of literature . . . we often have to 'stand back' from the poem to see its archetypal organization.' *Northrop Frye, Anatomy of Criticism*

Frye's suggestion is apposite to readers of Tilman's books – or those amongst them who might wish to consider more closely the power of the writing and the persona of the author. Take a step back from any of these traveller's tales and there comes into focus, instead of the fine brushwork of irony or the minute detail of a landscape, an extraordinary collation of images central to the quest-romance: the perfectly chaste hero; refusal of fellowship; the journey into the Waste Land; battle with an inhuman adversary; the eventual return of the hero to society, informed by the knowledge won from his quest. If we look at the whole of Tilman's career, taking the sailing books also into account, the resonances become even more marked, with death by water as the final stage in the archetypal quest for self.

I don't wish to put this forward as merely fanciful, because there is perhaps something central to Tilman's purpose as a writer here. Jung, in *The Archetypes and the Collective Unconscious*, defines an archetype as being 'essentially an unconscious content that is altered by becoming conscious and by being perceived, and . . . takes its colour from the individual consciousness in which it happens to appear. It is . . . something like the "pattern of behaviour" in biology.'

There is little doubt that in some way Tilman discerned such a pattern in the mode of life he came to adopt and to write about, and very frequently in his books there are references which point up the analogy between his own life and that of the quest-hero or similar archetypal figure: 'The Ancient Mariner', *Pilgrim's Progress*, Tennyson's 'Ulysses', Browning's 'Childe Roland', Housman's poem on 'the land of lost content'. At other times the sense comes directly from his own words:

> I felt I could go on like this forever, that life had little better to offer than to march day after day in unknown country to an unattainable goal.

The point can be over-stressed, but it has a part to play in the writer's creation of a persona. In an interview with Ronald Christ, Jorge Luis Borges made the following very interesting observation:

> When I was a young man I was always hunting for new metaphors. Then I found out that good metaphors are always the same. I mean you compare time to a road, death to sleeping, life to dreaming, and those are the great metaphors in literature because they correspond to something essential.

On standing back from these books, you see quite clearly that Tilman is using the metaphor of the journey for all that it's worth, because in his case it does 'correspond to something essential' – the desire of self for a fulfilment liberated from any anxiety not occasioned by the immediate or the imponderable, whilst still containing a vivid form of reality. I wrote in the introduction that these books are 'a form of restrained autobiography' – so they are, but they are also the record of a persona fiercely projected into the realms of the archetype:

> The needy Traveller, serene and gay,
> Walks the wild Heath, and sings his Toil away.

From this imaginative projection derives a great deal of the interest and power of Tilman's writing, but it also achieves a further purpose. By choosing the deliberately simplified and refined character of the archetype, anachronistic in an age of materialism, he creates for himself an important critical instrument. It is only through this fining down of personality that he can credibly sustain his ironic attacks upon the materialism of the age. The serious intent of Tilman's ironic humour should not be mistaken. It is very funny, is often quite light-hearted, but behind the characteristic *litotes* is a strenuous intelligence savagely indignant at the way things are going, and occasionally bursting out with barely-suppressed rancour:

> There is a good case for dropping bombs on civilians because so very few of them can be described as inoffensive . . .

On occasions like this he is reminiscent of no-one so much as of Swift, and the ironic stance should at no times be disregarded in a reading of these books.

Merely to read them for the irony and quest-imagery would be to disregard other of their best qualities, however. The style itself is one of the most pleasing features. It is graphic, lucid, and frequently has an aphoristic elegance, the restraint often having a heightening effect on comic situations:

> I hurried back to the main valley concerned to know whether the rest of the party had come down and gone on. Some Kazak women I met gathering dung merely looked surly; there was no sign of anyone having passed, nor any sign of movement up the valley. I started back and presently met a shepherd towing a sick sheep, accompanied by a nasty-looking blackguard with a rifle. We had nothing to say, but I was sociable and sat patiently smoking my pipe while they looked through the wrong end of my field-glasses and handled my ice-axe. Presently the armed gentleman indicated that he would like my shirt, so I got up to go. It wasn't a very good shirt, but it was the only one I had.

Or again, after what has obviously been a fraught attempt on Bogdo Ola, on the retreat from which Shipton had rolled, rather than lowered, their rucksacks down a slope with dire effects:

> The Primus once again refused to burn so we supped drily on a crust of bread in profound silence. The rucksack episode seemed a likely topic for conversation, but it was one on which only a very determined philosopher could have embarked dispassionately.

Tilman's erudition is also notably impressive, though lightly worn and never displayed simply for effect. Almost wherever he goes on his travels he is able to provide a full résumé of earlier exploration and activity in the area, often from the most recondite sources. His account of the first visitors to the

Ruwenzori in *Snow on the Equator*, or the remarks on Merzbacher in *China to Chitral* are good examples of this. His wide reading never leads him into over-literary style. Fresh, direct, and peppered with apt allusion and quotation, his books rank alongside such as Cobbett's *Rural Rides* or Borrow's *The Bible in Spain* not just as supremely entertaining descriptions of travel, but as minor classics of our literature. In an age obsessed by speed, security, and sensation, his blend of reflection, wit and wise sufficiency deserves to be more widely known and read.

APPENDIX B

Selected Bibliography

Books with mountaineering information or comment:

Nanda Devi by Eric Shipton (Hodder and Stoughton, 1936)
The account of the exploration of the Rishi Gorge to gain access to the Nanda Devi Sanctuary.

Everest: The Unfinished Adventure by Hugh Ruttledge (Hodder and Stoughton, 1937)

Blank on The Map by Eric Shipton (Hodder and Stoughton, 1938)
The main account of the Karakoram/Shaksgam expedition of 1937. It includes a chapter by Tilman on his explorations around Snow Lake.

Upon That Mountain by Eric Shipton (Hodder and Stoughton, 1943)
Shipton's account of many climbs with Tilman including those in East Africa, the Rishi Gorge exploration, Everest Reconnaissance 1935, the Karakoram (Shaksgam) travels of 1937 and Everest 1938.

Everest 1938 by H. W. Tilman (Cambridge University Press, 1948)
A record of a discussion at the Royal Geographical Society (Geographical Journal, December 1938) between members of the expedition is reprinted as Appendix A. Other Appendices in the deal with The Abominable Snowman (Tilman), The Use of Oxygen (Lloyd) and Geological and Some Other Observations (Odell).

Mountains of Tartary by Eric Shipton (Hodder and Stoughton, 1950)
Shipton's account of his Asian travels and climbs with Tilman

The Mountain Everest Reconnaissance Expedition 1951 by Eric Shipton (Hodder and Stoughton, 1952)

To the Third Pole by G. O. Dyhrenfurth (Werner Laurie, 1955)
This provides contemporary analysis of the early Everest expeditions with trenchant comments on the leadership errors of Shipton (1935) and Tilman (1938).

Tilman was just the right leader for a Spartan organisation of that kind. He swears by his 'Pemmican' and will have nothing to do with tinned foods or, in fact, most of the tastier means of subsistence. Be that as it may – members of this expedition have told me they have never been so hungry nor had to eat such ghastly fare in their lives . . . It was so cold and stormy that Tilman felt it necessary to wait before attempting any serious climbing. In this way the whole time advantage was lost in a great deal of to-and-fro movements, minor undertakings and withdrawals to a Rest-Camp in the Kharta Valley. That would not have mattered so much if this month had been used for scientific work; but the 'notoriously anti-scientific leader' [as dubbed by Odell] only made scathing jibes at all such activities, put difficulties in the way of scientific research, or forbade them outright.

Abode of Snow by Kenneth Mason (Rupert Hart Davis, 1955)

The World Atlas of Mountaineering by Wilfrid Noyce and Ian McMorrin (Thomas Nelson, 1969)

That Untravelled World by Eric Shipton (Hodder and Stoughton, 1969)
Shipton's autobiography with numerous references to Tilman.

The Ulysses Factor by J. R. L. Anderson (Hodder and Stoughton, 1970)
Studies of noted explorers with a chapter on Tilman.

In the Throne Room of the Mountain Gods by Galen Rowell (Sierra Club Books/Allen and Unwin, 1977)

High Mountains and Cold Seas:A Biography of H. W. Tilman by J. R. L. Anderson (Gollancz, 1980)

Everest by Walt Unsworth (Allen Lane, 1981)
A comprehensive history with thorough appraisals of both the 1935 and 1938 expeditions. Essential background reading to *Everest, 1938*

Journal articles:

The Mt. Everest Reconnaissance, 1935 by E. E. Shipton (The Alpine Journal, May 1936)
This is the most detailed account of the expedition with a collection of interesting photographs (Note: The photos of Nyönno Ri and Ama Drime have misleading captions.)

The Mt. Everest Reconnaissance, 1935 by Eric Shipton (The Geographical Journal, February 1936)
Another thorough report (reprinted as a pamphlet) with excellent photographs and a useful map.

Photographic Surveys in the Mount Everest Region by Michael Spender (The Geographical Journal, October 1936)
Further information from the 1935 Reconnaissance (reprinted as a pamphlet) with another collection of interesting photographs.

The Mount Everest Expedition of 1938 by H. W. Tilman (The Geographical Journal, December 1938)
The paper and discussion reprinted as Appendix A in *Everest 1938* (also as an RGS pamphlet, but with better illustrations).

Himalayan Apery by H. W. Tilman (The Alpine Journal, November 1955)

The Annapurna Himal and the South Side of Everest by H. W. Tilman (The Alpine Journal, May 1951)

Harold William Tilman (1898–1978) a Tribute by Peter Lloyd and Colin Putt (The Alpine Journal, 1979)

The Alpine and Geographical Journals have many other references.

Himalayan Journal Vols. VII, IX, X, XI and XV contain references to various expeditions.

Tilman's sailing books

Mischief in Patagonia (Cambridge University Press, 1957)
Mischief among the Penguins (Rupert Hart Davis, 1961)
Mischief in Greenland (Hollis and Carter, 1964)
Mostly Mischief (Hollis and Carter, 1966)
Mischief Goes South (Hollis and Carter, 1968)
In Mischief's Wake (Hollis and Carter, 1971)
Mischief's Last Days (a privately published pamphlet, c.1972)
Ice With Everything (Nautical Publishing Company, 1974)
Triumph and Tribulation (Nautical Publishing Company, 1977)

also:

The Sea and the Snow by Phillip Temple (Cassell, 1966)
An account of the Heard Island Expedition

Adventures Under Sail by Libby Purves (Gollancz, 1982)
An anthology of Tilman's writings on his sailing exploits selected from his eight books.

APPENDIX C

Tilman's Mountaineering Record 1929–50

Relevant pages in the text, books etc., are noted at the end of each item.

c.1929
The Lake District Introduction to rock-climbing during a holiday with his sister Adeline. They hired the guide J. E. B. Wright. (Source: *That Untravelled World* and photographic records.)

1930

East Africa Kilimanjaro Near success on Kibo and ascent of Mawenzi with Eric Shipton.   pages 38–45

East Africa: Mt. Kenya First ascent of West Ridge of Batian and traverse to Nelion with Eric Shipton. The pair also made an ascent of 'Midget Peak' and were lucky to escape disaster during the descent when Tilman fell, became unconscious, and had to be lowered to a ledge by Shipton who was unbelayed.   pages 45–53

1932

East Africa: Ruwenzori January. Ascents of the main summits of Mts Speke, Baker and Stanley (mostly 3rd ascents) with Eric Shipton.   pages 66–86

The Lake District: Accident on Dow Crag April. J. S. Brogden, Tilman and Miss V. Brown all fell while making an ascent of Jones's Route in Easter Gully. Brogden was killed and both Brown and Tilman injured, the former seriously. Tilman managed to descend (walking and crawling) to Coniston to get help ('a deed of wonderful endurance and heroism'). Subsequent analysis (FRCCJ. 1932) showed that both Tilman and Brogden were inadequately belayed and were dragged off when Brown (a novice) fell.

Alpine Holiday August. While still recovering from the Dow Crag accident Tilman travelled alone to the Alps and hired guides to make climbs in the Dauphiné and Mt. Blanc groups. Ascents recorded (in his diary) included Les Bans, the Meije, the Ecrins and Col des Avalanches; Aig.de l'M, Aig.du Tour, Col de la Fenêtre and Col du Chardonnet.

1933

East Africa: Kilimanjaro Solo ascent of Kibo to reach Kaiser Wilhelm Spitz (the highest point, that Shipton and he had failed to reach in 1930).   pages 99–104

1934

India: Nanda Devi Sanctuary May/June and September with Eric Shipton, Angtharkay, Pasang Bhotia and Kusang. Exploration of Rishi Gorge and surveying work in the Sanctuary including a reconnaissance of the South Ridge of Nanda Devi. In July and August the party crossed the Badrinath Range including the traverse of a difficult 18,000ft. pass.   see *Nanda Devi* by Eric Shipton

1935

Tibet: Mt. Everest Reconnaissance Expedition May/June with Eric Shipton (leader), Dan Bryant, Michael Spender, Charles Warren, Edwin Kempson, Edmond Wigram, Angtharkay, Rinsing, Pasang Bhotia, Kusang, Tensing Norgay (his first major expedition), Sen Tensing ('Foreign Sportsman') and eleven other Sherpa porters. Brief exploration of Nyönno Ri range including attempt on East Ridge of Nyönno Ri (with Warren and Kempson) reaching a height of 21,000ft. In the Everest region Tilman's main achievements were: first ascent of Kellas Rock Peak 23,000ft. (with Shipton and Bryant); reconnaissance of the West Ridge of Everest and the Khumbu Icefall from Lho La and ascent of Khumbutse, a traverse of col north of Changtse, and first ascents of two 22,000ft. peaks near south of Lhakpa La (all with Wigram). Tilman and Wigram climbed seventeen peaks during this expedition.   see Bibliography

1936

Sikkim: Attempt on Pandim and attempt to cross Zemu Gap April, with Pasang Kikuli and three other sherpas. The brief attempt to climb Pandim (22,010ft.) was abandoned in the face of dangerous stonefall. The party tried to reach Zemu Gap from the Tongshyong (south) side but objective dangers, and icefall and crevasse problems combined to defeat them.   pages 306–314

The Anglo-American Nanda Devi Expedition July–September, with Americans: W. F. Loomis (organiser), Charles Houston, H. Adams Carter and Arthur Emmons; and British: T. Graham Brown (UK organiser), Noel Odell, and Peter Lloyd. Sherpas included Pasang Kikuli and Kitar (who became ill and died during the expedition). The expedition made the first ascent of the mountain by a route up the South Ridge, the summit being reached by Tilman and Odell on August 29. Later Tilman, Houston and Kikuli made the first crossing of Longstaff's Col.

1937

India (now Pakistan) and China: The Karakoram – Shaksgam Expedition May–September with Eric Shipton, Michael Spender and John Auden (brothers of the distinguished poets) and Lhakpa Tensing, Sen Tensing, Angtharkay, Lobsang, Ila, Nukku and Angtensing. This outstanding survey expedition crossed the Mustagh Pass from the Baltoro to the Sarpo Laggo Glacier to reach the Shaksgam Valley. Here it extended the surveys made by Mason, reconnoitred the northern approaches to K2 and then penetrated the Karakoram glacier systems to the north-east of Snow Lake. The team divided into groups to maximise their explorations. Tilman, with Sen Tensing and Ila, following Crevasse Glacier to a high col leading to Snow Lake, breaking through the western wall of the Biafo Glacier by a difficult pass to the north of Sospun Brakk, and exploring the Garden, Cornice, Sospun and Hoh Lungma Glaciers before returning to Skardu.   see *Blank on the Map* by Eric Shipton

1938

Tibet: Mount Everest Expedition April–June. Tilman was leader with Frank Smythe, Eric Shipton, Charles Warren, Peter Lloyd, Noel Odell, Peter Oliver, Karma Paul (Tibetan liaison), Angtharkay, Kusang, Pasang Bhotia, Tensing Norgay, Nukku, Lhakpa Tsering, Ongdi Nurbu and Nurbu Bhotia and others. The expedition initially had to operate in very cold temperatures. This led to a premature retreat for recuperation after tents and supplies had been cached on the North Col. Later heavy snow conditions created problems. The North Col was regained by a new route up its western flank, and thereafter the climb followed the conventional route to Camp 6 at 27,300ft. Two summit attempts followed (Shipton and Smythe; Tilman and Lloyd) but little further progress was made in the deep and unstable snow on the upper section of the mountain.   pages 429–509

Sikkim: Ascent of Lachsi (21,100ft.) and traverse of the Zemu Gap November, with Renzing and Lhakpa Tenzing. Lachsi was climbed in misty weather and very warm conditions. Only Tilman and Renzing reached the summit – Lhakpa Tenzing waited for them at half height. The Zemu Gap was then traversed from north to south, the climbers making full use of abseil techniques to overcome the steep sections of the Tyongshyong side.   pages 314–323

1939

India (Assam): Attempt on Gori Chen (21,450ft.) April–June, with Wangdi Norbu, Nukku and Thundu. This arduous journey into the depths of the Assam Himalaya petered out on the lower slopes of Gori Chen. The party was ravaged by malaria and only reached the mountain by exercising sustained 'willpower'. The retreat was traumatic. Nukku died from fever and both Thundu and Tilman had to be carried out. 'A more unqualified failure has seldom been recorded' (Tilman).   pages 275–306

1941

Iraq and Iran In Kurdistan Tilman made a solo ascent, in winter, of a 6,500ft. peak ('of almost alpine standard') In the Zagros Mountains of Iran he climbed Bisitun (c.10,000ft.), a rock peak above Kermanshah.   pages 324–384

1942

Tunisia A night ascent of Zaghouan with a fellow battery commander 'George' using flares to illuminate the difficult sections of the ascent.   pages 337–342

1947

India (now Pakistan): Anglo-Swiss Rakaposhi Expedition April–July, with Hans Gyr, Robert Kappeler, Campbell Secord, Angdawa, Angtingtit, Phurbu and Ningma and others. Rakaposhi (25,550ft.) is a difficult but accessible mountain in the Karakoram near Gilgit. The party reconnoitred five different routes – two probes up the dangerous Biro Glacier, an attempt on the South West Ridge by a route from the Kunti Glacier and a line onto the North West Ridge directly from Darakush. The highest point reached (by Gyr and Tilman) was on the South West Ridge at c.20,000ft. below the Monk's Head. The fifth possible route by the South Ridge, or the glacier to the east of it, was investigated by crossing the Dainyor Pass but was found to be too difficult and complex.   pages 517–574

The expedition then moved to the Kukuay Glacier system in the Batura group north of Chalt hoping to find an easy pass to lead them into one of a number of possible glacier systems. All the passes were too difficult however.   pages 574–585

China: Mustagh Ata attempt August, with Eric Shipton and Gyalgen Sherpa. The trio came close to success on this 24,758ft. peak by an easy but long route. With Shipton frostbitten and all of them exhausted they retreated from c.24,300ft.   pages 597–605

1948

China: Bogdo Ola group July, with Eric Shipton, Lhakpa Sherpa and Agasha. The trio climbed to vantage points on the flanking ridges of the main mountain group including a peak of 17,000ft. on the East Ridge of East Peak.   pages 683–705

China: Chakar Aghil or Chakragil August and September. After making a brief reconnaissance with a non-climbing companion, Tilman returned with Shipton, Gyalgen and a local man, Mahmud, and made a determined attempt on the North Ridge of this 22,071ft. peak, reaching a height of 17,000ft. At this point Mahmud became ill and the party was forced to retreat.   pages 712–726

Chitral–Hindu Kush October–November. Sundry travels.   pages 726–738

1949

Nepal: Langtang, Ganesh and Jugal Himals May–September, with Peter Lloyd, O. Polunin, J. S. Scott, Tensing Norgay and others. A prolonged investigation of the glaciers and mountains of the area, involving the crossing or reaching of numerous passes, surveying, botanical work and geology. Lloyd and Tilman climbed Paldor (19,451ft.).   pages 745–805

1950

Nepal: British Annapurna Expedition April–July, Tilman was leader with Maj. J. O. M. 'Jimmy' Roberts, Col. D. G. Lowndes, Dr. C. H. (Charles) Evans, J. H. Emlyn Jones, W. P. Packard, Gyalgen, Da Namgyal and others. They explored the valleys and glacier systems around Manaslu, Himalchuli and the north side of the Annapurna group. Annapurna 4 (24,688ft.) was attempted and a high point of c.24,000ft. was gained by Evans and Packard. A peak of 22,997ft. north of the Marsyandi Khola was also attempted and a height of c.22,000ft. gained by Emlyn Jones and Packard.

pages 806–867

Nepal: Everest October–November, with Oscar Houston, Charles Houston, Mrs E. S. Cowles, Anderson Bakewell, Gyalgen, Da Namgyal, Pa Norbu and Saki. The party travelled to the Solu Khumbu where Tilman and Charles Houston continued to the Khumbu Glacier area where they viewed Everest from 18,000ft. on the slopes of Pumori.   pages 867–886